THE ROUTLEDGE COMPANION TO PRODUCTION AND OPERATIONS MANAGEMENT

This remarkable volume highlights the importance of Production and Operations Management (POM) as a field of study and research contributing to substantial business and social growth. The editors emphasize how POM works with a range of systems—agriculture, disaster management, e-commerce, healthcare, hospitality, military systems, not-for-profit, retail, sports, sustainability, telecommunications, and transport—and how it contributes to the growth of each.

Martin K. Starr and Sushil K. Gupta gather an international team of experts to provide researchers and students with a panoramic vision of the field. Divided into eight parts, the book presents the history of POM, and establishes the foundation upon which POM has been built while also revisiting and revitalizing topics that have long been essential. It examines the significance of *processes* and *projects* to the fundamental growth of the POM field. Critical emerging themes and new research are examined with open minds and this is followed by opportunities to interface with other business functions. Finally, the next era is discussed in ways that combine practical skill with philosophy in its analysis of POM, including traditional and nontraditional applications, before concluding with the editors' thoughts on the future of the discipline.

Students of POM will find this a comprehensive, definitive resource on the state of the discipline and its future directions.

Martin K. Starr is Distinguished Professor of Production and Operations Management Emeritus at Rollins College, and Emeritus Senior Professor of Operations Research, Management Science, and Operations Management at Columbia University, both in the USA. He is a past president of the Production and Operations Management Society (POMS) and the Institute for Operations Research and the Management Sciences (INFORMS). He is Director of Strategic Planning for POMS.

Sushil K. Gupta is Professor in the College of Business at Florida International University, USA, and an honorary professor at Universidad Ricardo Palma, Peru. He is one of the founding members and a past president of the Production and Operations Management Society (POMS) and serves on the advisory board of the *Production and Operations Management* journal. He is the Executive Director of POMS.

"This Companion is a masterpiece. By bringing together works of scholars from across the globe, Starr and Gupta have created a companion that reflects on POM achievements to date as well as exploration of its future. I have no doubt this text will prove an essential reference source for the whole POM community."

Andy Neely, *University of Cambridge, UK*

"These gifted editors have made a major contribution to the POM field, producing an innovative volume which will have a lasting effect on the profession of POM, practicing managers, and their academic thought leaders. The Companion is superbly balanced in its presentation of theory and practice. The breadth of coverage of this profession and its practices is remarkable and truly a first of its kind. Well done!"

Wickham Skinner, *Harvard University, USA*

"This book provides comprehensive coverage of the vast domain of POM, the discipline that forms the core of the global economy. The roster of contributors is made up of major POM thought leaders. This book ought to be read by everyone interested in POM and its kindred organizational functions."

Kalyan Singhal, *University of Baltimore, USA*

"A ground breaking presentation of the state of the art of Production and Operations Management, showing its relevance and application in a wide range of diverse areas. We see an outstanding set of international contributors who are leaders in this emerging field. This volume will be essential reading for both practitioners and academics."

John Buzacott, *York University, Canada*

"A timely and much needed compendium outlining the current state of POM literature, showing the paths for future practice and research. This is a comprehensive coverage of real-world POM practices and relevant technological advancements; a unique source of knowledge serving the needs of academics, early-career researchers, and practitioners alike."

Norma Harrison, *Macquarie University, Australia*

THE ROUTLEDGE COMPANION TO PRODUCTION AND OPERATIONS MANAGEMENT

Edited by Martin K. Starr and Sushil K. Gupta

NEW YORK AND LONDON

First published 2017
by Routledge
711 Third Avenue, New York, NY 10017

and by Routledge
2 Park Square, Milton Park, Abingdon, Oxon OX14 4RN

Routledge is an imprint of the Taylor & Francis Group, an informa business

© 2017 Taylor & Francis

The right of Martin K. Starr and Sushil K. Gupta to be identified as authors of the editorial material, and of the authors for their individual chapters, has been asserted in accordance with sections 77 and 78 of the Copyright, Designs and Patents Act 1988.

All rights reserved. No part of this book may be reprinted or reproduced or utilised in any form or by any electronic, mechanical, or other means, now known or hereafter invented, including photocopying and recording, or in any information storage or retrieval system, without permission in writing from the publishers.

Trademark notice: Product or corporate names may be trademarks or registered trademarks, and are used only for identification and explanation without intent to infringe.

Library of Congress Cataloging-in-Publication Data
Names: Starr, Martin K. (Martin Kenneth), 1927– editor. | Gupta, Sushil (Business scholar), editor.
Title: The Routledge companion to production and operations management / [edited by] Martin K. Starr, Sushil K. Gupta.
Other titles: Companion to production and operations management
Description: New York : Routledge, 2017. | Includes bibliographical references.
Identifiers: LCCN 2016039738 | ISBN 9781138919594 (hbk) |
    ISBN 9781315687803 (ebk) | ISBN 9781317419242 (web PDF) |
    ISBN 9781317419235 (ePub) | ISBN 9781317419228 (mobi/Kindle)
Subjects: LCSH: Production management. | Operations research. | Industrial management.
Classification: LCC TS155 .R6395 2017 | DDC 658.5—dc23
LC record available at https://lccn.loc.gov/2016039738

ISBN: 978-1-138-91959-4 (hbk)
ISBN: 978-1-315-68780-3 (ebk)

Typeset in Bembo
by CoVantage, LLC
Printed at CPI on sustainably sourced paper

We dedicate *The Routledge Companion to Production and Operations Management* to those POM researchers and professionals, from all over the globe, who are engaged in cutting edge research, disseminating knowledge, and improving organizational excellence. Their endeavors go a long way in making substantial contributions to improve the quality of life, to create a safer world to live in, and to sustain a healthy and beneficial environment for future generations.

CONTENTS

About the Editors   xxxii
Notes on Contributors   xxxv
Foreword   liii
Preface   liv

PART I
The Remarkable History of POM   1

1   Evolution of the POM Discipline   3
    Martin K. Starr, Sushil K. Gupta, and Christopher Tang
    1   Introduction to Evolving POM   3
    2   The Value of Historical Perspective for POM   4
    3   First POM Milestone—The Division of Labor   5
        3.1   The Holistic Production System of Volvo (Opposite to Division of Labor)   6
        3.2   Division of Labor Applied to Services   6
    4   Second POM Milestone—Interchangeable Parts (IP) and the Science of Tolerance Ranges   7
    5   Third POM Milestone—Statistical Quality Control (SQC) and Standardization   8
        5.1   Standardized Parts and Operations   9
    6   Four Industrial Revolutions—IR 1.0, IR 2.0, IR 3.0, and IR 4.0   10
        6.1   The First Industrial Revolution (IR 1.0), 1776 to 1840   10
        6.2   The Second Industrial Revolution (IR 2.0), 1840 to 1914   11
        6.3   The Third Industrial Revolution (IR 3.0), 1914 to 1999   12
        6.4   Industry 4.0: The Fourth Industrial Revolution (IR 4.0), 1999 and beyond   13
    7   Global Forces Acting on POM   15
    8   Global Competition: The Japanese Effect   15

    9 Outsourcing to China 16
   10 Sustainability—Social Responsibility—Crisis Management 18
   11 What is Next?—Industry 4.0 19
      11.1 Global Trade Processes 19
      11.2 Sharing Economy 20
      11.3 Data Analytics/Robotics—Phenomenon-Driven Research 20
   12 Conclusions 20
   References and Bibliography 21

2   Global Supply Chain Management   24
   Henrique L. Correa
   1 Introduction 24
   2 Technological Evolution 24
   3 Today's Competition: Between Supply Chains, Not Companies 25
   4 Historical Evolution of Supply Chain Management 25
      4.1 First Phase: The Operation Management Scope Is the Production Unit—"One Best Way" 25
      4.2 Second Phase: The Operations Management Scope Crosses Borders Between Functions 26
      4.3 Third Phase: The Operations Management Scope Crosses Borders Between Organizations—Supply Chains 26
      4.4 Fourth Phase: The Operations Management Scope Crosses National Borders—Global Supply Chains 27
      4.5 Fifth Phase: The Operations Management Scope Crosses the Borders of Organizations' Global Objectives—The Triple Bottom Line 27
   5 Everyone Wins With Good Supply Chain Management 27
   6 Supply Chain Management: Some Essential Concepts 28
      6.1 The Strategic "Make or Buy" Decision 28
          6.1.1 Transaction Cost Economics 29
          6.1.2 Resource-Based View of Strategy 30
          6.1.3 A Framework for the Strategic "Make or Buy" Decision 30
      6.2 Supply Chain Segmentation 31
          6.2.1 What Is the Right Supply Chain for Your Product? 32
          6.2.2 Aligning Competences in Supply Chains 34
          6.2.3 Avoiding Incentive Misalignment Among the Constellation of Partners in Supply Chains 34
      6.3 The Bullwhip Effect: Caused by Lack of Communication and Coordination Between Partners in Supply Chains 35
      6.4 Risk Assessment in Supply Chains 38
   7 Conclusion and Directions for Future Research 40
   References and Bibliography 40

PART II
Core POM Functions   43

3   Forecasting: State-of-the-Art in Research and Practice   45
Nada R. Sanders
- 1 Introduction to Forecasting in POM 45
  - 1.1 Forecasting Versus Planning 45
  - 1.2 Demand Management 46
  - 1.3 Impact on Costs 47
- 2 The Forecasting Process 47
  - 2.1 Steps in the Forecasting Process 47
  - 2.2 Factors in Method Selection 49
- 3 Forecasting Methodologies 50
  - 3.1 Categorization of Forecasting Methods 50
    - 3.1.1 Judgmental Forecasting Methods 51
    - 3.1.2 Statistical Forecasting Methods 52
  - 3.2 Combining Forecasting Methods 52
    - 3.2.1 Combining Judgmental and Statistical Methods 53
    - 3.2.2 The Role of Domain Knowledge and Contextual Information 55
- 4 The Future of Forecasting 55
  - 4.1 Information Access 56
  - 4.2 Big Data Analytics 56
  - 4.3 Information Sharing 57
- 5 Relevance for Managers 57
- 6 Research Opportunities 58
- 7 Conclusion 59
- References and Bibliography 59

4   Aggregate Production Planning   63
Lee Krajewski
- 1 Introduction 63
  - 1.1 The Importance of Aggregate Production Planning 63
  - 1.2 Dimensions of Aggregation 63
    - 1.2.1 Products 64
    - 1.2.2 Workforce 64
    - 1.2.3 Time 64
  - 1.3 Information Inputs 64
  - 1.4 Decision Variables and Supply Options 65
- 2 Historical Perspective of Aggregate Production Planning Research 66
  - 2.1 Linear Decision Rules 66
    - 2.1.1 Regular Time Wages 66
    - 2.1.2 Overtime Wages 67
    - 2.1.3 Hiring and Firing Costs 67

   2.1.4 Inventory and Backorder Costs 67
   2.1.5 Objective Function and the Rules 67
  2.2 Linear Programming 68
  2.3 Heuristics 69
  2.4 Evaluation of Early Aggregate Planning Models 70
  2.5 Goal Programming and Other Methodological Thrusts 70
 3 Disaggregation of Aggregate Production Plans 71
  3.1 Levels in Operations Planning and Scheduling 72
   3.1.1 Level 1 73
   3.1.2 Level 2 73
   3.1.3 Level 3 73
  3.2 Manufacturing 74
   3.2.1 Hierarchical Production Planning (HPP) 74
   3.2.2 Setups, Resource Profiles, and Distribution Plans 74
  3.3 Services 75
 4 Aggregate Production Planning in Practice 75
  4.1 Step 1: Roll the Plan Forward 76
  4.2 Step 2: Forecast and Demand Planning 76
  4.3 Step 3: Update the Sales and Operations Plan 76
  4.4 Step 4: Consensus Meetings 76
  4.5 Step 5: Executive S&OP Meeting 76
  4.6 Step 6: Update and Revise Final Plans 77
 5 Conclusions 77
  5.1 Future Research 77
   5.1.1 Employment Planning in Manufacturing 77
   5.1.2 Employment Planning in Services 77
   5.1.3 Aggregation 77
   5.1.4 Uncertainty 78
   5.1.5 Sustainability and Reverse Logistics 78
   5.1.6 Supply Chain Visibility 78
  5.2 Implications for Practitioners 79
 References and Bibliography 79

5 Scheduling in Manufacturing and Services   82
 Kangbok Lee and Michael Pinedo
 1 Introduction 82
  1.1 Classifications of Scheduling Problems 83
 2 Preliminaries and Fundamentals 84
  2.1 Computational Complexity of Scheduling Problems 84
  2.2 Solution Methodologies 85
 3 Scheduling in Manufacturing 86
  3.1 Job Shop Scheduling 86
   3.1.1 Scheduling Problems with the Total Weighted Completion Time Objective 86
   3.1.2 Scheduling Problems with the Total Completion Time Objective 87

3.1.3 Scheduling Problems with the Makespan Objective 88
3.1.4 Job Shop Scheduling with Additional Features 89
3.1.5 The Shifting Bottleneck Heuristic for Job Shop Scheduling 90
3.2 Resource Constrained Project Scheduling 91
4 Scheduling in Services 92
4.1 Personnel Scheduling 92
4.1.1 Mathematical Formulation 92
4.1.2 Impact of Breaks 93
4.2 Appointment Scheduling 94
4.2.1 Appointment Overbooking 94
4.2.2 Characteristics of Optimal Appointment Schedules 95
5 Managerial Implications 95
5.1 Design of Scheduling Systems 95
5.2 Dealing with Randomness 97
6 Conclusions and Future Research Directions 97
References and Bibliography 98

6   Inventory Management   101
Prem Vrat
1 Introduction 101
2 Functions of Inventory 102
3 Inventory Problem Formulation 103
    3.1 Inventory Policy 103
    3.2 Inventory Models 104
4 Inventory Research—A Historical Profile 106
5 Some Select Inventory Models 111
    5.1 The Classical EOQ Model 111
    5.2 Variants of the Classical EOQ Model 112
        5.2.1 A Generalized Type (1, 2, 3) System 114
        5.2.2 Inventory Model with Lost Sales Case 114
    5.3 Multi-Item Single Source EOQ Model: Coordinated Replenishment 115
    5.4 A Simple Model for Periodic Review Policy 115
    5.5 Inventory Models with Quantity Discounts 116
    5.6 Probabilistic Inventory Models with Demand and/or Supply Variability 117
        5.6.1 Inventory Models for Slow-Moving Items 119
6 Inventory Related Issues and Their Implications on Practicing Managers 120
7 Role of Professional Societies in Promoting Scientific Inventory Management 121
8 Some Suggested Areas for Future Research Efforts 122
9 Concluding Remarks 123
References and Bibliography 123

7   Quality Management   125
Peter W. Robertson, Martin K. Starr, and Sushil K. Gupta
1 Introduction 125

- 2 The Context of QM Successes and Failures 126
- 3 A Compelling Case for Achieving Quality Management Excellence in POM 127
- 4 A Brief History of Quality Management 128
  - 4.1 Key Figures 128
  - 4.2 After World War II 131
- 5 Present Situations 132
  - 5.1 Malcolm Baldrige National Quality Award 132
  - 5.2 ISO 9001 2015 132
  - 5.3 Quality Function Deployment (QFD) 133
  - 5.4 Statistical Process Control (SPC) 135
  - 5.5 Quality Improvement (QI) Story 140
  - 5.6 Six Sigma 140
  - 5.7 Lean 141
  - 5.8 Lean Six Sigma 141
  - 5.9 Design for Manufacture and Assembly (DFMA) 142
  - 5.10 Quality Risk Management and Quality Recovery Plans 142
  - 5.11 Quality Management Themes 142
  - 5.12 Quality Culture 143
- 6 Future Projections 143
- 7 Further Research Directions 144
- References and Bibliography 145

8 Facilities Design and Planning   147
Sunderesh S. Heragu and Ahmed Jamoussi
- 1 Introduction 147
- 2 Motivating Case Study 147
- 3 Flow Patterns and Flow Process Charts 149
  - 3.1 Flow Patterns 149
  - 3.2 Flow Process Chart 149
- 4 Facilities Layout 152
  - 4.1 Types of Layout 152
  - 4.2 Systematic Layout Planning 152
  - 4.3 Algorithms and Software for Layout Planning 153
    - 4.3.1 Layout Algorithms 153
    - 4.3.2 Software for Layout Design 153
- 5 Materials Handling 155
  - 5.1 Types of Material Handling Devices 155
  - 5.2 Automated MHDs Used in a Shipping Port 156
  - 5.3 Ten Principles of Materials Handling 157
- 6 Warehouse Design 158
  - 6.1 Warehouse Storage Policies 158
- 7 Trends in Facilities Design 160
  - 7.1 Material Handling and Logistics US Roadmap: Trends 160
    - 7.1.1 E-Commerce 160

       7.1.2   Competition among Third-Party Logistics Providers 161
       7.1.3   Mass Customization 161
       7.1.4   Urbanization 161
       7.1.5   Mobile and Wearable Computing 161
       7.1.6   Robotics and Automation 161
       7.1.7   Sensors and the Internet of Things 161
       7.1.8   Big Data and Predictive Analytics 162
       7.1.9   The Changing Workforce 162
       7.1.10 Sustainability 162
    7.2 Material Handling and Logistics US Roadmap: Capabilities by 2025 162
       7.2.1   Total Supply Chain Visibility 163
       7.2.2   Standardization 163
       7.2.3   High-Speed Delivery 163
       7.2.4   Low-Cost, Low-Impact Materials Handling and Logistics 163
       7.2.5   Planning and Optimization 164
       7.2.6   Impact of E-Commerce 164
       7.2.7   Collaboration 164
    7.3 Energy and Resource Efficient Manufacturing 164
    7.4 Leadership in Energy and Environmental Design 165
    7.5 Implications for Managers 165
    7.6 Directions for Future Research 166
  References and Bibliography 167

9 Manufacturing Strategy   169
   Raffaella Cagliano and Federico Caniato
   1 Introduction 169
   2 The Strategic Role of Manufacturing Operations 170
   3 Key Concepts in Manufacturing Strategy 171
      3.1 Manufacturing Strategy Content 171
      3.2 Manufacturing Strategy Process 172
   4 Manufacturing Paradigms 172
      4.1 The Most Relevant Manufacturing Paradigms 173
         4.1.1 World Class Manufacturing 173
         4.1.2 Lean Production 173
         4.1.3 Strategically Flexible Production 173
         4.1.4 Other Manufacturing Strategy Paradigms 173
         4.1.5 Smart Manufacturing: The Emerging Manufacturing Paradigm 174
      4.2 Manufacturing Paradigm Versus Strategic Choices: The Debate 174
   5 The Strategic Goals of Manufacturing Operations 175
      5.1 Strategic Trade-Offs and Cumulative Capabilities 175
         5.1.1 The Trade-Off Model 176
         5.1.2 The Cumulative Model 176
         5.1.3 The Integrative Model 176
      5.2 Strategic Configurations 177

6 Manufacturing Decisions 177
   6.1 Manufacturing Decisions from a Contingency Perspective 178
   6.2 Manufacturing Improvement Programs and Best Practices 178
7 Manufacturing Strategy and the Evolution of Technology 179
   7.1 Automation 180
   7.2 The Role of Information Technology 180
   7.3 Flexible Technologies 180
   7.4 Digital Technologies 180
   7.5 New Technologies 181
8 Global Manufacturing Strategies 181
   8.1 Enablers and Drivers 181
   8.2 Plant Location 182
   8.3 Manufacturing Networks 182
   8.4 Recent Trends 183
9 How to Research Manufacturing Strategy 183
   9.1 Large-Scale Surveys 183
   9.2 Limitations and Future Developments 184
10 New Challenges for Manufacturing Strategy 184
References and Bibliography 185

PART III
POM Process and Project Categories   195

10 Process Capabilities and Leveraging Advances in Science and Technology   197
Cheryl Gaimon, Manpreet Hora, and Karthik Ramachandran
   1 Introduction 197
      1.1 Process Capabilities and New Product Development 197
      1.2 Process Capabilities and Profitability 198
      1.3 Recent Advances in Process Capabilities 199
      1.4 Greenfield Versus Brownfield Change to Process Capabilities 199
   2 Managing Internal Knowledge to Develop Process Capabilities 200
      2.1 Integrating Product and Process Knowledge in a Single NPD Project 200
      2.2 Derivative and Radical NPD Projects 202
         2.2.1 A Radical NPD Project 202
         2.2.2 Funding Radical and Derivative NPD Projects 203
      2.3 Investments in Technical Support 203
   3 Managing External Knowledge to Develop Process Capabilities 204
      3.1 Alliances in a Supply Network 204
      3.2 Alliances with Competitors 204
         3.2.1 Trade-Offs in Coopetitive Development 205
      3.3 Acquiring Knowledge from Non-Competing Firms 205
   4 Future Opportunities for Research 206
      4.1 Leveraging Internal Knowledge 206

    4.2 Leveraging External Knowledge 207
        4.2.1 Alliances in a Supply Network 207
        4.2.2 Alliances with Competitors 207
        4.2.3 Acquiring Knowledge from a Non-Competing Firm 208
  5 Implications for Practitioners 208
  6 Conclusion 209
  References and Bibliography 210

11 Project Design and Management   214
Tyson R. Browning
  1 Introduction 214
  2 Looking Back at PM Research 215
    2.1 Activity Scheduling 215
    2.2 PM Tool Development 216
    2.3 Organizational Coordination 216
    2.4 Product Development (PD) and Innovation Management 217
    2.5 Project Portfolio Management (PPM) 217
    2.6 Other Empirical Research 218
    2.7 Perspective 218
  3 Looking Around: The Current Situation in PM Research 219
    3.1 Agile PM 220
    3.2 Factors Distinguishing Different Types of Projects and PM Methods 220
    3.3 People, Teams, Behaviors, and Knowledge Management 221
    3.4 Outsourcing and Partnering with Other Organizations 221
    3.5 Systems Views and Structural Models 222
    3.6 Measuring Progress and Value 223
  4 Looking Forward: Opportunities for Future PM Research 224
  5 Implications for Managers 226
  6 Conclusion 226
  References and Bibliography 227

12 From Lean Production to Operational Excellence   234
Pauline Found, Donna Samuel, and James Lyons
  1 Introduction 234
  2 Emergence of Lean Production 235
    2.1 Toyota Production System (TPS) 235
    2.2 Total Quality Management (TQM) 238
    2.3 Total Productive Maintenance (TPM) 239
  3 Evolution of Lean Production Research 239
    3.1 Lean and the Interactions with Traditional Cost Accounting 242
    3.2 Other Business Improvement Systems in OM 242
        3.2.1 Six Sigma 243
        3.2.2 Agile Manufacturing 243
        3.2.3 Theory of Constraints (TOC) 244

4 Contemporary and Future Research in Lean Operations Management 244
   4.1 Systems Thinking 245
   4.2 Operational Excellence 245
5 Future Research Directions 247
6 Conclusions 247
References and Bibliography 248

PART IV
Emerging Themes and New Research Domains of POM   253

13 Business Startup Operations   255
Nitin Joglekar, Moren Lévesque, and Sinan Erzurumlu
  1 Introduction 255
  2 What We Know about Business Startup Operations 257
    2.1 Review Articles 257
    2.2 Findings in Recent Publications 258
  3 Emergent Opportunities 264
    3.1 New Digital Technologies 264
      3.1.1 Connectivity Based Analytics 264
      3.1.2 Low-Cost Intelligent Robotics 266
    3.2 Business Model Innovations 266
    3.3 Research Implications 267
      3.3.1 Alignment between BMIs and OIs 267
      3.3.2 Platform Economics 269
    3.4 Managerial Implications 270
  4 Conclusion 271
  References and Bibliography 271

14 Sustainable Operations   276
Tharanga K. Rajapakshe, Asoo J. Vakharia, Lan Wang, and Arda Yenipazarli
  1 Introduction 276
    1.1 Why Focus on Sustainability? 276
    1.2 Operations/Supply Chain Management and Sustainability 277
      1.2.1 Product/Process Design and Sustainability 277
      1.2.2 Sustainability in Supply Chains 277
      1.2.3 Environmental Legislations 277
    1.3 Organization of This Chapter 278
  2 Product Design and Process Development 278
    2.1 Green Product Design and Environmental Performance 278
    2.2 Why Don't Consumers Buy Green Products? 279
    2.3 Innovation in Green Product Design 280
    2.4 Green Product Offering Strategies 280

3 Supply Chains 281
   3.1 Forward Supply Chains 281
      3.1.1 Product and Retail Competition 281
      3.1.2 Component Commonality and Remanufacturing 281
      3.1.3 Order Quantities and Customer Environmental Concerns 282
   3.2 Reverse Supply Chains 282
      3.2.1 Reverse Supply Chain Networks 282
      3.2.2 Managing the Collection Process 283
      3.2.3 Remanufacturing 283
4 Environmental Legislation 284
   4.1 Life-Cycle Assessment and New Product Introduction 284
   4.2 Extended Producer Responsibility (EPR) 285
   4.3 Policy Implications 286
5 Directions for Future Research 287
References and Bibliography 288

15 The Interdependence of Data Analytics and Operations Management 291
   Kaushik Dutta, Abhijeet Ghoshal, and Subodha Kumar
   1 Introduction 291
   2 Retail Operations 291
      2.1 Design Aspects of Recommender Systems 292
      2.2 Future Research on Recommender Systems 292
         2.2.1 Algorithm Design 292
         2.2.2 Recommendations Considering Trade-Offs 293
      2.3 Economic and Supply Chain Problems on Recommender Systems 293
         2.3.1 Effect of Recommendations on the Overall Supply Chain 293
         2.3.2 Information Sharing within a Supply Chain 294
   3 Mobile 294
      3.1 Existing Research on Using Data from Mobile Devices and Platforms 294
         3.1.1 Impact of Advertisements on Sales 295
         3.1.2 Location Determination of Users 295
      3.2 Future Research in the Space of Mobile Technology 295
         3.2.1 Operations of Mobile Phones 295
         3.2.2 Operations of Mobile Apps 296
         3.2.3 Operations of Mobile Network Service 296
   4 Online Advertising 296
      4.1 Advertisement Scheduling 297
      4.2 Real-Time Bidding Platforms 297
         4.2.1 The Ad Allocation Problem 297
         4.2.2 Audience Targeting in Mobile Apps 297

   4.2.3 Technology Challenges 298
   4.2.4 Auctioning Strategies 298
   4.2.5 Security and Privacy Research 298
 5 Smart Cities 298
  5.1 Existing Research on the Use of Big Data for City Planning 299
   5.1.1 City Transportation 299
   5.1.2 City Energy Needs 299
   5.1.3 Law Enforcement 300
  5.2 Future Research Directions for Smart Cities 300
   5.2.1 Potential Applications in Disaster Management 300
 6 Energy 301
  6.1 Generation and Distribution of Energy 301
  6.2 Energy Consumption 301
 7 Healthcare 302
  7.1 Existing Research in Healthcare 302
   7.1.1 Healthcare and Information Technology 302
   7.1.2 Device Manufacturing 303
   7.1.3 Role of Online Communities in Healthcare 303
  7.2 Potential Questions for Future Research 303
   7.2.1 Healthcare Information Exchange 303
   7.2.2 Privacy 303
   7.2.3 Online Communities 304
   7.2.4 Devices 304
 8 Implications for Managers 304
 9 Conclusions and Directions for Future Research 305
 References and Bibliography 305

16 The Evolution of Logistics Clusters 309
 Yossi Sheffi and Liliana Rivera
 1 Introduction 309
 2 Literature Review of Industrial Clusters 310
  2.1 Increased Productivity and Innovation 310
  2.2 Agglomeration Versus Dispersion 311
  2.3 Logistics Clusters 311
 3 Development of Logistics Clusters 312
 4 Logistics Clusters Benefits—Intra-Cluster Collaboration 312
  4.1 Transportation Capacity Sharing 312
  4.2 Warehouse Capacity Sharing 313
  4.3 Labor Sharing 313
  4.4 Information Sharing 313
 5 Logistics Clusters Benefits—Value-Added Services 314
  5.1 Postponement and Customization 314
  5.2 Retail Display Arrangement 315

        5.3 Kitting 315
        5.4 End-of-Runway Location 315
    6 Logistics Clusters Benefits—Innovation 316
        6.1 Environmental Innovation 316
        6.2 Intra-Organizational Inter-Cluster Innovation Transfer 316
    7 Logistics Clusters Benefits—Jobs 317
        7.1 Blue- and White-Collar Jobs 317
        7.2 Sub-Cluster Development and Jobs 317
        7.3 Education and Training 318
        7.4 Upward Mobility 318
    8 The Future of Logistics Clusters 318
        8.1 Factors Leading to Logistics Clusters Growth 319
        8.2 Factors Leading to Possible Decline of Logistics Clusters 319
    9 Implications for Practitioners and Policy Makers 320
        9.1 Considerations of Site Selection 320
        9.2 Globalization 320
        9.3 Support for Cluster Development: Zoning, Connectivity, and Finance 321
        9.4 Regulations and Taxes 321
        9.5 International Trade 321
    10 Future Research Opportunities 322
    References and Bibliography 323

17 Human Behavior in Operations   326
    Elliot Bendoly, Adam McClintock, and Rahul Pandey
    1 Introduction 326
    2 A Brief Historical Overview 327
        2.1 Early Rumbling of a Domain 327
        2.2 The BeOps Renaissance 328
    3 Contemporary Foundations from Aligned Domains 329
        3.1 Cognitive Psychology 329
            3.1.1 Common Biases 330
            3.1.2 Established Heuristics 332
        3.2 Group and Social Influences 333
        3.3 System Dynamics and Systems Thinking 334
    4 Designing for Behavior: Bridging OM Science and Practice 335
        4.1 Anticipating Cuts and Pastes 335
            4.1.1 Set Biases 336
            4.1.2 Trend Biases 336
            4.1.3 Casual Biases 337
    5 Conclusions 337
        5.1 Best Practices in Design for OM Tools 337
        5.2 Implications for Practitioners 338
        5.3 Directions for Future Research 339
    References and Bibliography 340

PART V
POM Interface with Other Functions 343

18 Management Accounting and Operations Management 345
   Thomas Hemmer and Eva Labro
   1 Introduction 345
   2 The Importance of Considering Incentives and Performance Measurement in Optimizing Operations 346
      2.1 Introduction to Performance Measurement and Incentives 346
         2.1.1 Agency Theory 346
         2.1.2 The Sufficient Statistic Condition 347
         2.1.3 Implications for Operations Management 348
      2.2 Throughput Maximization and Capacity Constraints 349
         2.2.1 An Operations Management Perspective on Throughput Maximization Under Capacity Constraints 349
         2.2.2 A Management Accounting Perspective on Throughput Maximization Under Capacity Constraints 350
         2.2.3 Alternate Solutions Proposed by the Management Accounting Perspective 351
            2.2.3.1 Profit Sharing 351
            2.2.3.2 Performance Measurement and the Balanced Scorecard 351
      2.3 Push Versus Pull Production 352
         2.3.1 An Operations Management Perspective on Push Versus Pull Production 352
         2.3.2 A Management Accounting Perspective on Push Versus Pull Production 352
            2.3.2.1 Incentives Under the Push System 352
            2.3.2.2 Incentives Under the Pull System 353
            2.3.2.3 A Measure of Intermediate Product Quality 353
      2.4 Implications for Practice 354
   3 The Importance of Considering Operations When Designing Cost Measurement Systems 354
      3.1 The Mechanics of Cost Measurement 354
         3.1.1 Traditional Costing Methods 354
         3.1.2 Activity-Based Costing 355
         3.1.3 Time-Driven Activity-Based Costing 355
      3.2 Operations Management Choices Affecting Cost Measurement Accuracy 356
         3.2.1 Validity of the ABC Hierarchy 356
         3.2.2 Cost of Product Variety 356
      3.3 Implications for Practice 357
   4 Directions for Future Research 358
      4.1 Service Sector Considerations 358
      4.2 Accounting Information Technology Advances 358
      4.3 Dynamic Cost Measurement in Specific Operations Environments 358
   References and Bibliography 359

19 POM and Finance 360
John R. Birge
1 Introduction 360
2 Impact of Financing Needs on Single Firm Operational Decisions 361
3 Impact of Financial Markets on Single Firm Operational Decisions 362
4 Impact of Financial Considerations on Supply Chain Operations 367
5 Impact of Operational Decisions on Financial Asset Prices 368
6 Empirical Results in Operations and Finance Interactions 368
7 Conclusions and Future Research Directions 370
References and Bibliography 370

20 POM and Marketing 374
Manoj K. Malhotra, Ramkumar Janakiraman, Saurabh Mishra, and Moonwon Chung
1 Introduction 374
2 Input Context-Multichannel Retailing as a Challenge to Customer Segmentation, Inventory Management, and Reverse Logistics 375
   2.1 Complex Market Segments 376
   2.2 Increased Inventory Volatility 377
   2.3 Returned and Remanufactured Products 377
3 Process Coordination: Intra-/Inter-Firm Issues in POM and Marketing Interface 378
   3.1 Focus on Micro-Level Process Integration with Data Rich Forecasting 378
   3.2 Joint Capability Planning 379
   3.3 Reverse Logistics and Sustainability 380
4 Output Consequence: Complementarity Between POM and Marketing for Building Shareholder Wealth 381
   4.1 Theoretical Frameworks for Research on Shareholder Wealth 381
   4.2 Current Research on Shareholder Wealth in POM and Marketing 382
5 Future POM and Marketing Interface Research Avenues 383
   5.1 Deepening Consumer Knowledge and Channel Dynamics Across Channels 383
   5.2 Designing Better Socially Responsible and Environmentally Sustainable Processes in POM and Marketing 385
   5.3 Fostering Complementarity Between POM and Marketing Capabilities 386
6 Implications for Practitioners 386
7 Conclusion and Future Research Directions 387
References and Bibliography 387

21 The Strategic Role of Human Resources in Enabling POM 392
Robert K. Prescott, Henrique L. Correa, and Adeola O. Shabiyi
1 Introduction 392
   1.1 Purpose of the Chapter 392
   1.2 Background 392

Contents

2 A Call for Synergy Between Human Resources and Production and Operations Management 393
   2.1 A Strategic Imperative—Review of the Literature 393
   2.2 Current Trends in Human Resources Management (HRM) 394
      2.2.1 Human Capital Research and Analytics 394
      2.2.2 Integrating HR Practices with POM 394
      2.2.3 Organizational Development (OD) and Human Resources (HR) in Production and Operations Management (POM) 394
   2.3 Best Practices in Human Resources Management (HRM) 395
      2.3.1 Internal HR Professionals and POM 395
      2.3.2 Human Resources (HR) and the Organizational Performance Linkage 396
      2.3.3 The HR–Performance Linkage and Geographic Implications 396
      2.3.4 The HR–Performance Linkage and Learning 397
   2.4 Current Issues in Production and Operations Management (POM) 397
      2.4.1 Human Resources (HR) and Production and Operations Management (POM) Research 397
      2.4.2 HR and Operations Practices and Organizational Performance 399
      2.4.3 Group Social Dynamics and Performance 399
      2.4.4 Cross-Functional Coordination, Information Systems Capability, and Performance 399
      2.4.5 Systems Thinking and Performance 400
3 Professional Perspective 400
   3.1 Explanatory Survey with HR and POM Leaders—"A Synthesis of Needs" 400
   3.2 Results 401
      3.2.1 How Is the Overall Role of SHRM Evaluated by Industry Production and Operations Leaders and Managers? 401
      3.2.2 How Is the Partnership Role of SHRM with POM Evaluated by Industry Human Resources Leaders and Managers? 401
      3.2.3 What Is the Contemporary Role of SHRM in POM? 402
      3.2.4 How Can SHRM Enable POM? 402
   3.3 Survey Conclusions 402
      3.3.1 HR and POM Partnership 402
      3.3.2 HR and POM Best Practices 403
      3.3.3 HR as a Change Agent 404
4 HR Enabling POM to Win the Talent War 404
5 Implications for Managers 407
6 Recommendations for Future Research 407
7 Conclusions 408
References and Bibliography 408

PART VI
POM Domains of Application   411

22 Operations Management in Hospitality   413
   Rohit Verma, Lu Kong, and Zhen Lin
   1 Introduction 413
   2 The Essence of Hospitality 414
   3 Product and Service Innovation in Hospitality 414
   4 Integrating Service Quality in Operational Processes 415
   5 The Role of Employees 415
   6 Demand and Capacity Management 416
   7 Yield and Revenue Management 416
   8 Ownership Structure, Franchising, and Cost of Operations 417
   9 Start-Up of New Locations and Managing Hospitality Projects 418
   10 Managing Risk and Disruption 419
   11 Role of Lean Thinking and Sustainable Operations in Hospitality 420
   12 The Role of New Media in Managing Hospitality Operations 420
   13 Directions for Future Research 421
   References and Bibliography 423

23 POM for Healthcare—Focusing on the Upstream: Management
   of Preventive and Emergency Care   427
   Vedat Verter
   1 Introduction 427
   2 POM for Preventive Care 430
      2.1 Preventive Care Processes 430
      2.2 A Basic Formulation for Designing Preventive Care Networks 431
      2.3 Extended Models for Preventive Care 432
   3 POM for Emergency Care 433
      3.1 Key Challenges in ED Management 434
      3.2 Simulation of ED Processes 435
      3.3 A Case Study in ED Triage 436
   4 Implications for Managers 439
   5 Conclusions and Future Research Directions 440
   References and Bibliography 440

24 Sports Operations Management: The Whole Nine Yards   443
   *David Bamford, Benjamin Dehe, Iain Reid, James Bamford,
   and Marina Papalexi*
   1 Introduction 443
   2 Past History 443

3 Present Situation 450
   3.1 Design of Sports Operations 451
   3.2 Planning and Control of Sports Operations 452
   3.3 Improvement of Operations 453
   3.4 Data in Sports 455
4 Future Projections and Opportunities 456
   4.1 Key Performance Indicators 458
   4.2 Implications for Practitioners 459
5 Conclusions 460
References and Bibliography 460

25 POM in Agriculture: Pastoral Farming in New Zealand — 467
David Gray and Nicola M. Shadbolt

1 Introduction 467
2 Normative Versus Descriptive Research 467
3 Tactical Management Process 468
   3.1 The Planning Process 470
      3.1.1 Informal Planning Process 470
      3.1.2 Formal Planning Process 472
4 The Plan 475
   4.1 The Predictive Planning Schedule 477
   4.2 Targets 478
   4.3 Contingency Plans 479
5 The Control Process 480
   5.1 Monitoring 482
      5.1.1 The Factors that are Monitored 482
      5.1.2 Monitoring Methods 483
      5.1.3 The Role of Information from the Monitoring Process 484
      5.1.4 Activation, Termination, and Frequency of Monitoring 485
   5.2 Decision Point Recognition 486
   5.3 Diagnosis 487
   5.4 Limits to Control and the Environment 489
   5.5 Control Responses 491
6 Implications for Practitioners 492
7 Conclusion 492
References and Bibliography 493

26 POM and the Military — 497
Keenan D. Yoho and Wayne P. Hughes Jr.

1 Introduction: Differentiating the Improvement of Arsenals from the Application of Weapons, Strategy, and Tactics in War 497
   1.1 Differentiating the Character of Operations Management in the Civilian and Military Contexts 497
   1.2 The Pirandello Principle 498

    2 Past History 498
        2.1 Bringing Advances in Military Operational Research to Civilian Operations Management 500
    3 Present Situation 501
        3.1 The Problems of Search, Optimization, and Exchange 501
    4 Future Projections as the Character of Conflict Changes 502
        4.1 High-End Warfare 503
        4.2 Warfare with Non-State Actors 503
    5 Implications for Managers 504
    6 Directions for Future Research 505
    References and Bibliography 505

27 Not-for-Profit Operations Management   510
    Qi Feng and J. George Shanthikumar
    1 Introduction 510
    2 Fundraising for Not-for-Profit Operations 511
        2.1 Funding Instability and Prediction 512
        2.2 Funding Restrictions and Contingencies 513
    3 Revenue Management and Pricing 514
    4 Resource Management 515
    5 Distribution of Product and Service 517
        5.1 The Choice of Product or Service Offering 517
        5.2 The Supply Process and Inventory Management 518
        5.3 Allocation and Consumer Behavior 520
    6 Performance Evaluation 520
    7 Implications for Managers 521
    8 Directions for Future Research 521
    References and Bibliography 522

28 Telecommunications and Operations Management   527
    Subodha Kumar, Kaushik Dutta, and Yonghua Ji
    1 Introduction 527
    2 Network Infrastructure 527
        2.1 Network Design and Interconnection 527
        2.2 Capacity Planning 528
        2.3 Capacity Allocation and Sharing 529
        2.4 Network Security Design 530
        2.5 Network Risk Management 530
        2.6 Future Research 531
    3 Network Operations 531
        3.1 Operations Management of Caching 531
        3.2 Content Delivery Network 533
            3.2.1 Content Distribution and Request Routing 533
            3.2.2 Allocation of Capacity 533

         3.2.3 Capacity Pricing 534
         3.2.4 Future Research 534
      3.3 Operations Management of Cloud Computing 534
         3.3.1 Job Scheduling in the Cloud 534
         3.3.2 Resource Optimization in the Cloud 535
         3.3.3 Future Research 535
   4 Applications of Telecommunications in Operations 536
      4.1 Humanitarian Operations 536
         4.1.1 Online Education 536
         4.1.2 Disaster Recovery and Rescue Operations 536
         4.1.3 Further Research 537
      4.2 Healthcare Operations 537
         4.2.1 Tele-Medicine 537
         4.2.2 Health Information Exchanges (HIEs) 537
         4.2.3 Future Research 538
      4.3 Homeland Security Applications 538
         4.3.1 Further Research 538
   5 Implications for Managers 539
   6 Conclusions and Directions for Future Research 539
   References and Bibliography 539

29 POM for Disaster Management   543
   Peter W. Robertson, Sushil K. Gupta, and Martin K. Starr
   1 Introduction 543
   2 Context 543
   3 Compelling Case for the Achievement of Disaster Management
     Excellence in POM 544
   4 Past History 547
   5 Present Situation 548
      5.1 Explanation of Figure 29.1—Disaster Management Cycle 548
      5.2 Present DM Taxonomies 548
      5.3 Present DM Typologies 550
   6 Future Projections 551
   7 Disaster Management Research 553
   8 Implications for Managers 555
   9 Future Research Directions 555
   References and Bibliography 556

30 The Impact of POM on Transport and Logistics   557
   Dongping Song
   1 Introduction 557
   2 Transport Modes and Features 558
      2.1 Road Transport 558
      2.2 Rail Transport 558

- 2.3 Air Transport 559
- 2.4 Water (Maritime) Transport 559
- 2.5 Pipeline Transport 559
- 2.6 Comparison of Transport Modes 559
- 3 Transport Systems and Key Performance Indicators (KPIs) 560
  - 3.1 Transport Systems 560
  - 3.2 KPIs 561
- 4 POM Research in Transport and Logistics 561
  - 4.1 Service Network Design 562
    - 4.1.1 Solution Techniques 563
  - 4.2 Fleet Sizing and Deployment 564
  - 4.3 Vehicle/Inventory Routing and Scheduling 565
    - 4.3.1 Vehicle Routing Problem (VRP) 565
    - 4.3.2 Inventory Routing Problem 566
    - 4.3.3 Cargo Routing Problem 566
    - 4.3.4 Schedule Design Problem 566
  - 4.4 Speed Management and Slow Streaming 567
  - 4.5 Empty Vehicle/Container Management 567
    - 4.5.1 Empty Vehicle Management 568
    - 4.5.2 Empty Container Management 568
  - 4.6 Disruption Management 568
  - 4.7 Crew Scheduling and Rostering 569
  - 4.8 Port/Terminal Management 570
  - 4.9 Emission Management 571
- 5 Implications for Managers 572
- 6 Directions for Future Research 572
  - 6.1 General POM Modelling Opportunities 572
    - 6.1.1 Objective Functions and Constraints 572
    - 6.1.2 Decision Integration 573
    - 6.1.3 Stochastic and Dynamic Operations 573
    - 6.1.4 Solution Techniques and Heuristic Rules 573
  - 6.2 Emerging ICT-Driven Opportunities 574
- References and Bibliography 574

31 POM and Retailing   579
Vishal Gaur
- 1 Introduction 579
- 2 A Historical Perspective of Research in Retail Operations 580
  - 2.1 Inventory Management 580
  - 2.2 Retail Supply Chains 582
  - 2.3 Customer Service 583
  - 2.4 Pricing and Clearance Markdowns 583
  - 2.5 Shelf Space Management 584

2.6 Assortment Planning 584
2.7 Financial Performance of Retailing Firms 585
3 Present Situation 586
   3.1 Store Execution and Workforce Management 587
   3.2 Online and Omnichannel Retailing 587
4 Directions for Future Research 588
   4.1 Availability of Individual Customer-Level High-Frequency Data Will Drive Research in New Decision Models and Experiments 589
   4.2 New In-Store Technologies Will Transform Retail Stores, Making Bricks and Clicks a Reality and Changing the Customer Experience 589
   4.3 Emerging Retail Formats, Warehouse Logistics, and Package Delivery Methods Will Create More Opportunities for Research 590
   4.4 Environmental Sustainability Will Grow as a Research Area in Retailing 590
   4.5 Merchandising and Sourcing Functions Will See Research in New Models 591
5 Implications for Practitioners 591
6 Conclusions 592
References and Bibliography 592

PART VII
Expert POM Practitioners' Perspectives   599

32 POM for the Hospitality Industry   601
   Lee Cockerell
   1 POM for the Hospitality Industry 601
   2 Mapping Customer Service—Managing Systems and Processes 601
   3 Management Is About Control 601
   4 Management Titles and POM Methods in the Hospitality Industry 602
   5 Walt Disney World® Principles for Success 602
      5.1 Chain of Excellence at Walt Disney World® 603
   6 Great Leader Strategies at Walt Disney World® 603
   7 The Disney World Purpose Statement 604
   8 Creating Disney World Magic 604
   9 Eliminate Hassles (Policies, Procedures, and Operating Guidelines) 604
   10 Stay Ahead of the Pack 605
   11 The Four Keys Model 606
   12 Learn to Tell a Good Story 606
      12.1 "Be Safe, Not Sorry!—Focused Attention Creates Positive Results" 607
      12.2 "Quality over Quantity . . . Quality Always Wins Out!" 607
      12.3 "Messy and Not Clean Look the Same to Guests/Customers" 607
      12.4 "9/11 Was the Saddest and Proudest Day of My Career" 608
      12.5 "How to Take the Wind Out of Hurricanes" 609

13 The Concept of POM: Find the Best Way to Do Everything and
   Then Do It That Way 609
References and Bibliography 610

33 Trends in Global Sourcing, Procurement, and Distribution
   Research and Practice   611
   Edwin Keh
   1 Global Trade's Role and Influence on Historical Developments 611
   2 The Modern Era of Global Trade 612
   3 Large-Scale Migration and Contract Manufacturing 613
   4 The Forces Influencing the New Global Trade—An Inflection Point 613
   5 Pollution and Other Costs to Consuming and Manufacturing 614
   6 New Consumption Models and the Complex Cycles
     of Global Sourcing 615
   7 Global Sourcing 616
   8 Procurement 617
   9 Costing 620
   10 Building Relationships Rather Than Making Transactions 621
   11 The Challenges of Distribution 622
   12 The Opportunities Ahead 622
   13 Effective Global Supply Chain Operations—A Product and Process
      Characteristics-Based Decision-Making Framework 623
      13.1 Product Characteristics 624
      13.2 Manufacturing Process Characteristics 624
   14 Implications for Future Research 630
   References and Bibliography 630

34 Best Practice: Supply Chain Optimization at Yihaodian   632
   Gang Yu and Ping (David) Yang
   1 Introduction 632
   2 Company Overview 632
   3 Industry Landscape and YHD's Supply Chain Strategy 633
   4 Supply Chain Models and YHD's Innovation 634
      4.1 Supplier Logistics Center (SLC) 635
      4.2 Pallet Pooling Service 637
      4.3 Aggregated Supplier Delivery 639
      4.4 Cross-Docking Logistics (CDL) 640
   5 Performance Improvements 641
   6 Future Development 641
      6.1 Collaborative Planning, Forecast, and Replenishment (CPFR) 642
      6.2 Data-Driven Supply Chain Management 642
   References and Bibliography 644

PART VIII
POM—The Next Era   **645**

35 The Evolutionary Trends of POM Research in Manufacturing   647
Tinglong Dai and Sridhar Tayur
  1 Introduction: Creating Wealth and Happiness, Massively 647
  2 Modern Manufacturing: An Orchestration of Technologies 649
  3 What Is Orchestrating Technology? 649
  4 Operational Innovations and PPOMs 650
    4.1 POM Inside the Factory 652
    4.2 POM Outside the Factory 654
    4.3 Interface Between the Inside and the Outside of the Factory 655
  5 Capital Versus Labor 657
  6 Implications for Managers 658
  7 Conclusion: The Future of POM and Manufacturing 659
  References and Bibliography 660

36 Future Trends for Research and Practice in the Management of
Global Supply Chains 663
Henrique L. Correa
  1 Introduction 663
    1.1 Increase in Volatility 663
    1.2 Increase in Complexity 664
    1.3 Increase in the Influence of Organized Society and Governments to Make Organizations Pursue the Triple Bottom Line (3BL) 664
  2 Implication of the Identified Trends for Practitioners 665
    2.1 Competencies to Deal with the Rise in Supply Chain Volatility 665
    2.2 Competencies to Deal with the Increase in Supply Chain Complexity 666
      2.2.1 The Use of Postponement 666
      2.2.2 Integration of Decision-Making Processes and Increased Collaboration 666
      2.2.3 The Use of New Technologies 667
      2.2.4 Segmentation of Supply Chains 667
    2.3 Competencies to Deal with the Increase in Pressure for 3BL 668
  3 Directions for Research in Supply Chain Management 669
    3.1 Supporting Theories 669
    3.2 Proposed Research Directions in Supply Chain Management 670
      3.2.1 Future Research Related to Increased Volatility 670
      3.2.2 Future Research Related to Increased Complexity 671
      3.2.3 Future Research Related to Increased 3BL Performance 672
  4 Conclusion 672
  References and Bibliography 673

37 Conclusions: Evaluation and Prognostications for the POM Domain   676
Sushil K. Gupta, Martin K. Starr, and Aleda Roth
  1 Summing Up the Accomplishments 676
  2 Reflections on the New Service Economy 677
  3 TRP—The Three Legs of the POM Stool 679
    3.1 POM Teaching and Learning 679
      3.1.1 POM in Business Schools 680
      3.1.2 Curriculum 680
      3.1.3 Teaching Materials 681
      3.1.4 Technology and Online 682
      3.1.5 Systems Approach/Interdisciplinary Teaching 683
      3.1.6 Experiential Learning 683
    3.2 Research and Modeling 684
      3.2.1 Models and Methodology 684
      3.2.2 Interdisciplinary Research 685
      3.2.3 Research Domains 686
      3.2.4 Publications Outlet 686
    3.3 New POM Practice Domains 686
      3.3.1 Emerging Application Areas 686
      3.3.2 Geographical Expansion 687
      3.3.3 POM and the Public Sector 687
        3.3.3.1 Regarding the First POM Interpretation 687
        3.3.3.2 Regarding the Second POM Interpretation 688
  4 Conclusions 688
  References and Bibliography 689
  Appendix 691

Index   693

ABOUT THE EDITORS

Vita of Dr. Martin K. Starr

Dr. Martin K. Starr is Distinguished Professor of Production and Operations Management Emeritus at the Crummer Graduate School of Business, Rollins College in Winter Park, Florida; also he is Emeritus Senior Professor of Operations Research, Management Science, and Operations Management at the Graduate School of Business at Columbia University in New York City.

As Director of the Center for Enterprise Management (CEM) at both schools, Dr. Starr spearheaded a series of comparative research studies of the performance of various manufacturing cultures over two decades starting in 1975. This resulted in understanding how Japanese manufacturing firms operating in the USA differed from their parent companies in Japan. Comparisons of Japanese, American, and European manufacturing firms operating in the USA revealed significant differences in their quality methods and process management. Later, CEM at Rollins conducted studies on how to reduce waste and effectuate lean and agile approaches to healthcare services in line with Efficient Healthcare Consumer Response (EHCR) criteria. Significant progress was made along various paths of the healthcare supply chain including the use of online telecommunications technology for homecare.

Dr. Starr has had a number of visiting professorships including The Hoover Fund Visiting Professor at the University of New South Wales in Sydney, Australia, the University of Cape Town, South Africa, the University of Southern California, and Ohio State University. Dr. Starr's activity with Executive Programs remains extensive. He has taught at Penn State at University Park, MIT—US Naval War College, Newport, RI, Rollins College Center for Management & Executive Education, Arden House for Columbia University, and many others. Additionally, he has made invited presentations at institutions such as the University of Western Ontario, Canada, Fundação Getúlio Vargas, São Paulo, Brazil, and Centro Studi D'Impresa, Valmadrera, Lecco, Italy.

Dr. Starr was elected a Fellow of the Production and Operations Management Society (POMS) in 2004. He is also a Fellow of INFORMS and Fellow of the American Association for the Advancement of Science (AAAS) since 1969. He is presently Director of Strategic Planning for POMS, and was President of POMS (1995–1996). He was President of TIMS (The Institute of Management Sciences; now INFORMS)—1974–1975; Editor-in-Chief of *Management Science* (Jan. 1967–June 1982); and Vice Dean, Graduate School of Business, Columbia University (1974–1975). He is now on the Board of various organizations including, the College of

Humanitarian Operations and Crisis Management, and POMS. In 1983 he received the George Kimball Medal for recognition of distinguished service to the profession of operations research and management science. In 2013 he received the *Sushil K. Gupta POMS Distinguished Service Award*.

Dr. Starr has authored 29 books on business topics, and over 100 papers. His research concerns knowledge creation and dissemination in POM (e.g., Commentary in *Production and Operations Management*, 2016, Vol. 25, Issue 9, pp.1489–1492), and modular production (Modular Production—a 45-year-old concept; Emerald; *International Journal of Operations & Production Management*, 2010, Vol. 30, Issue 1, pp.7–19). Dr. Starr has received teaching excellence awards from various schools including the Crummer GSB at Rollins and the GBS at Columbia University. *Production and Operations Management (POM)*, the flagship journal of POMS, published an article (2007) about his activities over the years—*Martin K. Starr: A Visionary Proponent for Systems Integration, Modular Production, and Catastrophe Avoidance* (by A. Roth and S. Gupta). "The Martin K. Starr Excellence in Production and Operations Management Practice Award" was instituted by POMS in 2006. Thus far, it has been awarded to twelve global leaders of operations management practice. He is co-Editor of the Special Issue on Humanitarian Operations and Crisis Management, *POM*, 2014.

Dr. Starr's consultancies have included Alabama Aircraft, American Express, AT&T, ABB, Boston Consulting Group, Bristol-Myers Squibb, Citibank, CNL, Chrysler, DuPont, Eastman Kodak, ExxonMobil, Fiat, GE Capital, Hendry Corporation, HP, IBM, Lever Brothers, McGraw-Hill Book Company, Merrill Lynch, Philips Electronics, Philips Healthcare, Unilever, United Nations, YPF de Argentina, and Young & Rubicam. Dr. Starr is presently Director of MKS Associates which offers POM, Supply Chain Management, and Analytics consulting services.

Dr. Starr holds the Bachelor of Science from Massachusetts Institute of Technology, Cambridge, MA. His MS and Ph.D. are from Columbia University in New York City.

Vita of Dr. Sushil K. Gupta

Dr. Sushil K. Gupta is a Professor and was simultaneously a Knight Ridder Center Research Fellow (2009–2015) in the College of Business, Florida International University (FIU), Miami, Florida, USA. He has taught at the Faculty of Management Studies (FMS), University of Delhi, Delhi, India (1969–1981), at the University of North Carolina, Greensboro, North Carolina, USA. (1981–1983), and at FIU (since 1983). Dr. Gupta has also served FIU as Vice Provost, Academic Affairs, and Associate Dean, College of Engineering. Dr. Gupta is an honorary professor at Universidad Ricardo Palma, Lima, Peru.

Dr. Gupta is a highly esteemed scholar in the field of Production and Operations Management. His research interests include production scheduling, mathematical modeling, project management, supply chain management, e-business, and disaster management. He has published in top-ranking professional journals including *Production and Operations Management, Management Science, IIE Transactions, European Journal of Operational Research, International Journal of Production Research, Omega, Computers and Industrial Engineering,* and *Socio-Economic Planning Sciences*.

Dr. Gupta is one of the founding members of the Production and Operations Management Society (POMS) and has played a key role in its initiation, development and growth. He was POMS Vice President for Member Activities (1994), POMS President (1996), and is currently serving as its Executive Director (since 1997). He also serves on the advisory board of *Production and Operations Management*—the flagship journal of POMS, POMS Board, and on the Board of POMS College of Humanitarian Operations and Crisis Management.

Dr. Gupta was elected a POMS Fellow in 2004. POMS also bestowed the honor on Dr. Gupta by awarding him the first POMS Distinguished Service Award in 2012. This award, starting in 2013, was renamed as the *Sushil K. Gupta POMS Distinguished Service Award* to honor Dr. Gupta for his dedicated services to POMS.

Dr. Gupta is very active in community service. The Association of Indians in America (AIA), the oldest national association of Asian Indians in America, founded in 1967, gave Dr. Gupta a special recognition award for his academic achievements and for promoting a better understanding between the people of India and the United States of America in 2013.

Dr. Gupta has been the recipient of many other prestigious awards that include: the "FIU Foundation Excellence in Research/Scholarship" award (1987), "Distinguished Scholarly Research Award" of the College of Business, FIU, (1984), "Fulbright Fellowship" to do research work at the Sloan School of Management, Massachusetts Institute of Technology, USA. (1977–1978), Commonwealth Scholarship for graduate work at the University of Toronto, Toronto, Canada, (1972–1974), and the Dr. V.K.R.V. Rao Gold Medal for his first place ranking in the MBA graduating class (1969), Delhi, India.

Dr. Gupta is a co-author of *Production and Operations Management Systems*, published by CRC Press/Taylor & Francis, 2014. He is also a co-author of *POMS—Production and Operations Management Software*, a software package published by Allyn & Bacon (1986) for an operations management course. In addition, he has written two books that include I, published by University of Delhi, Delhi, India (1979), and *Production Scheduling Techniques*, published by K.P. Bagchi and Company, Delhi, India (1981).

Dr. Gupta has developed a website for online learning of Production and Operations Management. He is very proficient in the use of Excel spreadsheets and has developed macro-based Excel spreadsheets to be used by instructors and students. He teaches fully online POM undergraduate and Corporate M.B.A. courses at FIU. Dr. Gupta has also received the teaching excellence award from the College of Business, FIU.

Dr. Gupta, in his capacity as the director of Corporate and Global Programs in the College of Engineering, initiated the development and promotion of the College of Engineering's corporate and global programs in many countries that include China, Colombia, Dominican Republic, India, Jamaica, Mexico, Peru, Taiwan, Turkey, Venezuela, and Yugoslavia.

Dr. Gupta holds the Bachelor of Technology in Mechanical Engineering from the Indian Institute of Technology, Bombay, India, M.B.A. from the Faculty of Management Studies (FMS), University of Delhi, India, Master of Applied Sciences in Industrial Engineering from University of Toronto, Canada, and Ph.D. from FMS, University of Delhi, India.

Dr. Gupta migrated to the USA. from India in 1981. He is a citizen of the USA.

CONTRIBUTORS

Dr. David Bamford is a Professor of Operations Management at the University of Huddersfield in England. Dr. Bamford is an experienced industrialist/academic with multiple publications to his name. Knowledge transfer projects across many sectors have been central to his academic career, and his research interests are focused towards operations improvement strategies in the application of operations management theories, strategic organizational change, leadership and quality management, and sports operations management.

Mr. James Bamford is an experienced academic and Senior Lecturer at the University of Huddersfield, UK, with a background in the health and service sectors. His research interests are focused towards operations management and improvement in the health sector, innovation, strategic organizational change, leadership, quality management, and sports operations management.

Dr. Elliot Bendoly is a Professor in the Management Sciences department Ohio State University's Fisher College of Business. Before joining Fisher, Dr. Bendoly was the Caldwell Research Fellow and Associate Professor at Emory University. He serves as Senior Editor at the *Production and Operations Management* journal (Behavioral Operations and Management of Technology departments) and as Associate Editor for the *Journal of Operations Management*. His own publications in *POM* and *JOM*, combined with his works in *Information Systems Research*, *MIS Quarterly*, and the *Journal of Applied Psychology*, represent no less than twenty-two published academic articles. An additional twenty-eight articles appear in other well-regarded peer reviewed outlets. Dr. Bendoly is the author of *Excel Basics to Black Belt* as well as the co-editor of *Strategic ERP Extension and Use*, *Handbook of Research in Enterprise Systems*, the *Handbook of Behavioral Operations Management*, and the forthcoming book *Visual Analytics for Management*.

Dr. John R. Birge is the Jerry W. and Carol Lee Levin Professor of Operations Management at the University of Chicago's Booth School of Business. Previously, he was Dean of the McCormick School of Engineering and Applied Science and Professor of Industrial Engineering and Management Sciences at Northwestern University. Dr. Birge has also served as Professor and Chair of Industrial and Operations Engineering at the University of Michigan, where he also established the Financial Engineering Program. He is former Editor-in-Chief of *Mathematical Programming, Series B*, and former President of the Institute for Operations Research and the

Management Sciences (INFORMS). His honors and awards include the IIE Medallion Award, the INFORMS Fellows Award, the MSOM Society Distinguished Fellow Award, the Harold W. Kuhn Prize, the George E. Kimball Medal, the William Pierskalla Award, and election to the US National Academy of Engineering. Dr. Birge received M.S. and Ph.D. degrees from Stanford University in Operations Research and an A.B. in Mathematics from Princeton University.

Dr. Tyson R. Browning is a Professor of Operations Management in the Neeley School of Business at Texas Christian University (TCU). Dr. Browning conducts research on managing complex projects and teaches MBA courses on project management, operations management, risk management, and process improvement. He earned a B.S. in Engineering Physics from Abilene Christian University as well as two Master's degrees and a Ph.D. from MIT. Prior to joining TCU in 2003, he worked at Lockheed Martin Aeronautics Company. He has also worked for the Lean Aerospace Initiative at MIT and Los Alamos National Laboratory and served as a consultant for several organizations, including BNSF Railway, General Motors, Seagate, and the U.S. Navy. His research appears in *California Management Review*, *IEEE Transactions on Engineering Management*, *Journal of Operations Management*, *Manufacturing & Service Operations Management*, *MIT Sloan Management Review*, *Production and Operations Management*, *Project Management Journal*, *Systems Engineering*, and other respected journals. He is also the co-author of a book on the Design Structure Matrix (DSM). Dr. Browning serves as a Department Editor for *IEEE Transactions on Engineering Management* and as an Associate Editor for the *Journal of Operations Management* and *Systems Engineering*.

Dr. Raffaella Cagliano is a full Professor at the School of Management of Politecnico di Milano and she teaches Organization Theory and Design at the Ph.D., postgraduate, and undergraduate levels. She is the Deputy Dean for Faculty Management and Director of the Specialized Masters at MIP Politecnico di Milano. She has been on the European Operations Management Association (EurOMA) Board since 2004, and she was the President of EurOMA between 2010 and 2013. She is a member of the Editorial Advisory Board of the *International Journal of Operations & Production Management* and Associate Editor of *Operations Management Research*. Her main research interests are related to manufacturing and supply chain strategies as well as work organization models and practices, placing particular emphasis on sustainable innovation. Dr. Cagliano is the author of over 150 publications, 35 of which are in international journals or books. She is also author/editor of four research books and two teaching books. Some of her papers have been awarded for their quality and relevance.

Dr. Federico Caniato is an Associate Professor at the School of Management of Politecnico di Milano, teaching supply chain and purchasing management in both undergraduate and graduate courses. Dr. Caniato is MIP Politecnico di Milano Graduate School of Business's Director of the Master in Supply Chain and Purchasing Management. Caniato's research interests lie in the fields of supply chain and purchasing management, and in recent years, he has focused on sustainability and supply chain finance. Dr. Caniato is the Director of the Supply Chain Finance Observatory, the leading research initiative in Italy, in close collaboration with the international Supply Chain Finance Community. He authored several international publications in various operations management journals, and he is Associate Editor of the *Journal of Purchasing and Supply Management*.

Moonwon Chung is currently a Ph.D. candidate in the Management Science Department at the Darla Moore School of Business, University of South Carolina, Columbia. He received his Master of Science in operations management from Seoul National University. Moonwon's research areas include buyer/supplier relationships, technology management, and service operations management. His methodological interests include applied econometrics, multilevel modeling, structural equation modeling, and response surface analysis. Currently, his work is under review in different journals of the field. He has also taught undergraduate courses on service science focusing on business analytic methods.

Mr. Lee Cockerell is CEO of Lee Cockerell, LLC. He worked as the Executive Vice President of Operations for Walt Disney World® Resorts for over ten years before retiring from the position. Prior to attaining that position, Mr. Cockerell worked as Director of Food and Beverage and Quality Assurance for the Disneyland Paris hotels and spent over twenty years working with the Marriot Corporation and Hilton Hotels. His responsibilities in those positions encompassed a diverse mix of operations, which included the management of twenty resort hotels, four theme parks, two water parks, five golf courses, a shopping village, a nighttime entertainment complex, and the ESPN Sports Complex. Additionally, Mr. Cockerell is also the author of four books: *Creating Magic: 10 Common Sense Leadership Strategies from a Life at Disney*, *The Customer Rules: The 39 Essential Rules for Delivering Sensational Service*, *Time Management Magic: How to Get More Done Every Day*, and *Creating Career Magic: How to Survive the Ups and Downs* (September 2016).

Dr. Henrique L. Correa is a Professor of Operations Management at Rollins College in Winter Park, Florida. He also teaches summer courses in POM and supply chain management in Brazil, Portugal, and Italy. Dr. Correa has consulted with established companies such as Unilever, Diageo, General Motors, PepsiCo, Natura, Hewlett-Packard, Embraer, 3M, Brazil Foods, Whirlpool, and Monsanto. Dr. Correa has published extensively in academic and professional journals. He has also authored and co-authored eleven books and textbooks in the fields of operations strategy, service operations, operations management, and global supply chain management. Between 2005 and 2007, Dr. Correa served as the Vice President for the Americas in the Production Operations Management Society. He was the 2011–2012 recipient of the Rollins College Bornstein Award for Faculty Scholarship. Dr. Correa holds a B.S. from the University of Sao Paulo, Brazil; an M.S. from the University of Sao Paulo, Brazil; and a Ph.D. from the University of Warwick, UK.

Dr. Tinglong Dai is an Assistant Professor of Operations Management at Johns Hopkins University's Carey Business School. His research areas include healthcare operations, marketing-operations interfaces, and operations research/computer science interfaces. In 2013, Dr. Dai received his Ph.D. from the Tepper School of Business, Carnegie Mellon University. Dr. Dai's research has been published in *Management Science*, *Manufacturing & Service Operations Management*, *Operations Research*, and *INFORMS Journal on Computing*. Additionally, he is on the Editorial Review Board of *Production and Operations Management*. Dr. Dai is the recipient of 2015 Johns Hopkins Discovery Award, a runner-up for the 2016 POMS Best Healthcare Paper Award, the winner of the 2012 POMS Best Healthcare Paper Award, and a runner-up for the 2012 INFORMS Pierskalla Award for the Best Paper in Healthcare. He has been quoted in a list of publications that includes the *Washington Post*, *Baltimore Sun*, *MedPage Today*, and *Pharmacy Times*, among others.

Dr. Benjamin Dehe is a Senior Lecturer in Operations Management at the University of Huddersfield, UK. He focuses his research and work in the application of operations excellence concepts and theories in manufacturing, built environment, and sport. Dr. Dehe's work has been published in national and international journals such as the *International Journal of Operations &*

Production Management, Expert Systems with Applications, the *International Journal of Quality & Reliability Management*, and the *International Journal of Productivity and Performance Management*.

Dr. Kaushik Dutta is an Associate Professor in the University of South Florida's (USF) Information Systems Decision Sciences Department. His current research interest is data analytics. Prior to joining USF, Dr. Dutta was a tenured associate professor at both the National University of Singapore (NUS) and Florida International University. Before starting on his academic path, he pursued a career in engineering, as the chief technology officer and vice president of engineering of Mobilewalla, a Madrona-funded and NUS-incubated company that developed big data based mobile advertisement platforms. Dr. Dutta has a Bachelor's in Electrical Engineering from Jadavpur University, a Master's in Computer Science from Indian Statistical Institute, and a Ph.D. in Management Information Systems from Georgia Institute of Technology.

Dr. Sinan Erzurumlu is an Associate Professor of Technology and Operations Management at Babson College. He received his Ph.D. in Management Science and Information Systems from McCombs School of Business and M.Sc. in Operations Research/Industrial Engineering from Department of Mechanical Engineering at the University of Texas at Austin. He holds a B.Sc. in Electrical and Electronics Engineering with distinction from Bogazici University in Turkey. His main areas of research and expertise include innovation management, technology development and commercialization, sustainability, and entrepreneurship. Dr. Erzurumlu studies the process of innovation to guide effective decision making for the development and growth of new ventures. His research has been published in several leading journals including *Production and Operations Management*, *IEEE Transactions*, *Decision Sciences*, *Resources Policy*, *International Journal of Innovation Management*, and *Omega*.

Dr. Qi Feng is the John and Donna Krenicki Chair in Operations Management at Krannert School of Management, Purdue University, Indiana. Previously, Dr. Feng was a faculty member at McCombs School of Business, The University of Texas (UT) at Austin. She received her Ph.D. in Operations Management from UT Dallas in 2006. Her main research interest lies in studying firms' sourcing decisions in the broad context of supply chain management. Dr. Feng's work focuses on individual firm's procurement, inventory, and pricing planning in uncertain environments and multiple firms' interactions in sourcing relationships. She also works in the areas of product development and proliferation management, resource planning, economic growth models, and information system management. Dr. Feng is currently a Department Editor for *Production and Operations Management*. She received the first prize in the INFORMS Junior Faculty Paper Competition in 2009, the Franz Edelman Award in 2009, and the Wickham Skinner Early-Career Research Accomplishment Award in 2012.

Dr. Pauline Found is a Professor of Lean Operations at the University of Buckingham and was formerly part of the Lean Enterprise Research Centre (LERC) at Cardiff University. Dr. Found is the co-author of *Staying Lean: Thriving, Not Just Surviving*, for which she holds a Shingo Research and Professional Publication Prize (2009). Dr. Found was educated at The Open University, Cardiff University, and Bristol University, and before joining LERC, she had spent eighteen years in senior management roles in industry. She is a Fellow of the Institute of Operations Management (FIOM) and a Member of the American Society of Quality (ASQ). She holds a Ph.D., MBA, B.Sc. (Hons), B.A., and Postgraduate Diploma in environmental management. She was President of the International POMS (Production and Operations Management Society) College of Behavior between 2009 and 2011.

Contributors

Dr. Cheryl Gaimon is the Regents' Professor and the Esther and Edward Chair in the Scheller College of Business at Georgia Tech, Atlanta, GA. Her research and teaching interests focus on developing the resource capabilities necessary for a firm to compete in environments characterized by developments in science and technology. Dr. Gaimon's specific interests include knowledge management and outsourcing, new product/process development, implementation of new technology, and sustainable operations. Her research has appeared in journals including *Management Science, Operations Research, Organization Science,* and *Production and Operations Management*. Dr. Gaimon is a Fellow of the Production and Operations Management Society (POMS). She received the Sushil K. Gupta POMS Distinguished Service Award in 2014. She served as the President of POMS between 2008 and 2009. She received the Distinguished Service Award for the Technology Management Section (TMS) of the Institute for Operations Research and the Management Sciences (INFORMS) in 2009. Dr. Gaimon currently serves as the Management of Technology Department Editor for *Production and Operations Management* and as Associate Editor for *Management Science*.

Dr. Vishal Gaur is the Emerson Professor of Manufacturing Management and a Professor of Operations, Technology, and Information Management at the Samuel Curtis Johnson Graduate School of Management at Cornell University. His research interests lie in retail operations and supply chain management, including topics such as inventory management, product variety, demand forecasting, store execution, and linking operations to financial performance. Dr. Gaur's research focuses on modeling data sets, such as aggregate publicly available firm-level or industry-level data, proprietary transaction-level data from firms, and online consumer browsing data, for solving problems in retailing and supply chains. Dr. Gaur served as a Department Editor for *POM* between 2010 and 2014, and currently serves as a Department Editor for *Management Science* and an associate editor for several journals. He received his Ph.D. from Wharton, University of Pennsylvania in 2001.

Dr. Abhijeet Ghoshal is an Assistant Professor at the Computer and Information Systems Department of the University of Louisville, Kentucky's College of Business. He received his Ph.D. from the University of Texas at Dallas. His research interests include operational and economic issues related to recommender systems. Dr. Ghoshal's work has appeared in *Information Systems Research, INFORMS Journal on Computing,* and *Journal of Management Information Systems*.

Dr. David Gray is a Senior Lecturer in Farm Management at Massey University in New Zealand. Dr. Gray's early research focused on the design of high-performing, pastoral-based farming systems using a range of modelling techniques. In recent decades, his research has shifted and he has adopted a qualitative case study-based approach to investigate a range of phenomena. This has included the tactical and operational management practices of high-performing, pastoral-based farmers; the risk management practices of pastoral-based farmers; and the resilience of pastoral-based farming systems. Dr. Gray has also investigated the consultancy and problem solving practices of expert farm management consultants and is currently undertaking a cross-case comparison of expert and novice consultants. More recent work has been undertaken into the areas of farmer learning and practice change, extension, and innovation systems.

Dr. Sushil K. Gupta is a Professor in the College of Business, Florida International University, Miami, Florida. His research interests include production scheduling, mathematical modeling, supply chain management, e-business, and disaster management. He has published in *Production* *and Operations Management, Management Science, EJOR,* and other reputed journals. He serves as a Senior Editor of *Production and Operations Management.* He has served as President of the Production and Operations Management Society (POMS) and is currently serving as its Executive Director. Dr. Gupta is a Production and Operations Management Society (POMS) Fellow. He has been a recipient of a Fulbright Fellowship, a Commonwealth Scholarship, and the POMS Distinguished Service Award. POMS created the Sushil K. Gupta POMS Distinguished Service Award to honor him for his dedicated service.

Dr. Thomas Hemmer is the Houston Endowment of Accounting at Jones GSB, Rice University and is currently an Editor at *The Accounting Review* and a Guest Editor at *Journal of Accounting Research.* Previously, Dr. Hemmer has been on the faculties of the University of Washington; the University of California, Los Angeles; the University of Chicago; the London School of Economics; and the University of Houston. Dr. Hemmer has taught a wide variety of Ph.D. courses on analytical economics-based accounting theory at a large number of research institutions across the US, Europe, and Asia. Dr. Hemmer studies information economics-based theory with a major focus on measurement and incentive problems in organizations as well as problems pertaining to the use and valuation of employee stock options. His current research focuses on optimal dynamic contracting, relative performance evaluation, and on the predicted distribution of unmanaged accounting earnings. Dr. Hemmer's research has been published in journals such as *The Accounting Review, Journal of Accounting Research, Journal of Accounting and Economics, Review of Accounting Studies, Journal of Labor Economics,* and *Economic Theory.*

Dr. Sunderesh S. Heragu is Regents Professor and Head of the School of Industrial Engineering and Management at Oklahoma State University where he holds the Donald and Cathey Humphreys Chair. Previously, he was the Duthie Chair in Engineering Logistics and Director of the Logistics and Distribution Institute at the University of Louisville. He has also worked at Rensselaer Polytechnic Institute and the State University of New York, Plattsburgh, and held visiting appointments at the State University of New York, Buffalo; the Technical University of Eindhoven; the University of Twente, in the Netherlands; and IBM's Thomas J Watson Research Center in Yorktown Heights, NY. He is author of the 4th edition of *Facilities Design* and has authored or co-authored over two hundred publications. He has served as Principal investigator or co-investigator on research projects totaling over $20 million funded by federal agencies such as the Department of Homeland Security, the National Science Foundation, the Defense Logistics Agency, and private companies such as General Electric. Dr. Heragu is a Fellow of the Institute of Industrial and Systems Engineers (IISE). He has received numerous awards including IISE's David F. Baker Distinguished Research Award, the Award for Technical Innovation in Industrial Engineering, and various best paper awards.

Dr. Manpreet Hora is an Associate Professor of Operations Management in the Scheller College of Business at Georgia Tech, Atlanta, GA. His research interests focus on operational risk and supply chain innovation. More specifically, his research empirically addresses specific challenges in three areas: (1) managing operational risk through capturing knowledge from low-frequency, high-impact operational failures; (2) building capabilities in global supply chain management and innovation; and (3) using knowledge in operational routines and process management. Dr. Hora's research articles have been accepted for publication in refereed journals including *Management Science,* the *Journal of Operations Management, Production and Operations Management,* and the *Journal of Management Studies.* He serves as a Senior Editor for *Production and Operations Management* and an Associate Editor for *Journal of Operations Management.*

Mr. Wayne Hughes Jr. is a retired Navy Captain whose teaching and research at the Naval Postgraduate School have centered on campaign analysis, operational logistics, naval tactics, and information warfare for thirty-seven years. While on active duty, he commanded a minesweeper, a destroyer, and a large training command. He contributed to operations analysis afloat and ashore, and was Deputy Director of the Systems Analysis Division (OP-96) for the Chief of Naval Operations. At the Naval Postgraduate School, he served in the Chairs of Applied Systems Analysis and Tactical Analysis and was Dean of the Graduate School of Operational and Information Sciences. He is a past President and Fellow of the Military Operations Research Society (MORS) and holds its Wanner Award for distinguished service. He was recognized as first Defence Technology Distinguished Fellow of the Republic of Singapore. In 2010, he received the Institute for Operations Research and Management Science (INFORMS) J. Steinhart Prize for lifetime contributions to military operations research.

Mr. Ahmed Jamoussi is pursuing his Master's in Business Administration at the Mediterranean School of Business in Tunisia. In Spring 2016, he was a visiting scholar in the School of Industrial Engineering and Management at Oklahoma State University and studied supply chain management and logistics. Jamoussi has done internships at the BG Group as a financial analyst; at Libya Oil, Tunisia, as Accounting and Payment Supervisor; and at J.F. Foundry, as Manager.

Dr. Ramkumar Janakiraman is an Associate Professor of Marketing and a Business Partnership Foundation Research Fellow at the Darla Moore School of Business at the University of South Carolina (USC). Dr. Janakiraman has a Ph.D. in Business Administration from the University of Southern California. His substantive research areas include social and digital media, multichannel retailing, big data, and marketing/operations interface. His methodological interests include microeconometrics, applied econometric modeling, and consumer learning/structural models. Dr. Janakiraman's research has appeared or forthcoming in leading marketing, information systems, strategy, and medical journals such as *Marketing Science*, *Management Science*, the *Journal of Marketing*, the *Journal of Marketing Research*, *Information Systems Research*, the *Journal of Consumer Psychology*, *Decision Sciences*, the *Journal of Management*, and the *Annals of Family Medicine*. He teaches graduate-level courses on marketing analytics, customer relationship management, and data mining as well as doctoral seminars on marketing models.

Dr. Yonghua Ji is an Associate Professor of Management Information Systems in the School of Business, University of Alberta. He received his Ph.D. in Management, with a major in MIS, from the University of Texas at Dallas. His current research interests include the economics of information security, real options, online e-commerce, and social networking. He has published in journals such as *INFORMS Journal on Computing*, *Information Systems Research (ISR)*, and *Production and Operations Management (POM)*. Dr. Ji is a Senior Editor of *POM* and regularly reviews papers for major journals such as *ISR*, *MIS Quarterly*, *POM*, and *Management Science*.

Dr. Nitin Joglekar is an Associate Professor of Operations & Technology Management and a Dean's Research Fellow at Boston University's Questrom School of Business. He holds a bachelor's degree from the Indian Institute of Technology, master's degrees in engineering from MIT and Memorial University (Canada), and a Ph.D. in Management Science from MIT Sloan School. Dr. Joglekar's interests span a wide range that includes product and process development, startup supply chain and innovative operations, technology management, connected health and self-care. He is currently a department editor for industry studies and public policy at *Production and Operations Management (POM)* and for Technology, Innovation Management &

Entrepreneurship at *IEEE Transactions on Engineering Management (IEEE-TEM)*. Dr. Joglekar's research findings have appeared in the *ACM Journal of Information and Data Quality, AIEDAM, IEEE-TEM, Journal of Applied Probability, Journal of Business Venturing, JPIM, Journal of Service Management, Managerial & Decision Economics, Management Science, POM, Research in Engineering Design, Service Science,* and *Systems Research & Behavioral Science.*

Mr. Edwin Keh is the CEO for the Hong Kong Research Institute for Textile & Apparel (HKRITA). He also is currently on the faculty at the Wharton School and serves as a visiting professor at the Hong Kong University of Science & Technology. Mr. Keh has had a long career in senior management roles in procurement for the consumer product and retail industries. Until 2010, he was the Senior Vice President, Chief Operating Officer of Walmart Global Procurement. Prior to that, he was the Managing Director of Payless Shoesource International, Donna Karan International, and Country Road Australia. Additionally, Mr. Keh was the 2011 recipient of the Production and Operations Management Society's Martin K. Starr Excellence in Practice Award. In 2015, he was also included in Debrett's "100 Most Influential" in Hong Kong.

Ms. Lu Kong is a first-year doctoral student in service operations management at the School of Hotel Administration (SHA) at Cornell University. After graduating from SHA with her M.S. in 2013, Ms. Kong worked for Marriott for one year before coming back for her Ph.D. study. Her research interests lie in service innovation, sustainable operations, social network, and the sharing economy. Currently, she is working on a project that explores the intersection between the hospitality industry and healthcare industry, the similarities and differences between those two industries, and how they can learn from each other. Ms. Kong's other research project explores how companies utilize customer feedback from social networks to improve service operations.

Dr. Lee Krajewski retired as a Professor from The Ohio State University where he won the Ohio State University Alumni Distinguished Teaching Award and supervised sixteen Ph.D. dissertations. His research interests are in the areas of manufacturing strategy and supply chain management. He co-authored three papers that won the Best Theoretical/Empirical Paper awards at three national Decision Sciences conferences. He also co-authored two papers that won the Stanley T. Hardy Award for the best paper in operations management. He won the Outstanding Faculty Research Award in the Fisher College of Business, The Ohio State University, in 1987. He is the co-author of two texts and three books. One text, *Operations Management: Processes and Supply Chains* is a leading text in the field, presently in its eleventh edition. He has written numerous articles appearing in the top journals in the field. He was the founding Editor of the *Journal of Operations Management* (1980–1983) and has served as Editor of *Decision Sciences*. He initiated and served as Director of the Center for Excellence in Manufacturing Management, now the Center for Operational Excellence, at The Ohio State University. Dr. Krajewski received his Ph.D. (1969) in Production Management from the University of Wisconsin-Madison.

Dr. Subodha Kumar is the Carol and G. David Van Houten, Jr. '71 Professor at the Mays Business School, Texas A&M University. He is also the Vice President of the Production and Operations Management Society (POMS) and the Institute for Operations Research and the Management Sciences' (INFORMS) ISS. Dr. Kumar's research interests include social media analytics, healthcare management, retailing, supply chain management, and Web advertisement. He has published several papers in reputed journals and refereed conferences. In addition, he has authored a book and has co-authored several book chapters and cases. He also has a patent. Dr. Kumar has been featured on the Indian School of Business Management Briefs, the University of Washington Television, and the *Industrial Engineer* Magazine. He is both the Deputy Editor and a Department Editor of *Production and Operations Management*, a Senior Editor of *Decision Sciences*, and an Associate Editor of *Information Systems Research*. Additionally, Dr. Kumar serves on the editorial boards of other journals and conferences. He has co-chaired the Workshop on Information Technology and Systems (WITS) in 2015 and INFORMS Conference on Information Systems and Technology (CIST) in 2011 and has been track and cluster chairs at leading conferences.

Dr. Eva Labro is an Associate Professor of Accounting and Michael W. Haley Distinguished Scholar at Kenan-Flagler Business School, University of North Carolina in Chapel Hill. She is a senior editor at *Production and Operations Management* for its POM-Accounting Interface and was previously on the faculty at the London School of Economics. Dr. Labro studies management accounting and how it interfaces with other areas of accounting and business with a specific focus on costing system design and the provision of management accounting information for both decision making and performance measurement. Her research has been published in journals such as *The Accounting Review*, *Journal of Accounting Research*, *Journal of Accounting and Economics*, *Manufacturing & Service Operations Management*, and *Production and Operations Management*. Dr. Labro is an award-winning researcher who has received the Impact on Management Accounting Practice Award three times—in 2011, 2013, and 2014—from the American Institute of Certified Public Accountants and the Chartered Institute of Management Accountants. She also received the 2011 Notable Contributions to the Management Accounting Literature Award.

Dr. Kangbok Lee is an Associate Professor at the Department of Industrial and Management Engineering, Pohang University of Science and Technology (POSTECH), Korea. He is a well-balanced scholar in solving real-world problems and doing academic research. During his working period in industry, he had extensive project experience in manufacturing and logistics. At Rutgers Business School, he worked for a project on pharmaceutical supply chain management with the U.S. Department of Homeland Security. Dr. Lee also taught a Production Operations Management course in the Business and Economics Department at York College in New York. He has published more than thirty papers in refereed journals, such as *Production and Operations Management*, *Omega*, the *European Journal of Operational Research*, *Discrete Applied Mathematics*, and the *International Journal of Production Economics*. He has served as an Associate Editor of *Journal of Scheduling* since 2012. His main research interests are scheduling, operations research, management science, and supply chain management.

Dr. Moren Lévesque is a Professor and the CPA Ontario Chair in International Entrepreneurship at York University's Schulich School of Business. Dr. Lévesque is currently a Department Editor at the *IEEE Transactions on Engineering Management* and a Senior Editor at *Production and Operations Management*. She holds a Ph.D. in Management Science from the University of British Columbia and M.Sc., B.Sc. in Mathematics from Université Laval. Her research applies the methodologies of analytical and quantitative disciplines to the study of decision making in new business formation. Dr. Lévesque's work appears in *Entrepreneurship Theory and Practice*, the *European Journal of Operational Research*, *IEEE Transactions on Engineering Management*, the *Journal of Business Venturing*, the *Journal of Management Studies*, *Long Range Planning*, *Organization Science*, *Production and Operations Management*, the *Strategic Entrepreneurship Journal*, and the *Strategic Management Journal*, among other research outlets.

Contributors

Ms. Zhen Lin is a first-year graduate student majoring in service operations management in the School of Hotel Administration (SHA) at Cornell University. Ms. Lin graduated from Nankai University in 2015 with a degree in tourism management. She developed an interest in the interaction between hospitality and health industry when she was doing undergraduate research on the development of mobile health and its impact on the healthcare industry. Now, Ms. Lin is conducting research to help improve the service quality of the mobile health industry both from the service provider's as well as consumer's perspectives.

Mr. James Lyons is currently the Vice President of Operations for Boston Scientific's Galway location. He has over twenty-six years' experience in electronics and medical device manufacturing. Prior to joining Boston Scientific, Mr. Lyons held the role of Worldwide Vice President of Program Management for Sanmina Corporation with responsibilities across more than fifty sites. Through his career, he has gained extensive experience in the areas of engineering, operations, and commercial management at companies such as Sanmina, MSL (now Celestica), Sensormatic (now Tyco), and SCI. Mr. Lyons holds a Bachelor's degree in Electronic Production from the University of Limerick and was awarded an honorary Professor in Operational Excellence by the University of Buckingham, UK. He is an advocate of continuous professional development in strategy, leadership, and operational excellence.

Dr. Manoj K. Malhotra is the Jeff B. Bates Professor and Chair of the Management Science Department at the Moore School of Business at the University of South Carolina (USC). He has also served as the founding director of the industry-based Center for Global Supply Chain and Process Management since 2005. Dr. Malhotra is the Senior Editor of *Decision Sciences* and the *POMS Journal*. Malhotra received an engineering undergraduate degree from IIT-Kanpur and Ph.D. from Ohio State University. Dr. Malhotra is a Fellow of the Decision Sciences Institute and the American Production and Inventory Management Society. He has co-authored a leading textbook and has published numerous articles in top-tier journals of the field such as *Decision Sciences*, the *European Journal of Operational Research*, *Interfaces*, *IIE Transactions*, the *Journal of Operations Management*, and *Production and Operations Management (POMS) Journal*, among others. He has received several research awards, including the 2002 and 2006 Stan Hardy Award for the best paper published in the field of operations management and the 2011 Decision Sciences Journal Best Paper Award. Apart from college- and university-wide teaching awards, Dr. Malhotra's research contributions have also been recognized through the USC Educational Foundation Research Award for Professional Schools.

Mr. Adam McClintock is an operations manager, supporting the Human Research Protections Program (HRPP) at The Ohio State University. Specifically, Mr. McClintock is a member of the staff responsible for assisting researchers and committee members supporting the Behavioral & Social Sciences, Biomedical Sciences, and Cancer Institutional Review Boards (IRBs). His work routinely analyzes operational processes to identify opportunities for continuous improvement and reduction in turnaround times. This often involves engaging cross-functional project teams in order to identify opportunities for improvement, analyzing possible solutions, and implementing changes for sustained improvements.

Dr. Saurabh Mishra is an Associate Professor of Marketing and a Desautels Faculty Scholar at the Desautels Faculty of Management, McGill University, Canada. Prior to joining McGill, he received his Ph.D. in Marketing from Indiana University, Bloomington, and worked as a post-doctoral researcher at the Kellogg School of Management, Northwestern University. Dr. Mishra's primary research interests are in marketing-operations management interface, with a particular focus on how these two business functions complement each other to inform shareholder wealth of organizations. He also works on understanding the financial value of corporate social responsibility and brands. Working in these areas, Dr. Mishra has published multiple articles in top-tier journals such as the *Journal of Marketing, Marketing Science,* and the *Journal of Operations Management.*

Mr. Rahul Pandey is a doctoral candidate in the Management Sciences department of the Fisher College of Business, at The Ohio State University. He studies managerial decision making in the context of supply chain resilience. Prior to Fisher, Mr. Pandey led a cross-functional team from R&D, production, central quality, and component suppliers to conduct a detailed study of entire brake assembly mechanism at Tata Motors assembly lines. Mr. Pandey was also actively involved in supplier Corrective and Preventive Action (CAPA), problem solving and onsite process audits and process improvements, and identified and analyzed trends of emerging quality issues with the preassigned group of suppliers, and the related root causes of quality nonconformance experienced.

Mrs. Marina Papalexi is a Ph.D. candidate and Research Assistant in Operations Management at the Business School, University of Huddersfield, UK. Her research focus is related to the application of operations management concepts and theories in supply chain and services in public and private sector. Mrs. Papalexi also has published a number of articles in peer-reviewed international journals.

Dr. Michael Pinedo is the Julius Schlesinger Professor of Operations Management at New York University's Stern School of Business. He received an Ir. degree in Mechanical Engineering from Delft University of Technology in 1973 and a Ph.D. in Operations Research from the University of California at Berkeley in 1978. His research focuses on the modeling of production and service systems, in particular planning and scheduling systems. He is the author of *Scheduling: Theory, Algorithms and Systems* (Springer) and *Planning and Scheduling in Manufacturing and Services* (Springer) and coauthor of *Queueing Networks: Customers, Signals and Product Form Solutions* (Wiley). Recently, his research has also focused on operational risk in financial services. He is co-editor of *Creating Value in Financial Services: Strategies, Operations, and Technologies* (Kluwer) and co-editor of *Global Asset Management—Strategies, Risks, Processes and Technologies* (Palgrave/McMillan). Dr. Pinedo has been actively involved in industrial systems development. He supervised the development and implementation of two scheduling systems for International Paper and participated in the development of systems at Goldman Sachs, Philips, Siemens, and Merck. Dr. Pinedo is Editor of the *Journal of Scheduling* (Springer), Department Editor of *Production and Operations Management*, and Associate Editor of *Annals of Operations Research.*

Mr. Ping (David) Yang is the Vice President of the JD Group. Prior to working with the JD Group, he was the VP of Yihaodian—a leading e-commerce company in China. Mr. Ping received his Bachelor of Science from the Central South University, a Master of Science from Fudan University, and an EMBA from the Shanghai Jiaotong University. Mr. Ping served as the IT Director of Group's China Headquarters of YRC Worldwide (US Fortune 500) and the IT Director of the Shanghai Waigaoqiao Free Trade Zone Development Co. Ltd. In 2012, he was awarded the honorable title as the "Top 10" Shanghai Computer Industry Technology Innovation Leader. Before attaining his position at the JD Group, David served as IT manager of IBM in China and as the IT manager of Shell in China. Mr. Ping has over fifteen years cross-experience in analysis, research and development, implementation and management for supply chain and related application system, including over ten years of experience as top management in a large enterprise group, multinational groups, and foreign invested enterprise. He has many years of practical experience in researching and developing supply-chain application software systems, and supply-chain Teradata-BI Tool, analyzing, and modeling.

Dr. Robert K. Prescott, SPHR, has spent twenty years in industry and sixteen years teaching in academic positions. Dr. Prescott is currently Graduate Faculty of Management at the Crummer Graduate School of Business at Rollins College in Winter Park, Florida, USA. In this role, Dr. Prescott is responsible for teaching graduate-level courses in the Executive Doctorate, MBA, and Masters of Human Resources (MHR) programs. His personal teaching expertise and research focuses on all aspects of human resource management, leadership, succession planning, organization behavior, training and development, career management, and enterprise consulting. He is a native of Birmingham, Alabama, and holds a B.Sc. in Marketing from the University of Alabama and a Ph.D. in Workforce Education and Development from The Pennsylvania State University. Dr. Prescott co-authored the books *The Strategic Human Resource Leader: How to Prepare Your Organization for the 6 Key Trends Shaping the Future* (Davies-Black, 1998), *HR Transformation: Demonstrating Leadership in the Face of Future Trends* (Davies-Black/SHRM, 2009), and the *Encyclopedia of Human Resource Management—Volume One* (Wiley, 2012).

Dr. Tharanga K. Rajapakshe is an Assistant Professor in the University of Florida's Department of Information Systems and Operations Management. She received her doctoral degree in Management Science from the University of Texas at Dallas. She received her bachelor's degree in Production Engineering from the University of Peradeniya, Sri Lanka. Dr. Rajapakshe also holds a master's degree (M.Sc.) in Supply Chain Management and a professional MBA from the University of Texas at Dallas. Dr. Rajapakshe's research interests focus on resolving novel issues that emerge in implementing socially responsible supply chains and in optimization theory and applications. She has published papers in top-tier journals in the area of operations management. Tharanga's teaching interests are in operations management, supply chain management, project management, logistics, and distribution.

Dr. Karthik Ramachandran is an Associate Professor of Operations Management in the Scheller College of Business at Georgia Tech, Atlanta, GA. He received his Ph.D. in Operations Management and M.Sc. in Operations Research from the University of Texas at Austin, and his B.Sc. in Mechanical Engineering from the Indian Institute of Technology, Madras, India. Previously, Dr. Ramachandran served as an Assistant Professor at the Cox School of Business at Southern Methodist University in Dallas, TX, and as a research associate at the Rady School of Business at the University of California, San Diego. Dr. Ramachandran's research focuses on operational issues related to new product design and development. He is primarily interested in the logistics of innovation such as how consumers, suppliers, and partners are affected by the innovative activities and design choices of an innovator. His work has been published in *Management Science, Manufacturing & Service Operations Management, Production and Operations Management,* and *IIE Transactions*.

Dr. Iain Reid is a Senior Lecturer at the University of Huddersfield, UK. Dr. Reid has over twenty years of experience working in the manufacturing sector, and his Ph.D. centers around knowledge sharing within engineer-to-order (ETO). He has numerous publications in the areas of operational agility, ETO supply chains, mass customization, and legal nimbleness. Prior to embarking upon an academic career, Dr. Reid worked as a Project Manager on an ERDF project supporting over a hundred manufacturing small and medium-sized enterprises on operational issues.

Contributors

Dr. Liliana Rivera is an Associate Professor at the Business Department at the Universidad del Rosario in Bogotá, Colombia and a Research Affiliate at the MIT Center for Transportation and Logistics. She has over ten years of experience in the design, evaluation, and improvement of supply chains, logistics, and economic systems. Dr. Rivera's main areas of interest are the analysis of supply chains in emerging markets and logistics clusters/hubs, including their impact on companies, workers, and local economies. Her work has been published in leading journals such as the *International Journal of Production Economics, Transportation Research Part A: Policy and Practice*, and the *International Journal of Physical Distribution and Logistics Management*. Dr. Rivera also has consulted with leading firms in these fields and government agencies. She has co-founded and served as director of Logistec Consultores, a company that offers consulting and technology solutions in areas related to logistics, supply chain management, economics, and public policy. Her educational background includes a Ph.D. and an M.Eng. in Logistics and Supply Chain Management from MIT as well as an M.A. and a B.A. in Economics from Universidad de Los Andes, Colombia.

Dr. Peter W. Robertson is a senior associate at the University of Wollongong in Australia. Dr. Robertson has forty years of industrial experience in operations and supply chain management, three years as an academic, and five years as a management consultant. Quality management has been a key component of each of those roles. Dr. Robertson completed his Ph.D. in Supply Chain Management & Logistics in 2005. His current research is centered on operations management, supply chain 4-element framework, logistics management, disaster management, project readiness, and asset management. Dr. Robertson is also interested in supply chain risk, both the identification and quantification of risk and preventive and contingent responses to such risks. Peter's particular interest is in the social (human) side of the above-mentioned fields such as the factors that determine individual and group purpose, passion and socio competencies, and the approach that best releases them.

Dr. Aleda Roth is the Burlington Industries Distinguished Professor in Supply Chain Management at Clemson University. She is an internationally recognized empirical scholar and thought leader in service and manufacturing strategy. Dr. Roth is a Fellow of the Production and Operations Management Society (POMS), the Manufacturing and Service Operations Management Society (MSOM), and Decision Sciences. She received the 2014 Award for the Advancement of Women in Operation Research and the Management Sciences (INFORMS) and was honored as a 2013 Texas A&M Institute for Advanced Study (TIAS) Eminent Scholar. Dr. Roth holds lifetime achievement awards from the POMS College of Service Management and the Academy of Management OM Division. Dr. Roth has held editorial leadership positions for the *POM* journal, *Management Science, M&SOM*, and others. Additionally, she was the first woman elected President of POMS. Dr. Roth received her doctorate in Production and Operations Management from The Ohio State University, where she also earned a Bachelor of Science in Psychology. She also holds a Master of Science in Public Health (MSPH) in biostatistics from the University of North Carolina at Chapel Hill.

Dr. Donna Samuel is Head of Lean Academy, S A Partners. She has recently completed her Ph.D. thesis on the past twenty-five years of the lean movement in the UK. She started her career in manufacturing but moved into the education sector where she spent many years at Cardiff University Lean Enterprise Research Centre (LERC) in a variety of teaching and research roles. She has delivered and managed lean and supply chain management courses at both graduate and undergraduate levels. Dr. Samuel has led and participated in a number of applied research projects in a variety of organizational contexts. The focus of her doctoral studies centered around the introduction of lean into nonconventional environments and some of the central debates within the broad lean movement.

Dr. Nada R. Sanders is Distinguished Professor of Supply Chain Management at the D'Amore-McKim School of Business at Northeastern University. Previously she served as the Iacocca Chair at Lehigh University and as West Chair and Professor of Supply Chain Management at the M.J. Neeley School of Business, Texas Christian University, where she was Research Director of the Supply and Value Chain Center. She holds a Ph.D. in Operations Management and Logistics and an MBA from the Fisher College of Business at The Ohio State University as well as a B.Sc. in Mechanical Engineering. Dr. Sanders is an internationally recognized thought leader and expert in forecasting and supply chain management, and has authored numerous articles published in top tier scholarly journals. She is author of the books *Big Data Driven Supply Chain Management* (Pearson, 2014) and *Foundations of Sustainable Business* (Wiley, 2014) as well as *Supply Chain Management: A Global Perspective* (2012) and is co-author of the book *Operations Management*, in its 6th edition. She is a Fellow of the Decision Sciences Institute and has served on the Board of Directors of the International Institute of Forecasters (IIF), Decision Sciences Institute (DSI), and the Production Operations Management Society (POMS).

Mr. Adeola Shabiyi has spent fifteen years in the industry as an Operations and Human Resources professional in food and confectionary manufacturing, financial services, and HR professional services in North America, Europe, and Africa. Mr. Shabiyi is currently the Global Human Resources Advisor for Anti Money Laundering Operations (AML Ops) at Citi based in Tampa, Florida, USA. In this role, Mr. Shabiyi is responsible for the advisory, strategy, and delivery of Human Resources practices that will enable AML Ops to be a best-in-class operation in the Citi Anti Money Laundering program. Mr. Shabiyi has primary expertise in Strategic Human Resources Management, executive coaching, talent management, and strategy. Mr. Shabiyi is a native of Lagos, Nigeria, and holds an HND in Business Administration from Yaba College of Technology, Lagos, Nigeria; a Master of Human Resources (MHR) from Rollins College, Winter Park, Florida, USA; and an MBA from the Thunderbird School of Global Management, Glendale, Arizona, USA and is currently an Executive Doctorate in Business Administration (EDBA) student at Rollins College focusing on human capacity.

Professor Nicola M. Shadbolt is a Massey University Professor of Farm & AgriBusiness Management who is focused on delivering research and education. Due to being a farmer for over thirty years, Professor Shadbolt has a depth and breadth of understanding of farming. Her research interests include cooperatives, their management and strategies, farm business analysis and performance indicators, ownership structures in dairying, investment and risk analysis, and overall strategic management by farmers. Professor Shadbolt currently serves as the Director of Fonterra Cooperative, as the Director of the International Food & Agribusiness Management Association, as the Director of Hopkins Farming Group Ltd, and as an Editor of *International Food and Agribusiness Management Review* and the *International Journal of Agricultural Management*. Professor Shadbolt represents New Zealand in the International Farm Comparison Network (IFCN) in Dairying. She is a Fellow of the New Zealand Institute of Primary Industry Management and the Australian Institute of Company Directors.

Dr. J. George Shanthikumar is the Richard E. Dauch Chair in Manufacturing and Operations Management and a Distinguished Chair Professor of Management. He was previously a Chancellor's Professor of Industrial Engineering and Operations Research at the University of

California, Berkeley. His research interests are in integrated interdisciplinary decision making, model uncertainty and learning, production systems, queueing theory, reliability, scheduling, semiconductor yield management, simulation, and stochastic processes. He has published over 300 papers on these topics and 3 books—*Stochastic Models of Manufacturing Systems* (with John A. Buzacott) and *Stochastic Orders and Their Applications* (with Moshe Shaked), and *Stochastic Orders* (with Moshe Shaked). He has extensively consulted for various companies including Applied Materials, Bellcore, IBM, KLA-Tencor, Nippon Telegraph and Telephone (Japan), Intel, Intermolecular, Reel Solar, Safeway, Southern Pacific Railways, Advanced Micro Devices, IBM, Intel, LSI, Motorola, Texas Instruments, Toshiba, Fujitsu, Taiwan Semiconductor Manufacturing Company, and United Microelectronics Corporation. He is an advisory consultant for Sensor Analytics and a member of the technical advisory board of Inter Molecular Inc. and Reel Solar, Inc.

Dr. Yossi Sheffi is the Elisha Gray II Professor of Engineering Systems at the Massachusetts Institute of Technology, where he serves as Director of the MIT Center for Transportation and Logistics. He is the author of numerous scientific publications and four award-winning books, translated to over a dozen languages. His latest book is *The Power of Resilience: How the Best Companies Manage the Unexpected* (MIT Press, October 2015). Outside the university, Dr. Sheffi has consulted with governments and leading manufacturing, retail, and transportation enterprises all over the world. He is also an active entrepreneur, who has founded and run five successful companies: PTCG, e-Chemicals, LogiCorp, Syncra, and Logistics.com. All his startups were acquired by leading enterprises. Dr. Sheffi was recognized in numerous ways in academic and industry forums, including CSCMP's the Distinguished Service Award, the Aragon International Prize, Salzberg Lifetime Award, the Eccles Medal, and many others, including book awards. He is a lifetime fellow of the UK's Cambridge University's Clair Hall and an Honorary Doctor (Doctor Honoris Causa) of Zaragoza University in Spain.

Dr. Dongping Song is a Professor of Supply Chain Management in the School of Management at the University of Liverpool. He studied and worked at Nankai University, Zhejiang University, Newcastle University, Imperial College, and Plymouth University. He is a Senior Member of IEEE and an Associate Editor of the *International Journal of Shipping and Transport Logistics*. He has managed several research projects in China, the UK, and the European Union. His research interests include modeling and optimization for manufacturing and transport logistics systems, especially in the presence of uncertainty. He has had papers published in journals including *IEEE Transactions on Automatic Control*, *Transportation Research Part B/E/D*, the *European Journal of Operational Research*, the *International Journal of Production Research*, *Naval Research Logistics*, and the *International Journal of Production Economics*.

Dr. Martin K. Starr is Distinguished Professor Emeritus of Operations Management at Rollins College in Winter Park, Florida, and Senior Professor Emeritus of the GBS, Columbia University in New York. His research interests include production modularity, disaster management, and decision theory. Dr. Starr has published in many journals as well as authoring recent POM texts. He is a Departmental Editor of *Production and Operations Management* and has served as President of POMS as well as TIMS. He is currently Director of Strategic Planning for POMS. Dr. Starr is a Fellow of the Institute for Operations Research and the Management Sciences (INFORMS) and the Production and Operations Management Society (POMS). He has been awarded the George E. Kimball Medal and the POMS Distinguished Service Award. POMS created the Martin K. Starr Excellence in Production and Operations Management Practice Award to honor exceptional POM practitioners.

Contributors

Dr. Christopher Tang is a University Distinguished Professor and the holder of the Edward W. Carter Chair in Business Administration at the UCLA Anderson School of Management at University of California, Los Angeles. Dr. Tang has published more than 100 articles in academic journals, magazines, and newspapers as well as five books. In addition to collaborating with students and colleagues, advising and mentoring many, including Ph.D. students, Dr. Tang has served as advisor to a number of corporate giants and startup companies. He has been a visiting professor at various international universities, such as the London Business School, and has taught various executive programs in Australia, Brazil, and the United Kingdom. Dr. Tang has been recognized with numerous UCLA teaching accolades, including the Dean's Excellent Service Award. He was elected a fellow by the Institute for Operations Research and the Management Sciences (INFORMS), Manufacturing and Service Operations Management Society (MSOM), and the Production and Operations Management Society (POMS). Dr. Tang was POMS' president in 2013, served on the editorial boards of many leading journals, and is the current Editor of *Manufacturing & Service Operations Management*.

Dr. Sridhar Tayur is the Ford Distinguished Research Chair and Professor of Operations Management at Carnegie Mellon University's Tepper School of Business. An *Academic Capitalist*, he is the founder and former CEO of SmartOps Corporation (acquired by SAP) and the founder of a social enterprise, OrganJet Corporation. An INFORMS Fellow, Dr. Tayur is widely known for his award-winning research and teaching in inventory theory, supply chain management, lean manufacturing, operations strategy, and healthcare and has published in *Operations Research*, *Management Science*, *Mathematics of Operations Research*, *Manufacturing & Service Operations Management*, and *Production and Operations Management*. He is co-editor of *Quantitative Models for Supply Chain Management*. Dr. Tayur has been featured in CBS News, HBS Case Studies, *Fortune*, *Forbes*, and *Atlantic* and has been recognized by the White House. Dr. Tayur founded RAGS Charitable Foundation, which supports documentary films and early stage medical research and which has gifted $1 million to Carnegie Mellon and has endowed an Institute Chair at IIT-Madras.

Dr. Asoo J. Vakharia is the McClatchy Professor and Director of the Center for Supply Chain Management in the Warrington College of Business Administration at the University of Florida. He has a Ph.D. in Operations Management from the University of Wisconsin. Dr. Vakharia's research primarily focuses on contemporary issues in supply chain management. He has published papers in several academic journals and serves as the Co-Department Editor for the *Production and Operations Management Journal*. Dr. Vakharia has extensive teaching experience having taught courses in management of service operations, operations strategy, international logistics, and MPC/ERP systems integration. His prior work experience includes managing the operations and financial aspects of a leather goods manufacturer and consulting for the banking industry. After joining academia, Dr. Vakharia has worked with several companies including AT&T Solutions Customer Care, e-Diets.com, Golden Eagle Distributors, Garrett Air Research, Motorola, Sweetheart Cups, Inc., University of Arizona Medical Center, and Vistakon, Inc.

Dr. Rohit Verma is the Dean for External Relations for the College of Business, Cornell University. He also serves as Executive Director of the Cornell Institute for Healthy Futures and the Singapore Tourism Board Distinguished Professor. Prior to his appointment at Cornell University, Dr. Verma was the George Eccles Professor of Management at the David Eccles School of Business, University of Utah. Dr. Verma has published over seventy-five articles in prestigious academic journals and has also written numerous reports for the industry audience. He is co-author of the *Operations and Supply Chain Management for the 21st Century* textbook and co-editor of *Cornell School of Hotel Administration on Hospitality: Cutting Edge Thinking and Practice*, a professional reference book that includes works of several of his colleagues at Cornell.

Dr. Vedat Verter is a James McGill Professor of Operations Management at the Desautels Faculty of Management of McGill University, Canada. He specializes on the application of business analytics for policy design and decision making in the public sector. His areas of research are transport risk management, sustainable operations, and healthcare operations management. His work in these areas is well recognized through top tier journal publications as well as invited presentations around the globe. In the area of healthcare, Dr. Verter focuses on preventive, primary, emergency, acute, and chronic care processes as well as their interaction. He is Director of McGill's MD-MBA Program and Founding Director of the NSERC CREATE Program in Healthcare Operations and Information Management, a Ph.D./PDF training program that is present in seven universities across Canada. Dr. Verter is also the Editor-in-Chief of *Socio-Economic Planning Sciences*, an international journal focusing on public sector decision making.

Dr. Prem Vrat is the Pro-Chancellor; Professor of Eminence and Chief Mentor at The North-Cap University, Gurugram, and held the position of Vice Chancellor at ITM University; Professor of Eminence (Management Development Institute, Gurugram); Director (Indian Institute of Technology, Roorkee); Vice Chancellor (Uttar Pradesh Technical University, Lucknow); Professor, and Director-in-charge (Indian Institute of Technology, Delhi); Professor and Division Chairman (Asian Institute of Technology, Bangkok); and Honorary Research Fellow (University of Birmingham). He received his Ph.D. from IIT Delhi. He has guided 39 Ph.D. theses and has published 450 research papers. He has authored/co-authored seven books and completed thirty-three consultancy assignments. He is a Fellow of the Indian National Academy of Engineering (INAE), National Academy of Sciences India (NASI), World Academy of Productivity Sciences (WAPS), Indian Institution of Industrial Engineering (IIIE), and Indian Society for Technical Education (ISTE). He has been conferred Doctor of Engineering (Honoris Causa), Distinguished Alumnus Award by IIT Kharagpur; the Distinguished Service Award by IIT Delhi; Outstanding Contribution Award for National Development by IIT Delhi Alumni Association; Lillian Gilbreth Award; thirteen best paper medals and prizes, including the National Systems Gold Medal (SSI) and the Life Time Achievement Award (SOM).

Dr. Lan Wang is currently an Assistant Professor at California State University's Department of Management. In 2014, she received her Ph.D. in Information System and Operations Management at University of Florida. In 2009, she received her Bachelor of Engineering in Industrial Engineering from Tsinghua University, Beijing. Dr. Wang's research primarily focuses on sustainability issues in supply chain management, interface between operations management with marketing and information systems, business analytics, management of technology. Dr. Wang has teaching experience in operations management, managerial statistics, decision science, and business analytics. Her prior working experience includes a stint as an industrial engineering intern at the Nissan Motor Corporation and as a supply chain consultant at the Chick-fil-A, Inc., headquarters.

Dr. Arda Yenipazarli is an Assistant Professor in the Department of Logistics & Supply Chain Management at Georgia Southern University. He earned his Ph.D. degree in Operations Management from the University of Florida. His primary research interests are in the areas of new product development, green supply chain management, sustainable technologies, and inventory management and theory. Dr. Yenipazarli's research investigates the profitability and efficiency of green operations launched in order to comply with environmental legislations and/or translate corporate sustainability liabilities into profits. His research also has implications for policy makers concerned with designing efficient environmental legislations. Dr. Yenipazarli's recent research has been published in the *European Journal of Operational Research*, the *International Journal of Production Economics*, *Annals of Operations Research*, the *International Journal of Production Research*, and *Operations Research Letters*. He serves as an ad-hoc referee for top-tier operations management journals. Dr. Yenipazarli also serves as the treasurer of Junior Faculty Interest Group (JFIG) of INFORMS since 2014 and is a member of the INFORMS Student Affairs Committee since 2015.

Dr. Keenan D. Yoho is an Associate Professor of Operations Management at Rollins College's Roy E. Crummer Graduate School of Business in Winter Park, Florida. His research and teaching is focused on the analysis of strategic, tactical, and operational alternatives under conditions of uncertainty and resource scarcity for the purpose of improving operational effectiveness and financial returns on investment. He has led studies for the Army, Air Force, U.S. Transportation Command, and the U.S. Office of the Secretary of Defense in the areas of transformation, operations, supply chain management, and acquisition to support active theaters of war. Prior to joining Rollins College, Dr. Yoho was part of a special team chosen to transform U.S. Special Operations Command and posture special operations forces around the globe to confront future security challenges.

Dr. Gang Yu is the co-founder and Executive Chairman of New Peak Group. Prior to founding New Peak Group, Dr. Yu was the co-founder and Chairman of Yihaodian—a leading e-commerce company in China. Dr. Yu has served as Vice President of Worldwide Procurement at Dell Inc. and Vice President of Worldwide Supply Chain at Amazon.com. Before Amazon, Dr. Yu served as Chair Professor at University of Texas at Austin, as Director of the Center for Management of Operations and Logistics, and as co-Director of the Center for Decision Making under Uncertainty. He is also the founder and former CEO of CALEB Technologies Corporation, a company later acquired by Accenture. Dr. Yu received a Bachelor of Science from Wuhan University, a Master of Science degree from Cornell University, and Ph.D. from the Wharton School of the University of Pennsylvania. Dr. Yu has published over eighty journal articles and four books, and he holds three US patents. Dr. Yu has received numerous international awards including the 2003 Outstanding IIE Publication Award from the Institute of Industrial Engineers, the 2012 Martin K. Starr Excellence in Production, and the Operations Management Practice Award from the Production and Operations Management Society (POMS).

Editorial Assistant

Ms. Zina Hutton is the editorial assistant for this project—the POM Companion. Ms. Hutton is a first year Master's student of Literature at Florida International University (FIU). Hutton graduated from FIU with her B.A. in History in 2012 and spent several years working in the Broward County School Board as an educator before returning to college in the quest for her graduate degree. Hutton currently works as a freelance editor and writer with publication credits in *Fireside Fiction* and the feminist news sites *The Mary Sue* and *Women Write about Comics*.

FOREWORD

The field of POMS has evolved at a rapid pace over the last decades. Summarizing the evolution would not be easy, but at the minimum, one can think of the tremendous expansion of the field in geographical coverage, discipline depth, inter-linkages with other fields, stakeholder perspectives, application bases, and the innovations of the field due to technological advancements.

The Routledge Companion to Production and Operations Management is a truly admirable publication. There are several distinctive contributions of the Companion. First, it provides, for the first time ever, an insightful historical perspective of the above evolution, allowing the readers to see how a field has grown, the approaches used by early researchers, and the continuing values of the field. Second, it is probably the most complete coverage of the expanded scope outlined in the evolution that I mentioned earlier. This is a complete treatment of all the important and exciting past, present, and future topics. Third, the Companion has been written by subject experts, and the collection of authors of the Companion is probably the Who's Who of the POM field.

I congratulate the editors for compiling the Companion. This is going to be a book that everyone in the POM field should read and use as a reference. What a first class accomplishment!

Dr. Hau L. Lee
Graduate School of Business
Knight Management Center
Stanford University, Stanford, CA, USA

PREFACE

This remarkable Production and Operations Management (POM) Companion highlights the fact that POM—as a field of study and research, including experimentation and practical implementation—can provide consequential business and social improvements. These improvements are sought by domestic and international organizations, global and local businesses, governments (of all types and sizes), and citizens who need help (in achieving sustainability, or during a disaster of any kind). This Companion shows that POM works well within an incredible range of systems (e.g., agriculture, disaster management, e-commerce, healthcare, hospitality, military systems, not-for-profit, retail, sports, sustainability, telecommunications, and transport). The POM companion helps to clarify how much POM has to contribute.

From a different perspective, but one that is equally compelling, we, as Editors, acknowledge that it has been a privilege to edit this book. What great admiration we have for our team of authors. They have worked diligently and put great amounts of their time into this book. We, as Editors, have watched as these thought leaders have toiled to achieve perfection and completion. We have received unstinted support from them even though their time is precious. It is a tribute to the POM field that when we set the highest standards for participation and invited these experts and visionaries of the POM field—they came forward to contribute their research and ideas.

We believe that support for this POM Companion will continue to be outstanding. Future revisions will be required to match the dynamics of this ever-changing domain as the POM field has much to offer in the future. We cannot predict what will occur. We know that visions of early POM scholars and practitioners have been surpassed. In straightforward words, POM methods apply to more types of organizational endeavors than we dreamed possible. Basic approaches have been extended and methodology has been fine-tuned. More powerful computer analytic capabilities employing increasingly creative statistical methods are producing more information than was ever thought possible. The real growth of the field is readily explained by the excellent return on investment obtained by solving a widening range of problems.

The POM Companion consists of eight parts. Part I is entitled "The Remarkable History of POM". Four authors participated in creating two outstanding chapters. Chapter 1, titled "Evolution of the POM Discipline," provides a unique panoramic vision of the POM field. Chapter 2, "Global Supply Chain Management," provides the vital background and balanced perspective of supply chain management development. These two chapters establish the critical foundation upon which the POM field has been built. They are essential chapters for all academics and practitioners, and especially for young scholars who have not been privy to such knowledge.

Part II, entitled "Core POM Functions" includes Chapters 3 through 9. It focuses on the main functions of POM. These seven incredible chapters, written by twelve authors, are: "Forecasting: State-of-the-Art in Research and Practice," "Aggregate Production Planning," "Scheduling in Manufacturing and Services," "Inventory Management," "Quality Management," "Facilities Design and Planning," and "Manufacturing Strategy." These expositions are up-to-date and provide present-day assessments and expectations of future functional applicability. Many combine pragmatic thinking with philosophical speculation. The readers will not be bored. Indeed, Part II provides an exciting opportunity to revisit and revitalize topics that have long been essential to POM. Real payoffs can be had if POM managers recognize the continuous development of these fundamental capabilities for both manufacturing and services.

Part III entitled "POM Process and Project Categories" has three inspiring chapters created by seven authors: "Process Capabilities and Leveraging Advances in Science and Technology," "Project Design and Management," and "From Lean Production to Operational Excellence. These authors have tackled fundamental approaches to deal with 21st Century disruptions of long-established POM traditions. This is the evolution of processes under the impetus of new technology. The applications of lean and agile methodologies are at the cutting edge. The chapter on project management could have had a subtitle: "This is not the PERT and CPM of yesterday." Young scholars, if you are champing at the bit, looking for great challenges, you will find them in Part III.

Part IV is entitled "Emerging Themes and New Research Domains of POM" and it vividly illustrates how growth of the POM field is accelerating. The emerging themes capture a significant part of "what is new." The five remarkable chapters created by 15 authors in Part IV are: "Business Startup Operations," "Sustainable Operations," "The Interdependence of Data Analytics and Operations Management," "The Evolution of Logistics Clusters," and "Human Behavior in Operations." These chapters illustrate how new domains appear which can create major disruptions in traditional ways of doing things. They also hold great promise of providing excellent returns on investment in research and development (R&D). We want to emphasize that POM has to make investments of its own, not only in the R of R&D but also in the D which translates into learning how to implement POM in new domains. These five chapters provide direction and motivation for experimentation and research on startups, sustainability, data mining, logistics clusters, and human behavior.

Part V is called "POM Interface with Other Functions." Four chapters created by 10 authors are: "Management Accounting and Operations Management," "POM and Finance," "POM and Marketing," and "The Strategic Role of Human Resources in Enabling POM." These four remarkable chapters are likely to set the tone for both POM pedagogy and research in the next decade. As Editors, we read and reviewed these chapters, learning new concepts that connected disparate ideas by unfolding unexpected compatibilities. Some chapters dug down deeply in pursuit of associating functionalities while others spanned so broadly that we found they linked more than two functions. That hardly surprised those of us who are committed systems thinkers. Again, young scholars in search of research topics will find them in abundance.

Part VI provides incredible proof of how far expansion of the POM field has progressed. It is called "POM Domains of Application" and is comprised of the greatest number of chapters of any part. Part VI has ten chapters written by twenty-three authors who have demonstrated the value of applying POM thinking to each of the ten areas represented by Chapters 22 through 31. Their topics are "Operations Management in Hospitality," "POM for Healthcare—Focusing on the Upstream," "Sports Operations Management," "POM in Agriculture," "POM and the

Military," "Not-for-Profit Operations Management," "Telecommunications and Operations Management," "POM for Disaster Management," "The Impact of POM on Transport and Logistics," and "POM and Retailing." If a teacher wants to truly understand the POM field and its many opportunities for each student to choose from, these ten chapters provide an amazing spectrum. For those studying POM, the application potentials are enormous and growing larger every day.

Part VII which is called, "Expert POM Practitioners' Perspectives," provides an interesting change of pace. Most authors of this POM Companion can walk on both sides of the street with ease, viz. teach a class and advise a business. However, all of us can be identified primarily either as an academician or a practitioner. Part VII lets the voices of four practitioners ring loud and clear. There are notable similarities among these three Chapters 32, 33, and 34. When recommendations for research are made, they are aimed at obtaining more effective management, better competitive positions, and greater control. They are right in sync with practitioners' goals. These three wonderful chapters, filled with anecdotes and lessons about leadership, are entitled: "POM for the Hospitality Industry," "Trends in Global Sourcing, Procurement, and Distribution Research and Practice," and "Best Practice: Supply Chain Optimization at Yihaodian." It is readily understandable why these four authors are widely recognized as experts.

The remaining Chapters 35, 36, and 37 in Part VIII succeed in bringing the POM Companion to an exciting conclusion. Part VIII is titled: "POM—The Next Era." The previous thirty-four chapters have done their bit to explore and extrapolate to "The Next Era." However, this purpose is completed with Part VIII. The three chapters—"The Evolutionary Trends of POM Research in Manufacturing," "Future Trends for Research and Practice in the Management of Global Supply Chains," and "Conclusions: Evaluation and Prognostications for the POM Domain"—pull no punches. What does that mean? "To pull no punches" is English colloquialism denoting "to hold nothing back." The six authors of Chapters 35, 36, and 37 state what they hope the future will become in unambiguous terms. The goal of Chapter 37 is to report as clearly and succinctly as possible what the contributors to the thirty-seven chapters of this POM Companion believe will be crucial for the future development of the POM field in teaching, research, and in various non-traditional applications. Their opinions were obtained from a survey conducted in the two months prior to submitting the manuscript for publication. Chapter 37 fulfills its mission to evaluate and prognosticate for the POM Domain.

Chapter 1 explained how some have heralded that POM is moving into Industry 4.0 (forecasting an era of artificial intelligence, Internet and the social media, etc.). As Editors we have said that our interest is not in forecasting the future of POM. Our preference is to influence what the future will become. We believe that all of the chapters in this POM Companion (topped off by keen perceptions and smart suggestions obtained from the survey) confirm the value of the design of this text based on reaching out to the thought leaders of the POM field. We have called upon these seventy POM visionaries to provide that influence and they have answered the call.

Martin K. Starr and Sushil K. Gupta
January 2017

PART I
The Remarkable History of POM

1
EVOLUTION OF THE POM DISCIPLINE

Martin K. Starr, Sushil K. Gupta, and Christopher Tang

1 Introduction to Evolving POM

Note that, for the purposes of this chapter and for the Companion as well, we have chosen to use the acronym POM to stand for Production and Operations Management, Operations Management, and Production Management, therefore embodying all possible usages in a single acronym.

Even as we start this chapter, we know that our interest in this chapter's mission is based upon using history to project the future. There are many advocates who say that only by knowing where you have been can you prognosticate where you are heading in the future. By describing POM's evolution, and recognizing the real drivers of the field, we may be able to prophesize the future. At the very least, we can discuss what POM is capable of becoming. Additionally, there is another major point that is concerned with how POM can fail and what POM should avoid.

This POM Companion only begins to map the surface of the evolving POM discipline. There are so many aspects to the field that even those of us who have been steeped in its development are somewhat dazzled by the variety. Each facet has its own group with intense advocacy and remarkable depth of investigation. This is true because POM represents a blending of Science and Art. There is the Science of technology and the Art of management. Taken together, and rendered properly, successful leadership arises.

We capitalize the first letters of Science and Art (S&A) because we are dealing with many applications of the generic structure of both S&A in the same way that Chemistry and Physics are both employers of legitimate Science. Similarly, both Painting and Sculpture utilize all of the most fundamental principles of Art. POM, as with architecture, uses both Science and Art to predict what will work and to forewarn what will not.

Looking back is instructive for other reasons as well. We can observe that the field of POM has gone through many changes that can be called evolutionary or revolutionary—depending upon the scholars' time frame. In this chapter, we choose several ways of viewing developments over the recent past. Our attention will be focused on the recent past because that will constitute the most relevant history for explaining foundations upon which the future of this field is likely to be constructed.

One approach identifies three milestone events (Sections 3, 4, and 5). A second approach examines the four industrial revolution eras (called IR 1.0, IR 2.0, IR 3.0, and IR 4.0) as found in Sections 6.1, 6.2, 6.3, and 6.4. These are two different ways of slicing the apple. Each provides insights and perspectives that are useful as frameworks for understanding why POM cuts across so many areas of application that are seemingly unrelated to each other except in the context of the rich fabric of a great society. We have to conclude that certain elements are common to all of these areas of application. Additionally, it will be very evident why, at first, POM was centered on manufacturing but then its applicability spread to services and many unconventional applications. At first, these milestones read as if they only apply to manufacturing, but that is misleading. As technology expands, so does vision. That is why we also use "industrial revolution eras" in this first chapter. The era perspective shows how services evolve to envelop and utilize the best of manufacturing processes and procedures.

Some of the elements of commonality are their dependency on competent process design to provide product supply that is scalable to the level of demand. Quite clearly, "products" in this context refer to both goods and services. Also evident is the commonality of the perception of product quality by the consumers of these goods and services. This measure of quality includes both speed of delivery and important product attributes. Although cost is seldom included as a quality attribute, it is a critical decision factor for most consumers. POM is involved in all three of these critical dimensions of process to product/service output performance. Each chapter in this POM Companion shows that the same commonalities apply to radically different domains of application (e.g., sports, military, healthcare, hospitality, disaster management, and farming in New Zealand).

Before concluding this "Introduction to Evolving POM," please note our strong preference towards influencing the future rather than trying to forecast what the future will look like. Unambiguously, we chose the strategy of achieving active impact rather than benefiting from passive forecasting. The thirty-seven chapters of this POM Companion should be viewed in this perspective. These chapters are meant to influence future developments rather than attempt to predict what the future will be like. That is why most chapters conclude with a section describing research opportunities for young scholars and why many chapters have a section that provides "implications for practitioners." Research that is intense and honest is useful on its own, but we also need brilliant insights and astounding breakthroughs that can be expanded upon for the future.

2 The Value of Historical Perspective for POM

The first steps out of the Stone Age came with the metalworking of copper (about 10,000 years ago). This actually precedes any real evidence of humanity's ability to read and write. Ages were named for the development of skills with materials starting with the Stone Age (9300 to 3300 BCE). Then, came the Bronze Age (3300 to 1300 BCE) followed by the Iron Age (1300 BCE to 700 CE). These numbers are approximate and depend on locations and contexts (e.g., scholars point to Early, Middle, and Late Iron Ages). All of this is definitely pre-POM and yet serves as a vital precursor to what POM may become in the Information Age (1950 CE and on).

We have no intention of describing (in any detail) production and operations developments during the Renaissance period of 1300 to 1600 CE. This rebirth of art and intellect began in Italy and spread across Europe, ending around 1600 CE with the major Reformation of church and state. However, centuries before 1300 CE, there was production of food and shelters, clothing, and other necessities such as shoes, water jugs, and kilns for cooking. Production of tools of war including ships, chariots, and means of hurling projectiles antedates Alexander the Great (356 BCE to 323 BCE).

As we move through eons of time, the year 1500 CE stands out as an important POM threshold because it signals the beginning of the artisan craft guilds. Often there was one guild for each trade (e.g., bakers, brewers, carpenters, cobblers, and stonemasons). Guilds imposed rationality and consistency on each trade's production. Most Guilds inspected product for violations of quality subject to standards set by the members, e.g., in parts of Europe the blending of gruit for beer was a closely held secret of the Gruit Guilds, which were responsible for high-quality beer. (Gruit—also from the Dutch word *gruyt*—a herb mixture used for bittering beer before the extensive use of hops.) The beer game aside, one can say that 1500 CE marks the first coherent efforts to organize a great variety of production systems in terms of supply and demand, cost and price, quality and quantity. It is interesting how often the motivations were beer and military factors.

3 First POM Milestone—The Division of Labor

The first major POM milestone occurred when the 18th century was about 75% completed. This milestone came in the form of a book that promoted the benefits of employing the division of labor in a factory setting. Written by Adam Smith, the book was entitled *An Inquiry into the Nature and Causes of the Wealth of Nations*. This two-volume treatise (published in the same year as the American Declaration of Independence) was followed by three new editions amended by Smith and a fourth edition in 1904—all of which had the same title (Smith 1776).

These texts examined the economics of national wealth, recognizing that the "specialization of jobs" in factories provided substantial commercial benefits. The "division of labor" is another way of describing this early effort to design for manufacturing (DFM) in terms of "the division of labor." DFM is related to process design that promotes job improvement by means of repetition of limited, circumscribed activities by individuals. Another major point that Adam Smith made was the way in which supply and demand achieve a state of equilibrium (he called it the invisible hand). In fact, it was the way in which the supply chain operated that caught Smith's attention. The name "supply chain" was unknown at that time, but the invisible hand referred to market forces as controlled by managers. Smith's *Wealth of Nations* put forward concepts that led to profound changes in the nature of production systems. It also foretold that remarkable societal cataclysmic changes were beginning to occur.

So often, this important book is mentioned without dissemination of its contents. To better understand why this publication was a landmark event and turning point, we believe that it helps to glimpse a part of its table of contents (as shown below). Here are a few of the chapter and section titles (we employ the British spelling for "labour" because that is the way it is written):

Volume I: *An Inquiry into the Nature and Causes of the Wealth of Nations*

 Book I: "Of the Causes of Improvement"

  Section I.1: "Of the Division of Labour"
  Section I.2: "Of the Principle which gives Occasion to the Division of Labour"
  Section I.3: "That the Division of Labour is Limited by the Extent of the Market"

 Book II: "Of the Nature, Accumulation, and Employment of Stock"
 Book III: "Of the different Progress of Opulence in different Nations"

  Section III.3: "Of the Rise and Progress of Cities and Towns. . . ."

 Book IV: "Of Systems of Political Economy"

Volume II: *An Inquiry into the Nature and Causes of the Wealth of Nations*

Book V: "Of the Revenue of the Sovereign or Commonwealth"

Section V.2: "Of the Sources of the General or Public Revenue of the Society"

This book was widely read. The thesis enabled risk-takers to assess the value of shifting their investments from the old style of doing business to a newer one that built factories (especially for the textile industry). It is a fair guess that Smith's work accelerated the rate with which a variety of POM-enabling events (e.g., inventions for textile mills) followed.

Methods for employing this "division of labor" have had major impacts on productivity enhancement, and they are often part of successful POM implementations at the present time. One of the first examples of how effective specialization can be was the way factory operations were designed at the Highland Park Ford plant in 1913. Henry Ford was a master at successfully implementing the "division of labor" concept on Ford's moving assembly (production) line.

This production system reduced the chassis assembly time from 12.5 hours to 1.5 hours with great cost reduction. This enabled Henry Ford to pay workers $5 per day, twice what they were originally being paid. At that pay scale, workers on the assembly line could buy a Model T with about four months of pay, and many of them became owners. Ford was applauded for enabling his workers to become customers.

3.1 The Holistic Production System of Volvo (Opposite to Division of Labor)

The holistic production system of the Volvo Uddevalla plant in Sweden (which opened in 1985) provided a counter example of job specialization. The very opposite of division of labor was used. Employees were part of an assembly team that was grouped around a single fixed position for auto assembly. Every employee was trained to do all of the jobs required to assemble a Volvo. The production method was called "naturally grouped assembly work." Employees moved around the car in well thought-out sequences to accomplish assembly. Unlike Ford assembly, the car chassis never moved.

What happened to this seven-year experiment is partially summarized in a report whose title is somewhat confusing, "The Uddevalla Plant: Why Did It Succeed with a Holistic Approach and why Did It Come to an End?" (Nilsson 2007). The report states that both the traditional (Ford-type) and the holistic approach were seen by management as having equivalent efficiencies and that the costs at Uddevalla were seen as higher. The report also states that this conclusion was not true, implying that costs were lower and efficiency was higher at Uddevalla. Quoting from the report, "Unfortunately the Volvo Uddevalla plant in its tragic premature closure will not be able to demonstrate the success of the model." This provocative conclusion seems to offer ample reason for future research on the validity of the division of labor thesis.

3.2 Division of Labor Applied to Services

It should be noted that "division of labor" has had an important influence on service systems as well as manufacturing. A few helpful examples come readily to mind. The use of specialists in the healthcare systems are the norm and not the exception. So many different skills are required in a hospital that it is even more diverse than a business school faculty. The pastry chef in a gourmet restaurant is not expected to cook the soup or serve fine wines. Call center designs are predicated on the advantages of separating requests and directing them to specialists in each type of query. Often, a robot sorter is used to direct calls to the right specialist.

There are ample opportunities to conduct important research on how best to use the division of labor to improve productivity in the service sector. General practitioners in the medical field are the generalists who can see the big picture. Specialists may understand particular parts of the body or mind, but the generalist's point of view is essential for proper diagnostics. This perspective is entirely applicable to managers of organizations who require input from staff specialists in order to reach decisions that reflect systems factors.

We would be remiss not to note that service robots have assumed an important role in many industries, reflecting years of development. Joe Engelberger—the so-called father of robotics—wanted to develop robots that could work in hazardous environments that were harmful to humans. He was chairman of the board and champion of robots at Transitions Research Corporation (TRC), which brought out Unimate, the first industrial robot in the U.S. in the 1950s. TRC specialized in service robots including HelpMate (a service bot that did the work of hospital orderlies).

Automated voice response systems have a commanding presence in taking reservations for airlines, restaurants, etc. Not only do they schedule appointments, but they also determine the best connective path for incoming calls. With the further development of artificial intelligence (AI), we can expect to obtain great diagnostics from computerized medical-assist programs. IBM's supercomputer Watson may be close to a tipping point in finding cures for diseases that have ravished both developed and underdeveloped economies. To conclude, it would appear that the application of the best "division of labor" in service organizations is a fertile area for scholarly research.

4 Second POM Milestone—Interchangeable Parts (IP) and the Science of Tolerance Ranges

Ford's assembly line could not have functioned if car doors had to be *customized* in order to fit each *unique* chassis. For the Ford system to work, all parts had to be *interchangeable*. Every door (e.g., the front seat driver's door), as it comes from the metal stamping machines, must fit the appropriate chassis door opening of the matching car model. Color is a different issue than tolerances. Color matching requires scheduling the same color door and chassis to meet at the right point in time and place on the production assembly line.

The concept of "interchangeable parts" assumes that components can be selected at random (from a batch of similar parts) and that they will fit together without requiring any make-fit work. It is important to note that make-fit procedures were the norm long before and even long after cotton gin inventor Eli Whitney (1765–1825) conceived of interchangeable musket parts. It was the only way that he could fulfill a 1798 Congressional contract to build 10,000 muskets for the U.S. Army by a given date.

Selective assembly is an alternative mode of assembly where pairs of parts having the best fit are selected. This option would override random selection when very tight tolerance matching is essential. For a deeper discussion and appropriate references, the Wikipedia article on "Interchangeable Parts" is a rather helpful starting point. Additionally, consider researching the article for "Honoré Blanc," another pioneer for interchangeable parts who, as the French counterpart of Eli Whitney, made a big impression on then American Ambassador to France, Thomas Jefferson.

Whitney developed specifications that would permit 10,000 of each part (e.g., triggers, stocks, barrels, etc.) to be substitutable for one another. One trigger was like another trigger, and that not only reduced the cost of assembling the muskets but allowed for rapid assembly. The idea of interchangeability was being developed in France and Sweden and quite possibly other places in

Europe as well. Wherever it was tried, it resulted in far better fabrication and assembly, which led to its adoption in factories after 1800. For this reason, at least in some circles, Whitney was known as a pioneer in the development of the American manufacturing system.

We are not born with the innate knowledge of how to design appropriate tolerance ranges so that part A fits "perfectly" into part B. For example, keys must fit the slot in the cylinder of locks just as doors must fit into doorframes. Logical use of fitting tools such as files would enable a worker to approximate what is required. This is called custom fitting. However, the method of gradually approaching a good fit incrementally is very costly and time consuming. Henry Ford's assembly line would not have achieved "mass production" of the Model T without the realization of the need for interchangeable parts. An extension of this knowledge has led to the meta-level of understanding that is required to achieve modular production (Starr 2010). Modular products have many varieties by simply interchanging components, e.g., cars with different engines and tires, phones with different memory levels. This is a higher degree of interchangeability than is achieved by standardization described in Section 5.1 below.

Engineers are trained to design tolerance ranges for interchangeability. The concepts that are required must take into account two additional phenomena. First, stamping dies (for example) wear down. This means that the sizes of components change over time (by usage) as they come off the production line. It is likely that the first door coming off the production line fits perfectly within the door frame of the first chassis that is constructed. That is because the tolerances are properly designed. Now, taking mechanical wear into account, the second door that is made is just a bit wider, and the chassis door frame maybe, just a bit narrower. The process of widening and narrowing continues until the door no longer is a perfect fit. Instead, it may wobble or cohere. Engineers know that it is time to replace the old and worn dies with new ones. No one is surprised. Designers, and workers on the assembly line, knew that this would happen. Eventually, stamping dies are always re-tooled or replaced. This production problem is well understood. It is competently addressed in most cases by quality control experts.

Now, let us turn to the second phenomenon, which was not understood until the early 1900s. That is when Milestone 3 was achieved and surpassed by Walter A. Shewhart who, in 1924, wrote a critical memorandum to his boss at Bell Labs (George Edwards) in which he developed the essential principles and fundamental concepts of statistical quality control (SQC).

5 Third POM Milestone—Statistical Quality Control (SQC) and Standardization

In an idealistic world, interchangeable parts would be identical. In a realistic world, that is not possible. This conundrum explains why Milestone 3 was such an elusive and critical next step that had to be traversed before the science of tolerance limits could be properly formulated by a host of statisticians with applied POM leanings and training.

Gratefully, we acknowledge that we do not have to repeat the biographic materials of these scientists because there is excellent coverage of twelve of the most important such individuals in Chapter 7, Section 4, which presents "Key Figures" in Quality Management.

We will, however, name these twelve pioneers who developed the fundamental concepts/methods related to the variability of production output. These are (in the order of their appearance in Chapter 7, Section 4): Frederick W. Taylor, William Sealy Gosset, Ronald Alymer Fisher, Henry Ford, George D. Edwards, Walter A. Shewhart, W. Edwards Deming, Armand V. Feigenbaum, Joseph M. Juran, Kaoru Ishikawa, Taiichi Ohno, and Philip B. Crosby. Each one of these outstanding practitioners and/or academics contributed to the accomplishments that were essential to achieve completion of the third Milestone.

When combined with empirical observations of the real world, probability theory showed that at some reasonable level of product dimension measurement some significant degree of variability would be observed. Shewhart showed how to measure, track, and control variability. Control could only be exercised if one could determine whether observed variability was an inherent part of the systems variability or an external and removable cause of variability.

There could be no correction (reduction of variability) of inherent statistical variability caused by endless numbers of trivial factors that add up to a significant amount of total variation. Gears heat up and expand at different rates. Each part of any machine provides its own unique underlying characteristics. For example, small vibrations from each and every machine element combine to produce a symphony of little causes.

Instead of inherent causes that cannot be eliminated are assignable causes that can be tracked, traced, and removed.

The statistical theory of variability is fundamental to fabrication of parts and components as well as to operations and activities, including time to maintain and repair a system as well as to service customers. For example, accident rates have been studied for stability where stability indicates that all assignable causes of variability have been removed. To illustrate, let's say that workers trip occasionally over a crack in the plant floor. Smoothing it out removes an assignable cause.

The variability of people's skills and behaviors are exemplified by the inability to drive a golf ball in an identical way—with exactly the same results every time you tee off. Workers using machines reflect the same phenomena in which machines, muscles, and vision each contribute some degree of variation. The distribution of total variability along many different dimensions must be understood to control the process and provide a satisfactory product to the customer.

5.1 Standardized Parts and Operations

Without standardization, costs increase and quality decreases substantially. For example, we take for granted the fact that the light bulbs we buy in the hardware store or supermarket fit the lamps in our homes. That is because in the U.S., the E26 is a standard light bulb screw base for a 110-volt outlet. The European variant, rated at 220 volts, is called E27 because it has a 27-mm diameter whereas the U.S. socket has a 26-mm diameter. An E26 bulb can fit into an E27 base, and vice versa. Often times, there are differences between European products based on metric system measures and U.S. products based on the English system of measurement.

There are at least ten different screw bases for light bulbs. That is a lot of choice within a convention, but there are other dimensional designations as well. The most common type of residential light bulb is the "A" shape. An A19 would signify that the width of the bulb at its widest point (in eighths of an inch) is 19 divided by 8, which equals 2.375inches in diameter. There are different sizes for different uses. For example, the Edison screw fitting is a system of screw mounts developed by Thomas Edison in 1909 under the Mazda trademark. Most have a right-hand, threaded metal base, which is turned clockwise to tighten in the socket. However, the New York City subway lightbulbs are turned counterclockwise to tighten, which keeps them from being stolen for use at home.

Typical incandescent A-type bulbs work with AC or DC. They are very inefficient, converting less than 2% to 3% of the energy they use into visible light; the remainder is converted into heat. Another measure of importance is how many lumens are delivered per watt, which is called luminous efficacy. The expected lifetime of such bulbs is in the thousands of hours and so, where the cost of replacing burnt-out bulbs is large, preference goes to LEDs. In many countries, regulations have been passed to phase out incandescent bulbs in the relatively near future.

We do not intend to present more than this cursory history of the light bulb (which, if properly pursued, is both fascinating and instructive). Dimensions and tolerances for screw bases are standardized in ANSI standard C81.67 and IEC standard 60061–1. Who are ANSI and IEC? ANSI refers to the American National Standards Institute, which is a private non-profit organization that oversees the development of voluntary consensus standards for products, services, processes, systems, and personnel in the U.S. The IEC is a similar organization (International Electrotechnical Commission) which sets international standards especially for electrical, electronics, and related technologies.

To the knowledge of any system of standards, we must now add the requirement that tolerances be understood. A lamp base of 26 mm must have an associated tolerance range for both the base and the socket into which the base screws. We will employ numbers that seem reasonable but are arbitrary (not related to any manufacturer of light bulbs). When tolerance ranges are proposed for a bulb base (such as 26.0 ± 0.1 mm), it connotes that the base diameter could be as narrow as 25.9 mm (26.0 − 0.1 = 25.9) or as wide as 26.1 mm (26.0 + 0.1 = 26.1).

The statistical variability of the system of production (persons and machines) will be expected to fall within that range (say) 99.5% of the time. If the base measures have a normal distribution with a mean of 26.0, it is quite feasible to determine if the given system is capable of achieving these results. It is also evident the socket maker must provide a tolerance range of diameters that will allow all bulbs that conform to be accommodated.

The three milestones have created an environment in which global trade is feasible for makers of bulbs and makers of lamps. The customer is able to buy the commodity of light at a very reasonable price. If all three milestones had not occurred with challenges met successfully, the world would be a much darker place.

We will now try taking a different cut at describing the evolution of the POM discipline. Instead of using critical events, we will describe a sequence of industrial revolution eras. The timeline consists of the four eras in Section 6. The first of these eras begins around 1760, which predates Adam Smith's publication of *The Wealth of Nations* by sixteen years. It is said that Smith was working on his manuscript for about nine years prior to its publication. Events were moving the Western World toward accelerated industrialization.

6 Four Industrial Revolutions—IR 1.0, IR 2.0, IR 3.0, and IR 4.0

Strictly speaking, industrialization is defined as the process by which a country (or group of nations) is transformed by a variety of forces from an agricultural society to one based on the manufacturing of goods and the production of services. Craftsmen who customize products are replaced by workers on an assembly line. At least, that is what was meant by the term "industrial" as in the First Industrial Revolution (which we will call IR 1.0 for reasons that will be obvious as we proceed).

6.1 The First Industrial Revolution (IR 1.0), 1776 to 1840

The textile industry was revolutionized by water power and steam power in the United Kingdom. Shortly after the American Revolution (1776), the same occurred in the emancipated colony across the Atlantic Ocean. Division of labor played an important part in disrupting the existing systems for producing textile products. Possibly, the most significant impact of this disruption was the increase in personal wealth. The standard of living for the general population started to increase, and it continued to do so beyond the conclusion of IR 1.0, which is generally stated to be 1840. We have spent ample time on the effects of the first industrial revolution.

Clearly, it created the foundation upon which POM was conceived and developed. The second industrial revolution had an even more profound effect.

6.2 The Second Industrial Revolution (IR 2.0), 1840 to 1914

The second phase is said by historians (who are in charge of such distinctions) to have begun in 1840 and continued until about 1914 which marked the start of World War I. During this period (which is also called the Technological Revolution), steam was adopted as a major power source for manufacturing as well as transportation. Iron making became a major industry as coke was substituted for charcoal. This change in production method created higher-quality iron and steel products, which were made at significantly lower costs. The effects rippled out, impinging on many products as well as on the construction of tall buildings and expansive railroad systems.

This was followed by electrification of factories. Telegraph lines changed the character of global communication. Automobiles were altering transportation. Paper production in conjunction with printing presses allowed for the mass production of newspapers and books. Petroleum became a source of energy that was portable for kerosene lamps and heaters. Mass produced pencils were a social phenomenon. Electric lights and fountain pens epitomized an era of unparalleled invention. IR 2.0 represented an exceptional time that affected large numbers of people.

Division of labor became ubiquitous for fabrication. It continued to characterize services. There was a clear distinction, however. Specialization in manufacturing applied to small subsets and sequences of the total activities required to make and assemble a product. Specialization for services was far more encompassing—as in healthcare and animal husbandry. The specialist was a generalist for a particular application.

Shoes are a good example of the transition that occurred with the advent of IR 2.0. Shoes had been crudely and custom made by shoemakers for ages. The right and left shoe were identical until about 1820. In 1812, Marc Brunel developed machinery for the mass production of boots for soldiers of the British Army. By 1815, manual labor was cheaper, and Brunel's system ceased to be used. However, Lyman Blake invented a shoe-stitching machine in 1856, and by 1864, it was known as the McKay stitching machine. By 1864, factories all over New England in the U.S. began to make shoes.

Iron made by rolling mills and hot blast furnaces (around 1830) was slow and costly. This was disrupted by the first inexpensive industrial process for the mass production of steel (Bessemer's process was patented in 1856). New capabilities of steel were explored allowing bridges to be built across greater spans than ever before. The Brooklyn Bridge was the world's longest suspension bridge at the time. It was completed in 1883 (McCullough 2012).

POM project management students are likely to profit by reading David McCullough's book referenced above as well as his book about the Panama Canal (McCullough 2001), which epitomized IR 2.0. This very difficult project was carried out in two stages. The French began in 1881, having completed the sea-level Suez Canal ten years earlier. Troubles abounded, and work was abandoned in 1888. A project group led by American engineers restarted the project in 1904. Locks were added because the tidal range at the Pacific was 20 feet, whereas it was only 1 foot on the Atlantic side. Completion occurred in 1914 after much loss of life due to yellow fever and malaria. The Panama Canal expansion project is near completion now and will lead to bigger ships requiring deeper harbors and greater container capabilities.

Although POM still did not exist as IR 2.0 ended, its most important precursor, industrial engineering, was being born in the early years of the 20th Century. In fact, industrial engineering became a major option at every engineering school in the U.S. after World War II.

Inventions during IR 2.0 came so regularly that it should have been named "the age of invention." In contrast, these days, 63% of all shoes are made in the People's Republic of China. We will get to such shifts in production locations, which are directly related to outsourcing labor-intensive work because of lower labor costs. "Outsourcing," which spans IR 3.0 and IR 4.0, has taken on serious pejorative connotations. There is little doubt that the emergence of powerful and inexpensive robotics during IR 4.0 will change this discourse.

6.3   The Third Industrial Revolution (IR 3.0), 1914 to 1999

The starting and ending dates for the Third Industrial Revolution are not agreed upon. The author, Jeremy Rifkin wrote a book called *The Third Industrial Revolution* (Rifkin 2011). In it, he contends that the Internet and renewable energy should be labeled as the third industrial revolution. It is our contention that the era between WWI and the end of the 20th Century deserves that label. The third Milestone was not fully developed until well after 1914. Instead, we have identified a new POM inspired (intellectual) movement, which is known as Industry 4.0 (as equivalent to IR 4.0).

The shift between IR 2.0 and IR 3.0 was an acceleration of existing trends plus a lot of new very disruptive technology. Using textiles as an example of acceleration of existing trends, the cottage industry's "putting-out system" was totally disrupted and obliterated. The main power source for everything that moved was steam made by burning coal. This was gradually, and then almost entirely, disrupted by electrification with many motors and engines being energized by petroleum products. Realization of *economies of scale* led to high-volume production systems sustained by increased capabilities of marketing to generate sufficient demand to support mass production.

During this era, industrial engineering (IE) was born. In the U.S., the first department of industrial and manufacturing engineering was established at Pennsylvania State University in 1909. In these early years of the 1900s, process analysis was being rationalized and legitimized by IE practitioners (who had never heard of POM). Great industrial engineers such as Frank Bunker Gilbreth Jr. and Lillian Moller Gilbreth were talking about process improvement both in the home and in the factory. Lillian gave lectures at MIT about efficiency in the kitchen. Time and motion studies were the method of studying process activities and the term efficiency expert had a glamorous ring to it. It sustained its vigor and importance for practitioners and academics alike into the third IR 3.0.

From 1914 to 1990, the computer evolved from a huge amalgam of vacuum tubes, patch cables, and switches to lightweight laptops with solid-state disks (SSDs) that were also called flash memory. Eventually, these advancements would lead to even smaller and lighter smart phones that had more power than the famous ENIAC at the University of Pennsylvania (1943–1945). The Advanced Research Projects Agency Network (ARPANET) is an important IR 3.0 step along the way. ARPA, the agency, was part of the United States Department of Defense, and it installed and maintained the network connecting many universities and defense establishments in the 1960s. This early packet switching network became the technical foundation of the Internet, something that we think of as a driving force for global communication and information searches. It may seem hard to believe that many opponents existed to this network, but this is due to how the Vietnam years had created plentiful public opposition to anything that involved the U.S. Department of Defense.

Let us continue our brief discussion of IR 3.0 with respect to energy. Petroleum became a major source of energy throughout this period, which made the Middle East into a power broker due to great reserves of traditional oil in the ground. New materials with petroleum bases were developed by chemists. Plastics emerged as a major new material for fabrication with thousands of new uses (including car doors and bumpers). Coincidentally, this was the era when jet planes cut travel time, therefore enabling international contacts. Huge container ships permitted giant amounts of cargo to be moved economically on a global scale.

With such a background, it makes sense that Japan, while striving to recover from WWII, launched (with the help of W. Edwards Deming and others—see Chapter 7, Section 4.1) an export drive that utilized the automobile industry to become a means for Japan to open very valuable markets in the U.S. Japanese production methods reduce costs and substantially increase the reliability of automobiles. Both of these factors were significant, but the increased reliability of automobiles was a major quality factor for the success of Japanese products.

The Japanese effect on world production methods had a major impact on the POM field, which was beginning to emerge as separate and distinct from industrial engineering (IE). We will consider this major influence by Japan on the POM field in Section 7 of this chapter.

The Operational Research Society was founded in the UK in 1948. The Operations Research Society of America (ORSA) was founded in 1952. The Institute of Management Sciences (TIMS) was founded in 1953. Mel Salveson wrote, "Prior to the formation of the Institute of Management Sciences, TIMS, the prevailing term that came closest to describing its evolving discipline and field of inquiry was *scientific management*" (Salveson 1997). This chapter in conjunction with Chapter 7, Section 4.1, identified Frederick W. Taylor as the so-called father of scientific management. Salveson continued to write, "However, scientific management was more a collection of admonitions as to what one ought to do to manage effectively. It was not a rigorous discipline nor an evolving body of knowledge based upon traditional scientific methods of research, inquiry, and experimentation." The challenge that Salveson (who was a founder of TIMS) described was a tipping point. TIMS was the beginning of the outright foundation for the Production and Operations Management Society (POMS). All of these societies were precursors to the POM field, but TIMS was directly involved in quantitative modeling and experimentation providing empirical results. There were still many more steps to take along the way.

APICS (originally, the American Production and Inventory Control Society) was founded in 1957. Churchman, Ackoff, and Arnoff published their *Introduction to Operations Research* in 1957 (Churchman et al. 1957). The military work of Blackett's Circus (Budiansky 2013) had crossed the paths of military needs for inventory and logistics with that of operations managers and project planners. The models created and reported in the prior references in this paragraph led directly to further developments some of which were reported by Elwood Buffa in his text entitled *Modern Production Management* (Buffa 1961). Inventory models and queuing systems had meaning for military minds as well as managers responsible for production.

Finally, it all came together when Kalyan Singhal established the Production and Operations Management Society (POMS) in June 1989. Christer Karlsson and Chris Voss were co-founders of the European Operations Management Association (EurOMA) in 1993.

6.4 Industry 4.0: The Fourth Industrial Revolution (IR 4.0), 1999 and beyond

As was true of IR 3.0, this designation of IR 4.0 is also disputed territory. It is our choice to date this future range of new disruptive technologies that are impacting the POM field over an unknown period of time. We believe it is reasonable to proclaim a fourth phase of the industrial revolution (IR 4.0). Each of the prior eras had characteristics that distinguish it from the prior periods.

This era promises new energy sources that may lead to inexpensive power. Rifkin describes people sharing (lateral) power with each other as in an "energy internet" (Rifkin 2011). Such transactions have the potential to revolutionize the POM domain in many ways. Inexpensive energy costs provide a new income source. They would be derived from alternative sources (not coal and petroleum) such as fusion, solar, wind, and tidal forces. We know that Tesla (led by Elon Musk) has built a huge new plant in Nevada to manufacture lithium batteries for cars and homes. Any means of storing energy more efficiently (with advanced battery designs) is game changing because such power can be used when the sun isn't shining and the wind isn't blowing. Such changes would revolutionize the cost structure of fabrication, transportation, home heating, and air conditioning as well as agriculture.

Day-to-day life may include driverless cars and deliveries by drones (see Kiva discussion below). The capability to make spare parts as needed using 3D additive printing is another game changer. It will alter a great variety of systems procedures that require stocking spare parts (e.g., airlines with a globally dispersed network). Military organizations like the U.S. Navy have enormous spare parts inventories.

In 2012, Amazon bought Kiva Systems for $775 million. Kiva makes robots that automate the entire picking and packing process at large warehouses. By the end of Q3 2015, Amazon had 30,000 bots working across 13 of its fulfillment center warehouses. The Kiva robots have significantly improved Amazon's packing and shipping efficiency and productivity. The Kiva robots are square-shaped, yellow machines that run on wheels. They're about 16 inches tall and weigh almost 320 pounds. They can run at a steady 5 mph and haul packages weighing up to 700 pounds. Here is a link that shows Kiva bots working together with people at an Amazon warehouse fulfillment center: www.youtube.com/watch?v=quWFjS3Ci7A.

In the bigger picture, robotics will likely be the main change agent during the Industry 4.0 era. Robots change the cost structure that has driven division of labor concepts and produced intense levels of outsourcing. With economies of scale, the lowering costs of robots will favor their use in place of outsourcing to locations where labor-intensive jobs can be done by so-called cheap labor. The paradox of low wages is that as soon as jobs move to low wage regions, the move itself starts a process of wage increases. Quality control gains the advantage of robot's extremely low inherent variability. The net effect will be for the manufacturing plant to move close to the market where the product is sold. The energy required to make and use robots will continuously decrease, which will be another factor promoting closeness to the market. Robots are designed to do labor-intensive jobs as they can work without stopping for anything except for maintenance. They do not need minimum wages and healthcare benefits. Further, the design of robotic systems will employ an increasing number of very bright and well-trained individuals. Many of them will be able to educate themselves inexpensively using online materials that will become the inventions of Industry 4.0.

For their September 19, 1994, issue, *Fortune* magazine ran a cover that proclaimed, "The End of the Job." In retrospect, it was a bit premature, but at least it eventually seemed to be coming true. Another magazine cover that might have been correct would be "The End of the Traditional College Education." POM currently faces many disruptions across a broad spectrum of its comfort zone. Adaptation in terms of what is taught and how it is taught seems to be called into play. The same holds for research. What is the research agenda (topics, methods, and timing)?

The Business 4.0 era might involve POM in space manufacturing. There are signs of a growing interest in a variety of space initiatives in that direction. Space colonization sounds like content coming straight from science fiction and a return to the throwback days of empires and kingdoms. Astronauts living in space for long periods of time sounded just as far out, and yet we take the people living on the International Space Station as a fact of life. In the same sense, new forms of transport are on the horizon. The rapid transit hyperloop is under serious development. POM faces many challenges that cannot, at this moment, be visualized. A flexible POM is required.

7 Global Forces Acting on POM

We have shown how a sequence of "industrial revolutions" has impacted POM practice and research. Now, we want to examine some of the particulars in greater detail. For example, during IR 3.0, the Toyota Production System (well known as TPS) played an important role in the development and refinement of many major ideas ranging from lean assembly production systems to company-wide quality control systems.

Since 1980, we have witnessed many manufacturing firms change from "vertically integrated" to "globally decentralized." During the end of IR 3.0, many developed countries shifted from "manufacturing-based economies" to "service-based economies." They shifted further to a "knowledge and information-based economy" with the advent of IR 4.0.

POM researchers have gone beyond traditional POM subject areas (scheduling, production planning, inventory control, quality control, etc. (Buffa 1961)). Specifically, POM researchers have ventured into "issue-oriented" topics: supply chains, healthcare, disaster management and humanitarian logistics, service management, and environmental sustainability as well as interfaces with marketing and finance among other areas. The expansion of POM research has led to the use of different research methods including economic analysis, empirical methods, behavioral experiments, and case studies.

Chapter 1 has described impacts on POM practice and research during four different industry revolutions, over some 240 years starting with 1776. With this background of three major milestones and four eras, we can now use Section 8 to discuss how global competition and Japanese production methods led to POM transformations.

8 Global Competition: The Japanese Effect

In the early 1980s, the United States was facing an economic crisis: the prime rate was over 20%, the unemployment rate was over 10%, and the 30-year mortgage rate exceeded 18% (instead of 3.88% as in 2015). The American car industry was losing market share to Japanese car companies. These challenges created strong motivation for POM action.

To improve the competitiveness of the U.S. manufacturing sector, many companies conducted company visits to Japan, did benchmark studies, used reverse engineering, etc. At the same time, there was widespread interest in Deming's 14 points (Deming 1986) and Crosby's "Quality is Free" (Crosby 1979). Additionally, practitioners and researchers identified several Japanese manufacturing strategies, e.g., TPS (Toyota's Production System) (Ohno 1988), SMED (Single-minute Exchange of Die) (Shingo 1985). Besides efficient production systems, there was a push for flexible manufacturing systems (FMS) (Draper 1984) and alternative product development methods so that firms could design and produce new products faster, cheaper, and better (Clark and Wheelwright 1993).

To learn how to implement the Toyota production system, General Motors (GM) formed a joint venture with Toyota (New United Motor Manufacturing, Inc. (NUMMI)). They agreed to produce GM's Nova and Toyota's Corolla in the idle Fremont, California, plant of GM. It turned out that Toyota ran the plant and GM was not given access to NUMMI planning methods. Because of the economic downturn in 2008 and a host of management issues, GM discontinued this joint venture in 2010. Within the year, the Tesla Factory moved into the same Fremont, California, plant to produce its Model S all-electric car.

To examine and evaluate lessons learned from Japanese production systems, FMS, and integrated product developments, various POM researchers embarked on groundbreaking research. One key article (Taguchi 1986) developed new statistical methods to improve manufacturing quality. Another article (Fine 1988) developed quality control models with learning, and incorporates the costs of quality (conformance and appraisal). Porteus (1985) and Spence and Porteus (1987) examined the implications of setup time reduction (e.g., SMED) on inventory planning and capacity planning, respectively. Deleersnyder et al. (1989) wrote one of the first papers to develop an analytical model for designing and managing a *kanban* controlled production system. Spearman et al. (1990) presented an alternative to a *kanban* system called CONWIP (constant work-in-process) that has certain practical advantages over push-and-pull systems.

The notion of flexibility in manufacturing received attention after showing how Seiko's flexible production system enabled the company to produce multiple types of watches on the same production line with minimum changeover time (or cost). Because the term "flexibility" was not well defined, Browne et al. (1984) provided a classification of flexible manufacturing systems. The reader is referred to Sethi and Sethi (1990) for a comprehensive review of the vast literature on flexibility including different types of flexibility and the interrelationships among them as well as various analytical models dealing with these flexibilities. Stecke (1983) was the first to define, formulate, and solve a set of five production planning problems arising from an FMS.

In the context of rapid new product development, Clark and Fujimoto (1989) studied product development projects in the automotive industry and found that, by using overlapping problem solving, Japanese automotive companies were able to shorten their product development cycle time and launch a new automobile twelve months faster than American firms using traditional methods. This finding spawned a new research interest in time-based competition (Stalk Jr. 1988).

9 Outsourcing to China

As American management learned more about Japanese production systems, it became clear that a stable environment (long-term commitment, job security) was necessary. Trust, teamwork, pride in one's work, collective problem solving, etc. are essential ingredients to successfully implementing various Japanese production systems. These ingredients posed major challenges to American management. By the mid-1980s, American corporations were not confident that they could compete against Japan with a Japanese-type production system. American managers felt the need to adopt a different operations strategy to compete globally.

By the early '90s, there were two developments that triggered calls for global sourcing. The first occurred when China opened up various Special Economic Zones, i.e., Pudong (Shanghai), Shenzhen (Guangzhou), etc., and three regions with less "red tape" and more tax benefits to attract Foreign Direct Investment. These zones offered strong economic incentives for American firms to explore the notion of off-shore manufacturing. When deciding whether to off-shore or not, each firm needed to take various types of costs (manufacturing, distribution, transportation, inventory, etc.) into consideration.

To design a global manufacturing network that consisted of manufacturing and distribution facilities in different countries, Cohen and Lee (1989) were the first to develop a global manufacturing network model that incorporated local content requirements, customs, and duties rates, and differential tax rates in different countries. Additionally, Huchzermeier and Cohen (1996) were the first to develop a stochastic dynamic programming formulation for the valuation of global manufacturing strategy options with switching costs under currency exchange rate risk. For a comprehensive discussion about global manufacturing, the reader is referred to the first book on this subject that combined text and cases (Dornier et al. 2008).

While off-shore manufacturing can enable firms to enjoy the benefit of tariff concessions and lower labor cost, Ferdows (1997) argued that such firms are not tapping the full potential of their foreign factories because they can sell into (and learn from) these new markets. It is certainly appealing to produce and sell different products globally. However, firms such as HP found it challenging to manage inventories where different country-specific requirements prevail (e.g., different languages for labels and manuals, packaging requirements, power supplies, etc.). The problems are compounded by forecasting difficulties.

To overcome such challenges, firms can exploit modular product structure of many products (e.g., electronics, printers, and computers have many modular components). Thus, a firm like HP can keep inventory of partially finished product as generic units and postpone the final assembly process until demand is specific at each global distribution center. Instead of producing a complete product at the factory, HP can customize the generic units into country-specific products at a later point in time so that the "postponement" strategy provides the benefits of risk pooling. However, operating costs (labor, transportation, customs, and duties rates) at different distribution centers can be very different around the globe. As such, careful analysis is needed to determine the best postponement strategy of a product. Lee (1996) and Lee and Tang (1997) were the first to develop models to explain the benefits of the postponement strategy and to determine the optimal postponement strategy under different situations.

When off-shore (global) manufacturing was gaining traction, there was a second development in digital communication abilities in the 1990s, i.e., rapid adoption of digital communication via email, Internet, and mobile phones. These communication technologies enabled companies to manage their global manufacturing more efficiently, which further accelerated the off-shore manufacturing movement. POM became deeply involved with telecommunication technologies (see Chapter 28 in this book).

Off-shore manufacturing and communication technologies created a golden opportunity for the United States to shift from a "manufacturing-based economy" to a "service-based economy" in the '90s (Karmarkar 2015). Specifically, we witnessed a sea change when companies such as HP began by off-shoring most of its manufacturing operations from the U.S. to Europe (Spain) and Asia (Singapore and Malaysia), and then followed by outsourcing their manufacturing operations to contract manufacturers such as Flextronics who operate heavily in China. By doing so, HP transitioned from computer manufacturer to provider of information technology services.

By the end of IR 3.0, most of the large American firms had become decentralized in the sense that they focused on certain operations (design, R&D, marketing, and sales) in the U.S. while delegating other operations (such as sourcing, fabrication, logistics, and distribution) to other companies. When operating in a decentralized system, most of the POM research literature became less relevant. This is because classic POM literature was developed for centralized planning based on full information and complete control of the decisions for all involved units.

However, in a decentralized system, various parties along the global supply chain belong to different companies, each of which has its own objectives. We know that different parties are reluctant to share their private information truthfully or to cooperate unselfishly unless there are incentives to do so. As such, the wave of global outsourcing created a new incentive for researchers to examine the implications of decentralized supply chains.

In an oft-cited POM research article, Lee, Padmanabhan, and Whang (1997) described the "bullwhip" phenomenon observed by P&G where a minor variability in downstream customer demand can create a huge variability in the order quantity observed by upstream partners along the supply chain. Clearly, the bullwhip effect can cause major inefficiencies in supply chain operations. Lee, Padmanabhan, and Whang (1997) identified four causes of the bullwhip effect. They explained how the identification of these causes can lead to prescriptions for alleviating the detrimental impact of the bullwhip effect. This research article paved the path for many POM researchers to develop ways to mitigate the bullwhip effect.

Lee, So, and Tang (2000) showed that the bullwhip effect can be dampened if downstream partners (e.g., retailers) are willing to share their demand information with upstream partners especially when the underlying demand possesses certain characteristics. The reader is referred to a review of the analysis of the bullwhip effect according to its causes conducted by Derbel et al. (2014) for details.

Intuitively speaking, better communication, cooperation, and coordination among different supply chain partners would be beneficial. However, in a decentralized supply chain, different partners are reluctant to communicate, cooperate, and coordinate unless there are economic incentives. Narayanan and Raman (2004) argue about the importance of incentive alignment among different supply chain partners. To achieve incentive alignment, one party (principal) needs to offer an incentive contract to entice the other party (agent) to behave in the interest of the principal (or the entire supply chain).

Besides mitigating the bullwhip effect and coordinating decentralized supply chains in the 1990s, global decentralized supply chains became more complex, which made them more vulnerable to disruptions with large unanticipated consequences (Craighead et al. 2007). Hendricks and Singhal (2003) were the first to establish the negative impact of supply chain disruptions on a firm's stock performance. The impact of supply chain disruptions (e.g., Mattel's toy recalls, Japan's earthquake, etc.) has led to growing interest in the area of "supply chain risk management." In a survey article, Sodhi et al. (2012) found that most research articles in this area tend to focus on ways to mitigate supply chain risks and that there is a lack of articles on ways to respond to risk events.

10 Sustainability—Social Responsibility—Crisis Management

Since the early 2000s (IR 4.0), two major forces are pressuring firms to pay attention to the *triple bottom line: profit, people, and planet* (Elkington 2002, also Chapters 14 and 36 in this book). First, there has been rapid growth in global supply chains (supply) and in global economic development (demand). The demand for natural resources (clean water, crude oil, woods, metals, etc.) continues to rise (especially in countries such as India and China), whereas the supply of these natural resources continues to diminish. At the same time, greenhouse gas emissions have been considered as a possible cause of climate change. This challenge has created a public concern over *environmental sustainability*.

Second, with growth slowing in developed countries since the recession in 2008, Western companies from the fast-moving consumer goods and other sectors are seeking to expand in emerging economies (Prahalad 2004). However, to develop the emerging market so that the poor producers can become their consumers, these companies need to help the poor to break the poverty cycle. This creates the motivation for companies to embark on *social responsibility*.

While more companies are developing products with the triple bottom line in mind, Agrawal and Toktay (2010) commented that environmental sustainability/social responsibility remains a nascent research area in the POM literature for the following reasons. First, while there are clear definitions for environmental sustainability (e.g., ISO 14000), there are no consistent measures for social responsibility—despite the newly established guidelines of ISO 26000 (Bloemhof and Corbett 2010). Second, it is challenging to measure a product's environmental and societal impacts. Third, there are conflicting economic, societal, and environmental factors and objectives of different partners along their respective supply chains.

POM research in the area of environmental sustainability tends to focus on the area of remanufacturing partly because it is directly related to manufacturing even though the flow is reversed.

Ferguson and Souza (2010) compiled an excellent collection of chapters that examine various issues arising from remanufacturing. See Chapter 14 in this book where various issues related to sustainability are discussed in detail.

Another aspect of environmental sustainability and social responsibility lies in the POM field's response to disasters. POM research on crisis management has grown globally at an exponent rate. The *POM Journal* established a new Department of Disaster Management in 2014 with Martin K. Starr as its Department Editor. Most POM journals are substantially involved in this emerging arena (see Chapter 29 in this book).

11 What is Next?—Industry 4.0

The Operations Management field has experienced constant evolution over the last 250 years. As we enter the Industry 4.0 era, the rate of change is accelerating. Wikipedia defines Industry 4.0 (or the fourth industrial revolution) as "the current trend of automation and data exchange in manufacturing technologies." The discussion goes on to describe "smart factories" utilizing cyber-physical systems that communicate with each other via the Internet of Things.

To Wikipedia's definition, we will add "smart warehouses" and "smart supply chains." The global distribution network thrives on the ability of cyber-systems to communicate with each other without involving any people. In the background, POM plans, delivers, installs, maintains, and upgrades these cyber-systems. That is "what is next."

This discussion is meant to assist young and up-and-coming POM researchers to choose *optimal career and field-beneficial paths*. At the same time that we have lauded flexibility, we have also acknowledged that we cannot predict the future. We do have a better chance of influencing it. In that regard, consider the following three (among many) exciting new POM areas to explore.

11.1 Global Trade Processes

As global supply chains operating in full swing since the 1990s, we observed the number of regional trade agreements has skyrocketed (e.g., NAFTA, Mercosur, ASEAN free trade agreements, etc.). These trade agreements were intended to set up rules and regulations to provide mutual benefits among specific trading partners. As things change, they need to be renegotiated and updated since these trade agreements offer lower custom duties for trading partners but higher duties for non-trader partners. Brexit negotiations represent a case in point.

Hausman et al. (2013) examined how global trade processes affect trade flows between two countries. Their study was based on cross-border trade flows across eighty countries, based on container flows of three specific types of products. The customs differentials among different trading partners with different requirements create a golden opportunity for POM researchers to find ways to design cost effective global supply chains.

To fully exploit the customs differentials of different countries under different requirements, one needs to examine the complete bill of materials of the product and to understand which parts or components will meet certain requirements associated with trade agreements among various trading countries. Finally, it is essential to design a global supply chain network that takes the costs associated with production, transportation, customs duties, etc., into consideration (e.g., negotiations related to TPPs [Trans-Pacific Partnership Agreements]) present another opportunity for POM researchers to examine the impact of TPP on all members of the global supply chain.

11.2 Sharing Economy

By leveraging information technologies (Internet, smart phones, email) that capture real-time data, Uber and Airbnb have disrupted traditional business models used by the taxi and hotel industries. Specifically, these two startups enable drivers and homeowners to earn extra income by driving passengers during their free time and by renting their vacant rooms without incurring large setup costs. By allowing more drivers and more homeowners to enter the market easily, it gives passengers and renters extra options at lower prices.

From the POM perspective, the real-time location data (about the supply of drivers and the demand of passengers) provides a research opportunity to explore how companies such as Uber can develop an effective dynamic pricing model to enable stochastic supply to match stochastic demand. While Uber sets its own price dynamically according to supply and demand, Didi Kuaidi, a taxi dispatching service in China, enables the passenger to set the price for taxi service instead. These two different pricing models raise interesting questions such as which pricing model is better, when, and for whom? As articulated by Netessine (2014), an excellent opportunity exists for POM researchers to examine and evaluate various innovative business models (see also, Girotra and Netessine 2014).

11.3 Data Analytics/Robotics—Phenomenon-Driven Research

Unlike Finance and Marketing, fields that have had an abundance of financial data and purchasing data, POM has suffered from the lack of operational transaction data for decades. With the advancement of information technologies, every company now has access to new forms of data. This gives POM researchers a golden opportunity to conduct exploratory data analysis so as to identify interesting phenomena, e.g., the bullwhip effect (Lee et al. 1997), to conduct descriptive analysis so as to explain certain phenomena (e.g., the sniping effect in online auctions, Ely and Hossain 2009), to conduct predictive analysis so as to improve forecasts (and consequences) of certain events. As articulated by Simchi-Levi (2014), data-driven research enables us to be more creative. POM will play an important role in the development of business analytics (see Chapter 15 in this book). For example, in healthcare, IBM's Watson supercomputer is scanning more medical records than could ever have been imagined. Computerized scheduling can alter the programs for doctors and nurses and for hospitals and clinics. Great efficiencies are in store (Green 2012).

Robotics will change the equation for out-sourcing and off-shore decisions. The decision mechanism must include a multiplicity of the right factors. POM is in an enviable position to determine the structure of this decision model. Who fashioned it before, during IR 3.0? Finance and Marketing dominated the situation without much consultation from POM. The system is bigger with Industry 4.0.

12 Conclusions

Because so much of POM's structure was built on the foundation of division of labor and work specialization, it is understandable that POM is a conservative discipline. Caution about change is expected behavior when technology and markets are stable. When this is not the case, a strategy for changing sensibly is in order.

The ability to react quickly with innovative solutions is not what POM teaches nor what it has researched. Disruption is opening up new vistas and great opportunities exist when the stable situation is disrupted. The equilibrium controls must be altered to meet new circumstances (Roth et al. 2016; Starr 2016).

Technology creates market and lifestyle disruptions with such regularity and severity that within any one person's lifetime, adaptability is essential. Adaptability to extremes may require re-engineering (REE) a system, i.e., making changes starting from scratch. POM did not adapt to REE (Hammer and Champy 1993) during IR 3.0 and preferred to work within the framework of *Kaizen* (which can be reassuring but misleading). As disruption becomes the "norm," POM has to learn to anticipate it; if possible, influence its direction; and do more than just cope reactively when it occurs (Champy 1995).

References and Bibliography

"About Joseph Engelberger—father of robotics" (n.d.) *Robotics Online*. Available from: www.robotics.org/joseph-engelberger/about.cfm.

Agrawal, V., & Toktay, L.B. (2010) "Interdisciplinarity in Closed-Loop Supply Chain Management Research," in M. Ferguson and G. Souza (eds.), *Closed Loop Supply Chains: New Developments to Improve the Sustainability of Business Practices*. Taylor & Francis Publishing, NY, pp. 197–214.

Anupindi, R., Sivakumar, S., Quelch, J., Rangan, V., Herrero, G., & Barton, B. (2007) "ITC's e-choupal: A platform strategy for rural transformation," in V. K. Rangan, J. Quelch, G. Herrero and B. Barton (eds.), *Business solutions for the global poor*. Jossey-Bass, San Francisco, CA, pp. 173–182.

Bloemhof, J. M., & Corbett, C. J. (2010) "Closed-loop supply chains: Environmental impact," *Wiley Encyclopedia of Operations Research and Management Science*. Wiley, New York.

Browne, J., Dubois, D., Rathmill, K., Sethi, S. P., & Stecke, K. E. (1984) "Classification of flexible manufacturing systems," *The FMS Magazine*, **2**(2): 114–117.

Budiansky, S. (2013) *Blackett's war: The men who defeated the Nazi U-boats and brought science to the art of warfare*. Alfred A. Knopf, New York.

Buffa, E. S. (1961) *Modern production management*. Wiley, New York.

Buffa, E. S. (1980) "Research in operations management," *Journal of Operations Management*, **1**(1): 1–7.

Buffa, E. S. (1984) *Meeting the competitive challenge: Manufacturing strategy for US companies*. Dow Jones-Irwin, New York.

Buffa, E., & Sarin, R. (1987) *Modern production: Operations management*. Kluwer, New York.

Cachon, G. P. (2003) "Supply chain coordination with contracts," *Handbooks in Operations Research and Management Science*, **11**: 227–339.

Champy J. (1995) *Reengineering management: The mandate for new leadership*. Harper Business, New York.

Chod, J., & Rudi, N. (2005) "Resource flexibility with responsive pricing," *Operations Research*, **53**(3): 532–548.

Chopra, S., & Sodhi, M. S. (2004) "Managing risk to avoid supply-chain breakdown," *MIT Sloan Management Review*, **46**(1): 53.

Churchman, C. W., Ackoff, R. L., & Arnoff, E. L. (1957) *Introduction to operations research*. John Wiley & Sons, New York.

Clark, K. B., & Fujimoto, T. (1989) "Lead time in automobile product development explaining the Japanese advantage," *Journal of Engineering and Technology Management*, **6**(1): 25–58.

Clark, K.B., & Wheelwright, S.C. (1993) *Managing New Product and Process Development*. Free Press, New York.

Cohen, M. A., & Lee, H. L. (1989) "Resource deployment analysis of global manufacturing and distribution networks," *Journal of Manufacturing and Operations Management*, **2**(2): 81–104.

Craighead, C. W., Blackhurst, J., Rungtusanatham, M. J., & Handfield, R. B. (2007) "The severity of supply chain disruptions: Design characteristics and mitigation capabilities," *Decision Sciences*, **38**(1): 131–156.

Crosby, P. B. (1979) *Quality is free: The art of making quality certain*. Signet, New York.

Deleersnyder, J., Hodgson, T. J., Muller-Malek, H., & O'Grady, P. J. (1989) "Kanban controlled pull systems: An analytic approach," *Management Science*, **35**(9): 1079–1091.

Deming, W. E. (1986) *Out of the crisis*. Massachusetts Institute of Technology. Center for Advanced Engineering Study, Cambridge, MA.

Derbel, M., Hachicha, W., & Masmoudi, F. (2014) "A literature survey of bullwhip effect (2010–2013) according to its causes and evaluation methods," *2014 International Conference on Advanced Logistics and Transport (ICALT)*, 173–178.

Dillon, A. P., & Shingo, S. (1985) *A revolution in manufacturing: The SMED system*. CRC Press, New York.

Dornier, P., Ernst, R., Fender, M., & Kouvelis, P. (2008) *Global operations and logistics: Text and cases*. John Wiley & Sons, New York.

Drake, D. F., & Spinler, S. (2013) "OM forum-sustainable operations management: An enduring stream or a passing fancy?" *Manufacturing & Service Operations Management*, **15**(4): 689–700.

Draper, C. (1984) *Flexible manufacturing systems handbook*. Automation and Management Systems Division, the Charles Stark Draper Laboratory Inc., Noyes Publication, Park Ridge, NJ.

Elkington, J. (1997) *Cannibals with forks: The triple bottom line of 21st century business*. Capstone Publishers, North Mankato, MN.

Ely, J. C., & Hossain, T. (2009) "Sniping and squatting in auction markets," *American Economic Journal: Microeconomics*, **1**(2), 68–94.

Esenduran, G., Kemahlioglu-Ziya, E., & Swaminathan, J. M. (2010) "The impact of take-back legislations on remanufacturing." Working paper. Ohio State University, Columbus, OH.

Ferdows, K. (1997) "Making the most of foreign factories," *Harvard Business Review*, **75**: 73–91.

Ferguson, M. (2010) *Strategic issues in closed-loop supply chains with remanufacturing*. Now Publishers, Boston, MA.

Ferguson, M.E., & Souza, G.C. (2010) *Closed-loop supply chains*. CRC Press, Boca Raton, FL.

Fine, C. H. (1988) "A quality control model with learning effects," *Operations Research*, **36**(3): 437–444.

Fisher, M. (2007) "Strengthening the empirical base of operations management," *Manufacturing & Service Operations Management*, **9**(4): 368–382.

Geoffrion, A.M. (1992) "Forces, trends, and opportunities in MS/OR," *Operations Research*, **40**(3): 423–445.

Gilbreth Jr., F. B., & Carey, E. G. (2013) *Cheaper by the dozen*. Open Road Media, New York.

Girotra, K., & Netessine, S. (2014) *The risk-driven business model: Four questions that will define your company*. Harvard Business Press, Boston, MA.

Graves, S. C. (1981) "A review of production scheduling," *Operations Research*, **29**(4): 646–675.

Green, L. V. (2012) "OM forum—the vital role of operations analysis in improving healthcare delivery," *Manufacturing & Service Operations Management*, **14**(4): 488–494.

Hammer, M., & Champy, J. (1993) *Reengineering the corporation: The manifesto for business revolution*. Harper Business, New York.

Hausman, W. H., Lee, H. L., & Subramanian, U. (2013) "The impact of logistics performance on trade," *Production and Operations Management*, **22**(2): 236–252.

Hendricks, K.B., & Singhal, V.R. (2003) "The effect of supply chain glitches on shareholder wealth." *Journal of Operations Management*, **21**(5): 501–522.

Huchzermeier, A., & Cohen, M. A. (1996) "Valuing operational flexibility under exchange rate risk," *Operations Research*, **44**(1): 100–113.

Jordan, W. C., & Graves, S. C. (1995) "Principles on the benefits of manufacturing process flexibility," *Management Science*, **41**(4): 577–594.

Karmarkar, U. (2015) "OM Forum—The service and information economy: Research opportunities," *Manufacturing & Service Operations Management*, **17**(2): 136–141.

Karnani, A. (2007) "The mirage of marketing to the bottom of the pyramid: How the private sector can help alleviate poverty," *California Management Review*, **49**(4): 90–111.

Lee, H. L. (1996) "Effective inventory and service management through product and process redesign," *Operations Research*, **44**(1): 151–159.

Lee, H. L., Padmanabhan, V., & Whang, S. (1997) "Information distortion in a supply chain: The bullwhip effect," *Management Science*, **43**(4): 546–558.

Lee, H. L., & Silverman, A. (2008) "Renault's Logan car: Managing customs duties for a global product," *HBS Premier Case Collection*. Product #: 700115-PDF-ENG. Harvard Business School Press.

Lee, H. L., So, K. C., & Tang, C. S. (2000) "The value of information sharing in a two-level supply chain," *Management Science*, **46**(5): 626–643.

Lee, H. L., & Tang, C. S. (1997) "Modelling the costs and benefits of delayed product differentiation," *Management Science*, **43**(1): 40–53.

McCullough, D. (2001) *The path between the seas: The creation of the Panama Canal, 1870–1914*. Simon and Schuster, New York.

McCullough, D. (2012) *The great bridge: The epic story of the building of the Brooklyn Bridge*. Simon and Schuster, New York.

Narayanan, V. G., & Raman, A. (2004) "Aligning incentives in supply chains," *Harvard Business Review*, **82**(11): 94–102, 149.

Netessine, S. (2014) "How we can Improve our Profession," presentation given at the INFORMS Conference, San Francisco, November 2014.

Nilsson, L. (2007) "The Uddevalla plant: Why did it succeed with a holistic approach and why did it come to an end?" in A. Sandberg (ed.), *Enriching production: Perspectives on Volvo's Uddevalla plant as an alternative to lean production*. Ashgate Publishing Company, Vermont.

Ohno, T. (1988) *Toyota production system: Beyond large-scale production.* CRC Press, New York.
Petersen, R., & Silver, E. (1979) *Decision systems for inventory management and production planning.* Wiley, New York.
Porteus, E. L. (1985) "Investing in reduced setups in the EOQ model," *Management Science*, **31**(8): 998–1010.
Prahalad, C. (2004) *Fortune at the bottom of the pyramid: Eradicating poverty through profits.* Wharton School Publishing, Philadelphia, PA.
Rifkin, J. (2011) *The third industrial revolution: How lateral power is transforming energy, the economy, and the world.* Macmillan, Basingstoke, UK.
Roth, A., Singhal, J., Singhal, K., & Tang, C. S. (2016) "Knowledge creation and dissemination in operations and supply-chain management," *Production and Operations Management*, **25**(9): (**forthcoming**).
Salveson, M. E. (1997) "The Institute of Management Sciences: A prehistory and commentary on the occasion of TIMS' 40th anniversary," *Interfaces*, **27**(3): 74–85.
Sandberg, Å. (1995) *Enriching production: Perspectives on Volvo's Uddevalla plant as an alternative to lean production.* Avebury, Aldershot, UK.
Sethi, A. K., & Sethi, S. P. (1990) "Flexibility in manufacturing: A survey," *International Journal of Flexible Manufacturing Systems*, **2**(4): 289–328.
Sheffi, Y., & Rice Jr., J. B. (2005) "A supply chain view of the resilient enterprise by Yossi Sheffi, and James B. Rice Jr.," *MIT Sloan Management Review*, **47**(1): 41–48.
Shingo, S. (1985) *A Revolution in Manufacturing: The SMED System.* Productivity Press, Cambridge.
Simchi-Levi, D. (2014) "OM forum—OM research: From problem-driven to data-driven research," *Manufacturing & Service Operations Management*, **16**(1): 2–10.
Singhal, K., & Singhal, J. (2012) "Opportunities for developing the science of operations and supply-chain management," *Journal of Operations Management*, **30**(3): 245–252.
Smith, A. (1937) *The wealth of nations.* Originally published in 1776 by Strahan and Cadell, Edinburgh, Scotland.
Sodhi, M. S., Son, B., & Tang, C. S. (2012) "Researchers' perspectives on supply chain risk management," *Production and Operations Management*, **21**(1): 1–13.
Sodhi, M. S., & Tang, C. S. (2011) "Social enterprises as supply-chain enablers for the poor," *Socio-Economic Planning Sciences*, **45**(4): 146–153.
Sodhi, M. S., & Tang, C. S. (2012) *Managing supply chain risk.* Springer Science & Business Media, New York.
Sodhi, M. S., & Tang, C. S. (2014) "Supply-chain research opportunities with the poor as suppliers or distributors in developing countries," *Production and Operations Management*, **23**(9): 1483–1494.
Spearman, M. L., Woodruff, D. L., & Hopp, W. J. (1990) "CONWIP: A pull alternative to kanban," *The International Journal of Production Research*, **28**(5): 879–894.
Spence, A. M., & Porteus, E. L. (1987) "Setup reduction and increased effective capacity," *Management Science*, **33**(10): 1291–1301.
Stalk Jr., G. (1988) "Time—The next source of competitive advantage," *Harvard Business Review*, **41**, July: 41–53.
Starr, M. K. (2010) "Modular production—a 45-year-old concept," *International Journal of Operations & Production Management*, **30**(1): 7–19.
Starr, M. K. (2016) "Commentary on knowledge creation and dissemination in operations and supply-chain management," *Production and Operations Management*, **25**(9): 1489–1492.
Stecke, K. (1983) "Formulation and solution of nonlinear integer production planning problems for flexible manufacturing systems," *Management Science*, **29**(3): 273–288.
Taguchi, G. (1986) *Introduction to quality engineering: Designing quality into products and processes.* Quality Resources, New York.
Tang, C. S. (2006) "Perspectives in supply chain risk management," *International Journal of Production Economics*, **103**(2): 451–488.
Tang, C. S., & Zhou, S. (2012) "Research advances in environmentally and socially sustainable operations," *European Journal of Operational Research*, **223**(3): 585–594.
Tang, C., & Tomlin, B. (2008) "The power of flexibility for mitigating supply chain risks," *International Journal of Production Economics*, **116**(1): 12–27.
Tsay, A. A., & Lovejoy, W. S. (1999) "Quantity flexibility contracts and supply chain performance," *Manufacturing & Service Operations Management*, **1**(2): 89–111.

2
GLOBAL SUPPLY CHAIN MANAGEMENT

Henrique L. Correa

1 Introduction

The term "supply chain management" has become a part of the business lexicon. Younger professionals and students may find it difficult to believe that it was not a widely known term just thirty years ago.

We define supply chain management (SCM) as the integrated management of the business processes (Poirier and Bauer 2000) associated with the direct and reverse (Stock and Boyer 2009) flows of physical goods, financial assets, and information (Elmuti 2002) from the producers of basic inputs to the final consumer's use (Handfield and Nichols 1999). More recently, supply chain management has also come to include the subsequent destination of goods (Souza 2013) and services. SCM seeks to optimize the creation of value for all customers (Cooper et al. 1997)—intermediary and final—and for other legitimate and relevant stakeholders (Walters and Lancaster 2000) in the chain (shareholders, employees, managers, the community, and the government).

The term was coined by consultants in the early 1980s (Lambert and Cooper 2000) and rose to prominence in the vocabulary of business in the 1990s. In comparison, modern concepts of production and operation management have been around for more than two hundred years, showing that the field of supply chain management is indeed new. What follows is a discussion of the main reasons for the growing interest in supply chain management. Most chapters conclude with a section titled "Implications for Managers." Chapter 2 embodies these "Implications" throughout and so there is no need for a concluding section.

2 Technological Evolution

Never before has technology evolved at such a fast pace. The technological changes in the industrial world have made it difficult for companies to use their internal resources alone to keep up with developments that influence their products and services. Companies have become increasingly dependent upon more technological specialized and advanced third parties. Therefore, companies now prefer to outsource substantial portions of not only their production operations but also of the development of their products and services and/or their component parts. This change has brought a tremendous increase in both the volume and intensity of trade and the need for communication and coordination between supplier and customer companies. Trade, communication, and coordination were in turn facilitated by internet and RFID technology. As supply chains have become more complex and information and communication technologies have become more available and affordable, supply chain management has become an important focus point for managers.

3 Today's Competition: Between Supply Chains, Not Companies

Several authors argue that competition in today's global market is no longer between companies, but between supply chains (Antai 2011). Some competing supply chains are self-contained and isolated, not sharing partners with the competing chains. One example is the footwear industry. Chinese footwear manufacturers have local supply chains and often do not share partners (except perhaps in retail) with the supply chains of a shoe manufacturer in Brazil. It is worthwhile to analyze the Chinese and Brazilian footwear manufacturers as competing supply chains rather than merely as competing companies.

A less obvious example can be found in the powdered detergent market. Two of the major players in this market are Unilever and Procter & Gamble. These two companies share most of their raw material suppliers in large chemical companies. They also share distributors, wholesalers, and major supermarket chains such as Carrefour and Wal-Mart, which distribute and sell products for both competitors. This could be viewed as evidence that their competition is between companies, *not* between supply chains.

However, while the two companies share many partners, the ways in which these companies manage their relationships with those shared partners to create greater or lesser efficiency, and better or worse cooperation, can be different and can differentiate one supply chain from the other. Many partner companies may be the same, but their supply chain relations may be different. These differences, for instance, show in terms of how much information is exchanged between the companies and their common distribution channel partners and to what extent decision processes about inventory replenishment are coordinated between the companies and their suppliers—who happen to be the same. Therefore, even in the less obvious case of powdered detergents, competition nowadays is indeed between supply chains and not between companies.

4 Historical Evolution of Supply Chain Management

Knowing the past helps us to understand the present and plan for the future. With this in mind, we will briefly describe the historical evolution of operations and supply chain management.

4.1 First Phase: The Operation Management Scope Is the Production Unit—"One Best Way"

At the turn of the 20th century, steel industry consultant Frederick Taylor (1911) believed that, if his scientific management principles were diligently applied to improve the method used to perform a task, then this process would come together as the "one best way" of realizing it.

Industrialist Henry Ford used the logic of scientific management and added other efficiency improvement techniques such as moving assembly lines to make Ford Motor Co. the greatest car manufacturer in less than twenty years. Nonetheless, this incredible rise in production efficiency came at the expense of product variety. For almost two decades, Ford only produced one model of car: the Model T. Ford, just like other "mass-producers" of the time, also executed most tasks internally. The level of outsourcing was very low and the idea that there was "one best way" of performing tasks and that efficiency should be sought mainly through economies of scale dominated the mass production era. This approach proved successful in the extremely cost-conscious market of the first part of the 20th century.

4.2 Second Phase: The Operations Management Scope Crosses Borders Between Functions

Nevertheless, markets ripened. Many countries saw their populations become more affluent and their markets more sophisticated in the first decades of the 20th century. Some market segments were willing to pay more for products as long as these offered better performance characteristics in some way, such as a higher quality, more alternatives to choose from, and greater customization. The need to adjust production choices and decisions to focus on the delivery of specific sets of performance characteristics led operations managers to challenge Taylor's (1911) assumption that there was "one best way" to perform tasks.

Operations managers realized the necessity of crossing the "functional border" between the operations function and the marketing/sales function for a better understanding of what precise combination of performance characteristics (cost, quality, delivery, flexibility, or service) would be needed to produce and deliver to compete in the target markets of the organization (Skinner 1969; Hill 1985). To deal with the required continuous harmonization between operations choices and decisions and the market, the concept of operations strategy was created and developed in the last third of the 20th century (Skinner 1969; Hayes and Wheelwright 1984; Hill 1985).

Operations strategy sought to respond to the need to integrate operations not only with marketing but also with various other functions and face hard choices. In order to do that, operations managers needed to deal with increasingly complex trade-offs when making decisions.

4.3 Third Phase: The Operations Management Scope Crosses Borders Between Organizations—Supply Chains

Throughout the 20th century, technological development and product complexity accelerated at an unprecedented rate (Utterback 1994). Manufacturers started realizing that relying only on internal resources made it very difficult to keep up with the evolution of all technologies involved in their products by relying only on internal resources. Companies began to delegate to specialized suppliers, first for the manufacturing and then for the conception and design of increasing portions of their products (Gottfredson et al. 2005). As the use of outsourcing intensified, operations managers were forced to adapt and learn to cross another border: the border between companies in supply chains (Correa 2014). This is because managers who decide to outsource activities to be performed by third parties (suppliers) need to learn new ways to coordinate the activities that they kept internally with the activities they outsourced across company borders. The scope of operations management widens yet again, the decision trade-offs become more complex and the necessary integration between decision processes of each company in the chain demands more complex management (see Mena et al. 2013).

The alignment of incentives (Narayanan and Raman 2004) between companies with diverse property ownership, for example, became mandatory—new mechanisms are needed to align the interests of the companies in the chain with the interests of the chain itself.

This requires new forms of contracting where risks, costs, and benefits are better and more rationally distributed between partners in the chain, with higher levels of trust, cooperation, and incentive alignment among the chain participants. The fates of all supply chain members are interlinked. If the companies work together to effectively deliver goods and services to consumers they will all win (Narayanan and Raman 2004, p. 3).

4.4 Fourth Phase: The Operations Management Scope Crosses National Borders—Global Supply Chains

Toward the end of the 20th century, the technological developments in telecommunications and transportation, aside from the globalizing actions of governments (reduction of trade tariffs and barriers), made it viable for companies to seek suppliers and other commercial partners wherever they were located (Trent and Monczka 2005). Supply chains became "global supply chains." While global supply chains promise enormous strategic benefits, managing operations across cultural, economic, and political boundaries is a formidable challenge. The scope of operations activities to be managed is quickly expanding to a worldwide scale. The management of trade-offs becomes yet again more complex. New elements were added to the decision-making scope of operations managers: time-zone differences, working standards, languages, culture, ethical standards, and diverse management systems and practices, among many others. On the one hand, these differences introduced a growing complexity to the necessary integration between the processes of partners in these now global networks. On the other hand, the differences brought great opportunities for significant differentiation in capabilities. Supply chain managers need to be masters in the art of managing complex trade-offs, now more than ever.

4.5 Fifth Phase: The Operations Management Scope Crosses the Borders of Organizations' Global Objectives—The Triple Bottom Line

By the beginning of the 21st century, a substantial change had begun to take shape. Until the 1990s, the management of global supply chains aimed almost exclusively for the economic prosperity of its members. The masters of trade-offs—global supply chain managers—tried to balance various conflicts aiming to increase the economic value of the chains and its members. However, a new widening of scope was occurring. Encouraged by the internet and its instruments, many stakeholders such as NGOs and government bodies, in the name of citizens and progressive shareholders (Wolf 2014), started to demand that corporations and their supply chains assume greater responsibility for environmental sustainability of the planet and for their social impact. As a consequence, many organizations are now adjusting their objectives accordingly. Moving away from aiming to maximize their results only in the traditional single "bottom line" (profit), these progressive companies are now striving to maximize their performance in the "triple bottom line" (3BL) (Elkington 1997), which consists of 1) economic prosperity (profit), 2) environmental sustainability (planet) and, 3) social responsibility (people) with evident implications to supply chain management (Wu et al. 2014).

Once more, the managers of global supply chains had their scope expanded. Trade-offs became even more complex. Now there is greater need and complexity in the sharing of information and in the integration of decision-making processes involved with the constituents of supply chains. This is the situation that we face today, a situation that brings exciting new challenges and opportunities for operations and supply chain managers and amazing research opportunities for scholars.

5 Everyone Wins With Good Supply Chain Management

One of the most attractive characteristics of successful supply chain management is that all parties win by working collaboratively instead of adopting the more traditionally contentious approach to business, where some members of the chain must lose in order for others to win. Let us look at how this "win-win" potential is possible by analyzing the model of a traditional negotiation.

Frequently, the many organizations comprising a supply chain not only have differing objectives but, more importantly, they have conflicting ones. When the executives of two companies that are part of a supply chain negotiate the purchase and sale of a product or service, each one has an interest in maximizing the financial outcome of the negotiation for their own company. Imagine a price negotiation between a manufacturer and one of its distributors. Because of the conflicting objectives, traditional negotiations are similar to an arm wrestling competition where for one to win the other one has to lose. This simple example of a "win-lose" relationship is called "zero-sum" (e.g., say the loser has to give the winner $10). The zero-sum outcome would be bad enough as a result in today's extremely competitive world. The situation, however, is worse because the result of the negotiation is not merely zero-sum but a negative sum.

A skilled professional in an arm wrestling-type negotiation will find ways to strengthen his/her metaphorical arm and will become more competitive through time, for example, by creating "information asymmetry." To do so, the negotiator understands that it is to his or her advantage not to share information. Indeed, some empirical studies suggest that the adoption of win-lose approaches in negotiations actually decrease future intentions to share information (Blome et al. 2014).

Some negotiators go as far as deliberately omitting or even distorting information that they do share or are required to share in order to gain an edge. For the same reasons, the opponent in the negotiation will also avoid sharing information. Since both parties are now avoiding the sharing of information, each makes the other work under greater levels of uncertainty. As a result, efficiency suffers across the board.

With more collaborative relationships where information and decision-making processes are shared and better integrated (Prajogo and Olhager 2012), supply chains perform better because collaboration results in reduced overall uncertainty and volatility. Therefore, this results in lower costs for all companies involved—a win-win situation. To achieve that, a management mechanism is needed through which information is shared, cooperation is fostered, and decisions and actions are both made and taken in a more coordinated fashion. Such a mechanism is supply chain management, and its successful deployment requires replacing zero-sum (win-lose) or lose-lose situations with win-win situations.

6 Supply Chain Management: Some Essential Concepts

Several concepts and effects are essential to understand the main challenges (and opportunities) faced by supply chain managers today.

6.1 The Strategic "Make or Buy" Decision

An important decision a company must make when developing its supply chain strategy is about which activities the company will perform itself and which will be outsourced (Kroes and Ghosh 2010). Traditionally, the decision to "make or buy" was based only (or predominantly) upon the costs incurred by one strategy as opposed to the other. The philosophy that cost should be the only factor in the decision to make or buy is a risky one. Now, it is widely understood and accepted that, in supply chains, the "make or buy" decision has strategic implications that are too serious to ignore. At least two bodies of knowledge are considered essential in supporting the make or buy decision in supply chains: transaction cost economics and the resource-based view of strategy (McIvor 2009).

6.1.1 Transaction Cost Economics

The area of economics that deals with transaction costs originated from the seminal work of Coase (1937), which aimed to understand why firms do things instead of purchasing them from third parties.

One transaction is the transfer of a product or service between technologically separated operating units. Transaction costs exist only because markets are imperfect. For example, market information is not 100% available, and people are not 100% effective or rational in their ability to analyze information and arrive at proper conclusions. Transaction costs include the cost of searching for information about a supplier, the cost of not perfectly understanding the information obtained, the cost of generating a quote, the cost of drawing up contracts, and the possible judicial costs to have contracts enforced.

Transaction analysis seeks efficiency in the management of such transactions or, in other words, it seeks to minimize transaction costs. According to industrial organization theory, transaction costs are driven by at least four factors (McIvor 2009):

- Asset specificity in the transaction
- Number of potential suppliers
- Overall uncertainty surrounding the transaction
- Frequency of transactions.

Transaction costs increase with asset specificity in the transaction. For instance, if I have a machine that can only process the raw material that I buy from a (specific) supplier, the supplier will likely adopt an "opportunistic" stance. The supplier will likely increase prices because he/she knows that I will think twice before buying raw material from a different supplier—because I would have to replace my current machine to be able to process the new supplier's raw material. The supplier's increase in price reflects an increase in my transaction costs.

In terms of the number of potential suppliers, fewer potential suppliers mean that these suppliers will likely use their "quasi-monopoly" condition to opportunistically increase their prices—and, again, a supplier's increase in price is directly reflected in the customer's increased transaction costs.

Transaction costs also increase with the level of uncertainty surrounding the transaction. If I do not have "perfect information" about many alternate potential suppliers, the few suppliers that I know will likely use opportunism to increase their prices, again reflecting in an increase in my transaction costs. As per the frequency of transactions, the more frequently a transaction occurs the higher the overall transaction costs incurred.

To summarize, the greater the level of asset specificity and uncertainty involved in a transaction, the frequency of transactions, and the presence of fewer potential suppliers in a market are all drivers of higher transaction costs between a company and a supplier.

The economic theory behind the analysis of transaction costs suggests that, when transaction costs rise, companies will attempt to mitigate those rising costs using vertical integration ("make"). In the same way, when the transaction costs are lower, there is an increased likelihood that companies will purchase ("buy") the item.

Considering transaction cost is a necessary but not sufficient part of this analysis (McIvor 2009). It is also necessary to consider the concepts related to the resource-based view of strategy.

6.1.2 Resource-Based View of Strategy

Resource-based theorists view the firm as a unique bundle of assets and resources that, if employed in distinctive ways, can create competitive advantage (Barney 1991). One of the most prominent concepts derived from the resource-based view of strategy is that of "core competencies." Hamel and Prahalad (1994) define competencies as a set of skills and technologies rather than a single skill or technology. A competence comprises the combined learning of teams and units across a broad range of company functions and therefore is rarely confined to a single unit or team. Hamel and Prahalad (1994) define three characteristics required for a specific competence to be labeled a core competence. This definition is important because core competencies are, according to the authors, the most valuable sources of sustainable competitive advantage for a company.

A core competence must provide a disproportionately large contribution to the value perceived by the final customer. In addition, a core competence must be competitively unique—a competence held in common by an entire industry should not be considered a core competence. Finally, a core competence should be able to enable the company that possesses it to open doors to future markets.

The notion of core competencies supports the idea that a company should not internally produce everything it sells. According to the resource-based view of strategy, items (goods or services) related directly to core competencies in an organization should not be outsourced. Other, non-core competence related activities can and, some authors suggest, should be outsourced to allow for the company to really focus on what it considers to be "core."

6.1.3 A Framework for the Strategic "Make or Buy" Decision

As discussed above, there are two main conceptual contributions to be considered when a company decides whether to make or buy (outsource) a certain activity related to the production of goods or services: transaction costs and core competencies. Figure 2.1 shows a simple framework for the making of make or buy decisions that takes both contributions into account.

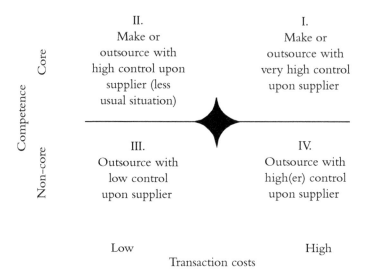

Figure 2.1 The "Make or Buy Decision" in Supply Chains

Quadrant I. Make or control 100%—In principle, activities within this quadrant should not be outsourced. These activities should be performed internally because they relate to one of the company's core competencies and is therefore crucial to its future competitiveness. Furthermore, because of the high transaction costs involved, outsourcing the activity could make the company vulnerable to opportunistic behavior on the part of its suppliers. This quadrant includes, for example, activities related to logistics intelligence within FedEx and integrated circuit design within Intel.

Quadrant II. Make or control (less common scenario)—In this quadrant, the activities are considered related to core competencies, but the transaction costs involved in outsourcing them are low. This should not be a common situation since by definition the skills needed to perform activities that are considered core competences cannot be widely spread. Only a handful of companies are likely to face this situation. For example, McDonald's requires just the right variety of potato for its French fries and requires those potatoes to meet strict quality standards. McDonald's French fries are world-famous, and maintaining their consistent quality is a core competence. However, when McDonald's expands into new countries, the company must create partnerships with local producers to cooperate in the cultivation of the proper type of potato, adapted to local conditions. In these situations, the outsourcing of the potato supply development takes the form of close partnerships. McDonald's is aware of the importance of keeping as much control as possible over this core process; however, the company is not interested in growing its own potatoes.

Quadrant III. Outsourcing with little control—This quadrant is where outsourcing is the simplest and most direct. Here, the outsourced activity does not directly involve core competencies and comes with low transaction costs when outsourced. These are nearly perfect market conditions for outsourcing, many competitors fighting for the preference of clients with comparable products. This outsourcing should also not require a high level of control by the company over the suppliers.

Quadrant IV. Outsourcing with high control—The activities here do not involve core competencies and, in principle, would not be candidates to be performed internally. However, the transaction costs are high. Imagine a microcomputer manufacturer such as HP or Dell. Producing operating system software for their computers is not among these companies' core competencies; however, their machines certainly require an operating system in order to function. There are few acceptable suppliers of operating systems (for example, Microsoft or Linux) for microcomputers. This means that, at least from the perspective of potential suppliers and asset specificity, the transaction costs are high. Microcomputer manufacturers such as Dell and HP outsource this non-core activity. However, the level of control over the outsourced processes (Wiengarten et al. 2013) that applies here is much higher than that of Quadrant III, because of the higher risk of the company becoming a victim of opportunism by the few available suppliers.

In supply chains, more than simply deciding whether to "make or buy," it is also essential for a company to elaborate on the nuances of its relationships with potential suppliers. Some recent studies have explored the changing role of supply chain managers as managers of relationships with partners in the chain (Wilson and Barbat 2015).

6.2 Supply Chain Segmentation

As discussed in the introduction to this chapter, there is no single best way to perform operations activities. This is because there is not a single way to compete in the marketplace. For the same reason, there is no single best way to design, manage, and perform supply chain activities. The development of a supply chain strategy must support, and be consistent with, the competitive market strategy of the business unit.

6.2.1 What Is the Right Supply Chain for Your Product?

Fisher (1997) argues that, when analyzing potential supply chain strategies, a company should first categorize its products and markets according to types. According to Fisher, the pattern of demand for a product is the most important variable to consider when categorizing products and markets served by a supply chain. According to this notion, product demand patterns determine the classification of a product as either functional or innovative.

Functional products are purchased by customers in their day-to-day lives from retail outlets such as supermarkets, convenience stores, and gas stations. These products meet basic needs that do not change frequently and generally have long life cycles and predictable demand. Functional products are less differentiated, and therefore, highly subject to price competition and to the use of low-cost competitive strategies (Porter 1980). These factors result in modest profit margins. With modest profit margins and price competition, these products require low production and delivery costs but high volume of production.

In an effort to avoid the uncomfortable situation of living with modest margins, many companies focus on introducing innovative products instead.

Innovative products, according to Fisher (1997) are differentiated products with more frequent product launches, shorter life cycles, and less predictable demand. Low price is not the primary motivation behind customers' interest in acquiring innovative products.

Electronic products such as Apple's innovative lines of iPads, iPhones, iWatches, and Mac computers often fall into this category. It is not rare for the profit margins on innovative products to be in the range of 20% to 80% or even more. Innovative products can potentially increase profitability, but constant innovation makes demand much less predictable and frequently leads to product shortages or excess inventory that may require markdown sales at the end of the season. These products usually compete using Porter's (1980) differentiation strategy.

The strategic supply chain characteristics necessary to produce and deliver innovative products are fundamentally different from the supply chain characteristics necessary to produce and deliver functional products (Fisher 1997).

One of the most important objectives of supply chain management is the continuous reconciliation of supply and demand. When demand is more stable and predictable, this reconciliation is usually easier. With unpredictable demand, companies must carefully manage their resources in order to be able to respond quickly to unexpected factors that cause imbalances between supply and demand. For products with consistent and predictable demand, there is less need for rapid response and their supply chains can concentrate their efforts on maintaining a continuous, uninterrupted, and efficient flow of products from producers to consumers.

The ways in which supply chain resources must be managed in order to handle functional products and the ways in which resources must be managed to handle innovative products are not only different but also often conflicting. That is why many companies are starting initiatives to segment their supply chains. For functional products, strategic supply chain management must emphasize efficiency. This keeps the costs of functional products low. For innovative products, the emphasis must be on responsiveness and flexibility in order to be able to quickly and dynamically match supply to unpredictable demand.

Figure 2.2 describes the strategic characteristics required for the efficient supply chain and the responsive supply chain.

When analyzing functional and innovative products and efficient and responsive supply chains, there is a natural match between the type of product and type of supply chain required, according to the matrix in Figure 2.3.

Characteristics	Efficient supply chains	Responsive supply chains
Objective	Supply predictable demand efficiently at the lowest possible cost	Respond quickly to unpredictable demand to minimize stock-out, markdowns, and obsolete inventory
Manufacturing goal	Keep high average utilization rates	Deploy excess buffer capacity
Inventory strategy	Maximize turns and minimize inventory cost through the chain	Deploy significant buffer stocks of parts or finished products
Response time	Shorten times as long as costs are not increased	Invest aggressively to reduce lead times
Choice of suppliers	Select suppliers mainly for cost and quality	Select suppliers mainly for speed, flexibility, and quality
Product design strategy	Maximize performance and minimize cost	Use modular design to postpone differentiation for as long as possible

Figure 2.2 Efficient Supply Chains Relating to Functional Demand Patterns and Responsive Supply Chains Relating to Innovative Demand Patterns

Source: Fisher 1997

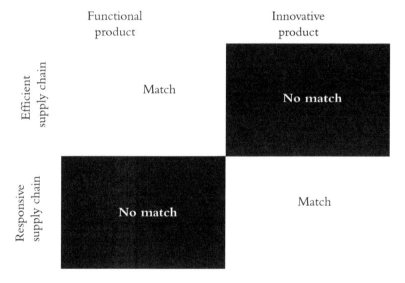

Figure 2.3 Matrix Matching the Two Product Categories and the Two Types of Supply Chains
Source: Fisher 1997

Supply chains planning to compete with functional products should organize their resources and processes according to the characteristics of efficient chains. Supply chains intending to compete with innovative products, however, must organize and manage resources and processes according to the characteristics of responsive chains. This requires extra resources with correspondingly higher costs, but the higher margins commanded by innovative products allow for that. Although Fisher's hypothesis (Fisher 1997) has not been fully tested empirically, there are recent empirical studies (for example, Godsell et al. 2011) and numerous anecdotal accounts that confirm the increasing use of supply chain segmentation, at least in the fast-moving consumer goods industry. Further research is certainly needed on this promising concept and its application.

6.2.2 Aligning Competences in Supply Chains

One important responsibility of supply chain management is to match the range of skills and capabilities possessed by the different companies within the supply chain with the many activities the chain needs to perform in order to satisfy its customers. An example can illustrate this idea. Think of the relationship between an insecticide manufacturer and a supermarket chain in Calcutta, India—a place that has warm temperatures most of the year.

Managers of the insecticide manufacturer are utterly focused on the insect-control industry. For example, they understand that two days of summer rain followed by two days of harsh sun and heat will lead to a rise in the mosquito population in certain areas of the city—thus increasing demand for bug spray in those areas.

Because the manufacturer's executives are focused on the industry and have great knowledge of the use of their products, they are adept at identifying patterns and predicting consumer demand trends for their products, maybe more so than retailers who sell their products to end users. When the weather or relevant conditions change, the supermarket manager has to evaluate their effect not for some, but for the around 30,000 items the supermarket sells—continuously!

The manufacturer's specific knowledge of its own product as well as its position in the supply chain places it in a better condition than the supermarket to forecast short-term sales (and consequently to manage inventory replenishment in the supermarket) of its products.

This means that it can sometimes make sense to reallocate the activities of forecasting consumer sales and managing inventory replenishment polices from the retailer to the manufacturer. This practice, one of the examples of the reallocation of activities to companies that are better positioned in the supply chain to execute them is called vendor-managed inventory, and it is widely used.

Individual companies frequently reshuffle their organizational structures, changing "who does what" inside the organization. What they are doing when they "reshuffle," is to try to achieve a better match between the capabilities required by certain activities and the capabilities present in the internal areas or departments that are allocated to perform them. Following the same rationale, supply chain activities often can and should be reallocated to companies with better capabilities to carry them out. This is only possible with the approach adopted by supply chain management, which considers the many companies that are required to work together to create and deliver products and services to consumers.

6.2.3 Avoiding Incentive Misalignment Among the Constellation of Partners in Supply Chains

One of the most daunting challenges in supply chain management is the challenge of managing a constellation of partners with potentially conflicting interests so that they work toward common objectives; indeed, managers sometimes complain that their partners seem unwilling to pursue the common good, even when doing so has obvious potential benefits for the supply chain.

When this happens, companies are likely to pursue divergent and sometimes incompatible goals. It should never be forgotten that, in a global supply chain, it is essential for the objectives and incentives of each partner to be aligned with the best interests of the entire chain, however, partners in the chain will only be interested in adding maximum value to the chain as a whole if they can retain a fair portion of the benefit achieved.

According to Narayanan and Raman (2004), there are three sources of incentive misalignment in global supply chain management:

- *Secret actions*—when a company does not have knowledge of the actions its partners are taking, it becomes difficult to persuade them to do what is best for the chain. Imagine Whirlpool, which needs retail sales clerks from retail chains like HH Gregg to help it sell its products because clerks have the greatest influence on consumers' buying choices. If *secret actions* are in place, because manufacturers like Whirlpool do not have the means to closely monitor the efforts the retailer is making to sell its products it is difficult to design effective incentives for the retailer that align the best interests of both companies.
- *No information sharing*—It is difficult to align incentives when there is not enough trust between members of the chain to allow for the sharing of information. When different partners do not know each other's profit margins, as is usually the case, it is much more difficult to come up with policies and contracts that prompt a fair distribution of benefits and give each company the incentives to behave in the best interest of the partnership and the supply chain as a whole.
- *Poor incentive system design*—Poorly designed performance measurement and incentive systems have the potential to induce dysfunctional behavior that contribute to misalign incentives in supply chains.

6.3 The Bullwhip Effect: Caused by Lack of Communication and Coordination Between Partners in Supply Chains

One of the important objectives of supply chain management is to reconcile supply and market demand. In some supply chains, a large part of the demand variation faced by individual supply operations is not caused by actual final consumer demand variations but rather by practices and decisions made by other supply chain participants. When practices and decisions internal to the supply chain cause other supply chain members, especially those upstream, to perceive amplified demand volatility, the result is called the bullwhip effect (Lee et al. 1997). This important effect is found in most supply chains (Mackelprang and Malhotra 2015).

The bullwhip effect is a dynamic phenomenon that causes even small downstream demand fluctuations in a supply chain to become distorted and gradually be perceived as increasingly larger fluctuations as information is conveyed upstream in the chain via customer-supplier relationships, usually in the form of orders.

The bullwhip effect can be seen in the simplified supply chain presented in Figure 2.4.

Imagine for the sake of simplicity that each of the companies in the supply chain in Figure 2.4 has a policy of keeping in inventory the equivalent of one month's worth of its

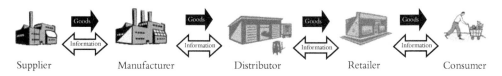

Figure 2.4 A Simplified Supply Chain

perceived demand. Imagine that the customer demand perceived by the retailer in this chain has remained stable for several months at 50 units per month. Since the chain works to meet the demand and keeps the equivalent of one month's worth of demand in stock, all the chain companies have a perceived demand of 50 units during Month 1. They deliver 50 units to their immediate customers, they purchase 50 units from their immediate suppliers, and they keep 50 units in stock.

This is shown in the first row, corresponding to Month 1, in the table in Figure 2.5. This table demonstrates what happens to the immediate demand perceived by each of the companies in the chain when a small variation occurs in demand at the consumer level. This change occurs when demand at the retail level increases from 50 to 53 units in Month 2 and remains at 53 units per month for the remaining 5 months shown in the table. The rows in the table represent months from 1 to 6 and the columns hold order and inventory level data at the end of each month, for each tier in the supply chain.

Observe that, when final consumer demand increases slightly from 50 units in Month 1 to 53 units in Month 2, the new inventory level demanded by the retailer's inventory policy for Month 2 becomes 53 units. This means the retailer's order to the distributor in Month 2 will be for 56 units: 53 units to meet consumer demand and another 3 units to increase the inventory level from 50 units to 53. The immediate demand perceived by the distributor in Month 2

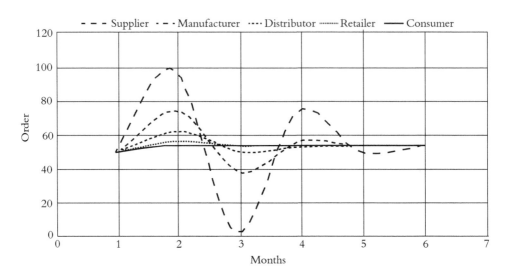

Figure 2.5 Simplified Illustration of the Bullwhip Effect on a Supply Chain with Four Links That Serves the Final Consumer

Source: Adapted from Slack et al. 2013

is therefore 56 units. Due to the distributor's own inventory policy also calling for them to keep one month's worth of demand in inventory, the distributor's system determines that its inventory level must increase from 50 to 56 units. To account for that, the distributor places an order to the manufacturer for 62 units: 56 units to meet the retailer's order and another 6 units to increase their own stock from 50 to 56 units. This distortion of actual consumer demand continues through the other supply chain nodes increasing in amplitude as the distortion moves upstream.

In Month 3, consumer demand is again 53 units. The retailer therefore orders 53 units from the distributor, who redefines the inventory level to be 53 units, causing it to place an order for only 50 units to the manufacturer (because three of the units required are taken from inventory, decreasing the inventory from 56 to 53 units). The effect propagates these new distortions all the way to the end of the chain. This continues to occur in subsequent months until the chain finally achieves stability in the form of the new demand baseline of 53 units that is universally adopted in the sixth month. Figure 2.5 shows how demand volatility (variation) is amplified as consumer demand information travels upstream in the chain as a result of distortions caused by adjustments being made to inventory levels at each stage in the chain. Note that this increased demand volatility must be satisfied by the supply side of each supplier-customer relationship in the chain and that satisfying it demands more resources and increases costs.

This simplified example demonstrates the bullwhip effect but in a much less severe way than what is found in real supply chains (see Wanphanich et al. 2010; Dominguez et al. 2014 for analyses of the bullwhip effect in more complex situations). This is because, in this example, the supply chain works with a single product; there are no competing chains, final consumer demand is relatively stable, and there are no requirements for minimum order quantities to be produced and shipped. In real supply chains, the bullwhip effect and its consequences are much more severe.

Under real-world business conditions, there are five causes of the bullwhip effect that are analyzed below, together with strategies to counter them (Lee et al. 1997; Correa 2014):

- The first cause of the bullwhip effect is uncoordinated forecast updating between stages of the chain. It is apparent in the example of Figure 2.5 that, when a chain company perceives an increase in its immediate demand, there is a tendency for this increase to be seen as indicative of a trend. This perception causes the company to review its demand forecasting and, based on that, to increase its inventory and place larger orders to its supplier; this behavior tends to flow upstream in the supply chain, perpetuating and increasing the distortion. One solution for this growth in volatility is to increase coordination and information exchange between the chain stages (Ciancimino et al. 2012) so that data about actual consumer demand is shared and therefore, more visible to all links in the chain, similarly to what Wal-Mart practices with its suppliers with its Retail Link tool. Retail Link is a large database of daily sales with great granularity maintained by Wal-Mart and to which suppliers can have access to better forecast demand and plan their operations and inventories. This way, companies upstream work with better knowledge of the (sell-out) market demand.
- The second is batching in production and/or transportation. Whenever batches form in production and/or transportation, there is distortion in the demand information from customer to supplier. Batch distortion occurs when, for instance, a retailer facing a stable daily market demand pattern for a product orders large replenishment batches from the distributor to save in transportation, say ordering a full truckload whenever the retailer inventory level falls below a certain quantity. The stable market demand is "distorted" when information travels upstream in the supply chain by the ordering policy of the retailer. The consequence is that

the distributor perceives a "lumpy" demand (large quantities ordered at once) coming from the retailer. Fighting to reduce batch distortion can help reduce demand volatility in supply chains. Supply chains can combat batch distortion both in production, via initiatives such as set up reduction (see Shingo 1985 for a good reference), and in transportation, via the use of shipping options that allow for the efficient transportation of smaller and more frequent quantities of products, such as by using third-party logistics providers and/or milk runs. The term "milk run" is a reference to traditional milkmen, who delivered milk to homes every morning. In modern logistics, it refers to a fixed regular schedule of periodic deliveries or pickups (Correa 2014).
- The third cause is related to price fluctuations. When price fluctuations occur, for example, with promotions, products with reasonably stable demand become less stable. For example, when the prices of diapers are reduced in a promotion, demand increases in the short term when the parents stockpile the product, but then demand drops, causing an artificial variation in sales that distorts perceived demand as information flows upstream in the chain. One solution is what retailers like Target do when using "everyday low prices" (EDLP) policies. They limit their use of promotions so as not to distort consumer demand data. The less the supply chain's demand fluctuates at the consumer level, the less dramatic the bullwhip effect will be for that chain.
- Next, we look at product rationing/opportunistic behavior as a cause for the bullwhip effect. Whenever there is a temporary rationing of a product for some reason, perhaps because of a surge in demand, accompanied by a simultaneous lack of production capacity to meet the surge, suppliers will often deliver only a part of the total orders they receive from each customer downstream in order to avoid leaving any one customer totally without the product. As a natural response, customers will artificially inflate their orders to obtain the full amount needed. This type of customers' action can distort the number of orders even further, intensifying the bullwhip effect. Supply chain managers need to analyze the chain's means of dealing with product shortages to ensure that that their policies will not induce undesirable behavior in customers that end up adding volatility to the chain.
- The final cause is related to delays in the flow of materials and information: Supply chains that process physical products depend upon the flow of the materials they require; long lead times to obtain such materials can create difficulties. Delays in information flow can also be problematic. The longer the lead times that are experienced in a supply chain, the greater the bullwhip effect will be in that chain (Saab and Correa 2005). A poorly thought-out decision to replace a nearby supplier with a supplier located on the other side of the world can expose the supply chain to considerable risk because of the longer lead times, both in the flow of information and materials, which increase the bullwhip effect. The solution here is to fight delays and to shorten lead times. This can be done either by maintaining closer (physical or organizational) relationships with suppliers or by increasing the agility with which information and materials flow through the chain.

6.4 *Risk Assessment in Supply Chains*

Risk assessment and risk management have been a matter of concern to global supply chain executives because with increasing complexity and globalization, supply chains have become much more intricate and interconnected. On the one hand, global supply chains offer enormous opportunities for cost reduction and access to talent and resources wherever they are located. On the other hand, risk substantially increases in global chains. Supply chains become longer with

Global Supply Chain Management

more inter-dependent links, and links that are potentially more diverse as well, with the result that complexity increases exponentially.

While in the past, supply chain managers were mainly concerned with costs and quality, ensuring a continuous flow of supply is now at least as important.

The vulnerability of a company or supply chain to a risk factor is a measurement of the potential a given risk has to cause significant harm to the organization.

In general, the mechanisms of risk management require some sort of method to evaluate the probability of the occurrence of a risk factor and some way to evaluate the impact of its occurrence considered simultaneously to define which priority actions should be adopted to reduce the probability of the chain being affected by the risk factor and/or to reduce the negative consequences for the chain, in case the factor manifests itself.

The joint consideration of the likelihood and consequence of possible risk factors (later described in this section) can be represented with a graphic as shown in the Vulnerability Map in Figure 2.6 and frequently used to assess the vulnerability of a company or a supply chain to certain risk factors.

In the Vulnerability Map, risk factors for a supply chain are identified and each risk factor is assessed in terms of its likelihood of occurrence and its impact on the supply chain, if and when it occurs. Based on the assessments of likelihood and impact (severity), all risk factors are then plotted on the Vulnerability Map. Then, based on where the risk factors fall on the map, the vulnerability of the supply chain to the risk factor is evaluated and actions are taken to mitigate the overall risk. The four quadrants of the Vulnerability Map are briefly discussed.

Quadrant 1: High Likelihood–Severe Consequence (High Vulnerability): Risk factors in this quadrant are those to which the operation is most vulnerable. Imagine that these risk factors could be the seizing of a nuclear power plant in Central Europe following the attacks in the Belgium Airport and Underground in 2016. Motivated by the attention from the Belgium attacks, several terrorist groups became interested in this type of action, increasing its likelihood. Obviously, the effects are almost impossible to calculate with precision, since substantial human losses can be involved, and those losses are also the most devastating. These risk factors deserve priority treatment both in terms of actions to reduce the likelihood of their occurrence via preventive measures and actions and preparations to make sure that the supply chains bounce back as quickly and inexpensively as possible whenever the risk factor in analysis causes a disruption.

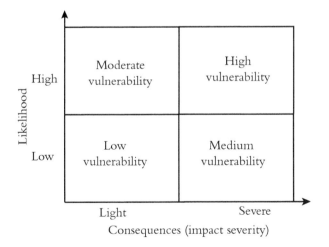

Figure 2.6 The Vulnerability Map

Quadrant 2: Low Likelihood–Severe Consequence (Medium Vulnerability): This includes the events with low likelihood but with severe potential impact. Imagine the incidence of a tornado striking a factory in Florida, in the US. Although the likelihood of a tornado hitting a specific location in Florida is low, the damage from an event like that would likely be very extensive, due to the destructive capacity of a tornado. Here, given that the likelihood of occurrence is already low, risk-mitigating actions should focus on increasing ability of the supply chain in analysis to recover once a disruption has occurred.

Quadrant 3: High Likelihood–Light Consequence (Moderate Vulnerability): This includes events that companies deal with on a daily basis, making use of their planning and control systems. Examples include moderate delays in the delivery of raw materials, equipment failures, accidents that occur while transporting products to a distribution center, among others. These incidents are likely to happen from time to time in most environments but cause only moderate impact. Companies routinely have safety stocks and other resources and control mechanisms on hand to deal with these issues.

Quadrant 4: Low Likelihood–Light Consequence (Low Vulnerability): The risk factors in this category certainly do not rank high in the priority list of risk managers for a supply chain. These are events that are not only unlikely but, should they occur, have a negligible impact. Issues and risk factors in this quadrant are substantially less consequential than risks in other quadrants and should not be priorities in terms of actions to mitigate risk.

7   Conclusion and Directions for Future Research

The management of global supply chains do not represent a disruptive change, such as a "volcanic eruption," but rather, they represent another stage of evolution in the expansion of scope that the area of POM has been experiencing since the beginning of the 20th century. This is important because, as it is an incremental process, this evolution does not require, strictly speaking, a totally new set of solutions but rather many of the solutions developed historically in other stages of this expansion can be used (and/or adapted) to meet current and future needs. This fact became apparent in our discussion of a number of fundamental concepts of supply chain management in the previous sections of this chapter. It is a fact, however, that this evolution is occurring in a more accelerated form than in previous phases, and it is also a fact that the levels of volatility, complexity, and social pressure on supply chains today and in the future do not have historical precedence, requiring all the competencies needed in the previous phases of evolution and some additional ones. Chapter 36 addresses the future research opportunities for POM in SCM.

Acknowledgements

I would like to thank my Graduate Assistant Bryan Basnight for his help with the literature review and formatting of this chapter.

References and Bibliography

Antai, I. (2011) "Supply chain vs supply chain competition: A niche-based approach." *Management Research Review*, **34**(10): 1107–1124.

Barney, J.B. (1991) "Firm resources and sustained competitive advantage." *Journal of Management*, **17**(1): 99–120.

Blome, C., A. Paulraj, and K. Schuetz (2014) "Supply collaboration and sustainability: A profile deviation analysis." *International Journal of Operations & Production Management*, **35**(4): 639–663.

Ciancimino, E., S. Cannella, and M. Bruccoleri (2012) "On the bullwhip avoidance phase: The synchronized supply chain." *European Journal of Operational Research*, **221**(1): 49–63.

Coase, R. (1937) "The nature of the firm." *Economica*, **4**(16): 386–405.

Cooper, M.C., D.M. Lambert, and J.D. Pagh (1997) "Supply chain management: More than a new name for logistics." *The International Journal of Logistics Management*, **8**(1): 1–14.

Correa, H.L. (2014) *Global supply chain management*. Atlas. São Paulo, Brazil. https://itunes.apple.com/us/book/global-supply-chain-management/id899237729?|=pt&ls=1&mt=11. Accessed October 22, 2015.

Dominguez, R., J.M. Framinan, and S. Cannella (2014) "Serial vs. divergent supply chain networks: A comparative analysis of the bullwhip effect." *International Journal of Production Research*, **52**(7): 2194–2210.

Elkington, J. (1997) *Cannibals with forks: The triple bottom line of 21st century business*. Capstone, Oxford, UK.

Elmuti, D. (2002) "The perceived impact of supply chain management on organizational effectiveness." *Journal of Supply Chain Management*, **38**(3): 49–57.

Fisher, M. (1997) "What is the right supply chain for your product?" *Harvard Business Review*, March–April: 105–116.

Godsell, J., T. Diefenbach, C. Clemmow, D. Towill, and M. Christopher (2011) "Enabling supply chain segmentation through demand profiling." *International Journal of Distribution & Logistics Management*, **41**(3): 296–314.

Gottfredson, M., R. Puryear, and S. Phillips (2005) "Strategic sourcing: From periphery to the core." *Harvard Business Review*, February: 1–9.

Guo, P., J.-S. Song, and Y. Wang (2010) "Outsourcing structures and information flow in a three-tier supply chain." *International Journal of Production Economics*, **128**(1): 175–187.

Hamel, G. and C.K. Prahalad (1994) "Competing for the future." *Harvard Business School Press*. Boston, MA.

Handfield, R. and E. Nichols (1999) *Introduction to supply chain management*. Prentice-Hall, Upper Saddle River, NJ.

Hayes, R.H. and S. Wheelwright (1984) *Restoring our competitive edge*. The Free Press, New York.

Hill, T. (1985) *Manufacturing strategy*. Milton Keynes. Open University Press, London.

Kroes, J.R. and S. Ghosh (2010) "Outsourcing congruence with competitive priorities: Impact on supply chain and firm performance." *Journal of Operations Management*, **28**(2): 124–143.

Lambert, D.M. and M.C. Cooper (2000) "Issues in supply chain management." *Industrial Marketing Management*, **29**(1): 65–83.

Lee, H., V. Padmanabhan, and S. Whang (1997) "The bullwhip effect in supply chains." *Sloan Management Review*, **38**(8): 93–102.

Mackelprang A.W. and M.K. Malhotra (2015) "The impact of bullwhip effect on supply chains: Performance pathways, control mechanisms, and managerial levers." *Journal of Operations Management*, **36**: 15–32.

McIvor, R. (2009) "How the transaction cost and resource-based theories of the firm inform outsource evaluation." *Journal of Operations Management*, **27**(1): 45–63.

Mena, C., A. Humphries, and T. Choi (2013) "Toward a theory of multi-tier supply chain management." *Journal of Supply Chain Management*, **49**(2): 58–77.

Narayanan, V.G. and A. Raman (2004) "Aligning incentives in supply chains." *Harvard Business Review*, November: 94–102.

Poirier, C. and M. Bauer (2000) *E-Supply chain*. Berrett-Koehker, San Francisco, CA.

Porter, M. (1980) *Competitive strategy*. The Free Press, New York.

Prajogo, D. and J. Olhager (2012) "Supply chain integration and performance: The effects of long-term relationships, information technology and sharing, and logistics integration." *International Journal of Production Economics*, **135**(1): 514–522.

Saab, J. and H.L. Correa (2005) "Bullwhip effect reduction in supply chain management." *International Journal of Logistics Systems and Management*, **1**(2/3): 211–226.

Shingo, S. (1985) *A Revolution in Manufacturing: the SMED System*, Productivity Press, Portland, OR.

Skinner, W. (1969) "Manufacturing: the missing link in corporate strategy." *Harvard Business Review*, May–Jun: 136–145.

Slack, N., A. Brandon-Jones, and R. Johnston (2013) *Operations management*. 7th edition. Pearson, Harlow, UK.

Souza, G.C. (2013) "Closed-loop supply chains: a critical review and future research." *Decision Sciences*, **44**(1): 7–38.

Stock, J.R. and S.L. Boyer (2009) "Developing a consensus definition of supply chain management: a qualitative study." *International Journal of Physical Distribution & Logistics Management*, **39**(8): 690–711.
Taylor, F.W. (1911) *The principles of scientific management*. Harper Bros, New York.
Trent, R.J. and R.M. Monczka (2005) "Achieving excellence in global sourcing." *Sloan Management Review*, **47**(1): 24–32.
Utterback, J. (1994) *Mastering the dynamics of innovation*. Harvard Business School Press, Cambridge, MA.
Walters, D. and G. Lancaster (2000) "Implementing value strategy through the value chain." *Management Decision*, **38**(3): 160–178.
Wanphanich, P., Kara, S., and Kayis, B. (2010) "Analysis of the bullwhip effect in multiproduct, multi-stage supply chain systems—a simulation approach", *International Journal of Production Research*, **48**: 4501–4517.
Wiengarten, F., M. Pagell, and B. Fynes (2013) "The importance of contextual factors in the success of outsourcing contracts in the supply chain environment: The role of risk and complementary practices." *Supply Chain Management: An International Journal*, **18**(6): 630–643.
Wilson, K. and V. Barbat (2015) "The supply chain manager as political-entrepreneur?" *Industrial Marketing Management*, **49**: 67–79.
Wolf, J. (2014) "The relationship between sustainable supply chain management, stakeholder pressure and corporate sustainability performance." *Journal of Business Ethics*, **119**(3): 317–328.
Wu, T., J. Wu, Y.J. Chen, and M. Goh (2014) "Aligning supply chain strategy with corporate environmental strategy: A contingency approach." *International Journal of Production Economics*, **147**(Part B): 220–229.
Yang, B. and Y. Yang (2010) "Postponement in supply chain risk management: A complexity perspective." *International Journal of Production Research*, **47**(7): 1901–1912.

PART II

Core POM Functions

3
FORECASTING
State-of-the-Art in Research and Practice

Nada R. Sanders

1 Introduction to Forecasting in POM

Forecasts lie at the heart of Production and Operations Management (POM). They serve as a key input to all POM decisions such as inventory management, production planning, and scheduling as well as operations strategy and product innovation. All these decisions are based on a forecast of the future, both long term at the strategic planning level as well as short-term disaggregate forecasts at the SKU level used for tactical decisions. Improving forecasting performance has been shown to lead to significant benefits in both POM and across the supply chain (Oliva and Watson 2011; Moritz et al. 2014). However, implementation of forecasting processes and associated technologies is a challenge. Methodological advancements, available technology, and information access have elevated forecasting capability. In practice, however, forecasting processes still rely heavily on human judgment (Lawrence et al. 2006). Forecasts within the practice of POM are usually produced as a combination of statistical forecasts and judgment (Fildes and Goodwin 2007), where an initial statistical forecast is adjusted judgmentally. Therefore, understanding forecasting requires comprehending both statistical and judgmental methods, as well as ways they can be combined in practice to improve performance.

Improving the practice of forecasting and extending relevant research requires understanding methodological capabilities and their use but also current challenges and shortcomings. In this chapter, we provide a state-of-the-art presentation of these critical issues. We begin with an overview of the practice of forecasting by looking at its far reaching impact on POM decisions and organizational costs, as well as its role in non-typical POM environments. We then discuss the forecasting process and factors guiding method selection. Next, we present a deep discussion of forecasting methodologies from judgment to statistical methods, to combination methodologies that have been shown to be particularly successful in both research and practice. Finally, we consider the future of forecasting, including the role of big data analytics and information, and implications for both managers and researchers.

1.1 Forecasting Versus Planning

Forecasting is the process of predicting future events. This can range from forecasting product demand, such as demand for the next iPhone, to forecasting the passage of a healthcare bill in

Congress. Any prediction of future events is a forecast. Forecasting is one of the most important business activities because it drives all other business decisions. Decisions such as which markets to pursue, which products to produce, how much inventory to carry, and how many people to hire are all based on forecasts.

Consider the full range of POM decisions, from inventory ordering, production planning, scheduling, to project management. They are all based on a forecast of demand. In fact, the computations for order quantities and safety stocks contain a demand component obtained through a forecast. These decisions are all part of the planning process often confused with forecasting (Armstrong 2001). Planning is the process of selecting actions in anticipation of a forecasted event. A forecast drives the plan that is made in response to the forecast. As organizations attempt to decrease their statistical variability, they generate forecasts and plan their resources accordingly.

Planning involves the following decisions:

- *Scheduling existing resources*: One important aspect of planning is deciding how to best utilize existing resources. This includes decisions regarding product variety and volumes produced, transportation and deliveries at right locations, labor allocation and utilization, facilities planning, and capital usage.
- *Determining future resource needs*: Organizations must also determine what resources will be needed in the future. These decisions depend on forecasts of emerging markets, future customer demands, technological advancements, and competition.
- *Acquiring new resources*: It takes time to acquire new facilities, new technologies, new equipment, and expand to new locations. Plans must be made well in advance, and procedures to acquire new resources and capabilities put in place ahead of time.

1.2 Demand Management

Forecasting and planning are intertwined and often confused in practice as companies have the ability to affect actual events, especially demand. This can be done through promotional campaigns and advertisements, offering incentives to sales staff and personnel, and through cutting prices. This is called "demand management" and is the process of attempting to modify demand. This is in contrast to supply management. Where supply management involves managing the supply base and sourcing decisions on the upstream side of the supply chain, demand management focuses on customers on the downstream side.

Demand management cannot occur without first having a forecast—a prediction of what future demand is going to be. Once a forecast and a resulting plan have been made, the organization may decide to "manage" the demand in order to better utilize its resources, and the plan is reconfigured accordingly. This is shown in Figure 3.1. The forecast is the starting point as an objective prediction of what is an iterative process. The plan follows the forecast as a course of action. However, demand management may modify the plan, such as with an advertising campaign, which then changes the forecast. They each impact each other as illustrated with two sided arrows.

The impact of forecasts also extends to the supply chain. Independent forecasting by members of the supply chain gives rise to the bullwhip effect (Forrester 1961), which is the increased volatility in orders as they propagate through the supply chain. The bullwhip effect occurs when each individual company in the supply chain forecasts its own demand, plans stock levels, and makes replenishment decisions independently of other companies in the chain (Chen et al. 2000; Lee et al. 1997; Lee et al. 2000). This creates volatility in orders, which makes forecasting more difficult, leads to increases in inventory throughout the supply chain, has a higher stock-out risk,

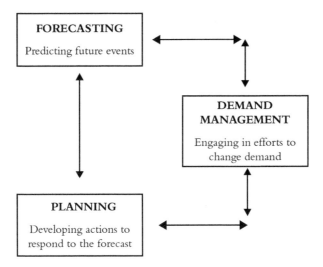

Figure 3.1 The Iterative Cycle of Forecasting, Planning, and Demand Management

and results in inefficient use of working capital and production capacity. Thus, forecasting has an impact on the entire supply chain. One strategy for mitigating the bullwhip effect is the sharing of forecast information with supply chain partners, discussed later in Section 4.3.

1.3 Impact on Costs

Forecasts not only impact POM decisions. They directly impact organizational costs. A number of studies have looked at the relationship between forecast error and organizational costs in the POM environment. Their collective finding is that forecast errors can increase organizational costs from 10% to 30%. Furthermore, this impact is dependent upon the characteristics of the organizational environment.

Although the initial studies in this area made many simplifying assumptions, such as single product production and a homogeneous workforce (Bowman 1963), they provided estimates of the strength of the relationship between forecast error and cost. Later studies further examined forecast errors in more realistic manufacturing settings. These studies confirmed that reducing forecast errors increases profitability and reduces cost roughly by 10%–30%. The impact, however, depends on the structure of the POM environment, such as inventory ordering decisions and workforce scheduling policies (Metters 1997; Sanders and Graman 2015). Collectively, these studies demonstrate that the impact of forecast errors varies based upon characteristics of the POM environment, underscoring the relationship between forecasting and planning and POM decisions.

2 The Forecasting Process

2.1 Steps in the Forecasting Process

Forecasts need to be credible in order to be justified to other parties that include management, suppliers, shareholders, and other stakeholders (Makridakis et al. 1983). To ensure credibility the forecasting process needs to follow an established set of steps regardless of what is being forecast or the model used (Armstrong 2001; Makridakis et al. 1982; Makridakis, Wheelwright, and Hyndman 2006). The steps are shown in Figure 3.2 and described below in the following sequence:

a) *Decide what to forecast*: Although seemingly simple, this initial step requires thought. A forecast provides an answer to a question and formulating the right question is critical. For example, there is an obvious difference between forecasting sales (dollars) versus demand (units). A little less obvious may be a scenario where a company forecasts demand to better manage inventory levels but finds that forecasting delivery lead times actually results in better performance. Forecasts are made in order to develop plans for the future, and it is important to first identify what forecasts are actually needed to develop them.

b) *Analyze data*: Before we can forecast, we must analyze data in order to identify patterns present and—as noted next—select the forecasting model most appropriate for the identified pattern. The most commonly observed data patterns are:

  i) *Level or horizontal*: This is the simplest pattern and exists when data fluctuate around a constant mean. It is the easiest to predict and is common for commodity products in the mature stage of the life cycle, such as table salt or toothpaste.
  ii) *Trend*: Trend is present when data exhibit an increasing or decreasing pattern over time. The simplest type of trend is a straight line, or linear trend, but a variety of trend patterns can exist such as exponential or logarithmic.
  iii) *Seasonality*: Seasonality is any pattern that regularly repeats itself. Most intuitive are demand patterns that fluctuate with the seasons, such as sale of ice cream or snow shovels. However, any pattern that regularly repeats itself is a seasonal pattern, including holiday retail sales or end of the month production rush.
  iv) *Cycles*: Cycles are patterns created by economic fluctuations. Examples include a recession, inflation, or even the life cycle of a product. The major distinction between seasonal patterns and cycles is that the latter do not have a repeating length or magnitude. As a result, they are most difficult to predict.

In addition, data inherently contains a certain amount of random variation. The greater the random variation, the harder it is to forecast as high degrees of randomness can obscure the pattern. Forecasting focuses on identifying the patterns in the data, attempting to smooth out the random variation, as shown below:

Data = Pattern   + Random Variation
Data = Level + trend + seasonality + cycles + Random Variation

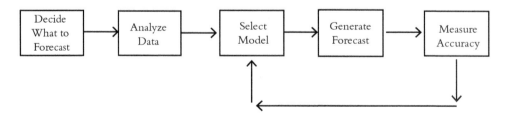

Figure 3.2 The Forecasting Process

a) *Select the forecasting model*: Once data patterns have been identified, we can select an appropriate forecasting model that is suitable for the identified data pattern. All models are not suited for every pattern. Generally, two or three different forecasting models are selected, and then they are tested on historical data to compare accuracy.
b) *Generate the forecast*: Once a model has been selected, the forecast is generated. This can be through any number of software packages, spreadsheets, or even via the use of paper and pencil.
c) *Measure accuracy*: After actual events have occurred, it is critical to measure forecast accuracy, a step often overlooked. Measuring accuracy provides information as to how well selected methods are performing enabling process improvement. Data patterns change over time, and models that once provided good results may no longer be adequate.

At the simplest level, forecast accuracy is computed as the difference between an actual and forecasted value taken as an average across the measured time periods called average error (AE). Here, both positive and negative errors are averaged. Although they cancel each other out, the net effect provides the direction of the forecast or the bias. There are many other metrics that can provide insights into data characteristics and method selection (Hyndman and Athanasopoulos 2013). One such metric is the mean absolute deviation (MAD), which is computed as the average of the sum of absolute errors, rather than algebraic errors. This provides a measure of average error regardless of sign or direction. Another metric is mean squared error (MSE), which is computed as the average of the squared errors. Through the process of squaring, larger errors are penalized. This is an effective metric in situations where large errors are important. There are many other metrics, and each provides unique insights into the forecasting process. Therefore, it is practical for forecasters to use multiple metrics.

2.2 Factors in Method Selection

Although there are many choices in forecasting methods, not all methods are appropriate for all forecasts. There are four factors to consider in method selection:

a) *Amount and type of available data*: Different forecasting methods require different types and quantities of data (Makridakis et al. 1983). Sophisticated quantitative methods, for example, may require large amounts of data, whereas simpler methods may not. In some cases—such as when forecasting new products—no historical data may be available. This factor plays a key role in the methods that can be selected. A note of caution, however, must be made here. Forecasts are only as good as the data they are based on, and the data must be credible. The old adage "garbage in, garbage out" is very applicable here. Therefore, all data must be checked for credibility and cleaned before use.
b) *Degree of accuracy required*: Sophisticated analytical methods may generate good forecasts but they may be costly to develop. The cost of the forecasting method needs to justify the importance of the forecast. For example, forecasting paper clips or rubber washers doesn't justify a costly method.
c) *Length of forecast horizon*: Some forecasting methods are better suited for short-term horizons, whereas others are better suited for the long term. It is important to select the method most appropriate for the horizon being forecast. For example, forecasting emergency room visits to a hospital during the month of December is going to require a very different forecasting method than forecasting demand for natural gas over the next ten years.

d) *Patterns in the data*: As already mentioned, critical to model selection is its appropriateness for the identified data patterns. In fact, a mismatch here virtually guarantees poor forecast performance. For example, it can be mathematically shown that forecasting a trend pattern with a model that does not address trend will result in a lagging of the forecast to the actual data (Makridakis, Wheelwright, and Hyndman 2006).

3 Forecasting Methodologies

There is a broad range of forecasting methodologies. Each one has its own strengths and weaknesses. In this section, we look at each category in more detail. We then delve into the topic of combining methodologies, a subject that has received a great deal of attention in the forecasting literature (Armstrong 2001).

3.1 Categorization of Forecasting Methods

Forecasting methods can be classified into two broad categories: judgmental and statistical. Judgmental methods are those based on subjective opinions and the judgment of individuals or groups of individuals, such as managers, sales staff, or customers. For example, asking customers whether they would buy a particular product is a type of judgmental forecasting method called "intention surveys." Another is called "sales force composite" when the sales staff make a group forecast of upcoming sales.

Judgmental methods are made by people; as a result, these methods are subject to human biases. Statistical forecasting methods, on the other hand, are based on mathematical modeling. These methods are objective and consistent, capable of handling large amounts of data and uncovering complex relationships.

Provided that good data is available, statistical methods are generally more accurate than judgmental methods (Lawrence et al. 2006). As shown in Table 3.1 however, both judgmental and statistical methods have their strengths and weaknesses. While statistical methods are objective and consistent, they require data in quantifiable form in order to generate a forecast. Often, such

Table 3.1 Comparing Qualitative and Quantitative Methods

I. Qualitative Forecasting Methods

Strengths	Weaknesses
✦ Responsive to change	✦ Cannot process large data
✦ Incorporates "soft" information	✦ Inconsistent
✦ Compensates for unusual events	✦ Inability to process complexity
✦ Provides a sense of "ownership"	✦ Biased (e.g., optimism, wishful thinking, political manipulation, lack of consistency)

II. Quantitative Forecasting Methods

Strengths	Weaknesses
✦ Can process complexity	✦ Accuracy dependent on data and model
✦ Objective	✦ Slow to respond to change
✦ Consistent	✦ Costly to model "soft" information
✦ Can process large data	✦ Requires technical understanding

data is not available, such as in new product forecasting or making long-range strategic forecasts. Also, statistical methods are only as good as the data on which they are based. Judgmental methods, on the other hand, have the advantage of being able to incorporate last-minute "inside" or "soft" information. This may be last-minute notice of a competitor's advertising campaign, a snowstorm delaying a shipment, or a heatwave increasing ice cream sales. Judgmental methods also offer users a sense of "ownership," which cannot be discounted, as it is these very users that are responsible for implementing plans to respond to forecasts (Lawrence et al. 2006; Goodwin et al. 2007). Their trust in the forecast is important for implementation.

Therefore, each method has its role in the forecasting process and a good forecaster learns to rely on both. In fact, there is ample evidence that merely relying on statistical forecasts generated via software can create problems. One notable case is a situation with Nike that occurred some years ago (Koch 2004). The company relied on automatically generated statistical forecasts without a judgmental check. The result was widespread inventory shortages of high-moving items and too much stock of low-moving items. Next, we will look at each category and discuss ways that they can be combined.

3.1.1 Judgmental Forecasting Methods

Numerous judgmental forecasting methods exist, ranging in degree of formality and structure. These methods can be useful in including information not available to the statistical model, such as information on special events or recent occurrences. However, these methods are fraught with human biases that include optimism, inconsistency, and political manipulation (Kahneman 2011; Hogarth 1987). As a result, they often exhibit large errors and exaggerations (Kahneman and Tversky 1979; Goodwin et al. 2007).

One such methodology is executive opinion where managers, executives, or sales staff meet and collectively develop a forecast. This method is often used to forecast sales, market trends, make strategic forecasts, or forecast new products. It can also be used to modify existing forecasts to account for special events, such as slowed spending during a recession or a special promotional campaign. The advantage here is the ability to quickly include the latest information in the forecast. However, the disadvantage is a risk of contaminating the forecast with the many human biases.

Another method is market research, which uses surveys and interviews to determine customer preferences and identify new product ideas. Although market research can be a good determinant of customer preferences, it has a number of shortcomings. One is the potential inadequacy of the survey questionnaire design. For example, subjects may be asked to identify a favorite hobby from a set of choices, such as gardening, fishing, cooking, or sports. The problem here is that the list is not exhaustive, and findings may incorrectly portray customer preferences.

One of the most popular judgmental methods is the Delphi technique designed to develop a consensus among a group of experts on a particular topic (Landeta and Barrutia 2011; Kauko and Palmroos 2014). Examples may include forecasting propagation of a disease, climate changes, or technological innovation. The process involves choosing anonymous experts in the field of inquiry. Questionnaires are sent to the experts, the findings summarized, and the process repeated with updated questionnaires that incorporate the initial findings. This process continues until consensus between the experts is reached. The Delphi technique is based on the assumption that agreement of experts on an outcome has a high likelihood of occurrence. The researcher's job is to extract this information and this role requires significant expertise. Although time consuming, the Delphi technique has been shown to be an excellent method for forecasting long-range product demand, technological change, and scientific advances in medicine.

3.1.2 Statistical Forecasting Methods

Statistical forecasting methods can be divided into two broad categories: time series and causal models. Although both are mathematical, the two categories differ in their assumptions and forecast development.

Time series models generate a forecast from an analysis of a "time series" of data. This is a simple listing of data points of the variable being forecast over time taken at regular intervals. For example, data of student enrollment per semester at a university over the past five years is an example of a time series. Time series models assume that forecasts can be made by modeling patterns present in the data. There are many types of time series models, from simple moving averages to models such as Holt-Winter's exponential smoothing that can address both trend and seasonal data patterns.

By contrast, causal models assume that the variable being forecast is related to other variables in the environment. For example, university enrollment may be related to unemployment rates, recession levels, or salary levels. In this case, the forecasting process involves identifying these relationships, expressing them in mathematical form, and using such correlative information to generate a forecast. A typical example would be regression models.

Time series models are generally easier to use than causal models. They are more readily available as forecasting software and easy to automate. Causal models, on the other hand, can be more complex, especially if relationships between multiple variables are being considered. However, time series models can often be just as accurate and have the advantage of simplicity. Numerous forecasting competitions have been conducted over the years where performance of different forecasting models is compared. Consistently, time series models such as exponential smoothing come out as top performers (Makridakis et al, 1982; Hyndman and Koehler 2006). Furthermore, time series models are easy to use and can generate a forecast more quickly than causal models, which require model building. For this reason, time series models are especially useful in the POM environment where demand for large numbers of SKUs must be forecast on a regular basis.

3.2 Combining Forecasting Methods

Much evidence exits to support the combining of two or more independent forecasts. In one of the earlier studies, Winkler and Makridakis (1983) used 1,001 series in order to show that mathematically combining quantitative forecasts reduces forecast errors. Numerous other studies have supported the finding that combining independent forecasts improves accuracy (Lobo and Nair 1990; Batchelor and Dua 1995; Webby, O'Connor, and Lawrence 2001). A literature review of 209 studies by Clemen (1989) documented the benefits of combining, which is well established today. The overall conclusion from these studies is that gains from combining are greatest when methods combined differ substantially and are based on different sources of information. Also, the constituent forecasts should be absent of bias or have biases that cancel each other out. Lastly, combining is most effective when the correlation between forecast errors of constituent forecasts is low, meaning that each forecast brings different information to the integration process (Armstrong 2001; Armstrong et al. 2015).

In an organizational setting, judgmental and statistical forecasts are typically based on different sources of information, making them ideal candidates for combining. The benefits of their mechanical integration have been supported by studies to date. For example, a study of forecasts of quarterly earnings used two judgmental and two quantitative methods for forecast generation (Lobo and Nair 1990). Combining the two judgmental methods reduced forecast error by 0.6%, as measured by the mean absolute percentage error (MAPE). Combining the two quantitative methods reduced MAPE by 2.1%. However, combining one judgmental and one quantitative method reduced MAPE by 5.2% on average.

3.2.1 Combining Judgmental and Statistical Methods

Historically, the forecasting literature has been divided on the relative value of judgmental versus statistical forecasting methods. A number of authors have suggested that judgment should not be given credibility due to high subjectivity (Bazerman 1998). Many studies have pointed to the shortcomings inherent in judgmental forecasting due to previously discussed limitations of human cognitive abilities (Hogarth 1987; Webby and O'Connor 1996). Other authors, however, have provided evidence to support the use of judgment in forecasting (Edmundson et al. 1988; Lawrence et al. 1985). In addition, studies of forecasting practices in business repeatedly show that practitioners rely heavily on judgmental forecasting methods (Dalrymple 1987; Mentzer and Cox 1984; Mentzer and Kahn 1995; Sanders and Manrodt 1994). As discussed earlier, the primary reason for this is that judgment is privy to the latest information on changes in the business environment. This may involve rumors of a competitor launching a promotion, a planned consolidation between competitors, or a sudden shift in consumer preferences due to changes in technology. Managerial judgment can be used to rapidly incorporate this information in the forecast. However, biases inherent in judgmental forecasting can create large and volatile swings of forecast errors, which can have serious customer service and inventory implications.

Today, most researchers agree that both judgmental and statistical forecasting methods each have their unique strengths and weaknesses. Statistical methods have the advantage of being objective, consistent, and capable of processing large amounts of data and considering relationships between numerous variables. However, they are only as good as the data upon which they are based. When changes occur in the data that are not incorporated in the model, the generated forecasts cannot be accurate. An ideal forecasting methodology is one that incorporates the advantages of both judgmental and quantitative forecasting approaches.

The literature review thus far provides support for the integration of judgmental and quantitative forecasts provided that certain criteria are met:

- Combined forecasts should be independently generated.
- Combined forecasts should have a low correlation of forecast errors, should be unbiased, or have biases that cancel each other out.
- Judgmental forecasts should be made in the presence of domain knowledge or based on specific information not available to the statistical model.

One integration methodology is to use judgment to adjust a statistically generated forecast based on contextual factors and is a common practice in business (Turner 1990; Moritz et al. 2014). In a survey of ninety-six US corporations, 45% of the respondents stated that they always made judgmental adjustments to quantitative forecasts with only 9% stating that they never made adjustments (Sanders and Manrodt 1994) with the remaining 54% stating that they sometimes made adjustments. The primary reason given for the practice of judgmentally adjusting quantitative forecasts is to incorporate the latest knowledge of the environment, product, or past experience into the forecast. The forecasting process is performed sequentially with the statistical forecasts generated first, and then adjusted based on judgment. One advantage of this approach is the ability to swiftly allow judgment to rapidly incorporate the latest information. Many studies have documented support for judgmental adjustment of statistically derived forecasts when contextual information is available (Sanders and Ritzman 2001; Fildes and Goodwin 1999). The recommendation is that judgmental adjustments should only be made when specific contextual information is available, including discontinuities in the data and pattern changes.

Another integration methodology is to mechanically combine two independently generated forecasts. The methods can be combined either objectively, such as with a simple average, or subjectively in light of specific contextual information. This type of integration has received much support from literature and has been shown to improve accuracy (Clemen 1989; Armstrong 2001). There is general agreement in the forecasting literature that even a combination forecast generated as a simple average of forecasts outperforms the individual forecasts being combined. Researchers generally prefer combining judgmental and statistical forecasts over judgmental adjustment, as the latter is more subject to judgment's negative effects (Armstrong 2001). Here, the constituent forecasts are made in parallel with the final forecast generated as a mathematical combination of the two minimizing the negative effect of bias. Still, the final forecast represents a merging of information upon which the constituent forecasts are based.

The simplest approach to combining forecasts is using an equal weighted arithmetic average of the individual methods. Numerous empirical studies have found this method to be as effective as using weighted averages or regression based weighting schemes (Makridakis and Winkler 1983; Clemen and Winkler 1986; Conroy and Harris 1987; Blattberg and Hoch 1990). Clemen's (1989) extensive literature review concludes that equal weighting provides improvements in accuracy for many forecasts. While using more elaborate weighting schemes has been shown to be successful in other studies (Lobo 1991), its complexity and time requirements render it less desirable for an organizational context.

Yet another way of combining forecasts is to use judgment in the selection and development of the statistical forecast. Judgment is used to select variables, specify model structure, and set parameters. Certainly, some judgmental inputs are required in the formulation of any statistical model. However, the integration methodology discussed here is one where judgment in the presence of domain knowledge can provide specific domain information that cannot be determined through statistical diagnostics. This methodology is often considered the least subject to the negative effects of judgmental biases while also including its benefits.

Bunn and Wright (1991) identified four areas in statistical model building where judgmental inputs can be important. These areas include the selection of variables, model specification, parameter estimation, and data analysis. Bunn and Wright (1991) suggest that while statistical diagnostics can be important in assisting with the identification of key causal variables, ultimately selection should be based on judgment. Specification of model structure and the estimation of parameters can easily be automated, especially when causal information can be quantified. Causal variables, such as the effect of an advertising campaign, can be automated by using techniques such as multiple regression. However, problems can arise when there are unaccounted "broken-leg" cues affecting the data (Kleinmuntz 1990). The "broken-leg cue," a commonly used term in the psychology and bootstrapping literature, describes cues that are rare but highly diagnostic (Meehl 1957). The idea comes from estimating physical performance of an individual but not knowing that suddenly the person has broken their leg—a rare event but one that clearly disrupts mobility. When there are "broken-leg" cues, modeling procedures will not be effective, and judgment becomes critical.

One approach to using judgment as an input to model building is the use of rule-based forecasting. Rule-based forecasting uses expert judgment to identify characteristics of the data and causal forces affecting change as inputs into the statistical procedure (Collopy and Armstrong 1992). The premise of rule-based forecasting is that forecasting methods need to be tailored to a specific situation and that expert judgment is best suited for this. Expert judgment can identify unusual patterns, direction of causal forces, and the functional form of the time series. Rule-based forecasting provides rules or instructions on how to weight forecasts from a set of forecasting methods, based on experts and prior research. Rule-based forecasting is especially useful when domain knowledge indicates that recent trends may not persist and that there are changes in the direction of causal forces.

3.2.2 The Role of Domain Knowledge and Contextual Information

While there is substantial support for integrating the above methodologies, simply integrating arbitrary judgment with documented statistical procedures can harm accuracy. Important factors that give credibility to judgment are domain knowledge and contextual information.

Domain knowledge is knowledge that practitioners gain through experience as part of their jobs. Becoming familiar with their environment, practitioners become attuned to many cause-effect relationships and environmental cues. Practitioners with domain knowledge understand which cues are significant and which may ultimately prove unimportant. Specific information available in the forecast environment is called contextual information, such as a price increase, an impending strike, or new policies that may affect forecasts. Domain knowledge enables the practitioner to evaluate the importance of specific contextual information (Webby, O'Connor, and Lawrence 2001).

The value of domain knowledge has been demonstrated in a number of studies. Edmundson et al. (1988) conducted a study to evaluate judgmental forecast performance of managers with three different levels of knowledge. The first level consisted of practitioners with considerable domain knowledge, having industry forecast experience and knowledge of the specific products being forecast. The second level was made up of practitioners with some domain knowledge, such as overall industry forecasting experience, but no knowledge of specific products. On the third level were students with no domain knowledge but with considerable technical knowledge, which is knowledge of forecasting methodologies. The study found that familiarity with specific products being forecast to be the most significant factor in improving forecast accuracy. Other studies have also found support for domain knowledge (Sanders and Ritzman 1995).

Domain knowledge has also been shown to be important in the judgmental adjustment of quantitatively derived forecasts. Studying judgmental revision of quantitative forecasts by individual experts with domain knowledge, Mathews and Diamantopoulos (1986; 1989) concluded that judgmental revisions of the quantitative forecasts led to improved accuracy. In another study, Mathews and Diamantopoulos (1990) compared judgmental adjustments made by product managers of a UK company to forecasts generated by a quantitative model. The study concluded that managers who had a higher understanding of market conditions for their products tended to generate better revisions. Similarly, Huss (1986) found that judgmental adjustment by company experts of trends in electricity sales outperformed econometric methods. However, even in the absence of domain knowledge, judgmental adjustment can be beneficial provided that it can bring information not available to the quantitative model, such as discontinuities or pattern changes in the data (Armstrong 2001; Armstrong et al. 2015).

4 The Future of Forecasting

Although the model categories and forecasting methods described in this chapter continue to be the state-of-the-art in forecasting, there are a number of trends that are changing the future. The first is information access, which has become more abundant than ever both in quantity and quality. Another is big data analytics, which is the computational ability to process and analyze the newly available data, providing unprecedented insights. Lastly, the sharing of information between entities and supply chain partners is improving accuracy and POM performance but is also creating risks such as security. In this section, we discuss these emerging trends and their impact on forecasting.

4.1 Information Access

Today, organizations have access to an unprecedented amount of data. These large volumes of data provide information needed for generating better forecasts. For example, sales data can be collected in real time through point-of-sale (POS) data, shortening the forecasting cycle and enabling companies to respond quickly to latest trends. Similarly, radio-frequency identification (RFID) tags gather data on inventories across supply chains, from quantities and location to ambient temperature and security breaches. These tags will number in the billions with 12 million RFID tags in 2011 projected to rise to 209 billion in 2021 (Manyika et al. 2011).

Increasingly, supply chains are combining data from different sources in order to coordinate activities across the POM environment. Marketing is generating huge volumes of POS data from retail stores that are automatically shared with suppliers for real-time stock level monitoring. RFID tags monitor inventory on shelves and in-transit coordinating with current stock levels for automatic order replenishment. Even greater benefits are achieved when companies are able to integrate data from other sources. This includes data from retailers beyond sales, such as promotion data including SKUs sold and prices. It also includes launch data—such as specific items associated with promotional ramp-up and ramp-down plans and inventory consequences.

4.2 Big Data Analytics

The gathering of large amounts of data is part of the trend of big data analytics, which has had a huge impact on forecasting. Big data refers to large datasets whose size is so large that the quantity can no longer fit into the memory that computers use for processing. This data can be captured, stored, communicated, aggregated, and analyzed. Analytics without big data are simply mathematical and statistical tools and applications. Many of these tools—such as correlation and regression analysis—have been around for decades. It is the combination of big data with statistical algorithms—or analytics—fueled by today's computing power that creates the ability to extract meaningful insights and turn information into intelligence. The availability of big data and the advancements in machine intelligence have created significant new opportunities given the size of memories and fast access to them.

Big data analytics has had a significant impact on forecasting especially in the area of predictive analytics. Predictive analytics is a "coined" name to emphasize that all available resources will be focused on making the desired prediction (Sanders 2014; Evans 2016). It creates the ability to foresee events before they happen by sensing small changes over time. For example, IBM's Watson computer uses an algorithm to predict best medical treatments (Hempel 2013), and UPS uses analytics to predict vehicle breakdown (Mayer-Schönberger and Cukier 2013). Sensors placed on machinery, motors, or infrastructure like bridges can monitor the data patterns they give off, such as heat, vibration, stress, and sound. These sensors can detect changes that may indicate looming problems ahead essentially forecasting an event.

These developments may significantly change our ability to forecast. They may also mean fewer "black swans." The term "black swans" is used to describe high-impact, low-probability events (Taleb 2007). Historically, we have assumed that these could not be predicted. However, with big data analytics that is rapidly changing. Big data analytics is improving forecasting so that the number of events that we used to consider unpredictable and purely random is getting smaller. We are now able to identify and spot changes in systems that indicate potential failure. Just consider the accuracy of the prediction of Hurricane Sandy provided by the NOAA weather satellite in 2012. Only a few years earlier, this type of event would have been considered a "black swan."

Spotting the abnormality early on enables the system to send out a warning so that a new part can be installed, preparation before an impending tsunami can be made, or the malfunction fixed. The goal is to identify a good proxy for the event that is being forecast, monitor the proxy, and use the information to predict the future. External events—such as weather or traffic or road construction—can be tracked, and the supply chain can respond. This ability is a game changer for forecasting, POM decision making, and risk management.

4.3 Information Sharing

Sharing this information with supply chain partners has been a recognized key element in mitigating the impact of forecast errors (Aviv 2007; Cachon 2001; Cachon and Lariviere 2001). As a result, many companies are engaging in efforts to improve forecast performance through information sharing (Chen and Lee 2009; Fildes and Kingsman 2011; Lee et al. 1997). The merits of information sharing along the supply chain are well known (Lee, So, and Tang 2000) and have received considerable attention in the POM literature (Lee et al. 1997). For example, Fildes and Kingsman (2011) report that the management of inventories and the effects of sharing forecast information across the supply chain as being a particularly important finding in their review of forecasting and operations research. Chen and Lee (2009) report that it may be useful for the supplier to know the buyer's forecast or some other aspect of demand information.

Sharing information has been shown to significantly reduce forecast errors. For example, in an empirical study of a two-stage supply chain Trapero et al. (2012) found information sharing to improve forecasting performance and result in a 6–8 percentage points lower forecast error. Byrne and Heavy (2006) considered a complex supply chain structure and conclude that information sharing could potentially lead to a reduction in supply chain cost savings of up to 9.7%. Similarly, Ali and Boylan (2010) found forecast sharing to lead to inventory cost savings of up to 49.4%.

This role of information has led to the development of formal sharing processes across the supply chain. One is Collaborative Planning, Forecasting, and Replenishment (CPFR), which is a collaborative process of developing joint forecasts and plans with supply chain partners. The distinguishing feature of CPFR is that members of the supply chain collaborate on business plans and jointly execute the processes of forecasting and replenishment. Trading partners jointly set forecasts, plan production, replenish inventories, and evaluate their success in the marketplace (see www.vics.org). Given the benefits of formal information sharing and the advent of ever more information through big data, we can anticipate an increase in these types of collaborations.

5 Relevance for Managers

Methodological advancements, available technology, and access to information often have made forecasting more confusing for managers. There are, however, some lessons that emerge through our presentation of the state-of-the-art of the field:

- Managers should not confuse forecasting and planning. Understanding and carefully separating these will provide greater objectivity and understanding of future events.

- Managers should follow the established forecasting process as described herein. Certainly, forecasts are rarely perfect. However, following this process will ensure good results and provide credibility to the forecasts.
- Managers should make sure that the data used is reliable and clean. It should not be assumed that more data is always better and managers should exercise caution with large data sets questioning its reliability.
- Managers should always measure forecast performance using multiple performance measures. This includes not only measuring overall forecast accuracy but also measuring forecast bias and maintaining a history of errors. Following the process described in Figure 3.2, these metrics should be used to reassess models used, better understand the data, and improve performance.

6 Research Opportunities

Numerous research opportunities exist to improve the practice of forecasting and contribute to the current knowledge base. One opportunity is in the role of information in reducing forecast errors. As previously discussed in Section 4, companies have access to an unprecedented amount of information. However, there continue to be many questions with regard to the role of this information. For example, a number of studies point to problems of sharing information across individual firms (Aviv 2007; Özer 2003; Toktay and Wein 2001). With no incentive for truthful information exchange, these authors conclude that information sharing may result in manipulation. Oh and Özer (2013) offer several examples of deliberately biased forecasts shared across the supply chain in several industries and caution against this practice. Collectively, these studies suggest that forecast sharing may not be a panacea as its benefits may be hindered by lack of truthfulness and incentives. This raises numerous research implications, such as how to share forecast information and ensure truthfulness. Related to that are security implications, as information sharing can also result in data leakage to undesirable parties.

There are numerous other research opportunities. One is studying the role of judgment and "soft information," especially in risk management. As forecasting systems become increasingly optimized and automated, what is the role of decision makers and how can they best have an input? Another research opportunity comes from looking at ways to optimize both the forecast and the appropriate supply chain performance. Research has clearly shown that the POM environment moderates the impact of forecast errors on costs. However, it is not clear which types of POM structures create greater resiliency, the ability to bounce back from disruptions and disasters, such as number and types of suppliers, inventory and postponement strategies, and other POM decisions.

Yet another research area is new product forecasting when there is no historical data. The advent of big data, especially unstructured data such as crowdsourcing, may have uses in forecasting new product demands and features but require more research. Crowdsourcing, which is defined as using social media to get many opinions and ideas, has gained large popularity, but it is not clear how to leverage it for forecasting.

Also, forecasting intermittent or "lumpy" demand continues to be a problem in POM (Prestwich et al. 2014) and better ways to address this would be important. Lastly, there are tremendous research opportunities in the area of metrics and forecast measurement. Indeed, measuring forecast performance is critical for greater understanding and continuous improvement. The development of better, more comprehensive, and easy to understand metrics, as well as frameworks to effectively use the metrics available is yet another area that would help evolve the practice of forecasting.

7 Conclusion

It should be evident from the discussion in this chapter that forecasting is as much of an art as it is a form of science. There are critical technical aspects to forecasting such as with data analysis and model selection. There are also behavioral aspects, as with most POM contexts, the managers are the people using generated forecasts for decision making. They must have confidence and belief in the forecast. In addition, forecast decisions are closely intertwined with planning in the form of a myriad of POM decisions. We have outlined many well-established tenets that should guide practitioners in their quest for better forecasts. However, many issues remain unresolved creating a broad spectrum of opportunities for scholars to improve on the theory and practice of forecasting in POM.

References and Bibliography

Ali, M.M. & Boylan, J. (2010) "The Value of Forecasting Information Sharing in the Supply Chain." *Foresight: The International Journal of Applied Forecasting.* **18**: 14–18.

Armstrong, J.S. (1985) *Long-range forecasting: From crystal ball to computer.* New York: John Wiley & Sons.

Armstrong, J.S. (2001) "Combining forecasting," in J.S. Armstrong (ed.), *Principles of forecasting.* Norwell, MA: Kluwer Academic Publishing.

Armstrong, J.S. & Collopy, F. (1989) "Integration of statistical methods and judgment for time series forecasting: Principles from empirical research," in G. Wright & P. Goodwin (eds.), *Forecasting with judgment*, pp. 1269–1293. New York: John Wiley.

Armstrong, J.S., Kesten, C.G., & Graefe, A. (2015) "Golden rule of forecasting: Be conservative." *Journal of Business Research*, **68**(8): 1717–1735.

Arkes, H.R. (2001) "Overconfidence in judgmental forecasting," in J.S. Armstrong (ed.), *Principles of forecasting.* Norwell, MA: Kluwer Academic Publishing.

Aviv, Y. (2001) "The effect of collaborative forecasting on supply chain performance." *Management Science*, **47**(10): 1326–1343.

Aviv, Y. (2007) "On the benefits of collaborative forecasting partnerships between retailers and manufacturers." *Management Science*, **54**(5): 777–794.

Batchelor, R. & Dua, P. (1995) "Forecaster diversity and the benefits of combining forecasts." *Management Science*, **41**(1): 68–75.

Bazerman, M.H. (1998) "The Impact of Personal Control on Performance: Is Too Much of a Good Thing Bad?" *Emerging management realities: proceedings of the 35th anniversary meeting, EAM, Eastern Academy of Management.* EAM.

Biggs J.R. & Campion, W.M. (1982) "The effect and cost of forecast error bias for multiple-stage production-inventory systems." *Decision Sciences*, **13**(4): 570–584.

Blattberg, R.C. & Hoch, S.J. (1990) "Database models and managerial intuition: 50% model + 50% manager." *Management Science*, **36**(8): 887–899.

Bowman, E.J. (1963) "Consistency and optimality in managerial decision making." *Management Science*, **9**(2): 310–321.

Bunn, D. & Wright, G. (1991) "Interaction of Judgmental and Statistical Forecasting Methods: Issues and Analysis." *Management Science*, **37**(1): 501–518.

Byrne P.J. & Heavy, C. (2006) "The impact of information sharing and forecasting in capacitated industrial supply chains; A case study." *International Journal of Production Economics*, **103**(1): 420–437.

Cachon, G.P. (2001) "Managing a retailer's shelf space, inventory, and transportation." *Manufacturing & Service Operations Management*, **3**(3): 211–229.

Cachon, G.P. & Lariviere, M.A. (2001) "Contracting to assure supply: How to share demand forecasts in a supply chain." *Management Science*, **47**(5): 629–646.

Chen, L. & Lee, H.L. (2009) "Information sharing and order variability control under a generalized demand model." *Management Science*, **55**(5): 781–797.

Chen, Y.F., Drezner, Z., Ryan, J.K., & Simchi-Levi, D. (2000) "Quantifying the bullwhip effect in a simple supply chain: The impact of forecasting, lead times and information." *Management Science*, **46**(3): 436–443.

Clemen, R.T. (1989) "Combining forecasts: A review and annotated bibliography." *International Journal of Forecasting*, **5**: 559–583.
Clemen, R.T. & Winkler, R.L. (1986) "Combining economic forecasts." *Journal of Business and Economic Statistics*, **4**: 39–46.
Collopy, F. & Armstrong, J.S. (1992) "Expert opinion about extrapolations and the mystery of the overlooked discontinuities." *International Journal of Forecasting*, **8**: 575–582.
Conroy, R. & Harris, R. (1987) "Consensus forecasts of corporate earnings: Analysts' forecasts and time series methods." *Management Science*, **33**(6): 687–705.
Croson, R., Schultz, K., Siemsen, E., & Yeo, M.L. (2013) "Behavioral operations: The state of the field." *Journal of Operations Management*, **31**(1–2): 1–5.
Dalrymple, D.J. (1987) "Sales forecasting practices: Results from a U.S. survey." *International Journal of Forecasting*, **3**(3): 379–391.
Danese, P. & Kalchschmidt, M. (2011a) "The role of the forecasting process in improving forecast accuracy and operational performance." *International Journal of Production Economics*, **131**: 204–214.
Danese, P. & Kalchschmidt, M. (2011b) "The impact of forecasting on companies' performance: Analysis in a multivariate setting." *International Journal of Production Economics*, **133**: 458–469.
Edmundson, R.J., Lawrence, M.J., & O'Connor, M.J. (1988) "The use of non-time series information in sales forecasting: A case study." *Journal of Forecasting*, **7**: 201–211.
Evans, J. (2016) *Business analytics: Methods, models, and decisions*. 2nd edition. Upper Saddle River, NJ: Pearson.
Fildes, R. & Goodwin, P. (1999) "Judgmental forecasts of time series affected by special events: Does providing a statistical forecast improve accuracy?" *Journal of Behavioral Decision Making*, **12**(1): 37–53.
Fildes, R. & Goodwin, P. (2007) "Against your better judgment how organizations can improve their use of management judgment in forecasting." *Interfaces*, **37**: 570–576.
Fildes, R., Goodwin, P., & Lawrence, M. (2006) "The design features of forecasting support systems and their effectiveness." *Decision Support Systems*, **42**: 351–361.
Fildes, R., Goodwin, P., Lawrence, M., & Nikolopoulos, K. (2009) "Effective forecasting and judgmental adjustments: An empirical evaluation and strategies for improvement in supply-chain planning." *International Journal of Forecasting*, **25**: 3–23.
Fildes R. & Kingsman, B. (2011) "Incorporating demand uncertainty and forecast error in supply chain planning models." *Journal of the Operational Research Society*, **62**(3): 483–500.
Fitzsimmons, J.A. & Fitzsimmons, M.J. (2005) *Service management: Operations, strategy and information technology*. 5th edition. Boston, MA: Irwin McGraw-Hill.
Forrester, J.W. (1961) *Industrial dynamics*. Cambridge, MA: MIT Press.
Franses, P.H. & Legerstee, R. (2010) "Do experts' adjustments on model-based SKU-level forecasts improve forecast quality?" *Journal of Forecasting*, **29**: 331–340.
Franses, P.H. & Legerstee, R. (2011) "Experts' adjustment to model-based SKU-level forecasts: Does the forecast horizon matter?" *Journal of the Operational Research Society*, **62**: 537–543.
Franses, P.H. & Legerstee, R. (2013) "Do statistical forecasting models for SKU-level data benefit from including past expert knowledge?" *International Journal of Forecasting*, **29**: 80–87.
Ginsburg, J. (2009) "Detecting influenza epidemics using search engine query data." *Nature*, **457**: 1012–1014.
Goodwin, P. (2005) "Providing support for decisions based on time series information under conditions of asymmetric loss." *European Journal of Operational Research*, **163**: 388–402.
Goodwin, P., Lee, W.-Y., Fildes, R., Nikolopoulos, K., & Lawrence, M. (2007) *Understanding the use of forecasting systems: An interpretive study in a supply-chain company*. University of Bath, School of Management Working Paper Series, 2007.14, Bath, UK.
Hempel, J. (2013) "IBM's massive bet on Watson." *Fortune*, October 7, pp. 81–88.
Hogarth, R. (1987) *Judgment and choice: The psychology of decision*. 2nd edition, Chichester, UK: Wiley.
Huss, W.R. (1986) "Comparative analysis of company forecasts and advanced time-series techniques using annual electric utility energy sales data." *International Journal of Forecasting*, **1**(3): 217–239.
Hyndman, R.J. & Athanasopoulos, G. (2013) *Forecasting: Principles and practice*, OTexts. Available from: www.otexts.org/fpp.
Hyndman, R.J. & Koehler, A.B. (2006) "Another look at measures of forecast accuracy." *International Journal of Forecasting*, **22**(4): 679–688.
Kahneman, D. (2011) *Thinking fast and slow*. Farrar, Straus & Giroux: New York.
Kahneman, D. & Tversky, A. (1973) "On the psychology of prediction." *Psychological Review*, **80**: 237–251.

Kahneman, D. & Tversky, A. (1979) "Prospect theory—Analysis of decision under risk." *Econometrica*, **47**: 263–291.
Kauko, K. & Palmroos, P. (2014) "The Delphi Method in forecasting financial markets—An experimental study." *International Journal of Forecasting*, **30**: 313–327.
Kleinmuntz, B. (1990) "Why we still use our heads instead of formulas: toward an integrative approach." *Psychological Bulletin*, **107**: 296–310.
Koch, C. (2004) "Nike rebounds." *CIO Magazine*, July 12, 2004.
Landeta, J. & Barrutia, J. (2011) "People consultation to construct the future: A Delphi application." *International Journal of Forecasting*, **27**: 134–151.
Lawrence, M.P., Edmundson, J.R.H., & O'Connor, M.J. (1985) "An examination of the accuracy of judgmental extrapolation of time series." *International Journal of Forecasting*, B(1): 25–35.
Lawrence, M.P., Edmundson, J.R.H., & O'Connor, M.J. (1986) "The accuracy of combining judgmental and statistical forecasts." *Management Science*, **32**(12): 1521–1532.
Lawrence, M.P., Goodwin, P., O'Connor, M., & Onkal, D. (2006) "Judgmental forecasting: A review of progress over the last 25 years." *International Journal of Forecasting*, **22**: 493–518.
Lawrence, M.P. & Makridakis, S. (1989) "Factors affecting judgmental forecasts and confidence intervals." *Organ. Behav. Hum. Decis. Process*, **42**(2): 172–187.
Lee, H.L., Padmanabhan, V., & Whang, S. (1997) "The bullwhip effect in supply chains." *Sloan Management Review*, **38**(3): 93–102.
Lee, H.L., So, K.C., & Tang, C.S. (2000) "The value of information sharing in a two-level supply chain." *Management Science*, **46**(5): 626–643.
Lee, T.S. & Adam Jr., E.E. (1986) "Forecasting error evaluation in material requirements planning (MRP) production systems." *Management Science*, **32**(9): 1186–1205.
Lee, T.S., Adam Jr., E.E., & Ebert, R.J. (1987) "An evaluation of forecast error in master production scheduling for material requirements planning systems." *Decision Sciences*, **18**(2): 292–307.
Lee, W.Y., Goodwin, P., Fildes, R., Nikolopoulos, K., & Lawrence, M. (2007) "Providing support for the use of analogies in demand forecasting tasks." *International Journal of Forecasting*, **23**: 377–390.
Legerstee, R. & Franses P.H. (2014) "Do experts' SKU forecasts improve after feedback?" *Journal of Forecasting*, **33**: 69–79.
Leitner, J. & Leopold-Wildburger, U. (2011) "Experiments on forecasting behavior with several sources of information—A review of the literature." *European Journal of Operational Research*, **213**: 459–469.
Lim, J.S. & O'Connor, M.J. (1995) "Judgmental adjustment of initial forecasts: Its effectiveness and biases." *Journal of Behavioral Decision Making*, **8**: 149–168.
Lim, J.S. & O'Connor, M.J. (1996a) "Judgmental forecasting with time series and causal information." *International Journal of Forecasting*, **12**: 139–153.
Lim, J.S. & O'Connor, M.J. (1996b) "Judgmental forecasting with interactive forecasting support systems." *Decision Support Systems*, **16**: 339–357.
Lobo, G.J. (1991) "Alternative methods of combining security analysts' and statistical forecasts of annual corporate earnings." *International Journal of Forecasting*, **7**: 57–63.
Lobo, G.J. & Nair, R.D. (1990) "Combining judgmental and statistical forecasts: An application to earnings forecasts." *Decision Sciences*, **16**: 339–357.
Makridakis, S. & Hibon, M. (2000) "The M3 competition: Results, conclusions and implications." *International Journal of Forecasting*, **16**(4): 451–476.
Makridakis, S. & Winkler, R.L. (1983) "Averages of forecasts: Some Empirical Results." *Management Science*, **29**(9): 987–996.
Makridakis, S., Anderson, A., Carbone, R., Fildes, R., Hibon, M., Lewandowski, R., Newton, J., Parzen, E., & Winkler, R. (1982) "The accuracy of extrapolation (time series) methods: Results of a forecasting competition." *Journal of Forecasting*, **1**: 111–153.
Makridakis S.G., Wheelwright, S.C., & Hyndman, R.J. (2006) *Forecasting: Methods and applications*, 4th edition. New York: John Wiley & Sons.
Makridakis, S.G., Wheelwright, S.C., & McGee, V.E. (1983) *Forecasting, methods and applications*. John Wiley & Sons, New York.
Manyika, J., Chui, M., Brown, B., Bughin, J., Dobbs, R., Roxburgh, C., & Byers, A.H. (2011) *Big data: The next frontier for innovation, competition, and productivity*. London: McKinsey Global Institute.
Mathews, B.P. & Diamantopoulos, A. (1986) "Managerial intervention in forecasting: An empirical investigation of forecast manipulation." *International Journal of Research in Marketing*, **3**, 3–10.

Mathews, B. P. & Diamantopoulos, A. (1989) "Judgmental revision of sales forecasts: A longitudinal extension." *Journal of Forecasting*, **8**, 129–140.

Mathews, B. P. & Diamantopoulos, A. (1990) "Judgmental revision of sales forecasts: Effectiveness of forecast selection." *Journal of Forecasting*, **9**, 407–415.

Mayer-Schönberger, V. & Cukier, K. (2013) *Big data, a revolution that will transform how we live, work, and think*. Boston, MA: Houghton Mifflin Harcourt.

Meehl, P.E. (1957) "When shall we use our heads instead of the formula?" *Journal of Counseling Psychology*, **4**(4): 268–273.

Mentzer, J.T. & Cox, J. (1984) "Familiarity, application and performance of sales forecasting techniques." *Journal of Forecasting*, **3**: 27–36.

Mentzer, J.T. & Kahn, K.B. (1995) "Forecasting technique familiarity, satisfaction, usage and application." *Journal of Forecasting*, **14**: 465–476.

Metters, R. (1997) "Quantifying the bullwhip effect in supply chains." *Journal of Operations Management*, **15**(2): 89–100.

Moon, M.A., Mentzer, J.T., & Smith, C.D. (2003) "Conducting a sales forecasting audit." *International Journal of Forecasting*, **19**: 5–25.

Moritz, B., Siemen, E., & Kremer, M. (2014) "Judgmental forecasting: Cognitive reflection and decision speed." *Production and Operations Management*, **23**: 1146–1160.

Nikolopoulos, K. & Fildes, R. (2013) "Adjusting supply chain forecasts for short-term temperature estimates: A case study in a Brewing company." *IMA Journal of Management Mathematics*, **24**: 79–88.

Oh, S. & Özer, Ö. (2013) "Mechanism design for capacity planning under dynamic evolution of asymmetric demand forecasts." *Management Science*, **59**(4): 987–1007.

Oliva, R. & Watson, N. (2011) "Cross-functional alignment in supply chain planning: A case study of sales and operations planning." *Journal of Operations Management*, **29**(5): 434–448.

Özer, Ö. (2003) "Replenishment strategies for distribution systems under advance demand information." *Management Science*, **49**(3): 255–272.

Prestwich, S.D., Tarim, S.A., Rossi, R., & Hnich, B. (2014) "Forecasting intermittent demand by hyperbolic-exponential smoothing." *International Journal of Forecasting*, **30**: 928–933.

Ritzman, L. P. & King, B.E. (1993) "The relative significance of forecast errors in multistage manufacturing." *Journal of Operations Management*, **11**(1): 51–65.

Sanders, N.R. (2014) *Big Data Driven Supply Chain Management*, Pearson FT Press.

Sanders, N.R. & Graman, G.A. (2009) "Quantifying costs of forecast errors: A case study of the warehouse environment." *OMEGA, The International Journal of Management Science*, **37**(1): 116–125.

Sanders, N.R. & Graman, G.A. (2015) "Bias magnification in supply chains: The mitigating role of forecast sharing." *Decision Sciences Journal*, **forthcoming**.

Sanders, N.R. & Manrodt, K.B. (1994) "Forecasting practices in U.S. corporations: Survey results." *Interfaces*, **24**: 91–100.

Sanders, N.R. & Ritzman, L. P. (1995) "Bringing judgment into combination forecasts." *Journal of Operations Management*, **13**(4): 311–321.

Sanders, N. R. & Ritzman, L. P. (2001) "Judgmental adjustment of statistical forecasts," in J.S. Armstrong (ed.), *Principles of forecasting*. Norwell, MA: Kluwer Academic Publishing.

Taleb, N.N. (2007) *The Black Swan*. New York: Random House.

Toktay, L.B. & Wein, L.M. (2001) "Analysis of a forecasting-production-inventory system with stationary demand." *Management Science*, **47**(9): 1268–1281.

Trapero, J.R., Kourentzes, N., & Fildes, R. (2012) "Impact of information exchange on supplier forecasting performance." *Omega*, **40**(6): 738–747.

Turner, D.S. (1990) "The role of judgment in macroeconomic forecasting." *Journal of Forecasting*, **9**: 315–345.

Webby, R. & O'Connor, M. (1996) "Judgmental and statistical time series forecasting: A review of the literature." *International Journal of Forecasting*, **12**(1): 91–118.

Webby, R., O'Connor, M., & Lawrence, M. (2001) "Judgmental time-series forecasting using domain knowledge," in J.S. Armstrong (ed.), *Principles of forecasting*. Norwell, MA: Kluwer Academic Publishing.

Winkler, R.L. & Makridakis, S. (1983) "The combination of forecasts." *Journal of the Royal Statistical Society (A)*, **146**(Part 2): 150–157.

4
AGGREGATE PRODUCTION PLANNING

Lee Krajewski

1 Introduction

The aggregate production plan refers to a plan of future aggregate resource levels that makes sure that supply is in balance with demand and costs are minimized. It is a plan that covers the intermediate term (as opposed to short term or long term) and is intended to minimize the effects of frequent changes to levels of resources such as materials and workers due to shortsighted planning. As we shall see in this chapter, the aggregate production planning problem has been, and still is, a practical problem that generates intense academic interest. We begin by emphasizing its importance for operations and then review its academic development, from its genesis in the 1950s until today. However, if aggregate plans are to have practical usefulness, they must produce feasible decisions for the key resources covered by the plan that can be used by the more detailed operational plans that follow. Consequently, we will review the "disaggregation" problem and follow that with a discussion of aggregate production planning in practice. We close the chapter with some thoughts on the future research directions of this important topic and its implications for practitioners.

1.1 The Importance of Aggregate Production Planning

In the term aggregate production plan, "production" refers to the production of goods or services. Consequently, the concept of an aggregate production plan applies equally to manufacturing as well as service firms. Its importance derives from the fact that it must reflect the operations strategy and the business plan, which is a projected statement of income, costs, and profits. The business plan embodies plans for market penetration, new product introduction, and capital investment. In this section we will describe what is aggregated, the information inputs to the plan, and the key decision variables or supply options that comprise the aggregate production plan.

1.2 Dimensions of Aggregation

The aggregate production plan shows how operations will support the operations strategy and the business plan over an extended time frame (usually twelve months) without getting bogged down in details. To that end, three planning dimensions are aggregated: products or services, workforce, and time.

1.2.1 Products

To avoid too much detail at this level of planning, products are aggregated into *product families*, which are groups of products that have similar demand, process, workforce, and material requirements. For example, an automobile manufacturer may produce trucks, SUVs, sedans, and electric cars. Each of these product types come in a variety of options and colors, creating thousands of potentially different products. Nonetheless, if we look at trucks, SUVs, sedans, and electric cars as separate product families, the products within each product family would have similar process, workforce, and material requirements. Planning for four product families is much easier than planning for thousands of different products.

1.2.2 Workforce

Employees can be grouped into categories and planned for accordingly. For example, at an auto manufacturer there are assembly workers and machinists, each group with its own set of skills, usage constraints, and wages. Planning for the amount of labor hours required is much simpler for two aggregate groups as opposed to thousands of individual employees. Similarly, for a service firm such as a cable communications company, employees may be categorized into service technicians, utility construction employees, and customer service representatives. Here, the aggregate production plan is called the aggregate employment plan because tangible products and inventories are not a part of the plan.

1.2.3 Time

The planning horizon of the aggregate production plan typically covers twelve months. Additionally, the plan is reviewed on a periodic basis. However, frequent changes to aggregate workforce levels and production rates could be disruptive. Consequently, time is aggregated into months or quarters so that decisions on production and labor are made monthly or quarterly, as opposed to daily or weekly. This is in order for the decisions to be compatible with the budgetary process and other financial plans and to avoid adding unnecessary volatility to the operating environment.

1.3 Information Inputs

The aggregate production plan has implications for an entire business and as such requires informational inputs from many functional areas. It is a dynamic plan that requires constant revision as supply, demand, product mix, and new product platforms manifest themselves over time. Figure 4.1 shows six of those areas, linked together through Information Technology. *Operations* must supply current machine capacities and plans for future increases or decreases, workforce capability and productivities, and the current staffing and inventory levels. *Accounting and Finance* provide cost data and the general financial condition of the firm, which may impinge on the strategy to be employed in the aggregate production plan. The *Materials and Suppliers* function has the data on supplier capabilities, limits on storage capacities, and raw material availability. The labor market conditions, which affect the ease of acquiring new employees, the training capacity,

Aggregate Production Planning

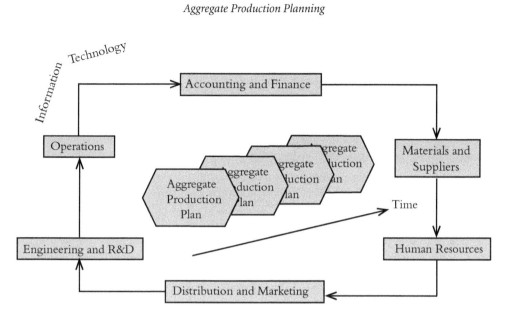

Figure 4.1 Functional Areas Providing Inputs to the Dynamic Aggregate Production Plan

which determines the time it takes for new employees to attain full productivity, and any ethical constraints on the use of overtime or excessive layoffs are inputs provided by *Human Resources*. *Distribution and Marketing* provide information on minimal inventories needed to maintain adequate safety stocks, demand forecasts, and the trends in the market for the firm's products or services. Finally, *Engineering and R&D* supply information on the introduction of new products, product design changes, and limits on machine capacities. It is clear that the aggregate production plan is complex and requires continual inputs from a variety of functional areas to be effective.

1.4 *Decision Variables and Supply Options*

For each period in the planning horizon, the aggregate production plan must specify the production quantity of each product or service family, the regular time workforce for each employee category, the amount of overtime, the amount of undertime (a situation that occurs when employees do not have enough work for the regular-time workweek but are retained nonetheless), the number of new hires, layoffs or part-time workers, the amount of subcontracted or outsourced work, vacation schedules, the inventory levels of each product family, and any planned backorders or stockouts. Given sales forecasts and goals, management manipulates these variables in order to meet the anticipated demand. The problem becomes more challenging if the firm faces a seasonal demand pattern because there are many options available to supply products or services, depending on the costs involved. In a manufacturing firm, seasonal inventory can be accumulated in low-demand periods for use in high-demand periods. Other options are available for both manufacturing and service firms. For example, the workforce capacity can be adjusted by hires and layoffs, or overtime can be used while keeping the regular-time workforce capacity unchanged. Undertime could be used to retain skilled employees during low demand periods. Part-time employees could be used in lieu of overtime. Another option is to use subcontractors to overcome short-term shortages in capacity, or to employ a strategy of outsourcing in long-term situations. Vacation schedules or planned shutdowns of plants can be scheduled so that they coincide with low-demand periods. It is no wonder that such a complex problem has been the topic of considerable academic research.

2 Historical Perspective of Aggregate Production Planning Research

In this section, we will provide an historical perspective to the research literature addressing the aggregate production planning problem. It is largely quantitative in nature, reporting the development and analysis of mathematical models utilizing a wide range of quantitative techniques. It will be impossible to cover all of the research devoted to the aggregate production planning problem here. Extensive literature reviews of the aggregate production planning problem can be found in the literature (e.g., Nam and Logendran 1992). Instead, we cover the genesis of this topic in the academic literature and discuss examples of the various methodological tendrils and formulations that followed.

2.1 Linear Decision Rules

The early 1950s provided the genesis for the aggregate production planning problem in the academic research arena. Often referred to as "production smoothing," the problem provided the attributes of substance and practicality that underlie sound research. One of the earliest and most comprehensive studies of the aggregate production planning problem was performed by Holt, Modigliani, and Simon (1955). The problem they consider derives a set of decision rules for production output and workforce levels such that expected costs are minimized over the planning horizon. Their study focused on a paint factory and used extensive data from 1949 to 1953 in order to develop the rules. This single work, and the book that followed with J. F. Muth as the third author (1960), became known as the HMMS model (the acronym for the work of Holt, Modigliani, Muth, and Simon) and set the stage for research for many years to come. Indeed, the principle result of this research, the Linear Decision Rules (LDR), reveals a concept of coordinated optimization of aggregate production, workforce, and inventory decisions that is natural and elegant, and has been used as a standard of comparison for many theoretical studies for decades afterwards (Schwarz and Johnson 1978; Sprague et al. 1990).

The problem is to minimize a total cost function which is the sum of a) regular time wages, b) overtime wages, c) hiring and firing costs, and d) inventory and back order costs. We will use the following notation:

W_t = number of workers required for period t
P_t = number of units to be produced in period t
I_t = inventory minus backlogs at the end of period t
R_t = demand requirements for period t
c_k = cost coefficients to be determined for a given plant, $k = 1, \ldots, 10$.

2.1.1 Regular Time Wages

The regular time wages are assumed to be a linear function of the workforce each period,

$$c_1 W_t \qquad [1]$$

where c_1 is the regular time wage rate per period.

Aggregate Production Planning

2.1.2 Overtime Wages

The overtime wages only occur when production exceeds the number of units the workforce can produce on regular time, c_3W_t, and thereby is only piece-wise linear with respect to the production rate in a given period. These costs can be approximated by a quadratic cost function:

$$c_2(P_t - c_3W_t)^2 + c_4P_t - c_5W_t \qquad [2]$$

2.1.3 Hiring and Firing Costs

The hiring and firing costs depend on changes in the workforce from period to period and can be approximated by a quadratic function:

$$c_6(W_t - W_{t-1})^2 \qquad [3]$$

2.1.4 Inventory and Backorder Costs

As inventory rises, holding costs increase. As inventory decreases, stockout and backorder costs increase. Once the "optimal" inventory level for a period has been determined, the costs can be approximated by the following quadratic function of the difference between the actual inventory and the optimal inventory in period t,

$$c_7(I_t - (c_8 + c_9R_t))^2 \qquad [4]$$

The optimal inventory, which is determined by a lot size formula, is a function of the demand in period t and can be approximated by $c_8 + c_9R_t$.

2.1.5 Objective Function and the Rules

The objective is to minimize

$$C_\tau = \sum_{t=1}^{\tau} c_1W_t + c_2(P_t - c_3W_t)^2 + c_4P_t - c_5W_t + c_6(W_t - W_{t-1})^2 + c_7(I_t - (c_8 + c_9R_t))^2) + c_{10} \qquad [5]$$

subject to

$$I_t = I_{t-1} + P_t - R_t \qquad t = 1, \ldots, \tau \qquad [6]$$

where c_{10} is the fixed cost and is the planning horizon. The solution procedure entails taking the partial derivatives of C_τ with respect to the decision variables for each period, P_t and W_t, and equating them to zero, producing 2τ equations in 2τ variables. Because the individual components of C_τ are either linear or quadratic, the resulting form of the solution will be a set of linear equations, called the Linear Decision Rules (LDR), dependent only on the initial conditions, the cost coefficients, and the periodic demands:

$$P_t = k_{1t}W_0 + k_{2t}I_0 + \sum_{j=1}^{\tau} \lambda_{jt}R_j + k_{3t} \qquad [7]$$

$$W_t = k_{4t}W_0 + k_{5t}I_0 + \sum_{j=1}^{\tau} \alpha_{jt}R_j + k_{6t} \qquad [8]$$

where the constants k_{it}, λ_{jt} and α_{jt} depend only on the original cost coefficients.

The HMMS model has been one of the most scrutinized and emulated models in the operations management literature. Nonetheless, the derivation of the rules is difficult and force-fitting quadratic equations to piece-wise linear costs often results in decisions that are only marginally better than informed managerial decisions (Schwarz and Johnson 1978; Lee and Khumawala 1974). In the remainder of this section, we will follow the methodological evolution of the aggregate planning problem for both manufacturing and service firms.

2.2 Linear Programming

The introduction of linear programming as a methodology for the aggregate production planning problem opened the floodgates for many applications. In one early application, Bowman (1956) noted that the aggregate production planning problem could be put into the framework of a transportation problem. The formulation involves keeping track of when an individual unit produced will satisfy a known demand. While the transportation method provides an integer solution, a general linear programming formulation would allow for a host of constraints on the decision variables that Bowman's model does not. Manne (1957) simplified the quadratic costs in the HMMS model by assuming that marginal production costs are constant and the workforce level is pre-determined for the duration of the planning horizon. He then approximated the total cost function with a piece-wise linear function, which then allowed for consideration of different work shifts, such as regular time and overtime. The decision variables are the production quantities on regular time and overtime and the inventory level for each period of the planning horizon.

Motivated by introducing the workforce as a decision variable and reducing the complexity of the HMMS model, Hanssmann and Hess (1960) developed a model that incorporated linear cost functions. The advantage to this model was that it allowed them to independently choose the unit costs of hiring and firing or inventory and backorders rather than trying to empirically fit a quadratic cost function to the change in workforce levels or inventory levels. Costs were modelled as step functions, relegating the objective to a piece-wise linear function that, after the definition of a new set of variables to deal with the step functions and the addition of three technical constraints for each period, could be minimized using linear programming. The model's major focus was on showing how to transform the HMMS model to a linear program that was much easier to solve using the computer technology of the time. As time passed and computer technology advanced, aggregate production planning models using linear programming, capable of incorporating many variables each period such as subcontracting, overtime, hires, fires, inventory, production, and workforce as well as a host of constraints and conditions on those variables, including integer variables, proliferated the literature (e.g., Chung and Krajewski 1987; Chopra and Meindl 2004; Kanyalkar and Adil 2007; 2010; Leung and Chan 2009).

Linear programming can also be used for the aggregate production planning problem in service organizations. It is referred to as the aggregate employment planning problem because those organizations are focused on workforce decisions and do not have inventories of produced goods. Nonetheless, the concept is the same. For example, Krajewski and Thompson (1975) developed an aggregate employment planning model for a telephone company that sought to minimize the costs of regular time wages, overtime wages, hiring and layoff costs, and subcontracting costs in light of a seasonal demand for its services. There were four employee groups, representing different skill sets, each with full and part time employees. Newly-hired employees first became part-time employees who progressed over time to full-time status. The four sets of constraints for each period consisted of (1) definitions of the number of employees in each group after hires, layoffs, attrition rates, and the rate of progression to full-time status was accounted for, (2) relationships ensuring that enough employee capacity, including overtime and planned delays, was available to meet demand for twenty-five different services each period, (3) limits on the amount of overtime that could be used each period, and (4) limits on the amount of delay in each service that would be tolerated each period. For a planning horizon of 12 months, there were more than 6,000 variables and 1,400 constraints, which would pose no particular problem with today's computing power. However, such a model would have posed a significant practical problem back in the day of Hanssmann and Hess. Present day computers eliminate this problem and open the vista for continued research into new methodologies and more elaborate models.

2.3 Heuristics

While the HMMS model and the resulting LDR provide an optimal solution to the aggregate planning problem, they do so by making stringent assumptions about the cost structure and the scope of the problem. Costs are assumed to be quadratic and the environment is assumed to have only a few constraints. Alternatively, linear programming models can recognize many complex constraints but must assume linear costs and relationships between the variables. While the attraction to the elegance and simplicity of the LDR was a driving force in the literature, the limitations of the LDR regarding the quadratic costs and the difficulty in deriving the rules set the stage for the development of heuristic approaches to the aggregate production planning problem. Bowman (1963) developed equivalent versions of the LDR in equations [7] and [8] that were deemed suitable for regression and used management's past decisions as data to estimate the coefficients for the rules. This approach avoids making assumptions about the form of the cost functions and takes advantage of the knowledge of experienced managers who are aware of the important performance criteria of a system. The rules, one for production and the other for the workforce, were dubbed the Management Coefficients Model (MCM). When compared to actual management performance in four companies, MCM was better in three of the cases, including the original paint company. MCM even beat the LDR in two of the cases, excluding the paint company. Bowman theorized that it is the *variance* in decision making, not the *bias*, which hurts because of the dish-shaped criteria surfaces. Therefore, decision rules with mean coefficients estimated from management's past behavior should be better than actual performance.

Jones (1967) developed an approach called Parametric Production Planning (PPP) which attempts to free the manager from classifying the cost function as either quadratic or linear. Following the lead of the LDR, Jones proposed two linear feedback decision rules: one for the workforce and one for the production each period. The workforce rule for the first period includes consideration of the current workforce level, the desired workforce to meet future demands, and the difference between the desired inventory level and the current inventory level. Given the workforce decision for the first period, the production rule considers the output that the workforce can produce, the desired production to cover future demands, and the difference between the desired inventory level and the current inventory.

Each rule contains two smoothing parameters, between zero and one, that are used to (1) average the current workforce or production capacity with the desired increase or decrease, and (2) place a weight on each demand forecast over the planning horizon for determining the average desired workforce or production levels. As the rules are applied, changes in the workforce level from period to period reflect hires or layoffs, while production in excess of the workforce capacity reflects overtime.

Jones used a grid search to find the best values of the parameters. For each trial, the workforce and production decisions were evaluated by the actual cost structure of the firm, something which was not limited to linear or quadratic functions. Compared to the LDR developed for the paint company, which is optimal for the assumed cost functions, PPP resulted in savings that were only 0.09% less than the same quadratic cost function. When compared to a linear programming solution of a problem with a linear cost function and linear constraints, the solution using PPP was 8% higher.

Smitten by the LDR for similar reasons, Taubert (1968) proposed the Search Decision Rule (SDR) to provide an option to determine production and workforce decisions in complex settings that does not rely on linear or quadratic cost assumptions. What the SDR loses in terms of optimality, it gains in terms of realism and simplicity. As with the LDR, a workforce and production decision must be made each period, from which the costs of wages, overtime, hires, layoffs, inventory, and the like can be determined. Over a planning horizon of τ periods there are 2τ variables. Taubert proposed that a computer search routine be used to explore the 2τ dimensional response surface of the model's cost function. He tested the approach with an objective function of 20 variables over a 10-period planning horizon and compared the results to the optimal LDR for the paint factory. Twenty periods were simulated and the total costs were only 0.1% more than the LDR even though the LDR had a 12-month planning horizon.

2.4 Evaluation of Early Aggregate Planning Models

Before we continue with the methodological evolution of the aggregate planning problem in the literature, it is important to note that many extensions to the LDR were reported in the literature. For example, multiple products (Bergstrom and Smith 1970; Chang and Jones 1970; Welam 1975), marketing variables (Damon and Schramm 1972; Leitch 1974; Tuite 1968), financial variables (Damon and Schramm 1972), and learning (Ebert 1976) were added to the LDR framework. The LDR was held up to be the standard bearer, the one used as a benchmark for performance. However, LDR had its limitations, and alternatives, such a MCM, PPP, and SDR that were not limited to quadratic cost assumptions, might actually be better in some scenarios. Lee and Khumawala (1974) found that to be the case. Using a firm in the capital goods industry, they simulated the application of these four approaches and concluded that the SDR outperformed the other models. However, the LDR and MCM approaches can perform well in certain circumstances. The key is to provide a realistic test situation within which the models can be evaluated for any given firm.

The elegance of the LDR aside, and the numerous extensions and articles written about it in the twenty years after its development, Schwartz and Johnson (1978) asked the profound question as to why there is no record of it ever being implemented in practice. They hypothesized that the LDR has not been implemented because most of the cost savings of the LDR can be achieved by improved inventory management alone. Using the originally reported cost comparisons of the LDR versus the paint company management's decisions, they show that virtually all of the savings of the LDR could have been achieved by a single one-time adjustment to the aggregate inventory buffer inventory. None of this detracts from the massive impact the LDR had on the development of the aggregate production planning literature. It does point out, however, that in addition to the potential superiority of improved inventory management, the LDR had other shortcomings in the implementation arena, including the inability to handle integer variables (Taubert 1968), the difficulty of constructing adequate aggregate cost functions that represent the firm's actual individual product and worker costs (Krajewski et al. 1973), and the problem of disaggregation (Zoller 1971), which will be explained in Section 3.

2.5 Goal Programming and Other Methodological Thrusts

Given the practical shortcomings related to the early efforts at modeling the aggregate production planning problem, academic researchers focused on more realistic formulations and more effective solution methodologies. One of their major criticisms was the singular focus on cost minimization in light of situations where management had other goals to consider, especially when those goals could not be reflected in dollars and cents. Goal programming (GP) was seen as a way to incorporate multiple goals in a linear programming format (e.g., Charnes and Cooper 1961; Rifai 1994; Romero 1991; 2004; Tamiz et al. 1998). The GP as a concept serves to introduce extra auxiliary variables called deviations that represent the distance between aspiration levels of goals, or targets, and the realized results. A GP model includes a set of technical constraints, as in a typical linear program, and a set of goal constraints with the auxiliary variables, which determine the best possible solution with respect to the goals. Each auxiliary variable can have its own coefficient in the objective function that signifies its priority as a goal. An early application of GP for the aggregate production planning problem focused on the LDR formulation, using the GP concept to approximate the quadratic cost curves (Goodman 1974). However, it was quickly realized that GP had the potential to add much more realism to the aggregate planning problem by incorporating conflicting goals in addition to minimizing cost or maximizing profit. For example, goals such as achieving production, employment, and inventory targets (Jaaskelainen 1969), maximizing customer service and plant/machine utilization (Krajewski 1984; Leung and Chan 2009), and quality and on-time deliveries (Jamalnia and Soukhakian 2009) are just a sample of the multiple goals reported in GP models for the aggregate production planning problem.

The aggregate production planning problem has been fertile ground for the application of diverse quantitative methodologies. For example, Jamalnia and Soukhakian (2009) modelled the objective "Total customer satisfaction should be *relatively high*" as a fuzzy goal in a hybrid GP approach. (See Narasimhan 1980, for details on the use of GP in a fuzzy environment.) Li et al. (2013) developed a belief-rule-based inference method for the aggregate production planning problem under uncertainty. Krajewski (1984) developed a heuristic procedure to solve a mixed-integer GP of an aggregate planning problem using data from an industrial-goods manufacturer. Finally, just when you think everything has been tried, Kumar and Haq (2005) combined a genetic global search algorithm with an ant colony algorithm, which is a heuristic optimization method typically used for job shop scheduling and shortest path problems using ideas borrowed from biological ants searching for food. Randomly wandering ants find a food source (solution to a problem) and follow a trail back to the nest, leaving markers for other ants to follow. The markers on the trail begin to evaporate over time, the longer the trail the more evaporation and the less likely other ants will follow. The shorter trails (least costly solutions) tend to be followed by more ants and the marker density becomes greater. Eventually all the ants follow a single path, which then becomes the solution to the problem. A hybrid model, consisting of a genetic algorithm combined with an ant colony algorithm for the aggregate planning problem, was better than either the genetic algorithm or the ant colony algorithm used separately.

3 Disaggregation of Aggregate Production Plans

The aggregate production planning problem, by virtue of the aggregation of many products and employee types into a smaller, more manageable number of decision variables, allows for the planning of resources over an intermediate time horizon. We have seen the intensity of the effort at modeling that problem with more realistic formulations and more powerful solution methodologies since the early days of the LDR. However, none of that will be useful in practice if the aggregate quantities cannot be translated into the plans and schedules for the individual products and employees represented in the plan. *Disaggregation* is the process of breaking apart aggregate decisions for production quantities and workforce sizes into feasible lower-level schedules. Marty Starr, while making the plenary address to the delegates at the Conference on Disaggregation at The Ohio State University, perhaps put it all into perspective in the following quote (see Ritzman et al. 1979):

> While doing research for this paper, I used the standard literature search which consists of looking up 'Aggregate' in the dictionary. My eye wandered to the entry above and I read 'to make worse, to exasperate; annoy.' And thus was born the slogan 'Aggregation is preceded by Aggravation." I thought, if that is so, then 'Disaggregation' should be preceded by pleasure. When I remarked on this twist of logic to a learned colleague, I was told that Anna Freud had observed that children take pleasure in taking things (e.g. butterflies) apart. She went on to point out that children are criticized for this taking apart and consequently grow up resisting the powerful learning experience of thoughtful disassembly.

We will now explore the thoughtful disassembly of aggregate production plans.

3.1 Levels in Operations Planning and Scheduling

Managers develop plans for their operations covering varying time spans, from the long term to the short term. These plans form a hierarchy: the long-term plans form an umbrella under which short-term plans exist (Krajewski et al. 2016). Figure 4.2 shows the levels of disaggregation and the plans that should be consistent relative to each other. As we will see in Sections 3.2 and 3.3, valid aggregate plans should incorporate data and constraints reflecting these lower-level plans to ensure the feasibility of the production quantities and the workforce sizes.

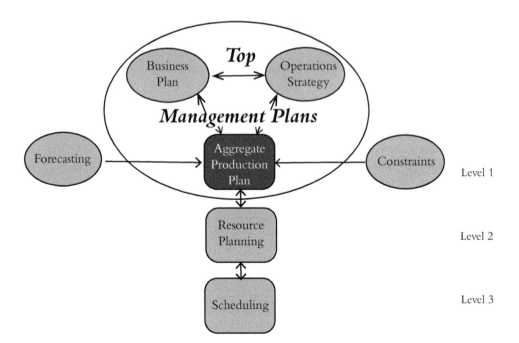

Figure 4.2 Disaggregation of Aggregate Production Plans

3.1.1 Level 1

The *aggregate production plan*, often referred to as the sales and operations plan in practice (Wallace and Stahl 2008) is at level 1 of the hierarchy and requires the inputs from a number of functional areas. First, there is the *business plan*, which is a projected statement of income, costs, and profits for the next one or two years. It is typically accompanied by budgets and cash flow projections that reflect the unified plans and expectations of a firm's operations, finance, sales, and marketing managers. These expectations include plans for market penetration, new product introduction, and capital investment. The aggregate plan must respond to these plans and expectations.

Second, the *operations strategy* is a statement of the way operations will implement the corporate strategy regarding the production of goods or services relative to the competitive dimensions the firm wants to emphasize. These competitive dimensions are reflected in priorities regarding cost, quality, time, and process flexibility, which affect the aggregate production plan regarding the use of seasonal inventory, backorders, overtime, hires and layoffs, vacation time, and subcontracting, for example.

Third, *forecasting* provides the demand projections that the aggregate production plan must address (see Chapter 3, Forecasting: State-of-the-Art in Research and Practice).

Finally, the aggregate production plan must adhere to various *constraints* on the resources at its disposal. For example, there may be restrictions on the use of overtime, part-time employees, layoffs, and vacations, and other human resource considerations. Further, there may be limitations on the production facilities, such as bottlenecks, plant capacity, and the like.

3.1.2 Level 2

At the next level, *resource planning* disaggregates the aggregate quantities of product or service families, workforce, and time to arrive at material and resource requirements over a time horizon of less than a year, broken down into time periods of days or weeks. For a manufacturing firm, the resource plan gets specific as to individual products, purchased materials, and resources. A major input is the master production schedule (MPS), which specifies the timing and size of production quantities for each product included in each product family. The material requirements plan (MRP) then determines the timing and size of orders for the components and purchased materials and workstation labor hours. Similarly, the resource plan for a service firm disaggregates projected service demands into daily or weekly requirements for the employees and service facilities using a bill of resources (Roth and Van Dierdonck 1995). Whether it is manufacturing or service, the aggregate production plan plays a direct role in the detailed planning that follows.

3.1.3 Level 3

Finally, *scheduling* translates the resource plan into specific operational tasks on a detailed basis (see Chapter 5 "Scheduling in Manufacturing and Services"). Given the resources provided by the aggregate plan, and the detailed requirements provided by the resource plan, facility, workforce, and job schedules can be developed. For example, an aggregate workforce plan may allocate fifteen police officers for the night shift in a particular district for a given month. The resource plan may determine the daily police protection requirements for a typical week, and the workforce schedule might assign eight of them to work Monday through Friday and the other seven to work Wednesday through Sunday to meet the varying needs for police protection in that district. Similarly, given the material requirements plan for a group of jobs in a manufacturing plant, the specific sequence of the jobs on a bottleneck machine can be scheduled.

Figure 4.2 implies that information flows in two directions: from the top down and the bottom up. If an aggregate plan cannot be developed to satisfy the objectives of the business plan with the existing resources, the business plan may have to be revised. Likewise, if a feasible material requirements plan or workforce schedule cannot be developed, the aggregate production plan may have to be revised. In the next two sections we will explore some of the research addressing the disaggregation of aggregate plans, which will demonstrate the importance of recognizing lower-level decisions in preparing a feasible aggregate production plan.

3.2 Manufacturing

This section first describes the initial attempts at developing aggregate production plans that recognize lower-level decisions and then shows some of the research that is based upon that earlier work and the direction is it taking.

3.2.1 Hierarchical Production Planning (HPP)

Much in the way the LDR was a catalyst for the early work in aggregate production planning, so was hierarchical production planning (HPP) a catalyst for the work on disaggregation (Hax and Meal 1975; Bitran and Hax 1977; 1981; Bitran et al. 1981; 1982). HPP follows the way in which decisions are made within the organizational hierarchy. Aggregate (strategic and tactical) decisions are made first and impose constraints within which more detailed (operational) decisions are made. In turn, the detailed decisions provide feedback to evaluate the quality of the aggregate decisions. HPP is as much a philosophy for solving the disaggregation problem as it is an actual technique. That is, the approach to solving the problem should be from the top down; the techniques used for solving sub problems could vary. There are three levels of aggregation:

- **Product types**: groups of products that have similar unit costs, direct costs, holding cost, productivities, and seasonality.
- **Families**: groups of products that belong to the same product type and share similar setups.
- **Items**: the final products delivered to the customer and the highest level of specificity; they differ in characteristics such as color, packaging, and size.

HPP develops an aggregate plan for product types, disaggregates it for product family production lots, and then disaggregates the family production to item quantities. There is management interaction at each stage of the process. Hax and Meal (1975) proposed a heuristic to perform the three levels of computations. Later, Bitran and Hax (1977) suggested the use of convex knapsack problems to disaggregate the product type quantities into family run quantities and then family run quantities into item run quantities.

3.2.2 Setups, Resource Profiles, and Distribution Plans

HPP did not consider setup costs in the aggregate plan. Chung and Krajewski (1987) formulated a mixed-integer programming model that incorporated setup costs at the aggregate planning level that interfaced with a goal programming model for the master production schedule (MPS) via a rolling horizon feedback mechanism. The MPS used resource planning profiles to ensure feasibility regarding work center capacities. Qiu et al. (2001) added setup costs at the aggregate level of the HPP model and incorporated an expert system to generate production plans and schedules for a fiber producer.

Inevitably, the evolution of problem solving in this area focused on expanding the problem scope to take advantage of the increased computing power available. Kanyalkar and Adil (2007; 2010) formulated a monolithic mixed-integer linear goal program (MILGP) that produced a time and capacity aggregated production plan, a detailed procurement plan, and a detailed distribution plan simultaneously to ensure the feasibility of all planning levels. Two heuristics were developed to solve the MILGP. Fahimnia et al. (2012) developed a mixed integer non-linear formulation (MINLF) that integrates the aggregate production plan and detailed distribution plan. They use a genetic algorithm, which is a search heuristic that mimics the process of natural selection, to solve a real-case scenario. This article contains many more references for the production-distribution disaggregation topic. See Mitchell (1996) for a detailed description of the genetic algorithm methodology.

3.3 Services

Aggregate planning for services differs from that of manufacturing because there are no tangible products to store as seasonal inventory. Typically, aggregate employment plans (also referred to as the staff-sizing problem) specify monthly employee levels (regular, part-time, temporary), overtime commitments, subcontracting needs, vacation plans, undertime levels, and hiring and layoff quantities (Ritzman et al. 1976). The aggregate staff sizes must be disaggregated into staff schedules, which specify for each employee a set of assigned work periods over a given time horizon. Other than creating monolithic models of the staff-sizing and staff-scheduling problems and using decomposition to arrive at feasible decisions (e.g., Ruefli 1971; Sweeny et al. 1978), several recursive approaches have been proposed. Top-down recursive approaches were developed by Nolan and Sovereign (1972) and Carlson et al. (1979) in which mathematical programs determine staff sizes and then, those results are tested in simulation models for feasibility regarding the staff schedules. If the staff-sizing plan was found to be infeasible, additional constraints are added to the mathematical program and a new staff plan generated.

A bottom-up approach suggested by Abernathy et al. (1973) uses a Monte Carlo simulation model to determine detailed work center requirements such that service levels will be met at a specified level of risk. These data provide constraints for a workforce allocation model. The resulting staff sizes are checked to determine if macro cost objectives are satisfied and, if not, new requirements are determined and the process repeats. Henderson et al. (1982) propose a recursive bottom-up approach that uses a heuristic staff scheduling model developed by Showalter et al. (1977) to generate a plot of service levels over a range of feasible staff sizes for each period of the planning horizon. From this analysis a target and a minimum staff size reflecting desired and minimal service levels are specified for each period for an aggregate employment goal programming model, which then specifies optimal staff sizes over the time horizon. In addition to a service goal, the model can incorporate goals on cost, mix of part-time and temporary employees, and workforce stability.

4 Aggregate Production Planning in Practice

Aggregate production planning is often referred to as sales and operations planning (S&OP) in practice (Wallace and Stahl 2008). The new title is meant to place emphasis on the fact that the aggregate plan is a top management plan, and not just the responsibility of operations management. S&OP enables top management to proactively manage customer service levels, inventory investment, and lead times for fulfilling customer orders, thereby giving them control over these strategic aspects of operating the business. S&OP is a six-step decision-making process that is dynamic and continuing, as aspects of the plan are updated periodically when new information becomes available and new opportunities emerge.

4.1 Step 1: Roll the Plan Forward

S&OP involves making monthly or quarterly decisions for a planning horizon that often extends a year or more into the future. Each period the plan is updated. This is often referred to as a "rolling horizon" in the aggregate production planning literature (e.g., Baker 1977; Chung and Krajewski 1987). Actual sales, production, inventory, and costs are recorded for the most recent past period and the database is prepared for the development of a new plan.

4.2 Step 2: Forecast and Demand Planning

Managers from sales and marketing provide forecasts of demand for each product family. The forecasts can be from statistical models of past demand patterns, tempered by the promotions and efforts at demand planning initiated by marketing. For service providers, the demand forecasts could be the result of a bottom up recursive approach (e.g., Abernathy et al. 1973; Henderson et al. 1982).

4.3 Step 3: Update the Sales and Operations Plan

Given the data from steps 1 and 2, the sales and operations plan is updated for each period of the planning horizon, recognizing any new constraints imposed by supplier shortages, plant capacities, storage limitations, and the like. Management may impose limitations on the amount of backorders, the use of subcontractors or outsourcing, and inventories. As there could be many plans that satisfy these constraints, the aggregate planning models discussed earlier can be helpful, especially those that can incorporate multiple goals such as cost, customer service, and workforce stability.

4.4 Step 4: Consensus Meetings

The process of updating the sales and operations plan typically results in several alternatives that differ in their achievement of the various goals. Plan stakeholders should hold a meeting with the goal of achieving consensus on how the firm will balance supply with demand. The plan would be presented at the executive S&OP meeting. The stakeholders include supply chain management, key suppliers and partners, supplier management, plant management, production control management, logistics management, and controller. Lacking consensus, several alternatives should be prepared. Further, an updated financial view of the total business can be prepared by accumulating the plans for each product family, converted to dollars.

4.5 Step 5: Executive S&OP Meeting

The recommendations for each product family are presented to the firm's president and vice presidents of each functional area. The plans are reviewed relative to the business plan, new product plans, and other corporate plans. The executives may ask for changes. For example, the demands planned for a product family may be too aggressive, or not aggressive enough. Consensus at this level means that everyone marches to the same drummer, whether they are in total agreement or not.

4.6 Step 6: Update and Revise Final Plans

The changes mandated at the executive S&OP meeting are incorporated in the final aggregate plan for each product family. The new plans are communicated to all the stakeholders, where the detailed schedules are prepared. However, the sales and operations plan is a dynamic plan that must be constantly reviewed and revised as necessary. Feedback loops made possible by information technology allow managers to use a rolling planning horizon to make revisions on a periodic basis.

5 Conclusions

Now that we have reviewed the problem of aggregate production planning and discussed its application in practice, we conclude with a discussion of future directions of research in this area and its implications for practitioners.

5.1 Future Research

This chapter has shown that the aggregate production plan is a key to the effective execution of a firm's operations strategy. While the analysis of the aggregate production plan had its origins in the 1950s, there are still six topics that could benefit from further research.

5.1.1 Employment Planning in Manufacturing

Aggregate plans, whether they are for manufacturing or service firms, include plans for employment levels, hires, layoffs, overtime, undertime, and vacations. With the advent of technology to operating processes, skilled labor is becoming in short supply. For example, the McKinsey Global Institute (McKinsey & Company 2012) projected a potential shortage of 40 million skilled manufacturing workers globally by 2020. Manufacturing firms will compete with service firms for this labor. Aggregate plans must incorporate the potential for hiring shortfalls and the need to entertain other sources of additional resources, such as placing more emphasis on offshore sources. For manufacturing firms, increased logistic lead times from offshoring may require additional inventories and more production during the off season. Further, firms may have to provide more extensive training to their new hires, increasing the lag time until they are fully productive.

5.1.2 Employment Planning in Services

Another employment planning topic worthy of future research is the growing expansion of services in manufacturing firms. Customers are increasingly looking to manufacturers for after-market services. Consequently, aggregate employment plans should recognize the additional resources manufacturing services may require as well as their timing. Finally, aggregate plans should incorporate any human resource policies the firm may have in place, such as limitations on layoffs and union-related limitations on the use of employees.

5.1.3 Aggregation

The consumer demand for products and services is constantly shifting and fragmenting. For example, new consumers in emerging economies often require very different products and services than their counterparts in more developed economies. This forces firms to provide more variety and stock keeping units (SKUs). The consumers in more established economies constantly demand more variety and faster product life cycles, all of which creates problems for producers who are trying to plan for adequate resources in the next six to eighteen months. One of the advantages of aggregate planning is to reduce the complexity of planning for a variety of products or services. In this emerging environment where fragmentation is necessary for competitiveness, new approaches for aggregating products, services, and employees is needed. This is especially true with the new strategic product platform concepts that are being utilized.

5.1.4 Uncertainty

When planning operations, the one thing for certain is that there will be uncertainty. It could come in the way of poor forecasts or evolving fragmentation of products or services, as mentioned in Section 5.1.3. Alternatively, the firm could be the victim of a massive natural disaster, such as a hurricane, which would affect its own operations or that of its suppliers. Each source of uncertainty has its own effect on the aggregate production plan. Future research should explore the ways to mitigate uncertainty in the aggregate production plan.

5.1.5 Sustainability and Reverse Logistics

Many firms now recognize the need to be responsible stewards of the earth's resources and have started planning for the entire birth to death cycle of products. A product begins at the new product development process, makes its way to the customer and then enters a reverse logistics process that either prepares the product for direct reuse (e.g., car rental), remanufactures it by tearing it down and rebuilding it with new parts as needed (e.g., diesel engine), or completely disassembles it and the useable parts cleaned, tested, and returned to the manufacturing process (Mollenkopf and Closs 2005; Ferguson 2010). Because of the reverse logistics process, each new product generates resource requirements beyond the point of its initial sale. Sustainability and the reverse logistics process pose interesting research opportunities regarding the aggregate production plan. Recognizing supplier capabilities throughout the birth to death life cycle and the logistical implications of material flows are important. Appropriate time lags and forecasts must be incorporated in the aggregate production plan to adequately plan for resources.

5.1.6 Supply Chain Visibility

Suppose the sales and operations plan for Firm X specifies the aggregate sales and production plan for the next 12 to 18 months. In addition to providing the operating targets for Firm X, it also provides a picture of the requirements for its direct suppliers, often called Tier One suppliers. Each of these suppliers must develop a sales and operations plan that provides requirements for their suppliers (Tier Two), and so on. The sales and operations plan for Firm X has a ripple-down effect on the entire supply chain. Viewing the problem myopically, Firm X could choose to use a chase strategy, seeking to follow the peaks and valleys of its seasonal demand pattern. Or, it could use a level strategy, using seasonal inventories to meet peaks in demands throughout the year.

Regardless of the strategy in play, the sales and operations plan for Firm X affects the cost of its supply, especially if it causes suppliers to react in ways that are not the most efficient. If Firm X has the most power in the supply chain, it can dictate its plan and require suppliers to react. If not, Firm X might have to revise its sales and operations plan to conform to what the supply chain can provide. Future research efforts could be directed at the sales and operations plan in a supply chain context in much the same way we did in Section 3.0 for synchronizing within-firm plans and schedules. That is, the aggregate production plan should recognize the aggregate production plans of key suppliers in the supply chain; each key supplier could be considered a sub problem to Firm X's aggregate plan. Recognizing multiple supplier tiers would add considerable complexity. Approaches such as bottom-up recursive planning might prove useful. The use of multiple criteria and the recognition of power in this context may also be fruitful. Further, the development of computer-based systems to handle the complexities of supply-chain visibility, along with the associated uncertainties and need to incorporate sustainability efforts, should be a primary research agenda.

5.2 *Implications for Practitioners*

Aggregate production planning has been, and will continue to be, a key activity in the planning cycles of manufacturing as well as service firms. Over time, the aggregate plan has morphed into the sales and operations plan or the aggregate employment plan depending on the firm. Its boundaries have expanded to include finance, marketing, sales, and human resources. Computing power has increased to the point where the granularity of the aggregate plan has reached lower level plans and schedules. All of this has helped to improve customer service and profitability. It is for these reasons that practitioners should look forward to the results of continued research on this topic.

References and Bibliography

Abernathy, W., N. Baloff, J. Hershey, and W. Wandel (1973) "A Three-Stage Manpower Planning and Scheduling Model: A Service Sector Example," *Operations Research*, **31**(3): 693–711.

Baker, K.R. (1977) "An Experimental Study of the Effectiveness of Rolling Schedules in Production Planning," *Decision Sciences*, **8**(1): 19–27.

Bergstrom, G.L. and B.E. Smith (1970) "Multi-Item Production Planning—An Extension of the HMMS Rules," *Management Science*, **16**(10): B614–B629.

Bitran, G.R. and A.C. Hax (1977) "On the Design of Hierarchical Production Planning Systems," *Decision Sciences*, **8**(1): 28–55.

Bitran, G.R. and A.C. Hax (1981) "Disaggregation and Resource Allocation Using Convex Knapsack Problems," *Management Science*, **27**(4): 431–441.

Bitran, G.R., E.A. Haas, and A.C. Hax (1981) "Hierarchical Production Planning: A Single Stage System," *Operations Research*, **29**(4): 717–743.

Bitran, G.R., E.A. Haas, and A.C. Hax (1982) "Hierarchical Production Planning: A Two-Stage System," *Operations Research*, **30**(2): 232–251.

Bowman, E.H. (1956) "Production Scheduling by the Transportation Method of Linear Programming," *Operations Research*, **4**(1): 100–103.

Bowman, E.H. (1963) "Consistency and Optimality in Managerial Decision Making," *Management Science*, **9**(2): 310–321.

Carlson, R., J. Hershey, and D. Kropp (1979) "Use of Both Optimization and Simulation Models to Analyze Outpatient Healthcare Settings," *Decision Sciences*, **10**(3): 412–433.

Chang, R.H. and C.M. Jones (1970) "Production and Workforce Scheduling Extensions," *AIIE Transactions*, **2**(4): 326–333.

Charnes, A. and W.W. Cooper (1961) *Management Models and Industrial Applications of Linear Programming*. New York: Wiley.

Chopra, S. and P. Meindl (2004) *Supply Chain Management Strategy, Planning, and Operation*. Upper Saddle River, NJ: Pearson Prentice Hall.

Chung, C.-H. and L.J. Krajewski (1987) "Interfacing Aggregate Plans and Master Production Schedules via a Rolling Horizon Feedback Procedure," *Omega International Journal of Management Science*, **15**(5): 401–409.

Damon, W.W. and R. Schramm (1972) "A Simultaneous Decision Model for Production, Marketing and Finance," *Management Science*, **19**(2): 161–172.

Ebert, R.J. (1976) "Aggregate Planning with Learning Curve Productivity," *Management Science*, **23**(2): 171–182.
Fahimnia, Behnam, Lee Luong, and Romeo Marian (2012) "Genetic Algorithm Optimisation of an Integrated Aggregate Production-Distribution Plan in Supply Chains," *International Journal of Production Research*, **50**(1): 81–96.
Ferguson, M. (2010) "Making Your Supply Chain More Sustainable by Closing the Loop," *The European Business Review*, (November/December): 28–31.
Goodman, D.A. (1974) "A Goal Programming Approach to Aggregate Planning of Production and Workforce," *Management Science*, **20**(12): 1569–1575.
Hanssmann, F. and S.W. Hess (1960) "A Linear Programming Approach to Production and Employment Scheduling," *Management Technology*, **1**: 46–51.
Hax, A.C. and H.C. Meal (1975) "Hierarchical Integration of Production Planning and Scheduling," in *Studies in Management Sciences, Volume 1, Logistics*, M.A. Geisler (ed.), New York: North Holland-American Elsevier.
Henderson, John C., Lee J. Krajewski, and Michael J. Showalter (1982) "An Integrated Approach for Manpower Planning in the Service Sector," *Omega the International Journal of Management Science*, **10**(1): 61–73.
Holt, C.C., F. Modigliani, and H.A. Simon (1955) "A Linear Decision Rule for Production and Employment Scheduling," *Management Science*, **2**(1): 1–30.
Holt, C.C., F. Modigliani, and J.F. Muth (1956) "Derivation of a Linear Decision Rule for Production and Employment," *Management Science*, **2**(2): 159–177.
Holt, C.C., F. Modigliani, J.F. Muth, and H.A. Simon (1960) *Planning Production, Inventories, and Work Force*. Upper Saddle River, NJ: Prentice Hall.
Jaaskelainen, Veikko (1969) "A Goal programming Model of Aggregate Production Planning," *The Swedish Journal of Economics*, **71**(1): 14–29.
Jamalnia, A. and M.A. Soukhakian (2009) "A Hybrid Fuzzy Goal Programming Approach With Different Goal Priorities to Aggregate Production Planning," *Computers and Industrial Engineering*, **56**(4): 1474–1486.
Jones, C.H. (1967) "Parametric Production Planning," *Management Science*, **13**(11): 843–866.
Kanyalkar, A.P. and G.K. Adil (2007) "Aggregate and Detailed Production Planning Integrating Procurement and Distribution Plans in a Multi-Site Environment," *International Journal of Production Research*, **45**(22): 5329–5353.
Kanyalkar, A.P. and G.K. Adil (2010) "A Robust Optimisation Model for Aggregate and Detailed Planning of a Multi-Site Procurement-Production-Distribution System," *International Journal of Production Research*, **48**(3): 635–656.
Krajewski, L.J. (1984) "Multiple-Criteria Optimization in Production Planning: An Application for a Large Industrial Goods Manufacturer," in *Production Planning and Scheduling: Mathematical Programming Applications*, (K. Lawrence and S. Zanakis, ed.), Norcross, GA: IIE Press.
Krajewski, L.J. and H.E. Thompson (1975) "Efficient Employment Planning in Public Utilities," *The Bell Journal of Economics*, **6**(1): 314–326.
Krajewski, L.J., M.K. Malhotra, and L.P. Ritzman (2016) *Operations Management: Processes and Supply Chains*, 11th ed. Upper Saddle River, NJ: Pearson.
Krajewski, L.J., V.A. Mabert, and H.E. Thompson (1973) "Quadratic Inventory Cost Approximations and the Aggregation of Individual Products," *Management Science*, **19**(11): 1229–1240.
Kumar, G.M. and A.N. Haq (2005) "Hybrid Genetic—Ant Colony Algorithms for Solving Aggregate Production Plan," *Journal of Advanced Manufacturing Systems*, **4**(1): 103–111.
Lee, W.B. and B.M. Khumawala (1974) "Simulation Testing of Aggregate Production Planning Models in an Implementation Methodology," *Management Science*, **20**(6): 903–911.
Leitch, R.A. (1974) "Marketing Strategy and Optimal Production Schedule," *Management Science*, **21**(3): 302–312.
Leung, S.C.H. and S.S.W. Chan (2009) "A Goal Programming Model for Aggregate Production Planning With Resource Utilization Constraint," *Computers and Industrial Engineering*, **56**(3): 1053–1064.
Li, B., H. Wang, J. Yang, M. Guo, and C. Qi (2013) "A Belief Rule-Based Inference Method for Aggregate Production Planning Under Uncertainty," *International Journal of Production Research*, **51**(1): 83–105.
Manne, A.S. (1957) "A Note on the Modigliani-Hohn Production Smoothing Problem," *Management Science*, **3**(4): 371–379.
Martha, J. and S. Subbakrishna (2002) "Targeting a Just-in-Case Supply Chain for the Inevitable Next Disaster," *Supply Chain Management Review*, (September/October): 18–23.

McKinsey & Company (2012) "Manufacturing the Future: The Next Era of Global Growth and Innovation," McKinsey Global Institute, www.mckinsey.com/mgi, downloaded January 10, 2013.

Mitchell, M. (1996) *An Introduction to Genetic Algorithms*. Cambridge, MA: MIT Press.

Mollenkopf, D.A. and D.J. Closs (2005) "The Hidden Value in Reverse Logistics," *Supply Chain Management Review*, (July/August): 34–43.

Nam, S.J. and R. Logendran (1992) "Aggregate Production Planning—A Survey of Models and Methodologies," *European Journal of Operational Research*, **61**(3): 255–272.

Narasimhan, R. (1980) "Goal Programming in a Fuzzy Environment," *Decision Sciences*, **11**(2): 325–336.

Nolan, R. and M. Sovereign (1972) "A Recursive Optimization and Simulation Approach to Analysis With an Application to Transportation Systems," *Management Science*, **18**(12): B676–690.

Qiu, M.M., L.D. Fredendall, and Z. Zhu (2001) "Application of Hierarchical Production Planning in a Multiproduct, Multimachine Environment," *International Journal of Production Research*, **39**(13): 2803–2816.

Rifai, A.K. (1994) "A Note on the Structure of the Goal Programming Model: Assessment and Evaluation," *International Journal of Operations & Production Management*, **16**(1): 40–49.

Ritzman, L.P., L.J. Krajewski, and M.J. Showalter (1976) "The Disaggregation of Aggregate Manpower Plans," *Management Science*, **22**(11): 1204–1214.

Ritzman, L.P., L.J. Krajewski, W.L. Berry, S.H. Goodman, S.T. Hardy, and L.D. Vitt, editors (1979) *Disaggregation: Problems in Manufacturing and Service Organizations*. Boston, MA: Martinus Nijhoff Publishing.

Romero, C. (1991) *Handbook of Critical Issues in Goal Programming*. Oxford: Pergamon Press.

Romero, C. (2004) "A General Structure of Achievement Function for a Goal Programming Model," *European Journal of Operational Research*, **153**(3): 675–686.

Roth, A.V. and R. Van Dierdonck (1995) "Hospital Resource Planning: Concepts, Feasibility, and Framework," *Production and Operations Management*, **4**(1): 2–29.

Ruefli, T. (1971) "A Generalized Goal Decomposition Model," *Management Science*, **17**(8): 505–518.

Schwarz, L.B. and R.E. Johnson (1978) "An Appraisal of the Empirical Performance of the Linear Decision Rule for Aggregate Planning," *Management Science*, **24**(8): 844–849.

Showalter, M.J., L.J. Krajewski, and L.P. Ritzman (1977) "Manpower Planning in U.S. Postal Facilities: A Heuristic Approach," *Journal of Computers and Operations Research*, **4**(4): 257–269.

Sprague, L.G., L.P. Ritzman, and L. Krajewski (1990) "Production Planning, Inventory Management and Scheduling: Spanning the Boundaries," *Managerial and Decision Economics*, **11**: 297–315.

Sweeny, D., E. Winofsky, P. Roy, and N. Baker (1978) "Composition vs. Decomposition: Two Approaches to Modeling Organization Decision Processes," *Management Science*, **24**(14): 4191–4199.

Tamiz, M., D. Jones, and C. Romero (1998) "Goal Programming for Decision Making: An Overview of the Current State-of-the-Art," *European Journal of Operational Research*, **111**(3): 569–581.

Taubert, W.H. (1968) "A Search Decision Rule for the Aggregate Scheduling Problem," *Management Science*, **14**(6): B343–359.

Tuite, M.F. (1968) "Merging Marketing Strategy Selection and Production Scheduling: A Higher Order Optimum," *JIE*, **19**(2): 76–84.

Wallace, T.F. and R.A. Stahl (2008) *Sales & Operations Planning: The How-To Handbook*, 3rd ed. Cincinnati, OH: T.F. Wallace & Company.

Welam, U.P. (1975) "Multi-Item Production Scheduling Models with Almost Closed Form Solutions," *Management Science*, **2**(9): 1021–1028.

Zoller, K. (1971) "Optimal Disaggregation of Aggregate Production Plans," *Management Science*, **17**(8): B533–549.

5
SCHEDULING IN MANUFACTURING AND SERVICES

Kangbok Lee and Michael Pinedo

1 Introduction

Scheduling is a decision-making process that is used on a regular basis in manufacturing and service industries. For example, scheduling plays an important role in the production of microelectronics manufacturing, in operator shift scheduling in call centers, and in the coordination of health care activities in hospitals. Scheduling processes in manufacturing industries tend to be different from scheduling processes in service industries. Scheduling processes in manufacturing industries are often more structured and better understood than those in service industries. The mathematical models that have led to the many scheduling algorithms that are applicable in manufacturing often fit very well within an established and well-organized framework. Scheduling in manufacturing industries may at times be referred to as machine scheduling, assembly line sequencing, or resource-constrained project scheduling. Scheduling processes in service industries vary in nature and may be more industry dependent. The service industries in which scheduling plays an important role include the transportation industries, the health care industry, the hospitality industries, and the entertainment industry. A scheduling process in any given service industry typically has its own peculiarities and idiosyncrasies.

Since it would be impossible to present an overview and a description of all the different types of scheduling processes that can take place in every possible manufacturing or services setting in a single chapter, in this chapter, we only consider four basic scheduling paradigms in detail. Two of these paradigms are prevalent in a variety of different manufacturing industries, and the other two, in various different service industries. In the conclusion, we refer to some other types of scheduling environments.

With regard to scheduling processes in manufacturing, we consider two important paradigms, namely,

(i) job shop scheduling and
(ii) resource constrained project scheduling.

Job shop scheduling plays an important role in a plethora of production environments (e.g., semiconductor manufacturing, printed circuit board manufacturing, and so on). Resource constrained project scheduling plays an important role in the manufacturing and construction of, for example, ocean liners and power plants.

With regard to scheduling processes in the service industries, we elaborate in what follows on two other paradigms, namely,

(i) personnel (shift) scheduling and
(ii) appointment scheduling.

Because of the typical and very variable demand for services in many different industries, shift scheduling in the service industries is significantly more challenging than shift scheduling in manufacturing. That is the main reason why research in personnel scheduling most often focuses on the service industries. Shift scheduling plays an important role in operator scheduling in call centers as well as in health care (e.g., nurse scheduling in hospitals). Appointment scheduling plays a crucial role in the scheduling of meetings, doctor appointments, surgeries, and so on.

There is an extensive amount of literature on scheduling theory and applications. In the last couple of decades, many books and survey papers appeared, covering all aspects of scheduling theory and applications. The more generally oriented books on scheduling include Baker and Trietsch (2009), Baptiste et al. (2001), Błazewicz et al. (2001), Brucker (2006), Brucker and Knust (2012), Pinedo (2009), and Pinedo (2016). The survey papers include those by Graves (1981) and Smith (1992).

1.1 Classifications of Scheduling Problems

In the literature, scheduling problems have been classified in various different ways. One way of classifying scheduling problems is based on when the exact data concerning a scheduling instance (i.e., release dates, processing times, etc.) become available to the scheduler. According to this criterion, there are two main classes of scheduling problems, namely, static problems and dynamic problems. Static scheduling assumes that all the information regarding the entire process (i.e., information with regard to the jobs as well as with regard to the machines) is already available at time zero and will not change over time. Therefore, the entire schedule can already be determined at time zero when the process starts. Dynamic scheduling assumes that new information may become available while the process evolves. For example, the exact processing time of a job may not be known beforehand, but it becomes known upon its completion. In a dynamic scheduling environment, a schedule is therefore being created while the process evolves. In the literature, static and dynamic scheduling problems are often also referred to as offline and online scheduling problems, respectively. Examples of static scheduling processes can often be found in production scheduling in manufacturing industries. The jobs to be processed within a scheduling horizon are selected in advance and all information concerning these jobs (e.g., their processing times) as well as all information concerning the machines (e.g., availability times) are known beforehand. Dynamic scheduling may occur, for example, in call centers. In such an environment, customers' calls are regarded as jobs and the information regarding a job only becomes known at the moment that the job comes in.

Another method of classifying scheduling problems is based on the probability distributions of quantities of interest, such as processing times, release dates, due dates, and so on. One can make a distinction between deterministic and stochastic scheduling. In deterministic scheduling, job characteristics such as release dates, processing times, and due dates are all known with certainty in advance. In stochastic scheduling, job characteristics such as processing times are known to be random variables from given probability distributions with known parameters. The actual processing time of a job only becomes known upon its completion. In deterministic scheduling, the value of an objective function can be computed precisely beforehand. In stochastic scheduling, one may only be able to compute the objective function in expectation. However, such an expectation is typically hard to compute. Scheduling problems in manufacturing tend to be more static and deterministic whereas scheduling problems in services tend to be more dynamic and stochastic. However, there are also settings that give rise to deterministic problems that are dynamic and settings that give rise to stochastic problems that are static.

This chapter focuses mainly on static (offline) deterministic scheduling problems. This class of problems has received most attention in the literature and the insights obtained through this research have often been useful in the analysis of related problems in the other classes of scheduling problems.

This chapter is organized as follows: In Section 2, we provide an overview of mathematical and computational preliminaries and the fundamental algorithmic frameworks that have wide applicability. In Section 3, we focus on selected topics in manufacturing scheduling, and in Section 4, we focus on selected topics in services scheduling. In Section 5, we discuss implementation issues, and in the last section, we present our conclusions and directions for future research.

2 Preliminaries and Fundamentals

2.1 Computational Complexity of Scheduling Problems

A schedule is a solution of a scheduling problem. It specifies when (at what time) and where (on which machine) each job is processed. In many scheduling problems, the objective function is to minimize a function of the completion times of the jobs. Two types of objective functions are common: (i) the sum of job values that are a function of their completion times (often referred to as a "min-sum" type of objective) and (ii) the maximum of job values that are a function of their completion times (often referred to as a "min-max" type of objective).

Static deterministic scheduling problems can be classified according to their computational complexity. Some scheduling problems tend to be relatively easy and can be solved without too much difficulty. In mathematical terms it is said that these easy problems can be solved in polynomial time because the running time to solve the problem is a polynomial function of the size of an instance of the problem (e.g., the number of jobs involved). Such problems are often referred to as tractable. That is to say that they can be solved fast in generating optimal schedules, using only a limited amount of computer time even when a large number of activities or jobs are involved.

Some of such tractable scheduling problems can be solved by applying a simple dispatching or priority rule. A classic example of a simple priority rule in a scheduling environment is the so-called Weighted Shortest Processing Time (WSPT) rule. Consider a single machine and n jobs. Job j has a processing time p_j and a weight (priority level) w_j, and its completion time in a schedule is denoted by C_j, $j = 1, 2, \ldots, n$. If the n jobs have to be scheduled on the machine in such a way that the total weighted completion time ($\Sigma_j w_j C_j$) has to be minimized, then the jobs have to be sequenced according to the WSPT rule (i.e., in decreasing order of w_j / p_j). The total weighted completion time is an example of an objective of the min-sum type. There are other and more complicated scheduling problems that are still tractable and also can be solved in polynomial time using algorithms that are a little bit more elaborate than simple priority rules. The techniques used for solving such "easy" scheduling problems may often be based on dynamic programming or linear programming techniques.

However, most static deterministic scheduling problems tend to be quite hard in practice and may not be solvable in polynomial time. Such problems are often referred to as intractable and are in mathematical terms called NP-Hard. (The concept of NP-Hardness is based on a formal mathematical definition that is beyond the scope of this chapter. However, it is generally believed that an algorithm for solving an NP-Hard problem cannot run in polynomial time.) NP-Hard problems can only be solved via elaborate and time-consuming optimization techniques.

Before describing the various solution approaches, it will be helpful to discuss the relationships between different problems as far as their complexities and solution methodologies are concerned.

Consider two scheduling problems. Let problem P_1 be a scheduling problem to minimize the total completion time on a single machine and let problem P_2 be a scheduling problem to minimize the total weighted completion time on a single machine. Thus, problem P_2 becomes problem P_1 when the weights of all jobs are made equal to one another. In such a case, we can say that problem P_1 is a special case of problem P_2 and problem P_2 is more general than problem P_1. In other words, problem P_2 is at least as hard as problem P_1. Specifically, if a special case is hard, then a more general case is hard too. Similarly, if a more general case is easy, then the special case will be easy as well. Such relationships are useful in determining the complexities of scheduling problems. As for solution methodology, a solution methodology for a general case is always applicable to a special case as well. On the other hand, a solution methodology for a special case may not be directly applicable to a more general case. It may need to be generalized; if it can be applied, the quality of the solution may be lower, or it may not be applicable at all, and an entirely different approach may have to be developed.

2.2 Solution Methodologies

Now, consider the solution methodologies. There are two criteria for evaluating the effectiveness of a solution methodology: the solution quality and the solution time. It is desirable to have a solution methodology that produces an optimal (or near-optimal) schedule in a very short amount of time. First of all, for tractable problems, we already know that they can be solved optimally in polynomial time. Thus, the research focuses on reducing the computation time mathematically and practically.

Intractable problems can only be solved via more elaborate optimization techniques. In the literature, the various techniques are typically categorized as (i) exact algorithms, (ii) approximation algorithms, and (iii) heuristic algorithms.

(i) Exact algorithms include Dynamic Programming as well as Branch-and-Bound techniques, which may be used for various forms of mathematical programming formulations, (e.g., Mixed Integer Programming (MIP) formulations, which may use various types of decision variables such as time-indexed variables or sequencing variables). Most exact algorithmic approaches are based on an efficient enumeration of the solution space while trying to avoid doing any unnecessary searches in the solution space. Only small instances can be solved optimally by exact algorithms within a reasonable time frame.

(ii) Approximation algorithms are often based on priority rules because of their ease of implementation and analysis. Sometimes, the problem is reduced to an easier problem that is similar in order to get an optimal solution for the modified problem and the optimal solution to the modified problem is then converted to a feasible solution to the original problem. Worst-case analysis is used mainly for evaluating the performance of approximation algorithms. It may be possible to show that the ratio of the objective function value of the solution obtained via an approximation algorithm to the optimal objective function value is no more than a certain value even though the optimal objective function value is not known. The minimum possible value of such a ratio is referred to as a worst-case performance ratio when offline scheduling problems are considered and as a competitive ratio when online scheduling problems are considered. We consider in the next section the application of the WSPT rule in an environment with m identical machines in parallel as an example of an approximation algorithm.

(iii) Heuristics have to be designed when problems are too complicated to allow for either exact algorithms or approximation algorithms. A heuristic may incorporate rules of thumb that are based on certain characteristics of the problem. It may also decompose the problem into subproblems and then solve these subproblems sequentially in order to gain computational efficiency with some sacrifice in the quality of the solution. Since in many cases it is hard to evaluate the solution quality of a heuristic in a theoretical manner, the performance of a heuristic is often evaluated through experimentation with randomly generated data sets and/or data sets from the real world. A metaheuristic is a higher-level procedure or heuristic that is designed to find, generate, or select a heuristic that may provide a sufficiently good solution to an optimization problem. Similar to heuristics, metaheuristics do not guarantee that a globally optimal solution will be found. However, since they may make relatively few assumptions with regard to the problem under consideration, they are, in practice, often used for a large variety of optimization problems. Metaheuristics include genetic algorithms, simulated annealing, and tabu search.

3 Scheduling in Manufacturing

Clearly there are a plethora of manufacturing environments where scheduling plays an important role. In this section, we consider two such environments, namely, job shop scheduling environments and resource constrained project scheduling environments. An example of the first one would be a semiconductor manufacturing facility and an example of the second one would be a shipyard that builds large cruise ships.

3.1 Job Shop Scheduling

A job shop typically consists of a number of machines that may be configured in any way, providing many different machine configurations to be considered. The simplest machine environment is clearly the single machine. An enormous amount of research has been done on single machine scheduling, see Abdul-Razaq et al. (1990), Koulamas (2010), and Adamu and Adewumi (2014), for example.

In this subsection, three classes of parallel machine scheduling problems are considered—basic problems, more general problems, and more practical problems. In the basic problem category, two types of objectives are of interest: min-sum objectives (e.g., the total weighted completion time and the total completion time) in Sections 3.1.1 and 3.1.2 and min-max objective (e.g., the makespan) in Section 3.1.3. In the category of more general problems, additional features such as due dates and release dates play a role as well in Section 3.1.4. Finally, a job shop scheduling is introduced along with a practically efficient solution methodology called the Shifting Bottleneck Heuristic in Section 3.1.5.

3.1.1 Scheduling Problems with the Total Weighted Completion Time Objective

Recall that for the single machine problem with the total weighted completion time objective, the WSPT rule is optimal. This problem is thus tractable. An immediate generalization of the single machine configuration is a configuration with m identical machines in parallel. Consider m machines in parallel and n jobs. A job can be processed on any one of the m machines, and the processing time of job j is p_j on any one of the machines. The objective is still the minimization of the total weighted completion time. Obviously, m machines in parallel is a more general setting than a single machine. This parallel machine scheduling problem with the total weighted completion time objective is known to be NP-Hard (Bruno et al. 1974), implying that the WSPT rule may not yield an optimal schedule. However, it is of course still possible to use the WSPT rule as an approximation scheme for the parallel machine case.

An application of the WSPT rule in a parallel machine environment can be described as follows: Sort the jobs in decreasing order of their WSPT ratio and assign them one after another to the machine that becomes available the earliest. In a schedule generated by the WSPT rule, all jobs assigned to the same machine follow one another in WSPT order. Thus, the WSPT rule is a reasonable approach for the parallel machine case even though it does not guarantee an optimal solution. An algorithm for a minimization problem is called a ρ-approximation algorithm if the objective function value of the schedule generated by the algorithm is at most ρ times the optimal objective function, and the value ρ is called the worst-case performance ratio. Indeed, it has been shown that the worst-case performance ratio of the WSPT rule is no more than $(1+\sqrt{2})/2 \approx 1.21$ (Kawaguchi and Kyan 1986).

Now consider a more general case where the processing time of a job depends on the machine on which the job is processed. In other words, if job j is processed on machine i, its processing time is p_{ij} time units. If the processing time of a job depends on both the job and the machine, then the machine environment is referred to as unrelated parallel machines. Since the identical parallel machine case is NP-Hard, the unrelated parallel machine case is clearly NP-Hard as well. The WSPT rule cannot now be applied because the processing time of a job depends on the machine.

Up to this point, we have only considered scheduling problems with the total weighted completion time objective in various different machine environments. Now consider their counterparts with the total (unweighted) completion time as objective; these are clearly special cases of the problems with the total weighted completion time objective. When an unweighted problem is considered, the WSPT priority rule becomes the SPT (Shortest Processing Time) rule because the weights of all jobs are equal to one another. Since the WSPT rule is optimal for the single machine scheduling to minimize total weighted completion time, the SPT rule is optimal for the single machine with the total completion time as objective.

3.1.2 Scheduling Problems with the Total Completion Time Objective

Then, what is the complexity of the problem with m identical machines in parallel and the total completion time objective? Conway et al. (1967) proved that the SPT rule is still optimal for the problem with m identical machines in parallel and the total completion time objective. What then is the complexity of the unrelated machines in parallel case? Actually, for this case the SPT rule is not even defined because the processing times vary over machines. In order to develop an algorithm for the problem with unrelated machines, either the SPT rule should be somehow generalized or a new idea needs to be developed.

The unrelated parallel machine scheduling problem with the total completion time objective can be formulated as a so-called weighted bipartite matching problem with n jobs on one side and mn positions on the other side (Horn 1973; Bruno et al. 1974). It can also be considered as an "assignment problem" or as a special case of the transportation problem. If job j is processed on machine i and there are $k-1$ jobs following job j on machine i, then job j contributes $k \times p_{ij}$ to the value of the objective function. There are well-known algorithms that run in polynomial time for the weighted bipartite matching problem: one of the more popular algorithms is the so-called Hungarian Method (Edmonds 1965; Hopcroft and Karp 1973). The unrelated parallel machine scheduling problem with the total completion time objective can therefore be solved in polynomial time.

Figure 5.1 shows the relationships between the special cases and the more general cases of the problems described above and their solution methodologies. Between the problems, arrows go from the more specialized problems to the more general problems. For the tractable problems, their polynomial time algorithms are presented while for the intractable problems, approximation algorithms are presented with their worst-case performance ratio.

3.1.3 Scheduling Problems with the Makespan Objective

Now consider a machine environment in which the makespan has to be minimized. When all jobs are available at time zero, the makespan on a single machine is always equal to the total processing time. The order in which the jobs are processed does not affect the makespan.

(i) *Identical machines in parallel and the makespan*: The simplest case is the case with identical machines in parallel. Scheduling identical parallel machines with the makespan objective is known to be NP-Hard, even for two machines in parallel. We can examine two priority rules for this problem with n jobs on m machines, namely, the List Scheduling (LS) rule and the Longest Processing Time (LPT) rule. List Scheduling is straightforward. Take the set of jobs in any order and for each job, allocate this job to the machine that has currently the smallest load. The worst-case performance ratio of the LS rule is known to be $2 - 1/m$ (Graham 1966). The LPT rule first sorts the jobs in decreasing order of their processing times and then applies the List Scheduling rule. The worst-case performance ratio of the LPT rule is known to be $4/3 - 1/3m$ (Graham 1969).

(ii) *Uniform machines in parallel and the makespan*: Consider parallel machines with different speeds. In the scheduling literature, such an environment is typically referred to as "uniformly related machines" or simply "uniform machines." In the uniform machines case, machine i has a speed s_i, and job j has a processing time p_j, and the time requirement (realized processing time) of job j on machine i is p_j / s_i. Thus, $p_{ij} = p_j / s_i$. However, when all s_i values are the same, then the problem reduces to identical machines in parallel. Applying LPT in a uniform machines environment may seem a reasonable approach. However, it may require a minor modification. In a uniform machines environment, a job should be tried out on every machine and then be assigned to the machine where it would have the minimum completion time. Several attempts have been made to determine the exact worst-case performance ratio of the LPT rule. (See Gonzalez et al.

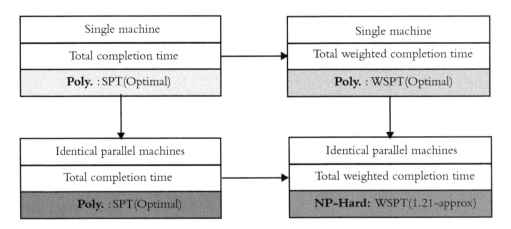

Figure 5.1 Relationships between Problems with Total Weighted Completion Time Objective

(1977), Dobson (1984), and Friesen (1987) for further information.) Kovács (2010) obtained the most recent results for this problem and showed that the worst-case performance ratio lies in the interval [1.54, 1.5773].

(iii) Unrelated machines in parallel and the makespan: In an unrelated parallel machine environment, the processing time of job j on machine i is p_{ij}. In this case, the LPT rule cannot be applied since it is not possible to sort the jobs according to their processing times. However, the problem can be formulated as an integer programming problem:

Minimize C_{max}

Subject to $\sum_{j=1}^{n} p_{ij} x_{ij} \leq C_{max}$ for $i = 1, \ldots, m$

$\sum_{i=1}^{m} x_{ij} = 1$ for $j = 1, \ldots, n$

$x_{ij} \in \{0, 1\}$ for $i = 1, \ldots, m$, for $j = 1, \ldots, n$

Even though the problem can be formulated easily as a mathematical program and has been studied extensively, the first applicable solution methodology was developed only in 1990. In general, an integer programming problem is hard to solve optimally. Lenstra et al. (1990) proposed a polynomial time algorithm that generates a schedule with a makespan that is guaranteed to be no longer than twice the optimum. The idea is to solve its linear programming relaxation (by relaxing the integrality constraints to non-negativity constraints) and to round the fractional solution in a clever way to an integer solution. This idea has been analyzed with regard to the quality of the solution as well as with regard to its computational time by Gairing et al. (2007), Shchepin and Vakhania (2005), and Arad et al. (2014).

In summary, the LPT rule as developed for the case of identical machines in parallel can be extended to the uniform machine case; however, it cannot be extended to the unrelated machines case.

3.1.4 Job Shop Scheduling with Additional Features

Job shop scheduling problems may have a variety of additional features. Job j may have a *release date* (denoted by r_j) when job j becomes available and may have a due date (denoted by d_j) by when job j is supposed to be completed. If the jobs have due dates, the maximum lateness (denoted by L_{max}) is often considered an objective of interest and the Earliest Due Date first (EDD) rule, which sequences the jobs in non-decreasing order of their due dates, is a possible algorithm. For a single machine scheduling problem with the maximum lateness as objective, the EDD rule is optimal (Jackson 1955). However, if the jobs have different release dates, then the problem turns out to be NP-Hard (Lenstra et al. 1977).

If a job can be interrupted at any time and resumed at a later point in time, it is said that preemptions are allowed. Precedence constraints imposed on the jobs may be described in the form of an acyclic graph (a directed graph with no cycles) $G = (V, A)$, where V is a set of nodes that represent the jobs and A is a set of directed arcs that denote the precedence constraints, i.e., pair i and j with $(i, j) \in A$ implies that job i must precede job j. Lageweg et al. (1976) studied various single machine scheduling problems with release and due dates, precedence constraints, and preemptions being allowed. This showed that some cases can be solved by the EDD rule. Since then, a significant amount of progress has been made, both theoretically as well as experimentally as seen in Grabowski et al. (1986), Gupta and Kyparisis (1987), and Uzsoy et al. (1992).

3.1.5 The Shifting Bottleneck Heuristic for Job Shop Scheduling

We will consider now a more complicated scheduling problem in a job shop environment with a practical solution approach, the so-called Shifting Bottleneck Heuristic (SBH). It is assumed that there are n jobs and m machines with each job having to follow a predetermined route (a sequence of machines) and with no recirculation. Job j comprises of a set of operations (i, j) which represents the processing of job j on machine i with its processing time denoted by p_{ij}.

The problem of minimizing the makespan in a job shop without recirculation can be represented by a so-called disjunctive graph. A disjunctive graph is defined as follows: A directed graph $G = (N, A, B)$ has a set of nodes N and two sets of arcs A and B. The nodes in N correspond to all operations (i, j) of the n jobs. The so-called conjunctive (solid) arcs in set A represent the routes of the jobs. If arc $(i, j) \rightarrow (h, j)$ is part of A, then operation (i, j) precedes operation (h, j). Two operations from different jobs that have to be processed on the same machine are connected to one another by two so-called disjunctive (dotted) arcs going in opposite directions; these disjunctive arcs belong to set B. All arcs from a node, conjunctive as well as disjunctive, have as length the processing time of the operation that is represented by that node. In addition, there is a source node U and a sink node V, which are dummy nodes. The source node U has n conjunctive arcs going to the first operations of the n jobs and the sink node V has n conjunctive arcs coming in representing all the last operations. The arcs from the source have length zero, see Figure 5.2.

A feasible schedule corresponds to a selection of one disjunctive arc from each pair of disjunctive arcs such that the resulting directed graph is acyclic. Such a selection determines a unique sequence of all the operations on each machine. It is known that the problem of minimizing the makespan is reduced to finding a selection of disjunctive arcs that minimizes the length of the longest path (i.e., the critical path) in the graph. However, since this problem has turned out to be very hard, many heuristic procedures have been developed. One of the best-known procedures is the Shifting Bottleneck Heuristic (SBH) developed by Adams et al. (1988).

The basic purpose of SBH is to determine the sequence of operations on the machines, machine by machine (Pinedo 2009). Let M denote the set of all machines, and let M_0 denote the set of machines whose operations already have a fixed sequence. In an iteration, a machine from $M - M_0$ is then chosen to be included in M_0. The graph has all conjunctive arcs and the fixed disjunctive arcs associated with M_0 (where M_0 initially is an empty set). With this graph, we can do in an iteration a forward and a backward pass using the Critical Path Method (CPM) and get for each operation its earliest possible starting time and its latest possible finishing time in order to ensure that the makespan is not going to be increased. Then, we consider for each machine in $M - M_0$ a single machine scheduling problem with the maximum lateness (L_{max}) objective where each operation's release date and due date are each operation's earliest starting time and latest finishing time, respectively. As stated previously, this single machine scheduling problem is NP-Hard; however, procedures have been developed that perform reasonably well in practice. The minimum L_{max} of such a single machine problem corresponding to a machine is a measure of the criticality of that machine. After solving all these single machine problems, the machine in $M - M_0$ with the largest maximum lateness, say machine h, is chosen in this iteration to be included next in set M_0 because this machine is in a sense the most critical, or the "bottleneck." If the disjunctive arcs that specify the sequence of operations on machine h are inserted in the graph, then the makespan of the current partial schedule is updated. In the next iteration, the entire procedure is repeated, and another machine is added to the current set $M_0 \cup \{h\}$. The procedure stops when all machines are in M_0 or the computed L_{max} is non-positive. Figure 5.2 depicts an example of a problem instance with three jobs and four machines in its disjunctive graph.

Table 5.1 An Example of a Problem Instance for Job Shop Scheduling

Jobs	Machine Sequence	Processing Times
1	1, 2, 3	$p_{11} = 10, p_{21} = 8, p_{31} = 4$
2	2, 1, 4, 3	$p_{22} = 8, p_{12} = 3, p_{42} = 5, p_{32} = 6$
3	1, 2, 4	$p_{13} = 4, p_{23} = 7, p_{43} = 3$

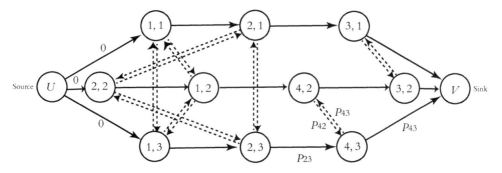

Figure 5.2 Disjunctive Graph for Job Shop with the Makespan as the Objective

This SBH idea can be extended to various other scheduling problems. For an example, see the problem of minimizing the total weighted tardiness in a job shop in Pinedo and Singer (1999).

3.2 Resource Constrained Project Scheduling

Resource constrained project scheduling fits within a framework of machine scheduling and also within a framework of project management. This type of problem, typically referred to as a Resource Constrained Project Scheduling Problem (RCPSP), has received an enormous amount of research attention over the years (as seen in Kolisch (1995) and Demeulemeester and Herroelen (2002) where a variety of formulations and solution methodologies for RCPSP are discussed).

RCPSP is one of the hardest scheduling problems around. However, some special cases can be solved in polynomial time. The most critical aspects of a project scheduling problem are its precedence constraints. The precedence relationships are expressed by an activity-on-node graph $G = (V, A)$ where V and A stand for the set of activities and the set of precedence relationships, respectively. In addition, the RCPSP is also subject to resource constraints. If we only consider precedence constraints and no resource constraints, the problem is actually easy.

A well-known method, referred to as the Critical Path Method (CPM), minimizes the total project duration (makespan) in project scheduling without resource constraints. This particular problem can actually also be formulated as a Linear Programming problem; a generalization of this problem can even be formulated as a Linear Programming problem. In project management, it is quite common for a project to be behind schedule or that the deadline for its completion has been moved earlier. Shortening the duration of a project is often called project crashing. In such a case, besides the makespan objective, there may be multiple objectives since crashing costs now have to be taken into consideration as well. The original processing time of job j is denoted by p_j^{max} and its lower bound of crashed processing time is denoted by p_j^{min}. If the processing time is shortened by x_j the crashing cost is $c_j x_j$. In some cases, there is a due date for each job (a milestone), and if job j cannot be completed on or before its due date d_j, a tardiness penalty is incurred equal to $w_j T_j$ where w_j is a unit tardiness penalty and $T_j = \max\{0, C_j - d_j\}$ is the tardiness of job j. The overall objective is now to minimize the sum of three objectives, namely, the total weighted tardiness, the total crashed cost, and the makespan. This problem can be formulated as the following Linear Program problem:

$$\text{Minimize} \quad \sum_{j=1}^{n} w_j T_j + \sum_{j=1}^{n} c_j x_j + C_{max}$$

$$\text{Subject to} \quad S_j + p_j \leq S_k \quad \text{for } (j, k) \in A$$

$$p_j \geq p_j^{min} \quad \text{for } j \in V$$

$$p_j = p_j^{max} - x_j \quad \text{for } j \in V$$

$$T_j \geq (S_j + p_j) - d_j \quad \text{for } j \in V$$

$$T_j \geq 0, x_j \geq 0, S_j \geq 0 \quad \text{for } j \in V$$

Therefore, project scheduling with linear crashing costs can be formulated as a Linear Programming problem and can thus be solved in polynomial time.

4 Scheduling in Services

This section focuses on two scheduling paradigms that are important in a variety of different service industries, namely, personnel scheduling (which is often also referred to as shift scheduling) and appointment scheduling. Personnel scheduling is, for example, very important in the scheduling of operators in call centers (which play an important role in financial services, transportation industries, and so on). The second paradigm considered is appointment scheduling, which is very important in the health care industry.

4.1 Personnel Scheduling

Personnel scheduling is very important in many service industries, since schedules have to be created in such a way that at all times operators will be available to meet a fluctuating and random demand, without causing too much queueing. This is very much in contrast with personnel scheduling in manufacturing, which is inherently much easier and less challenging. An enormous amount of research has been done on personnel scheduling. This has resulted in numerous survey papers and books by authors such as Tien and Kamiyama (1982), Burgess and Busby (1992), Nanda and Browne (1992), and Burke et al. (2004).

4.1.1 Mathematical Formulation

Consider the most basic personnel scheduling problem with cycles being fixed in advance. In certain settings a cycle may be a week, while in others it may be a day or a month. A predetermined cycle consists of m time intervals or periods. When scheduling operators in call centers, a cycle typically is a day with an interval or period being usually 15 minutes (however, the lengths of the periods within a cycle do not necessarily have to be all identical). During period

i, $i = 1, \ldots, m$, the presence of b_i personnel is required in order to meet anticipated (forecast) demand. The number b_i is, of course, an integer. Each work assignment pattern (type of shift) in a cycle has its own cost and the objective is to minimize the total cost of all the personnel assigned to the different shift patterns while meeting demand at all times. The problem can be formulated as follows: There are n different shift patterns and each employee is assigned to one and only one pattern. Shift pattern j is defined by a vector $(a_{1j}, a_{2j}, \ldots, a_{mj})$. The value a_{ij} is either 0 or 1; it is a 1 if period i is a work period for this shift pattern and 0 otherwise. Let c_j denote the cost of assigning a person to shift j and x_j the (integer) decision variable representing the number of people assigned to shift pattern j. The problem with minimizing the total cost of assigning personnel to meet demand can be formulated as the following integer programming problem:

Minimize $\quad c_1 x_1 + c_2 x_2 + \cdots + c_n x_n$

Subject to
$$a_{11} x_1 + a_{12} x_2 + \cdots + a_{1n} x_n \geq b_1$$
$$a_{21} x_1 + a_{22} x_2 + \cdots + a_{2n} x_n \geq b_2$$
$$\vdots$$
$$a_{m1} x_1 + a_{m2} x_2 + \cdots + a_{mn} x_n \geq b_m$$

$$x_j \geq 0 \quad \text{for } j = 1, \cdots, n, \text{ with } x_1, \cdots, x_n \text{ integer}.$$

In matrix form, this integer programming problem can be written as follows:

Minimize $\quad \overline{c}\,\overline{x}$

Subject to $\quad \mathbf{A}\overline{x} \geq \overline{b}$

$\overline{x}$ integer ≥ 0.

Such an integer programming problem in its most general form is known to be NP-Hard.

4.1.2 Impact of Breaks

However, the **A** matrix in practice may often exhibit a special structure. For example, shift j, $(a_{1j}, \ldots, a_{mj})$, may contain a contiguous set of 1's (a contiguous set of 1's implies that there are no 0's in between 1's). However, the number of 1's may often vary from shift to shift, since it is possible that some shifts have to work longer hours (or more days) than other shifts. Even though the integer programming formulation of the general personnel scheduling problem (with an arbitrary 0-1 **A** matrix) is NP-Hard, the special case with each column containing a contiguous set of 1's is easy. It can be shown that the solution of the linear programming relaxation is then always an integer. There are several other important special cases that are solvable in polynomial time.

However, in practice, the columns in the integer programming problem described above do not always contain a contiguous set of ones. The operators are often entitled to breaks (e.g., lunch breaks and coffee breaks). Such breaks imply that a column may have some zeroes sprinkled in between the ones. An integer programming problem with an arbitrary number of zeroes sprinkled in between the ones is known to be NP-Hard. However, if each particular shift has only one break, then it has been shown that the problem still can be solved in polynomial time. In the case that a shift has a lunch break as well as two coffee breaks, then a heuristic is often used: as a first step, the breaks are ignored. This implies that the columns in the integer programming problem have contiguous sets of ones. A solution is then obtained via Linear Programming. Since the breaks imply that in any period in actuality fewer operators will be available to serve the customers, the b_i vector of the Linear Programming problem is adjusted upwards to take this into account. A solution of the Linear Programming problem specifies the number of people that have to be hired for each shift type. After a solution has been generated via Linear Programming, the breaks are inserted through a straightforward break insertion heuristic.

Many papers have focused on a number of special cases of the problem described above; see Bartholdi et al. (1980), Burns and Carter (1985), Burns and Koop (1987), Emmons (1985), Emmons and Burns (1991), and Hung and Emmons (1993), for example.

4.2 Appointment Scheduling

Scheduling appointments is a common practice in many service industries, mainly in order to utilize resources efficiently and to avoid queueing. Many papers have appeared in the literature on appointment scheduling, mostly motivated by health care applications. Cayirli and Veral (2003) and Gupta and Denton (2008) provide overviews of the literature, research challenges, and opportunities. Hall (2012) provides a comprehensive review of models and methods used for scheduling the delivery of patient care in all parts of the health care system.

Outpatient clinics typically start empty at the beginning of a working day, operate for a finite amount of time (in the order 8–12 hours), and then shut down at the end of the day. An analysis of such an environment can be done through a variety of approaches, including stochastic programming, queueing theory, and stylized scheduling models.

Appointment scheduling systems are widely used as a tool for managing patient arrivals at health care facilities in order to match supply with demand. In practice, it is actually fairly common for patients not to show up for their scheduled services. Such a patient is then referred to as a no-show. No-shows result in under-utilization of valuable resources and limit the access for other patients who could have filled the empty slots. Meanwhile, patients nationwide experience difficulties in accessing medical appointments in a timely manner due to long backlogs.

4.2.1 Appointment Overbooking

Appointment overbooking is one operational strategy employed by health care providers to address the issue of no-shows and at the same time increase patients' access to care. However, overbooking may potentially result in an overcrowded facility that increases patients' waiting times and the system's overtime. Recent studies have demonstrated that a sensible practice of appointment overbooking can significantly improve the operational performance of a medical facility with patients experiencing shorter waiting times and better access to services. See LaGanga and Lawrence (2012), Robinson and Chen (2010), Zacharias and Pinedo (2014a), Zacharias and Pinedo (2014b), for example.

In a setting with patients that have similar characteristics, it is of interest to determine the number of patients to schedule every day and how to allocate these patients to the different time slots in a day. The sequencing of the patients is also of interest when patients have different characteristics (different no-show probabilities, different processing times, and different waiting costs). In most cases, finding an optimal schedule is analytically intractable. Thus, most of the literature uses enumeration, search algorithms, simulation-based techniques, and/or heuristics. For a formulation of an appointment scheduling model, see Zacharias and Pinedo (2014a; 2014b).

4.2.2 Characteristics of Optimal Appointment Schedules

Optimal schedules with overbooking tend to be front-loaded: More patients are scheduled towards the beginning of the working day (in order to get an empty system to start up), and the schedules tend to become somewhat less dense towards the end of the working day (clearly in order to avoid high overtime costs). Optimal schedules may therefore exhibit three phases: A start-up phase in which the overbooking level is above average (in order to ensure that the system will be able to start up without too much idle time in the beginning of the schedule), an intermediate phase with periodic overbookings, and an emptying out phase in which the overbooking level is below the average overbooking level.

For a more comprehensive numerical analysis, the reader is referred to Zacharias and Pinedo (2014b). It is evident, and intuitive, that the optimal overbooking level is increasing in the no-show rate. As the cost of waiting increases, the optimal schedules become less front-loaded, without necessarily observing a decrease in the overbooking level. Overbooking increases significantly with the number of parallel servers. That increase is more prevalent for higher no-show rates.

Variations of the model described above have been analyzed in various papers including Robinson and Chen (2010), LaGanga and Lawrence (2012), Zacharias and Pinedo (2014a), and Zacharias and Pinedo (2014b). Most of the appointment scheduling literature focuses on single-server models. Kaandorp and Koole (2007), Klassen and Yoogalingam (2009), Robinson and Chen (2010), and Millhiser and Veral (2015) consider the appointment scheduling problem with patients that have similar characteristics who arrive on time for their scheduled appointments, if they do show up. Begen and Queyranne (2011), Cayirli et al. (2012), LaGanga and Lawrence (2012), and Zacharias and Pinedo (2014a) account further for patient heterogeneity.

5 Managerial Implications

5.1 Design of Scheduling Systems

The implementation of a scheduling process in practice typically requires the development of a computerized system. Such a scheduling system must rely on and interact with a reliable database system that contains all the information regarding the orders on file (either customers or jobs) and the machine availability times. A scheduling system must also have at its disposal a scheduling engine that has a library of scheduling algorithms at its disposal, which includes priority rules and heuristic techniques (e.g., local search procedures, including simulated annealing and tabu search, which are very popular in practice). For a scheduling system to be effective, it typically must have also elaborate user interfaces that facilitate interactive optimization. For an example of a Gantt chart user interface, see Figure 5.3, which depicts the Gantt chart interface of the LEKIN system, an educational scheduling system developed at the Stern School of Business, New York University (NYU). Such an interface typically has drag-and-drop capabilities. These capabilities allow the scheduler to manually adjust a schedule that had been generated by the scheduling engine and check the feasibility of the revised schedule easily. Figure 5.4 depicts the user interface of a surgery scheduling system for a hospital.

In practice, any scheduling system must allow for a user-friendly way of manipulating an already existing schedule. There are many reasons why in practice existing schedules often have to be rescheduled. Usually, this is due to the occurrence of a random event, such as a machine breakdown, a sudden arrival of a high-priority job, and so on. However, there is a strong desirability that the new schedule is not too different from the already existing schedule (in order to avoid confusion).

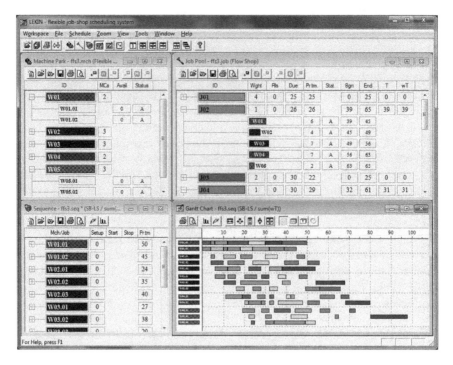

Figure 5.3 Interface of a Job Shop Scheduling System for a Manufacturing Application

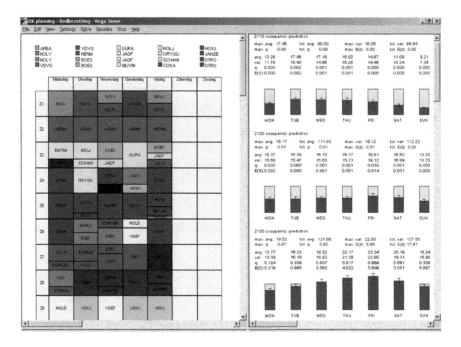

Figure 5.4 Interface of an Appointment Scheduling System (Operating Rooms in a Hospital)

5.2 Dealing with Randomness

In practice, there are many sources of randomness. Typically, processing times are not fixed but are rather random variables of which the distribution may or may not be known. Machines may be subject to breakdowns, which may make their availability periods random. New jobs or new appointments may come in at random and may have to be inserted in the schedule at once. In many scheduling environments, such random events may require frequent rescheduling. Since random events can have in practice a major impact on scheduling processes in many scheduling environments, it may not make sense to have an elaborate algorithm in place to construct a basic schedule when it is expected that the schedule will have to be changed soon afterwards. So even though the problem is very hard, it would not make that much sense to have an elaborate algorithm in place.

Thus, even if a deterministic version of a scheduling problem (assuming no randomness) is NP-Hard, a scheduler may use in practice only very simple and basic rules to generate a schedule. That is to say, he may use just a simple priority rule, even though the priority rule would not be optimal for the deterministic version of the problem. The priority rule may actually be theoretically optimal for certain stochastic counterparts of the problem.

Besides minimizing an objective function that is based on the completion times of the jobs, the scheduler may also want to maximize the robustness of the schedule. A schedule is robust if the necessary rescheduling triggered by a random event does not result in a schedule very different from the original schedule. There are several different measures of schedule robustness. For example, makespan variability, post-disturbance makespan, and various slack related functions are used in the literature.

There are several methods to make schedules more robust. A standard way is through the insertion of idle times (at times also referred to as buffer times), since scheduled idle times would mitigate the effects of machine breakdowns, unexpected arrivals of rush jobs, and so on.

6 Conclusions and Future Research Directions

Scheduling problems are clearly ubiquitous. In this chapter, we have only considered a sample of the many different types of scheduling problems that appear in practice. There are clearly many other types of scheduling problems.

For example, in manufacturing industries, scheduling plays an important role in assembly lines such as those used in the automotive industries. Assembly line scheduling has its own characteristics and requires specialized techniques. Scheduling plays also an important role in managing equipment maintenance activities; see Ait-Kadia et al. (2011), for example. Industrial robots that are designed to do a series of automated tasks require intricate scheduling techniques, see Dawande et al. (2007).

In the service industries, there are many other scheduling applications as well. This is clearly the case in transportation industries. Aircraft scheduling plays a very important role in the aviation industry (see Barnhart et al. (1998), Barnhart et al. (2003), Barnhart and Laporte (2006), Desaulniers et al. (1997), and Stojkovic et al. (2002)). In marine transportation, tanker scheduling is very important for the major oil companies, see Christiansen et al. (2004), Christiansen et al. (2006), and Perakis and Bremer (1992). Scheduling in public transport (e.g., train and bus scheduling) has received an enormous attention as well, that we see in works by Daduna et al. (1995) and Voss and Daduna (2001). In the entertainment industry, tournament scheduling is of the utmost importance in the sports industries (see Aggoun and Vazacopoulos (2004), Nemhauser and Trick (1998), Schaerf (1999), and Bartsch et al. (2006)). At universities, classroom scheduling and exam scheduling are very important (e.g., Burke et al. (1996)). Each one of the scheduling applications mentioned above has its own idiosyncrasies and leads to very specific problem formulations.

There are many avenues for future research in scheduling. Combinatorial optimization models, online scheduling models, stochastic scheduling models, as well as robust optimization applications will continue to receive significant research attention.

References and Bibliography

Abdul-Razaq, T.S., C.N. Potts, and L.N. Van Wassenhove (1990) "A survey of algorithms for the single machine total weighted tardiness scheduling problem," *Discrete Applied Mathematics*, **26**(2): 235–253.

Adams, J., E. Balas, and D. Zawack (1988) "The shifting bottleneck procedure for job shop scheduling," *Management Science*, **34**(3): 391–401. http://dx.doi.org/10.1287/mnsc.34.3.391

Adamu, M.O. and A.O. Adewumi (2014) "A survey of single machine scheduling to minimize weighted number of tardy jobs," *Journal of Industrial and Management Optimization*, **10**(1): 219–241.

Aggoun, A. and A. Vazacopoulos (2004) "Solving sports scheduling and timetabling problems with constraint programming," in *Economics, Management and Optimization in Sports*, S. Butenko, J. Gil-Lafuente, and P. Pardalos (Eds.), Springer, New York.

Ait-Kadia, D., J.-B. Menye, and H. Kane (2011) "Resources assignment model in maintenance activities scheduling," *International Journal of Production Research*, **49**(22): 6677–6689.

Arad, D., Y. Mordechai, and H. Shachnai (2014) "Tighter bounds for makespan minimization on unrelated machines." arXiv preprint arXiv:1405.2530.

Baker, K.R. and D. Trietsch (2009) *Principles of Sequencing and Scheduling*, J. Wiley, Hoboken, NJ.

Baptiste, P., C.L. Le Pape, and W. Nuijten (2001) *Constraint-Based Scheduling*, Kluwer Academic Publishers, Boston, MA.

Barnhart, C. and G. Laporte (Eds.) (2006) *Handbooks in Operations Research and Management Science, Volume 14—Transportation*, North-Holland, Amsterdam.

Barnhart, C., F. Lu, and R. Shenoi (1998) "Integrated airline schedule planning," in *Operations Research in the Airline Industry*, G. Yu (Ed.), Kluwer Academic Publishers, Boston, MA, pp. 384–403.

Barnhart, C., P. Belobaba, and A. Odoni (2003) "Applications of operations research in the air transport industry," *Transportation Science*, **37**: 368–391.

Bartholdi III, J.J., J.B. Orlin, and H.D. Ratliff (1980) "Cyclic scheduling via integer programs with circular ones," *Operations Research*, **28**: 1074–1085.

Bartsch, T., A. Drexl, and S. Kröger (2006) "Scheduling the professional soccer leagues of Austria and Germany," *Computers and Operations Research*, **33**(7): 1907–1937.

Begen, M.A. and M. Queyranne (2011) "Appointment scheduling with discrete random durations," *Mathematics of Operations Research*, **36**(2): 240–257.

Błażewicz, J., K.H. Ecker, E. Pesch, G. Schmidt, and J. Węglarz (2001) *Scheduling Computer and Manufacturing Processes*, 2nd Edition, Springer, Berlin.

Brucker, P. (2006) *Scheduling Algorithms*, 5th Edition, Springer, New York.

Brucker, P. and S. Knust (2012) *Complex Scheduling*, 2nd Edition, Springer, New York.

Bruno, J., E.G. Coffman Jr., and R. Sethi (1974) "Scheduling independent tasks to reduce mean finishing time," *Communications of the ACM*, **17**(7): 382–387.

Burgess, W.J. and R.E. Busby (1992) "Personnel Scheduling," in *Handbook of Industrial Engineering*, G. Salvendy (Ed.), pp. 2155–2169, J. Wiley, New York.

Burke, E. and M. Trick (Eds.) (2004) *The Practice and Theory of Automated Timetabling V*, Selected Papers from the 5th International Conference on the Practice and Theory of Automated Timetabling (held August 2004 in Pittsburgh, PA), *Lecture Notes in Computer Science*, Vol. 3616, Springer Verlag, Berlin.

Burke, E., D.G. Elliman, P.H. Ford, and R.F. Weare (1996) "Exam timetabling in British universities: A survey," in *The Practice and Theory of Automated Timetabling*, E. Burke and P. Ross (Eds.), *Lecture Notes in Computer Science*, Vol. 1153, Springer Verlag, Berlin.

Burns, R.N. and M.W. Carter (1985) "Work force size and single shift schedules with variable demands," *Management Science*, **31**(5): 599–608.

Burns, R.N. and G.J. Koop (1987) "A modular approach to optimal multiple shift manpower scheduling," *Operations Research*, **35**: 100–110.

Cayirli, T. and E. Veral (2003) "Outpatient scheduling in health care: A review of literature," *Production and Operations Management*, **12**(4): 519–549.

Cayirli, T., K. Khiong Yang, and S.A. Quek (2012) "A universal appointment rule in the presence of no-shows and walk-ins," *Production and Operations Management*, **21**(4): 682–697.

Christiansen, M., K. Fagerholt, and D. Ronen (2004) "Ship routing and scheduling—status and perspective," *Transportation Science*, **38**: 1–18.

Christiansen, M., K. Fagerholt, B. Nygreen, and D. Ronen (2006) "Maritime transportation," in *Handbooks in Operations Research and Management Science, Volume 14—Transportation*, C. Barnhart and G. Laporte (Eds.), pp. 189–284, North-Holland, Amsterdam.

Conway, R.W., W.L. Maxwell, and L.W. Miller (1967) *Theory of Scheduling*, Palo Alto-London.

Daduna, J.R., I. Branco, and J.M. Pinto Paixao (1995) *Computer Aided Scheduling of Public Transport. Lecture Notes in Economics and Mathematical Systems* No. 430, Springer Verlag, Berlin.

Dawande, M., H.N. Geismar, S.P. Sethi, and C. Sriskandarajah (2007) *Throughput Optimization in Robotic Cells*, Springer.

Demeulemeester, E.L. and W.S. Herroelen (2002) *Project Scheduling: A Research Handbook*, Kluwer Academic Publishers, Boston, MA.

Desaulniers, G., J. Desrosiers, Y. Dumas, M.M. Solomon, and F. Soumis (1997) "Daily aircraft routing and scheduling," *Management Science*, **43**(6): 841–855.

Dobson, G. (1984) "Scheduling independent tasks on uniform processors," *SIAM Journal on Computing*, **13**(4): 705–716.

Edmonds, J. (1965) "Paths, trees, and flowers," *Canadian Journal of Mathematics*, **17**(3): 449–467.

Emmons, H. (1985) "Work-force scheduling with cyclic requirements and constraints on days off, weekends off, and work stretch," *IIE Transactions*, **17**: 8–16.

Emmons, H. and R.N. Burns (1991) "Off-day scheduling with hierarchical worker categories," *Operations Research*, **39**: 484–495.

Friesen, D.K. (1987) "Tighter bounds for LPT scheduling on uniform processors," *SIAM Journal on Computing*, **16**(3): 554–560.

Gairing, M., B. Monien, and A. Woclaw (2007) "A faster combinatorial approximation algorithm for scheduling unrelated parallel machines," *Theoretical Computer Science*, **380**(1): 87–99.

Gonzalez, T., O.H. Ibarra, and S. Sahni (1977) "Bounds for LPT schedules on uniform processors," *SIAM Journal on Computing*, **6**(1): 155–166.

Grabowski, J., E. Nowicki, and S. Zdrzałka (1986) "A block approach for single-machine scheduling with release dates and due dates," *European Journal of Operational Research*, **26**(2): 278–285.

Graham, R.L. (1966) "Bounds for certain multiprocessing anomalies," *Bell System Technical Journal*, **45**(9): 1563–1581.

Graham, R.L. (1969) "Bounds on multiprocessing timing anomalies," *SIAM Journal on Applied Mathematics*, **17**(2): 416–429.

Graves, S.C. (1981) "A Review of production scheduling," *Operations Research*, **29**: 646–676.

Gupta, D. and B. Denton (2008) "Appointment scheduling in health care: Challenges and opportunities," *IIE Transactions*, **40**(9): 800–819.

Gupta, S.K. and J. Kyparisis (1987) "Single machine scheduling research," *OMEGA*, **13**: 207–227.

Hall, R. (2012) *Handbook of Healthcare System Scheduling*, Vol. 168, Springer, New York.

Hopcroft, J.E. and R.M. Karp (1973) "An $n^{5/2}$ algorithm for maximum matchings in bipartite graphs," *SIAM Journal on Computing*, **2**(4): 225–231.

Horn, W.A. (1973) "Minimizing average flow time with parallel machines," *Operations Research*, **21**: 846–847.

Hung, R. and H. Emmons (1993) "Multiple-shift workforce scheduling under the 3–4 compressed workweek with a hierarchical workforce," *IIE Transactions*, **25**: 82–89.

Jackson, J.R. (1955) *Scheduling a Production Line to Minimize Maximum Tardiness*, Research Report 43, Management Science Research Project, University of California, Los Angeles.

Kaandorp, G.C. and G. Koole (2007) "Optimal outpatient appointment scheduling," *Health Care Management Science*, **10**(3): 217–229.

Kawaguchi, T. and S. Kyan (1986) "Worst case bound of an LRF schedule for the mean weighted flow-time problem," *SIAM Journal on Computing*, **15**(4): 1119–1129.

Klassen, K.J. and R. Yoogalingam (2009) "Improving performance in outpatient appointment services with a simulation optimization approach," *Production and Operations Management*, **18**(4): 447–458.

Kolisch, R. (1995) *Project Scheduling under Resource Constraints*, Physica-Verlag (Springer Verlag), Heidelberg, Germany.

Koulamas, C. (2010) "The single-machine total tardiness scheduling problem: Review and extensions," *European Journal of Operational Research*, **202**(1): 1–7.

Kovács, A. (2010) "New approximation bounds for LPT scheduling," *Algorithmica*, **57**(2): 413–433.

LaGanga, L.R. and S.R. Lawrence (2012) "Appointment overbooking in health care clinics to improve patient service and clinic performance," *Production and Operations Management*, **21**(5): 874–888.

Lageweg, B.J., J.K. Lenstra, and A.H.G. Rinnooy Kan (1976) "Minimizing maximum lateness on one machine: Computational experience and some applications," *Statistica Neerlandica*, **30**(1): 25–41.

Lenstra, J.K., A.R. Kan, and P. Brucker (1977) "Complexity of machine scheduling problems," *Annals of Discrete Mathematics*, **1**: 343–362.

Lenstra, J.K., D.B. Shmoys, and É. Tardos (1990) "Approximation algorithms for scheduling unrelated parallel machines," *Mathematical Programming*, **46**(1–3): 259–271.

Millhiser, W.P. and E.A. Veral (2015) "Designing appointment system templates with operational performance targets," *IIE Transactions on Healthcare Systems Engineering*, **5**(3): 125–146.

Nanda, R. and J. Browne (1992) *Introduction to Employee Scheduling*, Van Nostrand Reinhold, New York.

Nemhauser, G.L. and M. Trick (1998) "Scheduling a major college basketball conference," *Operations Research*, **46**: 1–8.

Perakis, A.N. and W.M. Bremer (1992) "An operational tanker scheduling optimization system: Background, current practice and model formulation," *Maritime Policy and Management*, **19**: 177–187.

Pinedo, M. (2009) *Planning and Scheduling in Manufacturing and Services*, 2nd Edition, Springer, New York.

Pinedo, M. (2016) *Scheduling—Theory, Algorithms, and Systems*, 5th Edition, Springer, New York.

Pinedo, M. and M. Singer (1999) "A shifting bottleneck heuristic for minimizing the total weighted tardiness in a job shop," *Naval Research Logistics*, **46**(1): 1–17.

Robinson, L.W. and R.R. Chen (2010) "A comparison of traditional and open-access policies for appointment scheduling," *Manufacturing & Service Operations Management*, **12**(2): 330–346.

Schaerf, A. (1999) "Scheduling sport tournaments using constraint logic programming," *Constraints*, **4**: 43–65.

Shchepin, E.V. and N. Vakhania (2005) "An optimal rounding gives a better approximation for scheduling unrelated machines," *Operations Research Letters*, **33**(2): 127–133.

Smith, S.F. (1992) "Knowledge-based production management: Approaches, results, and prospects," *Production Planning and Control*, **3**: 350–380.

Stojkovic, G., F. Soumis, J. Desrosiers, and M. Solomon (2002) "An optimization model for a real-time flight scheduling problem," *Transportation Research Part A: Policy and Practice*, **36**: 779–788.

Tien, J.M. and A. Kamiyama (1982) "On manpower scheduling algorithms," *SIAM Review*, **24**: 275–287.

Uzsoy, R., C.Y. Lee, and L.A. Martin-Vega (1992) "Scheduling semiconductor test operations: Minimizing maximum lateness and number of tardy jobs on a single machine," *Naval Research Logistics*, **39**(3): 369–388.

Voss, S. and J.R. Daduna (2001) *Computer Aided Scheduling of Public Transport. Lecture Notes in Economics and Mathematical Systems*, No. 505, Springer Verlag, Berlin.

Zacharias, C. and M. Pinedo (2014a) "Appointment scheduling with no-shows and overbooking," *Production and Operations Management*, **23**(5): 788–801.

Zacharias, C. and M. Pinedo (2014b) "Managing customer arrivals in service systems with multiple servers," *Working Paper*, Stern School of Business, New York University, New York.

6
INVENTORY MANAGEMENT

Prem Vrat

1 Introduction

This chapter presents an overview of inventory management and highlights the role of effective inventory management in the overall competitiveness of the Production and Operations Management function. It identifies the concept, the need for, and determination of Optimal levels of inventories in an organization. Starting with the classical Economic Order Quantity (EOQ) model developed more than a hundred years ago, it presents a taxonomy of inventory models and outlines the current status of inventory research as well as future research trends. Selective inventory management and aggregate inventory analysis are presented in ways that enable management to get a macro view of inventory polices and facilitate its rationalization. The role of inventories in supply chains in a multi-echelon inventory system framework is outlined. Emerging trends in inventory related models—such as stock dependent consumption phenomenon and bio-inspired inventory systems—are suggested. Strategic interventions such as variety reduction, lead time reduction, vendor development can have enormous impact on inventory reduction along with trading of inventory with information.

Inventory of any kind is a "usable but idle resource". This definition contains inherent dichotomy in inventory planning and hence the need for optimization of inventory level. Inventory turnover ratio, defined as "the ratio of annual value of consumption of materials to the average value of inventory", can be a powerful performance indicator of not only the effectiveness of the materials management function but even the overall health of a business organization. It has been reported (Peterson and Silver 1981) that, in the same sector of business activity, a successful company in general will have inventory turnover ratio more than double that of its unsuccessful counterpart. This makes inventory management a very important function in the Production and Operations Management domain.

Inventories can exist in various forms: raw materials, bought-out components, in-process inventory, finished goods inventory, and maintenance as well as repair and operating supplies (MRO). The basic concept of inventories being a "necessary evil" applies to all its forms—necessary to enable production/operations to be sustained and evil because it reflects an organization's non-productive assets. In the "just-in-case" demand and supply environment of business operations, inventory levels are higher than those in a relatively stable and deterministic "just-in-time"

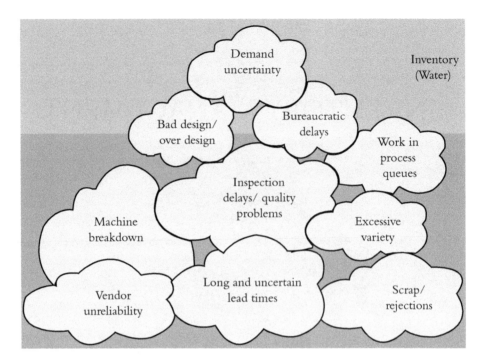

Figure 6.1 Problems Hidden by Inventory
Source: Adapted from Vrat 2014

environment. Inventories comprise of a significant part of the "working capital" of a company, and it is a terminological paradox that, from a resource management perspective, this "working capital" really does not work as it reflects non-productive forms of capital blocked.

2 Functions of Inventory

In any organization, inventory is needed to absorb the demand and supply variability. It functions like a shock-absorber in a mechanical system in order to decouple two sub-systems such as procurement and production or distribution and production sub-systems so that these can function, to an extent, independent of each other. Optimal inventory levels determine the right extent of the degree of decoupling inventories should provide. The larger the twin uncertainty of demand and supply, the greater the amount of inventory buffer needed to provide the right extent of decoupling. Inventories are also needed to get the economy of scale in the procurement function and are also sometimes used as a strategy to absorb demand fluctuations in aggregate production planning for time-varying demand. Quantity discounts, inflationary trends, and perishability aspects may also influence the inventory levels maintained by organizations.

However, inventories maintained by an organization reflect the symptoms of a problem and these often hide the causes that necessitate holding inventory as shown in Figure 6.1. Without removing the causes, reducing inventories will surface those problems. Therefore, addressing those causes will be a more rational way to inventory management rather than just reducing inventories, which may otherwise adversely affect production outputs, schedules, and customer satisfaction.

3 Inventory Problem Formulation

Typically, an inventory problem is to determine the right quantity of any material to meet an anticipated level of demand and place a timely procurement order to get the supplies in time. Thus, "how much to order" and "when to order" are two major decisions inventory managers have to make. These decisions are influenced by the conflicting nature of costs relevant to an inventory system. Naddor (1966) defines an inventory system as a system in which the following three types of costs are relevant:

a) Cost of carrying inventory (c_1)—the cost incurred in carrying a unit of inventory for a unit time period ($ per unit per year). This is also called "holding cost" and reflects the opportunity cost of holding a unit in stock for (say) one year. This cost reflects the cost of capital blocked in non-productive form and other cost components due to storage and warehousing, shrinkage, obsolescence, and perishability, etc.

b) Cost of shortage (c_2)—the cost imputed as opportunity cost of not meeting demand on time due to stock out. This is relatively more difficult to estimate due to a large number of intangible factors influencing the cost of shortage. But an approximate estimation is better than ignoring this cost all together from inventory planning process. Cost of shortage also depends upon the implications of such an experience—lost sales or customer backordering; as well as criticality of the item. It is expressed as $ / unit short or $ / unit short / unit time depending on whether it is a lost sales case or backlogging, respectively.

c) Ordering cost (c_3)—also known as replenishing cost; this cost incorporates all the administrative efforts, paperwork, progress chasing, and inspection costs of incoming materials received from the vendor. As an approximation, c_3 is assumed to be independent of the order quantity. Love (1979) has detailed the components of costs involved in estimation of cost parameters c_1, c_2, and c_3, which are invisible costs of managing materials.

3.1 Inventory Policy

An inventory policy is the standard operating procedure (SOP) employed to run an inventory system in repetitive purchase decisions. Depending upon the inventory policy selected, an appropriate inventory model needs to be developed to determine optimal values of inventory related decision variables. Generally, the following three polices are used in a majority of the situations:

a) **Continuous Review Policy:** Under this policy, the inventory status of an item is continuously monitored. When the stock status falls to a pre-determined level, called Reorder Point (R), a fixed order size (Q)—economically determined—is placed, and the process is repeated over an indefinite time horizon. Q and R are the two decision variables. Q is called Economic Order Quantity (EOQ) under optimal conditions, and the policy is also called (Q, R) policy.

b) **Periodic Review Policy:** Under this policy the inventory status of an item is periodically examined every T time period. Maximum stock level S and time period T are the two decision variables. If stock on hand at the time of review is x, then the order quantity will be Q = S − x. Obviously, this policy is quite sensitive to consumption in the immediate past review period, and Q is not optimally determined. One has to mandatorily order on every review even if the stock status is quite adequate. This policy is also called (S, T) policy.

c) **(s, S) Policy:** This is a refinement of the (S, T) policy for periodic review cases. The inventory status is periodically reviewed after every time period T. The maximum and minimum stock levels are S and s, respectively. If at the time of review stock on hand (x) is less than s, then a quantity Q = S − x is ordered like in (S, T) policy. However, if x ≥ s, then no order is placed, and the situation is reviewed at the next review period. For this reason, it is also called an "optional" replenishment policy because there is no mandatory replenishment at every review cycle. The three decision variables are s, S, and T. Figures 6.2A through 6.2C present these inventory policies graphically.

3.2 Inventory Models

Foundations of inventory theory were developed many years ago, and some of its benefits have been obtained over time. This chapter provides a renewed interest in the fundamental structure of inventory models. A model framework given by Naddor (1966) has been adopted in some of the models reviewed here.

Inventory models represent an inventory policy mathematically to optimize the value of decision variables in order to minimize the total system cost in operating an inventory policy. Three types of inventory models are type (1, 2); type (1, 3); and type (1, 2, 3) inventory systems if the optimization involves carrying and shortage costs, carrying and ordering costs, or all the three

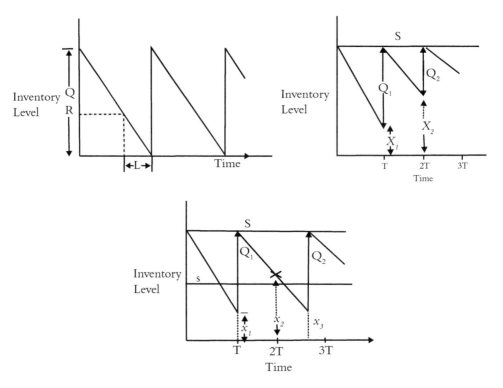

Figure 6.2 Examples of Inventory Policies: (clockwise from top left) Figure 6.2A (Q, R) Policy; Figure 6.2B (S, T) Policy; and, Figure 6.2C (s, S, T) Policy

Inventory Management

costs, respectively. Starting from a classical EOQ model for (Q, R) policy by Harris (1913), there exists a plethora of inventory models in inventory research, which ironically are itself inventory—a usable but idle resource—as very few companies, at least in less-developed economies, are really making use of these inventory models to optimize their inventory operations.

Literature on inventory models is so huge that it is practically impossible to cover, even synoptically, the majority of models in a chapter or even a book. However, a taxonomy of inventory models can help comprehend a fairly large spectrum of inventory models. Figure 6.3 presents a taxonomy of inventory models. Hollier and Vrat (1976) also proposed a classification of inventory systems on the lines of similar classification of queueing models.

Among the optimization approaches used to determine the optimal values of operating inventory decisions are the classical analytical models for optimization, which result in a closed form of optimal solution such as the classical Economic Order Quantity (EOQ) model, which employs classical conditions for optimality. This is the easiest way to determine optimal values of inventory decision but is limited to simple, often deterministic, situations. For discrete units, the method of finite differences may be possible. If there are resource constraints, such as space or

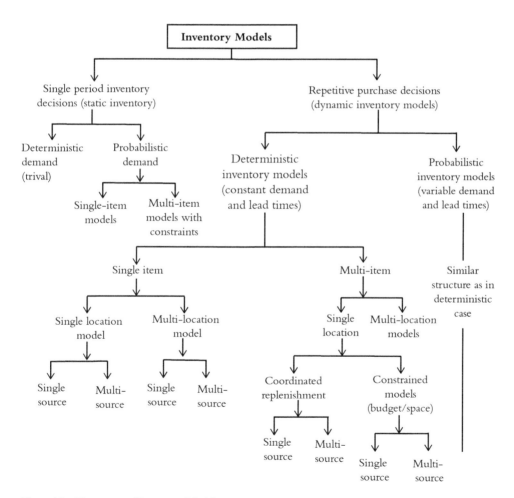

Figure 6.3 Taxonomy of Inventory Models

budget constraints, then Lagrange multipliers can be employed for a single constraint case, which may either lead to a closed form analytical solution or may be optimized through an iterative algorithm.

Probabilistic models are relatively more complex and difficult to optimize—at least analytically. But these are closer to real-life situations, at least in the globally competitive world of business in current times. Iterative search algorithms, numerical methods of optimization, have been employed for more complex models. Models for specific distribution pattern of demand and lead times conforming to standard distributions such as normal distribution and Poisson distribution are relatively easy to deal with when compared to more complex demand distribution patterns. However, simulation of inventory systems is possible for non-standard distribution pattern of demand and lead times as well as more complex system structure. For example, the optional replenishment policy (s, S, T) has been found to be the best amongst the three inventories polices identified in the previous section, but optimization of s, S, and T is quite complex for non-standard demand and lead time patterns and in such situations Monte Carlo simulation (Lewis 1970) may be the only option available for determining the optimal values of decision variables.

4 Inventory Research—A Historical Profile

Inventory research for developing scientific decision rules for optimization of inventory policy variables began a hundred years ago with the most classical model called the Economic Order Quantity (EOQ) model (Harris 1913). This is perhaps the simplest but most classic inventory model, which still holds its charm in current times because of the robustness of the model and insights it can provide to the inventory managers. Paradoxically, it is more popularly known as "Wilson's lot size" formula because of extensive application of this model by Wilson in British companies in the 1930s. It is however ironic that even this simple but robust model has not been widely used to rationalize inventory policies. Wilson's lot size formula has a large number of variants such as: models with planned backlogging, models with finite replenishment, and models with finite replenishment rate and planned backlogging.

Lost sales models that assume that demand not met instantaneously is lost are not many as compared to the planned backlogging models. However, with increasing customer impatience due to stiff market competition, the lost sales model may become prominent in times to come. Classical deterministic models are extended to multi-item inventory models with joint-replenishment or coordinated inventory policies and the models understandably demonstrate the benefits of coordinating procurement policy of multiple items procured from the same source. Fabrycky and Banks (1967) described models for procuring a single item from multiple sources as well as multiple items from multiple sources (SIMS and MIMS).

Resource constraint, such as available budget or space available for storage, has also been modeled with a view to determine optimal policies constrained by the budget or storage space, and the most classical method of Lagrange multipliers has been extensively used to develop decision rules for optimal policies in such situations. Another very popular class of inventory model incorporates the concept of "quantity discounts" known as inventory models with price-breaks—both all-unit discounts and incremental discounts. In the all-unit discount situation, all the units ordered are priced at the lower (discounted) price if the order quantity qualifies for the discount. In incremental discount case, only quantity exceeding the condition for discount is priced at the lower price and others at an undiscounted (higher) price. Obviously, the all-unit discount case has been more extensively used than incremental discount because of the inherently very strong motivation it has in the purchasing world.

Perishability of items by virtue of storage has also been extensively modeled by researchers with varying decaying characteristics. These have enormous application potential to reduce the wastage/expirations of items that remain in stock beyond their "shelf-life" period. This should motivate decision makers to impute a relatively higher cost of carrying inventory (c_1) depending upon the degree of perishability. This also results in a lowering of the quality even if still usable. However, such models are relatively few. Models that capture other "shrinking" features of stored items such as obsolescence, pilferage, evaporation loss during storage, and damage, which all impact on the material wastage due to inventory holding have not received as much attention of scholars as perishability has received. Gupta and Vrat (1986) initiated research on inventory models with stock-dependent consumption and selling rate, and in the past thirty years, this idea seems to have attracted enormous amounts of attention from researchers, with more than 300 research papers already published on this theme. However, not a single real-life case study employing these models has seemed to guide decision makers to reduce the indirect waste of materials induced by the unnecessary (stock induced) demand it generates just because we have the item on stock. This phenomenon has a direct linkage with waste of material if we look at waste as any "unnecessary input or undesirable output" from a system.

Multi-echelon inventory systems extend the concept of carrying inventory at multiple locations—hierarchical in structure but belonging to the same system. A large number of research papers have been contributed by a number of researchers with different types of system configurations—series, parallel, and arborescence (inverted tree) structures. The simplest models start with "base stock" inventory policy and develop more complex "push"- and "pull"-based inventory strategies. Hollier and Vrat (1976) have reviewed extensively the research on multi-echelon inventory control systems. Models employed range from analytical, iterative, heuristic, simulation, and system dynamics-based modeling approaches. Design of the system structure, which involves determining the number of echelons (levels), number of facilities at each echelon, and their location, constitute the strategic decisions, whereas types of inventory policy and optimal values of policy variables at each level are the operational decisions involved in a multi-echelon systems framework. A special context of multi-echelon inventory systems perceived for storage and repair of recoverable spares in hierarchically structured storage and maintenance workshops in a large repair-inventory system has also received much attention. METRIC (Sherbrook 1966) and MOD-METRIC (Muckstadt 1973) models are popular among repair-inventory systems. Such models are used in the context of transport corporations or in air force dealings with engines as rotable spares. Multi-echelon inventory systems can be considered to be forerunners of the concept of supply chain management (Shah 2009). The bullwhip effect or the "amplification effect" has been a much-researched concept in multi-echelon inventory systems and in supply chain contexts.

Another major research area in inventory management is in the field of lean-inventory or just-in-time (JIT) manufacturing. Due to global competition, remaining lean has become an operating necessity. A zero-inventory system is perhaps an ideal benchmark for managing an inventory system. This can be shown to be a special case of inventory models with finite replenishment rates when the supply rate matches the consumption rate. Mathematically, it can be shown that, when the rate of consumption matches the supply rate, a zero-inventory policy will be optimal at an infinite order quantity, but otherwise, supplies should be staggered to just meet the demand. Vrat (2011) has given an example of a perfect zero-inventory system, which can be nature's best benchmark in inventory management. Consumption of oxygen in the human body is the best fit of a zero-inventory system in which system operations are sustained without stock out and without any need to place an order for replenishment. A critical, fast-moving resource such as oxygen can sustain the human body forever without maintaining any inventory. Features such as staggered supplies, dedicated flow corridors, and a local source of supply with 100% dependability (which can match supply with demand just in time) are the characteristics of this example. This example can provide many insights to develop a JIT policy for organizations, and yet, it is a special case of a variant of the classical EOQ model.

Vendor Managed Inventory (VMI) outsources the inventory management function to the vendor. This includes the case where the item could be located near the point of consumption but belongs to the vendor till it is pulled out for consumption. Two major prerequisites for the success of VMI are: the trust between the vendor and the user and state-of-the-art technology including information and communication technology (ICT) at the ends of both vendor and user with real time information sharing. Trade-off between inventory and information is another topical area for inventory related research in current times.

At the macro level of the inventory control two very powerful concepts that have emerged are: a) Selective Inventory Management (SIM) and b) Aggregate Inventory Analysis (optimal policy/ exchange curve). Selective Inventory Management is perhaps the most used concept in business and industry and it is vital in order to have cost-effective inventory control. Before the application of models, an analyst must know where to use them as well as the degree of rigor required in inventory control. Three types of SIM being practiced are:

a) ABC analysis based on Pareto distribution of annual usage value;
b) VED—Vital (V), Essential (E), Desirable (D) analysis based on criticality of non-availability of stock;
c) FSN—Fast (F), Slow Moving (S), Non-Moving (N) analysis based on the frequency of demand.

ABC analysis is a very popular concept used in industry. Based on "Pareto's Law of Maldistribution", it divides the items into three categories A, B, and C depending upon their annual usage value—which is the monetary value of the annual material consumption of an item in stock. Annual usage value is the annual consumption in numbers multiplied by unit purchase price. Annual usage value may also be called annual dollar demand and is arranged in a descending order to plot the ABC curve as shown in Figure 6.4.

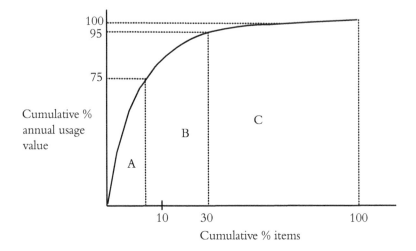

Figure 6.4   ABC Curve

Inventory Management

The ABC curve is the most universal manifestation of Pareto's Law. A-class items are those 10%–15% items which consume (say) 70%–75% of the annual material budget. B-class items are those (say) 20% items which consume (say) 20% of the annual material budget and C-class items are those (say) 70% items which consume only (say) 5% of the annual budget. It should be emphasized here that these figures of 10%, 75% etc. are only for the sake of illustration. In actual practice these figures may vary over a range. The governing principle is that A-class items are the significant few—while C-class items are the insignificant many. Obviously, for cost-effective inventory management, the major focus of scientific rigor should be on "A" class items; with a relaxed control for "B" class items. A vast majority of C-class items are not the candidates for scientific inventory control where the enlightened rule of thumb could be good enough. Thus an effective inventory management is possible by focusing only on 20% of the total items range and ignoring a vast majority (80%) for scientific scrutiny. This is also known as 20:80 rule meaning that 20% of items consume 80% of budget (significant few) and 80% consume only 20% budget (insignificant many). A-class items are the only items for which scientific inventory models described in the next section will be relevant. For B-class items, simple periodic inventory policy will do.

The second major development at the aggregate inventory level is the concept of "Optimal Policy Curve" by Starr and Miller (1975) and the "Exchange curve" concept by Peterson and Silver (1981) which look at the optimal trade-off or exchange between two conflicting aspects of inventory management—total inventory (TI) and total number of orders (TO). A rational policy will be one which minimizes TI for a given TO or minimizes TO for a given TI. Starr and Miller prove that for either of these formulations, the necessary conditions of optimality are:

$$(TI).(TO) = \text{constant } K = \frac{1}{2}\left(\sum_{i=1}^{i=n}\sqrt{D_i \cdot V_i}\right)^2 \text{ and } \frac{TI}{TO} = \frac{c_3}{i} = \text{constant if ratio } \left(\frac{c_3}{i}\right)$$

is essentially same for all items. Where c_3 = ordering cost; i = fraction of carrying cost; D_i = Demand of the ith item. V_i = Unit price of the ith item.

It can be seen that the relationship between TI and TO is a rectangular hyperbola. Figure 6.5 shows this curve and has been called an "Optimal Policy Curve" by Starr and Miller.

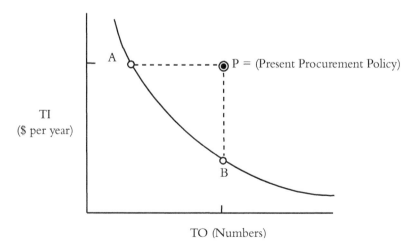

Figure 6.5 Optimal Policy Curve

If we know the annual usage value ($D_i \cdot V_i$) for the ith item, then constant K can be computed if there are total n items in the organization (i = 1 . . . n). With this, the optimal policy curve can be plotted. This serves as the optimal trade-off boundary between procurement efforts (TO) and the average investment in inventories (TI). If we are operating on any point on this curve, then it is assumed that the organization is able to have a rational trade-off between these conflicting aspects in scientific inventory management. This can now become a very useful "macro-level" tool to quickly detect the rationality of our current procurement policies. If we know the current number of procurement orders and current values of average inventory, then a point P on the Optimal Policy Curve represents the current practice.

If point P falls above the optimal policy curve as shown in Figure 6.5, then it reveals the opportunity to improve the inventory policies. Point P shows that current practice neither saves on procurement effort nor on the investment in inventories. The path of rationalization can be either moving from P to A suggesting the reduction in the procurement efforts (TO) with the same level of investment in inventories as at present. Alternatively, we may rationalize along the path PB, which can reduce the average investment in inventory with no additional procurement efforts (TO). Length "PB" can give the potential quantum of inventory reduction if an inventory rationalization project was initiated in the organization. Thus, this curve is a very ingenious way of determining the scope of an inventory reduction exercise, about the benefits that can come from such a step. Generally, companies may prefer path PB over PA. However, the Optimal Policy Curve only gives a macro view.

A major but relatively unrecognized approach to move from point P to B for individual items for determining rational inventory policy was proposed in 1965 by Murdoch, known by the name "Coverage Analysis" (Lewis 1970). This is a rough but ready approach to inventory rationalization without requiring the estimates of c_1, c_2, c_3 and without any elaborate mathematical treatment of the approach yet retaining the basic philosophy of EOQ. Coverage analysis is based on a randomly selected representative sample of items spanning over the entire item ranges based on annual usage value. This sample is grouped into 9–11 class intervals on the basis of increasing values of the annual usage. The class intervals are preferably chosen so that the square root of its mid-point is a whole number. Each item in the class interval is assumed to be represented by the mid-point as its annual usage value and the basic logic of coverage analysis is derived from the EOQ model.

A rational inventory policy is one in which the number of procurement orders are proportional to the square root of the mid-point of annual usage value in that class interval. The rational policy is arrived at by keeping the total number of orders the same as at present. If the total procurement orders in proposed policy are different, then a multiplier is found which will uniformly be applied on each class-interval to slash (if less than 1) or increase (if more than 1) to satisfy the constant procurement effort constraint. The items from the sample are grouped into the class intervals, and the numbers of orders for each group at present are found from the data collected from present practice. This approach along with Optimal Policy Curve could be the starting point of introducing scientific inventory control.

The concept of a coverage factor G as a ratio of Average inventory to Annual usage value is also defined by Lewis (1970). This can even be used as a quantifiable basis of grouping items into fast moving (G << 1), normal turnover stock (G < 1), and slow-moving stock (G > 2). G = 0 will be a non-stocked item (procured only after experiencing a demand) and G = ∞ will identify a dead stock. An appropriate coverage curve is plotted by plotting the number of orders on the x-axis and G on the y-axis. It may be seen from this that the coverage curve, in spirit, is similar to the optimal policy curve or the exchange curve. After the rationalized policy is proposed based on the sample analyzed, these then serve as a "decision-rule" for the entire item-range stocked in the organization even if they are not part of the random sample because the implicit assumption is that the sample represents the population. Hence, the representative nature of the sample for coverage analysis is critical for the success of the approach. Using the coverage factors, the possible inventory reduction through the process of rationalization can also be approximately estimated. Thus, a simple though approximate inventory management strategy could be to first detect, using optimal policy curve, if there is a need for inventory rationalization. If so, use the coverage analysis to find rational policy for each item to get the micro-level operating rule for each item. However, it must be accepted that the coverage analysis is a very rough but simple approach that can be attempted before any scientific model-based refinement is implemented which calls for estimation of cost parameter c_1, c_2, c_3 and other inventory related parameters. Section 5 attempts to give an overview of some select inventory models that can be used to further refine the inventory policy or gain better insights into scientific inventory management.

5 Some Select Inventory Models

In this section, we present some well-known inventory models for determining optimal inventory polices and gaining insights from them in order to better understand the implications of various parameters.

The most celebrated and classical model is the Economic Order Quantity (EOQ) model known as "Wilson's lot size" model. Erlenkotter (1989) has noted that this early classic model published in 1913 has been cited much later in book form (Whitin 1953). Though developed under highly simplifying assumptions, the EOQ model is still considered as a masterpiece among inventory models due to its robustness and usefulness.

5.1 The Classical EOQ Model

The EOQ model is a deterministic model with constant rate of demand and known lead times. In Naddor's classification, it is a type (1, 3) inventory system and is the optimal compromise between carrying costs and replenishment costs. Inventory status is perpetually reviewed, and decision variables are how much to buy (Q) and when to buy (R). The operating procedure is to "keep a continuous watch at inventory status—when the inventory level falls to predetermined level (R)—called reorder point, a fixed order size (Q) is ordered which is optimally determined EOQ". Here costs are assumed to be time invariant; replenishment is instantaneous, and no shortages are allowed. Unit price and the ordering cost are independent of the order size.

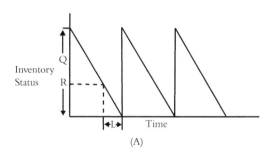
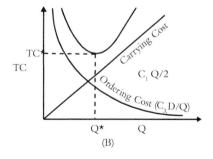

Figure 6.6 Economic Order Quantity (EOQ): Figure 6.6A—Inventory Graph for EOQ Policy; Figure 6.6B—Cost Behavior of EOQ Policy

Objective function is to minimize the total system cost TC comprising of carrying cost ($c_1 \cdot Q/2$) and ordering cost ($c_3 \cdot D/Q$). Purchase bill (V.D) is constant and hence not a function of decision variable Q. Thus, the classical model is:

$$\text{Find Q to minimize } TC = c_1 \cdot Q/2 + c_3 \cdot D/Q$$

Harris used a simple logic of optimality that under optimal Q, the two opposite costs are equal. Thus, $c_1 \cdot Q/2 = c_3 \cdot D/Q$ (This can also be obtained by optimality condition $\dfrac{dTC}{dQ} = 0$.)

This gives $Q^\star = \sqrt{\dfrac{2Dc_3}{c_1}}$ and $TC^\star = \sqrt{2Dc_1 \cdot c_3}$.

Sensitivity analysis of the EOQ model is very insightful and points out the robust nature of EOQ, for example, the EOQ may not be an optimal point but an optimal range that gives operational flexibility to the procurement manager for a marginal increase in total cost over its minimal cost. Q is assumed to be a continuous variable, but for operating convenience or for vendor's requirements, we may have to deviate from EOQ. Sensitivity analysis reveals how sensitive the total system cost is with respect to deviations from EOQ. If Q^1 is actual Q, T^1 as actual total cost with $Q^1 = bQ^\star$ where b is the sensitivity parameter; then it can be shown that $\dfrac{TC^1}{TC^\star} = \dfrac{1+b^2}{2b}$. If b = 1, then $TC^1 = TC^\star$.

Few important insights from the sensitivity analysis are: (a) with ±10% deviation from EOQ the total system cost increases only by about 0.5%; (b) relatively, the underestimation of EOQ is costlier than overestimation; (c) if $(TC^1/TC^\star) = p$; then $1 - 2bp + b^2 = 0$ and it gives Q_1 and Q_2 as the two values of Q for the same value of p as seen in Figure 6.7B. If p = 1.01, then optimal range of EOQ will be from $0.87Q^\star$ to $1.14Q^\star$, which provides adequate flexibility for the manager to choose the convenient order size. Similarly, if cost parameters are approximately estimated, then ±20% errors in parameters estimation (c_1 and c_3) will have the same effect as deviating Q by 10% provided these costs are consistently overestimated or underestimated.

5.2 Variants of the Classical EOQ Model

If we relax some assumptions of the EOQ model, the optimal order size will be some multiple of classical EOQ. If we permit planned backlogging with shortage cost c_2, then the inventory graph looks like as shown in Figure 6.8A in which S is the maximum stock level and B is the maximum backlog level.

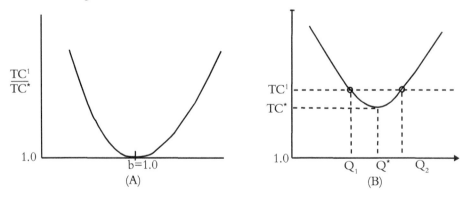

Figure 6.7 Sensitivity Analysis: Figure 6.7A Sensitivity Curve; Figure 6.7B Optimal Range of EOQ

The optimality conditions (Naddor 1966) gives:

$$Q^\star = \sqrt{\frac{2Dc_3}{c_1}} \cdots \sqrt{\frac{c_1+c_2}{c_2}}$$

$$S^\star = \sqrt{\frac{2Dc_3}{c_1}} \cdot \sqrt{\frac{c_2}{c_1+c_2}} \text{ and } B^\star = (Q^\star - S^\star);\ TC^\star = \sqrt{2Dc_3 \cdot c_1} \cdot \sqrt{\frac{c_2}{c_1+c_2}}$$

The major insight it provides is that if c_2 is finite, then planned backlogging leads to higher EOQ and reduced system cost. Hence, it is economically desirable.

If instantaneous replenishment (infinite rate of replenishment) is replaced with finite rate of replenishment with rate P (P > D) then the inventory graph looks like Figure 6.8B. The maximum stock level is S (S < Q).

This model gives optimal result as:

$$Q^\star = \sqrt{\frac{2Dc_3}{c_1\left(1 - D/P\right)}}$$

$$TC^\star = \sqrt{2Dc_1 \cdot c_3 \left(1 - D/P\right)}$$

Thus, staggered (finite rate) supplies improve the total system cost behavior. An interesting special case is when D = P, then $Q^\star = \infty$, $S^\star = 0$, and $TC^\star = 0$, which is a zero-inventory system

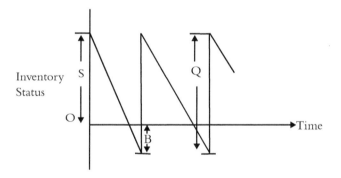

Figure 6.8A Inventory Graph for Planned Backlogging

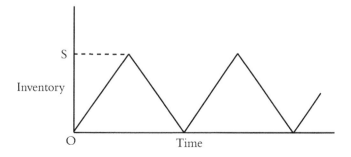

Figure 6.8B Inventory Graph for Finite Replenishment Rate

or JIT. Thus, the zero-inventory system is a classical EOQ model with staggered supplies with supply rate P = demand rate D. As stated earlier, the supply of oxygen in the human body is a perfect example of this.

5.2.1 A Generalized Type (1, 2, 3) System

In the generalized version of EOQ, all the three inventory related costs are relevant. Figure 6.8C depicts an inventory graph for it.

Naddor (1966) has shown that for optimality of type (1, 2, 3) inventory system:

$$TC^\star = \sqrt{2D\bar{c} \cdot c_3} \text{ and } Q^\star = TC^\star/\bar{c} \text{ ; } S^\star = TC^\star/c_1$$

Where $\bar{c} = \dfrac{1 - D/P}{\left(\dfrac{1}{c_1}\right) + \left(\dfrac{1}{c_2}\right)}$, which can be interpreted as adjusted value of carrying cost/unit

for staggered supplies and planned backlogging.

If $c_2 = \infty$, $P = \infty$, and the model reverts back to the classical EOQ.

5.2.2 Inventory Model with Lost Sales Case

This model assumes that demand not met immediately is lost because the customer will get it from elsewhere. This is emerging to be more relevant because of globally competitive markets with impatient customers. A lost sale will signify that profit margin is lost every time a shortage occurs. Naddor (1966) has shown that the optimal inventory policy under lost sales case is an "either or" policy. This means that either shortage should not permitted at all or the item should be a "non-stock" item. The conditions for this are: If $c_2 > \sqrt{2c_1c_3/D}$, then do not permit shortage, and if $c_2 " \sqrt{2c_1c_3/D}$, then do not stock the item at all. c_2 in this context can be perceived as the opportunity cost of procurement and storage of that item, and the profit margin should be more than this if the item needs to be sold. This concept can be very insightful for determining the lower bounds to the profit margin while fixing the selling price (Vrat 2014).

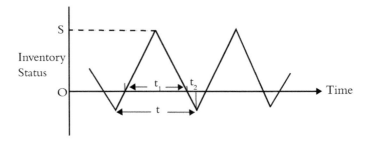

Figure 6.8C Generalized EOQ Inventory Graph

5.3 Multi-Item Single Source EOQ Model: Coordinated Replenishment

A very common situation encountered by materials managers is to determine the cost advantages of coordinating a joint replenishment of n items procured from the same source. Though obvious even intuitively, however, it has been proven (Naddor 1966) using deductive logic that the optimal policy is to have the same frequency of procurement for each item and to conceptualize a combined joint order of n items with quantity Q_i for the i item (i = 1 − n). If t is the time-interval between two orders and D_i is the demand for the ith item, c_{1i} is unit carrying cost for i^{th} item, and c_3 the ordering cost of placing a combined order, then the optimal time interval between two orders is given as:

$$t^\star = \sqrt{2c_3 / \left(\sum_{i=1}^{n} c_{1i} D_i\right)}$$

$$TC^\star = \sqrt{2c_3 \left(\sum_{i=1}^{n} c_{1i} D_i\right)}$$

From this, $Q_i^\star$ for i^{th} item $= D_i \cdot t^\star = D_i \sqrt{2c_3 / \sum_{i=1}^{n} c_{1i} D_i}$

If these items were procured independently, then using classical EOQ:

$$Q_i^* = \sqrt{\frac{2c_3 D_i}{c_{1i}}}; \quad TC_i^* = \sqrt{2c_3 D_i c_{1i}}$$

Total cost of individual ordering $= \sum Tc_i = \sum_{i=1}^{n} \sqrt{2c_3 D_i c_{1i}}$

Thus, the cost advantage of coordinating the procurement action is:

$$\Delta TC = \left[\sum_{i=1}^{n} \sqrt{2c_3 D_i c_{1i}} - \sqrt{2c_3 \sum_{i=1}^{n} c_{1i} \cdot D_i}\right]$$

If c_3 is marginally higher due to extra efforts in coordination, then Δ TC may reduce a bit and can be computed from above. It may be seen that the benefits can be quite substantial for coordinating the joint replenishment action.

5.4 A Simple Model for Periodic Review Policy

For B-class items, a simpler policy may be used. By prescribing the periodicity of review time interval as t_p, the decision variable is S, the maximum stock level. This then becomes type (1, 2) inventory system.

Figure 6.9 depicts such a simplified (S, t_p) inventory policy. If t_p is prescribed, order size Q is also prescribed as (D · t_p). The only decision variable is S, the optimal value of which is obtained

as $S^\star = D \cdot t_p \cdot \left(\dfrac{c_2}{c_1 + c_2}\right)$ and $TC^\star = \dfrac{1}{2} D \cdot t_p \left(\dfrac{C_1 \cdot C_2}{C_1 + C_2}\right)$

We could have prescribed S at S_p and optimize t, but it is more practical to know how frequently to review stock status than prescribing S.

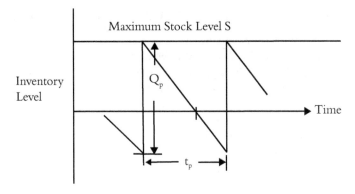

Figure 6.9 Periodic Review (S, t$_p$ policy)

5.5 *Inventory Models with Quantity Discounts*

As mentioned earlier in Section 5.4, a very practical situation encountered by the procurement manager is a quantity discount offered by a supplier to lure the customer to place larger order sizes. This is done by offering to lower the unit purchase price if order size is more than or equal to a threshold value prescribed. Price-breaks may be one or more and can be either "all-unit discount" or "incremental discount". In all units discounted, the reduced unit purchase price is applicable to all units purchased, whereas in the incremental discount case only the incremental order quantities beyond the threshold values will be offered at a lower price. Obviously, the "all-unit discounts" case has a higher motivation power for the buyer to increase the order size in order to avail himself of the discount on units purchased. Since the annual purchase bill will no longer be constant if order size influences it, the total system cost should include the total purchase cost—the visible cost of buying materials in addition to the invisible costs of carrying and replenishing inventories in the system. A manager who is driven by visible cost reduction alone may like to avail the opportunity of quantity discounts, but a higher order size will increase the cost of carrying inventory though it may decrease the ordering frequency for a given annual demand.

If a systems view is taken, the optimal decision could be even to reject the offer of discount or go for just the minimum order size which qualifies for the reduced unit purchase price. However, there is no single rule which supports the "accept or reject" the offer in all situations. The only generalized rule could be "it depends". Hence, based on specific situational parameters, the preferred policy has to be examined on case-by-case basis. A simple solution procedure can be prescribed to evaluate the total system cost in each case. For the generalized multiple-price break situation with an "all-unit discount", the following steps will lead to the optimal choice depending upon situational parameters—demand, unit carrying and ordering costs, number of price-breaks, discounts offered, and the threshold quantity condition imposed to avail the discount offer.

If n price-breaks exist (n = 1 or more), then the optimal choice has to be from (2n + 1) alternative options. Depending upon the situational parameters, any one of these (2n + 1) options could emerge as the optimal choice. Therefore, managers must avoid fixed responses to always accept or always reject the discount offer. The total cost must also include the purchase bill. The steps involved in reaching an optimal decision are:

a) Find EOQ with the smallest unit purchase price offer and check if it is valid (quantity is equal to or more than the condition imposed for the lowest unit price). If yes, stop as this is the preferred economic order quantity. If no, go to step 2.
b) Compute EOQ with the next highest unit purchase price and check if it is valid. If not, continue this process until the largest valid EOQ is found.
c) Compare the total system cost of this largest valid EOQ (inclusive of total purchase cost) and compare it with the total cost for all price-break points higher than this EOQ. The lowest cost option is the optimal choice.

5.6 Probabilistic Inventory Models with Demand and/or Supply Variability

The inventory models described above were deterministic models that assumed that the demand and lead time are always known and are kept constant. In reality, this may not be the case. Global markets and supply sources further increase the variability of the demand and supply environment. Intuitively, because of the "just-in-case" like condition, an additional amount of inventory will have to be in stock to absorb the twin variabilities. However, we must capture these variabilities and factor them in the determination of Reorder Point. In doing so, a concept of "safety stock" or "buffer stock" is used to optimally absorb these demands and lead time fluctuations. In a way, the buffer stock is the price one pays for planning under variability of demand and supply.

Let demand be randomly distributed with the expected value $\bar{D}$ and standard deviation of demand as σ_D. Similarly, let lead time L be also random with $\bar{L}$ as the expected lead time and the standard deviation of lead time as σ_L. Then, the twin variabilities can be factored into developing a distribution of lead time demand shown in Figure 6.10 for a normally distributed lead time demand. The demand during the lead time itself will be a random variable (x) with expected demand during the lead time as M and standard deviation σ. If R is the reorder point, then P (s) as the probability of shortage during a lead time is the shaded area to the right of the curve beyond R.

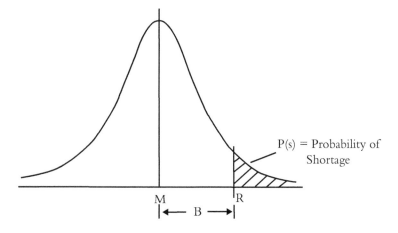

Figure 6.10 Lead Time Demand Distribution

R = Reorder Point = M + B (Expected demand during lead time + buffer stock for a Probability of shortage P(s))

Using moment generating functions of probability distributions (Vrat 2014):

$$M = \overline{D} \cdot \overline{L} \cdot \sigma = \sqrt{\overline{L} \cdot \sigma_D^2 + \overline{D}^2 \cdot \sigma_L^2}$$

If $K = \dfrac{X - M}{\sigma}$, then the reorder point R = M + K.σ.

Thus, buffer stock $B = K \cdot \sigma = K \cdot \sqrt{\overline{L} \cdot \sigma_D^2 + \overline{D}^2 \cdot \sigma_L^2}$

For normal distribution of lead time demand, the value of K can be obtained from standard normal tables corresponding to probability of shortage P(s) as the area to the right of curve at R and the Reorder Point $R = \overline{D} \cdot \overline{L} + K \cdot \sqrt{\overline{L} \cdot \sigma_D^2 + \overline{D}^2 \cdot \sigma_L^2}$.

This captures the twin variability to develop buffer stock policy for a prescribed service level (1 − P(S)) derived from the ABC-VED matrix. An ABC-VED matrix groups inventory items in a two-way classification based on ABC as well as VED category. A vital class A item will be (A, V), and a desirable class C item will be in the (C, D) category, and so on. This matrix (Vrat 2014) gives the service level desired. Tables are available for normal and Poisson distributions of lead time demand. However, for any non-standard distribution of lead time demand, either more generalized but well-tabulated distributions, such as a Pearson-type incomplete Gamma distribution, has to be assumed, or managers have to use normal approximation for lead time demand to be ≥ 10 and Laplace Distribution if it less than 10 as suggested by Peterson and Silver (1981).

The relationship between the buffer stock (B) and service level (1 - P(s)) is shown in Figure 6.11. Service levels at 50% can be obtained for normally distributed lead time demand even without any buffer stock. However, above a 90% service level, buffer size increases significantly for even a small increase in service level. Managers must avoid the 99% syndrome by aiming at 99% service level for all items because that may not be required but will increase inventories very significantly.

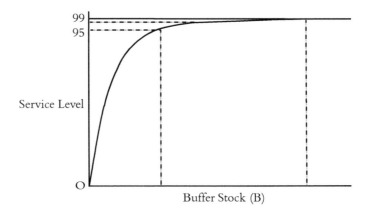

Figure 6.11 Service Level versus Buffer Stock Required

Some other interesting insights on the impact of variability on inventory are:

If $\sigma_D = 0$, $\sigma_L = 0$, and B = 0, then R = D.L, which is the deterministic case. If $\sigma_D = \sigma_D$ and $\sigma_L = 0$, then $B = K \cdot \sigma_D \sqrt{L}$; if $\sigma_D = 0$ and $\sigma_L = \sigma_L$, then $B = K.D.\sigma_L$

This reveals that in the case of probabilistic demand, the actual value of lead time, even if constant, matters in determining the buffer size. If lead time can be reduced from 4 weeks to 1 week, 50% buffer stock can be reduced for the same service level. However, for even deterministic demand, the lead time variability will directly influence the buffer size. As a result, a dependable reliable vendor is one of the greatest assets in reducing inventories. This leads to lead time reduction. Reduction of demand and lead time variability should be long-term strategies for inventory reduction.

5.6.1 Inventory Models for Slow-Moving Items

Models described from Sections 5.1 to 5.6 can only be used for fast-moving items that exhibit a regular consumption pattern. For expensive but slow-moving materials, these models are not applicable. For slow-moving items, the demand may occur only occasionally—say once or twice in a year. For less expensive items, it is a trivial issue. In contrast, even one extra item in stock is not desirable for very expensive items. Slow-moving items are encountered mainly for maintenance spares or special purpose materials required for project implementation: Mitchell as quoted in Lewis (1970) has proposed the following strategies in dealing with slow-moving, expensive spares:

A. If a spare is required on a particular date only such as for preventive replacement at scheduled maintenance date, do not stock it but place an order by offsetting the lead time and in case of variable lead time, offset further by safety lead time for a prescribed probability of delay beyond the due date required.
B. If the impending requirement comes in the form of a warning that is adequate for mounting an expedited procurement action, then do not stock but get the procurement process expedited the moment a warning signal is received. This is very useful on condition-based maintenance of equipment. Thus reduction of lead time should be the main focus of inventory reduction strategy for expensive but slow-moving materials.
C. If the requirement is sudden, or the warning time is less than the lead time, then only we need to stock the item. Optimal number of spares can be worked out numerically with 0, 1, or 2 spares only because of the slow-moving nature of spares, the optimal value will be mainly limited to 1 or 2. (S −1, S) policy has been found to be very useful in ordering one when one is consumed in such cases.

If a slow-moving but expensive spare is required by a number of project sites, then keeping a centralized pool of spares at a common location can cut down costs and risks. This risk pooling calls for the standardization of equipment and very efficient operations of central spare facility. Collaborative maintenance of central spare pool can reduce cost of carrying spares at each partner location in case the locations of demand point do not belong to the same company (Vrat 2014).

Sometimes an organization has to plan for stocking adequate number of expensive spares for the entire life of the equipment, or the project duration, because replenishment is not possible economically during the planning period. It is also called a "static inventory problem" (Starr and Miller 1975). Peterson and Silver (1981) define it as planning for a single relevant period. Models exist for consumable items such as spares as well as stocking for sales during short selling periods and also for multiple items with budget or space constraints.

For a single-item case for stocking for consumption such as spares, the optimality condition is that the cumulative probability of demand for the spare must first equal or exceed the service level given by ratios $\left(\dfrac{C_s - C}{c_s - g}\right)$ where C is the cost of the spare, c_s is the opportunity cost of shortage, and g is the salvage value of a surplus spare. Salvage value is the money received by disposing a surplus. If there is no salvage value, g = 0. If p (r) is the probability of exactly r spares required during planning period, then cumulative probability of up to n spares demanded is $\sum_{r=0}^{n} p(r)$, which can be estimated or can be obtained by Poisson distribution for given mean m obtained by m = (T/$_{MTBF}$), where T = planning period and MTBF = Mean Time Between Failures. Similar expressions can be obtained for stocking items for sale during short selling seasons as well as multiple items under budget constraints.

6 Inventory Related Issues and Their Implications on Practicing Managers

Although there is an abundance of mathematical models on inventory management in the literature, the general exposure of these models to the practicing managers is quite low. Even the rudimentary models such as EOQ and ABC-VED-FSN analyses are not very widely known to managers due to the lack of focus on training on scientific inventory management. The role conflict among various functional managers such as finance and production on what should be optimal inventory is also a cause for concern. Another major concern is the non-availability of inventory-related cost parameters and other data such as demand and lead time distributions. A systems perspective seems to be another missing link to look at the inventory management from a total systems point of view with visible and invisible costs included. Diagnostic analyses of low inventory turnover ratios need to be conducted to find out the root causes of low turnover ratio such as excessive variety, non-standardization, long and uncertain lead times, variation in units of procurement and units of issues from stores, and a lack of coordination of procurement of multiple items from one or multiple vendors. Inventory planning under budget, space, or capacity constraints is very real, but because of the complex modeling required, a practicing manager may not feel enthusiastic to use it.

Variability of demand, supply, quality, and costs are spots of uncertainty in smooth and lean inventory planning. Managers need to take long-term strategic initiatives to reduce these uncertainties. The investment of efforts in eliminating or reducing variability will have substantive long-term impact on inventory management. If designers could cut down variety (say 4 parts into 1), then by this act alone, a 50% inventory reduction can be attained (under certain situations).

Terminological mix-ups can lead to perceptual errors on the part of different functional managers to understand real functions of inventory. Financial management treats inventory as a "current asset", which at least psychologically calls it as an asset, whereas in reality (from a resources optimization point of view) it is hardly an asset. Similarly, a substantial part of working capital consists of inventory—which hardly "works" (as an idle resource). Such perceptual diversities may come in the way of all practicing managers looking at inventories from the same lenses and not through differently colored glasses. This calls for a major sensitization for all functional managers to understand inventory as a "necessary evil" and to aim to have no more than the optimal levels by looking at total system costs—both visible and hidden.

Non-availability of cost data in the form it is required for using inventory models is a major challenge in the use of scientific inventory models that require "invisible" cost data based on opportunity costs such as carrying cost, shortage cost, and replenishing cost. These are not easily available and may provide a ready excuse for not using these models. Volatility of the supply environment further makes it difficult because inventory models with fuzzy cost data are not common in the literature. However, macro-level approaches such as optimal policy curve concept—to detect the need for rationalizing procurement policies and coverage analysis to carry out micro-level rationalization for each item—can be a very good starting point that does not require any of the invisible costs data at all. Unfortunately, these concepts have not been largely published in inventory literature as the untapped potential they have to get started—even if these are approximate models. However, approximating estimates of shortage costs is better than ignoring these notions altogether.

In developing economies such as India, scientific approaches to materials management in general and inventory management in particular are not common. This is reflected by low inventory turnover ratios. Due to time-consuming bureaucratic procurement processes in conventionally managed companies, this problem is further compounded. Recent e-procurement and e-tendering initiatives are mitigating the problem of excessive inventory in public enterprises as compared to their private counterparts.

In business schools—at least in Indian scenarios—subjects like Production and Operations Management and Materials Management are not highly sought-after electives. Due to an emphasis on quantitative methods, learners may not be enthusiastic for them. As a result, there is greater "charm" in going for courses in strategy such as corporate social responsibility, marketing, and finance (though major finances are consumed in materials). Until business schools realize the importance of materials management (with inventory turnover ratio as a barometer of its performance), the practice of scientific inventory management will not be quite common. However, by developing appropriate computer based pedagogy—where most of the mathematics is done by computers—the lack of enthusiasm on the part of learners can be mitigated. Due to lack of holistic perspective in organizations, a potential inter-departmental conflict between marketing and purchase functions may arise due to a misconceived notion that the former earns revenue for the company while the latter consumes it.

There is lack of standards/norms of optimal range of inventory turnover ratios for various industries. Due to this lack, benchmarking the inventory management performance of a company in an industrial sector is difficult. Benchmarking with the role models in the industry can be a very effective way to improve performance on the inventory management front. This can be a potential area for further research.

7 Role of Professional Societies in Promoting Scientific Inventory Management

Professional societies such as the American Production and Inventory Control Society (APICS), the Production and Operations Management Society (POMS), and the International Society for Inventory Research (ISIR) have played important roles in promoting inventory research through their publications, conferences, and symposia. However, there is a need to focus on application-oriented research—something that is evidently not plentiful in the published literature. The research papers being published in the journals/conferences are so heavy in mathematical modeling that it may put off a manager to be interested in using them. That is why most research papers on inventory are themselves inventory—a usable but idle resource. The professional societies have a role in encouraging more case studies and application-oriented research that may encourage others to use scientific approaches to inventory management.

8 Some Suggested Areas for Future Research Efforts

There are several potential research areas for future research:

- Linking stock-dependent consumption phenomenon with waste management has enormous promise but has remained unaddressed. Vrat (2014) defines waste as "unnecessary input or undesired output from a system". Thus, stock-induced consumption becomes waste. Though models of inventory in this area are now plentiful, its application to real-life problems and linking it to waste is a promising research area.
- Inventory models with trade-off between inventory and information have potential promise in reducing inventory by leveraging the ICT (Information and Communication Technology). Studies to estimate the quantum of inventory reduction due to faster, better, and more reliable information can be very insightful.

Most inventory models have remained confined to the single-criterion optimization domain. Multiple criteria optimization with information vagueness may capture the ground reality much better particularly due to increasing globalization of business leading to multiple, often conflicting objectives under turbulent supply environments. Current inventory literature is inadequate to model such situations. VUCA (Volatile, Uncertain, Complex, and Ambiguous) demand and supply environment needs to be modeled from an inventory management perspective.

Role conflict among functional managers will inevitably require modeling for multiple, often conflicting, objectives. There is a need for researchers to develop models that capture role conflict and information vagueness simultaneously. Fuzzy goal programming-like approaches can be possibly explored to develop a decision support system that is more relevant in the current business environment.

Aggregate inventory analysis and its linkage with rationalization methodology such as coverage analysis have not been pursued by researchers even though these are very insightful at the macro level. Except for a few models, there is hardly any follow-up of research in the areas of optimal policy curve, coverage analysis particularly under demand and supply variability, supply disruptions, shortages, and perishable items. Aggregate inventory analysis under VUCA environment is a potential area for research.

More research on a mixture of partial backlogging and lost sales is needed. This includes research into cost parameter estimations such as shortage—both backlogging and lost sales—and parameters estimation for stock-dependent consumption. Research into perishability may help in efficient estimation of these parameters, which in turn can promote the use of scientific inventory models.

Multi-item, multi-echelon, coordinated replenishment policies under budget and/or space constraints will take inventory modeling to a more realistic domain. The development of software for user-friendly decision support systems with such models will take inventory management practice to the next orbit. Currently, there is very little evidence of managers practicing use of such models to improve their performance on inventory management.

There is a need to focus research on management of dead stock (surplus—obsolete—scrap) on much more scientific lines. Reverse supply chain management has been a good initiative and needs to be enriched. It is possible that "push" strategy may be more optimal than "pull" in management of dead stock.

There needs to be increased research into cost implications of role conflicts among functional managers. This could take the form of sensitivity analysis with respect to cost and demand dynamics, cost-benefit analysis of standardization, and a variety of reduction programs that can all be useful application-oriented research areas in inventory research.

Expensive, slow-moving materials have not been studied from an inventory modeling perspective. The trade-off between inventory provisioning and expedited lead times can be an insightful research area. Similarly, rotable spares, which constitute a significant percentage of stock value, have not been extensively studied (Vrat 2014). Rotable spares are non-consumable spares such as aircraft engines and are high-valued spares that keep on circulating through the closed loop system of spare store, maintenance facility, and in operational use fitted in the aircraft. Optimal initial provisioning of rotable spares is a vital area in the civil and military aviation industry.

9 Concluding Remarks

This chapter presented comprehensive coverage of inventory management as a very prominent area of study in Production and Operations Management (POM). Materials constitute the biggest single element of cost in POM, and an inventory turnover ratio is a barometer of performance for managing materials. The best-managed companies may have an inventory turnover ratio twice as much as those that are poorly managed. Thus, for global competitiveness, it is vital that inventories are managed well. The cost parameters relevant in inventory management and ways to estimate them was outlined. Formulating an inventory problem and models to solve an inventory problem are depicted through a taxonomy and a brief synoptic profile of the history of inventory research presented starting with the classical EOQ model developed by Harris (1913). Selective inventory control through ABC-VED-FSN analyses contributes to effective inventory management through selection of appropriate inventory models. Aggregate inventory analysis through optimal policy curve enables a quick detection of rationality or otherwise of the current inventory policy being followed in a company. Coverage analysis is a simple, though approximate, way to get started in the absence of cost estimates. A quick overview of various inventory models was presented to get a scientific insight into inventory modeling. Inventory models with variable demand and lead time need to capture the twin variabilities to translate them into buffer (safety) stock required for a stated level of service. It is advised to avoid the 99% syndrome while maintaining buffer stock. The role of professional societies such as POMS, APICS, ISIR, etc. for promoting inventory research is mentioned along with concerns and challenges in inventory management faced by practicing managers. Some areas in inventory research are outlined to enable scholars to pursue further research.

Acknowledgements

The author wishes to record his appreciation to Mr. Jatin Sharma and Mr. Lalit Narayan Lal of The NorthCap University, Gurugram, Haryana, India, for their assistance in preparation of the chapter.

References and Bibliography

Buchan, J. and E. Koenigsberg (1966) *Scientific Inventory Management*. Prentice Hall of India Ltd, New Delhi.

Burgin, T.A. and A.R. Wild (1967) "Stock Control: Experience and Usable Theory", *Operational Research Quarterly*, **18**(1): 35–45.

Chitale, A.K. and R.C. Gupta (2006) *Materials Management: Texts and Cases*. Prentice Hall International, New Delhi.

Erlenkotter, D. (1989) "Note—An Early classic Misplaced: Ford W. Harris's Economic Order Quantity Model of 1915", *Management Science*, **35**(7): 898–900.

Fabrycky, W.J. and J. Banks (1967) *Procurement and Inventory Systems: Theory and Analysis*. Reinhold Publishing Corporate, New York.

Gupta, R. and P. Vrat (1986) "Inventory Model for Stock Dependent Consumption Rate", *Opsearch*, **23**: 19–24.

Harris, F.W. (1913) "How Many Parts to Make At Once", *Factory: The Magazine of Management*, **10**(2): 135–136, 152.

Hollier, R.H. and P. Vrat (1976) "A Review of Multi-Echelon Inventory Control Research and Applications", Technical Report, Department of Engineering Production, University of Birmingham, UK.

Lewis, C.D. (1970) *Scientific Inventory Control*. Butterworths, London.

Love, S. (1979) *Inventory Control*. McGraw Hill Book Co., New York.

Muckstadt, J.A. (1973) "MOD-METRIC: A Multi-Item Multi-Echelon Multi-Indenture Inventory System", *Management Science*, **20**(4): 472–481.

Naddor, E. (1966) *Inventory Systems*. Wiley, New York.

Padmanabhan, G. and P. Vrat (1995) "EOQ Models for Perishables under Stock Dependent Selling Rate", *European Journal of Operational Research*, **86**(2): 281–292.

Peterson, R. and E.A. Silver (1981) *Decision Systems for Inventory Management and Production Planning*. Wiley, New York.

Shah, J. (2009) *Supply Chain Management*. Pearson Education, New Delhi.

Sherbrook, C.C. (1966) "METRIC: A Multi-Echelon Technique for Recoverable Items Control", *Operations Research*, **16**(1): 122–141.

Starr, M.K. and D.W. Miller (1975) *Inventory Control: Theory and Practice*. Prentice Hall of India, New Delhi.

Vrat, P. (2011) "Inventory Models and Human Body Food Supply Chain: Some Managerial Insights", *Industrial Engineering Journal*, **2**(27): 8–16.

Vrat, P. (2014) "Materials Management: An Integrated System Approach", *Springer Texts in Business and Economics*. Springer, India.

Whitin, T.M. (1953) *The Theory of Inventory Management*. Princeton University Press, Princeton, NJ.

7
QUALITY MANAGEMENT

Peter W. Robertson, Martin K. Starr, and Sushil K. Gupta

1 Introduction

Quality is typically defined as the assessment made by customers or end-users of a product or service as to how well said product or service matches and indeed exceeds their expectations (Gitlow et al. 1989). In turn, customers' quality expectations are usually centered on various product or service attributes such as fitness-for-purpose, reliability, durability, ease of use, lack of defects, and meeting in-service performance criteria.

Quality, then, can be considered as one of the key buying factors that potential customers assess before making a purchase decision. As such, good quality is a key value determinate and thus an important building block of competitive advantage (Reed et al. 2000).

In order to reliably deliver such quality attributes to customers, organizations are able to apply (if they so choose) quality practices, methodologies, and tools that have been developed over past decades. This quality organizing system and its application is referred to as Quality Management (QM) or (when applied holistically) as Total Quality Management (TQM). The acronym TQM implies a total customer focus (internal and external customers), a continuous process improvement mindset, and total involvement of everyone along the supply chain.

Therefore, if applied properly, quality management can ensure that an organization's products and services consistently achieve the attribute levels sought by customers (Finch 2006). Additionally, it needs to be stressed that customers perceive the quality of goods and services as a package of quality attributes whereby a failure on any single attribute can and often does represent for the customer, a quality failure overall. A further objective of QM is to reduce costs, creating an outcome that also builds customer satisfaction if such cost reductions, in total or in part, are passed along to the customer.

Quality management as a process usually includes quality planning (including design), quality control, quality assurance, and quality improvement. These processes are components of the International Standards Organization of Geneva (ISO) 9001 2015 quality management system as shown in Table 7.2. The ISO is an organization that has promulgated a family of quality management systems standards.

The issue of "proper" application of QM is important because not all attempts at QM have been successful (Samson and Terziovski 1999). This leads to questions that the management of the QM process utilizes (i.e., What are the critical QM success factors (enablers) that need to be carefully managed in order to assure actual business improvement?). Many authors (Reed et al.

2000) suggest these factors are (i) demonstrated, long-term commitment of top management; (ii) a strong customer focus; (iii) relevant training in QM concepts and techniques; (iv) cross-functional teamwork; and (v) a positive and supportive culture.

2 The Context of QM Successes and Failures

Especially in the industrialized world, the list of companies that have applied QM to their operations is substantial (Garvin 1991; Evans and Lindsay 1995). Many big-name companies that were struggling competitively and economically before their application of QM experienced significant turnaround in their market position and economic performance afterwards. Examples include: AlliedSignal, Motorola, General Electric, Xerox, Harley-Davidson, Porsche, Toyota, and Ford (Samson and Terziovski 1999).

At the same time, however, many companies that attempted QM applications later failed to achieve significant business improvement from their efforts. Such failures led to a degree of disillusionment with the process and gave many such companies an "excuse" to desist with their QM efforts. What then is the reason for this apparent QM paradox? Samson and Terziovski (1999) put such failures down to poor implementation and perhaps a lack of focus on important QM "soft" issues such as leadership commitment, customer focus, and teamwork alongside a positive and supportive culture. Reed et al. (2000) suggest that such "soft" factors are multidirectional (i.e., a gestalt). So, unless *all* factors are addressed with rigor, the likelihood of failure is high.

Readers are encouraged to peruse the following works in order to understand in more detail, the factors impacting QM initiative successes and failures:

(i) Samson and Terziovski (1999) provide a description of a study of 1,200 manufacturing companies in order to determine the relationship between use of TQM practices and firm performance. The authors found a significant positive relationship between the TQM elements of leadership, people management and customer focus, and firm performance. They also found "a good deal of variance" in their firm performance data that was not explained by the TQM elements alone.

(ii) Kaynak (2003) provides (a) a summary of work by previous authors on the relationship between TQM and firm performance, (b) a theoretical model of the relationship between TQM and performance measures, and (c) survey-based testing of several hypotheses set from the theoretical model. Good support for the proposed model was found confirming the positive relationship between the use of TQM and firm performance.

(iii) Schonberger's (2007) article is a must read for those wishing to understand the history, components, and the challenges that the operations management/TQM approach faces. This total system is often referred to as Japanese Production Management (JPM).

(iv) Ahire and Dreyfus (2000) provide a study of the quality practices in 418 manufacturing firms, establishing a positive relationship between design management and process management with both internal quality outcomes (scrap, rework, defects) and external quality outcomes (complaints, warranty claims, and market share).

(v) Su, Linderman, Schroeder, and Van de Ven (2014) provide a study of organizations that initially established high levels of quality performance only to lose it over time. They then examined the challenge of how to sustain a quality advantage. Using case studies, three main capabilities were identified in order to achieve sustainability of a quality edge. These examples include heightened meta-learning (reflection on, and enquiry into the process of learning itself, i.e., learning how to better learn), the ability to sense weak signals, and resilience to quality disruptions.

The other important contextual factor is that of time. The passage of time sees changing customer needs and expectations as well as increasing competitive intensity. Added to this are the need for statutory compliance, risk management, managing the complexity of global supply chains, community relations, R&D, new product/service launches, employee relations, and the need to build employee capability. Likewise, these latter issues are changing with time as well. So the resultant pressures on organizational leadership and their subordinates are significant. Therefore, companies need to find cleverly simple but effective approaches, methodologies, and tools in order to help this situation. Such approaches for QM are explored below.

3 A Compelling Case for Achieving Quality Management Excellence in POM

There are two main imperatives for the achievement of QM excellence in the practice of POM. First, QM should be an integral part of the POM management system (see Table 7.1) in order to ensure an enhanced business operational result. Second, QM can be used on the individual components of the POM management system itself, in order to continuously improve each component as well as the POM management system's overall effectiveness.

Taking these two imperatives in turn:

(i) As quality is one of the three key customer value components (the other two being cost and timeliness (Finch 2006)), it follows that the customer need for quality in products and services changes the POM priority from producing just for the sake of it, to producing goods and services that customers actually *want* to buy. To emphasize the point, a producer may make the cheapest product or service in the marketplace that can be reliably delivered with a very short leadtime, but if the quality is poor, then, while some customers may buy it once, over time sales of the low-quality item will dry up.

(ii) On the basis that QM has a legitimate position within the POM management system to help that system reliably deliver customer value, then, it also follows that the QM continuous improvement approach can and ought be applied to the processes within that POM system (Table 7.1), i.e., a QM approach to all POM processes. This is important because, as customers of the POM methodologies and processes, organizational leaders and their subordinates value processes that are efficient, fit-for-purpose, easy to apply and use, are reliable, non-complex, and timely in their application.

Table 7.1 POM Management System and Influence on Value and Business Outcomes

POM Management System	Value Components	Business Success Factors
Resource planning		Vision, strategy
Inventory management	Quality	
Capacity management		Customer value
Facilities management →	Cost →	
Workforce management		Processes and capabilities
Quality management	Timeliness	
Supply-chain management		Profit
Operating methodology		

Source: Adapted from Finch (2006)

4   A Brief History of Quality Management

Quality issues have existed for centuries. Examples can be found in several ancient documents such as the Code of Hammurabi from 1754 BCE wherein the quality requirements of house building are described along with the punitive consequences of poor workmanship (Gitlow et al. 1989). From around 1450 BCE, the Aztecs and ancient Egyptians used string measures to check the squareness of stone blocks. Craft guilds started their development during the thirteenth century CE and began to both set standards and utilize inspectors to check performance against those same standards (Gitlow et al. 1989).

The nineteenth century saw the beginning of our modern industrial system (Gitlow et al. 1989) with Fredrick W. Taylor developing his theory of scientific management. Within the next century, people such as Bill Gosset, Ron Fisher, Henry Ford, George Edwards, Walter Shewhart, W. Edwards Deming, Armand Feigenbaum, Joseph Juran, Kaoru Ishikawa, Taiichi Ohno, and Phil Crosby made significant contributions to the strategy, practice, and tools used in QM. A brief description of their major QM type contributions follows in chronological order in the next section.

4.1   Key Figures

Between 1890 and 1901, Frederick Winslow Taylor (1856–1915) developed an approach to operations management that became known as "Scientific Management". This approach specified that *the* best way of performing any task could be defined and set as a "standardized work method" for all to follow. Taylor described such efficiency techniques in his book *The Principles of Scientific Management* (1911). As his technique called for enforced standardization of tasks, enforced adoption of best implements and working conditions, and enforced cooperation from workers and managers, his ideas met with considerable resistance at the time, especially given that Taylor's methods addressed head-on the issue of "soldiering" (deliberate slowing of work rates) by employees. It is interesting to note however that Henry Ford adopted a number of Taylor's ideas—especially those that had to do with standards and utilization rates. However, Ford did insist on paying high wage rates for quality people. Turan (2015) describes the relevance of Taylor's principles to modern approaches to personnel selection and concludes that a number of Taylor's concepts are still valid.

Henry Ford (1863–1947) basically applied scientific management to the mass production of automobiles. Following suggestions from some of his key people, Ford introduced the moving (progressive) assembly line for the Ford Model T. Workers walked alongside a Model T chassis that was carried slowly by a conveyor. Parts were picked up from carefully placed bins (an early adoption of "just-in-time" (JIT)) and added to the chassis as it moved along. This process reduced the assembly time of a car from around 730 hours down to 1.5 hours, an incredible achievement for 1913. Quality was of crucial concern to Ford who insisted on high-quality components that had to be delivered on time. Ford integrated materials, logistics, people, processes, and standards in order to produce a product of reliable quality with greatly reduced assembly cycle times and minimal waste whilst meeting volume and cost requirements. Ford's book *Today and Tomorrow* (1926) was used extensively by Taiichi Ohno in developing the Toyota Production System (more recently described as "Lean" Production System).

William Sealy Gosset (1876–1937) went by the pen name "Student" because his employer at the time (Guinness of Ireland), for policy reasons, would not let him publish using his proper name. Gosset, a mathematician by training that worked in a quality control role, was studying the sensitivity of various types of barley used in the manufacture of Guinness to variations in soil and climatic conditions. He quickly realized that the normal curve was inadequate as a probability model for small samples. Recognizing that there was a greater probability of error when dealing with small samples, he empirically derived a different sampling distribution of the means for each sample size he was using. His derived set of distributions basically makes the rejection of the null hypothesis less probable. In his 1908 paper, "The Probable Error of a Mean", "Student" introduced the statistic t (originally called z but later changed to t by R. A. Fisher (below) on Gosset's suggestion) such that $t = \dfrac{M - \mu_0}{S_M}$ where M is the mean of the population under study, μ_0 is the mean of the norm population, and S_M is the standard error of the mean M.

Gosset's findings received little attention until they were published as part of R. A. Fisher's textbook some seventeen years later (Fisher 1925).

Ronald Alymer Fisher (1890–1962) published a number of statistical-type texts (Bennett 1989) including *Statistical Methods for Research Workers* in 1925 (Fisher 1925). This was a handbook primarily concerned with the methods of the design and analysis of experiments. In addition to building upon Gosset's earlier work, Fisher also included the development of methods suitable for small samples and the discovery of the precise distributions of many sample statistics including the t-distribution and later the t-test. Fisher also published *The Design of Experiments* in 1935 (Fisher 1935) and *Statistical Tables* in 1938 (Fisher 1938).

George D. Edwards (1890–1974) worked as director of quality assurance at Bell Telephone Laboratories from 1925 to 1955, and for a time in that role, he was Walter Shewhart's supervisor. Edwards was part of a team that developed sampling theory used in quality assurance. He was also the first president of the American Society for Quality Control from 1946 to 1948 (now called the American Society for Quality [ASQ]). The ASQ also administers the Malcolm Baldrige National Quality Award. It is interesting to note the connection between the four men who contributed so much to QM during the twentieth century: Shewhart worked for Edwards, Shewhart mentored both Deming and Juran, and they all worked at Western Electric (Bell Labs) for a period of time.

While working as a Bell Labs statistician for Western Electric, Walter Shewhart (1891–1967) classified variability into assignable (special or acute) causes and chance (common or chronic) causes, focusing on controlling processes as well as products. Shewhart recognized that data collected from a process could be analyzed, using statistical techniques, to determine if the process is stable and in control or not. In 1924, Shewhart prepared a memo for his manager, George Edwards, which included a very early version of a control chart. This memo outlined the essential principles and considerations that we now know as process quality control. During the 1990s, Shewhart's work was revisited (mostly by Motorola) and large parts of his teachings were incorporated into the Six Sigma approach (see below).

W. Edwards Deming (1900–1993) also worked and trained with Walter Shewhart at Western Electric, and he continued to champion Shewhart's ideas, methodologies, and theories throughout his career. After World War II, the U.S. Government asked Deming to work on Japanese reconstruction efforts. While working there, Deming further developed some of Shewhart's methodological approaches such as the Shewhart Cycle represented by the plan-do-check-act (PDCA) process. He also went on to describe a set of principles (Deming's so-called "14 points") that he stated management should apply in order to develop a quality culture within their organization (see *Out of the Crisis* by Deming (1986)).

Joseph M. Juran (1904–2008) was a contemporary of W. Edwards Deming and like Deming worked for a time at Bell Labs. Juran was also invited to Japan to help educate Japanese senior and middle managers on QM. Whilst Deming's focus was more on statistical process control, Juran focused on managing for quality. He did agree with Deming, however, that quality was achieved more through organization and management systems not only through techniques. He and Deming were in agreement that the main cause of poor quality is ineffective management. Juran developed an early quality management system (the Juran trilogy) that included:

- Quality planning (direction, guidance to employees to help them produce quality products and services)
- Quality control (evaluation of actual result against plan plus needed corrective actions)
- Quality improvement (identification of quality problems, their causes and solutions).

Juran wrote twelve books on QM, and readers are recommended to peruse *Quality Control Handbook* (Juran 1951/2010), *Quality Planning and Analysis* (Juran 1980), and *Juran on Leadership for Quality* (Juran 1989).

After graduation from the Nagoya Technical High School, Taiichi Ohno (1912–1990) joined the Toyoda family's Toyoda Spinning operation in 1932. In 1943, he moved to the Toyota motor company where he worked as a shop-floor supervisor in the engine shop and gradually rose through the ranks to become an executive. In what is considered to be an anachronistic snub, because he spoke publicly about the Toyota Production System that he largely developed—sometimes against internal ridicule within Toyota during the early years of its development—he was denied the normal executive track and in his later career was sent instead to consult with suppliers. In the operations management world, however, Ohno is revered as the father of the Toyota Production System (which became known as Lean Manufacturing in the U.S.) that integrates efficient operations management practices with QM. He devised the seven wastes *(muda* in Japanese) as part of this system. He wrote several books about the system, including *Toyota Production System: Beyond Large-Scale Production* (1988), *Just-in-Time for Today and Tomorrow* (1988), and *Workplace Management* (1988).

Born in Tokyo, the oldest of the eight sons, Kaoru Ishikawa (1915–1989) graduated from the University of Tokyo with an applied chemistry degree in 1939. After graduation, he worked as a naval technical officer from 1939 to 1941, and between 1941 and 1947, he worked at the Nissan Liquid Fuel Company. In 1947, Ishikawa started his academic career as an associate professor at the University of Tokyo, becoming a full professor in 1960. He worked with the quality control research group of the Japanese Union of Scientists and Engineers (JUSE) on the concept of the "leading hand" (*Gemba-cho*), which is a training concept that led to the design and introduction of operating quality circles in 1962. A quality circle comprises a group of workers doing the same or similar work, who identify, analyze, and solve work-related problems. With the help of Nippon Telephone & Telegraph, quality circles would soon become very popular and form an important link in any company's Total Quality Management system. Ishikawa wrote two books on quality circles, *QC Circle Koryo* (Ishikawa 1980) and *How to Operate QC Circle Activities* (Ishikawa 1985).

Ishikawa translated, integrated, and expanded the management concepts of W. Edwards Deming and Joseph M. Juran into the Japanese quality system. 1982 saw the development of the Ishikawa diagram or "Fishbone Chart" cause-and-effect diagram, which is widely used to help determine root causes of quality problems.

Armand Feigenbaum (1922–2014) was the Director of Manufacturing Operations at General Electric from 1958 to 1968 before setting up his own engineering firm General Systems. He also served as President of the American Society for Quality from 1961 to 1963. Feigenbaum wrote several books including *Quality Control* (Feigenbaum 1951). He proposed several QM concepts including:

- The "hidden" plant—the extra work performed in correcting mistakes is equivalent to a hidden plant within the factory.
- Lost accountability for quality—because quality is everybody's job, it may become nobody's job. Therefore, quality must be actively managed by nominated personnel and have visibility at the highest levels of leadership.
- Cost-of-quality—the quantification of the total costs of quality efforts plus the cost of correction of quality deficiencies.

After serving in the U.S. Navy, Philip B. Crosby (1926–2001) worked for a number of manufacturing firms before beginning a career at International Telephone and Telegraph (ITT). In 1979, he set up his own consulting company: Philip Crosby Associates. Crosby worked hard to lift both the education levels and attitudes of top management to quality, in particular that they take more active leadership roles. He also believed that quality professionals need to develop more business acumen and be energetic in sharing it. He is best known for developing the "Zero Defects" methodology, his fourteen quality improvement steps and the four absolutes of quality, namely, (i) a clear definition of quality requirements, (ii) clear and specific performance standards, (iii) a system to manage quality, and (iv) measurement methods that support the improvement process. Crosby was a prolific writer and wrote fourteen books describing his approaches to quality management. One of his early and very popular books, *Quality Is Free* (Crosby 1979), explained to senior managers, in terms they could understand, the requirements of an active quality management approach and how to deliver successful quality results. He reinforced the message that, whilst quality is free, it is not a gift. Other Crosby books worthy of study include *Let's Talk Quality* (Crosby 1989) and *Quality and Me: Lessons from an Evolving Life* (Crosby 1999).

4.2 After World War II

World War II saw a rapid development of quality technology. Materials and products required for the war effort were required in volume, but that volume also had to be right the first time. Thus, the practices of quality assurance, failure analysis, problem solving, quality in product design, and product testing all advanced. At the end of the war, however, the pressure was off and the emphasis on QM diminished (Gitlow et al. 1989).

In Japan, though, reconstruction was underway in earnest, and the Japanese leaders knew that Japan must be capable of producing and selling export-quality products. Japan therefore invited a number of QM specialists, including W. Edwards Deming, to help them embed quality principles into their processes in order to lift their product and service quality. To the chagrin of many U.S. companies, it turned out that the quality specialists were very successful in Japan. These specialists were so successful that, by the late 1970s, Japanese products were taking market share from their U.S. competitors (Finch 2006). U.S. manufacturers then began to play catch-up in order to improve their inferior quality.

QM as an operating philosophy continued to improve during the 1980s, 1990s, and 2000s. Statistically based techniques such as Six Sigma grew as did the QM aspects of programs such as the Toyota Production System (TPS or Lean), Lean Six Sigma, Operational Excellence, and Business Excellence. As Western companies started measuring, calculating, and reporting their cost-of-quality results (all the costs associated with assuring the quality of goods and services including all costs associated with scrap, waste, rework, inspection, warranty costs, failure costs, recalls, and rectification of failures) and realizing that such costs can be as high as 20% of operating budgets (Finch 2006), QM could no longer be ranked as a low priority by senior management.

5 Present Situations

Today, a number of reliable QM methodologies/frameworks/management systems exist for use in improving product and service quality. Perhaps the two most important of these are the frameworks provided by the Malcolm Baldrige National Quality Award and the quality management system contained within the Geneva-based International Standards Organization (ISO) ISO 9000 family of standards.

5.1 Malcolm Baldrige National Quality Award

The Baldrige Award (named after the then U.S. Secretary of Commerce in 1987) recognizes American organizations in all sectors of the economy for demonstrating performance excellence. It is not an international award as only organizations that are headquartered in the U.S. can apply for the award. Applicants for the award are evaluated against a "Criteria for Performance Excellence". The Baldrige Award (managed by the National Institute of Standards and Technology) thus considers seven main criteria in assessing an organization's performance excellence with regard to:

(i) Leadership
(ii) Strategy
(iii) Customers
(iv) Measurement, analysis, and knowledge management
(v) Workforce
(vi) Operations
(vii) Results.

Performance against each of the seven criteria is scored on two evaluation dimensions (i.e., process and results).

Link and Scott (2001) conservatively estimated the net private benefits associated with the Baldrige program to the U.S. economy as a whole at $24.65 billion. When compared to the social costs of the program of $119 million, the Baldrige Program's social benefit-to-cost ratio was, at that time, 207 to 1.

5.2 ISO 9001 2015

ISO 9001 2015 is one of the ISO 9000 family and was revised in 2015. It lists seven QM principles that the ISO suggests organizations apply. The QM principles "are a set of fundamental beliefs, norms, rules and values that are accepted as true and can be used as a basis for quality management" (ISO 9001 2015).

These seven principles thus form the quality management system recommended by ISO to reliably deliver value to customers (see Table 7.2). It is important to note, in relation to the discussion in Section 2, that of the seven principles shown, four of them are so-called "soft" factors.

Freely available on their website, importantly, the ISO makes available the particular actions that organizations should consider applying for each principle shown in Table 7.2. In addition, the full ISO 9001 2015 standard is available for a fee as are the guidelines for achievement of formal accreditation.

Because there are so many different QM approaches and methodologies, some key ones are described in the following sections.

Table 7.2 ISO 9001 2015 Quality Management Principles (ISO 2015)

	Principles	Details
ISO 9001 2015 Quality Management System	1. Customer focus	Meet customer requirements and strive to exceed customer expectations.
	2. Leadership	Establish unity of purpose and direction. Engage personnel in meeting quality objectives.
	3. People engagement	Competent, engaged, empowered people at all levels.
	4. Process approach	Understanding and managing interrelated systems as a coherent system. Includes quality planning, quality control, and quality assurance.
	5. Improvement	Ongoing focus on improvement using a range of QM improvement methodologies such as QI Story, Six Sigma, SPC, and the classic "Shewhart Cycle" of Plan, Do Check, Act (PDCA)—see more on these methods below.
	6. Evidence-based decision making	Decisions based on the analysis and evaluation of data and information.
	7. Relationship management	Active management of relationships with all key stakeholders.

Source: © ISO and Standards Australia Limited. Copied by P. Robertson with the permission of ISO and Standards Australia under License.

5.3 Quality Function Deployment (QFD)

First used by Mitsubishi in 1972, QFD is used to help with product and process design by translating customer needs into product and service designs that then influence process design. It consists of four phases and also makes use of a matrix commonly referred to as the "House of Quality". The four phases are:

(i) Phase I: Product planning—This consists of, first, listening to the "voice of the customer" in order to fully understand customer wants and needs (shown as row items in Figure 7.1). Second, the customers' needs and wants are translated into characteristics, capabilities, and targets of the product or service design (the "What's").
(ii) Phase II: Deployment—Product or service design characteristics are deployed down to technical design parameters at the component level (the "How's").

(iii) Phase III: Process planning—Process selection, equipment, and layouts are made in this phase. Checks are made to ensure that the necessary performance measure targets will be met.
(iv) Phase IV: Production planning—Translation of the process requirements into an overall control system capable of delivering to the specific targets defined previously (basically the system to be used to monitor and control the "What's").

When reading the House of Quality, the roof shows the degree of interrelationship between various columns that are Phase II design characteristics. For example, "Tank Level" and "Effectiveness Index" have an indirect relationship while "Survey Score" and "Effectiveness Index" have a direct relationship. Similarly, "Customer Expectations" are directly, indirectly, or not related to the characteristics/capabilities as shown. Current competitive position on each of the "Customer Expectations" is also displayed.

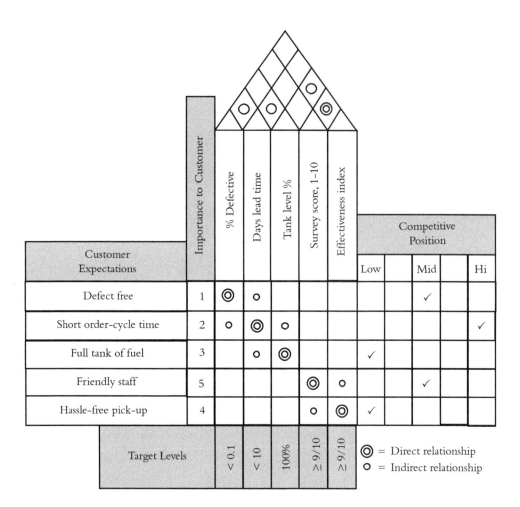

Figure 7.1 Illustrative House of Quality Example—New Car Purchase

5.4 Statistical Process Control (SPC)

Since the time of Gosset (see Section 4 above), quality practitioners have been collecting data and using statistics to analyze and understand it. Shewhart later applied the use of statistics as a process control tool. SPC thus represents the culmination of that development (i.e., it is a preventive approach to QM that measures processes in order to prevent problems that might lead to the creation of defects). There are three main phases to SPC, namely:

(i) A detailed understanding of the process and the specification limits of the product(s) produced.
(ii) Eliminating special causes of variation in order to stabilize the process by taking positive steps to remove and/or reduce causes of known variations, and
(iii) Ongoing monitoring using some or all of the tools described below in order to detect variations and changes to means.

To do this, SPC uses numerous statistically based tools such as:

(i) Run charts—A plot of a measured variable (*y*-axis) over time (*x*-axis), as shown in Figure 7.2.

Simple tests can be applied to run chart results to determine meaningful non-random trends or patterns such as:

- A Shift—Six or more consecutive points either above or below the median
- A Trend—Five or more consecutive points all going up or all going down
- A Run—A series of points in a row on one side of the median
- Astronomical Point—A point that is blatantly different to all the other points.

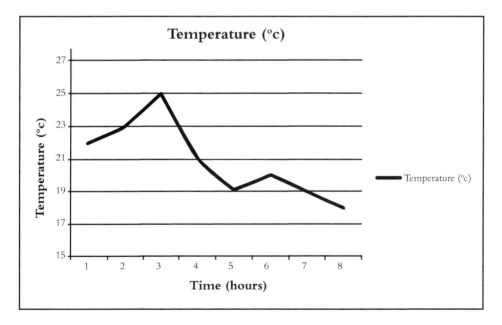

Figure 7.2 A Simple Run Chart

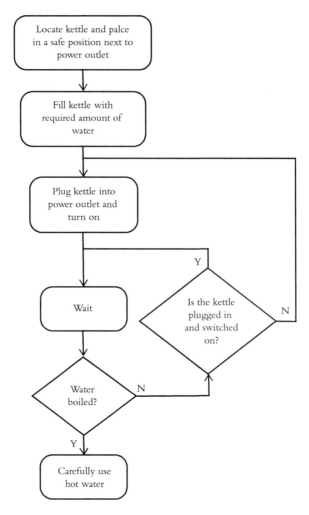

Figure 7.3 Process Flowchart Example—Boiling Water in a Kettle

(ii) Process flowchart—A sequential diagram of the steps and flows involved in a process. The example flowchart (Figure 7.3) is for the process of using an electric kettle to boil water.
(iii) Cause-and-effect diagram (also called a fishbone chart or Ishikawa diagram)—Used to help identify the root cause(s) of quality problems (can also be used for operational problem solving), as shown in Figure 7.4.
(iv) Pareto Charts—Simple bar graphs where the most frequently occurring category is placed on the left-hand side of the x-axis and then the next most frequent category is placed to the right of the first and so on until all categories appear in order of largest to smallest. This chart is used for the prioritization of quality problems.
(v) Histograms—again a simple bar chart but different to Pareto charts in that the x-axis depicts a scale such as time or weight (increasing or decreasing in value as we move from left to right). The categories are usually represented as either increasing or decreasing in value across the x-axis. As such, histograms give an appreciation of the variation in the plotted data.

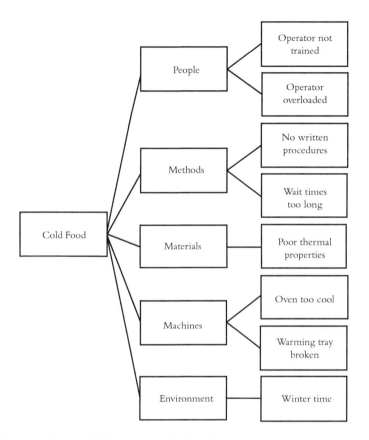

Figure 7.4 Example Cause and Effect Diagram for Food Served in a Restaurant

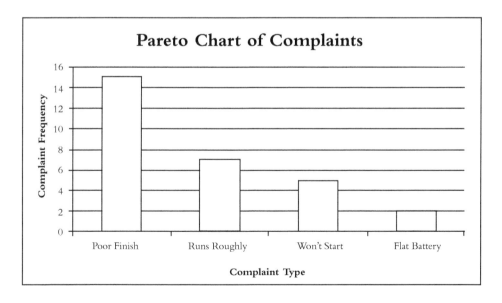

Figure 7.5 Pareto Diagram Example—Automobile Quality Complaints

(vi) Check Sheets—Simple data tally sheets used to tally items of interest, as shown in Figure 7.7.
(vii) Scatter Diagrams—Provides visibility on a possible relationship between a variable plotted on the *y*-axis and another plotted on the *x*-axis.
(viii) Control Charts—Plots the measures of process variable of interest over time, calculates and displays the upper and lower control limits (UCL and LCL) on the chart so that judgement can be made as to whether the process is within statistical control (often ±3σ about the mean (x-bar) on the chart) or out of statistical control.

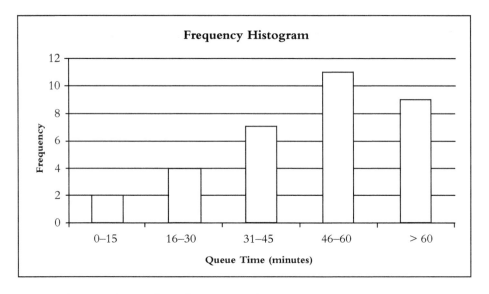

Figure 7.6 Histogram Diagram Example—Queuing Times

	Feature 1	Feature 2	Feature 3
Item A	III	I	
Item B		II	
Item C	II	ЖЕ	III
Item D		IIII	
Item E	II	III	IIII
Item F		ЖЕ	II

Figure 7.7 Check Sheet Example

Quality Management

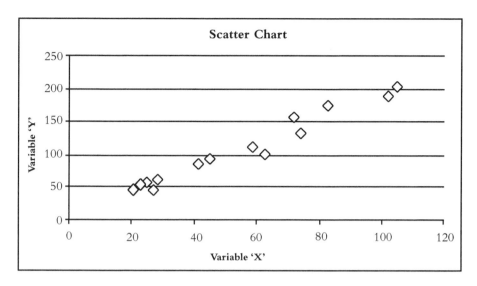

Figure 7.8 Scatter Chart Example

(ix) Process Capability—The ability of a process (such as shown in Figure 7.9) to be within the customer's upper and lower specification limits (USL and LSL). Usually calculated as an index, i.e., Cp, where:

$$Cp = \frac{USL - LSL}{6\sigma}$$

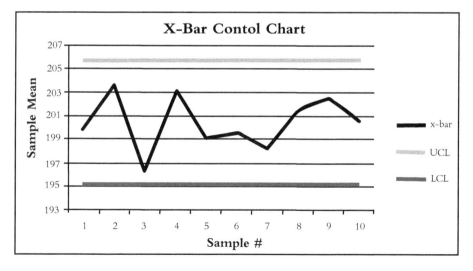

Figure 7.9 Control Chart Example

(x) For cases where the process mean is not centered between the USL and LSL the Cpk index is used (Note: the "k" stands for Katayori, which means shift of the process and measures the amount of potential capability lost due to poor centering of the process), i.e.:

$$Cpk = \min\left[\frac{\text{process mean} - \text{LSL}}{3\sigma}, \frac{\text{process mean} - \text{USL}}{3\sigma}\right]$$

5.5 Quality Improvement (QI) Story

This is basically an improvement "story" built around the PDCA cycle, as shown in Figure 7.10.

5.6 Six Sigma

Six Sigma is a quality improvement methodology that incorporates many statistical control features. Six Sigma strives to achieve a level of performance that is near perfection, i.e., 6σ quality is equivalent to a level of confidence of 99.9999998% or expressed another way, 3.4 defects per million opportunities. Six Sigma uses two main approaches, i.e.: (i) DMAIC (define, measure, analyze, improve, and control) for underperforming existing processes and (ii) DMADV (define, measure, analyze, design, and verify) is used for new products and services. These approaches are described in Figure 7.11.

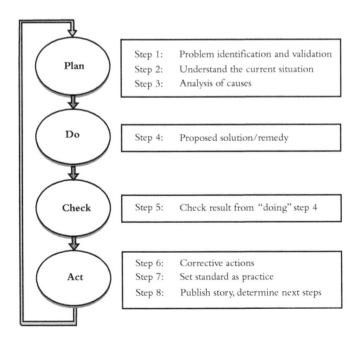

Figure 7.10 QI Story Using PDCA

DMAIC Process

Step	Activities
Define	Define problem & project objectives & describe the internal & external customers
Measure	Measure & understand current level of performance
Analyze	Determine root cause of identified problems
Improve	Identify/develop solutions to the identified problem & implement
Control	Set process control standards in place

DMADV Process

Step	Activities
Define	Define problem & project objectives & describe the internal & external customers
Measure	Measure & understand current level of performance
Analyze	Describe the processes that will meet customer requirements
Design	Design the new product or service
Verify	Determine if the new design is effective

Figure 7.11 Six Sigma DMAIC and DMADV Processes

5.7 Lean

Lean is an approach to the whole of operations not just QM. However, key QM methods are embedded in the Lean approach. Lean is essentially the Western label given to the Toyota Production System as developed by Taiichi Ohno and his people over the thirty-five-year period from 1947 to 1982. The refinement of Lean has continued in the East and West since that time. Lean is an integrated way of thinking and is in no way a "quick fix". It is rather an operating methodology that focuses on the following:

- The elimination of all forms of waste.
- The reduction of all cycle times including elimination of non-value-adding steps, the move to small lot sizes, and fast change-over times.
- Flowed deliveries using *kanbans* to manage inventory flows.
- *Kaizen* (continuous improvement).
- Quality management, because good quality reduces waste, QM engages the workforce and quality extends to housekeeping (Lean's 5S—sort, set-in-place, shine, standardize, and sustain) and asset management.
- Standardization of processes, methods, and parts.
- Protective capacity rather than carrying excess inventory.
- Improved plant and facilities layout.
- Error proofing of processes (*Poka-yoke*).
- Improvement teams.
- Relevant training.
- High levels of employee engagement.

The cultural requirements needed to successfully implement Lean are significant and basically the same as those needed to successfully implement QM (as explained in section 5.12).

5.8 Lean Six Sigma

This approach is the combination of Lean and Six Sigma methodologies. Its focus is on achieving customer satisfaction via quality improvement, reduced cycle times, and cost reductions. The proponents of Lean Six Sigma maintain that Lean by itself cannot bring a process under tight statistical control and that Six Sigma alone cannot dramatically improve process and order lead-time speed. Therefore, the two in combination are prima-facie an attractive option. Care needs to be taken with this approach, however, so as not to overload an organization's people with too much too quickly. Applied sensibly, however, a Lean Six Sigma approach does offer a complete solution to operations management and QM practitioners.

5.9 Design for Manufacture and Assembly (DFMA)

This is an important and more recent addition to Lean/QM methodologies/approaches. DFMA provides a methodical approach to the standardizing and simplification of designs of component parts (Boothroyd et al. 2002). It also focuses on reducing the costs of manufacture and costs of assembly of products and components.

The implementation of Lean/TQM becomes simpler also as DFMA reduces the number of products and the number of parts, thus requiring less skills, less technology, and fewer equipment types and processes.

5.10 Quality Risk Management and Quality Recovery Plans

Despite all expended QM efforts and duty of care precautions, sometimes things do go wrong despite best intentions (Johnston et al. 2008). Examples include Honda's faulty airbag problem of early 2015, Toyota's accelerator problems between 2009 and 2012, and, more recently, VW's 2015 emission control controversy. The length of the food recalls list shown at the U.S. Government's Food Safety site (www.foodsafety.gov/recalls/recent/) is both substantial and indicative of risk management and recovery in action. In 1990, Perrier recalled its bottled mineral water in the U.S. after traces of benzene were found in samples of the product. Tylenol, the leading pain killer producer in the U.S., had to recall its products in 1982 after capsules of the product were found to be laced with potassium cyanide.

Many companies today therefore have a quality recovery plan in place to protect customers (and thereby customer loyalty) when things go wrong (Michel et al. 2009).

Companies need to look upon such occurrences as opportunities for improvement and for making sure that every effort is made to look after customers affected by these at the organization's expense. A good recovery process is one that makes the customer feel as if everything within reason was done to recover the situation and that they want to come back to the company. as buying customers. For these reasons, a formal QM risk management assessment, including listing down preventive and contingent actions, is considered essential.

5.11 Quality Management Themes

More recent network analysis research carried out on articles published in the *Quality Management Journal* between 1993 and 2011 (Radziwill 2013) has identified seven main QM themes. These themes are:

(i) International aspects of quality management
(ii) Service quality
(iii) Quality culture
(iv) The impacts of quality management approach on business results
(v) Strategy development (using the Baldrige framework—see Section 5.1)

(vi) Validating the effectiveness of different approaches/techniques to quality management
(vii) The application of quality tools (such as quality function deployment (QFD) and Plan, Do, Check, Act (PDCA)) in different environments and industries.

Radziwill (2013) also identified the following unique emerging quality themes by analyzing articles published between 2009 and 2011:

(i) Teaching and learning in QM
(ii) Improving production quality through leadership and measurement of perceived quality along multiple dimensions
(iii) Understanding the linkages between supplier and service quality and voice of the customer and customer satisfaction.

So which QM framework or list of quality related issues should individual companies select to apply? Lakhal (2014) provides some guidance on this with research on 176 companies confirming organizations that adopt ISO 9000 practices *before* embarking on a concerted QM campaign, exhibit better organizational performance. Moreover, their research showed that ISO 9000 and QM practices each directly and positively impact organizational performance.

5.12 Quality Culture

The issue of a quality-minded culture is considered key to successful QM, and several authors have stressed the importance of developing and maintaining a quality culture (Gitlow et al. 1989; Samson and Terziovski 1999; Reed et al. 2000; Finch 2006; Latham 2013; Radziwill 2013). As reference and because space limitations prevent a full explanation here, Latham (2013, Parts I and II) presents an excellent and comprehensive study into leadership for quality and the leadership attributes found to facilitate performance excellence.

In managing culture, however, Livermore (2009) suggests that leaders need four main attributes:

(i) Motivation (drive)—This includes interest, presence, determination, and cultural flexibility.
(ii) Cognition (knowledge)—Awareness of organizational culture, the similarities and differences, and cultural type appropriateness.
(iii) Strategy—Ability to set sensible strategy based on awareness of requirements and understanding of existing and desired culture.
(iv) Behavior (actions)—Preparedness to act that is coupled with the simultaneous awareness of when to act and when not to act dependent on cultural understanding.

6 Future Projections

Great success in QM is not easy to achieve. Indeed, less than 10% of applicants for the Malcolm Baldrige National Quality Award over the twenty-year period to 2013 were successful (Latham 2013).

Additionally, quality improvement is not free. Organizations undertaking a quality improvement campaign can expect their costs to rise at the start. However, if the improvement campaign is carefully, sensibly, and closely managed, then the total cost of quality will reduce over time. This is mainly because costs associated with poor quality (scrap, rework, correction, recall, and rectification of failures) will reduce.

To be clear though, a QM campaign is a substantial undertaking for any organization as it consumes money and resource time. In addition, it has to be sustained in order to be effective. The requirements of quality planning; understanding customer needs and expectations; identifying QM focus; obtaining, assessing, and selecting resources; training; team formation; compilation of task briefs; data collection; data analysis; data publication; kick-off meetings; review meetings; team meetings; problem solving; resolution planning; implementation of improvement actions; checking and follow-up actions; monitoring; corrective actions; and the compilation and publication of quality stories can be exhausting processes especially if an organization takes on too much or tries to progress too rapidly chasing short-term results.

It is for these reasons that it is suggested that the future needs to bring both strong, determined leadership and QM principles and processes (e.g., those shown in Table 7.2) that are cleverly simply, efficient, robust, easy to understand, easy to apply, reliable, and that demonstrably deliver the required outcomes. This may well be a sizable task, but that is the challenge. We need academics, QM consultants, and perhaps retired POM practitioners to come up with such solutions to help organizations reduce the QM task overhead and, at the same time, raise management commitment.

There is a compelling case for this approach, because, if managed correctly and with an enabling quality mindset, the benefits of effective QM can be substantial and, in many cases, have made the difference between business survival over closure. It has been demonstrated in numerous examples that a sensible QM approach to product and service quality and particularly when coupled with process quality improvements (Finch 2006) does enhance the entire value offer to customers. This manifests ultimately in improved profitability levels and competitive advantage. A newly recognized competitive advantage in manufacturing, is seeing that it has a service function with its customers. The quality of that service function can make a big impact, e.g., Lexus versus Toyota and Lincoln versus Ford.

As such, it is suggested that while the attention to QM may wax and wane over time, it can never be disposed of and therefore will be an enduring and indeed crucial management function.

7 Further Research Directions

The following gaps in the reviewed material are recommended as opportunities for further research:

(i) The success or otherwise of any QM program will be largely shaped by the existence (or absence) of necessary preconditions. Not all of the necessary QM preconditions have been explored in the literature, and certainly, their relationships to one another and/or the sequence they must follow have not been quantitatively defined. This represents a rich research opportunity.
(ii) The validation of quality principles (e.g., those shown in Table 7.2) using different environments of customers and end-users, suppliers and supply chain partners, competitors, technologies, statutory requirements, and union influence (e.g., prevention of practice of multi-skilling and job-rotation).
(iii) What leverage (parameters and strength of) do customers have to insist that suppliers along the end-to-end supply chain comply with one of the number of quality methodologies and/or quality standards that exist (e.g., ISO 9001 2015)?
(iv) The issue of recalls has substantial implications, not only for individual organizations along the supply chain, but for the entire supply chain as well. How might the necessity for recalls be avoided in the first place? Given that a recall is necessary, how might it be better managed than past examples?

(v) The advantages or otherwise of making more use of information and communication technology (ICT), knowledge management, and neural networks as a QM tool especially for data collection, data analysis, data mining, data reporting, automation of QM plans, schedules and reports, information visibility, and problem solving.

(vi) The use of the Internet, company portals, and/or social media to build QM engagement, interaction, and collaboration and to speed the flow of QM type feedback along the supply chain. Unexpected consequences might include, for example, just how do reviews by customers on Amazon pages affect QM by companies?

(vii) QM and corporate social responsibility (CSR). Is there a case for concluding that heightened QM performance leads to enhanced CSR? Or, should CSR be used to bring more management attention and compliance to QM practices?

(viii) Many organizations throughout history have exhibited symptoms of organizational "amnesia", i.e., they have repeated mistakes made previously or forgotten how to solve repeating quality problems. How therefore might QM be used to improve organizational learning and in particular, assure organizational memory?

(ix) What approach would be best suited to an improvement program aimed at the development of a set of QM practices that are cleverly simply, efficient, robust, easy to understand, easy to apply, reliable, and that demonstrably deliver the required QM outcomes?

References and Bibliography

Ahire, S. L., and Dreyfus, P. (2000) "The Impact of Design Management and Process Management on Quality: An Empirical Investigation", *Journal of Operations Management* **18**(3): 549–575.

Bennett, J. H. (ed.) (1989) *Statistical Inference and Analysis: Selected Correspondence of R. A. Fisher*. Clarendon Press, Oxford, UK.

Boothroyd, G., Dewhurst, P., and Knight, W. (2002) *Product Design for Manufacture and Assembly*. Marcel Dekker, New York.

Crosby, P. (1979) *Quality Is Free*. McGraw-Hill, New York.

Crosby, P. (1989) *Let's Talk Quality*. McGraw-Hill, New York.

Crosby, P. (1999) *Quality and Me: Lessons from an Evolving Life*. Jossey-Bass, San Francisco, CA.

Deming, W. E. (1986) *Out of the Crisis*. Massachusetts Institute of Technology, Cambridge, MA.

Evans, J. R., and Lindsay, W. M. (1995) *The Management and Control of Quality*. 3rd ed. West Publishing, New York.

Feigenbaum, A. V. (1951) *Quality Control: Principles, Practice and Administration: An Industrial Management Tool for Improving Quality and Design and for Reducing Operating Costs and Losses*. McGraw-Hill, New York.

Finch, B. J. (2006) *Operations Now*. McGraw-Hill, New York.

Fisher, R. A. (1925) *Statistical Methods for Research Workers*. Oliver and Boyd, Edinburgh, Scotland.

Fisher, R. A. (1935) *The Design of Experiments*. Oliver and Boyd, Edinburgh, Scotland.

Fisher, R. A. (1938) *Statistical Tables*. Oliver and Boyd, Edinburgh, Scotland.

Ford, H. (1926) *Today and Tomorrow*. Productivity Press, Cambridge, MA.

Garvin, D. A. (1991) "How the Baldrige Award Really Works", *Harvard Business Review* **69**(6): 80–93.

Gitlow, H., Gitlow, S., Oppenheim, A., and Oppenheim, R. (1989) *Tools and Methods for the Improvement of Quality*. Irwin, Homewood, IL.

Ishikawa, K. (1980) *QC Circle Koryo: general principles of the QC circle*. QC Circle Headquarters, JUSE, Tokyo, Japan.

Ishikawa, K., (1985) *How to Operate QC Circle Activities*. QC Circle Headquarters, JUSE, Tokyo, Japan.

ISO 9001 (2015) "Quality Management Principles", www.iso.org/, accessed 8 Nov. 2015.

Johnston, R., and Stefan, M. (2008) "Three Outcomes of Service Recovery", *International Journal of Operations & Production Management* **28**(1): 79–99.

Juran, J. (1951/2010) *Quality Control Handbook*. 6th ed. McGraw-Hill, New York.

Juran, J. (1980) *Quality Planning and Analysis*. McGraw-Hill, New York.

Juran, J. (1989) *Juran on Leadership for Quality*. Free Press, New York.

Kaynak, H. (2003) "The Relationship between Total Quality Management Practices and Their Effects on Firm Performance", *Journal of Operations Management* **21**(4): 405–435.

Lakhal, K. (2014) "The Relationship between ISO 9000 Certification, TQM Practices and Organizational Performance", *Quality Management Journal* **21**(3): 38–48.

Latham, J. R. (2013) "A Framework for Leading the Transformation to Performance Excellence Part I", *Quality Management Journal* **20**(2): 12–33.

Latham, J. R. (2013) "A Framework for Leading the Transformation to Performance Excellence Part II", *Quality Management Journal* **20**(3): 19–40.

Link, A. N., and Scott, J. T. (2001, October) "Economic Evaluation of the Baldrige National Quality Program", Planning Report 01–3, National Institute of Standards and Technology, U.S. Department of Commerce, Washington, DC.

Livermore, D. (2009) *Leading with Cultural Intelligence: The New Secret to Success*. AMACOM, New York.

Michel, S., Bowen, D. E., and Johnston, R. (2009) "Why Service Recovery Fails: Tensions among Customer, Employee, and Process Perspectives", *Journal of Service Management* **20**(3): 253–273.

National Institute of Standards and Technology (2016), www.nist.gov/baldrige/index.cfm, accessed Jan. 2016.

Ohno, T. (1988) *Just-in-Time for Today and Tomorrow*. Productivity Press, Cambridge, MA.

Ohno, T. (1988) *Toyota Production System: Beyond Large-Scale Production*. Productivity Press, Cambridge, MA.

Ohno, T. (1988) *Workplace Management*. Productivity Press, Cambridge, MA.

Radziwill, N. M. (2013) "A Review of Research in the *Quality Management Journal*: Influential Resources, Key Themes, and Emerging Trends", *Quality Management Journal* **20**(1): 7–36.

Reed, R., Lemak, D. J., and Mero, N. (2000) "Total Quality Management and Sustainable Competitive Advantage", *Journal of Quality Management* **5**(1): 5–26.

Samson, D., and Terziovski, M. (1999) "The Relationship between Total Quality Management Practices and Operational Performance", *Journal of Operations Management* **17**(4): 393–409.

Schonberger, R. J. (2007) "Japanese Production Management: An Evolution—With Mixed Success", *Journal of Operations Management* **25**(2): 403–419.

Su, H-C., Linderman, K., Schroeder, R. G., Van de Ven, A. (2014) "A Comparative Case Study of Sustaining Quality as a Competitive Advantage", *Journal of Operations Management* **32**(7–8): 429–445.

Taylor, F. W. (1911) *The Principles of Scientific Management*. Harper and Brothers, New York.

Turan, H. (2015) "Taylor's 'Scientific Management Principles': Contemporary Issues in Personnel Selection Period", *Journal of Economics, Business and Management* **3**(11): 1102–1105.

U.S. Government (n.d.) "Food Safety", www.foodsafety.gov/recalls/recent/.

Womack, J. P., and Jones, D. T. (2003) *Lean Thinking*. Simon and Schuster, Bath, UK.

8

FACILITIES DESIGN AND PLANNING

Sunderesh S. Heragu and Ahmed Jamoussi

1 Introduction

Facilities Design and Planning can be broadly defined as the art and science of building facilities—buildings where people use material, machines, and other resources to produce a product or deliver a service (Heragu 2016). An air-conditioner manufacturer must order the required amount of raw materials and sub-assemblies, provide the required fabrication and assembly equipment, as well as plan and organize the various manufacturing steps so that the desired number of air-conditioners can be manufactured to meet the customer demand. A warehouse, on the other hand, does not manufacture any product, but uses people and/or equipment to both store incoming pallets and retrieve them as needed, based on specific customer orders (see Figure 8.1). Proper design, planning, and operation of facilities allow companies to meet customer demand quickly using a minimum amount of resources and at minimum cost.

It is true that the location, design, layout, and planning of facilities has gained more attention as an area of study in the past seventy-five years, but surely "organizations" in ancient civilizations must have thought about proper planning based on sound principles. For example, the Harappa and Mohenjo-Daro civilizations were built in 2500 BCE near the Indus river, but on a ridge to avoid being flooded. They had granaries with air-ducts, public baths, and a covered waste-water drainage system. Similarly, siting decisions, transportation of material, as well as the actual planning and construction of the Pyramid of Giza surely involved sound principles of Facilities Design and Planning. The same can be said about the Colosseum and other public buildings built by Rome during the Roman Empire.

2 Motivating Case Study

When the first White Castle opened in Wichita, Kansas, in 1921, the idea of fast-food restaurants was launched. The fast-food industry (now almost a hundred years old) is a worldwide success and a huge industry—notable not only in the United States but also, in recent years, Asian countries. This industry is estimated to be worth $250 billion worldwide and employs more than 4 million people in the United States alone.

Jimmy Johns (shown in Figure 8.2) is a fast-food chain that specializes in limited menu options, but very fast service. The simple, open layout of a typical Jimmy Johns store allows

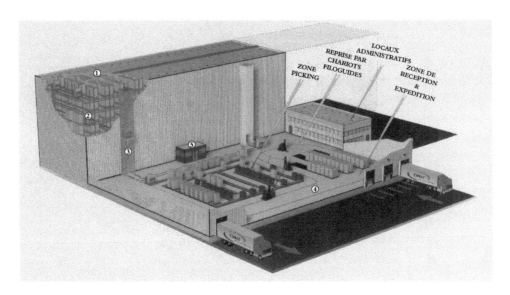

Figure 8.1 An Automated Warehouse Layout
Source: Courtesy of Savoye Logistics

Figure 8.2 Layout of a Jimmy Johns' Fast-Food Restaurant
Source: Courtesy of Certified General Contractors, Inc.

employees to keep the freaky-fast promise for walk-in, drive-through, and even delivery orders. Fast-food restaurants use process, material flow, layout, and technology to serve quickly, efficiently, and at low cost. For example, the 43,000 existing Subway stores have an assembly line layout with bread, meat, toppings, and dressing stations laid out in a sequence. The layout in McDonald's restaurants permits unskilled workers to perform a single task repetitively. One worker is typically dedicated to entering the orders and receiving payments. The orders are displayed on monitors at the grilling, frying, and assembly stations where one worker at each station knows exactly how to prepare their component of each order.

3 Flow Patterns and Flow Process Charts

3.1 Flow Patterns

It is important to identify the general flow patterns when building a facility. The pattern shown in Figure 8.3 depicts the flow of material, sub-assemblies, and assembly at the Nissan plant in Smyrna, Tennessee, from the metal stamping operation at the beginning until the final car assembly at the end. The multiple flow patterns shown in Figure 8.4, allow organizations to make sub-assemblies and feed them to the main assembly line in the correct sequence. The spine flow pattern in Figure 8.4b, allows a Volkswagen plant in Brazil to have suppliers of sub-assemblies housed under one roof. In fact, each "vertebrae" shown in the layout is owned and operated by a supplier who produces sub-assemblies for the car manufactured at this plant.

3.2 Flow Process Chart

A flow process chart is a visual display of the various operations a product undergoes in a facility. It shows the various processing steps, but also shows the product's travel and storage, as well as any delays it may encounter. Analyzing each step allows the analyst to determine the number of

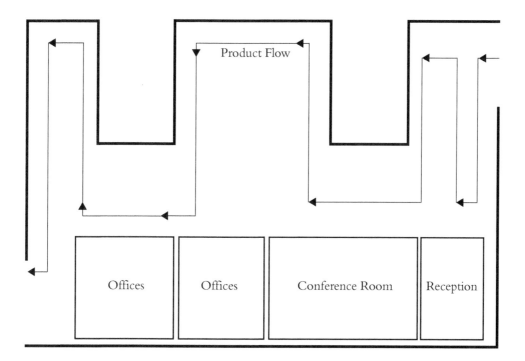

Figure 8.3 Flow Pattern of the Nissan Plant in Smyrna, TN (Adapted from Dilworth 1989)

value added and the number of non-value-added steps, thereby enabling them to devise more effective and efficient operations plans. The flow process chart shown in Figure 8.5 also shows the distance moved, operator and department identifiers, how a product is moved, and the transfer and operational batch size among other aspects of the processing steps.

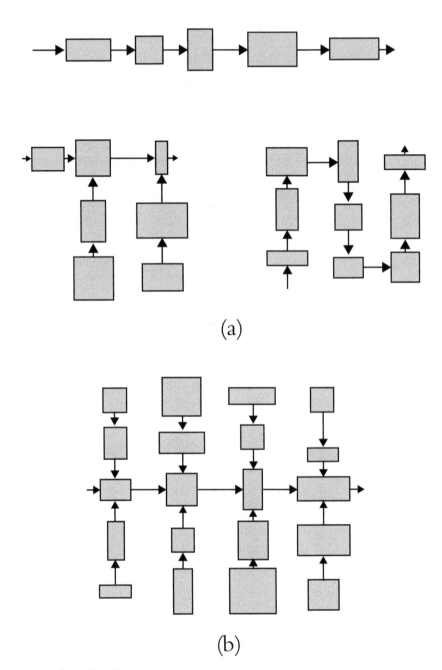

Figure 8.4 Multiple Flow Patterns

Source: Heragu 2016

FLOW PROCESS CHART

Subject Charted <u>TB03100 Face Panel</u> Chart No. <u>112XAG</u>
Drawing No._____ Part No._____ Chart of Method – <u>Present</u>
Chart Begins <u>Receiving</u> Charted By <u>N.L.</u>
Chart Ends <u>Steel Dept.</u> Date <u>Feb. 5/90</u> Sheet <u>1</u> of <u>1</u>

Dist. (ft)	Time	Chart Symbol	Oper ID	Dept ID	M/C ID	# of pieces	How moved	Process Description
	0.02	1 ▼	A1	S&R		100	Truck	Received material 0.022 wcs (51" x 102")
220	0.02	1 ➜	H2	MF1		100	Forklift	To crane bay area
		2 ▼		WIP1		100		Stored temporarily
20	0.02	2 ➜	H2	MF1		100	Conveyor	To hydra shear
	0.01	1 ●	M1	MF1	HS1	100		Cut to length (front panel)
50	0.02	3 ➜	H3	MF2	13G 142	95	Forklift	To machine #13G (100 ton press) or Komatsu (machine 142) or to HYMAC 101 (7" & over neck)
	0.01	2 ●	M2	MF2	101	95		Necking operation (punch hole)
160	0.03	4 ➜	H3	MF2		95	Forklift	To machine # 136
	0.03	3 ●	M2	MF2	136	95		Punch holes
240	0.01	5 ➜	H1	MF3		95	Forklift	To machine #155 or machine #104 or machine #111
	0.05	4 ●	M2	MF3	155	95		Braking operation
260	0.01	6 ➜	H1	WIP2		94	AGV	To marshalling area
		3 ▼		S&R		94		Temporary storage
150	0.01	7 ➜	H3	WIP3		94	AGV	To steel department

Summary

Event	Total	Time	Distance
● Operations	4		
■ Inspections	–	–	–
➜ Transportations	8		(min). 1100 ft.
▼ Storages	3		
▮ Delays			

Figure 8.5 Flow Process Chart
Source: Heragu 2016

4 Facilities Layout

Facilities layout is a topic that has received much attention as a research topic since the mid-1950s. In this section, we discuss four important topics in facilities layout.

4.1 Types of Layout

In general, the types of layouts seen in manufacturing and service facilities can be classified as: product, process, group-technology, fixed position, and hybrid layouts. In a product layout, processing equipment is arranged according to the sequence of operations required on the product manufactured. In a process layout, the equipment is grouped based on the operations they can perform, with machines that can perform the same operation housed in their own separate department. For example, all the milling machines are located in one department or location. Thus, these two types of layouts are on the opposite ends of a spectrum, with the others falling somewhere in between. The group-technology layout organizes departments by placing a set of dissimilar equipment capable of producing a family of parts (e.g., rotational parts) in one "cell." On the other hand, in a fixed-position layout, the product is fixed in one position and the equipment is brought to where the product is located, with aircraft assembly being one example. Hybrid layout, as the name indicates, has elements of one or more of the preceding layout types embedded in it. In the hybrid layout shown in Figure 8.6, a group-technology or cellular layout is located in the upper left corner. The process layout is on the upper right, and a product layout is at the bottom.

4.2 Systematic Layout Planning

Developed in the early 1960s, the Systematic Layout Planning (SLP) technique is a simple, yet effective way to develop rough layouts that can be refined further using modern software such as Sketchup and AutoCAD. Its simplicity is a prime factor that it has remained a popular layout development for more than fifty years. It offers a step-by-step guide on how to develop a layout, first by focusing on the layout of the major departments relative to one another and then by focusing on the layout of equipment within each department.

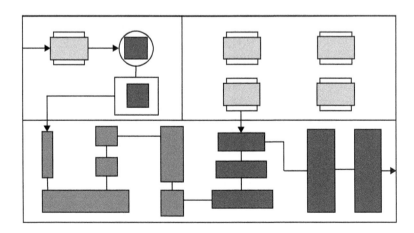

Figure 8.6 Hybrid Layout with Group-Technology, Process, and Product Layouts
Source: Heragu 2016

The SLP technique is explained in Figure 8.7. With manufacturing data on products, quantities, and routing (P-Q-R), a matrix representing the intensity of flow between machine pairs is constructed. Then, by considering the support services such as locker rooms, inspection stations, and other support services not directly used to manufacture a product, a relationship chart that captures qualitative, non-flow relationships is developed. Next, using the flow matrix and relationship chart, a relationship diagram is constructed. Machines are then connected by color coded lines that correspond to the desired closeness of the machine pairs—machine pairs that must be *absolutely* close to each other, *essential, important, ordinary*, and *unimportant*—A, E, I, O, U—representing the vowels of the English alphabet. Using color-coded lines, it is relatively easy to draw a relationship diagram that tells us which department pairs must be adjacent, which ones must not, and how the machines should be positioned relative to one another. Using the relationship diagram, machine dimensions, and spatial restrictions (if any) a space relationship diagram is constructed. This space relationship diagram is then used to develop three to five alternative layouts. The above-mentioned steps in SLP are illustrated in Figure 8.7.

4.3 Algorithms and Software for Layout Planning

In the past fifty years, several algorithms have been developed in order to solve the layout problem. Some of these have been developed specifically for the layout problem, while a majority have been to solve the quadratic assignment problem (QAP), which has been used to model the layout problem. As pointed out in Heragu (2016), due to the implicit assumption in formulating the layout problem as a QAP that all the departments are squares of equal size, the QAP and the algorithms developed to solve the QAP are not very useful in solving the layout problem.

4.3.1 Layout Algorithms

Algorithms for the layout problem can be classified as being construction or improvement algorithms. Construction algorithms develop a layout from scratch, often by adding one department to the layout at a time until all the departments are included. Improvement algorithms, on the other hand, begin with an initial layout and modify it using a specific protocol until no further improvement is possible. Newer algorithms such as ant colony optimization (Baykasoglu et al. 2006), simulated annealing (Heragu and Alfa [1992]), genetic algorithm (Kochhar et al. 1998), tabu search (Chiang and Kouvelis 1996), and neural network (Tsuchiya et al. 1996), mimic natural phenomena such as how ants that find a food source leave pheromone trails from the source to their colony allowing other ants to follow the same path, principles in forming good quality crystals, survival of the fittest principle, and biological neural network.

4.3.2 Software for Layout Design

Relative to layout software, software packages for layout have been developed since the 1960s. Some of these include ALDEP, CRAFT, BLOCPLAN, and PFAST. In the last two decades, some of the newer software programs that have been developed include Layout-iQ, VIP-PLANOPT, and FlowPath Calculator. Layout-iQ, and VIP-PLANOPT are capable of generating near-optimum layouts, whereas the others provide the user visual guidance on generating good layouts and for each layout that is generated by the user, they provide static performance measures. Heragu (2016) discusses many of the above state-of-the-art layout software packages.

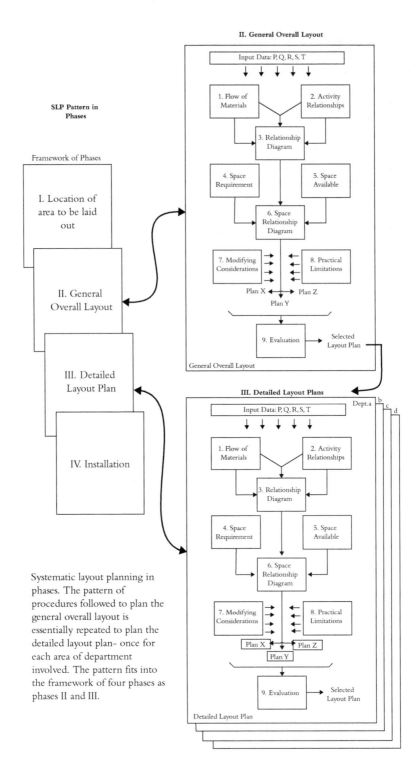

Figure 8.7 Systematic Layout Planning

Source: Redrawn with permission from Muther (1973)

Facilities Design and Planning

5 Materials Handling

Materials handling involves the transfer of material between various stages of processing efficiently using manual or automated devices. According to Tompkins et al. (2010), materials handling is about using the right method to provide the right amount of the right material at the right place, at the right time, in the right sequence, in the right position, and at the right cost. This is often referred to as the "right" definition of materials handling.

5.1 Types of Material Handling Devices

Several types of material handling devices (MHDs) are available. Each must be chosen not only based on factors such as the cost of the device, but also the size, weight, and the volume of loads it can handle. Devices that minimize annualized leasing or purchases costs as well as annual operating costs without sacrificing throughput requirements are preferred. Examples of some MHDs are shown in Figure 8.9. The most commonly used types are conveyors (Figure 8.8a), trucks (Figure 8.8b), automated guided vehicles (Figure 8.8c), hoists (Figure 8.8d), jibs, and cranes.

Figure 8.8 Different types of material handling devices (Figure 8.8a Courtesy of Bastian Solutions; Figure 8.8b Courtesy of Crown Corporation; Figure 8.8c Courtesy of Savant Corporation, and Figure 8.8d Courtesy of Ingersoll-Rand)

5.2 Automated MHDs Used in a Shipping Port

The shipping port of Rotterdam in the Netherlands utilizes a variety of MHDs to load containers arriving via truck and rail on a ship using straddle carriers, gantry cranes mounted on rails, automated guided vehicles, and overhead cranes as shown in Figure 8.9. Containers are brought into the port via trucks and hauled to the shipyard via straddle carriers (Figure 8.9a). Mobile gantry cranes, which are mounted on rails similar to those shown in Figure 8.9b, then move the containers to waiting automated guided vehicles (AGVs) (see Figure 8.9c), which in turn transport

(a) (b)

(c) (d)

Figure 8.9 Automated Loading and Unloading of Containers from a Ship
Source: Europe Combined Terminals B.V.

Facilities Design and Planning

the containers one at a time to the ship. Large gantry cranes shown in Figure 8.9d then load the containers on to the ship deck. Except for humans driving trucks into the shipyard and operating straddle carriers (see Figure 8.9a), the remainder of the loading and unloading of containers is entirely automated using mobile gantry cranes (Figure 8.9b), AGVs (Figure 8.9c), and overhead cranes (Figure 8.9d).

5.3   Ten Principles of Materials Handling

MHI, the nation's largest association for materials handling, logistics, and supply chains, has identified ten principles of materials handling. These principles are planning, standardization, work, ergonomics, unit load, space utilization, system, automation, environmental, and life cycle cost. Using a multi-media educational module, Heragu et al. (2003), introduce the learner to the ten principles, explain the key aspects of each, provide a real-world example of an improper application of the principle, and contrast it with a proper application, and extend each principle to domains outside of materials handling. A screenshot of some of the images seen in the multi-media educational tool are shown in Figure 8.10. The tool allows a self-paced learner to understand the various types of MHDs, their applications, the ten principles, and their key aspects.

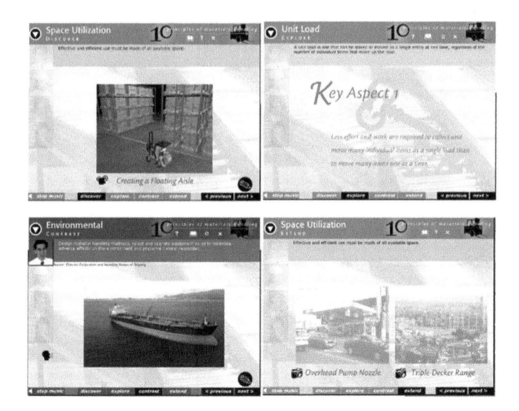

Figure 8.10   Ten Principles of Materials Handling Educational Module
Source: Developed by S.S. Heragu

6 Warehouse Design

Whereas some manufactured goods are made to order (e.g., Boeing planes), most are made to stock. This is because there is a lead time to make an item such as a television set or a mobile device and the length of this lead time may be so long that customers may not be willing to wait for the order to be placed and manufactured. Exceptions include high-demand items such as the Corvette or Tesla car. It is typically not possible to match demand with supply in most industries and therefore manufacturers generally make goods to stock. Thus, a warehouse, such as the one shown in Figure 8.1, is often used to store make-to-stock items so that a demand can be met when it occurs. Warehousing products is not a value-adding activity, but for the aforementioned reasons, is necessary. It is thus thought of as a necessary waste! A warehouse consists of an outer shell (the building), racks (for storage of products), and MHDs to store and retrieve items from the racks. Various types of warehouse MHDs exist, and these are illustrated in Figure 8.11. In Figure 8.11a, we have a pallet truck that maneuvers pallet loads into drive-through storage racks. Figure 8.11b illustrates an automated storage and retrieval system (AS/RS) capable of storing pallets on storage racks that are often a hundred feet deep and fifty feet tall. Figure 8.11c shows a set of robots used for automated order picking, and Figure 8.11d shows an AS/RS suitable for narrow aisles.

Designing a warehouse involves determining a footprint for the warehouse, its height, number of storage positions, types of storage, level of automation, desired throughput, and a myriad of other factors, some of which are inter-related. For example, the number of storage positions and the level of automation determine the warehouse dimensions. A warehouse with 50,000 storage spaces and one that requires high throughput (number of storage and retrieval transactions per hour) must often be automated. With an automated warehouse, it is possible to extend the warehouse dimensions vertically up to 75 feet. This means the horizontal dimensions or the footprint may be smaller than a manual warehouse with an equal number of storage spaces. In addition to designing a warehouse at minimum cost, designers must also be able to achieve the necessary throughput requirements at minimum operational costs. There are a number of operational problems that can be studied, and we examine a few in the next sub-section.

6.1 Warehouse Storage Policies

Products can be randomly stored in available storage locations in a warehouse or in designated locations. The two types of storage policies are referred to as random storage and dedicated storage policies, respectively. Random storage is widely used, especially in automated warehouses because it is simple to use, requires less space than dedicated storage, and allows faster replenishment. (Picking refers to the act of selecting or picking the required quantity and types of items in a pick list. Each pick list corresponds to a customer order. For example, a customer may have ordered three extra-large white T-shirts, four pairs of running socks of a certain brand, two wristbands of a particular kind, and two running shorts in large size of a particular type. The set of items in the order is called the pick list. Picking aisles for an order are the aisles that contain the items in the corresponding pick list and human or automated equipment enter and exit these aisles as needed in order to fulfill the order.) Dedicated policy allows operators to be more efficient in picking because they do not have to search for the SKU locations, but it requires more storage space. Other operational problems that arise in a warehouse include the sequence in which items in an order are to be picked, the routing policy to be used in picking items in an order, and whether items should be picked in batches. A variation of the dedicated policy, known as the cube-per order index storage policy stores products with a low cube-per order index (ratio of space occupied to ordering frequency) near the doors and those

Facilities Design and Planning

Figure 8.11 Warehouse MHDs (Figure 8.11a Courtesy of Advance Storage Products; Figures 8.11b and 8.11d Courtesy of Vanderlande Industries; Figure 8.11c Courtesy of Phoenix Pharmaceuticals)

with a high index to farther away locations (see Heskett 1963 and Malmborg and Bhaskaran 1990). The warehouse storage policies are explained in detail in Heragu (2016) and Tompkins et al. (2010), and the reader is referred to the two sources.

In warehouse management, it is important to understand the effect of the picking, storage, and routing process decisions on order picker travel. The order picker travel cost is a major component of order fulfillment costs. Numerous picking, storage, and routing policies must be evaluated to determine which process decision provides the greatest savings.

Order picking is the retrieval of stock keeping units (SKUs) in a warehouse and constitutes 50%–75% of the total operating costs for a typical warehouse (Coyle et al. 1996). Automation provides an opportunity to reduce labor costs, but many companies, especially in the United States, continue to use manual order picking due to a variety of factors including the variability in SKU shape, size, volume, the variability of demand, the seasonality of the products, and the large investment cost.

Order picking has been an important topic of research over the past several decades. Relative to the operational problems in a warehouse, the three that have received the most attention are identification of effective picking, storage, and routing policies. We discussed the storage policies briefly above. Picking policies determine how SKUs are assigned to a pick list and the sequence in which they are picked. Gibson and Sharp (1992) mention that combining several orders into batches (called batch-picking) can reduce total picking time, but it could be that the first order will have to wait until the last order arrives into the system, increasing the order wait times. Petersen and Aase (2003) described another policy called zone-picking which partitions the warehouse into zones. A set of pickers assigned to a zone only pick those SKUs in an order that are contained in their zone, one order at a time. Combining batch-picking and zone-picking results in wave-picking where each picker is responsible for SKUs in his or her zone for multiple orders.

7 Trends in Facilities Design

In this section, we discuss recent trends in facilities design and planning.

7.1 Material Handling and Logistics US Roadmap: Trends

Material handling and logistics is about moving goods from one location to another within the supply chain until it reaches the consumer's hands. The challenge faced by this industry today is to deliver goods faster than ever before. As a result, materials handling and logistics is becoming one of the most important and innovative industries worldwide. This field represents a broad sector of the US economy thanks to the tools and the technologies used to increase the productivity and to satisfy the customer's expectations.

In the summer of 2013, along with five association partners and eight publication partners, MHI organized four workshops in Atlanta, Chicago, Los Angeles, and Washington, D.C., that involved experts in the field of material handling and logistics from academia, industry, and government. The workshop participants were asked to predict what the industry would look like in 2025 and identify supporting trends, challenges, and capabilities faced by the industry. An outcome of the workshops was the development of the *Material Handling and Logistics US Roadmap*, which summarized the view of the participants relative to the charge they were given (Gue et al. 2014). This section and the succeeding sub-sections summarize the various trends, challenges, and capabilities contained in that publication.

7.1.1 E-Commerce

E-commerce continues to witness a rapid growth. By 2017, one in ten purchases will be made online. Not only are consumers spending more time online using handheld devices (and thereby making online purchases), but retailers also continue to make increasingly significant investments in e-commerce fulfillment. Order fulfillment times are expected to increase for picking, packing, and shipping as they are now measured in minutes rather than days. This increases the need for warehouse managers to optimize the type and quantity of inventory.

7.1.2 Competition among Third-Party Logistics Providers

The rise of third-party logistics (3PL) began several decades ago when companies wanted to outsource their transportation and logistics activities in order to focus more on their core competencies. Today, there is a significant amount of competition within the 3PL industry relative to price and services offered. 3PL companies must continually find ways to decrease costs while offering shorter delivery lead times, the ability to track and trace packages, accommodating minor changes to delivery times and locations, returns, and other factors that enhance the customer experience.

7.1.3 Mass Customization

Mass customization is defined in Gue et al. (2014) as the ability to produce and deliver a unique product that meets a customer's specifications at mass production prices. Not only will the products see greater customization in the future, but the channels they use to place orders as well as the delivery modes manufacturer and distributors will use to make and deliver them will also need to become diverse ranging from web orders to kiosk orders and delivery modes ranging from fixed-time (e.g., two-day shipping) to same-day delivery.

7.1.4 Urbanization

As more and more of the world's population continues to migrate to densely populated urban areas, congestion introduced because of the increased deliveries to urban areas, the increased complexity of the last-mile delivery, and the use of existing mass transit infrastructure for transport of goods will need to be addressed.

7.1.5 Mobile and Wearable Computing

Mobile computing allows us to get information, communicate, and make numerous decisions (including decisions to purchase goods or services) on the fly. Wearable computing devices such as a wristwatch, when coupled with a mobile device, not only allow customers to connect and know their locations, but they also allow companies to provide timely information about goods or services nearby.

7.1.6 Robotics and Automation

In addition to mobile and wearable computing devices, other emerging tools that will have a significant impact on logistics include robotics, autonomous control, and driverless vehicles. Robots are now available not only for manufacturing or warehousing operations, but for providing personal services at home as well. For example, consider the vacuum robot, which can clean an apartment when the occupant steps out. Not only are the capabilities of robots improving, but their costs are decreasing as well. Robots and autonomous vehicles can make and change decisions on their own depending upon the environment they are operating in. Driverless vehicles will significantly impact the way we travel and parcels are delivered in the future.

7.1.7 Sensors and the Internet of Things

According to Wikipedia, Kevin Ashton, a British technology pioneer invented the term "Internet of Things" or IoT, while he was with the Auto-ID center at the Massachusetts Institute of

Technology. The IoT is a network of physical devices that have sensors, software, and internet connectivity. These devices range from radio-frequency identification (RFID) tags, to appliances, automobiles, and even buildings. By exchanging information between themselves or a central server, each device can make local decisions for economic benefit without requiring human involvement. For example, a temperature sensor in a container mounted on a truck may be able to send directions to the truck's air-conditioning unit based on the external and internal temperatures so that the contents (e.g., perishable food) arrive fresh at the destination by consuming the optimal amount of energy.

7.1.8   Big Data and Predictive Analytics

The pervasiveness of sensors coupled with advances in computing hardware and software technology, wireless connectivity, and cloud data storage has led to an explosion in the amount of data that is collected, stored, and processed for economic benefits. While on one hand, data mining and data visualization tools can give us basic and advanced information about the data, data analytics tools help predict the future. For example, using data mining techniques, a company knows that customers who purchased an outdoor, four-burner gas grill are likely to purchase a stainless steel barbecue grilling tool set. Therefore, it can make a suggestion for the customer to buy that product or provide an incentive to do so.

Data analytics techniques such as machine learning or neural networks can even predict when an event might occur. For example, using heart rate data that is collected by a wearable sleep apnea arm-band, a statistical tool can not only determine how many times and when sleep apnea episodes occurred during the past one hour but can also predict when the next one will occur. In fact, with this knowledge, a small electric stimulus can then be sent to the patient so they change position, preventing an apnea attack and providing that patient with a more restful night! For details on this, see Wongdhamma (2015).

7.1.9   The Changing Workforce

The material handling and logistics industry along with the other industries must find ways of recruiting, training, and maintaining a workforce that is not only skilled but also motivated to excel in that industry. Industries need to find a way to tap into the populations that are currently underrepresented. Examples include people with disabilities, women, veterans, and workers under the age of 35.

7.1.10   Sustainability

The material handling and logistics industry must focus on creating economic value for all its stakeholders in a way that preserves the environment and improves social development. Value creation for customers and the resulting profitability for shareholders are well understood. Preserving the environment refers to limiting the impact on wildlife as well as minimizing the amount of pollution and solid waste that is generated. Social development includes improving education, healthcare, and the livelihood of human populations.

7.2   Material Handling and Logistics US Roadmap: Capabilities by 2025

Relative to the capabilities that the material handling and logistics industry must have to meet the challenges faced in 2025, participants of the US Roadmap workshop felt as though customers will demand greater value at a higher speed. Value refers to the timeliness, ability to make delivery changes made by the customer or necessitated by the environment, and the push to enhance the customer experience while being able to make deliveries quickly. The following sub-sections discuss the specific capabilities that will be required of the materials handling and logistics industry by 2025.

7.2.1   Total Supply Chain Visibility

Supply chain visibility will mean that it is not sufficient to know where a product was last tagged and traced. In the future, customers will want to also know that a hurricane problem in a hub located in a Gulf state has required the product to be re-routed through an airhub in Louisville, Kentucky. Details about the driver who will be delivering the product, their current location, as well as the precise delivery time also become important.

7.2.2   Standardization

Standardization is what has led the material handling and logistics industry to adopt containers for long-distance shipment of goods and pallets for unit-load handling. Similarly, the width of the Panama Canal (before its recent expansion) gave rise to the term Panamax ships, which have these maximum dimensions—950 feet length and 106 feet width. Post Panamax ships such as super tankers, container ships, and cruise ships have larger dimensions. In addition, the Panama Canal has undergone an expansion to increase the dimensions of the ships that can pass through the locks. Roadmap workshop participants felt that intermodal hubs in the future should be able to handle standardized pallets, cartons as well as containers, seamlessly. In addition, standardizing formats for exchanging and processing data emanating from sensors, open source access of data without company- or customer-specific information, cloud storage, software that can mine the data and process it for intelligent, and real-time decision making were all seen as important efforts towards standardizing how the product is handled and how the information is shared between multiple parties in a supply chain.

7.2.3   High-Speed Delivery

Nowadays, delivering in high speed has becoming obligatory in order to satisfy the needs of customers. In fact, the recent advances in delivery are all to provide items for consumers in the same day. This means that orders that have just been received will be delivered later the same day. However, such promises might be kept only within a very limited distance of the warehouse or retail outlet. Using strategically located warehouses, Amazon has offered same-day delivery in many cities.

7.2.4   Low-Cost, Low-Impact Materials Handling and Logistics

Material handling and logistics are a vital part of modern commerce. This is why they should operate at the lowest possible cost and should have the least possible negative impact on society. The financial burden is typically borne by the entities at the end of the supply chain. Therefore, cost reduction has always been the primary focus of the industry since its inception and will continue to be so into the indefinite future. This enables firms that execute logistics operations at a lower cost to enjoy a competitive advantage into perpetuity. Meanwhile, it's very important to keep in mind that material handling and logistics has a huge impact on the environment.

The use of trucks for transportation add to the carbon emission and traffic congestion. The primary focus here is obviously to develop some capabilities that will enable us to reduce the cost and to eliminate the negative impact on society.

7.2.5 Planning and Optimization

The set of planning and optimization tools developed by researchers today are not being fully utilized by industry. Standardizing such tools for network design, warehouse design and planning, and inventory control, in turn making them real-time optimization tools for current decision making and predictive analytics, will increase their acceptance by the practitioner community.

7.2.6 Impact of E-Commerce

As previously mentioned, the explosion of e-commerce will mean that distribution centers and warehouses will have to slash order fulfillment times dramatically; be able to handle multiple channels of distribution (to retail stores in large quantities, to individual homes or businesses in much smaller quantities); be designed for high-density storage; and be able to support high-speed order processing using automated, high-throughput, capable storage and retrieval systems.

7.2.7 Collaboration

Competitors in the distribution, transportation, and logistics industries will need to learn to be collaborators as well. When these companies collaborate, they will be able to share transportation resources so that trucks are filled to capacity and do not return empty. They will also be able to share warehouse resources such as storage space, automated material handling systems, human resources, and so on. Just like we have food and fuel service plazas along interstate highways that have multiple competing facilities under the same roof, one can imagine a logistics park that accommodates the needs of multiple vendors in one area using a common set of resources.

7.3 Energy and Resource Efficient Manufacturing

Energy and physical resources such as raw materials are required for manufacturing. However, in order to protect and preserve the environment, the manufacturing and service industries must use these raw materials in an efficient manner and utilize the least possible amount of energy and natural resources. Duflou et al. (2012) mention that, on a global scale, the energy consumption among the four primary end users of energy, namely, commercial, residential, transportation, and industrial sectors, are 7%, 14%, 27%, and 51%, respectively. Of the 51% consumed by the industrial sector, 90% is for manufacturing activities (Schipper 2006). Therefore, manufacturing accounts for approximately 46% of the global energy consumption and therefore is a significant part of the CO_2 emissions. Note that the manufacturing sector includes semi-continuous processes such as petroleum refining, metal and non-metallic mineral processing, chemical and paper processing.

Duflou et al. (2012) define energy and resource *efficiency* as the amount of resources required to produce a given level of output and define *effectiveness* as making wise choices on how resources are used. They cite the following example to illustrate the difference between the two. Consider the following two improvements. The wheel type in a grinding operation and the cutting fluid were changed so that the same grinding operation could be performed using less energy and fewer resources. A second improvement was to change the pat design and associated process plan so the grinding was entirely eliminated while still maintaining the functionality of the part manufactured. The first improvement relates to efficiency and the second to effectiveness. Duflou et al. (2012) survey 229 papers that focused on energy and resource efficiency in the manufacture of discrete parts.

7.4 Leadership in Energy and Environmental Design

Leadership in Energy and Environmental Design (LEED) is a rating system for evaluating the environmental performance of a building that was developed by the United States Green Building Council. Its use as a building certification tool has grown with more than 100,000 individuals who have been certified to have understood sustainable building practices (Gebken et al. 2009). LEED buildings use less water and energy while emitting much less greenhouse gases when compared to buildings that are not LEED compliant. They cover buildings that range from hospitals to homes, as well as the design, construction, operation, and maintenance of these buildings. For additional information on how buildings are being designed to not only be functional and aesthetic, but also to reduce the carbon footprint caused by its building and use, readers are encouraged to visit the US Green Building Council (USGBC) page on LEED compliance (2016).

7.5 Implications for Managers

The design and operations of facilities, whether they are manufacturing or service facilities, pose challenges to facilities designers. Here, we give a few examples of actual companies and how they design their facilities to give the reader an idea of the numerous decisions facility designers need to make.

Consider the "transparent factory" in Dresden, Germany. Located in the downtown area of an 800-year old city, the building shell and interiors are made of glass while the flooring is made of hardwood—Canadian maple! Although no stamping, welding, or painting operations take place in this facility, the Phaeton model is fully assembled here. Consider the myriad of design decisions that a facility designer has to make for this facility, which is intended to give a museum or a shopping-mall like experience for the customer who visits this plant to pick up their custom-ordered vehicle. These decisions range from having to make the factory blend in with the other downtown structures such as shopping malls, farmer's markets, and churches in this 800-year old city; having to transport sub-assemblies using enclosed, cargo trams; a speaker system emulating bird language for the building exterior so the birds do not crash into the glass walls; and many other decisions which enrich the experience of visitors and customers who walk into this facility.

Similarly, construction companies building high-rise apartment complexes in Panama City, Panama, must build apartments in odd-shaped lots in a way that each room in each apartment has a view of the Pacific Ocean. Thus, the first five floors in a high-rise typically have a lobby and stores in the main floor and parking on levels two through five. Constructing apartments from the sixth floor and up allows the residents to have a better view as well as reduced noise or pollution from the traffic below.

Companies such as Google provide numerous facilities within their campus so employees do not have to leave work early to utilize these facilities outside. Examples include dry-cleaning, baby-sitting, tennis courts, soccer fields, multiple fitness centers, massage rooms, micro-kitchens, and Lego stations.

In addition to designing facilities that permit the efficient movement of goods and material, the buildings need to consider the support facilities and the aesthetic aspects mentioned above.

In addition, they must meet local and national building codes as well as Occupational Safety and Health Administration (OSHA) regulations and the requirements of the Americans with Disabilities Act (ADA). As mentioned in Heragu (2016), facilities design is part art and part science. In addition to minimizing the total distance traveled and optimizing other objective performance measures, numerous qualitative aspects must be incorporated in the design.

7.6 Directions for Future Research

Future research in facilities design will focus on how facilities can be designed to optimize static design criteria such as building codes that have a longer-term impact, as well as shorter-term, stochastic operational criteria such as minimizing production cycle time. The design of offices, malls, and apartment buildings will focus more on aesthetics and energy conservation and much less on quantitative criteria such as minimizing the total distance traveled. On the other hand, the design of manufacturing plants will continue to focus on making the flow of materials and sub-assemblies smooth and efficient, and the design of warehouses will focus on making the order picking process fast and efficient. The miniaturization of machines (for example, 3D printers that can be placed on a desk), the breakthroughs in non-contact manufacturing (Asari 1993), and the use of new composites (Fujine et al. 1993) and lightweight materials (Arimond and Ayles 1993) will mean the footprint of machines in a manufacturing plant will be small and lightweight. These factors coupled with the availability of software tools for facilities planning, will make the facilities design problem more of an art than a science. The topics of facilities design and layout as well as materials handling, as they pertain to research, appear to have matured with not many research topics remaining from an operations management perspective. However, the area of warehouse design and operations is fertile and provides abundant opportunity for researchers and we name a few areas and relevant papers in the remainder of this section.

In the remainder of this section, we discuss future research areas relative to warehouse design and operations. Following the models presented in Francis and White (1974), Gue and Meller (2009) propose fishbone-like, warehouse aisle designs that also have been implemented in warehouses with random storage policy and human order-pickers. Warehouse design is constantly evolving with the introduction of automation and new technologies. For example, with the introduction of the autonomous vehicle storage and retrieval systems (AVS/RSs) technology, see Roy et al. (2012), models for determining the location of dwell points and cross-aisle locations have been proposed in Roy et al. (2015).

Queuing or queuing network models have been extensively used to evaluate the performance of automated warehouses in the past ten years. For example, Jia and Heragu (2009) used semi-open queuing networks to model systems in which an entering job or customer must be paired with another resource. Then, the resource remains paired with the job until its service is completed. Following that, the resource is available to pick up another job that is already waiting or it waits for the next job. Examples include automated warehouses in which a pallet that must be stored or retrieved must wait to be paired with an available autonomous vehicle (or vice versa). Other examples include a CONWIP system (see Hopp and Spearman 2008) in which each job must be paired with a Kanban card until all its operations are completed in a CONWIP loop. Jia and Heragu (2009) have shown that such systems, which have been traditionally modeled as open- or closed-queuing network models, are not accurate in estimating critical performance measures because they do not account for the time that a job may have to wait for a resource or vice versa. Hence, they propose modeling such systems as semi-open queuing networks. A number of papers have adopted this model for modeling the operational problems in warehouses with autonomous vehicles. Some examples include Heragu and Srinivasan (2008), Cai et al. (2014), Ekren and Heragu (2012), and Roy et al. (2015).

There has also been an increased interest in minimizing throughput time in manual order picking operations. De Koster (1994), De Koster et al. (2007), and Dekket et al. (2004) have developed analytical models that help minimize the throughput time. There is rich literature on warehouse operations and the reader is referred to Rouwenhorst et al. (2000), De Koster et al. (2007), and Roodbergen and Vis (2009), among other sources. To summarize, warehouse operations will continue to be an area of opportunity for researchers in the area of facilities design.

References and Bibliography

Arimond, J., and W.R. Ayles (1993), "Phenolics Creep Up on Engine Applications," *Advanced Materials and Processes*, **143**: 20.

Asari, M. (1993), "Electron Beam Hardening System," *Advanced Materials and Processes*, **143**: 30–31.

Baykasoglu, A., T. Dereli, and I. Sabuncu (2006), "An Ant Colony Algorithm for Solving Budget Constrained and Unconstrained Dynamic Facility Layout Problems," *Omega*, **34**(4): 385–396.

Benjaafar, S., S.S. Heragu, and S.A. Irani (2002), "Next Generation Factory Layouts: Research Challenges and Recent Progress," *Interfaces*, **32**(6): 58–76.

Bozer, Y.A., and M. Cho (2005), "Throughput Performance of Automated Storage/Retrieval Systems under Stochastic Demand," *IIE Transactions*, **37**(4): 367–378.

Bozer, Y.A., and J.A. White (1990), "Design and Performance Models for End-of-Aisle Order Picking Systems," *Management Science*, **26**(7): 852–866.

Cai, X., S.S. Heragu, and Y. Liu (2014), "Modeling and Evaluating the AVS/RS with Tier-to-Tier Vehicles Using Semi-Open Queuing Network," *IIE Transactions*, **46**(9): 905–927.

Chiang, W.C., and P. Kouvelis (1996), "An Improved Tabu Search Heuristic for Solving Facility Layout Design Problems," *International Journal of Production Research*, **34**(9): 2565–2585.

Coyle, J.J., E.J. Bardi, and C.J. Langley (1996), *The Management of Business Logistics* (6th Ed.). West Publishing, St Paul, MN.

De Koster, R. (1994), "Performance Approximation of Pick-to-Belt Orderpicking Systems," *European Journal of Operational Research*, **72**: 558–573.

De Koster, R., T. Le-Duc, and K.J. Roodbergen (2007), "Design and Control of Warehouse Order Picking: A Literature Review," *European Journal of Operational Research*, **182**: 481–501.

Dekker, R., R. de Koster, K.J. Roodbergen, and H. van Kalleveen (2004), "Improving Order-Picking Response Time at Ankor's Warehouse," *Interfaces*, **34**(4): 303–313.

Dilworth, J.B. (1989), *Production and Operations Management: Manufacturing and Non-Manufacturing*. Random House Publishing Company, New York.

Duflou, J.R., J.W. Sutherland, D. Dornfeld, C. Herrmann, J. Jeswiet, S. Kara, M. Hauschild, and K. Kellens (2012), "Towards Energy and Resource Efficient Manufacturing: A Process and Systems Approach," *CIRP Annals Manufacturing Technology*, **61**: 587–609.

Ekren, B., and S.S. Heragu (2008), "Simulation Based Performance Analysis of Autonomous Vehicle Storage and Retrieval System," *Simulation Modelling Practice and Theory*, **19**(7): 1640–1650.

Ekren, B., and S.S. Heragu (2012), "Performance Comparison of Two Material Handling Systems: AVS/RS and AS/RS," *International Journal of Production Research*, **50**(15): 4061–4074.

Ferrell, B. (n.d.), "Universities, Colleges Develop Programs to Prep Students for the Supply Chain Jobs of the Future," *Welcome to the US Roadmap for Material Handling and Logistics*. Available from: www.mhlroadmap.org/.

Francis, R.L., and J.A. White (1974), *Facility Layout and Location: An Analytical Approach*. Prentice-Hall, Inc., Englewood Cliffs, NJ.

Fujine, M., T. Kaneko, and J. Okijima (1993), "Aluminum Composites Replace Cast Iron," *Advanced Materials and Processes*, **6**: 20.

Gebken, R.J., R.D. Bruce, and S.D. Strong (2009), "Impact of the Leadership in Energy and Environmental Design Accredited Professional Credential on Design Professionals," *Journal of Professional Issues in Engineering Education and Practice*, **136**(3): 132–138.

Gibson D.R., and G.B. Sharp (1992), "Order batching procedures," *European Journal of Operational Research*, **58**(1): 57–67.

Gue, K., E. Akcali, A. Erera, B. Ferrell, and G. Forger (2014), "Material Handling and Logistics U.S. Roadmap," *Welcome to the US Roadmap for Material Handling and Logistics.* Available from: www.mhl roadmap.org.

Gue, K.R., and R.D. Meller (2009), "Aisle Configurations for Unit-Load Warehouses," *IIE Transactions*, **41**(3): 171–182.

Heragu, S.S. (2016), *Facilities Design* (4th Ed.). CRC Press, Clermont, FL.

Heragu, S.S., and A.S. Alfa (1992), "An Experimental Analysis of Simulated Annealing Based Algorithms for the Layout Problem," *European Journal of Operational Research*, **57**(2): 190–202.

Heragu, S.S., L. Du, R.J. Mantel, and P.B. Schuur (2005), "Mathematical Model for Warehouse Design and Product Allocation," *International Journal of Production Research*, **43**(5): 327–338.

Heragu, S.S., R.J. Graves, C.J. Malmborg, S. Jennings, and D. Newman (2003), "Multi-media Tools for Use in Materials Handling Classes," *European Journal of Engineering Education*, **28**(3): 375–394.

Heragu, S.S., and M. Srinivasan (2008), "Analysis of Manufacturing Systems via Semi-Open Queuing Networks," *International Journal of Production Research*, **49**(2): 295–319.

Heskett, J.L. (1963), "Cube-Per-Order Index—A Key to Warehouse Stock Location," *Transportation and Distribution Management*, **3**(1): 27–31.

Hopp W.J., and M.L. Spearman (2008), *Factory Physics* (2nd Ed.). McGraw-Hill, New York, NY.

Jia, J., and S.S. Heragu (2009), "Solving Semi-Open Queuing Networks," *Operations Research*, **57**(2): 391–401.

Johnson, M.E., and M.L. Brandeau (1992), "Stochastic Modeling for Automated Material Handling System Design and Control," *Transportation Science*, **30**(4): 330–350.

Kochhar, J.S., B.L. Foster, and S.S. Heragu (1998), "HOPE: A Genetic Algorithm for the Unequal Area Layout Problem," *Computers and Operations Research*, **25**(8): 583–594.

Malmborg, C.J., and K. Bhaskaran (1990), "A Revised Proof of Optimality for the Cube-Per-Order Index Rule for Stored Item Location," *Applied Mathematical Modelling*, **40**: 87–95.

Markus, F. (2003), "VW's Transparent Factory," *VW's Transparent Factory.* Available from: www.carand driver.com/features/vws-transparent-factory.

Muther, R. (1973), *Systematic Layout Planning.* Van Nostrand Reinhold Company, New York.

Petersen, C.G., and G. Aase (2003), "A Comparison of Picking, Storage, and Routing Policies in Manual Order Picking," *International Journal of Production Economics*, **92**(8): 10–19.

Roodbergen, K.J., and I.F.A. Vis (2009), "A Survey of Literature on Automated Storage and Retrieval Systems," *European Journal of Operational Research*, **194**: 343–362.

Rouwenhorst, B., B. Reuter, V. Stockrahm, G.J. van Houtum, R.J. Mantel, and W.H.M. Zijm (2000), "Warehouse Design and Control: Framework and Literatures Review," *European Journal of Operational Research*, **122**: 515–533.

Roy, D., A. Krishnamurthy, S.S. Heragu, and C.J. Malmborg (2012), "Performance Analysis and Design Tradeoffs in Warehouses with Autonomous Vehicle Technology," *IIE Transactions*, **44**(12): 1045–1060.

Roy, D., A. Krishnamurthy, S.S. Heragu, and C.J. Malmborg (2015), "Queuing Models to Analyze Dwell-Point and Cross-Aisle Location in Autonomous Vehicle-Based Warehouse Systems," *European Journal of Operational Research*, **242**(1): 72–87.

Schipper, M., Editor (2006), "Energy-Related Carbon Dioxide Emissions in the U.S. Manufacturing," U.S. Energy Information Administration Report #DOE/EIA-0573, available from: www.eia.gov/oiaf/1605/ggrpt/pdf/industry_mecs.pdf.

Tompkins, J.A., J.A. White, Y.A. Bozer, and E.H. Frazelle (2010), *Facilities Planning* (4th Ed.). Wiley, New York.

Tsuchiya, K., S. Bharitkar, and Y. Takefuji (1996), "A Neural Network Approach to Facility Layout Problems," *European Journal of Operational Research*, **89**(3): 556–563.

US Green Building Council (2016), "LEED." Available from: www.usgbc.org/leed

Wikipedia contributors (n.d.), "Internet of Things," *Wikipedia, The Free Encyclopedia.* Available from: https://en.wikipedia.org/w/index.php?title=Internet_of_things&oldid=725292973

Wongdhamma, W. (2015), "Statistical Data Mining Models for Predicting and Forecasting the Existence and Severity of Obstructive Sleep Apnea," Ph.D dissertation, School of Industrial Engineering and Management, Oklahoma State University, Stillwater, OK.

9
MANUFACTURING STRATEGY

Raffaella Cagliano and Federico Caniato

1 Introduction

Despite the fact that we live in the era of the Internet, social media and sharing economy, manufacturing still matters. Behind every Amazon, Uber, or Facebook, there are companies producing the goods that we are sharing, consuming, or chatting about in our daily lives.

According to a recent study by McKinsey & Co., manufacturing's share of the global GDP was 16% in 2010, with China topping the list at 33% (Manyika et al. 2012). There are 45 million manufacturing jobs in developed economies, and although this is significantly lower than the 62 million in 2000, this still represents 14% of the overall number of jobs in these countries (Manyika et al. 2012).

Manufacturing still matters. More so, it is ever more challenged by ongoing changes: evolving and ever more pervasive technologies, the globalization of markets and competition, changing customer needs, societal challenges, changing workforce characteristics, and expectations (e.g., John et al. 2001; Manyika et al. 2012; Chatha and Butt 2015). Having to face these challenges, manufacturing is under pressure to keep its promise as a major competitive weapon, especially in mature economies and developed countries. At the same time, companies in emerging countries are following the same steps that industry followed many years ago in the developed world, but at a different pace and with many distinctive features that require specific theories and practical knowledge.

Numerous studies support the idea that manufacturing can contribute significantly to business performance, especially by building strong manufacturing competencies (e.g., Cleveland et al. 1989; Vickery et al. 1993). The different avenues that can be taken by companies to achieve this result are described in the manufacturing strategy literature and theory development of the last five decades.

Manufacturing Strategy can be defined as "a projected pattern of manufacturing choices formulated to improve fundamental capabilities, and to support business and corporate strategy" (Miller and Hayslip 1989, p. 23). In particular, it refers to the definition of strategic goals. These goals then drive the adoption of practices and improvement programs, in order to improve performance from a medium- or long-term perspective.

In this chapter, we will mainly take an internal (company) perspective, and consider external partners as strategic interfaces to be managed rather than as the key players of the strategy itself.

From this perspective, manufacturing strategy complements, and needs alignment with, the supply chain strategy of a company, rather than being part of it.

Starting from these premises, this chapter aims to take a journey through the consolidated theories on manufacturing strategies which can be linked back to the seminal work of Skinner five decades ago (Skinner 1969). At the same time, we will consider the new challenges that manufacturing companies face in today's world and the new theories that are developing to provide guidance in this new context. In this way, we try to provide a comprehensive picture of the key concepts and the challenges that companies and researchers need to address when dealing with manufacturing strategy choices.

2 The Strategic Role of Manufacturing Operations

The contemporary concept of manufacturing strategy dates back to the late 1960s. However, older examples can be found in the principles of scientific management, promulgated by Fredrick Taylor (1911) and modified and elaborated by the industrialists of that time, among them Henry Ford. Indeed, the production at Ford, which applied the notions of product and work standardization to the assembly line, enabled the Ford Motor Company to gain a significant advantage over their competitors in the automotive industry (e.g., Hounshell 1984). Many companies interpreted the concepts of mass production in such a way as to determine the emergence of the so-called "one best way" to manage manufacturing systems. The only way for a company to differentiate itself from its competitors was to look into other functions, such as marketing or finance.

Through experience matured during years of teaching and case visits, Wickham Skinner developed his fundamental ideas about the role of manufacturing in a company's strategy, as expressed in a seminal paper of 1969 in the *Harvard Business Review*: "Manufacturing—missing link in corporate strategy" (Skinner 1969). Three basic concepts, which are the landmarks of manufacturing strategy theory even today, were put forward:

1. Different companies have different strengths and weaknesses and can choose to compete in different ways, and therefore should adopt different "yardsticks of success";
2. Similarly, different production systems have different operating characteristics;
3. Therefore, rather than adopting an industry-standard production system, the "task" for a company's manufacturing function is to construct a production system that, through a series of interrelated and internally consistent choices, reflects the priorities and tradeoffs implicit in its specific competitive situation and strategy.

(Hayes and Pisano 1996, p. 26)

From Skinner's seminal work, the theory of manufacturing strategy began to evolve (e.g., Skinner 1974; 1985; Hayes and Wheelwright 1984; Hill 1985; Voss 1992a). Despite the very important steps that rooted the importance of the manufacturing function within industrial companies, the dominant view was one where manufacturing had a mainly supportive role: the strategic management of manufacturing is "the effective use of manufacturing strengths as a competitive weapon for the achievement of business and corporate goals" (Swamidass and Newell 1987).

The observation of successful companies, however, suggested that the role of manufacturing strategy could go beyond this, becoming the main driver of the competitive strategy by creating unique capabilities. In particular, based on the observation of a number of manufacturing companies, Hayes and Wheelwright (1984) proposed a model where the strategic role of manufacturing evolves through four stages of increasing relevance:

- *Internally neutral*: manufacturing's goal is to minimize the negative impact on the overall company, by "doing as told" in a reactive fashion.
- *Externally neutral*: manufacturing has to catch up with competitors in order to maintain parity, usually by following industry practice.
- *Internally supportive*: manufacturing plays a supportive role in business strategy, and competitive priorities are the drivers of manufacturing choices in terms of structure and infrastructure.
- *Externally supportive*: manufacturing assumes a proactive role in building distinctive capabilities for competitive advantage. Competitive strategy is driven by manufacturing capabilities.

Empirical evidence at that time showed that the role of manufacturing in most companies was of the Stage 3 type (Schroeder et al. 1986; Wheelwright and Bowen 1996).

A significant change in perspective was introduced by the application of the Resource Based View to manufacturing strategy (e.g., Hayes and Upton 1998; Amundson 1998; Gagnon 1999). This paradigm underlines the key role of strategy in developing and leveraging unique operational resources for competitive advantage (Gagnon 1999). According to this perspective, the content of manufacturing strategy is defined based on those processes, technologies, organizational routines, knowledge, and skills that are needed to build the core capabilities that would allow a company to develop idiosyncratic manufacturing processes that differentiate it from competitors (Prahalad and Hamel 1990; Tranfield and Smith 1998). The perspective—as well as the manufacturing strategy process—is thus reversed (from "market to competencies" to "competencies to market"), therefore fostering the leadership role of manufacturing strategy in company's competitiveness. Empirical evidence widely supported this new perspective, showing the positive impact on firm performance (e.g., Schroeder et al. 2002; for a review, see Hitt et al. 2016).

3   Key Concepts in Manufacturing Strategy

Research into manufacturing strategy generally recognizes the distinction between the process of strategy definition and its content (e.g., Adam and Swamidass 1989; Leong et al. 1990; Voss 1992a). This distinction derives from the business strategy literature (Andrews 1971; Chandler 1962; Ansoff 1965). Fahey and Christensen (1986, p. 168) summarize the concept as "Content focuses on the specifics of what was decided, whereas process addresses how such decisions are reached in an organizational setting".

A number of models have been developed in the areas of both manufacturing strategy process and content. Research in these fields requires rather different approaches that are often carried out separately. Focusing on one subject or the other leads to greater insight into the problems and research questions that characterize each area. Unfortunately, this distinction led to the different evolution of knowledge in the two fields. Manufacturing strategy content was widely explored, while manufacturing strategy process received less attention, particularly in the early stages of empirical research. Few authors addressed the two subjects in the same study (e.g., Miller and Roth 1994; Schroeder et al. 1986; Kim and Arnold 1996; Cagliano and Spina 2000).

3.1   *Manufacturing Strategy Content*

Since Skinner's early work (1969), research on the content of manufacturing strategy distinguishes two broad categories of elements: (i) manufacturing objectives or goals and (ii) decision areas.

According to this model, the competitive environment drives the selection of a suitable business strategy that, in turn, determines mission statements for the manufacturing function. The basic manufacturing mission can be described in terms of competitive priorities—or manufacturing tasks. These tasks will then be translated into practice by taking a coherent set of decisions in a number of key areas, which are generally distinguished in structural and infrastructural decisions. More details about this model and its developments are provided in the following sections.

3.2 Manufacturing Strategy Process

The original formulation of the manufacturing strategy process model was proposed by Skinner (1969) and further developed by subsequent authors (Wheelwright 1978; Hill 1989; Fine and Hax 1985; Marucheck et al. 1990; Menda and Dilts 1997).

According to this model, manufacturing strategy is one of the functional strategies of a company. The manufacturing strategy process follows a top-down approach, in accordance with the hierarchy suggested in the traditional definition of corporate, business, and functional strategies (e.g., Chakravarthy and Lorange 1990). The comparison of industry factors with a company's characteristics helps to define business priorities. This in turn leads to the definition of the appropriate manufacturing tasks and manufacturing policies and choices.

An alternative view of the manufacturing strategy process involves a less structured approach, where strategy is formulated through a sequence of decisions informed by market requirements and by the need for external and internal fit (e.g., Papke-Shields et al. 2002; Paiva et al. 2008).

More recently, authors have suggested that a top-down approach is mostly applicable to the internally supportive manufacturing units of the Hayes and Wheelwright framework (Hayes and Wheelwright 1984), while externally supportive units require that manufacturing develops its capabilities autonomously and plays a driving role in building competitive advantage in the long term (Hayes 1985). From this new perspective, the strategy process starts from an analysis of the operating resources and competencies existing in the company. On this basis, a strategy is defined to reinforce or build the selected resources and capabilities so as to allow sustainable competitive advantage (Collis and Montgomery 1995; Gagnon 1999).

4 Manufacturing Paradigms

The development of manufacturing strategy theory cannot be seen as separate from other approaches to the study of production systems. One important stream of literature studied the evolution of the basic principles that underpin the different models and practices of manufacturing management over time. The two perspectives have been often seen as conflicting. The conceptualization of manufacturing strategic management does not include the existence of a common "best way"—or model—to manage and organize production systems. The main characteristics of the production system are defined in coherence with the competitive strategy of the company and the internal and external environment. The advocates of the strategic approach to manufacturing also often maintained that the servile imitation of successful managerial and organizational innovations causes companies to become similar, thus narrowing their strategic space (Hayes and Pisano 1994).

Various experiences in different countries and industries, however, demonstrated the existence of general rules of coherence between the levers that define manufacturing strategy. These levers depend on the characteristics of the market, the context, and the evolution of the industrial environment. These sets of coherent principles are often referred to as paradigms. After the established Fordist paradigm, other experiences were recognized as paradigms. Among these paradigms are World Class Manufacturing (Schonberger 1986), Lean Production (Womack et al. 1990), and Strategically Flexible Production (Spina et al. 1996).

4.1 The Most Relevant Manufacturing Paradigms

4.1.1 World Class Manufacturing

The World Class Manufacturing paradigm was first introduced by Hayes and Wheelwright (1984) and subsequently developed by Schonberger (1986) as well as many other authors (e.g., Giffi et al. 1990; Flynn et al. 1999). This paradigm concerns the ability to produce products for global markets that are of high quality, at low cost, and have high responsiveness and flexibility. These capabilities are reached through the implementation of best practices, that is, excellent managerial and organizational approaches, in every area of the operation. The key areas are workforce skills and capabilities, management technical competence, competing through superior quality, workforce participation, rebuilding manufacturing engineering, and incremental improvement approaches. Most of these practices were observed in leading companies in Japan, Germany, and the US. Just-in-time and total quality management practices were later included in the paradigm.

4.1.2 Lean Production

Lean Production refers to changes in production systems toward a model based on the key principle of reducing any kind of waste while streamlining production processes and adopting a total quality approach (e.g., Womack et al. 1990; Shah and Ward 2003). Lean production has been seen as a philosophy, a set of principles inspiring the design and management of production systems, as well as an approach comprising a wide variety of integrated practices, including just-in-time, total quality management, work teams, cellular manufacturing, and supplier integration. These practices are nowadays widely recognized as part of four different bundles: just-in-time (JIT), total preventive maintenance (TPM), total quality management (TQM), and human resource management (HRM) (Shah and Ward 2003).

4.1.3 Strategically Flexible Production

Strategically Flexible Production (Spina et al. 1996) was proposed as a set of coherent principles that summarize the most important changes that have occurred in production systems in the last decades of the past century. These are multifocusedness and strategic flexibility, that is, the pursuit of different goals simultaneously and the ability to rapidly shift from one set of goals to another; the integration of business processes along the value chain, inside and outside the company; and process ownership, that is, the ability to transfer decision making to the shop floor level, where problems arise. The three principles are described as complementary and are all required in order to obtain superior performance improvement capabilities.

4.1.4 Other Manufacturing Strategy Paradigms

Other models or paradigms have been discussed in the literature. These models or paradigms include agile manufacturing, mass customization, and servitization.

Agile manufacturing (Kidd 1994; Goldman et al. 1995; Yusuf et al. 1999) is an approach to manufacturing strategy and management aimed at addressing the challenge of the high volatility and uncertainty of business environments, including concepts such as virtual (e.g., Shukla et al. 1996) or holonic manufacturing (e.g., McFarlane and Bussmann 2000).

Mass customization (e.g., Pine 1999; da Silveira et al. 2001) is an approach that aims to provide individually designed products and services to every customer at reasonable cost through high process flexibility and integration.

Servitization (or servicing) refers to the innovation of abilities and processes aimed at offering Product-Service Systems, that is, bundles of goods, services, support, and knowledge, instead of just physical goods (Vandermerwe and Rada 1989; Chase and Garvin 1989; Voss 1992b; Baines et al. 2009a).

4.1.5 Smart Manufacturing: The Emerging Manufacturing Paradigm

At the turn of the century, a new wave of models and paradigms were put forward in order to synthesize the latest changes in manufacturing systems, especially the wide diffusion of new technologies such as advanced, human-centered automation, cyber-physical systems, interconnection through the Internet of Things, virtual/augmented reality, and big data analytics. These approaches have been called Smart Manufacturing (or Factory) (Zühlke 2010; Hessman 2013); Industry 4.0 (e.g., Kagermann et al. 2013); or the Factory of the Future (e.g., EU 2013), depending on the emphasis given to the various components. Knowledge of the reconfiguration of manufacturing strategies, organization, and management consequent to the adoption of these technologies is still in its infancy, and it will be one of the main avenues of research in manufacturing strategy in the years to come (see Section 7).

4.2 Manufacturing Paradigm Versus Strategic Choices: The Debate

Despite the different formulations proposed in the literature for the emerging paradigms, and going beyond debate over actual possibility to generalize contingent manufacturing models into strategic paradigms (see Bartezzaghi 1999), there is a key criticism of this approach. Most of the literature about paradigms tends to present normative solutions to manufacturing management that do not take into account either the specific contingencies that the company faces or the different strategies that the company may follow in order to gain competitive advantage.

Spina (1998) suggested a way to overcome the debate between paradigmatic and strategic views of manufacturing, by distinguishing three levels that describe manufacturing:

- *practices and techniques*: used to innovate production systems, they are the bricks that form the strategy and need adaptation to both the competitive environment and the internal context;
- *models*: coherent and systematic combinations of practices which are developed autonomously by the company to respond to their internal and external environment;
- *manufacturing paradigms*: a limited set of principles which underpin different techniques and bring together various manufacturing models. The principles defining the paradigms synthesize the common *modus operandi* of companies across different settings.

Using these conceptual categories, Spina (1998) asserted and empirically showed that strategic choices are possible—and necessary—to position a company against its competitors, even if they are adopting the same manufacturing paradigm.

Even the traditional exponents of the strategic school recognized that manufacturing strategy experienced a clear change in the reference paradigm around the beginning of the 1990s (Hayes and Pisano 1996; Clark 1996; Skinner 1996), since most of the concepts proposed in the early years had to be revisited.

5 The Strategic Goals of Manufacturing Operations

As mentioned in Section 2, one of the key components of a manufacturing strategy is the set of strategic goals, or competitive priorities, that a company pursues through manufacturing. Competitive priorities involve the translation of business strategy into tasks for the manufacturing function or capabilities that must be developed in order to fulfill its supporting role.

Manufacturing tasks were originally grouped into the broad categories of cost, quality, delivery, and flexibility (e.g., Hayes and Wheelwright 1984; Ward et al. 1998). These categories have been refined to more detailed levels in order to better understand connections and relationships (e.g., Slack 1983; Neely and Wilson 1992; Gerwin 1993; Garvin 1993). Specification of the most important competitive priorities was thought to be essential in order to better understand the specific improvements needed in manufacturing and, thus, to facilitate the planning of a coherent set of actions aimed at providing these improvements (Garvin 1993; Skinner 1996).

Over the years, new competitive dimensions have been highlighted such as time (e.g., Blackburn 1991; Stalk and Hout 1990); customer satisfaction (Chase and Garvin 1989); servicing (Armistead and Clark 1991); product innovation (Hayes et al. 1988); customization (e.g., Kotha 1995; Pine 1999); and, recently, environmental and social sustainability (Jimenez and Lorente 2001; Porter and Kramer 2006). This shift in the focus of manufacturing competitive priorities is fundamental to sustain the competitive advantage of manufacturing companies in developed economies, as the traditional cost-quality-delivery advantage is diminishing and new business models based on innovation, servitization, and sustainability are needed to attract and retain customers (Manyika et al. 2012; Kuivanen 2008; Chatha and Butt 2015).

Complementing this view, Hill (1985) proposed distinguishing competitive priorities in to those that drive the competition of the company in the marketplace, and the performance goals for manufacturing. The former are the performance dimensions on which the company wins orders or projects against its competitors ("order winners") or those that the company has to satisfy at a minimum level in order to stay in the market ("order qualifiers"). The latter are measurable performance goals for manufacturing.

A new wave of studies began in more recent years around the concept of manufacturing capabilities. In particular, Swink and Hegarty (1998) highlighted the necessity of discerning the differences between competitive priorities (called product differentiation dimensions), manufacturing performance goals (manufacturing outcomes), and manufacturing capabilities. Manufacturing capabilities are the activities that a company can do better than its competitors and are the basis for the development of superior products. This concept was developed within the stream of strategic literature focused on core competencies and capabilities (e.g., Prahalad and Hamel 1990; Stalk et al. 1992; Barney 1991). The concept of manufacturing capability has been used by many authors, many of whom maintain that decisions in manufacturing have to be made according to the core capabilities that a company wants to build in order to sustain future competitive advantage (e.g., Hayes and Pisano 1994; 1996; Hayes and Upton 1998; Jayanthi et al. 2009). Developing capabilities that create new opportunities for the competitive strategy of the firm is the main goal of manufacturing units that are in the externally supportive stage (Hayes and Wheelwright 1984; see Section 2).

5.1 Strategic Trade-Offs and Cumulative Capabilities

A very important issue that has been widely debated in the manufacturing strategy literature almost since the beginning, is the interaction between different manufacturing objectives. Three contrasting approaches in particular are present in the literature: the trade-off model, the cumulative model, and the integrative model (Boyer and Lewis 2002).

5.1.1 The Trade-Off Model

The trade-off model was first posited by Skinner in his early work (Skinner 1969; 1974). He asserted that no manufacturing unit can perform equally well on every performance measure and that manufacturing objectives need to be traded off against each other. The decisions that are made when developing manufacturing strategy result often in improvements in one performance dimension, while a second dimension is worsened. Managers therefore have to decide which performance is the most important for their company.

Trade-offs and their importance for manufacturing strategy have been widely studied, either by empirically testing them or by exploring their nature and motivations (see da Silveira 2005 for a review).

The success of Japanese manufacturing firms proved that these compromises are not always necessary, however, since their management practices allowed them to improve performance measures that were traditionally thought to be antithetical (Wheelwright 1981; Schonberger 1982; New 1992; Collins and Schmenner 1993). In a similar vein, other authors suggested that advances in manufacturing technology and organization minimize the effect of trade-offs and the need for focus (e.g., Goldhar and Jelinek 1983; Corbett et al. 1993).

5.1.2 The Cumulative Model

Taking a different perspective, Nakane (1986) suggested, and Ferdows and De Meyer (1990) supported with empirical evidence, that most companies follow definite sequences of improvement that aim at building capabilities in a cumulative way. The best sequence found is quality-time-cost-flexibility—this model is often referred to as the sandcone model (Ferdows and De Meyer 1990). A number of empirical tests in different contexts and with different contingent factors were subsequently performed, thus providing growing evidence to support the cumulative model (Amoako-Gyampah and Meredith 2007; Rosenzweig and Roth 2004; Größler and Grubner 2006). As pointed out by Schroeder et al. (2011), however, the cumulative model does not find undisputed support, and contingencies still prove to have a major impact.

In a similar vein, the concept of multifocusedness has also been put forward and tested, to contrast the trade-off view. Spina et al. (1996) used empirical evidence in order to show that companies that are "multifocused" aim to improve different goals simultaneously and obtain superior performance improvements if supported by adequate investments in process integration and worker empowerment. Rosenzweig and Easton (2010) later conducted a meta-analysis of the literature to contribute to the debate about the ability of manufacturing to focus on multiple competitive capabilities at the same time and use the theory of performance frontiers to justify the lack of empirical support to the trade-off model.

5.1.3 The Integrative Model

The debate about trade-offs versus cumulative competencies continued for several decades. In 1996, Skinner maintained that:

> While trade-off relationships change and performance on most criteria improves with new technologies, this does not mean that trade-offs go away. The trade-offs will be

different in kind, their mathematical relationships altered, and new different performance criteria become more important for success or failure.

(Skinner 1996, p. 9)

Along the same lines, Hayes and Pisano (1996) asserted the minor importance of "first order" trade-offs between performances when compared to the "dynamic, second order tradeoffs" which do not involve performance dimensions, but instead involves their rate of improvement. Similarly, Schmenner and Swink (1998) proposed that the trade-off model involves the importance placed on different competitive priorities, while the cumulative model involves the improvement of capabilities over time.

These authors are generally seen as proposing an integrative model (Boyer and Lewis 2002), that considers both previous models (trade-off and cumulative) to be valid, but at different logical levels.

5.2 Strategic Configurations

A complementary perspective has been adopted by a number of researchers in manufacturing strategy when dealing with the definition of a strategy's content. Specifically, manufacturing strategy is seen from a holistic perspective in this stream of studies, where the content is defined by an integrated set of goals and actions—a manufacturing strategy configuration.

The configuration view was widely adopted in the strategy and organization studies literature (e.g., Miles and Snow 1978; Mintzberg 1979; Porter 1980; for a review, see McGee and Thomas 1986 or Dess et al. 1993). Organizations are seen as a holistic synthesis of multiple, independent characteristics. Miller (1996) pointed out that configurations are particularly useful when the relationships between individual variables are too complex to be modelled.

Sweeney (1991), and later on Bozarth and McDermott (1998), reviewed studies in search of generic manufacturing strategies or configurations. The most influential conceptualization is one initially proposed by De Meyer (1990) and then worked on by Miller and Roth (1994), in Europe and North America, respectively. Using manufacturing tasks as grouping criteria, they identified three groups of companies: caretakers, those that competed first on price and second on reliability and consistency; marketeers that competed on product range and quality; and innovators, companies competing on product quality and innovativeness. De Meyer (1990) added a new configuration, the high-performance product, which competes on a wide range of dimensions, but primarily on flexibility. A number of subsequent works further tested this framework in different contexts and time periods (e.g., Kathuria 2000; Frohlich and Dixon 2001; Zhao et al. 2006; Sum et al. 2004). Cagliano et al. (2005) used longitudinal data to test the stability of manufacturing configurations over time. They were able to demonstrate that the existing manufacturing configurations did not change over more than a decade, while single companies showed a certain strategic flexibility, moving often from one configuration to the other over a relatively short period of time. Recently, this framework was extended to include the newer manufacturing goals: environmental and social sustainability (Longoni and Cagliano 2015). The analyses show that consideration of the new priorities translates into an extension of the existing configurations rather than a relevant change to them, since the new priorities are added to the existing configurations, according to the best strategic fit.

6 Manufacturing Decisions

Manufacturing objectives are achieved through a pattern of actions that move a set of control levers within main decision areas. Decisions are generally categorized as structural and infrastructural (Hayes and Wheelwright 1984). The former are the "brick-and-mortar" decisions about capital investment while the latter decisions deal with softer aspects of manufacturing such as management and organization.

Structural decisions include the design of production capacity and process technology, the selection of the factory type and location, vertical integration, and sourcing decisions. Infrastructural decisions have to do with operational policies, quality assurance, labor and staffing, performance measurement, and the introduction of new products.

The decision categories first suggested by Skinner (1969) were generally confirmed and enriched by subsequent contributions (Hayes and Wheelwright 1984; Buffa 1984; Fine and Hax 1985; Hill 1989). A number of studies empirically validated the conceptual categories proposed by the literature (e.g., Schroeder et al. 1986; Ward et al. 1988).

Most of the literature reported the choice of the manufacturing process as central to the development of manufacturing strategy (e.g., Hayes and Wheelwright 1984; Hill 1989) and that the other choices should be considered as part of process choice. In general, earlier studies placed a greater emphasis on structural decisions, according to a "static" view of manufacturing operations, where investments were the key strategic decisions.

The emergence of the new ideas about both corporate and manufacturing strategy asserted the importance, and even the centrality, of the infrastructural aspects of manufacturing strategy. Most authors underline the strong cumulative effect of infrastructural decisions, which determine the irreversibility of choices and their impact in the long run, due to path dependency (Hayes and Pisano 1996). The integration of structural and infrastructural choices was considered essential in order to build competitive advantage (e.g., Berry and Hill 1992; Misterek et al. 1992; Kinnie and Staughton 1991).

6.1 Manufacturing Decisions from a Contingency Perspective

Manufacturing choices are generally made in a contingent perspective, that is, choices are aligned to the business environment and the business strategy (external consistency or fit) and are internally coherent, that is, coherent within the manufacturing function and across functions in the company (internal consistency or fit) (Hayes and Wheelwright 1984).

Early examples of studies addressing external fit are Miller and Roth (1994) and Kotha and Orne (1989), which highlighted suitable strategies to fit business requirements and the external environment. Ward and colleagues empirically tested the links between the external environment, the competitive strategy, and manufacturing strategy (Ward et al. 1996; Ward and Duray 2000). Finally, after reviewing OM studies using a contingency approach, Sousa and Voss (2008) underline not only its importance, but also its limitations, and suggest a way forward for this type of research.

6.2 Manufacturing Improvement Programs and Best Practices

Internal fit between the elements of manufacturing is dependent upon the complex interactions of a wide range of interdependent variables that are at play when dealing with the main structural and infrastructural decisions. The challenge of internal coherence between manufacturing choices is often faced by proposing configurations of structural and infrastructural decisions that fit specific environments and strategic tasks, such as manufacturing improvement programs or manufacturing best practices.

Although the traditional framework, based on structural and infrastructural decisions is conceptually powerful, few studies have explored it empirically. Rather, manufacturing strategy content was explored in terms of best practices, or "ready-to-wear" strategic action programs. As Kim and Arnold (1996, p. 46) pointed out, "manufacturing executives are continuously looking at improvement programmes as the place where manufacturing strategy should be operationalized".

The best practice approach derives from the evidence that best practice leads to better operating performance (e.g., Hanson and Voss 1993; Voss 1995; Voss et al. 1997; Flynn et al. 1999; Laugen et al. 2005). Their popularity is explained by their accessibility and their *a priori* solution to the problem of internal consistency. As noted by Mills et al. (1995, p. 24), best practices, "can be considered as bundles of actions in certain majority view decision areas, which tend to work well together".

The literature reports a vast number of best practices. To the original list of programs implemented by Japanese firms, other actions were included over time for empirical exploration, including: concurrent/simultaneous engineering (e.g., Womack et al. 1990; Aggarwal 1995; Ahmed 1996); continuous improvement (Hayes et al. 1988; Harrison 1998; Garver 2003); advanced manufacturing technologies (e.g., Schonberger 1986; Gunn 1987; Hayes et al. 1988; Ettlie 1988; Giffi et al. 1990; Aggarwal 1995; Bates and Flynn 1996); and human resource management and organization (e.g., Schonberger 1986; Gunn 1987; Hayes et al. 1988; Ettlie 1988; Womack et al. 1990; Giffi et al. 1990; Bates and Flynn 1996). The most recent additions to the list involve the most advanced technologies (e.g., human centered automation, digital technologies, 3D printing, high precision technologies), and environmental (e.g., Sarkis 1998; Klassen and Whybark 1999; Kleindorfer et al. 2005) and social sustainability programs (Veleva and Ellenbecker 2001; Das et al. 2008).

The best practice approach has been widely debated. First of all, it may hamper the ability of managers to understand and design their own strategy aimed at building distinctive competitive advantage. Often programs are thought of as a panacea or cure-all for virtually all company problems. Instead, best practices should be tailored to the specific context and situation of a company, and incorporated into a coherent strategic framework rather than being seen as fixed recipes for the improvement of manufacturing (Mills et al. 1995).

The selection and adoption of manufacturing improvement programs should be oriented to build long-term capabilities from a strategic perspective (Hayes and Pisano 1994; 1996; Wheelwright and Bowen 1996). In this view, some authors discuss the complementarities between the best practice and the strategic choice approaches. Voss (1995) suggests that these two approaches should be used together in order to fully exploit manufacturing strategy development. Miller and Hayslip (1989) contend that strategic planning (i.e., decisions on structure and infrastructure) is the exclusive province of top management while improvement programs arise from the operating levels.

7 Manufacturing Strategy and the Evolution of Technology

Manufacturing strategy has always been strictly connected with the evolution of manufacturing technology and its adoption. Probably the most famous historical example is the case of the Ford Motor Company at the beginning of the 20th century. In order to make its Model T affordable to a large number of customers, Henry Ford designed a production system that was capable of producing many more cars at a much lower unit cost compared to competitors. In the company's factory at Highland Park, Ford developed the concepts of production mechanization and the assembly line. Combined with product standardization and work specialization, this gave birth to the concept of mass production (Chandler 1977).

Since the early days indeed, production technology has been considered a key dimension in the design of manufacturing systems that should be aligned with the manufacturing goals of the company and with the other structural and infrastructural decisions (see Section 6).

7.1 Automation

In the 1950s, production technology evolved into automation, the substitution of machines for manual work to pursue two fundamental goals: increasing productivity by reducing cycle time and improving quality by ensuring identical repetition of operations. Automation was associated with high production volumes, which justified the required investments since they allowed a shorter payback.

The evolution of technology clearly impacted products significantly, but for a given product technology, the choice of the process technology is associated with the manufacturing strategy, that is, with the strategic goals pursued by the company. Process automation was therefore associated with high volumes of low cost, standard products; and manual processing was associated with low volumes of high cost, customized products. Hayes and Wheelwright (1979) synthesized this concept very well in their well-known product-process matrix.

7.2 The Role of Information Technology

With the development of electronics, information technology (IT), and computers, manufacturing technology has changed significantly. The fundamental role of IT has been to change the way machines are programmed and controlled, allowing the development of concepts such as numeric control, computer aided design and manufacturing (CAD/CAM), material requirements planning (MRP), and many other systems. Information technology thus allowed the integration of multiple machines. This created interconnected production systems that could be better programmed and controlled, thus giving birth to the concept of Computer Integrated Manufacturing (CIM) (Gerwin 1982; Parthasharty and Yin 1996). Many authors, such as Rosenthal (1984), Beatty (1992), and Boyer et al. (1997), adopted the term "Advanced Manufacturing Technologies" (AMT) as a general concept representing the combination of mechanical and electronic manufacturing technologies.

7.3 Flexible Technologies

IT enabled a new strategic orientation towards automation: the quest for flexibility (Gerwin 1993). Essentially, computerized manufacturing was seen as a possible way to "escape" from the traditional concept of automation as a synonym for rigid, dedicated systems. Concepts such as Flexible Manufacturing Systems (FMSs) were introduced, emphasizing the ability to adapt to different products, with lower adjustment costs and set-up times (Nemetz and Fry 1988; Babbar and Rai 1990).

Despite claims of their flexibility, such systems failed at first to provide the promised benefits and to meet the challenges of increasingly fast, volatile, and changing products and markets, thus often resulting in systems with worse performance than those less integrated and automated (Meredith 1987; Boer et al. 1990).

The Toyota Production System was an alternative approach to automation and flexibility, combining automation with human work ("automation with a human touch"), instead of aiming at completely substituting machines for people. In this way, technology could enhance productivity while still allowing the flexibility inherent to human activities (Shingo and Dillon 1989).

7.4 Digital Technologies

Towards the end of the century, the role of technology in manufacturing evolved further, introducing the possibility of monitoring processes in real time, at first adopting tools such as barcodes, subsequently Radio Frequency Identification (RFID) and now the more general approach of the Internet of Things (IoT) (Huang et al. 2012; Wong et al. 2014; Meyer et al. 2011). At first monitoring was focused on tracking and tracing materials, parts, and products throughout the process, in order to control the progress of activities. More recently, the adoption of advanced sensors, capable of measuring size, shape, temperature, speed, etc., and connected through wired or wireless networks, allows comprehensive control of the entire process.

From a strategic perspective, these recent developments are in line with the pursuit of both quality, embedded in the process and controlled at the source, and responsiveness (i.e., the ability to respond to an increasingly unpredictable demand), by enabling the real-time visibility of flows and stocks. These technologies allow self-adjustment and self-optimization by machines, as well as a shift from reactive to predictive maintenance. This, therefore, affects the role of personnel, who can now monitor machines remotely and are required to develop new advanced skills in order to perform complex, decision-making tasks.

7.5 New Technologies

Green Technologies and Additive Manufacturing are the most recent developments that are expected to significantly modify the manufacturing processes.

With the increasing attention on environmental issues, the adoption of energy efficient and green technologies has become a priority for manufacturing strategy, in order to improve environmental sustainability as well as reducing energy costs (Dangayach and Deshmukh 2001; Chatha and Butt 2015).

Additive manufacturing (known as 3D printing), is expected to disrupt the conventional production models (Eyers and Potter 2015). This approach to production is based on adding layers of materials so as to obtain the desired product, on demand and in a short time, thus enabling distributed, flexible, and customized manufacturing. At the moment, additive manufacturing is mostly used for prototypes and very small production lots and is not yet a real alternative for large-scale production; however, it is indeed well suited to enable strategies oriented towards customization, leading to the so-called factory on demand (Noori and Lee, 2002), although this still has to demonstrate its potential.

We can conclude that the relationship between manufacturing strategy and technological evolution has always been strong and is still providing new and interesting challenges for both research and practice, opening the way to new developments.

8 Global Manufacturing Strategies

Manufacturing strategy research has today broadened its scope to consider multi-plant organizations, located in either one or multiple countries (often referred to as offshoring), and increasingly sourcing and selling internationally.

Given the focus of this chapter on manufacturing strategy, we will now examine decisions related to the location and management of production facilities, with direct (full or partial) ownership. We will not consider sourcing and distribution decisions, however, which are generally considered as part of a broader global supply chain strategy.

8.1 Enablers and Drivers

This phenomenon was possible thanks to a variety of enabling factors: the reduction or elimination of both trade and investment barriers, the development of emerging economies and their opening to international trade and investments, the improvement in transportation and communication infrastructures, and the enlargement of international trade agreements and organizations.

In addition to these enabling factors, other strategic drivers fostered the phenomenon, as theorized by Buckley and Casson (1976): the very different costs of labor, materials, and energy in different countries and continents encouraged the shift of production activities to low-cost countries (an efficiency-seeking strategy). In other cases, the opening and fast growth of vast new markets, with increasing income, in contrast to the slowing of mature markets, encouraged companies, not only to sell, but also to produce locally in order to quickly reach their target markets and to avoid logistics and customs costs (a market-seeking strategy). A third driver for moving production activities was the availability of scarce resources, which could be financial, material, or human, and in particular, high-skilled labor (a resource-seeking strategy). Finally, a fourth driver could be described as the search for complementary assets, capabilities, or products (strategic asset-seeking strategy).

8.2 Plant Location

It is therefore clear, as proposed since the early frameworks used in the field (see Section 6), that plant location is one of the key decisions in the definition of the manufacturing strategy. The models that can support companies in such decisions have been carefully investigated by several authors, often combining multiple variables. A major stream of research (e.g., Schmenner 1979; Aikens 1985; DuBois et al. 1993) proposed a "total cost" perspective, combining the multiple cost elements involved in manufacturing (production, transportation, custom duties, taxes, etc.).

A challenge arising from the internationalization of manufacturing is connected to national cultures, which affect the way and the effectiveness of transferring managerial and production methods. A well-known and much-studied case was the transfer of the Japanese production model to US plants, as shown by Schonberger (1982) and Liker et al. (1999). The study of the role of culture in designing and managing international manufacturing operations was, and still is, a relevant and promising research direction (Pagell et al. 2005).

8.3 Manufacturing Networks

Today many companies operate multiple plants, often in different countries, and therefore a network perspective is needed, considering the configuration of the network, the role of each plant, and the relationships among them.

Ferdows (1997), in his seminal work subsequently tested and extended by Vereecke and Van Dierdonck (2002) and Vereecke et al. (2006), conceptualized the role of the plant as a combination of two dimensions: the strategic reason for establishing a factory in a specific country (location advantage—as discussed above) and the site competence, which can range from being a simple production center, with no design or engineering responsibility, to being a center of excellence for the whole company. The combination of the two dimensions leads to the identification of six possible roles for each plant, which have to be defined consistently with the overall manufacturing network strategy of the company.

DuBois et al. (1993) proposed a framework for manufacturing network strategy that combines competitive priorities, manufacturing performance goals, market orientation, experience, and product characteristics. Shi and Gregory (1998) proposed a map of international manufacturing network configurations based on the level of geographic dispersion and coordination between international manufacturing operations, identifying the required strategic capabilities.

Rudberg and Olhager (2003) proposed a combined analysis of manufacturing networks and supply chains from an operations strategy perspective, analyzing coordination approaches according to the number of facilities and the level of vertical integration. Miltenburg (2009) proposed a definition consisting of six objects: generic international strategies, manufacturing networks, network manufacturing output, network levers, network capability, and factory types.

8.4 Recent Trends

Recently, a new research trend has emerged that focuses on the relocation of manufacturing operations around the world, as a consequence of changing factors and drivers at a global level, as well as new strategic orientations. Terms such as "reshoring/backshoring" (i.e., bringing back manufacturing operations in western countries) or "nearshoring" (i.e., moving manufacturing operations closer to the home country) have become popular in both research and practice (e.g., Kinkel and Maloca 2009; Kinkel 2012; Ellram et al. 2013; Gray et al. 2013). There has been strong emphasis on these topics, given their potential impact on the employment and the economy in mature countries, but whether this is a real and relevant phenomenon, or just political "hype," still has to be demonstrated.

9 How to Research Manufacturing Strategy

Manufacturing strategy was investigated over the decades using multiple methods, as reported in the various literature reviews published on the subject (Dangayach and Deshmukh 2001; Chatha and Butt 2015), including both conceptual and empirical papers, and both qualitative and quantitative methods, therefore exploiting the strengths of each method and compensating for their weaknesses.

Conceptual papers were very useful at the initial stages of research to define fundamental concepts and to formulate new theory to be subsequently tested by means of empirical studies. Today, conceptual papers are still a valid option with which to propose new theoretical developments, without neglecting the vast amount of literature already published. Conceptual papers today should be based on a sound theoretical basis, maybe combining different streams of research, even borrowing from other disciplines, to propose new directions and research propositions.

Empirical methodologies were adopted in the past with both an exploratory/descriptive purpose, as well as an explanatory/interpretative aim. Qualitative methods, such as case studies, have been very useful in the theory-building phase, allowing the analysis of complex phenomena and relationships between multiple variables, of different natures. They often allow the formulation of new models and research propositions. Quantitative methods, such as cross-sectional surveys on large samples, contributed most to the theory-testing phase, allowing hypotheses testing and the generalization of results.

Today, purely exploratory/descriptive studies may only be used to analyze very new and emerging phenomena, where for more consolidated phenomena, explanatory and theory-testing methods are required.

9.1 Large-Scale Surveys

A very important stream of research on manufacturing strategy is based on large-scale, multi-country surveys, thanks to the joint efforts of researchers from different universities, which allowed the gathering of very broad sets of data, with a very international perspective, in some cases also allowing longitudinal analyses thanks to the iteration of the survey over time.

The most important projects of this kind are:

- The Manufacturing Futures Project Survey (Miller 1982; De Meyer et al. 1989)
- World Class Manufacturing (subsequently renamed High Performance Manufacturing) (Flynn et al. 1997; Schroeder and Flynn 2001)
- The Global Manufacturing Research Group (Whybark and Vastag 1993; Whybark 1997; Whybark et al. 2009; Lee et al. 2015)
- The International Manufacturing Strategy Survey (Lindberg et al. 1998; Spina et al. 1996; www.manufacturingstrategy.net).

9.2 Limitations and Future Developments

Some authors have devoted their attention to reviewing the methodology adopted in researching manufacturing strategy and suggesting directions for improvement (Boyer and Pagell 2000; Barnes 2001). Some methodological limitations emerge. These limitations may be useful directions for future development. One limitation is the difficulty of conducting longitudinal studies. This is due to the lengthy data collection process from cause to effect. It is essential to be able to track the adoption of a specific manufacturing strategy, and then to be able to observe how it evolves over time while measuring results. A second limitation is the small number of papers adopting multiple methods, thus compensating their strengths and weaknesses, although this is also difficult to include in a single paper given the usual space limitations (and the effort required to conduct data collection). A third limitation is the small number of surveys addressing multiple respondents, which is also a challenging task, but may provide richer and more robust data. A fourth limitation is reliance on a single source of data, where the combination of multiple sources (e.g., both primary and secondary data) may enable triangulation and greater reliability.

10 New Challenges for Manufacturing Strategy

We now summarize the current and future challenges for manufacturing strategy, including those already mentioned in the previous pages, as well as some additions, to support young scholars in focusing their research efforts.

Our first challenge looks at flexibility, agility, and ambidexterity. We have already discussed the concepts of flexibility and agility (Gunasekaran 1998; Sharifi and Zhang 1999). More recently, however, a new challenge has emerged: the need to be simultaneously flexible and highly efficient. Borrowing a concept from the strategic management literature, the term "ambidexterity" has been used, referring to the ability to combine both the exploitation of current existing capabilities and the exploration of new ones (March 1991; Patel et al. 2012). It is still necessary to understand how firms can combine these two traditionally antithetical objectives.

Next is the servitization of a manufacturing/sharing economy. Servitization means that users are no longer owners of the product. While this business model is already quite common in business-to-business contexts, more recently it has also spread in consumer markets, thanks to the so-called sharing economy. One example is in the form of car sharing or bike sharing (users pick up cars or bikes that are available around the city for short-term rental, and drop them off where they want). The way this phenomenon affects manufacturing strategy, the way products are designed and produced, however, is still worth further exploration (Neely 2008; Baines et al. 2009a; Baines et al. 2009b).

The third challenge is sustainability (closed loop, circular economy, remanufacturing, cradle to cradle, etc.). This fundamental concept within the sustainability domain is the reduction of waste and the re-use, re-cycling, or re-manufacturing of products, thus creating closed-loop supply chains or, more in general, circular economy models. To make this happen, however, multiple enabling factors are needed, such as reverse logistic networks and economic incentives, but also an appropriate manufacturing strategy, starting from product and process design (Jayaraman et al. 1999; Östlin et al. 2008; Kumar and Putnam 2008; Zhu et al. 2011).

Next, we look at the changing nature of work. Challenges such as the aging of the population, the massive employment of millennials with their peculiar needs and competencies (native-digital), the globalization of the workforce as a consequence of the immigration flows, etc. are some of the many forces requiring a rethinking of the way work is designed and organized (e.g., Gratton 2011). At the same time, the evolution of manufacturing technology is continuously placing a number of challenges—but also opportunities—in front of workers, in terms of involvement, contribution, motivation, but also work intensity, strain, safety, and eventually well-being. The relationship between manufacturing strategy choices and work organization cannot be neglected in future research (Brown 1996; Askenazy 2001; Longoni et al. 2013; Longoni et al. 2014; Lampela et al. 2015).

Additive manufacturing/3D printing and virtual manufacturing are new forms of technology that also serve as challenges to marketing. These new technologies could enable and enhance the potential of the "old" idea of virtual manufacturing as a distributed set of independent organizations, collaborating on demand to deliver a customized product to the customer (Martinez et al. 2001; Noori and Lee 2002; Zhang et al. 2014; Eyers and Potter 2015). Will additive manufacturing make it happen for real?

Digitalization (the Internet of Things, big data analytics, etc.), our next challenge, is the development of digital technologies and their spread on the shop floor, as well as across all company functions, has opened new opportunities for manufacturing. The latest opportunities now include the possibility to monitor progress and performance in real time, thus collecting a huge amount of data and enabling self-optimizing and self-improving systems, thanks to new algorithms and computational power. The way this phenomenon will affect manufacturing strategies is still open to question (Zhong et al. 2015; Opresnik and Taisch 2015).

As already mentioned in Section 8, reshoring/backshoring/nearshoring as a phenomenon is still worth further investigation in order to understand its real potential and sustainability, as well as developing appropriate and consistent manufacturing strategies (Kinkel and Maloca 2009; Kinkel 2012; Ellram et al. 2013; Gray et al. 2013). The contribution of this phenomenon to regain competitiveness in the manufacturing industries of developed economies is a very important matter for study.

Acknowledgement

To Gianluca Spina, our mentor and constant source of inspiration.

References and Bibliography

Adam, E.F., and Swamidass, P.M. (1989) "Assessing Operations Management from a strategic perspective", *Journal of Management*, **15**(2): 181–203.

Aggarwal, S. (1995) "Emerging hard and soft technologies: Current status, issues and implementation problems", *Omega*, **23**(3): 323–339.

Ahmed, J.U. (1996) "Modern approaches to product reliability improvement", *International Journal of Quality & Reliability Management*, **13**(3): 27–41.

Aikens, C.H. (1985) "Facility location models for distribution planning", *European Journal of Operational Research*, **22**(3): 263–279.

Amoako-Gyampah, K., and Meredith, J.R. (2007) "Examining cumulative capabilities in a developing economy", *International Journal of Operations & Production Management*, **27**(9): 928–950.

Amundson, S.D. (1998) "Relationships between theory-driven empirical research in operations management and other disciplines", *Journal of Operations Management*, **16**(4): 341–359.

Andrews, K.R. (1971) *The Concept of Corporate Strategy*, RD Irwin, Homewood, IL.

Ansoff, H.I. (1965) *Corporate Strategy*, McGraw Hill, New York.

Armistead, C., and Clark, G. (1991) "A framework for formulating after-sales support strategy", *International Journal of Operations & Production Management*, **11**(3): 111–124.

Askenazy, P. (2001) "Innovative workplace practices and occupational injuries and illnesses in the United States", *Economic and Industrial Democracy*, **22**(4): 485–516.

Babbar, S., and Rai, A. (1990) "Computer integrated flexible manufacturing: An implementation framework", *International Journal of Operations & Production Management*, **10**(1): 42–50.

Baines, T.S., Lightfoot, H.W., Benedettini, O., and Kay, J.M. (2009a) "The servitization of manufacturing: A review of literature and reflection on future challenges", *Journal of Manufacturing Technology Management*, **20**(5): 547–567.

Baines, T.S., Lightfoot, H.W., Peppard, J., Johnson, M., Tiwari, A., Shehab, E., and Swink, M. (2009b) "Towards an operations strategy for product-centric servitization", *International Journal of Operations & Production Management*, **29**(5): 494–519.

Barnes, D. (2001) "Research methods for the empirical investigation of the process of formation of operations strategy", *International Journal of Operations & Production Management*, **21**(8): 1076–1095.

Barney, J. (1991) "Firm resources and sustained competitive advantage", *Journal of Management*, **17**(1): 99–120.

Bartezzaghi, E. (1999) "The evolution of production models: Is a new paradigm emerging?", *International Journal of Operations & Production Management*, **19**(2): 229–250.

Bates, K.A., and Flynn, E.J. (1996) "Innovation history and competitive advantage: A resource based view of manufacturing technology innovations", *Working Paper*, Management Department, Stern School of Business, New York.

Beatty, C.A. (1992) "Implementing advanced manufacturing technologies", *Sloan Management Review*, **33**(4): 47–60.

Berry, W.L., and Hill, T. (1992) "Linking systems to strategy", *International Journal of Operations & Production Management*, **12**(10): 3–15.

Blackburn, J.D. (1991) *Time Based Competition: The Next Battle Ground in American Manufacturing*, Business One Irwin, Homewood, IL.

Boer, H., Hill, M.R., and Krabbendam, J.J. (1990) "FMS implementation management: Promise and performance", *International Journal of Operations & Production Management*, **10**(1): 32–40.

Boyer, K.K., and Lewis, M.W. (2002) "Competitive priorities: Investigating the need for trade-offs in operations strategy", *Production and Operations Management*, **11**(1): 9–20.

Boyer, K.K., and Pagell, M. (2000) "Measurement issues in empirical research: Improving measures of operations strategy and advanced manufacturing technology", *Journal of Operations Management*, **18**(3): 361–374.

Boyer, K.K., Leong, G.K., Ward, P.T., and Krajewski, L.J. (1997) "Unlocking the potential of advanced manufacturing technologies", *Journal of Operations Management*, **15**(4): 331–347.

Bozarth, C., and McDermott, C. (1998) "Configurations in manufacturing strategy: A review and directions for future research", *Journal of Operations Management*, **16**(4): 427–439.

Brown, S.P. (1996) "A meta-analysis and review of organizational research on job involvement", *Psychological bulletin*, **120**(2): 235–255.

Buckley, P.J., and Casson, M. (1976) *The Future of the Multinational Enterprise*, Macmillan, London.

Buffa, E.S. (1984) *Meeting the Competitive Challenge: Manufacturing Strategy for U.S. Companies*, Irwin, Homewood, IL.

Cagliano, R., Acur, N., and Boer, H. (2005) "Patterns of change in manufacturing strategy configurations", *International Journal of Operations & Production Management*, **25**(7): 701–718.

Cagliano, R., and Spina, G. (2000) "How improvement programmes of manufacturing are selected: the role of strategic priorities and past experience", *International Journal of Operations & Production Management*, **20**(7): 772–792.

Chakravarthy, B., and Lorange, P. (1990) *Managing the Strategy Process*, Prentice-Hall, Englewood Cliffs, NJ.

Chandler, A. (1977) *The Visible Hand: The Managerial Revolution in American Business*, Harvard University Press, Cambridge, MA.

Chandler, A.D. (1962) *Strategy and Structure: Chapters in the History of the American Industrial Enterprise*, MIT Press, Cambridge, MA.

Chase, R., and Garvin, D.A. (1989) "The service factory", *Harvard Business Review*, **67**(4): 61–69.

Chatha, K.A., and Butt, I. (2015) "Themes of study in manufacturing strategy literature", *International Journal of Operations & Production Management*, **35**(4): 604–698.

Clark, K. (1996) "Competing through manufacturing and the new manufacturing paradigm: Is manufacturing strategy passè?", *Production and Operations Management*, **5**(1): 42–58.

Cleveland, G., Shroeder, R., and Anderson, J. (1989) "A theory of production competence", *Decision Science*, **20**(4): 655–668.

Collins, R.S., and Schmenner, R. (1993) "Factory focus for the 1990s", *European Management Journal*, **11**(4): 443–447.

Collis, D.J., and Montgomery, C.A. (1995) "Competing on resources: Strategy in the 1990s", in Michael, H.Z. (Ed.), *Knowledge and Strategy*, Routledge, London: 25–40.

Corbett, C., Van Wassenhove, L., and de Constance, B. (1993) "Trade-offs? What trade-offs?", *California Management Review*, **35**(4): 107–122.

da Silveira, G.J. (2005) "Improving trade-offs in manufacturing: method and illustration", *International Journal of Production Economics*, **95**(1): 27–38.

da Silveira, G., Borenstein, D., and Fogliatto, F.S. (2001) "Mass customization: Literature review and research directions", *International Journal of Production Economics*, **72**(1): 1–13.

Dangayach, G.S., and Deshmukh, S.G. (2001) "Manufacturing strategy: Literature review and some issues", *International Journal of Production Economics*, **21**(7): 884–932.

Das, A., Pagell, M., Behm, M., and Veltri, A. (2008) "Towards a theory of the linkages between safety and quality", *Journal of Operations Management*, **26**(4): 521–535.

De Meyer, A. (1990) "An empirical investigation of manufacturing strategies in European industry", *Manufacturing strategy—Theory and Practice, Proceeding of the 5th International Conference of the UK Operations Management Association*: 555–579.

De Meyer, A., Nakane, J., Miller, J.G., and Ferdows, K. (1989) "Flexibility: The next competitive battle the manufacturing futures survey", *Strategic Management Journal*, **10**(2): 135–144.

Dess, G.G., Newport, S., and Rasheed, A.M. (1993) "Configuration research in strategic management: Key issues and suggestions", *Journal of Management*, **19**(4): 775–795.

DuBois, F.L., Toyne, B., and Oliff, M.D. (1993) "International manufacturing strategies of US multinationals: A conceptual framework based on a four-industry study", *Journal of International Business Studies*, **24**(2): 307–333.

Ellram, L.M., Tate, W.L., and Petersen, K.J. (2013) "Offshoring and reshoring, an update on the manufacturing location decision", *Journal of Supply Chain Management*, **49**(2): 14–22.

Ettlie, J.E. (1988) *Taking Charge of Manufacturing*, Jossey-Bass, San Francisco, CA.

EU (2013) "Factories of the future", *Multi-annual roadmap for the contractual PPP under Horizon 2020*. http://effra.eu/attachments/article/129/Factories%20of%20the%20Future%202020%20Roadmap.pdf, retrieved on 5 November 2015.

Eyers, D.R., and Potter, A.T. (2015) "E-commerce channels for additive manufacturing: An exploratory study", *Journal of Manufacturing Technology Management*, **26**(3): 390–411.

Fahey, L., and Christensen, H.K. (1986) "Evaluating the research on strategy content", *Journal of Management*, **12**(2): 167–183.

Ferdows, K. (1997) "Making the most of foreign factories", *Harvard Business Review*, **75**: 73–91.

Ferdows, K., and De Meyer, A. (1990) "Lasting improvements in manufacturing performance: In search of a new theory", *Journal of Operations Management*, **9**(2): 168–184.

Fine, C.H., and Hax, A.C. (1985) "Manufacturing strategy: A methodology and an illustration", *Interfaces*, **15**(6): 28–46.

Flynn, B.B., Schroeder, R.G., and Flynn, E.J. (1999) "World class manufacturing: An investigation of Hayes and Wheelwright's foundation", *Journal of Operations Management*, **17**(3): 249–269.

Flynn, B.B., Schroeder, R.G., Flynn, E.J., Sakakibara, S., and Bates, K.A. (1997) "World-class manufacturing project: Overview and selected results", *International Journal of Operations & Production Management*, **17**(7): 671–685.

Frohlich, M.T., and Dixon, J.R. (2001) "A taxonomy of manufacturing strategies revisited", *Journal of Operations Management*, **19**(5): 541–558.

Gagnon, S. (1999) "Resource-based competition and the new operations strategy", *International Journal of Operations & Production Management*, **19**(2): 125–138.

Garver, M.S. (2003) "Best practices in identifying customer-driven improvement opportunities", *Industrial Marketing Management*, **32**(6): 455–466.

Garvin D.A. (1993) "Manufacturing Strategic Planning", *California Management Review*, **35**(4): 85–106.

Gerwin, D. (1982) "Do's and don'ts of computerized manufacturing", *Harvard Business Review*, **60**(2): 107–116.

Gerwin, D. (1993) "Manufacturing flexibility: A strategic perspective", *Management Science*, **39**(3): 395–410.

Giffi, C., Roth, V.A., and Seal, G.M. (1990) *Competing in World-Class Manufacturing: America's 21st Century Challenge*, Business One Irwin, Homewood, IL.

Goldhar, J.D., and Jelinek, M. (1983) "Plan for economies of scope", *Harvard Business Review*, **61**(6): 141–148.

Goldman, S.L., Nagel, R.N., and Preiss K. (1995) *Agile Competitors and Virtual Organizations*, Van Nostrand Reinhold, New York.

Gratton, L. (2011). *The Shift*, Collins, London.

Gray, J.V., Skowronski, K., Esenduran, G., and Rungtusanatham, J.M. (2013) "The reshoring phenomenon: What supply chain academics ought to know and should do", *Journal of Supply Chain Management*, **49**(2): 27–33.

Größler, A., and Grubner, A. (2006) "An empirical model of the relationships between manufacturing capabilities", *International Journal of Operations & Production Management*, **26**(5): 458–506.

Gunasekaran, A. (1998) "Agile manufacturing: Enablers and an implementation framework", *International Journal of Production Research*, **36**(5): 1223–1247.

Gunn, T.G. (1987) *Manufacturing for Competitive Advantage: Becoming a World Class Manufacturer*, Ballinger Publishing Company, Cambridge, MA.

Hanson, P., and Voss, C. (1993) *Made in Britain: The True State of Britain's Manufacturing Industry*, IBM United Kingdom.

Harrison, A. (1998) "Manufacturing strategy and the concept of world class manufacturing", *International Journal of Operations & Production Management*, **18**(4): 397–408.

Hayes, R.H. (1985) "Strategic planning—forward in reverse?", *Harvard Business Review*, **63**(6): 111–119.

Hayes, R.H., and Pisano, G.P. (1994) "Beyond world-class: The new manufacturing strategy", *Harvard Business Review*, **72**(10): 77–86.

Hayes, R.H., and Pisano, G.P. (1996) "Manufacturing strategy: At the intersection of two paradigm shifts", *Production and Operations Management*, **5**(1): 25–41.

Hayes, R.H., and Upton, D.M. (1998) "Operations-based strategy", *California Management Review*, **40**(4): 8–25.

Hayes, R.H., and Wheelwright, S.C. (1979) "Link manufacturing process and product life cycles", *Harvard Business Review*, **57**(1): 133–140.

Hayes, R.H., and Wheelwright, S.C. (1984) *Restoring Our Competitive Edge: Competing through Manufacturing*, John Wiley & Sons, New York.

Hayes, R.H., Wheelwright, S.C., and Clark, K.B. (1988) *Dynamic Manufacturing: Creating the Learning Organization*, The Free Press, New York.

Hessman, T. (2013) "The dawn of the smart factory", *Business Week*, **14**(February): 15–19.

Hill, T.J. (1985), *Manufacturing Strategy: The Strategic Management of the Manufacturing Function*, Macmillan, London.

Hill, T.J. (1989), *Manufacturing Strategy: Text and Cases*, Irwin, Homewood, IL.

Hitt, M.A., Xu, K., and Carnes, C.M. (2016) "Resource based theory in operations management research", *Journal of Operations Management*, **41**: 77–94.

Hounshell, D. (1984) *From the American System to Mass Production, 1800–1932: The Development of Manufacturing Technology in the United States* (No. 4), Johns Hopkins University Press, Baltimore, MD.

Huang, G.Q., Qu, T., Zhang, Y., and Yang, H.D. (2012) "RFID-enabled product-service system for automotive part and accessory manufacturing alliances", *International Journal of Production Research*, **50**(14): 3821–3840.

Jayanthi, S., Roth, A.V., Kristal, M.M., and Venu, L.C.R. (2009) "Strategic resource dynamics of manufacturing firms", *Management Science*, **55**(6): 1060–1076.

Jayaraman, V., Guide Jr., V., and Srivastava, R. (1999) "A closed-loop logistics model for remanufacturing", *Journal of the Operational Research Society*, **50**(5): 497–508.

Jimenez, J., and Lorente, J. (2001) "Environmental performance as an operations objective", *International Journal of Operations & Production Management*, **21**(12): 1553–1572.

John, C.H.S., Cannon, A.R., and Pouder, R.W. (2001) "Change drivers in the new millennium: Implications for manufacturing strategy research", *Journal of Operations Management*, **19**(2): 143–160.

Kagermann, H., Wahlster, W., and Helbig, J. (eds.) (2013) *Securing the Future of German Manufacturing Industry: Recommendations for Implementing the Strategic Initiative Industrie 4.0: Final Report of the Industrie 4.0 Working Group*, acatech e.V., Frankfurt am Main, Germany.

Kathuria, R. (2000) "Competitive priorities and managerial performance: A taxonomy of small manufacturers", *Journal of Operations Management*, **18**(6): 627–641.

Kidd, P.T. (1994) *Agile Manufacturing: Forging New Frontiers*, Addison-Wesley, Reading, MA.

Kim, J.S., and Arnold, P. (1996) "Operationalizing manufacturing strategy", *International Journal of Operations & Production Management*, **16**(12): 45–73.

Kinkel, S. (2012) "Trends in production relocation and backshoring activities: Changing patterns in the course of the global economic crisis", *International Journal of Operations & Production Management*, **32**(6): 696–720.

Kinkel, S., and Maloca, S. (2009) "Drivers and antecedents of manufacturing offshoring and backshoring—A German perspective", *Journal of Purchasing and Supply Management*, **15**(3): 154–165.

Kinnie, N.J., and Staughton, R.V.W. (1991) "Implementing manufacturing strategy—the HRM contribution", *International Journal of Operations & Production Management*, **11**(9): 24–40.

Klassen, R.D., and Whybark, D.C. (1999) "The impact of environmental technologies on manufacturing performance", *Academy of Management Journal*, **42**(6): 599–615.

Kleindorfer, P.R., Singhal, K., and Van Wassenhove, L.N. (2005) "Sustainable operations management", *Production and Operations Management*, **14**(4): 482–492.

Kotha, S. (1995) "Mass customization: Implementing the emerging paradigm for competitive advantage", *Strategic Management Journal*, **16**: 21–42.

Kotha, S., and Orne, D. (1989) "Generic manufacturing strategies: A conceptual synthesis", *Strategic Management Journal*, **10**: 211–231.

Kuivanen, R. (2008) "The future of manufacturing industry in Europe", *International Journal of Productivity and Performance Management*, **57**(6): 488–493.

Kumar, S., and Putnam, V. (2008) "Cradle to cradle: Reverse logistics strategies and opportunities across three industry sectors", *International Journal of Production Economics*, **115**(2), 305–315.

Lampela, H., Heilmann, P., Hurmelinna-Laukkanen, P., Lämsä, T., Hyrkäs, E., and Hannola, L. (2015) "Identifying worker needs in implementing knowledge work tools in manufacturing", *17th ILERA World Congress*, 7–11 September, Cape Town, South Africa.

Laugen, B.T., Acur, N., Boer, H., and Frick, J. (2005) "Best manufacturing practices: What do the best-performing companies do?", *International Journal of Operations & Production Management*, **25**(2): 131–150.

Lee, D., Rho, B.-H., and Yoon, S.N. (2015) "Effect of investments in manufacturing practices on process efficiency and organizational performance", *International Journal of Production Economics*, **162**: 45–54.

Leong G.K., Snyder D.L., and Ward P.T. (1990) "Research in the process and content of manufacturing strategy", *International Journal of Management Sciences*, **18**(2): 109–122.

Liker, J.K., Fruin, W.M., and Adler, P.S. (Eds.) (1999) *Remade in America: Transplanting and Transforming Japanese Management Systems*, Oxford University Press, New York.

Lindberg, P., Voss, C.A., and Blackmon, K. (1998) *International Manufacturing Strategies. Context, Content and Change*, Kluwer Academic Publishers, Dordrecht, The Netherlands.

Longoni, A., and Cagliano, R. (2015) "Environmental and social sustainability priorities: Their integration in operations strategies", *International Journal of Operations & Production Management*, **35**(2): 216–245.

Longoni, A., Golini, R., and Cagliano, R. (2014) "The role of new forms of work organization in developing sustainability strategies in operations", *International Journal of Production Economics*, **147** (PART A): 147–160.

Longoni, A., Pagell, M., Johnston, D., and Veltri, A. (2013) "When does lean hurt?—an exploration of lean practices and worker health and safety outcomes", *International Journal of Production Research*, **51**(11): 3300–3320.

Manyika, J., Sinclair, J., Dobbs, R., Strube, G., Rassey, L., Mischke, J., Remes, J., Roxburgh, C., George, K., O'Halloran, D., and Ramaswamy, S. (2012) *Manufacturing the Future: The Next Era of Global Growth and Innovation*, McKinsey Operations Practice, McKinsey Global Institute, New York.

March, J.G. (1991) "Exploration and exploitation in organizational learning", *Organization Science*, **2**(1), 71–87.

Martinez, M.T., Fouletier, P., Park, K.H., and Favrel, J. (2001) "Virtual enterprise—organisation, evolution and control", *International Journal of Production Economics*, **74**(1–3): 225–238.

Marucheck, A., Pannesi, R., and Anderson, C. (1990) "An exploratory study of manufacturing strategy process in practice", *Journal of Operations Management*, **9**(1): 101–123.
McFarlane, D.C., and Bussmann, S. (2000) "Developments in holonic production planning and control", *Production Planning & Control*, **11**(6): 522–536.
McGee, J., and Thomas, H. (1986) "Strategic groups: Theory, research and taxonomy", *Strategic Management Journal*, **7**: 38–48.
Menda, R., and Dilts, D. (1997) "The manufacturing strategy formulation process: Linking multifunctional viewpoints", *Journal of Operations Management*, **15**(4): 223–241.
Meredith, J.R. (1987) "Automating the factory: Theory versus practice", *International Journal of Production Research*, **25**(10): 1493–1510.
Meyer, G.G., Hans Wortmann, J.C., and Szirbik, N.B. (2011) "Production monitoring and control with intelligent products", *International Journal of Production Research*, **49**(5): 1303–1317.
Miles, R.E., and Snow, C.C. (1978) *Organization Strategy, Structure and Process*, McGraw-Hill, New York.
Miller, D. (1996) "Configurations revisited", *Strategic Management Journal*, **17**(7): 505–512.
Miller, J., and Roth, A. (1994) "A taxonomy of manufacturing strategies", *Management Science*, **40**(3): 285–304.
Miller, J.G. (1982) *Report on the 1982 Manufacturing Futures Survey*, Manufacturing Roundtable Research Report Series, Boston University, Boston, MA.
Miller, J.G., and Hayslip, W. (1989) "Implementing manufacturing strategic planning", *Planning Review*, **17**: 22–27.
Mills, J., Platts, K., and Gregory, M. (1995) "A framework for the design of manufacturing strategy processes: A contingency approach", *International Journal of Operations & Production Management*, **15**(4): 17–49.
Miltenburg, J. (2009) "Setting manufacturing strategy for a company's international manufacturing network", *International Journal of Production Research*, **47**(22): 6179–6203.
Mintzberg, H.T. (1979) *The Structure of Organizations*, Prentice Hall, Englewood Cliffs, NJ.
Misterek, S.D., Schroeder, R., and Bates, K.A. (1992) "The nature of the link between manufacturing strategy and organizational culture", in Voss, C.A. (Ed.), *Manufacturing Strategy: Process and Content*, Chapman & Hall, London.
Nakane, J. (1986) *Manufacturing Futures Survey in Japan: A Comparative Survey 1983–1986*, System Science Institute, Waseda University, Tokyo, Japan.
Neely, A. (2008) "Exploring the financial consequences of the servitization of manufacturing", *Operations Management Research*, **1**(2): 103–118.
Neely, A., and Wilson, J.R. (1992) "Measuring product goal congruence: An exploratory study", *International Journal of Operations & Production Management*, **12**(4): 45–52.
Nemetz, P.L., and Fry, L.W. (1988) "Flexible manufacturing organizations: Implications for strategy formulation and organization design", *Academy of Management Review*, **13**: 627–638.
New, C. (1992) "World-class manufacturing versus strategic trade-offs", *International Journal of Operations & Production Management*, **12**(4): 19–31.
Noori, H., and Lee, W.B. (2002) "Factory-on-demand and smart supply chains: The next challenge", *International Journal of Manufacturing Technology and Management*, **4**(5): 372–383.
Opresnik, D., and Taisch, M. (2015) "The value of big data in servitization", *International Journal of Production Economics*, **165**: 174–184.
Östlin, J., Sundin, E., and Björkman, M. (2008) "Importance of closed-loop supply chain relationships for product remanufacturing", *International Journal of Production Economics*, **115**(2): 336–348.
Pagell, M., Katz, J.P., and Sheu, C. (2005) "The importance of national culture in operations management research", *International Journal of Operations & Production Management*, **25**(4): 371–394.
Paiva, E.L., Roth, A.V., and Fensterseifer, J.E. (2008) "Organizational knowledge and the manufacturing strategy process: A resource-based view analysis", *Journal of Operations Management*, **26**(1): 115–132.
Papke-Shields, K.E., Malhotra, M.K., and Grover, V. (2002) "Strategic manufacturing planning systems and their linkage to planning system success", *Decision Sciences*, **33**(1): 1–30.
Parthasharty, R., and Yin, J.Z. (1996) "Computer-integrated manufacturing and competitive performance: Moderating effects of organization-wide integration", *Journal of Engineering and Technology Management*, **13**: 83–110.
Patel, P.C., Terjesen, S., and Li, D. (2012) "Enhancing effects of manufacturing flexibility through operational absorptive capacity and operational ambidexterity", *Journal of Operations Management*, **30**(3): 201–220.

Pine, B.J. (1999) *Mass Customization: The New Frontier in Business Competition*, Harvard Business Press, Boston, MA.

Porter, M., and Kramer, M.R. (2006) "The link between competitive advantage and corporate social responsibility", *Harvard Business Review*, **84**(12): 1–24.

Porter, M.E. (1980) *Competitive Strategy: Techniques for Analyzing Industries and Competitors*, The Free Press, New York.

Prahalad, C.K., and Hamel, G. (1990) "The core competence of the corporation", *Harvard Business Review*, **68**: 79–91.

Rosenthal, S. (1984) "Progress towards the factory of the future", *Journal of Operations Management*, **4**(3): 203–229.

Rosenzweig, E.D., and Easton, G.S. (2010) "Tradeoffs in manufacturing? A meta-analysis and critique of the literature", *Production and Operations Management*, **19**(2): 127–141.

Rosenzweig, E.D., and Roth, A.V. (2004) "Towards a theory of competitive progression: Evidence from high-tech manufacturing", *Production and Operations Management*, **13**(4): 354–368.

Rudberg, M., and Olhager, J. (2003) "Manufacturing networks and supply chains: An operations strategy perspective", *Omega*, **31**(1): 29–39.

Sarkis, J. (1998) "Evaluating environmentally conscious business practices", *European Journal of Operational Research*, **107**(1): 159–174.

Schmenner, R.W. (1979) "Look beyond the obvious in plant location", *Harvard Business Review*, **57**(1): 126–132.

Schmenner, R.W., and Swink, M.L. (1998) "On theory in operations management", *Journal of Operations Management*, **17**(1): 97–113.

Schonberger, R.J. (1982) *Japanese Manufacturing Techniques: Nine Hidden Lessons in Simplicity*, Free Press, New York.

Schonberger, R.J. (1986) *World Class Manufacturing: The Lessons of Simplicity Applied*, The Free Press, New York.

Schroeder, R., and Flynn, B. (2001) *High Performance Manufacturing: Global Perspectives*, Wiley, New York.

Schroeder, R., Anderson, J., and Cleveland G. (1986) "The content of Manufacturing Strategy: An empirical study", *Journal of Operations Management*, **6**(4): 405–415.

Schroeder, R.G., Bates, K.A., and Junttila, M.A. (2002) "A resource-based view of manufacturing strategy and the relationship to manufacturing performance", *Strategic Management Journal*, **23**(2): 105–117.

Schroeder, R.G., Shah, R., and Xiaosong Peng, D. (2011) "The cumulative capability 'sand cone' model revisited: A new perspective for manufacturing strategy", *International Journal of Production Research*, **49**(16): 4879–4901.

Shah, R., and Ward, P.T. (2003) "Lean manufacturing: Context, practice bundles, and performance", *Journal of Operations Management*, **21**(2): 129–149.

Sharifi, H., and Zhang, Z. (1999) "Methodology for achieving agility in manufacturing organisations: An introduction", *International Journal of Production Economics*, **62**(1), 7–22.

Shi, Y., and Gregory, M. (1998) "International manufacturing networks—to develop global competitive capabilities", *Journal of Operations Management*, **16**(2): 195–214.

Shingo, S., and Dillon, A.P. (1989) *A Study of the Toyota Production System: From an Industrial Engineering Viewpoint*, Productivity Press, New York.

Shukla, C., Vazquez, M., and Chen, F.F. (1996) "Virtual manufacturing: An overview", *Computers & Industrial Engineering*, **31**(1): 79–82.

Skinner, W. (1969) "Manufacturing—missing link in corporate strategy", *Harvard Business Review*, **47**(3): 136–145.

Skinner, W. (1974) "The focused factory", *Harvard Business Review*, **52**(3): 113–121.

Skinner, W. (1985) *Manufacturing: The Formidable Competitive Weapon*, John Wiley & Sons, New York.

Skinner, W. (1996) "Manufacturing strategy on the 'S' curve", *Production and Operations Management*, **5**(1): 3–14.

Slack, N. (1983) "Flexibility as a manufacturing objective", *International Journal of Operation and Production Management*, **3**(3): 4–13.

Sousa, R., and Voss, C.A. (2008) "Contingency research in operations management practices", *Journal of Operations Management*, **26**(6): 697–713.

Spina, G. (1998) "Manufacturing paradigms versus strategic approaches: A misleading contrast", *International Journal of Operations & Production Management*, **18**(8): 684–709.

Spina, G., Bartezzaghi, E., Bert, A., Cagliano, R., Draaijer, D.J., and Boer, H. (1996) "Strategically flexible production: The multi-focused manufacturing paradigm", *International Journal of Operations & Production Management*, **16**(11): 20–41.
Stalk, G., and Hout, T.M. (1990) *Competing Against Time*, The Free Press, New York.
Stalk, G., Evans, P., and Shulam, L. (1992) "Competing on capabilities: The new rules of corporate strategy", *Harvard Business Review*, **70**(2): 57–69.
Sum, C.C., Shih-Ju Kow, L., and Chen, C.S. (2004) "A taxonomy of operations strategies of high performing small and medium enterprises in Singapore", *International Journal of Operations & Production Management*, **24**(3): 321–345.
Swamidass, P.M., and Newell, W.T. (1987) "Manufacturing strategy, environmental uncertainty and performance: A path analytical model", *Management Science*, **33**(4): 509–524.
Sweeney, M.T. (1991) "Towards a unified theory of strategic manufacturing management", *International Journal of Operations & Production Management*, **11**(8): 6–22.
Swink, M., and Hegarty, H.W. (1998) "Core manufacturing capabilities and their links to product differentiation", *International Journal of Operation and Production Management*, **18**(4): 374–396.
Taylor, F.W. (1911) *The Principles of Scientific Management*, Harper and Row, New York.
Tranfield, D., and Smith, S. (1998) "The strategic regeneration of manufacturing by changing routines", *International Journal of Operations & Production Management*, **18**(2): 114–129.
Vandermerwe, S., and Rada, J. (1989) "Servitization of business: Adding value by adding services", *European Management Journal*, **6**(4): 314–324.
Veleva, V., and Ellenbecker, M. (2001) "Indicators of sustainable production: Framework and methodology", *Journal of Cleaner Production*, **9**(6): 519–549.
Vereecke, A., and Van Dierdonck, R. (2002) "The strategic role of the plant: Testing Ferdows's model", *International Journal of Operations & Production Management*, **22**(5/6): 492–514.
Vereecke, A., Van Dierdonck, R., and De Meyer, A. (2006) "A typology of plants in global manufacturing networks", *Management Science*, **52**(11): 1737–1750.
Vickery, S.K., Droge, C., and Markland, R.E. (1993) "Production competence and business strategy: Do they affect business performance?", *Decision Science*, **24**(2): 435–456.
Voss, C.A. (1992a) *Manufacturing Strategy: Process and Content*, Chapman & Hall, London.
Voss, C.A. (1992b) "Applying service concepts in manufacturing", *International Journal of Operations & Production Management*, **12**(4): 93–99.
Voss, C.A. (1995) "Alternative paradigms for manufacturing strategy", *International Journal of Operation and Production Management*, **15**(4): 5–16.
Voss, C.A., Åhlström, P., and Blackmon, K. (1997) "Benchmarking and operational performance: Some empirical results", *International Journal of Operations & Production Management*, **17**(10): 1046–1058.
Ward, P.T., and Duray, R. (2000) "Manufacturing strategy in context: Environment, competitive strategy and manufacturing strategy", *Journal of Operations Management*, **18**(2): 123–138.
Ward, P.T., Bickford, D.J., and Leong, G.K. (1996) "Configurations of manufacturing strategy, business strategy, environment and structure", *Journal of Management*, **22**(4): 597–626.
Ward, P.T., McCreery, J.K., Ritzman, L.P., and Sharma, D. (1998) "Competitive priorities in operations management", *Decision Sciences*, **29**(4): 1035–1046.
Ward P.T., Miller J.G., and Vollmann T.E. (1988) "Mapping manufacturing concerns and action plans", *International Journal of Operations & Production Management*, **8**(6): 5–17.
Wheelwright, S.C. (1978) "Reflecting corporate strategy in manufacturing decisions", *Business Horizons* (February): 57–66.
Wheelwright, S.C. (1981) "Japan—where operations really are strategic", *Harvard Business Review*, **59**(4): 65–74.
Wheelwright, S.C., and Bowen, H.K. (1996) "The challenge of manufacturing advantage", *Production and Operations Management*, **5**(1): 59–77.
Whybark, D.C. (1997) "GMRG survey research in operations management", *International Journal of Operations & Production Management*, **17**(7): 686–696.
Whybark, D.C., and Vastag, G., (Eds.) (1993) *Global Manufacturing Practices: A Worldwide Survey of Practices in Production Planning and Control*, Elsevier, Amsterdam.
Whybark, D.C., Wacker, J., and Sheu, C. (2009) "The evolution of an international academic manufacturing survey", *Decision Line*, **40**(3): 17–19.
Womack, J.P., Jones, D.T., and Roos, D. (1990) *The Machine That Changed the World*, Macmillan, London.

Wong, W.K., Guo, Z.X., and Leung, S.Y.S. (2014) "Intelligent multi-objective decision-making model with RFID technology for production planning", *International Journal of Production Economics*, **147**(PART C): 647–658.

Yusuf, Y.Y., Sarhadi, M., and Gunasekaran, A. (1999) "Agile manufacturing: The drivers, concepts and attributes", *International Journal of Production Economics*, **62**(1): 33–43.

Zhang, L., Luo, Y., Tao, F., Li, B.H., Ren, L., Zhang, X., Guo, H., Cheng, Y., Hu, A., and Liu, Y. (2014) "Cloud manufacturing: A new manufacturing paradigm", *Enterprise Information Systems*, **8**(2): 167–187.

Zhao, X., Sum, C.C., Qi, Y., Zhang, H., and Lee, T.S. (2006) "A taxonomy of manufacturing strategies in China", *Journal of Operations Management*, **24**(5): 621–636.

Zhong, R.Y., Huang, G.Q., Lan, S., Dai, Q.Y., Chen, X., and Zhang, T. (2015) "A big data approach for logistics trajectory discovery from RFID-enabled production data", *International Journal of Production Economics*, **165**: 260–272.

Zhu, Q., Geng, Y., and Lai, K.-H. (2011) "Environmental supply chain cooperation and its effect on the circular economy practice-performance relationship among Chinese manufacturers", *Journal of Industrial Ecology*, **15**(3): 405–419.

Zühlke, D. (2010) "Smart factory: Towards a factory-of-things", *Annual Reviews in Control*, **34**(1): 129–138.

PART III

POM Process and Project Categories

10
PROCESS CAPABILITIES AND LEVERAGING ADVANCES IN SCIENCE AND TECHNOLOGY

Cheryl Gaimon, Manpreet Hora, and Karthik Ramachandran

1 Introduction

This chapter focuses on the role of operations managers who define the process capabilities that critically impact a firm's competitive advantage. Process capabilities are embodied in manufacturing equipment, information technology (IT), workforce, distribution systems, materials, and procedures. For the purposes of this chapter, we establish two key characteristics of process capabilities. First, examples from managerial practice demonstrate how process capabilities drive the creation of new products, services, and business models as well as improvements in those that already exist. Second, these examples also demonstrate the importance of pursuing advances in science and technology to innovate process capabilities (Gaimon 2008).

The remainder of the chapter is devoted to developing a deep understanding of the research and managerial implications that lead to the successful innovation of process capabilities. We explore how advances in science and technology are pursued to innovate process capabilities in two contexts. In Section 2, we consider a firm that relies solely on its internal knowledge resources, whereas in Section 3, we consider a firm that relies on both internal and external knowledge resources. In Section 4, we suggest opportunities for future research. Implications to managerial practice are highlighted in Section 5. We conclude the chapter in Section 6. Consistent with the operations management orientation of this book, we generally focus on how advances in science and technology drive new process, as opposed to product, capabilities.

1.1 Process Capabilities and New Product Development

To successfully create new products, services, and business models, a firm must have a deep understanding of customer needs. Typically, market researchers obtain insights on consumer needs from surveys, focus groups, and feedback from sales workforce. However, while clearly important, a marketing-oriented focus is not sufficient to ensure success in the global marketplace. Rather, managers must have a systems oriented perspective that pursues advances in science and technology in response to or in anticipation of the need for both new product attributes (marketing) and new process capabilities (operations) (Kim and Mauborgne 2015).

The key element of the systems approach is integration. Integration of product and process considerations reduces the likelihood that market research identifies product attributes for which manufacturing processes do not exist. Advanced Micro Devices (AMDs) faced this challenge when it was unable to manufacture a series of advanced CPU chips it had successfully designed (Willcox 1999). Second, integration reduces the likelihood that the results from market research do not fully exploit the firm's unique process capabilities. Third, integration may suggest constraints on new product attributes to reduce the costs and risks needed for new process capabilities. By placing constraints on product design, Toyota manufactured the hybrid Prius in factories already producing gasoline powered vehicles (Tilin 2005; Nonaka and Peltokorpi 2006; Weber 2006). Fourth, constraining product design may be desirable to reduce the time and cost of new product introduction. Automobile manufacturers reduce the time and cost to introduce new models by relying on parts commonality and shared platforms (auto chassis) models (Kubota 2015).

1.2 Process Capabilities and Profitability

Beyond creating new products, services, and business models, process capabilities improve the profitability of a firm's existing product portfolio (Mattioli and Maher 2010). Advances in process capabilities reduce manufacturing costs by improving production efficiency (reduce setup times, direct labor, and yield loss). In services such as banking, insurance, and healthcare, advances in IT (referred to as the "machine tool" for services, Gaimon 2008) lower costs by both reducing the time for and improving the quality of processing transactions (Porter and Heppelmann 2014).

Advances in process capabilities, such as flexible manufacturing, also increase revenue by allowing a firm to rapidly changeover from the production of one high-volume product to another. This capability is particularly important in the pharmaceutical, electronics, and automotive industries where the demand for new high-volume products is uncertain, product life cycles are short, and high costs are incurred for new manufacturing facilities (Pisano and Rossi 1994; Gaimon and Morton 2005; Clark 2015). Additionally, by reducing the time and cost of changeover setups, flexible manufacturing provides the capability to economically produce a variety of small-mid volume products "simultaneously" in a single facility (Gerwin 1993; Carrillo and Gaimon 2002). At the extreme, flexible technology may enable mass customization (Gilmore and Pine 1997).

In services, advances in IT enable a firm to customize services while adjusting their capacity to manage demand variability (Aranda 2003). Manufacturers also increase revenue by bundling services with product offerings (Reinartz and Ulaga 2008). By leveraging IT capabilities, Caterpillar earns premium revenue by offering customers real-time monitoring of heavy farm machinery (Porter and Heppelmann 2014).

Advances in IT substantially impact a firm's extended supply chain by transforming business processes to enable real-time interactions among consumers, manufacturers, distributors, and retailers. The pasta maker, Barilla, uses a sophisticated replenishment system to reduce demand uncertainty, lower costs, improve time-to-market, and ensure consistent quality (Lee 2002). Retailers such as Zara rely on real-time monitoring systems to rapidly replenish fast-moving merchandise to reduce costs, improve revenue, and manage demand uncertainty (Harle et al. 2002; Bjork 2014). Airlines, hotels, and car rental agencies are exploiting advances in IT-based process capabilities with "revenue management" (a form of business analytics that determines both product availability and price to maximize revenue growth) (Talluri and van Ryzin 2006).

Lastly, advances in science and technology are particularly valuable because they may remain proprietary. Imitation by competitors may be limited because the disassembly of a finished good may not reveal the precise steps used in manufacturing (reverse engineering). Proprietary processes are leveraged in industries ranging from chemical and pharmaceutical (Pisano and Wheelwright 1995) to fashion (Pisano and Shih 2012).

1.3 Recent Advances in Process Capabilities

Advances in science and technology profoundly impact a firm's ability to provide new products, services, and business models and to improve those that already exist. Interactive communication technologies facilitate the real-time identification of major consumer trends (Bayus 2013). Advances in telecommunications technology and collaboration software integrate product and process development activities in diverse locations (Staats 2012). Rapid prototyping technology generates a large number of product and process concepts for further evaluation and testing, which reduces the cost and time to introduce new or to improve existing products and services, while increasing the likelihood of market success (Thomke 2001).

Recent advances in additive manufacturing (3D printers) allow a firm to offer custom products that were too complex and costly to produce with traditional manufacturing methods (*The Economist* 2012; D'Aveni 2015). However, while useful for high-end and low-volume custom products, advances in additive manufacturing that offer economies of scale are needed to economically produce low-price and high-volume commodity products (*The Economist* 2012).

Advances in robotic technologies reduce production costs so that firms can cost-effectively manufacture and distribute products worldwide to enhance their response to local customer needs and to reduce distribution costs (Hagerty 2015). Interestingly, even firms operating in countries known for low-cost labor are investing in robotics due to increasing wage rates (Markoff 2012). Retailers such as Amazon are introducing robotics in their fulfillment centers to meet increasing demand volume and to reduce order processing time (Love 2014). Nevertheless, advances in robotics and a deeper understanding of their applications are needed to reduce the investment cost, improve efficiency, improve fine motor capabilities, and enhance flexibility (Dou 2014).

1.4 Greenfield Versus Brownfield Change to Process Capabilities

To exploit advances in science and technology, a manager must decide whether to build a new manufacturing or service facility (greenfield) or to modify an existing facility (brownfield). According to Hargadon (2012, page 1), these terms "originated to describe the difficulties of modernizing existing factories relative to building new ones. Because brownfield factories were originally designed for particular modes of production, once major changes were needed, it was often easier to just find a green field to build a whole new factory than to upgrade an old one."

We extend the above interpretation of brownfield versus greenfield to include IT which serves as the "machine tool" in service industries (processing, tracking, and distribution) and plays a critical role in manufacturing industries (integrating producers, suppliers, and customers) (Gaimon 2008). Therefore, in a greenfield approach, new process capabilities may be obtained by building a new facility or introducing a new IT system. In contrast, when using a brownfield approach, new process capabilities result from upgrading an existing facility or an existing IT system.

The decision to pursue a greenfield approach versus a brownfield approach to process innovation is complex. Typically, if existing process capabilities can be easily re-deployed or upgraded, both the cost and time required for the brownfield approach are lower and the performance outcome is less uncertain. Unfortunately, it is often extremely difficult to anticipate a firm's ability to re-deploy or upgrade existing process capabilities. Moreover, the brownfield approach may limit performance improvement due to the constraints needed to ensure compatibility with existing manufacturing facilities or remaining legacy systems. In fact, Hargadon (2012) notes that many firms known for being highly innovative (Amazon, Google, and Facebook) benefited from introducing greenfield process capabilities, whereas established firms (GM) suffered from the constraints encountered when changing existing manufacturing facilities (brownfield).

The candy company Hershey's introduced a greenfield IT system (Enterprise 21) consisting of software and hardware from multiple vendors to manage a wide range of process capabilities (Laudon and Laudon 2013). Enterprise 21 went live all at once and in all locations in mid-July 1999; simultaneously, existing IT systems were shut down. While 40% of Hershey's annual sales occur between October and December, the greenfield system remained inoperable as of January 2000.

A great deal can be learned from the above example. Safeguards are needed to reduce the disruptions of implementing greenfield (or to a lesser extent, brownfield) process capabilities. For example, a manager may (i) rely on existing process capabilities as a backup until new processes are fully operational, (ii) perform extensive testing of new processes prior to full implementation, (iii) ensure workforce skills exist to operate and manage new processes, and (iv) have contingency plans in the event that new processes experience failure. In addition, (v) the appropriate timing strategy to innovate process capabilities is needed, as described next.

The speed with which a firm innovates its process capabilities (timing strategy) significantly impacts the cost, time, and performance realized (Carrillo and Gaimon 2000). Process capabilities can be radically changed either by building a new facility/IT system or by introducing a massive upgrade to an existing facility or IT system. Alternatively, process capabilities can be improved incrementally by introducing a series of smaller IT upgrades or smaller facilities. The incremental approach allows managers to exploit learning benefits to enhance the design, implementation, and overall performance of future changes in process capabilities (Carrillo and Gaimon 2000; Gaimon and Burgess 2003; Upton and Fuller 2004). The incremental approach also allows a manager to delay the full commitment to new process capabilities until uncertainties in future demand and advances in science and technology are resolved (Carrillo and Gaimon 2004; Burkitt 2015). Moreover, in practice, it is typically easier to manage the re-training and transition of the workforce when undertaking incremental improvements (Gaimon et al. 2011). However, the incremental approach may also slow the rate of performance improvement and reduce a firm's ability to meet rapidly increasing demand. Finally, due to the loss in economies of scale, a series of incremental investments in process capabilities may be more expensive.

2 Managing Internal Knowledge to Develop Process Capabilities

In this section, we consider a project where a manager relies on internal knowledge resources to enhance process capabilities in order to offer new or to improve existing products, services, or business models. In general, this is referred to as a new product (process) development (NPD) project. Essentially, an NPD project is a knowledge-oriented job shop where novel advances in science and technology are created by a highly skilled workforce whose efforts are supported by sophisticated IT systems. Of course, beyond the workforce and IT systems, we also consider how the external marketplace and internal incentives drive a successful NPD project.

2.1 Integrating Product and Process Knowledge in a Single NPD Project

Overlapping activities of product and process design teams facilitate the integration needed for a successful NPD project (Section 1.1). Integration requires that newly developed knowledge be transferred between teams of highly skilled workers responsible for both product and process design. In the context of NPD, knowledge development (KD) is a form of induced learning (deliberate activities are pursued and costs are incurred) in which product and process design teams generate knowledge about product attributes and process capabilities by performing problem solving activities including prototyping, simulation, experimentation, and testing (Argote 2013). Knowledge transfer (KT) between product and process design teams occurs when they participate in joint meetings, share documentation, or exchange information such as design drawings via telecommunications technology (Staats et al. 2011; Argote 2013).

Krishnan et al. (1997) were among the first to consider KT in NPD projects. To accelerate a firm's time-to-market, they suggest that the rate of KT from the product to the process design team should reflect: (i) the speed with which the product design converges to the final product attributes, and (ii) the nature of the problems that arise when process design decisions are made prematurely while the product design is evolving (Loch and Terwiesch 2005). However, since Krishnan et al. (1997) only consider the one-directional KT from a product to a process design team, they do not address the key problem of design for manufacturability. Moreover, given the focus on KT, the authors do not determine how a manager should pursue KD for each team during the NPD project.

More recently, Ozkan-Seely et al. (2015a) consider a manager who determines the rates of KD for a product and a process design team and the rates of KT between both teams (in both directions) throughout an NPD project. While the benefits from KD are instantaneous, the benefits of KT are lagged because of challenges faced by the source team to document knowledge and challenges faced by the recipient team to understand and apply knowledge (Szulanski 2000; Carlile 2002). Importantly, the authors capture the impact of absorptive capacity, which represents a firm's ability to recognize, assimilate, leverage, and deploy external knowledge (Cohen and Levinthal 1990). Specifically, empirical results on absorptive capacity are modeled as follows: (i) a more highly skilled team is better able to generate new knowledge from KD (Nonaka 1994; Carrillo and Gaimon 2004), and (ii) a recipient team benefits more from KT if the source team has more knowledge to transfer and if the recipient team has more knowledge to facilitate its application (Bhuiyan et al. 2004).

Ozkan-Seely et al. (2015a) describe their results in the context of Toyota's successful introduction of the Prius (Tilin 2005; Nonaka and Peltokorpi 2006; Weber 2006). The Prius differed from Toyota's other vehicles by using an electric motor in addition to the standard gasoline engine. Given the complex task of developing an entirely new system of electric motors, sensors, and other components, the initial level of knowledge for Prius' product design team was relatively small. However, by manufacturing the Prius in factories already producing gasoline powered vehicles, the initial level of process design knowledge was relatively large.

Toyota leveraged its process capability by front-loading KT to the product design team. Said differently, the Unit Production Technology Department transferred process design knowledge to the product design team at an initially large but decreasing rate over time. Therefore, early in the project, process design knowledge from Toyota's existing manufacturing capabilities provided direction for the product design team.

KD for the Prius' product design team initially occurred at a decreasing rate, reached a minimum, and later occurred at an increasing rate over time (U-shape). Early in the project, opposing forces drove Prius' product design team to pursue a large but decreasing rate of KD. The large rate was advocated to rapidly increase the initially small level of product design knowledge. But, since the early benefits of KT from the process design team were lagged, the product design team had incentive to delay higher rates of KD. Later in the project, as manufacturing process constraints were better understood (KT benefits were realized), Prius' product design team intensified KD, which occurred at an increasing rate, until final product attributes were established (fuel infrastructure, battery powered design, engine system). (KD for the Prius' process design team also followed a U-shape. However, early in the project, the process design team pursued more KD than that of the product design team in order to accelerate the rate of KT.)

The Prius example highlights two key managerial insights. First, it shows how a manager leverages a high (or compensates for a low) level of product or process design knowledge at the outset of an NPD project. Therefore, the manager must carefully select the initial members of both teams, and must invest in training to ensure that the necessary skills are available for future projects. Second, the Prius example demonstrates the importance of reducing the time lag for the recipient team to benefit from KT. The lag may be reduced by: (i) selecting team members with cross-functional skills, shared work experience, and trust (Goh 2002); (ii) establishing incentives and rewards to encourage the source team to codify knowledge and the recipient team to absorb knowledge (Clark and Fujimoto 1991); (iii) providing IT-based communication and collaboration capabilities to both teams (Staats et al. 2011); and (iv) reducing NPD project complexity (Gaimon et al. 2011).

2.2 Derivative and Radical NPD Projects

Beyond the challenge to integrate product and process design knowledge, we must also consider how NPD differs for a derivative or radical project (Wheelwright and Clark 1992). A derivative NPD project incrementally improves the performance of a product that already exists in the marketplace. The gain in profit, the development cost incurred, and the time required to complete a derivative project are relatively small. In contrast, a radical product, service, or business model creates a new market based on fundamental advances in science and technology (Kim and Mauborgne 2015). While offering the greatest opportunity to generate revenue, a radical NPD project consumes expensive R&D resources over a long period of time and is risky since advances in science and technology may not lead to successful new products (Christensen 2013).

It is reasonable to expect that the rates of KD and KT differ for a derivative versus a radical project. First, due to similarities with existing product attributes and process characteristics, more knowledge resources are available at the outset of a derivative as compared to a radical NPD project. Second, due to its incremental nature, the time lag required for a recipient team to understand and apply knowledge received from a source team is smaller for a derivative as opposed to a radical NPD project. Consistent with Ozkan-Seely et al. (2015a), we expect that the manager of a derivative project (i) front-loads KT in both directions and (ii) while KD is U-shaped, both the product and process design teams pursue relatively higher rates early in the project. However, since Ozkan-Seely et al. (2015a) assume deterministic conditions, the impact of uncertainty in the radical NPD project is unknown. The next two sub-sections are devoted to analyzing the challenges of managing a radical NPD project.

2.2.1 A Radical NPD Project

The *Big Dig* tunnel construction project in Boston was a radical NPD project that faced several unforeseen engineering challenges, which led to a massive cost overrun (over 300%) and significant delays (Murphy 2008). More recently, the U.S. Federal Government undertook a radical project to create the portal known as healthcare.gov, to serve as the backbone of the Affordable Care Act. According to Pipes (2014), the successful introduction of healthcare.gov faced challenges due to "bad management, poor oversight, lack of communication, and intense political pressure (which) combined to produce a technology failure of epic proportions."

The above examples demonstrate the delays and cost overruns typically encountered in a radical NPD project due to high degrees of uncertainty and complexity. Furthermore, the above examples demonstrate that, even if eventually successful, a radical NPD project may require that teams of highly skilled workers persevere through a series of intermediate failures in which project costs and deadlines balloon beyond initial targets.

Wu et al. (2014) explicitly consider the impact of incentives on the outcome of a radical NPD project. They assume the project is undertaken by highly skilled individuals who prefer immediate gratification over long-term happiness. The authors show that this behavioral bias may drive the rate of KD to be back-loaded (the rate increases over time throughout the project). Interestingly, according to Goldratt (1984), when individuals procrastinate in the early stages of a project and exert maximal effort closer to the project deadline, the project suffers from delays and undue resource consumption. Taken together, the above results demonstrate the important role of incentives as a driver of success in a radical NPD project.

2.2.2 Funding Radical and Derivative NPD Projects

Chao et al. (2009) analyze a portfolio manager's allocation of funding between derivative projects and a radical project. While derivative projects incrementally and continuously improve (by a known amount) the revenue stream from an existing product, the radical project potentially offers a large amount of revenue but consumes a considerable amount of R&D resources and is associated with high levels of technical and market uncertainty.

Chao et al. (2009) show how two funding mechanisms, commonly used by NPD portfolio managers, impact resource allocation. With the first mechanism, the manager receives a fixed amount of funding (budget) for its NPD portfolio. Under variable funding, the portfolio manager has the autonomy to control the allocation of NPD resources since the source of funding is the continuous revenue stream obtained from derivative products.

Chao et al. (2009) find that, when a portfolio manager controls funding, larger investments are made in derivative NPD projects as well as in the radical NPD project. However, autonomy has a critical downside: the portion of investment in derivative projects increases by a greater amount than does the portion of investment in the radical project. Therefore, a firm whose NPD portfolio manager controls his own budgets risks underperforming in situations where radical projects are necessary for long-term competitive advantage.

2.3 Investments in Technical Support

Beyond managing the highly skilled workforce, the NPD manager must also invest in IT such as computer-aided design, rapid prototyping, and telecommunications systems with collaboration software (Gino and Pisano 2006). Gaimon (1997) studies one such IT-worker system and finds the investment in IT increases the desirability of employing a larger workforce. Therefore, instead of the substitution of advanced technology for labor often observed in manufacturing, a complementary relationship exists.

In subsequent research, Gaimon et al. (2011) consider how workforce knowledge should be managed when a technology upgrade is introduced. The results offer important managerial insights. First, if rapid improvements in IT are anticipated, then a firm's increase in revenue from an IT upgrade may not be sustainable since superior IT capabilities will be available to competitors in the future. In other words, when the rate of technology advancement is high, the manager of the IT-worker system cannot solely rely on an IT upgrade to remain competitive. Alternatively, the manager may need to pursue a series of IT upgrades or rely more on advancing internal workforce skills (which may remain proprietary).

Second, Gaimon et al. (2011) recognize that, if an IT upgrade provides a large advancement in capability, then higher costs are incurred from workforce disruption since existing skills become obsolete and new skills are required. Their results suggest that, to cost effectively pursue a large increase in IT capability, the manager of an IT-worker system should work closely with the IT vendor to enhance the rate of increase in revenue and to curtail the costs of workforce disruption by ensuring technical compatibility and by providing customer training.

3 Managing External Knowledge to Develop Process Capabilities

The complexity and scope of knowledge necessary to successfully introduce new products, services, and business models based on advances in science and technology has dramatically increased (Oxley and Sampson 2004; Cassiman and Veugelers 2006). As a result, many firms engage in cooperative agreements (alliances or partnerships) to access external complementary resources to generate new knowledge (exploration) or to leverage existing knowledge (exploitation) (Hoang and Rothaermel 2010). For example, Proctor & Gamble's CEO stated that "we will acquire 50% of our technologies and products from outside" (Huston and Sakkab 2006). Naturally, depending on the nature of the alliance or partnership formed, financial resources may or may not be exchanged. In the remainder of this section, we consider three means by which a firm obtains external knowledge and the managerial implications of each.

3.1 Alliances in a Supply Network

Consistent with our operations management perspective, consider a firm's alliance with partners in its supply network (including customers, suppliers, and service providers) (Yli-Renko et al. 2001). Leveraging an extensive database in the electronics industry, Bellamy et al. (2014) examine how a firm's supply network enables it to develop and apply advances in science and technology. The authors explore the impact of (i) supply network accessibility (how quickly and effectively a firm can access different sources of knowledge from its network), and (ii) supply network interconnectedness (degree to which a firm's network partners have supply relationships with each other).

Bellamy et al. (2014) empirically show that a positive relationship exists between a firm's ability to benefit from advances in science and technology and supply network accessibility. Furthermore, the authors demonstrate that, with a high level of absorptive capacity (Section 2.1), a firm's supply network interconnectedness provides greater benefits from advances in science and technology.

Unfortunately, many firms do not obtain the anticipated benefits from its supply network (IBM Report 2007). This is partly due to the lack of alignment among partners in knowledge sharing agreements. Hora and Dutta (2013) study the role of depth and scope in a sample of 728 alliance partnerships between biotech firms and pharmaceutical companies. Depth refers to the extent that a firm engages in repeated alliances with the same partner, whereas scope refers to the breadth of knowledge shared in the alliance. Empirically, the authors show that, by increasing alliance depth and scope, the commercialization success of advances in science and technology improve. In particular, alliance depth enables a manager to build trust and thereby reduce transaction costs, and alliance scope facilitates KT to reduce development costs.

3.2 Alliances with Competitors

Ironically, the knowledge that a firm needs may only be available from a competitor (Arora and Fosfuri 2003). Under *coopetition*, a firm forms an alliance with a competitor whereby both firms simultaneously pursue competition and cooperation to launch new products, services, or business models (Brandenburger and Nalebuff 1997). Typically, a source firm (supplier) sells a portion of knowledge to his competitor (buyer) and later both firms compete in the same market (Anand and Khanna 2000). Coopetition occurs in many industries including automotive, electronics, and pharmaceuticals. Knowledge may be provided in the form of patents in addition to scientific or technical documentation. Samsung acquired patent rights from SanDisk and both firms used those patents to develop flash memory systems (Clark 2009). Toyota licensed its Prius hybrid technologies to Mazda, which plans to launch its own hybrid vehicle (Takahashi 2010).

3.2.1 Trade-Offs in Coopetitive Development

The revenue earned from selling knowledge to a competitor may compensate for the loss in proprietary value because it can be invested in other NPD projects (Brandenburger and Nalebuff 1997). Also, the supplier may benefit from the sale of knowledge if market response is uncertain (Appleyard 1996; Kulatilaka and Lin 2006). The buyer in coopetitive development also faces uncertainty regarding its own ability to integrate the supplier's knowledge, and the actual value of the knowledge given the supplier's opportunistic behavior (Gnyawali and Park 2011).

Interestingly, coopetition may be more lucrative than collaborating with a non-competing firm (Brandenburger and Nalebuff 1997). Loebecke et al. (1999) find that a buyer's ability to integrate knowledge from a supplier critically impacts the performance of both firms. Managerially, this result suggests the advantage realized by a firm that forms an alliance with a competitor whose knowledge is highly related. Ozkan-Seely et al. (2015b) consider coopetition between a leader (knowledge supplier) and a follower (knowledge buyer). Preliminary results show that the price charged by the leader and the amount of knowledge purchased by the follower differ depending on whether uncertainty resides in the marketplace, the technical ability of the supplier, or the buyer's absorptive capacity (Section 2.1). This suggests that, before a firm acquires knowledge from a competitor, it must carefully assess the sources of uncertainty.

3.3 Acquiring Knowledge from Non-Competing Firms

Beyond external knowledge obtained from its supply network or a competitor, a firm may also acquire knowledge from a non-competing firm. Knowledge outsourcing occurs when a buyer acquires and integrates knowledge from an external non-competing supplier such as a consultancy. According to Couto et al. (2008), the rate of knowledge outsourcing is increasing, particularly in sectors including product development, engineering services, R&D, and analytic knowledge services. U.S. census data (BEA 2013) indicates that the GDP value added by knowledge-intensive firms that drive advances in science and technology has more than doubled between 1998 and 2012. For instance, firms such as InnoCentive (Lakhani 2008) have greatly expanded the role of the consulting industry. While the operations management literature on component outsourcing has led to a deep understanding of procurement to ensure efficient quality, on-time performance, reliability, information sharing, and trust building, Cachon and Lariviere (2005) found that, despite its prevalence in practice, the literature on knowledge outsourcing is limited.

Lee et al. (2015) use game theory to analyze the situation where, to meet the need for more knowledge, a buyer (she) may develop knowledge internally (KD) and/or may outsource knowledge from an external non-competing supplier (he). The knowledge purchased by the buyer is specified as a deliverable in the form of knowledge "output" which may include design drawings, software, or a prototype. The fundamental questions addressed include the following: (i) What price should the supplier (leader) charge for outsourced knowledge? (ii) How much knowledge should the buyer (follower) develop internally versus outsource to the supplier?

The authors recognize that outsourcing may reduce the cost incurred by the buyer for internal KD (Carrillo and Gaimon 2000). However, the buyer's benefits from knowledge outsourcing may be limited by the supplier's high price and the buyer's lack of absorptive capacity (Section 2.1). The supplier's price is driven by, among other things, the amount of knowledge he has available versus the investment in internal KD the supplier must undertake to meet the buyer's demand for outsourcing.

In a key result, Lee et al. (2015) show that a buyer always benefits if she has a higher level of absorptive capacity; but a supplier's benefits are conditional. The authors also consider the situation where the buyer may not be certain of the extent to which her prior knowledge is applicable to meet her current needs; i.e., her project scope is uncertain. Counter to intuition from prior operational models, Lee et al. (2015) show that a buyer may benefit from project scope uncertainty because the supplier may be motivated to charge a lower price. Moreover, despite the lower price, the authors show that the supplier's profit may increase because the buyer pursues more outsourcing. Therefore, an important insight is obtained: under the right conditions, both the buyer and supplier benefit from project scope uncertainty.

4 Future Opportunities for Research

In this section, we suggest directions for future research.

4.1 Leveraging Internal Knowledge

The research in Section 2 explores a manager's use of internal knowledge for an NPD project. Much of that optimization research can be extended by explicitly recognizing the stochastic nature of revenue. This is particularly applicable for a radical NPD project (Chao et al. 2009). Empirical research is needed to better understand drivers of NPD uncertainty and how a manager can reduce the impact of uncertainty on time-to-market. Empirical and optimization research is needed to identify and exploit the complex relationships (grounded in organizational theory) among a manager's investments in KD, KT, and technical support which drive the IT-worker system responsible for the NPD project. Moreover, empirical and optimization research is needed to explore the implications of successful NPD in relation to the often contradictory incentives of top management, mid-level managers, and the knowledge workers who directly create the advancements in science and technology.

In the context of portfolio management, Chao et al. (2009) determine the funding allocation between a radical NPD project and derivative NPD projects. However, they do not examine the funding allocation between product and process design activities. Said differently, an opportunity exists to study how early and late investments in product versus process design should be allocated among a portfolio of products. Additionally, Chao et al. (2009) do not capture a key opportunity realized when radical and derivative NPD projects are linked. In ongoing research, Xiao (2012) recognizes that a portfolio manager may benefit from transferring a portion of the knowledge developed while pursuing a radical NPD project to introduce a new derivative product. Although KT potentially reduces the (stochastic) gain in revenue if the radical project were successful, it also increases the current revenue stream obtained from the derivative project and reduces the risk of investing in an unsuccessful radical project.

The potential benefits realized by a manager who invests in technical support of a highly skilled workforce are explored in Gaimon (1997) and Gaimon et al. (2011). However, that research does not focus on an IT-worker system in the context of an NPD project. Instead, it considers a manager who deterministically increases revenue by increasing output volume. Therefore, empirical research is needed to improve our understanding of performance drivers for an IT-worker system in NPD. Also, optimization research is needed to improve managerial decision making of the IT-worker system responsible for NPD. Empirical and optimization research is needed to better understand how market or technical uncertainty impacts the management of an NPD oriented IT-worker system.

Lastly, future research is needed exploring the unique challenges of motivating and managing a highly skilled and autonomous workforce at the individual and team levels (Wu et al. 2014). In the context of pursuing a radical NPD project, Huckman and Staats (2011) suggest the formation of fluid teams, where each team consisting of highly competitive individuals, bids to outwork other teams. They find that project performance improves if workforce efforts are smoothed over time. Taken together, Huckman and Staats (2011) and Wu et al. (2014) establish the need for a new set of operations principles and tools to manage the creative and autonomous workforce responsible for developing advances in science and technology.

4.2 Leveraging External Knowledge

In this section, we suggest research opportunities that deal with how a firm may leverage external knowledge to respond to the increasing complexity and distributed development of advances in science and technology.

4.2.1 Alliances in a Supply Network

The empirical results in Bellamy et al. (2014) indicate that absorptive capacity (Section 2.1) plays a key role in enabling a firm to benefit from advances in science and technology via the interconnectedness in its supply network. However, Ahuja's (2000) longitudinal study suggests that, under certain conditions, network interconnectedness may directly impact various measures of firm performance. Clearly, future research is needed to better understand the conditions that enable a firm to benefit from access to knowledge in its supply network.

Hora and Dutta (2013) empirically demonstrate that, to successfully commercialize advances in science and technology, a manager must consider the depth and scope of its alliance network. In addition, research opportunities exist in order to examine when firms should form alliances and at what future time the alliance goals should be met. These timing decisions are likely to be particularly important in industries such as the life sciences because the inherent scientific and technical uncertainty often leads to extensive delays for successful commercialization (Bhaskaran and Krishnan 2009). Furthermore, since substantial costs are incurred to coordinate, control, and sustain alliance relationships, future research is needed to unravel how such relationships should be managed to best facilitate improvements in a firm's process capabilities.

4.2.2 Alliances with Competitors

Research opportunities exist on the practical tradeoffs that occur when a firm forms an alliance with a competitor to develop advances in science and technology. First and foremost, future research is needed to improve our understanding of how to enhance the benefits and how to reduce the costs and risks of obtaining external knowledge from a competitor. Second, future research can provide a deeper understanding of how to pursue coopetition to develop derivative or radical NPD projects in different industries and in different competitive environments. Third, research is needed to inform a manager who acquires knowledge from a competitor on how performance is impacted by their past relationships and by both firms' organizational structures. Fourth, future research is needed to improve our understanding of how alliance formation is impacted by the size and dispersion of the marketplace and the levels of uncertainty or ambiguity in both the marketplace and the advancement of science and technology. Finally, considerable literature exists on the performance impact of different contractual agreements among supply chain partners (Cachon 2003). In contrast, research opportunities exist to improve our understanding of the impact of different contractual agreements when a firm acquires external knowledge from a competitor.

4.2.3 Acquiring Knowledge from a Non-Competing Firm

Erat and Krishnan (2011) consider a buyer that relies on non-competing external sources of knowledge (suppliers) to develop new products, services, and business models. They find that, beyond considering the price charged by the supplier, the buyer must carefully specify the nature of the knowledge to be acquired. This suggests two important opportunities for future research. First, a deeper understanding is needed to identify the attributes and to quantify the scope of knowledge required by a buyer. Second, future research can explore how a buyer quantifies the levels of knowledge of potential suppliers to facilitate its supplier selection decision.

In ongoing research, Rahmani and Ramachandran (2015) consider how the structure of incentives set by a buyer impacts the highly skilled workforce employed by a non-competing external supplier to conduct specialized searches for advances in science and technology. A buyer could either provide the supplier with a well-defined deliverable or retain the flexibility to request a better solution. Intuitively, retaining flexibility may reduce the buyer's risk of setting the deliverable too low. Interestingly, preliminary results suggest that the flexible incentive structure may drive the supplier to procrastinate, and thereby negatively impact the quality and timing of the buyer's deliverable. In our view, this research exemplifies the emerging literature that seeks a better understanding of operations principles for the "production of knowledge output."

Lastly, we note that Erat and Krishnan (2011), Lee et al. (2015), and Rahmani and Ramachandran (2015) introduce optimization models that consider how a manager should make decisions to maximize profit or to minimize cost. Given the nature of advances in science and technology, future research is needed that empirically defines and measures the multi-dimensional facets of knowledge; how knowledge is developed, transferred, and absorbed; and how knowledge is both a revenue and a cost driver. Lastly, experimental research is needed to provide deeper insights on the behavioral conditions under which all of the optimization models discussed in this chapter are most salient or simply do not apply.

5 Implications for Practitioners

Important implications for practicing managers are described throughout the chapter. In this section, we refer back to some of those insights and indicate the sub-section where the full discussion appears.

The chapter begins with industry examples to demonstrate the importance of the following:

- Process capabilities on firm performance in both manufacturing and service industries (including machine tools, distribution systems, and information technology (IT)) (Section 1.2).
- Advances in science and technology to improve process capabilities (Section 1.3).

- Integrating product and process development to create new or to improve existing products, services, or business models (Section 1.1).
- Comparing the benefits of building new process capabilities (new manufacturing facility or IT system) versus improving those that already exist (facility change or IT upgrade) (Section 1.4).

We explore how internal knowledge resources are used to generate advances in science and technology that lead to the successful introduction of new products, services, and business models and improvements in those that already exist. Insights to managerial practice include the following:

- Through a detailed discussion of the development of the Prius, we explore how Toyota leveraged its high level of process design knowledge and compensated for its low level of product design knowledge at the outset of the project (Section 2.1).
- We show how the frequently observed delays and cost overruns of radical new product development (NPD) projects may be the result of inappropriate incentives for the workforce (Section 2.2).
- We consider two NPD portfolio funding mechanisms found in practice and analyze their impact on (i) the investment in a radical project versus derivative projects, and (ii) the firm's long-term performance in highly dynamic markets (Section 2.2).
- We describe the potential risks encountered when a manager relies heavily on upgrading IT to improve the performance of the IT-worker system responsible for NPD (Section 2.3).

Industry examples are given demonstrating how a firm leverages external knowledge about advances in science and technology to innovate process capabilities. Implications to managerial practice are explored in relation to three sources of external knowledge.

First, the competitive advantage gleaned from knowledge in a firm's external supply network is enhanced if: IT is used as an enabler; employees are assigned explicit responsibility for KT; deep and long-term relationships in the supply network are nurtured; and careful consideration is given to the depth and scope of knowledge needed (Section 3.1).

Second, we consider a situation where competing firms form an alliance. Interestingly, the benefits realized when knowledge is obtained from an alliance with a competitor may be larger if the two firms have related knowledge. Also, the nature of the alliance may differ in response to market versus technical uncertainty (Section 3.2).

Third, a buyer always benefits from more absorptive capacity (e.g., from a greater ability to understand and apply outsourced knowledge from an external non-competing supplier); but the supplier derives benefits only under certain conditions. A buyer has more absorptive capacity if: (i) its workforce has the skills needed to understand and apply the knowledge outsourced from the supplier; (ii) its workforce has the necessary technical support (IT); (iii) incentives exist to limit the "not invented here syndrome" among its workforce; and (iv) trust exists between its workforce and the supplier (Section 3.3).

6 Conclusion

This chapter establishes that a firm's process capabilities play a critical role in the successful creation of new products, services, and business models, and the improvement of those that already exist. We describe how process capabilities enable a firm to generate revenue and reduce costs by determining its product portfolio, time-to-market, quality of output, and volume of output.

We explore how a firm leverages both internal and external knowledge resources to generate advances in science and technology that lead to innovations in process capabilities. Lastly, we suggest research opportunities and highlight important implications for managerial practice.

Acknowledgements

We offer our sincere gratitude to Sushil Gupta and Martin K. Starr for giving us the opportunity to write this chapter and for providing such thoughtful and detailed feedback on earlier drafts. Also, we gratefully thank Wayne Fu, one of our Ph.D. students, for his expert assistance.

References and Bibliography

Ahuja, G. (2000) "Collaboration Networks, Structural Holes, and Innovation: A Longitudinal Study," *Administrative Science Quarterly*, **45**(3): 425–455.

Anand, B.N. and T. Khanna (2000) "Do Firms Learn to Create Value? The Case of Alliances," *Strategic Management Journal*, **21**(3): 295–315.

Appleyard, M. (1996) "How Does Knowledge Flow? Interfirm Patterns in the Semiconductor Industry," *Strategic Management Journal*, **17**(2): 137–154.

Aranda, D.A. (2003) "Service Operations Strategy, Flexibility and Performance in Engineering Consulting Firms," *International Journal of Operations & Production Management*, **23**(11): 1401–1421.

Argote, L. (2013) *Organizational Learning: Transferring, Creating, Retaining Knowledge, 2nd Edition*. Springer, New York.

Arora, A. and A. Fosfuri (2003) "Licensing the Market for Technology," *Journal of Economic Behavior & Organization*, **52**(2): 277–295.

Bayus, B.L. (2013) "Crowdsourcing New Product Ideas Over Time: An Analysis of the Dell IdeaStorm Community," *Management Science*, **59**(1): 226–244.

BEA (Bureau of Economic Analysis) (2013) "Gross-Domestic-Product-(GDP)-by-Industry Data," www.bea.gov/industry/gdpbyind_data.htm, downloaded February 15, 2016.

Bellamy, M.A., S. Ghosh and M. Hora (2014) "The Influence of Supply Network Structure on Firm Innovation," *Journal of Operations Management*, **32**(6): 357–373.

Bhaskaran, S.R. and V. Krishnan (2009) "Effort, Revenue, and Cost Sharing Mechanisms for Collaborative New Product Development," *Management Science*, **55**(7): 1152–1169.

Bhuiyan, M., D. Gerwin and V. Thomson (2004) "Simulation of the New Product Development Process for Performance Improvement," *Management Science*, **50**(12): 1690–1703.

Bjork, C. (2014) "Zara Builds Its Business around RFID," *Wall Street Journal*, (September 17, 2014).

Brandenburger, A.M. and B.J. Nalebuff (1997) *Co-opetition: A Revolution Mindset That Combines Competition and Cooperation: The Game Theory Strategy That's Changing the Game of Business*. Currency Doubleday, New York.

Burkitt, L. (2015) "Wal-Mart Says It Will Go Slow in China," *Wall Street Journal*, (April 30, 2015).

Cachon, G.P. (2003) "Supply Chain Coordination with Contracts," *Handbooks in Operations Research and Management Science*, **11**(6): 227–339.

Cachon, G.P. and M.A. Lariviere (2005) "Supply Chain Coordination with Revenue-Sharing Contracts: Strengths and Limitations," *Management Science*, **51**(1): 30–44.

Carlile, P.R. (2002) "A Pragmatic View of Knowledge and Boundaries: Boundary Objects in New Product Development," *Organization Science*, **13**(4): 442–455.

Carrillo, J.E. and C. Gaimon (2000) "Improving Manufacturing Performance through Process Change and Knowledge Creation," *Management Science*, **46**(2): 265–288.

Carrillo, J.E. and C. Gaimon (2002) "A Framework for Process Change," *IEEE Transactions on Engineering Management*, **49**(4): 409–427.

Carrillo, J.E. and C. Gaimon (2004) "Managing Knowledge-Based Resource Capabilities under Uncertainty," *Management Science*, **50**(11): 1504–1518.

Cassiman, B. and R. Veugelers (2006) "In Search of Complementarity in Innovation Strategy: Internal R&D and External Knowledge Acquisition," *Management Science*, **52**(1): 68–82.

Chao, R., S. Kavadias and C. Gaimon (2009) "Revenue Driven Resource Allocation and Effective NPD Portfolio Management," *Management Science*, **55**(9): 1556–1569.

Christensen, C.M. (2013) *The Innovator's Dilemma: When New Technologies Cause Great Firms to Fail*. Harvard Business Review Press, Boston, MA.

Clark, D. (2009) "Samsung and SanDisk Forge Chip-Patent Agreement, Averting Litigation," *Wall Street Journal*, (May 28, 2009).

Clark, D. (2015) "Turning 50: Tech Axiom Moore's Law Shows Age," *Wall Street Journal*, (April 18, 2015).

Clark, K.B. and T. Fujimoto (1991) *Product Development Performance: Strategy, Organization and Management in the World Auto Industry*. Harvard Business School Press, Boston, MA.

Cohen, W.M. and D.A. Levinthal (1990) "Absorptive Capacity: A New Perspective on Learning and Innovation," *Administrative Science Quarterly*, **35**(1): 128–152.

Couto, V., A.Y. Lewin, M. Mani and V. Sehgal (2008) "Offshoring the Brains as Well As the Brawn. Companies Seek Intellectual Talent Beyond Their Borders," *Booz & Company. The Duke Center for International Business Education and Research*. Duke's Fuqua School of Business. Booz Allen Hamilton Inc. NY, (September 8, 2008).

D'Aveni, R. (2015) "The 3-D Printing Revolution," *Harvard Business Review*, (May 2015): 41–48.

Dou, E. (2014) "Robot Wars: Why China Is Outmanned in Electronics Automation," *Wall Street Journal*, (August 24, 2014).

Erat S. and V. Krishnan (2011) "Managing Delegated Search Over Design Spaces," *Management Science*, **58**(3): 606–623.

Gaimon, C. (1997) "Planning Information Technology—Knowledge Worker Systems," *Management Science*, **43**(9): 1308–1328.

Gaimon, C. (2008) "The Management of Technology: A Production and Operations Management Perspective," *Production and Operations Management, Focused Issue on the Management of Technology*, **17**(1): 1–11.

Gaimon, C. and A. Morton (2005) "Investment in Changeover Flexibility for Early Entry in High Tech Markets," *Production and Operations Management*, **14**(2): 159–174.

Gaimon, C. and R. Burgess (2003) "Analysis of Lead Time and Learning for Capacity Expansions," *Production and Operations Management*, **12**(1): 128–140.

Gaimon, C., G. Ozkan-Seely and K. Napoleon (2011) "Dynamic Resource Capabilities: Managing Workforce Knowledge with a Technology Upgrade," *Organization Science*, **22**(6): 1560–1578.

Gerwin, D. (1993) "Manufacturing Flexibility: A Strategic Perspective," *Management Science*, **39**(4): 395–410.

Gilmore, J.H. and B.J. Pine (1997) "The Four Faces of Mass Customization," *Harvard Business Review*, **75**(1): 91–101.

Gino, F. and G. Pisano (2006) "Teradyne Corporation: The Jaguar Project," *Harvard Business School Case*, 9-606-042. Harvard Business School, Boston, MA.

Gnyawali, D.R. and B-J.R. Park (2011) "Co-opetition between Giants: Collaboration with Competitors for Technological Innovation," *Research Policy*, **40**(5): 650–666.

Goh, S.C. (2002) "Managing Effective Knowledge Transfer: An Integrative Framework and Some Practice Implications," *Journal of Knowledge Management*, **6**(1): 23–30.

Goldratt, E.M. (1984) *Theory of Constraints*. North River Press, Great Barrington, MA.

Hagerty, J.R. (2015) "Meet the New Generation of Robots for Manufacturing," *Wall Street Journal*, (June 2, 2015).

Hargadon, A. (2012) "The Challenge of Innovating in Brownfield Versus Greenfield Markets," http://andrewhargadon.com/2012/03/the-challenge-of-innovating-in-brownfield-versus-greenfield-markets/, posted March 22, 2012, downloaded April 9, 2016.

Harle, N., M. Pich and L. Van der Heyden (2002) "Marks & Spencer and Zara: Process Competition in the Textile Apparel Industry," *INSEAD Case*, 601–010–1. INSEAD Case Publishing, Fontainebleau, France.

Hoang, H. and F.T. Rothaermel (2010) "Leveraging Internal and External Experience: Exploration, Exploitation, and R&D Project Performance," *Strategic Management Journal*, **31**(7): 734–758.

Hora, M. and D.K. Dutta (2013) "Entrepreneurial Firms and Downstream Alliance Partnerships: Impact of Portfolio Depth and Scope on Technology Innovation and Commercialization Success," *Production and Operations Management*, **22**(6): 1389–1400.

Huckman, R.S. and B.R. Staats (2011) "Fluid Tasks and Fluid Teams: The Impact of Diversity in Experience and Team Familiarity on Team Performance," *Manufacturing & Service Operations Management*, **13**(3): 310–328.

Huston, L. and N. Sakkab (2006) "Connect and Develop: Inside Procter & Gamble's New Model for Innovation," *Harvard Business Review*, **84**(3): 58–66.

IBM Report (2007) "A Marriage of Minds: Making Biopharmaceutical Collaborations Work," *IBM Institute for Business Value*.

Kim, W.C. and R. Mauborgne (2015) *Blue Ocean Strategy (Expanded Edition)*, Harvard Business Review Press, Boston, MA.

Krishnan, V., S.D. Eppinger and D.E. Whitney (1997) "A Model-based Framework to Overlap Product Development Activities," *Management Science*, **43**(4): 437–451.

Kubota Y. (2015) "Toyota Unveils Revamped Manufacturing Process," *Wall Street Journal*, (March 26, 2015).

Kulatilaka, N. and L. Lin (2006) "Impact of Licensing on Investment and Financing of Technology Development," *Management Science*, **52**(12): 1824–1837.

Lakhani, K.R. (2008) "InnoCentive.com (A)," *Harvard Business School Case*, 9–608–170. Harvard Business School, Boston, MA.

Laudon, K. and J. Laudon (2013) *Management Information Systems, Student Value Edition* (13th Edition), Prentice Hall, A Pearson Education Company, Upper Saddle River, NJ.

Lee, H.L. (2002) "Aligning Supply Chain Strategies with Product Uncertainties," *California Management Review*, **44**(3): 105–119.

Lee, J., C. Gaimon and K. Ramachandran (2015) "An Economic Model for Knowledge Outsourcing," Working Paper, Georgia Institute of Technology, Atlanta, GA.

Loch, C.H. and C. Terwiesch (2005) "Rush and Be Wrong or Wait and be Late? A Model of Information in Collaborative Processes," *Production and Operations Management*, **14**(3): 331–343.

Loebecke, C., P.C. Van Fenema and P. Powell (1999) "Co-opetition and Knowledge Transfer," *ACM SIGMIS Database*, **30**(2): 14–25.

Love, D. (2014) "Amazon Will Have 10,000 Robots Filling Customer Orders by the End of the Year," *Business Insider*, www.businessinsider.com/amazon-robotics-kiva-systems-2014-5, downloaded April 9, 2016.

Markoff, J. (2012) "Skilled Work, Without the Worker," *Wall Street Journal*, (August 19, 2012).

Mattioli, D. and K. Maher (2010) "At 3M, Innovation Comes in Tweaks and Snips," *Wall Street Journal*, (March 1, 2010).

Murphy, S.P. (2008) "Big Dig's Red Ink Engulfs State," *Boston Globe*, (July 17, 2008).

Nonaka, I. (1994) "A Dynamic Theory of Organizational Knowledge Creation," *Organization Science*, **5**(1): 14–37.

Nonaka, I. and V. Peltokorpi (2006) "Knowledge-Based View of Radical Innovation: Toyota Prius Case," Hage J.T. and M. Meenus, eds. *Innovation and Knowledge Growth*. Oxford University Press, Oxford, UK: 88–104.

Oxley, J.E. and R.C. Sampson (2004) "The Scope and Governance of International R&D Alliances," *Strategic Management Journal*, **25**(August–September Special Issue): 723–749.

Ozkan-Seely, G., C. Gaimon and S. Kavadias (2015a) "Dynamic Knowledge Transfer and Knowledge Development for Product and Process Design Teams," *Manufacturing & Service Operations Management*, **22**(2): 177–190.

Ozkan-Seely, G., C. Gaimon and S. Venkataraman (2015b) "Knowledge Management in Competitive NPD," Working Paper, Georgia Institute of Technology, Atlanta, GA.

Pipes, S. (2014) "The High and Rising Costs of the HealthCare.gov Fiasco," *Forbes*, (June 30, 2014).

Pisano, G.P. and S. Rossi (1994) "Eli Lilly Company: The Flexible Facility Decision," *Harvard Business School Case*, 9–694–074. Harvard Business School, Boston, MA.

Pisano, G.P. and S. Wheelwright (1995) "The New Logic of High-Tech R&D," *Harvard Business Review*, **73**(5): 93–105.

Pisano, G.P. and W.C. Shih (2012) "Does America Really Need Manufacturing?" *Harvard Business Review*, **90**(3): 94–102.

Porter, M.E. and J.E. Heppelmann (2014) "How Smart, Connected Products are Transforming Competition," *Harvard Business Review*, **92**(11): 64–88.

Rahmani, M. and K. Ramachandran (2015) "Dynamics of Delegated Search," Working Paper, Georgia Institute of Technology, Atlanta, GA.

Reinartz, W. and W. Ulaga (2008) "How to Sell Services More Profitably," *Harvard Business Review*, **86**(5): 90–96.

Staats, B.R. (2012) "Unpacking Team Familiarity: The Effect of Geographic Location and Hierarchical Role," *Production and Operations Management*, **21**(3): 619–635.

Staats, B.R., D.J. Brunner and D.M. Upton (2011) "Lean Principles, Learning, and Knowledge Work: Evidence from a Software Services Provider," *Journal of Operations Management*, **29**(5): 376–390.

Szulanski, G. (2000) "The Process of Knowledge Transfer: A Diachronic Analysis of Stickiness," *Organizational Behavior and Human Decision Processes*, **82**(1): 9–27.

Takahashi, Y. (2010) "Toyota, Mazda Reach Hybrid-License Deal," *Wall Street Journal*, (March 30, 2010).
Talluri, K.T. and G.J. van Ryzin (2006) *The Theory and Practice of Revenue Management*, **68**, Springer Science & Business Media.
The Economist (2012) "Special Report: Manufacturing and Innovation, A Third Industrial Revolution," (April 21, 2012): 3–20.
Thomke, S. (2001) "Enlightened Experimentation: The New Imperative for Innovation," *Harvard Business Review*, **79**(2): 66–75.
Tilin, A. (2005) "The Smartest Company of the Year: And the Winner is . . . Toyota Hot Cars," *Business 2.0*, **6**: 65–66.
Upton, D.M. and V.A. Fuller (2004) "The ITC eChoupal Initiative," *Harvard Business School Case*, 9-604-016. Harvard Business School, Boston, MA.
Weber, A. (2006) "The Hybrid Challenge," *Assembly Magazine*, www.assemblymag.com/articles/84379-the-hybrid-challenge, (June 1, 2006), downloaded April 9, 2016.
Wheelwright, S.C. and K.B. Clark (1992) *Revolutionizing Product Development: Quantum Leaps in Speed, Efficiency and Quality*. Free Press, New York.
Willcox, J.K. (1999) "Chip Makers Geared up for Year-end Battle," *Twice*, **14**(21): 36.
Wu, Y., V. Krishnan and K. Ramachandran (2014) "Managing Cost Salience and Procrastination in Projects: Compensation and Team Composition," *Production and Operations Management*, **23**(8): 1299–1311.
Xiao, W. (2012) "Essays on Knowledge Management," Doctoral dissertation, Georgia Institute of Technology, Atlanta, GA.
Yli-Renko, H., E. Autio and H.J. Sapienza (2001) "Social Capital, Knowledge Acquisition, and Knowledge Exploitation in Young Technology-Based Firms," *Strategic Management Journal*, **22**(6–7): 587–613.

11
PROJECT DESIGN AND MANAGEMENT

Tyson R. Browning

1 Introduction

A *project* is "a temporary endeavor undertaken to create a unique product, service, or result" (PMI 2013)—i.e., an attempt to do something new, once, and by a deadline. Projects comprise the opposite end of the spectrum of work from repetitive operations, where, at the extreme, the same thing is done over and over again. In contrast, projects are low-volume, high-variety operations (Maylor et al. 2015). However, projects come in many types and vary significantly in their degrees of novelty, complexity, innovation, dynamism, etc. Some projects seek to replicate previous projects, albeit under different circumstances. Other projects seek to create a recipe for a new product, process, or service, which will then be produced and delivered repetitively. Some projects seek to improve ongoing, repetitive operations. All projects contain some elements that are relatively well understood and perhaps even repetitive, but they all also have aspects that make them unique. Projects therefore tend to require a significant amount of creativity and innovation, as opposed to merely following established routines. (Projects thus have much in common with "white-collar" work (Hopp et al. 2009), although not all white-collar work is project work, nor vice versa.) Although projects and repetitive operations have some common characteristics and the dividing line between them is sometimes fuzzy, projects nevertheless require a distinctive perspective and analysis techniques. For example, while it is impossible to assemble two components on a production line when one is missing, it is often possible to do an activity in a project without one of its inputs (by using an assumption instead). In addition, it may be possible to build a model without having the exact values of all of its input variables or to do an analysis without knowing all of the factors completely, although doing so may increase the risk of later problems. Situations such as these give project managers additional degrees of freedom, albeit often at their peril, thus making for challenging decision problems (e.g., Loch and Terwiesch 2005). Projects permeate most modern organizations, and their effective and efficient execution can be a significant competitive lever.

Project management (PM) is "the application of knowledge, skills, tools, and techniques to project activities to meet the project requirements" (PMI 2013). PM includes determining a project's scope of work; identifying and scheduling activities; acquiring and assigning budgets and other resources; monitoring progress; managing people; and balancing time, cost, and results as a project unfolds. Relative to managing repetitive operations, PM tends to involve greater uncertainty, ambiguity, and dynamism. Although initial project *plans* are often erroneous, *planning* remains a fundamental basis for effective PM. (Even project control is essentially an act of replanning.) This chapter will suggest that projects can and should be *designed*—i.e., specified and customized based on deliberate choices regarding size, scope, cost, duration, resources, risk, deliverables, objectives, and managerial approach—and empowered to *adapt* to unforeseen circumstances and events.

Because PM includes a very wide array of transdisciplinary topics (Morris and Pinto 2004; Shenhar and Dvir 2007b; Kwak and Anbari 2009; Söderlund 2011b), this chapter is necessarily broad. Some universities offer an entire Master's degree in PM, where the curriculum overlaps with operations management (OM), operations research (OR), management science (MS), and decision science (DS) curricula. While PM research appears in many OM, OR, MS, and DS journals, other journals such as the *Project Management Journal* and the *International Journal of Project Management* address PM topics exclusively. Moreover, a myriad of topics in the much wider field of general management have a bearing on PM. For example, a great many PM-relevant papers may be found in the Academy of Management journals. On its own, PM has spawned professional societies and bodies of knowledge, such as the Project Management Institute (PMI) and its *Guide to the Project Management Body of Knowledge* (*PMBOK*) (PMI 2013), which outlines ten basic areas of PM: integration, scope, time, cost, quality, human resources, communications, risk, procurement, and stakeholder management. Each of these areas individually comprises many rich streams of research. Therefore, it would be impossible to address the vast literature pertinent to PM—with all of its history, topics, theories, findings, best practices, tools, and techniques—as well as comment on its future—in depth within a single chapter.

Rather, this chapter has the much more modest aim of providing a brief report on some important research findings, past and present, as they intersect with the work of scholars in the Production and Operations Management (POM) community. As much as possible, it will point readers to review papers and/or books that summarize particular topics. This chapter will also suggest some directions for future PM research. Hence, it is organized into three main sections: looking back, looking around, and looking forward at PM research. The intent is to provide doctoral students and established scholars with a perspective on the PM research landscape while emphasizing aspects that might not be obvious from a perusal of contemporary compendiums.

2   Looking Back at PM Research

Since their earliest days, humans have created and managed projects for construction and destruction, but it was not until the late 1950s that a delineated, supporting literature for PM began to emerge (e.g., Gaddis 1959; Malcolm et al. 1959). Many of the formal techniques for PM were initially codified through the systems- and OR-oriented approaches to management undertaken by U.S. military projects around that time (e.g., Hughes 1998; Cleland 2004). Formal PM was born out of necessity to address practical challenges. As PM approaches become more popular, they took under their wing other techniques for managing work (e.g., Gantt 1919). Over the last sixty years, PM research has taken a wide variety of approaches, emphasizing analytical and empirical methods and the development of PM tools and techniques. With no claim to comprehensiveness, this section highlights some important streams of this research.

2.1   Activity Scheduling

One of the most widely explored topics in PM concerns the scheduling of activity networks (*project processes*). Early approaches include the program evaluation and review technique

(PERT) and the critical path method (CPM) (Malcolm et al. 1959), used to estimate project duration and its variation. Unlike in repetitive processes—where the constraints are called bottlenecks, and metrics such as throughput and cycle time hold sway—in project processes, the constraint is one or more critical paths (composed of critical activities) that govern the key metric of overall project duration. The 1960s saw extensions to activity network methods that accounted for resource constraints and multiple projects—i.e., resource-constrained project scheduling (RCPS) and resource-constrained multi-project scheduling (RCMPS) (see Ballestín and Leus (2009) and Browning and Yassine (2016), respectively, for recent examples and citations)—as well as probabilistic networks that account for path contingency (e.g., Pritsker and Happ 1966; Taylor and Moore 1980). With heavy involvement from the OR community, this research emphasized network modeling, optimization, and the development of heuristics and meta heuristics for computationally-intensive (NP-hard) problems. These problems provided fertile ground for an enormous body of quantitative and analytical literature. Several authors (e.g., Elmaghraby 1995; Herroelen 2005; Hartmann and Briskorn 2010; Schwindt and Zimmermann 2015) have provided extensive reviews and discussions of aspects of this research. Project processes have also provided the basis for many other research topics such as resource loading and leveling (e.g., Woodworth and Willie 1975; Gather et al. 2011); network structure and complexity (e.g., Browning and Yassine 2010); task switching (by multi-project workers) and activity preemption (e.g., Bendoly et al. 2014); and activity overlapping, crashing, and other time-cost tradeoffs (e.g., Pilot and Pilot 1996; Roemer and Ahmadi 2004; Meier et al. 2015). However, beyond PERT/CPM, crashing, and a few basic priority rule heuristics for RCPS, the bulk of this research has not filtered into the mainstream of basic PM textbooks, guides, or practice.

2.2 PM Tool Development

Another huge category of research concerns the development of PM tools. Although many of these tools originated in research papers or government manuals, numerous books now provide comprehensive presentations of these tools and their various extensions and elaborations. Some of the most prominent tools include the project charter (e.g., Meredith et al. 2015); the work breakdown structure (WBS—e.g., Miller 2008); earned value management (EVM—e.g., Fleming and Koppelman 2010); risk management (e.g., Hillson 2006); critical chain scheduling (Goldratt 1997; Raz et al. 2003); stage gates (e.g., Cooper 2001; Chao et al. 2014); capability and maturity models (e.g., Ibbs and Kwak 2000; Chrissis et al. 2011; Mishra et al. 2014); and project evaluation, selection, and portfolio formation tools (e.g., Meredith et al. 2015). The *PMBOK* (PMI 2013) and various PM textbooks (e.g., Meredith et al. 2015) describe many additional tools. Over the years, empirical research has explored the efficacy and pervasiveness of various tools, often finding that only the simplest tools are widely used and that many tools are not used appropriately (e.g., Liberatore and Titus 1983; Besner and Hobbs 2008; Caughron and Mumford 2008). While not always connected to PM research, the development of PM software tools (e.g., Primavera® and Microsoft Project®) has significantly affected the practice of PM over the past few decades. These software tools deal primarily with activity scheduling and resourcing and intra- and inter-project coordination and are pervasive in many project-based organizations (e.g., Liberatore and Pollack-Johnson 2003).

2.3 Organizational Coordination

The challenge of organizing the people and teams performing projects in ways that facilitate their coordination motivates another stream of PM research (Söderlund 2011b). The now-ubiquitous *matrix* organizational structure (e.g., Galbraith 1973) emerged from roots in the field of PM, which had to innovate ways of performing short-term, cross-functional work within longer-term, functional organizations. Early on, scholars recognized the significance of coordination (or integrative) mechanisms, which in turn depend on activity relationships (i.e., the project process) and uncertainties (e.g., Thompson 1967; Galbraith 1973; Allen 1977; Allen and Henn 2007; Shenhar and Dvir 2007a). Some recent efforts along these lines have used design structure matrix (DSM) models to explore the targeting of integrative mechanisms such as co-location, electronic communication tools, heavyweight project managers (Clark and Wheelwright 1993), etc. (e.g., Eppinger and Browning 2012).

2.4 Product Development (PD) and Innovation Management

Another stream of PM research concerns PD and innovation management projects specifically. Although PD projects provided much of the initial impetus for the PM discipline (Gaddis 1959), increased understanding of the process of engineering design prompted a new set of project process models and perspectives, initially separate from those discussed in Section 2.1. PD is an iterative process (e.g., Smith and Eppinger 1997), often with many artificially overlapping activities, pervaded by rework (e.g., Cooper 1993; Mitchell and Nault 2007; Sosa 2014). In contrast to the natural parallelism of independent activities (assuming sufficient resources), artificial concurrency occurs when two or more activities are deliberately overlapped despite one- or two-way dependencies among them. This is often possible in projects, because an assumption can often act as a proxy for an activity's missing input. Yet, most of the models in Section 2.1 assume "100% yield" and acyclical processes. "Concurrent engineering" (overlapping product design with the design of its production process) and a desire to drastically decrease projects' durations increased the artificial overlap of otherwise sequential project activities (Starr 1992; Jayaram and Malhotra 2010), thus providing benefits while compounding rework (due to work done with only partial or preliminary inputs). Hence, a different breed of project process modeling frameworks emerged to deal with the realities of iteration, rework, activity overlapping, and other characteristics of complex PD processes—see Browning and Ramasesh (2007) for a review. One sub-stream of such models used temporal DSMs to capture cycles in the project process architecture, which revealed insights such as where greater rework was actually desirable to speed up a project (e.g., Eppinger and Browning 2012). Other researchers (e.g., Ford and Sterman 2003; Lyneis and Ford 2007) employed systems dynamics models to characterize projects not in terms of their activity structure but rather in terms of general amounts of work, rework, and other factors. However, most of the research in this stream of PD project management, while several decades old, has yet to make its way into mainstream PM textbooks and practitioner guides, probably because of its perceived complexity. Unfortunately, even the general concept of rework, which is ubiquitous in many other types of projects such as construction (e.g., Love et al. 2008), has so far received little assimilation into the mainstream PM guidance.

2.5 Project Portfolio Management (PPM)

Project portfolio management (PPM) deals with collections of simultaneous projects. According to Cooper et al. (2002), four goals in PPM are maximizing portfolio value, balancing the portfolio, aligning the portfolio with strategic business objectives, and optimally allocating resources. PPM tools include the Boston Consulting Group's product portfolio matrix, risk-reward diagrams, bubble diagrams, etc. (Rad and Levin 2006) that visualize the portfolio with respect to multiple criteria. PPM utilizes various project rating and scoring techniques (Fichman et al. 2005; Terwiesch and Ulrich 2008) as well as mathematical programming and optimization techniques such as non-linear, integer programs (Dickinson et al. 2001; Gutjahr et al. 2010); mixed-integer programs (Beaujon et al. 2001; Jiao et al. 2007); and dynamic programs (Kavadias and Loch 2004). Out of the technological innovation, PD, and entrepreneurship research published from 1954–2003 in *Management Science*, Shane and Ulrich (2004) found that "product planning and portfolios" comprising the second largest sub-stream yet had "found very little use in practice." Perhaps this is because most PPM research to date has focused on the strategic level (e.g., project selection), the purview of executives, rather than the operational level (e.g., project execution), the domain of project managers. Opportunities exist to extend the PPM literature towards portfolio execution and control at the level of the dynamic, operational decisions important to practicing managers (Verma and Sinha 2002; Anderson and Joglekar 2005; Bendoly et al. 2010; Verma et al. 2011; Browning and Yassine 2016), and there are still opportunities at the strategic level to improve the way projects are leveraged to execute business strategies (e.g., Hutchison-Krupat and Kavadias 2014; Maylor et al. 2015).

2.6 Other Empirical Research

PM has provided a rich field for a variety of empirical research. Quite a bit of this work has focused on the factors driving project and PM success and failure (e.g., Morris and Pinto 2004; Dilts and Pence 2006; Pinto 2007; Scott-Young and Samson 2008). Examples of key factors in such studies include planning, executive support, project manager capabilities, collaboration tools (e.g., Bardhan et al. 2013; Peng et al. 2014), and systems thinking (Frank et al. 2011; Bendoly 2014). Empirical researchers have explored varied topics such as the effects of information access (Bendoly and Swink 2007), the project life cycle (Söderlund 2011b), project termination (e.g., Dilts and Pence 2006), the effects of project changes (e.g., Dvir and Lechler 2004), how cooperative planning can reduce rework (Mitchell and Nault 2007), the causes of deviations from project plans (Munthe et al. 2014), the roles of tacit and explicit knowledge in process improvement projects (Anand et al. 2010), and the characteristics of a good project manager (e.g., Dvir et al. 2006). Other researchers have studied project monitoring (e.g., Vanhoucke 2010; 2011), information systems (Ahlemann 2009), project reviews (Rozenes et al. 2006), and the efficacy of blending varied styles of monitoring and control (Lewis et al. 2002). Topics such as team roles (e.g., Goodman and Goodman 1976) exemplify the myriad of pertinent connections with the broader management literature on topics such as teamwork, organizational effectiveness, human resources, etc. Indeed, the project is a common unit of analysis in many types of organizational and management research. However, research findings pertinent to PM have sometimes taken many years to migrate into the mainstream of PM knowledge, theory, and guidance (when they have at all).

2.7 Perspective

Looking back at PM research over the last sixty years suggests several generalizations. First, relevant PM research streams exist in many sub-disciplines of management. Söderlund (2011a) reviewed PM research in thirty leading journals and organized it into seven "schools of thought" (optimization, success factors, contingencies, behaviors, governance, relationships, and decisions) that "vary in terms of their main focus and use of the project concept, major research questions, methodological approaches and type of theorizing." Although it provides the benefit of many theoretical underpinnings and perspectives, this diversity also implies a fragmentation of basic concepts and definitions, thus prompting a need for greater awareness, cross-fertilization, and consolidation across the streams (Shenhar and Dvir 2007b; Söderlund 2011a).

Second, although originally practitioner-driven, academics found particular PM topics and models, such as the scheduling of activity networks, amenable to their preferred analytical approaches such as optimization. However, applying such methods required abstracting the complex reality of PM with many simplifying assumptions, such as: time and cost matter more than the quality of results, project goals are clear and stable, *a priori* it is possible to identify all of the activities required to reach the goal, decision makers are risk-neutral, and "soft" factors (e.g., worker morale, people issues) can be ignored. This tendency to distill and optimize simplified analytical models was driven by the preferences of researchers, but it also reflects the predilection of reviewers and editors to conform PM research to the conventions of other disciplines whose models are more naturally amenable to optimization (e.g., job shop scheduling).

Third, although PM is often described in terms of balancing project time, cost, and quality/scope/performance (e.g., PMI 2013), most research and tools have focused on the former two dimensions while neglecting the third, because it is more difficult to measure. Almost all of the scheduling literature, and tools such as EVM, do not explicitly address the quality of a project's results—or ignore it completely. (Mainstream tools such as EVM also ignore uncertainty, risk, and opportunity in all three dimensions.) Fourth, mainstream PM textbooks and guides have focused on standard, generic PM approaches applicable to all kinds of projects but do not yet provide clear guidance on how to tailor or scale methods by project characteristics such as size, type, risk, etc. A "one size fits all" mentality exists in the development and implementation of many PM methods and tools (Shenhar 2001). Lastly, it is worth noting that the perceptions of many practicing project managers seem to be influenced heavily by the current capabilities of PM software tools.

3   Looking Around: The Current Situation in PM Research

The current situation in PM research is a mix of old and new. The aforementioned streams endure to varying extents, but many perspectives are changing for several reasons. One of these reasons is that, despite the plethora of PM methods and tools, project failure rates remain stubbornly high (e.g., Standish 2001; Mishra et al. 2014). Why? One cause is the continued ignorance of many project managers about the methods and tools—or of how and when to use them effectively. Many project managers find themselves in that role without any formal preparation or awareness of PM methods. Yet many experienced and competent project managers are well aware of the conventional methods and tools but choose not to use them. This suggests another possible explanation for project failures—shortcomings of the methods and tools themselves, especially for particular types of projects and in particular situations. The effectiveness of PM methods and tools is likely contingent on project characteristics: some projects may need a very different set of methods and tools.

Two more causes of high project failure rates stem from the definition of success and information asymmetries. How challenging are a project's goals (Browning 2014)? How risky are they (Chao et al. 2014)? Were stakeholder expectations inflated to secure project approval (Flyvbjerg 2014)? Setting the bar too high, deliberately or otherwise, makes failure almost inevitable (and setting the bar too low leaves value "on the table"). Whatever the root causes of project failures, the fact that failure rates remain high calls into question the adequacy of the contemporary, mainstream methods, tools, and "discipline" of PM (in terms of capability and/or implementation), which implicitly claim to be normative, rational, and self-evidently correct (Williams 2005). This has sparked calls for a different way of thinking about PM research (e.g., Geraldi et al. 2008).

A second reason for recent changes in PM research is the desire of PM-centric scholars to increase its stature in the academic community (e.g., Söderlund and Maylor 2012). Originally practitioner-driven, PM journals are still seen as secondary by many academics. However, the quality and rigor of PM research and journals has improved greatly over the past twenty-five years (Turner 2010), and excellent PM research now appears in PM journals as well as in the elite OM, OR, MS, DS, and management journals.

On the other hand, technically rigorous academic research, published in elite journals, has often been guilty of providing little direct value to practicing project managers. "Practitioner-driven" should not be a pejorative term to academics when it refers to the topics and issues addressed by scholarly research. But addressing important PM topics and issues will require a change in prevailing research methods, including a retreat from the highly-restrictive and over-simplified assumptions made by many abstract models over the past 60 years (Williams 2003). What is the point of worrying about whether a model's solution is within ±3% of the optimum if the model's entire input is merely a forecast within ±50% of reality? Scholars need a new openness to improvisational approaches, action, and engaged research (e.g., Cicmil et al. 2006; Maylor et al. 2015), and richer models (which may not be amenable to closed-form solutions or optimization). These changes are already underway and have motivated some of the contemporary research streams highlighted in this section.

3.1 Agile PM

A reaction to the prevailing PM methods and tools sprung from practitioners in the late 1990s in the realm of software development. Going by several names, but most prominently as Agile PM (e.g., Highsmith 2009), these techniques deemphasize the use of formal PM processes and planning in favor of a "learn and adjust as you go" approach—albeit one with its own disciplines and conventions for teamwork and daily and weekly planning. Agile PM recognizes that a project's objectives are often much less clear than they might seem, that the right work to do is difficult to forecast far in advance, and that the early delivery of prototype results generates value-adding feedback for project direction. Agile PM has many proponents, and studies have shown positive outcomes (e.g., Serrador and Pinto 2015), particularly in the software industry, but researchers have yet to fully explore the theory, mechanisms, implications, limits, and contingencies of Agile PM. It may work less well outside of the world of software, which is much easier to redefine at various points during its development than hardware or physical construction. Large, complex, and safety-critical software projects also seem to require more careful planning than most Agile PM implementations propose (Boehm and Turner 2003).

3.2 Factors Distinguishing Different Types of Projects and PM Methods

On the academic side, researchers have advocated for a contingency-driven approach to PM—i.e., tailored approaches for different kinds of projects—e.g., PD and innovation projects (e.g., Pons 2008; Schultz et al. 2013) or software development projects that can benefit from code reuse (Liu et al. 2007). Scholars have sought to identify the key contingency factors (e.g., project size, risk, complexity, novelty, uncertainty, pace, etc.), resulting project typologies, and implications for PM (e.g., Shenhar 2001; Lewis et al. 2002; Crawford et al. 2005; Pollack 2007; Söderlund 2011b). For example, Chandrasekaran et al. (2015a) recommended managing projects differently based on their learning goals with respect to exploration versus exploitation. Zwikael et al. (2015) found that the effectiveness of planning is mediated by the amount of project risk. The degrees of novelty, complexity, uncertainty, ambiguity, and dynamism in projects have been highlighted as key contingency factors with implications for PM methods and approaches (e.g., Tatikonda and Rosenthal 2000; Geraldi et al. 2008; Collyer and Warren 2009; Lenfle and Loch 2010; Geraldi et al. 2011; Nair et al. 2011). Liu (2015) investigated different modes of project control in complex situations, and Chandrasekaran et al. (2016) studied how projects should alter management approaches under complexity and dynamism.

Many projects entail a high degree of uncertainty and ambiguity—i.e., "known unknowns" and "unknown unknowns" (or "unk-unks"). While the former are addressed by the conventional methods and tools for project risk management, the latter continue to surprise project managers and derail the best-laid plans. Recently, scholars (e.g., Loch et al. 2006) have provided insights on managerial techniques for projects fraught with unk-unks. Sommer and Loch (2004) distinguished two approaches, selectionism and learning, for executing a PD project depending on its amounts of complexity and uncertainty, and later (2009) they explored appropriate incentive contracts for projects with unk-unks. Complexity, complicatedness, and dynamism, as well as behavioral and cultural factors such as mindlessness and organizational pathologies, increase the likelihood of unk-unks lurking in a project's future (Ramasesh and Browning 2014). However, by understanding the influences of these driving factors, knowing where to look, and using the tools of directed recognition, it is possible to proactively convert many "knowable unk-unks" into "known unknowns" (Browning and Ramasesh 2015). For example, Loch et al. (2008) provided a rich case study showing how a firm diagnosed unk-unks in a new venture. Overall, we still need to learn much more about how PM methods should be tailored and scaled by project type (Winter et al. 2006).

3.3 People, Teams, Behaviors, and Knowledge Management

Other contemporary PM research has begun to address people, teams, and behavioral issues, such as motivation and authority. While providing some new findings specifically for project managers, this research rightly draws from deep streams of general management literature on these topics. For example, Cicmil et al. (2006) suggested the incorporation of social theories into PM, and Ravid et al. (2012) discussed PM issues regarding human resources and teams. Recent interest among OM scholars in experimental and behavioral topics has spread to PM research as well. For instance, Chandrasekaran and Mishra (2012) explored the effects of team autonomy and psychological safety of project workers. Wu et al. (2014) studied team members' tendencies to procrastinate, the need for managers to reward accomplishments early in a project, and the counter-intuitive benefits of diverse and fluid teams. Hutchison-Krupat and Chao (2014) used an experiment to highlight the importance of project risk characteristics, distributed responsibility, and an organization's cultural tolerance for failure in constructing incentives for project managers. Bendoly et al. (2010) used an experiment to examine project managers' psychological attachment to particular resource allocation solutions, finding a negative relationship between difficulty in work-planning and willingness to share resources. Sosa (2014) drew connections between personnel relationships and the task relationships that trigger rework. PM research also connects to the knowledge management literature—e.g., Anand et al. (2010)'s study of the effects of explicit and tacit knowledge in process improvement projects.

3.4 Outsourcing and Partnering with Other Organizations

Another stream of contemporary PM research studies outsourcing portions of a project and partnering with other organizations. Some key findings in this area are that contract structures indeed matter (MacCormack and Mishra 2015; Tang et al. 2015), that trust is necessary but not sufficient for success (e.g., Brinkhoff et al. 2015), that good planning and team stability help (Narayanan et al. 2011), and that partnering scale and scope matter (Mishra et al. 2015). Tripathy and Eppinger (2013) developed a quantitative model of work and coordination times for each organizational unit and used these to optimize the allocation of work across the units. As projects become more diverse and multi-national, partnering and outsourcing will continue to increase in importance for practicing project managers.

3.5 Systems Views and Structural Models

Some recent research has recognized projects as complex systems. For example, Section 2.3 noted PM research involving systems dynamics models, which have provided important insights into the effects of general feedback loops such as rework and schedule pressure. These holistic-view models continue to provide useful insights that transcend a reductionist paradigm (such as a WBS). Nevertheless, decomposition remains a valuable approach to understanding complex systems (Simon 1996), including projects. The main criticism of the reductionist/decomposition approach is that the value of a system is much greater than the sum of its parts. A significant amount of this additional value can be understood and explored, however, by accounting for relationships among the decomposed parts (e.g., Söderlund 2002; Williams 2005). For example, while not captured in a WBS, the input-output relationships among activities matter greatly. Although activity network models do capture some of these dependencies, they tend not to accentuate them nor allow their properties to vary (Browning and Ramasesh 2007).

Yet some richer, structural models are elaborating on the activity-deliverable paradigm for modeling a project's process system (where deliverables represent the typical outputs of project activities, which become inputs to other activities, giving rise to precedence relationships). For example, Meier et al. (2015) used a rich model of activities and relationships to explore project time-cost tradeoffs due to process architecture, iteration, crashing, overlapping, and work policy (rules about when to start and stop work), finding that the time-cost benefits of crashing and overlapping increase with increasing iteration, and that varied work policies (e.g., rushing and being wrong versus waiting and being late (Loch and Terwiesch 2005)) have enormous time-cost tradeoff implications.

Some scholars are porting complex adaptive systems (CASs) theory over to PM research, discussing how projects exhibit the characteristics of a CAS, such as self-organizing, connected agents that cause emergence and co-evolve with their environment (e.g., Johnston and Brennan 1996; Jaafari 2003; Browning 2007; Saynisch 2010). For example, departing from the conventional assumption that a project's activity network can and should be planned *a priori*, Lévárdy and Browning (2009) defined (1) a superset of general classes of activities, each with varied modes (i.e., options for alternative combinations of inputs, duration, cost, and expected benefits) and (2) simple rules for activity mode combination and self-organization. Simulating thousands of adaptive cases provided insights on the emergence of likely process paths across the project landscape, the patterns of iteration along the paths, and the paths' costs, durations, risks, and values. As these models demonstrate, the CAS paradigm provides a promising avenue for further PM research.

Meanwhile, others are looking at projects from the perspective of other subsystems besides their process, such as their result (e.g., a product design), organization, tools, and goals (Browning et al. 2006). Each of these subsystems has an architecture or structure that can be investigated to increase our understanding of important patterns such as modularity and cyclicality (e.g., MacCormack et al. 2006; Braha and Bar-Yam 2007; Starr 2010; Sosa et al. 2013). Some have studied two or more of these subsystems in tandem—e.g., product and organization (Sosa et al. 2004; Gokpinar et al. 2010)—and opportunities beckon to explore further implications of these subsystems individually and collectively (Eppinger and Browning 2012).

As models of projects become richer and more complex in themselves, they run into several difficulties such as being hard to populate, maintain, verify, validate, and understand. Little (1970) highlighted the tradeoff between simplicity and completeness in models—and noted that managers prefer the former. However, much as firms such as Dell Computer innovated hybrid production systems that provided advantages while departing from the diagonal of the product-process matrix (Hayes and Wheelwright 1979), research on *architecture frameworks* (AFs) points towards possibilities for modelers and managers to "have their cake and eat it too." By providing multiple, simple views of an underlying, complex model, AFs enable modeling experts and knowledge managers to capture and improve big, rich data sets while providing managers (and other users) with access to subsets of the data through simple visualizations of their own choosing (such as Gantt charts). By taking a more complete model and making it seem simple to users, while at the same time maintaining integration and synchronization of the information across all such views, AFs could provide a significant breakthrough in PM research and practice. AFs emerged from the field of information systems and are also used extensively by systems engineers, mainly for product systems, but recent work has demonstrated their efficacy for project process systems (Browning 2009) and in conceptualizing purpose-view alignment as a potential determinant of project success (Browning 2010). Future work could extend the AF approach to the project organization, tools, and goals subsystems, as well as to uniting models of all five project subsystems.

3.6 *Measuring Progress and Value*

Taking a system view of project processes has also produced insights about progress and value in projects, the measurement of which has been a long-standing challenge. Some contemporary projects use EVM (see Section 2.2) to plan and track progress, but this has the aforementioned shortcomings of ignoring technical performance (quality), uncertainty, and risk, as well as failing to distinguish perceived and actual progress (Cooper 1993). Viewing a project as a value-creation process (e.g., Winter et al. 2006; Winter and Szczepanek 2008), Browning et al. (2002) developed a method for planning and tracking the evolution of project performance attributes in terms of uncertainty and risk—recognizing that progress and the addition of value occur as a project eliminates the risks of not meeting its performance goals. Browning (2014) later extended this framework to fully integrate cost, performance, value, uncertainty, risk, and opportunity over project time. The framework views a project as the finite work done to decrease the portion of the project's (goal) value at risk, where reducing risk to zero implies having achieved the chosen goals. This view of adding value as removing "anti-value" (i.e., risks to value) has also informed process improvement approaches for innovative projects (e.g., Browning and Sanders 2012). Some have attempted to apply approaches such as Lean and Six Sigma (which were developed to improve repetitive processes) to project processes but have found this transference challenging. A systems view of project processes allows one to escape the reductionist question asked by Lean ("Is this a value-adding activity?") by acknowledging that value is an emergent property of the process system, not something that can be fully attributed to individual activities. (For example, a perfect, value-adding activity could not add value if it did its work based on faulty inputs or bad assumptions.) Therefore, value is not only a function of how individual activities are done but also of how activities work together in a process (which again signals the importance of the activity relationships). Some recent models (Browning and Ramasesh 2007; Lévárdy and Browning 2009) have begun to adopt this perspective on risk and value.

4 Looking Forward: Opportunities for Future PM Research

PM research continues to evolve. Some of the forces guiding the changes include the aforementioned desires to make PM research rigorous and relevant (which affects both topics and methods). Increasing the impact of PM research on practice will require scholars to improve observation, description, and understanding of the real challenges faced by project managers. This calls for rich field studies that account for project work, people, tools, goals, and contexts. It also begs for more nuanced studies to validate PM methods and tools and their implementations. Modeling will continue to provide valuable insights. However, the complexity of PM will require a greater openness to richer models that capture larger amounts of project data and co-evolve with their subject. Empirical research will continue to be essential for validating past and current practices, but research to develop new methods and tools will also be key, as relevance to practitioners depends not only on identifying "best practices" but also on developing "next practices." (The author first heard this expression from a practitioner at Lockheed Martin Corporation.) Just as projects must integrate across business functions, PM research must continue to span and integrate methods and theories from many relevant disciplines to hypothesize and test new practices. PM research can thereby contribute richly to the wider fields of OM and general management (Geraldi et al. 2008).

PM is an exciting and target-rich research area with no shortage of open questions. Sections 2 and 3 have already mentioned several important topics for future research: tactical portfolio management, strategic alignment of projects, guidance for tailoring PM approaches (including Agile PM) by project type, viewing a project as a complex adaptive system (CAS), investigating project subsystem architectures, and leveraging the concept of architecture frameworks (AFs). In addition to these, this section will now suggest several other promising areas of inquiry.

What are the criteria for judging project success? The opening paragraph of Section 3 mentioned that success depends partly on the chosen goals, how high "the bar" is set (Browning 2014). Projects have multiple objectives pertaining to their cost, duration, path, and scope and quality of results. Some of these results matter more than others. Some may change during or after the project. What initially seems like a catastrophic failure (e.g., the Sydney Opera House which was over budget, behind schedule, and initially deemed ugly by many) may later turn out to be a success—or vice versa (e.g., the Iridium satellite project, which elegantly met its requirements, but few actually wanted its result) (e.g., Shenhar et al. 2001; Jugdev and Müller 2005; Thomas and Fernández 2008). Moreover, executives judge success and failure differently than project managers (Dilts and Pence 2006). How are project objectives chosen? How can failures of project design be distinguished from failures of execution?

How can projects balance control and improvisation, formality versus discretion (Naveh 2007), following prescribed processes versus innovating better ones (Geraldi et al. 2008), and exploiting known approaches and best practices versus exploring next practices (Leybourne and Kennedy 2015)? What is the right amount of project structure and standardization (Browning 2007)? As a project's required level of innovation increases, conventional PM techniques seem to lose efficacy, but the process structure seems to retain its efficacy (Schultz et al. 2013). How can projects best be designed for adaptability to unforeseen future circumstances? How much investment in such adaptability is appropriate? How can projects increase their agility and flexibility (Lenfle and Loch 2010)? Can commitment network templates provide enablers of fast, generic, baseline project designs (Browning and Ramasesh 2007)? That is, can designing and pre-negotiating general agreements among various participants in a typical kind of recurring project accelerate project planning and adaptation?

Further research questions include the following:

- What are the most important and relevant theories for PM (Jugdev 2008; Söderlund 2011b)? How can appropriate theories be distinguished from practical methods and tools that may or may not depend on them (e.g., Schmenner and Swink 1998)?
- What is the right amount of investment of resources (time, money, personnel) in project planning? Too little planning (fire prevention) is associated with fire-fighting (Wearne 2014) and project failure, whereas too much could be a waste of resources, especially when a project is likely to change direction (and render a detailed plan obsolete). For example, Choo (2014) found a U-shaped relationship between the length of the Define (planning) phase in Six Sigma projects and their overall duration: a longer Define phase (more up-front planning) was associated with the faster execution of the rest of the project—to a point, past which further elongation of the Define phase correlated with longer projects.
- What is the right type of project planning? How can planning be more effective (Lawrence and Scanlan 2007; Leleur 2007; Salomo et al. 2007)?
- When and how should projects incentivize "fast failure" and early expenditures that save money later, versus delaying decisions and expenditures as long as possible?
- How can project value be defined, in terms of benefits and sacrifices, for highly uncertain R&D projects (e.g., Browning 2003; Maniak et al. 2014)? How can this value be balanced among the contrasting preferences of multiple stakeholders (workers, clients, sponsors, etc.) (e.g., Thyssen et al. 2010)?
- How important is clear prioritization across projects in a portfolio? What are the implications of unclear prioritizations for cooperation, coordination (Söderlund 2011b), and project value?
- A *program* is "a group of related projects . . . managed in a coordinated way to obtain benefits not available from managing them individually" (PMI 2013)—i.e., essentially a mega-project. How should program management be conceptualized in contrast to PM (Pellegrinelli et al. 2011)? What are its distinctive characteristics, challenges, methods, and tools?
- What are best and next practices for project management offices (PMOs—e.g., Meredith et al. 2015), the permanent, "functional" organizations that provide a number of support and guidance roles to an organization's various projects and project managers?
- How can project managers balance time, cost, and scope/quality/performance for maximum value (Browning 2003; Swink et al. 2006; Liberatore and Pollack-Johnson 2013; Browning 2014; Cohen and Iluz 2014)?
- Out of all the information that is or might be available to project managers, how should they distinguish signals from noise (Sanchez and Perez 2004; Haji-Kazemi et al. 2013; Ramasesh and Browning 2014)? Setting the filters too tightly will miss weak but important signals and early warning signs (e.g., Williams et al. 2012), while taking in too much information can cause overload. How should such methods account for distortions in project status reporting (Snow and Keil 2002)?
- What improvements are needed to software tools to enable improved PM practice? Could research findings be better disseminated into practice by embedding them in software tools?
- What are the best ways to deal with the tensions that emerge between temporary (i.e., project) and "permanent" organizations? Does the temporary nature of projects promote short-term thinking? What are the mechanisms for transitioning workers into and out of projects?

- How can and should knowledge and learning be managed across projects (Sydow et al. 2005; Browning 2009; Swan et al. 2010; Leybourne and Kennedy 2015)? To what extent can project knowledge be captured and reused on similar, future projects? Are particular methods, structures, tools, or incentives more or less helpful?
- How can projects be *designed* to fit desired characteristics of size, scope, cost, duration, resources, risk levels, risk preferences, objectives, and managerial approach?

This list is by no means comprehensive; it provides only a taste of the possibilities for future PM research.

5 Implications for Managers

Because of the temporary nature of projects, as well as their typical novelty, complexity, and uncertainty, project managers are some of the busiest managers in most organizations. Therefore, many project managers have little time or inclination to digest the latest results from PM research. To be of value to practicing managers, such research findings need to be easily and quickly applicable to new and ongoing projects. It is especially helpful when these findings are distilled into simple rules that managers can apply when making plans and decisions—along with specific guidance on when, where, and to what extent the findings apply—and when such results are embedded in the software tools used to support PM. However, the production of accessible research findings is greatly facilitated when practitioners share their current challenges and concerns through engagement with academics at conferences and symposia.

Of course, the onus is also on practicing managers to continue to learn and improve by discovering and implementing the cornucopia of useful findings emerging from contemporary PM research. General findings have long since concluded that the primary reasons for many project failures include lack of good planning, risk management, stakeholder support, and PM skills. Complexity, novelty, uncertainty, iteration, and rework all make effective planning more difficult, but, as noted at many points earlier in this chapter, much guidance already exists in the POM literature to ameliorate these challenges. Helpful findings on issues in ongoing projects such as project control, resource allocation, tracking progress, and delivering value have already been produced. Good practices for managing across projects, working with partner organizations, managing commitments, and managing organizational knowledge also exist in the literature—but as of yet have failed to be widely implemented in and across projects. Thus, while much further research on PM is needed, many insights from prior research have yet to be put into practice. Indeed, the existing literature is already rife with potential value for practicing project managers.

6 Conclusion

This chapter has provided a look around, back, and forward at PM research, yet all of this is just a sampling, merely "the tip of the iceberg." Hopefully, this perspective will prompt researchers and project managers to dig deeper into interesting areas, broaden their outlook, and contribute to a field that is both intellectually compelling and practically significant, with room for a variety of research methods. The goal of this chapter is to spark discussion and research—regardless of its eventual directions. It does seem especially useful, however, to encourage the development of methods and tools to help planners and managers *design* projects with more predictable size, scope, deliverables, cost, duration, resource needs, and risk levels; that apply the most appropriate managerial styles and techniques for their situation; and that empower more rapid adaptability to unforeseen situations.

References and Bibliography

Ahlemann, F. (2009) "Towards a Conceptual Reference Model for Project Management Information Systems," *International Journal of Project Management*, **27**(1): 19–30.

Allen, T.J. (1977) *Managing the Flow of Technology*, Cambridge, MA, MIT Press.

Allen, T.J. and G.W. Henn (2007) *The Organization and Architecture of Innovation*, Burlington, MA, Butterworth-Heinemann.

Anand, G., P.T. Ward and M.V. Tatikonda (2010) "Role of Explicit and Tacit Knowledge in Six Sigma Projects: An Empirical Examination of Differential Project Success," *Journal of Operations Management*, **28**(4): 303–315.

Anderson, E.G. and N.R. Joglekar (2005) "A Hierarchical Product Development Planning Framework," *Production and Operations Management*, **14**(3): 344–361.

Ballestín, F. and R. Leus (2009) "Resource-Constrained Project Scheduling for Timely Project Completion with Stochastic Activity Durations," *Production and Operations Management*, **18**(4): 459–474.

Bardhan, I.R., V.V. Krishnan and S. Lin (2013) "Team Dispersion, Information Technology, and Project Performance," *Production and Operations Management*, **22**(6): 1478–1493.

Beaujon, G.J., S.P. Marin and G.C. McDonald (2001) "Balancing and Optimizing a Portfolio of R&D Projects," *Naval Research Logistics*, **48**(1): 18–40.

Bendoly, E. (2014) "System Dynamics Understanding in Projects: Information Sharing, Psychological Safety, and Performance Effects," *Production and Operations Management*, **23**(8): 1352–1369.

Bendoly, E., J.E. Perry-Smith and D.G. Bachrach (2010) "The Perception of Difficulty in Project-Work Planning and its Impact on Resource Sharing," *Journal of Operations Management*, **28**(5): 385–397.

Bendoly, E. and M. Swink (2007) "Moderating Effects of Information Access on Project Management Behavior, Performance and Perceptions," *Journal of Operations Management*, **25**(3): 604–622.

Bendoly, E., M. Swink and W.P. Simpson III (2014) "Prioritizing and Monitoring Concurrent Project Work: Effects on Switching Behavior," *Production and Operations Management*, **23**(5): 847–860.

Besner, C. and B. Hobbs (2008) "Project Management Practice, Generic or Contextual: A Reality Check," *Project Management Journal*, **39**(1): 16–33.

Boehm, B. and R. Turner (2003) *Balancing Agility and Discipline*, New York, Addison-Wesley.

Braha, D. and Y. Bar-Yam (2007) "The Statistical Mechanics of Complex Product Development: Empirical and Analytical Results," *Management Science*, **53**(7): 1127–1145.

Brinkhoff, A., Ö. Özer and G. Sargut (2015) "All You Need Is Trust? An Examination of Interorganizational Supply Chain Projects," *Production and Operations Management*, **24**(2): 181–200.

Browning, T.R. (2003) "On Customer Value and Improvement in Product Development Processes," *Systems Engineering*, **6**(1): 49–61.

Browning, T.R. (2007) "Program Architecture and Adaptation," *Symposium on Complex Systems Engineering*, Santa Monica, CA, Jan. 11–12.

Browning, T.R. (2009) "The Many Views of a Process: Towards a Process Architecture Framework for Product Development Processes," *Systems Engineering*, **12**(1): 69–90.

Browning, T.R. (2010) "On the Alignment of the Purposes and Views of Process Models in Project Management," *Journal of Operations Management*, **28**(4): 316–332.

Browning, T.R. (2014) "A Quantitative Framework for Managing Project Value, Risk, and Opportunity," *IEEE Transactions on Engineering Management*, **61**(4): 583–598.

Browning, T.R., J.J. Deyst, S.D. Eppinger and D.E. Whitney (2002) "Adding Value in Product Development by Creating Information and Reducing Risk," *IEEE Transactions on Engineering Management*, **49**(4): 443–458.

Browning, T.R., E. Fricke and H. Negele (2006) "Key Concepts in Modeling Product Development Processes," *Systems Engineering*, **9**(2): 104–128.

Browning, T.R. and R.V. Ramasesh (2007) "A Survey of Activity Network-Based Process Models for Managing Product Development Projects," *Production and Operations Management*, **16**(2): 217–240.

Browning, T.R. and R.V. Ramasesh (2015) "Reducing Unwelcome Surprises in Project Management," *MIT Sloan Management Review*, **56**(3): 53–62.

Browning, T.R. and N.R. Sanders (2012) "Can Innovation Be Lean?" *California Management Review*, **54**(4): 5–19.

Browning, T.R. and A.A. Yassine (2010) "A Random Generator of Resource-Constrained Multi-Project Network Problems," *Journal of Scheduling*, **13**(2): 143–161.

Browning, T.R. and A.A. Yassine (2016) "Managing a Portfolio of Product Development Projects under Resource Constraints," *Decision Sciences*, **47**(2): 333–372.

Caughron, J.J. and M.D. Mumford (2008) "Project Planning: The Effects of Using Formal Planning Techniques on Creative Problem-Solving," *Creativity & Innovation Management*, **17**(3): 204–215.

Chandrasekaran, A., K. Linderman and R. Schroeder (2015a) "The Role of Project and Organizational Context in Managing High-Tech R&D Projects," *Production and Operations Management*, **24**(4): 560–586.

Chandrasekaran, A., K. Linderman, F. Sting and M. Benner (2016) "Managing R&D Project Shifts in High-Tech Organizations: A Multi-Method Study," *Production and Operations Management*, **25**(3): 390–416.

Chandrasekaran, A. and A. Mishra (2012) "Task Design, Team Context, and Psychological Safety: An Empirical Analysis of R&D Projects in High Technology Organizations," *Production and Operations Management*, **21**(6): 977–996.

Chao, R.O., K.C. Lichtendahl Jr. and Y. Grushka-Cockayne (2014) "Incentives in a Stage-Gate Process," *Production and Operations Management*, **23**(8): 1286–1298.

Choo, A.S. (2014) "Defining Problems Fast and Slow: The U-shaped Effect of Problem Definition Time on Project Duration," *Production and Operations Management*, **23**(8): 1462–1479.

Chrissis, M.B., M. Konrad and S. Shrum (2011) *CMMI for Development*, 3rd ed., Boston, MA, Addison-Wesley.

Cicmil, S., T. Williams, J. Thomas and D. Hodgson (2006) "Rethinking Project Management: Researching the Actuality of Projects," *International Journal of Project Management*, **24**(8): 675–686.

Clark, K.B. and S.C. Wheelwright (1993) *Managing New Product and Process Development*, New York, Free Press.

Cleland, D.I. (2004) "The Evolution of Project Management," *IEEE Transactions on Engineering Management*, **51**(4): 396–397.

Cohen, I. and M. Iluz (2014) "When Cost-Effective Design Strategies Are Not Enough: Evidence from an Experimental Study on the Role of Redundant Goals," *Omega*, **56**(1): 99–111.

Collyer, S. and C.M.J. Warren (2009) "Project Management Approaches for Dynamic Environments," *International Journal of Project Management*, **27**(4): 355–364.

Cooper, K.G. (1993) "The Rework Cycle: Benchmarks for the Project Manager," *Project Management Journal*, **24**(1): 17–21.

Cooper, R.G. (2001) *Winning at New Products*, 3rd ed., Reading, MA, Perseus.

Cooper, R.G., S.J. Edgett and E.J. Kleinschmidt (2002) *Portfolio Management for New Products*, 2nd ed., Cambridge, MA, Perseus Publishing.

Crawford, L.H., J.B. Hobbs and J.R. Turner (2005) *Project Categorization Systems*, Newtown Square, PA, Project Management Institute.

Dickinson, M.W., A.C. Thornton and S. Graves (2001) "Technology Portfolio Management: Optimizing Interdependent Projects Over Multiple Time Periods," *IEEE Transactions on Engineering Management*, **48**(4): 518–527.

Dilts, D.M. and K.R. Pence (2006) "Impact of Role in the Decision to Fail: An Exploratory Study of Terminated Projects," *Journal of Operations Management*, **24**(4): 378–396.

Dvir, D. and T.G. Lechler (2004) "Plans Are Nothing, Changing Plans Is Everything: The Impact of Changes on Project Success," *Research Policy*, **33**(1): 1–15.

Dvir, D., A. Sadeh and A. Malach-Pines (2006) "Projects and Project Managers: The Relationship between Project Managers' Personality, Project Types, and Project Success," *Project Management Journal*, **3**(5): 36–48.

Elmaghraby, S.E. (1995) "Activity Nets: A Guided Tour Through Some Recent Developments," *European Journal of Operational Research*, **82**(3): 383–408.

Eppinger, S.D. and T.R. Browning (2012) *Design Structure Matrix Methods and Applications*, Cambridge, MA, MIT Press.

Fichman, R.G., M. Keil and A. Tiwana (2005) "Beyond Valuation: 'Options Thinking' in IT Project Management," *California Management Review*, **47**(2): 74–96.

Fleming, Q.W. and J.M. Koppelman (2010) *Earned Value Project Management*, 4th ed., Newtown Square, PA, Project Management Institute.

Flyvbjerg, B. (2014) "What You Should Know About Megaprojects and Why: An Overview," *Project Management Journal*, **45**(2): 6–19.

Ford, D.N. and J.D. Sterman (2003) "The Liar's Club: Concealing Rework in Concurrent Development," *Concurrent Engineering: Research and Applications*, **11**(3): 211–219.

Frank, M., A. Sadeh and S. Ashkenasi (2011) "The Relationship among Systems Engineers' Capacity for Engineering Systems Thinking, Project Types, and Project Success," *Project Management Journal*, **42**(5): 31–41.

Gaddis, P.O. (1959) "The Project Manager," *Harvard Business Review*, **37**(3): 89–97.

Galbraith, J.R. (1973) *Designing Complex Organizations*, Reading, MA, Addison-Wesley.

Gantt, H.L. (1919) *Organizing for Work*, New York, Harcourt, Brace and Howe.

Gather, T., J. Zimmermann and J.-H. Bartels (2011) "Exact Methods for the Resource Levelling Problem," *Journal of Scheduling*, **14**(6): 557–569.

Geraldi, J., H. Maylor and T. Williams (2011) "Now, Let's Make It Really Complex (Complicated): A Systematic Review of the Complexities of Projects," *International Journal of Operations & Production Management*, **31**(9): 966–990.

Geraldi, J.G., J.R. Turner, H. Maylor, A. Söderholm, M. Hobday and T. Brady (2008) "Innovation in Project Management: Voices of Researchers," *International Journal of Project Management*, **26**(5): 586–589.

Gokpinar, B., W.J. Hopp and S.M.R. Iravani (2010) "The Impact of Misalignment of Organizational Structure and Product Architecture on Quality in Complex Product Development," *Management Science*, **56**(3): 468–484.

Goldratt, E.M. (1997) *Critical Chain*, Great Barrington, MA, The North River Press.

Goodman, R.A. and L.P. Goodman (1976) "Some Management Issues in Temporary Systems: A Study of Professional Development and Manpower—The Theater Case," *Administrative Science Quarterly*, **21**(3): 494–501.

Gutjahr, W.J., S. Katzensteiner, P. Reiter, C. Stummer and M. Denk (2010) "Multi-Objective Decision Analysis for Competence-oriented Project Portfolio Selection," *European Journal of Operational Research*, **205**: 670–679.

Haji-Kazemi, S., B. Andersen and H.P. Krane (2013) "A Review on Possible Approaches for Detecting Early Warning Signs in Projects," *Project Management Journal*, **44**(5): 55–69.

Hartmann, S. and D. Briskorn (2010) "A Survey of Variants and Extensions of the Resource-Constrained Project Scheduling Problem," *European Journal of Operational Research*, **207**(1): 1–14.

Hayes, R.H. and S.C. Wheelwright (1979) "Link Manufacturing Process and Product Life Cycles," *Harvard Business Review*, January: 133–140.

Herroelen, W.S. (2005) "Project Scheduling—Theory and Practice," *Production and Operations Management*, **14**(4): 413–432.

Highsmith, J. (2009) *Agile Project Management*, 2nd ed., Boston, Addison-Wesley.

Hillson, D., Ed. (2006) *The Risk Management Universe: A Guided Tour*, London: BSI.

Hopp, W.J., S.M.R. Iravani and F. Liu (2009) "Managing White Collar Work: An Operations Oriented Survey," *Production and Operations Management*, **18**(1): 1–32.

Hughes, T.P. (1998) *Rescuing Prometheus*, New York, NY, Pantheon.

Hutchison-Krupat, J. and R.O. Chao (2014) "Tolerance for Failure and Incentives for Collaborative Innovation," *Production and Operations Management*, **23**(8): 1265–1285.

Hutchison-Krupat, J. and S. Kavadias (2014) "Strategic Resource Allocation: Top-Down, Bottom-Up, and the Value of Strategic Buckets," *Management Science*, **61**(2): 391–412.

Ibbs, C.W. and Y.-H. Kwak (2000) "Assessing Project Management Maturity," *Project Management Journal*, **31**(1): 32–43.

Jaafari, A. (2003) "Project Management in the Age of Complexity and Change," *Project Management Journal*, **34**(4): 47–57.

Jayaram, J. and M.K. Malhotra (2010) "The Differential and Contingent Impact of Concurrency on New Product Development Project Performance: A Holistic Examination," *Decision Sciences*, **41**(1): 147–196.

Jiao, J.R., Y. Zhang and Y. Wang (2007) "A Heuristic Genetic Algorithm for Product Portfolio Planning," *Computers & Operations Research*, **34**(6): 1777–1799.

Johnston, R.B. and M. Brennan (1996) "Planning or Organizing: The Implications of Theories of Activity for Management of Operations," *Omega*, **24**(4): 367–384.

Jugdev, K. (2008) "Good Theory: Developing a Foundation for Project Management," *International Journal of Product Development*, **6**(2): 177–189.

Jugdev, K. and R. Müller (2005) "A Retrospective Look at Our Evolving Understanding of Project Success," *Project Management Journal*, **36**(4): 19–31.

Kavadias, S. and C.H. Loch (2004) *Project Selection under Uncertainty*, Boston, MA, Kluwer Academic Publishers.

Kwak, Y.H. and F.T. Anbari (2009) "Analyzing Project Management Research: Perspectives from Top Management Journals," *International Journal of Project Management*, **27**(5): 435–446.

Lawrence, P. and J. Scanlan (2007) "Planning in the Dark: Why Major Engineering Projects Fail to Achieve Key Goals," *Technology Analysis & Strategic Management*, **19**(4): 509–525.

Leleur, S. (2007) "Systemic Planning: Dealing with Complexity by a Wider Approach to Planning," *Emergence: Complexity & Organization*, **9**(1–2): 2–10.

Lenfle, S. and C. Loch (2010) "Lost Roots: How Project Management Came to Emphasize Control over Flexibility and Novelty," *California Management Review*, **53**(1): 32–55.

Lévárdy, V. and T.R. Browning (2009) "An Adaptive Process Model to Support Product Development Project Management," *IEEE Transactions on Engineering Management*, **56**(4): 600–620.

Lewis, M.W., M.A. Welsh, G.E. Dehler and S.G. Green (2002) "Product Development Tensions: Exploring Contrasting Styles of Project Management," *Academy of Management Journal*, **45**(3): 546–564.

Leybourne, S. and M. Kennedy (2015) "Learning to Improvise, or Improvising to Learn: Knowledge Generation and 'Innovative Practice' in Project Environments," *Knowledge and Process Management*, **22**(1): 1–10.

Liberatore, M.J. and B. Pollack-Johnson (2003) "Factors Influencing the Usage and Selection of Project Management Software," *IEEE Transactions on Engineering Management*, **50**(2): 164–174.

Liberatore, M.J. and B. Pollack-Johnson (2013) "Improving Project Management Decision Making by Modeling Quality, Time, and Cost Continuously," *IEEE Transactions on Engineering Management*, **60**(3): 518–528.

Liberatore, M.J. and G.J. Titus (1983) "The Practice of Management Science in R&D Project Management," *Management Science*, **29**(8): 962–974.

Little, J.D.C. (1970) "Models and Managers: The Concept of a Decision Calculus," *Management Science*, **16**(8): B466–B485.

Liu, D., M. Dawande and V. Mookerjee (2007) "Value-Driven Creation of Functionality in Software Projects: Optimal Sequencing and Reuse," *Production and Operations Management*, **16**(3): 381–399.

Liu, S. (2015) "Effects of Control on the Performance of Information Systems Projects: The Moderating Role of Complexity Risk," *Journal of Operations Management*, **36**(1): 46–62.

Loch, C.H., A. DeMeyer and M.T. Pich (2006) *Managing the Unknown*, New York, Wiley.

Loch, C.H., M.E. Solt and E.M. Bailey (2008) "Diagnosing Unforeseeable Uncertainty in a New Venture," *Journal of Product Innovation Management*, **25**(1): 28–46.

Loch, C.H. and C. Terwiesch (2005) "Rush and Be Wrong or Wait and Be Late? A Model of Information in Collaborative Processes," *Production and Operations Management*, **14**(3): 331–343.

Love, P.E.D., D.J. Edwards and Z. Irani (2008) "Forensic Project Management: An Exploratory Examination of the Causal Behavior of Design-Induced Rework," *IEEE Transactions on Engineering Management EM*, **55**(2): 234–247.

Lyneis, J.M. and D.N. Ford (2007) "System Dynamics Applied to Project Management: A Survey, Assessment, and Directions for Future Research," *System Dynamics Review*, **23**(2–3): 157–189.

MacCormack, A. and A. Mishra (2015) "Managing the Performance Trade-Offs from Partner Integration: Implications of Contract Choice in R&D Projects," *Production and Operations Management*, **24**(10): 1552–1569.

MacCormack, A., J. Rusnak and C.Y. Baldwin (2006) "Exploring the Structure of Complex Software Designs: An Empirical Study of Open Source and Proprietary Code," *Management Science*, **52**(7): 1015–1030.

Malcolm, D.J., J.H. Roseboom, C.E. Clark and W. Fazar (1959) "Application of a Technique for Research and Development Program Evaluation," *Operations Research*, **7**(5): 646–669.

Maniak, R., C. Midler, S. Lenfle and M. Le Pellec-Dairon (2014) "Value Management for Exploration Projects," *Project Management Journal*, **45**(4): 55–66.

Maylor, H., N. Turner and R. Murray-Webster (2015) "'It Worked for Manufacturing . . . !' Operations Strategy in Project-based Operations," *International Journal of Project Management*, **33**(1): 103–115.

Meier, C., T.R. Browning, A.A. Yassine and U. Walter (2015) "The Cost of Speed: Work Policies for Crashing and Overlapping in Product Development Projects," *IEEE Transactions on Engineering Management*, **62**(2): 237–255.

Meredith, J.R., S.J. Mantel Jr. and S.M. Shafer (2015) *Project Management*, 9th ed., New York, Wiley.

Miller, D.P. (2008) *Building a Project Work Breakdown Structure*, Boca Raton, FL, CRC Press.

Mishra, A., A. Chandrasekaran and A. MacCormack (2015) "Collaboration in Multi-Partner R&D Projects: The Impact of Partnering Scale and Scope," *Journal of Operations Management*, **33–34**: 1–14.

Mishra, A., S. Das and J. Murray (2014) "Managing Risks in Federal Government Information Technology Projects: Does Process Maturity Matter?" *Production and Operations Management*, **24**(3): 365–368.

Mitchell, V.L. and B.R. Nault (2007) "Cooperative Planning, Uncertainty, and Managerial Control in Concurrent Design," *Management Science*, **53**(3): 375–389.

Morris, P.W.G. and J.K. Pinto, Eds. (2004) *The Wiley Guide to Managing Projects*, Hoboken, NJ: Wiley.

Munthe, C.I., L. Uppvall, M. Engwall and L. Dahlén (2014) "Dealing with the Devil of Deviation: Managing Uncertainty during Product Development Execution," *R&D Management*, **44**(2): 203–216.

Nair, A., M.K. Malhotra and S.L. Ahire (2011) "Toward a Theory of Managing Context in Six Sigma Process-Improvement Projects: An Action Research Investigation," *Journal of Operations Management*, **29**(5): 529–548.

Narayanan, S., S. Balasubramanian and J.M. Swaminathan (2011) "Managing Outsourced Software Projects: An Analysis of Project Performance and Customer Satisfaction," *Production and Operations Management*, **20**(4): 508–521.

Naveh, E. (2007) "Formality and Discretion in Successful R&D Projects," *Journal of Operations Management*, **25**(1): 110–125.

Pellegrinelli, S., D. Partington and J.G. Geraldi (2011) "Program Management: An Emerging Opportunity for Research and Scholarship," in *The Oxford Handbook of Project Management*, P.W.G. Morris, J. Pinto and J. Söderlund, Eds., pp. 252–272.

Peng, D.X., G.R. Heim and D.N. Mallick (2014) "Collaborative Product Development: The Effect of Project Complexity on the Use of Information Technology Tools and New Product Development Practices," *Production and Operations Management*, **23**(8): 1421–1438.

Pilot, C. and S. Pilot (1996) "Modeling Time-Cost Trade-offs in CPM Networks," *Production and Operations Management*, **5**(3): 283–287.

Pinto, J.K. (2007) *Project Management*, Upper Saddle River, NJ, Pearson Prentice Hall.

PMI (2013) *A Guide to the Project Management Body of Knowledge*, 5th ed., Newtown Square, PA, Project Management Institute.

Pollack, J. (2007) "The Changing Paradigms of Project Management," *International Journal of Project Management*, **25**: 266–274.

Pons, D. (2008) "Project Management for New Product Development," *Project Management Journal*, **39**(2): 82–97.

Pritsker, A.A.B. and W.W. Happ (1966) "GERT: Graphical Evaluation and Review Technique: Part I. Fundamentals," *Journal of Industrial Engineering*, **17**(5): 267–274.

Rad, P.F. and G. Levin (2006) *Project Portfolio Management*, New York, IIL Publishing.

Ramasesh, R.V. and T.R. Browning (2014) "A Conceptual Framework for Tackling Knowable Unknown Unknowns in Project Management," *Journal of Operations Management*, **32**(4): 190–204.

Ravid, S., A. Shtub, A. Rafaeli and E. Glikson (2012) "From Project Management to Team Integration: Key Issues in the Management of the Human Resource in Projects," *Foundations and Trends in Technology, Information and Operations Management*, **6**(2): 89–160.

Raz, T., R. Barnes and D. Dvir (2003) "A Critical Look at Critical Chain Project Management," *Project Management Journal*, **34**(4): 24–32.

Roemer, T.A. and R. Ahmadi (2004) "Concurrent Crashing and Overlapping in Product Development," *Operations Research*, **52**(4): 606–622.

Rozenes, S., G. Vitner and S. Spraggett (2006) "Project Control: Literature Review," *Project Management Journal*, **37**(4): 5–14.

Salomo, S., J. Weise and H.G. Gemünden (2007) "NPD Planning Activities and Innovation Performance: The Mediating Role of Process Management and the Moderating Effect of Product Innovativeness," *Journal of Product Innovation Management*, **24**(4): 285–302.

Sanchez, A.M. and M.P. Perez (2004) "Early Warning Signals for R&D Projects: An Empirical Study," *Project Management Journal*, **35**(1): 11–23.

Saynisch, M. (2010) "Beyond Frontiers of Traditional Project Management: An Approach to Evolutionary, Self-Organizational Principles and the Complexity Theory—Results of the Research Program," *Project Management Journal*, **41**(2): 21–37.

Schmenner, R.W. and M.L. Swink (1998) "On Theory in Operations Management," *Journal of Operations Management*, **17**(1): 97–113.

Schultz, C., S. Salomo, U. de Brentani and E.J. Kleinschmidt (2013) "How Formal Control Influences Decision-Making Clarity and Innovation Performance," *Journal of Product Innovation Management*, **30**(3): 430–447.

Schwindt, C. and J. Zimmermann, Eds. (2015) *Handbook on Project Management and Scheduling*, Springer.

Scott-Young, C. and D. Samson (2008) "Project Success and Project Team Management: Evidence from Capital Projects in the Process Industries," *Journal of Operations Management*, **26**(6): 749–766.

Serrador, P. and J.K. Pinto (2015) "Does Agile Work?—A Quantitative Analysis of Agile Project Success," *International Journal of Project Management*, **33**(5): 1040–1051.

Shane, S.A. and K.T. Ulrich (2004) "Technological Innovation, Product Development, and Entrepreneurship in *Management Science*," *Management Science*, **50**(2): 133–144.

Shenhar, A. (2001) "One Size Does Not Fit All Projects: Exploring Classical Contingency Domains," *Management Science*, **47**(3): 394–414.

Shenhar, A. and D. Dvir (2007a) *Reinventing Project Management*, Boston, MA, Harvard Business School Press.

Shenhar, A.J. and D. Dvir (2007b) "Project Management Research—The Challenge and Opportunity," *Project Management Journal*, **38**(2): 93–99.

Shenhar, A.J., D. Dvir, O. Levy and A.C. Maltz (2001) "Project Success: A Multidimensional Strategic Concept," *Long Range Planning*, **34**(6): 699–725.

Simon, H.A. (1996) *The Sciences of the Artificial*, 3rd ed., Cambridge, MA, MIT Press.

Smith, R.P. and S.D. Eppinger (1997) "A Predictive Model of Sequential Iteration in Engineering Design," *Management Science*, **43**(8): 1104–1120.

Snow, A.P. and M. Keil (2002) "The Challenge of Accurate Software Project Status Reporting: A Two-Stage Model Incorporating Status Errors and Reporting Bias," *IEEE Transactions on Engineering Management*, **49**(4): 491–504.

Söderlund, J. (2002) "Managing Complex Development Projects: Arenas, Knowledge Processes and Time," *R&D Management*, **32**(5): 419–430.

Söderlund, J. (2011a) "Pluralism in Project Management Research: Navigating the Crossroads of Specialization and Fragmentation," *International Journal of Management Reviews*, **13**(2): 153–176.

Söderlund, J. (2011b) "Theoretical Foundations of Project Management: Suggestions for a Pluralistic Understanding," in *The Oxford Handbook of Project Management*, P.W.G. Morris, J. Pinto and J. Söderlund, Eds., Oxford, UK, Oxford University Press, pp. 37–63.

Söderlund, J. and H. Maylor (2012) "Project Management Scholarship: Relevance, Impact and Five Integrative Challenges for Business and Management Schools," *International Journal of Project Management*, **30**(6): 686–696.

Sommer, S.C. and C.H. Loch (2004) "Selectionism and Learning in Projects with Complexity and Unforeseeable Uncertainty," *Management Science*, **50**(10): 1334–1347.

Sommer, S.C. and C.H. Loch (2009) "Incentive Contracts in Projects with Unforeseeable Uncertainty," *Production and Operations Management*, **18**(2): 185–196.

Sosa, M.E. (2014) "Realizing the Need for Rework: From Task Interdependence to Social Networks," *Production and Operations Management*, **23**(8): 1312–1331.

Sosa, M.E., S.D. Eppinger and C.M. Rowles (2004) "The Misalignment of Product Architecture and Organizational Structure in Complex Product Development," *Management Science*, **50**(12): 1674–1689.

Sosa, M.E., J. Mihm and T.R. Browning (2013) "Linking Cyclicality and Product Quality," *Manufacturing & Service Operations Management*, **15**(3): 473–491.

Standish (2001) "Extreme CHAOS," The Standish Group International, Inc., Report.

Starr, M.K. (1992) "Accelerating Innovation," *Business Horizons*, **35**(4): 44–51.

Starr, M.K. (2010) "Modular Production—A 45-Year-Old Concept," *International Journal of Operations & Production Management*, **30**(1): 7–19.

Swan, J., H. Scarbrough and S. Newell (2010) "Why Don't (or Do) Organizations Learn from Projects?" *Management Learning*, **41**(3): 325–344.

Swink, M., S. Talluri and T. Pandejpong (2006) "Faster, Better, Cheaper: A Study of NPD Project Efficiency and Performance Tradeoffs," *Journal of Operations Management*, **24**(5): 542–562.

Sydow, J., L. Lindkvist and R. DeFillippi (2005) "Project-Based Organizations, Embeddedness, and Repositories of Knowledge," *Organization Studies*, **25**(9): 1475–1489.

Tang, C.S., K. Zhang and S.X. Zhou (2015) "Incentive Contracts for Managing a Project with Uncertain Completion Time," *Production and Operations Management*, **24**(12): 1945–1954.

Tatikonda, M.V. and S.R. Rosenthal (2000) "Technology Novelty, Project Complexity, and Product Development Project Execution Success: A Deeper Look at Task Uncertainty in Product Innovation," *IEEE Transactions on Engineering Management*, **47**(1): 74–87.

Taylor, B.W. and L.J. Moore (1980) "R&D Project Planning with Q-GERT Network Modeling and Simulation," *Management Science*, **26**(1): 44–59.

Terwiesch, C. and K. Ulrich (2008) "Managing the Opportunity Portfolio," *Research Technology Management*, **51**(5): 27–38.

Thomas, G. and W. Fernández (2008) "Success in IT Projects: A Matter of Definition?" *International Journal of Project Management*, **26**(7): 733–742.

Thompson, J.D. (1967) *Organizations in Action*, New York, McGraw-Hill.

Thyssen, M.H., S. Emmitt, S. Bonke and A. Kirk-Christoffersen (2010) "Facilitating Client Value Creation in the Conceptual Design Phase of Construction Projects: A Workshop Approach," *Architectural Engineering & Design Management*, **6**(1): 18–30.

Tripathy, A. and S.D. Eppinger (2013) "Structuring Work Distribution for Global Product Development Organizations," *Production and Operations Management*, **22**(6): 1557–1575.

Turner, J.R. (2010) "Evolution of Project Management Research as Evidenced by Papers Published in the International Journal of Project Management," *International Journal of Project Management*, **28**(1): 1–6.

Vanhoucke, M. (2010) "Using Activity Sensitivity and Network Topology Information to Monitor Project Time Performance," *Omega*, **38**(5): 359–370.

Vanhoucke, M. (2011) "On the Dynamic Use of Project Performance and Schedule Risk Information during Project Tracking," *Omega*, **39**(4): 416–426.

Verma, D., A. Mishra and K.K. Sinha (2011) "The Development and Application of a Process Model for R&D Project Management in a High Tech Firm: A Field Study," *Journal of Operations Management*, **29**(5): 462–476.

Verma, D. and K.K. Sinha (2002) "Toward a Theory of Project Interdependencies in High Tech R&D Environments," *Journal of Operations Management*, **20**(5): 451–468.

Wearne, S. (2014) "Evidence-Based Scope for Reducing 'Fire-Fighting' in Project Management," *Project Management Journal*, **45**(1): 67–75.

Williams, T. (2003) "The Contribution of Mathematical Modelling to the Practice of Project Management," *IMA Journal of Management Mathematics*, **14**(1): 3–30.

Williams, T. (2005) "Assessing and Moving on From the Dominant Project Management Discourse in the Light of Project Overruns," *IEEE Transactions on Engineering Management*, **52**(4): 497–508.

Williams, T., O.J. Klakegg, D.H.T. Walker, B. Andersen and O.M. Magnussen (2012) "Identifying and Acting on Early Warning Signs in Complex Projects," *Project Management Journal*, **43**(2): 37–53.

Winter, M., C. Smith, P. Morris and S. Cicmil (2006) "Directions for Future Research in Project Management: The Main Findings of a UK Government-Funded Research Network," *International Journal of Project Management*, **24**(8): 638–649.

Winter, M. and T. Szczepanek (2008) "Projects and Programmes as Value Creation Processes: A New Perspective and Some Practical Implications," *International Journal of Project Management*, **26**(1): 95–103.

Woodworth, B.M. and C.J. Willie (1975) "A Heuristic Algorithm for Resource Leveling in Multi-project, Multi-resource Scheduling," *Decision Sciences*, **6**(3): 525–540.

Wu, Y., K. Ramachandran and V. Krishnan (2014) "Managing Cost Salience and Procrastination in Projects: Compensation and Team Composition," *Production and Operations Management*, **23**(8): 1299–1311.

Zwikael, O., R.D. Pathak, G. Singh and S. Ahmed (2015) "The Moderating Effect of Risk on the Relationship Between Planning and Success," *International Journal of Project Management*, **32**(3): 435–441.

12
FROM LEAN PRODUCTION TO OPERATIONAL EXCELLENCE

Pauline Found, Donna Samuel, and James Lyons

1 Introduction

Production and Operations Management has seen many changes since it first emerged as an academic discipline. One of the most significant of these changes was the emergence of Lean Production and the worldwide interest in Japanese manufacturing processes. John Krafcik, a researcher from the Massachusetts Institute of Technology (MIT), first introduced the term "Lean Production" to the management lexicon (Krafcik 1988). Two years later, Womack et al. (1990) popularized it in the best-selling book *The Machine That Changed the World*, a book that is commonly referred to as the starting point of the Lean movement. In reality however, many of the concepts of Japanese manufacturing, the foundations of Lean, were already well established in the US by the early 1980s, albeit under different names. In *The Machine That Changed the World*, the authors contend that their findings revealed that there was a dramatic performance gap between Japanese and Western car producers and asserted that Lean production should be universally adopted, writing that "Our conclusion is simple: Lean production is a superior way for humans to make things. . . . It follows that the whole world should adopt Lean production, and as quickly as possible" (Womack et al. 1990, p. 225).

Lean is a term that is used to describe a demand-driven systems approach that is based on the shared experiences at Toyota Motor Corporation of developing the Toyota Production System (TPS) and integrating it with Total Quality Control (TQC) and Total Productive Maintenance (TPM) in a unique way to deliver customer value at the shortest lead-time. Lean is simply a system of time-compression developed by focusing on the end-to-end efficiency of flow, rather than the efficiency of resources, to deliver high-quality products and services that customers value in a way that shows respect for people (Modig and Åhlström 2015; Schonberger 2015). Despite the fact that there is evidence that the terminology of Lean is considered in some quarters to be dated and misunderstood due to its polymorphic nature, Lean has made a huge and significant contribution to OM studies. As seen by its successes, the concepts behind Lean are as valid in the 21st century as they were when the first mainstream usage of the term emerged twenty-five years ago.

In this chapter, we will look at the emergence and evolution of Lean Production through to the concepts of Operational Excellence that companies are striving to achieve today.

2 Emergence of Lean Production

The term "Lean" emerged from the study of the Toyota Production System (TPS) by researchers on the International Motor Vehicle Program (IMVP), a program that was founded at MIT in 1980. IMVP was, at that time, the largest international research consortium aimed at understanding the challenges facing the global automotive industry. Lean production is described as a counter-intuitive alternative to mass production that uses less of everything (i.e., resources, energy, manpower). It is derived from TPS, a system that had developed over a number of years from the collective and shared experiences of the people who had created the system and focuses on time-based competition (Stalk 1988) and systematic innovation (Spear 2009) through increasing the efficiencies of flow (Modig and Åhlström 2015). Whilst many of the principles behind TPS and the associated concepts of TQM and TPM originated in the US, the principles of Just-in-Time (JIT) and *Jidoka* derived from the original founders of Toyota.

2.1 Toyota Production System (TPS)

Sakichi Toyoda, the inventor of Japan's first power loom, is acknowledged to have developed the philosophy and methods of *Jidoka*: mistake-proofing (*Poka-yoke*) and autonomation (automation with a human touch). These principles influenced Sakichi's son Kiichiro Toyoda, causing him to develop the fully automated loom, something which led to the opening of The Toyoda Automatic Loom Works in 1926 and, from his interest in automobiles, to his founding the Toyota Motor Corporation in the late 1930s. The *Just-in-Time* (JIT) method derives from a comment by Kiichiro Toyoda on the best way to gather parts for automobile manufacturing.

The Second World War reconstruction of Japanese manufacturing, with its lack of available capital resources and severe economic slump saw these ideas extended and combined with a discipline of daily improvements (*Kaizen*). The new approach, created by Taiichi Ohno (1978; 1988), became known as the Toyota Production System (TPS) in the 1970s after twenty years' of trial and error experimentation by Ohno and colleagues. One such colleague was Kikuo Suzamura, a production engineer who was responsible for translating Ohno's ideas of a JIT pull system into practice (Shimokawa and Fujimoto 2009). *Kanban*, named by Toyota in 1964, is an enabling tool that underpins JIT by acting as an inventory control system (Monden 1983; Sugimori et al. 1977; Hopp and Spearman 2000). TPS is a management concept based upon JIT and Jidoka, which, according to Ohno, was focused initially on the goal of time-compression from order to cash, by the relentless elimination of waste to increase flow (Figure 12.1). During the post-war reconstruction of Japan Toyota faced financial difficulty and industrial unrest. TPS, with its focus on total cost management (Monden 1989) and respect for people, was part of the turnaround.

A strong focus of TPS was on eliminating all forms of waste—a process termed *muda*, *mura*, and *muri*. *Muda* is a Japanese term for futility that is used by Toyota to describe waste in the production process. Initially, Taiichi Ohno and Shigeo Shingo identified seven wastes (overproduction, over-processing, excessive motion, excessive inventory, excessive waiting time, excessive conveyancing transport, and defects) as targets for elimination. *Mura* is a word to describe unevenness that was addressed by leveled production, *Heijunka*, and the concept of *Takt* time (the rate of production required to meet the rate of demand). The third term used to describe waste is *muri*, a Japanese term for unreasonableness or over-burden. *Muri* can be avoided by implementing standardized work and having respect for people.

Central to and underpinning TPS was the concept of *Kaizen*, a concept that was adopted to facilitate the relentless pursuit of waste elimination and continuous improvement. Kaizen, which

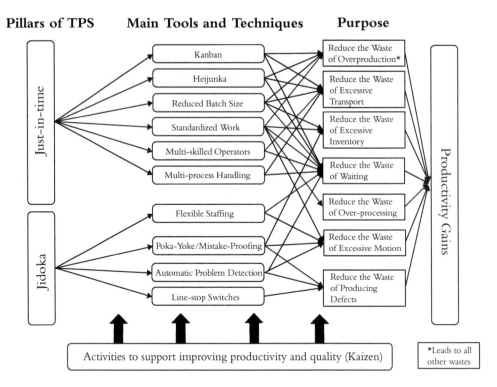

Figure 12.1 Schematic Representation of TPS

Source: Adapted from Shimokawa and Fujimoto 2009. © Copyright 2009, *The Birth of Lean*, p. 206, Lean Enterprise Institute, Inc., Cambridge, MA, lean.org. All rights reserved. Used with permission.

quite literally means change or changing (*kai*) for the better or good (*zen*), entered popular Western management terminology in the 1980s. Masaaki Imai first disseminated Kaizen within the field of OM (Imai 1986). Kaizen, as demonstrated by Imai at Toyota, represents both a philosophy and a set of tools. Many Japanese and, increasingly, Western facilities regard Kaizen as one of the main vehicles of problem solving and continuous improvement.

The philosophy and methods of TPS, which extended to Toyota's supply base in the 1970s and to its distribution and sales operations in the 1980s, became a competitive weapon as Toyota competed openly with US and European automakers by providing quality products and services that customers valued. However, it was not until the mid-1980s when Toyota went into a joint venture with GM to develop New United Motor Manufacturing Inc. (NUMMI) that US automakers and OM researchers really started to take notice. Toyota's business success and world-leading product quality are now established facts. This success is often attributed to the production system that Toyota developed during the 1950s and 1960s as a result of intense postwar competition.

Detailed chronologies of the events and publications that led up to the emergence of the TPS and subsequent Lean phenomena have been well documented. Table 12.1 offers a synthesis of these works and includes those events and publications considered to be the most important.

Table 12.1 Publications and Events Leading up to the Emergence of Lean

Year	Publications/Events
1925	Frank Woollard publishes "Some Notes on British Methods of Continuous Production."
1932	Taiichi Ohno joins Toyoda Loom Works as an engineer.
1937	Toyota Motor Corp. founded.
1937	Kiichiro Toyoda visits the US, in particular Ford, and begins TPS.
1940	Training Within Industry (TWI) program introduced for US military.
1930–1945	Ford use flow production to produce bombers at Willow Run.
1948	W. Edwards Deming first sent to Japan.
1950	Labor strikes bring Toyota to near bankruptcy. Kiichiro Toyoda resigns and hands business over to cousin Eiji Toyoda who visits Ford River Rouge plant.
1954	Frank Woollard publishes *Principles of Mass and Flow Production*.
1956	Ohno visits Ford River Rouge plant.
1970s	Business press identifies that Japan's exports are wreaking havoc.
1973	First oil crisis occurs.
1977	First English-language academic articles on TPS appeared.
1978	Ohno publishes *Toyota seisan hōshiki* (TPS) in Japanese. Vogul publishes *Japan as Number One: Lessons for America*.
1979	Second oil crisis occurs.
1979	IMVP starts at MIT.
1979	The Repetitive Manufacturing Group (RMG) is established by the American Production and Inventory Control Society (APICS) and included Schonberger and Hall.
1981	Monden publishes a series of articles on TPS in *Industrial Engineering*. Ohno and Kumagi publish a chapter on TPS. Ouchi publishes *Theory Z: How American Business Can Meet the Japanese Challenge*. Pascale and Athos publish *The Art of Japanese Management*.
1982	Schonberger publishes *Japanese Manufacturing Techniques*.
1983	Hall publishes *Zero Inventories*. Hewlett-Packard produce their widely sold and copied *Stockless Production at Greenly Division* video. Monden publishes *Toyota Production System*.
1984	Toyota enters into the New United Motor Manufacturing Inc. (NUMMI) joint venture with GM. First output of IMVP *The Future of the Automobile* published.
1985	The RMG splits from APICS and forms the Association for Manufacturing Excellence (AME).
1986	Imai publishes *Kaizen: The Key to Japan's Competitive Success*.
1988	Productivity Press publishes Ohno's book on TPS in English. Krafcik publishes "Triumph of the Lean Production System" and coins the term "Lean." Stalk publishes *Harvard Business Review* article, "Time: The Next Source of Competitive Advantage," expanding interest in TPS beyond manufacturing. Japanese Standards Association publishes Akao's book *Hoshin Kanri, Policy Deployment for Successful TQM* in Japanese (in English by Productivity Press in 1991).
1989	Shigeo Shingo publishes *A Study of the Toyota Production System*.
1990	Womack et al. publish *The Machine That Changed The World*.

Source: Adapted from Holweg 2007, Shah and Ward 2007, Schonberger 2007, and Bicheno and Holweg 2009

Although there was no mention of quality programs in *The Machine That Changed the World* it is clear that Toyota could not have achieved all its success without these. Both Total Quality Management (TQM) and its forerunner Total Quality Control (TQC), along with Total Productive Maintenance (TPM), were fundamentally linked to the high levels of quality and customer focus that are so associated with Toyota's success.

2.2   Total Quality Management (TQM)

Toyota was a relative latecomer to TPM, or as it was known as in 1960s, Total Quality Control (TQC). In contrast to the internally driven TPS, TQC was introduced via the US. The term originated from Armand Feigenbaum, who described TQC as an effective system for integrating the quality development, quality maintenance, and quality improvement efforts of the various groups in an organization to deliver full customer satisfaction (Feigenbaum 1956). However, TQC in the US meant something different to what was implemented by Toyota, which required the direct involvement of senior management across the whole organization, not just in engineering. Four key assumptions underpin TQC: that quality is less costly than poor workmanship, that employees care about quality and will improve it given the ability to do so, that organizations are systems of independent parts, and that senior managers create the system and are responsible for it. During the 1990s, the term TQM emerged from the principles of TQC as a common term among organizations to reflect a style of management that gives everyone in an organization responsibility for delivering quality to the customer (Dahlgaard-Park and Dahlgaard 2007).

Founders of the quality movement in Japan include W. Edwards Deming and Joseph Juran, two statisticians from the US who went to Japan in the 1950s to help with the post-war reconstruction. Whilst Deming focused on the use of statistical process control to reduce variation in processes, Juran started courses in quality management for senior and middle managers. Juran is responsible for introducing the Pareto Principle of the vital few and trivial many, the 80/20 rule, to Japanese manufacturers and demonstrating that it could apply universally to many management functions (Juran and Godfrey 1951).

Walter Shewhart originally developed the learning and improvement cycle that is used in problem solving at Toyota to support Kaizen. This same cycle was later published in a book edited by his student, W. Edwards Deming (Shewhart and Deming 1939). Dr. Deming modified the original cycle into a four-stage approach, which has been summarized as "PDCA" or Plan, Do, Check, and Act (or often, Plan, Do, Study, Act). Essentially, the approach first looks to identify the root cause of problems and then to eliminate the problem and achieve a higher level of performance. The Deming Application Prize for Quality was established in Japan to 1951 to honor W. Edwards Deming, who had contributed so much to Japan's proliferation of quality control and the philosophy of quality management (Mann 1985).

Nissan and Nippodenso (the company now known as Denso) had won Deming Application Prizes before Toyota formally adopted the TQC methodology as a company-wide program in 1961 and then went on to win the Deming Application Prize in 1965 (Shimokawa and Fujimoto 2009).

Unlike TPS, TQC was implemented as a top-down process and became part of the policy management system, known as *Hoshin Kanri*. TQC reinforced the *Genchi Gembutsu*, fact-based management that checks in the workplace to see the actual situation first-hand. This was built into the Quality Circles, introduced by Japanese quality guru, Ishikawa, and the TPS Kaizen improvements (Mann 1985).

2.3 Total Productive Maintenance (TPM)

Developed by Nakajima (1988), TPM is a systems approach first implemented in Nippodenso that is designed to optimize the performance, reliability, and productivity of plants and equipment by analyzing the reasons for stoppage to improve overall equipment effectiveness (OEE). In a JIT environment, equipment reliability and availability are critical in order to satisfy demand in a low inventory system. TPM is based on eight pillars: focused improvement; autonomous maintenance; planned maintenance; quality maintenance; cost deployment; early equipment management; training and education; and safety, health, and environment (Rich 2001). Elemental to TPM is 5S to reduce stoppages and delays due to searching for tools and other items. 5S is based on five Japanese words: *seiri, seiton, seiso, seiketsu,* and *shitsuke*. These words translate into sort, straighten, shine, standardize, and sustain, that represents five aspects of workplace organization.

It was against this backdrop that Lean Production emerged as an alternative to mass production in 1990. Lean, which emphasizes the socio-technical system of eliminating waste in all operational activities to provide value to the customer in the shortest possible lead-time, may be described as an organizational and managerial concept that advocates for the emulation of the systems in place at Toyota to other industries and sectors outside of Toyota and automotive manufacturing. It does this by focusing on customer value and the efficiencies of the "Flow" of products and services, compared to the efficiencies of "Resources"; equipment, either machines or IT systems; and people in a mass environment (Modig and Åhlström 2015). Lean has been one of the dominant logics in operations management since the 1990s and has influenced many organizations in different sectors, improving their production systems through simultaneously focusing on quality, productivity, efficiency, and flexibility by bringing together the concepts of TPS with that of TQM and TPM.

3 Evolution of Lean Production Research

Although Lean started as a description of TPS and focused heavily on Lean tools, evidence in the literature demonstrates that Lean has evolved over time. In doing so, it has spread well beyond the traditional Japanese automotive manufacturing roots to an enterprise-wide system focused on best practice and process improvement methodologies that has been adopted and adapted by both private and public sector organizations around the world. In a three-year study on the diffusion of Lean, Samuel (2012) established that the period between 1987–1995 was dominated by automobile and automotive supply chain publications. From 1995, publications on aerospace and electronics industries emerged. These were soon followed by publications on retail, construction, financial services, and health. This expansion into other areas was fueled by the publication of *Lean Thinking* (Womack and Jones 1996), which had introduced a core set of principles that could be adapted to any organization and had broadened the concept to other sectors.

The five Lean principles of customer value, value streams, flow, pull at the pace of customer demand, and the pursuit of perfection through continuous improvement represent a roadmap for those organizations attempting to implement Lean, or to emulate TPS. Since 2000, the body of Lean literature in all sectors has increased substantially and has extended from private sector manufacturing and service organizations to the public sector and public services in almost all departments from healthcare to education, welfare, and justice. In addition, more recent publications on innovation and new product/service development, leadership, culture, and IT have taken Lean beyond the traditional fields of operations and process improvement into more enterprise-wide areas from which the concept of operational excellence has emerged.

Over the years, however, many authors have noted a lack of a clear definition of Lean. This lack has contributed to the underdevelopment of Lean in academic research. Karlsson and Åhlström (1996) suggest that commentators on Lean have focused on visible aspects of the process while missing the invisible highly interdependent links of Lean systems as a whole. The conclusion is that this is due to the context-specific origins and the fact that Lean has evolved over time and that, as it continues to advance through experimentation by Toyota and other Lean organizations (Hines et al. 2004), "Lean" can be described as polymorphic, meaning different things to different people, at different moments in time (Samuel et al. 2015).

As with the definition, the scope and objectives of Lean have changed as it has evolved by experimentation. Different authors have different opinions on the characteristics with which it is associated. Shah and Ward (2003) describe four main practices, or bundles, that are part of Lean: JIT, TQM, TPM, and HRM. Pettersen (2009), however, disputes this and states that TQM and other bundles are different and not part of Lean despite the fact that many authors agree that they are critical constituents of the Toyota success story (Schonberger 2015).

Figure 12.2 shows the range of publications (1987–2013) that illustrates the diffusion of Lean publications in all forms of literature.

The period 1987 to 1996 is described as a period of theory building in the evolution of Lean (Lamming 1993; 1996; Womack and Jones 1994; Karlsson and Åhlström 1996; Hines and Rich 1997), which was dominated by academic research. The publication of *Lean Thinking* (Womack and Jones 1996) preceded a wealth of practitioner-oriented publications including Rother and Shook (1998), Spear and Bowen (1999), Liker (2004), and Bicheno and Holweg (2015). Additionally, there was a shift in empirical research from theory building with an emphasis on Lean tools towards theory testing and case study research to validate the models and concepts (Bhamu and Singh Sangwan 2014). Although Lean is often described as atheoretical, it was during this period that Schmenner and Swink (1998) articulated a theory that, although they did not refer to it as Lean, clearly described and underpinned Lean. It is a theory that seeks to

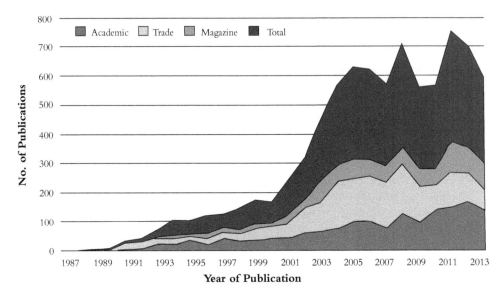

Figure 12.2 Lean Publications 1987–2013

Source: Adapted from Samuel et al. 2015

explain the phenomenon of why one factory or service operation is more productive, as measured by inputs and outputs, than another. They refer to this as the *Theory of Swift, Even Flow*, which they define as "the more swift and even the flow of materials through a process, the more productive that process is" (Schmenner and Swink 1998, p. 102). In a later publication, Schmenner (2012, p. 100) describes how the elements of Lean manufacturing fit together into a philosophy that is grounded in swift, even flow.

Lean has since been featured in all types of publication signifying the rise in practitioner interest as more and more organizations adopted Lean and Lean expanded beyond its roots in manufacturing process improvement to private and public sector services, innovation, and environmental studies (Shah and Ward 2003; 2007; Papadopoulou and Ozbayrak 2005; Bhasin and Burcher 2006; Holweg 2007; Hines et al. 2004; 2010; Piercy and Rich, 2009; Spear 2009; Mollenkop et al. 2010). This has been particularly evident in the interest in Lean applied to hospitals and healthcare (Papadopoulou et al. 2011).

Despite the unquestionable success of TPS, questions as to the sustainability of Lean practices were raised. This gave rise to a new wave of research resulting in a new set of literature. In this, many authors noted that successful Lean implementation is dependent on several organizational factors such as leadership and management strategies, employee behaviors, and engagement and investment in training, as well as external forces such as market situations, local and social cultures, and the availability of skilled people (MacDuffie 1995; Hines et al. 2010). Although the concept of "Respect for People" was recognized as a foundational principle of TPS (Sugimori et al. 1977), research interest in the organizational and leadership practices focused many authors on the behavioral concepts of Lean and books on Lean leadership (Emiliani 2007; Koenigsaecker 2009; Liker and Convis 2012) and Lean culture (Mann 2005; Liker and Hoseus 2008) emerged, which concentrated company attention on the management systems that support Lean. However, Ezzamel et al. (2001) question this and contend that the focus on *Poka-yoke* suggests that humans are not trusted to perform the task correctly, suggesting that Lean is based on McGregor's Theory X, whereas TPM is based on Theory Y.

The concept of Toyota Kata (Rother 2010) builds on the sentiment of Aristotle who said, "We are what we repeatedly do. Excellence, then, is not an act, but a habit" (Cited in Rother 2010, p. 238). Based on an extensive study of Toyota, Rother believes that it is the creation of habits and behaviors in the workforce that are at the root of Toyota's success as they have been able to create an improvement habit by using PDCA cycles repeatedly to move from the current state to a target condition that progressively moves forward towards an ideal future state that represents "True North," or perfection.

Throughout this time, there have been fierce critics of Lean. However, these were mainly focused on criticisms of the assertions made in *The Machine That Changed the World*, rather than on criticism of the concepts behind Lean. Delbridge (1995) criticized the arrogance of the claims made by Womack et al. (1990) and the generalized simplifications based on stereotypes and Western misconceptions. New (2007) takes a similar view, denouncing simple schema that seek to assert bald polarities between TPS and Taylorism. Similarly, Williams et al. (1992; 1994) argue that the "periodization" of craft, mass, and Lean, as used as one of the narrative devices in the book, is misleading.

Coffey (2006) is also critical of empirics within the IMVP study. This is due partly to methodological robustness, but primarily for what he perceives as a poor interpretation of data. He suggests that the role of automation was downplayed and that, if due account had been taken of Europe's weak overall results, automation would have offered far greater causal explanation. Coffey goes further to suggest that Lean is a historically counterfactual myth, formulated through a collective process of fictionalization, which is essentially politically motivated.

The assumption of universality is disputed by many, and Pettersen (2009) states that if, as claimed by Womack et al. (1990), Lean applies to any industry, then the Japanese would have distributed the knowledge throughout all domestic Japanese industry. The fact that it is represented only by other Japanese automakers—Nissan, Honda, and Mazda—counter this claim.

A number of authors noted the difficulty of measuring the success of Lean implementation efforts. Maskell and Baggaley (2004) argue that Lean implementation often leads to cost avoidance rather than cost reduction and that the accountant community lags behind the operations community in recognizing this. Therefore, the accounting community is often accused of hindering Lean implementation efforts. In particular, criticism revolves around the standard cost accounting methodologies. This is not confined to Western organizations though, as seen in a comment (Ohno 1988) where Ohno stated, "It was not enough to chase out the cost accountants from the plants. The problem was to chase cost accounting from my peoples' minds" (cited in Bell and Ozen 2016, p. 140). Clearly, this was also an issue that Toyota had to wrestle with.

3.1 Lean and the Interactions with Traditional Cost Accounting

Product costing information in traditional management accounting was designed primarily by engineers who understood the product process characteristics of their respective businesses. It was intended to serve two main management purposes: to check whether the product diversity was worthwhile and to check whether a particular division, location, or plant was profitable.

According to Johnson and Kaplan (1987), there was little or no effort made to reconcile financial accounting, reporting to the outside world, with the management accounting used internally to assist decision making and to motivate managers and supervisors. This cost accounting approach to management accounting was developed to support management decision making in the late nineteenth/early twentieth centuries during the beginning of the era of mass production (Johnson and Kaplan 1987; Johnson 1992). Compared with today, the cost structure of manufacturing operations in that era was characterized by a relatively high percentage of direct labor and low indirect costs.

Traditional management accounting conventions that focus on efficiencies and allocation of overheads do not support the Lean paradigm and, whilst alternative accounting approaches, such as Lean Accounting (Maskell and Baggaley 2004) and Flow Accounting (Darlington 2010) have been developed over the last twenty-five years, there is still dissatisfaction amongst academics and practitioners in developing an alternative approach to address this issue fully.

Since the 1980s, the debate in management accounting has become polarized between Activity Based Costing (ABC) and Throughput Accounting (TA). With ABC, managers are required to identify the major activities that pertain to the manufacture of specific products and allocate manufacturing overhead costs to activity cost pools. ABC is the foundation behind Lean Accounting (Maskell and Baggaley 2004). Throughput Accounting (TA) is the use of throughput (the rate at which the system generates money), inventory (all the money the system invests in things it intends to or could sell), and operating expense (all the money the system spends in turning inventory into throughput) as management decision tools to replace traditional cost management reports and analyses. TA is the foundation behind Flow Accounting, which focuses on reducing lead-time by identifying inactivity (IMA 1999; Darlington 2010).

3.2 Other Business Improvement Systems in OM

The most significant of the other improvement methodologies that emerged since 1990 are Six Sigma (SS), Agile Manufacturing (AM), and Theory of Constraints (TOC). They mostly have common aims (minimizing waste and resources, reducing lead-time, and increasing flow to improve customer satisfaction and financial results) and generally common origins (the quality evolution in Japan after the Second World War). In addition, they all represent ways of achieving a swifter and more even flow (Schmenner and Swink 1998). Most of these other improvement methodologies are both complementary and competitive to Lean. They are complementary in the sense they may be implemented alongside Lean. The competitive aspect comes into play in the sense that they compete with Lean in the market for business improvement methodologies. However, it is interesting to note that, due to the lack of a common definition of Lean, some Lean researchers believe that the concepts of SS, TOC, and Agile are all part of the philosophy of Lean while others see them as unique and separate. Hence, Lean Six Sigma (LSS) is a common term in more recent Lean literature and an accreditation system of belts, similar to that of SS exists for LSS.

Each of these methodologies will be described in the next sections and compared to Lean, before moving on to consider the present and future of Lean research.

3.2.1 Six Sigma

As discussed earlier in Section 2.2, the quality movement was central to Toyota's success and had been ongoing for many years, with the early focus being the evolution from statistical quality control to quality assurance and TQM.

Compared with TQM, SS is a relatively newer improvement methodology although it is now generally regarded as having overtaken TQM in the broader quality movement. SS was never intended to be a replacement to TQM, although the two concepts have common origins, aims, and other shared characteristics. SS is a data-driven method for achieving near perfect quality, which was originally developed by Motorola in 1987 and made popular by the well-publicized implementation at General Electric by Jack Welch. SS itself is a specific measure of quality, most commonly cited as 3.4% defects per million opportunities. The roots of sigma as a measurement standard can be traced back to Carl Gauss, who introduced the concept of the normal distribution curve, and to Walter Shewhart, who described 3 Sigma as a measure of output variation. The SS quality measure means operating at a level of quality that is defective only 0.0003% of the time. This measure acts as the goal of the SS process improvement methodology, although it is seldom achieved.

The methodology for achieving these process improvements is supported by the deployment of a SS hierarchy with champions referred to as black belts. Black belts are full-time project managers who, armed with knowledge of statistically based process improvement tools, implement improvement projects. Black belts follow a common project cycle known as DMAIC (define, measure, analyze, investigate, and control) which is a refinement of Deming's PDCA cycle.

After comparing TQM with SS, Schroeder et al. (2008) concluded that they differ in four key ways: first, SS has a greater focus on financial and business results; second, SS insists on following the structured DMAIC cycle; third, SS uses more specific metrics; fourth, SS uses several full-time improvement specialists (black belts).

3.2.2 Agile Manufacturing

Agile Manufacturing (AM) is, like Lean, an improvement strategy that emerged in the 1990s. AM arose from an industry-led team that was facilitated by the Iacocca Institute at Lehigh University, Pennsylvania. In contrast to Lean though, AM is described as focusing strategic efforts to achieve competitiveness through flexibility and does not have the same relentless commitment to reducing waste. It combines the purpose of Lean to reduce lead-time and achieve speed, with the ability to react to changes in demand quickly and hence more flexibly (Gunasekaran and Yusuf 2002). There is a debate now, however, as to whether this still applies. Lean has been proven to be appropriate to both high- and low-volume operations in both manufacturing and services and, with its focus on batch-size reduction, can respond with flexibility. Without a clear definition of either, it is difficult to discriminate.

However, in the software development arena, Agile methodologies have developed strongly with a clear set of principles around software development and project management that helps teams to respond quickly to unpredictability through incremental, iterative work cadences, known as sprints. Agile methodologies, as described in the Agile Manifesto, have a set of values and principles that represent an alternative to traditional, sequential project planning. Agile methodologies are used increasingly in all forms of innovation and the principles are diffusing into the business process improvement environment. Within an Agile environment, "Scrums" replace project meetings where the Product Owner, Team, and "Scrum Master" meet to build product increments within short iterations through empirical feedback and team self-management principles; Mary and Tom Poppendieck (2013) describe this as a Lean Mindset, and the values and principles of the Agile Manifesto are also argued as being complementary to that of contemporary Lean thinking.

3.2.3 Theory of Constraints (TOC)

TOC is a systems-management philosophy developed and made popular by Dr. Eliyahu Goldratt in the mid-1980s through the best-selling management book, *The Goal* (Goldratt and Cox 1984). The goal, according to Goldratt and Cox (1984), is to make money now as well as in the future. TOC defines three operational measures that determine whether operations are working toward that goal; throughput (T), inventory (I), and operating expense (OE). Of key importance in TOC is capacity management to identify bottlenecks or constrained resources. In a TOC environment, these are the resources that need to be scheduled to run at full capacity, all others have "catch-up capability." The concept of Drum, Buffer, Rope (DBR) as a means of scheduling production was developed by Goldratt (Goldratt and Cox 1984).

Several studies suggested that manufacturing organizations employing TOC exceed the performance of those using Lean (Mabin and Balderstone 2000). Additionally, several not-for-profit and government agencies around the world have also successfully adopted TOC, most notably parts of the UK National Health Service (NHS), the Israeli Air Force, and the US Department of Defense (Watson et al. 2007). While there are similarities between Lean and TOC, they are fundamentally different paradigms. Lean achieves process improvement through the removal of waste; TOC achieves improvement through increasing throughput. Like AM, however, TOC sees inventory as a way to buffer demand.

4 Contemporary and Future Research in Lean Operations Management

Despite significant research and huge investment of time and money over the past two decades, many organizations have struggled to implement and sustain operational improvement in any meaningful way. As we have seen, the 1990s was a time of paradigm flux as OM moved from a mass production paradigm to adopt the practices of Japanese manufacturing (Bartezzaghi

1999). This was also a period of convergence as functional silos were challenged as new business philosophies have emerged. In addition, the focus on resource efficiency shifted to that of flow efficiency, or effectiveness (Modig and Åhlström 2015).

The contemporary period has been termed the post-Lean era by OM researchers such as MacCarthy et al. (2013) who argue that the links between quality and process excellence are so well understood by managers today, that it is taken as axiomatic in most progressive organizations. As a result, the starting point of implementing Lean or any other improvement methodology has changed, not just in manufacturing but also in services, in both the public and private sector. There is also a plethora of models, frameworks, and roadmaps to choose, perhaps the most significant of these goes back to the roots of the quality movement and the teaching of Dr. W. Edwards Deming.

4.1 Systems Thinking

Dr. Deming talked of thinking in terms of a system and described the system of profound knowledge. The system of profound knowledge is a management philosophy grounded in systems theory (Mann 1985). The system is made up of interrelated components of people and processes with a clearly defined and shared destination or goal. Everyone shares an understanding of, and commitment to, the aim or purpose of the system. Organizations represent systems, and continuous improvement of the system depends on the leader's understanding of the interconnectedness and interdependence of the parts. Optimization of a system occurs when all interconnecting components are orchestrated to achieve the organization's goal.

One particular systems thinking approach commonly associated with Lean is the approach of John Seddon (2005). Seddon's approach uses a service process improvement methodology, the so-called Vanguard Method, that is based on the work of Deming (1982) and Senge (1990). Seddon argues that "Systems Thinking" underpins Lean and that TPS is a striking example of systems thinking applied to a business organization, which focuses on the interrelationship between the various parts of the organization. Having initially allied himself with the Lean movement by naming his approach "Lean Systems" (Jackson et al. 2008), Seddon is now publicly critical of the movement and has inspired debate and dissent within the Lean movement recently. He argues that by creating the label "Lean" to describe TPS, the movement has overemphasized the deployment of tools and techniques to the detriment of that of deeper understanding.

He concedes that organizations will improve by the use of such tools, but that the level of these improvements are insignificant when compared to the benefits from changing system conditions and norms, writing, "The danger with codifying method as tools is that by ignoring the all-important context it obviates the first requirement to understand the problem and, more importantly, to understand and articulate the problem from a systems perspective" (Seddon 2005, p. 190).

4.2 Operational Excellence

1990–2005 was an era of developing and testing theory around TPS and Lean, and one that saw the rise of career pathways of Lean professionals and the development of Lean teams in organizations. However, the last decade has seen a shift from the term Lean in major organizations towards that of *Operational Excellence*, a term made popular by the Shingo Institute to cover all improvement methodologies. This is consistent with Schonberger's thinking when he argued that management terms have a lifecycle approximating an "S" curve and that "Lean" had been in the ascendancy since "JIT" had started to decline in the late 1980s. He put this down to management fatigue, and suggested that the term Lean is undergoing a similar decline in the 2010s.

The term *Operational Excellence* was used by the Shingo Institute, as an award for the Shingo Prize, which builds on the work of Shigeo Shingo, one of the architects of Lean, particularly in the development of Single Minute Exchange of Die (SMED) that was fundamental to batch-size reduction and flexibility. One of Shingo's important contributions was the recognition of the importance of the interrelationship of the principles, systems, and tools. So, in contrast to Seddon's argument that Lean has focused solely on tools, Shingo and the concept of operational excellence taught the principles behind the tools in five key paradigm shifts:

1. Focus on results and behaviors.
2. Behaviors flow from the principles that govern results.
3. Principles underlie the culture that supports the results long term.
4. Creating principle-based cultures requires alignment of the management system.
5. The tools of Lean, TQM, JIT, SS, etc. are enablers and should be used strategically, appropriately, and cautiously to better drive ideal behavior and excellent results.

Although not confined to the Shingo Institute, or indeed to the Shingo Model, Operational Excellence (OE) is becoming a business function of 21st century organizations with Operational Excellence (Op Ex) teams replacing the Lean teams of the early 2000s. The research on OE, like Lean, is practice-led, but includes all the business improvement methodologies and represents a coalition of OM and Human Resource (HR) philosophies.

One OE model that has been developed by Boston Scientific in Galway, Ireland, addresses an issue that some of the managers of the company identified over the last decade. This is where the proliferation of models and the incomplete nature of any single method have made it quite difficult for an organization to navigate a sustainable path to deliver OE. Following an extensive study by one of the authors of this chapter (Lyons) on a range of existing OE methodologies and models in relation to their applicability to implementing and sustaining OE, he concluded that:

- There is an absence of an overarching transformation model that clearly identifies all of the necessary elements to implementing and sustaining operational excellence.
- There is an absence of clarity on the critical interdependence of the necessary elements of OE.
- There is a tendency for over-reliance on consultants' proprietary "big picture" understanding and their tacit experiential knowledge.

It was apparent to him that no one model/method identified all the necessary elements of implementing and sustaining OE. It also became apparent that the collective knowledge across a range of separate models and methodologies could be distilled into a single unified OE model that focused on the transformation of the organization's vision into results (Figure 12.3) in which the strategy, values, and principles drive the results through the appropriate tools, measures, technologies, supply chain structures, and skills based on a foundation of leadership and change management in a high-engagement culture.

The model, which illustrates clearly the functional convergence of OM with the other business functions and the convergence of all contemporary business improvement methodologies (Lean, Six Sigma, TOC, and Agile) in a systems approach became the foundation for Boston Scientific, Galway's strategic model and has been used successfully to develop the business and remain competitive in a harsh economic environment.

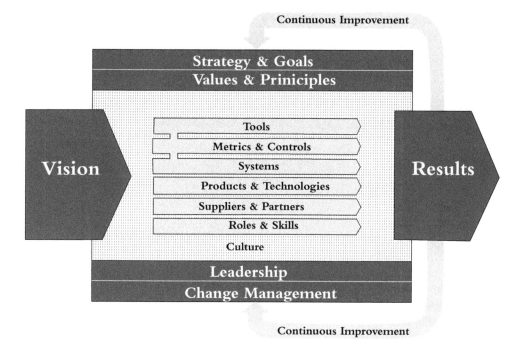

Figure 12.3 The Strategic Operational Excellence Model from Boston Scientific in Galway, Ireland

5 Future Research Directions

Future research into the application of the principles of Lean continue with studies of integrating concepts such as Lean and Green, working to develop a business system that is effective in reducing process waste and reducing the environmental impact (Pampanelli et al. 2014). This builds on the concepts of *Compression* (Hall 2011). Lean is predicated on the assumption of growth, but as shown by recent economic turmoil and the slowing down of the Chinese economy, the future may not be a growth future. How then can businesses remain competitive? This has serious implications for managers and can drive research into developing new OM business models that compete differently. Technology and innovation will present new research openings in the future with the widespread adoption of advanced manufacturing and Product-Service Systems (PSSs) where organizations will compete on the basis of their integrated product and service offering (Nadurupati et al. 2013).

Of particular interest in the Lean research community is Lean in the Digital Economy. The "Internet of Things" and the coming together of sensors and machines will change the way we operate and interact. This will be a major source of new products and services, created and produced in very different ways. If the introduction of Lean into OM was considered to be disruptive, this is likely to be the next disruption, with huge implications for OM research.

6 Conclusions

Clearly Lean has spread well beyond the traditional Japanese automotive manufacturing roots and has evolved over time from a generic description of TPS to a business improvement methodology focused on best practice and operational excellence. It has been adopted and adapted by public and private sector organizations around the world. Research in Lean has changed from theory development in the early 1990s based on understanding the TPS, to theory testing towards the end of the 20th century where the principles of Lean were tested in other organizations, both manufacturing and services, in the private and public sector. The early 21st century saw questions raised as to the sustainability of change and attention moved from the technical to the social systems. The view of Lean shifted from a tools focus to a management system focus and to a whole organizational system or philosophy focus (Bhasin and Burcher 2006). The paradigm shift from mass production was noted by Duguay et al. (1997) who argued that the era of mass production as the dominant production paradigm ended in the 1980s and was succeeded by a new customer-focused paradigm. They further argued that the proliferation of improvement methodologies in the late 1990s could be associated with paradigmatic chaos (Kuhn 1962 cited in Duguay et al. 1997) from which the new paradigm emerged, writing that "The decline of US mass producers has given rise to a variety of approaches better adapted to rapid change, such as flexible production, Lean production, mass customization and agile manufacturing" (Duguay et al. 1997, p. 1193). They contend that we have now entered the era (21st century) where Lean and flexible producers dominate.

This chapter builds on this and demonstrates that, despite the many criticisms of Lean and the lack of formal definition, Lean has emerged as a dominant global OM paradigm focused on reducing variability and compressing time in order to improve flow. The link between Lean and the Theory of Swift, Even Flow (Schmenner and Swink 1998) contributes to theory development in OM.

However, we believe that although managers have continued to pursue "operational excellence," they have adopted many of the Lean tools and techniques to achieve this. The Lean movement that was supported by governments, researched and criticized by other academics, could justifiably claim to be a paradigm shift in OM, whether it is called Lean, Operational Excellence, or simply the contemporary OM.

References and Bibliography

Bartezzaghi, E. (1999), "The Evolution of Production Models: Is a New Paradigm Emerging?" *International Journal of Operations & Production Management*, **19**(2): 229–250.

Bell, S.C. and M.A. Ozen (2016) *Lean IT: Enabling and Sustaining Your Lean Transformation.* CRC Productivity Press, New York.

Bhamu, J. and K. Singh Sangwan (2014) "Lean Manufacturing: Literature Review and Research Issues," *International Journal of Operations & Production Management*, **34**(7): 876–940.

Bhasin, S. and P. Burcher (2006) "Lean Viewed as a Philosophy," *Journal of Manufacturing Technology Management*, **17**(1): 56–72.

Bicheno, J. and M. Holweg (2015) *The Lean Toolbox: A Handbook for Lean Transformation*, 5th ed. PICSIE Books, Buckingham, UK.

Coffey, D. (2006) *The Myth of Japanese Efficiency: The World Car Industry in a Globalizing Age.* Edward Elgar Publishing Limited, Cheltenham, UK.

Dahlgaard-Park, S. and J. Dahlgaard (2007) "Excellence—25 Years Evolution," *Journal of Management History*, **14**(4): 371–393.

Darlington, J. (2010) "Accounting for Lean," *Lean Management Journal*, **7**(Nov/Dec): 20–25.

Delbridge, R. (1995) "Surviving JIT: Control and Resistance in a Japanese Transplant," *Journal of Business Studies*, **32**(6): 802–817.

Deming, W. (1982) *Out of the Crisis.* MIT Press, Cambridge, MA.

Duguay, C.R., S. Landry and F. Pasin (1997) "From Mass Production to Flexible/Agile Production," *International Journal of Operations & Production Management*, **17**(12): 1183–1195.

Emiliani, M.L. (2007) *Real Lean: Critical Issues and Opportunities in Lean Management.* The Center for Lean Management, LLC, Kensington, CT.

Ezzamel, M., H. Willmott and F. Worthington (2001) "Power, Control and Resistance in 'The Factory That Time Forgot'," *Journal of Management Studies*, **38**(8): 1053–1079.

Feigenbaum, A.V. (1956) "Total Quality Control," *Harvard Business Review*, **Nov–Dec**: 93–100.

Goldratt, E. and J. Cox (1984) *The Goal: A Process of Ongoing Improvement*. North River Press, Great Barrington, MA.

Gunasekaran, A. and Y.Y. Yusuf (2002) "Agile Manufacturing: A Taxonomy of Strategic and Technological Imperatives," *International Journal of Production Research*, **40**(6): 1357–1385.

Hall, R.W. (2011) *Compression: Meeting the Challenges of Sustainability through Vigorous Learning Enterprises*. CRC Press, Boca Raton, FL.

Harrison, G.C. (1919) "Cost Accounting in the 'New Industrial' Day," *Industrial Management*, **58**: 441–444.

Harrison, G.C. (1921) *Cost Accounting to Aid Production: A Practical Study of Scientific Cost Accounting*. Engineering Magazine Company, New York.

Hines, P. and N. Rich (1997) "The Seven Value Stream Mapping Tools," *International Journal of Operations & Production Management*, **17**(1): 46–64.

Hines, P., M. Holweg and N. Rich (2004) "From Strategic Toolkit to Strategic Value Creation: A Review of the Evolution of Contemporary Lean Thinking," *International Journal of Operations & Production Management*, **24**(10): 994–1011.

Hines, P., P. Found, G. Griffiths and R. Harrison (2010) *Staying Lean: Thriving, Not Just Surviving*. 2nd ed. Productivity Press, New York.

Holweg, M. (2007) "The Genealogy of Lean Production," *Journal of Operations Management*, **25**(2): 420–437.

Hopp, W. and M. Spearman (2000) *Factory Physics*, 2nd ed. McGraw-Hill, New York.

IMA. (1999) *Theory of Constraints (TOC): Management System Fundamentals*. Institute of Management Accounting, Statements on Management Accounting: Strategic Cost Management, www.imanet.org (accessed Dec. 2015).

Imai, M. (1986) *Kaizen: The Key to Japan's Competitive Success*. McGraw-Hill, New York.

Jackson, M., N. Johnston and J. Seddon (2008) "Evaluating Systems Thinking in Housing," *Journal of the Operational Research Society*, **59**: 186–197.

Johnson, H.T. (1992) *Relevance Regained: From Top Down Control to Bottom-Up Empowerment*. The Free Press, New York.

Johnson, H.T. and R.S. Kaplan (1987) *Relevance Lost*. Harvard Business School Press, Boston, MA.

Juran, J. and A.B. Godfrey (1951) *Juran's Quality Handbook*. McGraw-Hill, New York.

Karlsson, C. and P. Åhlström (1996) "Assessing Changes Towards Lean Production Management," *International Journal of Operations & Production Management*, **16**(2): 24–41.

Koenigsaecker, G. (2009) *Leading the Lean Enterprise Transformation*. CRC Productivity Press, New York.

Krafcik, J.F. (1988) "Triumph of the Lean Production System," *Sloan Management Review*, **30**(1): 41–51.

Lamming, R. (1993) *Beyond Partnership: Strategies for Innovation and Lean Supply*. Prentice Hall, Hemel Hempstead, UK.

Lamming, R. (1996) "Squaring Lean Supply with Supply Chain Management," *International Journal of Operations & Production Management*, **16**(2): 183–196.

Liker, J.K. (2004) *The Toyota Way: 14 Management Principles from the World's Greatest Manufacturer*. New York, McGraw-Hill.

Liker, J.K. and G.L. Convis (2012) *The Toyota Way to Lean Leadership: Achieving and Sustaining Excellence through Leadership Development*. McGraw-Hill, New York.

Liker, J.K. and M. Hoseus (2008) *Toyota Culture: The Heart and Soul of the Toyota Way*. McGraw Hill, New York.

Mabin, V. and S. Balderstone (2000) *The World of the TOC: A Review of the International Literature*. American Production and Inventory Control. The St. Lucie Press/APICS.

MacCarthy, B.L., M. Lewis, C. Voss and R. Narasimhan (2013) "The Same Old Methodologies? Perspectives on OM Research in the Post-Lean Age," *International Journal of Operations & Production Management*, **33**(7): 934–956.

MacDuffie, J. (1995) "Human Resource Bundles and Manufacturing Performance: Organisational Logic and Flexible Production Systems in the World Auto Industry," *Industrial and Labor Relations Review*, **48**(2): 197–221.

Mann, D. (2005) *Creating a Lean Culture: Tools to Sustain Lean Conversions*. Productivity Press, New York.

Mann, N.R. (1985) *The Keys to Excellence: The Story of the Deming Philosophy*. Prestwick Books, Los Angeles, CA.

Maskell, B. and B. Baggaley (2004) *Practical Lean Accounting: A Proven System for Measuring and Managing a Lean Enterprise*. Productivity Press, New York.

Modig, N. and P. Åhlström (2015) *This Is Lean: Resolving the Efficiency Paradox*. Rheological Publishing, Stockholm, Sweden.

Mollenkop, D., H. Stolze, W.L. Tate and M. Ueltschy (2010) "Green, Lean and Global Supply Chains," *International Journal of Physical Distribution & Logistics Management*, **40**(1–2): 14–41.

Monden, Y. (1983) *Toyota Production System: Practical Approach to Production Management*. 3rd ed. Institute of Industrial Engineers, Atlanta, GA.

Monden, Y. (1989) "Total Cost Management System in Japanese Automobile Corporations," in Monden, Y. and Sakurai, M. eds *Japanese Management Accounting*. Productivity Press, Cambridge, MA.

Moore, R. and L. Schienkopf (1998) *TOC and Lean Manufacturing: Friends or Foes?* Chesapeake Consulting Inc., Severna Park, MD.

Nadurupati, S.S., D. Lascelles, N. Yip and F.T. Chan (2013) "Eight Challenges of the Servitization." In Meier, H. ed. *Product-Service Integration of Sustainable Solution: Proc. of the 5th CIRP International Conference on Industrial Product-Service Systems, Bochum, Germany, March 14th–15th 2013*, Springer, Berlin.

Nakajima, S. (1988) *Introduction to TPM: Total Productive Maintenance*. CRC Productivity Press, Portland, OR.

New, S. (2007) Celebrating the Enigma: The Continuing Puzzle of the Toyota Production System. *International Journal of Production Research*, **45**(16): 3545–3554.

Ohno, T. (1978) *Toyota seisan hōshiki*. Diamond Inc., Tokyo, Japan.

Ohno, T. (1988) *Toyota Production System—Beyond Large Scale Production* (English translation). CRC Productivity Press, Portland, OR.

Oliver, N., R. Delbridge, D. Jones and J. Lowe (1994) "World Class Manufacturing: Further Evidence in the Lean Production Debate," *British Journal of Management*, **5**(SI): 53–63.

Pampanelli, A., P. Found and A.M. Bernardez (2014) "A Lean and Green Kaizen Model for a Production Cell," *International Journal of Cleaner Production*, **85**: 19–30.

Papadopoulou, T. and M. Ozbayrak (2005) "Leanness: Experiences from the Journey to Date," *Journal of Manufacturing Technology Management*, **16**(7): 784–805.

Papadopoulou, T., Z. Radnor and Y. Merali (2011) "The Role of Actor Associations in Understanding the Implementation of Lean Thinking in Healthcare," *International Journal of Operations & Production Management*, **31**(2): 167–191.

Pettersen, J. (2009) "Defining Lean Production: Some Conceptual and Practical Issues," *The TQM Journal*, **21**(2): 127–142.

Piercy, N. and N. Rich (2009) "Lean Transformation in the Pure Service Environment: The Case of the Call Centre Service," *International Journal of Operations & Production Management*, **29**(1): 54–76.

Poppendieck, M. and T. Poppendieck (2013) *The Lean Mindset: Ask the Right Questions*. Addison-Wesley, NJ.

Rich, N. (2001) *Total Productive Maintenance: The Lean Approach*. Tudor Business Publishing Ltd., Wirral, UK.

Rother, M. (2010) *Toyota Kata*. McGraw-Hill, New York.

Rother, M. and J. Shook (1998) *Learning to See*. Lean Enterprise Institute, Cambridge, MA.

Samuel, D. (2012) "Exploring UK Lean Diffusion in the Period 1988 to 2010," Ph.D. thesis, Cardiff University, Cardiff, UK.

Samuel, D., P. Found and S. Williams (2015) "How Did the Publication of the Book *The Machine That Changed The World* Change Management Thinking? Exploring 25 Years of Lean Literature," *International Journal of Operations & Production Management*, **35**(10): 1386–1407.

Schmenner, R.W. (2012) *Getting and Staying Productive: Applying Swift, Even Flow to Practice*. Cambridge University Press, Cambridge, UK.

Schmenner, R. and M. Swink (1998) "On Theory in Operations Management," *Journal of Operations Management*, **17**(1): 97–113.

Schonberger, R. (1982) *Japanese Manufacturing Techniques: Nine Hidden Lessons in Simplicity*. The Free Press, Simon & Schuster, New York.

Schonberger, R. (2007) "Japanese Production Management: An Evolution with Mixed Success," *Journal of Operations Management*, **25**(2): 403–419.

Schonberger, R. (2015) "Catching Lean's Drift: The Essential Message of Time-Based Competition," cover story *APICS Magazine*, **Jan/Feb**: 40–43.

Schroeder, R.D., K. Linderman, C. Liedtke and A.S. Choo (2008) "Six Sigma: Definition and underlying theory," *Journal of Operations Management*, **26**(4): 536–554.

Seddon, J. (2005) *Freedom from Command and Control: A Better Way to Make the Work Work, the Toyota System for Service Organisations*. 2nd ed. Vanguard Education Ltd., Buckingham, UK.

Senge, P. (1990) *The Fifth Discipline: The Art and Practice of the Learning Organisation.* Century, London.
Shah, R. and P. Ward (2003) "Lean Manufacturing Context, Practice Bundles and Performance," *Journal of Operations Management*, **21**(2): 129–149.
Shah, R. and P. Ward (2007) "Defining and Developing Measures of Lean Production," *Journal of Operations Management*, **25**(4): 785–805.
Shewhart, W.A. and W.E. Deming (1939) *Statistical Method from the Viewpoint of Quality Control.* Graduate School of Department of Agriculture, Washington, DC.
Shimokawa, K. and T. Fujimoto (2009) *The Birth of Lean: Conversations with Taiichi Ohno, Eiji Toyoda and Other Figures Who Shaped Toyota Management.* The Lean Enterprise Institute, Cambridge, MA.
Shingo, S. (1989) *A Study of the Toyota Production System from an Industrial Engineering Viewpoint.* Productivity Press, MA.
Spear, S. (2009) *Chasing the Rabbit.* McGraw-Hill, New York.
Spear, S. and H. Bowen (1999) "Decoding the DNA of the Toyota Production System," *Harvard Business Review*, **Sep–Oct**: 97–106.
Stalk, G. (1988) "Time—The Next Source of Competitive Advantage," *Harvard Business Review*, **July–Aug**: 41–51.
Sugimori, Y., K. Kusunoki, F. Cho and S. Uchikawa (1977) "Toyota Production System and Kanban System Materialization of Just-in-Time and Respect-for-Human System," *International Journal of Production Research*, **15**(6): 553–564.
Taylor, F. W. (1903), *Shop Management.* Harper & Brothers, New York.
Watson, K., J. Blackstone and S. Gardiner (2007) "The Evolution of a Management Philosophy: The Theory of Constraints," *Journal of Operations Management*, **25**(2): 387–402.
Williams, K., C. Haslam, S. Johal and J. Williams (1994) *Cars: Analysis, History, Cases.* Berghahn Books, Oxford, UK.
Williams, K., C. Haslam, J. Williams, A. Culter, A. Adcroft and S. Johal (1992) "Against Lean Production," *Economy and Society*, **21**(3): 321–354.
Woollard, F.G. (1925) "Some Notes on British Methods of Continuous Production," *Proc. of the Institution of Automobile Engineer*s 1924–25, **XIX**: 419–474.
Woollard, F.G. (1954) *Principles of Mass and Flow Production.* Ilife & Sons, London.
Womack, J.P. and D.T. Jones (1994) "From Lean Production to the Lean Enterprise," *Harvard Business Review*, **72**(2): 93–103.
Womack, J.P. and D.T. Jones (1996) *Lean Thinking: Banish Waste and Create Wealth in Your Corporation.* The Free Press, New York.
Womack, J.P., D.T. Jones and D. Roos (1990) *The Machine That Changed the World.* Rawson Associates, New York.

PART IV

Emerging Themes and New Research Domains of POM

13
BUSINESS STARTUP OPERATIONS

Nitin Joglekar, Moren Lévesque, and Sinan Erzurumlu

1 Introduction

Entrepreneurial business startups have been the lifeblood of the private economy sector with varying degrees across countries (Acs et al. 2008). Some of the most entrepreneurial countries exist in the developing world. For instance, the Global Entrepreneurship Monitor (GEM) ranks the top three countries as Uganda, Thailand, and Brazil, with China ranked 11th and the U.S. ranked 37th (GEM 2014). A 2015 study by the Kauffman Foundation shows that approximately 530,000 new businesses were started in the U.S. each month (Kauffman Foundation 2015). According to the U.S. Small Business Administration, small businesses have provided 55% of all jobs and 66% of all net new jobs since the 1970s (USSBA 2015). Amidst high activity and heightened interest in business startups, these businesses face severe organizational and fiscal constraints causing the failure of most within five years of their starting up. However, some exceptional startups, referred to as unicorns (CB Insights 2015), have shown spectacular valuation growth. Unicorns are defined as firms reaching well over $1 billion in valuation in a short period of time and becoming major economic/social entrepreneurship successes.

This chapter describes the contribution of the operations management (OM) field to entrepreneurship and startup practices. As examples of unique operational innovations (OIs) in startup settings, readers may recall well-documented news stories about two unicorns: the transportation firm Uber with its yield management strategies (Surowiecki 2014) and the hospitality firm Airbnb with its quality management practices (Pfeffer 2014). We define business startup operations as a configuration of resources and activities at nascent organizations that are geared to create, organize, and grow businesses based on the manufacturing of a product or delivery of a service.

We address several aspects of business startups in this chapter. First, startups are subject to three distinctive operational constraints on, or lack thereof, resources, routines (or processes), and reputation—also referred to as 3Rs in this chapter—that are affected by the capabilities of entrepreneurs as well as the uncertain, dynamic, and complex environment in which they operate (Zahra et al. 2011). Asset acquisition and process configuration also take shape as the startup progresses from opportunity discovery to commitment to organization growth—i.e., through the entrepreneurial value chain (Joglekar and Lévesque 2013)—contingent upon marketing acceptance, technology evolution, and execution efficacy. We explain these stages (i.e., discover, commit, organize, and grow) in detail in Section 2.

Second, the emerging operational structure of startup adds a unique layer of complexity and risk to activities associated with market development, technology development, and execution, whereas "established" firms already may have easy access to resources and well-organized routines. While lack of resources and routines generates inherent uncertainties, such uncertainties may not be easily overcome by startups that have not established a reputation or business history, making them highly vulnerable to vagaries of the venture lifecycle. Lack of reputation limits access to capital and startups may be unable to raise cash as needed. Their operational decisions are hence restricted by debt and other financial considerations (Berger and Udell 2003).

Third, while startups' efforts may be typically examined within small and medium-sized enterprises or SMEs—a glossary of relevant terms is provided in Table 13.1—we do not ignore entrepreneurial activities within large firms, which has also been referred to as intrapreneurship or corporate venturing. Family-owned businesses are a major segment of the SME literature (Sharma 2004), but we exclude specific startup issues related to such businesses for brevity. Lastly, akin to the domain of international entrepreneurship, we consider startups that create future goods and services through the discovery, enactment, evaluation, and exploitation of opportunities across national borders (Oviatt and McDougall 2005).

This chapter's organization and resulting contribution follow a two-part setup: what we know about startups and what we observe as emerging trends. We open by exploring the body of knowledge in the OM-entrepreneurship interface regarding venturing creation and technology commercialization throughout the entrepreneurial value chain. To establish what is already known about startup operations, we summarize published reviews covering the 2001–2011 period and then augment this summary with publications from the 2011–2015 period. This review effort has yielded five overarching principles—termed as the 3R Principles for startup operations—that we describe in the next section.

In the later part of this chapter, we take a close look at recent developments in lean operations, data analytics, and intelligent robotics that have pushed the boundaries of business practices and created opportunities for startups in new contexts (e.g., digital technologies and platforms) and new economies (e.g., circular economy—i.e., supply chains involving almost zero waste and pollution, either by design or intention). We use this evidence to argue that a central idea of entrepreneurial thinking involving constant improvisation and adaptation requires a tight alignment between evolving business model innovations (BMIs) and OIs. BMI refers to the way a firm generates revenues, limits costs, and provides its customers with a unique value proposition in a competitive marketplace (Girotra and Netessine 2013). OI refers to practices of solving problems and creating new opportunities through non-traditional applications of OM decisions such as inventory management, quality management, and supply chain design. These innovative operations based on novel technologies, such as digital connectivity-based capacity management practices in

Table 13.1 Glossary

BMI	Business Model Innovation
CBA	Connectivity-Based Analytics
LCIR	Low-Cost Intelligent Robotics
OI	Operational Innovation
Pivots	Changes in the Business Model
SMEs	Small and Medium-sized Enterprises
Unicorns	Firms that reach well over $1 billion in valuation in a short period of time
3Rs	Resources, Routines, and Reputation

emergent firms like Uber, are yet to be codified systematically through a body of formal studies in OM journals. We thus lay down anecdotal evidence on OIs in emergent businesses including the transshipment optimization model at Zipcar, yield management strategies at Uber, quality management practices at Airbnb, the reconfiguration of manufacturing systems at Rethink Robotics, and the reconfiguration of supply chain delivery at Kiva Systems.

We use this anecdotal evidence to point to potential research opportunities associated with 3R-related principles through the alignment between OIs, digital technologies, and platforms; connectivity-based analytics; and evolving business models and then discuss managerial implications of our findings in the startup operations context.

2 What We Know about Business Startup Operations

2.1 Review Articles

We draw upon a body of knowledge from mostly, but not limited to, OM-related research on how to create, organize, and grow business startup operations. We highlight two review articles featured in recently published special issues with focus on OM and entrepreneurship in the *Journal of Operations Management* (*JOM*) and the *Production and Operations Management* (*POM*) journal. We also draw upon a third review article from the *Journal of Management* on entrepreneurial decision making in order to provide perspective.

In the *JOM* 2011 special issue "Operations Management, Entrepreneurship, and Value Creation," Kickul et al. (2011) took a cross-disciplinary lens to OM and entrepreneurship. They highlight four issues for further consideration. First, OM may offer the best means to improve the efficiency of startups that produce or sell a good or service that is already available to other sources through supply chain management techniques. Second, large and small firms can explore comparative advantages to exploit: While large firms can offer the advantages of economies of scale and scope, smaller firms can be agile in creating new products or services. Third, OM can examine the viability of startups in terms of operational efficiency, customer service, and risk-management process analysis. Fourth, startups must also deal with governmental and administrative bureaucracies, which can be explored with the role of human behavior in OM.

In the 2013 special issue of the *POM* journal, "Technology Commercialization, Entrepreneurship & Growth Driven Operations," Joglekar and Lévesque (2013) provide a comprehensive review of research that brings out differing operational decisions specific to the discovery, commitment, organizing, and growth stages that form the entrepreneurial value chain. During the *discover stage* the entrepreneur can discover and assess the opportunity. At the *commit stage*, s/he begins committing her/his and other's human/financial resources to the newly formed venture. The *organize stage* is where ongoing and future needs are established and activities are organized to reach these needs and enable the opportunity to transform into a business that can release a product. At the *grow stage*, the product achieves some market success, and the venture itself must grow. They propose an evolutionary path for the use of resources, routines, and reputation—the 3Rs—that are often lacking in the four stages of the entrepreneurial value chain. Based on their literature review, they take a comprehensive view of operational decisions. They further identify threats and opportunities for emergent firms' decision making and unique operational tradeoffs, due to shortages of the 3Rs through the entrepreneurial value chain.

In addition to these focused issues on the operations-entrepreneurship interface, Shepherd et al. (2015) provide a review from mainstream entrepreneurship journals on judgment and decision making. Their focus is on key decisions in the primary activities of the entrepreneurial process and the entrepreneur's choices including opportunity-assessment, entrepreneurial-entry, opportunity-exploitation, and entrepreneurial-exit decisions; heuristics and biases in the entrepreneurial decision-making context; characteristics of the entrepreneurial decision maker; and environment as a decision context. In particular, entrepreneurs are diverse in terms of their background (i.e., knowledge, experience, abilities, attitudes, self-perception) and more biased towards taking risks in their decision making than non-entrepreneurs. They also operate in complex and dynamic environments and are heterogeneous in their perceptions of the environment, including industry, market, competitive, and institutional factors.

Therefore, conventional operational decisions, such as ordering capacity, must be adjusted by operations managers in startup settings to include 3R constraints and behavioral biases. These findings, with suitable adjustments to 3R decisions, are also applicable to intrapreneurial efforts in established technology and service firms such as 3M and Disney (Li 2008; Kenney et al. 2010). Antoncic and Hisrich (2001) have argued that intrapreneurship increases productivity, thus supporting a stronger work ethic and instilling pride in accomplishment. It can engender new products and services that are vital to economic survival and growth.

2.2 Findings in Recent Publications

To provide an update on how scholars in the OM and entrepreneurship fields have investigated business startup issues, we extend the 10 × 4 framework in Joglekar and Lévesque (2013: 1325–1326) by adding articles published between 2011 and 2015. We assemble a dataset of 38 articles at the OM-entrepreneurship interface published in seven journals (and after the review articles featured in Section 2.1): *Management Science, Production and Operations Management, Journal of Operations Management, Manufacturing & Service Operations Management, Entrepreneurship Theory & Practice, Journal of Business Venturing,* and *IEEE Transactions on Engineering Management.* We then offer (see Table 13.2) selected (i.e., one example per cell) questions and tradeoffs in a 10 × 4 matrix whose categories are consistent with the Joglekar and Lévesque's (2013) review. The ten rows represent well-established decision categories in the OM literature:

(i) Technology commercialization and adoption
(ii) Location, market selection, and network design
(iii) Product/service design and launch
(iv) Lean operations, flexibility, line balancing, and process design
(v) Scheduling, batching, and task design
(vi) Inventory and supply chain management
(vii) Quality, reliability, and process improvement
(viii) Aggregate, capacity, workforce, and integrated planning
(ix) Project, portfolio, and risk management
(x) Environmental sustainability.

The number of articles that fit in the "discover," "commit," "organize," and "grow" stages (the 4 columns of the 10 × 4 matrix) amount to 7, 5, 12, and 14, respectively. We categorize these articles into product- and/or service-oriented startups. For brevity, articles examining the manufacturing and/or supply chain associated with a product are included within product-oriented startups. For articles on software and information technology, we categorize them as either a product- or service-oriented startup depending on how the proposed technology serves customers. In this sample of thirty-eight articles, we classify twenty-nine as product-oriented and eight as both product- and service-oriented, with the remaining article classified as purely service-oriented. Each of the forty cells in Table 13.2, except for two cells where no relevant article is

Table 13.2 Exemplar Studies and Review Articles

Topics and Review Articles	Entrepreneurial Value Chain			
	Discover	Commit	Organize	Grow
Technology commercialization & adoption	Schmidt & Druehl (2005): When can a new technology substitute an existing product, based on depth and breadth (with respect to the reservation price curve) considerations?	Habib et al. (2013): What are the implications of the decision to spawn or to retain a new product for the nature and evolution of the firm?	Huang et al. (2013): Is ownership of intellectual property rights (IPRs) or downstream capabilities effective in encouraging entry into markets complementary to a proprietary platform by preventing the platform owner from expropriating rents from startups?	Galbraith et al. (2012): How do the evaluations of technical merit and commercial potential lead to successful funding of early stage technologies?
Location, market selection, & network design	Dahl & Sorenson (2012): What are the performance implications of entrepreneurs' location decisions?	Kouvelis et al. (2004): What are the tradeoffs in selecting global facility locations, while incorporating logistics, government subsidies, trade tariffs, and taxation issues?	Musteen & Ahsan (2013): What is the conceptual model of offshoring of knowledge-intensive, complex work by young, entrepreneurial firms?	Giloni et al. (2003): What are the tradeoffs in designing distribution systems to maximize profit with multiple time periods, with growing demand for capacity, while accounting for pricing and competition in various channels?
Product/service design & launch	Erat & Krishnan (2012): What are the drivers of outside agent's search dynamics? How do the awards, problem specification, and structure of the design space influence the number of searchers and breadth of induced search?	Lim et al. (2001): What are the conditions under which an entrepreneur can penetrate an established market via channels other than authorized distributors (a.k.a. gray marketing)?	Anderson & Parker (2013): How does a startup integrate its service or product with one or more complementary technologies in market entry?	Deligianni et al. (2014): What is the relationship between innovation and product diversification as growth strategies for new ventures?

(Continued)

Table 13.2 (Continued)

Topics and Review Articles	Entrepreneurial Value Chain			
	Discover	Commit	Organize	Grow
Lean operations, flexibility, line balancing, & process design	No article found in our sample of journals.	Atwater & Chakravorty (2002): When is 100% utilization of a primary constraint in drum-buffer-rope system not optimal?	Patel (2011): How can manufacturing flexibility help decouple activities required in task environments from those required in institutional environments, thereby mitigating the conflict of adopting flexible and rigid structures at the same time?	Gaimon and Burgess (2003): What is the impact of lead times and learning on capacity expansion plans?
Scheduling, batching, & task design	Kornish & Ulrich (2011): When efforts to generate ideas are conducted in parallel, how likely are the resulting ideas to be redundant and how large are the opportunity spaces?	◆Lévesque & Schade (2005): How should an entrepreneur allocate his/her time between leisure, a wage job and the newly formed venture, and how does he/she actually do it?	Thomke & Bell (2001): What are the optimal timing, frequency, and fidelity of sequential testing activities that are carried out to evaluate novel product concepts and designs?	Li et al. (2003): How does one acquire capacity in batches under uncertain technological growth?
Inventory & supply chain management	No article found in our sample of journals	Swinney et al. (2011): When the size of the market is unclear, how does a survival probability maximizing startup choose how much capacity to build?	Song et al. (2011): How can new ventures complement their resources and experience with supplier investment, to build positional advantages for their first product and increase marketplace performance?	◆Brettel et al. (2011): What are the factors that influence new entrepreneurial venture's choice of distribution channels, and what are the performance consequences of those choices?
Quality, reliability, & process improvement	Girotra et al. (2010): Can the quality of ideas be increased by managing the idea portfolio (e.g., size and variance) and teaming process sequence?	Tanrisever et al. (2012): How much should one invest in process improvement and production when the cash flow is subject to a probabilistic debt payback constraint?	◆Parker (2006): How much do entrepreneurs rely on their experience when making business decisions and on venture-performance information to learn about their true capabilities as well as their environment?	◆Yim (2008): Which one, quality shocks (i.e., technology shocks and innovations in the product/service, representing firm investments) or market shocks (industry business fluctuations), enhance the performance of rapid-growth startups to a larger extent?

Aggregate, capacity, workforce, & integrated planning	♦Chwolka & Raith (2012): What is the value of business planning before startup, or should the entrepreneur even bother to plan before making the decision of whether or not to enter the market?	Tatikonda et al. (2013): What is the role of operational capabilities in enhancing new venture survival during different phases of a venture's life cycle?	Azadegan et al. (2013): What is the role of operational slack on firm survival during its venture stage when its survival is significantly challenged by environmental threats?	Goodale et al. (2011): How do operations control variables act in concert with the determinants of corporate entrepreneurial activity to promote the innovation outcomes that facilitate long-term organizational success?
Project, portfolio, & risk management	Marion et al. (2012): How can large firms start "thinking small" to instill entrepreneurial spirit in their R&D teams?	♦Fairchild (2011): What are the effects of economic and behavioral characteristics on an entrepreneur's choice between a business angel and a venture capitalist?	♦Haeussler et al. (2011): How can new firms maximize the benefits of strategic alliances to gain access to knowledge, resources, and capabilities while reducing their risks?	♦Lévesque et al. (2012): In their attempt to grow, how do firms invest in resources (i.e., R&D and SG&A) while considering variations in these resources' growth rates?
Environmental sustainability	Girotra & Netessine (2013): How can a manager identify new business models by understanding the context of decision making in existing models and the associated inefficiencies?	Debo et al. (2006): How do firms plan for substitution between new and remanufactured products, subject to a constraint on the diffusion of remanufactured products due to the limited supply of used products that can be remanufactured?	Erzurumlu et al. (2014): How can operations design hedge risk and enhance project valuation in technology development and deployment stages for clean tech startups?	Noori & Chen (2003): How does one conduct scenario planning for the evolution of the demand for environmental products involving technology and operational uncertainty?

♦indicates an article from *Journal of Business Venturing* or *Entrepreneurship Theory & Practice*.

available, lists a research question on that particular OM topic at a specific stage of startup. The key issue associated with each of these questions is to demonstrate how the context for startup operations can yield managerial insights that are different from conventional findings for established firms. We refer the reader to each cited article to look for further insights. We next offer five 3R-related principles about the assembly and deployment of resources, operating routines, and (brand or market) reputation emerging from our review; we deploy the term "principles" to suggest that these observations apply across multiple cells.

Principle 1: Startups operate on the basis of multiple objectives and constraints in non-traditional ways. While startups establish stable routines and processes to meet conventional demands of institutional environments for growth, they explore non-traditional ways of utilizing operational resources and routines to overcome constraints and improve performance. For instance, startups can overcome capacity constraints with pricing (Shen et al. 2014), financial and technical constraints with co-development partnerships (Savva and Scholtes 2014), and fairness perception by involving experienced entrepreneurs (van Burg and van Oorschot 2013). Startups also deploy multiple objectives and constraints. For instance, at the commitment and organizing stages, a 3R-constrained startup can improve its performance by mobilizing resources (Villanueva et al. 2012), invest in process improvement and production (Tanrisever et al. 2012), develop capabilities with resources such as inventory and employees (Tatikonda et al. 2013), complement shortages with supplier involvement (Song et al. 2011), and seek to enhance survival likelihood by altering capacity investment timing (Swinney et al. 2011).

Principle 2: Startups utilize alternative and relatively unique sources and processes for idea generation at the discovery stage when compared to their established counterparts. A startup may, for example, use at the discovery stage an incremental OI to fine tune a product offering or a radical idea to reposition the revenue model (i.e., the manner in which it generates its revenue), while also looking for idea generation and validation through crowdsourcing. In fact, Mollick (2014) as well as Wooten and Ulrich (2015) discuss Kickstarter.com and 99designs.com as examples of idea generation and validation through crowdsourcing platforms. OM scholars have examined multiple ways of idea generation externally, especially in terms of the likelihood of redundancy when idea generation is conducted in parallel (Kornish and Ulrich 2011), strategic ambiguity in problem specification (Erat and Krishnan 2012), and breadth of solution space searched by outside agents (Franke et al. 2014). Research has shown that the characteristics of the external agents and search design could guide startups as they emerge.

Principle 3: Startups are nimble in the sense that they are likely to exhibit higher levels of flexibility, responsiveness, agility, and innovativeness than their established counterparts. Startups tend to be more agile in their responses to both internally and externally (market-based) tasks than established firms (Swinney et al. 2011; Marion et al. 2012) because uncertain, complex, and dynamic environments require more flexible and agile organizational structures. In the context of sustainability, Girotra and Netessine (2013) introduce a framework to facilitate such agility and innovativeness for BMIs. Taking production, demand, and competition uncertainties into consideration, startups can guide their agility and responsiveness with probabilistic survival analysis based on cash flow consideration (e.g., Tanrisever et al. 2012). Startups use manufacturing flexibility to decouple activities required in task environments from those required in institutional environments (Patel 2011) and operational slack in processes to lower the likelihood of venture failure (Azadegan et al. 2013).

Principle 4: External partnerships and brand/reputation stock can enhance the performance and growth of startups. Startups can obtain resources from strategic alliances (Haeussler et al. 2011) and knowhow from diverse external connections (Larraneta et al. 2011).

Regarding the configuration of routines, startups can manage technology selection and investment decisions with a strategic competitor (Bhaskaran and Ramachandran 2011); integration with a complementary technology (Anderson and Parker 2013); establishment of platform technologies (Huang et al. 2013; Bhargava et al. 2013); exploration and exploitation activities with suppliers (Chiu 2014); and offshoring complex activities (Musteen and Ahsan 2013).

Principle 5: Startups adjust their objectives and constraints to the particular stage of the entrepreneurial value chain. Startups not only employ a variety of operational decisions depending on their goals and operating environment but also pivot or, in other words, change these decisions as they grow due to the dynamic nature of their environments and operational demands (Tatikonda et al. 2013). Startups can elect not to maximize profit in the interest of conserving cash to maximize their survival likelihood or valuation. Such objectives yield operating policies that are incompatible with profit maximization-based mental models. In dynamic environments, startups can evaluate the commercialization potential of their technology not only with financial parameters (Galbraith et al. 2012), but also operational design (Erzurumlu et al. 2014) and control (Goodale et al. 2011) for each stage. Therefore, business planning can improve startup strategies by evaluating alternative actions (Chwolka and Raith 2011).

For those themes and decisions that are uniquely operative in either product- or service-oriented startups, we also identify four key operational considerations:

- **A dynamic resource strategy, particularly for capacity, elasticity, and flexibility, can impact the product-oriented startup's survival and productivity** because startups build their resources over time under the uncertainties surrounding the product, market, and associated growth rate. Swinney et al. (2011) finds an earlier timing of capacity investment for startups than established firms due to the threat of bankruptcy. Tatikonda et al. (2013) show that different constructs drive survival at different stages: Inventory flexibility is critical at the start, then profitability drives growth and operational productivity drives stability. Lévesque et al. (2012) consider the elasticity of accumulated resources to assess conditions where these resources might serve as substitutes for rather than complements to the cost of goods sold during periods of growth.
- Startups that accomplish a fit between their distribution channel system and transaction cost-, product-, strategy-, and competition-related variables perform better (Brettel et al. 2011). Erzurumlu et al. (2014) show that, in highly uncertain environments, startup valuation is higher when the startup can show proof of deployment feasibility. Hence, **product-oriented startups can increase valuation by designing their operations for the supply network or target markets.** While risk-minimizing startups can manage survival with vertical integration (de Figueiredo and Silverman 2012) and subsidies (Wei et al. 2013), performance-focused startups can improve their prospects with operational flexibility and slack, such as keeping cash on hand (Patel 2011; Azadegan et al. 2013); distribution channel choice (Brettel et al. 2011); manufacturing capabilities (Terjesen et al. 2011); resource elasticity (Lévesque et al. 2012); and product diversification (Deligianni et al. 2014). Reputational risks can be overcome through downstream alliance partnerships with mainstream industry players (Hora and Dutta 2013).
- **Product- and service-oriented startups can better understand the market by engaging in experimentation while incorporating the end consumer into the problem definition and development process at the discovery stage.** For instance, ideas can be generated through innovation contests open to the general public that are hosted on digital platforms like 99designs.com (Wooten and Ulrich 2015). This requires setting up open-ended design problems by employing a contest approach in which a search over a

solution space is delegated to outside agents. This approach can increase the innovation space (Erat and Krishnan 2012; Kornish and Ulrich 2011) and improve the solutions for highly intangible service innovations.

- **Service-oriented startups can improve their prospects at market entry by focusing on platform-based strategies or by integrating their service with one or more complementary technologies with uncertain cost-reduction potentials**. Anderson and Parker (2013) find that startups generally achieve higher expected returns by channeling their integration investment to only one complementary technology. In this instance, the main technology featured wind power plants, and the complementary technology to enhance the performance could be either storage batteries or gas turbine-based capacity for supporting the plant when the performance of the main plant degraded owing to low wind speed. This argument for focusing on the plant relates to, but is somewhat different from, the logic supporting the need for focus in conventional OM literature (Skinner 1974). This focus—i.e., on a single, complementary, technology-based plant strategy—is less applicable with increased transferability from one technology to another or when favorable financial conditions allow dual sourcing of complementary technologies.

3 Emergent Opportunities

New and specialized technologies have emerged rapidly and massively across multiple industries, ranging from clean energy (e.g., battery for clean energy storage; Erzurumlu et al. 2014) to healthcare and biotechnology (e.g., ways to sense and track the condition of a dialysis patient; Trisolini et al. 2004), that are altering conventional operations subject to 3R shortages. Some of these technologies have been the driver of unicorn firms' successes. Novel digital technologies, allied business models, and their implementation practices are changing the operating paradigms in startup operations and in some instances creating new startup opportunities within established firms. Therefore, we can draw upon evidence on OIs and BMIs by focusing on emergent startup best practices built on new digital connectivity and robotics. We study how these practices might shape or add to the five principles associated with the 3Rs of startup operations. We then touch upon ideas in relevant disciplines (e.g., information economics research) related to this evidence that point to germane theoretical questions in a broad class of startup operations.

3.1 New Digital Technologies

In order to illustrate the change driven by the OIs at startups, we identify two types of digital technologies that are altering operational practices in startups in a broad set of industries: (i) connectivity-based analytics (CBA) and (ii) low-cost intelligent robotics (LCIR). The usage of the former is more prevalent in services/IT-based startup operations while the latter is more evident in manufacturing/supply chain startup operations.

3.1.1 Connectivity Based Analytics

We consider two distinctive and highly regarded startup operations in the transportation service sector involving CBA: Zipcar and Uber. (Netessine and Tang 2009 offer a compendium of mainstream operations models using consumer-driven demand and information-technology-enabled sales mechanisms.) During its startup phase around 2000–2001, the key technology challenge at Zipcar (Hart et al. 2003) involved enabling a customer to pick up and drop off a rental automobile at geographically distributed locations. This was accomplished through a combination of digital technologies (e.g., web-based booking software along with the deployment of the Zipcard—a digital authentication-based connectivity capability that allows a customer to access the rental without the presence of service personnel and real-time updates on operational status based on individual transactions tracked through connectivity technologies); analytics (e.g., rental car tracking and capacity management); and physical operations (e.g., driving cars from a location with excess capacity to another location that needed this capacity). The startup phase created a number of operational challenges that can be viewed in terms of some of the operational decisions in Table 13.2, such as location selection and cost tradeoff during the acquisition of parking locations within selected cities, and the acquisition of different types of rentals (sedans versus vans) depending on demand.

Zipcar also had to deal with these operational challenges while facing 3R shortages: (i) dealing with resource constraints in terms of capacity acquisition and cash-flow-driven survival considerations, (ii) prioritizing in terms of choices that would build its reputation, and (iii) figuring out a process (routines) to setup and leverage high-frequency information generated by its CBA technology. Consistent with the startup strategy of pivoting around 3R shortages, Zipcar refined its operating model. Zipcar was highly cognizant of a classic operations tradeoff: the need to keep up utilization without increasing service delivery costs. It also had to solve a new class of transshipment problems (i.e., optimal shift of cars across locations in real time) based on CBA. In the initial business plan, Zipcar did not focus on specific market segments. After the initial years, Zipcar had to adjust these analytics during the scale up of its operations as it pivoted into specific market segments (e.g., specific geographies, corporate versus weekend customers).

Another example is the San Francisco-based transportation startup Uber, which has focused CBA technology toward the delivery of an on-demand taxi service. Unlike Zipcar, Uber does not face a transshipment problem but deals with its own 3R-related problems. Uber must track and classify geographically dispersed capacity while accounting for alternative pricing models and yield management considerations in real time, present the choices to discerning customers, and build its brand (Cachon et al. 2015). The deployment of the CBA technology based on 3R shortages thus offered new OIs and subsequent value to its customers. Although capacity tracking and yield management are classic operations problems, OIs emerge from the company's handling of high frequency of data gathering, managing dynamic consumer and driver interactions, and marshalling and optimizing geographically distributed information.

Similar to Zipcar's adoption of a successful operational model, Uber's model is spreading rather rapidly. Uber faces CBA-fueled competition in many locations (e.g., Lyft in the U.S., Didi Kuaidi in China, Ola in India, and GrabTaxi in Malaysia). This geographic heterogeneity brings up location specific legal and financial considerations that translate into unique operating challenges for yield management problems (e.g., the rise of Lyft has resulted in real-time order cancellations for Uber; Bradley 2015). Moreover, Uber's operational model and their use of CBA have rapidly spilled into many other industries ranging from home services (e.g., veterinarians) to food (e.g., groceries) (Schlafman 2014), making the "uberfication" of an industry a phenomenon. Both Zipcar and Uber are examples of companies identifying conventional operational challenges for a 3R-constrained startup and handling them with OIs built on a novel technology like CBA. Whereas Zipcar improves resource utilization and productivity with CBA, Uber becomes a highly flexible and resource-light transportation company. These two examples pose interesting questions for researchers and entrepreneurs. Which aspects of Zipcar's model and "uberfication" alter the entrepreneurial value chain's four stages? Which types of unique operational challenges might these models bring? We explore these questions in Section 3.3.

3.1.2 Low-Cost Intelligent Robotics

Now we turn our attention to the rapidly developing and highly influential LCIR technology. Its emergence and impact on employment and productivity, particularly in manufacturing and distribution networks, has created a lively debate (Brynjolfson and McAfee 2012). We describe two startups—Rethink Robotics and Kiva Systems—that have developed LCIR effectively to allow for OIs for flexibility, precision, quality, agility, and responsiveness in conventional manufacturing and distribution operations.

Boston-based Rethink Robotics provides affordable industrial robots to clients in a diverse set of industry sectors such as healthcare, manufacturing, university, and corporate R&D. The robots are human like in size, configured with two arms, a display screen face powered by tactile force sensors, and vision capability, at a $25,000 price tag (WSJ 2015). Rethink has built a series of elastic actuators into the robots to measure and control forces on their joints with greater precision, allowing these robots to perform tasks like placing a part into a machine by "feeling" when the part is at the right place (Guizzo 2015). With the deployment of artificial intelligence technology to learn new tasks with no programming, Rethink's LCIR technology is being positioned for OIs to automate complex assembly (e.g., automotive manufacturing) and serve SMEs' manufacturing operations (e.g., manufacturing operations can move away from low labor-cost-dominated sourcing considerations; Foroohar 2013).

The LCIR technology offered by Kiva Systems is also a source of OIs. Kiva is changing the supply and distribution chain dynamics by introducing mobile bots—an LCIR capable of locomotion—to replace conveyers and human-operated assembly and packing operations (Mountz 2012). Kiva's LCIR technology has enabled it to dramatically cut down cycle time and quality problems for third-party logistics and distribution. The acquisition of Kiva by Amazon in 2012 (rebranded as Amazon Robotics in 2015) changed the delivery operations of Amazon and allow for novel changes in the operation of customer order and delivery. The success of LCIR technology in this marketplace has spurred a number of similar startups. For example, SWISSLOG has done so in hospital logistics with a product set including Automated Tablet Packaging Systems, Automated Pharmacy Storage and Inventory Management Systems, and TransCar Automated Guided Vehicles.

3.2 Business Model Innovations

Although new technologies indicate innovation, they require change in firms' operational models. The implementation of OIs has led to BMIs in firms such as Zipcar, Uber, Rethink Robotics, Amazon Robotics (the revised brand name for Kiva Systems), and their SME partners. Recall from the introduction that BMI refers to the way a firm generates revenues, limits costs, and provides its customers with a unique value proposition (Girotra and Netessine 2013).

Amazon Robotics faced the challenge of not only proving the feasibility of its LCIR technology, but also the riskiness with the delivery of a reliable solution from an end-to-end supply chain perspective and one where potentially hidden costs can be limited. To convince major e-commerce firms such as Amazon, Gap, and Walgreens that its LCIR technology fits with their operating model of system reliability and cost containment, Amazon Robotics implemented a BMI by internalizing the acquisition and integration of all its offerings' components (i.e., hardware, software, and operational consultation) while guaranteeing customers a full refund if the projected logistics results did not materialize. Thus, one of the major challenges with new technology adoption is the alignment and updating (or pivoting) of operating decisions with the business model, and OIs associated with the underlying technologies must be examined in this context. Business startups often involve operational practices and OIs that become central to their survival, growth, and profitability. Business models regarding the formulation, handling, and adaptation of startup operations are thus central concerns to entrepreneurs, potential investors providing resources, suppliers formalizing the operational routines, channel partners affected by reputations, and customers.

Responsive fulfilment of medical prescriptions and containment of their cost have received considerable attention in a number of countries (Crow and Ward 2015). Startups funded in this space (PillPack, TinyRX, and ZappRX) have been leveraging OIs using CBA and LCIR technologies. PillPack is a pharmacy and packing distribution service that deploys CBA technology to collect data on individual patient prescriptions, to confirm medication prescriptions in real time, and to gather updates on refills. It creates small packages that bundle all the medicines a particular patient needs to take at a given time of the day. Assembled in a small box using LCIR technologies (see www.pillpack.com/how for an illustration), these packages are then mailed to the customer. In PillPack's business model, this service is delivered to the patient at the same cost as that charged by a regular pharmacy. PillPack does not receive any additional payment from the health insurance provider. Thus, management of operational issues such as conformance quality (i.e., putting the right medication into each package), distribution speed, and cost containment are the focus of CBA and LCIR technologies. They are also central to this startup's business model in order to solve a new class of 3R problems that extend beyond inventory and distribution.

Supply chain (i.e., packaging and distribution) design and oversight are not the only high leverage points for startups as they setup their business models. Other levers are design and branding. Song et al. (2015) describe methods to inform the evolution and launch of product design choices, subject to risk and innovation balance, based on crowdfunding. These design considerations that can alter design routines and resource acquisition balance have yet to be addressed in the literature. Similarly, a sharing-economy startup like Airbnb, which is a force in the hospitality and tourism industry, has instituted a distance education-based training program to teach its host families principles of service quality (Pfeffer 2014) because customer reviews affect reputation.

3.3 Research Implications

From a theory building perspective, three key implications emerge from the evidence presented in Sections 3.1 and 3.2: (i) OIs are becoming core differentiators for these emergent business models, and some of these innovations coevolve with adaptations/pivots in the business model, and (ii) since these BMIs might aim to create Uber-like platforms, an opportunity exists to draw upon the emergent platform economics literature to enrich the 3R principles in the startup operations domain. A platform in this context refers to intermediary based-on-software technologies that control information exchanges between demand and supply.

3.3.1 Alignment between BMIs and OIs

BMIs, especially in startup settings, are dynamic entities as shown in our proposed causal loop diagram (Sterman 2000) in Figure 13.1, where the sign of an arrow represents the sign of the correlation between the two constructs that it connects. One way to understand the loop in Figure 13.1 is to begin with a stock of BMIs (e.g., use of pricing to manage demand yield at Uber) and then trace the loop in the clockwise direction. A constant set of moves and countermoves exists that creates a gap between the extant BMIs and the competition's business model (e.g., as seen in the case of Uber and Lyft), resulting in a gap that engenders unique operational problems (e.g., shorter expectation of wait times by the customers). Over time, intensification of these problems creates opportunities for unique OIs (e.g., capacity management by surge pricing versus marshalling of extra capacity at prime time). However, lifecycle risks reduce the efficacy of such OIs. For instance, when Uber decided to grow its operations by adding new geographies, there was a sizable rise in the form of social media "horror stories" about surge pricing in many cities (Allan 2015).

Such risks have resulted in reconsideration of the approaches towards customer and driver satisfaction (i.e., created pivots) on the part of both Uber and Lyft. For instance, surge pricing might allow a driver to enjoy a higher rate, but Uber has instituted BMIs that forbid drivers control over when it is a surge and when it is not. These BMIs have accompanied OIs such as the design of Lyft interface that allows customers to tip the drivers, presumably based on service quality. When taken collectively, the linkages described here form a reinforcing loop that captures the co-evolution between BMIs and OIs. Many OIs leverage new information technologies, connectivity-based data and analytics, thus offering opportunities to develop new types of decision support models (e.g., transshipment and yield management models).

This alignment between BMIs and OIs has research implications. For instance, Amazon Robotics' decision to internalize all aspects of LCIR technology, based on the need to guarantee end-to-end service, requires commitment to multiple types of resources. Since Amazon Robotics did this, what are the implications for the organize stage of the entrepreneurial value chain

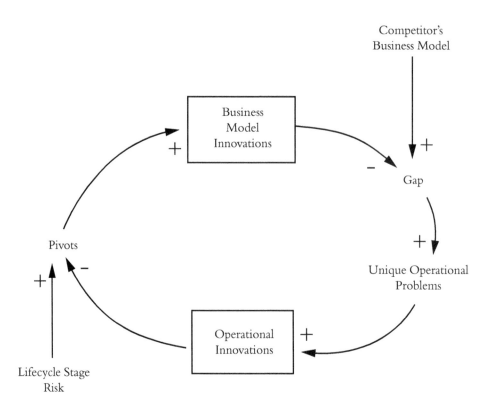

Figure 13.1 Dynamic View of the Alignment between Business Model Innovations (BMIs) and Operational Innovations (OIs)

(Joglekar and Lévesque 2013) in terms of hiring service professionals and setting up a distribution network? Amazon Robotics' business model was retail industry centric, whereas some of its competitors (e.g., SWISSLOG) focused on the healthcare industry. Is the decision to vertically integrate instead of sourcing components the optimal choice in such alternative business models? Will regulatory bodies approve of such information integration and supply chain choices instead of pushing for open standards promoting entrepreneurial activity?

3.3.2 Platform Economics

Given the selective nature of the technological opportunities described in Section 3.1 and 3.2, the theory implications we offer are a subset of a large class of research opportunities. In the case of CBA technology, we focus on the issue of platform economics (Eisenmann et al. 2011). In many BMIs associated with "uberfication," startups are interested in becoming a platform of choice for suppliers and consumers. Salminen (2015) lists a number of dilemmas faced by platform startups that are summarized in Table 13.3. This list is evolving over time. For instance, Airbnb has attempted to manage the role of reviews in shaping its reputation for quality by deploying 100 employees devoted exclusively to safety such that "hosts verify their IDs by connecting to their social networks and scanning their official ID or confirming personal details" (Hill 2015). Airbnb's quality management practices are now subject to public scrutiny and the efficacy of such practices offers a research opportunity that is yet to be analyzed in the POM literature.

This list is not exhaustive and several of the underlying tradeoffs have been studied in entrepreneurship literature (e.g., see Table 13.3 for the Peter Pan dilemma, where the decisions associated with this dilemma represent a classic dilution problem; Bhide 2000). However, these dilemmas are yet to be studied in the context of two-sided network dynamics. Moreover, from the perspective of startup operations, these dilemmas must be unpacked into a number of detailed decisions that have not been fully examined. If we take the Pioneer's dilemma, entry timing

Table 13.3 Dilemmas Faced by Platform Startups

Pioneer's dilemma	If the startup launches too early, it will pay the pioneer's cost and is likely to fail due to insufficient resources; if it launches too late, it is unable to capture users from incumbents.
Cold start dilemma	Without content, users are unwilling to join and generate content.
Lonely user dilemma	Without other users available at a given time, users are unable to use the platform.
Monetization dilemma	If access and usage of a platform is provided for a fee, users are unwilling to join; if access and usage is free, the platform is economically non-viable.
Remora's curse	If users or content is sourced from a host platform, the cold start problem can be solved; however, at the loss of power relating to customer relationships, monetization, and so on.
Pivot dilemma	If the startup accommodates its user's wishes in product development, it loses focus; if it does not, it loses the user.
Peter Pan dilemma	If the startup accepts external funding, it loses decisive authority and becomes vulnerable to hasty decisions; if it does not, it loses against competitors with funding.
Juggernaut dilemma	Due to lack of legitimacy, the startup is unable to convert enterprise clients which would grant it legitimacy.

Source: Salminen 2015

decisions have been studied in the startup literature (Armstrong and Lévesque 2002), but the consideration of network effects either on the supply side (Anderson and Parker 2013) or demand side (Bhargava et al. 2013) has only been studied at the growth stage. What are the implications of network effects using CBA technologies in the discovery, commit, and organize stages of the entrepreneurial value chain?

For instance, CBA technologies provide real-time updates on either supplier or customer choices. When should a fledgling startup commit to resources to develop analytics-driven features on the supply side and demand side? When do the resulting operational choices (e.g., either speedier access to SKU data or more types of SKUs offered in a retail operation) align with different stages of the startup's business model? An online retail customer at the commit stage may be happier with more detailed analytics on fashion or color trends, but will the suppliers also find the growth of such expertise among end customers to be useful? If they do, what are the implications for the organize stage of platform evolution in terms of showcasing the outcomes of the analytics-based findings?

3.4 *Managerial Implications*

We have identified five 3R-related principles in Section 2.2 in terms of what we know about startups operations. For ease of reference, these are summarized in Table 13.4. We now draw upon the alignment framework shown in Figure 13.1 to illustrate the implementation implications of these 3R principles.

Principles 1 and 2 call for identification of alternative objectives and resource deployment options, while Principle 3 calls for flexible routines. As an example, imagine a food supply chain and delivery startup with a BMI revolving around "uberfication." We assume that this startup's BMI is predicated upon both keeping low costs and promoting direct interaction between customers and supply chain partners that may use Uber-like mobile interfaces to order food. The need for exploring alternative objective functions for such a startup would imply either conservation of cash to increase its likelihood of survival, or investment in growth (by acquiring customers rapidly), rather than maximizing profit. Customer acquisition may require expanding resources for experimenting with specific product features, setting-up flexible operational routines, making commitment to low overhead processes, and outsourcing of infrastructure (e.g., plant and properties or logistic capabilities). The key OI at such a discovery stage might focus on experiments matching demand and supply through a low-cost food delivery (e.g., kiosks) mechanism. Customer acquisition and external partnerships may grow the brand's reputation, consistent with Principle 4. Principle 5 suggests that the startup may need to pivot and alter its objective function (e.g., move from cash conservation to profit maximization) after the initial discovery stage, while getting into the subsequent commit stage shown in Table 13.2. A key question around the pivot involves the types of OIs—e.g., setting up a wider distribution network and yield management routines that will enable this realignment of objectives.

This example offers a high-level description of pivots through the co-evolution of BMI and OIs based on the 3R principles, while going from the discover stage to the commit stage. Figure 13.1 also shows that BMI might sometimes be disrupted by competitive factors at any one stage—and such disruptions may require additional OIs (e.g., a reduction in unit cost through process improvement). Appropriate choices must also develop beyond the commit stage and into the organize and grow stages. Entrepreneurial managers might then have to focus on, for instance, detailed data (e.g., through CBA) and manage some of the operational decisions (e.g., location selection or network design) and allied tradeoffs shown in Table 13.2 until the next pivot in the entrepreneurial value chain comes about. Table 13.2's studies indicate that entrepreneurial

Table 13.4 3R Principles and Allied Operational Considerations

Principle 1	Startups operate on the basis of multiple objectives and constraints in non-traditional ways.
Principle 2	Startups utilize alternative and relatively unique sources and processes for idea generation at the discovery stage when compared to their established counterparts.
Principle 3	Startups are nimble in the sense that they are likely to exhibit higher levels of flexibility, responsiveness, agility, and innovativeness than their established counterparts.
Principle 4	External partnerships and brand/reputation stock can enhance the performance and growth of startups.
Principle 5	Startups adjust their objectives and constraints to the particular stage of the entrepreneurial value chain.
Operational considerations	• A dynamic resource strategy, particularly for capacity, elasticity, and flexibility, can impact the product-oriented startup's survival and productivity. • Product-oriented startups can increase valuation by designing their operations for the supply network or target markets. • Product- and service-oriented startups can better understand the market by engaging in experimentation while incorporating the end consumer into the problem definition and development process at the discovery stage. • Service-oriented startups can improve their prospects at market entry by focusing on platform-based strategies or by integrating their service with one or more complementary technologies with uncertain cost-reduction potentials.

managers should not manage these transitions between lifecycle stages using a conventional OM decision model (e.g., setting up the network to minimize cost, regardless of the startup's lifecycle stage) and waste the opportunity to leverage the alignment between BMI and OIs.

4 Conclusion

Economic and social opportunities associated with business startups' operations are large. These opportunities offer potentially high risks but also high rewards. Startup operations ought to be thought of differently in terms of available resources, organizational routines, and the need to have established reputations—the 3Rs. Moreover, an analysis of 3R ideas across the lifecycle of startup stages (a.k.a. entrepreneurial value chain of discover, commit, organize, and grow) yields different types of operating principles than pursued during steady state operations at established firms. Among others, survival constraints associated with cash flow considerations yield different capacity acquisition and process improvement strategies. The need for finding business models that are enabled and revised through operations innovations is growing. Novel digital technologies, particularly those involving connectivity-based analytics and deployment of low-cost intelligent robotics, provide fertile grounds for developing such operational-innovation-enabled startups.

References and Bibliography

Acs, Z.J., S. Desai and J. Hessels (2008) "Entrepreneurship, Economic Development and Institutions," *Small Business Economics*, **31**(3): 219–234.

Aggarwal, V. and D.H. Hsu (2014) "Entrepreneurial Exits and Innovation," *Management Science*, **60**(4): 867–887.

Allan, P. (2015) "Ride Sharing Showdown: Uber vs. Lyft," http://lifehacker.com/ride-sharing-showdown-uber-vs-lyft-1735886651, downloaded December 30, 2015.

Anderson, E.G. and G.G. Parker (2013) "Integration and Cospecialization of Emerging Complementary Technologies by Startups," *Production and Operations Management*, **22**(6): 1356–1373.

Antoncic, B. and R.D. Hisrich (2001) "Intrapreneurship: Construct Refinement and Cross-Cultural Validation," *Journal of Business Venturing*, **16**(5): 495–527.

Armstrong, M.J. and M. Lévesque (2002) "Timing and Quality Decisions for Entrepreneurial Product Development," *European Journal of Operational Research*, **141**(1): 88–106.

Atwater, J.B. and S.S. Chakravorty (2002) "A Study of the Utilization of Capacity Constrained Resources in Drum-Buffer-Rope Systems," *Production and Operations Management*, **11**(2): 259–273.

Azadegan, A., P.C. Patel and V. Parida (2013) "Operational Slack and Venture Survival," *Production and Operations Management*, **22**(1): 1–18.

Berger, A.N. and G.F. Udell (2003) "Small Business and Debt Finance," in: Acs, Z.J. and Audretsch, D.B. (Eds), *Handbook of Entrepreneurship Research: An Interdisciplinary Survey and Introduction*, 299–328. Kluwer Academic Publishers, Boston, MA.

Bhargava, H.K., B.C. Kim and D. Sun (2013) "Commercialization of Platform Technologies: Launch Timing and Versioning Strategy," *Production and Operations Management*, **22**(6): 1374–1388.

Bhaskaran, S.R. and K. Ramachandran (2011) "Managing Technology Selection and Development Risk in Competitive Environments," *Production and Operations Management*, **20**(4): 541–555.

Bhide, A. (2000) *The Origin and Evolution of New Businesses*. Oxford University Press, Oxford; New York.

Bradley, R. (2015) "Lyft's Search for a New Mode of Transport," *Technology Review*, www.technologyreview.com/s/541791/lyfts-search-for-a-new-mode-of-transport/, downloaded December 1, 2015.

Brettel, M., A. Engelen, T. Muller and O. Schilke (2011) "Distribution Channel Choice of New Entrepreneurial Ventures," *Entrepreneurship Theory and Practice*, **35**(4): 683–708.

Brynjolfson, E. and A. McAfee (2012) *Race against the Machine: How the Digital Revolution Is Accelerating Innovation, Driving Productivity, and Irreversibly Transforming Employment and the Economy*. Digital Frontier Press, Boston, MA.

Cachon, G., K. Daniels and R. Lobel (2015) "The Role of Surge Pricing on a Service Platform with Self-Scheduling Capacity," Social Science Research Network (SSRN), http://papers.ssrn.com/sol3/papers.cfm?abstract_id=2698192.

CB Insights, "50 future unicorns predicted by CB Insights," *Company Mosaic*, www.cbinsights.com/research-future-unicorn-companies, downloaded November 30, 2015.

Chiu, Y. (2014) "Balancing Exploration and Exploitation in Supply Chain Portfolios," *IEEE Transactions on Engineering Management*, **61**(1): 18–27.

Chwolka, A. and M.G. Raith (2012) "The value of business planning before start-up—A decision-theoretical perspective," *Journal of Business Venturing*, **27**: 385–399.

Crow, D. and A. Ward (February 10, 2015) "Healthcare: The Race to Cure Rising Drug Costs," *Financial Times*.

Dahl, M.S. and O. Sorenson (2012) "Home Sweet Home: Entrepreneurs' Location Choices and the Performance of Their Ventures," *Management Science*, **58**(6): 1059–1071.

Debo, L., B. Toktay and L.N. Van Wassenhove (2006) "Joint Life-Cycle Dynamics of New and Remanufactured Products," *Production and Operations Management*, **15**: 498–513.

de Figueiredo, J.M. and B.S. Silverman (2012) "Firm Survival and Industry Evolution in Vertically Related Populations," *Management Science*, **58**(9): 1632–1650.

Deligianni, I., I. Voudouris and S. Lioukas (2014) "The Relationship between Innovation and Diversification in the Case of New Ventures: Unidirectional or Bidirectional?" *IEEE Transactions on Engineering Management*, **61**(3): 462–475.

Eisenmann, T., G. Parker and M. van Alstyne (2011) "Platform Envelopment," *Strategic Management Journal*, **32**(12): 1270–1285.

Erat, S. and V. Krishnan (2012) "Managing Delegated Search over Design Spaces," *Management Science*, **58**(3): 606–623.

Erzurumlu, S.S., J. Davies and N. Joglekar (2014) "Managing Highly Innovative Projects: The Influence of Design Characteristics on Project Valuation," *IEEE Transactions on Engineering Management*, **61**(2): 349–361.

Fairchild, R. (2011) "An Entrepreneur's Choice of Venture Capitalist or Angel-Financing: A Behavioral Game-Theoretic Approach," *Journal of Business Venturing*, **26**: 359–374.

Foroohar, R. (2013) "How 'Made in the USA' Is Making a Comeback," http://business.time.com/2013/04/11/how-made-in-the-usa-is-making-a-comeback, downloaded December 1, 2015.

Franke, N., M.K. Poetz and M. Schreier (2014) "Integrating Problem Solvers from Analogous Markets in New Product Ideation," *Management Science*, **60**(4): 1063–1081.

Gaimon, C. and R.H. Burgess (2003) "Analysis of Lead Time and Learning for Capacity Expansions," *Production and Operations Management*, **12**(1): 128–140.

Galbraith, C.S., A.F. DeNoble and S.B. Ehrlich (2012) "Predicting the Commercialization Progress of Early-Stage Technologies: An Ex-Ante Analysis," *IEEE Transactions on Engineering Management*, **59**(2): 213–225.

GEM (2014) "Global Entrepreneurship Monitor Report," http://gemconsortium.org/docs, downloaded January 15, 2016.

Giloni, A., S. Seshadri and P.V. Kamesam (2003) "Service System Design for the Property and Casualty Insurance Industry," *Production and Operations Management*, **12**(1): 62–78.

Girotra, K. and S. Netessine (2013) "Business Model Innovation for Sustainability," *Manufacturing & Service Operations Management*, **15**(4): 537–544.

Girotra, K., C. Terwiesch and K.T. Ulrich (2010) "Idea Generation and the Quality of the Best Idea," *Management Science*, **56**(4): 591–605.

Goodale, J.C., D.F. Kuratko, J.S. Hornsby and J.G. Covin (2011) "Operations Management and Corporate Entrepreneurship: The Moderating Effect of Operations Control on the Antecedents of Corporate Entrepreneurial Activity in Relation to Innovation Performance," *Journal of Operations Management*, **29**(1–2): 116–127.

Guizzo, E. (2015) "Rethink Robotics' Sawyer Goes on Sale, Rodney Brooks Says 'There May Be More Robots,'" http://spectrum.ieee.org/automaton/robotics/industrial-robots/rethink-robotics-sawyer-robots, downloaded December 1, 2015.

Habib, M.A., U. Hege and P. Mella-Barral (2013) "Entrepreneurial Spawning and Firm Characteristics," *Management Science*, **59**(12): 2790–2804.

Haeussler, C., H. Patzelt and S.A. Zahra (2011) "Strategic Alliances and Product Development in High Technology New Firms: The Moderating Effect of Technological Capabilities," *Journal of Business Venturing*, **27**(2): 217–233.

Hart, M., M. Roberts and J. Stevens (2003). *Zipcar: Redefining the Business Model*. Case #803096-PDF-ENG. Harvard Business School Press, Boston, MA.

Hill, S. (2015) "The Two Faces of Airbnb," www.businessinsider.com/the-two-faces-of-airbnb-2015-10, downloaded February 29, 2016.

Hora, M. and D.K. Dutta (2013) "Entrepreneurial Firms and Downstream Alliance Partnerships: Impact of Portfolio Depth and Scope on Technology Innovation and Commercialization Success," *Production and Operations Management*, **22**(6): 1389–1400.

Huang, P., M. Ceccagnoli, C. Forman and D.J. Wu (2013) "Appropriability Mechanisms and the Platform Partnership Decision: Evidence from Enterprise Software," *Management Science*, **59**(1): 102–121.

Joglekar, N. and M. Lévesque (2013) "The Role of Operations Management across the Entrepreneurial Value Chain," *Production and Operations Management*, **22**(6): 1321–1335.

Kauffman Foundation (2015) "The Kauffman Index Startup Activity National Trends 2015," www.kauffman.org/~/media/kauffman_org/research%20reports%20and%20covers/2015/05/kauffman_index_startup_activity_national_trends_2015.pdf, downloaded November 30.

Kenney, M., N.M. Khanfar and B.G. Mujtaba (2010) "The Value of Creating, Maintaining and Sustaining an Intrapreneurial Culture: An Analysis of 3M's Strategic Positioning," *International Journal of Arts and Sciences*, **3**(13): 332–346.

Kickul, J.R., M.D. Griffiths, J. Jayaram and S.M. Wagner (2011) "Operations Management, Entrepreneurship, and Value Creation: Emerging Opportunities in a Cross-Disciplinary Context," *Journal of Operations Management*, **29**: 78–85.

Kornish, L. and K. Ulrich (2011) "Opportunity Spaces in Innovation: Empirical Analysis of Large Samples of Ideas," *Management Science*, **57**(1): 107–128.

Kouvelis, P., M.J. Rosenblatt and C.L. Munson (2004) "A Mathematical Programming Model for Global Plant Location Problems: Analysis and Insights," *IIE Transactions*, **36**: 127–144.

Larraneta, B., S.A. Zahra and J.L.G. Gonzalez (2011) "Enriching Strategic Variety in New Ventures through External Knowledge," *Journal of Business Venturing*, **27**(4): 401–413.

Lévesque, M., N. Joglekar and J. Davies (2012) "A Comparison of Revenue Growth at Recent-IPO and Established Firms: Influence of SG&A, R&D and COGS," *Journal of Business Venturing*, **27**(1): 47–61.

Lévesque, M. and C. Schade (2005) "Intuitive Optimizing: Experimental Findings on Time Allocation Decisions with Newly Formed Ventures," *Journal of Business Venturing*, **20**(3): 313–342.

Li, L. (2008) "A Review of Entrepreneurship Research Published in the Hospitality and Tourism Management Journals," *Tourism Management*, **29**(5): 1013–1022.

Li, S., R. Loulou and A. Rahman (2003) "Technological Progress and Technology Acquisition: Strategic Decision under Uncertainty," *Production and Operations Management,* **12**(1): 102–119.

Lim, G.H., K.S. Lee and S.J. Tan (2001) "Gray Marketing as an Alternative Market Penetration Strategy for Entrepreneurs: Conceptual Model and Case Evidence," *Journal of Business Venturing,* **16**: 405–427.

Marion, T., D. Dunlap and J. Friar (2012) "Instilling the Entrepreneurial Spirit in Your R&D Team: What Large Firms Can Learn from Successful Start-ups," *IEEE Transactions on Engineering Management,* **59**(2): 323–337.

Marx, M., J.S. Gans and D.H. Hsu (2014) "Dynamic Commercialization Strategies for Disruptive Technologies: Evidence from the Speech Recognition Industry," *Management Science,* **60**(12): 3103–3123.

Mollick, E. (2014) "The Dynamics of Crowdfunding: An Exploratory Study," *Journal of Business Venturing,* **29**(1): 1–16.

Mountz, M. (December, 2012). "Kiva the Disruptor," *Harvard Business Review,* https://hbr.org/2012/12/kiva-the-disrupter.

Musteen, M. and M. Ahsan (2013) "Beyond Cost: The Role of Intellectual Capital in Offshoring and Innovation in Young Firms," *Entrepreneurship Theory and Practice,* **37**(2): 421–434.

Netessine, S. and C. Tang (2009) *Consumer-Driven Demand and Operations Management Models: A Systematic Study of Information-Technology-Enabled Sales Mechanisms.* Springer Science & Business Media, New York.

Noori, H. and C. Chen (2003) "Applying Scenario-Driven Strategy to Integrate Environmental Management and Product Design," *Production and Operations Management,* **12**(3): 353–368.

Oviatt, B.M. and P.P. McDougall (2005) "Defining International Entrepreneurship and Modeling the Speed of Internationalization," *Entrepreneurship Theory and Practice,* **29**(5): 537–554.

Papanikolaou, D. (2015) "Cloudcommuting: Games, Interaction, and Learning," http://dimitris-papanikolaou.com/files/dpapanikolaou_idc13.pdf, downloaded December 1, 2015.

Parker, S.C. (2006) "Learning about the Unknown: How Fast Do Entrepreneurs Adjust Their Beliefs?" *Journal of Business Venturing,* **21**: 1–26.

Patel, P.C. (2011) "Role of Manufacturing Flexibility in Managing Duality of Formalization and Environmental Uncertainty in Emerging Firms," *Journal of Operations Management,* **29**(1–2): 143–162.

Pfeffer, J. (2014, November) "How to Make a Fortune without 'Doing' Anything: The Uber, Airbnb Story," *Fortune,* http://fortune.com/2014/11/24/uber-airbnb-sharing-economy-fallacy, downloaded November 30, 2015.

Renaissance Capital, www.renaissancecapital.com/ipohome/press/ipoavgage.aspx, downloaded November 30, 2015.

Salminen, J. (2015) "Dilemmas of Platform Startup. Proceedings of 2015 Platform Symposium," Boston University, Questrom School of Business, http://questromworld.bu.edu/platformstrategy/files/2015/06/platform2015_submission_10–1.pdf, downloaded December 1, 2015.

Savva, N. and S. Scholtes (2014) "Opt-Out Options in New Product Co-development Partnerships," *Production and Operations Management,* **23**(8): 1370–1386.

Schlafman, S. (2014) "Uberification of the US Service Economy," http://schlaf.me/post/81679927670, downloaded November 15, 2015.

Schmidt, G.M. and C.T. Druehl (2005) "Changes in Product Attributes and Costs as Drivers of New Product Diffusion and Substitution," *Production and Operations Management,* **14**(3): 272–285.

Sharma, P. (2004) "An Overview of the Field of Family Business Studies: Current Status and Directions for the Future," *Family Business Review,* **17**(1): 1–36.

Shen, W., I. Duenyas and R. Kapuściński (2014) "Optimal Pricing, Production, and Inventory for New Product Diffusion under Supply Constraints," *Manufacturing & Service Operations Management,* **16**(1): 28–45.

Shepherd, D.A., T.A. Williams and H. Patzelt (2015) "Thinking about Entrepreneurial Decision Making: Review and Research Agenda," *Journal of Management,* **41**(1): 11–46.

Skinner, W. (1974). "The Focused Factory," *Harvard Business Review,* **52**(3): 113–121.

Song, C., J. Luo, K. Otto-Hoelttae, W. Seering and K. Otto (2015) "Risk and Innovation Balance in Crowdfunding New Products. In: *DS 80–8 Proceedings of the 20th International Conference on Engineering Design* (ICED 15), Milan, Italy, July 27–30, 2015.

Song, L.Z., M. Song and A. Di Benedetto (2011) "Resources, Supplier Investment, Product Launch Advantages, and First Product Performance," *Journal of Operations Management,* **29**(1–2): 86–104.

Sterman, J. (2000) *Business Dynamics: Systems Thinking and Modeling for a Complex World.* Boston, MA: Irwin/McGraw-Hill.

Surowiecki, J. (2014) "In Praise of Efficient Price Gouging," *Technology Review*, August 19, www.technologyreview.com/s/529961/in-praise-of-efficient-price-gouging/.

Swinney, R., G. Cachon and S. Netessine (2011) "Capacity Investment Timing by Start-Ups and Established Firms in New Markets," *Management Science*, **57**(4): 763–777.

Tanrisever, F., S. Erzurumlu and N. Joglekar (2012) "Production, Process Investment and the Survival of Debt Financed Startup Firms," *Production and Operations Management*, **21**(4): 637–652.

Tatikonda, M.V., S. Terjesen, P.C. Patel and V. Parida (2013) "The Role of Operational Capabilities in Enhancing New Venture Survival: A Longitudinal Study," *Production and Operations Management*, **22**(6): 1401–1415.

Terjesen, S., P.C. Patel and J.G. Covin (2011) "Alliance Diversity, Environmental Context and the Value of Manufacturing Capabilities among New High Technology Ventures," *Journal of Operations Management*, **29**(1–2): 105–115.

Thomke, S. and D.E. Bell (2001) "Sequential Testing in Product Development," *Management Science*, **47**(2): 308–323.

Trisolini, M., A. Roussel, E. Zerhusen, D. Schatell, S. Harris, K. Bandel and K. Klicko (2004). "Activating Chronic Kidney Disease Patients and Family Members through the Internet to Promote Integration of Care," *International Journal of Integrated Care*, **4**: 1–13.

USSBA, www.sba.gov/content/small-business-trends-impact, downloaded December 1, 2015.

van Burg, E. and K.E. van Oorschot (2013) "Cooperating to Commercialize Technology: A Dynamic Model of Fairness Perceptions, Experience, and Cooperation," *Production and Operations Management*, **22**(6): 1336–1355.

Villanueva, J., A.H. Van de Vende and H.J. Sapienza (2012) "Resource Mobilization in Entrepreneurial Firms," *Journal of Business Venturing*, **27**(1): 19–30.

Wei, M.M., T. Yao, B. Jiang and S.T. Young (2013) "Profit Seeking vs. Survival Seeking: An Analytical Study of Supplier's Behavior and Buyer's Subsidy Strategy," *Production and Operations Management*, **22**(2): 269–282.

Wooten, J. and K. Ulrich (2015) "Idea Generation and the Role of Feedback: Evidence from Field Experiments with Innovation Tournaments," SSRN Working Paper #1838733, Social Science Research Network (SSRN) database, http://ssrn.com.

WSJ, "Rethink Robotics Raises $26.6M to Go Global with Its Robots," http://blogs.wsj.com/venturecapital/2015/01/08/rethink-robotics-raises-26-6m-to-go-global-with-its-robots/, downloaded December 1, 2015.

Yim, H.R. (2008) "Quality Shock vs. Market Shock: Lessons from Recently Established Rapidly Growing U.S. Startups," *Journal of Business Venturing*, **23**(1): 141–164.

Zahra, S. A., S.G. Abdelgawad and E. W. Tsang (2011) "Emerging Multinationals Venturing into Developed Economies: Implications for Learning, Unlearning, and Entrepreneurial Capability," *Journal of Management Inquiry*, **20**(3): 323–330.

14
SUSTAINABLE OPERATIONS

Tharanga K. Rajapakshe, Asoo J. Vakharia, Lan Wang, and Arda Yenipazarli

1 Introduction

1.1 Why Focus on Sustainability?

The emerging focus on sustainability can be traced back to several observations regarding the consumption and availability of natural resources. First, from an absolute perspective, the total consumption of these resources has grown substantially. This can be attributed to significant increases in world population (due to reduced mortality rates that stem from medical advances). Second, the increase in per capita incomes of individual consumers (driven in part by the fact that two of the largest populated economies, China and India, have started to develop industrial bases) has also led to an increase in the consumption rate of these resources. Third, there is a finite supply of several natural resources, and this has led to dire predictions on when the current consumption will exhaust the availability of these resources. Finally, even for natural resources that can be replenished, there are two issues of concern: either the replenishment lead times are very long, or the increase in availability can only be achieved through the adoption of approaches (e.g., fracking) that are not environmentally sustainable.

Given these observations, becoming more *sustainable* seems justified since a commonly accepted definition of the term integrates three critical aspects: (a) the ability to be used without being completely used up or destroyed (e.g., a fusion reaction); (b) the use of methods that do not completely use up or destroy natural resources (e.g., recycling of water); and (c) the ability to last or continue for a long time (e.g., use of solar energy).

A broad perspective of sustainability covers the four interconnected domains of ecology, economics, politics, and culture. Since the early 2000s, firms have started to pay attention to the triple bottom line: profit, people, and the planet (Elkington 1997). These three forces are articulated by Tang and Zhou (2012). As the demand for natural resources continues to rise, the economic activities have generated and will continue generating vast wastes and pollutants to the environment (e.g., electronic waste or e-waste and greenhouse gas emissions). Consumer-advocacy groups have raised concerns about various unethical practices as companies begin outsourcing or offshoring their manufacturing operations to developing countries. With growth slowing in developed countries, fast-moving consumer goods providers are seeking to expand in emerging economies. The reader is referred to Tang and Zhou (2012) for a comprehensive review on broad sustainability using triple bottom line.

1.2 Operations/Supply Chain Management and Sustainability

From an operations/supply chain (O/SC) perspective, the seminal works of Corbett and Kleindorfer (2001) and Kleindorfer et al. (2005) note that there are significant opportunities for O/SC researchers and practitioners in the domain of sustainability. The specific issues that have been addressed can be categorized as those relating to product/process development and design, (forward and reverse) supply chain management, and environmental legislation.

1.2.1 Product/Process Design and Sustainability

"Green" is often used under the umbrella of sustainability. Although *green* was historically associated with regeneration, fertility, and rebirth for its connections to nature, it is also used as a symbol of environmental protection and social justice by political groups. From an O/SC perspective, it is associated with "green" product development and introduction. The general evidence associated with product/process development is confounded by market reactions; this is well illustrated in a 2010 article in the *New York Times* (September 18, 2010) titled "Can Green Products Deliver?" In this case, consumers were not satisfied with the visual "performance" (i.e., after product use, dishes did not appear to be sparkling!) of a new dish washing product that was better for the environment. There is also anecdotal evidence of successes associated with "green" products such as (a) GE experiencing a 21% growth in its *ecomagination* product line to $17 billion in 2008 sales and (b) P&G realizing $13 billion in cumulative sales from its sustainable innovations product group.

1.2.2 Sustainability in Supply Chains

The notion of sustainability in supply chains is motivated by industry observations that see a growing public concern regarding environmental issues. This has led to the introduction of environmental mandates (e.g., carbon generation caps), increases in the availability of greener products and services, contractual agreements which comprise some elements of green, and more rigorous specifications for green components in conventional products (through, for example, eco-labeling). Corporate social responsibility (CSR) programs reflect firm-level responses to these revised sustainability standards. The essential premise of these programs is that long-term success is a function of the joint consideration of profitability, social, and environmental issues. Firm-level success in sustainability-based contractual arrangements between supply chain partners is documented in the case of Wal-Mart, a company that estimates annual savings of approximately $200 million in combined freight and diesel fuel consumption costs simply by reducing packaging content in one toy product line.

Reverse supply chains provide two sustainability benefits: (a) they can extend the life of existing products, which leads to a smaller consumption of current resources; and (b) they can simultaneously minimize the generation of waste for disposal through recycling efforts. O/SC research and practice in this critical domain primarily focus on product and process design to facilitate recycling efforts as well as examining the impact of extending product life through remanufacturing efforts.

1.2.3 Environmental Legislations

Environmental legislations with a focus on sustainability is an emerging area which is receiving greater attention by O/SC practitioners and researchers. The United States has a long history of monitoring and regulating clean air/water, pesticide use, and emissions. European countries (and especially Germany), on the other hand, also have stringent standards imposed on waste management. The political difficulties associated with mandating similar electronic waste-focused *federal* legislation in the United States has led individual states to take the lead in developing and implementing alternative legislation. Examining the efficacy of alternative legislative practices (typically directed at e-waste) is obviously of interest for O/SC researchers and practitioners.

1.3 Organization of This Chapter

The remainder of this chapter is organized as follows. Using the above categorization, Sections 2, 3, and 4 discuss current research and practice in the areas of product/process development and design, (forward and reverse) supply chains, and environmental legislation, respectively. Finally, Section 5 concludes this chapter with directions for future research.

2 Product Design and Process Development

In this section, we describe prior research studies that have addressed key sustainability issues relating to product design and process development.

2.1 Green Product Design and Environmental Performance

Green products that are capable of performing the same function as traditional ones only with significantly less environmental impact could be more expensive than their traditional counterparts. This extra expense is due to lack of scale economies and/or due to the use of more expensive materials or new technologies. If this is the case, success in green product development and introduction would be a function of market conditions (e.g., customer learning and behavior change), technology and operational capabilities (e.g., biotechnology for generic products and better technology for EVs), and the regulatory environments. Given the high degree of Market-Technology-Regulatory (MTR) uncertainties for green product development, Noori and Chen (2003) propose a scenario-driven methodology for designing and developing new green products that jointly analyzes the market, technology, and regulatory conditions in dynamic environments. The proposed methodology employs scenario analysis and back casting to analyze the complex and uncertain future states of new product development and uses continuous monitoring to deal with the changing environment. On the basis of the development process of biotechnology products in a major Canadian spice and seasoning company, a case study is presented to demonstrate how to apply the methodology for developing genetically engineered products.

In order to find the most efficient way to combine product specifications and attributes to achieve better environmental performances through product design, Chen et al. (2012) propose a two-stage network Data Envelopment Analysis (DEA) approach for evaluating the green product design that includes two internal modules: an industrial design module where engineering specifications (inputs) can be combined into product attributes (outputs); and a biodesign module where the links between key product attributes and environmental performances/consequences are examined. The data of product specifications, attributes, and indices of vehicle emissions performances in the vehicle emissions testing database published by the United States' Environmental Protection Agency (EPA) are used to demonstrate how the approach can be applied to evaluate the sustainable design performances in both public and private sectors. The test results show that designing a green product does not imply a compromise between traditional and environmental attributes. Due to the interrelated nature of subsystems (i.e., material selection, product reengineering, and expanding the technology frontier), the authors posit that product specifications and attributes can be combined most efficiently so that they lead to lower environmental impacts and/or better environmental performances.

Raz et al. (2013) focus on a profit-maximizing firm that pursues design changes in the manufacturing and use life-cycle stages of its product. Products are differentiated based on product life-cycle length (i.e., functional versus innovative products) and also by the environmental impact during their life-cycle stages (i.e., higher manufacturing stage environmental impact versus higher use stage environmental impact). Using a newsvendor framework, optimal quantity and effort decisions and their environmental impacts are characterized. Through an application of their framework to other products categorized based on life-cycle analysis (LCA), the authors show that functional products will require higher effort investment in manufacturing stage than in use stage, whereas the opposite is true for innovative products. This research also shows that while unit environmental impact is an increasing function of eco-efficient innovations, total environmental impact can either increase or decrease since this is driven by production quantities.

Chen and Liu (2014) study the pricing and design decisions of firms for green product design with virgin and recycled material contents in a duopoly. Products are composed of two materials: a recycled material and a virgin material. The external market is divided into two mutually exclusive segments each of a fixed size: a brown market segment and a green market segment. The firm that targets the brown market segment is referred to as the brown firm, while the firm targeting the green market segment as the green firm. Competition between firms takes place in a two-stage, non-cooperative game. In the first stage, each firm designs the mix of recycled and virgin material contents of its own product. In the second stage, after observing the other firm's product design choice, the two firms set their prices under a specific type of price leadership. Two cases are used to summarize the two possible price leaderships (i.e., the leader and follower firm) arrangements: the brown firm is the leader while the green firm is the follower; and vice versa. The analysis in the paper characterizes financial incentives for sustainable product design and the authors show that: (a) the brown segment's base level of efficient quality (i.e., the quality level that maximizes the differences between product valuations and production costs for brown segment customers) provides an "anchor product position" for the price leader no matter whether it is the brown or green firm; and (b) when the brown firm is the price leader and the green firm is the follower, a higher volume of recycled materials are used in product design.

2.2 Why Don't Consumers Buy Green Products?

Public opinion polls consistently indicate that some customers are willing to pay a premium for green products and would prefer to choose a green product over a non-green product. However, observations show that customers keep purchasing those products that are less friendly to the environment. One underlying reason behind this value-action gap could be related to the way green products force customers to make trade-offs between traditional attributes (e.g., price, quality, and performance) and environmental attributes (e.g., ease of disposal and environmentally friendly content). Olson (2013) analyzes the attitudinal and behavioral impact of such trade-offs on customers' preferences and choice of green products. Preferences for hybrid automobiles are contrasted with preferences for LED TVs through a full-profile conjoint analysis, which reveals attribute importance in the decision making process for these green products. Using data collected from customers in Norway and/or members of Norwegian organizations, the author finds that customers would choose a green product over one that is less friendly to the environment when all other things are equal. The value-action gap observed in the customer market stems from the trade-offs between environmental and traditional attributes. The reduction in preference is observed to be less for LED TVs in comparison to hybrid automobiles which leads the author to conclude that a green product offering a compensatory advantage on a traditional attribute (i.e., the LED TV) attracts a broader spectrum of customers, while a product which does not (i.e., the Hybrid automobile) only attracts customers who are willing to pay a premium price. For both product categories, however, potential buyers of the greenest technologies tend to choose energy-thirsty specifications on negatively correlated conventional attributes, which in turn offsets some of their choices' environmental benefits.

2.3 Innovation in Green Product Design

Customer demand for green products is increasingly pronounced to create far-reaching opportunities for businesses to promote their greener offerings and introduce profitable new ones. Lin et al. (2013) examine how market demand affects green product innovation and firm performance in the context of the Vietnamese motorcycle industry. Their study is focused around two issues: the impact of market demand on a firm's green product innovation and the impact of green product innovation on firm performance. Four major motorcycle manufacturers have been surveyed, and the authors find that there is a positive correlation between market demand and both green product innovation and firm performance. In addition, green product innovation performance has a positive correlation with firm performance. The study also finds that in a highly competitive market, green product innovation is required to achieve a competitive advantage.

2.4 Green Product Offering Strategies

Prior work in this stream develops customer-centric models with a view to providing strategic and policy guidelines. More specifically, consumer preferences toward green products are modeled using traditional quality-based utility models that assume that the consumers' willingness to pay for a product is increasing in quality and declining in price.

Chen (2001) proposes a quality-based model for green product design and consumer choice, and analyzes the strategic decisions of a monopolist on product development and market segmentation. Products are characterized in terms of two attributes: a traditional attribute and an environmental attribute. Analogously, the market consists of two segments: an ordinary segment comprised of consumers who only value the traditional attributes in products and a green segment consisting of consumers who value both the traditional and environmental attributes. Therefore, two product strategies are considered: (a) a status quo strategy (or mass-marketing strategy) where a single product is introduced to serve both market segments; and (b) a green product development strategy (or market-segmentation strategy) in which a single product is developed specifically for each segment. The author shows that both product strategies would lead to equivalent total environmental quality. When an external environmental standard is imposed, on the other hand, the paper shows that there exists a "danger zone" within which a stricter environmental standard may actually result in lower levels of total environmental quality.

Using a product differentiation model, Yenipazarli and Vakharia (2015a) evaluate alternate green product strategies that a monopolist firm can choose and implement in order to integrate environmental benefits into its product design. Product attributes are classified into two distinct aggregate dimensions (i.e., brown and green). Based on empirical evidence, customers are segmented into three distinct mutually exclusive groups: Traditionals, Fence-Sitters, and Greens. Using this framework, the authors evaluate three single-product strategies: Greening-Off, under which a product defined by a single brown attribute is offered; Greening-Out, where a new product defined in terms of a single environmental attribute is offered; and Greening-Up, under which the firm redesigns its current brown product to incorporate green attributes so that the product offering is defined in terms of two attributes. The key results stemming from this research are that greening up an existing brown product is not necessarily better at reducing the environmental impact, and that both environmental performance and profits can be simultaneously optimized through a focus on serving some but not all market segments.

In a follow-up study, Yenipazarli and Vakharia (2015b) analyze tactical and strategic implications of expanding a brown product line with a new green product. The focus of this research is on examining preferred product introduction strategies under aggregate capacity constraints and by considering two green product pricing choices: low- and high-priced green product. The authors find that the two-level pricing structure can decrease the adverse effects of cannibalization of green product introduction when adequate capacity is available. On the other hand, when capacity is limited, a firm can never protect its products from the threat of cannibalization by merely revising the pricing structure and this can lead to the firm not having an incentive to introduce a green product.

3 Supply Chains

A multitude of papers examine issues related to the management of sustainable supply chains. These contributions are described in this section and are categorized in terms of whether they focus on forward or reverse supply chains.

3.1 Forward Supply Chains

3.1.1 Product and Retail Competition

Liu et al. (2012) examine the impact of customers' willingness to pay higher prices for environmentally friendly products and competition intensity levels—between partially substitutable products made by different manufacturers and the competition between retail stores—on the profits of different supply chain players. Three supply chain network structures are considered: (a) a simple structure with no product or retail competition (i.e., there is a single manufacturer and a single retailer); (b) a structure with only product competition (i.e., two competing manufacturers and a single retailer); and (c) a structure with both product and retail competition (i.e., two competing manufacturers and two competing retailers). Using a Stackelberg leader-follower setting (Stackelberg 2011), each supply chain network structure is analyzed. The analysis indicates that when customers' environmental awareness increases, the profits of retailers and the green manufacturer increase. The profits for a manufacturer offering only brown products can be increased through a reduction of costs for environmentally friendly production or if it is possible to increase product differentiation with a view to reduce product competition. In contrast, the manufacturer offering green products will find a loss of profit if it does not have a significant cost advantage or customers are not willing to pay a higher premium for its products. Under stronger retail competition, retailers are usually worse off while the green manufacturer is usually better off.

3.1.2 Component Commonality and Remanufacturing

Subramanian et al. (2013) study how an original equipment manufacturer's (OEM's) choice of whether to implement component commonality is affected by secondary market considerations. Three scenarios are analyzed: (a) the benchmark scenario with manufacturing only, (b) a scenario with the OEM remanufacturing; and (c) a scenario with third-party remanufacturing. Product offerings are of two types; i.e., high-end and low-end with given exogenous original product qualities. To evaluate commonality-related trade-offs under OEM remanufacturing and under third-party remanufacturing, it is assumed that the high-end product is remanufactured. The authors use this setting to investigate how remanufacturing could lead to a reversal of the OEM's commonality decision. Relative to when the OEM produces and sells only new products, the authors show that cost reduction and cannibalization effects of commonality may lead to a different strategy choice under remanufacturing. Other specific findings stemming from this work are that under third-party remanufacturing: (a) commonality may result in a cost reduction for both the OEM and the third party and hence, component commonality may not be preferred by the OEM if the remanufacturing cost reduction is substantial; and (b) the cannibalization effect of commonality may instead be beneficial to the OEM, because its low-end product becomes more competitive relative to the third-party's remanufactured product.

3.1.3 Order Quantities and Customer Environmental Concerns

Zhang et al. (2015) study the effects of customer environmental awareness (CEA) on order quantities for traditional and green products and on coordination of a supply chain with one manufacturer and one retailer. The manufacturer produces two substitute products: a green product and a traditional product. Using a multi-product newsvendor model, three supply chain scenarios are considered: centralized, decentralized, and decentralized with a returns contract. The key results of their study are that the order quantity of the green product increases with CEA, while the impact of CEA on the order quantity of a traditional product depends on the difference between environmental qualities of traditional and green products; the retailer serves as the conduit to develop a market for green products since the retailer's profit increases monotonically with CEA; and the partial return credit contract for unsold products would provide a win-win solution in terms of green product development for both the manufacturer and the retailer.

3.2 Reverse Supply Chains

Blackburn et al. (2004) note that reverse supply chains are typically organized to manage activities related to used product acquisition; the transportation of used products to sorting facilities; the inspection, sorting, and disposition of collected products; remanufacturing (or refurbishing) of returns; and the creation of secondary markets for remanufactured products. In addition, the issue of reverse supply chain networks is also of relevance. In this section, we highlight the major contributions related to network design, managing the collections process, and remanufacturing.

3.2.1 Reverse Supply Chain Networks

Fleischmann et al. (2001) propose a reverse supply chain network with four levels: (i) plants where new products are manufactured and/or recovery takes place; (ii) warehouses for distribution of new and/or recovered products; (iii) consolidation centers; and (iv) customers. New and/or recovered products are shipped to customers via warehouses while returns are shipped to recovery facilities (or disposal) via consolidation centers. All the returns are sent first to testing centers and then shipped to different facilities. The goal of the firm is to minimize total costs, which include the fixed cost of opening sites and variable costs of transportation, handling, and production. The objective is subject to the constraints of flow balancing at each plant and required disposal rate, and the problem is solved by mixed-integer linear programming (MILP).

Wang et al. (2016a) focus on whether remanufacturing activities in a reverse supply chain should be carried out by the firm (i.e., in-house) or subcontracted to a third party (i.e., outsourcing). Their research is motivated by industry observations of GameStop, which, at the time, outsourced remanufacturing of game consoles to a third party and was contemplating whether this activity should be carried out in-house. Their analysis considers the relative cost-effectiveness of the two approaches, uncertainty in the input quality of the collected/returned used products, consumer willingness-to-pay for remanufactured products, and the extent to which the remanufactured product cannibalizes demand for new product. The authors identify "conflict" scenarios in which the in-house strategy maximizes profits, but outsourcing is better for the environment. To resolve this conflict, a profit-sharing mechanism is proposed where, under certain conditions, outsourcing becomes the retailer's more profitable strategy while retaining an environmental advantage over the in-house approach. As a final extension, the authors also investigate how the outsourcing dominance region for profit maximization would be influenced by differences in bargaining power between the channel partners. Using an egalitarian bargaining framework, the authors show that the congruence and conflict regions for each strategy choice are similar to those obtained under the Stackelberg leader/follower setting.

3.2.2 Managing the Collection Process

Savaskan et al. (2004) explore the problem of who should collect used products and consider a two-echelon supply chain structure with a manufacturer and a retailer and compare the profitability of different collection modes: (a) manufacturer, (b) retailer, and (c) an independent third party. They find that the preferred collecting agent is the retailer, followed by the manufacturer, and the third party.

Souza et al. (2002) discuss various reasons and time scales of the enormous returns. Trade-in programs as a source of returns for remanufacturing is also of high relevance to reverse supply chains. Ray et al. (2005) assume that traded-in products can be remanufactured (so they have a value) and that consumers also have a feel for the value of their used product. They derive optimal trade-in discounts under three different policies: a discount dependent on the used product's age, a discount independent of the product age, and no trade-in discount. Li et al. (2011) propose a methodology for forecasting trade-ins based on customer segmentation and signals (return merchandise authorizations, or RMAs).

Guide et al. (2006) use queuing networks to demonstrate the value of speed in recovery on profitability for time-sensitive consumer returns such as consumer electronics. Their analysis indicates that drivers for network design are product value, price decay, return rate, and proportion of unused returns.

3.2.3 Remanufacturing

Should an OEM offer a remanufactured version of its product? This question has been analyzed by several papers, and most of them use a vertical differentiation framework that incorporates the price trade-off between competing products of equivalent or unequal quality. Two implications of offering a remanufactured product are also considered: a market expansion effect, because the remanufactured product which usually has a lower price reaches a segment of consumers who are not willing to pay for the new product; and a cannibalization effect, as some consumers who would have previously purchased the new product switch to the remanufactured product.

Debo et al. (2005) analyze conditions under which it is profitable for a manufacturer to produce a remanufacturable product in a discrete-time, infinite-horizon framework for an industry in which the manufacturer holds a monopoly in the markets for new and remanufactured products. A discounted profit-optimization problem is developed where the manufacturer's goal is to maximize the net present value of introducing a remanufacturable product, calculated over the life-cycle of this product. The key results of this work are: high production costs of the single-use product, low remanufacturing costs, and low incremental costs to make a single-use product remanufacturable are the key drivers for investment in remanufacturing; the larger the number of low-end customers (i.e., customers with a low willingness-to-pay for new products) in the market, the lower the remanufacturing potential; and the customer profile and fixed costs interact to determine the optimal level of remanufacturability such that if the fixed costs are higher, the optimal remanufacturability level is lower and the market has more high-end customers. The authors extend their monopoly setting to one where the manufacturer produces only the new product (i.e., it has a monopoly position) but used products are remanufactured by multiple independent competing remanufacturers. In this scenario, the authors show that the optimal level of remanufacturability offered by the manufacturer is lower than that in the monopoly model and it decreases as the number of competing remanufacturers increases.

Ferguson and Toktay (2006) study the trade-offs between cannibalization of new product demand stemming from introducing a remanufactured product and the collection and manufacturing activities which can extend product life. They adopt a two-period setting where remanufacturing in the second period is constrained by the number of cores stemming from new product sales in the first period. The authors first identify conditions under which the firm would choose not to remanufacture its products. Then, they characterize the potential loss of profits stemming from external remanufacturing competition and analyze two third-party entry-deterrent strategies: remanufacturing and preemptive collection. In some cases, the authors find that some remanufactured-branded consumer products do not cannibalize new sales and thus can be used as a strategic deterrent to low-cost competitors. Examples of studies which have extended this analysis are as follows: Vorasayan and Ryan (2006) who focus on the impact of demand uncertainty; Ferrer and Swaminathan (2006) who examine the case where the OEM's new and remanufactured products are perfect substitutes and the OEM compete with a third-party offering remanufactured product with an inferior quality; and Majumder and Groenevelt (2001) who provide an extension for the case of linearly decreasing demand as a function of price.

Atasu et al. (2008) examine a setting where there is a market segment which has identical valuations for both the remanufactured and new products. They focus on a case where an OEM creates both new and remanufactured products and competes with a low-cost producer of new product. Their key result is that if the consumers have a lower valuation for the competitive product, the competitor will not have any competitive advantage. Pince et al. (2012) show that an OEM will always offer a remanufactured product if such a product can be used to meet demand for warranty replacements.

4 Environmental Legislation

4.1 Life-Cycle Assessment and New Product Introduction

Mayers et al. (2005) focus on the Waste Electrical and Electronic Equipment (WEEE) directive within the European Union (EU). Using life-cycle assessment and costing, they are unable to identify a dominant waste management scenario as compared to landfilling. They also find that contrary to belief, the use of targets in the directive would not necessarily lead to increased eco-design efforts on the part of manufacturers. Their key conclusion is to call for a revision of the scope of the directive by instead focusing on developing environmental objectives and standards for treatment and recycling processes.

Plambeck and Wang (2009) examine the impact of e-waste (electronic waste) regulation on new product introduction and design for remanufacturability, depending on the level of competition and on the form of regulation. Two specific legislations; i.e., fee upon sale and fee upon disposal, are considered. The authors identify the conditions under which a unique equilibrium for a new product introduction process can be characterized both in a monopoly and in a duopoly setting. The effects of the two e-waste regulations on the new product introduction process, quantity of e-waste, design for remanufacturability, and manufacturer profits are examined. Specifically, it is shown that fee-upon-sale types of e-waste regulation cause manufacturers to increase their development time and expenditure, resulting in increases in the incremental quality for each new product. Such a regulation also increases manufacturers' profits since customers pay a higher price for each new product as they anticipate using these products for longer. However, the authors find that fee-upon-sale types of e-waste regulation discourage manufacturers to design new products that are remanufacturable. While the social welfare increases in a duopoly, it decreases in a monopoly if and only if e-waste costs are small. In contrast, fee-upon-disposal types of e-waste regulation encourages design for remanufacturability but simultaneously forces manufacturers to introduce new products too rapidly, which in turn generates more e-waste.

4.2 Extended Producer Responsibility (EPR)

Although there are a multitude of legislative practices with an environmental focus that have been proposed, Lifset (1993) contends that all such practices internalize externalities by changing the behavior of producers as well as consumers, and in the long run should promote environmentally oriented technological change. From an economic policy perspective, Palmer and Walls (1997) study Extended Producer Responsibility (EPR)-type legislation that mandate the use of specific secondary materials content in manufacturing. They find that such policies need to be coupled with additional taxes on the final product and other production inputs so as to generate the optimal disposal amount.

Gui et al. (2016) provide an in-depth analysis of implementing an Extended Producer Responsibility (EPR) program in the state of Washington in the United States. They are able to provide guidelines on how to achieve effective and efficient EPR implementations with a focus on design incentives, reuse and refurbishing, product scope, downstream material flows, and operational efficiency. Atasu et al. (2009) derive efficiency conditions for EPR-type legislation. In addition to these legislations being perceived as alleviating fairness concerns, they also incentivize eco-design producers to create larger environmental benefits.

Subramanian et al. (2009) examine the impact of EPR policy parameters on product design. They model a manufacturer supplying a remanufacturable product to a single customer who obtains a fixed utility (or revenue) per period from the product. Three questions are addressed in this paper. First, they address the issue of whether EPR programs provide adequate incentives to manufacturers to design green products. An integrated supply chain is considered in which the average supply chain profit has to be maximized per period. They find that higher charges for environmental impact during product use can lead to better remanufacturability that reduces the end-of-life environmental impact of the product. Additionally, as the customer bears a larger share of charges during product use, the manufacturer is shown to have a greater incentive to design the product to be more remanufacturable. Second, they investigate how contracts can be structured to improve supply chain profitability and environmental product design. A decentralized supply chain under symmetric and asymmetric information is modeled where the manufacturer and the customer are independent entities who privately maximize their profits. For the case of symmetric information, it is shown that coordination leads not only to higher supply chain profits as expected but also to environmentally more favorable product design. Third, they examine how customer attributes affect incentives for product design and supply chain coordination. They show that a supply chain with an efficient customer lowers the manufacturer's incentive to design the product with greater remanufacturability, since remanufacturing and disposal costs are incurred less often.

Atasu and Subramanian (2012) turn their attention to comparing collective and individual producer responsibility (CPR and IPR, respectively) models of EPR. Their primary focus is on design for product recovery (DfR) and find that IPR leads to superior DfR incentives since CPR could lead to free-riding. In a follow-up study, Gui et al. (2013) examine collective implementations of EPR. Since current cost allocation mechanisms in these implementations might lead to higher costs for certain producers, this could lead to a market fragmentation. To address this problem, they propose and validate a cost allocation mechanism, which induces participation and simultaneously maximizes efficiency. Atasu et al. (2013) comparatively evaluate two legislative practices: a tax model, where the social planner specifies a take-back fraction and charges the OEM a recovery fee; and a rate model, where it is the responsibility of the OEM to ensure compliance with the take-back fraction. They are able to show that the impacts of this type of legislation can be significantly different, and hence, stakeholder preferences vary across practices.

4.3 Policy Implications

There is another stream analyzing how the policy instruments impact the incentive of supply chain members as well as the environmentally favorable design. The typical objective in this stream of research is for the social planner to maximize net social surplus subject to resource constraints, material balance constraints, and production functions. Toffel (2003) provides an excellent overview of developments in take-back legislation and their likely impacts on organizational decision making. Runkel (2003) examines how EPR influences the choice of product durability and social welfare. Several researchers have examined the economic and social efficiencies of various policy instruments such as taxes, subsidies, standards, and take-back requirements (e.g., Calcott and Walls (2000), Eichner and Pethig (2001), Fullerton and Wu (1998), Palmer and Walls (1997), and Dinan (2005)). An environmentally favorable design implies lower material consumption, higher fraction of product recycled, or lower cost of recycling. A consistent finding is that a combined tax/subsidy, where there is a consumption good tax and a recycling subsidy (such as in a deposit-refund system) can yield the socially optimal product design and quantity of waste.

Yenipazarli (2015) studies the impact of emissions taxations on the optimal production and pricing decisions of a manufacturer who could remanufacture its own product. The conditions under what the manufacturer's decision to remanufacture under an emission regulation reduces its environmental impact while at the same time increasing its profits are characterized. On the policy side, the conditions under what emissions taxes can be instituted to realize the economic, environmental, and social benefits of remanufacturing are also characterized. The analyses are subsequently extended to an emissions trading setting where emissions are regulated using tradable permits, and the economic implications of remanufacturing under emissions trading vis-à-vis emissions taxation are studied.

Wang et al. (2016b) examine the strategic and policy implications of two diametrically opposed legislative practices for regulating and financing e-waste disposal. The first practice (characterized as "Producer Pays") imposes a fixed market share based fee and a per-unit disposal fee on an OEM, while the second practice (characterized as "Anticipatory Protection") charges a per-unit fee to each consumer of an electronic product. To analyze the impact of each legislation, they typify current practices by considering an OEM who offers two competing products: a new product and a remanufactured product. The two legislative practices are evaluated in the context of multiple stakeholder objectives: product prices, OEM profits, and consumer and environmental surplus. Their results reveal that, in most cases, there is a parametric trade-off in the choice of legislative practices. By structurally characterizing this trade-off, the authors identify dominance regions for each strategy choice. Regions where a single strategy choice would be the preferred choice of both a social planner and the OEM are also identified by the authors. From a policy perspective, the authors provide guidelines on how the per-unit fee for the OEM should be structured by the social planner so that both the former and latter players prefer a specific legislative practice.

5 Directions for Future Research

Irrespective of the vast literature on product/process design, we identify the following areas as promising avenues for future thought. The majority of product/process development literature focuses on the demand-side impact on the manufacturer's decisions. Although the existing work incorporates certain aspects of the supply side, there is still ample room for new and insightful research that focuses on:

- *Integrating product/process development with component recovery.* Product design changes impact the recovery of core (remanufacturable) components. Hence, the testing of the returned products, disassembly costs, and manufacturing process re-engineering all play a role in the product/process design decisions.
- *Interplay between modularity and sustainable product design.* Disassembly operations for products should be integrated along with process changes. The higher the complexity of the product, the higher the benefit due to integrating the design decisions with the disassembly decisions. Although product modularity and its impact on the supply side decisions has been well studied, sustainable product design could influence these decisions extensively.

The existing work on supply chain design can further be strengthened by bridging the gap between the logistics network design and reverse channel design. Most of the existing work includes the decisions of the consumers and various supply chain partners in the presence of green products. In this context, opportunities for future research include:

- *Impact of supply chain decisions on the overall logistics network.* The decisions on who should perform the remanufacturing operations, which channel is used to collect the used products, which channel is used in marketing the products, etc., alter the demand characteristics as well as the logistics requirements. Consequently, supply chain partners may need to rethink their logistics decisions including facility location, demand forecasting, and transportation.
- *Examining the impact of a firm's sustainability initiatives on supply chain partners.* There is the possibility that a focus on sustainability within a firm might result in a transfer of knowledge/benefits to supply chain partners. As a consequence, a firm's investment on such an initiative may ultimately benefit its competitors. Such a linkage needs to be integrated in a firm's investment on environmentally friendly practices as well as operational and strategic decisions.

Finally, in the area of environmental legislations, two specific future research opportunities are:

- *Fit of environmental legislations with industry type.* Legislations may force the supply chain partners to modify the logistics network to avoid possible penalties and to reduce the carbon footprint. In this context, studies that develop frameworks for environmental legislative practice based on their applicability under distinct industry settings would serve as valuable tools.
- *Policy guidelines for social planners.* Since social planners are often struggling with assessing the policy implication when designing environmental legislations, it would be helpful to conduct research that provides insights into how multiple-stakeholders in supply chains are impacted by specific legislations. This would of course vary by industry types and thus, frameworks developed would be particularly useful in formulating these policy guidelines.

References and Bibliography

Akçay, Y., T. Boyaci, and D. Zhang (2013) "Selling with money back guarantees: The impact on prices, quantities, and retail profitability," *Production and Operations Management*, **22**(4): 777–791.

Atasu, A. and R. Subramanian (2012) "Extended producer responsibility for e-waste: Individual or collective producer responsibility?" *Production and Operations Management*, **21**(6): 1042–1059.

Atasu A., Ö. Özdemir, and L. N. Van Wassenhove (2013) "Stakeholder perspectives on e-waste take-back legislation," *Production and Operations Management*, **22**(2): 382–396.

Atasu, A., L. N. Van Wassenhove, and M. Sarvary (2009) "Efficient take-back legislation," *Production and Operations Management*, **18**(3): 243–258.

Atasu, A., M. Sarvary, and L. N. Van Wassenhove (2008) "Remanufacturing as a marketing strategy," *Management Science*, **54**(10): 1731–1746.

Blackburn, J. D., V. D. R. Guide, G. C. Souza, and L. N. Van Wassenhove (2004) "Reverse supply chains for commercial returns," *California Management Review*, **46**(2): 6–22.

Calcott, P. and M. Walls (2000) "Can downstream waste disposal policies encourage upstream 'design for environment'?" *American Economic Review*, **90**(2): 233–237.

Chen, C. (2001) "Design for the environment: A quality-based model for green product development," *Management Science*, **47**(2): 250–263.

Chen, C. and L. Q. Liu (2014) "Pricing and quality decisions and financial incentives for sustainable product design with recycled material content under price leadership," *International Journal of Production Economics*, **147**(C): 666–677.

Chen, C., J. Zhu, J.-Y. Yu, and H. Noori (2012) "A new methodology for evaluating sustainable product design performance with two-stage network data envelopment analysis," *European Journal of Operational Research*, **221**(2): 348–359.

Corbett, C. J. and P. R. Kleindorfer (2001) "Environmental management and operations management: Introduction to part 1 (manufacturing and ecologistics)," *Production and Operations Management*, **10**(2): 107–111.

Debo, L., L. B. Toktay, and L. N. Van Wassenhove (2005) "Market segmentation and product technology selection for remanufacturable products." *Management Science*, **51**(8): 1193–1205.

Dinan, T. M. (2005) "Economic efficiency effects of alternative policies for reducing waste disposal," *Journal of Environmental Economics and Management*, **25**(3): 242–256.

Eichner, T. and R. Pethig (2001) "Product design and efficient management of recycling and waste treatment," *Journal of Environmental Economics and Management*, **41**(1): 109–134.

Elkington, J. (1997) *Cannibals with forks: The triple bottom line of 21st century business*, Capstone Publishing, Ltd., Oxford, UK.

Ferguson, M. and B. Toktay (2006) "Effect of competition on recovery strategies," *Production and Operations Management*, **15**(3): 351–368.

Ferguson, M., V. D. R. Guide Jr., and G. C. Souza (2006) "Supply chain coordination for false failure returns," *Manufacturing & Service Operations Management*, **8**(4): 376–393.

Ferrer, G. and J. Swaminathan (2006) "Managing new and remanufactured product," *Management Science*, **52**(1): 15–26.

Fleischmann, M., P. Beullens, J. M. Bloemhof-Ruwaard, and L. N. Van Wassenhove (2001) "The impact of product recovery on logistics network design," *Production and Operations Management*, **10**(2): 156–173.

Fullerton, D. and W. Wu (1998) "Policies for green design," *Journal of Environmental Economics and Management*, **36**(2): 131–148.

Gui, L., A. Atasu, O. Ergun, and L. B. Toktay (2013) "Implementing extended producer responsibility legislation," *Journal of Industrial Ecology*, **17**(2): 262–276.

Gui, L., A. Atasu, O. Ergun, and L. B. Toktay (2016) "Efficient implementation of product take-back legislation with collective producer responsibility," *Management Science*, **62**(4): 1098–1123.

Guide, V. D. R., Jr., G. C. Souza, L. N. Van Wassenhove, and J. D. Blackburn (2006) "Time value of commercial product returns," *Management Science*, **52**(8): 1200–1214.

Kleindorfer, P. R., K. Singhal, and L. N. Van Wassenhove (2005) "Sustainable operations management," *Production and Operations Management*, **14**(4): 482–492.

Li, K. J., D. K. H. Fong, and S. H. Xu (2011) "Managing trade-in programs based on product characteristics and customer heterogeneity in business-to-business markets," *Manufacturing & Service Operations Management*, **13**(1): 108–123.

Lifset, R. J. (1993) "Take it back: Extended producer responsibility as a form of incentive-based environmental policy," *Journal of Resource Management and Technology*, **21**(4): 163–175.

Lin, R. J., K. H. Tan, and Y. Geng (2013) "Market demand, green product innovation, and firm performance: Evidence from Vietnam motorcycle industry," *Journal of Cleaner Production*, **40**(1): 101–107.

Liu, Z., T. D. Anderson, and J. M. Cruz (2012) "Consumer environmental awareness and competition in two-stage supply chains," *European Journal of Operational Research*, **218**(4): 602–613.

Majumder, P. and H. Groenevelt (2001) "Competition in remanufacturing," *Production and Operations Management*, **10**(2): 125–141.

Mayers, C. K., C. M. France, and S. J. Cowell (2005) "Extended producer responsibility for waste electronics: An example of printer recycling in the United Kingdom," *Journal of Industrial Ecology*, **9**(3): 169–189.

Noori, H. and C. Chen (2003) "Applying scenario-driven strategy to integrate environmental management and product design," *Production and Operations Management*, **12**(3): 353–368.

Olson, E. L. (2013) "It's not easy being green: The effects of attribute tradeoffs on green product preference and choice," *Journal of the Academy of Marketing Science*, **41**(2): 171–184.

Palmer, K. and M. Walls (1997) "Optimal polices for solid waste disposal: Taxes, subsidies and standards," *Journal of Public Economics*, **65**(2): 193–205.

Pince, C., M. Ferguson, and L. B. Toktay (2012) "Extracting maximum value from consumer returns: Allocating between selling refurbished product and meeting warranty demand," *Technical Report*, Working paper, Georgia Institute of Technology, Atlanta, GA.

Plambeck, E. and Q. Wang (2009) "Effects of e-waste regulation on new product introduction," *Management Science*, **55**(3): 333–347.

Ray, S., T. Boyaci, and N. Aras (2005) "Optimal prices and trade-in rebates for durable, remanufacturable products," *Manufacturing & Service Operations Management*, **7**(3): 208–228.

Raz, G., C. T. Druehl, and V. Blass (2013) "Design for the environment: Life-cycle approach using a newsvendor model," *Production and Operations Management*, **22**(4): 940–957.

Runkel, M. (2003) "Product durability and extended producer responsibility in solid waste management," *Environmental and Resource Economics*, **24**(2): 161–182.

Savaskan, R. C., S. Bhattacharya, and L. N. Van Wassenhove (2004) "Closed-loop supply chain models with product remanufacturing," *Management Science*, **50**(2): 239–252.

Shulman, J. D., A. T. Coughlan, and R. C. Savaskan (2011) "Managing consumer returns in a competitive environment," *Management Science*, **57**(2): 347–362.

Souza, G. C., M. E. Ketzenberg, and V. D. R. Guide Jr. (2002) "Capacitated remanufacturing with service level constraints," *Production and Operations Management*, **11**(2): 231–248.

Stackelberg, H. V. (2011) *Market structure and equilibrium*, (translated into English by Bazin, Urch & Hill), Springer, New York.

Subramanian, R., M. E. Ferguson, and L. B. Toktay (2013) "Remanufacturing and the component commonality decision," *Production and Operations Management*, **22**(1): 36–53.

Subramanian, R., S. Gupta, and B. Talbot (2009) "Product design and supply chain coordination under extended producer responsibility," *Production and Operations Management*, **18**(3): 259–277.

Tang, C. S. and S. Zhou (2012) "Research advances in environmentally and socially sustainable operations," *European Journal of Operational Research*, **223**(3): 585–594.

Toffel, M. W. (2003) "The growing strategic importance of end-of-life product management," *California Management Review*, **45**(3): 102–129.

Vorasayan, J. and S. Ryan (2006) "Optimal price and quantity of refurbished products," *Production and Operations Management*, **15**(3): 369–383.

Wang, L., G. Cai, A. Tsay, and A.J. Vakharia (2016a) "Design of the reverse channel for remanufacturing: Must profit maximization harm the environment?" *Working Paper*, California State University, East Bay, Hayward, CA.

Wang, L., T. Rajapakshe, and A.J. Vakharia (2016b) "Producer pays versus consumer pays legislations: A strategic analysis," *Working Paper*, California State University, East Bay, Hayward, CA.

Yenipazarli, A. (2015) "Managing new and remanufactured products to mitigate environmental damage under emissions regulation," *European Journal of Operational Research*, **249**(1): 117–130.

Yenipazarli, A. and A.J. Vakharia (2015a) "Green, greener or brown: Choosing the right color of the product," *Annals of Operations Research*, **226**(1): 669–694.

Yenipazarli, A. and A.J. Vakharia (2015b) "Pricing, market coverage and capacity: Can green and brown products co-exist?" *European Journal of Operational Research*, **242**(1): 304–315.

Zhang, L., J. Wang, and J. You (2015) "Consumer environmental awareness and channel coordination with two substitutable products," *European Journal of Operational Research*, **241**(1): 63–73.

15
THE INTERDEPENDENCE OF DATA ANALYTICS AND OPERATIONS MANAGEMENT

Kaushik Dutta, Abhijeet Ghoshal, and Subodha Kumar

1 Introduction

With the recent proliferation of data, data analytics has become popular across many domains. Data analytics and operations management (OM) techniques are inextricably intertwined. Several operations research techniques, particularly mathematical programming and time-series-based predictive methods, are being used to derive insights from historical data. In this chapter, we explore the applications of these techniques in various domains.

In each section, we describe the existing research on the use of big data and analytics on the topic, which is then followed by future research directions according to the interests of OM researchers. In the retail domain, we analyze the role of big data applications for recommender systems operations, the impact of recommender systems on supply chains, and the research problems that exist regarding recommender system design. The section on digital advertisements discusses various research questions related to optimization and simulation models in the space of advertisement placement, targeting, and auctioning in online environments. The mobile section describes the application of big data and analytics for advertisement through mobile phones, problems faced by mobile network providers, and better mobile-app design. In the section on so-called "smart cities," we discuss the research problems pertaining to the transformations that occur due to the applications of big data and analytics on city operations, such as transportation, parking, energy needs, and the general health of the city. Next, the energy management section ponders upon the application of data analytics in the domain of the generation, distribution, and consumption of energy. Finally, the healthcare section discusses how big data is used for electronic healthcare record systems.

In no way is this an exhaustive set of data analytics applications. Rather, it provides a representative view of how operations research-based data analytics techniques have been applied so far in pursuing improved operations. Additionally, we also identify a few research areas in each of these domains that require further development and application of data analytics.

2 Retail Operations

Big data has significantly affected the landscape of retail business. Organizations use big data and analytics to develop and test models that not only reduce their costs more effectively and increase revenues but also make them attractive to customers in the market and dilute the effect of competition (Janakiraman et al. 2013; Mehra et al. 2013; Kumar et al. 2014). Recommender systems are one of the important tools that help organizations to make personalized recommendations by using data and analytics in order to learn the preferences of customers (Murthi and Sarkar 2003). These systems serve as decision aids for customers (Hauble and Trifts 2000); a recommender system reduces a customer's search effort by predicting the products that customers are likely to purchase and recommends them proactively. Therefore, instead of searching a large number of products in an online shopping environment, customers can focus on the recommended products and select one that they prefer most.

2.1 Design Aspects of Recommender Systems

Recommender system design has been an active area of research for more than two decades. The constant increase in the variety of available data and improvements in analytics techniques have kept this line of research alive. The common practice for design evaluation has been to measure the performance improvements over previous designs based on one or more performance metrics. A large portion of the extant literature focuses on improving the *accuracy* of recommender systems (Ricci et al. 2011).

Another widely cited, but moderately studied, metric for measuring the performance of a recommender system is the *diversity* of recommendations made by the system, which measures the ability of a recommender system to push consumers towards niche products instead of pushing them to a few popular products. Researchers have already established that e-commerce websites increase diversity more than the traditional catalog channels (Brynjolfsson et al. 2011). The presence of a recommender system, however, may not lead to an increase in diversity when compared to diversity stats where recommender systems are absent. Rigorous analysis through an analytical model and simulation-based empirical analysis shows that the collaborative-filtering based systems may in fact reduce the diversity of products recommended to customers (Fleder and Hosanagar 2009). To counter this undesired effect of recommender systems, several optimization-based algorithms are proposed for systems that use collaborative filtering and matrix factorization (Adomavicius and Kwon 2014).

2.2 Future Research on Recommender Systems

Although the research literature concerned with the recommender system design is rich, a lot still needs to be done. Future research may continue to explore methods to further improve recommender systems based on the two performance metrics mentioned above.

2.2.1 Algorithm Design

Optimization-based approaches have been used for making predictive models for product recommendations (Ghoshal et al. 2015). With the availability of large amounts of opinions expressed by users about almost everything on Facebook, Twitter, Yelp, etc., researchers may focus on incorporating them into recommendations in real time. Past researchers have shown that using structured data that incorporates ratings from multiple sources improves prediction accuracy. However, using unstructured data for improving the recommendation accuracy poses multi-dimensional challenges.

First, efficient algorithms must be developed to convert unstructured data into structured data that can be integrated into the existing data. The concerns that need to be addressed are how to reconcile data to match records from different sources that follow disparate standards, how to recognize noise in the data and filter it out, and how to verify the correctness of the data. This line of research requires incorporating linguistics knowledge, natural language processing, data processing, and validation.

Next, research should progress towards developing methods for quickly incorporating public opinions to revise the models used for making individual predictions. Once converted to structured data, data from multiple sources is then used to revise the model parameters. As the amount of data generated per unit time increases, so does the need for algorithms that can quickly update the model parameters. Further, algorithms should also learn the changing preferences of customers and accordingly update the model parameters. For example, a system should be able to infer that a school-age child is moving to a college from relevant blogs, review posts, comments, etc., and recognize changes in this student's needs and preferences. Accordingly, the recommendations should change to avoid making irrelevant suggestions. Probabilistic and *hidden Markov process* models have been used in the past to learn changes in the customer preferences (Sahoo et al. 2012).

2.2.2 Recommendations Considering Trade-Offs

The challenges mentioned above are typical in systems meant to increase accuracy or diversity. However, increases in diversity of products pose many new roadblocks in the path of developing recommender systems. It is well known that, with an increase in the diversity of recommendations, the predictive accuracy of the system decreases (Adomavicius and Kwon 2014). Thus, a trade-off is necessary between the diversity and accuracy. Future research should consider trade-offs based on the utilities of improving diversity and accuracy, where the utility functions would represent economic quantities. For example, how should the trade-off be balanced so that sales are maximized, or customer satisfaction is maximized, or inventory stock-outs are minimized? Future research may also focus on how to develop methods that scale well with increases in the sizes of datasets and the variety of data while improving the balance between diversity and accuracy.

2.3 Economic and Supply Chain Problems on Recommender Systems

Both research literature and popular press provide evidence that recommender systems increase product demand and sales. Empirical research using data from premier online retailers who provide recommendation services shows that recommender systems can help build customer loyalty and increase switching costs of the customers (Pathak et al. 2010). Over time, with an increasing number of products purchased by the customers, recommender systems build customers' profiles that incrementally improve the accuracies of the recommendations for all customers, thereby increasing the switching costs of the customers.

2.3.1 Effect of Recommendations on the Overall Supply Chain

A related, but scarcely researched area in this context, is the effect of recommendations on the overall supply chain. Apart from increasing sales, it also creates a "pull effect" on the supply side of the organization. For example, consider a situation in which Netflix recommends a recently released movie to a large number of customers. If Netflix does not carry an inventory with high enough number of DVDs to fulfill the demand, then the customers become dissatisfied if they order the movie and Netflix is unable to supply it (Demirezen and Kumar 2016). Netflix's recommender system is tuned to avoid such a situation. When a large number of users are likely to order a specific movie simultaneously (e.g., a recently released and popular movie), Netflix proactively recommends other movies to some of these subscribers that are available in its inventory and are most likely preferred by the customers. This way, Netflix diverts the demands of movies to the ones it carries and skews the demand pattern of the movies in its favor (Liedtke 2012).

In this context, future research may focus on developing recommender system models to avoid inventory stock-outs similar to that in Demirezen and Kumar (2016). In fact, for service providers like Netflix, who also stream movies in addition to sending DVDs through the mail, the predictive models should consider diverting the demands to movies that can be streamed instantaneously to fulfill customer demands while making sure that the customer remains satisfied with the service. A similar research question may be raised in the reverse direction—how can an organization predict the demands of products that may be ordered by the customers so that they can be stocked in the warehouses in advance?

2.3.2 Information Sharing within a Supply Chain

Firms' ability to learn customer preferences from real-time data and use them for predictions has significant implications for the supply chain. For example, Xia et al. (2012) proposed an analytical model for predicting the sales of fashion products. Another potential area of research in this stream centers on the exploration of coordination mechanisms between a firm and its suppliers when the firm has the knowledge about customer preferences. How much information must the firm share with the supplier so that the supplier can plan properly for supplying the raw material just-in-time?

3 Mobile

The emergence of smartphones and handheld devices such as iPhones, iPads, and iPad minis, have suddenly created a deluge of data. According to a Nielsen report (Nielsen 2014), users now spend more time online on mobile devices than on computers. In particular, the young generation uses mobile devices to stay online far more than computers (Alleyne 2011). This trend of using mobile devices to stay online will only increase with the launch of gadgets such as smartwatches and Google Glass. Thus, mobile devices are bound to change the way customers consume products and services. As a result, organizations need to develop approaches to learn these new patterns of consumption in order to stay relevant and competitive.

3.1 Existing Research on Using Data from Mobile Devices and Platforms

Research in this domain is scarce as this trend is very recent, something that provides a significant opportunity for future research. Thirty percent of all online transactions happen through mobile devices (Berthene 2015), which makes mobile devices a hot channel for product and services advertising. Empirical analysis on competition between iOS and Android platforms to determine customer preferences towards these platforms shows that, interestingly, while the in-app ability to complete transactions increases the preference towards the platform, in-app advertising decreases that same preference (Ghose and Han 2014). This finding may have a significant impact on the advertising strategies of the firms. Firms now have to be smarter in showing ads that are particularly relevant. For instance, ad targeting may be based on the geographical locations and timing. Several researchers have explored this direction of research. The research can be grouped into two main categories: impact of advertisements on sales and location determination of users.

3.1.1 Impact of Advertisements on Sales

Regarding the impact of mobile advertisements on sales, interestingly, researchers found that pushing advertisements in smartphones in a very crowded place may increase the responses from target users. For example, users in crowded trains are more likely to respond to mobile advertisements than users in non-crowded trains. This is because, in crowded trains, users get more immersed and engaged with the mobile phones due to severe space constraints (Andrews et al. 2015). Additionally, mobile advertisements have a delayed sales effect, i.e., users may respond to a mobile ad after approximately twelve days (Fang et al. 2015). Hence, the sales impact of mobile ads may be severely underestimated if the delayed sales impact is not considered. Furthermore, combining temporal targeting and geographical targeting individually increases sales purchases (Luo et al. 2014). Surprisingly, the sales effects of employing these two strategies simultaneously are not straightforward. When targeting proximal mobile users, Luo et al. (2014) find a negative sales–lead time relationship.

3.1.2 Location Determination of Users

In the context of location determination, Chen et al. (2011) propose a system to predict the route of a user based on historical data. This system uses data-mining algorithms to extract the patterns of trajectories (routes) of a user, which are used to predict the future routes that the user may consider. Provost et al. (2015) propose a method to find same and similar users using location-visitation data in a mobile environment. They also propose a new design that uses consumer-location data from mobile devices to build a "geo-similarity network" among users. Additionally, Wang et al. (2006) propose an approach to determine a group of users who are in close proximity.

3.2 Future Research in the Space of Mobile Technology

Since the adoption of technology is growing, the scope of future research is immense. In the arena of advertising on mobile phones, most researchers use econometric methodologies to establish the value of advertising and study the factors that tend to increase the response. In this vein, future research should consider designing systems that can utilize this knowledge for targeting the consumers to maximize sales. For instance, mobile phones typically have small screens, and determining the optimal locations of the advertisements is an important problem for research. Along with that, another important issue to solve revolves around determining the right time and place for showing the advertisement.

3.2.1 Operations of Mobile Phones

Mobile phones are also used for viewing movies and listening to songs, causing several operational problems to exist in this context. Since these applications require mobile devices to transfer large amounts of data, telecommunications companies will have to develop optimal plans for allocation of bandwidth at different times of the day and at different locations. Related to this issue, telecommunication companies need to develop pricing policies for providing these services and determine caps on the maximum usage of services every month. For example, AT&T offers different plans to users based on the maximum amount of data that can be downloaded/uploaded from a device in a month. Are these plans (with caps) optimal for every customer? Should customers be rewarded for using less data and freeing some bandwidth (customers pay more if they use more data than as in the contract)? What are the social implications of a reward mechanism if users consume less data than the maximum as per the plan contract in a month? Perhaps service providers will also benefit from such a scheme of rewarding customers for underutilizing the bandwidth. These questions may be answered by analyzing the data about the usage patterns of customers.

3.2.2 Operations of Mobile Apps

Service providers who provide online video viewing services on mobile devices through apps such as Netflix, Hulu, and Amazon have a different set of problems to solve. The primary objective of these companies is to provide uninterrupted service to all consumers. They may be interested in better design of their apps. Users' video viewing patterns may be determined by using data mining techniques on the historical viewing patterns, something that may be used for better cache management policies for the apps. How much cache should an app use in order to show uninterrupted video while avoiding becoming a data-hogging app? Also, how can the app efficiently download a portion of the movie/music in the background when the phone is not in use? Cache management from browsers have been studied in the past (Tan and Mookerjee 2002); these policies may be further improvised by considering the historical data about the customers to fit in the contexts of mobile devices.

3.2.3 Operations of Mobile Network Service

Telecommunication service providers are trying to optimize the usage of data over the network by reducing the data download/upload speeds of the users who transfer disproportionately large amounts of data. Their goal is to discourage some users who burden the network and slow down the speed in the network for all users. Usually, the impact is concentrated in a localized network (i.e., one data-hogging user impacts some users around them but cannot impact the network of the entire country). There may be several approaches to addressing this problem of managing usage of data by the customers. One way is that the service provider dynamically decides on how much of a reduction in speed should be done for a data-hogging user in a local network based on the overall usage of data in the network at a specific time of the day. Right now, the policy is static and depends on identifying users who use data significantly more than the population (such as the top 5% of data users) in a month (Chowdhry 2014). Another policy (which already exists) hinges on designing data price contracts in a tiered manner where the price of data is dependent on the level of use. The question remains: How do these policies compare with each other? A hybrid approach may be that the customer may be charged extra for transferring disproportionate amounts of data over the network based on the overall burden on the network, which the network provider will know and not the customer. Perhaps this information asymmetry will discourage customers from using disproportionate amounts of data.

4 Online Advertising

Digital advertisement is growing at a rapid pace. In 2015, the total worldwide ad spending reached $569.65 billion (Media Buying 2015). In digital advertisement, the majority of the negotiation and the placement of the advertisement happens programmatically. That has opened up a new avenue for application of data analytics techniques.

4.1 Advertisement Scheduling

The problem with advertisement scheduling includes the decisions about which advertisement to deliver, who the advertisement will be delivered to, and when will the advertisement go live. This is modeled as a placement problem where there is a schedule of length L consisting of several slots where ads can be placed and a collection of ads must be scheduled in that time frame. In a simplistic model, each slot is assumed to be homogenous, whereas in complex models, various slots are assumed to represent advertisement placeholders with different width and heights. Similar problems for traditional media were addressed earlier with OM techniques. However, one of the key differences between the previously addressed problem and the problem in-hand for digital advertisement is the real-time nature of the problem and the scale. With digital advertising, at any time, any advertisement system can deal with thousands of potential ads and millions of users. On top of that, every online ad placement decision needs to be taken within 200 milliseconds (IAB 2014). This makes the problem more challenging and worthy of fresh looks in this newer context.

This is typically an optimization problem where the revenue of the publisher is maximized with varied constraints. Kumar et al. (2006) develop this problem as a revenue-maximization problem. They show that this problem maps to an NP-Hard problem and develop different heuristics. On the other hand, Freund and Naor (2004) develop it as a profit-maximization problem. They map the problem to a job scheduling problem and solve it by combining Knapsack Relaxation with a greedy heuristic. Kumar et al. (2007) incorporate a more complex pricing mechanism in the optimization model. They consider a scenario where advertisers pay based on both the number of exposures and the number of clicks. They also map the problem to a variation of the Knapsack problem and develop a heuristic. Most recently, Mookerjee et al. (2016) developed a predictive model of a visitor clicking on a given ad. Using this prediction, they developed a decision-model that uses a threshold to decide whether or not to show an ad to the visitor. For a review of optimization issues in web and mobile advertising, please refer to Kumar (2016).

4.2 Real-Time Bidding Platforms

Most of the above research focuses on the advertisement placement with the assumptions that all these advertisement slots have equal prices. However, with programmatic advertisement platforms, pricing advertisement slots based on auction is becoming a popular approach. This method has been adopted by Google AdWords (Mehta et al. 2007), where slots associated with a particular word are auctioned to advertisers. Real-time bidding (RTB) (Mookerjee et al. 2012; Ebbert 2015) is the platform through which such auctions are carried out.

4.2.1 The Ad Allocation Problem

There are several open problems in this context: How do we design better online algorithms to allocate and serve ads from several competing sources operating within finite time and resource constraints? How can we model the mobile ad-auctioning process on exchanges as a non-cooperative game for which an equilibrium can be searched, where none of the party will gain anything by changing its strategy? What is the equilibrium strategy for each bidder?

4.2.2 Audience Targeting in Mobile Apps

The problem with audience profiling in the context of web display ads is due to the presence and active use of web cookies to track audience history. However, the absence of such cookie-driven capabilities in mobile phones makes it difficult to do the same sort of tracking for mobile app users. An interesting research challenge for the data science researchers could be to conceptualize new and innovative identity metrics for mobile devices. Based on these identity metrics, devices and perhaps even users could be effectively identified and targeted. The key research question challenging researchers in this domain of work can be summarized as follows: In absence of panel-based techniques to measure app popularity, how can we design and develop newer strategies to capture unbiased audience data from mobile apps?

4.2.3 Technology Challenges

A frequently cited question that seems to have come up in recent debates is whether RTB imposes a certain additional latency on the app usage. Indeed, a number of app developers have shunned away from trading on the exchanges via demand-side platforms (DSPs) as they feel that the delay incurred might compromise the user app experience. How do we develop systems that are optimized for handling high-volume and high-velocity data streams from disparate sources and how do we use these systems to evaluate this real-time data in an unbiased fashion?

4.2.4 Auctioning Strategies

Auctioning over ad exchanges typically uses a generalized second-pricing (GSP) strategy. In the GSP-type auction, the DSP with the highest bid gets the top position but pays the bid amount of the second-highest bidding DSP. However, most existing works on static auctioning make the naïve assumptions that all bidders are aware of each other's valuation of the impressions. However, this is patently untrue in the context of ad serving as the evaluating strategy of each bidder is decided in real-time based on three factors: the remaining budget, the degree of match with the impression, and the recency of the last ad served under the same campaign (i.e., advertisers prefer to space out their ad serving over time) (Mookerjee et al. 2014). This calls for an increased focus on using many different types of auctioning strategies to see which performs better in the context of RTB. Researchers working with the economic aspects of digital media might find it increasingly fruitful to expand existing work in this area and answer the following key research question: What is a dominant and successful bidding strategy for programmatic buying of mobile ads?

4.2.5 Security and Privacy Research

In today's world, advertisements are highly personalized. This is because end-user devices (such as mobile phone and smartwatch) are inherently private devices. The key questions here that might pique the interest of researchers working in the security and privacy domains are as follows: How do we develop privacy-preserving technologies and protocols to measure audience information in mobile apps? How do we ensure anonymization of private data before passing it on to other stakeholders (ad networks, ad exchanges, etc.) in the mobile advertising supply chain?

5 Smart Cities

The use of big data for building smart cities has gained momentum due to the availability of state-of-the-art technology at affordable costs and availability of data and business analytics techniques. As the processing speed and storage capacities of devices increase along with the decrease in device sizes, city planners now find it feasible to use technology for the automation of public services (Booker 2014). However, academic research demonstrating the use of big data and analytics for city planning is still scant.

5.1 Existing Research on the Use of Big Data for City Planning

Increasingly, smart cities use digital devices and infrastructure that produce big data (Kitchin 2014). Smart city advocates argue that such data enables real-time analysis of city life, creates new modes of urban governance, and provides the raw material for envisioning and enacting cities that are more efficient, sustainable, competitive, productive, open, and transparent. Technical breakthroughs (e.g., IBM's Watson supercomputer) aid in analyzing large amounts of data for decision making. In Washington, D.C., a software system analyzes the city's water system—pipes, valves, and drains—in order to predict the possible time of failure of the systems so that the repairs can be planned (Woody 2011). Furthermore, the horizon of decision making will become shorter and frequency of decision making will increase, i.e., city planners will shift to short-term (dynamic) planning from long-term (static) planning (Batty 2013). Big data will become the source of information at every decision horizon. The significantly improved computational capabilities will enable the processing of information quickly by the city planners, thereby enabling adjustments in city planning more frequently than before. Such decision problems may include preparing the cities for weather related events; planning suitable manpower for various routine city operations (such as transportation services, flow of goods, and utilities); event planning in the cities; infrastructure development planning; and city expansions.

5.1.1 City Transportation

One of the important operations components in any city is transportation. Driverless trains are common at airports as they run on dedicated links between multiple hubs (terminals, for example). However, the automation of cars and public transports on the road will significantly change how cities operate. According to Brynjolfsson and McAfee (2012), autonomous vehicles are one of the many technologies that should be noticed in the near future. As they mention, Google's experiment with autonomous cars has received worldwide attention from customers and policy-makers alike. Google used its vast collections of maps and street view data to create software based on artificial intelligence algorithms that can drive a car successfully on the road without any human intervention.

Planning for vehicle parking is another important function of city planners. In large cities like Pittsburgh, a system like ParkPGH that can predict the location of parking garages with space available can save significant amounts of time and energy (Fabusuyi et al. 2014). Apart from cars, bicycles are another important mode of transportation in many cities, particularly in environmentally conscious countries like the Netherlands. Erdogan et al. (2015) propose an algorithm for efficient rebalancing of the bicycles across stations, where the number of bicycles in each station has to be restored to its target value by a truck through pickup and delivery operations.

5.1.2 City Energy Needs

In the context of managing energy needs, PowerTAC is a system designed to simulate the demand and supply of energy in the market and test various policies to help in improving the balance of demand and supply of energy that eventually leads to efficient generation and use of electricity (Ketter et al. 2013). Smart Electric Grid may critically rely on advances in intelligent decentralized control mechanisms (Peters et al. 2013). Researchers have proposed a novel class of autonomous broker agents for retail electricity trading that can operate in a wide range of Smart Electricity Markets, and are capable of deriving long-term, profit-maximizing policies. In another important direction of energy management, cloud computing based technologies are used for using energy efficiently in schools (Priceschool 2015).

5.1.3 Law Enforcement

The use of big data also helps improve decision making for law-and-order in cities. There is increasing evidence of the use of real-time data and analytics for helping law enforcement patrol parties. Efficient algorithms are used for deciding patrol sectors based on performance attributes such as workload and response time (Camacho-Collados et al. 2015). The Los Angeles Police Department even relies on predictive models that crunch data in real time to determine where to send officers to thwart would-be thieves and burglars (Risling 2012).

5.2 Future Research Directions for Smart Cities

Future research may explore several directions in the domain of smart cities development. With the availability of mobile community-based apps (such as Waze), users can tag traffic incidents, jams, and accidents that are happening on the roads in real-time. How can we design a system that uses this real-time information to plan emergency vehicle routes as well as the allocation of resources during an emergency? Predictive models may determine the likely places in the cities where incidents may happen and when on particular days to manage their operations in a better way. Development of such systems is an important area of research requiring use of text, photos, audio, and video analysis.

Autonomous vehicles are very likely to use these real-time data to plan routes and help in improving the flow of traffic within cities. However, an important question that the policy-makers are struggling with is: how to design the vehicle insurance contracts and amend the traffic rules to include the autonomous vehicles? When an incident happens, should the driver be held liable? Insurance companies are struggling with the question of deciding the premiums for autonomous vehicles. Should the premiums be lowered (and to what extent) with the human driver out of the driver's seat, since machines are less likely to make mistakes? Simulations using data on driving related incidents, driving habits of the users, localities where the drivers frequent and live, crime statistics of the areas where a driver usually drives the car, etc., should be used to answer these questions. Such use of data on deciding premiums is not unusual; companies like Progressive and State Farm have programs that decide premiums based on data collected about driving habits of a person. However, the abundance of data available will help in making better predictive models and answering the questions regarding the new age of autonomous vehicles.

5.2.1 Potential Applications in Disaster Management

Real-time data collection and analytics may also help in disaster recovery situations. Tomnod used crowdsourcing to identify the parts of a missing Malaysian jet (Fishwick 2014). Deployment of such systems statewide may help in identifying people in distress when disasters strike; using satellite images, thousands of users may tag places. Such data may be used to develop models that help in deciding where the rescue teams should focus to evacuate victims. Researchers may focus on design, deployment, and use of such systems on a large scale. Several open questions exist in this domain. What are the incentives for states to participate in a central disaster recovery management system? How much supplies should be kept in inventory to meet the demands of disasters (Manoj et al. 2016)? In anticipation of disasters, how should companies spread their orders for raw materials so that the cost of managing multiple vendors is minimized while reducing the risk of non-availability of raw materials? In a well-known incident in 2011, computer manufacturers were not able to meet demands in the market because Thailand, where most of the hard-disks are manufactured, was flooded after the tsunami. The past data on natural disasters can be used to assess risks and to decide where the temporary warehouses should be located (Manoj et al. 2016)? More discussions on disaster management can be found in Chapter 29.

6 Energy

Energy shortage and increasing consumption of energy have become major concerns in today's world. The application of data analytics and optimization techniques for generation, distribution, and use of energy has become a popular approach to respond to these concerns. Several research approaches are being carried out in this direction. However, it is still a very nascent area that needs further discussion and research as it grows.

6.1 Generation and Distribution of Energy

The placement of generation units is a classic optimization problem that has been well-studied in electrical engineering literature. However, with the increased popularity of renewable and alternative energy sources, as smaller (and micro-size) generation units become popular (every household with a solar unit becomes a micro-generation station), the use of these resources and the distribution of the power in the grid become an interesting research area. Such research needs to rely on optimization model and techniques, but also on data analytics to bring clarity derived from real-data to the system.

Typically, there is uncertainty about the renewable energy source. For example, wind power depends on the speed of air flow, while solar energy depends on the intensity of sunlight. Additionally, if energy generated locally is consumed by a household, the household will act as the consumer of the energy, whereas if the consumption is lower than the amount generated, they will act as the generating unit. In such scenarios, data analytics on historical data and predictive analytics can be used to predict and optimize the energy generation and distribution in the grid. This is a complex issue that involves technical, legal, and political challenges, which becomes clear from the recent controversy related to Nevada's decision of decreasing the price of excess solar energy fed back to the grid (Kaften 2016).

6.2 Energy Consumption

As the generation and distribution of energy is optimized, the consumption of energy also needs to be addressed. The management of energy consumption requires collecting detailed data about energy consumption, running analytics, and identifying the opportunities where reduction in energy consumption is possible. The optimization of energy consumption has mainly focused on two aspects: optimizing the energy consumption in data-centers and optimizing the energy consumption in buildings.

Marwah et al. (2009) explore the role of data analysis, visualization, and knowledge discovery techniques in improving the energy consumption of a data center. Researchers have also proposed ways to reduce the energy cost of data centers by storing energy during low-demand time in a battery and use it during high-demand time (Yao et al. 2014).

Another growing area centers on the application of data analytics and optimization techniques to manage the energy utilization of factories and office buildings. Singh et al. (2013) developed a cloud-based architecture that provides consumers with fast access and fine-grained control over their usage data, as well as the ability to analyze this data with data analytics and optimization algorithms. Another utilization of data analytics techniques in energy management is the knowledge about how to retrofit old buildings to make them high-energy performing buildings (Hong et al. 2014).

7 Healthcare

Healthcare operations have been an important area of POM research for a very long time. However, the availability of data about patients, diseases, service providers, and healthy people through sources such as social media and searches, and the digitization of services through the large scale use of IT have suddenly invigorated this area of research. On top of that, the US government's recent attempts to improve healthcare services through the Patient Protection and Affordable Care Act (PPACA), which is considered by some as one of the greatest healthcare reforms in history since Medicare in 1965 (Obamacarefacts 2015), have made this domain a very important area of research.

7.1 Existing Research in Healthcare

Although this area of research is old, we choose to discuss the research that has happened in the last few years.

7.1.1 Healthcare and Information Technology

The main objective of PPACA is to make healthcare services affordable to everyone. One of the several ways to make this possible is to cut healthcare costs (which has increased as a percentage of GDP from 9% in 1980 to 17% in 2014 (Economist 2015)) and improve quality of care (Youn et al. 2015). In this direction, Healthcare Information Exchange (HIE) is considered to be an important initiative (Demirezen et al. 2016). Some recent studies use econometric analysis on large-scale archival data to understand the impact of HIE. A study of the adoption, use, and involvement of clinical practices by Yaraghi et al. (2015) shows that the position of a physician in a network of patients is an important determinant of HIE adoption and use. Another study examines the privacy related questions of consumers on disclosing their information for digitization (Anderson and Agarwal 2011). They found that the type of information requested and the timing for when the information is sought play key roles in the willingness to provide information by the patients.

Some other studies have studied and analyzed the impact of IT on regular operations of hospitals and clinics. For example, Bardhan et al. (2015) develop a predictive model to determine when and whether a readmission will occur, and how often readmissions will occur. They find that health IT usage, patient demographics, visit characteristics, payer type, and hospital characteristics are significantly associated with patient readmission risk. For improving care at clinical-levels through dynamic decision making, Meyer et al. (2014) propose a decision-tree based predictive model to improve treatment strategies for Type-2 diabetes patients.

7.1.2 Device Manufacturing

Healthcare can be conceptualized as a bundle of goods, services, and experiences—including diet and exercise, drugs, devices, invasive procedures, new biologics, travel and lodging, and payment and reimbursement (Sinha and Kohnke 2009). Using a case of cardiovascular diseases, they propose a framework to provide insights to the organizations that deal with the design of supply chain for the healthcare sector. Within the supply chain of medical devices, factors affecting recalls of devices is an important topic to study (Thirumalai and Sinha 2011). Researchers find that, at an aggregate level, the costs of introducing poor quality products in the market are not severe.

7.1.3 Role of Online Communities in Healthcare

Yan and Tan (2014) show that the social support exchanged in an online healthcare community improves patients' mental health. Another study examines the driving forces behind patients' social network formation and evolution (Yan et al. 2015). This study finds that the firsthand disease experience increases the probability that patients will find others with similar concerns and establish communication ties. Kostkova et al. (2014) use user-generated content and social media for predicting disease spread by exploiting the two-way communication nature of Twitter. This study demonstrates the role of the social network for early warning by detecting an upcoming spike in an epidemic before the official surveillance systems.

7.2 Potential Questions for Future Research

Given the focus on reduction of healthcare costs and increase of coverage, researchers may study several problems related to participation and adoption of HIEs, health insurance exchange, efficient and proper use of expensive medical devices, tracking of diseases through online channels, social networks of patients, etc.

7.2.1 Healthcare Information Exchange

Regarding HIEs, one of the major hurdles is the fragmented nature of these exchanges and difficulty in sharing information across all hospitals and clinics across the country. The development of standard working procedures, protocols, and interface designs, in consultation with physicians, nurses, and other stakeholders, is essential to make full information exchangeability a reality. This stream of research may take cues from many government departments, such as Department Homeland Security and Social Security Administration, which already have functioning systems where information can be exchanged across state borders. A big challenge in establishing a large-scale HIE is: How to involve private clinics and hospitals?

Studies should focus on various factors and incentives for hospitals and clinics to participate in HIE (Demirezen et al. 2016). Also, hospitals and clinics widely differ in the quality of services and the demographics of patients they serve. How do these factors affect the incentives of service providers to participate in an HIE? Such studies would require large amounts of data from various healthcare service providers spread across different geographical areas. Part of the data may already exist in their IT systems, and surveys may be employed to collect more data.

7.2.2 Privacy

Another area of concern is the patients' willingness to share information. Often, patients are concerned that if health records and related information are shared by the hospitals and clinics with outside parties such as retailers (who sell drugs) and insurance companies, these companies may exploit them by increasing the prices of drugs and insurance rates. An interesting and important research question focuses on developing the data-sharing policies. On one hand, data-sharing about patient illnesses may significantly improve the quality of service through advance planning. It may also reduce overall premiums, because data-sharing may reduce the uncertainties regarding health of customers and enable the insurance companies to plan beforehand. However, sharing personal information about patients may not always be necessary for planning. Several privacy preserving data-mining and data-sharing methods have been developed in the retail context (Li and Sarkar 2014). Such methods may be developed for sharing information about patients' health as well.

7.2.3 Online Communities

In the context of online communities for patients, many research questions have significance from the point of view of predicting disease trends. These online communities share experiences with each other, provide emotional support, suggest doctors and treatments, etc. Most of this information exists in text form. Systems may be developed to analyze these discussions to develop correlational and predictive models to get early warnings regarding increased instances of life threatening diseases like cancer, diabetes, and genetic disorders. Such a system will not only provide trends of the spread of disease, but also help in planning for future allocation of funds for drugs research, hospital, and service expenses.

7.2.4 Devices

With the development and adoption of health-monitoring technologies embedded in devices, such as Apple Watch, Android Watch, and pacemakers that can communicate wirelessly with other devices, it is now possible to develop methods to predict the health of the users and generate warning signs in case the vital signs look abnormal. Future research should focus on designing systems that are fast and efficient in analyzing the data incoming in real time and using models to generate predictions for the next few hours. Patients with prior histories of severe illnesses will especially benefit from these systems. The models in such systems should be self-learning, as the health conditions of users may change with time, and the model parameters need to adjust with the physical changes in the body. For example, metabolic rates after heavy exercise and after a meal are different for people between the ages of 25 and 40. Additionally, there may be a difference between two persons of the same age based on their current body weights, daily routines, etc. Thus, such models must incorporate self-learning characteristics, as in artificial intelligence algorithms. Variants of techniques such as Neural Networks and Bayesian learning may be used for developing such systems as they are typically used in self-learning systems.

8 Implications for Managers

Data-based decision making is the new mantra of management in the new age, which is a result of the growth in data availability, the new techniques to analyze them, and the increasing marketing competition. Accordingly, there is a growing need for operations managers to be able to use these techniques, at least at a basic level, and crunch data for making informed decisions. These data analytics techniques are often the core engines for various strategic initiatives, such as advertising, health monitoring of patients, performance monitoring for equipment (e.g., G.E. monitors the performances of aircraft engines it supplies to aircraft manufacturers in real time), retail business, and city operations. Therefore, operations managers of the current century must handle data and use analytics irrespective of their functional areas. Data analytics help managers stay ahead of the competition, create customized solutions for consumers, proactively act when systems are about to fail, anticipate the needs of consumers, create relevant products, and make optimal internal decisions to achieve all these objectives.

9   Conclusions and Directions for Future Research

In this chapter, we have described various applications of OM-based data analytics techniques. Increasing volumes and variety of data is facilitating the development of data analytics tools for decision making, especially the tools based on mathematical programming and statistical analysis. This chapter broadly outlines how these techniques have been applied in the contexts of retail, mobile, energy, advertising, smart city, and healthcare. We describe the extant literature on using OM-based data analytics approaches to solve decision problems in these domains. We also present several relatively new issues that need fresh attention given the availability of big data and new tools for data analytics. The discussions in this chapter are by no means exhaustive; rather, each of the subsections in this chapter needs separate in-depth attention. Our objective in this chapter is two-fold: First, after reading this chapter, organizations and managers should be encouraged to apply OM-based decision tools in solving data driven problems that could help them make better decisions. Second, this chapter should encourage researchers to investigate cutting-edge problems and issues relevant to future managers.

References and Bibliography

Adomavicius, G. and Y. Kwon (2014) "Optimization-Based Approaches for Maximizing Aggregate Recommendation Diversity," *INFORMS Journal on Computing*, **26**(2): 351–369.

Alleyne, R. (2011) "The Young Generation Are 'Addicted' to Mobile Phones," *The Telegraph*, www.telegraph.co.uk/technology/8458786/The-young-generation-are-addicted-to-mobile-phones.html, accessed on Nov. 26, 2011.

Anderson, C.L. and R. Agarwal (2011) "The Digitization of Healthcare: Boundary Risks, Emotion, and Consumer Willingness to Disclose Personal Health Information," *Information Systems Research*, **22**(3): 469–490.

Andrews, M., X. Luo, Z. Fang and A. Ghose (2015) "Mobile Ad Effectiveness: Hyper-Contextual Targeting with Crowdedness," *Marketing Science*, **35**(2): 218–233.

Bardhan, I., J.H. Oh, Z. Zheng and K. Kirksey (2015) "Predictive Analytics for Readmission of Patients with Congestive Heart Failure," *Information Systems Research*, **26**(1): 19–39.

Batty, M. (2013) "Big Data, Smart Cities and City Planning," *Dialogues in Human Geography*, **3**(3): 274–279.

Berthene, A. (2015) "Mobile Now Accounts for 30% of Online Transactions," *MobileStrategies360*, www.mobilestrategies360.com/2015/06/26/mobile-now-accounts-30-e-commerce-transactions, accessed on Nov. 26, 2015.

Booker, E. (2014) "Cities Get Smart with Big Data," *DataInformed*, http://data-informed.com/cities-get-smart-big-data/, accessed on Nov. 26, 2015.

Brynjolfsson, E., Y. Hu and D. Simester (2011) "Goodbye Pareto Principle, Hello Long Tail: The Effect of Search Costs on the Concentration of Product Sales," *Management Science*, **57**(8): 1373–1386.

Brynjolfsson, E. and A. McAfee (2012) "Winning the Race with Ever-Smarter Machines," *MIT Sloan Management Review*, **53**(2): 53–60.

Camacho-Collados, M., F. Liberatore and J.M. Angulo (2015) "A Multi-Criteria Police Districting Problem for the Efficient and Effective Design of Patrol Sector," *European Journal of Operational Research*, **246**(2): 674–684.

Chen, L., M. Lv, Q. Ye, G. Chen and J. Woodward (2011) "A Personal Route Prediction System Based on Trajectory Data Mining," *Information Sciences*, **181**(7): 1264–1284.

Chowdhry, A. (2014) "Verizon to Slow Down 4G LTE for Top 5% Data Users Starting in October," *Forbes*, www.forbes.com/sites/amitchowdhry/2014/07/26/verizon-to-slow-down-4g-lte-for-top-5-data-users-starting-in-october/, accessed on Nov. 26, 2015.

Demirezen, E.M. and S. Kumar (2016) "Optimization of Recommender Systems Based on Inventory," *Production and Operations Management*, **25**(4): 593–608.

Demirezen, E.M., S. Kumar and A. Sen (2016) "Sustainability of Healthcare Information Exchanges: A Game-Theoretic Approach," *Information Systems Research*, Article-in-Advance.

Ebbert, J. (2015) "Define It—What Is Real-Time Bidding?" *AdExchanger*, http://adexchanger.com/online-advertising/real-time-bidding/, accessed on March 11, 2015.

Economist (2015) "Will Obamacare Cut Costs?" *The Economist*, www.economist.com/news/united-states/21645855-growth-americas-health-care-spending-slowing-will-obamacare-cut-costs, accessed on Nov. 26, 2015.

Erdogan, G., M. Battarra and R. Wolfler (2015) "An Exact Algorithm for the Static Rebalancing Problem Arising in Bicycle Sharing Systems," *European Journal of Operational Research*, **245**: 667–679.

Fabusuyi, T., R.C. Hampshire, V.A. Hill and K. Sasanuma (2014) "Decision Analytics for Parking Availability in Downtown Pittsburgh," *Interfaces*, **44**(3): 286–299.

Fang, Z., B. Gu, X. Luo and Y. Xu (2015) "Contemporaneous and Delayed Sales Impact of Location-Based Mobile Promotions," *Information Systems Research*, **26**(3): 552–564.

Fishwick, C. (2015) "Tomnod—The Online Search Party Looking for Malaysian Airlines Flight MH370," *The Guardian*, www.theguardian.com/world/2014/mar/14/tomnod-online-search-malaysian-airlines-flight-mh370, accessed on Nov. 26, 2015.

Fleder, D. and K. Hosanagar (2009) "Blockbuster Culture's Next Rise or Fall: The Impact of Recommender Systems on Sales Diversity," *Management Science*, **55**(5): 697–712.

Freund, A.J. and J. Naor (Seffi) (2004) "Approximating the Advertisement Placement Problem," *Journal of Scheduling*, **7**(5): 365–374.

Ghose, A. and S. P. Han (2014) "Estimating Demand for Mobile Applications in the New Economy," *Management Science*, **60**(6): 1470–1488.

Ghoshal, A., S. Kumar and V. Mookerjee (2015) "Impact of Recommender Systems on Competition between Personalizing and Non-Personalizing Firms," *Journal of Management Information Systems*, **31**(4): 243–277.

Haubl, G. and V. Trifts (2000) "Shopping Environments: The Effects of Interactive Decision Aids," *Marketing Science*, **19**(1): 4–21.

Hong, T., L. Yang, D. Hill and W. Feng (2014) "Data and Analytics to Inform Energy Retrofit of High Performance Buildings," *Applied Energy*, **126**: 90–106.

IAB (2014) "Open RTB API Specification Version 2.3," www.iab.com/wp-content/uploads/2015/05/OpenRTB_API_Specification_Version_2_3_1.pdf, accessed on Apr. 21, 2016.

Janakiraman, R., Y. Liu, R. Bezawada and S. Kumar (2013) "A Structural Model of Consumers' Perception of Channel Fit and Consumer Channel Choice: Evidence from a Multichannel Retailer," *Conference on Information Systems and Technology (CIST)*, October 5–6, Minneapolis, MN.

Kaften, C. (2016) "Nevada PUC Hikes Costs for Commercial, Residential Rooftop Solar," retrieved April 4, 2016, from www.energymanagertoday.com/nevada-puc-hikes-costs-for-commercial-residential-rooftop-solar-0121119/.

Ketter, W., J. Collins and P. Reddy (2013) "Power TAC: A Competitive Economic Simulation of the Smart Grid," *Energy Economics*, **39**: 262–270.

Kitchin, R. (2014) "The Real-Time City? Big Data and Smart Urbanism," *GeoJournal*, **79**(1): 1–14.

Kostkova, P., M. Szomszor, and C. St. Louis (2014) "#swineflu: The Use of Twitter as an Early Warning and Risk Communication Tool in the 2009 Swine Flu Pandemic," *ACM Transactions on Management Information Systems*, **5**(2): 8:1–8:25.

Kumar, A., A. Mehra and S. Kumar (2014) "Can Facilitating Multichannel Usage Improve Customer Value for Firms?" *Conference on Information Systems and Technology (CIST)*, November 8–9, San Francisco, CA.

Kumar, S. (2016) *Optimization Issues in Web and Mobile Advertising: Past and Future Trends*. Springer, New York.

Kumar, S., M. Dawande and V. Mookerjee (2007) "Optimal Scheduling and Placement of Internet Banner Advertisements," *IEEE Transactions on Knowledge and Data Engineering*, **19**(11): 1571–1584.

Kumar, S., V.S. Jacob and C. Sriskandarajah (2006) "Scheduling Advertisements on a Web Page to Maximize Revenue," *European Journal of Operational Research*, **173**(3): 1067–1089.

Li, X. and S. Sarkar (2014) "Digression and Value Concatenation to Enable Privacy-Preserving Regression," *Management Information Systems Quarterly*, **38**(3): 679–698.

Liedtke, B.M. (2012) "Netflix Works on Improving Recommendations," *USA Today*, http://usatoday30.usatoday.com/tech/news/story/2012-04-09/netflix-recommendations-video/54133648/1, accessed on Nov. 26, 2015.

Luo, X., M. Andrews, Z. Fang and C.W. Phang (2014) "Mobile Targeting," *Management Science*, **50**(3): 352–364.

Manoj, U.V., S. Kumar and S. Gupta (2016) "An Integrated Logistic Model for Predictable Disasters," *Production and Operations Management*, **25**(5): 791–811.

Marwah, M., R. Sharma, R. Shih, C. Patel, V. Bhatia, M. Mekanapurath, R. Velumani and S. Velayudhan (2009) "Data Analysis, Visualization and Knowledge Discovery in Sustainable Data Centers," *Proceedings of the 2nd Bangalore Annual Compute Conference (COMPUTE '09)*, Bangalore, India.

Media Buying (2015) "Mobile Ad Spend to Top $100 Billion Worldwide in 2016, 51% of Digital Market," www.emarketer.com/Article/Mobile-Ad-Spend-Top-100-Billion-Worldwide-2016-51-of-Digital-Market/1012299, accessed on Apr. 21, 2016.

Mehra, A., S. Kumar and J.S. Raju (2013) "Showrooming and the Competition between Store and Online Retailers," *Summer Institute in Competitive Strategy (SICS)*, June 24–28, Berkeley, CA.

Mehta, A., A. Saberi, U. Vazirani and V. Vazirani (2007) "AdWords and Generalized Online Matching," *Journal of the ACM*, **54**(5): XXX.

Meyer, G., G. Adomavicius, P.E. Johnson, M. Elidrisi, W.A. Rush, J.M. Sperl-Hillen and P.J. O'Connor (2014) "A Machine Learning Approach to Improving Dynamic Decision Making," *Information Systems Research*, **25**(2): 239–263.

Mookerjee, R., S. Kumar and V. Mookerjee (2012) "To Show or Not Show: Using User Profiling to Manage Internet Advertisement Campaigns," *Interfaces*, **42**(5): 449–464.

Mookerjee, R., S. Kumar and V. Mookerjee (2016) "Optimizing Performance Based Internet Advertisement Campaigns," *Operations Research*, Article-in-Advance.

Mookerjee, R., S. Kumar, V. Mookerjee and C. Sriskandarajah (2014) "Demand-Supply Optimization in Mobile Advertising," *Proceedings of the 24th Annual Workshop on Information Technologies and Systems (WITS)*, December 17–19, Auckland, New Zealand.

Murthi, B.P.S. and S. Sarkar (2003) "The Role of the Management Sciences in Research on Personalization," *Management Science*, **49**(10): 1344–1362.

Nielsen (2014) "How Smartphones are Changing Consumer's Daily Routines, Around the Globe," *Nielsen*, www.nielsen.com/us/en/insights/news/2014/how-smartphones-are-changing-consumers-daily-routines-around-the-globe.html, accessed on Nov. 26, 2015.

Obamacarefacts (2015) http://obamacarefacts.com/, accessed on Nov. 26, 2015.

Pathak, B., R. Garfinkel, R.D. Gopal, R. Venkatesan and F. Yin (2010) "Empirical Analysis of the Impact of Recommender Systems on Sales," *Journal of Management Information Systems*, **27**(2): 159–188.

Peters, M., W. Ketter, M. Saar-Tsechansky and J. Collins (2013) "A Reinforcement Learning Approach to Autonomous Decision-Making in Smart Electricity Markets," *Machine Learning*, **92**(1): 5–39.

Priceschool (2010) "Customer Solution Case Study Primary School's Energy Management Transformed by Cloud-based Insights," *priceschool.info*, https://customers.microsoft.com/Pages/Download.aspx?id=21110, accessed on Nov. 26, 2015.

Provost, F., D. Martens and A. Murray (2015) "Finding Similar Mobile Consumers with a Privacy-Friendly Geosocial Design," *Information Systems Research*, **26**(2): 243–265.

Ricci, F., L. Rokach, B. Shapira and P.B. Kantor (2011) *Recommender System Handbook*. Springer, New York.

Risling, G. (2012) "'Predictive Policing' Technology Lowers Crime in Los Angeles," *Huffingtonpost*, www.huffingtonpost.com/2012/07/01/predictive-policing-technology-los-angeles_n_1641276.html, accessed on Nov. 26, 2015.

Sahoo, N., P.V. Singh, T. Mukhopadhyay (2012) "A Hidden Markov Model for Collaborative Filtering," *Management Information Systems Quarterly*, **36**(4): 1329–1356.

Singh, R.P., S. Keshav and T. Brecht (2013) "A Cloud-based Consumer-centric Architecture for Energy Data Analytics," *Proceedings of the Fourth International Conference on Future Energy Systems (e-Energy '13)*, pp. 63–74.

Sinha, K.K. and E.J. Kohnke (2009) "Health Care Supply Chain Design: Toward Linking the Development and Delivery of Care Globally," *Decision Sciences*, **40**(2): 197–212.

Tan, Y. and V.S. Mookerjee (2002) "Analysis of a Least Recently Used Cache Management Policy for Web Browsers," *Operations Research*, **50**(2): 345–357.

Thirumalai, S. and K.K. Sinha (2011) "Product Recalls in the Medical Device Industry: An Empirical Exploration of the Sources and Financial Consequences," *Management Science*, **57**(2): 376–392.

Wang, Y., E. Lim and S. Hwang (2006) "Efficient Mining of Group Patterns from User Movement Data," *Data and Knowledge Engineering*, **57**(3): 240–282.

Woody, T. (2011) "If Watson Can Win Jeopardy, Can IBM Make Cities Smarter?" http://grist.org/smart-cities/2011-03-02-if-watson-can-win-jeopardy-can-ibm-make-cities-smarter/, accessed on Nov. 26, 2015.

Xia, M., Y. Zhang, L. Weng and X. Ye (2012) "Fashion Retailing Forecasting Based on Extreme Learning Machine with Adaptive Metrics of Inputs," *Knowledge-Based Systems*, **36**: 253–259.

Yan, L., J. Peng and Y. Tan (2015) "Network Dynamics: How Can We Find Patients Like Us?" *Information Systems Research*, **26**(3): 496–512.

Yan, L. and Y. Tan (2014) "Feeling Blue? Go Online: An Empirical Study of Social Support among Patients," *Information Systems Research*, **25**(4): 690–709.

Yao, J., X. Liu and C. Zhang (2014) "Predictive Electricity Cost Minimization through Energy Buffering in Data Centers," *IEEE Transactions on Smart Grid*, **5**(1): 230–238.

Yaraghi, N., A.Y. Du, R. Sharman, R.D. Gopal and R. Ramesh (2015) "Health Information Exchange as a Multisided Platform: Adoption, Usage, and Practice Involvement in Service Co-Production," *Information Systems Research*, **26**(1): 1–18.

Youn, S., G. Heim, S. Kumar and C. Sriskandarajah (2015) "Relationship between Variation in Medical Charges and Quality of Care: An Empirical Analysis for Payment Reform Models," *Healthcare Conference: Patient-Centric HealthCare Management in the Age of Analytics*, Bloomington, IN.

16

THE EVOLUTION OF LOGISTICS CLUSTERS

Yossi Sheffi and Liliana Rivera

1 Introduction

The logistics function encompasses activities such as transportation, warehousing, planning, and facilities location (Kasilingman 1998). The demand for logistics services arises from the need to move materials, parts, and products in space and in time—through a supply chain of intermediate facilities and players, to final consumers, as well as returns and responsible discarding. This process has to be accomplished in a time-efficient, high-quality (Groothedde et al. 2005; Stank and Goldsby 2000), and cost-effective manner (Xu and Hancock 2004), which is what logistics management is focused on. Logistics management is a fundamental supporting role for any industrial sector associated with physical products. An efficient logistics sector promotes high level-of-service and low-cost delivery and thus is a key to industrial competitiveness. Interestingly, logistics facilities and operations tend to cluster in the same geographical locations.

Sheffi (2012) defines logistics clusters as spatial agglomerations (that is, a collection of items in the same geography) of logistics operations and firms. These include logistics services providers such as transportation carriers, warehouse operators, and third-party logistics providers (3PLs). These providers are defined as firms providing multiple logistics services, usually integrated or bundled together by the provider for use by customers (CSCMP 2013), logistics divisions (and distribution centers) of manufacturers and retailers, and companies with logistics-intensive operations such as automobile manufacturers or bulk commodities distributors. Because efficiency in logistics can deliver competitive advantages and agglomeration can enable efficiency in logistics, logistics clusters have gained the attention of private enterprises and governments worldwide.

This unique, popular, and successful type of agglomeration is being developed all around the world through massive capital investments. For instance, in Zaragoza, Spain, the Government of Aragon invested €680 million to develop the Plataforma Logística de Zaragoza (PLAZA), which has become the core of the Zaragoza logistics cluster and the largest logistics park in Europe. Logistics parks are organizations with clearly defined ownership and geographic property boundaries. This is in contrast to a logistics cluster that is an amorphous agglomeration of companies and facilities with logistics-intensive operations that have fuzzy borders and no central management (Sheffi 2012). Similarly, the Panamanian government's five-year plan includes an expected investment of more than $2 billion to position the country as the logistics hub for the Americas, based on logistics clusters at both ends of the expanded Panama Canal. In the United States, the

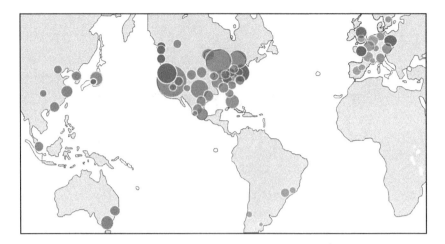

Figure 16.1 Logistics Clusters Map
Source: Prologis 2015

Dallas Logistics Hub was developed with an investment of more than $500 million, including $113 million from public sources (Hethcock 2010). As seen in Figure 16.1, new clusters are being developed, and existing logistics clusters are also expanding their scale and scope. Such is the case, for example, of the logistics clusters in Singapore, Rotterdam, Dubai, Los Angeles, New York, Miami, Memphis, Atlanta, Chicago, and others (Rivera et al. 2014).

2 Literature Review of Industrial Clusters

For almost a century, economists have studied industrial agglomeration in different contexts. Marshall (1890) identified three positive externalities associated with industrial clusters: knowledge sharing, the development of specialized labor pools, and the development of a suppliers' base. Weber and Friedrich (1929) argued that agglomerated companies enjoy benefits from external economies of scale, specifically those provided by localization economies (Hoover 1937) that arise when firms from a particular sector co-locate.

2.1 *Increased Productivity and Innovation*

More recently, a branch of literature argues that, in addition, intra-cluster competition (see Section 4) fosters an increase in productivity and innovation, thus positioning co-located companies a step ahead of non-clustered firms and fostering new business creation within clusters (Porter 1998; Delgado et al. 2010). In addition, the close proximity allows for collaboration, which allows clustered companies to act as if they were formally bonded with each other but still keep their flexibility. This allows companies to enjoy some of the benefits of large companies (reach and resources), while avoiding large-company problems (slow decision-making and bureaucracy). An explanation of the clustering trend (Feser 2008; Ellison et al. 2010) states that clusters provide higher collective learning as well as tacit knowledge exchange. (Collective learning is the process of learning through a synergy that has been developed after interaction and communication (Granberg and Ohlsson 2005; King and Rowe 1999) while tacit knowledge exchange involves knowledge that cannot be verbalized or articulated and is closely related to intuition and personal experience (Nonaka et al. 2000).) Both of these types of knowledge exchange have been shown as keys to fostering innovation (Keeble and Wilkinson 2000; Maskell 2001; Leamer and Storper 2001). By and large, the benefits of industrial clusters grow as the clusters themselves become larger. The larger freight volumes in and out of a logistics cluster mean lower transportation costs (because carriers can use large conveyances at high utilization) and better transportation level of service (owing to higher service frequencies and more direct services). Not only do the interactions between companies grow and the opportunities to collaborate multiply, but companies in the cluster enjoy more sway with local government to get the regulations and public investment they need. The result is a positive reinforcing feedback loop. The more benefits there are, the more firms join the cluster. This causes the benefits to grow further, therefore attracting even more firms. Governments are typically supportive because, as industrial clusters grow, their activities lead to regional growth (Baptista 1998) and have a positive impact on firms' competitiveness (Huo 2012).

2.2 Agglomeration Versus Dispersion

It should be noted, however, that another branch of the literature argues for the decreased relevance of industrial clustering. The argument rests on the power of modern information and communications technology which represent "the end of geography" (O'Brien 1992) and the "death of distance" (Cairncross 1997), possibly reducing the advantages of co-location. Another argument is that the agglomeration of firms causes an increase of land and labor prices as clusters grow, inducing a negative externality that encourages firms to leave clusters (Henderson and Shalizi 2001; Glasmeier and Kibler 1996; Teubal et al. 1991). These authors even argue that the clustering effect has been replaced by dispersion economies (Polenske 2003) that arise when firms relocate from clusters to dispersed areas.

The academic literature includes only a few articles specifically about logistics clusters, with little mention of their prevalence. Rivera et al. (2014) study this phenomenon in the US, finding qualitative and quantitative evidence that logistics companies and logistics operations of manufacturers, retailers, and distributors have clustered and that those clusters have been growing over time. Such growth of clusters is a strong indicator of the success of such clusters and that any economic dispersion forces are weaker than the agglomeration benefits. Van Den Heuvel et al. (2013) studied the concentration of logistics-related jobs in three provinces in the Netherlands and also chronicled a trend of increased clustering.

2.3 Logistics Clusters

Most of the literature related to logistics clusters is specific to ports or airports and does not address the logistics sector in general (i.e., the interrelationships of water, air, rail, and road systems in the context of manufacturing, warehouse, and distribution networks). Haezendonck (2001), Klink and De Langen (2001), and De Langen (2002; 2004) investigated maritime clusters, concluding that the concentration of maritime activities in clusters is likely to increase over time. The economics of hubs for maritime and airfreight are similar. Martin and Román (2003) document the agglomeration of airfreight carriers in hub airports, while Lindsay and Kasadra (2011) developed the concept of the "aerotropolis," a full urban development that comes into being around an airport.

Finally, Wu et al. (2006) argue that China's economic advantage goes beyond labor costs and can be explained, in significant measure, by the presence of "supply clusters." These clusters provide all the logistics services needed for the management of global supply chains and have contributed significantly to improving China's manufacturing competitiveness.

3 Development of Logistics Clusters

Logistics clusters typically develop around two types of locations. The first is a terminal location where shipments are moved between modes of transportation, such as around ports, airport, rail hub, and intermodal yards. The second is a central location with good surface accessibility. For example, the Rotterdam logistics cluster has developed due to the port and the large volume of trade that goes through it, while the Zaragoza Logistics Cluster is strategically located in the epicenter of the four largest cities in Spain with good road and rail access.

Many logistics clusters have a long history. For example, Singapore started as a free port and the logistics cluster grew around the port, while Chicago initially started as a trading hub for Western furs and grew to become the hub of commodity exchanges and a significant logistics cluster. Cluster-building strategies are popular with government because the belief is that the government just has to seed the process and let the "flywheel" do its magic, and the cluster will grow on its own. For example, the Zaragoza cluster started because the local government wanted to diversify the local economy, which was dependent on the automotive industry. The government bought the land and attracted Zara to the park, after which several local banks and many other logistics operations joined.

The role of governments in the development and nurturing of logistics clusters is more important than with other industrial clusters because these clusters require large tracts of land, and government-controlled regulation of trade, transportation, taxation of inventory, and other regulatory edicts affecting logistics operations. Governments are also responsible for infrastructure development as well as the provision of education and training for potential employees.

4 Logistics Clusters Benefits—Intra-Cluster Collaboration

In addition to the benefits accruing to any industrial cluster, logistics clusters offer four categories of advantages for the individual firms and the regional economies where they develop (Sheffi 2012; Rivera et al. 2016; Rivera et al. 2015b). The first is intra-cluster collaborations described in this section. The others are value-added services, innovation, and job growth, all described in subsequent sections.

The co-location of firms in a logistics cluster enables the development of natural cooperative linkages. Logistics companies (or, more generally, logistics operations) typically serve many different industries. However, the operations performed by the logistics function—e.g., receiving, handling, storing, packing, shipping, transporting, and tracking—are the same regardless of "what is in the box." Thus, logistics companies serving different industries in the same locations are not really direct competitors. The results include both vertical collaborations (which are to be expected in any cluster) but also horizontal collaborations between logistics companies (Sheffi 2012; Rivera et al. 2015a). Similarities of goals and activities induce the formulation of joint strategies, solutions, or tactics. Moreover, the commonality of logistics assets (e.g., conveyances and warehouses) enable sharing of capacity; commonality of types of logistics labor (e.g., drivers, forklift operators, and pick-and-pack workers) enable sharing of labor; and commonality of logistics knowledge enables internal knowledge transfers. Importantly, geographical proximity means shared language, culture, and customs, which encourages informal ties between employees of different companies.

4.1 Transportation Capacity Sharing

The geographical proximity in logistics clusters enables time- and cost-efficient consolidation of loads from neighboring companies. Clustered firms can bundle loads going to a similar destination and use a direct service (which does not require consolidation hubs) to deliver freight. Such consolidation-by-partnering is applicable to all transportation modes: air, land, and ocean freight. For example, Finnish and Russian companies routinely perform joint air cargo and warehousing activities within the Northwest Russian Transport Logistics Cluster (Pekkarinen 2005).

An example of airplane capacity sharing is described by Sheffi (2012) at the Zaragoza Logistics Cluster, between Zara, a clothes retailer, and Caladero, a fish distributor. Clothes from Spain fly to South Africa on a jointly leased 747, which flies back a load of fish to Zaragoza. Furthermore, since fish packed in ice are heavy, Zara uses the surplus volume capacity on the northbound leg to transport wool, which is a light, fluffy cargo. Zara and Caladero benefit from their spatial proximity because they are able to reduce the cost per unit of transporting their goods in a fast and effective conveyance.

4.2   Warehouse Capacity Sharing

Logistics clusters have vast expanses of warehouses and distribution facilities. Warehouse utilization, however, fluctuates due to variations in demand. Thus, a given firm may have under-utilized space at one time or may be in need of extra space at another time. To reduce costs, firms within a cluster can lend or borrow warehouse space from neighbors. For instance, the Vermont Teddy Bear Company, a handcrafted toy maker, faces peak demand just before Valentine's Day. To cope with such orders, the company uses the space of neighboring facilities in the UPS logistics campus in Louisville, Kentucky.

Such co-locations enable smooth space exchanges without the need to train new workers, obtain new transportation contracts and or make other adjustments, which would be required if the distribution center or warehouse space exchange involved a different location. In general, companies are inclined to share their facilities and productive assets in order to achieve cost reductions and improved efficiency (Chapman et al. 2003).

4.3   Labor Sharing

Sharing employees between companies and facilities within the cluster is a common practice. The sharing is possible because of the similarity of required skills, the often non-competing nature of firms (e.g., a toy distributor and home goods distributor), frequent interactions between firms that engender trust, and the proximity of facilities. Human resource sharing is important for agglomerated businesses because it reduces recruitment and training costs, thereby increasing efficiency. Naturally, such an exchange is particularly easy when a single 3PL manages several facilities within a cluster.

For example, Exel, a logistics services provider, manages eight distribution centers (DCs) in the Alliance*Texas Logistics Park. Exel routinely shares workers between its managed DCs in order to ensure optimal performance for the different businesses it serves. The firm even created a special software tool to coordinate among DC managers who need workers and those who have extra ones in any given period. The software not only determines valid exchanges in terms of qualifications but also accounts for the work hours, charges to the correct customer, and completes the financial accounting involved.

4.4   Information Sharing

The increasing complexity of systems, services, and products has turned knowledge codification into a challenging task. Information management plays a key role in the profitability and growth of logistics operations. Logistics clusters enable company managers to have casual encounters and chance conversations which are often the basis for developing trust, leading to knowledge-sharing and formal collaborations. Shared information may include supplier requirements, customer support needs, and benchmarking data; firms may also share information about their distribution methods and routes (Rivera et al. 2015a).

This type of information exchange was observed in Air Logistics Park Singapore (ALPS), where DHL and UPS share information about customers' peculiar needs when the customer changes providers. For example, DHL had to transfer a Phillips Health Care contract for regional freight to UPS. Although DHL and UPS compete with one another, they both have incentives to ensure a smooth transfer of these contracts, something that entails sharing information about clients, routes, special requirements, and schedules. Both companies are conscious that the contracts may be transferred back to them in the next bidding process and thus they take advantage of the geographical proximity to easily coordinate such transitions (Sheffi 2012).

5 Logistics Clusters Benefits—Value-Added Services

Logistics companies typically perform many value-added activities while products spend time in their DCs. These include postponement and customization, tagging, kitting, labeling, managing returns and repairs, and preparing for retail display. Appold (1995) argues that offering value-added services increases the competitiveness of logistics establishments. Certainly, it increases the customer "stickiness" and the revenue derived from a given client. In general, it is argued that spatially concentrated firms are more likely to capture greater value in their production processes to create new products, materials, and value-adding services (Ettlie and Reza 1992). This is certainly the case for logistics clusters. As managers mention, "local value-added is the driving dimension behind a number of further operational decisions and dimensions. . . . It even determines the investments required for setting up co-located facilities" (Reichart and Holweg 2008).

Such value-added services are not only unique to logistics clusters, but they are more prevalent in such clusters as compared to dispersed locations due to the following four reasons: (i) the cross-fertilization of ideas, (ii) the ability to cooperate in the provision of value-added services, (iii) the availability of cost-effective and high-service transportation in a cluster (which helps deliver the processed goods to their destination), and (iv) the availability of specialized suppliers required for such services.

5.1 Postponement and Customization

Postponement is the practice of mass customization—shipping semi-finished goods to a distribution center and then making a late-stage adjustment or addition to the product after demand for the differentiated product is better known or orders are at hand. This allows companies to combine low-cost, long-lead time manufacturing processes (production in Asia with ocean-freight shipment) with high-service, short-lead product differentiation processes (e.g., colors, monograms, sizing, and custom assembly followed by local distribution) and just-in-time delivery. It also enables companies to respond to a sudden change in demand while reducing inventory carrying costs at the same time (Sheffi 2012).

For instance, Reebok sells replicas of National Football League (NFL) players' jerseys. Reebok cannot predict fans' demand for the apparel of particular teams and players because demand fluctuates week-to-week depending on player and team performance on the field. To satisfy demand during a surge in popularity while avoiding excess inventory, Reebok adopted a postponement strategy. The company manufactures blank jerseys overseas and sends them to its Indianapolis distribution center where it can add team's colors and players' names based on a given team's and player's popularity. The location of Reebok's distribution center within the 1,500-firm-strong Indianapolis logistics cluster allows for fast distribution. The Indianapolis logistics cluster attracts many transportation carriers—including FedEx, which has a regional hub there—leading to high level of service for outbound transportation, supporting the postponement strategy.

5.2 Retail Display Arrangement

Retail display arrangement involves organizing merchandise in specially constructed marketing displays that sit in the aisles of retail stores to increase visibility and sales, typically during promotions. It also involves the production of end-of-aisle and point-of-purchase displays, graphic design of promotional material, and so forth. Companies specializing in these types of activity can be found in most logistics clusters. For example, the Louisville area boasts twenty-five companies offering slatwall (panels made with horizontal grooves that are configured to accept a variety of merchandising accessories and are used in retail display fixtures).

In some cases, 3PL firms that operate several facilities in a cluster develop the local expertise to offer retail display production for their customers. For example, Exel in Alliance*Texas Logistics Park, builds, delivers, and installs retail displays.

5.3 Kitting

Kitting is the separation or joining of certain products or product parts to form a new, more saleable item. Firms use kitting to create product bundles (e.g., camera + lens or value-for-money multi-packs), provide product samples (e.g., a sample fabric softener with detergent), or to add promotional or seasonal accessories. For example, UPS Supply Chain Solutions, located in the logistics cluster in Louisville, handles Nikon's logistics activities. UPS receives Nikon's photographic equipment and creates kits with batteries, chargers, lenses and other equipment based on each retailer's requirements or promotional plans.

Kitting is a postponement activity that relies on the efficient transportation services available outbound from a cluster location. Such service enables last-minute promotional adjustments by retailers without creating an undue cost burden on the supplier or the 3PL.

5.4 End-of-Runway Location

Operating in a logistics cluster reduces the round-trip journey for maintenance, diagnostic services, and repair, creating a unique service offering (Sheffi 2012). For example, Flextronics operates a repair depot for laptops made by several manufacturers. It selected Memphis for the repair depot in order to allow customers to send laptops in need of repair as late as 8pm in most US cities by FedEx. The company fixes 1,500 to 2,000 laptops every night, which are then flown back to the customers 36 hours later. Therefore, a laptop dropped at a FedEx retail facility by 8:00pm on Monday in Boston, will arrive at Memphis by midnight, be at the Flextronics facility by 1:00am Tuesday, where technicians will have about 22 hours to work on it. Before midnight Tuesday, it will get back to the Memphis facility and be in Boston on the owner's desk at 8:30am Wednesday.

Such a turnaround is possible because of the FedEx hub, which is the center of the Memphis logistics hub. Similar opportunities are available to shippers located in and around Louisville, where the UPS world hub is located. When Christmas shopping includes shoes from Zappos.com, customers can place orders by December 23rd, and as long as the order was placed before 4:00 pm Eastern time, it will arrive on December 24th anywhere in the United States. This works because the Zappos fulfillment center is part of the Louisville logistics cluster developed around the UPS Worldport.

6 Logistics Clusters Benefits—Innovation

As cited in the literature review section, a number of authors describe how industrial clusters foster higher rates of innovation, knowledge creation, and knowledge transfer within the cluster. The same is true of logistics clusters. However, logistics clusters offer two special innovation benefits in the form of environmental innovations and inter-cluster transfers of innovation.

6.1 Environmental Innovation

In general, logistics clusters improve the efficiency of transportation activities owing to the use of larger conveyances and higher utilization of these conveyances, both of which generally reduce total freight transportation environmental emissions. However, while reducing environmental impact globally, clusters can create local environmental nuisances for the communities around them as a result of concentrated fumes leading to health effects. Through community pressure and enabled by the concentration of resources, logistics clusters became a hotbed of environmental innovation (e.g., Port of Singapore biodiesel plant, or the Ports of LA/LB Clean Air Action Plan) that may not have occurred if the emissions were more diffused in a world without logistics clusters.

Innovation activities around the Port of Los Angeles—spurred by environmental lawsuits and regulation—illustrate this phenomenon. Investments in new green technologies around the port range from alternative fuel vehicles (as of 2012, the Port of Los Angeles had some 900 alternative fuel vehicles in use) to speculative innovations such as algae-based biofuels. The port also instituted operational changes for the drayage trucks servicing the ports, resulting in 89% reductions in truck emissions. Environmental innovations are then shared among the other co-located companies. For example, VYCON Inc. has developed a new flywheel energy storage system for regenerative braking and hybrid drivetrains on dockyard cranes that is being deployed to Los Angeles' mass transit system.

6.2 Intra-Organizational Inter-Cluster Innovation Transfer

Logistics clusters differ from other industrial clusters in a subtle, additional way: the way that innovative ideas are disseminated. Whereas industrial clusters agglomerate industrial activities in a concentrated region of production, logistics activities must be performed over distance and between clusters. Moreover, logistics operators spend much of their time in several clusters. Many global logistics firms (e.g., FedEx, UPS, Maersk) operate across the world and are able to transmit innovation across logistics clusters by replicating practices developed in one cluster to other clusters. Local firms can then benefit from such new knowledge. Even regional logistics firms (e.g., a US railroad such as BNSF) operate across multiple clusters (e.g., the Ports of LA and Long Beach; Alliance, Texas; Chicago, Illinois; and others).

In the EffizienzCluster LogistikRuhr in Germany, 160 companies and 12 scientific institutions work together on innovation and research that centers on a wide range of environmental, operational, transportation, and design issues. The innovations developed in EffizienzCluster LogistikRuhr have far-reaching implications that transcend national boundaries. For instance, in the education and training fields, the cluster has been working on the eQual 2.0 project (a vocational training plan that addresses the educational needs of logistics companies by applying a constructionist approach through a learner-centered program). Some further examples of innovative projects are smartNRW, which aims to develop an "Optimal Tag Type and Position Evaluator" to determine the best type of tag and its position on the outer package of consumer goods, and ResIH, which seeks to raise the efficiency in intra-logistics and maintenance in chemical parks. The logistics cluster shares knowledge and best practices with top European logistics institutions that work within other logistics clusters such as the Zaragoza Logistics Center in Spain, the Dutch Institute for Advanced Logistics in the Netherlands, and the Verein Netzwerk Logistik in Austria. Moreover, many of the companies participating in EffizienzCluster LogistikRuhr—companies such as UPS, CHEP, and DB Schenker—have global footprints, thus innovations developed within the cluster become deployed around the world.

7 Logistics Clusters Benefits—Jobs

The regional economic benefits of logistics clusters arise from the clusters' role as job creation engines. Sheffi (2012) identifies five traits of the logistics clusters jobs that contribute to this. First, most distribution activities must be performed locally to provide competitive service levels, which implies that they cannot be offshored. Second, logistics clusters foster economic activity beyond distribution and transportation, such as the value-added services described above, which increases regional job creation (and in many cases with higher salaries). Third, logistics clusters offer low transportation costs and high transportation service levels, which attracts other industries such as manufacturing. Fourth, logistics clusters offer jobs for unskilled or low-skill workers but also prize these workers' operational experience, which creates opportunities for upward mobility. Finally, logistics clusters serve many different industries, and therefore, the regional employment is not dependent on the business cycle of a single industry.

Logistics clusters have massive amounts of impact on the economy. For instance, the development of Alliance★Texas Logistics Park has had a total economic impact of $36.4 billion for the region from 1990 through 2008. By 2008, the park accounted for the creation of 28,000 direct jobs (both white and blue collar), 1,700 construction jobs, and 63,388 indirect jobs (Sheffi 2010). Another example is Memphis Airport. Most of the 220,000 people who work at the airport work in logistics-related jobs. In fact, one in three jobs in the greater Memphis area is tied to logistics.

7.1 Blue- and White-Collar Jobs

Logistics clusters offer a spectrum of employment opportunities. Blue-collar workers perform most of the operational activities of the sector such as picking, packing, sorting, stocking, loading, and driving. However, those entry-level workers have the opportunity to be promoted to high-income, mid- or top-management positions because the industry favors managers who have frontline operational experience. In addition, the industry offers a multitude of white-collar jobs in information technology and systems engineering as well as customer service. Being located in a cluster enables workers to move between companies as their careers develop.

7.2 Sub-Cluster Development and Jobs

Logistics clusters can give rise to sub-clusters of other industries. For example, the logistics clusters in Louisville, Kentucky (UPS's hub), and Memphis, Tennessee (FedEx's hub), attracted a number medical devices firms who relocated there in order to improve their lead times for time-critical medical supplies. This started a positive feedback loop that attracted more such firms, including specialized suppliers, and a new medical devices cluster developed.

Along the Panama Canal, sub-clusters of vessel and container repair, construction, and refurbishment have thrived within the logistics cluster. Rotterdam Car Center is another example of a cluster-in-cluster. Located in Brittanniëhaven, it benefits from having both the Rotterdam port and a logistics cluster nearby.

Most of the activities performed in such sub-clusters, as well as in the adjoining logistics cluster, are value-added activities that require higher-paid workers with specific skills such as pharmacists, marine engineers, or laptop repair technicians, generating well-paying jobs in the region. For instance, in Alliance★Texas Logistics Park, ATC's cellphone repair operations employ many information technology technicians who have specialized skills and education.

7.3 Education and Training

In order to fulfill the specialized worker demand of the logistics industry, logistics clusters have developed training programs with local universities or colleges. For example, the Tarrant County College Corporate Training Center was created by the Alliance★Texas Logistics Park and the local Tarrant County College in order to provide trained workers for the park. This collective initiative guarantees a permanent supply of qualified logistics workers for the agglomerated firms while increasing the employees' competence. Similar efforts take place in the logistics clusters across the world, including places like Louisville, Zaragoza, and Singapore.

7.4 Upward Mobility

In many cases, the logistics industry recruits people with low levels of education and gives them the opportunity to progress in the labor market. Clusters seem to enhance this phenomenon because of the concentration of firms. For example, workers in several firms in the Zaragoza cluster started "on the floor" and moved up to managerial positions either at the same firm or in another firm in the cluster (Rivera et al. 2016).

The classic example of upward mobility is UPS, which has a strong "promote-from-within" culture. The company trains entry-level workers and enables them to develop a career within the firm. An Accenture's 2006 report states that 54% of UPS's current full-time drivers were once part-time employees; 68% of its full-time management employees rose from non-management positions; and 78% of its vice presidents started in non-management positions (Thomas et al. 2006). In addition to these statistics, many other logistics firms are managed by former UPS employees.

Finally, large seasonal fluctuations in logistics volumes lead to the hiring of part-time or temporary personnel. The new workers gain experience in the industry, and firms can assess the performance of these workers who might then be offered permanent work, training, and opportunities for promotions. In this sense, temporary jobs in logistics are an entry point for permanent and well-paid jobs. This phenomenon is particularly strong in logistics clusters because the seasonality of such jobs means that workers in the area can count on such temporary jobs and schedule their other work and life arrangements accordingly. Furthermore, the experience that workers gain during temporary work at one company can open doors to other local companies.

8 The Future of Logistics Clusters

Logistics clusters have been growing owing to a positive feedback loop driving their success. However, there are some factors that may reinforce the growth effects, while others may provide a countervailing force.

8.1 Factors Leading to Logistics Clusters Growth

Any growth in globalization and international trade is likely to increase the importance of all logistics clusters. However, small logistics clusters suffer during recessions while large ones actually grow as a result. The reason is that their advantages—especially in terms of costs—lead shippers to route freight through the largest clusters, while smaller ones lose business.

Tariff and non-tariff barriers have been reduced after the creation of the World Trade Organization (WTO), with total trade increasing over the last ten years (WTO 2014). This has been the major force behind economic growth, because it links the most cost-effective sources from anywhere in the world with end markets everywhere in the world (Zakery 2011). However, it has increased the complexities of global supply chains and created more cost pressures owing to global competition, thus increasing the need for further efficiencies such as those offered by logistics clusters. At the end of 2015, however, certain political and economic factors converged to reduce the growth of trade below the global GDP growth—if such a trend takes hold, one expects again the largest clusters to keep attracting operations while smaller ones languish.

Logistics clusters, as the nodes of global supply networks where shipments are consolidated and de-consolidated, help businesses achieve economies of scale in production while maintaining their flexibility to handle temporal and spatial variations in demand. Thus, logistics clusters are pivotal in the global value chain to efficiently handle international trade volumes. At the same time, logistics clusters foster the growth of international trade by making it more efficient, creating a global economic self-reinforcing positive feedback loop. Such an effect may be observed in Dubai, where the development of logistics infrastructure and free zones like Port Rashi, Jebel Ali Port, and Dubai International Airport in the 1970s and 1980s led to a positive impact in the foreign trade that increased from US$39 billion in 2000 to US$362 billion in 2013 (Invest Bridge Capital 2015).

The economics of conveyances also favor the growth of logistics clusters. Both fuel-efficiency and labor-efficiency considerations favor larger conveyances over smaller ones. Yet larger conveyances implicitly increase the need for logistics clusters to perform consolidation, deconsolidation, and transshipment operations.

Large conveyances moving between logistics clusters also reduce the carbon footprint per ton moved. Thus, further environmental pressures may lead to growth of logistics clusters. In fact, the German government encourages the development of logistics clusters mainly for environmental reasons, pushing for more intermodal transportation, which is only economically feasible with large volumes of freight, requiring cluster-to-cluster moves.

Increasing customer demands for fast "same day" or "within the hour" deliveries will also likely favor the development of logistics clusters—in this case, places that are close to urban centers. This is due to the fact that such clusters can have enough outbound deliveries (e-commerce in particular) to justify a cost-effective transportation delivery service.

8.2 Factors Leading to Possible Decline of Logistics Clusters

Despite such possible drivers of logistics clusters' formation and growth, other factors may point to possible declines in clustering. Protectionist and anti-trade regulation present risks for the logistics industry. Any restrictions on global trade will lead to decreased need for international logistics and therefore logistics clustering.

Low fuel prices decrease the need for efficient transportation and therefore the need for clustering. However, low fuel prices may also have a countervailing effect by encouraging global trade and therefore the need for logistics clusters. A rise in local sourcing, possibly motivated by environmental concerns, would reduce freight volumes over long distances and with it the need for logistics clustering.

Logistics clusters may also contract and even disappear. The most frequent reason for such phenomena is that the local stakeholders are working in cross-purposes and do not cooperate. Such was the fate of the New Orleans oil processing and oil logistics cluster, which lost its pre-eminent position to Houston, which is now (by far) the largest oil logistics cluster in the US. In other cases, "when you build it, people simply don't come." An investment in a logistics cluster launched during 2008 in Winston-Salem, North Carolina, struggled. Computer maker Dell Inc. closed a manufacturing plant there in 2009, and other operations did not move in.

In some cases, logistics clusters simply run out of space. Such is the case in Barcelona, Spain, where the city now abuts the warehouses and distribution centers. In other cases, typically with maritime clusters, the high value of ocean-front condominiums and apartments pushes away any industrial activity.

9 Implications for Practitioners and Policy Makers

This chapter raises awareness of the benefits of logistics clusters for logistics companies and companies that depend on logistics, namely manufacturers, distributors, and retailers. Implications for company managers include considerations of site selection, globalization, and value-added activities. This paper also presents information on logistics clusters that may help improve regional and national public policy design and execution. Implications include support for cluster development, specifically in terms of zoning, connectivity and finance, regulations and taxes, and international trade

9.1 Considerations of Site Selection

By choosing to locate in a logistics cluster, managers can benefit from high connectivity, reliable infrastructure, available human capital, and administrative efficiency. In many cases, such clusters also host educational institutions with specialized programs geared to the cluster's needs, as well as research organizations and consulting firms specializing in logistics and supply chain management. Companies in a cluster also have the power to influence regulations owing to the influence of the cluster with local government.

Although optimal location software packages are frequently used to decide on facility location for warehouses, distribution centers, and fulfillment centers, these packages capture only some of the benefits of logistics cluster locations. These include low transportation costs and, possibly, high transportation level of service. What these software applications do not capture are dynamic effects. Thus, they do not capture the ability to exchange space, equipment, and employees when the business expands or contracts. They also cannot capture the potential for cooperation among cluster firms for increased efficiency and service levels. Finally, they cannot capture the ability of clusters to become better with time on many dimensions, owing to the positive reinforcing feedback loop that controls their growth.

9.2 Globalization

As long as international trade and globalization grow, the relevance of logistics activities and logistics clusters to companies who source from international suppliers or sell into international markets is likely to remain high. As other authors have stated, "globalization poses a challenge to companies since it greatly influences the business environment and it has been identified as the main influencing factor in the logistics sector growth" (Kleindorfer and Visvikis 2007, p. 18).

9.3 Support for Cluster Development: Zoning, Connectivity, and Finance

Logistics clusters depend on certain conditions, conditions that are controlled by local and central governments. Foremost among these condition requirements is a large space, something that requires favorable zoning regulations. Logistics clusters also require high levels of physical accessibility (Van Den Heuvel et al. 2014) and connectedness—road, rail, air, and water transportation infrastructure—many of which are created, operated, and maintained through large-scale investment of public funds. Even in the case of private logistics infrastructure (e.g., private railroads or port facilities), freight often travels via public infrastructure such as road networks to manufacturers, warehouses, and retailers.

Many countries are developing their public infrastructure with an emphasis on improving their logistics competitiveness, as is the case of China, India, and the United Arab Emirates. Interestingly, the 2015 US transportation bill pays strong attention to logistics, including $10.8 billion for freight-specific projects. This is the first time the US Congress has funded a freight program in the transportation bill (Transportation for America 2015), including the creation of the Nationally Significant Freight and Highway Projects discretionary grant program, funded at $4.5 billion over five years, and the establishment of a new National Highway Freight Program (NHFP) with resources up to $6.2 billion over five years. The bill also creates a Port Performance statistics program, in order to collect data to help provide recommendations to improve port efficiency (American Association of State Highway and Transportation Officials 2015).

9.4 Regulations and Taxes

Regulations and taxes affect the economics of logistics and logistics clusters development. Regulations impact land uses for logistics and the costs of logistics due to permissible conveyance size, conveyance operations, freight movement restrictions, and other factors. Government-mediated land uses regulations and processes impact not only the ease of development of port, airport, and warehouse facilities but also affect rights-of-way by which goods can move via road and rail into and out of the cluster. Taxes (or tax incentives) impact site selection decisions by companies deciding where they might locate warehouses and value-added activities. Governments also help ensure the economic sustainability of logistics operations in a cluster through efficient administrative processes (e.g., conveyance registration, or customs processes for imported goods), and the stability of rules and incentives for soft infrastructure development like research centers and educational institutions.

9.5 International Trade

Governments have an important role to play in international trade because it is controlled by international and government-to-government agreements. For example, the recent explosive growth of logistics clusters in Mexico (the largest ones being in Reynosa, Juarez, Monterey, Tijuana, Guadalajara, and Mexico City) followed the establishment of about sixty bilateral trade agreements; most other countries, including the US, Canada, and China follow the same trend (WTO, 2015).

Governments are also responsible for the development of free trade zones and special economic zones where certain activities can enjoy preferential tax treatment. Finally, governments can help promote logistics cluster development through external relationships such as trade missions and harmonization of regulations.

Logistics clusters are especially relevant to policy makers in developing economies, in which the effectiveness of export-led growth policies are strongly dependent on the efficient operation of export logistics. Emerging BRIC countries (Brazil, Russia, India, and China) as well as CIVETS (Colombia, Indonesia, Vietnam, Egypt, Turkey, and South Africa) countries have become hotbed locations for new logistics clusters acting as important nodes of global trade.

Countries such as Panama, Singapore, Holland, Belgium, Dubai, and even Germany have made logistics a major pillar of their economies by creating key infrastructural waypoints in global supply chains. In turn, the development of logistics clusters "attracts workers, entrepreneurs, investment, companies, political interest and intellectual capital" (Sheffi 2012, p. 38), which fosters regional economic growth. Governments and societies then benefit from logistics clusters through their wide spectrum of employment opportunities, upward mobility, economic growth, and the lower dependency on the business cycles of particular industries.

10 Future Research Opportunities

Rising global trade has generated a higher demand for logistics services, favoring the spatial agglomeration of logistics activities. The increasing prevalence of logistics clusters contrasts with the paucity of literature in the field, which represents an opportunity for scholars. Our study summarizes selected benefits of agglomeration of logistics such as collaborative sharing of assets, value-added services, upward mobility, job creation, and environmental innovation. Future research may address the following issues:

- Assessing and measuring the relative importance of other potential benefits for companies in logistics clusters. For example, one such element argued in the literature on industrial districts is innovation (e.g., Albino et al. 2006). Another is capital formation—the higher rate of new business formation—which has been observed in many industrial clusters (Porter 1998).
- Obtaining an in-depth understanding of how location decisions evolve over time and are influenced by prior experience, current incentives, or changing regulations (e.g., hours-of-service regulations for truck drivers or changes in conveyance sizes).
- Settling the debate on the relative effects of agglomeration economics versus dispersion economics in logistics cluster development and logistics-related land use patterns. Data-driven analysis based on more than the US and Holland can help here.
- Analyzing intra- and inter-cluster relationships in order to describe the process of trade-network building, for instance horizontal collaboration practices emerge both inside clusters and between them (for more detail, see Rivera et al. 2015a).
- Examining the co-evolution of logistics agglomeration and urban agglomeration through sharing of (or contention for) infrastructure between freight and personal transportation.
- Extending research on logistics clusters by conducting analyses on clusters at a smaller unit of analysis that helps understand the clustering effect at a more granular level (see, for instance, Rivera et al. 2015b).
- Developing robust methodologies for sharing the costs and benefits of conveyance sharing arrangements; how costs and benefits can be shared if a jointly loaded conveyance off-loads in different places or if it performs multiple deliveries; how to deal with the

fact that one company's costs may go up while others' costs decrease to the benefits of the whole but not everyone's.
- Collecting qualitative and quantitative data to measure the impact of logistics clusters on the operational efficiency of companies. Local, regional, and national economic data could help estimate the effects of logistics clusters on economic outcomes.

References and Bibliography

Albino, V., Carbonara, N. and Giannoccaro, I. (2006) "Innovation in industrial districts: An agent-based simulation model," *International Journal of Production Economics*, **104**(1): 30–45.

American Association of State Highway and Transportation Officials (2015) "AASHTO summary of the new surface transportation bill Fixing America's Surface Transportation (FAST) Act." http://fast.transportation.org/Documents/AASHTO%20Summary%20of%20FAST%20Act%202015-12-16%20FINAL.pdf, downloaded January 25, 2016.

Appold, S. (1995) "Agglomeration, interorganizational networks, and competitive performance in the U.S. metalworking sector," *Economic Geography*, **71**(1): 27–74.

Baptista, R. (1998) "Clusters, innovation and growth: A survey of the literature," in G. Swann, M. Prevezer, D. Stout (Eds.), *The Dynamics of Industrial Clustering: International Comparisons in Computing and Biotechnology*, Oxford University Press, Oxford.

Cairncross, F. (1997) *The Death of Distance*, Orion Business Books, London.

Chapman, R.L., Soosay, C. and Kandampully, J. (2003) "Innovation in logistic services and the new business model: A conceptual framework," *International Journal of Physical Distribution & Logistics Management*, **33**(7): 630–650.

CSCMP (2013) "Supply chain management terms and glossary," https://cscmp.org/sites/default/files/user_uploads/resources/downloads/glossary-2013.pdf, downloaded January 10, 2016.

De Langen, P. (2002) "Clustering and performance: The case of maritime clustering in the Netherlands," *Maritime Policy Management*, **29**(3): 209–22.

De Langen, P. (2004) "Analyzing the performance of seaport clusters," in: Pinder, D., Slack, B. (Eds.), *Shipping and Ports in the Twenty-First Century*. Seoul, Korea, pp. 82–98.

Delgado, M., Porter, M. and Stern, S. (2010) "Clusters and entrepreneurship," *Journal of Economic Geography*, **10**(4): 495–518.

Ellison, G., Glaeser, E.L. and Kerr, W. (2010) "What causes industry agglomeration? Evidence from coagglomeration patterns," *American Economic Review*, **100**(3): 1195–1213.

Ettlie, J.E. and Reza, E.M. (1992) "Organizational integration and process innovation," *The Academy of Management Journal*, **35**(4): 795–827.

Feser, E. (2008) "Clusters and the design of innovation policy for developing economies," in U. Blien, G. Maier (Eds.), *The Economics of Regional Clusters: Networks, Technology and Policy*, Edward Elgar, Cheltenham, UK, pp. 191–213.

Glasmeier, A.K. and Kibler, J. (1996) "Power shift: The rising control of distributors and retailers in the supply chain for manufactured goods," *Urban Geography*, **17**(8): 740–757.

Granberg, O. and Ohlsson, J. (2005) "Collective learning in teams," *Journal of Swedish Educational Research*, **10**: 227–243.

Groothedde, B., Ruijgrok, C. and Tavasszy, L. (2005) "Towards collaborative, intermodal hub networks: A case study in the fast moving consumer goods market," *Transportation Research: Part E*, **41**(6): 567–583.

Haezendonck, E. (2001) *Essays on Strategy Analysis for Seaports*, Garant Publishers, Leuven, Belgium.

Henderson, J.V. and Shalizi, Z. (2001) "Geography and development," *Journal of Economic Geography*, **1**(1): 81–105.

Hethcock, B. (2010) "Dallas Logistics Hub woos investors," *Dallas Business Journal*, www.bizjournals.com/dallas/print-edition/2010/11/19/dallas-logistics-hub-plan-draws.html, downloaded February 2, 2016.

Hoover, E.M. (1937) "Spatial price discrimination," *Review of Economic Studies*, **4**(3): 182–191.

Huo, B. (2012) "The impact of supply chain integration on company performance: An organizational capability perspective," *Supply Chain Management: An International Journal*, **17**(6): 596–610.

Invest Bridge Capital (2015) www.investbridgecapital.com/real-estate/, downloaded June 10, 2015.

Kasilingman, R.G. (1998) *Logistics and Transportation, Design and Planning*, Kluwer Academic Publishers, Kluwer Academic, London.

Keeble, D. and Wilkinson, F. (2000) *High-Technology Clusters, Networking and Collective Learning in Europe*, Ashgate, Aldershot, UK.

King, I.W. and Rowe, A. (1999) "Space and the not-so-final frontiers: Re-presenting the potential of collective learning for organizations," *Management Learning*, **30**: 431–48.

Kleindorfer, P.R. and Visvikis, I. (2007) *Integration of Financial and Physical Networks in Global Logistics*, Risk Management and Decision Processes Center Working Paper, University of Pennsylvania, Philadelphia, PA.

Klink, H.A.v. and De Langen, P.W. (2001) "Cycles in industrial clusters: The case of the shipbuilding industry in the Northern Netherlands," *Tijdschrift Sociale en Eonomische Geografie*, **92**(4): 449–463.

Leamer, E.E. and Storper, M. (2001) "The economy geography of the internet age," *Journal of International Business Studies*, **32**(4): 641–665.

Lindsay, G. and Kasadra, J. (2011) *Aerotropolis: The Way We Will Live Next*, Farrar, Straus and Giroux, New York.

Marshall, A. (1890) *Principles of Economics*, Macmillan, London, New York.

Martin, J. and Román, C. (2003) "Hub location in the South-Atlantic airline market: A spatial competition game," *Transportation Research Part A: Policy Practice*, **37**(10): 865–888.

Maskell, P. (2001) "Knowledge creation and diffusion in geographic clusters," *International Journal of Innovation Management*, **5**(2): 213–238.

Nonaka, I., Totama, R. and Nagata, A. (2000) "A firm as a knowledge-creating entity: A new perspective on the theory of the firm," *Industrial and Corporate Change*, **9**(1): 1–20.

O'Brien, R. (1992) *Global Financial Integration: The End of Geography*, Council on Foreign Relations Press, New York.

Pekkarinen, O. (2005) "Northwest Russian transport logistics cluster: Finnish perspective," Northern Dimension Research Centre, Lappeenranta University of Technology, Lappeenranta, Finland.

Polenske, K. (2003) "Clustering in space versus dispersing over space: Agglomeration versus dispersal economies," Symposium 2002. Universities of Trollhätten/Uddevalla, Trollhätten, Sweden.

Porter, M. (1998) "Clusters and the new economics of competitiveness," *Harvard Business Review*, **76**(6): 77–90.

Prologis (2015) "The evolution of logistics real estate clusters," www.prologis.com/docs/research/supply_chain/LogisticsClustersWhitePaper_August2015.pdf, downloaded January 15, 2016.

Reichart, A. and Holweg, M. (2008) "Co-located supplier clusters: Forms, functions and theoretical perspectives," *International Journal of Operations & Production Management*, **28**(1): 53–78.

Rivera, L., Gligor, D. and Sheffi, Y. (2016) "The benefits of logistics clusters," *International Journal of Physical Distribution and Logistics Management*, **46**(3): 242–268.

Rivera, L., Gligor, D., Saenz, M. and Sheffi, Y. (2015a) "The role of logistics clusters in facilitating horizontal collaboration mechanisms," MIT Center for Transportation and Logistics Working Paper, Cambridge, MA.

Rivera, L, Sheffi Y. and Knoppen, D. (2015b) "The process of agglomeration within logistics clusters and the impact of firm size on collaboration and value added services," MIT Center for Transportation and Logistics Working Paper, Cambridge, MA.

Rivera, L., Sheffi, Y. and Welsch R. (2014) "Logistics agglomeration in the US," *Transportation Research Part A: Policy and Practice*, **59**: 222–238.

Sheffi, Y. (2010) "Logistics intensive clusters: Global competitiveness and regional growth," MIT Center for Transportation and Logistics Working Paper, Cambridge, MA.

Sheffi, Y. (2012) *Logistics Clusters: Delivering Value and Driving Growth*, MIT Press, Cambridge, MA.

Stank, T.P. and Goldsby, T.J. (2000) "A framework for transportation decision making in an integrated supply chain," *Supply Chain Management: An International Journal*, **5**(2): 71–78.

Teubal, M., Yinnon, T. and Zuscovitch, E. (1991) "Networks and market creation," *Research Policy*, **20**(5): 381–392.

Thomas, R., Linder, J. and Dutra A. (2006) "Inside the value-driven culture at UPS," *Accenture Outlook Journal*, September 2006.

Transportation for America (2015) "Think FAST—the good, the bad and the ugly in Congress' new five-year transportation bill," http://t4america.org/2015/12/02/think-fast-the-good-the-bad-and-the-ugly-in-congress-new-five-year-transportation-bill/, downloaded January 25, 2016.

Van den Heuvel, F.P., De Langen, P.W., Van Donselaar, K.H. and Fransoo, J.C. (2013) "Spatial concentration and location dynamics in logistics: The case of a Dutch province," *Journal of Transport Geography*, **28**: 39–48.

Van den Heuvel, F.P., Rivera, L., Van Donselaar, K.H., De Jong, A., Sheffi, Y., De Langen, P.W. and Fransoo, J.C. (2014) "Relationship between freight accessibility and logistics employment in US counties," *Transportation Research Part A: Policy and Practice*, **59**: 91–105.
Weber, A. and Friedrich C.J. (1929) *Theory of the Location of Industries*, University of Chicago Press, Chicago.
WTO (2014) "Statistics database: Time series," http://stat.wto.org/StatisticalProgram/WSDBViewData.aspx?Language=E, downloaded October 2, 2015.
WTO (2015) "Participation in regional trade agreements," www.wto.org/english/tratop_e/region_e/rta_participation_map_e.htm
Wu, L., Yue, X. and Sim, T. (2006) "Supply clusters: A key to China's cost advantage," *Supply Chain Management Review*, **10**(2): 46–51.
Xu, J. and Hancock, K.L. (2004) "Enterprise-wide freight simulation in an integrated logistics and transportation system," *IEEE Transactions, Intelligent Transportation Systems*, **5**(4): 342–346.
Zakery, A. (2011) "Logistics future trends," in Farahani, R., Rezapour, S. and Kardar, L. *Logistics Operations and Management*, Elsevier, London, pp. 93–105.

17
HUMAN BEHAVIOR IN OPERATIONS

Elliot Bendoly, Adam McClintock, and Rahul Pandey

1 Introduction

Analytical treatments of operations management have been applied tirelessly over the years to model operating contexts and derive theoretical "best solutions" within them. Ironically, despite noble intentions to assist managers and professionals, such efforts have systematically undermined the critical role of these decision makers through explicit and implicit assumptions in formulation (Bendoly et al. 2015). In many of these studies, managers are assumed to be perfectly rational beings, with unconstrained information processing capabilities and who are unbiased in their actions and responses. These assumptions provide the means to simplify and solve otherwise overly complex real-world problems while also unfortunately restricting the applicability and effectiveness of otherwise mathematically sophisticated research efforts.

Bendoly et al. (2006) identify and categorize these assumptions into three broad categories: intentions, actions, and reactions. Decision makers in many analytical models are typically expected to maximize all efforts and resources to achieve a set of goals (Gino and Pisano 2008) and are often characterized as deterministic, predictable, independent, emotionless, and stationary (Boudreau et al. 2003).

For example, in supply chain coordination and cost management studies, it is often assumed that the sharing of certain information always adds clarity to decision making (reducing the bounds on rational processing). However, in practice, a supplier may be active in multiple competing supply chains. In such scenarios, the sharing of certain information with the assumed intention of benefiting a particular supply chain may be flawed. A supplier may retain social, political, or even philosophical bias towards a subset of supply chain partners that may not be explained by financial utility and its maximization. It may also realize that sharing selected, filtered information with a subset of its supply chain may enable it to induce action by those partners or even accentuate its implied power position relative to certain partners. Ulterior motives and subsequent actions in support of these motives by any supply chain player can significantly undermine the best intentions of agreements maintained among them. It complicates the ability to model these scenarios and prescribe action to management. Nevertheless, such motives often play a very real role in supply chain dynamics. As a field, we ignore them and make other behavior-simplifying assumptions at our own peril.

Certainly, contemporary research in Operations Management has shown that this need not be the case. In an age where computational power is at an unprecedented level, recent studies in OM (many of which we will highlight in this chapter) take a step back and appreciate that most decisions are, after all, still made by people. Simply assuming someone needs a hammer to fix a problem doesn't make a hammer the right tool for the job. It also doesn't imply that if used, the manner of such use can be easily anticipated or even yield benefit. With this critical perspective, and in order to explore the place of the human decision maker in operations management, we adapt the definition of behavioral operations management from Bendoly et al. (2015, pp. ix):

> Behavioral operations management explores the interaction of human behaviors and operational systems and processes. Specifically, the study of behavioral operations management has the goal of identifying ways in which human psychology and sociological phenomena impact operational performance, as well as identifying the ways in which operations policies impact such behavior.

Behavioral operations management aims to bridge the disconnect between academic research and practical applicability or the usefulness of such research in solving real world operations management problems. Behavioral Operations (BeOps) create value for both researchers and practitioners in that it addresses and analyzes the fundamental entity in any operational setting: the people. For scholars, it provides a means to accurately develop and solve for an operations problem while taking into account the managers making decisions, employees, and customers. Such consideration while solving a problem allows practitioners to confidently refer to these models and implement them in an organization.

However, the question remains: How do we account for and incorporate human decision makers, and subsequently interpret the results? With the growth in the availability of large quantities of related data, new opportunities exist for intrepid researchers interested in further closing the gap between complex math-theoretic modeling and practical relevance. In order to get to this next level, we need to start with an appreciation of the foundations the have supported the last two decades of BeOps research.

The aim of this chapter is to provide a review of the history of Behavioral Operations as a research domain. It is not to rehash existing review pieces on the subject but rather to provide a unified description of the fundamental elements underlying progress behind this area of research and ultimately to provide some guidance for future research and practice informed by this domain. With that said, let's go back briefly to the beginning of things.

2 A Brief Historical Overview

2.1 Early Rumbling of a Domain

Distinct from other management disciplines, Operations Management has been referred to as notably multi-theoretical at its earliest foundations (Gino and Pisano 2008), spanning perspectives from flow focus and value generation (Gilbreth and Gilbreth 1922; Ford 1926) to the relatively more recent transformative focus (e.g., Starr 1966). Facilitated by the openness of the field to alternative theoretical lenses and areas of consideration, some of the earliest work in Operations Management in fact inspired research streams in the associated field of industrial psychology (e.g., studies by Mayo 1949 of what became known as the Hawthorne Effect; studies reviewed by Kanigel 1997).

Further instrumental in laying the groundwork for what would ultimately become the domain of Behavioral Operations was the seminal introduction of concepts from related fields, such as the bounded rationality perspective (Simon 1956; 1957; Festinger 1957). Simon defined this by writing:

> The capacity of the human mind for formulating and solving complex problems is very small compared with the size of the problems whose solution is required for objectively rational behavior in the real world—or even for a reasonable approximation to such objective rationality.
>
> *(Simon 1956, p. 135)*

Indeed, individual cognitive limitations to process information, social psychological factors wherein decision makers are influenced by cooperating and/or competing environments, and the complexity of the task combined with limited mental capability to form an accurate mental model play a significant role in most OM decision-making processes. An understanding of these phenomena and the importance of incorporating them in operational settings has certainly gained traction among OM scholars and continues to motivate new research. Subsequent work in the field of Behavioral Economics was similarly heavily influenced by these concepts (cf. Kahneman and Tversky 1979). Little (1970) also seems to have alluded to these limitations, limitations that might be exacerbated by insufficiently specified mathematical models of operations that otherwise would falsely convey control. We will talk more on the influence of these perspectives on contemporary BeOps research in Section 3 as well.

Research and practical considerations of operational system improvement also latched on fairly early to the notion that the study of actual managerial decisions could be directly informative of both their context and mechanisms for enhancement (Bowman 1963). While case-based, grounded-theory development may certainly be a mechanism through which the observation of managerial behavior can inform future research, it is also a perfectly suitable approach for practice. Rather than strictly considering the mechanical nature of an industrial system, understanding what drives individual managers to stop process runs when they do, or to modify them, may be incredibly informative when attempting to identify the nature of floating process bottlenecks and/or failures in incentive structures.

2.2 The BeOps Renaissance

Though these early contributions ultimately proved highly influential, it wasn't until the early 1990s that consistent signs in dedicated OM outlets emerged of a movement to re-examine operating systems through behavioral lenses. These works spanned the consideration of the critical role of social organizational systems as they overlap and interact with operational processes (Huber and Brown 1991), to the methodological consideration of Japanese tabletop experiments (Robinson and Robinson 1994), to investigations into the use of new computerized decision support technologies in OM contexts (Robinson and Swink 1995). Such works energized a latent interest by the field to peer into the often complicated, bounded rational thought processes of managers and those they supervised.

Take for example the shift in focus with regards to research into the *bullwhip effect*, the information distortion in terms of disproportionate increase in order variance compared to the market demand variance as one moves upstream in a supply chain. The effect has been studied for quite some time with notable references to human behavior (Forrester 1961; Sterman 1989). Yet, until the early 2000s, scholars were still largely analyzing the operational causes rather than behavioral nuances in these settings (Lee et al. 2004), suggesting strictly mechanistic strategies to alleviate these problems (Chen et al. 1998; Cachon and Lariviere 1999; Cachon 1999; Sogomonian and Tang 1993). However, in the last decade, a major shift in focus seems apparent. For example, Croson and Donohue (2006) recently identified underweighting of in-transit inventory due to cognitive limitation and decision bias as one of the behavioral factors of the bullwhip effect. Narayanan and Moritz (2015) provide further support that cognitive limitation contributes to the bullwhip effect. Similarly, Wu and Katok (2006) established bounded rationality and decision makers' constrained insights and limited knowledge as contributing factors. Recently, Croson et al. (2014) provided evidence to suggest that decision makers' perception of other supply chain members as unreliable, defined as *coordination risk*, can motivate them to deviate from optimal strategy, thereby facilitating the bullwhip effect.

In these and alternate settings, such as newsvendor contexts, decision makers are consistently shown to inadequately anchor their projections on previous experiences and deviate from the optimal order quantities. Risk-averse decision makers have been shown to systematically order less and charge higher prices when faced with uncertain customer demand (Agrawal and Seshadri 2000). Even with a known demand distribution, decision makers make choices that do not adhere to a profit-maximization objective, with decisions perhaps better explained as "regret" minimization in some instances. Schweitzer and Cachon (2000) found that decision makers are biased towards the mean order quantity, anchoring their choices on previous orders/demands and making insufficient adjustment and resulting in non-optimal order quantities. Gurnani et al. (2014) state that decision makers tend to deviate from the optimal strategy for procurement decision and establish bounded rationality as a contributing factor for the deviation. Increasingly across the board, behavioral factors are taken into account while modeling multi-echelon supply chains to study capacity allocation (Chen et al. 2015; Chen et al. 2012), demand forecasting (Ebrahim-Khanjari et al. 2012), and inventory management (Hartwig et al. 2015).

These are only a couple of examples of the explosion of behavioral studies in a topical area of interest to Operations Management.

3 Contemporary Foundations from Aligned Domains

Although it may be heartening to see the energy behind the growth in Behavioral Operations research over the last decade, it must be emphasized that it owes much of its development to research progress in aligned research efforts. These include developments in the research domains of cognitive psychology, social and group dynamics, and more broadly, system dynamics and systems thinking. We can neither responsibly look back on the recent work in BeOps, nor look forward to research opportunities for the domain without a strong appreciation of what these aligned research areas have contributed.

3.1 Cognitive Psychology

The study of cognitive science is fundamental to a better understanding of decisions made in business settings because very often the mental processes involved in reasoning, problem solving, perception, and decision making are complex and not easy to decipher. Psychological research has developed and furthered a number of general theoretical bases, all focused on structures and processes within an individual's mind, in order to explain the systematic deviations in individual decision making that would otherwise seem irrational. In particular, cognitive psychology addresses the individual's limited mental capacity to cope with increasing levels of complexity and to develop accurate mental models of complex real word problems.

Bounded rationality (Simon 1957; Festinger 1957), referred to earlier in Section 2.2, sheds light on decision making in organizational settings in that decision makers constantly shift through information, choices, and options to arrive at an alternative that is *satisficing* rather than optimal. The satisficing phenomenon arises as decision makers have a limited amount of time and resources that can be employed towards a search for the best alternative. As a result, when they arrive at an alternate good enough for the problem, the search stops. Even when the decision makers make a conscious effort to follow a formal rational process to arrive at an optimal solution, there is significant cost associated with searching for the best alternate. Additionally, the mental limitations on the degree of complexity decision makers can handle and the need to arrive at an alternate within the limited time constraint restricts the boundaries of the search process.

The suboptimality of decision making in real-world managerial problems as seen from the conceptual understanding of bounded rationality and the cognitive limitation of the human mind implies the following: a) that satisficing rather than searching for an optimal solution will dominate and that this dominance arises due to the fact that decisions will always be made in the presence of incomplete information and limited understanding (mental models) of the complex environment, b) that cognitive limitations to the information processing capability of the human mind will constrain the consideration of all possible solutions to the problem and that the decision makers will most likely never be able to consider and evaluate the merit of all possible solutions, and c) that the decision to settle for a solution will be based on some heuristics developed by the decision makers which will be based on an insufficient and incomplete representation of the complex problem.

From an operational perspective, bounded rationality and cognitive limitation are essentially constraints that can be distinguished by their respective exogenous and endogenous natures. Specifically, bounded rationality is typically discussed as a constraint imposed by the external environment on the decision maker. Individuals are forced to make decisions with incomplete information because they are not *given* complete information. Cognitive limitation is endogenous to the decision maker. Even in the presence of sufficient information, individuals may not be able to comprehend some of that information, may not understand how information is related, and/or may not have the cognitive faculties to systematically leverage the information for translation into an ideal decision. It is important to note that exogenous influences such as the providing of excessive information beyond that which is critical or providing information in a way that is positively or negatively framed, can certainly impact perception in the presence of cognitive limitations. However, it is only because of the existence of endogenous cognitive limitations that such exogenous (including math model) influences appear relevant.

From an Input-Process-Output (IPO) perspective, the impact of bounded rationality in decision making can be observed in both the effective inputs of decision making as well as in the nature of the decision-making process. Specifically, the inputs to decision making are most readily discussed as being colored by the biases that individuals develop based on the information available and their available cognitive resources. In the presence of bounded rationality, a wide range of perceptual and interpretational biases may be relevant to an individual decision maker, several of which are outlined in Figure 17.1, with distinctions in predominant reference by Economics and Psychology disciplines.

3.1.1 Common Biases

Loss aversion refers to an individual's tendency to place higher value on and be influenced more by losses than gains. In terms of dollar value, losing a dollar hurts more than gaining a dollar helps. Loss aversion suggests that individuals will be more resistant to set a challenging target

Human Behavior in Operations

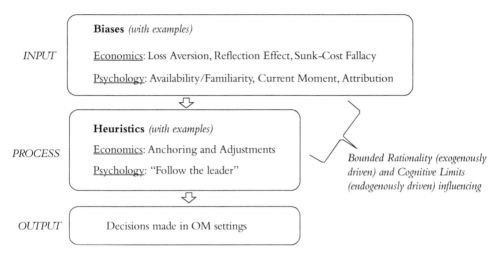

Figure 17.1 An Input-Process-Output View of Biases and Heuristics

when the chances of underperforming and overperforming the target are equally likely. In a buyer-supplier relationship, for example, if a supplier anticipates that there is a likelihood that it might not meet the buyer's expectations, the risk of missing the target will overweigh the gains from achieving (or overachieving) the target. In such cases, the supplier may bargain for a target that is much lower than its potential, thereby limiting the supply chain performance. Recently, loss aversion has helped motivate OM research in the area of supply chain contracts and channel efficiency (Davis 2015; Davis et al. 2014).

The *reflection effect* relates individuals' loss aversion bias to their risk preference with respect to loss and gain expectations. In short, individuals are more risk seeking in losses and risk averse in gains. The now very popular and widely cited Tversky and Kahneman (1981) experimental study clearly demonstrated the risk-seeking versus risk-averse nature of decision makers. The study highlights that individuals make risk-averse choices when the problem is framed as gains whereas individuals make risk-seeking choices when the same problem is framed in terms of losses (specifically with an interest in avoiding these losses). That is not to say that individuals are loss seeking—but rather that individuals are more willing to consider riskier options that might avoid impending losses when faced with the prospect of such losses. Recent considerations of such biases include multi-echelon system investigations (cf. Narayanan and Moritz 2015).

The *Sunk-Cost Fallacy* refers to individuals' tendency to further invest time, money, or resources to an unprofitable product or unfavorable situation just because the initial investment made on it cannot be recovered. While the situation, from a rational thinking perspective, does not warrant any further investment, the initial sunk investment will bias the individual in making seemingly irrational decisions. As academic researchers, we are all familiar with this. It's difficult to put down a research study even after our favorite outlets have given us a pass; we invest more time even though the return to our time could be higher elsewhere. Arguments regarding the Sunk-Cost Fallacy have recently been applied to the management of informational goods (Wei and Nault 2014) and project management (Dilts and Pence 2006).

Availability or familiarity bias refers to individuals' greater weightage on recent events or information, events that were experienced personally, or events that are remembered or recalled easily while making a decision. For example, the Toyota recall of millions of cars due to a brake pedal issue and the General Motors ignition key problem that garnered unprecedented public attention will weigh heavily on potential customers even if the Toyota's and GM's cars available in the market are void of those or any defects.

Current moment bias relates to immediate payoffs versus payoffs in the long run. Individuals are biased in their decision towards payoffs that can be realized immediately or in the near future even though they may be inferior to the payoffs that can be achieved in the long run.

Attribution bias arises when individuals attempt to employ biased reasoning and logic to infer and draw meaning out of other's behavior. For instance, in a supply chain coordination game a supplier will most likely blame the buyer for lack of coordination in demand and inventory management resulting in additional inventory cost or lost sales as compared to the inherent difficulty and complexity in forecasting accurate demand and market fluctuation. Recent OM research applications have suggested that the salience and likelihood of witnessing such biases increase as the complexity of organizational structure and the lack of clarity or uncertainty regarding operational interdependencies increase (Repenning and Sterman 2002; Ramasesh and Browning 2014).

3.1.2 Established Heuristics

Apart from perception and interpretation at the input level, the manner in which inputs are translated into decision outputs can also be influenced by bounded rationality and cognitive limitations. For the sake of present and future discussion, we plant a flag here by unambiguously using the term "heuristic" to describe these *translational processes* in contrast to the use of the term "bias" (the extant literature is a mess of inconsistent interchangeability with these terms). To be clear, heuristics need not involve specific biases, although the selection of one heuristic over another often alludes to individual preferences in a given context.

A *heuristic* is a general rule-of-thumb that individuals employ to arrive at a solution. When solving for problems or making decisions for situations, individuals constantly make use of mental shortcuts in order to overcome the complexity of the real-world problems. Such mental shortcuts allow individuals to make a feasible, although not necessarily optimal, decision within the limited time, information, and computation capacity. For example, the phenomenon of satisficing is essentially a manifestation of heuristics in decision making.

Scholars continue to employ heuristics to understand and solve for problems in OM settings. Recent research has analyzed the role of heuristics in formulating simple and implementable decision rules to complex problems such as resource capacity and allocation planning (Nagarajan and Rajagopalan 2008). Individuals often employ a wide variety of heuristics based on the complexity and attributes of the problem. Some of these such as the *anchoring and insufficient adjustment heuristic*, the *availability heuristic*, and the *affect heuristic* have proven very useful to untangle the individual's decision-making process. Bendoly et al. (2010) provide an introductory platform and references to some of the seminal studies in heuristics that could help readers better appreciate the extent to which heuristics are prominent in operations management. While the intention here is not to provide a detailed review on the list of heuristics, the *anchoring and insufficient adjustment heuristic* is known to influence a wide range of operational decision making and plays a significant role in behavioral operations management studies.

Anchoring and insufficient adjustment refers to the human tendency to analyze information and make decisions based on a relative reference to some anchor, generally a mental shortcut developed as a result of previous experiences and information. In the process, individuals first compare and estimate the set of information or situation to a suitable anchor, which may or may not be relevant to the problem and then make an, often minimal and insufficient, adjustment to arrive at a final value. Operations management literature has seen this form of heuristic manifest in various operational settings such as demand order generation (Schweitzer and Cachon

2000), inventory management (Croson and Donohue 2006), and forecasting (Harvey 2007), and recently, in supply chain coordination contracts, lower than expected theoretical efficiency, and supplier-retailer coordination were attributed to anchoring and constant insufficient adjustments (Goncalves et al. 2005; Loch and Wu 2008; Castenada and Goncalves 2015). Biases may trigger as well as influence the workings of the heuristic, shifting the level of an anchor and the magnitude of the adjustment.

Another heuristic commonly observed is generally referred to as *follow the leader*. It essentially involves setting aside one's own reasoning and thought process and adopting the opinion, suggestion, or guidance from external sources that could be an individual, group, automated systems, etc. The willingness to adopt may be either due to the lack of decision-making capability and/or unquestionable belief and faith in the "leader." Goddard et al. (2011) demonstrated how individuals very easily place their faith on the "leader"—the automated systems—and readily adopt to the suggestions made by the systems. The "follow the leader" heuristic is prominent in group settings where individuals very frequently set aside their beliefs in order to arrive at a consensus among the group. This is despite the possibility that the consensus arrived at is worse than the belief held by the individual. Rather than debating the pros and cons of suggestions put forward, the individuals in the group may, due to various reasons (fear of rejection, disrupting harmony in the group, etc.), adopt the dominant view in the group, which might not necessarily be the best decision for the group.

It is critical to point out here that the presence of individual heuristics does not mean that mathematical models intended to inform decision makers are not useful. Often, mathematical models can be useful in reminding individuals of factors or dynamics that they might otherwise overlook. What is critical however, is that since mathematical models of complex settings are often incomplete themselves (often omitting behavioral dynamics of others in a system), managers cannot expect those they supervise to strictly adhere to them in decision-making processes. Knowing the heuristics workers and managers use, as well as one's tendencies in solving problems, remains invaluable.

Given the profound influence of social and group settings on individual decision making, in the next section, we consider the influence of the group and social environment on an individual's actions.

3.2 *Group and Social Influences*

Building on the last point in the previous section, while biases and heuristics are results of information availability and an individual's cognitive limitations, available information and the nature of individual cognition does not exist in a vacuum. Available information can be influenced by a wide range of actors—supervisors, co-workers, and clients for example—not to mention underlying operational processes that collect and disseminate information. The tendency for aspects of such information to appear familiar and suitable for use, or for aspects to become associated with other elements of information in the formation/modification of causal assumptions, can also be highly influenced by interactions with such actors and processes. This comes both from a sociological perspective as well as an organizational incentive structure perspective.

Individual behaviors and actions are influenced by people around them and social stimuli, specifically, motivation and feedback. Social psychology illuminates how motivation from the group and social environment encourages individuals to act and make particular choices. Motivation in turn arises from the belief individuals hold, the objective they aspire to achieve, and the feedback about their goals and objectives received from the people around them. In operations, motivation and feedback suggesting a friendly environment can induce cooperation among the members whereas indication of a hostile environment from the social environment may motivate the players to compete even though it might not be in the best interest of the members. For instance, Loch and Wu (2008) demonstrated that supply chain partners tend to deviate from the self-seeking profit maximization motive towards decisions that would foster the relationship when the social feedback suggest cooperation. Apart from motivation, goal setting, feedback and control, and interdependence are other important aspects of social psychology.

Goal setting theory states that individuals can be systematically directed to achieve a set of goals and objectives through appropriate motivation and specific feedback. However, the individual should first be motivated enough to accept a goal. Goal acceptance is easier when the set goal is unambiguous, measureable, and the individual efforts can significantly affect the outcome. A clear and challenging goal creates motivation for the individual. This motivation, combined with relevant feedback, appropriate and sufficient knowledge, and skills, leads to better task performance and goal attainment (Bendoly 2013; 2011).

Proponents of *social control theory* (cf. Ross 1901; Ngo 2011) have long advocated that goal attainment and individual effort works more efficiently and effectively for a closed-loop system, as compared to an open system, where continuous and specific feedback received from the environment allow individuals to make adjustments to their behaviors and efforts to adjust and remove any discrepancies. It is essential that feedback received is specific, meaningful, and actionable so as individuals can act on it to better align with the goal.

Interdependence in social or work settings arises when individuals acknowledge that their goal attainment can be significantly influenced both positively and negatively by the actions or inactions of the individuals or workers around them. No interdependence will exist if the individual believes that the goal can be achieved regardless of the state of the environment, in terms of coworkers' level of achievement of their goals, cooperation or competition, and level of support. The most common forms of interdependence studied and widely used in the literature are outcome interdependence and task interdependence. Outcome interdependence relates to the individual perception that the ability to achieve the goal is linked to other individuals' ability to achieve their goal, and task interdependence relates to individual perception that the ability to perform a task depends on the knowledge, skills, and efforts of other individuals (Wageman and Baker 1997). Belief in such interdependence often alludes to beliefs in non-zero-sum games.

3.3 *System Dynamics and Systems Thinking*

Framing, or the manner in which the presentation of information influences its interpretation, is a topic that is often discussed as relevant to decision making. Although framing can be initiated and reinforced by external sources, the actions taken by individual decision makers can also influence the framing they face in subsequent decision scenarios. Critical to such dynamics is the notion of feedback, which in turn motivates a broader discussion of the systematic nature of decision-making contexts as well as the individual decision makers present in these contexts. As discussed in the previous section, the presence of multiple decision makers in a single context adds a considerable level of complexity. However, it also emphasizes the importance of timing in that one individual's decisions and subsequent actions have the *potential* to influence those of others provided that it precedes these other decisions and has a means by which to exogenously influence them—*outputs* feeding back to influence *inputs* and *processes* of the decision makers as well as those around her/him.

The fields of system dynamics and systems thinking have in a related way had a long history of considering the critical role that feedback can have in the dynamics of systems (Forrester 1961; 1971). The field of system dynamics seeks to understand the non-linear behavior of complex systems, by understanding how actions flow through the system, as well as how feedback is given and received (a point recently emphasized by Gladwell's popular 2006 book). Due to his work as a professor at the MIT Sloan School of Management, Jay Forrester is widely acknowledged as the father of system dynamics. Forrester emphasized the importance that feedback has in influencing the dynamic interaction between inputs and outputs, and their effect on processes. Another one of Forrester's beliefs is that those individuals who are intimately involved with systems and processes—namely, managers—have some innate understanding of the factors that effect change in a system. Their intuition often leads them to enact change that has unintended consequences (Meadows and Wright 2008). This further emphasizes the importance of feedback and systems thinking.

Systems thinking is more dynamic than simple problem solving in that it considers the actions, reactions, and interactions of different problem solving approaches. This is counter to the traditional, linear approach to problem solving which ignores these complexities (Bendoly 2014). If we think of system dynamics models as similar to hardware in a computer, then systems thinking can be viewed as the operating protocols that guide how such structures (either codified or tacit) might be used in practice. Systems thinking helps us guide the use of inputs, processes, and outputs in complex system frameworks to produce superior outcomes.

Again, this requires adequate feedback and information sharing about the system, with participants in the system. We often seek to identify the root cause of a system event, assuming that the changing of the root cause can affect the outcomes. This falls back into the linear causality mindset and ignores the interactions that occur after initiation of the system. This is where feedback is more important than the linear root cause. Similarly, chemical reactions are often preceded by a short-lived event that initiates the reaction. However, once the process has begun, what caused the reaction is less relevant than what is necessary to sustain or restrain the reaction to our desired end. Again, this is where the notion of flows and feedback remains important in understanding and managing complex processes, such as chemical reactions or business systems.

4 Designing for Behavior: Bridging OM Science and Practice

Ultimately, OM science has an interest in conveying the best state-of-the-art models, guidelines, and prescriptions as possible to practice. Accepting that there will tend to be limitations in the completeness of data and computational capabilities, it is nevertheless worth considering how to ensure the most effective design and use of OM support tools.

To be clear, human biases and heuristics are not limited to the contexts that OM models are meant to provide insights into. They also affect the designers of these models and the likely users of these models. Clearly, there is virtue in getting these individuals to think systematically about complex problems, but that is easier said than done. What can we do to facilitate ideal levels of systematic consideration while managing to avoid losing decision makers in details? Ironically one of the most critical bodies of knowledge relevant to this question is one that has been largely overlooked in OM studies, namely, that provided by the fields and subfields of Design.

4.1 Anticipating Cuts and Pastes

Let's consider the kind of biases that effect individuals as they attempt to design tools or extrapolate beyond what sophisticated but limited tools provide. Rather than focusing on the nature of biases as they might apply broadly, let's consider the specific forms that biases can take with regards to the design and use of decision support tools encapsulating OM models and prescriptions. There are three levels of extrapolation that may take place in the discretionary use of decision support tools that are also ostensibly relevant in discussion of designer tendencies (see Bendoly and Clark 2016): set biases (biases that relate to how decision makers view the form of the data involved in multi-dimensional problems), trend biases (biases relating to how individuals view the tendency and manner by which this data changes), and causal biases (biases that describe how decision makers perceive changes in data to be interdependent). We will discuss each in turn.

4.1.1 Set Biases

Set biases include fairly widespread generalizations (among both practitioners and academics) regarding the distributions that data sets embody. Homogeneity, for example, is a highly common bias. Individuals tend to believe that a single data set in fact contains data specific to only a single population, rather than more than one population that might have distinct attributes. Uniformity and normality are also fairly typical assumptions regarding the makeup of individual subpopulations in observed and available data intended for decision support. Unless given reason to suspect otherwise, individuals will tend to assume that the "mean" of an attribute is one that half the population is above and the rest below (which of course is only true with perfectly symmetric populations). Normal, and lacking that, Uniform distributions, are what individuals have the most experience with through education and the popular press. It is therefore no surprise that these associated biases (along with homogeneity) play out in many decisions, supported by management tools or otherwise.

How is does this bias apply to OM tool designs, and particularly to fallacies in human behavioral consideration? Unlike the field of marketing for example, OM models in particular have a tendency to assume managers and workers can be characterized by fairly monolithic population characteristics (i.e., are fairly homogeneous, without major discontinuities in behavioral traits). Descriptions of individual consumers arriving to service operations settings are often less rigidly defined in contemporary work, but the view of how workers and managers might respond to varying conditions still remains oddly and largely predicated on similarity expectations. These set biases are then often built into OM models. Even when they are not built in, their impact is often not evident to users of those tools (e.g., worker/manager heterogeneity is often not a key performance indicator in decision support tools).

4.1.2 Trend Biases

While set biases involve the cognitive misinterpretation of the distribution of the data set as a whole, trend biases are misinterpretations of discrete patterns formed within a data set. In OM models, this is the realm in which erroneously specified forecasting structures can undermine supply chain, revenue management, project management, and a host of other support tools. Practitioners often oversimplify trends (i.e., unboundedness, stasis) by ignoring trends outside of the data range under observation. One common trend bias is linearity, in which trends observed in a data set are assumed to have a linear relationship. This bias ignores correlative relationships between points in the data set outside of the range of observation that may be non-linear. It also does not account for the possibility of outliers.

Continuity bias is another common trend bias. This occurs as a result of the assumption that trends in a data set are continuous, based on the observations of a particular segment of a data set. This bias extrapolates a relationship observed in a particular segment of a data set to the entirety of the set. Again, this bias ignores the possibility of an overall non-linear relationship and/or distinct clusters of subpopulations. These trend biases are founded in other fundamental biases, such as unboundedness and stasis. The interpreter may fall victim to unboundedness when they suspend belief in a single finite set of solutions and seemingly valid solutions can extend infinitely in either a positive or negative direction. Stasis is an erroneous assumption that data sets do not contain differentiation outside the relevant range of observation.

4.1.3 Causal Biases

Unlike set and trend biases, which distort the construct and distribution of data sets as well as how patterns are recognized, which affect the predictive analytics, causal biases affect perceptions of interdependence and how conclusions are drawn. That is to say, the set and trend biases may lead to erroneous assumptions about the correlation between two variables, whereas causal biases may lead to the unfounded belief that a change in one variable causes a change in the other variable. As the adage goes, "correlation does not equal causation."

Consider the well-established immediacy effect bias (Kirby and Herrnstein 1995; Weber and Chapman 2005), which assumes that causal factors are in close temporal proximity to the onset of the outcome (e.g., the rainstorm yesterday caused the seedling to sprout). Or consider the non-coincidence bias, which, on the other hand, assigns causality to any number of human and non-human factors that may or may not have the potential to affect outcomes. Such biases are often allowed to emerge due to the same cognitive dissonance (conflict between expectations and perceptions) behind the phenomenon known as "just-world bias," which maintains predictability in the world. We can continue to list these biases in passing, but the implication is a broad and singular one: Ultimately, there is a tendency for both model designers, as well as the users of these tools, to misattribute "cause" in the models built and used. Largely, the tendency is to assign causality to what is most immediately apparent.

Yet as indicated earlier, details presented to users of OM model-driven decision support tools should be tempered. Overloading individuals with descriptions can also be a recipe for poor use. The Law of Pragnanz (Kohler 1947), a foundational concept in discussion of design, offers some reinforcement to this perspective. Specifically, the law suggests that when people are given a set of ambiguous elements, they interpret the elements in the simplest way. Here "simplest" refers to arrangement having fewer rather than more elements, having symmetrical rather than asymmetrical composition, and generally observing the other Gestalt principles of perception (see the seminal work of Koffka 1935). The less clutter in the design, the less noise the practitioner will need to sort through to perceive the object of the model. This makes it easier for the designer to highlight what is and is not important.

To reiterate, given the choice between functionally equivalent designs, the simplest design should be selected, with cautions regarding over simplification.

5 Conclusions

5.1 Best Practices in Design for OM Tools

How can these caveats regarding the role of managerial and worker behavior on operational dynamics, and the biases of model designers and users with regard to the systematic consideration of these dynamics, be applied? Most critically, how can they be applied to the design of decision support tools with the intent of more intelligently informing managers and working in operational settings? To consider this question, we can draw again from aligned domains, such as the field of Semiotics (going back to Pierce 1868). As discussed in Bendoly's work in the *Journal of Business Logistics* (2016), the components of Pierce's Semiotic framework, and its adaptations, suggests that different messages require different levels of objective-abstract connections. These in turn necessitate different levels of complexity in the design. The most effective OM models will end with both a well thought out back-end as well as a strong visually representative front-end that is at least as sophisticated as its intent. That is to say, that the intended use and messaging of tools should be no more sophisticated than the analytical capabilities that the tool provides to its intended user (e.g., a purchasing manager, a revenue manager, etc.).

This is certainly not strictly an OM modeler's responsibility. Front-end interface developers must also understand the nature of intended messaging and use, as well as the nature of the back-end capabilities, in order to facilitate effective matches where possible. If the architecture of the tool interface, including all visual representations of data, predictions, and prescriptions, does not accurately convey the message, then key decision makers will not be effectively supported. Done well, however, such alignment between intent, design, and execution can inspire a virtual cycle of organizational learning regarding operational dynamics (per enacted sensemaking; Weick 1988). After all, effective OM models and associated support tools are developed and maintained through iteration rather than representative of final destinations.

5.2 Implications for Practitioners

As we highlight the need for a healthy culture of organizations, or the people behind the tools of the OM systems, we should consider the importance of perceived locus of control. Most effective OM systems will inevitably have some degree of interactivity. As interactivity increases, users of the model will undoubtedly accept some degree of responsibility for their role in the effective or ineffective use of the system. In his discussion of Rotter's studies of locus of control, Gray (1999) suggests that those with higher internal loci of control—at least in Western cultures—are more proficient problem solvers. This is validated by several recent studies, such as one that notes those who believe they can influence use and action are more effective learners and problem solvers and perceive higher ease of use of computer systems than internals (Hsia et al. 2012). Whereas another study confirms that internals have higher degrees of visual working memory as users of visual systems (Maxcey-Richard and Hollingsworth 2013) such as OM models. Both studies highlight how important it is for designers to have a degree of understanding about how users visually and cognitively process OM systems (e.g., intrascopic biases, set biases, trend biases, causal biases, etc.) in order to develop effective models. Without an understanding of common user errors, one is vulnerable to designing a system rife with perceptual traps for the end user. The end result is likely to be a system that is ineffective or at best, inefficient.

Now consider the flexibility-usability tradeoff, which suggests that flexibility and usability are inversely related. This implies that as operational systems become capable of addressing additional needs, they become more unwieldy for the user. Accommodating flexibility requires increased design complexity to perform a more diverse set of functions, but is achieved at the cost of efficiency. There are also associated monetary costs and additional development time. Lidwell et al. (2010) suggest that increased specialization (and resulting decreased efficiency) should increase only with increasing levels of uncertainty in future needs of users. As an example, they contrast the personal computer to modern video game systems. The personal computer is designed to perform a wide array of unspecified functions, whereas video game systems very efficiently perform a narrow range of functions at a high level of performance. The desired level of complexity from the perspective of the user is dependent on the anticipated need for flexibility. If the OM system is and always will be a specific purpose, extra bells and whistles may be viewed as clutter or artifacts. This, in turn, may lead the user to devalue the tool.

To the extent that OM systems rely on user perception, which they must by definition, the importance of both business acumen and psychological deftness converge. One cannot communicate important business concepts or measures without an understanding of the underlying business. On the other hand, those concepts cannot be communicated in the form of theoretical models without some understanding of the psychology of perception—particularly, the biases that users are likely to fall victim. In designing effective OM systems, a designer must be cognizant of the biases the users may exhibit at both the macro level in the makeup of data sets (e.g., set biases) and in the interpretation of the data within datasets. This applies to both actual or perceived trends and the likelihood that users interpret, as well as possible errors in causal attributions.

Unless they are aware of them, designers set users up for failed application of OM models, and ultimately poor business decisions. Going a step further, when developing the level of interactivity, designers must consider the psychology of users of the models, as well as their intended use of the specific models. Ease of use will allow users a better mastery of the models, which will lead to improved decision making and ultimately, a more effective model. Finally, the complexity of a system must be proportionate to the level of uncertainty of the future needs of the system. In other words, to paraphrase a quote attributed to Einstein (1934), although the incorporation of sophisticated considerations may constitute the backend, effective OM support tools should be designed to be as simple to work with in practice as possible—no simpler. The overarching design goal should be to inform and empower. Nontransparent operational mandates are ones that serve few practical interests in the end.

Returning once again to the earliest pragmatic approaches to learning from managerial behavior (e.g., Bowman 1963), it is clearly to the benefit of practice to place greater emphasis on developing an understanding of how the individual actors critical to their operations perceive of and cope with the complexity within which decisions are made. Not only can this information be leveraged in internal planning, it can also be communicated to tool designers that firms partner with in the development of modeling-based decision support systems. It may be that the best means by which to safeguard against flawed assumptions is for managers to provide a clearer voice regarding their behavioral context to those mathematicians and computer scientists for which human behavior is strictly an afterthought at best.

5.3 *Directions for Future Research*

Where does this leave the future of Behavioral Operations research? To say that the field has only scratched the surface and that we have only seen the tip of the iceberg, would be an understatement. Operating systems are incredibly complex structures. We make them so. Our designs in practice emerge from the confluence of complex reasoning and the conditions we are both truly constrained by as well as those that we simply imagine exist. As long as we have managers pushing the frontier of what can be done in practice, we will have questions regarding whether the reason behind those decisions were biased by factors that may have mislead these decisions.

We recognize that many of these questions continue to be unresolved today:

- How do managers and their workers cope with new operational developments (predominantly technology tool driven) that expose them to higher levels of information regarding operational processes?
- Are there tendencies to filter and aggregate otherwise overwhelming amounts of content in ways that are problematic (or conversely notably savvy)?
- Are certain organizations, or the developers they engage with, particularly capable in ensuring that tools are designed to capture key behavioral dynamics, capturing systematic effects

while also packaging information and prescriptions in ways that are clear, effective, and not fundamentally misleading?
- How are changes in the social norms impacted by phenomena both internal and external to work environments influencing the choices managers and workers make in adopting, adapting, or simply quietly and grudgingly accommodating changes while consciously seeking circumventions?
- What contemporary best practices can be identified in tool development and organizational use and adoption?

Future research in Behavioral Operations must proceed not only along the interface of Operations Management contextual design and the psychological/social realm that is the human condition. It must also proceed with a close eye on how both of these are being increasingly augmented by the role of technology. It is at this multi-disciplinary interface that the greatest future contributions to BeOps research and application await us. It is also one in which we should not shy from engaging our colleagues in the other aligned management and non-management disciplines towards such advancement. We can no more assume that silo-based, discipline-specific research is a solution to practical research contributions than we can any longer assume humans are rational profit maximizers. We have gotten over this first hurdle; we should be able to tackle the next.

References and Bibliography

Agrawal, V. and S. Seshadri (2000) "Impact of Uncertainty and Risk Aversion on Price and Order Quantity in the Newsvendor Problem," *Manufacturing & Service Operations Management*, **2**(4): 410–423.

Bendoly, E. (2011) "Linking Task Conditions to Physiology and Judgment Errors in RM Systems," *Production and Operations Management*, **20**(6): 860–876.

Bendoly, E. (2013) "Real-time Feedback and Booking Behavior: Moderating the Balance between Imperfect Judgment and Imperfect Prescription," *Journal of Operations Management*, **31**(1–2): 62–71.

Bendoly, E. (2014) "Systems Dynamics Understanding in Project Execution: Information Sharing Quality and Psychological Safety," *Production and Operations Management*, **23**(8): 1352–1369.

Bendoly, E. (2016) "Fit, Bias and Enacted Sensemaking in Data Visualization: Frameworks for Continuous in Operations and Supply Chain Management Analytics," *Journal of Business Logistics*, **forthcoming**.

Bendoly, E. and S. Clark (2016) *Visual Analytics for Management: Translational Science and Applications in Practice*. Taylor and Francis/Routledge, New York.

Bendoly, E., R. Croson, P. Goncalves and K. Schultz (2010) "Bodies of Knowledge for Research in Behavioral Operations," *Production and Operations Management*, **19**(4): 434–452.

Bendoly, E., K. Donohue and K.L. Schultz (2006) "Behavior in Operations Management: Assessing Recent Findings and Revisiting Old Assumptions," *Journal of Operations Management*, **24**(6): 737–752.

Bendoly, E., W. van Wezel and D.G. Bachrach (Eds.) (2015) *The Handbook of Behavioral Operations Management: Social and Psychological Dynamics in Production and Service Settings*. Oxford University Press, Oxford, UK.

Boudreau, J., W. Hopp, J.O. McClain and L.J. Thomas (2003) "On the Interface Between Operations and Human Resources Management," *Manufacturing & Service Operations Management*, **5**(3): 179–202.

Bowman, E.H. (1963) "Consistency and Optimality in Managerial Decision Making," *Management Science*, **9**(2): 310–321.

Cachon, G.P. (1999) "Managing Supply Chain Demand Variability with Scheduled Ordering Policies," *Management Science*, **45**(6): 843–856.

Cachon, G.P. and M.A. Lariviere (1999) "Capacity Choice and Allocation: Strategic Behavior and Supply Chain Performance," *Management Science*, **45**(8): 1091–1108.

Castenada, J. and P. Goncalves (2015) "Kicking the 'Mean' Habit: Joint Prepositioning in Debiasing Pull-to-Center Effect," (Bendoly, Van Wezel, Bachrach, (Eds.)) *The Handbook of Behavioral Operations Management: Social and Psychological Dynamics in Production and Service Settings*. Oxford University Press.

Chen, F., Z. Drezner, J.K. Ryan and D. Simchi-Levi (1998) "The Bullwhip Effect: Managerial Insights on the Impact of Forecasting and Information on Variability in a Supply Chain," (pp. 417–439) in *Quantitative Models for Supply Chain Management* (S. Tayur, R. Ganeshan, M. Magazine (Eds.)). Springer, New York.

Chen, Y., X. Su and X. Zhao (2012) "Modeling Bounded Rationality in Capacity Allocation Games with the Quantal Response Equilibrium," *Management Science*, **58**(10): 1952–1962.

Chen, Y. and X. Zhao (2015) "Decision Bias in Capacity Allocation Games with Uncertain Demand," *Production and Operations Management*, **24**(4): 634–646.

Croson, R. and K. Donohue (2006) "Behavioral Causes of the Bullwhip Effect and the Observed Value of Inventory Information," *Management Science*, **52**(3): 323–336.

Croson, R., K. Donohue, E. Katok and J. Sterman (2014) "Order Stability in Supply Chains: Coordination Risk and the Role of Coordination Stock," *Production and Operations Management*, **23**(2): 176–196.

Croson, R., K. Schultz, E. Siemsen and M.L. Yeo (2013) "Behavioral Operations: The State of the Field," *Journal of Operations Management*, **31**(1): 1–5.

Davis, A. (2015) "An Experimental Investigation of Pull Contracts in Supply Chains," *Production and Operations Management*, **24**(2): 325–340.

Davis, A., E. Katok and N. Santamaria (2014) "Push, Pull, or Both? A Behavioral Study of How the Allocation of Inventory Risk Affects Channel Efficiency," *Management Science*, **60**(11): 2665–2683.

Dilts, D. and K. Pence (2006) "Impact of Role in the Decision to Fail: An Exploratory Study of Terminated Projects," *Journal of Operations Management*, **24**(4): 378–396.

Ebrahim-Khanjari, N., W. Hopp and S.M.R. Iravani (2012) "Trust and Information Sharing in Supply Chains," *Production and Operations Management*, **21**(3): 444–464.

Einstein, A. (1934) "On the Method of Theoretical Physics," *Philosophy of Science Association*, **1**(2): 163–169.

Festinger, L. (1957) *A Theory of Cognitive Dissonance*. Stanford University Press, Stanford, CA.

Ford, H. (1926) *Today and Tomorrow*. Productivity Press, Portland, OR.

Forrester, J. (1961) *Industrial Dynamics*. MIT Press and John Wiley & Sons, Inc., New York.

Forrester, J. (1971) "Counterintuitive Behavior of Social Systems," *Technology Review*, **73**(3): 52–68.

Gilbreth, F.B. and L.M. Gilbreth (1922) "Process Charts and their Place in Management," *Mechanical Engineering*, **44**(1): 38–41.

Gino, F. and G. Pisano (2008) "Toward a Theory of Behavioral Operations," *Manufacturing & Service Operations Management*, **10**(4): 676–691.

Gladwell, M. (2006) *The Tipping Point*. Little Brown and Company, New York.

Goddard, K., A. Roudsari and J.C. Wyatt (2011) "Automation Bias—A Hidden Issue for Clinical Decision Support System Use," *International Perspectives in Health Informatics. Studies in Health Technology and Informatics*, **164**: 17–22.

Goncalves, P., J. Hines and J. Sterman (2005) "The Impact of Endogenous Demand on Push-Pull Production Systems," *System Dynamics Review*, **21**(3): 187–216.

Gray, P. (1999) *Psychology*. Worth Publishing, New York.

Gurnani, H., K. Ramachandran, S. Ray and Y. Xia (2014) "Ordering Behavior under Supply Risk: An Experimental Investigation," *Manufacturing & Service Operations Management*, **16**(1): 61–75.

Hartwig, R., K. Inderfurth, A. Sadrieh and G. Voigt (2015) "Strategic Inventory and Supply Chain Behavior," *Production and Operations Management*, **24**(8): 1329–1345.

Harvey, N. (2007) "Use of Heuristics: Insights from Forecasting Research," *Thinking and Reasoning*, **13**(1): 5–24.

Hsia, J., C. Chang and A. Tseng (2012) "Effects of Individuals' Locus of Control and Computer Self-efficacy on Their e-Learning Acceptance in High-Tech Companies," *Behavior and Information Technology*, **33**(1): 51–64.

Huber, V.L. and K.A. Brown (1991) "Human Resource Issues in Cellular Manufacturing: A Sociotechnical Analysis," *Journal of Operations Management*, **10**(1): 138–159.

Kahneman, D (2011) *Thinking Fast and Slow*. Farrar, Straus and Giroux, New York.

Kahneman, D. and A. Tversky (1979) "Prospect Theory: An Analysis of Decision under Risk," *Econometrica*, **47**(2), 263–292.

Kanigel, R. (1997) *The One Best Way: Frederick Winslow Taylor and the Enigma of Efficiency*. MIT Press, Cambridge, MA.

Kirby, K.N. and R.J. Herrnstein (1995) "Preference Reversals Due to Myopic Discounting of Delayed Reward," *Psychological Science*, **6**(2): 83–89.

Koffka, K. (1935) *Principles of Gestalt Psychology*. Harcourt Press, New York.

Kohler, W. (1947) *Gestalt Psychology*. Liveright, New York.

Lee, H.L., V. Padmanabhan and S. Whang (2004) "Information Distortion in a Supply Chain: The Bullwhip Effect," *Management Science*, **50**(12 supplement): 1875–1886.
Lidwell, W., K. Holden, J. Butler and K. Elam (2010) *Universal Principles of Design: 125 ways to Enhance Usability, Influence Perception, Increase Appeal, Make Better Design Decisions, and Teach through Design*. Rockport Publishers, Beverly, MA.
Little, J.D.C. (1970) "Models and Managers: The Concept of a Decision Calculus," *Management Science*, **16**(8): 466–485.
Loch, C.H. and Y. Wu (2008) "Social Preferences and Supply Chain Performance: An Experimental Study," *Management Science*, **54**(11): 1835–1849.
Maxcey-Richard, A. and A. Hollingsworth (2013) "The Strategic Retention of Task-Relevant Objects in Visual Working Memory," *Journal of Experimental Psychology: Learning, Memory, and Cognition*, **39**(3): 760–772.
Mayo, E. (1949) *Hawthorne and the Western Electric Company: The Social Problems of an Industrial Civilization*, Routledge, New York.
Meadows, D. and D. Wright (2008) *Thinking in Systems: A Primer*. Chelsea Green Publishing, White River Junction, VT.
Nagarajan, M. and S. Rajagopalan (2008) "Inventory Models for Substitutable Products: Optimal Policies and Heuristics," *Management Science*, **54**(8): 1453–1466.
Narayanan, A. and B.B. Moritz (2015) "Decision Making and Cognition in Multi-Echelon Supply Chains: An Experimental Study," *Production and Operations Management*, **24**(8): 1216–1234.
Ngo, F.T. (2011) "Role-taking and Recidivism: A Test of Differential Social Control Theory," *Justice Quarterly*, **28**(5): 667–697.
Pierce, C.S. (1868) "Upon Logical Comprehension and Extension," *Proceedings of the American Academy of Arts and Sciences*, **7**: 416–432.
Ramasesh, R.V. and T.R. Browning (2014) "A Conceptual Framework for Tackling Knowable Unknown Unknowns in Project Management," *Journal of Operations Management*, **32**(4): 190–204.
Repenning, N. and J. Sterman (2002) "Capability Traps and Self-Confirming Attribution Errors in the Dynamics of Process Improvement," *Administrative Science Quarterly*, **47**(2): 265–295.
Robinson, A.G. and M.M. Robinson (1994) "On the Tabletop Improvement Experiments of Japan," *Production and Operations Management*, **3**(3): 201–216.
Robinson, E.P. and M.L. Swink (1995) "A Comparative Model of Network Design Methodologies," *Journal of Operations Management*, **13**(3): 169–181.
Ross, E.A. (1901) *Social Control: A Survey of the Foundations of Order*. The Macmillan Company, London.
Schweitzer, M.E. and G.P. Cachon (2000) "Decision Bias in the Newsvendor Problem with a Known Demand Distribution: Experimental Evidence," *Management Science*, **46**(3): 404–420.
Simon, H.A. (1956) "Rational Choice and the Structure of the Environment," *Psychology Review*, **63**(2): 129–138.
Simon, H.A. (1957) *Models of Management*. John Wiley & Sons, New York.
Sogomonian, A.G. and C.S. Tang (1993) "A Modeling Framework for Coordinating Promotion and Production Decisions within a Firm," *Management Science*, **39**(2): 191–203.
Starr, M. (1966) "Evolving Concepts in Production Management," in Elwood S. Buffa, (Ed.) *Readings in Production and Operations Management*. John Wiley, New York, pp. 28–35.
Sterman, J.D. (1989) "Modeling Managerial Behavior: Misperceptions of Feedback in a Dynamic Decision Making Experiment," *Management Science*, **35**(3): 321–339.
Tversky, A. and D. Kahneman (1981) "The Framing of Decisions and the Psychology of Choice," *Science*, **211**(4481): 453–458.
Wageman, R. and G. Baker (1997) "Incentives and Cooperation: The Joint Effects of Task and Reward Interdependence on Group Performance," *Journal of Organizational Behavior*, **18**(2): 139–158.
Weber, B. and G. Chapman (2005) "The Combined Effects of Risk and Time on Choice: Does Uncertainty Eliminate the Immediate Effect? Does Delay Eliminate the Certainty Effect?" *Organizational Behavior and Human Decision Processes*, **96**(2): 104–118.
Wei, D. and B. Nault (2014) "Monopoly Versioning of Information Goods When Consumers Have Group Tastes," *Production and Operations Management*, **23**(6): 1067–1081.
Weick, K.E. (1988) "Enacted Sensemaking in Crisis Situations," *Journal of Management Studies*, **25**: 305–317.
Wu, D.Y. and E. Katok (2006) "Learning, Communication, and the Bullwhip Effect," *Journal of Operations Management*, **24**(6): 839–850.

PART V
POM Interface with Other Functions

18
MANAGEMENT ACCOUNTING AND OPERATIONS MANAGEMENT

Thomas Hemmer and Eva Labro

1 Introduction

In this chapter, we would like to outline the benefits gained for practice from looking at the Operations Management phenomenon through multiple angles, in particular by including Accounting, performance measurement, and incentives angles. Furthermore, we will explore the opportunities for interdisciplinary contributions to both the academic Operations Management and Accounting literature. Accounting focuses on the role of accounting information in assessing, valuing, and predicting the performance of firms and individuals. Furthermore, Financial Accounting is concerned with the role of such information to improve external (to the firm) decision making such as lending decisions by banks and trading decisions by financial market participants. Management Accounting, on the other hand, focuses on the role of accounting information internally within the firm.

If the reader will allow us some sweeping generalizations, we would characterize Managerial Accounting research as originally being very focused on the role of information to improve internal decision making up until the mid-sixties (Kaplan 1984). Over time, the focus of this research has shifted to the role of such information in measuring performance within the firm and providing incentives to align employees' actions with the firm's strategy. We would argue, however, that the pendulum has swung out a little too far. While the majority of what we teach in our Management Accounting courses is decision-making oriented in order to prepare our students for their roles in the workforce, the amount of research to support our teaching needs and update our teaching materials on this front is much more limited. Operations Management research, on the other hand, has continued to study the role of information in decision making (e.g., how to reduce the bullwhip effect by improved information sharing), and it would be valuable to bring some of that focus back to Accounting research.

Overall, Operations Management has typically been much more concerned with decision making and, until fairly recently, usually not considered the behavior of humans under incentives provided by performance measures. The main focus has been on accomplishing process and operations improvement by dealing with exogenously imposed challenges such as, for example, randomness of demand, outages, and defects. Operations Management research and practice have not been focused on how to best measure aspects of an exogenously determined process. Instead, the focus lands on the endogeneity that arises when measures are used not just to capture the properties of the process but to incentivize and inform decision makers that are responsible for managing the process. As such, this perspective of Accounting research provides an important vantage point for thinking through the interactions among performance measurement options, human behavior when responding to these incentives, and the resulting optimal structure of operations. Given the readership of the book, our chapter will focus on what an Accounting perspective can signify for Operations Management. We argue that both areas are inseparable.

In Section 2, we will discuss the importance of considering incentives and performance measurement in Operations Management. Using the illustrative cases of two typical Operations Management settings (throughput maximization and the choice between push and pull production), we will outline how the performance measurement perspective adds many tools to the operations manager's toolbox and how opportunities for joint optimization of operations and performance measurement arise. We will also discuss the role for Management Accounting in devising additional performance measures (such as those included in a balanced scorecard which typically reports performance measures for four different perspectives: financial, learning and growth, internal, and operational) to which incentives can be linked and how this affects how to best solve an operations problem.

In Section 3, we take the opposite perspective and discuss how the organization of operations affects what can and cannot be measured by Accounting. Here, our focus falls on cost measurement techniques such as Activity-Based Costing and Time-Driven Costing. We explain how Operations Management affects the accuracy of such cost measurement. This will in turn influence the operations management decisions based on these reported costs, suggesting that Accounting and Operations Management are joined at the hip. To be clear, some practitioners and researchers are already wrestling with issues on this interface (such as many of the works referenced in this chapter), and we do not aim to provide an exhaustive reference list of those that do (e.g., additional references include Hansen and Mouritsen (2007) and Chao et al. (2014)). Rather, we hope that our chapter will further stimulate Operations Management researchers and practitioners to consider Accounting and performance measurement issues, and vice versa, by outlining some avenues for research and practice which we believe will be most fruitful.

2 The Importance of Considering Incentives and Performance Measurement in Optimizing Operations

2.1 Introduction to Performance Measurement and Incentives

2.1.1 Agency Theory

Agency theory is the economic framework that underlies the majority of hypotheses building on performance measurement topics in Accounting research (with the next substantial theoretical framework used on this topic being behavioral/psychological). In its very basic form, a Principal with utility function G contracts with a risk averse Agent with utility function U to exert unobservable effort in return for a wage, which is a function of the observable outcome x_i. A self-interested Agent will only behave in the way desired by the Principal when his pay structure is set up in such way that Principal's and Agent's incentives align. A discrete outcome (N different x_i values)—binary input measure (a_h for high effort, a_l for low effort) version of the classic agency model by Hölmstrom (1979) is specified as follows:

$$Max_{S(x)} \sum_{i=1}^{N} G(x_i - S(x_i)) p(x_i \mid a_h)$$

s.t.

$$\sum_{i=1}^{N} U(S(X_i)) p(x_i | a_h) - V(a_h) \geq \underline{U} \quad \text{(IR)}$$

$$\sum_{i=1}^{N} U(S(X_i)) p(x_i | a_h) - V(a_h) \geq \sum_{i=1}^{N} U(S(X_i)) p(x_i | a_l) - V(a_l) \quad \text{(IC)}$$

$V(a)$ is the cost of effort of the Agent, and p is the conditional probability of achieving a particular outcome, given the level of effort exerted. The Principal's (e.g., CEO or shareholders of the firm) objective is to maximize his residual, while offering the Agent (e.g., a worker in the firm) a wage that satisfies both his individual rationality (IR) constraint, which ensures that the Agent at least earns his reservation utility $\underline{U}$ and incentive compatibility (IC) constraint. This makes the Agent prefer to put in high effort rather than low effort (since the problem is set up such that the Principal always prefers high effort). Forming the Lagrangian for this optimization problem, and taking the first order condition (FOC) with respect to $S(x_i)$, we obtain:

$$\frac{dL}{dS(x_i)} = 0 \Leftrightarrow$$

$$-G'(x_i - S(x_i)) p(x_i | a^h) + \lambda U'(S(x_i)) p(x_i | a^h) + \mu U'(S(x_i)) (p(x_i | a^h) - p(x_i | a^l)) = 0$$

This expression further simplifies to:

$$\frac{dL}{dS(x_i)} = 0 \Leftrightarrow \frac{G'(x_i - S(x_i))}{U'(S(x_i))} = \lambda + \mu \frac{p(x_i | a^h) - p(x_i | a^l)}{p(x_i | a^h)}$$

In this expression, the term $\frac{p(x_i | a^h) - p(x_i | a^l)}{p(x_i | a^h)}$ is the likelihood ratio, which shows the precision with which the outcome x_i indicates that the effort level exerted was a^h. Viewing x_i as a performance measure of the Agent's effort, the precision of the performance measure determines its quality and hence impacts the weight placed on the measure in the contract $S(x_i)$. All else being equal, a measure with higher precision is preferred since it reduces the risk that is imposed on the (typically considered) risk-averse Agent.

2.1.2 The Sufficient Statistic Condition

Holmström (1979) goes on to show that any publically observed piece of information that does not satisfy the sufficient statistic condition generates value for an agency. When y is publically observable, using both x and y (instead of x alone) in the performance evaluation will lead to a Pareto improvement, if and only if it is *not* the case that x is a sufficient statistic for y. Mathematically, the sufficient statistic condition holds when $p(x, y | a) = p(y | x) \times p(x | a)$. In this case, nothing is learned from observing the additional performance measure y that we don't already learn from observing x and hence y will not be used. To see this, substitute the sufficient statistic condition in the likelihood ratio (Labro 2015):

$$\frac{p(y_j | x_i) p(x_i | a^h) - p(y_j | x_i) p(x_i | a^l)}{p(y_j | x_i) p(x_i | a^h)} = \frac{p(x_i | a^h) - p(x_i | a^l)}{p(x_i | a^h)}$$

This is good news for Accounting, since many of the accounting numbers (such as profit and cost) we provide do not satisfy the sufficient statistic condition. The availability of information to populate particular performance measures will, as a result, have an influence on how incentives can be structured.

2.1.3 Implications for Operations Management

What does all this mean for Operations Management? Because the availability of information to populate particular performance measures affects the provision of incentives, it will also influence how operations should optimally be structured in conjunction with such optimal incentives. (Management) Accounting may help by removing information constraints and thus make particular Operations Management structures more effective. For example, throughput can be increased if measures and incentives can be established to work on the right parts at the right time (Hopp and Spearman 2000, 368). As explained in Section 3, Activity-Based Costing (ABC) and Time-Driven Activity-Based Costing (TD-ABC) improve measurement of costs while appropriate contribution margin calculations will support throughput optimization.

Furthermore, when ignoring incentives and performance measurement considerations, observations of production processes' attributes such as capacity utilization, quality, and throughput volatility may lead to faulty conclusions about appropriate corrective actions. However, once incentives and performance measurement are considered, it becomes clear that aspects such as performance variance are endogenous responses to incentives embedded in the process design, and that the best way to deal with those is through changes in such incentives, rather than through Operations Management changes. As we will illustrate next, if we take the view that performance variance is created endogenously by incentives rather than exogenously, we will develop a comprehensive understanding of how to structure Operations Management practices optimally (Cachon 2012).

In the remainder of this section, we develop simple models of two typical Operations Management settings that illustrate the role of incentives and performance measurement outlined above in optimizing operations: throughput maximization with capacity constraints and push versus pull production. While the single-Agent, single-task model presented above is simplified, these two Operations Management settings introduce additional complexities that illustrate the continuing development of agency theory.

The model of throughput maximization with capacity constraints centers on a multi-tasking extension of the agency model whereby the role of information in providing performance measures of the different tasks is key. The multi-tasking literature was jumpstarted by Hölmstrom and Milgrom (1991). In essence, this literature extends the basic agency model where the Agent chooses the amount of effort to provide on a single-task to a model where the Agent not only chooses his level of effort but also the allocation of effort to multiple tasks. Of crucial importance in the Principal's ability to motivate both high effort levels and effort allocation to the appropriate tasks is the quality of the available performance measures of each task.

In a multi-tasking setting where there exists a precise performance measure of one task, yet the precision of the performance measure of the other task is very low, the Agent will choose to only exert effort on the task that is accurately measured where his effort level has a high likelihood of impacting this task's performance measure positively (if observed and rewarded by the Principal). The Agent will exert little, if any, effort on the task with an imprecise performance measure, since it is highly likely that even if he puts in high effort, this performance measure may not reflect that. Hence, the Agent will not provide a "balanced" effort on both tasks. Management Accounting can play an important role here, in that it can construct more precise performance measures of various tasks, allowing for a more appropriate effort allocation. It is this idea that inspired Management Accounting researchers to think about the role of the Balanced Scorecard (which reports scores on a set of "balanced" performance measures) in facilitating such effort allocation.

The model of push versus pull production, on the other hand, is exemplary of a multi-agent extension where multiple employees exert effort to produce an output. In the model presented in Section 3 of the seminal Hölmstrom (1982) paper that jumpstarted this literature, multiple Agents chose their effort levels, each obtaining a score on an observable, yet uncertain, performance measure of their output. Hölmstrom (1982) shows that something similar to the sufficient statistic result on the value of additional performance measures that we introduced earlier holds in this multi-Agent context. Say there are two Agents that provide effort a_1 and a_2, respectively, and each Agent's performance is reflected in their performance measures, y_1 and y_2, respectively. Unless you can write that $g(y_1, y_2 | a_1, a_2) = h_1(y_1, y_2 | a_2) \times p_1(y_1 | a_1, a_2)$, it is optimal to also base Agent 1's compensation on the performance measure of Agent 2, as this improves risk sharing.

For each of these Operations Management settings, we first derive insights from a view without incentives and performance measurement (traditional view) and discuss the decisions an operations manager in this firm may take. Next, we derive the insights from a perspective that includes incentives and performance measurement (a view through an Accounting lens) discussing the avenues that are suggested before comparing and contrasting these with the earlier recommendations.

2.2 Throughput Maximization and Capacity Constraints

2.2.1 An Operations Management Perspective on Throughput Maximization Under Capacity Constraints

The first Operations Management example of throughput maximization under capacity constraints models a firm (Principal) with a production technology that relies on some unlimited production factors, such as materials which can be bought at any point in any quantity and two potentially constraining production factors, labor L and machine space M, which are batch resources. The laborer (Agent) exerts efforts on multiple tasks (say, two: L_1 and L_2). Two types of outputs of differing size are created: q_s is the quantity of the (physically) small product, and q_b is the quantity of the big product, which is twice as high as the smaller product. The machine produces a batch of products at the time and is configured with adjustable shelf space to allow for different combinations of product sizes to be combined during the batch processing. The firm's objective is to maximize contribution margin, and the decision variables are the quantities of each product produced and the shelf configuration. In particular, the operations manager has to choose how many shelves that can hold big (M_b) versus small products (M_s) are put in the machine. Each shelf can hold a_i products. The following linear program is solved:

$$Max_{q_i, M_b, M_s} \sum_i (p_i - vc_i) q_i$$

subject to

$$\sum_i (l_{i1} + l_{i2}) q_i \leq L$$
$$m_b q_b \leq a_b M_b$$
$$m_s q_s \leq a_s M_s$$
$$2M_b + M_s \leq M$$

whereby p_i is the price of product i, vc_i is the variable cost of product i such as materials used, l_{ij} is the units of labor capacity resource of task j consumed by one unit of product i, m_i is the units of shelf space consumed by one unit of product i, and L and M are the labor and machine capacity resources currently in place.

To make the model more concrete, you can think of an example of a clay pottery where an artist (the Agent) uses clay and other unlimited materials to create outputs like vases (big size) and bowls (small size). The Agent's two tasks are creatively coming up with original designs (L_1) and shaping the clay (L_2) readying it for placement on the shelves that are subsequently put in the oven (the machine) for baking. Solving this linear program, the firm finds that the shadow price to the labor constraint is zero (the labor constraint is slack) and hence that the Agent has some idle capacity. However, the machine space constraint is binding and has a positive shadow price. This is the result of the vases and bowls needing a very long time in the oven and the inability of the artist to produce any further outputs while he waits, as the quality of the products decreases dramatically if they cannot immediately enter the oven.

Note that the optimal solution will result in a restriction on small and big products sharing the same shelf since that would entail suboptimal shelf space. However, this could potentially stifle the artist's creativity, as it constrains the products that the artist can design. For example, if the shelves allocated to vases are already filled, the artist has no choice but to come up with a design for a bowl. From a traditional Operations Management perspective, the manager of this firm may want to expand the capacity on the constrained machining resource. However, because this is a batch resource, it may be very costly to do so, and a cost-benefit analysis would need to be provided. Furthermore, if the operations manager is concerned about reduced creativity in the designs, he may relax the constraints on size-allocated shelf space, which would result in an even bigger need to buy additional oven capacity, as combining big and small products on the same shelf makes suboptimal use of the existing capacity.

2.2.2 A Management Accounting Perspective on Throughput Maximization Under Capacity Constraints

Next, consider this situation from the perspective of the incentives of the Agent who provides the effort on multiple tasks (L_1 and L_2). The artist has incentives to minimize throughput in the oven, as the artist is a batch resource that is left idle at the end of their shift each time the oven resource constraint binds, as it is the firm's policy that the artist can go home because clay cannot be molded that long prior to baking. If the Agent deliberately uses the shelf space suboptimally, he can shorten his time at work. Incentives are such that idle labor capacity is *created*. (See Boudreau et al. (2003) for the example of a power plant where throughput was much lower than predicted by the operations model because human factors were overlooked.)

Can these incentives be changed by tying the Agent's pay to performance measures such as volume? The Agent performs effort on multiple tasks. L_2, the task of shaping clay to put on the oven shelves is fairly and easily measureable. In addition, using the volume of objects produced as a performance measure would incentivize the Agent to make many products. However, the task of coming up with an original design for the products (L_1) is very hard to measure and the Principal is unable to assess the level of creativity applied until he learns of the customers' reaction to the designs in the future and their willingness to pay. As explained earlier, in a multi-tasking setting where there exists a precise performance measure of one task, yet the precision of the performance measure of the other task is very low, the Agent will choose to only exert effort on the task that is accurately measured (Hölmstrom and Milgrom 1991). So, when the Principal incentivizes volume, the Agent will not spend any time to come up with creative designs.

2.2.3 Alternate Solutions Proposed by the Management Accounting Perspective

When approaching the issue from an incentives perspective, the solutions that the manager may consider are very different from the solution proposed by an Operations Management perspective, where the plan is to increase the capacity on the bottleneck resource, and may indeed not require such investment.

2.2.3.1 Profit Sharing

Because the creativity in the design will affect the quantity of the products sold and the price at which they are sold, a profit sharing arrangement may offer appropriate incentives to the Agent since profit will drop if creativity in the designs decreases. Profit provides an aggregate performance measure that encompasses both tasks of the Agent, creativity, and volume of production, and incentivizes both as a result. The drawback of this solution, though, is that many other things that are outside of the control of the Agent will also affect profit (e.g., the state of the economy). As a result, the Principal will have to pay a large risk premium to the risk-averse Agent under such an agreement. In particular, this may be prohibitive in very large organizations with many employees.

2.2.3.2 Performance Measurement and the Balanced Scorecard

An alternate solution is to have the management accountant of the firm devise a reasonably precise performance measure of the hard to measure task. In our example, this task involved the creativity of the worker, a hard to measure aspect of performance. However, it would be possible to organize focus groups of customers that provide a bi-yearly assessment of the creativity of designs of the products that workers produced. Such measures can then be incorporated, next to volume, in the incentive pay offered to the Agent. In another setting, one could think about the quality of the produced output being harder to measure than the quantity of the output, yet measures of defects per million in a manufacturing setting or patient satisfaction in a healthcare setting can be collected next to product or patient volume.

Balanced Scorecards will incorporate a measure of each task the Agent is requested to work on (Kaplan and Norton 1992). The Balanced Scorecard is a strategic performance management tool that defines what the Principal defines as "performance" (the tasks to work on) and the target level of achievement on each task, providing a quantification of strategy. Of course, while the Balanced Scorecard offers an excellent way to clearly communicate the company's strategy to employees, there are some complications that may result in implementation problems. First, it is hard to achieve the right "balance" in assigning appropriate weights to each of the performance measures. The Balanced Scorecard typically includes performance measures of tasks in four different perspectives (financial, learning and growth, internal processes, and customers), but assigning weights to each of these perspectives remains more of an art than a science. Second, even if the management accountant is able to devise a performance measure of each task, it is highly unlikely that every task is measured with the same level of precision. Therefore, the Agent will still prefer to spend more effort on those tasks that are measured with more accuracy, as his effort will directly translate into his performance measurement score.

On the other hand, effort on less precisely measured tasks entails more risk, as there is more noise in the translation from effort to the performance score, and the Agent will choose to spend less time on this task. (The earlier example where there was no performance measure available of the creative design task is an extreme example of this case since the performance measure of this task exhibits infinite noise.) In mathematical terms, the numerator of the likelihood ratio

$(p(x_i | a^h) - p(x_i | a^l))$ is smaller for tasks with less precise performance measures since the performance score x_i is not a good reflection of the level of effort put in. If the difference between $p(x_i | a^h)$ and $p(x_i | a^l)$ is small, an Agent who puts in very little effort can score almost as high on the performance measure as an Agent who puts in high effort. Hence, the Principal cannot distinguish the high effort Agent easily from the low effort Agent, which is very risky for the high effort Agent. Measures with a smaller likelihood ratio are receiving less weight in the incentive pay structure of the Agent, since they attract a larger risk premium.

2.3 Push Versus Pull Production

Next, we enhance the basic agency model by introducing multiple Agents, based on a simplified version of the model in Hemmer (1998). Two Agents are working in sequence to produce a finished product. Agent I performs the initial tasks, passes the intermediate product onto Agent F, after which F performs the final tasks.

2.3.1 An Operations Management Perspective on Push versus Pull Production

To the operations manager, the natural question is whether a push or a pull system is preferred. In a push system, Agent I initiates production, while Agent F is simply responsible for keeping up with the flow. In a pull system, the responsibility to initiate production rests with Agent F, while Agent I is responsible for meeting the demand from F. The parameters that enter a decision on whether to organize the production as push versus pull from a traditional Operations Management perspective are the benefits of low inventory holding costs and the ability to rapidly adjust to demand shocks versus low risk of stock-outs and improved information flow. The first two are typically better under a pull environment, while the latter two are typically better under a push environment.

2.3.2 A Management Accounting Perspective on Push versus Pull Production

The incentives and performance measurement perspective may get the operations manager to think about other parameters that impact the choice between a push or pull environment. Typically, the quality of the work of Agent I on the intermediate product affects Agent F's ability to finish the product. For example, think about Agent I sanding chairs, while Agent F paints them. The smoothness of the sanding and thoroughness of the dusting by Agent I affect not only the quality of the final products, but also the speed with which Agent F can paint the chairs. Under which production organization would it be easier to give Agent I incentives to do a quality job on the intermediate product? Let Agent I be a multi-tasker, who allocates effort to both speed and quality, while Agent F can only supply speed. As before, Agent I's tasks have different levels of measurability. While the time that each Agent spends is a very precise measure of speed, it is very hard to measure intermediate quality.

Whether or not the operation is organized as a push or a pull system will affect the options management has to incentivize the Agents.

2.3.2.1 INCENTIVES UNDER THE PUSH SYSTEM

Under a push system, time is a highly accurate measure of whether Agent F meets contractual obligations, so he can be paid a risk-free flat wage if he keeps up with Agent I's production. However, since no measure of quality exists, Agent I can only be paid based on volume. Hence, he will not allocate much effort to quality as that doesn't impact his incentive pay positively. Following the assumption in Hölmstrom and Milgrom (1991), Agent I is benevolent, which entails that he will supply some limited effort on quality "for free," up to a certain level. This is a natural way to think about Agents allocating effort to things that are not contractually part of their incentive pay. Most humans do wish to be at least somewhat of a good "citizen" in the workplace and will allocate some effort to parts of their job that are not strongly incentivized.

2.3.2.2 Incentives Under the Pull System

Under a pull system, Agent F is assigned the responsibility to initiate production. However, Agent I controls the choice of quality of the intermediate product supplied, thereby affecting the speed of Agent F. Hence, the expected production volume is determined jointly by Agent I's choice of quality supplied and Agent's F choice of speed. This means that the production volume now becomes a measure of quality as well. By offering both Agents a contract that is increasing in volume, the Principal can incentivize quality input by Agent I. (One could interpret this as a group incentive whereby the entire team gets paid on the same measure: volume.) Contract parameters can be chosen in such a way that Agent I will exert more effort on quality than the level he benevolently supplies. Because there is no measure of quality in the push system, it is impossible for the Principal to get more than such benevolent level under that production organization. In sum, other parameters than those considered in the traditional Operations Management view now enter into the decision of how to organize production optimally as either push or pull: the level of quality benevolently provided by I, the benefit to the organization of I allocating more effort than this benevolent level to quality, and the productivity of I's quality enhancing effort.

2.3.2.3 A Measure of Intermediate Product Quality

So far, we have assumed that the quality of the intermediate product is impossible to separately measure. Hence, in the push system no measure of quality is available, whereas in the pull system volume can serve as a measure of quality. Imagine that the company's management accountant can produce a measure of intermediate quality, such as the evenness of the chair's surface or the amount of dust remaining on the chair. The noise in this performance measure will determine whether this additional information is of value. However, the level of precision required for the measure to be of value and the yardstick to compare it to are different in a push versus a pull organization. In the push system, the new measure of quality can potentially complement the volume measure of speed. However, the higher the benevolent level of quality provided by Agent I in the push system, the more precise the performance measure of quality should be before the Principal will use it. In the pull system, the new measure of quality is a substitute for the volume measure, which already provides information about intermediate quality. Hence, for the Principal to wish to make this substitution in the incentive pay scheme, the new intermediate quality measure needs to be a more precise measure of this construct than volume.

Consequently, the availability of such a performance measure of intermediate quality (or the creation thereof by the management accountant) determines how operations should be organized. If performance measurement can be done right, pull production outperforms push production, as it can create higher value to the organization by incentivizing more effort on quality. If not, push production outperforms pull production. Hence, performance measurement and incentive systems need to be optimally matched with how production is organized. Empirically, we observe substantial cross-sectional variation in success or failure of companies that adopt pull production, even though the Operations Management mechanics of their implementation are the same (e.g., Shah and Ward 2003). The (in)ability to match a pull production environment with the right performance measurement system can potentially explain such variation.

2.4 Implications for Practice

Broadening the operations manager's perspective to include incentives and performance measurement increases the number of tools in his toolbox that he can use to improve operations. Operations Management tools such as capacity acquisition and allocation, production scheduling, throughput planning, and organizing production to be pulled or pushed are to be complemented with performance measurement and incentive pay tools, and jointly optimized. Furthermore, variation that may seem random when considering a narrow Operations Management perspective may actually be predictable when the human incentive side of the issue is also considered. The construction of (accounting) performance measures may increase the degrees of freedom that the operations manager has to organize production processes.

3 The Importance of Considering Operations When Designing Cost Measurement Systems

Section 2 described how accounting performance measures affect the optimal design of Operations. This section reverses the causality, and develops on how Operations Management choices affect the accounting measurement function. In particular, we will illustrate how the way in which operations are managed can affect the accuracy of cost measurement. Before doing so, we first need to introduce the mechanics of cost measurement.

3.1 The Mechanics of Cost Measurement

In most organizations, costing systems serve many different needs such as product pricing, product line decisions, capacity planning and allocation, performance measurement and control, project scheduling, project selection, and benchmarking. In order to improve decision making and performance management, managers try to understand how costs behave and how cost objects consume resources by means of cost functions. A cost function is a mathematical description of how cost changes with changes in volume or in the level of an activity or process relating to that cost (Labro 2006). Cost objects are the products, services, distribution channels, customers, or any other part of the business that a manager may wish to understand how much of the firm's resources it consumes. Costing is therefore in essence an estimation or approximation exercise: within a relevant range, management accountants seek to derive a linear function that approximates the underlying true cost behavior. Various cost measurement techniques have been developed to make this approximation.

3.1.1 Traditional Costing Methods

Traditional costing methods estimate cost as a linear function of volume (Horngren et al. 2014). Along with other management experts, Kaplan and Johnson (1987) and Cooper and Kaplan (1987) have claimed that these traditional costing methods were systematically distorting product costs, leading to wrong decisions being taken on the basis of these costs. They critiqued the simplicity of only considering costs to be either variable with volume or fixed and disapproved of the exaggerated use of direct labor hours as an allocation base for the indirect costs in a "new" production environment where fewer hours of direct labor were used. In addition, a bigger share of the costs in this "new" production environment was indirect and therefore had to be allocated using some allocation base. Picking the wrong allocation base in this setting has disastrous consequences.

3.1.2 Activity-Based Costing

Activity-Based Costing (ABC) was coined as a more accurate costing method where allocation bases are chosen to better reflect the cause and effect relationship in resource consumption patterns. ABC estimates changes in cost as a function of changes in level of activity, where an activity is any discrete task that an organization undertakes to make or deliver a product or service. New cost drivers (factors that cause or drive an activity's cost; in essence the same as the old term "allocation bases"), other than volume-based drivers such as direct labor hours and direct machine hours, were now used to allocate the cost of the resources aggregated in these activity cost pools. Examples include the number of set-ups to allocate the cost of the set-up activity, the number of purchasing orders to allocate the cost of the procurement activity, the number of machine insertions to allocate the cost of the machining activity, the number of inspections to allocate the cost of the inspection activity, and the number of different components to allocate the cost of maintenance of the Bill of Materials.

The final innovation of ABC was to introduce the ABC hierarchy: an understanding that costs are driven by (and hence variable with respect to) activities that occur at different levels. The typical hierarchy considers four levels: unit, batch, product- (or service-) sustaining, and facility-sustaining. The hierarchical level at which a particular cost is classified indicates when this cost becomes variable. Costs on the unit level are the costs that traditionally are called variable costs and are incurred per unit (e.g., price). Costs on the batch level are incurred each time a batch is delivered or brought to the production line (e.g., inspection and set-up costs). Product-sustaining costs are incurred to enable the production and sale of a particular product (e.g., product design and product advertising). Facility-sustaining costs are costs that are fixed in the short run. They only become variable when the facility is closed down or reduced in size.

This ABC hierarchy helps management identify which costs are incremental for different types of decisions. For example, if the decision concerns whether or not to produce one extra unit of a product, only the unit level costs (such as the material to use in the unit) are relevant. However, for the introduction of a new service to the firm's service mix, all costs up to the service-sustaining costs (such as service development and service specific marketing) are to be considered.

3.1.3 Time-Driven Activity-Based Costing

A more recent cost method innovation is Time-Driven Activity-Based Costing (TD-ABC) (Kaplan and Anderson 2004). TD-ABC was introduced because of a perceived dissatisfaction with the complexity and low maintainability of ABC systems, which were argued to be particularly harmful in industries subject to rapid change. Two simplifications are proposed in this method. First, TD-ABC systems only use time as a cost driver, and hence are particularly suitable for businesses where time spent by the employees and human capital of the firm is a big percentage of resources, such as in the service sector. Cost rates per unit of time of each resource can then be calculated.

Second, TD-ABC introduces the notion of time equations. A time equation collects information on the quantity (in units of time) of each resource that supports an activity that is required to produce a unit of the cost object. Next, the cost rates per unit of time can be multiplied in to calculate the cost of the cost object. While no survey evidence is currently available about the widespread adoption of this technique, case studies illustrating its use have been published. The first TD-ABC implementations were mostly in the service sector, such as in healthcare and banking. Also distribution features TD-ABC implementations, since an understanding of what drives delivery time is crucial. (Like the number of deliveries, a transaction cost driver doesn't capture all the variation in delivery effort that a duration cost driver, like the time spent delivering, reports.) However, the idea of time as a cost driver can extend to time spent on machinery or in facilities or warehouses. For more detail on the mechanics of each of these techniques and numerical examples, we refer to Balakrishnan et al. (2012).

3.2 Operations Management Choices Affecting Cost Measurement Accuracy

With the mechanics of the cost measurement techniques explained, we are now ready to study how Operations Management choices may affect the accuracy of these costing methods.

3.2.1 Validity of the ABC Hierarchy

Ittner et al. (1997) explain how Operations Management choices affect the validity of the ABC hierarchy. From an Accounting perspective, the implication of the ABC hierarchy is that total costs associated with product-sustaining activities are independent of any of the cost drivers on lower levels in the hierarchy (batch or unit). Additionally, the setup cost of a single batch is independent of the number of units produced in that batch. That is, for the ABC hierarchy on which ABC cost measurement is based to be an accurate reflection of the truth, the batch-level cost should not depend on the size of the batch (volume, or unit-level).

In contrast, decision rules used by operations managers introduce associations among the cost hierarchy categories and between these classifications and total manufacturing costs. For example, Economic Order Quantity (EOQ) models in their simplest form calculate optimal economic order quantity in units as $Q_o = \sqrt{\dfrac{2DS}{H}}$, whereby D is demands in units over the time period, S is the ordering cost per order in dollars and H is the inventory holding cost per unit over the time period. That is, the optimal batch size Q_0 is a function of trade-offs between order costs (which are incurred at batch level) and inventory holding costs (which are incurred at unit level). Hence, EOQ rules used by the procurement function entail that the number of batches is positively associated with production volume since the total number of batches represents the product's production volume divided by the constant reorder point. This invalidates the assumption of the ABC hierarchy that the batch and unit level costs are independent. Such endogenous production scheduling based on EOQ models thus makes variation in costs associated with production batches empirically indistinguishable from variation due to production volume (Anderson and Sedatole 2013).

3.2.2 Cost of Product Variety

As a second example, consider the cost of product variety. A big proportion of product variety costs are accounted for in the ABC hierarchy at product-level as they relate to the spending on product-specific development resources and marketing campaigns, and as such should be captured by a well-specified ABC system. However, the choice of operations managers to invest in flexible automation (or not) also affects a firm's understanding of its cost of product variety (Ittner et al. 1997). Firms that are making large fixed cost investments in flexible automation systems (typically considered facility-level costs) reduce batch set-up costs to close to zero. Firms that are making no such investments and continue to rely on manual set-ups (the costs of which are measured at batch-level) are likely to see a strong association between product variety and batch-level costs.

Firms that have flexible automation systems are unlikely to observe such association between breadth of product offering and batch-related costs. However, in such firms, batch level and facility-level costs are negatively correlated, again invalidating the assumption of independence of levels in the ABC hierarchy. Furthermore, if firms endogenously respond to the need for offering product variety by adopting flexible automation systems, their cost measurement system may underestimate the resulting costs since a regression analysis will not document any batch cost level variation (as these are close to zero) nor any fixed investment cost variation (by definition, since these costs are fixed) that is associated with an increase in product variety.

The way in which operations are organized can also affect the general accuracy of the cost measurement system, defined as the level of error with which cost object's costs are measured by the costing system. Consider the distinction between a job shop organization and a process shop organization. In a job shop, small batches of a variety of products are manufactured and most of the products produced require a unique set-up and sequencing of steps. In a process shop, larger batches of more similar products are manufactured using a similar setup and common sequencing of steps. These two ways of organizing production are typically considered the extreme ends of a continuum. In a production organization that leans more toward a job shop there is little sharing of resources across products, whereas a system that is closer to a process shop is characterized by a lot of resource sharing with most products making use of the same set of resources (even if the pattern of resource consumption varies somewhat across products).

Balakrishnan et al. (2011) find that in job shops, a more sophisticated cost system with more cost pools is required than in process shops in order to achieve the same overall level of cost measurement accuracy. The reason is the following: At every step in cost calculations, measurement errors can be made. However, some errors may offset. While one error over-costs a cost object, another error may under-cost it, resulting in an overall fairly accurate approximation of the cost of the cost object (Datar and Gupta 1994). The likelihood that costing errors offset each other is much higher in a process shop because the various products share resources, which means that over- and under-allocations are more likely to cancel out. In a job shop, however, the likelihood that errors offset each other is much smaller, and hence a more sophisticated costing system needs to be put in place to achieve the same level of accuracy.

3.3 *Implications for Practice*

The various prior studies and examples mentioned suggest that to understand the validity of costing assumptions and the accuracy of cost measurement, we must take into account the production environment that is being measured. The same cost measurement technique may produce more or less accurate cost numbers in different environments. Furthermore, operations managers may take deliberate actions to change the way in which production is organized. First, such decisions are likely based on reported costs and hence subject to this measurement concern. Second, these actions to change the Operations Management environment will in turn not only affect the actual (unobservable) resource consumption but also the accuracy and the bias with which the cost system can measure, approximate, and report this resource consumption. Managers should be aware that in some production environments costs are likely to be reported with higher inaccuracy than in others. For example, job shop environments and firms relying heavily on EOQ type ordering policies likely have a higher than average level of errors in reported costs.

4 Directions for Future Research

We see a lot of opportunities for academic research on both the performance measurement/incentives and Operations Management interface, as well as on the interface between cost measurement and Operations Management.

4.1 Service Sector Considerations

We surmise that the importance of performance measurement and incentives in Operations Management will increase even more with a shift away from research studying the manufacturing sector towards the service sector, which has increased significantly in economic importance over the last couple of decades. As a percentage of total inputs, material and machine cost make up a smaller amount than labor in the service sector, so incentives to align human behavior with the strategy of the firm are even more important. Time and cost measurement is of utmost importance in the service sector more generally. For example, they are crucial inputs to effective project planning (e.g., in construction and maintenance). Furthermore, most services resemble a pull environment with the arrival of the client triggering the service and decisions being made by people on the spot when serving these customers. We know from Section 2.3, that getting performance measurement right is of utmost importance in such pull environments. Opportunities for empirical work are potentially bigger in the service sector too, since many service industries are regulated, and regulation typically goes hand in hand with an increase in data availability. Prime examples are banking, healthcare, and airline travel.

4.2 Accounting Information Technology Advances

With rapid accounting information technology advances, informational constraints on what can be measured as a performance measure are relaxed, allowing for changing Operations Management structures that increase value generation. For example, do we empirically observe that when accounting performance measurement quality is improved, organizations shift towards more pull production? While a call for studying how performance measurement affects operations is not new (Melnyk et al. 2004), most Operations Management research has focused on how data quality affects operations decision making (e.g., Hazen et al. 2014).

4.3 Dynamic Cost Measurement in Specific Operations Environments

Further research on how to tailor cost driver analysis and cost measurement to particular operations environments will be fruitful. Here, too, the service sector poses a very different operations environment with different cost measurement implications that we have not studied sufficiently. For example, recently we started seeing more Time-Driven-Based costing implementations (with time spent by resources as the sole cost driver) in human resource intensive sectors such as healthcare and distribution.

Furthermore, Operations Management is in constant flux and over time many changes occur with how operations are organized in response to changing technological, environmental, or demand parameters. Cost measurement has historically taken a very static perspective and makes a snapshot of resource consumption patterns by products or services at a set point in time. Understanding the impact of operational changes on cost measurement and improving dynamic cost measurement are important to further both academic literature and practice.

References and Bibliography

Anderson, S. W., and K. L. Sedatole. 2013. Evidence on the Cost Hierarchy: The Association between Resource Consumption and Production Activities. *Journal of Management Accounting Research* **25**: 119–141.

Balakrishnan, R., E. Labro, and K. Sivaramakrishnan. 2012. Product Costs as Decision Aids: An Analysis of Alternative Approaches (Part 1). *Accounting Horizons* **26** (1): 1–20.

Balakrishnan, R., S. Hansen, and E. Labro. 2011. Evaluating Heuristics Used When Designing Product Costing Systems. *Management Science* **57** (3): 520–541.

Boudreau, J., W. J. Hopp, J. O. McClain, and L. J. Thomas. 2003. On the Interface between Operations and Human Resources Management. *Manufacturing & Service Operations Management* **5** (3): 179–202.

Cachon, G. P. 2012. What is Interesting in Operations Management? *Manufacturing & Service Operations Management* **14** (2): 166–169.

Chao, R. O., K. C. Lichtendahl Jr., and Y. Grushka-Cockayne. 2014. Incentives in a Stage-Gate Process. *Production and Operations Management* **23** (8): 1286–1298.

Cooper, R. and R. Kaplan. 1987. How Cost Accounting Systematically Distorts Product Costs. In *Accounting & Management Field Study Perspectives*, edited by W. J. Bruns, Jr., and Robert S. Kaplan. Boston, MA, Harvard University Press, 204–228.

Datar, S. M., and M. Gupta. 1994. Aggregation, specification, and measurement errors in product costing. *The Accounting Review* **69** (4): 567–591.

Hansen, A., and J. Mouritsen. 2007. Management Accounting and Operations Management: Understanding the Challenges from Integrated Manufacturing. In *Handbook in Management Accounting Research*, edited by C. S. Chapman, A. Hopwood, and M. D. Shields. Amsterdam, Netherlands: Pergamon Press, 729–752.

Hazen, B. T., C. A. Boone, J. D. Ezell, and A. Jones-Farmer. 2014. Data Quality for Data Science, Predictive Analytics, and Big Data in Supply Chain Management: An Introduction to the Problem and Suggestions for Research and Applications. *International Journal of Production Economics* **154**: 72–80.

Hemmer, T. 1998. Performance Measurement Systems, Incentives, and the Optimal Allocation of Responsibilities. *Journal of Accounting and Economics* **25**: 321–347.

Hölmstrom, B. 1979. Moral Hazard and Observability. *Bell Journal of Economics* **10** (1): 74–91.

Hölmstrom, B. 1982. Moral Hazard in Teams. *Bell Journal of Economics* **13** (2): 324–340.

Hölmstrom, B., and P. Milgrom. 1991. Multitask Principal-Agent Analyses: Incentive Contracts, Asset Ownership, and Job Design. *Journal of Law, Economics, & Organization* **7**: 24–52.

Hopp, W. J., and M. L. Spearman. 2000. *Factory Physics*. 2nd ed. New York: McGraw-Hill.

Horngren, C. T., S. M. Datar, and M. Rajan. 2014. *Cost Accounting: A Managerial Emphasis*. 15th ed. Pearson Higher Education, New York.

Ittner, C. D., D. F. Larcker, and T. Randall. 1997. The Activity-Based Cost Hierarchy, Production Policies and Firm Profitability. *Journal of Management Accounting Research* **9**: 143–162.

Kaplan, R. S. 1984. The Evolution of Management Accounting. *The Accounting Review* **59** (3): 390–418.

Kaplan, R. S., and D. P. Norton. 1992. The Balanced Scorecard—Measures that Drive Performance. *Harvard Business Review* Jan–Feb: 71–79.

Kaplan, R. S., and H. T. Johnson. 1987. *Relevance Lost: The Rise and Fall of Management Accounting*. Boston, MA: Harvard Business School Press.

Kaplan, R. S., and R. S. Anderson. 2004. Time-Driven Activity-Based Costing. *Harvard Business Review* **82** (11): 131–138.

Labro, E. 2006. Analytics of Costing System Design. In *Contemporary Issues in Management Accounting*, edited by A. Bhimani. Oxford: Oxford University Press.

Labro, E. 2015. Hobby Horses Ridden. *Journal of Management Accounting Research* **27** (1): 133–138.

Melnyk, S. A., D. M. Stewart, and M. Swink. 2004. Metrics and Performance Measurement in Operations Management: Dealing with the Metrics Maze. *Journal of Operations Management* **22**: 209–217.

Shah, R., and P. T. Ward. 2003. Lean Manufacturing: Context, Practice Bundles, and Performance. *Journal of Operations Management* **21**: 129–149.

19
POM AND FINANCE

John R. Birge

1 Introduction

Production and operations management research has provided a number of classic models such as the EOQ formula (Harris 1913), the news vendor model (as in Arrow et al. 1951), the HMMS model (Holt et al. 1960), the Wagner-Whitin model (Wagner and Whitin 1958), Clark and Scarf's (1960) echelon inventory model, and more recent examples such as Lariviere and Porteus's (2001) selling-to-a-news vendor and the various channel coordination models described in Cachon (2003), among many others. Common themes in these models are the assumptions of infinite liquidity (i.e., sufficient cash for any expenditure) and the absence of risk considerations (at least as related to operational decisions) in the evaluation of cash flows. Both of these assumptions conflict with practical observations of finite liquidity and premiums applied to cash flows on the basis of risk contribution (that cannot be eliminated by diversification).

In certain situations, such as the perfect market assumed in Modigliani and Miller's classic work (1958), the available liquidity assumption is not constraining since any firm with a value-enhancing project can obtain financing (whether in debt or equity, which makes no difference as Modigliani and Miller show). This observation yields a separation of operational from financial decisions that would justify the operational models that ignore liquidity concerns; however, as Modigliani and Miller later observed (1963), market imperfections, such as tax, distress, transaction, and agency costs, negate the irrelevance result and remove the wedge separating operations from finance.

In addition to illuminating the need to consider liquidity in practical situations, the financial market also provides information on the value of future cash flows that explicitly considers the role of risk in those cash flows. The relevant risk level generally depends on a firm's operational decisions so that valuing uncertain cash flows then depends explicitly on operational considerations such as production, procurement, and capacity. In this case, the valuation of uncertain cash flows for an operational decision requires specific consideration of how those decisions would affect financial valuation.

This chapter briefly explains the issues involved in the interactions between the operational and financial decisions of firms. This chapter also covers some of the results in the area in terms of models that provide a structure for a firm's consistent decision making, that uncover properties of decisions and how they differ from results ignoring the financial context, and empirical results that explore how finance and operations interact in practice. The intent of the chapter is to be instructive while giving examples in many areas and not an exhaustive list of results.

The chapter also focuses on work that explicitly recognizes financial market conditions and the distinction between market and unique risks (i.e., that do not treat all variations in cash flows as equivalent). The following section presents the basic theory surrounding the integrated nature of finance and operations in imperfect markets. Section 3 describes how the valuation of future cash flows depends on operational considerations and the inconsistency in approaches based on exogenously determined discount rates. Section 4 describes how supply chain decisions and interactions between firms are also affected by financial considerations and how these issues impact supply chain efficiency and how operational "hedging" activities differ from financial market hedging activity. Section 5 considers the role that operations management plays in the financial risk of a firm (i.e., the causality from operations to finance). Section 6 describes some of the empirical results that have appeared on the topic. Finally, Section 7 summarizes the results and provides directions for further work for modelers, theorists, and empirical researchers.

2 Impact of Financing Needs on Single Firm Operational Decisions

As a starting point for operational models, consider the basic EOQ model to determine the optimal order quantity ($Q^\star$ solved as $Q^\star = \sqrt{\frac{2aK}{h}}$) of a firm facing constant known demand at rate a with a fixed charge K for every order and an inventory holding cost proportional to the amount of inventory as h times the amount of inventory. An implicit assumption for that model is that the firm has sufficient liquidity to finance an initial $K + cQ^\star$, assuming a constant marginal cost c for each unit ordered in addition to the fixed order cost. Even if the assumption (sometimes mentioned) that the selling price or other value from the product will be sufficient to cover the total ordering cost (and ensure a profit) is met, the firm may still not have sufficient cash to finance the initial working capital.

In a perfect market world, as explained by Modigliani and Miller (1958), the firm's lack of liquidity alone would not affect the EOQ (again assuming sufficient return in each order period to cover the total ordering cost). The firm can obtain funding either by offering some share (equity) of the total profits or by borrowing whatever amount the firm is short (debt). The perfect market ensures that a willing investor or lender would be available and would not interfere with the firm's profits from the ordering decision.

As noted above however, in reality, markets are not perfect and the firm would face some additional cost for financing this inventory. If no external financial market exists (i.e., the cost of additional debt or equity is infinite), the firm could order no more than its initial cash can support but may then only order up to the free cash flow from the cycle that ends when inventory is depleted. That may not be sufficient to cover the ordering cost. A model to determine the minimum long-run average cost now takes a different form. First, the firm can determine a sustainable cycle that will support the ordering cost indefinitely and then, it can decide whether a strategy exists to build up sufficient capital to finance this policy or, if more than sufficient capital is available, whether larger order quantities can be sustained.

For the minimum average cost self-financing cycle with revenues of p per unit of demand, the firm would solve:

$$\min_{Q \geq 0} \frac{aK}{Q} + \frac{hQ}{2} \tag{1}$$

$$\text{s.t. } K + cQ \leq pQ - \frac{hQ^2}{2a}, \tag{2}$$

where we assume the revenue and holding charges occur at the end of the period. This then implies that, if the positive Q satisfying the constraint, given by:

$$Q^{\min} = (p-c)h/(2a) + h\sqrt{(p-c)^2 + 8aK/h/(2a)}, \tag{3}$$

is smaller than $Q^\star$, then $Q^{\min}$ becomes the optimal feasible strategy, assuming that the firm can support an initial order and policy to reach a cash level of $K + cQ^{\min}$. Another strategy is then needed to build sufficient cash or to maximize the amount of cash that can be supported (and, hence, a lower overall Q than $Q^{\min}$). This then requires an additional optimization.

If the firm has more than $K + cQ^{\min}$ available, then the firm can order up to Q^{cash} that solves (1 and 2) with $K + cQ^{cash} \leq C$, where C is the firm's initial cash position. This value then increases with C until $Q^{cash} > Q^\star$, at which point, the original EOQ is again optimal.

The result is that, with no external financing possibility, the EOQ can change substantially. When the firm can obtain financing with some costs or perhaps benefits (for example, from the tax deductibility of debt), the results for the EOQ would then be reflected in a change in the formula. As long as the overall average profit is positive, the original EOQ formula applies if all the quantities remain fixed and known. A lender may also guarantee payment by securing the debt with some form of collateral, such as a debt covenant requiring sufficient assets (i.e., cash, inventory, accounts receivable, or fixed assets that are pledged to the lender). Buzacott and Zhang (2004) show how such asset-based financing can affect a firm's operating decisions. Alan and Gaur (2011) provide another example of a study of how a firm's operational decisions are affected by this form of financing. Babich and Sobel (2004) also consider a firm (deciding a time for an IPO) with a riskless loan and an extension that assumes losses in fixed assets in the event of inadequate liquidity for loan repayment. A dynamic version of repeated losses in the event of inadequate liquidity also appears in Li et al. (2013). In contrast to these models, when demand has risk and the firm may default on any unsecured loan amount, operational and financial decisions then interact with the broader financial market as described in the following section.

3 Impact of Financial Markets on Single Firm Operational Decisions

When firms face risk, operational decisions should reflect risk preferences consistent with the decision maker's objective. Firm managers are generally obligated to make decisions in the best interest of the firm owners. As agents of the owners, or principals, agents may act otherwise, requiring the principal to apply penalties or some form of monitoring to control the agent. In such cases, principal-agent theory (e.g., Hölmstrom (1979) and Plambeck and Zenios (2000) for an operational example) provides a process to design a mechanism that ensures the agent acts according to the principal's goals. Assuming a firm-owner objective, if the owners are shareholders of a public firm, then the decisions should reflect risk preferences consistent with those of the financial market. This observation implies that uncertain cash flows affected by the operational decisions of a public firm should be viewed from a financial market perspective.

As a simple example with uncertain cash flows, consider the basic news vendor model in which a firm must commit to a purchase or order decision in advance of observing demand. The cash flow revenue is then uncertain and requires consistent evaluation. A basic assumption of a market without financial frictions (e.g., no transaction or other costs for trading) is that the cash flows from these decisions cannot be exchanged costlessly with other cash flows in the market with zero current net cash flow to produce non-negative net cash flows in all future states of the world with strictly positive cash flows in some non-trivial (positive probability) set of states (i.e., the market does not admit arbitrage possibilities). This assumption provides the basis for the financially consistent valuation of uncertain cash flows from operational decisions (see Birge (2015) for an explanation).

The absence of arbitrage in a market with no frictions is the ability to adjust the probability distribution of the future cash flows to reflect risk so that then all future cash flows can be discounted with the market's valuation of risk-free cash flows (i.e., discounted with the so-called *risk-free* rate that applies to assumed zero-risk investments such as US treasury bills). This probability distribution is known as a risk-neutral or equivalent martingale measure. The equivalence of its existence with the absence of arbitrage is known as the Fundamental Theorem of Asset Pricing and is a result of linear programming duality (see Harrison and Kreps (1979) for a general discussion and Birge (2015) for a simple derivation in the operational context).

For the news vendor context, we consider an initial purchase quantity x at cost c and future sales $y(\xi) = \min(x, \xi)$ at price p (for now, assumed known or representing a price commitment from the seller) that depends on a random demand ξ with original (or natural) cumulative distribution function F. The financial market's value for the future cash flows $py(\xi)$ can reflect risk by finding the market's utility for this future cash flow. The Fundamental Theorem of Asset Pricing states that this is possible by transforming the distribution F to an equivalent risk-neutral distribution F_n and then treating the expectation, $E_{F_n}\left[py(\xi)\right]$, as a certain cash flow.

This process requires finding the equivalent representation of F_n. As explained in Birge (2000) and Birge (2015), this distribution can be found using the capital asset pricing model (CAPM) described in Sharpe (1964) and Lintner (1965). A key point in this derivation is to recognize that investors can diversify against idiosyncratic risks, which only relate to a specific investment and, therefore, can be fully diversified by investors, and systematic risks that cannot be diversified. This distinction particularly means that a utility that does not distinguish between these forms of risk is inconsistent for valuing the cash flows of any public firm (Birge 2015). The CAPM implies that the transformation of the distribution to a risk-neutral equivalent form only depends on the systematic risk of the cash flow.

An example from Birge (2015) to illustrate the difference in values considers two identical cash flows (A and B) that occur at a time $t = 1$ where both have mean \$100 and standard deviation of \$20. In the news vendor context, we might imagine that ξ for Cash Flow A actually depends on a single salesperson's effectiveness, which is not related to the market but only depends on the salesperson's unknown idiosyncratic ability. Cash Flow B, however, is the result only of consumer reaction to the firm's posted prices and is the result of (certain) production at a fixed posted price in response to uncertain demand, which is highly correlated with the market. From the CAPM, the cash flow in A, because it has zero correlation with market risk, is simply discounted with the risk-free rate as having value:

$$v_A = \frac{100}{1+r_f}, \qquad (4)$$

where r_f is the riskfree rate.

Cash Flow B, however, is correlated with market risk. The CAPM implies that Cash Flow B should be discounted for the amount of market or systematic risk as follows:

$$v_B = \frac{100}{1+r_f}\left(1 + r_f - \lambda_m CoV\left(\tilde{B}/100, \tilde{r}_m\right)\right), \qquad (5)$$

where $\tilde{r}_m$ is the market return, in which the overhead tilde (~) denotes a random variable with a mean value denoted with an overhead bar as $\bar{r}_m$, and λ_m is known as the *market price of risk*, given as:

$$\lambda_m = \frac{\bar{r}_m - r_f}{\sigma_m^2}. \tag{6}$$

The difference in the additional discounting in $\left(1 + r_f - \lambda_m CoV\left(\tilde{B}/100, \tilde{r}_m\right)\right)$, between A and B can be 3% annually for typical products such as trucks. Products with higher correlation with the market could have annual premiums higher than 10% above a cash flow with equivalent variance but no market correlation.

From the equivalence with a risk-neutral distribution, this result implies that the expectation of B with respect to the equivalent risk-neutral distribution is given as:

$$\mathbb{E}_{F_n}[B] = \mathbb{E}_F[B]\left(1 + r_f - \lambda_m CoV\left(\tilde{B}/\mathbb{E}_F[B], \tilde{r}_m\right)\right). \tag{7}$$

Finding F_n will permit solving for future cash flows that maintain a consistent correlation with the market return. As Birge (2000) describes, this occurs when the future demand distribution evolves as a lognormal distribution where the mean follows a geometric Brownian motion with constant correlation with the value of the market portfolio. The result is that the equivalent risk-neutral distribution can be found by discounting the cash flow by shifting the mean of the future cash flow by the additional premium $\delta = \lambda_m CoV\left(\tilde{B}/\mathbb{E}_F[B], \tilde{r}_m\right) - \left(1 + r_f\right)$ while maintaining the cash flow's volatility or variance. With r_f corresponding to continuous compounding (i.e., using e^{-r_f} in place of $\frac{1}{1+r_f}$, for the news vendor problem (see Birge and Zhang (1999)), setting $r_f = 0$ for simplicity, this implies for continuous F that the classic optimal solutions $x^\star = F^{-1}\left(\frac{p-c}{p}\right)$ is replaced by:

$$x_r^* = F^{-1}\left(\frac{(1-\delta)p - c}{(1-\delta)p}\right), \tag{8}$$

where $1-\delta$ is replaced with $e^{-\delta}$ for continuous discounting and the subscript r indicates that the solution includes risk aversion consistent with the market's premium for risk.

This form of adjustment for risk then involves identifying uncertainties that correlate with the market and adjusting for the risk premiums in their expectations to obtain risk-neutral equivalence. This applies to the price and cost parameters as well as to demand. Berling and Rosling (2005) provides examples showing how market risk in these parameters can affect EOQ and news vendor solutions, noting that the decision can be more sensitive to selling price and cost risk than to demand risk. The approach also applies in dynamic models over multiple periods. Birge (2000) shows that, in linear models, the risk-neutral equivalence allows solution of linear models for incorporating risk in long-term capacity plans where demand risk may be quite substantial and that the risk-neutral equivalent distribution can be obtained by adjusting constraints in this structure instead of transforming the probability distribution.

While these results apply for markets without imperfections, the general principles can be applied in imperfect markets assuming that the imperfections are idiosyncratic (and, hence, not priced in the market). As an example, we consider a news vendor with limited cash (less than cx) to support initial investment, following Xu and Birge (2004). This model assumes a proportional tax rate τ on profit and that a fraction α of any remaining assets of the firm are lost in the event that the firm defaults on a loan (following Leland (1994) and other work in financial economics). The firm can finance the inventory either with debt or by selling shares to other investors (equity). We assume that interest payments i can be deducted (assuming positive profits).

The news vendor problem in this case is to maximize the value of the firm. Assuming full information (or that bankers can monitor or control the firm manager's actions costlessly), the news vendor model becomes:

$$V\star = -\min_{(x,D,r,s_b,s_p)\geq 0} cx - \int_0^{s_b}\gamma y g(y)dy - \int_{s_b}^{s_p} y g(y)dy$$
$$- \int_{s_p}^{x}(y - \tau(y - cx - iD))g(y)dy$$
$$- \int_{x}^{\infty}(x - \tau(x - cx - iD))g(y)dy \tag{9}$$

s.t. $D - \int_0^{s_b}\gamma y g(y)dy$
$$- (1+i)D\int_{s_b}^{\infty} g(y)dy = 0, \tag{10}$$

$$s_b - D(1+i) = 0, \tag{11}$$

$$s_p - cx - iD = 0, \tag{12}$$

where g denotes the density of demand, γ is the fraction recovered in the event of default on the debt, s_b is the bankruptcy point or minimum demand level to re-pay the loan, and s_p is the profit point or minimum demand level to earn positive profits (and to owe taxes). The objective represents the (negative of the) net value of the firm overall where cx is expended and then returns fall into one of four groups according to the demand realization: default, losses without default, taxed profits with production below capacity, and taxed profits with production at capacity. The complicating factor in this model is the constraint (10) that represents fair pricing of the loan. This constraint effectively assumes that the financial market is competitive and that no information asymmetries exist (or the bank can costlessly monitor production and infer the demand distribution) so that the interest rate i is set to make a loan of value D have a zero net present value.

We can write the optimization problem in (9)–(12) in terms of x and D with $i(D)$ determined by (10) after substituting for s_b and s_p with the expressions in (11) and (12). The result is that an interior optimal solution occurs at the solution of the following two first-order conditions:

$$(1-\tau)\int_x^{\infty} g(s)ds + c\tau\int_{s_p}^{\infty} g(s)ds - c = 0; \tag{13}$$

$$\tau\left(i + D\frac{\partial i}{\partial D}\right)\int_{s_p}^{\infty} g(s)ds - (1-\gamma)\left(1 + i + D\frac{\partial i}{\partial D}\right)s_b g(s_b) = 0. \tag{14}$$

The first condition (13) includes the standard news vendor optimality condition with the addition of $c\tau(1 - F(s_p))$ as the marginal value of the tax deduction for the cost of the capacity x which only has value when the firm is profitable. The absence of a deduction in the event of a loss creates a distortion to reduce investment below a no-tax solution even in the absence of debt. With debt, the breakeven point rises, reducing the effective tax deduction of the capacity cost and further reducing investment; expected profit, however, increases as the firm gains the interest rate deduction. The second condition reflects the marginal benefit of this debt for tax purposes in the first term and the marginal cost from the deadweight loss in the event of default on the debt in the second term.

As shown in Xu and Birge (2004), these conditions lead to a capacity on debt such that firms cannot borrow beyond an upper bound $\bar{D}$, regardless of interest rate. The conditions also imply a first order impact of the capacity decision on the optimal debt level through the tax benefit term while the debt level has effectively a second-order impact on the optimal capacity level since it is only the change in the break-even level from the interest payment that enters the first equation in (14). As explored in Xu and Birge (2004), this difference in relative influence implies that, while operational and financial decisions are dependent in this framework, correctly identifying the operational decision $x^\star$ is more critical than determining the optimal financial structure through optimal debt $D^\star$.

The equations in (14) also lead to a potentially non-monotonic relationship between the leverage ratio, $D^\star/V^\star$, and c (or the profit margin) in which high debt levels can occur at both low and high margins since, at low margins, $x^\star$ is also low, leading to little variation in revenues and low default risk to support higher leverage, and at high margins, low chances of losses overall reduce default risk and again can support high leverage. Section 5 discusses predictions from these observations and empirical results that support these observations.

Relatively few papers in the literature explicitly consider such tradeoffs and particularly the firm's operational commitment to a production or capacity level (and selling price) in advance of realizing demand. Dotan and Ravid (1985) is an example that considers a model in which production and financing decisions are endogenous, but the variation in revenues is not affected by the production scale (i.e., higher variation with higher capacity as in the news vendor framework). Lederer and Singhal (1994) also consider operational and financial decisions in a model of financing and technology choice in which production follows demand realizations. Additional examples include Mauer and Triantis (1994), whose model also assumes instantaneous production and, while including market imperfections, predicts a limited connection between financial and operational decisions. Among other papers, Hennessy and Whited (2005) provides a dynamic tradeoff model that includes capital investment. While these models assume competitive capital markets for loans as generally assumed in financial models, Dada and Hu (2008) considers a situation with a single lender who can strategically offer an interest rate to a producer.

These results are generally related to risk management of the firm and incentives for firms to reduce risk or to hedge positions. Hedging can enhance value by ensuring that firms can profitably take advantage of investment (or production) opportunities. Froot et al. (1993) provides a basic model of how investment and borrowing are interrelated in this framework. Financing can also exercise control over management actions to prevent over- and under-investment (and hence increase value) as in Stulz (1990).

Operational actions, such as shifting production from one region to another to take advantage of favorable exchange rates (see, e.g., Kogut and Kulatilaka 1994; Huchzermeier and Cohen 1996; Dasu and Li 1997; Kazaz et al. 2005; Aytekin and Birge 2009) can also be viewed as a hedging mechanism. In general, these models consider the valuation of flexible forms of capacity investment that enable production to shift in response to demand, rate, and price changes. Van Mieghem (2003) provides an overview of this literature and discusses how such operational hedges can interact with financial instruments. Combinations of operational and financial hedges are also discussed in Ding et al. (2007) and compared in Chod et al. (2010), Chowdhry and Howe (1999), and Hommel (2003). The general conclusion is that operational hedges that can adjust quantities in response to demand or price changes have an advantage over financial hedging instruments that generally have payoffs depending on prices alone. Their payoffs are then generally not directly available in the market and, hence, provide some rent to the firm as owner of the relevant assets.

4 Impact of Financial Considerations on Supply Chain Operations

Financial considerations can affect interactions among firms in a supply chain in different ways from the impact on a single firm. In particular, as observed in Rajan and Zingales (1995), financing from supply chain partners (trade credit) is the leading source of short-term borrowing for public firms. While many theories for trade credit exist (e.g., Petersen and Rajan (1997)), an operationally important aspect of trade credit is that it can improve supply chain efficiency by reducing issues such as double marginalization (the addition of margins from both retailers and suppliers that can result in inefficient production quantities) and improving coordination. As shown in Yang and Birge (2011), trade credit can provide a risk-sharing mechanism so that upstream firms share in the risk of the downstream firms' demand and can use the leverage of their trade credit offer to induce the downstream firm to order an efficient quantity.

In the model in Yang and Birge (2011), which follows the selling-to-a-news vendor model in Lariviere and Porteus (2001), a supplier offers a two-part contract with two prices to the buyer; w_c if the buyer pays immediately upon delivery and w_t if the buyer delays payment until after demand is realized and revenues are collected. The buyer solves a problem similar to (9)–(10) with now an additional source of financing from the supplier, potentially in addition to external debt from a third party such as a bank. In a model without taxes or equity financing, their result is that, like other two-part tariffs in the operations management literature (Cachon 2003), the two-part trade credit contract can enable channel coordination and eliminate double marginalization. In addition, trade credit is used before bank lending. Again, this has empirical implications that are discussed in Section 5.

Models of trade credit usage in supply chains appear as early as Haley and Higgins (1973), which only considers the suppliers' financing incentive (as opposed to external financing). In general, the overall coordination of product and cash flows across a supply chain represents a complex optimization problem that is explored in Gupta and Dutta (2011), which focuses on the timing of trade credit payments and cash management. A paper that considers both trade credit and bank financing in comparison is Kouvelis and Zhao (2012), which does not include costs of financial distress. In this case, Kouvelis and Zhao (2012) also shows that trade credit is preferred to bank financing (while not considering a portfolio of both bank and trade credit financing). Gupta and Wang (2009) and Lee and Rhee (2011) also consider models of trade credit in the news vendor framework without distress costs and, in which, the supplier can vary the financing terms. Supply chain financing and inventory risk are considered with potential default in Lai et al. (2009), in which, if the supplier is willing, the buyer can pre-order products at a fixed wholesale price or wait for demand realization and sell on consignment. In the presence of financial constraints, the supplier may choose to offer pre-ordering even if this would not be offered otherwise. Deferred payment as a form of trade credit is also considered in Caldentey and Haugh (2009), which examines the buyers' advantage in engaging in financial hedging to assist in fulfilling the supplier's payment obligation. Other papers on trade credit influence in the supply chain are reviewed in Seifert et al. (2013).

5 Impact of Operational Decisions on Financial Asset Prices

The previous two sections concerned the influence of financial market theory on operational decisions. Operational decisions can also have an impact on financial asset prices. These impacts can be viewed as directly implied by the results above. For example, as a firm increases capacity, it increases its exposure to the broader market and, hence, its correlation with the market. That should then increase the discount that investors apply to this firm's expected cash flows according to CAPM. This implies that firms with a higher capacity relative to demand than others should also have higher returns to their shares.

Similar reasoning implies that firms with more flexible resources or alternate suppliers have a natural operational hedge that should lower their exposure to market risk. The result of lower market risk should then be lower returns for firms with larger hedges. This again has empirical implications that are discussed in Section 6.

The key observation in this process is that operational hedges, such as alternative suppliers and flexible production resources, can improve value both in terms of future expectations and in the present value of those expectations (due to lower market risk exposure). Operational hedges often take the form of options that are contingent on future realizations of random variables. Aytekin and Birge (2009), for example, consider the valuation of capacity in multiple markets with different currency and random exchange rates. The option to produce in a market with favorable exchange rates creates an operational hedge that has value for the firm.

While techniques from financial option valuation also apply to operational options, most traded financial options are functions of the price of an underlying resource and not of an underlying demand. A direct option on an asset that correlates perfectly with the underlying demand is generally not available. An option could be constructed that mimics a factor proportional to the market risk fraction, but market imperfections may make such an option expensive relative to the firm's operations (indeed, otherwise, the firm could add no value from its unique resources). Using unique resources, operational hedges then generally provide incremental value relative to a corresponding financial hedge. As Chowdhry and Howe (1999) observe, it is the combination of price and quantity flexibility that underlies the operational value.

6 Empirical Results in Operations and Finance Interactions

The results mentioned above have a variety of testable empirical implications. The news vendor model and supply chain generalizations, such as Graves et al. (1998) and Chen and Lee (2009), for which Bray and Mendelson (2015) provides empirical support, have implications for the capital structure of firms. As noted above, the results in Xu and Birge (2004) imply that a potential U-shaped relationship exists between firm profitability (as a fraction of sales) and firm leverage (its fraction in debt). Xu and Birge (2006) provide some evidence that this is the case by using the leverage and reported (positive) operating margin of public US firms. The model in Xu and Birge (2004) is expanded in Birge and Xu (2011) to include fixed costs that act as operating leverage and effectively replace debt in the firm's capital structure. That paper also argues that firms with highly negative operating margins (which were not explored in the empirical results in Xu and Birge (2006)) must have high future expectations to support their continued existence. Those expectations must then involve relatively higher future expected margins for surviving firms with current highly negative operating margins. This logic then implies a cubic form of the relationship between profitability and leverage in which leverage first increases as profits increase from highly negative to zero and then follows the U-shaped pattern previously observed. The paper presents empirical evidence that this pattern appears in the cross-section of all public firms and is persistent across time.

One could try to do this historically for similar cash flows, e.g., previous years' sales of the same product and to provide the sales estimates as rates of increase over the previous years' sales. Indeed, Gaur and Seshadri (2005) find that such estimates can be quite useful in predicting sales. A key implication of this modeling framework is that the capacity decision endogenously determines the firm's cash flow risk and, hence, the cost of debt. In models where firm value evolves exogenously or price risk is simply a multiplier on production capacity, this effect is lost. Operational decisions of the firm, such as capacity levels, are bound with the firm's risk and should not be separated from other decisions that affect firm risk. Recognizing this interdependence reveals relationships that do not appear in exogenous-value driven firm models.

Much of the empirical evidence of operational and financial interactions has appeared in the finance literature. Direct evidence of the impact of financial markets, for example, appears in Kashyap et al. (1994), which shows that firms reduce inventories when credit tightens. Other papers address the issue of hedging and firms' use of operational resources. Financial hedging's effect on firm values is supported in the study in Allayannis et al. (2001), which examines the use of foreign exchange derivatives. Kim et al. (2006) consider both financial and operational hedging and show that firms with more operational flexibility use less financial hedging and that hedging increases value. Blome and Schönherr (2011) provide case studies that demonstrate the value of supply chain risk management strategies.

The impact of supply chain disruptions on firm value is explicitly considered in Hendricks and Singhal (2005), which uses an event study of disruptions to show that supply chain issues have a lasting impact on a firm's financial performance as reflected in its stock return. The impact of customers on a firm's performance is also examined in Cohen and Frazzini (2008), which show that shocks to a firm's customers have a delayed impact of that firm's returns, indicating a form of slow diffusion of information. Both supplier and customer effects are considered in Wu and Birge (2014), which show that supplier shocks may also have a lagged impact on a firm while, after the publication of Cohen and Frazzini (2008), customer effects may no longer exhibit a delay. In addition, Wu and Birge (2014) provide evidence of the impact of a firm's hedging policies by relating returns to overall position in the network of all firms. The results indicate that manufacturers, which have an additional incentive to that of downstream retailers to hedge operationally to protect against individual suppliers' disruptions affecting all operations, have lower returns as they become more central in the network of firms while retailers, wholesalers, and distributors have higher returns for higher centrality. The implication of these findings is that manufacturers' hedging incentive reduces their exposure to systematic risk (and hence the risk premium associated with that risk) while retailers and logistics providers have incentives to build on existing relationships and increase systematic risk as they become more central in the network.

Many papers have also examined the impact of trade credit on firms' operational performance. Petersen and Rajan (1997) show that firms with less access to financial institutions use more trade credit and that firms may use trade credit as a form of price discrimination. Cuñat (2007) examines the extent of trade credit in UK firms and shows higher trade credit for emerging firms. Yang and Birge (2011) show that trade credit is generally used by firms before short-term borrowing in support of its role in supply chain coordination. Boissay and Gropp (2013) consider a different effect of trade credit across a supply chain in terms of absorbing liquidity shocks, demonstrating this effect for French firms. In contrast to these papers focused on buyers' borrowing, for a supplier financing perspective, Klapper (2006) considers factoring in which a supplier may use accounts receivable to obtain financing from a financial institution, showing that factoring increases in countries with greater development and accessible credit information.

7 Conclusions and Future Research Directions

Due to unavoidable market imperfections including taxes and financial distress costs, operational and financial decisions are interconnected. This chapter discusses the reasons for these connections and their implications for the operational decisions of firms individually and collectively within a supply chain. The relationships also have implications for the performance of firms and their valuations in the financial market. Models of these effects provide insight into firm decisions and hypotheses that can be tested empirically as discussed in Section 6.

The discussion above does not address competition, which can also have an influence on a firms' operational and financial decisions and their interrelationship. Competition can, however, have an impact on firms' operational decisions such as supplier choices as in Babich et al. (2007). This area has received relatively little attention in the literature overall and provides significant potential for further research. Interactions of multiple suppliers and their competing interests to provide financing to firms represents a related area of high potential.

Relatively little work has also considered the interaction of agency issues, such as managerial control, in relationship to operational and financial control. Such issues as those discussed in Jensen and Meckling (1976) also play a role in the interactions of firms' financial and operational decisions (as, for example, in Xu and Birge (2006)) and may guide decisions such as the form of managerial compensation. This area also represents fertile ground for additional research.

Joint consideration of financial and operational interactions is essential for effective management. Modeling these interactions requires an appreciation of the structure of operational decisions, including the commitment and deployment of resources and prices, as well as understanding of market consideration of risk and financial flows. Combining these elements provides perspective on firms' decisions and can help in guiding and improving them. Research has, however, been limited to date in comparison to specific operational decisions of a firm. As such, the area of operational and financial decisions provides many opportunities for further research, new insights, and impact on operational practice.

Acknowledgement

This work was supported by the University of Chicago Booth School of Business, Chicago, IL.

References and Bibliography

Alan, Y. and V. Gaur (2011) "Operational investment and capital structure under asset based lending: A one period mode," Research paper, Johnson School Series, Cornell University, Ithaca, NY. Available at SSRN: http://ssrn.com/abstract=1716925.

Allayannis, G., J. Ihrig, and J. Weston (2001) "Exchange-rate hedging: Financial vs. operational strategies," *American Economic Review*, **91**: 391–395.

Arrow, K., T. Harris, and J. Marschak (1951) "Optimal inventory policy," *Econometrica*, **19**: 250–272.

Aytekin, A. and J. Birge (2009) "Optimal investement and production across markets with stochastic exchange rates," Technical report, University of Chicago Booth School of Business, Chicago, IL. Available at SSRN: http://ssrn.com/abstract=652561.

Babich, V., A. Burnetas, and P. Ritchken (2007) "Competition and diversification effects in supply chains with supplier default risk," *Manufacturing & Service Operations Management*, **9**(2): 123–146.

Babich, V. and M. Sobel (2004) "Pre-IPO operational and financial decisions," *Management Science*, **50**(7): 935–948.

Berling, P. and K. Rosling (2005) "The effects of financial risks on inventory policy," *Management Science*, **51**(12): 1804–1815.

Birge, J.R. (2000) "Option methods for incorporating risk into linear capacity planning models," *Manufacturing & Service Operations Management*, **2**(1): 19–31.

Birge, J.R. (2015) "Operations and finance interactions," *Manufacturing & Service Operations Management*, **17**(1): 4–15.

Birge, J.R. and X. Xu (2011) "Firm profitability, inventory volatility, and capital structure," Working paper, University of Chicago Booth School of Business, Chicago, IL. Available at SSRN: http://ssrn.com/abstract=1914690.

Birge, J.R. and R.Q. Zhang (1999) "Risk-neutral option pricing methods for adjusting constrained cash flows," *Engineering Economist*, **44**: 36–49.

Blome, C. and T. Schönherr (2011) "Supply chain risk management in financial crises—a multiple case-study approach," *International Journal of Production Economics*, **134**: 43–57.

Boissay, F. and R. Gropp (2013) "Payment defaults and interfirm liquidity provision," *Review of Finance*, **17**: 1853–1894.

Bray, R.L. and H. Mendelson (2015) "Production smoothing and the bullwhip effect," *Manufacturing & Service Operations Management*, **17**(2): 208–220.

Buzacott, J.A. and R.Q. Zhang (2004) "Inventory management with asset-based financing," *Management Science*, **50**(9): 1274–1292.

Cachon, G. (2003) "Supply chain coordination with contracts," in Graves, S. and de Kok, T., editors, *Handbooks in Operations Research and Management Science*, Chapter 11, pages 229–340, North Holland, Amsterdam, Netherlands.

Caldentey, R. and M. Haugh (2009) "Supply contracts with financial hedging," *Operations research*, **57**(1): 47–65.

Chen, L. and H.L. Lee (2009) "Information sharing and order variability control under a generalized demand model," *Management Science*, **55**(5): 781–797.

Chod, J., N. Rudi, and J.A. Van Mieghem (2010) "Operational flexibility and financial hedging: Complements or substitutes?" *Management Science*, **56**(6): 1030–1045.

Chowdhry, B. and J.T.B. Howe (1999) "Corporate risk management for multinational corporations: Financial and operational hedging policies," *Eur. Finance Rev.*, **2**: 229–246.

Clark, A.J. and H. Scarf (1960) "Optimal policies for a multi-echelon stochastic inventory system," *Management Science*, **6**(4): 475–490.

Cohen, L. and A. Frazzini (2008) "Economic links and predictable returns," *Journal of Finance*, **63**: 1977–2011.

Cuñat, V. (2007) "Trade credit: Suppliers as debt collectors and insurance providers," *Review of Financial Studies* **20**(2): 491–527.

Dada, M. and Q. Hu (2008) "Financing newsvendor inventory," *Operations Research Letters*, **36**: 569–573.

Dasu, S. and L. Li (1997) "Optimal operating policies in the presence of exchange rate variability," *Management Science*, **43**: 705–722.

Ding, Q., L. Dong, and P. Kouvelis (2007) "On the integration of production and financial hedging decisions in global markets," *Operations Research*, **55**(3): 470–489.

Dotan, A. and S.A. Ravid (1985) "On the interaction of real and financial decisions of the firm under uncertainty," *Journal of Finance*, **40**(2): 501–517.

Froot, K.A., D.S. Scharfstein, and J.C. Stein (1993) "Risk management: Coordinating corporate investment and financing policies," *Journal of Finance*, **48**(5): 1629–1658.

Gaur, V. and S. Seshadri (2005) "Hedging inventory risk through market instruments," *Manufacturing & Service Operations Management*, **7**(2): 103–120.

Graves, S., D. Kletter, and W. Hetzel (1998) "A dynamic model for requirements planning with application to supply chain optimization," *Operations Research*, **46**: S35–S49.

Gupta, D. and L. Wang (2009) "A stochastic inventory model with trade credit," *Manufacturing & Service Operations Management*, **11**(1): 4–18.

Gupta, S. and K. Dutta (2011) "Modeling of financial supply chain," *European Journal of Operational Research* **211**: 47–56.

Haley, C. and R. Higgins (1973) "Inventory policy and trade credit financing," *Management Science*, **20**(4): 464–471.

Harris, F.W. (1913) "How many parts to make at once," *Factory, The Magazine of Management*, **10**(2): 135–136, 152.

Harrison, J.M. and D.M. Kreps (1979) "Martingales and arbitrage in multiperiod securities markets," *Journal of Economic Theory*, **20**: 381–408.

Hendricks, K.B. and V.R. Singhal (2005) "Association between supply chain glitches and operating performance," *Management Science*, **51**(5): 695–711.

Hennessy, C.A. and T.M. Whited (2005) "Debt dynamics," *The Journal of Finance*, **60**(3): 1129–1165.

Hölmstrom, B. (1979) "Moral hazard and observability," *The Bell Journal of Economics*, **10**: 74–91.
Holt, C., F. Modigliani, J. Muth, and W. Simon (1960) *Planning, Production, Inventories, and Work Force*. Englewood Cliffs, NJ: Prentice Hall.
Hommel, U. (2003) "Financial versus operative hedging of currency risk," *Global Finance J.*, **14**: 1–18.
Huchzermeier, A. and M.A. Cohen (1996) "Valuing operational flexibility under exchange rate risk," *Operations Research*, **44**: 100–111.
Jensen, M. and W. Meckling (1976) "Theory of the firm: Managerial behavior, agency costs and ownership structure," *Journal of Financial Economics*, **3**(4): 305–360.
Kashyap, A., O. Lamont, and J.C. Stein (1994) "Credit conditions and the cyclical behavior of inventories," *Quarterly Journal of Economics*, **109**: 565–592.
Kazaz, B., M. Dada, and H. Moskowitz (2005) "Global production planning under exchange-rate uncertainty," *Management Science*, **51**(7): 1101–1119.
Kim, Y.S., I. Mathur, and J. Nam (2006) "Is operational hedging a substitute for or a complement to financial hedging?" *J. Corporate Finance* **12**: 834–853.
Klapper, L. (2006) "The role of factoring for financing small and medium enterprises," *Journal of Banking and Finance*, **30**(11): 3111–3130.
Kogut, B. and N. Kulatilaka (1994) "Operating flexibility, global manufacturing, and the option value of a multinational network," *Management Science*, **40**(1): 123–139.
Kouvelis, P. and W. Zhao (2012) "Financing the newsvendor: Supplier vs. bank, and the structure of optimal trade credit contracts," *Operations Research*, **60**(3): 566–580.
Lai, G., L. Debo, and K. Sycara (2009) "Sharing inventory risk in supply chain: The implication of financial constraint," *Omega*, **37**(4): 811–825.
Lariviere, M. and E. Porteus (2001) "Selling to the newsvendor: An analysis of price-only contracts," *Manufacturing & Service Operations Management*, **3**(4): 293–305.
Lederer, P.J. and V.R. Singhal (1994) "The effect of financing decisions on the choice of manufacturing technologies," *The International Journal of Flexible Manufacturing Systems*, **6**: 333–360.
Lee, C.H. and B.-D. Rhee (2011) "Trade credit for supply chain coordination," *European Journal of Operational Research*, **214**: 136–146.
Leland, H.E. (1994) "Corporate debt value, bond covenants, and optimal capital structure," *Journal of Finance*, **49**: 1213–1252.
Li, L., M. Shubik, and M.J. Sobel (2013) "Control of dividends, capital subscriptions, and physical inventories," *Management Science*, **59**(5): 1107–1124.
Lintner, J. (1965) "The valuation of risk assets and the selection of risky investments in stock portfolios and capital budgets," *Review of Economics and Statistics*, **47**: 13–37.
Mauer, D.C. and A.J. Triantis (1994) "Interactions of corporate financing and investment decisions: A dynamic framework," *Journal of Finance*, **49**: 1253–1277.
Modigliani, F. and M.H. Miller (1958) "The cost of capital, corporation finance, and the theory of investment," *American Economic Review*, **48**: 261–297.
Modigliani, F. and M.H. Miller (1963) "Corporate income taxes and the cost of capital: A correction," *American Economic Review*, **53**: 433–443.
Petersen, M. and R. Rajan (1997) "Trade credit: Theories and evidence," *Review of Financial Studies*, **10**(3): 661–691.
Plambeck, E.L. and S.A. Zenios (2000) "Performance-based incentives in a dynamic principal-agent model," *Manufacturing & Service Operations Management*, **2**(3): 240–263.
Rajan, R. and L. Zingales (1995) "What do we know about capital structure? Some evidence from international data," *The Journal of Finance*, **50**: 1421–1460.
Seifert, D., R. Seifert, and M. Protopappa-Sieke (2013) "A review of trade credit literature: Opportunities for research in operations," *European Journal of Operational Research*, **231**: 245–256.
Sharpe, W.F. (1964) "Capital asset prices: A theory of market equilibrium under conditions of risk," *Journal of Finance* **19**: 425–442.
Stulz, R. (1990) "Managerial discretion and optimal financing policies," *Journal of Financial Economics*, **26**(1): 3–27.
Van Mieghem, J.A. (2003) "Capacity management, investment and hedging: Review and recent developments," *Manufacturing & Service Operations Management*, **5**: 269–302.
Wagner, H. and T.M. Whitin (1958) "Dynamic version of the economic-lot-size formula," *Management Science*, **5**(1): 89–96.

Wu, J. and J.R. Birge (2014) "Supply chain network structure and firm returns," Working paper, The University of Chicago Booth School of Business, Chicago, IL. Available at SSRN: http://ssrn.com/abstract=2385217.

Xu, X. and J.R. Birge (2004) "Joint production and financing decisions: Modeling and analysis," Technical report, Working paper, The University of Chicago Graduate School of Business, Chicago, IL, October 2004. Available at SSRN: http://ssrn.com/abstract=652562.

Xu, X. and J.R. Birge (2006) "Equity valuation, production, and financial planning: A stochastic programming approach," *Naval Research Logistics*, 43: 641–655.

Yang, S.A. and J.R. Birge (2011) "How inventory is (should be) financed: Trade credit in supply chains with demand uncertainty and costs of financial distress," Working paper, University of Chicago Booth School of Business, Chicago, IL, January 2011. Available at SSRN: http://ssrn.com/abstract=1734682.

20
POM AND MARKETING

Manoj K. Malhotra, Ramkumar Janakiraman, Saurabh Mishra, and Moonwon Chung

1 Introduction

Since Shapiro's (1977) article "Can Manufacturing and Marketing Coexist?", scholars have pursued the study of Production and Operations Management (POM) and marketing interfaces. Based on systems theory, prior studies have classified interface research into three domains: 1) Input; the situational context in terms of individual, function, interdepartmental, organization, product, and market, 2) Process; the level (Strategic, Tactical, and Operational) of decision-making interaction, and 3) Output; the tangible result of the interface (Parente 1998). In this chapter, we describe developments in each domain.

Recent studies have shifted our attention to the multichannel retail setting, as it poses a challenging context where firms have to manage issues in customer targeting, increased inventory fluctuations, and product returns. In the domain of process, we delineate process coordination and forecasting issues in sales and operations planning (S&OP), interfirm joint capability decision making, and managing closed loop supply chains. On the output side, we assert that performance metrics derived from a single business function (e.g., operations, marketing, or finance) are insufficient. Instead, we propose the need for assessing shareholder value as a complementary output metric, which not only captures the performance of each function as a whole, but also takes into account the institutional concerns regarding sustainability and corporate social responsibility (CSR).

We develop Figure 20.1 to show how the POM and Marketing interface come together within the input-process-output typology commonly found in operations management. We call it the Triple C (Context, Coordination, and Consequence) framework. The input represents the context within which Marketing starts playing an important role in distributing a firm's goods and services to its customers, the process represents the coordination of different processes within POM that drive value for the customer, and output represents the consequence of how well the interface creates value for the shareholders. The relevant topics within each leg of the Triple C framework are shown in Figure 20.1, which we discuss next in greater detail.

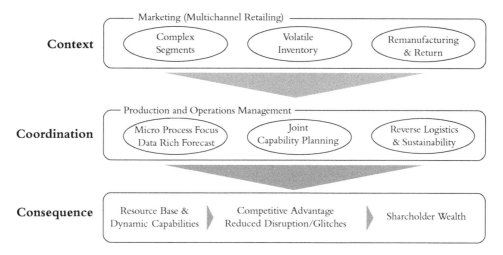

Figure 20.1 Triple C Framework for POM and Marketing Interface

2 Input Context-Multichannel Retailing as a Challenge to Customer Segmentation, Inventory Management, and Reverse Logistics

The integration of POM functions with Marketing continues to prove a point of considerable attention in multi-channel retailing literature. As firms ramp up their online presence, new channels for retailing and distribution emerge, placing a far greater strain on operations decision-makers who are tasked with implementing feasible channel-specific marketing initiatives. Online shopping provides consumers with unparalleled ability to compare prices, sort desired products across many attributes, and read critic and user-generated reviews for valuable insights. Retailers like Amazon, and even traditional players like Wal-Mart (that's increasingly diversifying into online distribution modes), often provide low-price shipping coupled with consumer-friendly return policies. While firms' marketing departments communicate the tremendous value provided to consumers through these multi-channels, significant POM challenges emerge as well.

Take for example the unique marketing mix of eyeglass and sunglass brand Warby Parker, which includes free delivery and return for a five-day trial of a box of five consumer-selected frames for potential patrons to choose, fostering a unique product trial experience (www.warbyparker.com/home-try-on). However, delivering multiple frames to consumers all at once gives rise to operational challenges in inventory management, repackaging, and product return forecasting. The key to such service implementation depends on devising novel and cost-efficient methods to deliver personalized products through untraditional channels.

Conversely, providing increased customer value across channels presents many opportunities for firms to recoup their investments, with evidence existing in the very same eyeglass and sunglass industry. Over the past few years, Warby Parker has strategically introduced showrooms across the United States, recognizing the potential benefits of a multi-channel approach. Adding to the literature addressing the impact of a multi-channel approach on sales (Forman et al. 2009; Avery et al. 2012), Bell et al. (2015) demonstrated that within its trading area, the showroom introduction increased sales for Warby Parker both overall and through the web channel. From a POM perspective, showrooms experienced an increased conversion in the channel sampled, which led to decreased returns, whereby orders fell by 6.1% while sales only fell by 4.5% (Bell et al. 2015).

The traditional consumer shopping process of in-person product evaluation and purchase continues to shift into a multi-channel framework where products may be explored in a brick-and-mortar store but purchased online. Preventing product stock outs at retailer locations becomes even more challenging if price matching between multiple channels is implemented, allowing consumers to utilize feature-sorting interfaces online for research and brick-and-mortar stores for procurement. Undoubtedly, the emergence of multi-channel retailing provides an improved value proposition for consumers, who can now decrease search costs and circumvent the traditional product acquisition processes through direct home shipping.

Online retailers like Amazon, which offers superb selection and often free two-day shipping, may stimulate online purchasing indirectly by encouraging customers to use brick-and-mortar locations as informal showrooms. Lower offline consumer purchase intentions push firms to more closely evaluate their retail store environment and stocking strategies. Such product and service marketing context requires the integration of several separate firm functions across the supply chain. Research in consumer segmentation, inventory management, and product return policies provides a rationale for firms to create a strong link between POM and Marketing in an evolving retail space.

The current multichannel retailing research in POM and Marketing falls into three distinct categories, related to complex market segments, increased inventory volatility, and returned and remanufactured goods. Each of these categories is explored in the following subsections.

2.1 Complex Market Segments

While retailers across channels strive to stimulate consumer purchases, some segments may be more profitable to target in specific channels. Using a game theoretic model, Hsiao and Chen (2014) deduced that grocery shoppers who preferred purchasing through a physical channel and were classified as within an intermediate profitability region (between highly profitable and relatively unimportant), were the most desirable consumers for manufacturers to "poach" from physical channels. On a related note, Prasad et al. (2011) demonstrated that marketing efforts focused on advanced selling are less fruitful for retailers when consumers are more risk averse. Advance selling can take the form of an example by Tang et al. (2004), where bakeries in Hong Kong provided price discounts to encourage customers to purchase cakes for a festival a month in advance in order to reduce inventory risk. Such benefits put emphasis on understanding the factors that contribute to consumers' expected utilities, as they drive advance purchase decisions.

As online search engines and advanced user interface provide richer information (e.g., historical price trends) to consumers, the characteristics of these segments may shift to become more strategic (forward-looking). As a result, the effectiveness of prior established practices such as quick-response, can generally be lower and even damaging depending on pricing strategies or consumer return policies (Swinney 2011).

Geographical properties also tend to affect the multi-channel effectiveness. Through a field experiment that began with the introduction of an informational website, Pauwels et al. (2011) showed that the negative revenue effects of introducing an informational website proved more likely to appear for customer groups living closer to the physical store. While some consumer segments showed increased sales, other segments used the website as an alternative to physically frequenting the store. It can also affect a firm's operational decisions on optimal staffing.

Understanding consumer preferences across segments can provide insights in resolving channel conflict. In an online and catalog multichannel setting, Brynjolfsson et al. (2009) showed that competition was more intense between Internet and brick-and-mortar retailers when selling mainstream products, but far less intense by comparison when selling niche products (products not amongst those cumulatively generating 80% of total sales). Therefore, regarding distribution strategies, it is important for the manufacturer to consider target segments and positioning of the product that drives intra-brand competition across channels.

2.2 Increased Inventory Volatility

Firms constantly strive to reduce optimal levels of inventory by fostering better communication throughout the supply chain and aligning product distribution strategies. Alan et al. (2014) used longitudinal analysis of portfolio returns to demonstrate that inventory management performance as measured by inventory turnover, gross margin returns on inventory, and adjusted inventory turnover, can predict future near-term stock returns. This emphasizes the importance of inventory management. However, recent distribution decisions in practice are not easily explained by POM efficiency logic. Gateway PC shifted their focus to online sales after closing 188 offline retail stores in 2004, while GM and Chrysler closed approximately 30% of their dealerships (Lee et al. 2013). Such decisions show increasing concerns of intra brand competition and customer substitution between online and offline channels. Moreover, as online channels do not provide the touch and feel of products, there is an increase in likelihood of product returns (Ofek et al. 2011) and obscuring of true product demand. Product returns also lead to a number of negative events, one of them being the increase in phantom products that are physically present in the store, but only in unobservable storage spaces due to mishandling of a returned product. Estimated sales losses due to these invisible products amount to $560–960 million per year in the US supermarket industry (Ton and Raman 2010). Scholars have suggested the use of different accounting methods, RFID tracking, store environment redesign, and change in distribution structure (DeHoratius and Raman 2008) to tackle this problem.

While consumers often examine products in store and purchase online, it is common for product pick-up to happen within a brick-and-mortar location. Gallino and Moreno (2014) examined the related interface between operations and marketing in a similar purchase process, finding that implementation of a buy-online, pick-up in store (BOPS) product reduced online sales and increased in-store sales and traffic. They concluded that a cross-selling effect might have emerged, where customers who used the BOPS functionality bought additional products once in the stores. By analyzing online cart abandonment and in-store conversion rates, Gallino and Moreno (2014) demonstrated that BOPS implementation might have increased "research online, purchase offline" consumer behavior.

2.3 Returned and Remanufactured Products

The issue of product returns is a still an underdeveloped research topic, one that requires understanding the combined issues of cross-functional integration of marketing and operations (Malhotra and Sharma 2002), and reverse flow of products. Mollenkopf et al. (2007) argue that product returns should be investigated by taking a holistic view, where firms should try to get a better understanding of the total costs of returns, develop cross function teams to interact with customers, and pay close attention to the quality of the product and service dimension that is relevant to the intermediary customers in the supply chain.

The marketing actions of a retailer related to promotional offerings and pricing decisions are often made before consumer demand can be assessed (Iyer et al. 2007), something which often leads to increased product returns. Therefore, a stream of Marketing and POM interface research focuses on what to do with returned products, or reduce the return likelihood. Akçay et al. (2013) demonstrated that money-back-guaranteed policies that sell returned products in an open-box format resulted in decreased initial stocking quantities, diminished retailer inventory risk, and reduced procurement costs. The effects were found to be greater for innovative new products in a multichannel setting. Their model takes into account retailer decisions related to procurement quantity, new product and open-box product pricing, and the refund amount provided. These decisions require proper coordination between POM and Marketing functions.

Products purchased during certain seasons, for specific purposes, and in new channels can also provide insight into product return likelihood. Using data from a business-to-consumer multi-channel retailer, Petersen and Kumar (2009) demonstrated that on average, products purchased during the holiday season were more likely to be returned. For consumers who purchased more through channels new to them but within familiar product categories, product returns decreased. Consumers were also more likely to return products from new categories when purchasing them in a new channel.

Methods for implementing operationally-efficient return policies must therefore take into account not only the product category, but also the consumer profile, time, and channel of purchase. With a focus on identifying their most valuable consumers, firms can develop methods to push traffic to certain channels for certain consumers. Chen and Bell (2012) demonstrate this idea by showing the results of an analytical model, where a firm offers a full refund scheme and no return scheme in a single market to generate sub segments. These sub markets can use alternative distribution channels for various geographic locations with multiple prices. They conclude that new products with uncertain customer expectations perform better with a full refund policy, and mature products with low uncertainty are better off with a no-returns policy or distributed through a dual channel. Segmenting a market using customer returns can be a profit maximizing policy, though research on more sophisticated segmentation schemes is needed.

3 Process Coordination: Intra-/Inter-Firm Issues in POM and Marketing Interface

In order to cope with the downstream changes due to the rise of multichannel retailing, firms can build competency by focusing on the details of process integration to make better forecasts, make joint decisions, and expand supply chain perspectives by including end-of-life or returned products. In this section, we discuss the POM research findings in each respective domain.

3.1 Focus on Micro-Level Process Integration with Data Rich Forecasting

The focus on micro-level processes is important because there can be information deficiency in decision-making processes, and people are vulnerable to political barriers, functional limitations, and biases (Oliva and Watson 2009). Even with a well-defined system, this subjective element can affect the choice and outcome of a process. Through a case study of Sales and Operations (S&OPs) planning, a cross functional process performed to balance demand and supply and to align all business function plans with the strategic business plan (Ling and Goddard 1988), Oliva and Watson (2011) propose that the incentive structures of each function depend on how each detailed sub processes are specified and carried out. In an interorganizational, multichannel setting, there are still voids in research on designs of micro-level processes in collaborative activities such as Efficient Consumer Response (ECR) and Collaborative Planning, Forecasting, and Replenishment (CPFR) that synchronize and coordinate forecasts and plans across supply chain partners. If the processes are still ambiguously specified on a case-by-case basis, the implementation cost can be very high due to safeguarding costs of relationship specific assets, and there can be considerable cynicism in practice due to negative inequity and power play (Corsten and Kumar 2005).

Alongside process integration, additional sources of information can contribute to better forecasts. For example, the hospitality and tourism industry has been utilizing social media data as a crucial information source to improve demand predictions (Noone and McGuire 2011; Sigala et al. 2012). For example, HKhotels closely monitors customer reviews on TripAdvisor and uses this data to enhance value for customers by adjusting items in the breakfast buffet, as well as providing additional wine and cheese services in the evening. Wyndham Hotels and Resorts on the other hand, previously put effort into developing a micro-site to attract female travelers in order to gain insights into the services and amenities that matter to female travelers (now-defunct "Women on Their Way" website).

Due to the advancements in online communication technologies, recent forecasting methods incorporate web content volumes, online search records, stock market valuations, advertising and marketing activities, advance selling volumes, and social media viral traffic data (Xiong and Bharadwaj 2014). Recognizing such rich sources of information available online, POM research on predictive models can guide firms on how to interpret and utilize these content rich data to reduce the uncertainty in daily operations and decision making. As an example, Huang and Mieghem (2014) evaluate the case where a firm features their products online, but takes orders offline. They show that using online clickstream variables can help predict the propensity, amount, and timing of offline orders. As a result, the estimated reduction in inventory holding and backordering costs can be as high as 3% to 5%.

3.2 Joint Capability Planning

From a financial strategy perspective, integrating POM and Marketing functions proves to be critical in a variety of contexts. Particularly with regards to firm investment decisions, extant research has demonstrated that short-term and long-term implications abound for imprudent internal firm communication and POM coordination. Liu et al. (2010) examined supply reliability in a retail context that included joint marketing and inventory decisions. For products with a lower marketing costs function, the value for increasing supply reliability was always higher. Investment in new technologies was demonstrated as more financially beneficial when marketing costs related to increasing consumer demand were lower.

Relatedly, Shockley et al. (2015) employed a service operations management strategy to examine strategic design responsiveness ("the degree to which retailers dynamically coordinate investments in human and structural capital with the complexity of their service and product offerings") in a key area where marketing and operations functions are intertwined. They found that delayed applications of strategic investments did produce short-term financial benefits, but operational performance ultimately suffered. These results thus provided empirical support for the financial implications of an uncoordinated marketing and operations interface in the chain retail store context. In fact, in their analysis of ACSI customer satisfaction data, Shockley et al. (2015) found that decreasing labor force intensity faster than proportional margins was significantly and negatively associated with forward customer satisfaction scores.

Service capacity decisions within the supply chain require attention for the supply chain members to enhance joint profitability. In the case of after-sales service where the sales volume is affected by the retailer's service level commitment, the retailer faces make-or-buy decisions for the service capacity. Li et al. (2014) found that the outsourcing market encourages retailers to make higher levels of service commitment and have the manufacturers lower their wholesale price. Moreover, if the manufacturer is willing to share the cost to build service capacity with the retailer, profits of both parties tend to increase, especially when combined with different pricing strategies. Cachon and Feldman (2015) propose a pricing strategy of charging a high price only when the demand is high, and offering discounts otherwise. Although this strategy offers discounts more frequently than price commitment strategies, it happens to be more profitable, and reduces the need for overbuying capacity (higher levels of inventory). These findings are contrary to suggestions that advocate limiting markdowns and acquiring excess capacity. Periodic and infrequent communication between POM and Marketing decision makers within an organization does not work well in a traditional retail framework, and the deficiencies of such an approach likely prove even more pronounced in a multi-channel setting.

When consumers do elect to visit brick-and-mortar stores, conversion rates (the ratio of the number of transactions to traffic in the store) become critically important to retailers. Using apparel retailer data, Perdikaki et al. (2012) found that conversion rate declined with increasing store traffic, and that lower conversion rates led to a decrease in future traffic growth. However, when store traffic and staffing levels were close to their means, increasing average traffic per hour by one unit increased average sales volume. Retail firms must be able to balance demand across different channels; increasing just the store traffic yields diminishing returns in conversion rates. Marketing strategy is critical in identifying what consumers could be serviced effectively through online channels, lessening the operations-related strain of variable staffing and potential stockouts for brick-and-mortar retailers.

3.3 Reverse Logistics and Sustainability

As for the POM response on dealing with returned products, we discuss supply chain designs for reverse flow of products. The reverse supply chain needs to acquire products from end-users, transport those products to their disposition point. It also needs to test, sort, and inspect the product's condition, as well as refurbishing and remarketing the products (Guide et al. 2003). Together, the forward and reverse supply chains comprise a closed loop supply chain (Guide and Wassenhove 2009), proper design of which can allow firms to deal with not only product returns, but also product recalls and remanufactured products. Studies have looked into the determinants of product recalls and returns, and have found that the quality of the product itself is not a sufficient predictor of such incidences. In addition, innovative firms that focus heavily on R&D or maintain a broad SKU line will experience higher probabilities of product recalls (Thirumalai and Sinha 2011). Other studies have looked into the pricing schemes and product designs for remanufactured products (Chen and Chang 2013; Wu 2012). Regarding an important decision of what and how much to remanufacture, prior studies have attempted to identify optimal acquisition and sorting policies (Galbreth and Blackburn 2006; Ferguson et al. 2009). If a firm can manage to pool knowledge from multiple retail channels, the combined market knowledge about acceptability and consumer preferences of remanufactured products can enhance the effectiveness of such policies.

Another way firms have found useful in redistributing remanufactured or refurbished products is through specialized online retail channels that adopt "one deal a day" business models. An example is Woot.com, a deep discount retailer selling consumer electronics, wine, t-shirts, and remanufactured products (Wang et al. 2009). Selling through these channels rely on a psychological effect known as "the scarcity principle" (Lynn 1991). By placing limitations on the deals, consumers are induced with a sense of urgency, which increases the purchase tendency, shortens searches, and results in greater customer satisfaction (Sodero 2012). Such channels with innovative business models prove to be effective in dealing with excessive returns and remanufactured inventories.

4 Output Consequence: Complementarity Between POM and Marketing for Building Shareholder Wealth

One of the primary objectives of firms is to maximize the financial wealth of their shareholders. Therefore, it is important to ask whether the value of marketing and POM integration yields significant shareholder wealth. However, despite its importance, research on shareholder wealth has chiefly been the domain of scholars in finance. This is unfortunate, as limited attention on shareholder wealth in POM and Marketing has resulted in an under-appreciation of these business functions in the C-suite.

It is not that scholars in POM & Marketing have not considered financial performance in their investigations. However, a significant portion of this research has centered on accounting-based metrics rather than measures of shareholder wealth. Accounting-based metrics by definition are backwards-looking and provide limited guidance towards the future outlook of firms. Both POM and marketing can significantly impact forward-looking metrics that form components of shareholder wealth, underscoring more research attention on these. Indeed, marketing is focused on understanding and influencing customer needs and demands, and POM ensures that the supply chains of firms are aligned to optimally and efficiently meet the customer needs and demands. As such, the two business functions of POM and marketing have the potential to complement each other and positively inform firm value. A recent study by Inman et al. (2011) supports this complementarity by showing that marketing performance mediates the indirect relationship between firm operational and financial performances. This complementarity can give rise to key organizational capabilities that can enhance future financial flows of firms.

Based on these observations, we next describe the key theoretical frameworks that can be used to investigate the shareholder wealth of firms, along with an overview of some of the research that has already been conducted on this topic in POM and Marketing.

4.1 Theoretical Frameworks for Research on Shareholder Wealth

To evaluate how POM-marketing influences shareholder wealth in a complementary fashion, multiple theories can be called upon to develop a grounded view. However, one theory that has proven highly relevant and has been increasingly utilized by scholars is the resource-based view (RBV) of the firm (e.g., Barney 1991). According to RBV, competitive advantage resides in firm resources that have four characteristics—such resources are 1) valuable, 2) inimitable, 3) non-substitutable, and 4) heterogeneously distributed across firms. RBV thus suggests that if POM and Marketing allow firms to create resources with these four key characteristics, they will help firms derive higher prospective cash flows that enhance shareholder wealth.

While RBV stresses resource possession, the dynamic capabilities theory has recently underscored the point that firms also need to help unlock the value residing in their resources (e.g., Morgan et al. 2009). According to this theory, capabilities involve complex patterns of skills and knowledge that are embedded in firm routines and are difficult for competitors to acquire or duplicate (Eisenhardt and Martin 2000; Teece et al. 1997). Dynamic capabilities allow firms to acquire, integrate, and deploy valuable resources better than competition and lead to enduring competitive advantage (Peng et al. 2008) associated with greater financial flows that impact shareholder wealth (Shankar 2012), and also help firms achieve success in new product development and introductions. The importance of dynamic capabilities is becoming more relevant as the rate of change in technological advancements increase, and institutional concerns such as product safety (Beske et al. 2014), environmental issues (Mathiyazhagan et al. 2014), and humanitarian operations assert strong pressures in markets.

Similarly, supply chain synergies can create intelligence, which allows for enhanced market responsiveness (Schoenherr and Swink 2015). For example, Bang and Olufsen (B&O) was able to develop a new mobile phone by tapping into their supplier's (Samsung) technology base via close collaboration. Such close collaborations lead to early involvement of suppliers in new product development, which is fundamental in leveraging supplier capabilities and increasing supply chain responsiveness. Such a shift leads to the creation of a dynamic capability that stems from downstream customer focus (Roh and Min 2014). Examples of tapping into supply chain synergies provide support for the notion that proper alignment of POM and Marketing capabilities can serve as a competitive advantage that can enhance firm performance (Moorman and Slotegraaf 1999; Peng et al. 2008).

Marketing scholars have started to build on the dynamic capabilities theory to highlight the value of marketing capabilities. In this vein, leveraging stochastic frontier analysis in order to capture capabilities using objective data (Dutta et al. 1999; Narasimhan et al. 2006), studies have explored the complementary role of marketing capability in elevating shareholder wealth from key resources. For instance, in the context of mergers and acquisitions, marketing capability of firms has been shown to enhance the value residing in brands (Bahadir et al. 2008), and affect the valuation of brand acquisitions and disposals by firms (Wiles et al. 2012). For example, Unilever announced their brand portfolio slimming strategy in 2000, and eliminated hundreds of brands including Elizabeth Arden and Golden Griddle Syrup. This narrower focus allowed Unilever to streamline their procurement process, increase cost efficiency, and eventually contribute to shareholder wealth. Similarly, the key role played by marketing capability in elevating shareholder value from advertising resources (Xiong and Bharadwaj 2013) and from Corporate Social Responsibility (CSR) has been established (Mishra and Modi 2016).

Still, much of the extant research in these two fields has developed in isolation of each other, resulting in limited understanding of how POM and Marketing resources and capabilities financially complement each other. The finance literature provides useful metrics and empirical frameworks to capture shareholder wealth, and future researchers can draw upon these and to make further empirical investigations on this important topic (see Srinivasan and Hanssens (2009) for an excellent summary). Together, RBV and dynamic capabilities theories are key lenses that scholars in POM and marketing can utilize to investigate shareholder wealth, and evaluate the complementarities between POM and Marketing capabilities and resources. We now turn towards highlighting some research topics in this area.

4.2 Current Research on Shareholder Wealth in POM and Marketing

Utilizing RBV and dynamic capabilities theory, scholars have underscored the value of POM and Marketing resources and capabilities to firms. Indeed, given the central role of these two business functions in the value chain, they are expected to allow for valuable resources such as brands, innovations, and CSR that will make more customers buy firm offerings and do so with higher certainty (e.g., Mizik and Jacobson 2008; Luo and Bhattacharya 2009; Zhang et al. 2014). POM and Marketing are also responsible for adoption and utilization of enterprise-level systems which allow firms to better anticipate/forecast customer demands while managing production and operations more efficiently to help lower the level and variability of a firm's future cash flows (Hendricks et al. 2007), thereby increasing shareholder wealth. POM and Marketing capabilities in turn can afford firms the opportunity to convert their resources into valuable outputs more efficiently than competition, leading to gains in firm value (Dutta et al. 1999).

Underscoring the value relevance of POM, scholars have shown how specific supply chain resources add to firm value. For example, in a series of studies Hendricks and Singhal (2001; 1997) show that Total Quality Management (TQM) and quality improvement programs allow for short and long run stock market gains for firms. Similarly, scholars have also validated the link between firm adoption of ERP, SCM, and CRM systems and stock prices to underscore the financial value of these resources (Hendricks et al. 2007), and on industry exchanges between supply chain partners as key resources driving firm value (Mitra and Singhal 2008).

In addition to highlighting the value of resources, POM scholars have also investigated losses associated with supply chain risks to motivate managers to pay more attention towards lowering the probability of upstream disruptions. For instance, supply chain glitches that result in production or shipment delays have been shown to negatively affect stock returns (Hendricks and Singhal 2003). Similarly, excess inventory announcements, which indicate firm's inability to match supply with demand, have been documented to reduce shareholder wealth (Hendricks and Singhal 2009). Focusing on inventories, another study has shown that although inventory efficiency is good for shareholder wealth, too much efficiency can expose firms to supply chain risks that detract from firm value (Modi and Mishra 2011). Highlighting the virtues and risks of inventory efficiency, a study by Kesavan and Mani (2013) has shown that abnormal inventory growth has an inverted U-shaped relationship with one-year ahead earnings of firms.

Similar to POM, scholars in marketing have also considered the financial implications of marketing resources. For example, studies have established how brands, brand equity, and brand strategies affect stock returns and risks (e.g., Mizik and Jacobson 2008; Bharadwaj et al. 2011; Krasnikov et al. 2009; Rao et al. 2004). In addition, researchers have also highlighted the value relevance of other customer-based resources such as customer satisfaction (e.g., Fornell et al. 2006; Mittal et al. 2005), customer-life time value, and customer equity (e.g., Gupta et al. 2004). The shareholder implications of marketing mix resources, including advertising (McAlister et al. 2007), distribution (e.g., Geyskens et al. 2002), and products (e.g., Sorescu et al. 2007) have been established as well.

5 Future POM and Marketing Interface Research Avenues

The discussion thus far has created the Triple C framework for better understanding and placing extant research in the POM-Marketing interface in its proper perspective. Even though we have alluded to potential research opportunities throughout this chapter, we focus next on a few specific avenues that seem relevant and fruitful, and which are summarized in Table 20.1.

5.1 Deepening Consumer Knowledge and Channel Dynamics Across Channels

Future research opportunities on the topic of multi-channel retailing and its need for integrated POM and Marketing are fruitful and diverse. Product returns, for example, place a strain on the POM side of retail firm management, necessitating a closer examination of how returns repositioned as open-box products are perceived by consumers. Increased multi-channel retail activity will require evaluating which products on what retail channel could benefit most from money-back-guarantees. These insights can only be gathered through considering the phenomenon from both a POM and Marketing perspective.

Hsiao and Chen's (2014) findings that different consumer segments provide varying levels of value to manufacturers and retailers could promote research on how upstream supply chains

Table 20.1 POM and Marketing Interface Research Topics

Topic	Input (Context)	Process (Coordination)	Output (Consequence)
	Multichannel Retail	*Coordination & Integration*	*Shareholder Value*

Recent Developments	• Consumer Characteristics and Segmentation
	• Inventory Volatility
	  • Phantom Product
	• Money Back Guarantees and Product Returns
		• Micro-Level Process Integration
		• Data Rich Forecasting
		  • Social Network Service
		  • Geographical Information Systems
		  • Search Records
		• Joint Capability Planning
		• Reverse Logistics & Sustainability
			• Framework
			  • Resource Based View + Dynamic Capability
			• Metrics
			  • Stock Price
			  • Tobin's Q
			  • Market-to-Book Ratio
			• Risk Management
			  • Robust Performance
			  • Supply Chain Disruptions
			  • Event Study

Future Topics	• Segment Profitability
	• Geographic Profiling
	• Advance Selling
	• Channel Conflict and Supplier Encroachment
	• Co-op Advertising
		• Designing Corporate Social Responsible & Sustainable Processes
		  • Lean and Green
		  • Base of Pyramid Operations
			• POM and Marketing Complementarity Impact on Shareholder Wealth
			• Brand Equity for Risk Protection
			• Information Systems and Shareholder Wealth
			• More Dynamic Capabilities

can use quantitative marketing techniques to determine ideal consumer profiles for new Internet channel efforts. Allowing consumers to choose their own channel to operate in has been shown to be detrimental in certain circumstances (Perdikaki et al. 2012), implying that new research must not only identify which segments are the most profitable for firms to target, but which product lines within each firm should be highlighted for those consumers.

On a macro level, Brynjolfsson et al. (2009) demonstrated that multi-channel firms must analyze local markets, providing an opportunity for retailers to vary targeting efforts based on the consumer geographic and channel profiles. Future research can explore if products that are considered niche in some markets (and typically appear online only) may in fact benefit from a presence in brick-and-mortar stores in specific locations, stimulating "online-only" niche-product-consumers to visit stores in person.

Relatedly, it may be worthwhile to more closely explore the beneficial impact of advance selling under different retailer and consumer-specific scenarios. Prasad et al. (2011) noted that discounts provided to stimulate advance selling must be adjusted downward if return policies prove too liberal, providing consumers with easy returns. Given the profoundly negative effects that product stock outs have on brick-and-mortar retailers, analyzing consumer perceptions of full and partial refunds may yield insights as to how marketers can decrease trial risk for consumers while lessening back-end operations pressure on inventory management. If advance buying proves appealing to consumers and is coupled with an excessively loose return policy, product stock outs may discourage future store traffic.

Finally, there is a need for research in understanding competitive and cooperative behaviors between upstream suppliers and downstream retailers. Recently, a phenomenon called supplier encroachment has garnered the attention of scholars. Many upstream manufacturers have invested in establishing direct channels such as online stores, catalog sales, and factory outlets during the past couple of decades. Supplier encroachment refers to the market infiltration behavior that can increase the competition between the supplier and their resellers. Prior studies have shown that supplier encroachment allows the supplier to control the selling price in the retail market, and reduce their wholesale price. As a consequence, the problem of double marginalization, which causes sub optimal joint profits due to mark-up in wholesale price, can be mitigated, and benefit both the supplier and retailer (Arya et al. 2007). More recent studies show that depending on how the information and knowledge of the selling process is distributed between the buyer and supplier, supplier encroachment can lead to lose-lose or lose-win outcomes (Li et al. 2014). Still our understanding in this matter is incomplete, and there is a need for empirical research to address the consequences of such channel conflicts and encroachment behaviors. On the other hand, there is also potential for cooperative behaviors that can take place, an example being cooperative (co-op) advertising. Co-op advertising is a commonly adopted practice where the manufacturer pays a portion of the retailer's advertising costs. Many companies such as IBM, Apple, and Intel are known to use this strategy. Prior studies mostly analyze this arrangement under the rationality assumption, and conclude that co-op advertising does not lead to channel coordination (Bergen and John 1997). However, recent developments show that the manufacturer can coordinate the channel via co-op advertising schemes when firms care about the difference between each member's profits, and are willing to sacrifice their own profits in order to achieve fair payoffs (Yang et al. 2013). This can be another fruitful area of research, which requires more evidence based empirical approaches.

5.2 Designing Better Socially Responsible and Environmentally Sustainable Processes in POM and Marketing

Should managers care for philanthropy? Some studies based on risk management theory posit that corporate philanthropy can generate positive moral capital among stakeholders that can also provide shareholders with insurance-like protection for a firm's relationship based intangible assets, and that this protection contributes to shareholder wealth (Godfrey 2005). As a result, CSR is increasingly becoming an important component of corporate strategy, with firms reporting their socially responsible efforts publicly. Moreover, the concept of triple bottom line (i.e., economic, environmental, and social) is gaining prevalence among managers and key stakeholders (Kleindorfer et al. 2005). Within CSR, POM scholars have looked at environmental issues (e.g., Angell and Klassen 1999; Corbett and Klassen 2006; Jacobs et al. 2010), the relationship between lean and green (e.g., Rothenberg et al. 2001), and the impact of sustainability on key firm stakeholders (Sarkis et al. 2010). In marketing, the focus has mostly been on the effect of CSR on consumers (e.g., Brown and Dacin 1997; Bhattacharya and Sen 2003; Chernev and Blair 2015), with some work evaluating how CSR affects shareholder wealth (e.g., Luo and Bhattacharya 2009; Mishra and Modi 2016).

Despite these rich insights, there remains significant potential for understanding complementarity between POM and Marketing in fostering CSR. For instance, marketing frameworks on how CSR influences consumers can be combined with POM insights to evaluate the effect of CSR on other firm stakeholders, particularly channel partners. Channel members are needed for facilitating the socially responsible agenda of firms, and articulating their role in the CSR-financial value relationship can be very useful for practice. Research can also look at if lean aligns with green, and how these two concepts relate to elevating shareholder wealth.

An avenue of CSR research that requires attention from POM-marketing researchers is to identify strategies that effectively reach the base of the pyramid (BOP) (Karmani 2007; Prahalad 2005). As growth opportunities are limited in developed markets and CSR is a paramount issue, firms that successfully tap into this highly potent customer base in BOP markets will make significant contributions to shareholder wealth. Future research should address how MNCs can evolve in BOP markets over time by utilizing their POM and Marketing competencies.

5.3 Fostering Complementarity Between POM and Marketing Capabilities

Building on branding research in marketing and research on lean in POM, it will be worthwhile to investigate the chain-of-effects linking lean and brands with shareholder wealth. The answers here will be non-trivial, and likely depend on a host of contingency factors, which remain to be explored. As an example, it is likely that the effect of lean would be contingent on how effectively a lean focus is communicated to key stakeholders, underscoring the role of advertising as a complementary resource.

A second path of inquiry relating lean and brands can focus on the buffering role of brand equity in attenuating the risks arising from inventory efficiency. As discussed, POM scholars have cautioned against an excessive focus on lean, as this may expose firms to unexpected negative events and shocks (Hendricks and Singhal 2003). Marketing researchers have highlighted that brand equity provides a cushion to firms against negative events (e.g., Bharadwaj et al. 2011). A compelling follow-up question then is: Are high brand equity firms also protected from external supply chain shocks as they maintain a lean focus, and if so how?

In addition to lean and brands, future studies can also focus on understanding how different types of SCM and CRM systems influence marketing resources to elevate shareholder wealth. One potential consequence of effective CRM implementation could be an increase in customer satisfaction, as this can allow firms to identify high value customers and better understand their needs to form more enduring customer relationships. SCM systems can similarly ensure that customer needs are met in a timely and predictable manner. Customer satisfaction is a valuable firm resource that generates shareholder wealth (e.g., Rego et al. 2013).

Finally, extant research has not provided much evidence towards the value potential of key organizational capabilities. Given the complementary role of marketing and POM, it is likely that capabilities of these two functions would positively reinforce each other to enable valuable firm resources. This can result in higher levels of customer satisfaction due to better management of the value chain catering to customer needs and wants. Similarly, these two capabilities can help attenuate the negative effect of external shocks (e.g., supply chain disruptions, product recalls, etc.) on shareholder wealth. Furthermore, the two capabilities can have a positive role in facilitating CSR and its effect on future firm cash flows. Uncovering these relationships can underscore the importance of POM and Marketing managers working more closely with each other in building their core competencies, and ensuring sustainable competitive advantage.

6 Implications for Practitioners

By tying research streams from multiple disciplines, practitioners can gain a clearer understanding of root causes that affect shareholder wealth. Also, the constant strive for relevance in research can provide a more detailed prescription on how process coordination can be achieved based on technological shifts or change in market demand.

We proposed shareholder wealth as one measure that can partly capture the value of marketing and POM dynamic capabilities residing within the firm. This long term forward-looking performance measure can guide managers' attention towards building sustainable competitive advantages rather than pursuing immediate consequences. The 3C framework (Context, Coordination, and Consequence) presented in this chapter also presents several relevant insights for practitioners as listed below.

- It is always important to pay attention to the market and customers, as they are key determinants of how the context is formed and dynamics are embedded.
- Process and coordination efforts should also evolve constantly because the context is dynamic in nature. Combined with excellence in market sensing and adaptation, well-aligned processes complement the formulation of dynamic capabilities.
- Often firms focus on managing the consequences. However, consequences are only products of the input context and the coordination of processes.

7 Conclusion and Future Research Directions

Research in the area of Production and Operations Management (POM), set in various contexts ranging from outsourcing decisions, service failures, firm innovation, process improvement, and supply chain integration, has underscored the importance of relating operations to financial performance and firm value. At the same time, research in the interdisciplinary areas of POM and Marketing has highlighted the joint effect of operations and marketing capabilities on customer and firm value.

Drawing from recent findings in the literature, we have developed and presented in this chapter a 3C (Context, Coordination, and Consequence) framework that connects the demand side fluctuations with financial outcomes. Relevant POM research within this framework encompasses micro-level process integrations with data-rich forecasting, joint capability planning, and reverse logistics within the context of multichannel retailing. Using this framework, we have shown how POM and Marketing interface research can help address radical shifts in the business landscape such as the emergence of online retail channels, identification and management of complex consumer segments, volatile inventories, and increased product returns. Within this context, multi-channel retailing with a mix of online and offline, direct and indirect sales, forward and reverse, drastically impacts a firm's daily decisions. Due to an increase in complexity and volatility, firms should put more effort in coordination, both internally and externally. Measuring and managing the performance of such settings is truly a difficult task, and we propose a focus on shareholder value as an alternative that also considers the institutional pressures. Firms that successfully manage this complexity will be able to achieve competitive advantage, while firms that fail to do so will experience supply and demand mismatches and disruptions, which, in the end, will adversely impact the shareholder value of the firm.

We hope future research will adopt the multidisciplinary perspectives and theoretical lenses highlighted in this chapter to yield findings that advance both theory and practice, and provide a deeper understanding of how the POM-Marketing interface can help firms expand their strategic options. Research opportunities at the interface of these disciplines should be focused on aligning complex market segments with supply capabilities, resolving channel conflicts through cooperation, coordinating corporate social responsibility (CSR) and sustainability initiatives, and creating dynamic POM and Marketing capabilities.

References and Bibliography

Akçay, Y., T. Boyacı and D. Zhang (2013) "Selling with Money-Back Guarantees: The Impact on Prices, Quantities, and Retail Profitability," *Production and Operations Management*, **22**(4): 777–791.

Alan, Y., G.P. Gao and V. Gaur (2014) "Does Inventory Productivity Predict Future Stock Returns? A Retailing Industry Perspective," *Management Science*, **60**(10): 2416–2434.

Angell, L.C. and R.D. Klassen (1999) "Integrating Environmental Issues into the Mainstream: An Agenda for Research in Operations Management," *Journal of Operations Management*, **17**(5): 575–598.

Arya, A., B. Mittendorf and D.E. Sappington (2007) "The Bright Side of Supplier Encroachment," *Marketing Science*, **26**(5): 651–659.

Avery, J., T.J. Steenburgh, J. Deighton and M. Caravella (2012) "Adding Bricks to Clicks: Predicting the Patterns of Cross-Channel Elasticities Over Time," *Journal of Marketing*, **76**(3): 96–111.

Bahadir, S.C., S.G. Bharadwaj and R.K. Srivastava (2008) "Financial Value of Brands in Mergers and Acquisitions: Is Value in the Eye of the Beholder?" *Journal of Marketing*, **72**(6): 49–64.

Barney, J. (1991) "Firm Resources and Sustained Competitive Advantage," *Journal of Management*, **17**(1): 99–120.

Bell, D., S. Gallino and A. Moreno (2015) "Showrooms and Information Provision in Omni-Channel Retail," *Production and Operations Management*, **24**(3): 360–362.

Bergen, M. and G. John (1997) "Understanding Cooperative Advertising Participation Rates in Conventional Channels," *Journal of Marketing Research*, **34**(3): 357–369.

Beske, P., A. Land and S. Seuring (2014) "Sustainable Supply Chain Management Practices and Dynamic Capabilities in the Food Industry: A Critical Analysis of the Literature," *International Journal of Production Economics*, **152**: 131–143.

Bharadwaj, S.G., K.R. Tuli and A. Bonfrer (2011) "The Impact of Brand Quality on Shareholder Wealth," *Journal of Marketing*, **75**(5): 88–104.

Bhattacharya, C.B. and S. Sen (2003) "Consumer-Company Identification: A Framework for Understanding Consumers' Relationships with Companies," *Journal of Marketing*, **67**(2): 76–88.

Brown, T.J. and P.A. Dacin (1997) "The Company and the Product: Corporate Associations and Consumer Product Responses," *Journal of Marketing*, **51**(1): 68–84.

Brynjolfsson, E., Y. Hu and M.S. Rahman (2009) "Battle of the Retail Channels: How Product Selection and Geography Drive Cross-Channel Competition," *Management Science*, **55**(11): 1755–1765.

Cachon, G.P. and P. Feldman (2015) "Price Commitments with Strategic Consumers: Why It Can Be Optimal to Discount More Frequently . . . than Optimal," *Manufacturing & Service Operations Management*, **17**(3): 399–410.

Chen, J. and P.C. Bell (2012) "Implementing Market Segmentation using Full-Refund and No-Refund Customer Returns Policies in a Dual-Channel Supply Chain Structure," *International Journal of Production Economics*, **136**(1): 56–66.

Chen, J.M. and C.I. Chang (2013) "Dynamic Pricing for New and Remanufactured Products in a Closed-Loop Supply Chain," *International Journal of Production Economics*, **146**(1): 153–160.

Chernev, A. and S. Blair (2015) "Doing Well by Doing Good: The Benevolent Halo of Corporate Social Responsibility," *Journal of Consumer Research*, **41**(6): 1412–1425.

Corbett, C.J. and R.D. Klassen (2006) "Extending the Horizons: Environmental Excellence as Key to Improving Operations," *Manufacturing & Service Operations Management*, **8**(1): 5–22.

Corsten, D. and N. Kumar (2005) "Do Suppliers Benefit from Collaborative Relationships with Large Retailers? An Empirical Investigation of Efficient Consumer Response Adoption," *Journal of Marketing*, **69**(3): 80–94.

DeHoratius, N., A. Raman (2008) "Inventory Record Inaccuracy: An Empirical Analysis," *Management Science*, **54**(4): 627–641.

Dutta, S., O. Narasimhan and S. Rajiv (1999) "Success in High-Technology Markets: Is Marketing Capability Critical?" *Marketing Science*, **18**(4): 547–568.

Eisenhardt, K.M. and J.A. Martin (2000) "Dynamic Capabilities: What Are They?" *Strategic Management Journal*, **21**(10–11): 1105–1121.

Ferguson, M., V.D. Guide, E. Koca and G.C. Souza (2009) "The Value of Quality Grading in Remanufacturing," *Production and Operations Management*, **18**(3): 300–314.

Forman, C., A. Ghose and A. Goldfarb (2009) "Competition Between Local and Electronic Markets: How the Benefit of Buying Online Depends on Where You Live," *Management Science*, **55**(1): 47–57.

Fornell, C., S. Mithas, F.V. Morgeson III and M.S. Krishnan (2006) "Customer Satisfaction and Stock Prices: High Returns, Low Risk," *Journal of Marketing*, **70**(1): 3–14.

Galbreth, M.R. and J.D. Blackburn (2006) "Optimal Acquisition and Sorting Policies for Remanufacturing," *Production and Operations Management*, **15**(3): 384.

Gallino, S. and A. Moreno (2014) "Integration of Online and Offline Channels in Retail: The Impact of Sharing Reliable Inventory Availability Information," *Management Science*, **60**(6): 1434–1451.

Geyskens, I., K. Gielens and M.G. Dekimpe (2002) "The Market Valuation of Internet Channel Additions," *Journal of Marketing*, **66**(2): 102–119.

Godfrey, P.C. (2005) "The Relationship between Corporate Philanthropy and Shareholder Wealth: A Risk Management Perspective," *Academy of Management Review*, **30**(4): 777–798.

Guide Jr, V.D.R. and L.N. Van Wassenhove (2009) "OR FORUM-The Evolution of Closed-Loop Supply Chain Research," *Operations Research*, **57**(1): 10–18.

Guide Jr, V.D.R., T.P. Harrison and L.N. Van Wassenhove (2003) "The Challenge of Closed-Loop Supply Chains," *Interfaces*, **33**(6): 3–6.

Gupta, S., D.R. Lehmann and J.A. Stuart (2004) "Valuing Customers," *Journal of Marketing Research*, **41**(1): 7–18.

Hendricks, K.B. and V.R. Singhal (1997) "Does Implementing an Effective TQM Program Actually Improve Operating Performance? Empirical Evidence from Firms that Have Won Quality Awards," *Management Science*, **43**(9): 1258–1274.

Hendricks, K.B. and V.R. Singhal (2001) "Firm Characteristics, Total Quality Management, and Financial Performance," *Journal of Operations Management*, **19**(3): 269–285.

Hendricks, K.B. and V.R. Singhal (2003) "The Effect of Supply Chain Glitches on Shareholder Wealth," *Journal of Operations Management*, **21**(5): 501–522.

Hendricks, K.B. and V.R. Singhal (2009) "Demand-Supply Mismatches and Stock Market Reaction: Evidence from Excess Inventory Announcements," *Manufacturing & Service Operations Management*, **11**(3): 509–524.

Hendricks, K.B., V.R. Singhal and J.K. Stratman (2007) "The Impact of Enterprise Systems on Corporate Performance: A Study of ERP, SCM, and CRM System Implementations," *Journal of Operations Management*, **25**(1): 65–82.

Hsiao, L. and Y.J. Chen (2014) "Strategic Motive for Introducing Internet Channels in a Supply Chain," *Production and Operations Management*, **23**(1): 36–47.

Huang, T. and J.A. Van Mieghem (2014) "Clickstream Data and Inventory Management: Model and Empirical Analysis," *Production and Operations Management*, **23**(3): 333–347.

Inman, R.A., R.S. Sale, K.W. Green and D. Whitten (2011) "Agile Manufacturing: Relation to JIT, Operational Performance and Firm Performance," *Journal of Operations Management*, **29**(4): 343–355.

Iyer, G., C. Narasimhan and R. Niraj (2007) "Information and Inventory in Distribution Channels," *Management Science*, **53**(10): 1551–1561.

Jacobs, B.W., V.R. Singhal and R. Subramanian (2010) "An Empirical Investigation of Environmental Performance and the Market Value of the Firm," *Journal of Operations Management*, **28**(5): 430–441.

Karmani, A. (2007) "The Mirage of Marketing to the Bottom of the Pyramid," *California Management Review*, **49**(4): 91–111.

Kesavan, S. and V. Mani (2013) "The Relationship between Abnormal Inventory Growth and Future Earnings for US Public Retailers," *Manufacturing & Service Operations Management*, **15**(1): 6–23.

Kleindorfer, P.R., K. Singhal and L.N. Van Wassenhove (2005) "Sustainable Operations Management," *Production and Operations Management*, **14**(4): 482–492.

Krasnikov, A., S. Mishra and D. Orozco (2009) "Evaluating the Financial Impact of Branding Using Trademarks: A Framework and Empirical Evidence," *Journal of Marketing*, **73**(6): 154–166.

Lee, E., R. Staelin, W.S. Yoo and R. Du (2013) "A 'Meta-Analysis' of Multibrand, Multioutlet Channel Systems," *Management Science*, **59**(9): 1950–1969.

Li, G., F.F. Huang, T.C.E. Cheng, Q. Zheng and P. Ji (2014) "Make-or-Buy Service Capacity Decision in a Supply Chain Providing After-Sales Service," *European Journal of Operational Research*, **239**(2): 377–388.

Li, Z., S.M. Gilbert and G. Lai (2013) "Supplier Encroachment under Asymmetric Information," *Management Science*, **60**(2): 449–462.

Ling, R.C. and W.E. Goddard (1988) *Orchestrating Success: Improve Control of The Business with Sales & Operations Planning*. Essex Junction, VT: Oliver Wight Limited Publications.

Liu, S., K.C. So and F. Zhang (2010) "Effect of Supply Reliability in a Retail Setting with Joint Marketing and Inventory Decisions," *Manufacturing & Service Operations Management*, **12**(1): 19–32.

Luo, X. and C.B. Bhattacharya (2009) "The Debate over Doing Good: Corporate Social Performance, Strategic Marketing Levers, and Firm-Idiosyncratic Risk," *Journal of Marketing*, **73**(6): 198–213.

Lynn, M. (1991) "Scarcity Effects on Value: A Quantitative Review of the Commodity Theory Literature," *Psychology & Marketing*, **8**(1): 43–57.

Malhotra, M.K. and S. Sharma (2002) "Spanning the Continuum between Marketing and Operations," *Journal of Operations Management*, **20**(3): 209–219.

Mathiyazhagan, K., K. Govindan and A. Noorul Haq (2014) "Pressure Analysis for Green Supply Chain Management Implementation in Indian Industries using Analytic Hierarchy Process," *International Journal of Production Research*, **52**(1): 188–202.

McAlister, L., R. Srinivasan and M. Kim (2007) "Advertising, Research and Development, and Systematic Risk of the Firm," *Journal of Marketing*, **71**(1): 35–48.

Mishra, S. and S.B. Modi (2016) "Corporate Social Responsibility and Shareholder Wealth: The Role of Marketing Capability," *Journal of Marketing*, **80**(1): 26–46.

Mitra, S. and V.R. Singhal (2008) "Supply Chain Integration and Shareholder Value: Evidence from Consortium Based Industry Exchanges," *Journal of Operations Management*, **26**(1): 96–114.

Mittal, V., E.W. Anderson, A. Sayrak and P. Tadikamalla (2005) "Dual Emphasis and the Long-Term Financial Impact of Customer Satisfaction," *Marketing Science*, **24**(4): 544–555.

Mizik, N. and R. Jacobson (2008) "The Financial Value Impact of Perceptual Brand Attributes," *Journal of Marketing Research*, **45**(1): 15–32.

Modi, S.B. and S. Mishra (2011) "What Drives Financial Performance–Resource Efficiency or Resource Slack? Evidence from US Based Manufacturing Firms from 1991 to 2006," *Journal of Operations Management*, **29**(3): 254–273.

Mollenkopf, D., I. Russo and R. Frankel (2007) "The Returns Management Process in Supply Chain Strategy," *International Journal of Physical Distribution & Logistics Management*, **37**(7): 568–592.

Moorman, C. and R.J. Slotegraaf (1999) "The Contingency Value of Complementary Capabilities in Product Development," *Journal of Marketing Research*, 239–257.

Morgan, N.A., R.J. Slotegraaf and D.W. Vorhies (2009) "Linking Marketing Capabilities with Profit Growth," *International Journal of Research in Marketing*, **26**(4): 284–293.

Narasimhan, O., S. Rajiv and S. Dutta (2006) "Absorptive Capacity in High-Technology Markets: The Competitive Advantage of the Haves," *Marketing Science*, **25**(5): 510–524.

Noone, B.M., K.A. McGuire and K.V. Rohlfs (2011) "Social Media Meets Hotel Revenue Management: Opportunities, Issues and Unanswered Questions," *Journal of Revenue & Pricing Management*, **10**(4): 293–305.

Ofek, E., Z. Katona and M. Sarvary (2011) "'Bricks and Clicks': The Impact of Product Returns on the Strategies of Multichannel Retailers," *Marketing Science*, **30**(1): 42–60.

Oliva, R. and N. Watson (2009) "Managing Functional Biases in Organizational Forecasts: A Case Study of Consensus Forecasting in Supply Chain Planning," *Production and Operations Management*, **18**(2): 138–151.

Oliva, R. and N. Watson (2011) "Cross-Functional Alignment in Supply Chain Planning: A Case Study of Sales and Operations Planning," *Journal of Operations Management*, **29**(5): 434–448.

Parente, D.H. (1998) "Across the Manufacturing-Marketing Interface Classification of Significant Research," *International Journal of Operations & Production Management*, **18**(12): 1205–1222.

Pauwels, K., P.S.H. Leeflang, M.L. Teerling and K.R.E. Huizingh (2011) "Does Online Information Drive Offline Revenues?" *Journal of Retailing*, **87**(1): 1–17.

Peng, D.X., R.G. Schroeder and R. Shah (2008) "Linking Routines to Operations Capabilities: A New Perspective," *Journal of Operations Management*, **26**(6): 730–748.

Perdikaki, O., S. Kesavan and J.M. Swaminathan (2012) "Effect of Traffic on Sales and Conversion Rates of Retail Stores," *Manufacturing & Service Operations Management*, **14**(1): 145–162.

Petersen, J.A. and V. Kumar (2009) "Are Product Returns a Necessary Evil? Antecedents and Consequences," *Journal of Marketing*, **73**(3): 35–51.

Prahalad, C.K. (2006) *The Fortune at the Bottom of the Pyramid*. Upper Saddle River, NJ: Pearson Education.

Prasad, A., K.E. Stecke and X. Zhao (2011) "Advance Selling by a Newsvendor Retailer," *Production and Operations Management*, **20**(1): 129–142.

Rao, V.R., M.K. Agarwal and D. Dahlhoff (2004) "How is Manifest Branding Strategy Related to the Intangible Value of a Corporation?" *Journal of Marketing*, **68**(4): 126–141.

Rego, L.L., N.A. Morgan and C. Fornell (2013) "Reexamining the Market Share-Customer Satisfaction Relationship," *Journal of Marketing*, **77**(5): 1–20.

Roh, J., P. Hong and H. Min (2014) "Implementation of a Responsive Supply Chain Strategy in Global Complexity: The Case of Manufacturing Firms," *International Journal of Production Economics*, **147**: 198–210.

Rothenberg, S., F.K. Pil and J. Maxwell (2001) "Lean, Green, and the Quest for Superior Environmental Performance," *Production and Operations Management*, **10**(3): 228–243.

Sarkis, J., P. Gonzalez-Torre and B. Adenso-Diaz (2010) "Stakeholder Pressure and the Adoption of Environmental Practices: The Mediating Effect of Training," *Journal of Operations Management*, **28**(2): 163–176.

Schoenherr, T. and M. Swink (2015) "The Roles of Supply Chain Intelligence and Adaptability in New Product Launch Success," *Decision Sciences*, **46**(5): 901–936.

Shankar, V. (2012) "Marketing Strategy and Firm Value," *Handbook of Marketing Strategy*, Cheltenham, UK: Edward-Elgar.

Shapiro, B.P. (1977) "Can Manufacturing and Marketing Coexist?" *Harvard Business Review*, **55**(5): 104–111.

Shockley, J., L.A. Plummer, A.V. Roth and L.D. Fredendall (2015) "Strategic Design Responsiveness: An Empirical Analysis of US Retail Store Networks," *Production and Operations Management*, **24**(3): 451–468.

Sigala, M., E. Christou and U. Gretzel (2012) *Social Media in Travel, Tourism and Hospitality: Theory, Practice and Cases*. Farnham, UK: Ashgate Publishing, Ltd.

Sodero, A. (2012) "The Effect of Social Interactions on Demand and Service Levels of Online Retailers in the Social Shopping Context," Doctoral dissertation, Arizona State University, Phoenix, AZ.

Sorescu, A., V. Shankar and T. Kushwaha (2007) "New Product Preannouncements and Shareholder Value: Don't Make Promises You Can't Keep," *Journal of Marketing Research*, **44**(3): 468–489.

Srinivasan, S. and D.M. Hanssens (2009) "Marketing and Firm Value: Metrics, Methods, Findings, and Future Directions," *Journal of Marketing Research*, **46**(3): 293–312.

Swinney, R. (2011) "Selling to Strategic Consumers when Product Value is Uncertain: The Value of Matching Supply and Demand," *Management Science*, **57**(10): 1737–1751.

Tang, C.S., K. Rajaram, A. Alptekinoğlu and J. Ou (2004) "The Benefits of Advance Booking Discount Programs: Model and Analysis," *Management Science*, **50**(4): 465–478.

Teece, D.J., G. Pisano and A. Shuen (1997) "Dynamic Capabilities and Strategic Management," *Strategic Management Journal*, **18**(7): 509–533.

Thirumalai, S. and K.K. Sinha (2011) "Product Recalls in the Medical Device Industry: An Empirical Exploration of the Sources and Financial Consequences," *Management Science*, **57**(2): 376–392.

Ton, Z. and A. Raman (2010) "The Effect of Product Variety and Inventory Levels on Retail Store Sales: A Longitudinal Study," *Production and Operations Management*, **19**(5): 546–560.

Wang, B., L.C. Liu, K.S. Koong and S. Bai (2009) "Effects of Daily and 'Woot-Off' Strategies on E-Commerce," *Industrial Management & Data Systems*, **109**(3): 389–403.

Warby Parker (2016) Home Try-On. Available from: www.warbyparker.com/home-try-on.

Wiles, M.A., N.A. Morgan and L.L. Rego (2012) "The Effect of Brand Acquisition and Disposal on Stock Returns," *Journal of Marketing*, **76**(1): 38–58.

Wu, C.H. (2012) "Product-Design and Pricing Strategies with Remanufacturing," *European Journal of Operational Research*, **222**(2): 204–215.

Xiong, G. and S. Bharadwaj (2013) "Asymmetric Roles of Advertising and Marketing Capability in Financial Returns to News: Turning Bad into Good and Good into Great," *Journal of Marketing Research*, **50**(6): 706–724.

Xiong, G. and S. Bharadwaj (2014) "Prerelease Buzz Evolution Patterns and New Product Performance," *Marketing Science*, **33**(3): 401–421.

Yang, J., J. Xie, X. Deng and H. Xiong (2013) "Cooperative Advertising in a Distribution Channel with Fairness Concerns," *European Journal of Operational Research*, **227**(2): 401–407.

Zhang, G.P., J. Yu and Y. Xia (2014) "The Payback of Effective Innovation Programs: Empirical Evidence from Firms that Have Won Innovation Awards," *Production and Operations Management*, **23**(8): 1401–1420.

21
THE STRATEGIC ROLE OF HUMAN RESOURCES IN ENABLING POM

Robert K. Prescott, Henrique L. Correa, and Adeola O. Shabiyi

1 Introduction

1.1 Purpose of the Chapter

The ideals of engaged scholarship (Van de Ven 2007) encourage the collaboration between academics and practitioners with a view to creating practitioner-meaningful research underpinned by the rigor of scientific methodology. The quest for this collaboration transcends the vocation of academics and industry practitioners, moving into business disciplines. Empirically, there are many interdisciplinary studies among strategy, management, accounting, marketing, sales, finance, and operations management. Examples include Birts et al. (1997) who presented the story of a research exercise that encompassed the disciplines of finance, accountancy, marketing, organizational behavior, and strategy as well as the work of Karmarkar (1996) which brought together models, methods, and techniques from marketing and operations. However, interdisciplinary studies between Human Resources (HR)—the division of a company that focuses on activities relating to employees—and other major business disciplines are not as popular. Considering the opportunity that exists in this area of research, this chapter covers many different avenues. We start by looking at the impact of Strategic Human Resources Management (SHRM) as well as the concepts and practices that guide and align Human Resource Management (HRM). Next, we focus on the function in organizations designed to maximize employee performance of an employer's strategic objectives philosophy. We also look towards enabling Production and Operations Management (POM), a process which combines and transforms various resources used in the production/operations subsystem of the organization in order to create Sustained Competitive Advantage (SCA)—a long-term competitive advantage for the business.

1.2 Background

Barney (1991) put forward a model for analyzing how firm resources could potentially generate sustained competitive advantage. Firm resources include all assets, capabilities, organizational processes, firm attributes, information, knowledge, etc. controlled by the firm that enable the firm to conceive of and implement strategies that improve its efficiency and effectiveness (Barney 1991). These firm resources were categorized into three—Physical Capital Resources (technology, plant and equipment, stores, etc.); Human Capital Resources (experience, training, talent, insights of individual managers, team dynamics, workers in the firm, etc.); and Organizational Capital Resources (formal reporting structure, coordinating systems, tactical processes, etc.) (Barney 1991). With respect to human capital resources, Rastogi (2000) indicated that, in today's volatile business environment, the competitive advantages of firms are temporary. Top management does not, and cannot, have all the answers to increasingly complex and rapidly changing problem situations facing the firm. In such a context, people of an organization constitute its core resource for continuous competitiveness. This resource comprises people's individual and collective learning and knowledge, skills and expertise, creativity and innovation, competencies, and capabilities (i.e., people's continuous capacity for providing customer-valued outcomes) (Rastogi 2000). Additionally, Barney (1991) also alluded to this context in his research.

Furthering the human capital resources discussion, Hatch and Dyer (2004) stated that, in the resource-based view of the firm, human capital is frequently assumed to contribute to competitive advantage due to its inimitability based on its intangible, firm-specific, and socially complex nature. Consistent with this view, they found that investments in firm-specific human capital have a significant impact on learning and firm performance. More specifically, human capital selection (education requirements and screening), development through training, and deployment significantly improve and increase instances of learning by doing, which in turn improves performance.

Shaw et al. (2013) indicated that the focus on human capital as a source of competitive advantage has intensified the need for organizations not only to understand and win the talent war but has also led to a tighter integration between strategic management (SM) and SHRM from the Resource-Based View (RBV). Note that strategic management refers to the formulation and implementation of the major goals and initiatives taken by a company's top management while Strategic Human Resources Management refers to the application of a bundle of valuable tangible or intangible resources at the firm's disposal. The RBV has shifted the focus of SM literature on sources of competitive advantage from external factors, such as industry positions, to idiosyncratic internal factors, such as human capital accumulations (Shaw et al. 2013). With the generally held belief that SHRM facilitates the acquisition, development, deployment (or mobility), retention, and transition (or separation) of Human Capital Resources (HCR), it becomes imperative to study how SHRM enables POM with a view to creating a SCA.

Targeted dimensions of focus in this chapter include the strategic rationale for both disciplines, SHRM and POM, in working together in synergistic ways. These ways include the functional connection points of HR practices and supply chain operations, the enabling thoughts and perspectives from industry production and operations leaders as well as frameworks for thinking, analyzing, and implementing HR function practices that enable POM. The strategic opportunity in this work is to further extend the discussion on the interaction between HR and POM and provide a framework for transforming that interaction into sustainable competitive advantage for the business.

2   A Call for Synergy Between Human Resources and Production and Operations Management

2.1   A Strategic Imperative—Review of the Literature

In this section, we present a discussion of the literature related to the HR competency dimensions of the study using multiple empirical studies identified for review and presented in topical order of research.

2.2 Current Trends in Human Resources Management (HRM)

A number of trends are surfacing in the field of HRM. Important trends worthy of consideration here are human capital research and analytics, integrating HR practices with other functions, and the role of organization development in the HR function. These trending topics are discussed within the strategic context of enabling POM in the delivery of sustained competitive advantage to the business.

2.2.1 Human Capital Research and Analytics

Fink (2010) looked at the trending issue of Human Capital Analytics (HCA)—techniques to help articulate the impact of human capital investments—while also writing about the need to understand work being done in the analytics world. As organizations seek to transition to a more data-driven profession, there is little available information to guide them on the most useful approach to integrating HCA into daily organizational practices (Fink 2010). Fink also sought to understand the leading-edge data analytics practices of peers at respected organizations, so as to adapt, extend, or be inspired by their work. This study found that linkages across multiple and multi-functional data sets are quite useful. The linking of recruiting and staffing data to performance data within 12 and 24 months of hiring a new employee helps to improve the quality of hire (Fink 2010). It also helps in the development and validation of selection procedures that ensure it is tied to succession planning and ultimately an end-to-end recruitment of talent.

Furthermore, capturing different dimensions, of culture and Employee Value Proposition (EVP)—a unique set of offerings, associations, and values to positively influence target candidates and employees—helps to inform decision making. From a methods standpoint, organizations use regression analysis, a family of statistical methods designed to test a conceptual or theoretical model known as Structural Equation Modeling (SEM), discrete choice analysis, latent growth curve modeling, and ethnographic methods to establish linkages and patterns in order to gain insights (Fink 2010). While HR tends to be the primary user of these analytics, the POM function benefits extensively by using HRA in the attraction, development, deployment, and retention of talent as well as organizational practices that lead to increased employee engagement and productivity.

2.2.2 Integrating HR Practices with POM

Menon (2012) studied management and HR practices that lead to executives' satisfaction with the performance of an organization's supply chain and with employee wellbeing. The objective of this study was to develop recommendations for practicing managers. Menon (2012) tested hypotheses linking executives' satisfaction with supply chain performance to non-traditional HR practices like flexible job descriptions and teamwork training. The results of the study identified specific HR practices, such as flexible job descriptions, teamwork training, and the use of performance metrics to determine rewards are significantly related to satisfaction with supply chain performance.

2.2.3 Organizational Development (OD) and Human Resources (HR) in Production and Operations Management (POM)

Organizational Development (OD) is a field of research, theory, and practice dedicated to organizational change and performance. Schein (2010) studied the role of OD in the HR function as an innovation-oriented function and labeled it as a current trend which helps to facilitate needed cultural changes in the organization and across the business functions (Schein 2010).

According to Schein (2010), results assert a failure to recognize the following five important trends between HR and OD:

- All of the organizational functions are becoming more complex and technologically sophisticated (e.g., POM leading to the creation of subcultures based on different occupational technologies such as SCM).
- The rapid evolution of information technology has changed the nature of work and the nature of organizing in dramatic ways, stimulating innovation in OD and challenging some of the most sacred cows of the HR culture.
- The world is becoming more of a global village in which the interdependencies between countries and between organizations are increasing dramatically (e.g., global supply chains).
- Due to the complexity that arises from cultural diversity, culture is a group's learned response to the problem of survival in the external environment and the problem of internal integration (e.g., process management).
- The fundamental function of organizations is being reexamined around the issues of social responsibility and business ethics.

The implications of these five factors for both OD and HR are staggering, but the impact is not the same on both functions. OD has always been the more innovation-oriented function while HR is typically expected to be stable and conservative. In order to determine how employees are paid and disciplined, companies require systems that are reasonably transparent and predictable (Schein 2010). This therefore delineates the strategic and tactical roles of OD/HR in partnership with POM.

Schein (2010) highlights "The Professional HR Manager" role. This is the role in which HR managers became change agents and process consultants, advising managers on the most efficient and effective end-to-end organizational and HR processes to enable POM achieve its goals. This role focuses on learning about best practices of the profession externally and implementing such within the organization. To fulfill this role, the HR manager has to have new and powerful influence along with change agent skills. In particular, he or she has to be able to think of the organization in broader systemic terms and be able to get that perspective across to the executive suite. This role is important for POM because it will help lead the paradigm shift from a local to global functional context. Schein (2010) recommends a study to evaluate how much of HR and OD responsibilities have transitioned from HR and OD professionals to line managers. Recommended questions should elicit patterns, motivations, trends, current status, and future projections.

2.3 Best Practices in Human Resources Management (HRM)

The appropriateness of the concept of "best practices" in modern management has been debated extensively (Stavrou et al. 2010). Despite that, this next section will do a review of literature on some contemporary best practices such as the evolution of the HR role into internal consulting and the linkage between HRM and organizational performance. While this article does not specifically focus on POM performance, the functional context of POM is a subset of organizational performance, hence the relevance of the section.

2.3.1 Internal HR Professionals and POM

Grima and Trepo (2011) assessed the benefits that Internal Manager-Clients (IMCs)—people managers within the organization—draw from their relationships with Internal Consultants (INCs)—HR managers who are employees of the firm responsible for collaborating with people managers—in terms of skill transfer, intervention success, and implementation. They articulate a consulting relationship between HR and POM, thereby referring to people managers as IMCs, Internal HR managers as INCs, and external HR consultants as External Consultants (EXCs)—contracted non-employees of the firm. They also looked at what other elements IMCs value in their relationship with INCs (Grima and Trepo 2011). Results showed that IMCs value a low-cost internal provider who can deliver high-quality service in terms of both time commitment to the IMC and diversity of the contributions (Grima and Trepo 2011). Essentially, INCs delivered greater value than EXCs. INCs were considered better than EXCs in complex tasks because INCs connected IMCs to more sources of organizational innovation (Grima and Trepo 2011). The relevance of this study to POM is that it established the higher value contribution of internal HR professionals in helping to anticipate and solve the various business issues and challenges POM professionals encounter.

2.3.2 Human Resources (HR) and the Organizational Performance Linkage

The linkage between HRM and organizational performance came under review in Safdar (2011). The study sought to extend the theoretical and methodological debate on the issue of the linkage between HRM and performance. There were three questions asked in this survey: (1) what is HRM, (2) what is performance, and (3) what is the nature of the link between HRM and performance? Results of the study showed a lack of consensus on the definition of HRM. The survey defined performance as the achievement of predetermined goals and outputs. While POM is seen as human-centric, the output focus of the function (e.g., tonnage of products made per shift of eight hours or freight travel time from point A to point B) underscores the performance emphasis of the function—hence, the emphasis on the HRM–performance linkage. A finding of the study that performance management relates to the coordination and measurement of individual performance in line with organization's goals and objectives support this thought (Safdar 2011). Results also show that the nature of the link between HRM and performance is enhanced when outcome variables closely linked to HR interventions of multiple individual HR practices or systems/bundles of practices are used, for example, attitudinal outcomes (e.g., employee motivation, commitment, and trust); behavioral outcomes (e.g., employee turnover, absence); productivity (output per unit effort); and the quality of services or products (Safdar 2011).

2.3.3 The HR–Performance Linkage and Geographic Implications

Stavrou et al. (2010) explore the importance of geographic context on the link between HRM and firm performance. Hypotheses tested related to regional geographic differences and performance of unique HR functions. The results revealed three regions in Europe: the North-Western region, the Anglo-Irish region, and the Central Southern region. While the relationship of the training and development bundle to performance is highest in the Anglo-Irish region, it is lowest in the Central-Southern region. In high-performance-oriented cultures, training and development are highly connected to performance. Conversely, in the opposite sets of cultures, training and development are connected to factors other than performance (Stavrou et al. 2010). It also shows that no perfect or universal set of best practices exists, but rather a combination of "best practice" and "best fit" depending on bundle and region (Stavrou et al. 2010). Overall, the results confirm the value of a combination of the "best fit" and "best practice" approach to the HRM–performance link: the correlation between HRM practices and performance is sometimes consistent across Europe while other times it varies with region (Stavrou et al. 2010). The results raise issues about the universal applicability of HRM performance research and have implications for the standardization of HRM policies and practices within internationally operating organizations (Stavrou et al. 2010).

2.3.4 The HR–Performance Linkage and Learning

Over the past several years, there have been intensive discussions about the role of HRM as a key asset in today's organizations (Theriou and Chatzoglou 2014). However, a central issue in this line of research refers to the limited empirical exploration of the causal mechanisms through which these HR practices lead to greater firm performance. Theriou and Chatzoglou (2014) empirically sought to examine the relationships between best HRM practices such as Knowledge Management (KM), the systematic management of an organization's knowledge; Organizational Learning (OL), a way in which the organization sustainably improves its utilization of knowledge; and Organizational Capabilities (OC)—the collective skills, abilities, and expertise of an organization, as well as their impact on organizational performance using Structured Equation Modeling (SEM). Results indicate that manufacturing firms pursuing best HRM practices achieve higher performance through the interaction of these practices with KM and OL and the creation of OC. A significant positive relationship exists between best HRM practices, KM, and OL processes. Additionally, a positive relationship between OL and KM is also demonstrated, as KM is positively related to OC and a significant positive relationship is shown between OC and organizational performance.

2.4 Current Issues in Production and Operations Management (POM)

Having discussed trends and best practices in HRM, understanding contemporary issues in POM is necessary in order to be able to establish the connection between the two functions but, more importantly, how HR enables POM.

2.4.1 Human Resources (HR) and Production and Operations Management (POM) Research

Empirical studies and top management now recognize the significant impact of superior operations and Supply Chain Management (SCM)—the active management of supply chain activities—competency on financial performance. SCM has emerged as a strategic organizational process driven by human interaction. Hohenstein et al. (2014)'s work provides insights and analysis of HRM issues in SCM research published in leading academic journals. Their study had three goals: to analyze HRM/SCM issues published in leading SCM journals, to identify different HRM research streams in the SCM literature, and to propose areas for future research (Hohenstein et al. 2014). Research questions asked in their research are: (1) how HRM issues in SCM research developed in recent times and (2) how can HRM literature in SCM research be classified into different research streams? Their paper employs a systematic literature review methodology, categorizing the selected journal articles based on an analytical framework that contains seven HRM/SCM research streams derived from the extant literature (Hohenstein et al. 2014, p. 440). The streams and their definitions are:

- Knowledge, Skills, and Abilities (KSAs)—"competencies that a manager possesses to carry out tasks in a competent manner for effective work performance and to add value for competitive advantage"

- Training and Development—"the systematic acquisition and development of necessary skills, knowledge, and abilities by managers and employees to successfully perform a task/job or to improve work performance"
- HRM Impact on Performance—"the pattern of global HRM deployments and practices that relate to overall organizational performance (theoretically or empirically) and that significantly impact SCM success"
- Education and Teaching—"integrated, effective, and high-quality SCM curricula that apply appropriate instructional methods to produce higher quality graduates and to help students gain the competencies that industry demands to compete in global business"
- Hiring and Recruiting—"creating the largest pool of qualified and talented employees with the desired skills, knowledge, and abilities by using appropriate selection techniques"
- Compensation and Pay—"financial returns, such as fixed and variable payments, tangible services and benefits that employees receive for their work contribution"
- Global Mindset—"a diverse bundle of experiences, perceptions, and insights to effectively manage and compete in the dynamic and globally oriented economy."

Results reveal that several researchers argue that SCM is a human-centric discipline and stress the strategic importance of HRM in this context. This is in line with the findings that indicate HRM's increasing significance in SCM, pertaining to recruiting and retaining the most qualified and talented employees (Hohenstein et al. 2014). The first research stream was skills, knowledge, and abilities. The majority of articles focus on the competencies that supply chain managers need in order to add value and contribute to firms' competitive advantage. They are problem solving, managing ambiguity, and being strong multi-level communicators and global citizens. The second research stream was training and development. Internal, executive, or post-secondary training programs can assess proficiencies and provide employees with best practices while increasing the necessary competencies for certain positions in order to ensure superior job performance. The third research stream was HRM impact on performance. HRM becomes an important source of competitive advantage globally through recruiting, retaining, developing, and managing valuable supply chain employees. The fourth research stream was education and teaching. SCM education and teaching are changing in order to meet the more demanding qualification criteria of SCM positions in industry. The fifth research stream was hiring and recruiting.

The growing global demand for managerial SCM talent is pressing on a comparatively small pool of potential candidates. As skills, knowledge, and abilities are assessed as predictors of superior job performance, employee selection and hiring decisions often rely on these attributes. The sixth research stream was compensation and pay. Due to the predicted future shortage of SCM talent, compensation levels are expected to rise according to supply chain managers' increasing value. The seventh research stream was global mindset. Global orientation, open-mindedness, and understanding cultural diversity are core attributes for supply chain managers working amid increasing globalization and shifting target markets. These lead to global organizations with multicultural differences (Hohenstein et al. 2014).

The conclusion, based on the structured literature review of 109 academic peer-reviewed articles, advances the present body of SCM literature by selecting, classifying, and analyzing HRM/SCM literature published in leading academic journals from 1998 to 2014. As such, this paper provides key insights on where research has been and where additional future research on the important topic of the HRM/SCM interface is needed (Hohenstein et al. 2014).

2.4.2 HR and Operations Practices and Organizational Performance

de Menezes et al. (2010) focus on the integration of HRM and OM practices and its potential impact on performance. The assumption is that there is a philosophy or culture underlying the integration of HRM and OM practices, whose principles are not only concerned with eliminating waste and adding value for customers (lean production), but also entail the pursuit of continuous improvements (de Menezes et al. 2010). Four propositions were tested: (1) OM and HRM practices that are associated with the lean production concept are integrated; (2) the integration of OM and HRM practices associated with the lean production concept is linked to performance; (3) there is a pattern in the evolution of lean practices, so firms can be classified according to their adoption stages; and (4) there is an association between stages of evolution and performance. Results show a significant correlation in practice use over a 24-year period (i.e., OM or HRM practices were not being adopted independently but were integrated). Second, integrated OM and HRM practices are positively linked with productivity. Third, results indicate that there are three clearly identifiable stages in the evolution of lean practices. Finally, that continuous improvement is achieved through a longer period of integrating practices suggests first-mover advantage (de Menezes et al. 2010).

2.4.3 Group Social Dynamics and Performance

Bendoly et al. (2010) sought to clarify the role of individual behavioral traits in driving project dynamics and performance, consequently adding to decision makers' understanding of the levers they might utilize in project management contexts. For POM practitioners, some of the findings are particularly revealing. Excellent technical skills and intuition certainly may be insufficient to drive performance if not accompanied by appropriate levels of interpersonal interaction within project groups. However, individuals that value such interactions will likely seek such interactions out. Additionally, it seems that the same individuals who believe in their ability to control and positively impact outcomes as well as feeling a sense of responsibility in group work may be the very ones most critical in driving project agendas. These may not be the most skilled workers. Rather, high-level managers overseeing project organization should take care to ensure a range of training opportunities exist to shore up any deficits in such individual attributes that could stymie project flow and performance (Bendoly et al. 2010).

2.4.4 Cross-Functional Coordination, Information Systems Capability, and Performance

Bendoly et al. (2012) indicate that coordination efforts that access and align relevant cross-functional expertise are regarded as an essential element of innovation success. These efforts have been further augmented through complementary investments in information systems, which provide the technological platforms for information sharing and coordination across functional and organizational boundaries. Somewhat overlooked has been the critical mediating role of the intelligence gained through these efforts and capabilities (i.e., the value added by the intelligence gained in improving the success rate of innovation ideas). This study finds that internal and external coordination are both synergistically complemented by Information Systems (IS)—an integrated set of components for collecting, storing, and processing data—capabilities in their impact on the creation of high-quality actionable intelligence, a crucial mediating factor for the enhancement of New Product Development (NPD)—the development process for a new product or service—performance. Market dynamics appear to be relevant as far as the applicability of this intelligence toward NPD performance is concerned, with many of their effects accentuated in more dynamic market environments (Bendoly et al. 2012).

2.4.5 Systems Thinking and Performance

Bendoly (2014) states that systems thinking has proven useful in project management planning activities and has been suggested as a critical driver of a range of beneficial organizational behaviors. Yet, empirical evidence on the myriad of ways in which systems thinking can impact internal project dynamics and performance remains limited. This study focuses on one aspect of systems thinking in particular: the ability to recognize and understand the dynamics of systems and their features (e.g., feedback and delay). Results show that all hypotheses tested are supported:

- H1: In group project contexts, the system dynamics understanding possessed by a group will have a significant positive impact on performance.
- H2: The relationship between group system dynamics understanding and project performance is partially mediated by the quality of information shared in the group setting.
- H3: The similarity in system dynamics understanding among members of a project team and project performance is partially mediated by the degree of psychological safety among members of the team.

A final issue worth further consideration stems from the study's fundamental focus on System Dynamics Understanding (SDU)—a method for understanding, designing, and managing change—as an aspect of the larger systems thinking concept (Bendoly 2014).

3 Professional Perspective

The presented literature review rightly underscores key elements of the SHRM, POM, and SCA linkage. To triangulate the findings and conclusions from the literature review, this section discusses a study conducted on senior business leaders in HR and POM in order to see if the same or similar conclusions are produced.

3.1 Explanatory Survey with HR and POM Leaders— "A Synthesis of Needs"

To advance the discussion of the interaction between HR and POM, hearing directly from functional leaders in HR and POM, through a simple illustrative survey (however not intended to be statistically significant or representative of managers' views) on how well the interaction has performed and expectations for the future, is a beneficial endeavor. A questionnaire composed of open-ended, closed-ended, and scale questions was used to elicit the professional opinion of participants on the impact of SHRM on POM to deliver SCA. The response rate was 40% and then the responses were subsequently analyzed using a bottom-up narrative analytical approach. The professionals surveyed were functional leaders in POM, HR, HR Operations, or directly related subfunctions with a minimum professional experience of fifteen years in POM, HR, or both. They occupied decision-making positions within their organization, which were medium to large organizations with clearly delineated HR and POM functions or departments.

This survey intended to confirm the findings from the literature review, especially as HR assumes the conscience of the organization, bringing in new knowledge and practices into the various functions within the organization to be able to achieve expected superior performance (Schein 2010). To achieve this purpose, four research questions were developed. The need to get real insights from professionals by soliciting an evaluation of the value contribution of the interaction between HR and POM, and vision of the future formed the basis for the research questions (RQs). The four research questions are:

(1) How is the overall role of SHRM evaluated by industry production and operations leaders and managers?
(2) How is the partnership role of SHRM with POM evaluated by industry Human Resources leaders and managers?
(3) What is the contemporary role of SHRM in POM?
(4) How can SHRM enable POM?

3.2 Results

3.2.1 How Is the Overall Role of SHRM Evaluated by Industry Production and Operations Leaders and Managers?

All respondents who indicated Operations as their functional area evaluated the role of SHRM favorably. 83% of responses describe HR as either a change agent, helping to define behaviors necessary to deliver enterprise wide change initiatives or strategic partners helping to align HR strategy and tactics to business plans. In addition, 89% of responses indicate interaction with HR at very critical points of employee life cycle (i.e., staffing and recruiting, training and development, retention and deployment). In the words of a managing director for regional operations of a global financial services company: "We are in an operating situation where there are significant changes to the size of the workforce. HR works with us to understand these trends ahead of time and help create the right managerial strategies to address the same." The same respondent, in sharing an example of a business accomplishment facilitated by strategic HR partnership, said:

> I have been in startup business situations where HR successfully partnered with me in terms of attracting and retaining the right talent within the organizational constraints. The partnership helped ensure that the business could be launched on time and we had a bunch of high performing employees in place to grow it.

3.2.2 How Is the Partnership Role of SHRM with POM Evaluated by Industry Human Resources Leaders and Managers?

This is a self-evaluation by HR leaders and managers on how well SHRM has interacted with POM. 100% of respondents who indicated Human Resources as their functional area evaluated their SHRM role in POM favorably. Those same respondents also worked at least closely with Operations professionals, with 75% of respondents being dedicated partners to the operations professionals. This aligns with perceived clarity of purpose expressed by the HR respondents that indicated interaction with Operations was strategic and that Operations professionals had an understanding of Strategic Human Resources. One of the respondents, a Director of HR at a global insurance services firm said:

> In my experience, most of the business leaders I provide HR counsel to understand that HR is an important component of how they manage their teams. Examples include organization design, resource planning, culture, recognition, reward, talent planning/succession, and motivation. I have had some leaders that do not understand the role of strategic HR, but luckily these have been fewer than the ones that do.

3.2.3 What Is the Contemporary Role of SHRM in POM?

In articulating the contemporary role of SHRM in POM, respondents indicated contemporary issues to include the retention of talented people, optimizing workforce diversity, continuous training and development of workforce, skills shortage, employee work ethics, product quality, and keeping employees motivated and engaged in an increasingly competitive market environment. In addition, they also indicated a need for these other issues: offering flexible work arrangements especially in business environments where customers need to be served "round the clock" and employees want a "9-to-5" job, consistent and open communication, continuous deployment of modern technology, and staying current with the legal requirements for working. Respondents indicated that SHRM plays a major role in resolving these contemporary issues by helping managers develop career paths for employees and line managers, providing training and development strategies to keep workforces highly skilled, coaching managers on respective employment laws to ensure compliance, facilitating talent management and succession planning to ensure the long-term sustainability of the organization. It also helps managers design challenging and rewarding jobs, helps partners with managers to develop creative solutions to changing workforce dimensions, and ensures open communication with staff on organization goals and strategies to help staff connect their work to the bigger organizational goals.

3.2.4 How Can SHRM Enable POM?

Respondents articulated the role of SHRM in enabling POM creates a sustained competitive advantage around the following themes—attracting, developing, and retaining talent; helping to keep operating costs low through innovative HR practices; and employee initiatives. Proactive redesign of organizational structure and jobs to deliver changing business priorities and workforces. SHRM also enables the use of data in decision making and action and in helping to build leadership capabilities.

3.3 Survey Conclusions

The results of this research study show HR as a value contributor and a major stakeholder in achieving organizational goals. Conclusions are summarized in themes below.

3.3.1 HR and POM Partnership

With respect to Section 3.2.1, both operations leaders and managers evaluated the role of SHRM positively and they consider HR to be a strategic and change partner in the business. This is not surprising as the clamor for HR to be a strategic business partner has been ongoing for more than four decades. Schein (2010, p. 8) indicated in a 1975 article for the *Journal of the College and University Personnel Association* that:

> I outlined what at that time seemed to be the major change that the HR function was undergoing (Schein 1975). I noted that HR Managers were of necessity, becoming change agents and process consultants. This role shift was in part the result of the professionalization of the function. More was known about employee motivation, career development, leadership and management development, and it was often the role of the HR manager to bring the research knowledge and practice into the organization.

The constant communication of this strategic partnership imperative has impressed itself in the organizational subconscious, which is an evident answer to Section 3.2.2 in the evaluation of the partnership role of SHRM with POM by HR and Operations professionals alike as favorable and value adding. As professionals in both functions identify contemporary issues and future challenges centering around talent availability and retention, workforce development, optimizing workforce diversity, business operating costs, a thriving work environment with flexibility, and the employment legal framework, POM professionals expect SHRM to evolve solutions and practices around these themes to create a sustained competitive advantage for the organization.

3.3.2 HR and POM Best Practices

In Sections 3.2.3 and 3.2.4, the contemporary role of SHRM in POM and how SHRM can enable POM revolve around the customized best practices that HR can partner with POM in designing, to address various contemporary issues identified in the data analysis and results part of the chapter, Section 3.2.3. The survey response alluded to the changes in size and nature of the workforce. Operations professionals look up to their HR colleagues to understand the trends driving these changes ahead of time and help create the right people strategies to address them. The workforce is getting more technology savvy, more oriented toward immediate gratification, and more likely to perform various life and work activities on a mobile device. These have triggered the need for strategies in the different stages of the Employee Life Cycle (ELC)—the various stages of the employment process from recruitment to termination—to optimize the opportunities, potentials, and value of the predominant workforce characteristics (as opposed to generation) in each ELC stage. Many scholars have studied the various generations in the workforce and developed profiles of who they are, what they do, their affinities, how to work with them, and strategies for getting the best out of the different generations. A best practice these scholars recommend is to define a set of characteristics, competencies (with required minimum proficiencies), and skills (all hereafter referred to as "capabilities") needed by the organization in the various stages of the ELC and articulate strategies to deliver these capabilities to the organization in the most efficient way.

This approach is recommended as the changing nature of global business, driven by technology is producing a dynamic of workforce capabilities rebalancing. This is when a capability or bundle of capabilities that used to be a unique strength of a particular workforce generation becomes a base competency across all or many workforce generations, ceasing to be a competitive edge for a particular workforce generation. For example, because baby boomers are living longer due to healthcare innovations, they are staying in the workplace longer and recognize that, for them to continue to be useful in the workplace, they need to build their technology capabilities. While the prevalence of baby boomers who have reinvented themselves do not compare to technology savvy generation "Ys" or "millennials," the reality of the situation is not lost on the other generations. Now, being "technology savvy" (which used to largely be a Unique Selling Proposition (USP)—the factor or consideration presented by a seller as the reason that one product or service is different from and better than that of the competition) of generation "Ys" and "millennials" is now a base competency available in any generation. The differentiator is technical knowledge of a particular software, database, programming language, process, or methodology.

Some of the strategies HR has deployed in the learning and development function to regularly provide real-time learning to the workforce is a series of "how to" videos that run from a few seconds to a few minutes. They teach employees how to use a tool, run a process, use a certain functionality in Excel, etc. This strategy mirrors the various "do-it-yourself" videos on YouTube and the teaching methodology on online learning portals like KhanAcademy.com. For some big institutions in large industries like financial services or manufacturing, strategies deployed to reinvent tenured employees in the decline stage of their career is to leverage them in areas of work that require significant historical backdrop. Examples include community relations, regulatory functions, operational areas of the organization that still depend on knowledge of old methods and processes to function.

In the areas of talent, respondents are either seeing high turnover or higher threats of losing talents and demand HR to help articulate strategies for retaining them. Some ideas now available in the workplace include the computation of a talent risk factor and threshold, which flags for when a company is at the risk of losing a talent. The risk factor and threshold is computed based on real-life scenarios and industry and environmental dynamics. While this is a backstop as organizations are expected to be in constant interaction with their talents, developing and deploying them accordingly, the talent risk factor and threshold gives organizations an edge in recognizing situations and circumstances that may cause the loss of a talent and subsequently remedy it. Another approach to developing and keeping people is building a culture that expects people to change jobs after 24–36 months in a role. This is different from setting a minimum timeframe for which an employee can be in a job before they can move. This "culturally encouraged self-obligatory job change" strategy forces employees to think of their self-development and career growth regularly. It embeds a personal culture of self-improvement and to the extent that the organization can provide career opportunities and has resources and systems that facilitate the acquisition, synthesis, use, sharing, and feedback of information; this is a great way of building a learning organization as decisions in learning organizations are driven by data and intelligence derived from cross-pollination activities.

3.3.3   HR as a Change Agent

Operations Managers and their HR colleagues need to develop strategies that drive engagement and ownership through initiatives that make the organization a great place to work, supported by a rewards and recognition program. Employees are encouraged to bring to the workplace ideas and activities they do in their own time to enrich their lives and share with other members of staff. They are encouraged to design activities, learning programs, and job improvement ideas that help the employees become what they want to be in the workplace or that make their work easier to perform. These actions strengthen the community, sense of belonging, and the culture of the organization. These are all elements necessary for companies to retain the best talent and grow into a high performing organization.

Summarily, the survey revealed similar key points identified in the literature review. POM professionals are concerned about performance and productivity, managing change seamlessly, talent acquisition, development, retention, motivation, and optimal deployment, putting in place an effective and efficient rewards and recognition program, lean manufacturing, and labor outsourcing. In a similar vein, a recurring response in the survey was for POM professionals to have greater partnership with HR in order to address these key concerns in a strategic and beneficial manner for the organization.

4   HR Enabling POM to Win the Talent War

Menon's (2012) view of HR thinking of human capital requirements as a whole system is underpinned by Hohenstein et al. (2014) in that the POM function and subfunctions like supply chain

The Strategic Role of HR in Enabling POM

management, manufacturing, distribution, and logistics are all human-centric disciplines. Due to the human-centric nature of these functions, the need to recruit and retain the best talent becomes imperative. The seven research streams as articulated by Hohenstein et al. (2014) underline how HRM can impact POM and, subsequently, create sustained competitive advantage. Having established the criticality of the human being (employee) in the HRM–performance linkage (Bendoly et al. 2010), the employee typically goes through a four-stage employee life cycle (Smither 2003) (see Figure 21.1). Therefore, overlaying the subjects of the seven research streams (see Figure 21.2) of Hohenstein et al. (2014) on the employee life cycle reveals an interaction model (see Figure 21.3) between HRM and POM that delivers sustained competitive advantage (SCA). This interaction model places different responsibilities on HR as an INC and the manager as an IMC (Grima and Trepo 2011).

As Grima and Trepo (2011) stated, HR (INC) is low cost yet adds high value to IMCs and to the organization because INCs deliver a high level of commitment, diversity of thought, and contribution and are always willing to follow up due to a shared responsibility for results. Again, substantiating Schein (2010)'s view of the fourth role of the HR manager, where they are not only change agents but the organizational conscience and a powerful influence that brings knowledge, new attitudes, and new practices into the organization. From an industry standpoint, the manager has responsibility for the employee (Maheras 1966). With this interaction model, the IMC comes to the table with people; processes; the work environment; and organizational thoughts, issues, and plans, while HR as the internal consultant comes to the table with knowledge, skills, and best practices or best fit ideas applicable to improve performance. When coming to the table, HR is empowered with intelligence gotten from HR data analytics (Fink 2010) and is able to be innovative (Bendoly et al. 2012) in creating solutions, recommending practices, or partnering with managers to integrate OM and HR practices (de Menezes et al. 2010) that will deliver superior performance and continuous improvement.

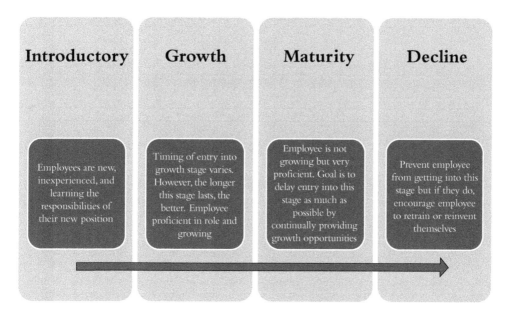

Figure 21.1 Employee Life Cycle

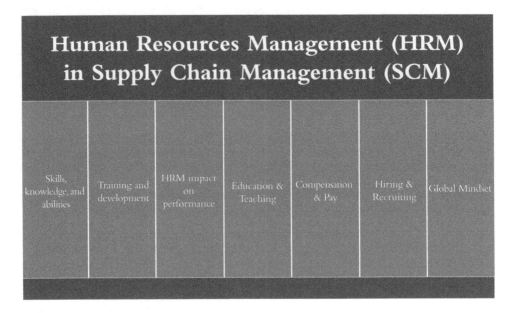

Figure 21.2 HRM in SCM Analytical Framework

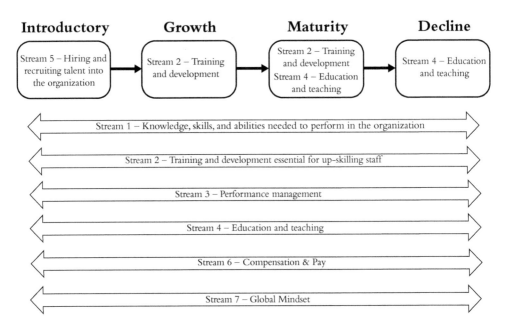

Figure 21.3 HRM–POM Interaction Model

As HR and manager work on best fit and best practice ideas especially for a global operation, the cultural context should not be overlooked, as Stavrou et al. (2010) indicated that HRM bundles of competitive advantage and performance are contingent on geographic context. Therefore, there is no universal set of best practices but a combination of best practice and best fit that depends on the geographic region and situation (Stavrou et al. 2010). Finally, organizational learning is important, as this is the medium used for transferring knowledge and creating organizational capabilities that truly set the business on a path of sustained competitive advantage. Whether it is HR interacting with Operations or Finance interacting with technology, an organization has to develop a learning culture intertwined with behaviors that facilitate learning, sharing, application, and feedback. It is only then that higher performance can be achieved, when HRM practices are integrated with knowledge management, organizational learning culture, and the creation of organizational capabilities (Theriou and Chatzoglou 2014).

5 Implications for Managers

Managers need to understand that to consistently deliver superior performance, they need to have a well-articulated people strategy that impacts every stage of the employee life cycle. They need to develop this in partnership with their HR colleagues, defining all the issues and constraints as well as the desired outcomes. Managers need to understand that there is no universal set of best practices but that they constantly have to work towards a combination of best practices and best fits. They need to study every situation desiring of a solution and customize solutions or leverage existing solutions accordingly without sacrificing efficiency and effectiveness. This is particularly instructive as the shelf life of a value adding idea is unimaginably short, an indication of the constantly changing business dynamics and environment that thereby necessitates a proactive and responsive approach to managing people, process, environment, and the interaction of these three variables. However, as short as the shelf life of ideas may be, the need to have an engaged and productive workforce that generates creative solutions and ideas which delivers sustained superior performance to the organization is a fundamental that remains unchanged. This is especially true for the sustainability of the organization. In addition, managers need to evolve flexible practices like having flexible job descriptions, cross-functional or cross-team trainings, and flexible work arrangements, etc. to be able to keep employees engaged and committed to the organization. In partnership with HR, leverage intelligence derived from HR data analytics in making people and process related decisions and actions. Finally, it is important to embed a meritocratic culture in the organization. Compensation should be linked to performance and clearly differentiated (Menon 2012). Top performers in the organization should get the best of everything while low performers should be challenged to deliver improved work.

6 Recommendations for Future Research

The following ideas are suggested for future research. First, we suggest leveraging the seven HRM/SCM research streams and the employee life cycle, a study of the streams in each stage of the employee life cycle in order to determine its impact on performance. Next, researchers should look into how flexible job descriptions, teamwork training, and the use of performance metrics to determine rewards have truly helped to integrate supply chains and improve executives' satisfaction of their organization's supply chain performance. There should be a focus on a study to evaluate how much of HR and OD responsibilities have transitioned from HR and OD professionals to line managers. Recommended questions should elicit patterns, motivations, trends, current status, and future projections. We also recommend comparison between INCs and EXCs from IMCs perspective. As is an expanded study of the geographic contexts of the HR—performance linkage among a larger set of countries and continents, in order to explore in greater scale the "best fit, best practice or both" argument. Next, studies should center on the application of mixed methods research such as case studies in combination with quantitative methods in order to adequately explain supply chain phenomena from the seven streams. Lastly, we believe that further study on both the role of global mindset in the success of SCM performance and the application of multi-method to social factor influence in team settings are necessary.

7 Conclusions

This study has explored several dimensions of the SHRM–POM–SCA framework through literature review and a survey. Findings and conclusions from both exercises reveal several things. First, the need for the connection point for SHRM and POM to be able to deliver SCA is in talent and the integrated organizational practices of HR and POM. Next, we discovered that the issues of talent availability and clarity around the linkage between HRM and performance are prevalent. From the survey results, it was evident that finding practical ways to deal with the evolving work population is an issue of grave concern to managers. Issues of work ethic and flexible work arrangements regularly come up when discussing this issue (Menon 2012). Following that, HR as an internal consultant facilitates the creation and use of practices that continue to deliver top talent to the business, through either external recruitment, internal mobility or training, and development. HR also facilitates integrative practices and ideas that help the business to create a work environment that people want to work in while also getting work done in a seamless and collaborative manner. The manager has full responsibility and accountability for the people and their welfare. And lastly, training, learning culture, knowledge management, intelligence, and partnership are themes that keep recurring in this study. This underscores the importance of constant development and organizational learning if the business wants to create a sustained competitive advantage.

References and Bibliography

Barney, J. (1991) "Firm Resources and Sustained Competitive Advantage," *Journal of Management*, **17**(1): 99–120.

Bendoly, E. (2014) "Systems Dynamics Understanding in Projects: Information Sharing, Psychological Safety, and Performance Effects," *Production and Operations Management*, **23**(8): 1352–1369.

Bendoly, E., A. Bharadwaj and S. Bharadwaj (2012) "Complementary Drivers of New Product Development Performance: Cross-Functional Coordination, Information System Capability and Intelligence Quality," *Production and Operations Management*, **24**(4): 653–667.

Bendoly, E., D. Thomas and M. Capra (2010) "Multilevel Social Dynamics Considerations for Project Management Decision Makers: Antecedents and Implications of Group Member Tie Development," *Decision Sciences*, **41**(3): 459–490.

Birts, A., L. McAulay, M. Pitt, M. Saren and D. Sims (1997) "The Expertise of Finance and Accountancy: An Interdisciplinary Study," *British Journal of Management*, **8**(1): 75–83.

de Menezes, L. M., S. Wood and G. Gelade (2010) "The Integration of Human Resource and Operation Management Practices and Its Link with Performance: A Longitudinal Latent Class Study," *Journal of Operations Management*, **28**(6): 455–471.

Edmondson, A. (1999) "Psychological Safety and Learning Behavior in Work Teams," *Administrative Science Quarterly*, **44**(2): 350–383.

Fink, A. A. (2010) "New Trends in Human Capital Research and Analytics," *People & Strategy*, **33**(2): 14–21.

Grima, F. and G. Trepo (2011) "Internal Consultants: Why do clients use them and for what benefits?" *European Management Journal*, **29**(2): 144–154.

Hatch, N. and J. Dyer (2004) "Human Capital and Learning as a Source of Sustainable Competitive Advantage," *Strategic Management Journal*, **25**(12): 1155–1178.

Hohenstein, N. O., E. Feisel and E. Hartmann (2014) "Human Resources Management Issues in Supply Chain Management Research," *International Journal of Physical Distribution & Logistics Management*, **44**(6): 434–463.

Karmarkar, U. S. (1996) "Integrative Research in Marketing and Operations Management," *Journal of Marketing Research*, **33**(2): 125–133.

Krajicek, D. (2014) "Big Data's Next Step," *Marketing Insights*, **26**(1): 10–11.
Maheras, T. G. (1966) "Concepts of Law and the Manager," *Industrial Management*, **8**(8): 3–5.
Menon, S. T. (2012) "Human Resources Practices, Supply Chain Performance and Wellbeing," *International Journal of Manpower*, **33**(7): 769–785.
Rastogi, P. N. (2000) "Sustaining Enterprise Competitiveness—Is Human Capital the Answer?" *Human Systems Management*, **19**(3): 193–203.
Safdar, R. (2011) "HRM: Performance Relationship: Need for Further Development?" *International Journal of Public Administration*, **34**(13): 858–868.
Schein, E. H. (2010) "The Role of Organizational Development in the Human Resources Function," *OD Practitioner*, **42**(4): 6–10.
Shaw, J. D., T. Y. Park and E. Kim (2013) "A Resource-Based Perspective on Human Capital Losses, HRM Investments, and Organizational Performance," *Strategic Management Journal*, **34**(5): 572–589.
Smither, L. (2003) "Managing Employee Life Cycles to Improve Labor Retention," *Leadership & Management In Engineering*, **31**(1): 19–23.
Stavrou, E. T., C. Brewster and C. Charalambous (2010) "Human Resource Management and Firm Performance in Europe through the Lens of Business Systems: Best Fit, Best Practice or Both?" *The International Journal of Human Resources Management*, **21**(7): 933–962.
Theriou, G. N., and P. Chatzoglou (2014) "The Impact of Best HRM Practices on Performance—Identifying Enabling Factors," *Employee Relations*, **36**(5): 535–561.
Van de Ven, A. H. (2007) *Engaged Scholarship*, Oxford, UK: Oxford University Press.

PART VI

POM Domains of Application

22
OPERATIONS MANAGEMENT IN HOSPITALITY

Rohit Verma, Lu Kong, and Zhen Lin

1 Introduction

According to the World Travel and Tourism Council, the Travel, Tourism, and Hospitality industries collectively generate 9.8% of the world's GDP while supporting 284 million jobs. Within the United States, the direct contribution of travel and tourism to GDP was US$488 billion (2.7% of total GDP) in 2015 and is forecasted to rise by 2.8% in 2016, and to rise by 3.7% per annum (pa), from 2016–2026, to US$722.3 billion (3.2% of total GDP) in 2026. Considering both direct and indirect impact, the total contribution of travel and tourism to GDP was US$1.5 trillion (8.2% of GDP) in 2015, a total that is forecast to rise by 3.0% in 2016, and to rise by 3.4% pa to US$2.2 trillion (9.3% of GDP) by 2026. During 2015, the total contribution of travel and tourism to employment, including indirect jobs, was 9.6% of total employment (14,248,000 jobs). This is expected to rise by 2.0% in 2016 to 14,527,000 jobs and rise by 2.4% pa to 18,493,000 jobs in 2026 (11.4% of total). The lodging sector of travel, tourism, and hospitality alone accounts for over 53,000 hotel properties, 4.9 million guest rooms, and US$176 billion in sales just within the United States. These statistics from the World Travel and Tourism Council demonstrate the size and value of the travel, tourism, and hospitality operations within the context of the global economy.

While the travel sector, especially within airline operations, has received attention within the operations management research, relatively few articles have been published in the mainstream operations management journals that focus on hospitality operations. We reviewed *Management Science*, *Production and Operations Management*, *Journal of Operations Management*, *Manufacturing & Service Operations Management*, and *Operations Research* for published articles that used keywords such as "hospitality," "hotel," or "restaurant." We were able to find only twenty-four articles that met the above criteria (See Table 22.1 and Table 22.2 at the end of the chapter).

Given the size of the hospitality sector in terms of revenue and employment, more research needs to be conducted within the operations management discipline in order to explore unique aspects of this industry. Therefore, the purpose of this chapter is to present an overview of different topics and concepts from hospitality that provide opportunities for research to the operations management community.

The rest of this chapter is organized in several sub-sections that explore different aspects of hospitality operations.

2 The Essence of Hospitality

To study hospitality operations, first one must understand the meaning of hospitality. While many people may define hospitality as providing service to customers, in fact, there are subtle differences between the two concepts. Hospitality is a word derived from *hospes* in Latin, which means "host" or "guest." Therefore, hospitality means taking care of customers' feelings and emotions, going above and beyond just meeting their stated needs. In fact, although the words "hospitality" and "hospital" invoke very different emotions, they stem from the same root word in Latin described earlier. The two industries have evolved quite differently over the centuries, but they continue to share many common characteristics. For example, both industries need to take care of the unique needs of their guests by proving comfortable lodging, food-service, privacy/security, and many other similar amenities and supplementary services. Each industry can provide unique opportunities for companies operating in the other industry because of evolving customer preferences/business dynamics and changing regulations and policies. Many new industry segments are emerging at the interface of hospitality and healthcare, including senior housing and care, wellness and medical tourism, and concierge medicine.

The hospitality industry consists of a variety of service operations (Ottenbacher et al. 2009), including lodging, hotel, restaurant, tourism, convention and entertainment industries, etc. With the fast growth of the global economy and new communications technology, customers from all around the world are traveling not merely for business reasons but also for leisure and experience purposes. Therefore, managing their operations to create a memorable guest experience has become extremely important for hospitality firms during the recent years. Multiple dimensions, such as the service environment, customers' expectations, actual service quality, and even guests' personalities, influence the customer experience in hospitality. Consequently, managing guest experience within hospitality is a very complex task. Therefore, effective hospitality operations management must include improving guest awareness of positive emotions and distracting their attentions from negative aspects in order to minimize passive influences on overall experience (Pizam and Shani 2009).

3 Product and Service Innovation in Hospitality

Unlike in the manufacturing industry, innovation in the hospitality industry is more difficult to define, measure, and even facilitate. However, to keep up with the rapidly changing market and competition, it is necessary for hospitality firms and the hospitality industry to develop a new product, innovate services to adapt to new customer demands, and therefore remain competitive (Hassanien and Dale 2012). Current research on this topic within hospitality generally falls into two categories. The first set of papers studies the measurement of service innovation in the hospitality industry. These papers suggest that innovation can take place at multiple levels in hospitality including service concepts, primary processes, service environment, technology and service interaction, and in supporting processes (Hertog et al. 2011). Taking a step further, some new studies have identified the characteristics that contribute to the success of service development (Kitsios et al. 2011). The other group of studies puts emphasis on how to facilitate product and service innovation in the hospitality industry. For example, encouraging knowledge sharing and establishing a learning oriented strategy are demonstrated to be useful (Hua et al. 2009). From the individual perspective, both front-line employees and managers play important roles in new service development. Managers should always hold a positive attitude and grant extrinsic reward plus creativity training to motivate innovative ideas or behaviors.

4 Integrating Service Quality in Operational Processes

As demonstrated by past research studies, service quality is closely related to customer satisfaction and is the key to attract and retain guests. Therefore, it is essential for every service company to provide consistent, standard, and excellent quality that can meet guests' expectations by launching effective quality assurance programs (e.g., "transaction-focused" and "relationship-focused"). If customer expectations cannot be met due to various reasons, errors will appear. Therefore, both programs are designed with the purpose of eliminating errors and recovering from service failures. Relationship-focused systems are more advanced since they not only provide solutions to fix mistakes, but they also find out why the errors happen in order to then prevent them from happening again.

In the process of quality assurance, both employees and customers play vital roles. Therefore, it is important to train our employees, especially those front-line workers who deal with customers face to face, to understand the complaining cues in guests' gestures, languages, and behaviors. With efficient complaint management, we can always eliminate errors in time and restore customers' satisfaction.

Current studies have paid significant attention to service quality from various perspectives. For example, since the SERVQUAL (service quality) measurement is proved to be inadequate in fully assessing quality, one recent research study found out the dimensions of customer perception and built a new quality model based on it for travel agencies (Caro and Garcia 2008). One other research paper came up with additional useful measurements for destination quality management (Narayan et al. 2008). Another study (Ha and Jang 2010) focuses on the relationship between service quality and satisfaction. Higher service quality can improve satisfaction and then loyalty, as shown by the research centered on traditional restaurants in Korea, and guest perception of the environment influences that relationship (Ha and Jang 2010). As with the inevitable service failure, successful and unsuccessful recovery have different impacts on customer repurchase behavior and satisfaction (Swanson and Hsu 2011). As demonstrated in the new research, higher commitment and empowering employees are more helpful in motivating them to provide excellent service with high quality (Clark et al. 2009).

5 The Role of Employees

From the topics discussed earlier, it should not be difficult to recognize the importance of service employees, especially front-line workers in the hospitality and tourism industries. Service employees generally serve several roles in daily operations. First, since they interact with customers face to face, their behavior and service quality greatly influence customers' experiences. Studies have shown that the satisfaction and loyalty of employees directly relate to the satisfaction of customers, while indirectly relating to financial performance (Chi and Gursoy 2009). In other words, satisfied and loyal employees can improve guest satisfaction and bring additional and loyal customers that would then improve performance. Clearly, employees are the source of guest information (Huang et al. 2014). Second, from the business perspective, employees also play important roles in the development of companies. For example, current research has shown that engaged employees can not only improve customer satisfaction but can also improve innovation and develop brands (Slatten and Mehmetoglu 2011).

In addition to studying the roles of service employees, many studies also focus on how to motivate employees to perform their roles and go above and beyond what is required of them. Although some studies point out that intrinsic incentives are more important in motivating employees (Chiang and Jang 2008), it is still critical to combine extrinsic and intrinsic rewards together in order to create a culture in which employees can get meaningful training, be fully motivated to engage, and have enough autonomy to excel (Alonso and O'Neill 2011).

6 Demand and Capacity Management

The goal of demand and capacity management is to maximize revenue, so both of them are closely related to yield and revenue management (see Section 7). Even though demand and capacity management always come up together in business and academic research, they are essentially different concepts. Companies require different strategies to manage both well.

Demand management requires the cooperation of different departments within a company since it involves pricing, promotion, distribution, and customer relationships. As shown in previous studies in the hotel industry, the setting of prices, occupancy, and the consequent revenue are greatly influenced by all the hotels within the same competitive sets (Kimes and Anderson 2011). In other words, if one hotel sets a higher price, the demand will drop significantly since customers can always find a substitute but with a lower price, so the revenue will also drop. However, if all hotels within the competitive set raise their prices, the revenue is more likely to decrease slightly.

With the development of the Internet, electronic demands have become an important source of demand and it has changed the distribution channels greatly. As a result, the hospitality industry went through several periods: the Global Distribution System, Internet era, the SoLoMo (Social, Location, and Mobile), before finally entering the hybrid stage (Thakran and Verma 2013).

There are many different approaches to analyzing capacity management within hospitality by focusing on short- or long-term strategies (Pullman and Rodgers 2010). Related research materials published during the past five years focuses mostly on studying the capacity of different types of restaurants and providing applicable decision-support models. Hwang et al. (2010) have shown that by combining marketing and operations in analyzing capacity organizations, researchers achieve better results than just focusing on one discipline (Hwang et al. 2010). Another study identified the thresholds of resources, such as a table, server, and cook, and different stages of services that affect customers' expectations on waiting (Hwang and Lambert 2009). From those research studies, it is clear that, although each approach has its own advantages and disadvantages, it is important to select the most proper analytical technique to develop strategies and even combine them to take every aspect into consideration based on different situations.

7 Yield and Revenue Management

Yield or revenue management was popularized by American Airlines about two decades ago. In the hotel industry, revenue management is all about selling the right rooms to the right customers, at the right time. To achieve this goal, hotels should have the ability to segment their consumers and prices, then allocate room inventory accordingly across those segments. To be more specific, the task requires the revenue manager to forecast the demand using existing reservations on hand (ROH). A booking curve (used to estimate demand) can be drawn using ROH as a function of days before arrival (DBA).

Typical ways to segment the customers include by their booking channels, by the number of days they are staying, and by the day of week they are staying. For example, a special "early booking" price can be set to target those who would like to book long before their arriving date. In addition, instead of a fixed price for all rooms, variable prices can be set. For example, a hotel can sell 30 rooms at $150, 50 rooms at $100, and 80 rooms at $80 to target different customer segments simultaneously. In addition to variable pricing, hotels also widely use dynamic pricing. That is, instead of setting unchanged prices, a hotel can change its price over time in response to demand. Usually, hotels decrease price to stimulate demand and increase price when demand is strong. However, this strategy must be used carefully, since with decreased prices, hotels need higher occupancy to break even. If the revenue gain by increasing occupancy cannot offset the revenue lost by decreasing the price, the hotel should think twice before decreasing price.

Easy access to the Internet and the simplicity of its use greatly influence revenue management in hospitality. Since most hotel rates can be found online, consumers are able to compare room rates between different hotels from different channels. Under these circumstances, opaque pricing (i.e., when the brand name of the specific hotel, airline, etc. remains hidden until after the purchase has been completed for a discounted price) can allow hotels to keep higher rates on regular channels as well as target price-sensitive customers using competitive and private rates. For example, a channel using opaque pricing will hide the property names, only posting some segmentation attributes (e.g., location, facilities, and star levels). Only after the room is sold, will the customer find out what property they are staying at. Hotels can also use search engines to manage their exposure on the Internet.

Using online travel agents (OTAs) helps hotels targeting price-sensitive customers, thus increasing the number of reservations. Some OTAs allow hotels to pay and get specific exposure such as taking up top slots in search engine results. A recent study by Anderson (2009) shows that using OTAs can also increase reservation volume at non-OTA channels. Revenue per available room (RevPAR) is widely used to measure hotel revenue performance. In addition, a hotel should look into the performance of hotels in its competitive set.

A study based on a survey of 487 professionals shows that RM in hospitality will become more strategic and more strongly driven by technology. In addition, survey respondents think that the organization of the RM function is going to become more centralized and that the skills required for a successful revenue manager are going to be a combination of analytical and communication abilities. As a consequence of RM, performance measurement will move to total revenue or gross operating profit rather than using RevPAR (Kimes 2011). Noone et al. (2011) try to identify the influence and opportunity that social media brought to RM. They argue that social media provides the ideal platform and data source to support RM's efforts to build a business strategy, expand RM into other revenue-generating assets, and become more customer-centric. Wang (2012) argues that in practice, companies may find it difficult to accommodate both customer relationship management and revenue management due to potential management conflicts.

8 Ownership Structure, Franchising, and Cost of Operations

Owners often do not operate hotel properties themselves. Conversely, restaurant owners are more likely to operate their own properties. Being familiar with hospitality ownership structure helps participants view the managerial issues from the point of view of owners. There are several forms of ownership. Each has its own advantages and disadvantages: proprietorship, partnership, limited liability companies, and corporations. Typically, there are four types of entities: owner, lender, operator or manager, and franchisor. Typical ownership and operating structures of the U.S. hospitality industry are:

- The owner is also the manager under the affiliation of a franchise company. This structure allows the most flexibility for the owners. However, the associated costs of affiliation can be very high, and it might not be the most effective way for the owner to manage the property.

- The owner contracts with a management firm that has its own brand, such as Marriott, Hilton, Hyatt, etc. to run operations on their properties.
- The owner is the manager and has their own affiliation. The costs of management and affiliation are the lowest under this structure. However, the brand and the managers may not be the best fit for the property and its marketing target.
- The owner is independent and manages the property. Under this structure, the cost is low and motivation is high, since the manager is the owner. However, without a well-established brand name, the marketing power may be low.
- The owner hires a management company to operate the hotel and contracts separately with a franchise company for the affiliation. The cost is highest under this structure, but the owner can choose the location, management team, and affiliation to optimize the brand fit.

Today, it is rare to see publicly listed firms that are owners of the property, have their own brand, and operate their business. This is where franchise comes in. In the relationship between franchisor and franchisee, the franchisee purchases the right to use the concept created by the franchisor as well as the right to sell goods under the franchisor's brand image. Franchising is expected to and normally offers better results, efficiency, and cost savings for both parties.

Franchise fees in the hotel industry are different than in other industries. The franchisor collects an initial fee at the signing of the franchise agreement that is normally based on the number of rooms. Then franchisors charge a royalty fee based on a percentage of gross revenue. Other fees include training program fee, software and hardware, and so on, also calculated by a certain percentage of gross revenue. When signing their contract, both franchisors and franchisees want the other side to bear higher financial risk. Also, as the owner of the property, franchisees may want to preserve some operational control. Both sides need to decide their proper rights and responsibilities during negotiation.

Corporate social responsibility (CSR) remains a hot topic in recent years. How does the relationship between CSR and managerial ownership look in the hospitality industry? In their study, Paek et al. (2013) found that managerial ownership has a significant impact on the community, environment, and product dimensions, while it has a negative impact on employee relations and diversity dimensions. Roh and Yoon (2009) investigated franchisee's satisfaction based on franchisor's pre-opening support and ongoing business support. They found that franchisees were generally not satisfied with franchisors' ongoing support but that they were satisfied with central purchasing support from their franchisors. As many franchisors are increasing the diversity of their brands, Roh and Choi (2010) explored the efficiency of brands under the same franchisor in the restaurant industry. They concluded that the efficiency of each establishment and brand differed significantly from each other. Going "green" may help hotels build a positive brand image as well as save operation costs. Rahman et al. (2012) found that at the time of the study, chain hotels were stronger adopters of green practices than independent hotels were, and hotels in the Midwest were found to be the most environmentally friendly in terms of their use of no-cost or low-cost green practices.

9 Start-Up of New Locations and Managing Hospitality Projects

For any hospitality projects or start-ups, a relationship between two categories needs to be formed: those who provide financial capital and those who provide services, materials, and labor. Then the development process shall begin: first coming up with a renovation idea, then accessing the site, considering the feasibility, reviewing current and future contracts, making the improvements, and then finally finishing the project. During this process, many issues need to be considered. First, the demand driver needs to be identified. Which customer segments have yet to be served by the existing businesses? Do significant seasonal demand differences exist? Which hotels are part of your true competitor set? Additionally, local government should be contacted for all the support they can provide, given the benefits a hotel can provide for the local community. Then, occupancy should be estimated, and brands should be properly positioned. As an owner, one should carefully choose from a major chain brand, a small chain brand, or an independent operation to suit the local market. The chain brand's website usually provides a massive amount of information such as franchisee benefits and requirements in order to help potential franchisors to determine whether the brand is a good fit.

Once the market investigation is clear, a consultant (company) should conduct a feasibility study. This study should examine the project itself, the market and competitors, the demand generators, and the occupancy. The study should also forecast the financial performance within a certain number of years and estimate the value of the hotel. After the feasibility study, a financial review must be conducted. This study's results would allow for an estimate of the loans and profit. When all the paperwork and preparation are done, the next thing is construction. An experienced construction team is needed to build the hotel according to the franchisor brand and local market. Before the property opening, staff should be retained, certain approvals should be obtained from local authorities such as building department and fire department, and some properties will conduct preopening sales.

Hotel innovation projects are of great importance for managements. As a result, it remains to be a hot topic in academia. Lopez et al. (2011) explored the factors that encourage innovation in hospitality firms. They found that external factors (such as government assistance programs) had little effect on hospitality innovation, whereas internal factors (such as large firm size, membership in a business group, willingness to change, and a sufficiently bureaucratic framework to manage and institutionalize any innovations) have a significant positive relationship with innovation. When planning a start-up hotel, location is another big issue. Yang et al. (2012) investigated how existing hotels in Beijing choose their locations, finding that star rating, years after opening, service diversification, ownership, agglomeration effect, public service infrastructure, road accessibility, subway accessibility, and accessibility to tourism sites are important factors of location choice. In addition, they argued that downscale hotels do not usually seek the benefits of agglomeration effects and upscale ones are more sensitive to accessibility.

As they realize the importance of the environment, more hospitality firms are making an effort to become "green." Sozer (2010) argued that the efficiency of the resource use starting from the building design to the end-users in hotel facilities is typically low, and the resulting environmental impacts are greater than those caused by other types of buildings of similar size. Thus, decisions taken during the architectural building design play as important a role in reducing these environmental impacts as does the management of the building.

10 Managing Risk and Disruption

Hotel investors face not only risks associated with commercial real estate investments, but they also face risks associated with the hospitality industry. The first major difference is that instead of the long-term tenant, hotels have short-term guests. The rate charged can be higher or lower than the owners initially projected. Lacking tenant commitment brings substantial risks for hotel investors. The risks then increase the costs of investment. Hotel mortgages and loans are higher when the risks are considered higher—which is known as a risk premium. As a result, investors will look for extra returns to cover the higher rates.

11 Role of Lean Thinking and Sustainable Operations in Hospitality

Lean production is a sociotechnical production system whose main objective is to eliminate waste by concurrently reducing or minimizing supplier, customer, and internal variability. This concept was originated from the automobile industry but can be applied to other industries. Lean thinking refers to more than techniques and approaches. It is a mindset for all employees and managers to eliminate waste in all process operations. In *The Machine That Changed the World*, Womack et al. (1991) made the following points about the principles of lean production: The entire production mechanism should be customer driven. That is, the whole process should create value for customers. From the micro perspective, each step in production should be implemented and evaluated based on its role in value creation. And they should be seamlessly and efficiently integrated to deliver value to customers. This principle is not only applicable to the on-site production; it is also of vital importance to the whole flow from designing to product delivery. And the flow should be continuously improved towards perfection. Efforts have been made to implement Lean and Six Sigma into hospitality organizations. In Lancaster's work (2011), he seeks to explore the types of operations in hospitality that have used Lean or Six Sigma and provides a plan and framework to successfully implement those systems. Working with a sample of small and medium-sized hotels in Europe, Vlachos and Bogdanovic (2013) found that hotels do apply value mapping techniques, and similarities were found in hotel operations regardless of location. They argued that many value stream mapping techniques (such as process activity mapping, supply chain response matrix, production variety funnel, and so on) could help in detecting and eliminating waste (both upstream and downstream) in the value chain. As mentioned before, buildings in the hospitality industry are not energy efficient. Does the implementation of sustainable techniques influence traveler's choices? Prud'homme and Raymond (2013) found that the hotel's adoption of sustainable development positively influences customer's satisfaction. Additionally, the level of customer satisfaction varies according to the hotel's size and type of ownership. Sirakaya-Turk et al. (2014) argued that the effect of the value of sustainable approaches is mediated by the travelers' environment behaviors. They suggested that management should segment customers into "strong-sustainers" and "centrists-sustainers" groups and only send sustainable messages to "strong-sustainer" group.

12 The Role of New Media in Managing Hospitality Operations

During the past few years, new media has become a great marketing tool that no industry can afford to ignore. New media has significantly changed customer behavior and marketing communications. Old or new, the measurements of successful media marketing remain the same: whether or not the new media 1) boosts sales, 2) increases market share, 3) improves effectiveness for complementary media, and 4) helps build long-term customer relationship and loyalty. Usually, hotels and restaurants use an online travel agency (OTA) as one of their distribution channels. The position of display on those OTA websites can significantly affect the booking numbers. Sometimes, using OTA can even increase direct booking from the official websites of the hotels or restaurants. As mentioned in the "revenue management" section, position of display in search engines can be a form of effective advertising which boosts sales. Firms can manage their display by contracting with search engine companies.

In a way, OTAs and search engines are already "old" technologies. Social media (online communities) and mobile media (including mobile apps) play an important role in hospitality marketing and are already seen as "new technologies." One big difference is that, on social media, customers not only communicate with companies, they also communicate with each other in a public way, which is known as "peer-to-peer" reviews. Companies can use social media to engage customers and manage this channel by monitoring and responding to their reviews. Mobile applications provide "space" for marketers to communicate with customers whenever and wherever they want. As we can see in real life, many hotels have launched their own apps in which customers can find relevant hotel information, booking information, comments on experience from other customers, and so on. With the help of these apps, customers can gather information easily and have better experiences during their stays. All media channels provide opportunities for companies to 1) encourage loyal customers to refer new customers and 2) find new customers directly through their interests.

Given the ever-growing importance of social media and search engines, discovering their interrelationships can provide much important information for new media marketing. Xiang and Gretzel (2010) found that social media constitutes a substantial part of the search results, indicating that search engines direct travelers to social media sites. Evidence generated from this study shows that traditional travel information providers are facing incredible challenges. As for customer preference of information gathering sources, Verma et al. (2012) found out in their study that business travelers mostly rely on their companies' recommendations, search engines, and OTAs to gather information, whereas leisure travelers rely on recommendations of friends and colleagues, travel-related websites, and search engines. However, the researchers also found that, after the information is gathered, both business and leisure travelers tend to use company websites and OTAs to book their rooms.

It seems all evident that hospitality firms need to build and retain customer relationships via social media, but the question remains—how far should companies go? In his article, Witham (2011) talked about what activities are appropriate and what will offend consumers. In terms of performance, how exactly does social media influence sales? Anderson (2012) pointed out that transactional data from Travelocity illustrate that, if a hotel increases its review scores by 1 point (out of 5), the hotel can increase its price by 11.2% and still achieve the same occupancy and market share.

13 Directions for Future Research

The purpose of this chapter was to provide a broad overview of operations management and related concepts specific to the hospitality industry. We reviewed published research on hospitality from major operations management journals and found that, despite the size and importance of this industry, these topics are generally under-researched. Therefore, we believe that many opportunities exist for additional research and scholarship in the rapidly evolving hospitality, travel, and tourism industry. In this chapter, we identify and describe eleven different multi-disciplinary research themes related to the hospitality sector. Operations and supply chain management scholars can provide many unique insights to addressing these important research topics which also have significant influence in enhancing the practice of hospitality around the world.

Table 22.1 Empirical Study on Operations in Hospitality in JOM, POM, MS, and MSOM Journals

Author	Year	Journal	Key word	Category
Bendoly, Elliot	2013	JOM	Hospitality	Feedback/behavior
Baker, Timothy; Collier, David	2003	POM	Hotel	Revenue management
Gu, Bin; Ye, Qiang	2014	POM	Hotel	Social media/response
Anderson, Chris; Xie, Xiaoqing	2012	POM	Hospitality pricing	Opaque pricing
Bodea, Tudor; Ferguson, Mark; Garrow, Laurie	2009	MSOM	Hospitality	Revenue management
Allon, Gad; Federgruen, Awi; Pierson, Margaret	2011	MSOM	Restaurant	Waiting time
Baum, Joel A.C.; Ingram, Paul	1998	MS	Hospitality	Survival
Kalnins, Arturs; Chung, Wilbur	2006	MS	Hotel	Survival
Lehman, David; Kovács, Balazs; Carroll, Glenn R.	2014	MS	Restaurant	Evaluation
Kalnins, Arturs; Mayer, Kyle	2004	MS	Restaurant	Survival
Tan, Tom Fangyun; Netessine, Serguei	2014	MS	Restaurant	Productivity

Table 22.2 Non-Empirical Study on Operations in Hospitality in JOM, POM, MS, and MSOM Journals

Author	Year	Journal	Keyword	Category	Methodology
Queenan, Carrie Crystal; Ferguson, Mark	2007	POM	Hotel reservation systems	Revenue management	Review paper
Bodea, Tudor; Ferguson, Mark	2009	MSOM	Hospitality	Revenue management	Empirical + modeling
Alexandrov, Alexei; Lariviere, Martin A.	2012	MSOM	Restaurant, hotel	Reservation	Modeling
Veeraraghavan, Senthil; Debo, Laurens	2009	MSOM	Restaurant	Behavior/queue	Theoretical
Vulcano, Gustavo; van Ryzin, Garrett; Maglaras, Costis	2002	MS	Hospitality	Revenue management	Modeling
Gallego, Guillermo; van Ryzin, Garrett	1994	MS	Hospitality	Pricing	Modeling
Kinberg, Yoram; Rao, Ambar G.; Sudit, Ephraim F.	1980	MS	Hospitality marketing	Demand	Modeling
Kim, Byung-Do; Shi, Mengze; Kannan, Srinivasan	2004	MS	Hotels	Reward program	Modeling
Yingjie Lan; Huina Gao; Ball, Michael O.; Karaesmen, Itir	2008	MS	Hotels	Revenue management/demand	Modeling/competitive analysis
Lin, Grace; Yingdong Lu; Yao, David	2008	OR	Hospitality	Pricing	Modeling

Author	Year	Journal	Keyword	Category	Methodology
Bitran, Gabriel; Mondschein, Susana	1995	OR	Hotel	Revenue management	Modeling
Bitran, Gabriel; Gilbert, Stephen	1996	OR	Hotel	Reservation	Modeling
Levin, Yuri	2008	OR	Hotel	Revenue management/pricing	Modeling
Bertsimas, Dimitris; Shioda, Romy	2003	OR	Restaurant	Revenue management	Modeling

References and Bibliography

Alexandrov, A. and A.M. Lariviere (2012). "Are reservations recommended?" *Manufacturing & Service Operations Management*, **14**(2): 218–230.

Allon, Gad, A. Federgruen, and M. Pierson (2011). "How much is a reduction of your customers' wait worth? An empirical study of the fast-food drive-thru industry based on structural estimation methods," *Manufacturing & Service Operations Management*, **13**(4): 489–507.

Alonso, A. and M. O'Neill (2011). "What defines the 'ideal' hospitality employee? A college town case," *International Journal of Hospitality & Tourism Administration*, **12**(1): 73–93.

Anderson, C. (2009). "The billboard effect: Online travel agent impact on non-OTA reservation volume," *Cornell Center for Hospitality Research Report*, **9**(16): 6–9.

Anderson, C. (2012). "The impact of social media on lodging performance," *Cornell Hospitality Report*, **12**(15), 6–11.

Anderson, C. and S. Kimes (2011). "Revenue management for enhanced profitability, an introduction for hotel owners and asset managers," *The Cornell School of Hotel Administration on Hospitality*: 192–206.

Anderson, C.K. and X. Xie (2012). "A choice-based dynamic programming approach for setting opaque prices," *Production and Operations Management*, **21**(3): 590–605.

Baker, T.K. and D. Collier (2003). "The benefits of optimizing prices to manage demand in hotel revenue management systems," *Production and Operations Management*, **12**(4): 502–518.

Baum, Joel A.C. and P. Ingram (1998). "Survival-enhancing learning in the Manhattan hotel industry, 1898–1980," *Management Science*, **44**(7): 996–1016.

Bendoly, E. (2013). "Real-time feedback and booking behavior in the hospitality industry: Moderating the balance between imperfect judgment and imperfect prescription," *Journal of Operations Management*, **31**(1): 62–71.

Bertsimas, D. and R. Shioda (2003). "Restaurant revenue management," *Operations Research*, **51**(3): 472–486.

Bitran, G.R. and S. Gilbert (1996). "Managing hotel reservations with uncertain arrivals," *Operations Research*, **44**(1): 35–49.

Bitran, G.R. and S. Mondschein (1995). "An application of yield management to the hotel industry considering multiple day stays," *Operations Research*, **43**(3): 427–443.

Bodea, T., M. Ferguson, and L. Garrow (2009). "Data set-choice-based revenue management: Data from a major hotel chain," *Manufacturing & Service Operations Management*, **11**(2): 356–361.

Boyer, K. and R. Verma (2009). "Lean enterprise," in *Operations and Supply Chain Management for the 21st Century* (pp. 447–475). South-Western Cengage, Mason, OH.

Caro, L. and J. Garcia (2008). "Developing a multidimensional and hierarchical service quality model for the travel agency industry," *Tourism Management*, **29**: 706–720.

Carroll, B. (2011). "Demand management." Retrieved 5/25/2016, from School of Hospitality Administration, Cornell University, Ithaca, NY: http://scholarship.sha.cornell.edu/articles/253.

Chi, C. and D. Gursoy (2009). "Employee satisfaction, customer satisfaction, and financial performance: An empirical examination," *International Journal of Hospitality Management*, **28**: 245–253.

Chiang, C. and S. Jang (2008). "An expectancy theory model for hotel employee motivation," *International Journal of Hospitality Management*, **27**: 313–322.

Clark, R., M. Hartline, and K. Jones (2009). "The effects of leadership style on hotel employees' commitment to service quality," *Cornell Hospitality Quarterly*, **50**(2): 209–231.

Corgel, J., J. Deroos, and K. Fitzpatrick (2011). "Developing and renovating hospitality properties," in *The Cornell School of Hotel Administration on Hospitality* (pp. 309–320). John Wiley & Sons, Hoboken, NJ.

Corgel, J., R. Mandelbaum, and R. Woodworth (2011). "Hospitality property ownership where you fit in," in *The Cornell School of Hotel Administration on Hospitality* (pp. 247–269). John Wiley & Sons, Hoboken, NJ.

Deroos, J. (2011). "Gaining maximum benefit from franchise agreements, management contracts, and leases," in *The Cornell School of Hotel Administration on Hospitality* (pp. 293–308). John Wiley & Sons, Hoboken, NJ.

Deroos, J. (2011). "Planning and programming a hotel," in *The Cornell School of Hotel Administration on Hospitality* (pp. 321–332). John Wiley & Sons, Hoboken, NJ.

Fernández, L., M. Concepción, A. Serrano-Bedia, and R. Gómez-López (2011). "Factors encouraging innovation in Spanish hospitality firms," *Cornell Hospitality Quarterly*, **52**(2): 144–152.

Gallego, G. and G. van Ryzin (1994). "Optimal dynamic pricing of inventories with stochastic demand over finite horizons," *Management Science*, **40**(8): 999–1020.

Gu, B. and Q. Ye (2014). "First step in social media: Measuring the influence of online management responses on customer satisfaction," *Production and Operations Management*, **23**(4): 570–582.

Ha, J. and S. Jang (2010). "Effects of service quality and food quality: The moderating role of atmospherics in an ethnic restaurant segment," *International Journal of Hospitality Management*, **29**: 520–529.

Hassanien, A. and C. Dale (2012). "Drivers and barriers of new product development and innovation in event venues: A multiple case study," *Journal of Facilities Management*, **10**(1): 75–92.

Hertog, P., F. Gallouj, and J. Segers (2011). "Measuring innovation in a 'low-tech' service industry: The case of the Dutch hospitality industry," *The Service Industries Journal*, **31**(9): 1429–1449.

Hua, M., J. Horng, and Y. Sun (2009). "Hospitality teams: Knowledge sharing and service innovation performance," *Tourism Management*, **30**: 41–50.

Huang, Z., C. Zhao, L. Miao, and X. Fu (2014). "Triggers and inhibitors of illegitimate customer complaining behavior: Anecdotes from frontline employees in the hospitality industry," *International Journal of Contemporary Hospitality Management*, **26**(4): 544–571.

Hwang, J., L. Gao, and W. Jang (2010). "Joint demand and capacity management in a restaurant system," *European Journal of Operational Research*, **207**: 465–472.

Hwang, J. and C. Lambert (2009). "The use of acceptable customer waiting times for capacity management in a multistage restaurant," *Journal of Hospitality & Tourism Research*, **33**(4): 547–561.

Kalnins, A. and W. Chung (2006). "Social capital, geography, and survival: Gujarati immigrant entrepreneurs in the US lodging industry," *Management Science*, **52**(2): 233–247.

Kalnins, A. and K. Mayer (2004). "Franchising, ownership, and experience: A study of pizza restaurant survival," *Management Science*, **50**(12): 1716–1728.

Kim, B.D., M. Shi, and K. Srinivasan (2004). "Managing capacity through reward programs," *Management Science*, **50**(4): 503–520.

Kimes, S. (2011). "The future of hotel revenue management," *Journal of Revenue & Pricing Management*, **10**(1): 62–72.

Kimes, S. and Anderson, C. (2011). "Hotel revenue management in an economic downturn." Retrieved 5/25/2016, from School of Hospitality Administration, Cornell University, Ithaca, NY: http://scholarship.sha.cornell.edu/articles/254.

Kinberg, Y., A. Rao, and E. Sudit (1980). "Optimal resource allocation between spot and package demands," *Management Science*, **26**(9): 890–900.

Kitsios, F., M. Doumpos, E. Grigoroudis, and C. Zopounidis (2009). "Evaluation of new service development strategies using multicriteria analysis: Predicting the success of innovative hospitality services," *Operational Research*, **9**(1): 17–33.

Lan, Y., H. Gao, M.O. Ball, and I. Karaesmen (2008). "Revenue management with limited demand information," *Management Science*, **54**(9): 1594–1609.

Lancaster, J. (2011). "Lean and Six Sigma in hospitality organizations: Benefits, challenges, and implementation," *UNLV Theses/Dissertations/Professional Papers/Capstones*: Paper 1150. University of Nevada, Las Vegas, NV.

Lehman, D., B. Kovács, and G. Carroll (2014). "Conflicting social codes and organizations: Hygiene and authenticity in consumer evaluations of restaurants," *Management Science*, **60**(10): 2602–2617.

Levin, Y., J. McGill, and M. Nediak (2008). "Risk in revenue management and dynamic pricing," *Operations Research*, **56**(2): 326–343.

Lin, G.Y., Y. Lu, and D. Yao (2008). "The stochastic knapsack revisited: Switch-over policies and dynamic pricing," *Operations Research*, **56**(4): 945–957.

Liu, P. and D. Quan (2011). "Measuring hotel risk and financing," in *The Cornell School of Hotel Administration on Hospitality* (pp. 333–350). John Wiley & Sons, Hoboken, NJ.

Narayan, B., C. Rajendran, and L. Sai (2008). "Scales to measure and benchmark service quality in tourism industry," *Benchmarking: An International Journal*, **15**(4): 469–493.

Noone, B., K. McGuire, and K. Rohlfs (2011). "Social media meets hotel revenue management: Opportunities, issues and unanswered questions," *Journal of Revenue & Pricing Management*, **10**(4): 293–305.

Ottenbacher, M., R. Harrington, and H.G. Parsa (2009). "Defining the hospitality discipline: A discussion of pedagogical and research implications," *Journal of Hospitality & Tourism Research*, **33**(3): 263–283.

Paek, S., Q. Xiao, S. Lee, and H. Song (2013). "Does managerial ownership affect different corporate social responsibility dimensions? An empirical examination of US publicly traded hospitality firms," *International Journal of Hospitality Management*, **34**: 423–433.

Pearo, L. and B. Carroll (2011). "New media: Connecting with guests throughout the travel experience," in *The Cornell School of Hotel Administration on Hospitality* (pp. 370–387). John Wiley & Sons, Hoboken, NJ.

Pizam, A. and A. Shani (2009). "The nature of the hospitality industry: Present and future managers' perspectives," *Anatolia: An International Journal of Tourism and Hospitality Research*, **20**(1): 134–150.

Prud'homme, B. and L. Raymond (2013). "Sustainable development practices in the hospitality industry: An empirical study of their impact on customer satisfaction and intentions," *International Journal of Hospitality Management*, **34**: 116–126.

Pullman, M. and S. Rodgers (2010). "Capacity management for hospitality and tourism: A review of current approaches," *International Journal of Hospitality Management*, **29**: 177–187.

Queenan, C.C., M. Ferguson, J. Higbie, and R. Kapoor (2007). "A comparison of unconstraining methods to improve revenue management systems," *Production and Operations Management*, **16**(6): 729–746.

Rahman, Imran, R. Dennis, and S. Svaren (2012). "How 'green' are North American hotels? An exploration of low-cost adoption practices," *International Journal of Hospitality Management*, **31**(3): 720–727.

Roh, E. and K. Choi (2010). "Efficiency comparison of multiple brands within the same franchise: Data envelopment analysis approach," *International Journal of Hospitality Management*, **29**(1): 92–98.

Roh, E. and J. Yoon (2009). "Franchisor's ongoing support and franchisee's satisfaction: A case of ice cream franchising in Korea," *International Journal of Contemporary Hospitality Management*, **21**(1): 85–99.

Sirakaya-Turk, E., S. Baloglu, and H. Mercado (2014). "The efficacy of sustainability values in predicting travelers' choices for sustainable hospitality businesses," *Cornell Hospitality Quarterly*, **55**(1): 115–126.

Slatten, T. and M. Mehmetoglu (2011). "Antecedents and effects of engaged frontline employees: A study from the hospitality industry," *Managing Service Quality*, **21**(1): 88–107.

Sozer, H. (2010). "Improving energy efficiency through the design of the building envelope," *Building and Environment*, **45**(12): 2581–2593.

Swanson, S. and M. Hsu (2011). "The effect of recovery locus attributions and service failure severity on word-of-mouth and repurchase behaviors in the hospitality industry," *Journal of Hospitality & Tourism Research*, **35**(4): 511–529.

Tan, T.F. and S. Netessine (2014). "When does the devil make work? An empirical study of the impact of workload on worker productivity," *Management Science*, **60**(6): 1574–1593.

Thakran, K. and R. Verma (2013). "The emergence of hybrid online distribution channels in travel, tourism and hospitality," *Cornell Hospitality Quarterly*, **54**(3): 240–247.

Veeraraghavan, S. and L. Debo (2009). "Joining longer queues: Information externalities in queue choice," *Manufacturing & Service Operations Management*, **11**(4): 543–562.

Verma, R., D. Stock, and L. McCarthy (2012). "Customer preferences for online, social media, and mobile innovations in the hospitality industry," *Cornell Hospitality Quarterly*, **53**(3): 183–186.

Vlachos, I. and A. Bogdanovic (2013). "Lean thinking in the European hotel industry," *Tourism Management*, **36**: 354–363.

Vulcano, G., G. van Ryzin, and C. Maglaras (2002). "Optimal dynamic auctions for revenue management," *Management Science*, **48**(11): 1388–1407.

Wang, X. (2012). "Relationship or revenue: Potential management conflicts between customer relationship management and hotel revenue management," *International Journal of Hospitality Management*, **31**(3): 864–874.

Withiam, G. (2011). "Social media and the hospitality industry: Holding the tiger by the tail," *Cornell Hospitality Roundtable Proceedings*, **3**(3): 6–15.

Womack J., D. Jones, and D. Roos. *The Machine That Changed the World: The Story of Lean Production*. Free Press, New York, 1991.

Xiang, Zheng, and U. Gretzel (2010). "Role of social media in online travel information search," *Tourism management*, **31**(2): 179–188.

Yang, Y., K. Wong, and T. Wang (2012). "How do hotels choose their location? Evidence from hotels in Beijing," *International Journal of Hospitality Management*, **31**(3): 675–685.

23

POM FOR HEALTHCARE—FOCUSING ON THE UPSTREAM

Management of Preventive and Emergency Care

Vedat Verter

1 Introduction

The health sector accounts for a significant portion of gross domestic product (GDP) around the globe, particularly in developed countries. According to the Organization for Economic Co-operation and Development (OECD)'s Health Statistics (2015), the U.S. spent 16.4% of its GDP in 2013 (excluding capital expenditure) in the healthcare sector, while the spending average of the thirty-four OECD countries in the same sector was 8.9%. This has remained unchanged since 2009 as health-spending growth matched economic growth. OECD estimates the per capita health spending in the U.S. was $8,713 in 2013. In Canada, where the per capita health spending is about half of that of the United States', hospitals account for 30% of the overall costs. Hospitals are then followed by drugs and physicians, each with about a 15% share (Canadian Institute for Health Information (CIHI) 2015). As a result of hospital consolidation and bed closures as well as sustained transition from inpatient to outpatient care, there has been a significant reduction in hospital spending since the '90s—now stabilized at its current level. This suggests that there may not be any more "low-hanging fruit" for further cutting hospital costs via macro-level policies. Although continued efforts at the governmental level for improving the health sector are still necessary, they are not sufficient for achieving tangible success on the ground. To increase the efficiency of care delivery processes and the quality of care, healthcare providers and decision makers must implement health policies through concerted and sustained efforts at the operational level. Healthcare processes are dynamic and complex systems. Their design and improvement often involve pushing the frontiers of research in engineering and management.

There is a consensus among the stakeholders concerning the overarching objectives of healthcare: health outcomes, accessibility, quality, and cost of care. Although the plethora of stakeholders may have different individual prioritizations of these objectives, no one would find a health system that performs worse than a certain threshold in any of these attributes. There is, however, a widespread disagreement as to how the goals mentioned above can be attained, since the preferred path to these targets depends on the organization of the health system in a country or state (i.e., the extent of private/public ownership, the insurance and reimbursement systems in effect, single/multiple payers, and the various access barriers to healthcare).

For the purposes of this chapter, it is important to also highlight the difference between the care providers' and POM experts' viewpoints. The physicians and nurses are predominantly trained in a disease-oriented fashion, which constitutes their mindset for providing the best care to the patients. On the other hand, the POM experts—who may be the administrators or the consultants to the administrators—are trained in a process-oriented fashion that tends to downplay the differences with regard to the disease condition of the patients in an effort to come up with generalizable managerial insights. It is evident from our and other scholars' experiences that POM can make a positive impact for the care providers, patients, and administrators to the extent that the attention to health outcomes and process performance are balanced and the tradeoff between generalizability and individuality in patient care is treated carefully at the operational level (Ibrahim et al. 2016; Hulshof et al. 2012).

From a process perspective, the journey of each individual through the healthcare continuum involves one or more care phases, each with differentiating characteristics. A non-exhaustive list of these phases includes preventive care, primary care, pre-hospital (i.e., ambulance) care, acute (i.e., hospital) care, rehabilitative care, community-based care, chronic care, home care, long-term care, and palliative care. We will discuss the features of three of these phases (i.e., preventive, primary, and emergency care) and their implications for process design and improvement in the remainder of this chapter. At the outset, however, we must point out the significance of the interaction among these phases.

For example, the lack of access to primary care physicians increases the burden on the emergency departments (EDs), since EDs are the only facilities where the patients have a legal right to access healthcare. Recently, Sarnak and Ryan (2016) found out that about one of five patients (19% of all patients) aged 65 and older with at least three chronic conditions in the U.S. and Canada reported an avoidable ED visit that could have been treated by a family physician. Interestingly, the causes for this lack of access are quite different in the U.S. and Canada. In the U.S., the major challenge is formed by financial barriers due to the unaffordability of insurance, whereas in Canada the limited availability of primary care resources is a fundamental access barrier. Nevertheless, the overall impact of a problem at the upstream primary care phase on the downstream emergency care is quite similar from a patient-centric viewpoint.

In this chapter, we will focus on some of the process related challenges currently faced by the health sector and demonstrate how POM can be helpful. Notwithstanding the fact that healthcare systems vary around the world, POM methodology takes the macro system structure given and aims at supporting the strategic, tactical, and operational decisions concerning healthcare delivery. The lack of collaboration across the healthcare continuum is a significant impediment to patient care. A number of large-scale organizations such as Kaiser Permanente, the Cleveland Clinic, and the Mayo Clinic in the U.S. and King's Health Partner's in the U.K. have made great strides toward providing integrated care to their patients under one roof. Nonetheless, there remains a lot more work to be done for the public at large to benefit from such initiatives. In Quebec, for example, Bill 10 has reorganized the healthcare landscape in order to improve integration as recently as April 2015. So far, the implementation outcomes have yet to be seen.

There is a rich series of POM literature (Hulshof et al. 2012) offering a number of methods for designing integrated health networks as well as for improving the effectiveness at the implementation stage. Another major challenge is the disentanglement of the internal versus external determinants of performance at each phase of the care continuum. POM methodology can be also effective in identifying the most promising interventions through internal factors that are under the jurisdiction of the managers at each phase, whereas having a quantitative handle on the impact of external factors on their own system (e.g., the impact of lack of access to primary care on ED, as discussed above) would increase their ability to convince their superiors in releasing some of the burden.

This chapter is not intended to be a comprehensive literature review on healthcare operations management. There are a number of significant challenges in this domain that are out of the scope of the chapter.

POM can make a positive contribution concerning these issues as well. For example, the misalignment of the incentives provided to the care providers and the overall system objectives constitutes a significant challenge for the managers. It is well established that whether the physicians are reimbursed on a "fee for service" or on a "capitation" basis influences the type and volume of patients they serve. Supply chain coordination literature presents alternative ways to align the incentives through the healthcare service chain as well as for the different stakeholders. We include only the issues directly related to the configuration of the care delivery processes in this chapter and provide a narrative review that aims at demonstrating the potential value of POM. A comprehensive literature review on healthcare operations management would require multiples of the space allocated to a single book chapter. To make this point and to demonstrate the increasing scholarly activity in this domain, Figure 23.1 depicts the proliferation of the number of papers published in the most relevant journals during a twenty-five-year time horizon.

The potential value of POM for process design and improvement at two of the upstream layers of the healthcare continuum constitutes the focus of this chapter. This is due to the attention *preventive care* and *emergency care* received from POM scholars. This attention has led to the development of a rather solid methodology and application base. In contrast, the POM literature on primary care is fledgling, despite the significance of this upstream phase—something we discuss briefly in the last section. We provide a detailed discussion of the prevailing POM methodology

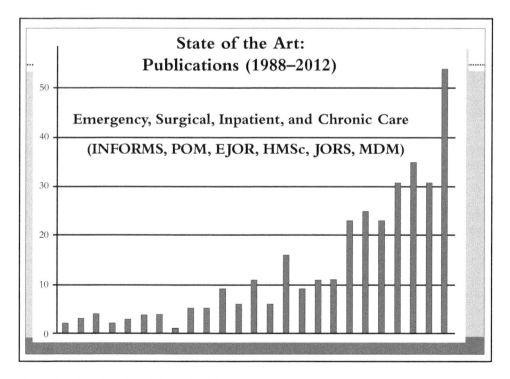

Figure 23.1 The Number of Papers Published
Source: Verter 2013

for preventive care in Section 2. Section 3 presents the current challenges in emergency care, discusses a case study, and directs the reader to the core papers within the abundance of literature in this domain. Section 4 discusses the implications for managers, and Section 5 concludes the paper with an outlook for the needed developments in POM methodology concerning the upstream phases of the healthcare continuum.

2 POM for Preventive Care

We start by providing a fundamental understanding of the preventive care processes. We continue with a basic formulation in Section 2.2, and discuss its extensions as well as other modeling frameworks in Section 2.3

2.1 Preventive Care Processes

Preventive care is based on the premise that it is easier and more humane to prevent health conditions, such as many forms of cancer, rather than to treat them. With preventive care, it is also more likely that the patient will fully recover as a result of early diagnosis. Thus, there are three types of preventive care programs: (i) *primary prevention* reduces the likelihood of diseases in people with no symptoms, such as flu shots; (ii) *secondary prevention* identifies and treats people with risk factors or are at very early stage of diseases, such as colonoscopy to detect early forms of colon cancer; and (iii) *tertiary prevention* treats symptomatic patients in an effort to decrease complications or severity of disease, such as sugar control in a diabetic in order to mitigate vision and nerve problems.

The differentiating characteristics of preventive care are as follows: (i) it is a *user-choice* environment in terms of the allocation of clients to facilities, where the regulators typically do not control the patronage of the facilities; (ii) the clients' willingness to participate in preventive programs could decrease significantly when either access is inconvenient or there is congestion at the facilities leading to unreasonable wait times; and (iii) each facility needs to capture a certain volume of clientele to satisfy a *minimum workload* requirement that ensures the quality of the service.

The substantial savings in the costs of diagnosis and therapy as well as the relatively lower capital investment associated with preventive care programs have been recognized for a long time (Walker 1977). Although it is well established that preventive care programs can save lives and contribute to a better quality of life by reducing the needs for radical treatments, they do not constitute a priority for many governments that are preoccupied with responding to the urgent needs of patients. Under these circumstances, increasing the number of people receiving preventive care services has been an integral part of many healthcare reform programs (Goldsmith 1989). Note that the individuals seeking preventive services have more flexibility as to when and where to receive care. Consequently, early empirical work demonstrated that the accessibility of the facilities is an important factor for the success of a preventive care program. Zimmerman (1997) found through a survey that the convenience of access to the facility was a very important factor in a client's decision to have prostate cancer screening. Facione (1999) revealed that the perceptions of lack of access to services were related to the decrease of mammography participation.

From a POM perspective, the underlying problem involves the design of a preventive care facility network in a way that would maximize the level of participation. The number of facilities to be established as well as the location, capacity, and service mix of each facility constitute the primary structural decisions. Of course, there are also infrastructural decisions to be made in this context, particularly concerning the skillset of the care providers at each facility. The prevailing POM literature uses the time spent to receive preventive services as a proxy for accessibility of healthcare facilities (Zhang et al. 2012). This includes the time spent in transportation to the facility and the total time spent at the facility (i.e., waiting and care).

2.2 A Basic Formulation for Designing Preventive Care Networks

We will use the model by Zhang et al. (2009), where each facility is represented by an $M/M/1$ queue, as the basis for illustration. To formulate the problem, they used the following notation:

y_j = 1 if a facility is located at demand node j, 0 otherwise
x_{ij} = 1 if clients from node i require service from facility j, 0 otherwise
N = set of demand nodes, indexed by i
X = set of alternative facility sites, indexed by j
λ = overall rate of demand for the preventive service (assuming Poisson distribution)
$1/\mu$ = average service time (assuming exponential distribution)
h_i = fraction of clients residing at node i
a_{ij} = fraction of clients from node i who would patronize facility j
R_{min} = minimum workload at each operational preventive care facility

The implicit assumption is that all individuals from the same node request service from the same facility. Also, in the long run, the clients will gather sufficient information about the total time required to obtain preventive healthcare services at the facilities in their vicinity, and hence, each user will choose the facility by which they would receive the service the fastest. To this end, Zhang et al. (2009) denote the travel time tij and the expected waiting time for the service $\bar{W}_j$. Assuming a linearly decreasing participation function, $a_{ij} = A_{ij} - \gamma(t_{ij} + \bar{W}_j)$, where $\bar{W}_j = 1/\left(\mu - \lambda \sum_{i \in N} h_i a_{ij} x_{ij}\right)$ and A_{ij} and γ are the intercept and slope of the participation function, respectively. The resulting nonlinear binary formulation is as follows:

$$\text{Maximize } \lambda \sum_{i \in N} h_i \sum_{j \in X} a_{ij} x_{ij} \tag{1}$$

Subject to

$$\sum_{j \in X} x_{ij} = 1 \qquad i \in N \tag{2}$$

$$x_{ij} \leq y_j \qquad i \in N, j \in X \tag{3}$$

$$R_{min} y_j \leq \lambda \sum_{i \in N} h_i a_{ij} x_{ij} \leq \mu \qquad j \in X \tag{4}$$

$$x_{ij}(t_{ij} + \bar{W}_j)t_{ik} \leq \bar{W}_k + M(1 - y_k) \qquad i \in N, j, k \in X \tag{5}$$

$$a_{ij} x_{ij} \geq 0 \qquad i \in N, j \in X \tag{6}$$

$$x_{ij}, y_j = 0, 1 \qquad i \in N, j \in X \tag{7}$$

The objective function (1) maximizes the total number of people expected to participate in the preventive care program. Constraints (2) impose the single-facility service requirements on each demand node. Constraints (3) ensure that clients can require service only from open facilities. Constraints (4) guarantee the stability of the queue and impose minimum workload on the open facilities. Constraints (5), where M represents a big number, are the closest facility assignment constraints in terms of minimum total time to receive service, whereas constraints (6) prohibit negative values for participation.

The above model was used for determining which breast cancer screening centers in Montreal, Canada, should be included in the Health Ministry's program to subsidize mammograms for women between the ages of 50 and 69 (originally discussed in Verter and Lapierre 2002). Zhang et al. (2009) demonstrated that the incorporation of congestion would considerably increase the accuracy of the estimates for the participation level to the program. They also showed that centralizing system capacity at the locations preferred by the clients would be a better policy than pushing for decentralization by accrediting a larger number of small facilities. Their methodology can be used in making decisions concerning the total system capacity as well as the investments in raising public awareness with regard to preventive healthcare programs. That is, the allocation of some resources on health promotion projects targeted to potential clients can be considered as an effective means of increasing participation. This should, of course, be considered as a complementary to the optimization of the facility network configuration.

In a follow-up paper, Zhang et al. (2010) extend the basic model by also optimizing the capacity (i.e., the number of servers) at each facility and allowing for the people from the same population zone to receive preventive care at different facilities, as long as the total (travel + wait + service) times required for receiving care are the same. They developed a bi-level formulation, where the lower level represents the user choices, whereas the upper level determines the structural decisions pertaining to the preventive care facility network. The lower level aims at reaching user equilibrium, where all clients are content with the facility choices. The lower-level problem is incorporated in the upper level via a variational inequality. Using their multi-server model on the Montreal case mentioned above, Zhang et al. (2010) were able to demonstrate that capacity pooling (i.e., centralizing the system capacity in a few large facilities) may raise participation by reducing the mean waiting time. Note that the minimum workload requirement also favors centralization, since it may not be feasible to accredit many single-server facilities. Interestingly, they also show that Zhang et al. (2009)'s findings using a single server model, pertaining to the value of the centralization strategy, hold true only when the number of servers is not too restricted. For the Montreal case, when there are less than ten mammography workstations available, however, rather than striving for capacity pooling by adding one server to an existing facility, it is better to increase the spatial coverage by locating a new facility in another high-density area.

2.3 *Extended Models for Preventive Care*

The stream of literature presented in the previous section has been extended in many ways. In particular, Aboolian et al. (2016) studies the problem of determining the overall capacity at each site rather than the number of servers. They reformulated the nonlinear model as a mixed-integer program by replacing the service rates with the waiting times that are approximated using tangent line approximation. By studying Toronto's twenty-two-hospital network (Berman et al. 2007), they observed that the capability of the Ontario government to increase participation in its services by simply increasing accessibility is limited. They also showed that a gradual capacity expansion strategy could be robust as long as the system is originally conceived with an overall capacity that is above a threshold level. Zhang et al. (2012) incorporated probabilistic user choice to account for the facility attributes that attract patients other than accessibility. Using the Montreal case, they demonstrated the similarity between the optimal-choice and probabilistic-choice models concerning the trade-off between capacity pooling and spatial coverage. The resulting network configurations obtained from the two models, however, are quite different. This emphasizes the significance of accurately representing the user choice in preventive care facility network design.

One of the challenges that is not explicitly taken into account by the above papers is that many screening facilities also provide diagnostic services. Therefore, the capacity of such facilities needs to be allocated between the urgent diagnostic needs of a group of patients and the preventive needs of the asymptomatic patients to be screened. In the context of colonoscopy procedures, Güneş et al. (2015) studied the impact of preventive care on reducing the future demand for diagnostic services. By integrating the disease progression and operations perspectives in a system dynamics model, they were able to assess alternative resource allocation policies. They showed that if the diagnostic service capacity could be set to keep the average waiting time for diagnosis below two weeks, then the remaining capacity can be dedicated to screening. Örmeci et al. (2016) analyzed the long-term impact of preventive care, mentioned above, through a partially endogenous random environment. They explored the operational-level colonoscopy scheduling policies using a Markov decision process (MDP). Interestingly, Örmeci et al. (2016) and Güneş et al. (2015) both confirm the current practice of prioritizing the diagnostic services, although under certain—albeit less often—circumstances patients with lower waiting costs (i.e., screening) need to be given priority.

In an effort to personalize the screening decisions, a stream of papers utilize the partially observable Markov decision process (POMDP) framework, where the true state of the cancer being screened for is not observable. Erenay et al. (2014) incorporated age, gender, and risk of having colorectal cancer in a POMDP to optimize colonoscopy screening policies so as to maximize the patient's total quality-adjusted life years. Ayer et al. (2012) and Maillart et al. (2008) developed a POMDP for breast cancer screening, whereas Zhang J. et al. (2012) used the same framework for prostate cancer screening. All of these studies provide a favorable comparison between the proposed screening policy and the current clinical guidelines and highlight the effect of aging on the optimal screening policies. There is a long road for these personalized screening policies to be implemented by practitioners in a wide scale, since this would require their validation through extensive randomized control trials. Nonetheless, POM can certainly claim a significant contribution towards more effective and efficient design of the needed control trials as well as towards empowering the individual physicians (whose patient-centric decisions can override the guidelines) with more accurate knowledge concerning the potential benefits of personalized screening policies.

3 POM for Emergency Care

We first provide a brief account of the key process challenges emergency department (ED) managers face in providing timely and quality care to patients. The literature on the use of POM in the context of ED process design and improvement is vast. A recent comprehensive review based on 350 papers can be found in Saghafian et al. (2015). Due to the complexity of the ED processes, a vast majority of the prevailing studies resort to simulation for the purposes of modeling, analysis, and improvement. Thus, Section 3.2 is devoted to the simulation of ED process and a new case study at the ED of a large tertiary hospital is presented in Section 3.3.

The recent trend in using POM for emergency care involves the use of optimization methods by taking advantage of stylistic models. In particular, Mandelbaum et al. (2012) studied the patient admissions from an ED to the inpatient wards by means of a queuing model with a single centralized queue and several server pools. They proposed a randomized most-idle routing policy for patient admissions. Under the proposed policy, a patient is assigned to one of the available wards, with probability that equals the fraction of available beds in that ward out of the total number of available beds in the system. Saghafian et al. (2012) studied the impact of streaming ED patients based on predictions concerning the disposition decision after receiving care (i.e., whether they will be discharged or admitted to the hospital). They underline the importance of sharing ED resources across streams and not earmarking them to the patient streams. Saghafian et al. (2014) showed that estimating the complexity of the required care during the ED triage could lead to considerable reductions in both the risk of adverse events and the average length of stay. These two papers also determine the conditions under which the virtual streaming and complexity-augmented triage policies would be effective.

3.1 Key Challenges in ED Management

The ED constitutes the point of entry to a hospital for all patients—except those who are scheduled for elective surgeries. According to Schuur and Venkatesh (2012), ED is the first point of contact for nearly half of all hospital admissions in the U.S. Nonetheless, emergency care is sufficient for the significant majority of the patients who present at the ED and eventually get discharged home. ED managers are faced with a multitude of challenges including overcrowding, resource reductions, limited bed capacity, long waiting times, and low staff morale. These issues are becoming more pronounced due to the increasing number of ED visits and never-ending budget cuts from the health sector at large.

The Canadian Association of Emergency Physicians (CAEP) (2013) defined overcrowding as "demand surpassing the ability of an ED to provide quality care within acceptable time frames". This definition implies that ED overcrowding corresponds to an "access block", to use POM terminology. The most significant impact of overcrowding is on the ability to deliver emergency care in a timely manner (Derlet and Richards 2000; Derlet et al. 2001). Overcrowding often leads to an increase in the number of interruptions the caregivers endure while caring for a patient. This makes them feel overextended and has the potential to cause adverse patient outcomes. Another important effect of overcrowding is patient morale and satisfaction. Delays in patient treatment may unnecessarily increase their time spent on stretchers in the ED. Patients who experience disheartening waiting times, are often forced to lie in crowded corridors which robs them of both privacy and a sense of dignity. Overcrowding has also led to an increase in patients leaving without being seen by medical personnel as well as ambulance diversions whereby critical patients may be denied access to the closest ED, and rerouted to other centers (Schull et al. 2003).

The optimization of staffing decisions is another key challenge for the ED managers, where the prevailing POM methodology can be very helpful. The visits of the ambulance and walk-in patients are unscheduled, whereas most EDs are staffed through a fixed schedule. The number of physicians and nurses is predetermined and does not fluctuate depending on patient volume. This often results in either the under or over staffing of units. Many EDs are thus left scrambling to meet the demands of a crowded and hectic unit. Staffing the ED with the appropriate type and number of personnel needed to meet these demands is essential. The ED managers must also take into consideration the efficient utilization of existing personnel. Non-medical tasks, often performed by highly trained physicians and nurses, are well known to decrease efficiency. Examples of such tasks include looking for charts, tracking down laboratory results, arranging for admission, or rewriting information. It is well known that these additional tasks cause unnecessary disruptions in patient care and frequently result in increased job stress and risk for medical errors (Wears and Leape 1999).

3.2 Simulation of ED Processes

A process view of the patient flow through the ED is depicted in Figure 23.2. The first step for all patients (irrespective of the mode of arrival) is triage, where a triage nurse evaluates the patient's medical condition to identify the need for an ED bed as well as the priority for seeing a physician. The next step is registration upon which patients wait in the waiting area until an ED bed (or an ambulatory treatment space, if appropriate) becomes available. ED treatment starts with the initial physician and nurse assessments. An ED physician may request one or several lab tests (i.e., blood/fluids or imaging), keep the patient under observation, or decide to consult a specialist. Such consultations often include a clinical examination of the patient by the specialist as well as additional lab tests. The last step is the disposition decision by which the patient is either admitted to the hospital by a specialist for further treatment or discharged home. Many of the admitted

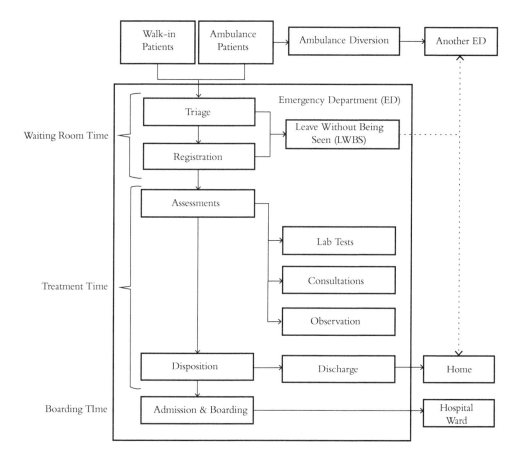

Figure 23.2 Process Flow in the ED Process (Klein 2013)

patients wait in the ED for an inpatient bed, which is called "ED boarding" (i.e., an access block for the newly arriving ED patients).

There are number of process challenges concerning the flow of patients through an ED. First, the triage and assessment operations are based on priority queues: At triage, ambulance arrivals have priority over walk-in arrivals, and at the first assessment, patients are often prioritized according to their triage code. Second, it is entirely possible for a new patient arrival to pre-empt the current task an ED physician is performing. For example, in the event of the arrival of a patient requiring resuscitation, the physician will have to pause caring for the current patient, which may require restarting the entire task upon performing the resuscitation. Third, and perhaps most importantly, ED physicians depend on their specialist counterparts for consultation and, if necessary, hospital admission of the patients. In some hospitals, the consultation requests from ED may not constitute the top priority for specialists who need to also provide care at the inpatient wards as well as the outpatient clinics and (in surgical specialties) operate in the surgical theatres. In addition, the specialist who is sent to the ED may need to consult someone with more experience or different specialty. Last, but not least, many EDs do not have dedicated laboratories and imaging facilities to conduct the necessary blood/urine tests and diagnostic scans a patient may require. It is due to these differentiating characteristics of the ED that patient flow is a rather complex phenomenon, one where POM has ample opportunity to bring value to management.

Computer simulation lends itself naturally for modeling the ED processes with such complexity. A major advantage of simulation in modeling EDs, over analytical techniques (which we will discuss later in this section) is its ability to represent variability in *individual* patient characteristics. Note that patient visits to EDs are mostly unscheduled and present irregular peaks and troughs in the number of patients as well as in the acuity of their illness or injury. For tractability, analytical methods require the aggregation of patients into homogenous groups. This thereby ignores the individual differences within each group. In our experience, such stylized representations seem to hinder the usefulness of analytical techniques in detailed operational modeling of EDs; at least for the decision makers with a medical background.

As addressed by Sinreich and Marmor (2005), an important aspect of ED simulation is the structure and collection of the necessary data as well as its level of detail. Saunders et al. (1989) is one of the earliest ED simulation models to reflect the underlying complexity. They built a rather sophisticated model (relative to the state of technology at the time) that assigned an individual nurse to each patient; incorporated the patients' movements on several pathways simultaneously; and represented tests, treatments, and procedures in detail. They used sensitivity analysis in studying the factors that determine the patient's waiting time and used severity as the only patient characteristic. In contrast, McGuire et al. (1994) categorized patients on both severity and broad category of diseases. McGuire used simulation to test several operating alternatives in a Sun Health Alliance Hospital, with the objective of reducing patient length of stay (LOS). The most comprehensive framework, to date, is developed by an Israeli team of scholars, who made significant strides toward simulation-based real-time decision-support systems for EDs (Zeltyn et al. 2011).

3.3 *A Case Study in ED Triage*

In order to demonstrate the potential value of simulation, we report on the triage module of a comprehensive simulation platform that was developed by our multi-disciplinary research team for the ED of a tertiary hospital in Montreal, Canada (Verter et al. 2012). This ED has about 66,000 patient visits annually. Patient triage, performed by a registered nurse (RN) immediately upon arrival, aims to rapidly identify patients with urgent (possibly life-threatening) conditions and to determine the most appropriate treatment area in ED. Both the U.S. and Canada use five-level triage codes, where a lower code indicates a higher level of urgency. The Canadian triage scores are based on the target time the patient needs to be first seen by a physician, whereas the U.S. emergency severity index is associated with the expected resource utilization of the patient in the ED.

For the purposes of this project, the triage was observed over a 15-week period during weekday shifts (8:00 to 16:00) for an average of 8 hours/day. During this period, 537 ambulance and 3,205 walk-in patients were observed. We also extracted data from the ED administrative database: socio-demographic, patient arrival patterns, and triage severity. During the data collection period, the one full-time RN and a second RN available for about 5 hours throughout the day were assigned to triage. Figure 23.3 depicts the observational data concerning the distribution of arrivals, service times, and wait times depending on the mode of arrival.

The triage module was built using the ARENA software (www.arenasimulation.com), and the simulation model was validated through comparing the simulated wait time with those depicted in Figure 23.3. Two remarks are warranted here: (i) at the time of data collection, the triage performance was far below the Canadian Triage Acuity Standards (CTAS), which stipulate that 95% of the code II patients should be seen by a physician within 15 minutes of arrival, and the first physician assessment for 90% of code III patients should occur within half an hour; and (ii) the bimodal shape of the triage wait times for the walk-in patients (i.e., with a kink around two hours) is due to the multiple ambulance arrivals within short time windows.

As noted earlier, our baseline involves 1.5 RNs, each triaging both ambulance and walk-in patients, where the former group has priority. The ED chief was interested in increasing the triage staffing to 2 RNs and wanted to know the impact of the following two possible interventions: (i) dedicating one RN to ambulance patients and one RN to walk-ins (i.e., un-pooling) and (ii) performing a 1-minute pre-triage screening to fast track eligible patients to a rapid assessment zone. Table 23.1 shows the mean and standard deviation of the triage wait times as well as the nurse utilization levels for the four scenarios we have studied.

The benefits of capacity pooling are well established in the general POM literature (Cachon and Terwiesch 2012). Although we knew the direction of change when the RNs are dedicated, the simulation model informed the ED chief as to the level of reduction in the wait times for the ambulance patients and the level of associated increase in the mean and variability of the wait times to be experienced by the walk-in patients. Clearly, pre-triaging all arrivals is beneficial for both patient groups. Although combining pooling with pre-triage (i.e., the fourth scenario) brings the triage wait times to levels that would enable the ED to achieve the CTAS standards, the expected nurse utilization of 39% constituted a sticking point in an environment plagued with limited resources.

After a lengthy discussion period, the ED management was convinced to keep the nurses pooled and to implement the pre-triage as well as the rapid assessment zone ideas. By depicting how the problematic right-hand tale of the wait time distributions would be curtailed as a result of these interventions, Figure 23.4 was instrumental in achieving the administrators' buy-in.

We also studied the impact of a dynamic nurse staffing policy for ED triage, where the second RN is called in only when the triage waiting line reaches a predetermined threshold level. Although this strategy further reduces the wait times (albeit not significantly) while keeping the triage nurse utilization at high levels, it was not acceptable to the ED chief due to the perceived complexity of implementation.

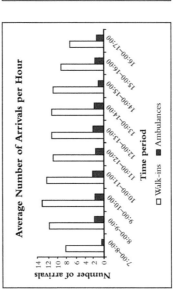
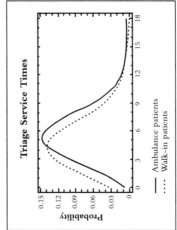
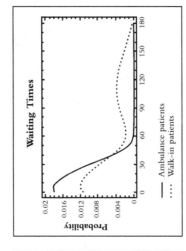

Figure 23.3 Triage Data: Patient Arrivals, Service Times, and Wait Times

Table 23.1 Scenario Analysis for Triage Process Design

Scenario	Triage Wait Time (Min.) Ambulance	Triage Wait Time (Min.) Walk-in	Nurse Utilization
Baseline (1.5 Pooled RNs)	3.6 ± 5.9	18 ± 29	71%
2 Dedicated RNs + Regular Triage	1.5 ± 3.8	68 ± 108	Walk in 90% Ambulance 25%
2 Dedicated RNs + Pre-triage	1.4 ± 3.7	9 ± 13	Walk in 53% Ambulance 25%
2 Pooled RNs + Pre-triage	0.68 ± 1.66	2.25 ± 3.7	39%

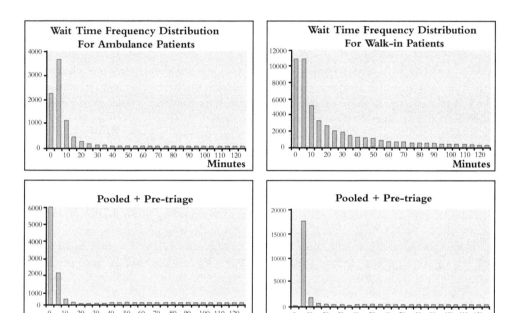

Figure 23.4 The Impact of Triage Scenarios on the Distribution of Wait Times

4 Implications for Managers

Individuals with medical or nursing training and experience have been managing healthcare facilities for a very long time. Notwithstanding the increasing number of management professionals recruited to positions with decision-making authority, the management and policy-making positions in the health sector are still largely occupied by people without any formal exposure to the fundamentals of management. Hence, the health sector is plagued by the prevalence of "management by intuition" and/or "management based on experience". However, the previously discussed complexities associated with the dynamics of healthcare delivery operations often render the intuitive solutions sub-optimal. In addition, the "low hanging fruit" often does not result in the envisioned benefits in such complex systems. This is why it is essential that the managers of healthcare facilities take advantage of detailed analyses through the use of POM methodology in improving healthcare delivery. In facilities of sufficient size, we would advocate for an in-house team of POM experts, rather than resorting to one of the reputable consulting companies. The advantage of this approach, in our experience, is that the POM team will own the process improvement problem as seen through the continuous improvement of the delivery process.

5 Conclusions and Future Research Directions

This chapter highlights the usefulness of POM in designing and improving preventive and emergency care processes. In closing, we comment on some of the remaining research challenges in these two domains and point out the use of POM for primary care as a fruitful research avenue that is largely untapped.

Concerning preventive care, the prevailing studies cited in Section 2 represent accessibility in terms of the patient's distance to or time in the facility. There is empirical evidence that there are additional factors that attract patients to a preventive care facility, such as the friendliness of the staff and the availability of parking. In addition, these studies are not applicable to representing preventive care services that work with appointments (i.e., they are geared toward walk-in services). One of the main challenges associated with modeling appointment systems is the fact that wait times for appointments are often not commensurate with the travel times to and the service times at the facilities. Research on overcoming these issues would be a welcome contribution, particularly from the perspective of practical applicability.

There are a number of challenges facing researchers concerning the use of POM for emergency care. Although an abundance of ED simulation models have been reported in the scholarly literature (Saghafian et al. 2015), their uptake by the ED managers has not been stellar. To the best of our knowledge, a very significant majority of the simulation models have been used for decision-making episodes only once or twice rather than becoming an integral part of the toolkit of ED managers. The suite of ED simulation models developed by Mandelbaum and his team (Zeltyn et al. 2011) (which are being used in Israel at multiple hospitals) is the only exception to this that we know of. There is a need for a concerted effort to understand the reasons behind this low uptake in practice. In addition, top-tier POM journals are typically not interested in publishing such application-oriented simulation work, unless there is a methodology contribution. This certainly constitutes a concern. Thus, the recent trend we mention at the beginning of Section 3 involving the dual use of analytic and simulation approaches for tackling specific processes at the ED rather than the entire ED process seems to be the best approach to push frontiers of research at this time.

An important upstream phase of the healthcare continuum that we did not discuss in this chapter is primary care. This is not an oversight but mainly a reflection of the state of using POM for designing and improving primary care processes. The first point of contact for a patient with the health system should be primary care. Despite its significant impact on the overall population health, primary care has been largely unstudied by POM researchers. To this end, the recent paper by Güneş et al. (2014) on matching patient and physician preferences and the research by Graber-Nadich et al. (2015) on the regulator's perspective concerning primary care are merely initial steps. There is a lot of work that remains to be done in this important domain.

References and Bibliography

Aboolian, R., O. Berman and V. Verter (2016) "Maximal accessibility network design in the public sector," *Transportation Science*, **50**(1): 336–347.

ARENA Software, www.arenasimulation.com.

Ayer, T., O. Alagoz and N.K. Stout (2012) "A POMDP approach to personalize mammography screening decisions," *Operations Research*, **60**(5): 1019–1034.

Berman, O., D. Krass and M.B.C. Menezes (2007) "Facility reliability issues in network *p*-median problems: Strategic centralization and co-location effects," *Operations Research*, **55**(2): 332–350.

Cachon, G. and C. Terwiesch (2012) *Matching Supply with Demand: An Introduction to Operations Management*. 3rd edition. McGraw Hill, New York.

Canadian Association of Emergency Physicians (2013) "CAEP position statement: Emergency department overcrowding and access block," http://caep.ca/sites/caep.ca/files/caep/PositionStatments/edoc_document_final_eng.pdf

CIHI (2015) "National health expenditure trends 1975 to 2013," Canadian Institute for Health Information, https://secure.cihi.ca/estore/productSeries.htm?pc=PCC52

Derlet, R.W. and J.R. Richards (2000) "Overcrowding in the nation's emergency departments: Complex causes and disturbing effects," *Annals of Emergency Medicine*, **35**(1): 63–68.

Derlet, R.W., J.R. Richards and R.L. Kravitz (2001) "Frequent overcrowding in U.S. emergency departments," *Academic Emergency Medicine*, **8**(2): 151–155.

Erenay, F.S., O. Alagoz and A. Said (2014) "Optimizing colonoscopy screening for colorectal cancer prevention and surveillance," *Manufacturing & Service Operations Management*, **16**(3): 381–400.

Facione, N.C. (1999) "Breast cancer screening in relation to access to health services," *Oncology Nursing Forum*, **26**: 689–696.

Graber-Nadich, A., M. Carter and V. Verter (2015) "Primary care facility network development—the regulator's perspective," *Journal of Operational Research Society*, **66**: 1519–1532.

Goldsmith, J. (1989) "A radical prescription for hospitals," *Harvard Business Review*, **67**(3): 104–111.

Güneş, E.D., E.L. Örmeci and D. Kunduzcu (2015) "Preventing and diagnosing colorectal cancer with a limited colonoscopy resource," *Production and Operations Management*, **24**(1): 1–20.

Güneş, E.D., H. Yaman, B. Cekyay and V. Verter (2014) "Matching patient and physician preferences in designing a primary care facility network," *Journal of the Operational Research Society*, **65**(4): 483–496.

Hulshof, O.J.H., N. Kortbeek, R.J. Boucherie, E.W. Hans and P.J.M. Bakker (2012) "Taxonomic classification of planning decisions in health care: A structured review of the state of the art in OR/MS," *Health Systems*, **1**: 129–175.

Ibrahim, R., B. Kucukyazici, V. Verter, M. Gendreau and M. Blostein (2016) "Designing personalized treatment: An application to anticoagulation therapy," *Production and Operations Management*, **25**(5): 902–918.

Klein, M. (2013) "Emergency department operations management: An overview and outlook," Working Paper, McGill University, Montreal, Canada.

Maillart, L.M., J.S. Ivy, S. Ransom, K. Diehl (2008) "Assessing dynamic breast cancer screening policies," *Operations Research*, **56**(6): 1411–1427.

Mandelbaum, A., P. Momcilovic and Y. Tseytlin (2012) "On fair routing from emergency departments to hospital wards: QED queues with heterogeneous servers," *Management Science*, **58**(7): 1273–1291.

McGuire, F. (1994) "Using simulation to reduce length of stay in emergency departments," *Proceedings of the Winter Simulation Conference*, December 11–14, 1994; 861–867.

OECD Health Statistics (2015), www.oecd.org/health/health-data.htm.

Örmeci, E.L., E.D. Güneş and D. Kunduzcu (2016) "A modeling framework for control of preventive services," *Manufacturing & Service Operations Management*, **18**(2): 227–244.

Saghafian, S., G. Austin and S.J. Traub (2015) "Operations research/management contributions to emergency department patient flow optimization: Review and research prospects," *IIE Transactions on Healthcare Systems Engineering*, **5**(2): 101–123.

Saghafian, S., W.J. Hopp, M.P. Van Oyen, J.S. Desmond and S.L. Kronick (2012) "Patient streaming as a mechanism for improving responsiveness in emergency departments," *Operations Research*, **60**(5): 1080–1097.

Saghafian, S., W.J. Hopp, M.P. Van Oyen, J.S. Desmond and S.L. Kronick (2014) "Complexity-augmented triage: A tool for improving patient safety and operational efficiency," *Manufacturing & Service Operations Management*, **16**(3): 329–345.

Sarnak D.O. and J. Ryan (2016) *How High-Need Patients Experience the Health Care System in Nine Countries*. The Commonwealth Fund, www.commonwealthfund.org/publications/issue-briefs/2016/jan/high-need-patients-nine-countries.

Saunders, C.E., P.K.Makens and L.J. Leblanc (1989) "Modeling emergency department operations using advanced computer simulation systems," *Annals of Emergency Medicine*, **18**(2): 134–140.

Schull, M.J., L.J. Morrison, M. Vermeulen and D.A. Redelmeier (2003) "Emergency department overcrowding and ambulance transport delays for patients with chest pain," *Canadian Medical Association Journal*, **168**(3): 277–283.

Schuur, J.D. and A.K. Venkatesh (2012) "The growing role of emergency departments in hospital admissions," *New England Journal of Medicine*, **367**: 391–393.

Sinreich, D. and Y. Marmor (2005) "Emergency department operations: The basis for developing a simulation tool," *IIE Transactions*, **37**(3): 233–245.

Verter, V. (2013) "Healthcare operations management: An overview and outlook," plenary talk at Canadian Operations Research Society meeting, Vancouver, Canada, May 27–29, 2013.

Verter, V., A. Gutman, M. Afilalo and A. Colacone (2012) "Emergency department simulation for tackling overcrowding," presented at the INFORMS Phoenix, AZ, October 14–17, 2012.

Verter, V. and S.D. Lapierre (2002) "Location of preventive health care facilities," *Annals of Operations Research*, **110**: 123–132.

Walker, K. (1977) "Current issues in the provision of health care services," *Journal of Consumer Affairs*, **11**: 52–62.

Wears R. and L.L. Leape (1999) "Human error in emergency medicine," *Annals of Emergency Medicine*, **34**: 370–372

Zeltyn S., Y.N. Marmor, A. Mandelbaum, B. Carmeli, O. Greenshpan, Y. Mesika, S. Wasserkrug, P. Vortman, A. Shtub, T. Lauterman, D. Schwartz, K. Moskovitch, S. Tzafrir, F. Basis (2011) "Simulation-based models of emergency departments: Operational, tactical, and strategic staffing," *ACM Transactions on Modeling and Computer Simulation (TOMACS)*, **21**(4): 24.

Zhang, J., B.T. Denton, H. Balasubramanian, N.D. Shah and B.A. Inman (2012) "Optimization of PSA screening policies: A comparison of the patient and societal perspectives," *Medical Decision Making*, **32**(2): 337–349.

Zhang, Y., O. Berman and V. Verter (2009) "Incorporating congestion in preventive healthcare facility network design," *European Journal of Operational Research*, **198**: 922–935.

Zhang, Y., O. Berman and V. Verter (2012) "The impact of client choice on preventive healthcare facility network design," *OR Spectrum*, **34**: 349–370.

Zhang, Y., O. Berman, P. Marcotte and V. Verter (2010) "A bilevel model for preventive healthcare network design with congestion," *IIE Transactions*, **42**(12): 865–880.

Zimmerman, S. (1997) "Factors influencing Hispanic participation in prostate cancer screening," *Oncology Nursing Forum*, **24**: 499–504.

24
SPORTS OPERATIONS MANAGEMENT
The Whole Nine Yards

David Bamford, Benjamin Dehe, Iain Reid, James Bamford, and Marina Papalexi

1 Introduction

The majority of research related to operations management in the sports industry is relatively immature and underdeveloped. This is despite the fact that the sports sector is a regular focus of study in other disciplines such as economics, tourism, sociology, and medicine. There is a lack of theory-driven sports operations management research. Most examinations on the topic are conducted in isolation and are not linked to the wider operations management theory base (Moxham et al. 2014). This is rather a missed opportunity as sports provide a potential for rich data and findings, given that it is not limited to leagues and competitions, but includes the sporting facilities sector, which incorporates gyms and pools that are offered for public usage. For example, in the US, the total fitness club-industry revenue is sizable and is estimated to be $24.2 billion per annum (Statista 2015). In addition to revenue, other benefits of sports facilities usage include lower healthcare requirements, lower crime rates, better quality of life, and contributions to social redevelopment (Taylor and Godfrey 2003). In this chapter, we seek to present the opportunity to engage in applying core operations management techniques within sports (the whole nine yards!), and to do so, we will cover three areas: i) past history, ii) present situation, and iii) future projections and opportunities. We have purposefully avoided a single sport focus; deciding to present the opportunities across a wider range of disciplines as shown in Tables 24.1 and 24.2 in which several sports are represented with references for the motivated reader to follow up on.

2 Past History

In an interesting article published in the *Journal of the Operational Research Society*, Wright (2009) reviewed "50 years of OR in sport" and highlighted four themes: i) tactics and strategy, ii) scheduling, iii) forecasting, and iv) "other". We have adapted this table and created themes that are sport specific, such as American football, basketball, cricket, etc. (shown in Table 24.1). Wright (2009) identified that most research that had been published was not highly theoretical or mathematical and that much of the research was "one off in nature", therefore making the topic somewhat incoherent and rather confused.

Table 24.1 Themes from 50 Years of OR Research in Sport

Sport	Author	Area	Theme
American Football	Silverman and Schwartz (1973)	When teams should lose on purpose	Tactics & Strategy
	Brimberg et al. (1999)	Where to place punt returners	Scheduling
	Urban and Russell (2003)	Case study—exact optimization	Tactics & Strategy
Australian Rules Football	Clarke and Norman (1998)	Giving up points for advantage	Tactics & Strategy
Badminton	Percy (2007b)	Gambling	Forecasting
Baseball	Freeze (1974)	Effect of rules changes	Other
	Hirotsu and Wright (2003)	Batting order	Tactics & Strategy
	Cooper et al. (2008)	Dynamic Programming	
	Russell and Leung (1994)	Player contribution	
	Evans et al. 1984	Case study—heuristics	Scheduling
	Evans 1988	Scheduling sports officials	
Baseball (Amateur)	Vasko (2003)	Player selection	Tactics & Strategy
Basketball	Annis (2006)	Professional fouls	Tactics & Strategy
	Nemhauser and Trick (1998)	Case study—exact optimization	Scheduling
	van Voorhis (2002)		
	Wright (2006)		
	Albright and Winston (1978)	Case study—metaheuristics	Other
Cricket	Swartz et al. (2006)	Effect of rules changes	Tactics & Strategy
	Norman and Clarke (2007)	Batting order	
	Clarke and Norman (1999; 2003)	Protecting batsmen	
	Clarke (1988)	Dynamic programming	
	Armstrong and Willis (1993)	Scoring rates	
	Willis and Terrill (1994)	Case study—heuristics	Scheduling
	Wright (1994; 2005)	Case study—metaheuristics	
	Wright (1991; 2007)		
	Duckworth and Lewis (1998)	Scheduling sports officials	
	Carter and Guthrie (2004)	Calculating the winner	Other
	Wright (1992)	Fair fixtures	

Sport	Reference	Problem	Category
Cross Sport	Elf et al. (2003)		Scheduling
	Miyashiro and Matsui (2006)	Break minimization	
	Briskorn and Drexl (2009)		
	Rasmussen and Trick (2007)		
	Duarte et al. (2007)	Scheduling sports officials	
	Easton et al. (2001)	Travelling tournament	
	Lim et al. (2006)		
	Ribeiro and Urrutia (2007)		
	Glickman (2008)	Probability of winning a knockout tournament	Other
		Tournament design	
Curling	McGarry (1998)	When to be aggressive or cautious	Tactics & Strategy
Cycling	Kostuk et al. (2001)	Route choice	Tactics & Strategy
Darts	Scarf and Grehan (2005)	Which numbers to aim for	Tactics & Strategy
	Kohler (1982)	Design of dart boards	Other
Disabled Sports	Eiselt and Laporte (1991)	Handicapping systems	Other
Golf	Percy (2007a)	Fair handicapping	Other
Horse Racing	Pollock (1974)	Gambling	Forecasting
Ice Hockey	Lo et al. (1995)	When to substitute the Goalkeeper	Tactics & Strategy
	Washburn (1991)	Case study—exact optimization	Scheduling
Long Jump	Fleurent and Ferland (1993)	How close to the take off line to aim for	Tactics & Strategy
Orienteering	Sphicas and Ladney (1977)	Route choice	Tactics & Strategy
Olympic Games	Hayes and Norman (1984)	Predicting success	Forecasting
	Condon et al. 1999		
	Heazlewood 2006		
Pentathlon	Ladany (1975b)	Optimising training schedules	Tactics & Strategy
Pole Vaulting	Ladany (1975a)	Starting height	Tactics & Strategy
	Hersh and Ladany (1989)		
Rugby Union	Thompson (1999)	Case study—tabu search	Scheduling
Running	Norman (2004)	Uphill energy needs	Tactics & Strategy
	Davey et al. (1994)	Uphill route choice	
Skating	Kuper and Sterken (2004)	Choice of clothing	Tactics & Strategy

(Continued)

Table 24.1 (Continued)

Sport	Author	Area	Theme
Soccer	Boon and Sierksma (2003)	Player contribution	Tactics & Strategy
	Sierksma (2006)		
	Wright and Hirotsu (2003)	Professional fouls	
	Hirotsu and Wright (2002)	Timing of substitutions	
	Audas et al. (2002)	When a manager should be sacked	
	Bruinshoofd and ter Weel (2003)		
	Hope (2003)		
	Tena and Forrest (2007)		
	Della Croce and Oliveri (2006)	Case study—exact optimization	Scheduling
	Bartsch et al. (2006)	Case study—heuristics	
	Biajoli et al. (2004)	Case study—metaheuristics	
	Kendall (2008)		
	Gil Lafuente (2004)	Scheduling sports officials	
	Zakarya et al. (1989)		
	Yavuz et al. (2008)		
	Dixon and Robinson (1998)	Gambling	Forecasting
	Fitt et al. (2006)		
	Flitman (2006)		
	Bennett et al. (1980)	Hooliganism	Other
	Buraimo et al. (2008)	How match attendance is effected by TV coverage	
	Saltzman and Bradford (1996)	League structures	
	Scarf and Xin (2008)	Measures of importance of a match	

Sports Facilities	Taylor and Keown (1978)	Urban planning	
Squash	Clarke and Norman (1978)	Mathematical modelling	Tactics & Strategy
	Wright 1988		
Swimming	Nowak et al. (2006)	Team selection	Tactics & Strategy
Table Tennis (Amateur)	Schonberger et al. (2004)	Scheduling fixtures	Scheduling
Tennis	Della Croce (1999)	Case study—heuristics	Scheduling
	Klassen and Magnus (2003)	Gambling	Forecasting
	Barnett and Clarke (2005)		
Volleyball	Lee and Chin (2004)	When to choose to serve	Tactics & Strategy
Weight Lifting	Lilien (1977)	What weights to choose	Tactics & Strategy
Yachting	Golding (2002)	Route choice	Tactics & Strategy
	Philpott et al. (2004)	Gambling	Forecasting

Source: Adapted from Wright 2009

From a review of Table 24.1, there is a disproportionate focus on professional sports rather than amateur sports (with only two articles being published that examined amateur sports) indicating that there is a distinct lack of research into amateur sporting activities. The vast majority of the research focuses on a single sport. Consequently, there is a lack of cross-sport or industry-wide research into the key themes identified by Wright (2009), which might provide more generic recommendations that could be of more use to practitioners. Wright also found a divide between North America and the rest of the world—as you might expect, North American journals tended only to publish articles on North American Sports such as American football (Note: to avoid confusion, the word "football" will refer to American football, otherwise "soccer" will be used), baseball, and ice hockey, and the rest of world tended to publish articles on non-American sports (e.g., soccer, cricket, darts). In addition to amateur sports, Wright identified that research focusing on sports fans and the effects of operations management on them was a potential area for future research.

Kauppi et al. (2013) conducted a robustly structured literature review that looked at what operations management research had been published with sports as the focus. The review found studies ranging from an analysis of the Olympic Games to more localized studies of fitness clubs and soccer leagues and identified nine key themes: Capacity, Layout, Forecasting, Purchasing and Supply Chain Management, Distribution, Quality, Project Management, Process Design, and Strategy. We have adapted this table and created themes that are sport specific such as basketball, golf, ice hockey, etc. This is summarized in Table 24.2. The review's results showed a field of research that had highly distinctive characteristics warranting specialist research (Chadwick 2011) yet was still largely in its infancy, with limited evidence of cumulative learning or any recognized body of knowledge.

Like Wright (2009), Kauppi et al. (2013) also observed a "scatter gun" approach to much of the research, it being rather "one-off in nature". However, there appears to be a move to broaden the focus to include health and fitness clubs, sports facilities, and resorts, as well as large and unique events such as the Olympic Games. They also identified that the following list of topics have been studied within sports: loyalty, pay equity, and structure; motivation and performance; the relationship of managerial succession to organizational performance; new product development; human resources strategy; and the resource-based view of the firm (Wolfe et al. 2005). Other research identified in the article includes public financing in building sports stadia (Baade and Matheson 2006), gambling (Sauer 2005; Forrest and McHale 2007), marketing issues such as sponsorship (Olson 2010), the effects of attitude importance (Pritchard and Funk 2010), ticket pricing, and consumer options (Sainam et al. 2010).

Kauppi et al. (2013) also observed a geographical bias in the research, agreeing with Machuca et al. (2007) who argue that not enough attention is paid in operations management journals to conduct research in significant sectors found in developing countries, such as tourism, leisure, culture, and sport. They suggest that most of the major sports operations management research is narrow in focus and coverage. This is surprising considering the effects of operations management failures in sport, particularly when this failure can be highly visible to a global audience. The key themes identified in Table 24.2 are also proposed as the areas for focus in future research, and the unique opportunities that sporting events provide for experimental research in operations management are discussed, as very few papers appear to cite both operations management and sport-focused journals, which indicates that there is a gap between the two fields. They also found that there was a lack of theory-driven sports operations management research. Here, hypotheses and causalities that are drawn from literature are tested with empirical data. They concluded by stressing the need for a wider, more theoretically based and vigorously conducted research agenda for sports operations management.

Table 24.2 Key Themes and Opportunities for Sports Operations Management Research

Sport	Author	Area	Theme
Basketball	Burden and Li (2009)	Outsourcing sport marketing	Purchasing and supply chain management
	Kelley and Turley (2001)	Evaluating quality	Quality
Elite sports	de Bosscher, et al. (2009)	Elite athletes	Strategy
Fitness clubs	Alexandris et al. (2001)	Revenue and service quality	Quality
	Chang and Chelladurai (2003) Moxham and Wiseman (2009)	Evaluating quality	
Golf	Heim and Ketzberg (2011)	Redesign	Layout
	Tesone et al. (2009)	Production systems	
		Input-transformation-output framework	Process design
	Collier and Meyer (1998; 2000)	Service system design	
Health clubs	Bodet (2006)	Repeat purchases and service quality	Quality
Ice hockey	Greenwell et al. (2002)	Customer satisfaction	Capacity
Industry-wide	Smith and Stewart (2010)	Use of technology	Distribution
	Mawson (1993)	Application of TQM	Quality
Olympic Games	Sampson (2006)	Availability and utilization of labor	Capacity
	Minis et al. (2006)	Logistics	Purchasing and supply chain management distribution
	Lowendahl (1995) Pitsis et al. (2003)	Uncertainty, complexity and uniqueness	Project management
	Beis et al. (2006)	Analysis of venue operations	Forecasting (operational planning)
Skateboarding	Kellett and Russell (2009)	Customer experience	Layout
Skiing	Pullman and Moore (1999) Pullman and Thompson (2003)	Multiple facilities	Capacity
	Davis and Heineke (1994)	Queuing	Process design
	Foster et al. (2000)	Environment vs. customer service	Strategy
Soccer	Lonsdale (2003)	Value and relationships in networks	Purchasing and supply chain management
	Cross and Henderson (2003)	Resource-based view	
	Cross and Henderson (2003)	On-field performance	Strategy
	Sampson (2006)	Availability and utilization of labour	Capacity
Sporting events	Emery (2010)	Organization of events	Strategy
Sports clubs	De Knop et al. (2004)	Evaluating quality	Quality
Sports facilities	Misener and Doherty (2009)	Organizational capacity	Capacity
	Taylor and Godfrey (2003)	Income and cost performance	
		Evaluating quality	Quality
Sports resorts	Voss et al. (2008)	Experience-centric services	Strategy
Sports services	Tsitskari et al. (2006)	What and how to measure	Quality
Surfing	Getz et al. (2001)	Service mapping	Quality

Source: Adapted from Kauppi et al. 2013

Kauppi et al. (2013) carried out a systematic literature review across operations/supply chain management and sports management journals using relevant key words and identified thirty-four papers for a small-scale co-citation analysis. As a result of this review, they found that only Chelladurai and Chang (2000), Chang and Chelladurai (2003), and Collier and Meyer (1998) were actually cited by other authors—three times, six times, and once, respectively. The first two papers focus on aspects of quality in sport services and their citation goes some way towards building a body of knowledge. However, the rather surprising lack of further co-citation across the remaining thirty-one papers suggests that the theoretical and practical transfer of knowledge within the sports OM literature is chronically underutilized. Most articles that appeared in journals classified as sport focused did not contain any references to the OM journals used in the systematic literature review, likewise most articles that appeared in the OM journals made no reference to sport journals. The existing research appears to be largely exploratory, searching for interesting phenomena and insights to report. Consequently, there is a lack of theory-driven sports operations management research where hypotheses and causalities drawn from literature are tested with data. In addition, the survey scales used in studies are not well developed and refined, as demonstrated by the very few instances of confirmatory or even exploratory factor analysis to refine scales in the papers reviewed. The lack of survey items displayed in many studies also does little to promote continuity and scale development. The review highlighted the need for a wider, more theoretically based, and rigorously conducted research agenda for sports operations management.

3 Present Situation

The majority of people all over the world have some interest in sports. They enjoy it as a participant or as a spectator (Bamford et al. 2015), and sports can be considered as a leisure activity, ceremony, celebration, or a business (Chadwick 2011). Although it benefits individuals as they can develop a healthier and higher-quality life, it provides a financial interest as well. Countries such as the UK, Canada, and Australia have increasingly allocated funds to sports activities (Houlihan 2005) and at the same time, sport has a financially intensified economy (Dutta 2015). According to Sport England (2015), the sports industry generated a Gross Value Added (GVA) of £20.3 billion, which represent about 2% of the English total. On top of the amount of the direct income earnings, sports have considerably influenced the tourism sector (Biddiscombe 2004). Sport mega-events (such as World Cups and Olympic Games) are an important reason for travelling and tourism.

According to Saltzman (2011), sports tourism accounts for 10% of the international tourism market. Therefore, the sport significant economic contribution and its popularity have attracted researchers' attention from many disciplines. There have been a number of reported papers focusing on a variety of topics, including financing of stadium construction (Baade and Matheson 2006); ticket pricing and consumer options (Sainam et al. 2010); sponsorship (Olson 2010); and the effects of attitude on performance (Pritchard and Funk 2010). However, from an operations management (OM) perspective, academic research studies still remain limited (Bamford et al. 2015). Hence, this section aims to stimulate the OM community interest and promote further engagement in this area. We will focus on the role of OM in the sports industry from a design, planning and control, and improvement perspective and examine how the OM practices can enhance the efficiency and effectiveness of sport events and clubs' processes, keeping spectators, fans, athletes, and other key stakeholders satisfied.

Moreover, the particular characteristics of the sports sector differentiate it from other industrial sectors, which have led scholars to look at this area from an OM perspective. Bamford et al. (2015) and Moxham et al. (2014) have analyzed and created a list of the sport sector's

Table 24.3 Sport Characteristics and Definitions

Sport Characteristics	Definitions	Impact
Uncertainty of on-pitch outcome	The unpredictability of outcome associated with a contest.	It can affect the perceived quality of the sporting experience and have consequences for the management of off-field operations.
Limited organizational control over the product	The product specifications, such as competition duration and format, are outside of the control of the individual sporting organization.	This limits the ability of the sporting organization to make decisions about the sports product and can restrict opportunities for differentiation.
Enforced collaboration to create competitions	Sporting rivals must collaborate to organise competitive events.	It can influence the production and delivery of the sporting event.
Significance of on-pitch performance	Winning is the most important objective for a professional club.	The on-pitch performances influence the resources of the club to manage its off-pitch processes as well as the quality perceived.
Spectator co-creation	Fans are both producers and consumers of the sporting experience.	Co-creation creates complexity for sports operations managers as fans not only purchase and consume the product, they also help to create the atmosphere which gives strength to the product.

Source: Adapted from Moxham et al. 2014

characteristics: uncertainty of outcome, limited organizational control over the product, enforced collaboration to create competitions, significance of on-pitch (on the sports field or area of play) performance, spectator co-creation—where fans are producers and consumers; these are described in Table 24.3. Moreover, it is worth mentioning that these characteristics are independent of the sport.

It seems relevant to clarify here that we are differentiating the sports environment into two distinctive parts: on-pitch and off-pitch. On-pitch refers to what happens on the field of play, inside the stadium, whereas off-pitch refers to the processes and operations outside the field of play and around the stadium. This distinction is important even if they impact each other.

These characteristics create complexity for sport managers who try to control the operations through the implementation of different tools and techniques. Therefore, this section highlights some of the practices and initiatives that we have come across and classify them into three categories: i) design of sports operations, ii) planning and control of sports operations, and iii) improvement of sports operations.

3.1 Design of Sports Operations

Generally speaking, design activity is considered to be one of the most important areas in operations management as it influences so many decisions behind the management of queuing, capacity, inventory, and quality. Sports organizations are willing to design their venues and services according to their customers and fans' demands. However, they are often limited by the type of their facilities, venues, and stadiums and the wider strategic objectives of the organization, the market, and organizational and human issues (Bamford and Forrester 2010). Therefore, designing effective and efficient operations requires the adoption of appropriate systems and often-large capital investments. Moreover, due to the nature of the sport sector, regular introduction and design of innovative new products and services is necessary. For instance, recently, Jacksonville Jaguars fans were able to enjoy watching a game while sitting in a pool inside the stadium. The club intended to attract and satisfy its fans by replacing 9,500 seats in the north end zone with a 2-level party deck including 2 pools and 16 cabanas (Jacksonville Jaguars 2014). The team's senior vice president of sales, Chad Johnson, highlighted that the team has sold 65% of the in-stadium cabanas for the 2014 season. By designing unique and innovative services, Jacksonville achieved the second-highest population turnover of an NFL city after Washington, D.C. (Jacksonville Jaguars 2014). It would be extremely relevant to identify how this design decision came up in the first place: was it an idea that emerged from the fans or was it part of the wider vision from the management team?

As part of the design activities and decision making, clubs can engage with their fans to capture and understand their requirements better in hopes of being able to translate them within the design features. However, in sport, this seems even more difficult than in other industries and this might be related to its special characteristics and nature. From our research, we have found out that the fans *co-creation* is a difficult characteristic to manage in relation to design decisions. For instance, Leigh Centurions, a Rugby club in the UK (note: Rugby is similar to American Football. It was invented in 1823 at Rugby School, England), decided to move into new facilities in 2008, a state-of-the-art stadium was designed with a total capacity of 12,500 seats to meet the current and future club's strategy. The club believed that this would inflate the home game attendance, as some study suggested (Greenwell et al. 2002); however, the average home attendance from 2008 to 2011 was of 2,222 with a high variation (standard deviation = 592) between games, and the change of stadium did not lead to the expected increase in the attendance (Bamford and Dehe 2013). It took the club longer to engage with new fans and increase attendance notably by aligning and designing an overall operations strategy around aspects of innovation, value for money, communication and marketing, and on-pitch performances. It is quite clear in this example that a mixture of the specific characteristics of sport greatly influences the outcome of a design decision, namely, the significance of on-pitch performance and spectator co-creation.

As explained in Bamford et al. (2015), clubs and sports organizations can draw from operations management concepts and models to improve the layout, queuing, process, and job design to enhance fans and spectators' throughput and optimize the service design to increase infrastructure utilization.

3.2 Planning and Control of Sports Operations

Having designed and installed a system, the sports organization needs to plan and control its activities on a day-to-day basis. An effective control of operations requires a "closed-loop" system where outputs can be compared to inputs and the differences monitored (Bamford and Forrester 2010). Planning and control activities often include scheduling, capacity control, cost control, and the management of people. In the sports industry, activities of planning and controlling have not been given much attention especially for the off-field operations.

Scheduling is one of the key challenges, and it is related to another key characteristic of sports: *the limited control over the product*. Sports teams and clubs can have limited control over the operating procedures and schedules for sporting events. Sports are subject to local, national, and international laws and external operating criteria, many of which are not present in many other industries as suggested in Moxham et al. (2014). Moreover, Bamford et al. (2015) explained that scheduling issues were also associated with a mixture of off-pitch and on-pitch decisions such as i) the availability of the resources, ii) the inability to control the weather conditions and the fixture timing, and iii) the uncertainty of the player selection.

The majority of clubs have to deal with over capacity or under capacity issues. For example, the Singapore SEA Games Organising Committee decided to implement a yield management strategy and to over-sell the tickets, which is common practice (over-issue tickets by about 5%) in order to increase the revenue generated (Sha 2015). However, on an occasion, they sold 25%–35% more tickets than the stadium's capacity, which had caused a number of problems such as unsatisfied fans waiting outside along with health and safety issues. On the other hand, Bamford (2015) stated than "most sports stadiums only use a very small percentage of the available aggregated capacity for its main purpose". He explained that "a typical football [Soccer] club will only have around 23 home games in a season which leaves plenty of empty seats for over 300 days". Sports managers, attempting to create a sustainable business model, are looking for business opportunities to use their core asset, attracting customers throughout the whole year and not only during match days. Multi-stakeholder engagement enhances clubs' financial security, introducing new activities. For example, Scunthorpe United's new soccer stadium includes a hotel gym, bar, and offices. As a result, clubs are becoming financially independent and the communities can enjoy the variety of facilities offered.

3.3   *Improvement of Operations*

Sports organizations focus on improving their operations through performance measurement. Although more attention has been put on financial measures and on measuring the on-pitch success (e.g., the winning ratio, number of goals or points per game, etc.), clubs and sports organizations acknowledge the significance of off-pitch performance measurement and its relation with OM issues (Franco-Santos et al. 2007). Hudson et al. (2001) suggested key characteristics of a successful performance management system. These included derivations from strategy, links to strategic goals, easy to maintain and relevant, clearly defined with an explicit purpose, simple to understand and use, providing fast and accurate feedback and stimulate continuous improvement.

From some of our research, we have found that clubs and sports organizations often use engagement tools and techniques such as questionnaires and surveys to capture their customers and fans' opinions, monitor these indicators against their performance management systems, identify areas for improvement and drive process improvement. For instance, Bamford and Dehe (2015) reported on a service quality study undertaken during the Paralympic Games in London 2012. They surveyed 250 athletes in order to capture their perceptions and satisfactions of the games against a framework composed of ten criteria: i) Paralympic village, ii) competition venues, iii) transport, iv) catering, v) volunteers and staff, vi) ceremonies, vii) pre-game information, viii) medical and healthcare, ix) arrival and departures, and x) anti-doping, and 73 sub-criteria. The research demonstrated that, although the athletes were delighted by the games' organization, the themes considered as the most important by the athletes did not perform the best, which led the authors to identify some areas for improvement and make recommendations for future sport mega-events. This was feedback given to the World Academy of Sport (WAoS), an organization that works in narrow collaboration with the International Paralympic Committee (IPC), which were able to develop a coherent performance picture of the 2012 Paralympics.

Moreover, Bamford and Dehe (2013) worked in collaboration with Leigh Centurions, who wanted to place the fans at the center of the club's ongoing operational and business strategy. The club needed to understand the fan base and use evidence to improve the home game attendance figures, which is often used as a key indicator for clubs. Therefore, a survey was designed for the fans (N = 511) to express their expectations in order to improve the service quality. The research contributed to informing and shaping the future operations strategy of the club. It was relevant to notice the following, on a scale from 1 to 6 (6 being the highest): "seeing a committed team with lots of fighting spirit" (mean = 5.78), "seeing an exciting and attractive game style" (mean = 5.29), and "experiencing a cheerful atmosphere in the stadium" (mean = 5.10) were the three first expectations that the respondents had. This also demonstrated the impact of the different sports' characteristics: uncertainty of outcome, enforced collaboration to create competitions, significance of on-pitch performance, and spectator co-creation. Fewer expectations were about "having entertaining activities before the game and at half time" (mean = 3.37), "having children's activities before the game" (mean = 3.26), and "having business networking opportunities" (mean = 2.50), as Table 24.4 shows.

The study also analyzed the factors and initiatives influencing attendance. From the survey as illustrated in Table 24.5, "Good value for money" (mean = 4.50), "a successful team" (mean = 4.08) and "club and players involvement in the local community" (mean = 3.97) were the primary factors that would influence home game attendance. On the other hand, "large group discount", "match day entertainment activities", and "dedicated transport to ground" were not seen as key characteristics.

For the club, evidencing these fan expectations and measuring the factors influencing attendance was extremely powerful to start establishing a baseline and setting up an improvement strategy. As part of the improvement initiatives, clubs and institutions have also engaged with different groups of stakeholders in open-ended questions such as "Are there any improvements that you would like to see implemented?" and "What do you think are the improvement priorities?". Managers and players are asked these types of questions in order to develop critical thinking and create some improvement ideas. In addition to these questions, brainstorming activities have been set up in order to trigger quality improvement initiatives. For instance, during the

Table 24.4 Fans' Expectations

Items	N	Mean	Standard Deviation
See a committed team with lots of fighting spirit	511	5.78	0.712
See an exciting and attractive game style	511	5.29	0.947
Experience a cheerful atmosphere in the stadium	511	5.10	1.092
Watch the game in a high quality stadium	511	4.98	1.222
Experience easy access to the stadium	511	4.96	1.278
Share with other fans the same passion after the game	511	4.43	1.566
Enjoy a relaxing time at the game	511	4.34	1.445
Attend a game with lot of tries	511	3.98	1.319
Spend quality time with your family	511	3.92	1.782
Have entertaining activities before the game and at half time	511	3.37	1.584
Have children's activities before the game	511	3.26	1.66
Have business networking opportunities	511	2.50	1.661

Source: Bamford and Dehe 2013

Reliability Cronbach alpha = 0.79

Table 24.5 Factors and Initiatives Influencing Attendance

Items	N	Mean	Standard Deviation
Good value for money	509	4.50	1.605
A successful team	509	4.08	1.533
Club and players involvement in the local community	507	3.97	1.681
The visiting teams reputation and quality	502	3.83	1.633
Early bird offers	504	3.66	1.891
High player profile	507	3.62	1.496
Stories on the club in the local paper	505	3.37	1.75
Family ticket discount	502	3.35	1.944
Advertising in the local paper	504	3.24	1.805
Pre- and post-game events in the village bars	503	2.94	1.684
Pre-match game	511	2.94	1.675
Large group ticket discount	504	2.79	1.861
Match day entertainment activities	509	2.78	1.619
Dedicated transport to ground	503	2.57	1.778

Source: Bamford and Dehe 2013

Reliability of the scale Cronbach's alpha = 0.92

Olympic and Paralympic games, taskforce groups were set up to reflect on i) the logistics and transportation processes, ii) the logistics in and around the venues, and iii) how to create seamless services for the athletes and the press. Another representative example of off-field operations improvement was during a triathlon where "10% of spectators who attended and participating to the event were invited to complete a survey asking a range of questions about their opinion on the quality of the catering" (Bamford et al. 2015).

Finally, a more established improvement technique used in the sports industry to improve off-pitch operations is the benchmarking. Benchmarking has been considered as one of the most widely adopted management techniques also in the sports industry. This gives organizations or clubs the opportunity to assess their current operations and compare them to the industry and/or to best practices (Rigby and Bilodeau 2009). By applying benchmarking, sports organizations have been able to identify key areas for improvement. For instance, some of the authors are currently working with a professional soccer club to optimize their sponsors' relationships and partners' portfolio. As part of this project, a benchmarking exercise is being undertaken. This allows also facilitating a knowledge transfer process and sharing best practices within the sports industry.

Based on the above analysis, it can be seen that the improvement initiatives still remain at an embryonic level when compared to other sectors, hence, this call for developing further empirical research in this area.

3.4 Data in Sports

We recognize and acknowledge the importance of on-pitch performance and its impact onto a club management. We also believe that there is substantial room for the operations management communities. Therefore, OM models could be also created for analyzing what is happening on the field of play and influencing the design, planning and control, and improvement of on-pitch processes. To do so, data collection and data analysis is critical. Without the required information it is difficult to capture the current situation and go beyond the management, coaching staff, and fans' "gut feeling". According to Bamford et al. (2015) "league tables, rankings and medal tallies add increased levels of scrutiny to sport operations". Teams have increasingly adopted analytical approaches in order to improve their on-pitch efficiency. Coaches have used data such as players' physical and mental tests to identify potential draft picks (Iansity and Snively 2015). The Baltimore Ravens hired a director of soccer analytics in 2012; during the same year, the Jacksonville Jaguars created a soccer technology and analytics group (Iansity and Snively 2015). Using advanced statistics, team managers are able to capture trends and adjust decision making in real time (Battista 2012).

Therefore, it is suggested that we use operations management and operational research models and theories in order to investigate the sport data analytics and technology utilization phenomenon that have emerged in the past five years and assess how professional clubs can enhance their learning organization and their on-pitch performances. Since 2003 and the book *Moneyball: The Art of Winning an Unfair Game,* by Michael Lewis (2003), the use of data and technology in professional clubs has been growing. The book describes "the Oakland A's' secret of success in baseball", not by the accumulation of athletic superstars, high-tech gear, or rabid fan bases, but by analyzing the mundane and banal data that had slowly been accumulated over years of competition, as Dutcher (2014) explained. However, no academic studies have yet fully demonstrated and measured its impact (Coleman 2012). Millington and Millington (2015) also suggested that the area is still very under-researched. Moreover, sports analytics, sports technologies, definitions, and uses remain very disparate between sports and within sports. It seems relevant to start shedding some light on this global phenomenon. For instance, it is well established that the use of statistics in the NBA and in the MLB leagues in the US is substantial and that the coaching staff collects real-time data during a game to make tactical changes, to the point that Ross (2015) reported "that some people say that analytics are taking the fun out of it". On the other hand, other sports such as soccer seem to be lagging behind, even if there are some applications.

As described above, operations management (OM) and operations research (OR) techniques can be used to transform the data into information and support decision makers to enhance their knowledge and optimize the design, planning and control, and improvement decisions, which will lead to increase on-pitch performances.

4 Future Projections and Opportunities

Future projections and opportunities in regards POM in sports depends upon the opportunity to use a number of elements, including the nine key themes: Capacity, Layout, Forecasting, Purchasing and Supply Chain Management, Distribution, Quality, Project Management, Process Design, and Strategy (Kauppi et al. 2013). These projections also depend upon the ability to operate in an agile and possibly opportunistic manner so as to be able to respond to market needs. Accordingly, flexible mechanisms are necessary to respond to sports environment dynamics. Wright (2009) acknowledged that sophisticated OR software will probably make further inroads into the scheduling of fixtures and officials (and possibly other things such as training facilities), not only for professionals, but also at amateur level. Meanwhile, other academics will continue to create and solve new variants of their theoretical problems. From the structured literature review by Kauppi et al. (2013), the research opportunities within the sports industry are proposed in Figure 24.1. Furthermore, flexible mechanisms are necessary to respond to sports environment dynamics. Kauppi et al. (2013) presents a conceptual framework that addresses the issue of developing POM in sports through a number of interacting factors such as the customer dynamics, business environment, technology, and supporting the dynamic characteristics of POM in sports.

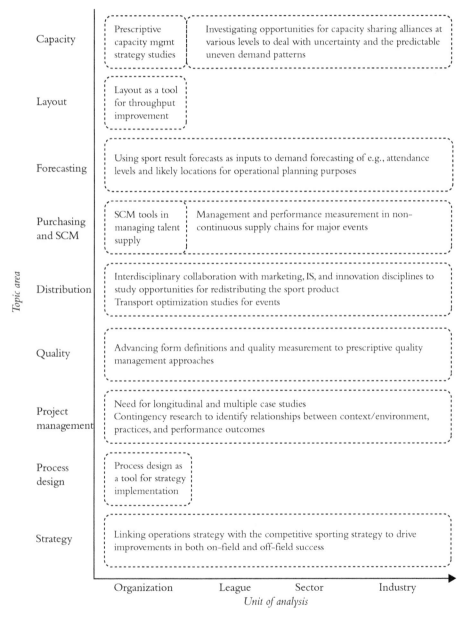

Figure 24.1 Future Research Opportunities within Sports Industry Operations Management
Source: Kauppi et al. 2013

This future proofing also needs to understand the root cause characterized by Bamford et al. (2015) and Moxham et al. (2014) as:

- Uncertainty of outcome
- Product-led industry
- Limited organizational control over the product
- Enforced collaboration to create competitions
- Significance of on-pitch performance
- Spectator co-creation, where fans are producers and consumers.

These interacting factors move to capture the lower-end market through service offerings of competition through "cost/price" or through opportunity and/or moving towards up-market and hence co-creation for which it means being "innovative" to supersede the competition by exceeding expectations. The result of the initial analysis highlights the relevant issues that such a framework needs to address in the design of sports operations, planning, and control of sports operations as well as the improvement of sports operations. A number of models and methods were conceptualized through a holistic approach to a future-proof POM in sport and an implementation approach, with a view to developing a structured framework, is proposed. In particular, an approach is proposed for strategy assessment in which the growth strategy is assessed by evaluating possible strategies.

Through extending the proposed model and developing implementation tools, it is possible to provide practical insight into the complexities of POM in sport. For example, Woratschek et al. (2014) propose a "sports value framework" (SVF) that aims to enable a better understanding of sport management phenomena and improve management decisions and the value of co-creation in sport management. In addition to these academic-focused opportunities, when the application of OM theory is adopted within the sports industry the results could lead to better-managed stadiums and competitions. This would provide a more rewarding experience for larger numbers of fans cheering on teams, players performing to the peak of their ability, and in addition, greater profitability of clubs. In addition, the selection of players would also then be based on statistical evidence rather than gut feeling by coaches and managers, moving away from the cult of personality and more towards what the Sky cycling team achieved (Moore 2013). They identified the athletes they needed on the basis of their podium potential through defined performance metrics.

4.1 Key Performance Indicators

This use of key performance indicators is taken straight from operations management theory and, when correctly applied, it has the potential to create sports services provisions that are reliable and repeatable, an application of core operations management process design and control. This will raise the fans' expectations about the level of service they should expect. For the organizers, it can make the total event experience more seamless by design. Another aspect is that operations management techniques can be used to boost playing standards, thereby providing a more rewarding spectacle. There is a direct correlation between what happens on the pitch and the spectators' experience. So the next stage is to see how we can tangibly use numbers, metrics, and business analysis to improve the on-field performance, thereby creating a virtuous circle of improvement. When we get that right, then we really will provide a missing link as glimpsed in the Michael Lewis (2003) book and the 2011 movie *Moneyball*. The film was based on the true story of the Oakland Athletics baseball team's 2002 season and their manager who achieved success by assembling a team using metrics and performance indicators. But is there a danger that sports will be robbed of its romance? No, the passion that players and athletes put into their sport can never be broken down into dry statistics. Fans watch sporting events for the unpredictability of the outcome, the emotion, and the beauty of the physical performance. Furthermore, team identification has been researched from the perspective of the consumer (Swanson and Kent 2015) in which the study proposes that employees working in professional sport may also be fans of their respective teams and provides insight on the role of team identification in the workplace environment.

4.2 Implications for Practitioners

Operations management can aid the athlete and players by ensuring they are at the right place, with the right kit, and at the right time to turn in a winning performance. We can ensure, by design, that the little details that could distract from a peak performance are minimized. Operations management has the potential to increase the satisfaction of the spectators and to facilitate the longevity and sustainability of the sports stadiums. The following is a suggested framework for applying these concepts:

- *Design*: designing an overall operations strategy around aspects of innovation, value for money, communication and marketing, and on-pitch performances, enhance fans and spectators' throughput, and optimize the service design to increase infrastructure utilization. As mentioned above, the sports industry in England generated a Gross Value Added (GVA) of £20.3 billion, and sport tourism accounts for 10% of the international tourism market (Saltzman 2011).
  - Future Focus:
    - Fan *co-creation* and capital investment, such as the case of Leigh Centurions, a Rugby League club in the UK that decided to move facilities in 2008 to meet the current and future club's strategy. NFL team the Jacksonville Jaguars achieved the second-highest population turnover of an NFL city by designing unique and innovative services (Jacksonville Jaguars 2014).
- *Planning*: scheduling issues are also associated with a mixture of off-pitch and on-pitch decisions such as i) the availability of the resources.
  - Future Focus:
    - Fan engagement increasing attendance by aligning and designing an overall operations strategy through innovation, value for money, communication and marketing, and on-pitch performances.
    - Big Data, English soccer team Manchester City FC SAP tie-up, revolutionizing both their playing and fan operations (Wilson 2015).
    - Yield management strategy to over-sell the tickets, in order to increase the revenue generated (Sha 2015).
- *Control*: ii) the inability to control the weather conditions and the fixture timing, and iii) the uncertainty of the player selection.
  - Future Focus:
    - Scheduling issues were also associated with a mixture of off-pitch and on-pitch decisions such as i) the availability of the resources, ii) the inability to control the weather conditions and the fixture timing, and iii) the uncertainty of the player selection.
    - Utilization of social media, use of technology, apps.

- *Improvements*: derivation from strategy, link to strategic goals, relevant and easy to maintain, provide fast and accurate feedback, and stimulate continuous improvement.

- Future Focus:

  - Performance measures and social impact, home game attendance figures, value, team success, involvement in the community. For example, the Paralympic Games in London 2012 proposed a framework composed of ten criteria: i) Paralympic village, ii) competition venues, iii) transport, iv) catering, v) volunteers and staff, vi) ceremonies, vii) pre-game information, viii) medical and healthcare, ix) arrival and departures, and x) anti-doping.
  - Understanding the fan base such as analyzing home game attendance figures.
  - Coaches using and analyzing players' physical and mental tests to identify potential draft picks (Iansity and Snively 2015).

For this to succeed, a calculated approach is required. This calculated approach takes into account a wider, more theoretical knowledge base emulating the research agenda for sports operations management from its operational performance and social dynamics through engagement. The aspects of POM in sports can enhance the efficiency and effectiveness of sport events, stakeholders' satisfaction, and fan loyalty through a lens of POM.

5 Conclusions

In this chapter, we have sought to present the opportunity to engage in applying core operations management techniques within sports and in doing so covered three areas: i) past history, ii) present situation, and iii) future projections and opportunities. We have tried to communicate both the prospects for engagement and the genuine excitement that exists within this dynamic sector. POM has an opportunity, and perhaps a duty to society, to provide the application of our proven and evidence based methodologies for design, planning, control, and improvement in sports operations management. It's time to "get in the game"!

References and Bibliography

Albright, S.C. and Winston, W. (1978). "A probabilistic model of winners' outs versus losers' outs rules in basketball". *Operations Research*, **26**(6): 1010–1019.

Alexandris, K., Dimitriadis, N. and Kasiara, A. (2001). "The behavioural consequences of perceived service quality: An exploratory study in the context of private fitness clubs in Greece". *European Sport Management Quarterly*, **1**(4): 280–299.

Annis, D.H. (2006). "Optimal end-game strategy in basketball". *Journal of Quantitative Analysis in Sports*, **2**(2): 1.

Armstrong, J. and Willis, R.J. (1993). "Scheduling the cricket World Cup—A case study". *Journal of the Operational Research Society*, **44**(11): 1067–1072.

Audas, R., Dobson, S. and Goddard, J. (2002). "The impact of managerial change on team performance in professional sports". *Journal of Economics and Business*, **54**(6): 633–650.

Baade, R. and Matheson, V. (2006). "Have public finance principles been shut out in financing new stadiums for the NFL?" *Public Finance and Management*, **6**(3): 284–320.

Bamford, D. (2015). "Sports stadiums—do communities and the needs of business-to-business engagement fit?" Available from: www.bqlive.co.uk/2015/05/27/sports-stadiums-do-businessesandcommunitiesbothfit/?utm_source=Room501+Ltd&utm_medium=email&utm_campaign=5712811_BQB+YK+Mon+01+Jun+2015&utm_content=sports&dm_i=1SK3,3EG17,CH4X3P,C608H,1

Bamford, D. and Dehe, B. (2013). "Servicescape in Sports: Levels of fan satisfaction in a UK Rugby League Club". I *Proceedings of 20th International Annual EurOMA Conference*, Dublin, Ireland.

Bamford. D. and Dehe, B. (2015). "Service quality at the London 2012 Games—a Paralympics Athletes Survey". *International Journal of Quality and Reliability Management*, Vol(Issue): in press.

Bamford, D. and Forrester, P. (2010). *Essential guide to operations management*. Hoboken, NJ: John Wiley & Sons.

Bamford, D., Moxham, C., Kauppi, K. and Dehe, B. (2015). "Going the distance—Sport operations management in the public and third sectors". In: Z.J. Radnor, N. Bateman, A. Esain, M. Kumar, S.J. Williams and D.M. Upton (eds), *Public service operations management: a research handbook* (pp. 13–29). Abingdon: Routledge.

Barnett, T. and Clarke, S.R. (2005). "Combining player statistics to predict outcomes". *IMA Journal of Management Mathematics*, **16**: 113–120.

Bartsch, T., Drexl, A. and Kroger, S. (2006). "Scheduling the professional soccer leagues of Austria and Germany". *Computers & Operations Research*, **33**(7): 1907–1937.

Battista, J. (2012). "More N.F.L. Teams hire statisticians but their use remains mostly guarded". *New York Times*. Available from: www.nytimes.com/2012/11/25/sports/football/more-nfl-teams-hire-statisticians-but-their-use-remains-mostly-guarded.html?_r=0.

Beis, D., Loucopoulus, P., Pyrgiotis, Y. and Zografos, K. (2006). "PLATO helps Athens win gold: Olympic Games knowledge modelling for organizational change and resource management". *Interfaces*, **36**(1): 26–24.

Bennett, P.G., Dando, M.R. and Sharp, R.G. (1980). "Using hypergames to model difficult social issues: An approach to the case of soccer hooliganism". *Journal of the Operational Research Society*, **31**(7): 621–635.

Biajoli, F.L., Souza, M.J.F., Chaves, A.A., Mine, O.M., Cabral, L.A.F. and Pontes, R.C. (2004). "Scheduling the Brazilian soccer championships: A simulated annealing approach". In: Burke, E.K. and Trick, M.A. (eds). *Fifth International Conference on the Practice and Theory of Automated Timetabling*. Pittsburgh, PA. Springer-Verlag: Berlin.

Biddiscombe, R. (2004). *Business of sport tourism*. Sport Business Group Ltd., London.

Bodet, G. (2006). "Investigation of customer satisfaction in a health club context by an application of the Tetraclasse model". *European Sport Management Quarterly*, **6**(2): 149–165.

Boon, B.H. and Sierksma, G. (2003). "Team formation: Matching quality supply and quality demand". *European Journal of Operational Research*, **148**(2): 277–292.

Brimberg, J., Hurley, W.J. and Johnson, R.E. (1999). "A punt returner location problem". *Operations Research*, **47**(3): 482–487.

Briskorn, D. and Drexl, A. (2009). "A branch-and-price algorithm for scheduling sport leagues". *Journal of the Operational Research Society*, **60**(1): 84–93.

Bruinshoofd, A. and ter Weel, B. (2003). "Manager to go? Performance dips reconsidered with evidence from Dutch football". *European Journal of Operational Research*, **148**(2): 233–246.

Buraimo B., Forrest, D. and Simmons, R. (2008). "Insights for clubs from modelling match attendance in football". *Journal of the Operational Research Society*. Advance online publication 9 January 2008, doi: 10.1057/palgrave.jors.2602549.

Burden, W. and Li, M. (2009). "Minor league baseball: exploring the growing interest in outsourced sport marketing". *Sport Marketing Quarterly*, **18**(3): 139–149.

Carter, M. and Guthrie, G. (2004). "Cricket interruptus: Fairness and incentive in limited overs cricket matches". *Journal of the Operational Research Society*, **55**(8): 822–829.

Chadwick, S. (2011). "Editorial: The distinctiveness of sport: Opportunities for research in the field". *Sport, Business and Management: An International Journal*, **1**(2): 120–123.

Chang, K. and Chelladurai, P. (2003). "System-based quality dimensions in fitness services: Development of the scale of quality". *The Service Industries Journal*, **23**(5): 65–83.

Chelladurai, P. and Chang, K. (2000). "Targets and standards of quality in sport services". *Sport Management Review*, **3**(1): 1–22.

Clarke, S.R. (1988). "Dynamic programming in one-day cricket—Optimal scoring rates". *Journal of the Operational Research Society*, **39**(4): 331–337.

Clarke, S.R (1993). "Computer forecasting of Australian Rules football for a daily newspaper". *European Journal of Operational Research*, **44**(8): 753–759.

Clarke, S.R and Norman, J.M. (1978). "What chance playing up to 10; they may be better if you think again". *The Squash Player*, July, pp 50–51.

Clarke, S.R and Norman, J.M. (1998). "When to rush a 'behind' in Australian Rules football: A dynamic programming approach". *Journal of the Operational Research Society*, **49**(5): 530–536.

Clarke, S.R. and Norman J.M. (1999). "To run or not to run? Some dynamic programming models in cricket". *Journal of the Operational Research Society*, **50**(5): 536–545.

Clarke, S.R and Norman, J.M. (2003). "Dynamic programming in cricket: Choosing a night watchman". *Journal of the Operational Research Society*, **54**(8): 838–845.

Coleman, J. (2012). "Identifying the 'Players' in Sports Analytics Research". *Interfaces*, **42**(2). Available: http://interfaces.journal.informs.org/content/42/2/109.abstract

Collier, D.A. and Meyer, S.M. (1998). "A service positioning matrix". *International Journal of Operations & Production Management*, **18**(12): 1223–1244.

Collier, D.A. and Meyer, S.M. (2000). "An empirical comparison of service matrices". *International Journal of Operations & Production Management*, **20**(6): 705–729.

Condon, E.M., Golden, B.L. and Wasil, E.A. (1999). "Predicting the success of nations at the summer Olympics using neural networks". *Computers & Operations Research*, **26**(13): 1243–1265.

Cooper, W.W., Ruiz, J.L. and Sirvent, I. (2008). "Selecting non-zero weights to evaluate effectiveness of basketball players with DEA". *European Journal of Operational Research*, **195**(2): 563–574.

Cross, J. and Henderson, S. (2003). "Strategic challenges in the football business: A SPACE analysis". *Strategic Change*, **12**: 409–420.

Davey, R.C., Hayes, M. and Norman, J.M. (1994). "Running uphill: An experimental result and its applications". *Journal of the Operational Research Society*, **45**(1): 25–29.

Davis, M. and Heineke, J. (1994). "Understanding the roles of the customer and the operation for better queue management". *International Journal of Operations & Production Management*, **14**(5): 21–34.

De Bosscher, V., De Knop, P., Van Bottenburg, M., Shibli, S. and Bingham, J. (2009). "Explaining international sporting success: An international comparison of elite sport systems and policies in six countries". *Sport Management Review*, **12**(3): 113–136.

De Knop, P., Van Hoecke, J. and De Bosscher, V. (2004). "Quality management in sports clubs". *Sport Management Review*, **7**(1): 57–77.

Della Croce, F. and Oliveri, D. (2006). "Scheduling the Italian Football League: An ILP-based approach". *Computers & Operations Research*, **33**(7): 1963–1974.

Della Croce, F., Tadei, R. and Asioli, P.S. (1999). "Scheduling a round robin tennis tournament under courts and players availability constraints". *Annals of Operations Research*, **92**: 349–361.

Dixon, M.J. and Robinson, M.E. (1998). "A birth process model for association football matches". *Statistician*, **47**: 523–538.

Duarte, A.R., Ribeiro C.C., Urrutia S. and Haeusler E.H. (2007). "Referee assignment in sports leagues". *Lecture Notes Computer Science*, **3867**: 158–173.

Duckworth, F.C. and Lewis, A.J. (1998). "A fair method for resetting the target in interrupted one-day cricket matches". *Journal of the Operational Research Society*, **49**(3): 220–227.

Dutcher, J. (2014). "Book Review: Moneyball: The Art of Winning an Unfair Game" available from https://datascience.berkeley.edu/moneyball-book-review/

Dutta, S. (2015). *English Premier League: Caught up in a sponsorship mess*. Research Centers Headquarters, Bangalore, India.

Easton, K., Nemhauser, G.L. and Trick, M.A. (2001). "The traveling tournament problem: Description and benchmarks". *Lecture Notes in Computer Science*, **2239**: 580–584.

Eiselt, H.A. and Laporte, G. (1991). "A combinatorial optimization problem arising in dartboard design". *Journal of the Operational Research Society*, **42**(2): 113–118.

Elf, M., Junger, M. and Rinaldi, G. (2003). "Minimizing breaks by maximizing cuts". *Operations Research Letters*, **31**(5): 343–349.

Emery, P. (2010). "Past, present, future major sport event management practice: The practitioner perspective". *Sport Management Review*, **13**(2): 158–170.

Evans, J.R. (1988). "A microcomputer-based decision support system for scheduling umpires in the American baseball league". *Interfaces*, **18**(6): 42–51.

Evans, J.R., Hebert, J.E. and Deckro, R.F. (1984). "Play ball—The Scheduling of sports officials". *Perspect Comput*, **4**(1): 18–29.

Fitt, A.D., Howls, C.J. and Kabelka, M. (2006). "Valuation of soccer spread bets". *Journal of the Operational Research Society*, **57**(8): 975–985.

Fleurent, C. and Ferland, J.A. (1993). "Allocating games for the NHL using integer programming". *Operations Research*, **41**(4): 649–654.

Flitman, A.M. (2006). "Towards probabilistic footy tipping: A hybrid approach utilising genetically defined neural networks and linear programming". *Computers & Operations Research*, **33**(7): 2003–2022.

Forrest, D. and McHale, I. (2007). "Anyone for tennis (betting)?". *The European Journal of Finance*, **13**(8): 751–768.

Foster, S.T. Jr, Sampson, S. and Dunn, S. (2000). "The impact of customer contact on environmental initiatives for service firms". *International Journal of Operations & Production Management*, **20**(2): 187–203.

Franco-Santos, M., Kennerley, M., Micheli, P., Martinez, V., Mason, S., Marr, B., Gray, D. and Neely, A. (2007). "Towards a definition of a business performance measurement system". *International Journal of Operations & Production Management*, **27**(8): 784–801.

Freeze, R.A. (1974). "An analysis of baseball batting order by Monte Carlo simulation". *Operations Research*, **22**(4): 728–735.

Getz, D., O'Neill, M. and Carlsen, J. (2001). "Service quality evaluation at events through service mapping". *Journal of Travel Research*, **39**: 380–390.

Gil Lafuente, J. (2004). "The best systems for appointing referees". In: Butenko, S., Gil Lafuente, J. and Pardalos, P.M. (eds). *Economics, Management and Optimization in Sports*. Springer-Verlag: Berlin, 101–120.

Glickman, M.E. (2008). "Bayesian locally optimal design of knockout tournaments". *Journal of Statistical Planning and Inference*, **138**(7): 2117–2127.

Golding, M. (2002). "Tactics and planning in round the world yacht racing". Presented at the OR Society Southern OR Group One-day Event on OR in Sport, January, Oxford, UK.

Greenwell, T.C., Fink, J.S. and Pastore, D.L. (2002). "Assessing the influence of the physical sports facility on customer satisfaction within the context of the service experience". *Sport Management Review*, **5**: 129–148.

Hayes, M. and Norman, J.M. (1984). "Dynamic programming in orienteering: Route choice and the siting of controls". *Journal of the Operational Research Society*, **35**(9): 791–796.

Heazlewood, T. (2006). "Prediction versus reality: The use of mathematical models to predict elite performance in swimming and athletics at the Olympic Games". *Journal of Sports Science and Medicine*, **5**: 541–547.

Heim, G. and Ketzenberg, M. (2011). "Learning and relearning effects within innovative service designs: An empirical analysis of top golf courses". *Journal of Operations Management*, **29**(5): 449–461.

Hersh, M. and Ladany, S.P. (1989). "Optimal pole-vaulting strategy". *Operations Research*, **37**(1): 172–175.

Hirotsu, N. and Wright, M.B. (2002). "Using a Markov process model of an association football match to determine the optimal timing of substitution and tactical decisions". *Journal of the Operational Research Society*, **53**(1): 88–96.

Hirotsu, N. and Wright, M.B. (2003). "A Markov chain approach to optimal pinch hitting strategies in a designated hitter rule baseball game". *Journal of the Operations Research Society of Japan*, **46**(3): 353–371.

Hope, C. (2003). "When should you sack a football manager? Results from a simple model applied to the English Premiership". *Journal of the Operational Research Society*, **54**(11): 1167–1176.

Houlihan, B. (2005). "Public sector sport policy: Developing a framework for analysis". *International Review for the Sociology of Sport*, **40**(2): 163–185.

Hudson, M., Smart, A. and Bourne, M. (2001). "Theory and practice in SME performance measurement systems". *International Journal of Operations & Production Management*, **21**(8): 1096–1115.

Iansity, M. and Snively, C. (2015). "Deflategate and the National Football League". The Business School. Harvard, the Case Center.

Jacksonville Jaguars (2014). "Jaguars to have poolside cabanas". Available from: http://espn.go.com/nfl/story/_/id/11055495/jacksonville-jaguars-poolside-cabanas-stadium

Kauppi, K., Moxham, C. and Bamford, D. (2013). "Should we try out for the major leagues? A call for research in sports operations management". *International Journal of Operations & Production Management*, **33**(10): 1368–1399.

Kellett, P. and Russell, R. (2009). "A comparison between mainstream and action sport industries in Australia: A case study of the skateboarding cluster". *Sport Management Review*, **12**(2): 66–78.

Kelley, S.W. and Turley, L.W. (2001). "Consumer perceptions of service quality attributes at sporting events". *Journal of Business Research*, **54**(2): 161–166.

Kendall, G.X. (2008). "Scheduling English football fixtures over holiday periods". *Journal of the Operational Research Society*, **59**(6): 743–755.

Klaassen, F.J.G.M. and Magnus, J.R. (2003). "Forecasting the winner of a tennis match". *European Journal of Operational Research*, **148**(2): 257–267.

Kohler, D. (1982). "Optimal strategies for the game of darts". *Journal of the Operational Research Society*, **33**(10): 871–884.

Kostuk, K.J., Willoughby, K.A. and Saedt, A.P.H. (2001). "Modelling curling as a Markov process". *European Journal of Operational Research*, **133**(3): 557–565.

Kuper, G.H. and Sterken, E. (2004). "Do skating suits increase average skating speed?" Working Paper, Groningen University, Netherlands. Available from www.ub.rug.nl/eldoc/ccso/200404.

Ladany, S.P. (1975a). "Optimal starting height for pole-vaulting". *Operations Research*, **23**(5): 968–978.

Ladany, S.P. (1975b). "Optimization of pentathlon training plans". *Management Science*, **21**(10): 1144–1155.

Lee, K.T. and Chin, S.T. (2004). "Strategies to serve or receive the service in volleyball". *Mathematical Methods of Operations Research*, **59**(1): 53–67.

Lewis, M. (2003). *Moneyball: The Art of Winning an Unfair Game*. W.W. Norton, New York.

Lilien, G. (1977). "Optimal weightlifting". In: Ladany, S.P. and Machol, R.E. (eds). *Optimal Strategies in Sports*. North-Holland: New York, pp 101–112.

Lim, A., Rodrigues, B. and Zhang, X. (2006). "A simulated annealing and hill-climbing algorithm for the traveling tournament problem". *European Journal of Operational Research*, **174**(3): 1459–1478.

Lo, V.S.Y., Bacon-Shone, J. and Busche, K. (1995). "The application of ranking probability models to racetrack betting". *Management Science*, **41**(6): 1048–1059.

Lonsdale, C. (2004). "Player power: Capturing value in the English football supply network". *Supply Chain Management*, **9**(5): 383–391.

Lowendahl, B.R. (1995). "Organizing the Lillehammer Olympic Winter Games". *Scandinavian Journal of Management*, **11**(4): 347–362.

Machuca, J., Gonzalez-Zamora, M. and Aguilar-Escobar, V. (2007). "Service operations management research". *Journal of Operations Management*, **25**(3): 585–603.

Mawson, L.M. (1993). "Total quality management: Perspectives for sport managers". *Journal of Sport Management*, **7**: 101–106.

McGarry. T. (1998). "On the design of sports tournaments". In: Bennett, J.M. (ed.). *Statistics in Sport*. Arnold: London, pp 199–217.

Millington, B. and Millington, R. (2015). "The datafication of everything: Toward a sociology of sport and big data". *Sociology of Sport Journal*, **32**(2): 140–160.

Minis, I., Parashi, M. and Tzimourtas, A. (2006). "The design of logistics operations for the Olympic Games". *International Journal of Physical Distribution and Logistics Management*, **36**(8): 621–642.

Misener, K. and Doherty, A. (2009). "A case study of organizational capacity in non-profit community sport". *Journal of Sport Management*, **23**(4): 457–482.

Miyashiro. R. and Matsui. T. (2006). "Semidefinite programming based approaches to the break minimization problem". *Computers & Operations Research*, **33**(7): 1975–1982.

Moore, R. (2013) *Sky's the Limit*. Harper Sport, London.

Moxham, C. and Wiseman, F. (2009). "Examining the development, delivery and measurement of service quality in the fitness industry: A case study". *Total Quality Management and Business Excellence*, **20**(5): 467–482.

Moxham. C, Bamford. D, Dehe. B. and Kauppi. K. (2014). "Well played? Examining strategy and performance in off-field sporting operations". *Proceedings of European Operations Management Association (EurOMA) Conference*, Palermo, Italy.

Nemhauser, G.L. and Trick, M.A. (1998). "Scheduling a major college basketball conference". *Operations Research*, **46**(1): 1–8.

Norman, J.M. (2004). "Running uphill: Energy needs and Naismith's rule". *Journal of the Operational Research Society*, **55**(3): 308–311.

Norman, J.M. and Clarke, S.R. (2007). "Dynamic programming in cricket: Optimizing batting order for a sticky wicket". *Journal of the Operational Research Society*, **58**(12): 1678–1682.

Nowak, M., Epelman, M. and Pollock, S.M. (2006). "Assignment of swimmers to dual meet events". *Computers & Operations Research*, **33**(7): 1951–1962.

Olson, E. (2010). "Does sponsorship work in the same way in different sponsorship contexts?". *European Journal of Marketing*, **44**(1/2): 180–199.

Percy, D.F. (2007a). "Handicapping systems for disabled Alpine skiing". In: Percy, D.F., Scarf P.A. and Robinson C.L. (eds). *Proceedings of the 1st International Conference on Mathematical Modelling in Sport*. Salford University: Salford, UK, pp 157–162.

Percy, D.F. (2007b). "A mathematical analysis of badminton scoring systems". *Journal of the Operational Research Society*, **60**: 63–71.

Philpott, A.B., Henderson, S.G. and Teimey, D. (2004). "A simulation model for predicting yacht match race outcomes". *Operations Research*, **52**(1): 1–16.

Pitsis, T.S., Clegg, S.R., Marosszeky, M. and Rura-Polley, T. (2003). "Constructing the Olympic dream: A future perfect strategy of project management". *Organization Science*, **14**(5): 574–590.

Pollock, S.M. (1974). "A model for evaluating golf handicapping". *Operations Research*, **22**(5): 1040–1050.

Pritchard, M. and Funk, D. (2010). "The formation and effect of attitude importance in professional sport". *European Journal of Marketing*, **44**(7/8): 1017–1036.

Pullman, M.E. and Moore, W.L. (1999). "Optimal service design: Integrating marketing and operations perspectives". *International Journal of Service Industry Management*, **10**(2): 239–260.

Pullman, M.E. and Thompson, G. (2003). "Strategies for integrating capacity with demand in service networks". *Journal of Service Research*, **5**(3): 169–183.

Rasmussen, R.V. and Trick, M.A. (2007). "A Benders approach for the constrained minimum break problem". *European Journal of Operational Research*, **177**(1): 198–213.

Ribeiro, C.C. and Urrutia, S. (2007). "Heuristics for the mirrored traveling tournament problem". *European Journal of Operational Research*, **179**(3): 775–787.

Rigby, D. and Bilodeau, B. (2009). "Management tools and trends". Bain & Company, 1–14.

Ross, T.F. (2015). "Welcome to Smarter Basketball: The rise of big data is pitting the old school against the new school as the NBA undergoes its analytics revolution". *The Atlantic*. Available from: www.theatlantic.com/entertainment/archive/2015/06/nba-data-analytics/396776/

Russell, R.A. and Leung, J.M.Y. (1994). "Devising a cost effective schedule for a baseball league". *Operations Research*, **42**(4): 614–625.

Sainam, P., Balasubramanian, S. and Bayus, B. (2010). "Consumer options: Theory and an empirical application to a sport market". *Journal of Marketing Research*, **47**(3): 401–414.

Saltzman, D. (2011). "Agents can score big with fans and athletes". Available from: www.travelmarketreport.com/content/publiccontent.aspx?pageID=1365&articleID=4887&LP=1 Travel Market Report, (accessed: 21st August 2013).

Saltzman, R.M. and Bradford, R.M. (1996). "Optimal realignments of the teams in the National Football League". *European Journal of Operational Research*, **93**(3): 469–475.

Sampson, S.E. (2006). "Optimization of volunteer labor assignments". *Journal of Operations Management*, **24**(4): 363–377.

Sauer, R. (2005). "The state of research on markets for sports betting and suggested future directions". *Journal of Economics and Finance*, **29**(3): 416–426.

Scarf, P. and Grehan, P. (2005). "An empirical basis for route choice in cycling". *Journal of Sports Sciences*, **23**(9): 919–925.

Scarf, P. and Xin, S. (2008). "The importance of a match in a tournament". *Computers & Operations Research*, **35**(7): 2406–2418.

Schonberger, J., Mattfeld, D.C. and Kopfer, H. (2004). "Memetic algorithm timetabling for non-commercial sport leagues". *European Journal of Operational Research*, **153**(1): 102–116.

Sha, A. (2015). "Story behind stadium gate jams—SINGSOC over-catered on seats?". The Online Citizen. Available from: www.theonlinecitizen.com/2015/06/story-behind-stadium-gate-jams-singsoc-over-catered-on-seats/

Sierksma, G. (2006). "Computer support for coaching and scouting in football". *Sports England*, **9**(4): 229–249.

Silver, N. (2014). "The search for intelligent life". ESPN.com. Available from: http://espn.go.com/espn/story/_/id/10476210/nba-mlb-embrace-analytics-nfl-reluctant-espn-magazine

Silverman, D. and Schwartz, B.L. (1973). "How to win by losing". *Operations Research*, **21**(2): 639–643.

Smith, A. and Stewart, B. (2010). "The special features of sport: A critical revisit". *Sport Management Review*, **13**(1): 1–13.

Sphicas, G.P. and Ladany, S.P. (1977). "Dynamic policies in the long jump". In: Ladany, S.P. and Machol, R.E. (eds). *Optimal Strategies in Sports*. North-Holland: New York, 101–112.

Sport England (2015). Economic value of sport in England. www.sportengland.org/research/benefits-of-sport/economic-value-of-sport/

Statista (2015). "U.S. fitness center / health club industry revenue from 2000 to 2014 (in billion U.S. dollars)". Statista—The Statistics Portal. Available from: www.statista.com/statistics/236120/us-fitness-center-revenue/ accessed 21st July 2015.

Swanson, S. and Kent, A. (2015). "Fandom in the workplace: Multi-target identification in professional team sports". *Journal of Sport Management*, **29**(4): 461–477.

Swartz, T.B., Gill, P.S., Beaudoin, D. and deSilva, B.M. (2006). "Optimal batting orders in one-day cricket". *Computers & Operations Research*, **33**(7): 1939–1950.

Taylor, B.W. and Keown, A.J. (1978). "Planning urban recreational facilities with integer goal programming". *Journal of the Operational Research Society*, **29**(8): 751–758.

Taylor, P. and Godfrey, A. (2003). "Performance measurement in English local authority sports facilities". *Public Performance and Measurement Review*, **26**(3): 251–262.

Tena, J.D. and Forrest, D. (2007). "Within-season dismissal of football coaches: Statistical analysis of causes and consequences". *European Journal of Operational Research*, **181**(1): 362–373.

Tesone, D.V., Jackson, L.A. and Fjelstul, J. (2009). "Charting production systems for golf and club operations". *Journal of Retail and Leisure Property*, **8**(1): 67–76.

Thompson, J. (1999). "Kicking timetabling problems into touch". *OR Insight*, **12**(3): 7–15.

Tsitskari, E., Tsiotras, D. and Tsiotras, G. (2006). "Measuring service quality in sport services". *Total Quality Management*, **17**(5): 623–631.

Urban, T.L. and Russell, R.A. (2003). "Scheduling sports competitions on multiple venues". *European Journal of Operational Research*, **148**(2): 302–311.

van Voorhis, T. (2002). "Highly constrained college basketball scheduling". *Journal of the Operational Research Society*, **53**(6): 603–609.

Vasko, F.J. (2003). "Play ball—Equally: Math programming lends a hand to little league baseball". *OR Insight*, **16**(2): 16–19.

Voss, C., Roth, A.V. and Chase, R. (2008). "Experience, service operations strategy, and services as destinations: Foundations and exploratory investigation". *Production and Operations Management*, **17**(3): 247–266.

Washburn, A. (1991). "Still more on pulling the goalie". *Interfaces*, **21**: 59–64.

Willis, R.J. and Terrill, B.J. (1994). "Scheduling the Australian state cricket season using simulated annealing". *Journal of the Operational Research Society*, **45**(3): 276–280.

Wilson, B. (2015). "Manchester City's data-driven vision for players and fans". BBC online, available from: www.bbc.co.uk/news/business-33277924.

Wolfe, R., Weick, K., Usher, J., Terborg, J., Poppo, L., Murrell, A., Rukerich, J., Core, D., Dickson, K. and Simmons, J. (2005). "Sport and organizational studies: Exploring synergy". *Journal of Management Inquiry*, **14**(2): 182–210.

Woratschek, H., Horbel, C and Popp, B. (2014). "The sport value framework—a new fundamental logic for analyses in sport management". *European Sport Management Quarterly*, **14**(1): 6–24.

Wright, M.B. (1988). "Probabilities and decision rules for the game of squash rackets". *Journal of the Operational Research Society*, **39**(1): 91–99.

Wright, M.B. (1991). "Scheduling English cricket umpires". *Journal of the Operational Research Society*, **42**(6): 447–452.

Wright, M.B. (1992). "A fair allocation of county cricket opponents". *Journal of the Operational Research Society*, **43**(3): 195–201.

Wright, M.B. (1994). "Timetabling county cricket fixtures using a form of tabu search". *Journal of the Operational Research Society*, **45**(7): 758–770.

Wright, M.B. (2005). "Scheduling fixtures for New Zealand Cricket". *IMA Journal of Management Mathematics*, **16**(2): 99–112.

Wright, M.B. (2006). "Scheduling fixtures for Basketball New Zealand". *Computers & Operations Research*, **33**(7): 1875–1893.

Wright, M.B. (2007). "Case study: Problem formulation and solution for a real-world sports scheduling problem". *Journal of the Operational Research Society*, **58**(4): 439–445.

Wright, M.B. (2009). "50 years of OR in sport". *Journal of the Operational Research Society*, **60**(1): 161–168.

Wright, M.B. and Hirotsu, N. (2003). "The professional foul in football—Tactics and deterrents". *Journal of the Operational Research Society*, **54**(3): 213–221.

Yavuz, M., Inan, U.H. and Figlah, A. (2008). "Fair referee assignments for professional football leagues". *Computers & Operations Research*, **35**(9): 2937–2951.

Zakarya, Z., Hertz, A. and de Werra, D. (1989). "Un systeme informatique pour les calendriers d'arbitrage d'une association sportive". Report of the Department de mathematiques, Ecole Polytechnique Federate de Lausanne, Switzerland.

25
POM IN AGRICULTURE
Pastoral Farming in New Zealand

David Gray and Nicola M. Shadbolt

1 Introduction

The Maori word for New Zealand is *Aotearoa*, and a literal translation of the term is "the land of the long white cloud". This sets the context for this chapter as those familiar with farming will know that clouds (rain or imminent rain) are excellent for forage production and pastoral farming. They're not so good for crop production. So, pasture as forage is New Zealand's dominant crop, and it provides the feed input to dairy, sheep, beef, deer, and goat producers.

From a POM perspective, the challenges created by livestock farming are universal with respect to livestock inventory (this inventory that can age, die, and reproduce). However, with pastoral farming systems, it is the input inventory that has its unique challenges. Determining how much feed is available is the first challenge as that is a factor of pasture growth rates that is affected by rainfall, soil temperature, and previous management of the sward. Planning for feed to match the known demand from breeding and finishing livestock is, therefore, fraught with uncertainty and requires a wide range of contingency plans in case the feed is either not there or there in abundant quantities at diminishing quality. This chapter takes a specific focus on feed inventory management in order to illustrate the challenges to POM that exist in pastoral farming and the methods that New Zealand farmers use to overcome them.

2 Normative Versus Descriptive Research

Management can be studied from two viewpoints in the context of farming: normative and descriptive (Ilbery 1978). Normative studies seek to determine how a rational person would make decisions in a given situation and to provide prescriptive advice on how best to make decisions. Normative research on the management and decision-making processes dominated the farm management literature through until the 1990s (Jacobsen 1993; Ohlmer et al. 1998; Rougoor et al. 1998). During this time, numerous authors have argued that greater emphasis should be placed on descriptive research and that until this occurs, and the gap between theory and practice is closed, farmers will continue to view much of the farm management research as irrelevant (Ohlmer 1998; Rougoor et al. 1998; Nuthall 1999). For example, Nielson (1961) was concerned that much of the theory in farm management was based on agricultural economics and that this had resulted in a largely normative research approach, that is, the focus was on what managers *ought to do*, rather than what they *actually do*.

Despite this and other similar criticisms (Johnson 1963; Burns 1973; Jackson 1975; Nix 1979; Andison 1989; Malcolm 1990) made throughout the history of the discipline, it is only within the last few decades that the processes used by farmers to make management decisions has been researched (e.g., Jacobsen 1993; Ohlmer 1998; Rougoor et al. 1998; Nuthall 1999). Although the early descriptive work of Johnson et al. (1961) challenged some of the normative views of management at the time, the impact of this study on United States agriculture was not great. In fact, farm management research in the United States has remained predominantly normative in nature. In contrast, European researchers developed this area through the 1990s (Attonaty and Soler 1991; Cerf et al. 1993; Fleury et al. 1996; Aubry et al. 1998; Ohlmer et al. 1998). This more recently emerged descriptive research into farm management has enriched the discipline and some of the research in this area in relation to tactical management is described in the following sections in relation to pastoral farming in New Zealand.

In the following sections, the tactical management processes used by pastoral-based livestock farmers is described and compared with the literature, both normative and descriptive. The planning processes used by farmers are discussed. The product of farmers' planning processes, the plan, and its components: goals, predictive schedule of events, targets, and contingency plans are compared with other reported research. Aspects of the control process that are compared with the literature include the monitoring process, decision point recognition, diagnosis, and control response selection.

3 Tactical Management Process

The tactical management process used by farmers can be represented as a cyclical process of planning, implementation, and control, in much the same manner as proposed by Barnard and Nix (1979) and Boehlje and Eidman (1984). While the process is cyclic, planning decisions are made irregularly (Figure 25.1), and the ratio of implementation to control decisions is a function of the level of uncertainty in the environment. This model is more useful than the decision-making model (Hardaker et al. 1970; Osburn and Schneeberger 1983; Kay 1981; Boehlje and Eidman 1984), which fails to capture the importance of management control. The model reported here is similar to those reported in the descriptive tactical management literature (Cerf et al. 1993; Fleury et al. 1996; Aubry et al. 1998). In essence, farmers have a plan, implement it, and then use control decisions or "*regulations*" (Aubry et al. 1998) to manage deviations from the plan due to uncertainty in the environment.

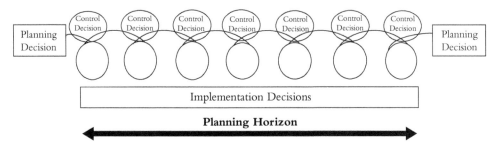

Figure 25.1 Representation of the Tactical Management Process Used by Farmers from a Decision-Making Perspective

Source: Adapted from Gray 2001

As proposed by Simon (1960) and Gorry and Morton (1971), the tactical decisions made by farmers are predominantly "structured" in nature. It was only under extreme conditions or where a new input or management practice was used that farmers use less structured decision-making processes. In these instances, rather than automatically drawing on their heuristics to select a plan or control response, farmers either undertake a less "structured" planning process, or in the case of control decisions, diagnostic and/or evaluation processes are used that lead to learning and the introduction of a new control response. These "unstructured" decisions are analogous to Scoullar's (1975) problem-solving process that he proposed managers would use in novel situations, where a knowledge, rather than a performance gap existed.

Little useful information is provided in the normative literature on how to determine the planning horizon for a particular plan. Other than suggesting that tactical plans should have shorter planning horizons than strategic plans (Wright 1985), the literature suggests that decisions on the planning horizon be left to the manager's judgement (Reisch 1971; Hanf and Schiefer 1983; Wright 1985). Hanf and Schiefer (1983) also highlighted the trade-off that occurs between reducing uncertainty and lessening the manager's appreciation of longer-term consequences as the planning horizon is shortened.

Both the criteria used for setting their planning horizons, and the means by which the problem of interdependency and consequences was overcome, has been identified for farmers. A farmer's planning horizon primarily reflects seasonal changes in the physiological state of the pastures, the balance between pasture growth and livestock feed demand and the goals associated with these changes. Similar results were reported by Mathieu (1989), who found that on a French pastoral farm in the Jura Mountains, the year could be separated into three phases on the basis of relative pasture growth rates, which are a function of the physiological status of the sward and the climate. Other descriptive studies (Gladwin 1979; Cerf et al. 1993; Siddiq and Kundu 1993) have reported the importance of climate to the annual calendar of operations adopted by farmers, but they have not discussed this in relation to planning horizons.

Some farmers also used a critical event, calving, to reduce the length of their mid-year planning horizon and simplify the planning process. Proximity to a critical event (e.g., drying off) also influences farmers' choice of the plan termination date. Because farmers' planning horizons are primarily a function of seasonal changes in the feed balance, each period has different goals and associated tasks for achieving these goals. Similarly, Cerf et al. (1993) reported that farmers separated the year into different periods according to the tasks required for production. For farmers, extreme climatic conditions (dry spring, early autumn rains) that shifted the seasonal change-point, precipitated modifications to their planning horizons. A strategic decision such as changing farms could also prompt a change in planning horizon.

Farmers have developed a simple means of overcoming the problem of interdependency and consequences (Reisch 1971; Kennedy 1974; Hanf and Schiefer 1983). Within the plan, they set terminating targets that specified the farm's state at the end of each planning horizon. These terminating targets are designed to ensure optimum system performance, *ceteris paribus*, in the next planning period. The targets are selected on the basis of the farmer's knowledge of cause-and-effect relationships in system performance and ensured short-term gains were not obtained in the current planning period at the expense of longer-term production.

Rather than undertake a full planning process at regular intervals, farmers developed a plan at the start of each planning period and then used the control process to cope with uncertainty. This achieved the same outcome as the rolling planning process (Kennedy 1974; Hanf and Schiefer 1983) but reduced the input required by farmers. Plans are revised, but on an irregular basis in response to strategic decisions, extreme conditions, or the imminence of a critical decision (e.g., drying off).

Previous authors' (Kennedy 1974; Jolly 1983; Wright 1985; Parker 1999) criticism of the farm management discipline's focus on planning to the detriment of control is well supported by empirical research into farmer practice. Farmers spend limited time on tactical planning, instead relying on control in order to cope with uncertainty in the environment. These findings support the view of Wright (1985) and Kaine (1993) that in situations where uncertainty is high, greater emphasis will be placed on control relative to planning. The interdependence of planning and control (Anthony 1965) was demonstrated by Gray (2001) who identified that important components of his case farmers' plans were essential for control: these were their targets (or standards) and associated contingency plans and decision rules. A case farmer is the farmer that was investigated during a case study.

3.1 The Planning Process

Farmers in New Zealand have been found to use either (i) "informal and qualitative" or (ii) "formal and quantitative feed budgeting" approaches to planning. Other farmers have been found to alternate between the two (Gray et al. 2003). Most of the literature has tended to identify farmers as using one approach or the other. The work of Gladwin (Gladwin and Murtaugh 1980; Gladwin and Butler 1984) and that of the French (Mathieu 1989; Cerf et al. 1993; Fleury et al. 1996; Aubry et al. 1998) suggested that farmers used an informal qualitative heuristic-based planning approach. Other studies (Jacobsen 1993; Ohlmer et al. 1998; Catley et al. 2000) also found that the majority of farmers used an informal qualitative approach and that few developed formal written plans for their farms. Similarly, survey research (Parker et al. 1993; Nuthall 1996; Nuthall and Bishop-Hurley 1999) has tended to report on the use—or non-use—of formal quantitative planning approaches by farmers. However, this research has not explored the transition from one approach to the other. The other interesting point was that, although budgeting is widely recognized in the discipline as an important planning aid for resource allocation (Barnard and Nix 1979; 1983; Osburn and Schneeberger 1983; Kay and Edwards 1994), to the point that Boehlje and Eidman (1984) referred to it as a "fundamental planning tool", it was only used for part of the year by high-performing farmers in a study by Gray et al. (2003). During the spring and summer, farmers in the study by Gray et al. (2003) argued that they perceived no additional benefit to formal planning, particularly given the high level of uncertainty over this period relative to what they currently did. Rather, the additional planning and pasture measurement would incur additional time costs.

3.1.1 Informal Planning Process

Similar to the process described in several other studies (Gladwin and Murtaugh 1980; Gladwin and Butler 1984; Mathieu 1989; Cerf et al. 1993; Fleury et al. 1996; Aubry et al. 1998), New Zealand pastoral farmers use a predominantly informal, qualitative, and heuristic-based planning process. However, as seen in Figure 25.2, some important differences were identified. The "typical" plan was modified in response to prior learning, a form of historical control, previously made strategic and "atypical" tactical decisions, and the state of the farm at the start of the planning period. The state of a farm at the start of a planning period can have a major influence on the structure of a farmer's plan (Figure 25.2). For example, at the start of the summer in a study by Gray (2001), the state of the farm was quantified in terms of the pasture, supplement, forage crop, and herd resources. If the farm state was fairly typical for that time of year, then the "typical" plan was implemented. This process was largely subconscious. However, if the farm state was significantly different from normal for that time of year (e.g., due to drought), the case farmers

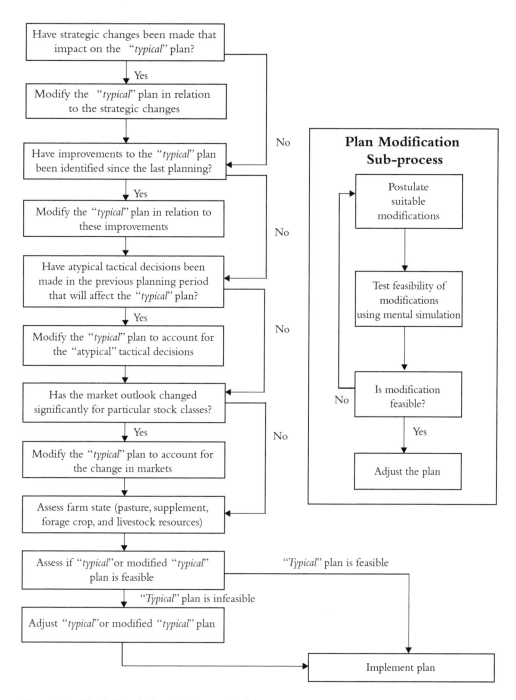

Figure 25.2 The Informal Planning Process Used by Farmers
Source: Gray 2001

knew that their typical plans would not be feasible. In this situation, they proposed some changes to the plan in relation to their planning heuristics (sequence and timing of events, level, and type of inputs, and target selection) so that their summer goals for the plan would be met. A mental simulation was then run to test the efficacy of the changes. If the adjusted plan proved feasible, it was implemented. If not, further changes were investigated. Sometimes this iterative process was completed over several days. The time taken was dependent on the nature of the farm state and the severity of the changes required to achieve the summer goals. This problem was compounded if a major change to the typical plan had already been made due to strategic or historical control reasons. A more formal quantitative approach to planning was used in such situations. These results suggest that farmers have a broadly defined set of conditions within which their "typical" plan is robust, but if conditions fall outside this range, the plan is modified.

Gray (2001) reported that the planning process used by the farmers in his study for a "typical" year was largely subconscious or "pre-attentive" (Gladwin and Butler 1984) and as such, it avoided the cognitive effort and stress involved in more formal planning (Gladwin and Murtaugh 1980; Gladwin and Butler 1984). This finding supports the views of Simon (1960) as well as Gorry and Morton (1971) that effort declines as decisions become more structured and that this structuredness eventuates from the repetitive nature of the decisions, a factor more likely to occur at the tactical and operational than the strategic level of decision making.

3.1.2 Formal Planning Process

The "expert" farmers in Gray's (2001) study changed from an informal qualitative to a formal quantitative planning approach in autumn. In the literature, however, farmers have been classified as either using or not using formal quantitative planning approaches rather than both (Parker et al. 1993; Nuthall 1996; Ohlmer et al. 1998; Nuthall and Bishop-Hurley 1999). A relatively simple planning aid, a feed budget, provided assistance to the planning process but required a series of "pre-decisions" to be made, as also described by Reisch (1971), before the mechanical process of computation began. It also highlights why Wright (1985) distinguished the cognitive process a manager undertakes when developing a plan from the use of planning aids. The effective use of planning aids depends upon the user's knowledge of the planning process and their production system. Someone with limited knowledge and experience of pastoral systems (a novice) would struggle to use a simple feed budget effectively.

The farmers in Gray's (2001) study believed that the feed budget enhanced a manager's planning process and resultant plan. Given the importance of the planning period in this study, the low capital and time cost (up to one hour), and the usefulness of the planning aid, the low adoption rate of formal feed budgeting by New Zealand pastoral farmers (Parker et al. 1993; Nuthall 1996; Nuthall and Bishop-Hurley 1999) is surprising. This is especially so, given Wright's (1985) belief that planning effort is proportional to the perceived net benefit from planning. However, there is another cost associated with formal feed planning, and that is the need for a two to three-hour pasture walk every five to fourteen days for control purposes. This increases the "cost" when compared to the much quicker informal visual assessment practiced by farmers. Survey data supports farmers' preference for non-formal approaches, with the most important reason given for non-adoption being the time requirements of formal feed planning and monitoring (Nuthall and Bishop-Hurley 1999).

In the study by Gray (2001), the farmers had a good understanding of the likely range of conditions they could expect. Contingency plans were "stored" mentally as could be expected given the tactical nature of the plans and the expertise of the case farmers. Other studies (Gladwin and Murtaugh 1980; Gladwin and Butler 1984; Mathieu 1989; Cerf et al. 1993; Fleury et al.

1996; Aubry et al. 1998) have also reported that farmers have pre-defined contingency plans, which are activated when conditions deviate from the plan as proposed by Boehlje and Eidman (1984). Importantly, farmers have contingency plans to deal with both upside and downside risk and they tend to rank them in terms of priority of use (as seen in Table 25.1) (Gray et al. 2006).

The farmers in Gray's (2001) study used the final step in the formal planning process, the modification of plans in the light of control results (Barnard and Nix 1979; Boehlje and Eidman 1984), during both the summer and autumn to cope with uncertainty. Several authors (Reisch 1971; Kennedy 1974; Hanf and Schiefer 1983; Jolly 1983; Boehlje and Eidman 1984; Wright 1985) have argued that control and plan revision are important because of the dynamic nature of the planning process. Results from other similar studies (Mathieu 1989; Cerf et al. 1993; Fleury et al. 1996; Aubry et al. 1998) support this view. The case farmers in Gray's study (2001) did not formally analyze or account for risk in their planning procedures. For example, as reported by researchers such as Gladwin (1989) and Ohlmer et al. (1998), these farmers did not use probabilities to assess the level of risk associated with alternative plans. One farmer used conservative pasture growth rates to provide some flexibility, and both case farmers retained silage (maize or grass) in reserve to cope with extreme conditions. Risk was mainly managed through the farmers' control process. A wide choice of options provided them with the flexibility to cope with deviations from the plan.

In a study of an expert sheep and cattle farmer, Gray et al. (2006) found that the farmer uses an iterative feed planning process to develop the feed plan (as seen in Figure 25.3). The process begins in January when the farmer determines which areas will be allocated to sheep and cattle for the spring. The cattle are allocated the easier contour country and the sheep the steeper country. The farmer decides, on the basis of the performance of these blocks over the last twelve months, whether they are growing more grass than in the past. If he thinks the blocks are producing more pasture, he will adjust the spring stocking rate accordingly for each stock class. For example, in year one of the study, the farmer believed his cattle country was growing

Table 25.1 Contingency Plans for Dealing with Winter Feed Problems

Feed	Deficit	Feed	Surplus
Reduce Feed Demand	*Increase Feed Supply*	*Increase Feed Demand*	*Reduce Feed Supply*
1. Reduce intake of R2yr bulls	1. Feed balage reserve	1. Increase ewe intakes	1. Reduce urea application
2. Place R2yr bulls in the pine plantation	2. Feed forage crop earlier	2. Increase hogget intakes	
3. Reduce dry hogget intake	3. Apply urea early	3. Increase R1yr bull intakes	
4. Sell 100 "surplus" dry hoggets	4. Apply additional urea	4. Increase thin R2yr cattle intakes	
5. Reduce single-bearing ewe intakes late winter		5. Buy cattle in earlier	
6. Reduce intake of tail end R1yr bulls		6. Buy in additional cattle	
7. Sell R2yr cattle			

Source: Gray et al. 2006

more pasture than in the past and as a result, he decided to increase his cattle stocking rate by 0.8–1.0 csu/ha (cattle stock unit per hectare). If the farmer does not believe the blocks are producing more pasture than normal, he will use the same spring stocking rate as in the previous year.

Once the block area and stocking rates are determined, the farmer calculates, given his desired ratio of older to younger cattle, how many cattle he can winter (Figure 25.3). He then estimates the likely lambing percentage for the ewes based on their current live weight relative to historical data and expected feed conditions through autumn. This information is then used

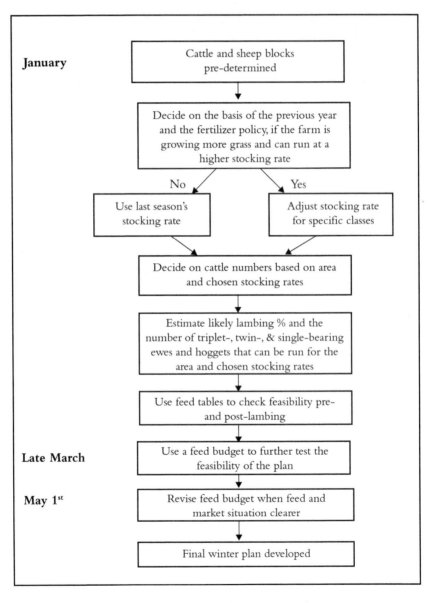

Figure 25.3 The Feed Planning Process Used to Develop the Winter Plan
Source: Gray et al. 2006

to estimate the proportion of triplet-, twin-, and single-bearing ewes that would be on-hand at set stocking ten days prior to the start of lambing. From this, given his stocking rate assumptions and the allocated sheep area, the farmer works out how many sheep he can winter. The feasibility of this initial plan is then tested by estimating the feed demand of each stock class from set stocking to lambing and then from lambing to balance date to determine if the expected pasture growth rates will be sufficient to match feed demand and meet the pasture cover targets for balance date (Figure 25.3). If the plan does not appear feasible, adjustments will be made to stock numbers.

In the next step in the process (Figure 25.3), the farmer completes a formal feed budget (using an Excel spreadsheet developed by a local consultant) for the period late March to balance date in late September to further test the feasibility of the plan and estimate the level of average pasture cover required at May 1st to make the plan work. If the plan is not feasible because there is an insufficient amount of feed on-hand, alternative plans using additional nitrogen or delaying the purchase of cattle in late winter and early spring are investigated. If the plan suggests surplus feed is available, the farmer will investigate options such as retaining cattle for longer before sale and/or reducing autumn nitrogen inputs. On May 1st, when the farmer has a clearer idea of the feed and market situations, the feed budget is revised. The outcome from the planning process, the plan, is discussed next.

4 The Plan

The "typical" or "modified typical" plan used by the farmers comprised a set of heuristics that determined the activities, their sequence and timing, the type and level of inputs, and the intermediate targets in the plan (Gray et al. 2003). In effect, they reflect the cognitive processes farmers have to undertake to develop their "typical" plan over time. Wright (1985) believed that these cognitive processes are central to planning. The heuristics used for planning by farmers could be classified into the categories identified by Aubry et al. (1998): sequencing, activation and termination or time range, arbitration, and mode establishment decision rules. The sequencing rules could be further subdivided into obligatory and non-obligatory heuristics. Similarly, the mode establishment decision rules could be separated into type, level, and combination of input determining heuristics. Limited evidence of grouping rules (Aubry et al. 1998) was found in the study by Gray (2001). Unlike cropping (e.g., Aubry et al. 1998), and the more diverse alpine pastoral livestock farms (e.g., Fleury et al. 1996), the case farmers tended to treat their paddocks as homogenous entities over the summer-autumn in the study by Gray (2001). Target selection heuristics, not identified by Aubry et al. (1998) were used by farmers to select intermediate and terminating targets for control purposes.

Farmers' knowledge of cause and effect relationships within the production system and the short- and long-term consequences of their actions formed the basis for the development of planning heuristics (Gray 2001). This corresponds with Papy's (1994) view that interaction occurs between a farmer's knowledge model and their plan (action model) and that this interaction is two-way. The planning heuristics used by farmers appears to be based on the economic principle of marginality (Gray 2001), that is, they will adjust inputs to the point at which marginal cost of the inputs equals the marginal value of the outputs they create. Similar results were reported by Jacobsen (1993). As with Aubry et al. (1998), the priority of resource use within the farmers' plans in Gray's (2001) study was based on the criteria of "impact on final yield". However, the farmers were considering the effect, not only in terms of impact on the current, but also next season's milk yield, where next season's yield had priority. A farmer's concern for longer-term productivity was also reported by Buxton and Stafford Smith (1996).

The planning heuristics identified by Aubry et al. (1998) make explicit the important planning decisions a farmer must make. These include:

- What activities should be included in the plan?
- How should the activities be sequenced?
- When should an activity be activated and terminated?
- What inputs, or combination of inputs should be used?
- What level of inputs should be used?
- What targets should be set to control the implementation of the plan?

Making these cognitive processes associated with planning explicit enables farmers to reflect on the structure of their own plan and to compare this with those of others. It also provides researchers with a basis for understanding and comparing farmers' plans, as illustrated by the focus of the French work (Mathieu 1989; Cerf et al. 1993; Fleury et al. 1996; Aubry et al. 1998).

The plans used by farmers contain five important components: the goals for the planning period, a predictive schedule of events, a set of targets for controlling the implementation of

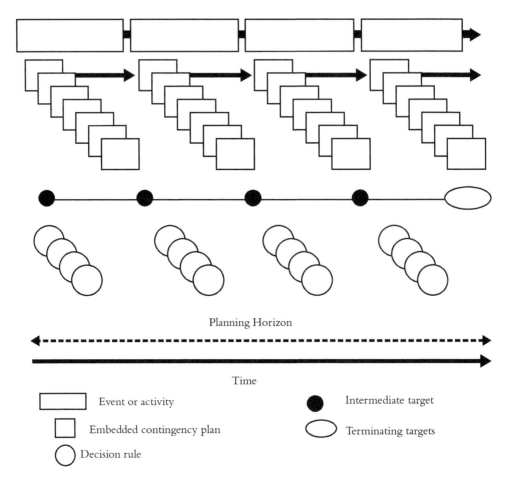

Figure 25.4 A Diagrammatic Representation of a Farmer's Plan
Source: Gray 2001

the plan, a rich set of contingency plans that could be implemented if a deviation from the plan occurred, and a set of decision rules that are used in conjunction with the targets to implement the plan, or if a deviation occurs, implement a suitable contingency plan (as seen in Figure 25.4).

This structure in Figure 25.4 is identical to those reported from several other studies (Gladwin and Murtaugh 1980; Gladwin and Butler 1984; Gladwin et al. 1984; Mathieu 1989; Cerf et al. 1993; Fleury et al. 1996; Aubry et al. 1998) although the terminology is different in several instances. The French (Sebillotte 1993; Papy 1994) referred to the plan as a "cognitive action model". Sebillotte (1993) described this as a representation of "the mental image a farmer has of the actions required to attain certain objectives". Gladwin (Gladwin and Murtaugh 1980; Gladwin and Butler 1984) referred to the plan as a "predefined plan" or "script". Both identified goals, a predictive schedule of events, and an associated set of intermediate targets as important components of farmers' tactical plans. Neither made reference to contingency plans. Gladwin (Gladwin and Murtaugh 1980; Gladwin and Butler 1984) called these "embedded sub-plans" and found that farmers used decision rules to determine whether to implement the plan, or one of the "embedded sub-plans". In contrast, the French (Mathieu 1989; Cerf et al. 1993; Fleury et al. 1996; Aubry et al. 1998) coined the term "regulations", which incorporates both the decision rules and the contingency plans.

Implicit within the literature are the components one would expect in a plan. For example, Boehlje and Eidman (1984) discuss the process of planning and mention the need to clarify goals, set out procedures, define targets, and develop contingency plans. However, the nature of what exactly a plan should comprise is not discussed. This is one of the criticisms raised by Reisch (1971) and Wright (1985) of the planning literature in farm management. In the following sections, the components of farmers' plans that are important for achieving the goals of the planning period are discussed and compared with the literature.

4.1 *The Predictive Planning Schedule*

Farmers have a "typical" plan that contains a predictive planning schedule of the events or activities to be undertaken to achieve targets (Gladwin and Murtaugh 1980; Gladwin and Butler 1984; Mathieu 1989; Cerf et al. 1993; Fleury et al. 1996; Aubry et al. 1998). Five factors influenced the nature of a farmers' predictive planning schedule and these accounted for between-year and across-farmer differences: values, strategic decisions, learning, prior tactical decisions, and the state of the farm at the start of the planning period. Values influenced the farmers' strategic choices, which in turn influenced the structure of the predictive planning schedule. Other authors have reported the influence of values (Gasson 1973) and attitudes towards intensification (Fleury et al. 1996) on farmers' plans. Gray (2001) found that over a three-year period, one farmer's predictive planning schedules diverged considerably, primarily as a result of strategic decisions designed to increase feed inputs over the summer-autumn. In contrast, another farmer was prevented from pursuing this approach by his "low-input" philosophy. Through learning (Aubry et al. 1998), new or improved management practices are identified by farmers and introduced into their predictive planning schedules. Prior tactical decisions also influenced the predictive planning decision. The state of the farm at the start of the planning period could precipitate changes to the "typical" plan.

Farmers' predictive planning schedules have inherent flexibility. Although some activities in a farmer's plan are date specific (e.g., pregnancy testing, sowing new grass), the timing of most activities is specified by condition-dependent heuristics. The latter reduced the need for plan revision in response to changing conditions, i.e., if conditions were below average, the heuristic triggered the next event in the plan earlier. Similar results have been found in other descriptive studies (Mathieu 1989; Cerf et al. 1993; Fleury et al. 1996; Aubry et al. 1998).

4.2 Targets

The third component of a farmer's plans is their targets (or standards) (Figure 25.5). These were used in two main ways: first to trigger the implementation of the activities specified in the plan and second to identify when the implementation deviated from the plan. In the latter case, suitable contingency plans were adopted to minimize the impact of the deviation. This is the same as the role attributed to targets in the normative (Barnard and Nix 1979; Kay 1981; Boehlje and Eidman 1984; Kay and Edwards 1994; Parker 1999) and descriptive literature (Mathieu 1989; Fleury et al. 1996; Aubry et al. 1998) although the former tend to only mention their role in relation to deviations from the plan.

As seen in Figure 25.5, a novel typology of target types was developed from a study by Gray (2001). Two main types of targets were used in tactical management: terminating and intermediate. The former were specified at the end of a planning period and acted as "sustainability" constraints in much the same way as Barnard and Nix (1979) described for "husbandry" constraints. In contrast, intermediate targets were applied between the start and end of the planning horizon. Mathieu (1989), Fleury et al. (1996), and Aubry et al. (1998) identified these as intermediate objectives. They can be separated into three types: benchmark dates, milestones, and thresholds. Benchmark dates specify the date at which a certain activity or event must be implemented. Milestones, on the other hand, are projected steps on the way to a final terminating target, for example, intermediate average pasture cover targets. Threshold targets, if exceeded, trigger an activity or event. Aubry et al. (1998) mentioned that farmers used dates and "states of progress of work" to activate events within the plan, or contingency plans, but did not place these in a typology. Mathieu (1989) separated intermediate objectives into production, animal requirement, and forage state targets. She also described "regulations" to adjust forage regrowth speed, and forage regrowth duration, but did not mention targets or objectives for these factors. Intermediate targets were identified for production, animal requirements, forage state, climatic events, and

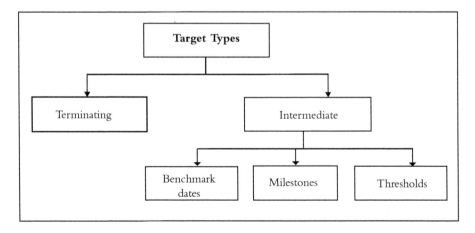

Figure 25.5 A Typology of Target Types
Source: Gray 2001

regrowth duration (rotation length). These had associated benchmark date targets. Some of these can be viewed as sub-categories of the "milestone" and "threshold" categories.

Intermediate targets had three roles: controlling the implementation of the plan, ensuring the terminating targets were met, and optimizing system performance. Except for the first, little mention is made of other roles in the literature, although the third role is often implied (e.g., Parker 1999). Targets changed from one planning period to the next (Gray 2001). Thus, milk production was the primary target for summer, while average pasture cover took over this role in the autumn plan (Gray 2001).

Many of the targets used by farmers are flexible. As Fleury et al. (1996) notes, they could be adjusted to suit the conditions. The adjustment of targets is viewed as a normal control response in the normative literature (Boehlje and Eidman 1984). However, some targets were non-negotiable within a season. These were the terminating conditions for the autumn plan including the targets set for calving or balance date (pasture cover and/or cow condition score). They were non-negotiable because they were critical for ensuring optimum production in the next season. Other studies have identified situations where farmers have negotiable terminating targets (Burrows 2013), but this has consequences for production in the subsequent planning period.

4.3 Contingency Plans

Boehlje and Eidman (1984) recommended that farmers prepare a set of contingency plans for different forecasted scenarios. In contrast, farmers' contingency plans tend to be developed through time from experience (Gray 2001). Farmers have a wide range of options to cope with different conditions and their contingencies tend to be developed to cope with both upside and downside risk. Pastoral farmers tend to face two types of feed situations: a deficit (downside risk) or a surplus (upside risk). As seen in Figure 25.6, two "types" of responses were available for each of these "situations" and these were mirror images of each other. Thus, in a feed deficit situation, farmers can implement contingency plans that would increase feed supply, reduce feed demand, or produce a combination of these responses. In a feed surplus situation, they would do the opposite. These control responses are used in the manner proposed by Makeham and Malcolm (1993) to minimize the impact of adverse situations and exploit favorable circumstances.

Contingency plans were either sourced from existing resources (e.g., cow condition, stored feeds) or externally (e.g., nitrogenous fertilizer, grazing, maize silage, greenfeed maize). The latter

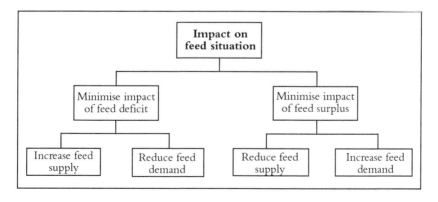

Figure 25.6 Typology of Contingency Plans Used by Farmers
Source: Gray 2001

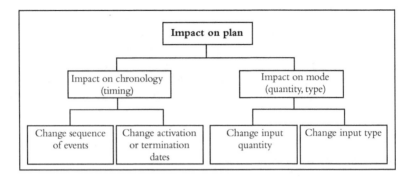

Figure 25.7 An Alternative Typology for the Contingency Plans Used by the Case Farmers
Source: Gray 2001

increased the farmers' "system" variety to cope with uncertainty (Dalton 1982). The typology in Figure 25.6 is useful when comparing different pastoral-based systems, and it could be applied to other tactical management fields such as cashflow management, water budgeting, and labor management. However, at a more abstract level, the typology shown in Figure 25.7 may provide a more useful framework in relation to tactical management. It defines the impact a contingency plan can have on the plan when implemented, rather than its impact on the problem situation. The categories in this typology are similar to those identified by Aubry et al. (1998) for planning heuristics.

5 The Control Process

The control process used by the farmers is shown in Figure 25.8 (Gray 2001). Other studies (Gladwin and Butler 1984; Gladwin et al. 1984; Mathieu 1989; Cerf et al. 1993; Fleury et al. 1996; Aubry et al. 1998; Gray et al. 2003) have also shown that farmers monitor a range of indicators and compare these to intermediate objectives or targets in their plans. When an indicator reaches a threshold value, a decision point is identified. Decision rules are then used to determine what action to take. This may be to continue the implementation of the plan, or it may be to modify the plan in some way. At each decision point in the plan, farmers had a set of sub- or contingency plans. Decision rules are used to select the contingency plan that would best minimize the impact of any deviation from the plan.

The control process used by farmers is also similar to that advocated in the normative literature (Barnard and Nix 1979; Kay 1981; Boehlje and Eidman 1984; Kay and Edwards 1994; Parker 1999). The recording and storage of monitored information is assumed in most models of control (Barnard and Nix 1979; Kay 1981; Boehlje and Eidman 1984; Kay and Edwards 1994), although Dalton (1982) viewed it as a separate function of management. Much of the data collected by farmers is not recorded. This is not surprising given the quantity of information and the subjective, qualitative nature of much of it. Gray (2001) reported that limited analysis was undertaken on the data collected by the farmers in his study, and where this did occur, it comprised mainly of the calculation of means or ratios as proposed by Barnard and Nix (1979). Information, stored in memory or in some documented form (e.g., a farm diary), was later used for other management functions such as contingency plan selection, diagnoses, evaluation, and planning as proposed by Boehlje and Eidman (1984).

Mauldon (1979) stated that control encompasses the decision of whether or not to depart from the current plan. This was a key part of farmers' control processes, and as with the normative

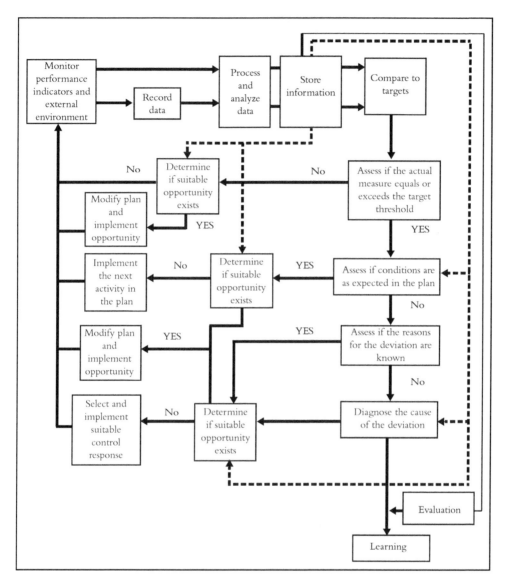

Figure 25.8 The Control Process Used by Farmers
Source: Gray 2001

model, they compared the monitored information to their targets (or standards). If the performance indicators were below (or above) the targets, then farmers continued to monitor the implementation of the plan, much in the same way as proposed in the normative literature. However, when one of the performance indicators matched or exceeded a target, a decision point was reached to either continue to implement the plan or adopt a contingency for it. For both options, secondary indicators were used for option selection. Relative to the normative literature (Barnard and Nix 1979; Kay 1981; Boehlje and Eidman 1984; Kay and Edwards 1994; Parker 1999), which focuses on identifying deviations and the need for management control, farmers put additional input into the use of targets to control implementation (Gray 2001).

David Gray and Nicola M. Shadbolt

Farmers use a diagnostic process to identify the reasons for a deviation from the plan, and an evaluation process to assess the efficacy of a management decision (Figure 25.8). An important distinction in this model is that two processes, diagnosis and evaluation, were identified. In the normative literature, these two processes are encompassed under a general term, "*evaluation*" (Barnard and Nix 1979; Mauldon 1979; Boehlje and Eidman 1984; Parker 1999). The results also support the views of Johnson (1954), Mauldon (1979), Makeham and Malcolm (1993), and Parker (1999) that learning is an important outcome of the evaluation process (Figure 25.8). Once the cause of a deviation from the plan was identified, farmers implement an appropriate control response (Figure 25.8). This was again consistent with the normative literature (Barnard and Nix 1979; Kay 1981; Boehlje and Eidman 1984; Kay and Edwards 1994; Parker 1999).

5.1 Monitoring

A farmer's monitoring process is comprised of the factors that were monitored, the method of monitoring, the roles the monitored information played, the means by which, and reasons why monitoring frequency changed, and dealing with errors. These aspects are discussed in more detail in the ensuing sections.

5.1.1 The Factors that are Monitored

Farmers monitor a large number of factors in relation to production management. For example, Gray (2001) identified that the farmers in his study monitored between twenty-eight and forty-one factors over the summer-autumn period. Landais and Deffontaines (1989) reported a similar breadth of monitoring. As seen in Figure 25.9, the factors monitored by the farmers in Gray's (2001) study were both internal (those which the case farmers have control over) and external (those outside their control). This approach aligns with Kennedy (1974) and Boehlje and Eidman (1984) who suggested a systems approach for identifying factors to monitor and separate

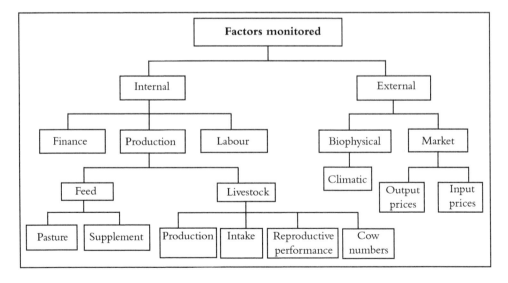

Figure 25.9 A Typology of the Factors Monitored by Farmers
Source: Gray 2001

these on the basis of whether variables were endogenous or exogenous. Boehlje and Eidman (1984) recommended identifying areas of control on the basis of enterprises or activities. They separated these into production, servicing, and marketing enterprises but did not separate internal and external factors. As such, climate would be incorporated under production.

5.1.2 Monitoring Methods

As seen in Figure 25.10, Gray (2001) classified the monitoring methods used by farmers into a typology. The objective, subjective distinction was made by Parker (1999). Gray (2001) found that subjective methods could be further separated into quantitative and qualitative methods. A subjective, quantitative method was one where a quantitative value was placed on a subjective assessment of a factor, such as pasture, condition, and yield scoring. The converse applied to subjective qualitative measures such as the visual assessment of pasture on-hand or cow body condition where no numeric value was used.

Indirect measures have also been found to be important in farmers' monitoring systems and these were sometimes used in preference to a direct measure (e.g., use of milk production to measure pasture cover over summer) (Gray 2001). The effective use of these indirect measures required an in-depth understanding of the cause-and-effect relationships within the production system.

Subjective, qualitative methods can be separated into two sub-categories: conscious and pre-attentive (Gray 2001). The former applies where farmers consciously made a visual assessment of a factor of interest. The latter applies where a factor was monitored subconsciously. The state of the factor (e.g., cow condition) was not registered consciously by the case farmers unless they were either asked about it, or it crossed some threshold. For example, a farmer began to monitor his herd more intensively when average body condition score fell below a desired level. Most measures used by farmers in Gray's (2001) study were subjective. They were considered to

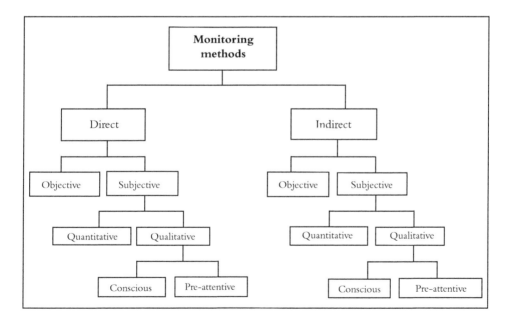

Figure 25.10 A Typology of the Monitoring Methods Used by Farmers
Source: Gray 2001

be timely, rapid, and required no capital outlay. They also had acceptable accuracy because they were calibrated against accurate objective measures. Parker (1999) argued that farmers were more likely to adopt subjective indicators, provided their accuracy was established through calibration to standards, because they were convenient and faster to measure. He also suggested that a proportion of farmers replaced objective measures with subjective measures once they had learned the association between relevant indicators. Thus, farmers learn visual "cues" that are associated with system performance. These then replace the objective measures. Another advantage of subjective measures was that they provide multivariate information whereas the information provided by objective measures tends to be univariate (Paine 1997).

5.1.3 The Role of Information from the Monitoring Process

Monitored information played several important roles in relation to farmers' tactical management (as seen in Figure 25.11). These were planning, decision point recognition, triangulation, early warning prediction, control response selection, and learning (diagnosis and evaluation). Gray (2001) observed that, prior to the start of each planning period, farmers used their monitoring systems to collect information about the farm state for planning purposes.

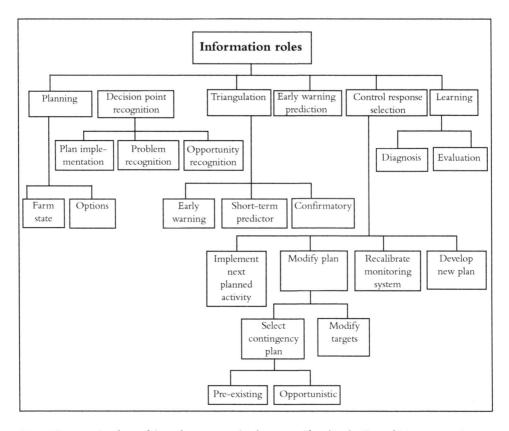

Figure 25.11 A Typology of the Roles Monitored Information Played in the Tactical Management Process Used by Farmers

Source: Gray 2001

The use of monitoring information for decision point recognition may be for one of three purposes: to recognize when to implement the next activity in the plan, to recognize that there is a significant deviation from the plan (problem recognition), or to recognize an opportunity. The majority of the indicators used for decision point recognition could be classified as lead indicators as defined by Parker (1999) after Kaplan and Norton (1996a,b,c), that is, they indicate progress towards the achievement of the plan.

The third role played by the monitored information was triangulation where it was used to ensure the veracity of the monitoring system. This prevented reliance on a single measure that may have been incorrect, a problem identified by Osburn and Schneeberger (1983). It also allowed subjective measures to be calibrated correctly against objective measures such as milk production or average pasture cover. Four methods of triangulation were used by the case farmers in Gray's (2001) study. In effect, the case farmers had created a monitoring "network" that ensures information is timely, accurate, and inexpensive. This "network" has been created through a detailed knowledge of their production systems, confirming Kennedy's (1974) and Wright's (1985) views that the development of an effective control system is dependent on a farmer having a detailed understanding of his or her system.

In Figure 25.11, we see that the fourth role played by the farmers' monitored information was a form of early warning prediction (Gray 2001). Harsh et al. (1981) also discussed the role of information in making predictions to identify problems in advance: a critical aspect for coping with climatic uncertainty.

Information was also used for control response selection (Gray 2001). Once a decision point had been identified through a primary indicator, secondary indicators were used to determine whether to implement the next activity in the plan, or a control response. If it was the latter, the secondary indicators in conjunction with heuristics were then used to select the most appropriate control response. Boehlje and Eidman (1984) mentioned the role of heuristics in the selection of control responses.

Finally, as shown in Figure 25.11, information monitoring was used for learning. Diagnosis was used where the cause of a deviation from the plan was unknown, whereas evaluation was used to assess the outcome of some aspect of the plan. Evaluation is recognized as an important function in the management process (Barnard and Nix 1979; Mauldon 1979; Boehlje and Eidman 1984; Parker 1999), but only Harsh et al. (1981) explicitly discussed the role of diagnostic information in identifying the cause of a problem and identifying opportunities for improvement in farm performance.

5.1.4 Activation, Termination, and Frequency of Monitoring

The farmers in Gray's (2001) study had developed heuristics to determine the activation, termination, and frequency of monitoring. Most factors were monitored at a subconscious or "pre-attentive level" on a daily basis as they went about their normal farm operations, similar to those described by Gladwin and Murtaugh (1980). Four factors were found to activate (or terminate) the conscious monitoring of a factor as suggested in Figure 25.12. Threshold values that activated (or terminated) monitoring of a factor were either direct or indirect measures of the factor. A threshold was either an absolute value, or a "rate of change" in the factor.

The farmers in the 2001 study monitored most factors on a daily basis using subjective, qualitative methods. Other factors (e.g., herd and pregnancy testing) were monitored infrequently (one to three times) over the summer-autumn. Intermediate monitoring intervals (two to fourteen days) were used for the more formal methods (subjective, quantitative, or objective). However,

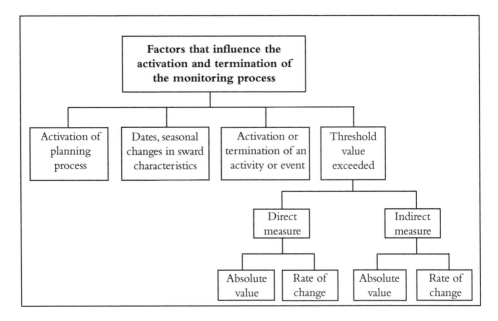

Figure 25.12 Factors That Influence the Activation and Termination of the Monitoring Process
Source: Gray 2001

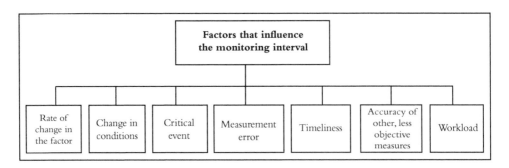

Figure 25.13 Factors That Influence the Monitoring Interval
Source: Gray 2001

the actual monitoring interval was not rigidly set but was influenced by several factors (see Figure 25.13). Generally, the less stable the factor, the shorter the monitoring interval (Kennedy 1974).

5.2 Decision Point Recognition

The most important role played by the information collected through farmers' monitoring systems was its use to determine decision points during the implementation of the plan. Gladwin and Butler (1984) reported that the first decision point used by a decision maker is whether or not to implement the plan. The next decision point occurs at any point in the plan where more than one sub-plan can be embedded and a choice has to be made. This is similar to the definition

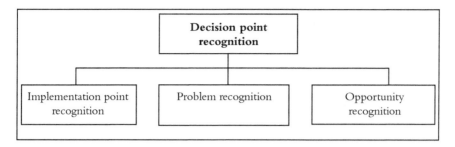

Figure 25.14 A Typology of Decision Point Recognition Processes
Source: Gray 2001

Gray (2001) uses where he defines a decision point: "any point in the implementation phase where farmers must decide between the implementation of: (i) the next activity in current plan, (ii) a control response, or (iii) an opportunity". As such, there were three types of decision point recognition processes: implementation point recognition, problem recognition, and opportunity recognition (See Figure 25.14).

When a primary indicator met or exceeded a target, it was the secondary, not primary, indicators that were used by the case farmers to identify a problem. A problem existed if the secondary indicators showed that conditions at the time differed from those predicted in the plan. Similar results were reported by Gladwin and Butler (1984), who found that a farmer's choice between implementing the plan and introducing a contingency plan was dependent on the conditions at the time of the decision.

5.3 *Diagnosis*

Diagnosis was undertaken by farmers in situations where the actual outcome differed significantly from their expected outcome. Although several authors (Mauldon 1979; Barnard and Nix 1979; Boehlje and Eidman 1984) in the normative literature mention the need to identify the reasons for a deviation from the plan, few explicitly refer to this process as diagnosis. Diagnosis is more commonly recognized in decision-making models where it is normally termed as problem detection or a definition (Kay 1981; Boehlje and Eidman 1984; Kay and Edwards 1994). In one of the few descriptive studies, albeit on strategic decision making, Ohlmer et al. (1998), reported that farmers undertook problem detection. However, little detail was provided about the nature of the farmers' problem detection processes in this publication.

The process the farmers in Gray's (2001) study used to determine when to undertake a diagnosis is shown in Figure 25.15. A plan was developed which contained "planned" milestones and associated outcomes. The plan was then implemented and the "actual" milestones, and associated outcomes (a function of the environment and case farmers' implementation and control processes) were monitored. Monitored information on the state of the farming system and the environment were used, along with the case farmers' system models, to predict "expected" milestones and associated outcomes. These expectations were updated as new information became available. Deviations from the plan were identified when the measured milestones or outcomes differed significantly from those predicted in the plan. If no deviation was identified, then the implementation of the plan continued. However, if a significant deviation was identified, the case farmers then determined whether the deviation was significantly different from their expectations. If it

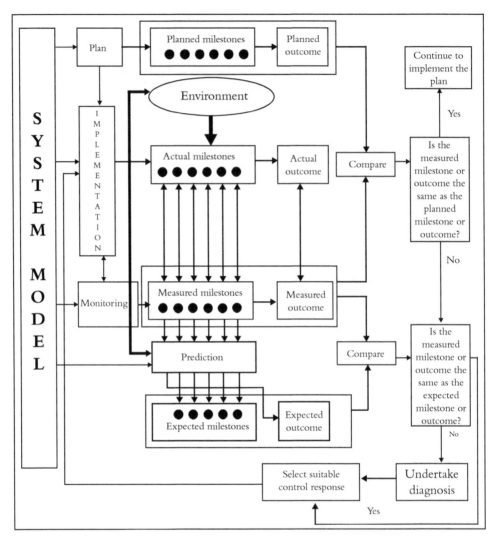

Figure 25.15 The Process Used by the Case Farmers to Determine When to Undertake a Diagnosis
Source: Gray 2001

was not, then a suitable control response was selected. However, if it was, then this deviation, not the deviation from the plan, initiated the diagnostic process.

Mauldon (1979) and Barnard and Nix (1979) discuss the need to identify the cause of a deviation between actual and planned performance. However, no mention is made of the role of expectations in this process. This is an important finding because it is only when an expectation is not met, rather than a planned level of performance, that determines when diagnosis is undertaken. This explains why the case farmers undertook limited diagnosis during the study despite experiencing considerable climatic variation. The process of using system models to predict expectations from information collected through the monitoring system meant that the case farmers knew the outcome (or next milestone) and the reason why it had deviated from the plan before it occurred. As such, there was no need for diagnosis. However, where the case farmers' expectations were not met, diagnosis was promptly undertaken to identify the cause of the inaccurate prediction. Ohlmer et al. (1998) also reported that farmers either knew the cause of a deviation from the plan or, if they did not, diagnosis was undertaken. No mention was made of diagnoses in earlier studies of farmers' tactical management (e.g., Mathieu 1989; Cerf et al. 1993; Fleury et al. 1996; Aubry et al. 1998).

Several reasons have been identified as to why the farmers' fail to predict a milestone or outcome (Gray 2001). The first was that their system models are not well enough developed to accurately predict outcomes under certain conditions. This occurs where environmental conditions are outside a farmers' experience or when new inputs or management practices are used. A second reason is that the monitoring system is providing inaccurate information upon which the predictions are based. This often occurred under unusual environmental conditions and again reflected a limitation in the case farmers' system models. The final reason was that the plan was not implemented as expected. This occurred when someone other than the case farmer implemented the plan incorrectly.

Because diagnosis was found to be about expectations not being met rather than planned outcomes, the reasons for a deviation as mentioned above are quite different from those proposed to account for a deviation from the plan. For example, Barnard and Nix (1979) identified four reasons why the actual outcome might deviate from the plan. These were that the underlying assumptions in the plan were wrong, the targets were not achievable, or changes in either the socio-economic or biophysical environment had occurred. These are problems to do with planning or changes in the environment. In this study, the reasons for a deviation from expectations were due to problems associated with system knowledge, accuracy of the monitoring system, and implementation. The planning problems mentioned by Barnard and Nix (1979) could be considered a sub-set of problems related to incomplete or incorrect system knowledge.

The above results support Scoullar's (1975) view that managers perform two types of decision-making processes, those for routine decisions, and those for novel decisions. This is similar to Simon's (1960) programmed and unprogrammed decisions and Gorry and Morton's (1971) structured and unstructured decisions. Scoullar (1975) believed that a problem, as opposed to a routine decision, was a gap between actual and desired knowledge, not between actual and desired performance. For the case farmers, this is the nature of the problems they diagnosed. It is the knowledge, not the performance gap, that they are interested in closing when they initiate diagnosis.

The diagnostic process used by the case farmers is shown in Figure 25.16. If an outcome differed significantly from expectations, then the case farmers drew on their system knowledge to hypothesize possible causes. If their system models were inadequate for this process, they consulted with their peers or a local expert and then developed their hypotheses. The most likely true hypothesis was then selected and the means by which it could be tested, devised. Data was retrieved from either the case farmers' memory or their recording system to test the hypothesis. If it was confirmed, the process was complete, but if it was refuted, the process was repeated with the next most likely hypothesis. Descriptive studies that report the use of diagnoses by farmers (e.g., Ohlmer et al. 1998) provide no information about the process applied. Similarly, in the normative literature, Lee and Chastain (1960) describe a three-step model that comprises of recognizing alternative problem definitions, analyzing alternative problem definitions, and defining the problem. However, they provide little insight into how each step is undertaken.

5.4 Limits to Control and the Environment

The inherent uncertainty within a manager's environment is an important determinant of the limits to control (Ashby 1961). Therefore, any study of farmers' management practices should

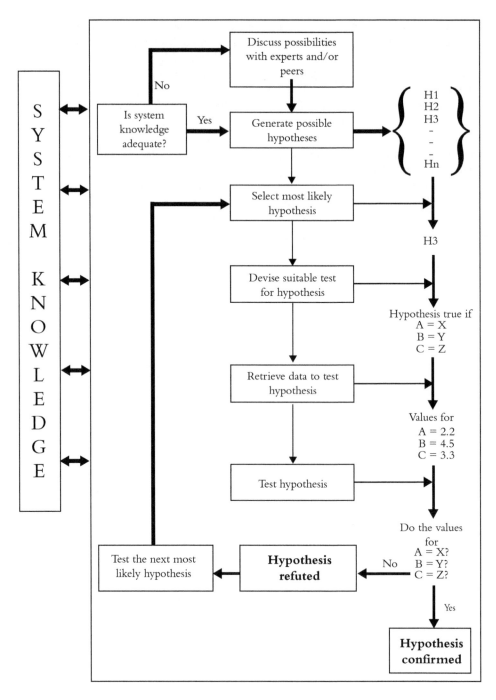

Figure 25.16 The Diagnostic Process Used by Farmers
Source: Gray 2001

provide some description of the nature of the environment in which they operate. Production risk dominated other sources of risk (seen in Figure 25.17) over the summer-autumn period. The supply of their main source of feed, pasture, was climate-driven, and the farmers felt they had limited ability to "control" this. Wright (1985) and Mathieu (1989) both identified climate as a major source of variation on farms. Although the case farmers set precise production objectives for budgeting purposes, they did not expect to achieve these objectives due to climatic conditions. This is in line with Wright's (1985) and Kaine's (1993) views that where managers have insufficient system variety to offset the variety in the environment, they will set broad, imprecise objectives.

5.5 *Control Responses*

Any deviations from Gray's (2001) case farmers' plans would be accounted for by five key reasons:

(i)   The underlying assumptions in the farmers' plans were incorrect.
(ii) Targets in the plan were not achievable.
(iii) Changes in the biophysical environment had occurred.
(iv) The monitoring system was inaccurate.
(v)   The plan was implemented incorrectly.

Three of these reasons (i–iii) were also proposed by Barnard and Nix (1979). They also identified changes in the socio-economic environment as a reason for deviations from the plan. However, this aspect did not influence the case farmers' plans, and this is in part a reflection of the production management focus of the study. The results could have been quite different if the research focus had been finance or marketing. The primary cause of deviations from the plan was the weather.

The Gray (2001) case farmers used three of the four types of control responses defined in the literature (Mauldon 1979; Dalton 1982; Boehlje and Eidman 1984) to cope with the variation in the environment. These were preliminary, concurrent, and historical control. They did not use an "elimination of disturbances" control response. However, these results are a function of case selection because some New Zealand dairy farms use irrigation of pastures for this purpose. Concurrent control was the predominant type of control used by the case farmers as would be

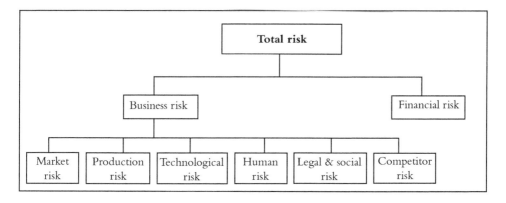

Figure 25.17   Sources of Risk Faced by Farmers
Source: Gray 2001

expected for tactical management. Preliminary control was used to prevent the occurrence of animal health problems such as bloat and facial eczema and forage crops and silage were fed during periods when pasture growth rates were most variable. Historical control was used as Mauldon (1979) proposed, after learning had taken place.

The most common form of concurrent control was plan modification. Modification of the monitoring system, viewed as a form of historical control by Boehlje and Eidman (1984) was used concurrently to ensure the accuracy of the case farmers' monitoring system.

The control responses used by farmers can also be considered from a risk management perspective (Jolly 1983). Risk management responses used by farmers can be classified as those that mitigate risk impacts and maintain short-run flexibility. Martin and McLeay (1998) reported that over 70% of the pastoral farmers in their survey used short-run flexibility to manage risk. Both maintaining flexibility and having feed reserves have ranked in the top four risk responses in many studies (Shadbolt et al. 2013; Boggess et al. 1985; Patrick et al. 1985; Wilson et al. 1993; Martin 1994; 1996).

As proposed by Boehlje and Eidman (1984), the final step in the control process was the specification of the control response. The control response selection process in Gray (2001) is similar to that reported in several tactical management studies (Gladwin and Butler 1984; Mathieu 1989; Cerf et al. 1993; Fleury et al. 1996; Aubry et al. 1998). These studies reported that at each decision point, farmers had a set of sub-plans or ("regulations") and used heuristics to select the most appropriate sub-plan for the conditions at the time.

6 Implications for Practitioners

This chapter provides a model of the tactical management process against which practitioners can compare their own management practices and reflect on areas for improvement. Detailed knowledge of the production system and environment were identified as critical for effective tactical management in the field of production. As such, this area is important for farmer education. An important distinction is made between planning aids and the cognition behind planning. It is the latter that is much more important in the development of effective plans despite limited research being undertaken in this area by the discipline. The chapter has also highlighted the importance farmers place on control relative to planning, again an area that has tended to receive limited attention in the literature.

The chapter identifies important areas of a farmer's production management that should be evaluated. For example, in relation to planning, they could consider their choice of a "typical" plan, the heuristics underlying the plan structure in terms of sequencing, timing, input and target selection rules, the contingency plans they have to cope with variation, and their choice of intermediate and terminating targets. Similarly, under control, they could consider the effectiveness of their monitoring system, what they monitor, how they monitor, and the frequency of monitoring, the means by which they select control responses and identify opportunities. The management process also has an important role in relation to learning and therefore is central to improving farmers' management skills and productivity.

7 Conclusion

Management can be thought of as a cyclic process involving irregular planning decisions followed by regular, repetitive, and less major implementation and control decisions. The interdependence of planning and control is central to management. Under conditions of high uncertainty, farmers placed greater effort on control than planning. To facilitate control, plans incorporated targets, contingency plans, and contingency plan selection rules. Decision rules, monitoring, and learning processes played an important role in coping with a changing and unpredictable environment.

As expected, the majority of tactical decisions undertaken by farmers are of a structured nature. Instances of unstructured decisions were identified and these were in situations where a knowledge gap existed. Such unstructured decisions required the use of diagnostic, evaluation, and learning processes. Because of this, farmers tend to spend limited time on planning, using a "typical" plan based on experience. Plan structure rather than planning *per se* is the focus at the tactical level. The effectiveness of a farmer's plan is a function of the heuristics used to develop the plan, highlighting the importance of the cognitive aspect of planning.

A small proportion of New Zealand farmers use formal planning techniques or "planning aids", and they may alternate between these and informal heuristic-based techniques throughout the year. However, the majority of farmers are using heuristic-based techniques. Although farmers normally draw on a "typical" plan each year, strategic decisions, learning (or historical control), atypical tactical decisions made in the previous planning period, and the state of the farm at the start of the planning period, in combination with heuristics and mental simulation, can result in the modification of a tactical plan in any one year.

The control process is important for plan implementation, control selection, and opportunity finding. Farmers tend to use a complex and holistic monitoring process. That is, they monitor a wide range of factors to obtain a more complete picture of the state of their farms. This could include pasture mass, clover content, sward color, the clumpiness of the sward, animal behavior, rumen fill, and body condition. In contrast, extension agents would recommend simpler monitoring systems such as measuring pasture mass and weighing stock. "Expert" farmers use their intimate knowledge of the production system to develop low-cost, timely, and accurate monitoring systems. Critical to the successful implementation of a farmers' plan is the range of contingency plans they have to manage both upside and downside risk along with decision rules and priority rankings that help them select the most suitable contingency for the situation. The final conclusion in relation to this chapter is that empirical research into the tactical management processes of farmers is critical for the development of theory and management techniques that are relevant to practitioners.

References and Bibliography

Andison, N. B. (1989) "Getting beyond the management illusion," *Canadian Journal of Agricultural Economics*, **37**: 743–746.
Anthony, R. N. (1965) *Planning and Control Systems: A Framework for Analysis*. Boston, MA: Harvard.
Ashby, W. R. (1961) *An Introduction to Cybernetics*. London: Chapman and Hall Ltd.
Attonaty, J. and Soler, L. (1991) "Renewing strategic decision-making aids," *European Review of Agricultural Economics*, **18**: 423–442.
Aubry, C., Papy, F. and Cappillon, A. (1998) "Modeling decision-making processes for annual crop management," *Agricultural Systems*, **56**(1): 45–65.
Barnard, C. S. and Nix, J. S. (1979) *Farm Planning and Control*. Second edition. Cambridge, UK: Cambridge University Press.
Boehlje, M. D. and Eidman, V. R. (1984) *Farm Management*. New York: John Wiley & Sons.
Boggess, W. G., Anaman, K. A. and Hanson, G. D. (1985) "Importance, causes and management responses to farm risk: Evidence from Florida and Alabama," *Southern Journal of Agricultural Economics*, **17**: 105–116.
Burns, E. O. (1973) "Random thought of some problems of professional communication," *The Australian Journal of Agricultural Economics*, **17**: 93–103.
Burrows, J. (2013) *How New Zealand dairy farmers integrate cow body condition scoring into their management practice: A case study report*. Honours dissertation. Palmerston North, New Zealand: Massey University.
Buxton, R. and Stafford Smith, M. (1996) "Managing drought in Australia's rangelands: Four weddings and a funeral," *Rangeland Journal*, **18**(2): 292–308.

Catley, J. L., Hurley, E. M., Cameron, E. A. and Hall, A. J. (2000) "Decision-making behaviour of New Zealand cut flower growers," *Journal of Applied Systems Studies*, **1**(2): 268–289.

Cerf, M., Papy, C., Aubry, J. M. and Meynard, J. M. (1993) "Agronomic theory and decision tools." In: Brossier, J., de Bonneval, L. and Landais, E. (Eds.), *Systems Studies in Agriculture and Rural Development*, pp. 343–356. Paris: INRA Editions.

Dalton, G. E. (1982) *Managing Agricultural Systems*. London: Applied Science Publishers.

Fleury, T., Dubeuf, B. and Jeannin, B. (1996) "Forage management in dairy farms: A methodological approach," *Agricultural Systems*, **53**: 199–212.

Gasson, R. (1973) "Goals and values of farmers," *Journal of Agricultural Economics*, **24**: 521–542.

Gladwin, C. H. (1989) "Indigenous knowledge systems, the cognitive revolution, and agricultural decision making," *Agriculture and Human Values*, **6**: 32–41.

Gladwin, C. H. (1979) "Cognitive strategies and adoption decisions: A case study of non-adoption of an agronomic recommendation," *Economic Development and Cultural Change*, **28**(1): 155–173.

Gladwin, C. H. and Butler, J. (1984) "Is gardening an adaptive strategy for Florida family farmers?" *Human Organization*, **43**(3): 208–216.

Gladwin, C. H. and Murtaugh, M. (1980) "The attentive-pre-attentive distinction in agricultural decision making." In: Barlett, P. F. (Ed.), *Agricultural Decision Making: Anthropological Contributions to Rural Development*, pp. 115–135. New York: Academic Press.

Gladwin, C. H., Zabawa, R. and Zimet, D. (1984) "Using ethnoscientific tools to understand farmers' plans, goals, decisions." In: Matlon, P., Cantrell, R., King, D. and Benoit-Catlin, M. (Eds.), *Coming Full Circle: Farmer Participation in the Development of Technology*, pp. 27–40. Ottawa, Canada: IRDC.

Gorry, G. A. and Morton, M. S. (1971) "A framework for management information systems," *Sloan Management Review*, **13**(1): 55–70.

Gray, D. I. (2001) *The tactical management processes used by pastoral-based dairy farmers: A multiple-case study of experts*. Unpublished Ph.D. thesis. Palmerston North, New Zealand: Massey University.

Gray, D. I., Parker, W. J., Kemp, E. A., Kemp, P. D., Brookes, I. M., Horne, D., Kenyon, P. R., Matthew, C., Morris, S. T., Reid, J. I. and Valentine, I. (2003) "Feed planning—Alternative approaches used by farmers," *Proceedings of the New Zealand Grassland Association*, **65**: 211–217.

Gray, D. I., Reid, J. I., Kemp, P. D., Kenyon, P. R., Morris, S. T., Brookes, I. M., Matthew, C. and Horne, D. (2006) "High sheep performance on hill country: Critical winter management decisions." In: Kemp, P. D. (Ed.), *Agronomy New Zealand: Proceedings of the Thirty-sixth Annual Conference*, 16 October, Dunedin, New Zealand, **36**: 12–23. Massey University, Institute of Natural Resources.

Hanf, C. H. and Schiefer, G. (1983) "Introduction to planning and decision models." In: Hanf, C. H. and Schiefer, G. W. (Eds.), *Planning and Decision in Agribusiness: Principles and Experiences. A case study approach to the use of models in decision planning*, pp. 7–21. Oxford: Elsevier Scientific Publishing Company.

Hardaker, J. B., Lewis, J. N. and McFarlane, G. C. (1970) *Farm Management and Agricultural Economics: An Introduction*. London: Angus and Robertson.

Harsh, S. B., Connor, L. J. and Schwab, G. D. (1981) *Managing the Farm Business*. Englewood Cliffs, NJ: Prentice-Hall.

Ilbery, B. W. (1978) "Agricultural decision making: A behavioural perspective," *Progress in Human Geography*, **2**: 448–466.

Jackson, R. (1975) "Decision analysis and farm management: The need for a new perspective," *Review of Marketing and Agricultural Economics*, **43**: 146–150.

Jacobsen, B. H. (1993) "Farmers' decision making behaviour—Empirical findings from Denmark," *Proceedings of the 9th International Farm Management Congress*, 11–17 July, Budapest, pp. 107–116.

Johnson, G. L. (1954) "Managerial concepts for agriculturalists: Their development, present status, importance, shortcomings, and usefulness," *Bulletin 619*. Lexington: Kentucky Agricultural Experiment Station, University of Kentucky.

Johnson, G. L. (1963) "Stress on production economics," *Australian Journal of Agricultural Economics*, **7**: 12–26.

Johnson, G. L., Halter, A. N., Jensen, H. R. and Thomas, D. W. (1961) *A Study of the Managerial Processes of Midwestern Farmers*. Ames, Iowa: Iowa State University Press.

Jolly, R. W. (1983) "Risk management in agricultural production," *American Journal of Agricultural Economics*, **65**(5): 1107–1113.

Kaine, G. (1993) *Planning and Performance: An Exploration of Farm Business Strategy and Perceptions of Control*. Armidale, NSW, Australia: The Rural Development Centre, University of New England.

Kaplan, R. S. and Norton, D. P. (1996a) *Translating Strategy into Action: The Balanced Scorecard.* Boston, MA: Harvard Business School Press.

Kaplan, R. S. and Norton, D. P. (1996b) "Using the balanced scorecard as a strategic measurement system," *Harvard Business Review,* **74**(1): 75–85.

Kaplan, R. S. and Norton, D. P. (1996c) "Linking the balanced scorecard to strategy," *California Management Review,* **39**(1): 53–79.

Kay, R. D. (1981) *Farm Management: Planning, Control and Implementation.* New York: McGraw-Hill.

Kay, R. D. and Edwards, W. M. (1994) *Farm, Management.* Third edition. New York: McGraw-Hill.

Kennedy, J. O. S. (1974) "Control systems in farm planning," *European Review of Agricultural Economics,* **1**(4): 415–433.

Landais, E. and Deffontaines, J. (1989) "Analysing the management of a pastoral territory: The study of the practices of a shepherd in the southern French alps," *Etudes et Recherches sur les Systemes Agraires et le Developpement,* **16**: 199–207.

Lee, J. E. and Chastain, E. D. (1960) "The role of problem recognition in managerial adjustment," *Journal of Farm Economics,* **42**(3): 650–659.

Makeham, J. P. and Malcolm, L. R. (1993) *The Farming Game Now.* Cambridge, UK: Cambridge University Press.

Malcolm, L. R. (1990) "Fifty years of farm management in Australia: Survey and review," *Review of Marketing and Agricultural Economics,* **58**(1): 24–55.

Martin, S. K. (1994) "Risk perceptions and management responses to risk in pastoral farming in New Zealand," *Proceedings of the New Zealand Society of Animal Production,* **54**: 363–368.

Martin, S. (1996) "Risk management strategies in New Zealand agriculture and horticulture," *Review of Marketing and Agricultural Economics,* **64**(1): 31–44.

Martin, S. and McLeay, F. (1998) "The diversity of farmers' risk management strategies in a deregulated New Zealand market," *Journal of Agricultural Economics,* **49**: 218–233.

Mathieu, A. (1989) "A view point on herbage systems in farms: The management programme. Application to spring pasture in the Jura mountains," *Etudes et Recherches sur les Systemes Agraires et le Developpement,* **16**: 129–136.

Mauldon, R. G. (1973) "Financial control within commercial family farms," *Australian Journal of Agricultural Economics,* **17**(1): 33–42.

Nielson, J. (1961) "Improved managerial processes for farmers," *Journal of Farm Economics,* **43**(5): 1250–1261.

Nix, J. (1979) "Farm management: The state of the art (or science)," *Journal of Agricultural Economics,* **30**: 277–291.

Nuthall, P. L. (1996) "Feed practices on New Zealand farms," *Agricultural Economics Research Unit Discussion Paper,* No. 144. Christchurch, New Zealand: Canterbury, Lincoln University.

Nuthall, P. L. (1999) "Management ability (The forgotten resource): Its assessment and modification," *Proceedings of the 43rd Australian Agricultural and Resource Economics Society,* Christchurch, New Zealand, 20–22 January, p. 20.

Nuthall, P. L. and Bishop-Hurley, G. J. (1999) "Feed planning on New Zealand farms," *Journal of International Farm Management,* **2**(2): 100–112.

Ohlmer, B. (1998) "Models of farmers' decision making—Problem definition," *Swedish Journal of Agricultural Research,* **28**: 17–27.

Ohlmer, B., Olson, K. and Brehmer, B. (1998) "Understanding farmers' decision making processes and improving managerial assistance," *Agricultural Economics,* **18**: 273–290.

Osburn, D. D. and Schneeberger, K. C. (1983) *Modern Agricultural Management.* Second edition. Reston, VA: Reston Publishing Company.

Paine, M. S. (1997) *Doing it together: Technology as practice in the New Zealand dairy sector.* Ph.D. thesis. Wageningen, Netherlands: University of Wageningen.

Papy, F. (1994) "Working knowledge concerning technical systems and decision support." In: Dent, J. B. and McGregor, M. J. (Eds.), *Rural and Farming Systems Analysis: European Perspectives,* pp. 222–235. Wallingford, UK: CAB International.

Parker, W. J. (1999) "Farm performance measurement—Linking monitoring to business strategy," *Proceedings of the New Zealand Society of Animal Production,* **59**: 6–13.

Parker, W. J., Gray, D. I., Lockhart, J. S., Lynch, G. A. and Todd, E. A. G. (1993) "Drying off management and the use of management aids on seasonal supply dairy farms," *Proceedings of the New Zealand Society of Animal Production*, **53**: 127–131.

Patrick, G. F., Wilson, P. N., Barry, P. J., Boggess, W. G. and Young, D. L. (1985) "Risk perceptions and management responses: Producer generated hypotheses for risk modelling," *Southern Journal of Agricultural Economics*, **17**: 231–238.

Reisch, E. M. (1971) "Recent advances in farm planning in Europe and North America." *Fourteenth International Conference of Agricultural Economists: Policies, Planning and Management for Agricultural Development*, pp. 199–216. Oxford, UK: International Association of Agricultural Economists.

Rougoor, C. W., Trip, G., Huirne, R. B. M. and Renkema, J. A. (1998) "How to define and study farmer's management capacity: Theory and use in agricultural economics," *Agricultural Economics*, **18**: 261–272.

Scoullar, B. B. (1975) "Towards a definition of management process," *Sociologia Ruralis*, **15**(4): 259–272.

Sebillotte, M. (1993) "Analysing farming and cropping systems and their effects: Some important concepts." In: Brossier, J., de Bonneval, L. and Landais, E. (Eds.), *Systems Studies in Agriculture and Rural Development*, pp. 273–290. Paris: INRA Editions.

Shadbolt, N. and F. Olubode-Awosola (2013) *New Zealand Dairy Farmers and Risk: Perceptions of, Attitude to, Management of and Performance under Risk and Uncertainty*. Research Report, Palmerston North, New Zealand: Centre of Excellence in Farm Business Management. Available from: www.onefarm.ac.nz

Siddiq, E. A. and Kundu, D. K. (1993) "Production strategies for rice-based cropping systems in the humid tropics." In: *International Crop Science I*, pp. 155–162. Madison, WI: Crop Science Society of America.

Simon, H. A. (1960) *The New Science of Management Decision*. New York: Harper and Row.

Wilson, P. N., Dahlgran, R. D. and Conklin, N. C. (1993) "'Perceptions as reality' on large-scale dairy farms," *Review of Agricultural Economics*, **15**(1): 89–101.

Wright, V. E. (1985) *Farm planning: A farm business perspective*. Unpublished Ph.D. thesis. Armidale, NSW, Australia: University of New England.

26
POM AND THE MILITARY

Keenan D. Yoho and Wayne P. Hughes Jr.

1 Introduction: Differentiating the Improvement of Arsenals from the Application of Weapons, Strategy, and Tactics in War

The early attempts at efficient management of large-scale operations in support of military power may be traced back to the Venetian Arsenal. Established in the 1100s, this employed a type of assembly line to mass produce galleys (Lane 1973). The industrial revolutions of England in the eighteenth century and the United States in the late nineteenth century engendered tremendous growth in the application of scientific principles to industrial problems and processes. The development of interchangeable parts and the division of labor into specified, discrete tasks facilitated the refinement of production operations at a level of precision that was impossible before.

In the United States, Frederick Taylor developed "best methods," time studies, and made tremendous contributions to "shop management" (see Taylor 1911; 1912 for the original and enduring works). Frank and Lillian Gilbreth shot more than 250,000 feet of 35mm film, capturing the movements of workers, which led to the development of the motion study methodology used in conjunction with Taylor's time studies to develop the practice used by industrial engineers today (see Gilbreth and Gilbreth 1917, for a collection of their publications). The publications of Harris (1913) inspired a flurry of work in production and inventory planning that carries on today, and Shewhart (1931) ushered in methods for controlling quality through the use of statistical methods that would carry on through the work of Feigenbaum (1945), Deming (1982), Juran (1988), Ishikawa (1990) and contribute to the development of Ohno's (1988) Toyota Production System. All of these methods and innovations resulted in the capacity of national arsenals to make greater quantities of reliable and even more destructive weapons at a lower cost. This fundamentally changed the nature and scope of war from 1914 onward. The production efficiency and quality of national arsenals has never been greater at any point in history.

1.1 Differentiating the Character of Operations Management in the Civilian and Military Contexts

Differentiating operations research from operations management or management science has concerned scholars for some time (see Miser 1997, for example). In the end, however, we conclude that if they are not different moods of one personality, then they are close cousins of the same species. What distinguishes operations management in the military context from the civilian context is that the focus is on fighting under extremely volatile and dynamic conditions. The contributions of Frederick Taylor (1911) differ fundamentally from those of Morse and Kimball (1951), who collected the most effective methods and approaches to operational problems that were so successful during World War II and introduced them to the broader scientific and industrial community. Taylor was focused on repetitive processes in a controlled environment that would result in a *best method* resulting in long-run gains. Morse and Kimball's work, however, focused on *effective methods* that tended to provide a decision maker with *a scientific basis for a decision* in a deadly, dynamic environment that would yield some immediate advantage. Another distinguishing feature of operations methods in the military context is that new methods and models may be adopted almost immediately because the focus is on fighting more effectively and winning in an existential competition.

Operations management in a civilian context has non-lethal competition as its context. However, a wartime enemy is much more compelling in his lethality, and the rate of change that must be made to counter an enemy's actions has a much shorter time constant. Intelligence and information is vital but cannot be perfect, and the often-lethal countermeasures by which we try to slow down the enemy's knowledge and decisions are not available in a civilian context.

1.2 The Pirandello Principle

Military applications of operations management confront what Machol (1977) described as the *Pirandello principle* where "numbers which are quite reasonable to obtain in theory, [cannot] be obtained in practice" because it is infeasible. In military operations, battlefield data is notoriously unreliable and "dirty." The "fog of war" and the presence of danger inhibit accurate collection. Hit probabilities, casualties, and damage measurements are unreliable or mixed in their accuracy. But combat data is better than controlled tests and simulations, and good enough to get first-order approximations. The military analysts' rule is "when there is a war on, study the war." This implies that operations analysts must be forward deployed with the forces that are operating and fighting at the scene of the action.

We have described how the industrial revolution brought methods used to build and improve the efficiency and quality of arsenals. We have also differentiated between the practice of developing and improving arsenals with the application of methods to improve military operations which must necessarily include the application of weapons as well as strategy and tactics development. We will now address past history beginning in the early twentieth century and how operations analysis evolved in support of war.

2 Past History

Prior to World War II, there was a tradition of applying quantitative methods, as well as deliberate and advance operational planning, to military operations. This application of quantitative methods was especially successful for logistics planning when the timely movement of troops and their supplies to a specific site or theater of war could be measured with relative precision (i.e., accurate within a factor of two or less). Lynn (1993) and van Creveld (1980) give impressive examples of how the profession of military logistics developed during modernity.

World War I proved to the world that warfare was now an industrial endeavor. The complexities encountered while implementing and utilizing new and innovative weapons such as the airplane, machine gun, chemical agents, armored tank, wireless radio, and the submarine would require bringing to bear scientific discipline in order to realize the full destructive power of these technologies. Many veterans from World War I would go on to apply their experience as well as their scientific training to the problems encountered in World War II.

The accelerated rate of technological change from the years 1939 through 1945 placed significant demands on warring nations to increase the rate of adoption, implementation, and adaptation in the most destructive and controlled manner possible to better their chances of winning. After the attack on Pearl Harbor in December 1941, most American warship classes changed their functions. For example, aircraft carriers with their longer range of attacks replaced battleships as the capital ships in every fleet that had them (Hughes 2000). Battleships became primary naval gunfire ships to support the many opposed amphibious assaults in the Pacific and European theaters. New employments entailed changes in the way analysis in support of tactics and battle planning was conducted.

Many of the core methods used in operations analysis during this time were developed many years before the war. Notably, the works of Babbage, Bridgman, Feller, Lanchester, Pearson, and Von Neumann were influential. The 1930s witnessed such advances in mathematical and statistical methods as game theory (von Neumann 1928), sequential sampling (Dodge and Romig 1929), confidence limits (Fisher 1932), the formula for $M/G/1$ queues (Pollaczek 1930; Khintchine 1932), control charts (Shewhart 1931), continuous time Markov processes (Chapman 1928; Kolmogorov 1931), hypothesis testing (Neyman and Pearson 1933), martingales (Lévy 1934), matroids (Whitney 1935), the design of experiments (Fisher 1935), and Turing machines (Turing 1936). However, it was during the war that new operations methods were developed as well as advances in computers.

The British led the way to better tactics that increased supply and troop convoy survivability, exploited radar, sonar, voice radio, aircraft homing devices, developed airborne identification methods as to friend or foe, and the employment of chaff as well as other decoys. The British Anti-Aircraft Command Research Group—known also as "Blackett's Circus"—were a motley crew of physicists, physiologists, mathematicians, and a surveyor working under the leadership of P.M.S. Blackett (who went on to win a Nobel Prize in physics in 1948) that made significant headway in the application of science to all aspects of war at the time (Budiansky 2013; Kirby 2003). The United States followed in April 1942 by creating the U.S. Antisubmarine Warfare Operations Research Group (ASWORG). The ASWORG was staffed by civilians working under a Navy admiral (Gass and Assad 2005). Then, in October 1942, the United States also deployed a civilian team to support the Eighth Air Force in Britain (Jewell 1977). The declassified work by Koopman (1946) on search and screening is worthy of several hours reading, not only for its historical significance, but also for the elegance and thoroughness of its exposition and applicability to emerging problems.

The defining characteristics of the early military operations giants were (1) familiarization with the technologies and tactics that allowed them to make quantitative recommendations that saved lives and enhanced weapon performance; (2) acknowledgment that analysis of *war* alone could not cover all aspects of the decisions, actions, and results for war; and (3) the way that analysts had to work directly under the decision maker and his top staff with no layers between them and the commander to be effective due to both factors. It became obvious during the war and thereafter, that if the decision maker was not astute enough to recognize how military operations methods of research and management could help them, as well as its limits, then the analyst teams—even the best ones—were wasting their time and must go somewhere their assistance would improve combat effectiveness.

Keenan D. Yoho and Wayne P. Hughes Jr.

2.1 Bringing Advances in Military Operational Research to Civilian Operations Management

Shortly after the war, scientists who worked on operational problems sought to introduce the rest of the world to the rapid developments that had been made in methodologies and the results achieved that helped improve the efficiency and efficacy of combat. The 1950s and 1960s witnessed the publication of several works devoted to expounding the methods of operations management, research, and analysis (see, for example, Morse and Kimball 1951; Kaufman 1963). However, there was a struggle to reconcile how or whether to bring the new methods and approaches into the disciplinary fold that constituted the monastic structure of academe. Kittel (1947) was one of the early prognosticators of the potential impact of these new methods on industrial society with a publication in *Science*. Hindrichs (1953) proposed a philosophy for operations analysis that would bridge military operations research with business, management, and general industrial problems. Churchman et al. (1957) provided a timely survey of operations research methods and their applications that expanded upon wartime work and is to this day an extremely useful introduction to the subject. Beer (1967) introduced the term *management science* and defined it as "the business use of operations research." However, the views on the emerging field of operations research were not all welcoming or enthusiastic (Mood 1953). In spite of the discussions regarding where operations research "belonged" as a discipline or field, its influence and methods spread into finance, commerce, production, and transportation industries.

The creation of the operations curriculum and the award of Masters Degrees at the Naval Postgraduate School in Monterey, California, gave coherence and structure to the operations discipline, for both military and commercial purposes. After 1962 when the Department of Operations Research was chartered, it was accompanied by a greatly expanded officer student population. Simultaneously, systems analysis and management science curricula were established in order to create complementary disciplines as well. The work on operational military problems continued at a rapid pace after the war at places like the RAND Corporation in Santa Monica, California. RAND exemplified a place for scientists to work together on the interdisciplinary problems faced by the United States during the Cold War. Scientists not on permanent staff would retreat to the sunny beaches of Southern California for the summers to work in a vibrant atmosphere that seemed to produce an endless fountain of new ideas that directly addressed military problems. It was here that the work of Dantzig, Arrow, Aumann, Schelling, Koopmans, Nash, Kahn, Enthoven, Baran, Marshall, Bellman, Hitch, Speier, von Neumann, the Wohlstetters, and many others found fertile ground for their intellectual seeds to bloom. In the United States, the first Military Operations Research Symposium took place in 1957 with support from the Office of Naval Research and was held at least once a year until the Military Operations Research Society (MORS) was created in 1966 and continues to convene an annual meeting and publishes the *Military Operations Research Society (MORS) Journal* dedicated to the subject of military operations research.

From 1950 through the 1970s, advances in analytic methods and algorithms, as well as computing machines, encouraged analysts to take on larger and more complex problems. Dantzig (1957) showed that some of the most important decision problems in war and industry could be stated as linear programs. His development of the simplex method allowed for fast solutions. The post-war development of operations research, systems analysis, and policy analytical works shaped far-reaching subjects as military basing (Wohlstetter et al. 1954), intelligence (Wohlstetter 1962), and strategic conflict, especially between two competitors. This resulted in further development, and elaboration upon, von Neumann's early work in game theory (Nash 1950; Flood 1952; Luce and Raifa 1957; Schelling 1960; Dresher 1961). Miser and Quade's contribution to the area of systems analysis is well known and established in their seminal handbook containing three volumes (Miser and Quade 1985; 1988; Miser 1995; 1997). It was also during this period that systems analysis gained ever-increasing influence in the national policy circles. Operations research and analysis in their original forms were not about procurement and programming but about *fighting* more effectively. Systems analysts, beginning with McNamara, Hitch, and Enthovan in the 1960s, had ever-increasing influence in Washington, D.C., and often claimed more predictive power with their methods than they could deliver—particularly in making macro-planning, programming, budgeting, and execution (PPBE) decisions.

We have described how, at the dawn of World War II, it was broadly recognized that the analysis of war alone was insufficient for winning wars. The rate of technological change increased significantly and war was now a technical business from both the standpoint of weapons as well as methods of application and concepts of operation. After World War II, systems analysis developed out of the early analytic, operational approaches, which shaped strategic developments in the programming of military force sizes and capabilities. Today, it is understood that there is a dialectic between the practice of operations management in the context of military and non-military settings, and that the applications advance and expand as a result of the cross-fertilization over time. We will now address the present situation and how operations management has been used to support contemporary wars.

3 Present Situation

More than thirty-five years ago, Bonder (1979) wrote, "The relevance of current mathematical developments in OR is continually questioned and, perhaps more significant, the techniques and methods are being developed by individuals who have more of a disciplinary allegiance to mathematics and economics than to operations research." Operational (or operations) research took shape from 1939 to 1945 in response to fundamental changes in the technology and resulting conduct of war. Today, operations research as it exists outside of military application barely resembles what it was when it began more than seventy years ago, containing much more emphasis placed on sophistication of methods regardless of efficacy (Ackoff 1999). However, within institutions that focus primarily on military problems, there have been refinements on past methods as well as new developments that have contributed to both operational and cost effectiveness during recent wars and conflicts. Much of the applied operations work in support of the military is of little interest to the academic community because the methods may not be entirely new (mathematical programming is widely used) or the problems are not easily solved in a closed-form, analytic expression; as computing has advanced, algorithms and approximate approaches that produce fast, feasible and "good enough" solutions are preferred by decision makers that must act quickly. Some approaches may be so interdisciplinary or novel that they do not easily fit within the orderly and cautious bounds of the peer-reviewed journals and find better homes in books; the Delphi method (Brown 1968), the focus group and Guttman scale (Stouffer et al. 1950), and the Monte Carlo method (Ulam et al. 1947) come to mind.

3.1 The Problems of Search, Optimization, and Exchange

The problems of search, optimization, and exchange were particularly pressing during World War II and they remain so today. Morse and Kimball (1951) identify many of the fundamental problems addressed at the time as well as measures of effectiveness. Sweep rates of patrol and search include submarines searching for ships and ships and aircraft searching for submarines. Exchange rates address the ratio of enemy and own losses such as during air-to-air combat or convoy versus submarine actions. Comparative effectiveness addresses the effect of weapons (such as whether to use submarines or aircraft to destroy ships). The evaluation of equipment performance addresses the effectiveness of new weapons or weapon applications during the course of a war. Determining optimal routes for transporting troops and supplies inspired the development of the transportation problem (Hitchcock 1941; Koopmans 1949). These problems, and of course, the atomic bomb, required a high degree of interdisciplinary work and swift application. Today, the problem of search, optimization, and exchange are extremely relevant. Precision strike weapons necessitate military formations become smaller, more dispersed, and heavily armed.

The wars in Iraq (1991–1992 and 2003–2011) and Afghanistan confronted decision makers with problems of search (for people and improvised explosives), logistics, and pacification. The first two were well studied in previous conflicts—particularly World War II—and the last was covered by the seminal works of Gwynn (1934), Galula (1964), Trinquier (1964), and Kellen (1970). The search for people and improvised explosives took on a different approach from the past given the availability of empirical data collected from unmanned systems (or drones), sensors, and first-hand reporting from soldiers in the field. The amount of empirical data being collected aided the effort to find targets, identify patterns of activity and behavior, and focus resources to neutralize or kill the enemy. The need to quickly and effectively address improvised explosive device (IED) attacks became particularly urgent and the use of empirical data gave rise to behavioral analysis that resulted in some success during the second Iraq war of 2003–2011 (Davis et al. 2013). The U.S. solidified its reputation as having the world's greatest man hunting capability evidenced by a continuous cycle of successful raids that killed or captured high-ranking figures within Al Qaeda and its splinter groups across Iraq and Afghanistan. The man hunting capability, too, was built upon earlier scientific models of problem solving. Anyone familiar with the find, fix, finish, exploit, analyze (F3EA) cycle used by special operations forces under General Stanley McChrystal (2011; 2013) will recognize the similarity to Shewhart's plan, do, check, act (PDCA) cycle (Shewhart 1931; Deming 1982). The availability of data also made streamlining the logistics operations much easier and faster as combat operations evolved (Peltz et al. 2015; Peltz et al. 2005a; 2005b) and algorithms were developed, resulting in unprecedented inventory service levels in the history of the U.S. Army (Peltz et al. 2008; Girardini et al. 2004; Peltz and Robbins 2007). As the nature of warfare is changing, there remain many problems in the areas of sourcing, interoperability, resiliency, stock positioning, basing, and integration of unmanned systems that remain to be addressed (Yoho et al. 2013) and we will discuss some of these in Section 6.

4 Future Projections as the Character of Conflict Changes

The current and past application areas of operations management in the military context are in the following seven areas: (1) battle planning, (2) wartime operations, (3) weapon procurement, (4) force sizing, (5) human resource planning, (6) logistics planning, and (7) national policy analysis. A comprehensive discussion of each is addressed in Hughes (1997). Battle planning includes the preparation for wartime operations, based on friendly and enemy orders of battle as well as the existing strategic or tactical environment. Wartime operations are concerned with the actual conduct of war and are distinguished from battle planning by available, current, wartime data and known, immediate military objectives. Weapon procurement involves the selection from among competing weapon systems or characteristics for procurement decisions. Force sizing involves the decision of how many weapons systems of which types to (1) operate, (2) support, and (3) procure in the future, either in the defense establishment as a whole or in a major component such as the army or the nuclear weapons arsenal. Human resource planning involves the design and operation of manpower, personnel, training, and assignment systems. Logistics planning includes the design and operation of all manner of military logistic support. And finally, national policy analysis addresses supra military actions that influence, or are influenced by, military considerations such as arms treaties or subsidies of commercial transportation.

Five of these seven topics (planning, operations, procurement, human resource planning, and logistics planning) are also important in a non-military context, but the costs, consequences, and planning horizons tend to be much different. Ship building plans, traditional aircraft design, and even small arms development may take place over decades whereas capital investment decisions in the non-military setting are typically shorter. For both the military and non-military settings, the application areas will likely remain the same, but the problems within them will change as will the need to solve the problems of trade-offs given the interdependencies between them all. Future warfare will be conducted in two domains: (1) what may be called "high-end" or conventional warfare between two peer or near-peer actors possessing missiles and other precision strike weapons and (2) warfare with non-state actors capable of carrying out military, para-military, or terror operations both within and outside their geographic span of control.

4.1 High-End Warfare

What might be called "high-end" or conventional warfare will require the use of salvo equations (Hughes 1995) to illustrate potential losses and survival where precision weapons are used by two peer or near-peer combatants possessing precision strike weapons. Additionally, campaign analyses such as those described by Kline et al. (2010) supported by wargaming will be critical to developing and maintaining sharp thinking about security, conflict, and combat; these types of analyses often point to where more refined mathematical, computational, and/or analytic work should focus. The war games played at the Naval War College—more than 300 between 1919 and 1940—illustrated that the prevailing U.S. strategy that was intended to guide any campaign against the Japanese in the Pacific was unexecutable (Hughes 2012). The influence of Boyd (1976; 1996) who introduced the OODA (observe, orient, decide, act) loop has never been more present as the need for making *good enough* decisions quickly is paramount, and Boyd's echo of "he who can handle the quickest rate of change survives" remains valid.

4.2 Warfare with Non-State Actors

The newest category of military operations analysis is in methods of conducting irregular warfare and fighting non-state actors to include terrorist and trans-national criminal organizations. As the nature of conflict and stability has changed, there are opportunities to apply operational analytics to security in arenas beyond the military battlefield. The methods of village stability operations (CJSOTF-A 2011; Galula 1963; Jones 2010; Krepinevich 1986; Petit 2011; and Shackleton 1975) as well as behavioral analysis to predict attacks, has crossed over from warfare into policing in order to prevent crime, improve the effective use of resources, and to track potential terrorists (Levine and Tisch 2014). The use of mathematical models to predict whether a terror cell is still functional after a number of operatives have been removed will continue to be important (Farley 2003).

We are in the age of what Arquilla and Ronfeldt call *netwar* (Arquilla and Ronfeldt 1996; 1997; 2001). The analytical techniques needed will likely be patterned after antisubmarine warfare analysis, which emphasizes search theory techniques. In irregular warfare, as in antisubmarine warfare, usually if you can find your enemy, you can track him, and if you can track him, you can kill or neutralize him. There are likely continued opportunities to apply game theory to important military problems at the operational and tactical levels as it has been in the past (Haywood Jr. 1954). However, the classic two-player games that proved useful for analyzing strategic competitions such as the Cold War struggle between the U.S. and Soviet Union will have to be expanded upon to include multiple players—many of whom are not rational—with sometimes competing and other times complementary objectives. Approaches and models that consider ethology rather than the purely rational calculating, and maximizing *homo economicus*, will be useful. Finally, the development of algorithms and models that contribute to the effective development of swarming autonomous systems as well as the defeat of swarming autonomous systems will be in great demand throughout the remainder of this century. Swarming behavior has been studied in the natural sciences to understand group behavior of ants, locusts, bees, birds, and fish. However, it is also a serious area of study with respect to the future of war. Edwards (2000) and Arquilla and Ronfeldt (2005) discuss the application of swarming in warfare as well as its implications for the future of war.

5 Implications for Managers

Growing computer power has enhanced the ability to explore ever more complicated problems and variations on friendly and enemy choices. Among these are spreadsheet applications and geographic information systems (GISs) to include the simplest available through a web browser, and presentation software that permits the swift preparation of presentations, either artfully simple and communicative or robust with visual display and graphical exposition of relationships. Google Maps has, almost unnoticed, become one of the most powerful aids to analysis, just as electronic maps have become valuable for planning operations. Because future conflict will require coordination and cooperation of allies and partners to function as a coordinated network, the ability to bring together information quickly and develop concrete pictures that translate across time and language barriers will be critical. However, like all innovations in communication technology, the power to gather and disseminate data quickly brings with it the danger of both information overload and enemy intrusion, so we emphasize the value of analyst experience and quality over brute force and comprehensive quantity.

Finally, there are opportunities to capitalize on management techniques that allow organizations to execute important warfighting processes more efficiently and effectively. For example, developing methods and processes that allow for searching for the enemy, fixing the enemy's location, killing or immobilizing them, and then exploiting what we may learn from the engagement in order to make new decisions that are cheaper, better, and/or faster are highly desirable. Advances in this area would combine key aspects of what we have learned from the application of repeatable, data-driven scientific processes (such as Shwehart's PDCA cycle), "lean manufacturing" (eliminating waste, visual management, and reducing handoffs and bottlenecks), Boyd's OODA loops, and search and eliminate targeting cycles such as find, fix, finish, exploit, analyze, and disseminate (F3EAD). This area will likely be the sole burden of managers and warfighters. Academicians will steer clear of the process domain because it is a subject not aligned with their primary evaluation metric: the peer-reviewed academic journal. The academic journals almost never publish applied articles focused on process or the "how"; note that Shewhart (1931) published his PDCA cycle in a book, Boyd (1996) presented his OODA loop in lectures, "lean manufacturing" was documented in a book (Womack and Roos 1990), and the F3EAD process emerged in practice and was later documented in news (Gray 2014) and trade press (Flynn et al. 2008). However, there is significant opportunity in this management and process domain to increase the speed, efficiency, and effectiveness of all military operations that will be critical for winning in the new warfare environment.

6 Directions for Future Research

Research opportunities for military applications are nearly boundless, because operations and systems analysis are techniques limited only by the imaginations of receptive decision makers and the artful and communicative skills of the analysts. There are two categories that we see as fertile ground for advancement: (1) methodological development that may extend optimization techniques, the scope of data analysis, and data culling (to include what is being called "big data") for useful presentation in support of critical decisions in a timely way and (2) substantive work, with growing interest in defeating drug running, containing terrorist attacks, and irregular warfare operations—these are all defensive operations. For the offense, a fertile field with many applications is in swarming autonomous systems as well as the support of special operations, with new and more effective ways to conduct clandestine or surprise attacks in support of legitimate authority.

The methodological field is widening in terms of opportunity largely due to the increased speed and decreased cost of computing that has occurred over the last several decades. The influential text by Holt et al. (1960) came as a result of U.S. Navy funding and included, among other significant contributions, optimal linear decision rules and exponentially weighted moving average forecasting methods (Gass and Assad 2005). However, there were many problems pointed out by the authors that could not be easily solved through analysis alone but would benefit from computational studies if there were enough computing power available in the future (Rappold and Yoho 2008). Many problems have been waiting for computing to catch up in terms of power and cost. Today, there is ample computing power available at reasonably low costs to address very complex problems and come up with computationally efficient and managerially satisfactory solutions. Again, in armed conflict, the optimal solution is not as important as having a better, cheaper, and/or faster solution than your opponent. Both the problem framing and solution benefit the decision-making process most when it can be comprehended visually. The importance of useful data presentation cannot be overstated. The speed and cost of computing, as well as the availability of shared, distributed networks, support that ability to bring together lots of information into singular "views" that are meaningful and support effective and efficient decision making.

Work that addresses networks and the complexity of systems with multiple actors will be beneficial for identifying promising directions for applied operations analysis and management. Moffat (2003) has contributed a good primer on this area and would be a good place for scholars interested in making contributions, but are new to the area, to begin. Substantive work that takes networks of cooperating agents as its subject will find a wide field of application in security studies. As conflict and long-run competition take place increasingly outside of the domain of high-intensity warfare, approaches that develop solutions for defending against networks intent on attacking will be useful. On the other hand, approaches that are focused on developing effective attacks using a network of distributed but lethal actors will also be useful particularly as warfare becomes increasingly unmanned and autonomous.

References and Bibliography

Ackoff, R. L., (1999) *Ackoff's Best: His Classic Writings on Management*. John Wiley & Sons, New York.

Arquilla, J. and Ronfeldt, D., (1996) *The Advent of Netwar*. MR-789-OSD. RAND Corporation, Santa Monica, California.

Arquilla, J. and Ronfeldt, D., (1997) *In Athena's Camp: Preparing for Conflict in the Information Age*. RAND Corporation, Santa Monica, California.

Arquilla, J. and Ronfeldt, D., (2000) *Swarming and the Future of Conflict* (No. RAND/D8-311-OSD). RAND Corporation, Santa Monica, California.

Arquilla, J. and Ronfeldt, D., (2001) *Networks and Netwars: The Future of Terror, Crime, and Militancy.* RAND Corporation, Santa Monica, California.

Arquilla, J. and Ronfeldt, D., (2005) "Netwar revisited: The fight for the future continues," in Bunker, R. (ed.) *Networks, Terrorism and Global Insurgency.* Routledge, New York, pp. 8–19.

Assad, A. A. and Gass, S. I., (2011) *Profiles in Operations Research: Pioneers and Innovators* (Vol. 147). Springer Science & Business Media, New York.

Beer, S., (1967) *Management Science: The Business Use of Operations Research.* Aldus Publishers and Doubleday Science Series, London.

Beer, S., (1994) *Decision and Control: The Meaning of Operational Research and Management Cybernetics.* John Wiley & Sons, Ltd., London.

Bernstein, P. L., (1998) *Against the Gods: The Remarkable Story of Risk.* John Wiley & Sons, New York.

Bonder, S., (1979) "Changing the future of operations research," *Operations Research*, **27**(2): 209–224.

Boyd, J., (1976) "New Conception for Air-to-Air Combat," Professional Briefing. Accessed at: http://dnipogo.org/john-r-boyd/.

Boyd, J., (1996) "The Essence of Winning and Losing," Professional Briefing. Accessed at: http://pogoarchives.org/m/dni/john_boyd_compendium/essence_of_winning_losing.pdf.

Brown, B., (1968) *Delphi Process: A Methodology Used for the Elicitation of Opinions of Experts, P-3925*, RAND Corporation, Santa Monica, California.

Budiansky, S., (2013) *Blackett's War: The Men Who Defeated the Nazi U-Boats and Brought Science to the Art of Warfare.* Vintage Books, New York.

Chapman, S., (1928) "On the Brownian displacements and thermal diffusion of grains suspended in a non-uniform fluid," *Proceedings of the Royal Society of London. Series A, Containing Papers of a Mathematical and Physical Character*, **119**(781): 34–54.

Churchman, C. W., Ackoff, R. L., and Arnoff, E. L., (1957) *Introduction to Operations Research.* John Wiley & Sons, New York.

Combined Joint Special Operations Task Force Afghanistan (CJSOTF-A), (2011) *Village Stability Operations and Afghan Local Police: Bottom-up Counterinsurgency*, Headquarters, Combined Joint Special Operations Task Force-Afghanistan, Bagram Airbase, Afghanistan. Accessed at: http://stabilityinstitute.com/wp-content/uploads/CJSOTF-A_VSO_ALP_Handbook01APR11-FINAL.pdf.

Dantzig, G., (1957) *Concepts, Origins, and Use of Linear Programming, P-980*, RAND Corporation, Santa Monica, California.

Davis, P., Perry, W., Brown, R. A., Yeung, D., Roshan, P., and Voorhies, P., (2013) *Using Behavioral Indicators to Help Detect Potential Violent Acts A Review of the Science Base, RR-215-NAVY*, RAND Corporation, Santa Monica, California.

Deming, W. E., (1982) *Out of the Crisis.* M.I.T. Press, Boston, Massachusetts.

Dodge, H. F. and Romig, H. G., (1929) "A method of sampling inspection," *Bell System Technical Journal*, **8**(4): 613–631.

Dresher, M., (1961) *Games of Strategy: Theory and Applications.* Prentice-Hall, Englewood Cliffs, New Jersey.

Edwards, S. J. A., (2000) *Swarming on the Battlefield: Past, Present, and Future, MR-1100-OSD*, RAND Corporation, Santa Monica, California.

Farley, J. D., (2003) "Breaking Al Qaeda cells: A mathematical analysis of counterterrorism operations (A guide for risk assessment and decision making)," *Studies in Conflict & Terrorism*, **26**(6): 399–411.

Feigenbaum, A. V., (1945) *Quality Control: Principles, Practice and Administration; An Industrial Management Tool for Improving Product Quality and Design and for Reducing Operating Costs and Losses*, McGraw-Hill Industrial Organization and Management Series.

Fisher, R. A., (1932) "Inverse probability and the use of likelihood," *Mathematical Proceedings of the Cambridge Philosophical Society*, **28**(3) 257–261.

Fisher, R. A., (1935) *The Design of Experiments.* Oliver and Boyd, Edinburgh, United Kingdom.

Flood, M., (1952) *Some Experimental Games, RM-789–1*, RAND Corporation, Santa Monica, California.

Flynn, M. T., Juergens, R., and Cantrell, T. R., (2008) "Employing ISR SOF best practices," *Joint Forces Quarterly*, **50**: 56–61.

Galula, D., (1963) *Pacification in Algeria: 1956–1958, MG-478-1*, RAND Corporation, Santa Monica, California.

Galula, D., (1964) *Counterinsurgency Warfare: Theory and Practice.* Frederick A. Praeger Publishers, New York.

Gass, S. I. and Assad, A. A., (2005) *An Annotated Timeline of Operations Research: An Informal History.* Springer Science and Kluwer Publishing Company, Boston, Massachusetts.

Gilbreth, F. and Gilbreth, L., (1917) *Applied Motion Study: A Collection of Papers on the Efficient Method to Industrial Preparedness*. Sturgis and Walton Company, New York.

Girardini, K., Lackey, A., Leuschner, K., Relles, D., Totten, M., and Blake, D., (2004) *Dollar Cost Banding: A New Algorithm for Computing Inventory Levels for Army Supply Support Activities*, MG-128-A, RAND Corporation, Santa Monica, California.

Gray, K., (2014) "The general who led a new kind of warfare to take on Al-Qaeda," Wired.co.uk, December 10, 2014. Accessed at: www.wired.co.uk/magazine/archive/2015/03/features/new-art-of-business.

Gwynn, C. W., (1934) *Imperial Policing*. MacMillan & Company Limited, London.

Harris, F. W., (1913) "How many parts to make at once," *Operations Research*, **38**(6): 947–950.

Haywood Jr., O. G., (1954) "Military decision and game theory," *Journal of the Operations Research Society of America*, **2**(4): 365–385.

Hindrichs, G., (1953) "Toward a philosophy of operations research," *Philosophy of Science*, **20**(1): 59–66.

Hitchcock, F., (1941) "The distribution of a product from several sources to numerous localities," *Journal of Mathematical Physics*, **20**: 224–230.

Holt, C., Modigliani, F., Muth, J., and Simon, H., (1960) *Planning Production, Inventories, and Work Force*. Prentice-Hall, Englewood Cliffs, New Jersey.

Hughes, W. P., Jr., (1995) "A salvo model of warships in missile combat used to evaluate their staying power," *Naval Research Logistics*, **42**(2): 267.

Hughes, W. P., Jr., (Ed.) (1997) *Military Modeling for Decision Making*. Military Operations Research Society, Alexandria, Virginia.

Hughes, W. P., Jr., (1998) "Some comments on the state of operations analysis," *Phalanx*, **31**(1): 6–7.

Hughes, W. P., Jr., (2000) *Fleet Tactics*. Naval Institute Press, Annapolis, Maryland.

Hughes, W. P., Jr., (2012) "Naval operations: A close look at the operational level of war at sea," *Naval War College Review*, **65**(3) 23–47.

Ishikawa, K., (1990) *Introduction to Quality Control*. 3A Corporation, Tokyo, Japan.

Jewell, W. S., (1977) "The analytic methods of operations research," *Philosophical Transactions of the Royal Society of London A: Mathematical, Physical and Engineering Sciences*, **287**(1346): 373–404.

Johnson, E., (1960) "A new application of operations research," *Operations Research*, **8**(3): 423–424.

Jones, S. G., (2010) "It takes the villages: Bringing change from below in Afghanistan," *Foreign Affairs*, **89**(3): 120–127.

Juran, J., (1988) *Juran on Planning for Quality*. Free Press, New York.

Kaufman, A., (1963) *Methods and Models of Operations Research*. Prentice-Hall, Englewood Cliffs, New Jersey.

Kellen, K., (1970) *Conversations with Enemy Soldiers in Late 1968/Early 1969: A Study of Motivation and Morale*. RM-6131-1-ISA/ARPA. RAND Corporation, Santa Monica, California.

Khintchine, A., (1932) "Mathematical theory of a stationary queue," *Matematicheskii Sbornik*, **39**(4): 73–84.

Kirby, M., (2003) *Operational Research in War and Peace: The British Experience from the 1930s to 1970*. Imperial College Press, London.

Kittel, C., (1947) "The nature and development of operations research," *Science*, **105**(2719): 150–153.

Kline, J., Hughes, Jr., W., and Otte, D., (2010) "Campaign analysis: An introductory review," in Cochran, J., (Ed.), *Wiley Encyclopedia of Operations Research and Management Science*. John Wiley & Sons, Inc., New York.

Kolmogorov, A., (1931) "Uber die Analytishcen Methoden in der Wahrscheinlichkeitsrechnung," *Mathematische Annalen*, **104**: 415–458.

Koopman, B. O., (1946) *Search and Screening*. Operations Evaluation Group, Office of the Chief of Naval Operations, Navy Department, Washington, D.C.

Koopmans, T., (1949) "Optimum utilization of the transportation system," *Econometrica: Journal of the Econometric Society*, **17**: 136–146.

Krepinevich, A. F., (1986) *The Army and Vietnam*. Johns Hopkins University Press, Baltimore, Maryland.

Lane, F. C., (1973) *Venice: A Maritime Republic*. Johns Hopkins University Press, Baltimore, Maryland.

Levine, E. S. and Tisch, J. S., (2014) "Analytics in action at the New York City Police Department's Counter-terrorism Bureau," *Military Operations Research*, **19**(4): 5–14.

Lévy, P., (1934) "Proprietes Asymptotiques des sommes de variables aleatoires enchainees," *Comptes rendus de l'Académie des Sciences*, **199**: 627–629.

Luce, R. and Raifa, H., (1957) *Games and Decisions*. John Wiley & Sons, New York.

Lynn, J. A., (1993) *Feeding Mars: Logistics in Western Warfare from the Middle Ages to the Present*. Westview Press, Boulder, Colorado.

Machol, R., (1977) "Principles of operations research—2. The Pirandello principle," *Interfaces*, **7**(4): 85–86.
McChrystal, S., (2011) "It takes a network: The new front line of modern warfare," *Foreign Policy*, February 21, 2011.
McChrystal, S., (2013) *My Share of the Task*. Penguin, New York.
McCloskey, J. F., (1987) "The beginnings of operations research: 1934–1941," *Operations Research*, **35**(1): 143–152.
McCloskey, J. F., (1987) "U.S. operations research in World War II," *Operations Research*, **35**(6): 910–925.
Miser, H. J., (Ed.) (1995) *Handbook of Systems Analysis: Cases*, Volume III, John Wiley & Sons Ltd., New York.
Miser, H. J., (1997) "The easy chair: Is it possible to have a good definitional description of operations research and management science?" *Interfaces*, **27**(6): 16–21.
Miser, H. J. and Quade, E. S., (1985) *Handbook of Systems Analysis: Overview of Uses, Procedures, Applications and Practice*. Volume I, John Wiley & Sons Ltd., New York.
Miser, H. J. and Quade, E. S., (1988) *Handbook of Systems Analysis: Craft Issues and Procedural Choices*. Volume II, John Wiley & Sons Ltd., New York.
Moffat, J., (2003) *Complexity Theory and Network Centric Warfare*. U.S. Department of Defense Command and Control Research Program, Information Age Transformation Series, Washington, D.C.
Mood, A. M., (1953) "Review of methods of operations research by Philip M. Morse, George E. Kimball," *Journal of the Operations Research Society of America*, **1**(5): 306–308.
Morse, P. M. and Kimball, G. E., (1951) *Methods of Operations Research*. The Technology Press, M.I.T. and John Wiley & Sons, Inc., New York.
Nash, J., (1950) "Equilibrium points in n-person games," *Proceedings of the National Academy of Sciences*, **36**: 48–49.
Neyman, J. and Pearson, E., (1933) "On the problem of the most efficient tests of statistical hypotheses," *Philosophical Transactions of the Royal Society of London. Series A, Containing Papers of a Mathematical or Physical Character*, **231**: 289–337.
O'Hanlon, M., (2009) *The Science of War: Defense Budgeting, Military Technology, Logistics, and Combat Outcomes*. Princeton University Press, Princeton, New Jersey.
Ohno, T., (1988) *The Toyota Production System: Beyond Large-Scale Production*. Productivity Press, Portland, Oregon.
Peltz, E., Halliday, J., Robbins, M., and Girardini, K., (2005a) *Sustainment of Army Forces in Operation Iraqi Freedom: Battlefield Logistics and Effects on Operations, MG-344-A*, RAND Corporation, Santa Monica, California.
Peltz, E., Robbins, M., Girardini, K., Eden, R., Halliday, J., and Angers, J., (2005b) *Sustainment of Army Forces in Operation Iraqi Freedom: Major Findings and Recommendations, MG-342-A*, RAND Corporation, Santa Monica, California.
Peltz, E. and Robbins, M., (2007) *Leveraging Complementary Distribution Channels for an Effective, Efficient Global Supply Chain, DB-515-A*, RAND Corporation, Santa Monica, California.
Peltz, E., Girardini, K., Robbins, M., and Boren, P., (2008) *Effectively Sustaining Forces Overseas While Minimizing Supply Chain Costs: Targeted Theater Inventory, DB-524-A/DLA*, RAND Corporation, Santa Monica, California.
Peltz, E., Kassing, D., Yost, C., Robbins, M., Girardini, K., Nichiporuk, B., Schirmer, P., Halliday, J., and Bondanella, J., (2015) "Mobilization, deployment, and sustainment in Operation IRAQI FREEDOM," in Perry, W., Darilek, R., Rohn, L., and Sollinger, J., (Eds), *Operation IRAQI FREEDOM: Decisive War, Elusive Peace*, RAND Corporation, Santa Monica, California.
Petit, B., (2011) "The fight for the village: Southern Afghanistan, 2010," *Military Review*, May–June. Accessed at: http://usacac.army.mil/CAC2/MilitaryReview/Archives/English/MilitaryReview_20110630_art 007.pdf.
Pollaczek, F., (1930) "Über eine Aufgabe der Wahrscheinlichkeitstheorie," *Mathematische Zeitschrift*, **32**: 64–100.
Quade, E. S., (Ed.), (1964) *Analysis for Military Decisions*. Rand McNally and Company, Chicago, Illinois.
Rappold, J. A. and Yoho, K. D., (2008) "A model for level-loading production in the process industries when demand is stochastic," *Production Planning & Control: The Management of Operations*, **19**(7): 686–701.
Schelling, T., (1960) *The Strategy of Conflict*. Harvard University Press, Cambridge, Massachusetts.
Shackleton, R., (1975) *Village Defense: Initial Special Forces Operations in Vietnam*. Phoenix Press, Arvada, Colorado.

Shewhart, W. A., (1931) *Economic Control of Quality of Manufactured Product*. Van Nostrand Publishers, New York.

Stouffer, S. A., Guttman, L., Suchman, E. A., Lazarsfeld, P. F., Star, S. A., and Clausen, J. A., (1950) *Measurement and Prediction: Studies in Social Psychology in World War II*, Vol. 4, Princeton University Press, Princeton, New Jersey.

Taylor, F. W., (1911) *The Principles of Scientific Management*. Harper Brothers, New York.

Taylor, F. W., (1912) *Shop Management*. Harper Brothers, New York.

Taylor, J. G., (1974) "Solving Lanchester-type equations for 'modern warfare' with variable coefficients," *Operations Research*, **22**(4): 756–770.

Taylor, J. G. and Brown, G. G., (1976) "Canonical methods in the solution of variable-coefficient Lanchester-type equations of modern warfare," *Operations Research*, **24**(1): 44–69.

Taylor, J. G., (1979) "Optimal commitment of forces in some Lanchester-type combat models," *Operations Research*, **27**(1): 96–114.

Taylor, J. G. (1979) "Prediction of zero points of solutions to Lanchester-type differential combat equations for modern warfare," *SIAM Journal on Applied Mathematics*, **36**(3): 438–456.

Taylor, J. G. and Brown, G. G. (1983) "Annihilation prediction for Lanchester-type models of modern warfare," *Operations Research*, **31**(4): 752–771.

Trinquier, R., (1964) *Modern Warfare: A French View of Counterinsurgency*. Frederick A. Praeger Publishers, New York.

Turing, A., (1936) "On computable numbers, with an application to the Entscheidungsproblem," *Proceedings of the London Mathematical Society*, **2**(42): 230–265.

Ulam, S., Richtmyer, R. D., and von Neumann, J., (1947) *Statistical Methods in Neutron Diffusion*, Report LAMS-551, Los Alamos Scientific Laboratory, Los Alamos, New Mexico.

van Creveld, M., (1980) *Supplying War: Logistics from Wallenstein to Patton*. Cambridge University Press, Cambridge, England.

von Neumann, J., (1928) "Zur Theorie de Gesellschaftsspiele," *Mathematische Annalen*, Vol. 100, pp. 295–320. Translated by Sonya Bargmann in A. W. Tucker and R. D. Luce (eds), *Contributions to the Theory of Games*, Vol. 4, Annals of Mathematics Study, No. 40, Princeton University Press, Princeton, New Jersey, 1959, pp. 13–42.

Washburn, A. and Kress, M., (2009) *Combat Modeling*. Springer, New York.

Whitney, H., (1935) "On the abstract properties of linear dependence," *American Journal of Mathematics*, **57**: 509–533.

Wohlstetter, A., Hoffman, F., Lutz, R. J., and Rowen, H. S., (1954) *Selection and Use of Strategic Air Bases, R-266*. RAND Corporation, Santa Monica, California.

Wohlstetter, R., (1962) *Pearl Harbor: Warning and Decision*. Stanford University Press, Stanford, California.

Womack, J. P. and Roos, D. T., (1990) *The Machine That Changed the World*. Free Press, New York.

Yoho, K. D., Rietjens, S., and Tatham, P., (2013) "Defence logistics: An important research field in need of researchers," *International Journal of Physical Distribution & Logistics Management*, **43**(2): 80–96.

27
NOT-FOR-PROFIT OPERATIONS MANAGEMENT

Qi Feng and J. George Shanthikumar

1 Introduction

In recent years, not-for-profits and nonprofits have become more frequent topics in our teaching and research. This chapter is intended to summarize the existing research development in not-for-profit operations as well as providing directions for further contributions that can be made by operations management researchers. To define the scope of "not-for-profit operations management," we should first articulate the distinction between not-for-profit and nonprofit.

The emergence and growth of the nonprofit sector in the last few decades have made it an important part of modern economy. By 2013, there were over 1.4 million nonprofit organizations in the United States (National Center for Charitable Statistics, n.d.). The nonprofit sector, consisting of private, voluntary, and nonprofit organizations and associations, is often referred to as the "third sector" after the public sector (i.e., government and its agencies) and the business sector (i.e., for-profit corporations). Today, nonprofit organizations span over local (e.g., community organizations), national (e.g., social, health, or educational services), and international (e.g., international nongovernmental organizations, global civil societies) levels, playing a crucial role in areas including welfare provisioning (e.g., disaster relief, humanitarian aid, and food stamps), education, community development, international relations, environment, and culture (Anheier 2014).

The objective of a nonprofit organization is not to benefit a narrow group of owners but a broader public, which is similar to that of a government. At the same time, a nonprofit must also ensure income and expense match over time, which is similar to business. However, nonprofits are distinct often because of their value (e.g., religious, political, humanitarian, moral, etc.), seeking nonmonetary returns such as faith, believers, adherents, or members rather than monetary returns (Young and Steinberg 1995). Economists have identified the primary roles of nonprofits as service-providers who provide various functions in delivering products and services to designated populations especially those with minority preferences, vanguards who experiment and pioneer new approaches, processes, or programs in service delivery, value guardians who foster and help express diverse values, and advocacies who give voice to the minority and particularistic interests and values for effecting changes and improvement in social and other policies (Kramer 1981). These roles allow nonprofit organizations to complement the public and business sectors. Thus, nonprofit organizations, forming a separate sector in an economy, distinguish themselves from organizations in the public sector and those in the business sector with tax being the most noticeable distinction.

Naturally, the major operations of nonprofit organizations are not for profit. As we speak of not-for-profit operations in this chapter, however, we are not limited to those activities performed by nonprofit organizations. In fact, many not-for-profit activities, for example, funding, organizing, or facilitating the logistics for disaster reliefs, may involve government agencies and private firms. Moreover, a nonprofit organization may also perform for-profit operations (e.g., generating revenue by serving high-income customers to subsidize the service to the low-income ones), though making money is not the ultimate goal. *Not-for-profit operations management* refers to managing the process of product or service delivery that is not aiming toward (eventual) profitability but toward certain welfare, social, environmental, or cultural values.

Though the nonprofit sector is an extensively studied area in economics, sociology, and political science, only fairly recently have researchers in the operations management field begun to pay considerable attention to not-for-profit operations. Because not-for-profit operations cover a wide range of activities and concern a large number of products and services, which each reveal some unique operational characteristics, operations management research can contribute in many important dimensions. It would be overly ambitious to complete a comprehensive discussion of not-for-profit operations within this chapter. Our intention is to offer some understanding of the major operational issues and provide some guidance for future research. In particular, we focus on the management of fundraising (Section 2), revenue (Section 3), resource (Section 4), distribution (Section 5), and performance (Section 6).

2 Fundraising for Not-for-Profit Operations

Though profitability is not its ultimate goal, a not-for-profit operation, like any business activities, needs funds in order to realize its intended value. Foster et al. (2009) summarize ten funding models of the nonprofit organizations based on the donor's value proposition and the recipient's value proposition. Funds can come from two areas: donation and revenue. This depends on whether they are directly related to the product or service provided through the operation. Most donative or philanthropic resources (e.g., gifts, grants, and public subsidies) are not direct revenue from the product or service of the operation as the beneficiaries are different from the donors. In addition to these fund sources, many nonprofit organizations also generate revenue either by directly charging a fee or price for the product or service, or by collecting membership dues from the intended beneficiaries or other customers. In this section, we mostly focus on the first type of funds and the discussions on the second type is postponed to Section 3, as it is closely related to the research on revenue management.

As donative funds consist of the major support for not-for-profit operations, fundraising is an important function. There are five typical fundraising sources (Carpenter n.d.):

(i) *Foundation support*: An example is the Bill & Melinda Gates Foundation, the largest private foundation. The foundation aims at enhancing healthcare and reducing extreme poverty globally and, in America, expanding educational opportunities and access to information technology.
(ii) *Corporate support*: Many large corporations with specific giving departments regularly contribute to specific need in the community.
(iii) *Individual support*: Donations can come from individuals who may or may not be connected with the nonprofit organization.

(iv) *Government support*: Often in the form of grants from specific government agencies.
(v) *Planned giving*: Examples include a donor putting a nonprofit organization as a beneficiary in his/her will or when a donor makes a multi-year giving commitment.

There are several important aspects of the fundraising process that need to be understood for the success of the operation.

2.1 Funding Instability and Prediction

Due to their dependence on philanthropic resources, the incomes of not-for-profit operations are heavily affected by fluctuations in the economy. The chronic resource insufficiency is a constant challenge faced by most nonprofit organizations (Salamon 1995). Typically, a period of economic downturn is accompanied by a decrease in funding and an increase in demand for not-for-profit products and services. Such an economic environment, on the one hand, forces nonprofit organizations to seek alternative sources for income generation (e.g., charging for the products or services offered; see Section 3. On the other hand, these nonprofit organizations should plan their programs and spending based on the projected income flow (Section 4). For either purpose, the ability to understand philanthropy and forecast the future funds becomes crucial.

The literature on fundraising is vast. Bekkers and Wiepking (2011) provide a survey of over 500 research studies on philanthropy across many different disciplines. Many of the studies present predictive approaches to identify qualitatively significant attributes of the donors that are related to their giving. Demographics (e.g., donors versus nondonors, male donors versus female donors, income level), donor patronage (e.g., major contributors versus regular donors), and contribution frequency (e.g., consistent versus occasional donors) are among the most analyzed attributes to characterize the heterogeneity in donors. With identified attributes, statistical methods are used to estimate predictive models for giving. Segmentations of potential donors are identified using tools like logit analysis (e.g., Lindahl and Winship 1992), classification and regression tree (e.g., Weerts and Ronca 2008), and finite-mixture models (e.g., Durango-Cohen and Balasubramanian 2015). Studies also assume different donation behavior in each segment and use descriptive approach to explain. Bekkers and Wiepking (2011) summarize eight mechanisms as the most important forces that drive charitable giving: awareness of need, solicitation, costs and benefits, altruism, reputation, psychological benefits, values, and efficacy. A more recent paper by Durango-Cohen and Balasubramanian (2015) also gives examples of studies focusing on different reasons for philanthropy.

Though results obtained from this rich body of literature help to give a mostly *qualitative* guide for selecting fundraising sources, there are several open issues remaining unsolved where researchers in operations management can greatly contribute.

First of all, among the researchers there are debates on whether or not certain variables are significantly related to giving behavior. For example, Lindahl and Winship (1992, p. 54) underscore their findings by claiming that "the variables that were in question in past studies were not significant." From the operational perspective, however, one would probably care less about *who* would give, rather *how much* funds would be available and *when*, because the answers to the former, though good to know, do not provide an immediate implication to resource and process planning toward realizing the intended value. Unfortunately, the prediction models in the existing studies mostly seek static estimates. Even the ones built in time-dimension do not offer the predictive ability to understand the future donative income flow.

The second aspect concerns how to directly translate the historical contribution data into a *prescriptive* solution for fundraisers and a *quantitative* description of the associated outcome. For example, a nonprofit organization can effectively select donors and generate funds by identifying means of building trust with potential donors (Sargeant and Lee 2004), understanding and inducing peer pressure among donors in giving (Meer 2011), making use of the tiered funding structure (McCardle et al. 2009), or leveraging conventional market variables like advertising and pricing (Weisbrod and Dominguez 1986). To be able to offer a prescriptive solution, one needs a data-driven model that links the data with the actions. Such a modeling approach should allow one to quantify the uncertainty associated with different funding sources so that one can then design appropriate resource planning strategies.

2.2 Funding Restrictions and Contingencies

Fundraising activities require effort and resources. However, excessive spending on fundraising can cause concerns from funders. It is typical that funders require reports on fund spending, not only tracking how effective the programs run but also monitoring the expense structures. For example, many foundations would not fund or renew funding if an organization's administrative and fundraising expense is above a certain percentage of the total expense. A typically recommended expense structure consists of program expenses between 70%–85%, administrative expenses between 10%–15%, and fundraising expenses between 5%–10% of total expenditures (Carpenter n.d.). In other words, funders use the ratio of expenses directly toward the intended value to total expense as a measure of operational efficiency. At the operational level, this imposes a resource or effort constraint on optimizing effective fundraising activities. Moreover, funding or renewal contingent on spending structure suggests that the nonprofit organizations should take a dynamic view of their operations. There is a delicate balance in how much resources to allocate in the current period to generate potential current and future funds while not hurting the efficiency measured in the current period to reduce the funders' giving incentive.

Other than expense structure, funders or donors may also impose other constraints or contingencies. One phenomenon is earmarking, which has become increasingly common in charitable giving. For example, the Donor Direct policy implemented by the Red Cross bounds it to spend donations only toward the donor-specified purposes. In particular, most of disaster response funding is earmarked (Pedraza-Martineza et al. 2011). Funders see earmarking as a way to ensure that the money goes to what they intend to support and not toward excessive overheads (e.g., upgrading office furniture or the lifestyle of an executive). Recipients, however, complain that such a policy often leads to insufficient funds for needs especially those with low media coverage and donor awareness, while having to use up excessive funds in designated areas to avoid reduced future contribution by the donor. For example, relief organizations, who cannot pay to build wells for clean drinking water, may receive plenty of support for a specific crisis that gets tremendous public attention; hospitals, having difficulty funding kidney research, may obtain generous funds for breast cancer research instead (Strom 2008).

Toyasaki and Wakolbinger (2014) set up an analytical model to understand the effect of earmarking on the interaction among an aid agency and multiple donors. They find that, for emergencies with strong media attention and donor interest, allowing for earmarking of donations is likely to reduce fundraising activities of organizations with low fundraising costs, and is likely to encourage fundraising activities among organizations with high fundraising costs. There are many open questions that need to be answered here. The most important one is the design of a mechanism to coordinate the aid agency and the donors. Though there is a large literature on supply chain coordination, the focus is very different. The unique feature of coordinating fundraising activities lies in the nonmonetary objectives of the aid agency and the donors. Another aspect worth studying is the collaboration among agencies involved in related activities. For example, disaster relief is often a joint effort by many agencies. At different times, some may have more flexible funding sources while others may have more earmarked funds. A carefully designed fund pooling mechanism can help improve the overall operational efficiency.

For certain programs, funding can be staged. Donors may track the progress of the project to decide whether or not to continue the support. In many situations, recipients may find that multiple rounds of fundraising for small contributions can lead to a higher overall amount of funds (Vesterlund 2006). However, staged funding leads to uncertainty in available resources during the program implementation. In a related study, Devalkar and Sohoni (2015) suggest that endogeneity of funding stream can be created when the donors choose to fund projects showing early positive outcomes. To obtain funding, however, the program directors may sacrifice operational efficiency to start the project earlier than needed, leading to suboptimal program implementation and resource management. In fact, similar observations have been made in capacity investment for new product manufacturing. For example, Tanrisever et al. (2015) find companies looking for capacity financing would be better off by first building a small capacity to reduce the marginal cost, because production cost reduction allows the firm to reduce the cost of financing the full capacity expansion.

All the aforementioned considerations and alike impose constraints or inter-temporal dependency on fundraising activities. The existing models in the operations literature involving the dynamics of limited funds often assume exogenous uncertainty in fundraising (e.g., Natarajan and Swaminathan 2014; Taylor and Xiao 2014b; Devalkar et al. 2016) with Devalkar and Sohoni (2015) and Natarajan and Swaminathan (2016) as exceptions. There is certainly room for more development along these dimensions.

3 Revenue Management and Pricing

Though the major support of not-for-profit operations comes from donative funds, revenue raised by charging for the product or service offered is becoming increasingly a large portion of the budget. Obviously, fee-charging helps to mitigate the uncertainty in fundraising and supplement funding deficiency during economic downturn. Funds from revenue are also flexible in the sense that they are not subject to donors' restrictions (e.g., earmarking). The advocates for fee-charging practice further suggest that such practice allows for accountability of the nonprofit organization in meeting the needs of the beneficiaries, instead of focusing on the requirement and satisfaction of the funders (Gary et al. 2004). Of course, charging may not be possible for certain not-for-profit operations, especially those intended to benefit the general population than a specific group of individuals (e.g., research institute, environmental advocates, human rights campaigns). From the perspective of the beneficiaries or customers, fee-charging can also have a positive impact. Paying a modest price for the product or service can create ownership or buy-in for the customers, increase the quality of the product or service perceived by the customers (Yoken and Berman 1984), and preserve the dignity of the customer.

There are several typical ways to charge the fees (see, e.g., http://strengtheningnonprofits. org/resources/guidebooks/Understanding_Fee-for-service_Models.pdf). A *mandatory fee* is a fixed price, lower than its market counterpart, predetermined based on specific criteria. Example organizations that charge mandatory fees include public universities and hospitals. Sometimes, a product or service can be offered at no cost while the customer is encouraged to make a *voluntary donation* or pay a *requested fee*. The difference between the two is that the amount of payment is determined by the customer in the former, while it is specified to the customer in the latter. Some organizations charge a *membership due* for all products and services available to members for free or at a reduced cost.

To optimize the use of products and services, a portfolio of fee structures or prices can be used to segment the customers into specific characteristics, e.g., timing of concert ticket purchase (Tereyagoglu et al. 2016). Income level is the most commonly used criterion because it enables the customers to contribute to the not-for-profit operations based on their financial ability. de Vericourt and Lobo (2009) formulate a dynamic model to analyze such a practice by an eye surgery hospital in India, where revenue generated from high-income customers is used to subsidize and offer free service to low-income customers. They analyze how to price the service to revenue-generating customers and how much resources to reserve for mission-serving customers. Lu and Shen (2015) studied a similar practice but tackle the problem from a different angle. They allow uncertainty in the service time and focus on surgical time allocation between the two segments of customers with a chance constraint over time. The modeling framework set up by de Vericourt and Lobo (2009) and Lu and Shen (2015) can be extended to other fee-charging structures, for example, voluntary donation by revenue generating customers. Moreover, considerations of uncertain philanthropic funds, the cost of product or service, and the customers' affordability can be included into the model to formulate a comprehensive revenue management strategy for the not-for-profit operations.

Many of the issues extensively studied in the context of profit-maximizing firms may have different representations in the context of not-for-profit operations. For example, like a for-profit firm, the nonprofit organization can use price as an instrument to signal the quality of its service or product, though the ultimate goal is not profit making. Quality can also influence the willingness of a revenue-generating customer to voluntarily support those who need the same service but cannot afford it.

As pricing schemes are often the central decision in revenue management, it is inevitable to take the market into consideration. Prices for similar or substitutable products or services available in the market can affect the price expectations of customers from different segments. Output, price, and quality are common levers in competition. Economists have developed analytical models in order to understand the competitive environment of nonprofit organizations. For example, Calem et al. (1999) analyze output competition between hospitals and thus the service prices are induced by the output decisions; Harrison and Lybecker (2005) study price competition between nonprofit and for-profit hospitals; and Liu and Weinberg (2004) analyze price competition between a for-profit firm and a nonprofit organization in a Stackelberg framework. Nevertheless, these analyses are done in static settings. There is a need for modeling work to understand the competition dynamics faced by nonprofit organizations and help these organizations effectively manage their operations to address the fluctuations in funding source and service need at different stages of an economic cycle.

4 Resource Management

Resource management for not-for-profit operations shares many similarities with its for-profit counterparts. Both aim at achieving a certain objective by efficiently utilizing and allocating resources involving budget and operating capacity (e.g., manpower, vehicles, equipment, and rooms). However, there are critical differences too. The most apparent one is the objective. Though cost minimization can be important for both, the not-for-profit operations often have their unique features that do not appear in most for-profit operations.

For example, during the fundraising process, a nonprofit organization attempts to obtain the largest donation without exceeding a certain spending percentage. At the same time, resource distribution must allow trust and relationship building with donors and funders (Sargeant and Lee 2004). When managing revenue from high-income customers, a nonprofit aims at maximizing the well-being of low income customers and thus has to carefully allocate the limited operating capacity between the two (de Vericourt and Lobo 2009; Lu and Shen 2015). When planning the material flow of the product to be distributed, a nonprofit organization may need to carefully distribute the limited, uncertain funds over the planned supporting period (Natarajan and Swaminathan 2014). When spending funds on different activities, a nonprofit may be constrained by how to use funds based on the donors' request (Toyasaki and Wakolbinger 2014). When distributing insufficient resources to needy groups, the nonprofit organization must carefully evaluate the negative consequences of shortage induced by prioritizing allocation (Azhar and Lejeune 2016). Each of these aspects brings a new dimension to the conventional resource planning, where both analytical and empirical modeling can contribute.

We highlight one specific area, workforce management. A unique feature of workforce planning in not-for-profit operations is the heavy involvement of volunteers and members, in addition to the paid workforce. For example, organizations like the Girl Scouts and the Salvation Army rely mostly on their regular members and long term and episodic volunteers (Drucker 1989), and the Red Cross depends heavily on the contribution of spontaneous volunteers in disasters (Wolczynski et al. 2015). Unlike in the planning for a regular workforce, labor cost is not the major concern for assigning and scheduling volunteers, as they are provided none or very little monetary compensation. Volunteers reveal great heterogeneity in their incentives, skills, and capabilities, which are *a priori* uncertain to the planner. As many of them have a short working period, volunteers can only perform tasks with specific and limited focus, without legal liability (e.g., confidentiality of a rescued victim or of a rehabilitated young criminal), and not requiring extensive training. Operational methods can help in matching volunteer resources with the need and scheduling of volunteers' time based on their arrival and availability. Examples of research in this area include Sampson (2006), Falasca and Zobel (2012), Lodree et al. (2015), Wolczynski et al. (2015), and Sonmez et al. (2016).

For regular or long-term staffing, task assignment or scheduling can often be separated from hiring, as the former concerns day-to-day operations, while the latter is a tactical or even strategic decision. With volunteers, however, resource allocation and acquisition have more intricate connections. In many practices, volunteer and task arrivals are parallel rather than sequential, and future arrivals of both are highly uncertain. Matching the volunteer resources with the needed tasks can be highly dynamic and it requires a careful coordination between recruiting and assignment decisions. On the one hand, an excessive number of volunteers can reduce efficiency because the volunteers' unfamiliarity with the task and team members can lead to a great complexity in management, supervision, and coordination. Volunteers who are underutilized or mismatched with tasks reveal reduced propensity to contribute in the future, which can have a profound impact on the reputation of the organization. On the other hand, insufficient volunteering hinders the operation to realize its intended purpose. Overly utilizing volunteer resources often leads to deterioration of quality, which can also result in reduced future commitment.

Moreover, purposive or missionary incentives are critically important for members and volunteers to contribute their time and effort. Volunteer motivation can be multifaceted along values, understanding, career, social, and prospective dimensions (Clary et al. 1996). Successful volunteer acquisition and task assignment require an appropriate assessment of the volunteering incentive. Thus, the process of volunteer acquisition must take into account the assignment of the volunteers that can fulfill their feelings of satisfaction, which, in turn, help to incentivize good performance and future participation. This gives rise to a new angle of study in resource management.

Volunteer evaluation is another dimension that can help in planning such a resource, where prescriptive empirical work can add value. Different angles can be taken to analyze historical data of programs and participating volunteers. At the recruiting stage, one can identify the appropriate attributes of volunteers, who are likely to efficiently perform the needed task. Identifying potential "fit" volunteers allows for effective design of acquisition strategy in terms of ways to approach and attract such resources. A deeper issue to explore is how task assignment and the interactions among team members affect the performance and satisfaction of a certain kind of volunteer. Prescriptive models addressing these issues can become very handy for managing volunteer resources.

5 Distribution of Product and Service

Like in any other operation, the process of distributing product and service in not-for-profit operations concerns what to offer, who supplies the materials, how to distribute the product, and who consumes it. We discuss these aspects in the following subsections.

5.1 The Choice of Product or Service Offering

The first question is: what product or service will the organization offer and in what forms? Answers to this question, however, may change over time. The means to achieve the mission of a nonprofit evolve with the economic and social environment which reshapes the need of the beneficiaries, the "customer" of the product or service offered. The growth of an organization may allow it to broaden its offerings to better achieve its mission as well as increase its efficiency in production and distribution with economies of scope. One example is the Girl Scouts' expanded training program in business and science in addition to the traditional homemaking skills. In another vein, adapting computers for disabled people could not have been offered by any organization twenty years ago.

A new product or service to be introduced needs a thorough analysis to understand how it impacts all the stakeholders involved. Product or service proliferation management models can be developed.

One emerging phenomenon is the increased use of cash to replace in-kind provision, particularly in disaster relief. During the 2007–2008 food crisis in Swaziland, cash transfers were used in addition to regular food distribution to the drought-affected population (Devereux and Jere 2008). Cash transfer programs have been adopted in the Philippines to deliver assistance in humanitarian emergencies (Poisson 2011). Ethiopia, a country with a population of over eight million food insecure people, has implemented programs to facilitate predictable income transfer to replace part of the food ration (Kebede 2006). The decisions regarding whether or not to offer cash and what portion of the provision to be offered in cash involve many trade-offs that can be analyzed using operations models.

From the beneficiaries' viewpoint, cash has its attraction compared with in-kind provision. With cash, the beneficiaries can purchase alternative food items to meet their specific dietary preference without being restricted by the offered ones. Alternatively, spending on food may be saved for essential nonfood items (e.g., health, clothing, and education) or investment in assets and livelihoods (e.g., fertilizers for farming, boats for fishing, and cookers for street food vending) to improve the living condition in the long run. However, there are drawbacks with cash as well. The market availability and price for food can be fluctuating, leading to uncertainties in buying power. Cash distribution can be impossible in remote areas where a banking system is not accessible or areas with little attraction for trade.

From the execution perspective, cash is often easier to distribute than physical goods, as the latter often involves sophisticated procurement and logistics planning. However, cash, as opposed to food, may not ensure that its intended purpose is served. Cash may be more vulnerable to corrupt diversion, looting, or theft than food. Additionally, cash can offer too much flexibility to the beneficiary as it may be used on anything including inappropriate purposes (e.g., alcohol and cigarettes). Thus, there is a risk that such an aid program may have negative side effects to the society.

The choice between cash and in-kind can have a significant impact on the local market, which cannot be ignored in assessing the temporal effect of the policy. Empirical evidence suggests that cash injection leads to price increase in the local market. For example, Devereux and Jere (2008) find that the food price inflation is much higher than predicted in regions where half the food ration is replaced by cash. Their study also finds that the stocks for both food and nonfood items increase as well, suggesting the market is responsive to the increased cash. Compared with food, cash transfers lead to very different dynamics of the supply chains for food and nonfood products during the disaster recovery periods.

5.2 The Supply Process and Inventory Management

Like business operations, a not-for-profit operation needs to source products and services in order to achieve its goals. While cost efficiency may not always be an objective and specific constraints need to be imposed, the developments in conventional procurement and inventory management can be borrowed to manage the material flow in not-for-profit operations. For example, Prastacos (1984) summarizes the research on procurement and inventory management for hospital blood banks. He presents statistical methods for demand and supply fitting as well as analytical models for determining procurement policies and inventory levels based on cost-minimization objectives, which are very similar to the conventional forecasting and perishable inventory models but with application to blood bank data. Duran et al. (2011) model the configuration of the supply network with stockpiling for emergency relief items. Their method allows for an evaluation of how stockpiling policies affect emergency response time, a critical determinant of human suffering and life loss in many disasters. Arifoglu et al. (2012) model the uncertain supply of vaccination as a stochastic proportional yield of production. Though the supplier is a profit maximizer, the social planner (i.e., the offering agency) focuses on the social welfare. Natarajan and Swaminathan (2014) apply periodic-review inventory model to analyze the effect of uncertain philanthropic funds on the procurement strategy over a finite horizon. Balcik and Ak (2014) analyze cost efficient selection of suppliers who differ in their commitment requirements, reserve capacities, pricing schedules, and geographic coverage when sourcing for humanitarian relief.

Many areas in the not-for-profit supply processes need to be analyzed and such analyses can add new dimensions to operations literature. We discuss two of those areas. One concerns subsidizing producers or suppliers and the other concerns collecting from supply networks.

The commercial markets for products and services offered by not-for-profit operations often give limited access to a low socioeconomic population, a certain minority population, or even the general population. Consumption of such products and services by inaccessible populations often generate positive social benefit. Thus, governments and nonprofit organizations may offer *subsidies* to the producers or suppliers to reduce their costs and thus induce increased outputs and reduced prices. Governments in developing countries often subsidize food producers (e.g., cereal mills) in order to increase supply (Tuck and Lindert 1996). The distribution of health products to the poor is commonly subsidized by government or nonprofit organizations. Examples include ready-to-use therapeutic food (Natarajan and Swaminathan 2014), contraceptives (Behrman 1989; Kearney and Levine 2009), recommended malaria drugs (Sabot et al. 2009), vaccines (Chick et al. 2008; Whittington et al. 2012), and eyeglasses (Karnani et al. 2011).

Subsidy programs are also offered to suppliers to popularize products with improved social value even in developed countries. For example, subsidies are given to restaurants, both fast food and sit-down establishments, for offering vegetables, fruits, and healthy beverages to entice consumers reducing the high caloric intake that may contribute to obesity and other health problems (An 2012; Powell et al. 2013). Sometimes a subsidy may not be directly offered to the producer or supplier. Instead, it is given in forms of a price subsidy or rebate to the consumers to induce consumption. This is a typical way to encourage adoption of new technological products (Kalish and Lilien 1983) or environmentally friendly products (Hirte and Tscharaktschiew 2013; Cohen et al. 2016). Price subsidy to consumers, though not paid directly to the producers or suppliers, usually induces an increased supply of the product or service.

In the economics literature, government subsidy has been extensively researched and the focus is often given to its effect on social welfare and local economy. Recently, researchers in operations management started paying attention to subsidy programs. These studies touch on the effect of subsidies on the supplier's output decisions (Taylor and Xiao 2014b; Berenguer et al. 2016) and technology investment (Krass et al. 2013), as well as coordination with the suppliers (Mamani et al. 2012; Chick et al. 2008; Raz and Ovchinnikov 2015). Subsidies can influence the supply process in many other dimensions. For example, a program subsidizing farmers can devise proper incentives to induce production of the appropriate mix of products for the target population.

Though many aid products are produced by designated suppliers, *collection* is a common means of sourcing for many not-for-profit operations. For example, food bank gleaner volunteers pick up donations from farmers, the Salvation Army collects donations at different locations through collection sites or pickup trucks, and organ procurement organizations acquire the deceased's organs from donor families. Collection processes involve a great deal of uncertainty because the time, amount, type, and quality of the donated physical items are highly unpredictable. For example, the arrival of gleaning foods and the availability of pickup volunteers are both stochastic processes, leading to a high risk of food wastage (Sonmez et al. 2016). Different constraints exist in different collection processes. Items such as food and organs are highly perishable, while quality checks to ensure food safety and transfer requirements of organs take time. Many of the collection processes must comply with restrictions and regulations. For example, it is mandated that fresh frozen plasma be manufactured only from male blood donors (Williamson and Devine 2013). The existing studies on sourcing through collection often examine the supply processes at an aggregate level. For example, Prastacos (1984) presents models of blood collection based on estimated supply quantity at each collection location and develops heuristic policies by assuming perfect supply estimates. Sonmez et al. (2016)'s model gleaning foods and gleaner volunteers as two exogenous stochastic processes. In practice, however, the donors and donated items can reveal significant heterogeneity among one another. Matching collection with diverse need is an important consideration in these sourcing processes to reduce waste of the donations and increase the welfare of the beneficiaries. There has not been much analytical and empirical work developed to understand the supply network for such collection processes and quantify efficient and effective collection strategies. Arikan et al. (2015) is an example of an exception. They analyze the donor and recipient data for kidney transfer to understand the organ procurement process and evaluate alternative policies.

5.3 Allocation and Consumer Behavior

The product or service offered by a not-for-profit operation is eventually handed over to the needy people. Allocation of the product and service among the target beneficiaries or customers is a common decision to be made. Sometimes, allocation can be a consequence of a differentiated pricing scheme (recall our discussion in Section 3), while in other situations, the allocation is a direct result of decisions on logistics distribution and inventory rationing.

As in their for-profit counterpart, understanding the characteristics of the customer within different segments is the starting point for making product and service allocation decisions in not-for-profit operations. Heterogeneity among the customers can be often identified based on factors like demographics, the extent of need for aid, location, and social interaction. In aiding the drought-affected people suffering from food shortages, the amount of aid is distributed according to the need, and the form of distribution (i.e., food or cash) is determined based on accessibility to financial services and trade (Devereux and Jere 2008). Distribution by food banks often attempts to balance need, nutrition, and local preference. Mismatch in the amount and type can lead to waste or spoilage (Teron and Tarasuk 1999). Medical resource allocation decisions must consider the medical conditions of the patients (Atasu et al. 2016). Effective distribution of limited products like vaccines and antibiotics for contagious diseases must take into account factors like the population density, age mix, income level, and health conditions so that the medicine distribution can effectively reduce disease spreading and save lives. In all these examples, there are opportunities for developing models to understand the inherent trade-offs using operations management tools. For example, Natarajan and Swaminathan (2016) develop an analytical model to understand dynamic distribution to patients classified into different health states, aiming at minimizing the disease-adjusted life periods lost. Bravata et al. (2006) develop a simulation model to understand how the distribution of medical supplies between local and regional sites impact the mortality of a potential anthrax attack.

Different allocation policies may induce very different behaviors of the customers or beneficiaries, which in turn determines the effectiveness of the policy. For example, personal decisions on vaccination injection can lead to different risk evaluation of an epidemic (Arifoglu et al. 2012); individuals' choices of clean energy cooking methods can affect the health of the entire population (Hatten 2009); consumers' awareness can be influenced by the execution of a subsidy program and, in turn, affecting the adoption of a socially desirable product (Taylor and Xiao 2014a).

6 Performance Evaluation

Researchers from different disciplines have produced an extensive literature to evaluate the performance of nonprofits at the industrial or organizational level. For example, Steinberg (1986) attempts to evaluate the implicit objective underlying the behavior of nonprofits by estimating the marginal donative product of their fundraising. He concludes that welfare, education, and arts firms act as service maximizers, while health firms are budget maximizers. Calem et al. (1999) and Gaynor and Vogt (2003) suggest that output maximization is a common objective.

Accounting researchers have found expense misreporting is common among nonprofit organizations (e.g., Krishnan et al. 2006). Keating et al. (2008) conclude that many nonprofits misreport fundraising expenses by putting it as a component of net revenue rather than expenses. Privett and Erhun (2011) use an analytical model to explain that such a misreporting incentive is driven by the common practice that the funders use the ratio of program expense to total expense to evaluate the efficiency of the nonprofits. They conclude that fund allocation based on reported efficiency does not result in efficient funding allocation.

Aside from organizational level evaluations, the most commonly used form of evaluation in practice is program evaluation. It is a result based evaluation of the extent to which a program meets the specific needs (Fine et al. 2000). We take two examples from Anheier (2014): Performance indicators of a vocational rehabilitation and employment training program may include the number of participants placed in employment who retained their job for 150 days, average hourly wage, average work hours per week, the percentage of employers satisfied with the program, etc. An environmental program may be evaluated by the amount of material recovered, the amount of recycled material diverted from landfills, and percentage of citizens satisfied with the recycling program. Excellent performance on these indicators often attract funding on similar or related programs. However, there are concerns in focusing on program evaluations. As Campbell (2002) points out, overly focusing on program outcomes can induce program developers to overlook the social value in a longer horizon or in a larger scope. There is certainly a need for research that introduces system and dynamic views in evaluating not-for-profit operations and identify process improvement opportunities.

7 Implications for Managers

We have discussed several key aspects of not-for-profit operations management. While we focus on its unique features when compared with for-profit operations management, it is clear throughout this chapter that many of the methodologies and theories developed for for-profit operations can provide helpful guidance to managing the not-for-profit operations. We highlight four key messages to the leaders in not-for-profit operations:

- Integrating cash flow with operational planning and execution is particularly relevant and crucial to not-for-profit operations.
- Human resources may not be incentivized by monetary compensation schemes. Instead, task assignment and performance evaluation must take into account the heterogeneity in the motivations of the workforce.
- Not-for-profit operations management must deal with different constitutions with varying objectives. Coordination among different parties becomes more important and less straightforward compared to that among for-profit entities.
- Reaching out to beneficiaries through not-for-profit operations is less of a competitive act than a cooperative one. Resource sharing among different parties becomes particularly valuable for fulfilling their long-term mission.

8 Directions for Future Research

Not-for-profit operations cover a wide range of activities as well as diverse types of institutions and organizations. It is impossible to cover all the operational features or issues in a short chapter. This area, playing increasingly important roles in our economy and society, has gathered increasing attention by operations management researchers. Our intention is to offer some thoughts on research opportunities for not-for-profit operations and guide the directions to expand the dimensions of operations management studies. We have discussed the following potential research areas:

- Prediction of funding levels, identification and classification of funding sources, quantification of fund raising strategies and integrating fundraising with operational design
- Dynamic revenue management and pricing scheme design that allows for coping with fluctuation in funding levels and competition for funds
- Product and service portfolio management to achieve the intended missions and to adapt to the changing needs of the beneficiaries
- Design of supply networks, inventory allocation, and incentive schemes for product and service offering
- Policy design for product and service distribution to heterogeneous needy beneficiaries to achieve the intended objectives and avoid negative social outcomes
- Systematic and dynamic approach to evaluate operational performance.

Many aspects, which can be important for specific context, are not highlighted in our discussion. Though we do not devote a separate section on coordination of decisions, it is crucial to achieve operational efficiency because not-for-profit operations involve many stakeholders and highly decentralized decision making. Coordination is needed for aligning the incentive of the funders or donors with the recipient in fundraising (Privett and Erhun 2011; Toyasaki and Wakolbinger 2014), synchronizing the material flow of product or service in logistic distribution (Dolinskaya et al. 2011), matching the procurement process with the consumption process in supply management (Arora and Subramanian 2016), and building partnership with government agencies (Salamon 1987).

Due to decentralized operations, information plays a pivotal role in many situations. When an agency attempts to increase consumption of a product with social benefit, one question to ask is whether to spend on subsidizing the producer or on providing appropriate information to customers (Ashraf et al. 2013). Designing a distribution policy can be challenging when aid may be offered to individuals whose type may not be verifiable (Blackorby and Donaldson 1988). For example, it is prohibitively expensive to distinguish an individual who would use cash aid for alcohol from one who would spend on food for kids, or an individual who is not a rape victim from one who is.

With the increasing influence of not-for-profit operations on our economy and society, the need for understanding such operations and formulating appropriate strategies and policies opens up many opportunities for operations researchers. It is our hope that this short chapter would generate interest among the operations community, and good research work with potential practical impact would follow.

References and Bibliography

An, R. (2012) "Effectiveness of subsidies in promoting healthy food purchases and consumption: A review of field experiments," *Public Health Nutrition*, 16(7): 1215–1228.

Anheier, H. K. (2014) *Nonprofit Organizations: Theory, Management, Policy*. London; New York: Routledge.

Arifoglu, K., S. Deo, and S. M. R. Iravani. (2012) "Consumption externality and yield uncertainty in the influenza vaccine supply chain: Interventions in demand and supply sides," *Management Science*, 58(6): 1072–1091.

Arikan, M., B. Ata, J.J. Friedewald, and R. P. Parker. (2015) "What drives the geographical differences in deceased donor organ procurement in the United States," *Working paper*.

Arora, P., and R. Subramanian. (2016) "Improving societal outcomes in the organ donation value chain," *Production and Operations Management* (**forthcoming**).

Ashraf, N., B. K. Jack, and E. Kamenica. (2013) "Information and subsidies: Complements or substitutes?" *Journal of Economic Behavior & Organization*, **88**: 133–139.

Atasu, A., B. Toktay, and W. Yeo. (2016) "Efficient medical surplus discovery," *Production and Operations Management* (**forthcoming**).

Azhar, A., and M. Lejeune. (2016) "Resource deployment and donation allocation for epidemic outbreaks," *Production and Operations Management* (**forthcoming**).

Balcik, B., and D. Ak. (2014) "Supplier selection for framework agreements in humanitarian relief," *Production and Operations Management*, **23**(6): 1028–1041.

Behrman, J. R. (1989) "The simple analytics of contraceptive social marketing," *World Development*, **17**(10): 1499–1521.

Bekkers, R., and P. Wiepking. (2011) "A literature review of empirical studies of philanthropy: Eight mechanisms that drive charitable giving," *Nonprofit and Voluntary Sector Quarterly*, **40**(5): 924–973.

Berenguer, G., Q. Feng, J. G. Shanthikumar, and L. Xu. (2016) "The effects of subsidies on increasing consumption through for-profit and not-for-profit newsvendors," *Productions and Operations Management*. DOI: 10.1111/poms.12632

Blackorby, C., and D. Donaldson. (1988) "Cash versus kind, self-selection, and efficient transfers," *American Economic Review*, **78**(4): 691–700.

Bravata, D. M., G. S. Zaric, J. E. Holty, M. L. Brandeau, E. R. Wilhelm, K. M. McDonald, and D. K. Owens. (2006) "Reducing mortality from anthrax bioterrorism: Strategies for stockpiling and dispensing medical and pharmaceutical supplies," *Biosecur Bioterror*, **4**(3): 244–262.

Calem, P. S., A. Dor, and J. A. Rizzo. (1999) "The welfare effects of mergers in the hospital industry," *Journal of Economics and Business*, **51**: 197–213.

Campbell, D. (2002) "Outcomes assessment and the paradox of nonprofit accountability," *Nonprofit Management and Leadership*, **12**(3): 243–259.

Carpenter, H. (n.d.) *Nonprofit Operations Toolkit*. www.mtnonprofit.org/%uploadedfiles/tertiary_information/starting_a_nonprofit/nonprofitoperationstoolkit3rdedpub.pdf

Chick, S. E., H. Mamani, and D. Simchi-Levi. (2008) "Supply chain coordination and influenza vaccination," *Operations Research*, **56**(6): 1493–1506.

Clary, E. G., M. Snyder, and A. A. Stukas. (1996) "Volunteers' motivations: Findings from a national survey," *Nonprofit and Voluntary Sector*, **25**(4): 485–505.

Cohen, M. C., R. Lobel, and G. Perakis. (2016) "The impact of demand uncertainty on consumer subsidies for green technology adoption," *Management Science*, **62**(5): 1235–1258.

de Vericourt, F., and M. S. Lobo. (2009) "Resource and revenue management in nonprofit operations," *Operations Research*, **57**(5): 1114–1128.

Devalkar, S., and M. Sohoni. (2015) "Payment for results: Signaling efficiency in non-profit operations," *Working paper*, Indian School of Business, Hyderabad, India.

Devalkar, S., M. Sohoni, and P. Arora. (2016) "Ex-post funding: How should a resource-constrained non-profit organization allocate its initial funds?" *Production and Operations Management*. DOI: 10.1111/poms.12633

Devereux, S., and P. Jere. (2008) "Choice, dignity and empowerment? Cash and food transfers in Swaziland: An evaluation of Save the Children's emergency drought response." www.savethechildren.org.uk/sites/default/files/docs/SavetheChildren_Emergency_Drought_Response_Evaluation_08_1.pdf.

Dolinskaya, I. S., Z. Shi, K. R. Smilowitz, and M. Ross. (2011) "Decentralized approaches to logistics coordination in humanitarian relief," in T. Doolen, E. Van Aken, eds., *Proceedings of the 2011 Industrial Engineering Research Conference*, May, Reno, NV.

Drucker, P. E. (1989) "What business can learn from nonprofits," *Harvard Business Review*, (July–August): 88–93.

Duran, S., M. A. Gutierrez, and P. Keskinocak. (2011) "Pre-positioning of emergency items for CARE international," *Interfaces*, **41**(3): 223–237.

Durango-Cohen, E. J., and S. K. Balasubramanian. (2015) "Effective segmentation of university alumni: Mining contribution data with finite-mixture models," *Research in Higher Education*, **56**(1): 78–104.

Falasca, M., and C. Zobel. (2012) "An optimization model for volunteer assignments in humanitarian organizations," *Socio-Economic Planning Sciences*, **46**: 250–260.

Fine, A. H., C. E. Thayer, and A. Coghlan. (2000) "Program evaluation practice in the nonprofit sector," *Nonprofit Management and Leadership*, **10**(3): 331–339.

Foster, W. L., P. Kim, and B. Christiansen. (2009) "Ten nonprofit funding models," *Stanford Social Innovation Review*. https://ssir.org/articles/entry/ten_nonprofit_funding_models

Gary, C. M., S. M. Oster, and C. Weinberg. (2004) "To fee or not to fee?" *Nonprofit Quarterly* (June 21). https://nonprofitquarterly.org/2004/06/21/to-fee-or-not-to-fee-and-related-questions/

Gaynor, M., and W. B. Vogt. (2003) "Competition among hospitals," *RAND Journal of Economics*, **34**(4): 764–785.

Harrison, T. D., and K. M. Lybecker. (2005) "The effect of the nonprofit motive on hospital competitive behavior," *Contributions in Economic Analysis & Policy*, **4**(1): 1–15.

Hatten, M. L. (2009) "Subsidy schemes for the dissemination of improved stoves: Experiences of GTZ HERA and energising development," *Gesellschaft für Technische Zusammenarbeit* (GTZ), Eschborn, Germany.

Hirte, G., and S. Tscharaktschiew. (2013) "The optimal subsidy on electric vehicles in German metropolitan areas: A spatial general equilibrium analysis," *Energy Economics*, **40**: 515–528. http://strengtheningnonprofits.org/resources/guidebooks/Understanding_Fee-for-service_Models.pdf

Kalish, S., and G. L. Lilien. (1983) "Optimal price subsidy policy for accelerating the diffusion of innovation," *Marketing Science*, **2**(4): 407–420.

Karnani, A., B. Garrette, J. Kassalow, and M. Lee. (2011) "Better vision for the poor," *Stanford Social Innovation Review*. https://ssir.org/articles/entry/better_vision_for_the_poor

Kearney, M. S., and P. B. Levine. (2009) "Subsidized contraception, fertility, and sexual behavior," *The Review of Economics and Statistics*, **91**(1): 137–151.

Keating, E. K., L. M. Parsons, and A. A. Roberts. (2008) "Misreporting fundraising: How do nonprofit organizations account for telemarketing campaigns?" *The Accounting Review*, **83**(2): 417–446.

Kebede, E. (2006) "Moving from emergency food aid to predictable cash transfers: Recent experience in Ethiopia," *Development Policy Review*, **24**(5): 579–599.

Kramer, R. (1981) *Voluntary Agencies in the Welfare State*. Berkeley, CA: University of California Press.

Krass, D., T. Nedorezov, and A. Ovchinnikov. (2013) "Environmental taxes and the choice of green technology," *Production and Operations Management*, **22**(5): 1035–1055.

Krishnan, R., M. H. Yetman, and R. J. Yetman (2006) "Expense misreporting in nonprofit organizations," *The Accounting Review*, **81**(2) 399–420.

Lindahl, W., and C. Winship. (1992) "Predictive models for annual fundraising and major gift fundraising," *Non-profit Management and Leadership*, **3**(1): 43–63.

Liu, Y., and C. B. Weinberg. (2004) "Are nonprofits unfair competitors for businesses? An analytical approach," *J. Public Policy Marketing*, **23**(1): 65–79.

Lodree, E. J., L. B. Davis, and R. A. Cook. (2015) "Managing relief center convergence following large-scale disaster events," *Working paper*, Culverhouse College of Commerce, Tuscaloosa, AL.

Lu, M., and S. Shen. (2015) "Not-for-profit surgery block allocation with cross-subsidization," *Working paper*, Purdue University, West Lafayette, IN.

Mamani, H., E. Adida, and D. Dey. (2012) "Vaccine market coordination using subsidy," *IIE Transactions on Healthcare Systems Engineering*, **2**(1): 78–96.

McCardle, K. F., K. Rajaram, and C. S. Tang. (2009) "A decision analysis tool for evaluating fundraising tiers," *Decision Analysis*, **6**(1): 4–13.

Meer, J. (2011) "Brother, can you spare a dime? Peer pressure in charitable solicitation," *Journal of Public Economics*, **95**: 926–941.

Natarajan, K. V., and J. M. Swaminathan. (2014) "Inventory management in humanitarian operations: Impact of amount, schedule, and uncertainty in funding," *Manufacturing & Service Operations Management*, **16**(4): 595–603.

Natarajan, K. V., and J. M. Swaminathan. (2016) "Multi-treatment inventory allocation in humanitarian health settings under funding constraints," *Production and Operations Management*. DOI: 10.1111/poms.12634

National Center for Charitable Statistics. (n.d.) *Number of Nonprofit Organizations in the United States, 2003–2013*. http://nccsweb.urban.org/PubApps/profile1.php?state=US

Pedraza-Martineza, A. J., O. Stapleton, and L. N. Van Wassenhove. (2011) "Field vehicle fleet management in humanitarian operations: A case-based approach," *Journal of Operations Management*, **29**(5): 404–421.

Poisson, G. (2011) *Cash transfer programming in emergencies: Cash transfer mechanisms and disaster preparedness in the Philippines*. Oxfam House: The Cash Learning Partnership. www.cashlearning.org/downloads/resources/calp/Cash%20Transfer%20Mechanisms%20in%20the%20Philippines_web.pdf

Powell, L. M., J. F. Chriqui, T. Khan, R. Wada, and F. J. Chaloupka. (2013) "Assessing the potential effectiveness of food and beverage taxes and subsidies for improving public health: A systematic review of prices, demand and body weight outcomes," *Obesity Reviews*, **14**: 110–128.

Prastacos, G. P. (1984) "Blood inventory management: An overview of theory and practice," *Management Science*, **30**(7): 777–800.

Privett, N., and F. Erhun. (2011) "Efficient funding: Auditing in the nonprofit sector," *Manufacturing & Service Operations Management*, **13**(4): 471–488.

Raz, G., and A. Ovchinnikov. (2015) "Coordinating pricing and supply of public interest goods using government rebates and subsidies," *IEEE Transactions on Engineering Management*, **62**(1): 65–79.

Sabot, O. J., A. Mwita, J. M. Cohen, Y. Ipuge, M. Gordon, D. Bishop, M. Odhiambo, L. Ward, and C. Goodman. (2009) "The impact of subsidized artemisinin-based combination therapies distributed through private drug shops in rural Tanzania," *PLoS ONE*, **4**(9). http://journals.plos.org/plosone/article?id=10.1371/journal.pone.0006857

Salamon, L. M. (1987) "Partners in public service: The scope and theory of government-nonprofit relations," in *The nonprofit sector: A research handbook*, pp. 99–117. New Haven, CT: Yale University Press.

Salamon, L. M. (1995) *Partners in Public Service: Government-Nonprofit Relations in the Modern Welfare State*. Baltimore, MD: Johns Hopkins University Press.

Sampson, S. (2006) "Optimization of volunteer labor assignments," *Journal of Operations Management*, **24**(4): 363–377.

Sargeant, A., and S. Lee. (2004) "Trust and relationship commitment in the United Kingdom voluntary sector: Determinants of donor behavior," *Psychology & Marketing*, **21**(8): 613–635.

Sonmez, E., D. Lee, M. I. Gomez, and X. Fan. (2016) "Improving food bank gleaning operations: An application in New York State," *American Journal of Agricultural Economics*, **9**(2): 549–563.

Steinberg, R. (1986) "The revealed objective function of nonprofit firms," *Rand Journal of Economics*, **17**(4): 508–526.

Strom, S. (2008) "Here's my check; spend it all at once," *New York Times* (January 20). www.nytimes.com/2008/01/20/weekinreview/20strom.html?_r=0

Tanrisever, F., N. Joglekar, S. S. Erzurumlu, and M. Lévesque. (2015) "Managing market friction via cost-reduction investment," *Working paper*, Qeustrom School of Business, Boston University, Boston, MA.

Taylor, T. A., and W. Xiao. (2014a) "Donor product-subsidies to increase consumption: Implications of consumer awareness and profit-maximizing intermediaries," *Working Paper*, University of California, Berkeley.

Taylor, T. A., and W. Xiao. (2014b) "Subsidizing the distribution channel: Donor funding to improve the availability of malaria drugs," *Management Science*, **60**(10): 2461–2477.

Tereyagoglu, N., P. Fader, and S. Veeraraghavan. (2016) "Pricing theater seats: The value of price commitment and monotone discounting," *Production and Operations Management*. DOI:org/10.1111/poms.12611

Teron, A. C., and V. S. Tarasuk. (1999) "Charitable food assistance: What are food bank users receiving?" *Canadian Journal of Public Health*, **90**(6): 382–384.

Toyasaki, F., and T. Wakolbinger. (2014) "Impacts of earmarked private donations for disaster fundraising," *Annals of Operations Research*, **221**: 427–447.

Tuck, L., and K. Lindert. (1996) "From universal food subsidies to a self-targeted program: A case in Tunisian reform," *World Bank Discussion Papers*, **1**(351). http://documents.worldbank.org/curated/en/785181468778457225/pdf/multi-page.pdf

Vesterlund, L. (2006) "Why do people give?" in *The Nonprofit Sector*, R. Steinberg and W. W. Powell eds., 2nd edition, pp. 568–587. New Haven, CT: Yale University Press.

Weerts, D., and J. Ronca. (2008) "Characteristics of alumni donors who volunteer at their alma mater," *Research in Higher Education*, **49**: 274–292.

Weisbrod, B. A., and N. D. Dominguez. (1986) "Demand for collective goods in private nonprofit markets: Can fundraising expenditures help overcome free-rider behavior?" *Journal of Public Economics*, **30**(1): 83–96.

Whittington, D., M. Jeuland, K. Barker, and Y. Yuen. (2012) "Setting priorities, targeting subsidies among water, sanitation, and preventive health interventions in developing countries," *World Development*, **40**(8): 1546–1568.

Williamson, L. M., and D. V. Devine. (2013) "Challenges in the management of the blood supply," *The Lancet*, **381**(9880): 1866–1875.

Wolczynski, J., M. Mayorga, and E. Lodree. (2015) "The optimal assignment of spontaneous volunteers," *Working paper*, North Carolina State University, Raleigh, NC.

Yoken, C., and J. Berman. (1984) "Does paying a fee for psychotherapy alter the effectiveness of treatment?" *Journal of Consulting and Clinical Psychology*, **52**(2): 254–260.

Young, D. R., and R. S. Steinberg. (1995) *Economics for Nonprofit Managers*. New York, Foundation Center.

28
TELECOMMUNICATIONS AND OPERATIONS MANAGEMENT

Subodha Kumar, Kaushik Dutta, and Yonghua Ji

1 Introduction

Operational research and data analytics techniques have been applied in telecommunication in many forms over the years. Some of the key decisions that need to be taken in are: (1) What is the optimal placement of network devices and data across the network for efficient access by application? (2) What should be the capacity of the data storage distributed across the network? (3) When and how should the data flow from the storage to the application (and from the application to the storage)? (4) What are the recent telecommunication applications in areas such as humanitarian and healthcare operations? Some of these problems have proven to be NP-hard. Consequently, these problems have been addressed by developing mathematical programming models and finding the near-optimal solutions. With the recent popularization of cloud-based virtualized systems, these problems have received renewed interest in the newer context. Traditional network analysis has long since been restricted to local areas or within a limited geographical distribution. However, with the popularization of cloud-based systems, the placement and management of data and resources have spread across a globally distributed network. So, addressing the problems related to optimization of network applications in cloud environments requires a fresh look. Operations management is in a strong position to deal with these new applications.

2 Network Infrastructure

2.1 Network Design and Interconnection

Computer network infrastructure refers to a group of computer systems interconnected by a telecommunication infrastructure, such as routers, switches, and backbones. The arrangement of computers, the associated network components, and backbones form a network topology. As companies are constantly investing in network infrastructure in order to take advantage of new technology, creating and maintaining an efficient and robust network infrastructure become an important task from the network planning standpoint. One important first step in the process of building network infrastructure is to design a sound network topology, i.e., the structure of how nodes such as computers and routers are connected to local-area and other networks via links such as metal wires and optical fiber cables. Chamberland et al. (2000) study the topological design of two-level networks, where the term "two-level" refers to two major subnetworks—access and backbone networks. In this context, an access network links a network user to a network via switches whereas a backbone network connects switches together. These two networks are often designed separately by telecommunication companies.

Chamberland et al. (2000) propose a mixed 0–1 linear programming model to include the location of modular switches (composed of a base, ports, and multiplexers); the configuration of ports and multiplexers; and the topology of access networks and a backbone network. They find two well-known NP-hard problems as the corresponding special cases of the two problems, dynamic packet routing (DPR) and dynamic packet transmission (DPT), generated according to the topology constraints of a ring or tree network. Hence, it is unlikely to find polynomial-time algorithms to resolve these two problems. Therefore, Chamberland et al. (2000) propose a greedy heuristic to find a satisfactory solution that also serves as a starting point for the tabu search heuristic. Their numerical examples show that the tabu algorithm is excellent in terms of performance, producing solutions within 1.5% of the optimal solution on average.

Similar to other capital investment projects, building network infrastructure also faces uncertainties. A new form of technology (e.g., cloud storage and computing) could be available for businesses, and the design of the network should always be prepared to take such technology into consideration. Demand at certain nodes could change due to network failure or modification of a node (e.g., to be a more powerful server). To deal with uncertainty in network design problems, the notion of flexibility has received a lot of attention (Kogut and Kulatilaka 1994; Chow and Regan 2011; Chow et al. 2011; Dong et al. 2013). Two examples of applying real options to network design are (1) the deferral options link capacity expansion (Chow and Regan 2011) and (2) the valuation of network infrastructure investment portfolio (Angelou and Economides 2008).

2.2 Capacity Planning

Capacity planning (an essential POM role) is also an important problem in the telecommunication industry, similar to its position in the manufacturing industry. However, the differences between these two industries are that the transmission capacity surplus cannot be stored as inventory and the unsatisfied demand cannot be backordered. This is also characteristic of services and, in that regard, it is noteworthy that we call the telecommunication devices (such as routers and switches) "servers." Network capacity investment can be very costly since it involves adding expensive fiber optics links and larger servers, and therefore the network capacity planning becomes increasingly important. As traffic volume can grow over time due to consumer demand and competition, it is important to decide where and when to add link capacity over a multi-period planning horizon (Dutta and Lim 1992). In this multi-period capacity and flow application (MPCFA) problem, the topology of the network can change as new codes are added to the network. It can be formulated as an integer programming problem that is combinatorially explosive. Hence, using several lower-bound tightening methods with Lagrangian relaxation methods, Chang and Gavish (1995) propose heuristics that reduce the gap between a primal solution and the lower bound. Since analytical solutions often do not exist in such multi-period capacity expansion problems, the search heuristics (combined with artificial intelligence methods such as genetic algorithms) can yield improvements over the previous results (Kouassi et al. 2007).

Facing independent service providers who make capacity and pricing decisions according to their own objectives in a large-scale network, a central network designer can improve network performance in two ways (Korilis et al. 1995): (1) In the capacity provision phase, the designer can allocate the communication link capacities in a system-wide efficient way. Surprisingly, the designer should withhold some capacity resources in equilibrium as adding capacity can cause congestions and degrade user performance; and (2) in the run time phase, the manager can implement a routing strategy that yields the best Nash equilibrium by anticipating user's non-cooperative reactions.

In the context of a loss network where network services are either downgraded or blocked when the link capacity is fully utilized, non-cooperative routing by service providers becomes an interesting issue to study since the uniqueness of the loss network can yield some new theoretical results. Two solution concepts most often studied in a non-cooperative routing game are (Altman et al. 2002): the Nash equilibrium, in the case of a finite number of service providers, and the so-called Wardrop equilibrium, which is used when there are many players. Altman et al. (2002) show that, in loss networks, the equilibria are not unique, even for the simple case of parallel links. This contrasts with previous theoretical results. In the special case of parallel link topology with equal bandwidth requirement per call, they present some simple ways of obtaining both equilibria.

2.3 Capacity Allocation and Sharing

In a capacity provision network, service providers coordinate through a capacity allocation hub. One provider can share excess capacity with others for a certain fee. Service providers can be shown to have strong incentives in cooperative allocation and surplus sharing (Du et al. 2008), something that plays an important role in network infrastructure planning. Interestingly, a network of more than two service providers can provide opportunities for intermediation and improve the efficiency of allocation through successive trading. A centralized allocation can yield socially optimal allocation that is arbitrage free.

For a single seller of storage capacity, such as Amazon.com, the seller can either provide a spot market with dynamic prices, or it can offer forward contracts to hedge against future demand uncertainty (Das et al. 2011). Both pricing strategies can yield higher revenue than fixed pricing alone. In addition, forward contracts can reduce risks against revenue uncertainty without lowering the seller's revenue. A seller can also extend its selling horizon to a finite planning horizon and use dynamic forward contracts for risk hedging (Du et al. 2013). In such contracts, a seller and client interact through offers and responses as a pair of nested dynamic programs; a seller can learn client's demand and risk propensity. Sellers can use dynamic pricing contracts to gain higher revenue than by using spot markets or static forward pricing.

With multiple sellers and buyers of computing resources, such as CPU and storage, an auction is a useful way to provide economic incentives for buyers and sellers to exchange computing resources (Wolski et al. 2001; Bapna et al. 2008; 2011). A centralized procedure can allocate resources fairly in polynomial time with perfect information (Bapna et al. 2008). In a stochastic grid problem with uncertain job times, the use of a clock auction facilitates the discovery of resource prices and can be used as a decentralized mechanism for demand clearing (Bapna et al. 2011; Bichler et al. 2013). The complementarity of CPU and storages requires a combinatorial call auction that allows specification of both CPU and storage requirements and the pricing of both resources in order to avoid an exposure problem that is typical in combinatorial auctions. For service capacity, such as network transmission subject to congestion, simple price adjustment processes might fail to clear demand or be subject to strategic manipulation; instead, an iterative auction mechanism can maximize the social welfare and induce participants to reveal their true demands (Barrera and Garcia 2015).

2.4 Network Security Design

Organizations are increasingly using computer network to run their operations on enterprise systems, store their valuable data on database servers, and access their systems over the Internet. As more computers are connected to the Internet, how to detect computer intrusions and threats in a timely fashion has become an important topic in computer security (Bhuyan et al. 2014). An intrusion detection system (IDS) uses a supervised learning approach (by using training data and outputs) to build a model of normal network traffic. The obtained model is then used to detect anomalous events among incoming network events (Mookerjee et al. 2012). Network anomaly detection methods include statistical methods, clustering, and genetic algorithms (GAs). In addition, intrusion detection methods can be combined to improve the system performance. For example, one can use an ensemble of Bayesian networks (BNs) and Classification and Regression Trees (CARTs) to identify important features in building an efficient and effective IDS (Chebrolu et al. 2005). An IDS can also run in a distributed environment where each network node trains its classification algorithm based on the local training data and cooperates by communicating the learned models over the network (Folino et al. 2010).

More recent research and industrial attentions have been attracted to the rising of the Internet of Things (IOT). As network devices become widely available, more and more physical objects with embedded sensors are connected together in a wired or wireless sensor network. These devices can collect and exchange data continuously, some of which can be very important: health, home security, and human location. The performance and security of those underlying sensor networks will crucially affect the success of IOT. The network security issues become an important concern when designing a wireless sensor network (WSN) (Chen et al. 2009). Some of the challenges facing the design of WSN are that sensors are limited in computing capacity and are easy to be compromised via nodes' open programming interfaces. Countermeasures can be designed from the physical layer to transport layer. At the physical layer, passive protections by coatings and seals are more common so that signals are kept inside sensors and links. At a higher layer, such as the transport layer, one countermeasure could be package authentication and encryption.

2.5 Network Risk Management

In addition to outside security threats, one important source of security threats comes from internal employees due to their intentional or unintentional actions that can cause security breaches. One effective way to minimize internal risks is through access control mechanism with role-based access control (RBAC). This has been the dominant and most flexible access control mechanism (Xia et al. 2014). In the RBAC model, a role can have several permissions; each user will be assigned a set of roles to perform his or her job requirements. One of the most important RBAC problems has been to uncover a complete set of roles from existing user permissions. Role mining problems (RMPs) are concerned with problems of finding an optimal set of roles, a user-role assignment and a role-permission assignment that minimize certain cost functions, given a set of users, a set of permissions and a user-permission assignment (Vaidya et al. 2010). Once a set of roles has been discovered, how can one build a set of new roles that minimize the cost of managing such role systems? Often one needs to design approximation methods to solve such role refinement problems (RRPs) (Xia et al. 2014).

2.6 Future Research

In the area of network design, past research has focused on the goal of minimizing cost when there is demand uncertainty (Chow and Regan 2011). Future research should study how to build redundancy as a backup option when there could be threats of network attacks and intrusions to bring down networks, as in many real-world scenarios. In the area of capacity planning, a fruitful direction would be to re-examine the capacity expansion problems with cloud technology. For example, by dealing with increased demand instead of adding new nodes to the existing network (Kouassi et al. 2007), one might be able to remove certain nodes. This would mean that the demand could be satisfied through capacity purchased from cloud providers (such as Amazon.com). When selling capacity to a group of buyers, a capacity provider can use forward contracts to hedge against future demand uncertainty (Das et al. 2011). One interesting question to study is whether a capacity provider should allow the trading of forward contracts among buyers. That is, will it enhance the provider's profit since buyers might purchase more capacity and trade the surplus later on? Or would the provider's profit decrease since buyers could buy capacity later on through the trading of forward contracts? Does it enhance social welfare?

There are a lot of challenges that remain to be solved by the joint effort of information systems (IS) and operations management (OM) communities in the area of network security and risk management. Next, let us look at some interesting problems in this area.

First, how can one incorporate IT controls into the design of security systems? Past research has focused on designing effective intrusion detection systems. It would be interesting to see how controls (such as profiling and encryption) can work together with IDSs rather than being separate research subjects. The readers can refer to Ji et al. (2016) for one such example where profiling is combined with IDS.

Second, network security should be viewed in a broader context as security breaches can affect partners in a supply chain at various levels. Therefore, security design should consider the interconnection between the focal firm (such as Wal-mart) and its business partners (such as suppliers), and protect such interconnections as well. Game theory would be useful to study the coordination between a focal firm and its partners in security investment.

Finally, as firms outsource their network operations to third parties (Ji et al. 2016) or buy networking capabilities through cloud marketplace, their security consideration should include the understanding of cloud providers' strengths and weaknesses. This might call for redesign of a firm's existing network infrastructure. For example, firms might want to prioritize their information processes and run their sensitive operations in a cloud if cloud providers have better security measures in place.

3 Network Operations

3.1 Operations Management of Caching

Caching is one of the network applications that is used to improve the performance of applications involving multiple nodes (computers) in the computer network. The key concept of caching involves getting and storing the data geographically near to where it will be used or accessed. Due to high connectivity in the present day's Internet, the geographical distance is directly linked to network distance between two nodes in the computer network. The details of caching across various parts of the network have been described in Datta et al. (2003). There are several operational problems in caching that have been addressed extensively in the literature.

First, let's look at Cache Location Identification. In the case of distributed applications where data is accessed from various locations, it becomes important to distribute data across various caches distributed over the network. To optimize the resources, these caches are shared by applications from multiple locations. In such a scenario, the placement of the cache across the network depends on what is being accessed by which application and from where. Krishnan et al. (2000) minimize the cost of deployment of the cache across various locations with the constraint of meeting the SLA (service level agreement) for data access by application nodes. They consider network conditions to solve the problem using a greedy algorithm and a dynamic algorithm.

Next is the problem of Cache Storage Management. Cache has limited storage capacity. The data found in the cache can be accessed much faster than retrieving the data from primary storage like a database. With that limited storage, the decision problem of which data to store in the cache becomes important. Choosing the data to store in the cache appropriately improves the application performance. There have been several research studies on storage management of cache that have applied operational research techniques to determine optimal cache size and to identify element in the cache to evict. Aggarwal et al. (1999) describe various caching policies. They formulate the cache eviction policy as an optimization problem and demonstrate that it is a version of the knapsack problem, which is NP-hard. Then, they discuss and propose several greedy heuristics based on various cost factors of fetching the object versus keeping the object in the cache.

The problem of location and storage has been addressed together by several researchers. For example, Tang and Chanson (2002) propose the combined problem as a reduction of total cost in the network. They develop a scheme by which the data can be placed across a select set of network nodes with limited storage capacity. They apply dynamic programming to solve this problem. They also consider coordination among cache nodes to achieve higher performance of the application. Koskela et al. (2003) develop a storage management scheme by using the rich feature of the object to cache. In addition to object size, they use many other features of objects (such as historical popularity of the object and HTML structure) to classify the objects. Objects in each class are managed separately by the LRU (least recently used) cache policy.

Caching programmatic objects within the application is also a very popular technique to improve the performance of applications that require network communication, such as connecting a database server or web services. However, one of the key features of caching programmatic objects is "which object to cache"—a two-level decision process. In the first step, objects are selected at application design time whose instances may be a candidate for caching at runtime. In the second step, at runtime for object instances of cacheable objects, decisions are taken whether to cache the object instance or not. This decision process is formulated as an integer programming problem in Dutta et al. (2006). They develop a genetic algorithm based solution and demonstrate the accuracy with the Lagrangian relaxation bound of the problem.

Another problem that concerns caches, is that of future research. Research on caching has matured. However, with the advent of big data systems there is a renewed interest in caching on the part of telecom and IT professionals. Some of the open problems on caching that are related to big data systems are:

(1) How the data and the computation should be distributed across multiple nodes that will allow completing the map-reduce type of distributed computation in the most efficient time?
(2) Typically, similar types of data are accessed together. So, how should data clustering and data placement be made (together) to make data consumption efficient?

(3) Big data systems are characterized by velocity, variety, and volume. In such a dynamic environment, existing approaches of deciding storage and location of cache nodes in networks will not work. Each requires separate attention.

The present network based distributed systems are cloud-centric where physical machines are not that important. Applications in the cloud are capable of running on any machine in the set of virtualized computers. The exact number of virtual machines is decided at runtime based on the performance of the application and the deadlines of jobs to run.

3.2 Content Delivery Network

A content delivery network (CDN) is a system of distributed servers that deliver web content according to the geographical proximity of the users (Zakas 2011). It consists of thousands of servers that are placed strategically across the globe. Content exists as multiple copies on these servers. CDN management software dynamically calculates which server is located nearest to the requesting client and delivers content from that server to the requesting user. Akamai is the pioneer in the creation of content distribution networks. The details of Akamai are available in Nygren et al. (2010).

3.2.1 Content Distribution and Request Routing

The CDN needs to address two problems at the same time: content distribution (or location of the content) and to which cache node the user requests will be routed. Ercetin and Tassiulas (2003) formulate the problem as a minimization problem, where they minimize the user latency to access data by distributing the data across various cache nodes and directing an incoming user request to the most efficient node (less network latency, i.e., less delay in serving the content at the network node). They propose a scheme where the CDN users pay for their usage of the storage. They demonstrate that achieving global optimum for a CDN is cost prohibitive; rather, it is possible to obtain near-optimal solutions. The CDNs are particularly popular for streaming services, such as IPTV and video-on-demand services. Sofman and Krogfoss (2009) address the problems related to streaming services on CDN. They formulate the problem of optimal cache placement and size determination as a cost minimization problem. Their model depends on basic parameters: traffic, topology, and cost parameters. Laoutaris et al. (2005) develop an optimization problem to allocate storages in CDN nodes. They consider node locations, node sizes, and object placement in their problem formulation. They develop several greedy heuristics to solve the problem, and compare their solutions with the LP relaxation solution of the IP problem to demonstrate the accuracy of the heuristics.

3.2.2 Allocation of Capacity

There has been an exponential increase in the number of user requests to access content on the Internet. To satisfy this demand, content providers are opting for CDNs. It is very important for CDNs to determine the storage capacities of its servers (Uderman et al. 2011). An over-dimensioned server may be good for content delivery purposes because it can serve the client requests fast and efficiently. However, over-dimensioned servers are costly to maintain and they usually have a high probability of under-usage. On the other hand, a sub-dimensioned storage capacity can be cost-effective, but it usually leads to lower average performance. Economically optimal capacity allocation requires market-driven prices. Hence, an equilibrium is required to be established between storage capacity and pricing. Moreover, CDNs should incorporate Quality of Service (QoS) constraints in their functions. Cache slicing improves the Quality of Experience (QoE) of CDN services, because slicing enables the CDN to act as a set of CDNs, one for each content provider, instead of a big CDN where content providers compete for resources (Moreira et al. 2015).

3.2.3 Capacity Pricing

Most CDN firms use traditional volume-based pricing. However, studies have shown that a pricing policy that accounts for both the mean and variance in traffic, such as the percentile-based pricing, is more profitable than the volume-based pricing (Hosanagar et al. 2008). In recent times, CDNs have started allowing content providers to deliver entire websites through distributed CDN servers. For such services, CDNs' pricing functions should incorporate volume discounts to content providers. Moreover, CDNs should invest in technology to ensure security of contents. It should be noted that any security concern with content delivery will result in lower prices (Hosanagar et al. 2004).

3.2.4 Future Research

Research is being conducted to develop a cost-effective optimal solution for the Storage Capacity Allocation Problem (Uderman et al. 2011). Further research is required to reduce the time taken by contents to reach the requesting users and to minimize the user latency. Also, more research is required to improve the security of content and the QoS in CDNs.

3.3 Operations Management of Cloud Computing

3.3.1 Job Scheduling in the Cloud

There are different kinds of research about the application of the cloud framework to variations of scheduling jobs with context-specific constraints and optimization criteria. Kllapi et al. (2011) develop a scheduling problem for data processing workflow. A data processing workflow consists of querying, searching, information filtering, retrieval, data transformation and analysis, and other data manipulation tasks. These tasks are represented by data processing graphs. Each of the nodes in the data processing graph has a deadline to meet and requires certain time to complete. Kllapi et al. (2011) propose a number of nested search algorithms to find both the optimal and near-optimal alternatives. Kumar et al. (2009) address the problem of job scheduling in a computational grid. They demonstrate that the problem maps to a three-partition problem, and therefore, the problem is strongly NP-hard. They propose a greedy heuristic and then demonstrate that the heuristic can obtain a solution within 1%–2% of the lower bound obtained from the LP relaxation of the problem.

Not all jobs in cloud and grid computing are critical in nature. Organizations run a number of batch jobs on a regular basis that can be temporarily pre-empted and restarted based on resource availabilities. Many of the current cloud organizations are centered on providing cheap computing nodes at very low spot prices with the conditions that if the demand of the node rises, the existing running job in the node will be pre-empted and the node will be acquired by the central unit for allocating it to more demanding applications at a higher price (on demand or reserve price). Chaisiri et al. (2012) develop an optimization model for scheduling tasks in such an environment. The assumption here is that the low priority jobs can be pre-empted to make way for high priority jobs in a resource constraint situation. They propose several algorithms to obtain more efficient and cost-effective scheduling in such an environment.

3.3.2 Resource Optimization in the Cloud

Dutta and VanderMeer (2011) develop an integer programming model to allocate resources for continuously running applications. The resources allocated in each duration are based on the demand of the application, which is the number of active users at that duration. Resources are allocated and deallocated to the application in dynamic fashion. At the beginning of each time interval, decisions are taken about which resources will be taken out and which resources will be assigned to which applications. They apply dynamic slope scaling procedure to solve this problem. This procedure provides solutions within 4% of the LP relaxed solution.

Ghanbari et al. (2012) address the problem of resource allocation in a private cloud. They minimize the total cost of the resources to be used in supporting a set of applications with the constraint of maintaining the applications' desired SLAs. Chaisiri et al. (2012) address a more complex scenario of the public cloud where computing nodes can be acquired in reserve mode (where consumers pay for a fixed price for a fixed duration) or on-demand (where consumers use the computing node as and when needed, and pay only for the duration it is used). This is due to uncertainty in the application demand and resource requirements in the future. Chaisiri et al. (2012) develop this problem as a stochastic programming model. They propose a solution for the stochastic problem that optimally combines the reserve nodes along with the on-demand node to not only minimize the cost but to also address the uncertainty in demand of the application.

3.3.3 Future Research

As can be seen from the prior discussions in this chapter, many of the problems in the context of cloud and grid computing environments have similarities to traditional machine shop scheduling problems. However, the scale of cloud environments requires revisiting many of the old problems. One example is that in a typical cloud environment, IT operations deal with thousands of machines and several thousands of computing jobs across an organization. Additionally, computing jobs usually have many dependencies. For example, a computing job may require a set of other computing jobs to finish before starting itself. Further, another computing job may be distributed in nature, which indicates that multiple nodes are required. A computing job may also need some other computing jobs to run in parallel to finish a task in coordinated fashion. In summary, the interdependencies among computing jobs are usually much more complex than those in traditional machine shop jobs.

Furthermore, as the cloud is becoming a generic commodity resource, how can scheduling of jobs happen that span across multiple cloud systems? Instead of relying on a single cloud system, organizations are now deploying more than one cloud system along with their own private cloud. Selecting resources across all these available options that meet the applications' SLA requirement and minimizes the long-term cost of the organization is a challenging task.

Each cloud entity has its own pricing mechanism with various levels of services. All these needs should be considered in selecting computing node across multiple cloud systems.

4 Applications of Telecommunications in Operations

4.1 Humanitarian Operations

A new concept of humanitarian technology—use of information and communication technology (ICT) to aid humanitarian efforts—has developed due to the increased use of high-tech tools in humanitarian operations. Such efforts include activities as online education, disaster recovery, and rescue operations. ICT has improved the people's quality of life and is now an irreplaceable part of human development (Garshnek and Burkle 1999; Chan et al. 2004).

4.1.1 Online Education

With the advances in ICT, online learning provides people with an affordable, learning-on-demand opportunity (Zhang and Nunamaker 2003). The course design is an important factor that contributes to the success of an online course. It should be flexible and should offer a personalized way to learn (Garrison and Cleveland-Innes 2005). In recent years, the demand for higher education is growing at a rapid pace. The Internet has played a key role in the development of online education by providing scalable connectivity between different geographic locations and by providing a ubiquitous user interface platform for various distributed learning software applications (Alavi and Leidner 2001; Wan and Fang 2006). Research has identified three major factors critical to the success of online education: technology, role of instructor, and how adept the students are with the technology (Volery and Lord 2000). Universities and corporations are making huge investments on infrastructure and information technologies for online education to foster better learning.

4.1.2 Disaster Recovery and Rescue Operations

ICT plays a significant role in mitigating the tremendous human suffering and property damage caused by disasters (Ei Sun 2003). Proper coordination and rapid dissemination of adequate information is required amongst the deployed teams as well as between command centers and ground units. However, in reality, many rescue operations suffer due to lack of communicational channels. Most disasters usually result in complete or partial collapse of telecommunications infrastructures. Research in this area has developed several frameworks, creating a synergy between telecommunication systems, organizational proceedings, and information flow, which may be followed in disaster rescue operations (Patricelli et al. 2009). Wireless systems play an important role in disaster recovery and rescue operations. Wireless mobile ad hoc networks (MANETs) (Subbarao 2000) and automotive accident management systems (Azaro et al. 2006) may be deployed in disaster areas for efficient rescue operations. These can facilitate emergency telecommunication even in hostile conditions with limited resources. In recent times, the Internet has also played a vital role in disaster recovery operations. For example, during the 2010 Haiti earthquake rescue effort, US government agencies employed social media technologies as the main knowledge sharing mechanisms (Yates and Paquette 2011). If a disaster can be predicted in advance, it provides some critical lead time for preparation. For such situations, recent studies have proposed an integrated logistics model for disaster management and rescue operations (Gupta et al. 2016; Manoj et al. 2016).

4.1.3 Further Research

Future research is strongly required to understand the qualitative nature of online interaction in terms of teaching and learning approaches, and how technology can assist students' learning. Apart from that, research efforts are ongoing to improve the design structure of online courses (Alavi and Leidner 2001; Garrison and Cleveland-Innes 2005). More research is required to develop systems and frameworks that will ensure continuous flow of dynamic and complex information during disaster recovery and rescue operations. Poorly designed information systems (e.g., insufficient flow of information) can hamper rescue operations in disaster zones (Patricelli et al. 2009). Moreover, several of the existing technologies fail to adapt to large scale human assistance operations (Bui et al. 2000). Research should be conducted in making these technologies more scalable. Apart from these, effort should be made to generate monetary donations and financial support to stock up resources and store them in accessible physical locations under appropriate conditions so that they can be used efficiently and effectively in case of a disaster (Vestal et al. 2015).

4.2 Healthcare Operations

One of the most prominent applications of telecommunication in healthcare operations is tele-medicine (Garshnek et al. 1997; Garshnek and Burkle 1999). This is a growing field that is not only affordable but also easily accessible. Hence, it is rapidly gaining popularity among healthcare providers as well as patients. Another application of telecommunication in healthcare that is also gaining momentum is Healthcare Information Exchange (HIE) (Kuperman 2011).

4.2.1 Tele-Medicine

Tele-medicine is the use of telecommunication and information systems to exchange medical information from one site to another. This convergence of wireless technologies and mobile communications enables remote access to a physician to address a health concern, thus promising better services to patients (Pattichis et al. 2002). Tele-medicine continues to gain popularity as an alternative to urgent or emergency care for minor health issues, such as colds and fever. Moreover, tele-medicine helps provide quality healthcare services to under-staffed remote sites (Garshnek and Burkle 1999). The more user-friendly an application is, the more it is accepted by patients and doctors. If they are well designed, applications will contain appropriate clinical content (Vollenbroek-Hutten and Hermens 2010). Since the Internet is used in providing tele-medicine, special care must be taken to ensure the safety of patients and medical data as the Internet has a number of security issues (Wang 1999). Although tele-medicine has been used in developed countries for some years now with mixed success, only 0.1% of the potential tele-medicine demand from the developing world is being satisfied (Wootton 2008).

4.2.2 Health Information Exchanges (HIEs)

HIEs allow healthcare providers to store, access, and share critical medical information of patients over the Internet (HealthIT.gov 2016). By facilitating interoperability of automated health data, it saves precious time and improves the standard of healthcare provided to patients

(Kuperman 2011). Moreover, HIEs enhance patient safety as they have the potential to eliminate 18% of the patient safety errors and almost 70% of adverse drug events (Kaelber and Bates 2007). Viewing the potential of HIEs, most of the US government federal policies support adoption of HIE (Vest and Gamm 2010).

4.2.3 Future Research

Although the application of tele-medicine is growing in popularity, these applications often lack a constructive feedback system about the content and design of these applications. Research in incorporating effective feedback strategies into tele-medicine systems is still in its infancy (Vollenbroek-Hutten and Hermens 2010). Future research in this field should be focused on extending the scope of tele-medicine, such as tele-surgery and application of robotics in healthcare services (Satava 2005).

There are a number of hurdles in the way of implementing HIEs. First, there is no particular business model. Second, there is a complete lack of trust and control among different entities in HIEs (Vest and Gamm 2010). Studies are underway to offer insightful guidelines to improve the sustainability of HIEs and to increase the degree of participation in these networks (Demirezen et al. 2016).

4.3 Homeland Security Applications

For every nation, protecting its people and major infrastructure assets from natural threats as well as threats of terrorism is of immense importance. With the rise in occurrences of violent events, countries are leaning more towards innovative technologies that they can use to limit human and economic losses.

In ensuring the security of civil infrastructures, such as bridges and dams, low-power but high-performance wireless monitoring systems are used to rapidly assess their structural integrity and environmental conditions (Kiremidjian et al. 2004). Such systems act as a decision support unit for interpretation and communication of information to various decision makers. These are built on advanced sensor and wireless technologies and are extremely useful for mitigating threats. Low-cost radar surveillance systems are used to protect borders and inland waterways, providing continuous surveillance as they are highly effective in countering terrorism and smuggling operations (Weber et al. 2004). To prevent security threats from harmful chemicals, wireless radio-frequency identification (RFID) tags, adapted for chemical sensing, are used to rapidly and efficiently detect agents (Potyrailo et al. 2012). Wireless mesh networks (WMNs) are often used for ensuring public safety in case of crisis management (Portmann and Pirzada 2008). These wireless networks have self-organizing and self-configuring capabilities and can provide wireless broadband connectivity at affordable cost. Hence, these are helpful for continuous communication in the wake of a crisis.

4.3.1 Further Research

With advances in technology, more improved and higher performing applications are being developed for homeland security. In the past, the WMNs did not perform well in terms of scalability and the quality of service required for protecting public safety. Hence, more research is required to increase scalability and improve quality of service of the WMNs (Portmann and

Pirzada 2008). A major drawback of continuous radar surveillance is the high cost of human effort associated with monitoring sensor displays. Research is needed to minimize the human element in monitoring.

5 Implications for Managers

With the growing popularity of media-based content (such as video and audio), the demand on the IT network is growing exponentially. The IT managers are struggling to support more traffic and reduce response time within the existing infrastructure. Hence, they are always looking for the optimal use of network infrastructure. This chapter highlights some of the applications of operations management techniques that may help them in achieving this goal. For example, in the design and deployment of networks, we discuss how the existing traffic pattern can be taken into account to optimize the network layout. Further on, in network operations, we discuss how the caching can improve the utilization of existing networks. In the context of cloud-based systems, we discuss how business processes can be allocated and run in a more efficient manner using the existing cloud infrastructure. These are some of the questions for which IT managers are increasingly trying to find answers. This chapter discusses research streams addressing these questions. This chapter also discusses the use of telecommunications in various operations, such as humanitarian operations, education, and disaster recovery. The research in these areas are of profound practical interest to managers.

6 Conclusions and Directions for Future Research

Many of the problems discussed in this chapter have been widely discussed and addressed in past research. However, in the newer context of cloud-based systems, data intensive applications require fresh attention. For example, with respect to network security, it is important to study how operations management and operations research techniques can be used for auditing and security in cloud environments. Cloud-based big data infrastructure opens up a new set of problems in operations due to the enormous number of computing nodes and locations involved. Similarly, robust wireless technologies and satellite-based communications have opened up the possibility of new research and development in the context of humanitarian operations and disaster management in remote parts of the world. This chapter discusses many such future research problems that require the merging of telecommunication infrastructures and efficient operations.

References and Bibliography

Aggarwal, C., J.L. Wolf, P.S. Yu. (1999) "Caching on the World Wide Web," *IEEE Transactions on Knowledge and Data Engineering*, **11**(1): 94–107.

Alavi, M., D.E. Leidner. (2001) "Research commentary: Technology-mediated learning—a call for greater depth and breadth of research," *Information Systems Research*, **12**(1): 1–10.

Altman, E., R.E. Azouzi, V. Abramov. (2002) "Non-cooperative routing in loss networks," *Performance Evaluation*, **49**(1–4): 257–272.

Angelou, G.N., A.A. Economides. (2008) "A decision analysis framework for prioritizing a portfolio of ICT infrastructure projects," *IEEE Transactions on Engineering Management*, **55**(3): 479–495.

Azaro, R., F.G.B. De Natale, M. Donelli, A. Massa, E. Zeni. (2006) "Optimized design of a multifunction/multiband antenna for automotive rescue systems," *IEEE Transactions on Antennas and Propagation*, **54**(2): 392–400.

Bapna, R., S. Das, R. Day, R. Garfinkel, J. Stallaert. (2011) "A clock-and-offer auction market for grid resources when bidders face stochastic computational needs," *INFORMS Journal on Computing*, **23**(4): 630–647.

Bapna, R., S. Das, R. Garfinkel, J. Stallaert. (2008) "A market design for grid computing," *INFORMS Journal on Computing*, **20**(1): 100–111.

Barrera, J., A. Garcia. (2015) "Auction design for the efficient allocation of service capacity under congestion," *Operations Research*, **63**(1): 151–165.

Bhuyan, M.H., D.K. Bhattacharyya, J.K. Kalita. (2014) "Network anomaly detection: Methods, systems and tools," *Communications Surveys & Tutorials, IEEE*, **16**(1): 303–336.

Bichler, M., P. Shabalin, G. Ziegler. (2013) "Efficiency with linear prices? A game-theoretical and computational analysis of the combinatorial clock auction," *Information Systems Research*, **24**(2): 394–417.

Bui, T., S. Cho, S. Sankaran, M. Sovereign. (2000) "A framework for designing a global information network for multinational humanitarian assistance/disaster relief," *Information Systems Frontiers*, **1**(4): 427–442.

Chaisiri, S., L. Bu-Sung, D. Niyato. (2012) "Optimization of resource provisioning cost in cloud computing," *IEEE Transactions on Services Computing*, **5**(2): 164–177.

Chamberland, S., B. Sansò, O. Marcotte. (2000) "Topological design of two-level telecommunication networks with modular switches," *Operations Research*, **48**(5): 745–760.

Chan, T.C., J. Killeen, W. Griswold, L. Lenert. (2004) "Information technology and emergency medical care during disasters," *Academic Emergency Medicine*, **11**(11): 1229–1236.

Chang, S.-G., B. Gavish. (1995) "Lower bounding procedures for multiperiod telecommunications network expansion problems," *Operations Research*, **43**(1): 43–57.

Chebrolu, S., A. Abraham, J.P. Thomas. (2005) "Feature deduction and ensemble design of intrusion detection systems," *Computers & Security*, **24**(4): 295–307.

Chen, X., K. Makki, K. Yen, N. Pissinou. (2009) "Sensor network security: A survey," *Communications Surveys & Tutorials, IEEE*, **11**(2): 52–73.

Chow, J.Y.J., A.C. Regan. (2011) "Real option pricing of network design investments," *Transportation Science*, **45**(1): 50–63.

Chow, J.Y.J., A.C. Regan, F. Ranaiefar, D.I. Arkhipov. (2011) "A network option portfolio management framework for adaptive transportation planning," *Transportation Research Part A: Policy and Practice*, **45**(8): 765–778.

Das, S., A.Y. Du, R. Gopal, R. Ramesh. (2011) "Risk management and optimal pricing in online storage grids," *Information Systems Research*, **22**(4): 756–773.

Datta, A., K. Dutta, H. Thomas, D. VanderMeer. (2003) "World wide wait: A study of Internet scalability and cache-based approaches to alleviate it," *Management Science*, **49**(10): 1425–1444.

Demirezen, E., S. Kumar, A. Sen. (2016) "Sustainability of healthcare information exchanges: A game-theoretic approach." *Information Systems Research*, **forthcoming**.

Dong, L., P. Kouvelis, P. Su. (2013) "Global facility network design in the presence of competition," *European Journal of Operational Research*, **228**(2): 437–446.

Du, A.Y., S. Das, R. Ramesh. (2013) "Efficient risk hedging by dynamic forward pricing: A study in cloud computing," *INFORMS Journal on Computing*, **25**(4): 625–642.

Du, A.Y., X. Geng, R. Gopal, R. Ramesh, A.B. Whinston. (2008) "Capacity provision networks: Foundations of markets for sharable resources in distributed computational economies," *Information Systems Research*, **19**(2): 144–160.

Dutta, A., J.-I. Lim. (1992) "A multiperiod capacity planning model for backbone computer communication networks," *Operations Research*, **40**(4): 689–705.

Dutta, K., S. Soni, S. Narasimhan, A. Datta. (2006) "Optimization in object caching," *Informs Journal on Computing*, **18**(2): 243–254.

Dutta, K., D. VanderMeer. (2011) "Cost-based decision-making in middleware virtualization environments," *European Journal of Operational Research*, **210**(2): 344–357.

Ei Sun, O. (2003) "Information and communication technology in the service of disaster mitigation and humanitarian relief." *The 9th Asia-Pacific Conference on Communications (APCC)*, Sept. 21–24, Penang, Malaysia.

Ercetin, O., L. Tassiulas. (2003) "Market-based resource allocation for content delivery in the Internet," *IEEE Transactions on Computers*, **52**(12): 1573–1585.

Folino, G., C. Pizzuti, G. Spezzano. (2010) "An ensemble-based evolutionary framework for coping with distributed intrusion detection," *Genetic Programming and Evolvable Machines*, **11**(2): 131–146.

Garrison, D.R., M. Cleveland-Innes. (2005) "Facilitating cognitive presence in online learning: Interaction is not enough," *American Journal of Distance Education*, **19**(3): 133–148.

Garshnek, V., F.M. Burkle. (1999) "Applications of telemedicine and telecommunications to disaster medicine: Historical and future perspectives," *Journal of the American Medical Informatics Association: JAMIA*, **6**(1): 26–37.

Garshnek, V., L.H. Hassell, H.Q. Davis. (1997) "Telemedicine—Breaking the distance barrier in health care delivery," *AIAA Student Journal*, **35**(1): 2–8.

Ghanbari, H., B. Simmons, M. Litoiu, G. Iszlai. (2012) "Feedback-based optimization of a private cloud," *Future Generation Computer Systems*, **28**(1): 104–111.

Gupta, S., M. Starr, R.Z. Farahani, N. Matinrad. (2016) "Disaster management from a POM perspective: Mapping a new domain," *Production and Operations Management*, **forthcoming**.

HealthIT.gov. (2016) "Health Information Exchange (HIE)." Retrieved Feb. 2016, www.healthit.gov/providers-professionals/health-information-exchange/what-hie.

Hosanagar, K., J. Chuang, R. Krishnan, M.D. Smith. (2008) "Service adoption and pricing of Content Delivery Network (CDN) services," *Management Science*, **54**(9): 1579–1593.

Hosanagar, K., R. Krishnan, M. Smith, J. Chuang. (2004) "Optimal pricing of Content Delivery Network (CDN) services." *Proceedings of the 37th Annual Hawaii International Conference on System Sciences (HICSS)*, Jan. 5–8, Big Island, Hawaii.

Ji, Y., S. Kumar, V.S. Mookerjee. (2016) "When being hot is not cool: Managing hot lists in information security. *Information Systems Research*, **forthcoming**.

Kaelber, D.C., D.W. Bates. (2007) "Health information exchange and patient safety," *Journal of Biomedical Informatics*, **40**(6): S40–S45.

Kiremidjian, G.K., A.S. Kiremidjian, J.P. Lynch. (2004) "Wireless structural monitoring for homeland security applications," *NDE for Health Monitoring and Diagnostics*, 82–90.

Kllapi, H., E. Sitaridi, M.M. Tsangaris, Y. Ioannidis. (2011) *Schedule Optimization for Data Processing Flows on the Cloud*. Association for Computing Machinery (ACM), New York.

Kogut, B., N. Kulatilaka. (1994) "Operating flexibility, global manufacturing, and the option value of a multinational network," *Management Science*, **40**(1): 123–139.

Korilis, Y.A., A.A. Lazar, A. Orda. (1995) "Architecting noncooperative networks," *IEEE Journal on Selected Areas in Communications*, **13**(7): 1241–1251.

Koskela, T., J. Heikkonen, K. Kaski. (2003) "Web cache optimization with nonlinear model using object features," *Computer Networks*, **43**(6): 805–817.

Kouassi, R., M. Gendreau, J.-Y. Potvin, P. Soriano. (2007) "Heuristics for multi-period capacity expansion in local telecommunications networks," *Journal of Heuristics*, **15**(4): 381–402.

Krishnan, P., D. Raz, Y. Shavitt. (2000) "The cache location problem," *IEEE/ACM Transactions on Networking*, **8**(5): 568–582.

Kumar, S., K. Dutta, V. Mookerjee. (2009) "Maximizing business value by optimal assignment of jobs to resources in grid computing," *European Journal of Operational Research*, **194**(3): 856–872.

Kuperman, G.J. (2011) "Health-information exchange: Why are we doing it, and what are we doing?" *Journal of the American Medical Informatics Association: JAMIA*, **18**(5): 678–682.

Laoutaris, N., V. Zissimopoulos, I. Stavrakakis. (2005) "On the optimization of storage capacity allocation for content distribution," *Computer Networks*, **47**(3): 409–428.

Manoj, U.V., S. Kumar, S. Gupta. (2016) "An integrated logistic model for predictable disasters," *Production and Operations Management*, **25**(5): 791–811.

Mookerjee, R., S. Kumar, V.S. Mookerjee. (2012) "Managing hot-lists in intrusion detection and prevention systems," *Conference on Information Systems and Technology (CIST)*, Oct. 13–14, 2015, Phoenix, AZ.

Moreira, A., E. Azevedo, J. Kelner, D. Sadok, A. Callado, V. Souza. (2015) "An adaptable storage slicing algorithm for content delivery networks," *2015 IFIP/IEEE International Symposium on Integrated Network Management (IM)*, May 11–15, 2015, Ottawa, Canada.

Nygren, E., R.K. Sitaraman, J. Sun. (2010) "The Akamai network: A platform for high-performance internet applications," *ACM SIGOPS Operating Systems Review*, **44**(3): 2–19.

Patricelli, F., J.E. Beakley, A. Carnevale, M. Tarabochia, D.K.J.E. Von Lubitz. (2009) "Disaster management and mitigation: The telecommunications infrastructure," *Disasters*, **33**(1): 23–37.

Pattichis, C.S., E. Kyriacou, S. Voskarides, M.S. Pattichis, R. Istepanian, C.N. Schizas. (2002) "Wireless telemedicine systems: An overview," *Antennas and Propagation Magazine, IEEE*, **44**(2): 143–153.

Portmann, M., A.A. Pirzada. (2008) "Wireless mesh networks for public safety and crisis management applications," *IEEE Transactions on Internet Computing*, **12**(1): 18–25.

Potyrailo, R.A., N. Nagraj, C. Surman, H. Boudries, H. Lai, J.M. Slocik, N. Kelley-Loughnane, R.R. Naik. (2012) "Wireless sensors and sensor networks for homeland security applications," *TrAC Trends in Analytical Chemistry*, **40**: 133–145.

Satava, R.M. (2005) "Telesurgery, robotics, and the future of telemedicine," *European Surgery*, **37**(5): 304–307.

Sofman, L.B., B. Krogfoss. (2009) "Analytical model for hierarchical cache optimization in IPTV Network," *IEEE Transactions on Broadcasting*, **55**(1): 62–70.

Subbarao, M.W. (2000) "Mobile ad hoc data networks for emergency preparedness telecommunications-dynamic power-conscious routing concepts." Submitted as an interim project for Contract Number DNCR086200 to the National Communications Systems, www.itl.nist.gov/div892/pubs/subbarao-ncs.pdf.

Tang, X., S.T. Chanson. (2002) "Coordinated en-route Web caching," *IEEE Transactions on Computers*, **51**(6): 595–607.

Uderman, F., T. Neves, C. Albuquerque. (2011) "*Optimizing server storage capacity on Content Distribution Networks.*" XVI Workshop de Gerência e Operação de Redes e Serviços, May 30–Jun. 3, Campo Grande, Brazil.

Vaidya, J., V. Atluri, Q. Guo. (2010) "The role mining problem: A formal perspective," *ACM Transactions on Information and System Security*, **13**(3): 1–31.

Vest, J.R., L.D. Gamm. (2010) "Health information exchange: Persistent challenges and new strategies," *Journal of the American Medical Informatics Association: JAMIA*, **17**(3): 288–294.

Vestal, E., M. Vanajakumari, S. Kumar. (2015) *Brazos Valley Food Bank: Fostering Partnership, Feeding Hope.* Ivey Publishing London, Ontario, Canada.

Volery, T., D. Lord. (2000) "Critical success factors in online education," *International Journal of Educational Management*, **14**(5): 216–223.

Vollenbroek-Hutten, M.M.R., H.J. Hermens. (2010) "Remote care nearby," *Journal of Telemedicine and Telecare*, **16**(6): 294–301.

Wan, Z., Y. Fang. (2006) "The role of information technology in technology-mediated learning: A review of the past for the future," *Proceedings of Americas Conference on Information Systems (AMCIS)*, Aug. 4–6, Acapulco, Mexico.

Wang, C.X. (1999) "Security issues to tele-medicine system design." *Southeastcon '99*, Mar. 25–28, Lexington, KY.

Weber, P., A. Premji, T.J. Nohara, C. Krasnor. (2004) "Low-cost radar surveillance of inland waterways for homeland security applications," *Radar Conference, 2004*, Apr. 26–29, Philadelphia, PA.

Wolski, R., J.S. Plank, J. Brevik, T. Bryan. (2001) "Analyzing market-based resource allocation strategies for the computational grid," *International Journal of High Performance Computing Applications*, **15**(3): 258–281.

Wootton, R. (2008) "Telemedicine support for the developing world," *Journal of Telemedicine and Telecare*, **14**(3): 109–114.

Xia, H., M. Dawande, V. Mookerjee. (2014) "Role refinement in access control: Model and analysis," *INFORMS Journal on Computing*, **26**(4): 866–884.

Yates, D., S. Paquette. (2011) "Emergency knowledge management and social media technologies: A case study of the 2010 Haitian earthquake," *International Journal of Information Management*, **31**(1): 6–13.

Zakas, N.C. (2011) "How content delivery networks (CDNs) work," nczonline.net, https://www.nczonline.net/blog/2011/11/29/how-content-delivery-networks-cdns-work/.

Zhang, D., J.F. Nunamaker. (2003) "Powering e-learning in the new millennium: An overview of e-learning and enabling technology," *Information Systems Frontiers*, **5**(2): 207–218.

29
POM FOR DISASTER MANAGEMENT

Peter W. Robertson, Sushil K. Gupta, and Martin K. Starr

1 Introduction

The United Nations defines a *disaster* as a "serious disruption to the functioning of a community or a society" (UNISDR 2015). Disasters are events that cause widespread and negative human, material, economic, or environmental issues. Such negative impacts exceed the ability of the affected community or society to cope effectively using its own resources i.e., external help is required by the community/society to respond and recover from the disaster.

The Red Cross and Red Crescent societies define *disaster management* as the organisation and management of resources and responsibilities for dealing with all humanitarian aspects of emergencies, in particular mitigation, preparedness, response, recovery, and development in order to lessen the impact of disasters (IFRC 2015).

2 Context

Recently, disaster management (DM) has gained major importance for Production and Operations Management (POM) due to the global media spotlight that now illuminates extensive tragedies and informs the world about the countless numbers of human lives lost or at risk. Calamities are becoming increasingly devastating because the world is changing, populations are growing, and networks of interconnected systems are multiplying.

Operations management is the only field that can be called upon to deal directly with the fundamental systems and variables that characterise disasters. Studies of disaster management reveal the application of the basic tools familiar to and developed by POM over many years. However, when applied to catastrophic systems, these tools of necessity must be employed in new and different ways.

One major difference between traditional POM and POM-disaster management is that, for the latter, profit motives are not relevant. Rather, the objectives are to provide relief to victims and to save as many lives as possible. Understanding the disaster-driven supply chain is essential to maximise humanitarian benefits therefore. The application of POM principles to DM apply to all phases of the DM cycle (Figure 29.1) and especially well to achieving success with preparedness, response, and recovery.

Unfortunately, as discussed below, the uptake of POM practices in the DM field has been quite slow and lags behind the private sector.

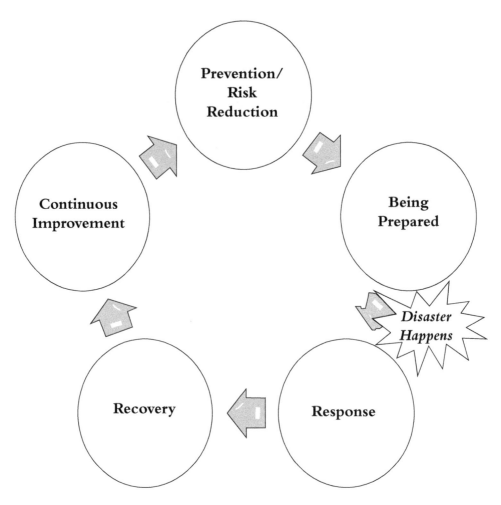

Figure 29.1 Disaster Management Cycle (see also Section 5.1)

3 Compelling Case for the Achievement of Disaster Management Excellence in POM

Superficially, it seems almost redundant to attempt an explanation of the importance of disaster management. After all, wouldn't such an attempt be nothing more than stating the blatantly obvious? That is, as disasters (or emergencies) represent a threat to human and/or animal life, a threat to structures, infrastructure, and/or the environment, then surely management of them must be, by default, important?

The economic cost of disasters is enormous as Table 29.1 illustrates for the US only.

More important than economic cost alone, is the loss of human life caused by disasters. As Table 29.2 shows, when looking at natural disasters and then specifically focusing on the top ten natural disasters that have resulted in deaths, the results are shocking. Please note that Hurricane Katrina is added for comparison. (The total property damage in Hurricane Katrina is estimated

Table 29.1 Damage Cost Statistics from US Disaster Events 1990 to 2016

Disaster Type	Number of Events	Total Deaths	Damage (US$ billion)
Drought	12	N/A	39.135
Earthquake	16	69	33.443
Epidemic	4	317	N/A
Extreme Temperature	20	1,728	8.915
Flood	196	1,737	86.530
Landslide	3	58	0.200
Storm	334	5,969	541.012
Wildfire	61	139	16.965

Source: An adaptation based on data found at http://emdat.be

Table 29.2 Top Ten Natural Disasters Impacting Human Life

Natural Disaster	Location	Year	Deaths
Yellow River Flood	China	1931	1 to 4 million
Yellow River Flood	China	1887	0.9 to 2 million
Bhola Cyclone	Bangladesh	1970	0.5 to 1 million
Shaanxi Earthquake	China	1556	830,000
Cyclone	Coringa, India	1839	300,000+
Kaifeng Floods	China	1642	300,000
Tangshan Earthquake	China	1976	242,000
Banqiao Dam Flood	China	1975	231,000
Ocean Earthquake + Tsunami	Indian Ocean	2004	230,000
Earthquake	Aleppo, Syria	1138	230,000
Hurricane Katrina*	United States	2005	1,245

Source: Compiled from Listverse.com (2007) data

at $108 billion (2005 USD) making it one of the costliest natural disasters in the history of the United States, https://en.wikipedia.org/wiki/Hurricane_Katrina.)

If human-made disasters are added to the consideration, then the results become horrendous. For example, it is estimated that 50 million people died as a result of World War II alone (War Chronicle 2016). For reference, the Centre for Research on the Epidemiology of Disasters (CRED) maintains an International Disaster Database (EM-DAT) containing descriptive information on more than 18,000 disasters since 1900. In summary, given the threat to human, animal, and plant life, the impact on human assets and the environment, as well as the sheer economic cost of disasters, then the line of thought that disaster management is important appears valid.

So why then is disaster management addressed in such a disparate way around the globe? Why are there no observed international standards when indeed several international DM bodies exist with the charter to do just that? Why are there no globally agreed upon and applied definitions, methodologies, processes, and management structures? Why is there no international coordination of data capture, data analysis, and reporting on all forms of disasters? And why does there exist such variability in approach between various countries, states within countries, and municipalities within states to disaster management?

Even the corporate approach is seemingly patchy. For example, 60% of small US based businesses do not have a formal disaster (or emergency) management plan (Boston University 2015). Additionally, and again for the US alone, 20%–40% of small businesses that close as a result of a disaster, never reopen (Smith and Matthews 2015). This leads therefore to a parallel question to the one of DM importance per se: "Given that, prima facie, disaster management is important from the point of view of protecting human life, animal life, property, and the environment, then why isn't its management a shining light example to all other management issues?"

There are many answers to the above questions with commonality around culture, socio-economic differences, education levels, availability of resources, "not invented here" syndrome, different risk types for different areas and the variable frequency (experience) of dealing with disasters.

But what is the value that POM brings to DM?

The short answer is that the following POM methodologies and philosophies are indeed relevant to the field of disaster management and provide a rich set of proven practices that can be applied to assist/enhance DM performance (see also Table 29.4):

(1) POM strategic plan and alignment with DM strategy
(2) Forecasting of demand (i.e., disaster forecasting)
(3) Capacity planning, operations planning, and scheduling
(4) Supply chain design including facility locations, layouts, inventory positions, and logistics
(5) POM staffing (includes numbers, training/competency requirements, locations, equipment needed, communication protocols, roles and structures, responsibilities, and accountabilities (RACI diagram))
(6) POM quality management
(7) POM lean philosophy and lean methodologies
(8) Supply chain agility
(9) Design of products and services (DPS)
(10) Materials requirements planning (MRP)
(11) Inventory management (in total)
(12) Procurement management
(13) Supply chain coordination
(14) Modelling and simulation
(15) POM/supply chain process mapping, process improvement
(16) Cost management
(17) Data collection, storage, analysis, and reporting
(18) Supply chain visibility (how can everyone who needs to know, see what's going on along the end-to-end DM supply chain in real time?)
(19) Key measures and targets (KPIs) plus reporting requirements.

Table 29.3 below illustrates the estimated extent of benefit that each POM practice brings to each phase of the disaster management cycle. As can be seen, the benefits of utilising POM practices to help with the individual phases of disaster management are potentially extensive. In particular, the phases "Preparedness," "Response," and "Recovery" could be substantially underpinned by POM practices if they were competently applied and supported to these phases.

An explanation of the nineteen POM practices is presented in Table 29.4.

Table 29.3 Estimated Benefits of POM Practices to the Phases of Disaster Management

POM Practice	Disaster Management Phases				
	Prevention	Preparedness	Response	Recovery	Improvement
Capacity planning	★★	★★★	★★★	★★★	★★
Forecasting	★★	★★★	★★★	★★★	★
Inventory Management	★	★★★	★★★	★★★	★
"Lean" Approach	★★	★★★	★★★	★★★	★★
MRP	★	★★★	★★★	★★★	★
Procurement Management	★★	★★★	★★★	★★★	★★
Product/Service Design	★	★★★	★★★	★★	★
SC Agility	★★	★★★	★★★	★★	★★
SC Coordination	★	★★★	★★★	★★★	★
SC Cost Management	★★	★★★	★★	★★★	★
SC Data Management	★★	★★★	★★★	★★★	★★
SC Design	★★	★★★	★★★	★★★	★★
SC Modelling	★★★	★★★	★★★	★★★	★★
SC Performance Management	★★	★★★	★★★	★★★	★
SC Process-mapping	★★	★★★	★★★	★★	★★
SC Quality Management	★★	★★★	★★★	★★★	★★
SC Staffing	★★	★★★	★★★	★★★	★★
SC Visibility	★★	★★★	★★★	★★★	★★
Strategic Planning	★★★	★★★	★★★	★★★	★★★

Key: Minor Benefits (★), Medium Benefits (★★), Major Benefits (★★★)

4 Past History

Disaster risk, which is oftentimes expressed as a function of hazard dimension multiplied by vulnerability (risk = hazard ★ vulnerability), has in the past been discounted somewhat by the low probability of major disaster type events (Riede 2014). The vulnerability still existed, but earlier societies adapted more after a disaster event than before it. If as experienced more recently however, the frequency of disaster events increases (especially human-induced disasters) and population growth and clustering increases vulnerability, then the impact of disasters is likely to increase even with improvements to resilience due to improved technology (albeit perhaps limited in effect) and better preparedness (Bankoff 2007).

Until recent times, limited formal disaster management structures or arrangements were in place. Countries or municipalities rather relied on their defence forces that were able to provide some level of response to disasters and emergencies. Taking the state of Queensland in Australia as an example, a series of natural disasters including the 1974 Brisbane Floods and the destruction of Darwin by Cyclone Tracy in the same year highlighted the need for the state to develop a disaster management system that would ensure broad and effective coordination of disaster management. Therefore, in 1975, Queensland enacted specific disaster legislation i.e., the State Counter Disaster Organisation Act, which established two principal arms:

(1) The State Counter Disaster Organisation as the umbrella body to ensure effective coordination and collaboration in the event of disasters
(2) The State Emergency Service (SES) to provide response resources to disasters as they happen.

The legislation also stipulated special legal powers to enhance the preservation of human life such as ordering an evacuation or the commandeering of assets. The application of POM practices to DM however, lagged behind such governmental responses. Indeed, POM in DM didn't start to appear in any formal way until the 1990s.

5 Present Situation

Managing disasters is an intense undertaking, so much so that disaster professionals cannot carry the task of achieving disaster recovery ability alone and thus the DM load needs to be a shared responsibility across society (Weichselgartner and Kelman 2014). As well, in recent years the disaster management system has been required to respond to new threats, which has placed additional difficulties and demands on disaster management response groups. New human induced threats include damage to technology and critical infrastructure, storage and transportation of hazardous materials, and biosecurity risks from the spread of infectious diseases through human pandemics and terrorism.

Two separate studies carried out in 2006 and 2015 suggest that of all the operations research (OR) techniques available, mathematical programming has been given the most attention in DM (Hoyos 2015) (47%) and that was chiefly applied (46%) to the response phase of the DM cycle and predominantly focussed on cost minimisation of facility and material locations. For additional information on the frequency of usage for various techniques, see the survey paper by Gupta et al. (2016) that is discussed in Section 7.

Due to a lack of understanding about how POM practices work and their benefit, POM in disaster management has struggled for identity and priority (Gupta et al. 2016). This has led to a "fire-fighting" mentality in many disaster response organisations. More recently, this situation has changed somewhat, but it still has a way to go before it can be claimed that POM practices are considered and used as crucial disaster management processes.

5.1 Explanation of Figure 29.1—Disaster Management Cycle

I. Prevention—actions taken to prevent a disaster, minimise the chance of it happening, or attenuate its negative effects
II. Preparedness—being ready—preparations made to minimise impact and to prepare for rapid deployment of response and rescue operations
III. Response—a disaster event has happened, so the response phase is about provision of help and assistance to affected people and their assets
IV. Recovery—return to normalcy. This includes reconstruction, restoration of services, transport corridor openings, return of people to their homes when safe to do so
V. Improvement—longer-term building of a safer and sustainable livelihood through continuous improvement to education, infrastructure solutions, and social resilience.

5.2 Present DM Taxonomies

EM-DAT (the International Disaster Database) distinguishes two generic categories for disasters: natural and technological. The natural disaster category is divided into five sub-groups, which in turn cover fifteen disaster types and more than thirty sub-types. The technological disaster category is divided in three sub-groups that in turn cover fifteen disaster types. The EM-DAT taxonomy can be viewed at the EM-DAT website (www.emdat.be/new-classification).

Disaster Taxonomy	Nature	Weather Event	Deep Chill			
			Heatwave			
			Flood	landslide		
			Drought			
			Storm	snow/ice storm		
				wind storm		
				dust/sand storm		
				thunderstorm	lightening strike	fire
				hurricane/cyclone		
				tornado		
			Fog			
		Landslide				
		Avalanche				
		Earthquake				
		Tsunami				
		Pestilence	Epidemic			
			Pandemic			
			Crop Disease			
			Insect Plague			
	Human	War				
		Terror	Kidnapping			
			Beheading			
			Shooting			
			Bombing			
			Power supply damage			
			Water supply damage			
			Air travel safety			
			Port/shipping safety			
			Chemical threat	Gas/Chemical agents		
			Bio-Chemical threat	Anthrax		
			Nuclear device			
		Explosion	Design Error	Incompetence		
				Negligence		
				Malevolence		
			Construction Error	Incompetence		
				Negligence		
				Malevolence		
			Operational Error	Incompetence		
				Negligence		
				Malevolence		
			Maintenance Error	Incompetence		
				Negligence		
				Malevolence		
		Crash	Design Error	Incompetence		
				Negligence		
				Malevolence		
			Construction Error	Incompetence		
				Negligence		
				Malevolence		
			Operational Error	Incompetence		
				Negligence		
				Malevolence		
			Maintenance Error	Incompetence		
				Negligence		
				Malevolence		
		Fire	Design Error	Incompetence		
				Negligence		
				Malevolence		
			Construction Error	Incompetence		
				Negligence		
				Malevolence		
			Operational Error	Incompetence		
				Negligence		
				Malevolence		
			Maintenance Error	Incompetence		
				Negligence		
				Malevolence		
		Power Outage	Design Error	Incompetence		
				Negligence		
				Malevolence		
			Construction Error	Incompetence		
				Negligence		
				Malevolence		
			Operational Error	Incompetence		
				Negligence		
				Malevolence		
			Maintenance Error	Incompetence		
				Negligence		
				Malevolence		
		Environmental Damage				
		Economic Damage				
		Political-Dogma Damage				
		Over-Population Damage				

Figure 29.2 Example of a Disaster Taxonomy

Such classifications usually include disaster categories and types as shown in Figure 29.2. Importantly, as such "trees" are taken further to the right then we get closer to disaster causes.

5.3 Present DM Typologies

DM typologies attempt to classify disasters according to their probability of occurrence, their geographic scope, emergence pattern, spread rate, and impact. An example typology is shown in Figure 29.3.

Currently, responsibility for DM rests with numerous groups at various levels i.e., international, national, state, and local. Examples include the International Emergency Management Society, The International Association of Emergency Managers, International Recovery Platform, Red Cross/Red Crescent, United Nations, World Bank, and the European Union. In addition, most countries have a national agency (e.g., the Federal Emergency Management Agency (FEMA) in the USA) as well as numerous state and local based disaster agencies.

Unfortunately, not all of these groups act as a coherent body and their roles vary between both the phases of a disaster (e.g., preparedness vs. response) and their principal focus (e.g., humanitarian relief vs. DM managers vs. data repositories and practice advocates). Even greater differences exist between nations and between states within nations.

Consequently, a globally agreed approach (including methodology, protocols, coordination, standards, practices, desired outcomes, measures and targets, monitoring and reporting, and continuous improvement) to DM represents a significant opportunity for both the DM community and of course the people affected by disasters. Additionally, a globally agreed approach to DM represents a significant opportunity for POM in operationalising POM processes to help better manage the disaster management cycle shown at Figure 29.1.

Disaster Typology	Probability	Highly Unlikely	$p<0.15$
		Unlikely	$0.15 \leq p < 0.45$
		Neutral (50:50)	$0.45 \leq p < 0.55$
		Likely	$0.55 \leq p < 0.85$
		Highly Likely	$p > 0.85$
	Geographical Scope	Local	
		Regional	
		Statewide	
		National	
		Multi-National	
		Global	
	Emergence Pattern	Undetectable	
		Slowly Evolving	
		Evolving	
		Sudden	
		Instantaneous	
	Spread Rate	Very Slow	
		Slow	
		Moderate	
		Rapid	
		Very Rapid	
	Impact	Very Low	Minor injuries to small % of affected population, minimal property damage
		Low	
		Moderate	
		High	
		Catastrophic	Numerous fatalities to large % of affected population, extensive property damage

Figure 29.3 Example of a Disaster Typology

6 Future Projections

The long-term goal for POM in DM is to provide the knowhow and processes that ensure that the right product or service is delivered at the right time, to the right place, in the right quantity at the right quality, and, perhaps excepting the first seventy-two hours after a disaster event happening, for the right cost.

It should be recognised, however, that, whilst private sector supply chains have developed the capabilities and staffing to achieve such a goal, the dynamics faced in dealing with an actual disaster are quite different. That is, in responding to an actual disaster, the level of uncertainty is greater. Needs keep changing, the level of complexity ratchets higher (many more groups involved with varying political agendas, ideologies, and religious beliefs), time pressures are more intense, staff stress levels are heightened, and media attention is incessant, all beyond that of a normal commercial supply chain. (For example, see Gupta et al. (2016)'s survey paper and the references listed there.)

Therefore, DM supply chains need to exhibit competent agility and adaptability in response to such highly dynamic situations. In turn, to exhibit such characteristics, a disaster supply chain needs to have (1) sufficient numbers of skilled, experienced, and competent POM practitioners who (2) have ready access to relevant knowledge and situational information, (3) robust POM practices and processes, (4) needed tools and materials in strategic locations, and (5) who operate in a coordinated and collaborative way with all disaster-related stakeholders. Moreover, these attributes need to be applied to *all* phases of the DM cycle.

To stress the point, disaster organisations that purposely build capabilities around the above five success elements will likely achieve their disaster management goals; those that don't, won't.

POM practices available to help DM are briefly described at Table 29.4.

Table 29.4 Brief Description of POM Practices

POM Practice	Description
Strategic planning	(i) For all types of disaster, an agreed description of future desired state, goals, objectives, targets, strategies, leadership, organisational structure, and strategy alignment. (ii) For specific disaster types, specific goals, and strategies for each of the five phases of the disaster management cycle (Figure 29.1).
Forecasting	Forecasting of timing and severity of likely disaster events before any occurrence so that mitigation actions can be taken. Demand and capacity forecasting using time series analysis or modelling for post-disaster event occurring so that materials and resources can be deployed as required.
Capacity planning	Balancing disaster forecast demand against forecast capacity and adjusting flows and/or alternate capacity opportunities accordingly to maximise disaster response quality.
SC Design	Design of SC flows, inventory points, facility locations & layouts, and control systems that best meet disaster mitigation and response requirements.

(Continued)

Table 29.4 (Continued)

POM Practice	Description
Requisite SC staffing	Organisational design for entire disaster management community—including RACI model of roles, clear position descriptions, leadership styles per cycle phase (e.g., command & control, democratic, consensus).
Disaster SC quality management	TQM ISO9001 based approach to all disaster management SC processes, products & services.
"Lean" approach	For the disaster management supply chain, elimination of all forms of waste, reductions to all cycles times, simplification of all processes, minimisation of all costs, "pull" inventory via "*kanbans*."
SC agility	SC attributes enabling nimbleness and dexterity in responding to the many changes that happen before and especially after disaster events.
Product/service design	Matching the requirements of disaster response teams and those affected by disasters with the products and services they need.
MRP	Materials requirements planning of all dependent & independent demand along the disaster management supply chain.
Inventory management	The right stock keeping units (SKUs), at the right stocking point, at the right time, in the right amount before the disaster event and during the disaster response.
Procurement management	Management of demand, ordering, receipt, testing, and payment of incoming supplies including vendor interface & information flows also before the disaster event and during the disaster response.
SC coordination	Techniques for engaging, responding, & relationship building with all relevant disaster management SC partners.
SC modelling	Simulation modelling of disaster management supply chain's flows, material stocks, delivery against demand, and costing.
SC process-mapping	Process improvement via mapping to simplify and streamline SC disaster management processes.
SC cost management	From disaster mitigation to response, modelling and forecasting of costs, cost budgeting, & management of costs to budget, cost reductions, and yield improvements.
SC data management	Specification, capture, storage, distribution, and analysis of all relevant SC specific disaster management data.
SC visibility	"Glass Pipeline Effect"—all relevant SC data for the disaster to be managed is visible to all those who need to see it in real time.
SC performance management	For the disaster to be managed and based on sustainability of economics, social and environmental outcomes, the specific SMART SC measures, targets including monitoring, reporting, and any necessary corrective actions for all phases of the disaster management cycle.

7 Disaster Management Research

From a POM perspective, disaster management is of recent origin. Gupta et al. (2016) have done a comprehensive review of disaster management research from 1957 to 2014—a span of fifty-seven years. They found 267 relevant papers in major Operations Management, Management Science, Operations Research, Supply Chain Management, and Transportation/Logistics journals. The growing interest of researchers in disaster management is depicted in Figure 29.4 that shows a three-year moving average of papers published on disaster management in these journals. The research picked up in 2014, and 150 out of 267 (56.18%) papers were published during the years (2011–2014).

Figure 29.5 gives the number of papers published in each journal. The three primarily POM-centered journals (*Production and Operations Management, Manufacturing & Service Operations Management*, and the *Journal of Operations Management*) only published twenty-one papers (7.86% of total publications). Clearly, disaster research has missed the attention of mainstream POM researchers. A department of "Disaster Management" has been created by the *Production and Operations Management* journal to fill this void and to encourage DM research.

Gupta et al. (2016) noticed that the disaster management field tends to be described as "humanitarian logistics" or "humanitarian operations," and the words "humanitarian logistics" appear to be synonymous with "disaster management." In fact, they are not! Disaster management is much wider and more inclusive. Humanitarian logistics is just one of the functions. Other functions include prevention/mitigations, evacuations, casualty management, and restoration/recovery.

Gupta et al. (2016) categorised papers into the following six administrative functions: humanitarian logistics (73), decision-making process (57), prevention and mitigation (49), evacuation (38), casualty management (24), and restoration/recovery (8). The numbers in parentheses show the count of papers.

In addition, there were eight survey-type papers. Four of these survey papers include Altay and Green III (2006), Galindo and Batta (2013), Abidi et al. (2014), and Day (2014). Altay and Green III (2006) and Galindo and Batta (2013) focus on reviewing research studies that use POM

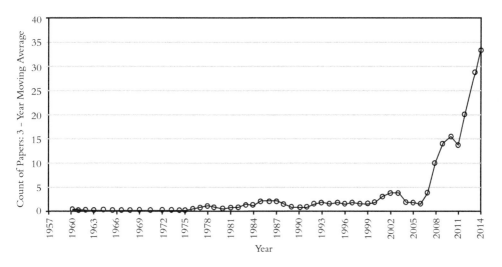

Figure 29.4 Three-Year Moving Average of the Count of Papers Published
Source: Gupta et al. 2016

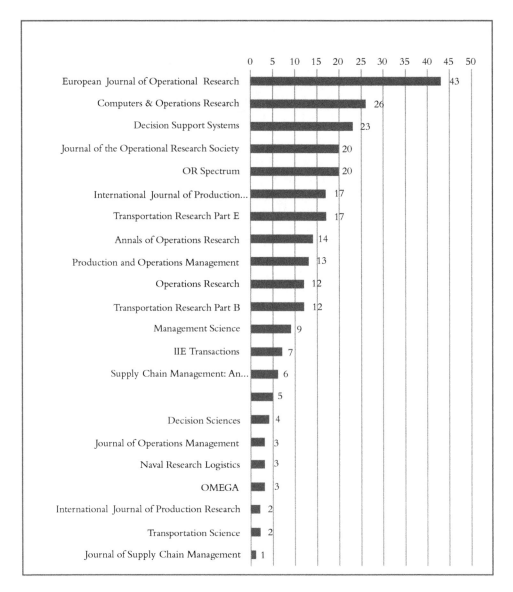

Figure 29.5 Count of Papers by Journal
Source: Gupta et al. 2016

techniques for managing disasters, whereas Abidi et al. (2014) study performance measurement, and Day (2014) studies resilience in disaster management.

Gupta et al. (2016) reviewed the data in more detail for years from 2011 to 2014 and found that the following data analysis techniques have been used in the research papers reviewed: Bidding Models (2), Decision Analysis (12), Expert Systems (6), Fuzzy Systems Analysis (3), Game Theory (10), Heuristics (4), Mathematical Programming (70), Network Flow Models (2), Queueing Theory (2), Simulation (15), Statistical Analysis (3), and Utility Theory (8). The numbers in parentheses show the paper counts. In some instances, one technique followed the other technique; for example, a heuristics model followed a mathematical programming formulation. There were nine other miscellaneous techniques that included differential equations, nonlinear differential equations, lab-based experiments, a viable system model, text data mining, structuration theory, and pattern theory.

The readers are encouraged to read Gupta et al. (2016) to find more research findings about the type of disasters (hurricanes, floods, earthquakes, etc.) and the time of disaster (before, after, and during).

8 Implications for Managers

The managers can benefit from disaster research if they can find answers to the specific functions that they are performing and for the specific type of disaster.

Gupta et al. (2016) advised readers to:

> Take, for example, the evacuation function. Evacuation includes many activities that include among others: how far in advance to issue warning signals, what is the impact of these signals, movement of traffic, use of public transportations and/or private cars for evacuation and shelter location. Some people do not evacuate in spite of warnings. So understanding individual behavior and the influence of social networks is important. Experience with near-miss events also plays an important role. An administrator will be able to identify appropriate research and make strategic and operational decisions based on research findings.

Gupta et al. (2016) also state:

> The administrators' interest in different types of disasters may be based on their work related responsibilities. For example, an administrator in Florida will have more interest in hurricanes whereas an administrator in California will have more interest in earthquakes. Similarly, there are specially qualified people who deal with disasters involving hazardous materials (HAZMAT) and those who deal with terrorism. These disasters have different origins and different impacts. Terrorism is preventable if the surveillance system is strong and warning signals are analyzed in time and preventive action is taken; HAZMAT is a result of human error and negligence; whereas hurricanes are natural disaster and inevitable.

9 Future Research Directions

The following research opportunities are suggested:

(1) What is the case for and what would be the preferred manner of achieving an agreed global approach to DM? Who are the key "players" and decision makers?
(2) Of the international DM type organisations that exists today, what is the level of understanding by their key staff of POM processes? If this level of understanding is found to be low, then how might it be lifted?
(3) How might POM type organisations better "sell" their offer to disaster organisations so that the uptake of POM practices in DM actually improves?

(4) How might private companies learn from the high need for flexibility and adaptability that is experienced by DM organisations in every disaster?
(5) How might POM organisations specifically help communities lift their social resilience to disasters?
(6) The researchers should study the prevailing DM processes in DM agencies like FEMA and then develop models in support of the current processes; or must have convincing results for administrators to change the existing processes.
(7) More research is needed in prevention/mitigation, repair/restoration, and the surge capacity of hospitals.
(8) Models that help in making integrated decisions (see, e.g., Vanajakumari et al. 2016) in humanitarian logistics need to be developed.

References and Bibliography

Abidi, H., de Leeuw, S., & Klumpp, M. (2014) "Humanitarian supply chain performance management: A systematic literature review," *Supply Chain Management: An International Journal*, **19**(5/6): 592–608.

Altay, N., & Green III, W. G. (2006) "OR/MS research in disaster operations management," *European Journal of Operational Research*, **175**(1): 475–493.

Bankoff, G. (2007) "Comparing vulnerabilities: Toward charting an historical trajectory of disasters," *Historical Social Research/Historische Sozialforschung*, **32**(3): 103–114.

Boston University Metropolitan College Online Graduate Programs in Management (2015) "Boston University's Online Master of Science in Manager Degree." Available from: http://msmonline.bu.edu/survive-a-natural-disaster/.

Day, J. M. (2014) "Fostering emergent resilience: The complex adaptive supply network of disaster relief," *International Journal of Production Research*, **52**(7): 1970–1988.

EM-DAT, "Country profile." Available from: www.emdat.be/country_profile/index.html [Accessed 07 Aug 2016].

Galindo, G., & Batta, R. (2013) "Review of recent developments in OR/MS research in disaster operations management," *European Journal of Operational Research*, **230**(2): 201–211.

Gupta, S., Starr, M., Zanjirani Farahani, R., & Matinrad, N. (2016) "Disaster management from a POM perspective: Mapping a new domain," *Production and Operations Management*, **25**(10): 1611–1637.

Hoyos, M. C., Morales, R. S., & Akhavan-Tabatabaei, R. (2015) "OR models with stochastic components in disaster operations management: A literature survey," *Computers & Industrial Engineering*, **82**: 183–197.

IFRC (2015) "Disaster and crisis management." *IFRC, International Federation of Red Cross and Red Crescent Societies*. Available from: www.ifrc.org/en/what-we-do/disaster-management/ [Accessed 19 Dec 2015].

Listverse.com, "Top 10 deadliest natural disasters." Available from: http://listverse.com/2007/09/07/top-10-deadliest-natural-disasters/ [Accessed 21 July 2016].

Riede, F. (2014) "Towards a science of past disasters," *Natural Hazards*, **71**(1): 335–362.

Smith, A.B., & Matthews, J.L. (2015) "Quantifying uncertainty and variable sensitivity within the US billion-dollar weather and climate disaster cost estimates," *Natural Hazards*, **77**(3): 1829–1851.

UNISDR (2015) "Terminology." *UNISDR News*. Available from: https://www.unisdr.org/we/inform/terminology [Accessed 19 Dec 2015].

Vanajakumari, M., Kumar, S., & Gupta, S. (2016) "An integrated logistic model for predictable disasters," *Production and Operations Management*, **25**(5): 791–811.

War Chronicle (2016) "Estimated war dead: World War II." Available from: http://warchronicle.com/numbers/WWII/deaths.htm [Accessed July 2016].

Weichselgartner, J., & Kelman, I. (2014) "Geographies of resilience: challenges and opportunities of a descriptive concept," *Progress in Human Geography*, **39**(3): 249–267.

Wikipedia contributors, "Hurricane Katrina," *Wikipedia, The Free Encyclopedia*. Available from: https://en.wikipedia.org/w/index.php?title=Hurricane_Katrina&oldid=728612805 [Accessed July 2016].

30
THE IMPACT OF POM ON TRANSPORT AND LOGISTICS

Dongping Song

1 Introduction

Transportation is a service industry that enables the movement of people and/or goods from one location to another. There is a wide range of specific demands for transport, which are differentiated by time of day, day of week, month of year, journey purpose, type of cargo, importance of speed, frequency, safety and security, and so on (Ortuzar and Willumsen 2011). A transport service has to match this differentiated demand. Transportation takes a link function perspective to connect the origin and the destination arising from the transport demand. The management of transportation concerns managing a range of activities including vehicle fleet sizing, routing, scheduling, maintenance, fuel costing, communications, technology implementations, traveler and cargo handling, and carrier selection. The goals of transportation are to achieve high utilization, cost reduction, and safe and on-time transport.

According to the Council of Supply Chain Management Professionals (https://cscmp.org/supply-chain-management-definitions), logistics management is that part of supply chain management that plans, implements, and controls the efficient, effective forward and reverse flow and storage of goods, services, and related information between the point of origin and the point of consumption in order to meet customers' requirements. Logistics includes inbound, outbound, internal, and external movements along the supply chain, which essentially takes a channel perspective. The goals of logistics are to achieve cost efficiency, service effectiveness, and customer requirements along the supply chain process, in which the latter two goals include quality factors.

As a discipline, transportation has a long history. On the other hand, logistics is relatively new and emerged as a discipline about three decades ago. It could be argued that transportation differs from logistics in two aspects: focus point and managerial function. In the first aspect, transport often takes the "individual focus" emphasizing on individual functions and pursuing its own goals or competitiveness usually from the carrier's perspective. Logistics takes the "integrated system" viewpoint, emphasizing not only transportation but also logistics flows in the entire supply chain. Therefore, logistics often takes the supply chain's or the customer's perspective. Second, transportation concerns the managerial functions such as fleet management, contracting, routing, scheduling, and cargo handling, normally in a specific segment of transportation.

Logistics covers the entire transportation journey (that may involve multiple transport modes) while also considering additional managerial activities such as consolidation, storage, warehousing, packaging, repacking, repairing, re-use, and documentation. However, in the last two decades, we have seen the convergence of transport and logistics. This reflects in the overlap between the goals of transportation and the goals of logistics. Nevertheless, some transport sectors are still rather fragmented, and transport service providers may largely focus on their own operational efficiency without much consideration from the supply chain system's perspective (e.g., in the shipping sector).

Production and operations management (POM) concerns planning, organizing, coordinating, and controlling the processes of the business operations in the creation of goods or services efficiently and effectively. POM involves managing all the resources such as people, equipment, technology, and information that are required in the creation of goods and services. POM is the central core function of every company in both manufacturing and service industries. The application of POM in transport and logistics would facilitate the achievement of these goals. In this chapter, we will discuss the impact of POM on transport and logistics.

2 Transport Modes and Features

Transportation modes are the means to achieve the mobility of people or goods. They are generally organized into five categories: road, rail, air, water, and pipeline. Each mode has its own features and may be adapted to serve specific types of demands. This section briefly discusses the features of different transport modes, which is helpful for mode selection and multimodal arrangement.

2.1 Road Transport

Road transport dominates passenger and goods transport for relatively short distance. From the road user's viewpoint, the main advantage of road transport is accessibility and flexibility. It can access almost any location and is flexible in vehicle routing with short notice. In the business aspect, it has a relatively low entry capital cost. Special equipment is available for certain types of commodities (e.g., frozen foods or glassware). From the logistics perspective, many road haulers have broadened into or become part of logistics companies undertaking a range of activities, e.g., warehousing, repackaging, and order processing.

2.2 Rail Transport

Rail transport is more suitable for longer-distance journeys in larger countries or international land journeys (e.g., across Europe). It has advantages of reliability and fixed routes with timetables, which can facilitate the planning of business operations such as production, distribution, and inventory management. The accessibility of rail transport is rather low because many locations are not rail-connected and therefore may require road transport to finish the journey. In the business aspect, it has relatively low operating costs but high entry costs because it requires the investment of tracks, terminals, and trains. Special equipment is available, particularly for bulk cargo (e.g., bulk powder wagons, tank wagons). Rail transport has a much smaller environmental impact (such as emissions) than road transport. McKinnon (2007) estimated the carbon intensity of freight transport modes based on the UK data, and reported that the CO_2 emissions per ton-km were about 1,600 grams, 150 grams, 35 grams, 15 grams, 5 grams for by air, truck (heavy goods vehicles), water, rail, and pipeline, respectively.

2.3 Air Transport

Air transport is mainly for passengers and cargoes that are time sensitive, valuable, or perishable. The biggest advantage of the air transport mode is the fast speed in long distance, which supports just-in-time production and distribution. However, air transport is disrupted by weather conditions more often than other modes are. The accessibility of air transport is rather limited because of the restricted number of airports. In the business aspect, the entry costs (for equipment) and operating variable costs (airport terminal usage costs) are high. ERA (2014) provided statistics on the risk of fatality for a passenger travelling over a given distance using different transport modes. It reported that the fatality risk for a passenger on average (defined as the fatalities per billion km) is about 0.06, 0.13, 0.20, and 3.14 by airline, railway, coach, and car respectively. This indicates that air is the safest mode.

2.4 Water (Maritime) Transport

Maritime transport is the most effective mode to move large quantities over long distances. Maritime transport includes inland waterways, coastal shipping, and international ocean transport. Traditionally, maritime freight transport is mainly for products of low value and high density such as coal, wood, and liquid. With containerization, high-value manufactured goods have been consolidated into containers and moved by container ships. The main features of maritime transport are its capability, the smaller environmental impact (compared to road and air), and the existence of a wide range of ships available for different types of cargoes. The accessibility of maritime transport is limited to certain ports with necessary infrastructure. In the business aspect, the entry costs are relatively low for domestic water carriers but quite high for international ocean carriers.

2.5 Pipeline Transport

Pipeline transport is very effective for the limited range of products (e.g., oil, gas, water) that require a continuous flow, particularly when moving large quantities over long distances. Pipeline routes tend to link isolated areas of production to major refining and manufacturing centers (to transport oil) or to major populated areas (to transport gas). The continuous supply is the main feature of pipeline transport. The accessibility of goods via pipeline transport is highly limited. Once built, it is difficult to adjust the pipeline network in response to demands. In the business aspect, it is very expensive to install pipelines (incurring high fixed costs) but cheap to operate.

2.6 Comparison of Transport Modes

The characteristics of the above different transport modes are summarized in Table 30.1. The attributes are explained as follows:

- Transport cost per unit is related to the travel distance. Literature showed that threshold values exist for the preference of transport modes, e.g., short distance is in favor of road, medium distance for rail, and long distance for water.
- The time attribute refers to the transit time.

Table 30.1 Comparison of Characteristics of Transport Modes

Attribute	Road	Rail	Air	Water	Pipeline
Fixed cost	Low	High	Very high	High/low	High
Operating cost	High	Low	Very high	Very low	Very low
Time	Short	Medium	Very short	Very long	Continuous
On-time reliability	Low	Medium	Medium	Very low	High
Accessibility	Very high	Low	Low	Low	Very low
Frequency	High	Low	Medium	Very low	Continuous
Capability	Low	Medium	Low	Very high	Medium
Goods flexibility	Medium	High	Low	Very high	Very low
Safety	Medium	High	Very high	Medium	Medium
Emission	High	Low	Very high	Low	Very low

- The on-time reliability attribute can actually be divided into two types: absolute reliability and relative reliability. The absolute on-time reliability is defined as the absolute deviation from the schedule, whereas the relative on-time reliability is defined as the ratio of the deviation to the transit time. It is worth noting that the relative on-time reliability for water could be high due to its very long transit time, although its absolute on-time reliability may be very low.
- The accessibility attribute refers to the ability and flexibility to visit any location.
- The frequency attribute represents how often the transport service is provided and available.
- The capability attribute refers to the handling capacity.
- Goods flexibility indicates the ability of carrying different types of commodities.
- The safety attribute reflects the level of possible loss and damage.
- The emission attribute refers to the environmental impact from the transport mode.

In the freight transport, Lloyds Marine Intelligence Unit (MIU) conducted a comprehensive analysis based on the UN trade data and found that 75% of the world trade was carried by sea, and 0.3% by air in terms of volume, while 60% of the world trade was carried by sea, and 10% by air in terms of value (Mandryk 2009). The above statistics show that sea transport moves the majority of world trade, and air transport moves the goods with the highest value density. Within the sea transport industry (including tanker, dry bulk, container, and general cargo), Lloyds MIU found that about 52% of cargoes by value was carried by container ships, while only 10% of cargoes by volume was carried by container ships. Container shipping has experienced a rapid development in the last two decades.

3 Transport Systems and Key Performance Indicators (KPIs)

3.1 Transport Systems

From the modelling perspective, transport systems may be classified into three types: taxi-type transport, industrial-type transport, and liner-type transport.

- Taxi-type transport is negotiated for each trip with specific origin and destination such as taxi on road and tramp shipping at sea.

- Industrial-type transport is organized by the carrier with possible multiple collections and deliveries along the journey. The carrier may own the cargo on vehicle. Typical examples are the truck movements between distribution centers and stores, and the tanker vessel movements in the sea.
- Liner-type transport has to follow the published schedules. Examples include bus service, train service, airline service, and liner shipping services. Clearly, three types of transport systems have quite different management scopes.

3.2 KPIs

To represent the goals of transport and logistics systems, the literature often adopts four performance measures: cost, asset utilization, reliability, and responsiveness/flexibility. The first two are service providers' internal-facing measures for efficiency, while the last two are external customer-facing measures for service effectiveness (Lai et al. 2002). The traditional key performance indicators (KPI) in transport can be categorized into two groups: operational efficiency and service effectiveness. The former emphasizes on cost reduction and asset utilization/efficiency, whilst the latter emphasizes on service differentiation and quality of service.

In the last two decades, another group of KPIs has emerged and attracted much attention, which represents the social and environmental impacts of transport. This group appears to have become more important due to the greater concerns about climate change and sustainability. The applications of POM in transport and logistics are therefore focusing on evaluating and optimizing one or multiple of the above three groups of KPIs in a specific transport system. Representative studies will be discussed in the next section.

4 POM Research in Transport and Logistics

The management decisions in transport and logistics systems can generally be divided into three levels: strategic, tactical, and operational planning (Crainic and Laporte 1997; Crainic 2000; Wieberneit 2008). At the strategic planning level, the decisions focus on the infrastructure of facility (location, layout, and capacity); the physical structure and size of resources (personnel and equipment); and the customer service types and tariff policies (contracting and pricing). Typical questions include where terminals and hubs should be built/selected, what type of fleet mix should be used, and what kind of contractual agreements should be made with other firms.

At the tactical planning level, the main decision is the transport network design, which focuses on the allocation of existing resources to meet transport service demands effectively and efficiently. In general, at this planning level, the customer demand is treated as external input data. The aim is to best match the service supply with the service demand. Fleet sizing and deployment, vehicle routing, and scheduling are among the common planning issues. In most cases, the service network has been operating and cannot be re-designed from scratch. A sub-problem is how to assign the customer demands over the existing service network.

At the operational planning level, the planners are required to deal with the dynamic environment, in which the time dimension has to be considered. Customers may make changes with short notice. Uncertainties exist in various aspects that may cause the physical operations to deviate from the plan. Disruptive events require operators to respond in real-time mode. The planners may design the service operations taking into account the dynamic and uncertain nature of the transport environment (introducing buffer time or contingency planning); on the other hand, the planners have to be flexible and adaptive in response to disruptive events (e.g., re-routing and rescheduling vehicles).

POM methods have been applied extensively to deal with various planning issues in the transport and logistics industry. Note that it is impossible to cover all aspects of POM research in transport and logistics in this chapter. We will discuss the representative extant POM studies in a range of selected topics. These topics are selected due to their importance and representativeness in the transport and logistics industries. Nevertheless, we attempt to provide good coverage of many well studied and some newly emerging topics.

More specifically, we will select the following planning issues: service network design, fleet sizing and deployment, vehicle/inventory routing and scheduling, speed management and slow steaming, empty vehicle/container management, disruption management, crew scheduling and rostering, port/terminal management, and emission management. It should be noted that (i) some planning issues are more general than others (e.g., service network design may include fleet deployment and vehicle routing as sub-problems); (ii) some issues may partially overlap with others and sometimes be considered jointly (e.g., vehicle routing and empty vehicle management; speed management with emission management); and (iii) some issues are common in many transport sectors (e.g., service network design, vehicle routing, and scheduling), whereas others may be more specific to one transport sector (e.g., slow steaming in maritime transport).

4.1 Service Network Design

Service network design usually takes the carrier's perspective. This is natural as the transport service provider is responsible to set up a network consisting of nodes (ports, terminals, depots) and links (connections between nodes) and deploy a fleet of vehicles (truck, train, plane, and vessel) to provide transport services. A service route can be defined as a sequence of nodes that a certain type of vehicle visits. A service network consists of a set of service routes.

The objective of service network design is to optimize the service networks by rationalizing the coverage of ports, service routes and transit time, which is a trade-off between meeting customer requirements and service operational cost. In a broad perspective, management decisions in service network design include: how many service routes should be opened, how a service route should be structured in terms of port rotation and schedule, with which frequency the service route should be used, which type of vehicles and how many should be deployed in a service route, how the demands should assigned over the service network, and how the human resources are allocated to execute the transport services. In this view, service network design includes fleet deployment, vehicle routing, inventory routing, and crew scheduling as sub-problems, but these sub-problems may be treated in a simplified and/or aggregated level.

In a narrow perspective, service network design mainly concerns the route structure generation or selection. Woxenius (2007) summarized six generic route structures for transport network design problems:

(i) Direct link structure is exemplified by taxis and tramp shipping. It is also suitable for moving large quantities of commodities, which justifies the utilization of the vehicle.
(ii) Corridor route structure is suitable for high-density flow along an artery. The nodes in the corridor may represent big cities or ports along a river. The nodes off the corridor are served by short capillary services.
(iii) Hub-and-spoke structure is often used to connect a distribution center to a large number of stores. The hub node can also act as a cross-dock point to link any two spoke nodes.

(iv) Connected hub structure is generally applicable for large countries or international transportation.
(v) Static route design aims to construct a set of regular services. The sequence of nodes in the route and the schedule (timetables) of visits has to be determined in advance.
(vi) Dynamic route design is responding to actual demand with flexible routing between origin and destination nodes, under which the vehicle's route from origin node to destination node varies over time.

A summary of examples of applications of the above generic route structures in passenger and freight transportation is given in Table 30.2. It should be pointed out there is no clear cut distinction between these route structures, and multiple route structures could be applied to the same transport sector, e.g., direct links, corridor (conveyor belt) routes, connected hubs, and static routes are all adopted in the container shipping industry.

Table 30.2 provides useful information to simplify the service route design problems in some specific transport sectors or for some specific purposes. Service network design problem is a common problem arising from both passenger and freight transportation and in all transport modes, for example:

- In road transport mode, public transit network design and its approaches were discussed in the survey papers, Ceder and Wilson (1986), Guihaire and Hao (2008), and Farahani et al. (2013). The planning process can be decomposed into a sequence of five sub-problems in a hierarchical structure, e.g., network design, frequencies setting, timetable development, bus scheduling, and driver scheduling.
- In the air transport mode, airline network design problem with routing pattern selection and service scheduling was addressed in Lederer and Nambimadom (1998).
- In the container shipping sector, the network design problem aims to select ports and construct service routes in a way that the customer demands can be served efficiently by the vessel fleet, cf. recent review papers (e.g., Christiansen et al. (2007); Brouer et al. (2014); and Tran and Haasis (2015)).

4.1.1 Solution Techniques

Mathematical models for service network design mainly employ integer programming, mixed integer programming, non-linear programming based on three frameworks: node-arc (or link-based), path-based, and tree formulation (Kim and Barnhart 1999). Integer decision variables are often essential to select nodes, links, routes, or paths. Continuous variables may be used to represent the flow volumes. Non-linearity may arise from the constraints or the objectives. Service

Table 30.2 Typical Applications of the Different Transport Network Designs in Transport Services

Direct Link	Corridor	Hub-and-Spoke	Connected Hubs	Static Routes	Dynamic Routes
Taxi service	Intercity train service	Domestic airline traffic	Intercontinental airline traffic	Urban public transport systems	Airport limousine service
Full truckload service	Transport on inland waterways	Air transport of express cargo	Container liner shipping	Container liner shipping	Partial load truck service

Source: Based on Woxenius 2007

network design problems are often tackled in a multi-stage hierarchical procedure through decomposing the original problem into a series of sub-problems.

Due to the complexity of the underlying problem, exact optimal solutions are often difficult to obtain for realistic size of the problems. It is common to use heuristics, metaheuristics, or approximation methods to seek the sub-optimal solutions. Such methods may be classified into five groups (Guihaire and Hao 2008):

- Specific and ad-hoc heuristics (e.g., based on greedy principle or simple rules)
- Neighborhood search methods (e.g., Tabu Search)
- Evolutionary search methods (Genetic Algorithms)
- Bound-based approximation methods (e.g., Column Generation; Lagrangian Relaxation)
- Hybrid search methods that combine two or more solution methods.

In the above methods, simulation is often used to evaluate the performance of a given solution. It is worth noting that sometimes service network design problems could be greatly simplified if industrial specific characteristics could be utilized (Song and Dong 2013).

4.2 *Fleet Sizing and Deployment*

Fleet sizing and deployment consists of two components: supply capacity management and fleet deployment/redeployment. The former concerns determining the fleet size and mix and the capacity leasing or purchasing or laying up (idling) decisions. The latter involves determining how the fleet is to be deployed or redeployed in the service network.

Part of fleet sizing and deployment decisions may be incorporated into service network design problem (e.g., the number of vehicles deployed in a particular route is highly related to the frequency of the service). On the other hand, fleet sizing and mix may be regarded as an input and constraint to the service network design problem. In that sense, fleet sizing and mix is treated as a strategic planning issue at a higher level. The fleet sizing and deployment aims to manage the supply capacity, composition, and deployment to better satisfy customer demands. Quite often, vehicle routing is jointly considered with fleet sizing and deployment either in an integrated way or in a hierarchical way.

Hoff et al. (2010) provided a survey on fleet sizing and mix problem combined with vehicle routing. They took the industrial aspects of the fleet composition and routing and covered two main transport modes: land-based and maritime transportation. In the following, we take the maritime transport as an example to give a brief review of the existing research on fleet sizing and deployment problems. Interested readers can refer to two survey papers by Christiansen et al. (2007) and Pantuso et al. (2014) for more relevant literature on the shipping industry.

Dantzig and Fulkerson (1954) were among the first to study the fleet sizing and deployment problem. They used linear programming to formulate a problem of determining the minimum number of tanker vessels required to meet a fixed schedule of transporting Navy fuel oil. Nicholson and Pullen (1971) considered a planning problem of phasing out a fleet of existing ships and the replacement policy (by charter ships). Mourao et al. (2001) applied integer linear programming to determine the optimal number of ships to be assigned to a given hub-and-spoke system. Bendall and Stent (2005) performed real option analysis on three scenarios in a hub-and-spoke system facing uncertain demand in order to determine the best deployment scenario (which specifies the number of ships and the frequencies of calls at ports).

Fleet deployment/assignment over a given set of liner service routes including lay-up (idle) and hire decisions was first addressed in Perakis and Jaramillo (1991). Gelareh and Meng (2010) considered fleet deployment including ship sailing speed decision for liner shipping operations. Meng and Wang (2010) developed a chance constrained programming model for the liner ship fleet deployment problem with uncertain demand. Meng and Wang (2011) studied the ship fleet deployment in a long-haul liner service route with fixed demand including the decisions of the ship sailing speed and the service frequency. Wang and Meng (2012d) extended the fleet deployment problem allowing transshipment operations. Meng et al. (2012) further extended the work in a situation with uncertain demand. A two-stage stochastic integer programming model is proposed, and the sample average approximation method is used to solve the problem.

Vessel sharing, slot exchanging, and slot purchase are quite common in the liner shipping industry. A generalization of a ship fleet deployment problem is the service capacity planning in a given shipping network. In this direction, Dong et al. (2015) considered a joint shipping service capacity planning and dynamic container routing problem with demand uncertainty. A two-stage stochastic programming model with recourse is formulated and solved using an adapted progressive hedging algorithm.

Shipping companies have to adjust their service networks in response to the change of demand patterns and/or the deployment of new ships. Adjustments of the service network may include adding new services, removing services, or modifying existing services. Whenever these adjustments take place, some vessels will be redeployed (i.e., repositioned) to a different service in order to replace another vessel. Tierney et al. (2015) addressed the ship fleet repositioning problem with the aim of maximizing profits during the ship phasing-in and phasing-out process without disrupting cargo flows and respecting the service schedules. A mathematical model is formulated and solved using a simulated annealing algorithm.

The common POM methods used in the fleet sizing and deployment issue include: linear programming, integer programming, dynamic programming, mixed integer programming, and simulation. As the fleet sizing and deployment is targeting on matching service supply with customer demand, uncertainty in demand is sometimes considered explicitly, in which chance constrained programming, stochastic programming with sample average approximation method, real option analysis has been applied.

4.3 Vehicle/Inventory Routing and Scheduling

Vehicle/inventory routing and scheduling are generally operational level decisions, although schedule (timetable) design can be regarded as a tactical decision. Due to the wide coverage and variants of the problems in this area, we classify the problems into four groups. The first group includes the classic vehicle routing problem (VRP) and its direct extensions. It aims to design the optimal delivery or collection routes from one or several depots to a number of geographically scattered customers subject to side constraints. Vehicle routing usually takes the carrier's perspective. The second group is inventory routing problem. It integrates vehicle routing, inventory management, and delivery scheduling decisions, which essentially takes both carrier and customer's perspectives. The third group is cargo routing problem or shipment assignment problem. It aims to determine the cargo path in a given service network. Cargo routing can take either carrier or customer's perspective to optimize a performance criterion. The fourth group is schedule design problem, which aims to specify the arrival and departure times of the vehicles. The studies on the above four groups are discussed briefly below.

4.3.1 Vehicle Routing Problem (VRP)

In VRP, normally each non-depot node in the service network is visited exactly once by exactly one vehicle. All vehicle routes start and end at the depot node and some side constraints are satisfied. Common side constraints include vehicle capacity, number of non-depot nodes on any route, total time of the route, time windows of the visits, and precedence relationships.

There have been a huge number of studies published on VRP since its introduction by Dantzig and Ramser (1959). Readers can refer to the following survey papers and the references therein, e.g., Lenstra and Kan (1981); Laporte (1992); Meng et al. (2014); Lahyani et al. (2015); Ritzinger et al. (2016). VRP is highly industrially relevant and can arise from air transport, rail transport, as well as maritime transport modes. In fact, VRP is regarded as one of the success stories of POM (Hoff et al. 2010). Apart from a plethora of academic research on VRP, many software tools have been developed in the market. Exact algorithms for the VRP include direct tree search methods, dynamic programming, and integer linear programming. Well known heuristic algorithms have been developed (e.g., the Clarke and Wright algorithm). However, more often, metaheuristic methods are applied to solve NP-hard VRP problems.

4.3.2 Inventory Routing Problem

Inventory routing problem was initiated from Bell et al. (1983). They integrated inventory management of industrial gases at customer locations with vehicle scheduling and dispatching. Moin and Salhi (2007) took the supply chain management viewpoint and provided a survey on inventory routing. Recently, Coelho et al. (2014) provided a review of inventory routing and its development. They noticed that the main application area of inventory routing is in maritime logistics (e.g., ship routing and inventory management (Ronen 1993; Christiansen et al. 2004)).

In terms of solution methods to inventory routing problems, exact algorithms (e.g., branch-and-cut algorithms) have been applied in some cases. However, because the basic inventory routing problem is also NP-hard (Coelho et al. 2014), it often returns to metaheuristics, hybrid metaheuristics, or matheuristic algorithms (which combine heuristics with mathematical programming).

4.3.3 Cargo Routing Problem

The focus in this group lands on cargo routing rather than vehicle routing. When both cargo and vehicle routing are decision variables, the problem may be regarded as the first group VRP or the service network design problem. We limit this group with cargo routing and assuming the vehicle routes are fixed. When taking the carrier's perspective, the cargo routing problem is about how to efficiently utilize the existing service supply subject to customers' requirements. When taking the shipper's perspective, cargo routing can be regarded as a shipper or a freight forwarder organizing trips for a set of shipments. This may involve selecting the transport modes, the carriers, and the routes in order to transport the shipments from origins to destinations efficiently.

Cargo transport is a one-way operation, whereas vehicle routing usually needs to consider the return journey. Cargo routing may involve multiple transport modes, carriers, and vehicles, while vehicle routing usually concerns a single vehicle or a fleet of vehicles operated by the same carrier. Container routing can be regarded as one example of cargo routing in a given service network. A number of studies have been published in this area in the last decade (e.g., Song et al. 2005; Agarwal and Ergun, 2008; Brouer et al. 2011). Path-based and link-based network flow models have been developed to tackle the problem.

4.3.4 Schedule Design Problem

Schedule design problem may be treated as a sub-problem in service network design. In particular, all static service network design problems involve a timetable development and optimization (e.g., bus service, train service, liner shipping service). In practice, transport systems are always subject to uncertainty caused by congestion and weather conditions. Therefore, schedule design should consider time uncertainty in the transport system to ensure reasonable service reliability, which implies the need of setting up the total buffer time and the assignment of buffer time among different legs of the schedule.

In the container shipping sector, Wang and Meng (2012b) developed a mixed-integer, non-linear, stochastic model for the liner ship route scheduling problem with sea contingency and uncertain port time in order to minimize the ship cost and bunker cost. Wang and Meng (2012a) considered the robust schedule design problem for a liner ship route. The objective is to achieve the optimal trade-off between buffer time allocation and schedule robustness in terms of reliability, integrity, and stability. Qi and Song (2012) designed an optimal container ship schedule in a service route with uncertain port times by minimizing an expected objective function consisting of fuel consumption and delay penalty.

4.4 Speed Management and Slow Streaming

Speed management is less relevant to air, train, and road transport modes, because these types of vehicles often operate at their designed speeds and there is not much benefit or flexibility to deviate from the designed speed. On the other hand, speed management is an important issue in maritime transport. Fuel consumption cost can account for 75% of the ship operating costs, and reducing the cruising speed by 20% can reduce daily bunker consumption by 50% (Ronen 2011).

Slow steaming refers to the practice of operating cargo ships at significantly less than their designed speeds. Since the global economic crisis in 2008, slow steaming in the container shipping industry has become a popular practice. Slower speed implies extra vessels should be deployed in a single route to maintain the service frequency (normally weekly service). Hence, it can not only reduce the ship operating cost, but also absorb spare vessels and mitigate the overcapacity issue. In addition, reducing fuel consumption implies the reduction of emissions, which is beneficial to the environment and society.

Ronen (2011) presented a cost model to analyze the trade-off between reducing ship speed and adding extra ships to a container service route by minimizing the annual operating cost of the route. Wang and Meng (2012c) optimized vessel speed on each leg of each ship route in a shipping network considering container routing. Psaraftis and Kontovas (2013) presented a comprehensive review on the models in which ship speed is one of the decision variables in maritime transportation. They classified the models according to a set of parameters, including optimization criterion, shipping market, decision maker, fuel price, freight rate, fuel consumption function, ship fleet, cargo inventory costs, port-related variables, and emissions.

Cariou (2011) discussed the sustainability of slow steaming. He stated that slow steaming could only be sustained given a bunker fuel price of at least $350 per ton for the main container trades, based on a simple cost model. However, slow steaming depends on multiple factors including ship supply, trade demand, and freight rates. This is why slow steaming is still widely adopted now although the bunker fuel price has been below $350/ton for most of the time since January 2015.

4.5 Empty Vehicle/Container Management

Trade imbalance is a common phenomenon in freight transportation, which generates a significant number of empty vehicle movements. This phenomenon arises from many transport sectors (e.g., empty truck movements on road, empty wagons and railcars on railways, empty motor carrier movements on road, empty vessel sailing at sea (called ballast voyages), empty container movements at sea and on road/railway). Empty runs not only incur a financial burden to the carriers, but they also create congestion and emissions for the society. Therefore, efficiently managing empty vehicle/container movements is an important issue in transport and logistics. We discuss this issue in two groups: empty vehicle management and empty container management. The second group differs from the first group because containers have to be carried by trucks, trains, or vessels. In addition, empty container management has emerged as a popular and challenging topic recently.

4.5.1 Empty Vehicle Management

Empty vehicle management may be incorporated into the service network design and/or fleet deployment problem. This is because empty vehicle movements are derived from the loaded vehicle movements, and it is natural to consider them together. Dejax and Crainic (1987) reviewed the literature on empty flows and fleet management in freight transportation. A number of models have been developed (e.g., non-linear network programs (Beaujon and Turnquist 1991); multistage dynamic networks (Cheung and Powell 1996); logistics queueing networks (Powell and Carvalho 1998); and inventory control policies (Song 2005; Song and Earl 2008)).

4.5.2 Empty Container Management

Empty container management is closely associated with container fleet sizing, container purchasing, container leasing and off-leasing, and empty container repositioning, in which empty container repositioning (ECR) is the predominant component. ECR has attracted much attention in the last two decades partially due to the rapid growth of container shipping and the severe imbalance of trade demands globally and regionally. It was reported that shipping companies spent about US$110 billion per year in managing their container fleets (e.g., purchase, maintenance, repairs), of which US$16 billion (or 15%) for repositioning empty containers (Rodrigue et al. 2013). Empty containers in the transport system have a similar function to the inventory in production-inventory system as both are transported and stored in a space-time dimension to satisfy external customer demands.

In terms of the modelling techniques, ECR models in the literature may be classified into two streams (Song and Dong 2015). The first stream adopts the network flow models and often applies mathematical programming to produce a set of arc-based (or O-D based) matrices, which specify the quantity of empty containers to be moved on an arc (i.e., from one node to another node) in the network. The underlying concept is flow balancing, i.e., the container flows out of a node should be equal to the flows into the same node (Crainic et al. 1993; Brouer et al. 2011; Song and Dong 2012). The second stream adopts the inventory control models to produce decision-making rules, which are able to determine the amount of empty containers to be repositioned into/out of a node dynamically by utilizing the information of inventory levels of empty containers in the system (Dong and Song 2009; Long et al. 2012; Dang et al. 2013). Braekers et al. (2011) provided a literature review on empty container repositioning models at different planning levels (i.e., strategic, tactical, and operational levels). Song and Dong (2015) gave a survey on ECR problems from the supply chain perspective and as well as from the modelling technique perspective.

4.6 Disruption Management

Disruption management refers to dynamically recovering a predetermined operational plan when various disruptive events prevent the original plan from being executed smoothly (Yu and

Qi 2004). In the transportation industry, disruption management is usually an operational or real-time decision on adjusting transportation plans and operations in response to unusual events that may have just occurred or will occur in the near future. Common disruptive events include vehicle breakdowns, accidents, bad weather, industry actions, and severe delays. If the same type of disruptive events becomes regular, then it is possible to model their occurrence using probability distribution based on historical data. In such a case, tactical level planning (e.g., timetable design) can accommodate this type of uncertainty through robust planning and/or adding buffer time. In general, disruptive events are regarded as occasional and one-off events, which are tackled on a real-time basis.

Research on disruption management in transport industries has mainly focused on the airline sector. Clausen et al. (2010) provided a survey on airline disruption management. They defined a disruptive situation as a state during the execution of the current operation, where the deviation from the plan is sufficiently large to impose a substantial change. One challenge of disruption management is to define an appropriate objective. In fact, there are multiple objectives that should be considered. These examples include: delivering the passengers and their luggage to their destinations on-time with the booked service level; minimizing the total costs including excess crew costs, costs of compensation, hotel and accommodation to disrupted passengers and crew, and tickets on other airlines; minimizing the reputation damage (passenger dissatisfaction), and recovering the plan and schedule as soon as possible (Kohl et al. 2007). These objectives are conflicting and some are difficult to quantify. The generation of a good recovery plan is very complicated due to the rearrangement of many resources such as crews, aircraft, passengers, slots, schedules, hotels, cargoes, etc. The majority of the mathematical models and solution methods for solving the airline recovery problems are similar to those that are used for planning purposes (Clausen et al. 2010). Commonly used mathematical models include set partitioning models, set covering models, multicommodity network flow models. In practice, real-time decisions by large airlines are usually made in a sequential mode with respect to sub-problems, e.g., rescheduling the aircraft, rescheduling crews, then deal with ground problems, followed by the impacts on passengers (Clausen et al. 2010).

In maritime transport, particularly in liner shipping, a few studies have addressed disruption management recently. Brouer et al. (2013) sought the optimal recovery measure (e.g., speeding up, port omission, swapping ports of call) under a given disruptive scenario in container shipping. Li et al. (2015) presented nonlinear programming models and dynamic programming algorithms to determine the optimal operational action to catch up a delayed journey in liner shipping. Both Brouer et al. (2013) and Li et al. (2015) focus on schedule recovery after a disruptive event, which are deterministic models and do not consider future new delays. Li et al. (2016) formulated a stochastic model to adjust vessel schedules considering both regular uncertainties and disruptive events on a real-time basis.

4.7 Crew Scheduling and Rostering

Crew scheduling and rostering is an operational level decision, which concerns the assignment of a group of workers to performing a set of tasks. The aim is to minimize total labor costs subject to a wide variety of constraints imposed by safety regulations and labor negotiations. Crew scheduling problems arise from multiple transport sectors (e.g., freight and passenger air transport, bus and rail transit, truck and rail freight transport). Regardless of the transport sector, the common features for crew scheduling and rostering are (i) both temporal and spatial dimensions are involved (i.e., specifying the starting time and location and the finishing time and location for each task) and (ii) the tasks to be performed by crew are pre-specified in a timetable. A task may be a flight leg in airlines, a trip between two or more consecutive segments in a train journey, or a trip between two or more consecutive stops in a bus line (Ernst et al. 2004). Crew scheduling and rostering may be treated as a sub-problem in a service network design problem (e.g., bus network design) or jointly with vehicle routing problem.

Most of the literature in this area focused on the airline sector. Crew costs represent the largest single cost factor for the airlines only second to fuel costs. Readers can be referred to survey papers such as Arabeyre et al. (1969), Barnhart et al. (2003), and Gopalakrishnan and Johnson (2005). The most popular approach to airline crew scheduling and rostering is the decomposition technique. The overall problem is laid out into two stages: (i) crew pairing and (ii) crew rostering. Crew pairing is a process of generating a number of feasible pairings/duties from the given timetable, and selecting the more appropriate one. Crew rostering is to sequence the selected pairings into rosters that will be assigned to individual crew. Recently, more effort has been committed to develop integrated models (e.g., Weide et al. 2010).

In the bus transit sector, driver schedules and rosters are constructed from given bus timetables. Different from airlines, the time scale is much smaller in which tasks are often called duties that can be performed by a crew without long rests. Wren and Rousseau (1995) presented an overview of bus driver scheduling problem and the solution methods. Multi-objective bus driver scheduling problem was addressed in Lourenco et al. (2001). There have also been some attempts to integrate crew scheduling and vehicle scheduling in a single model (e.g., Freling et al. 2003). Applications of crew scheduling and rostering in the railway sector is relatively new (Ernst et al. 2001).

It should be noted that most crew scheduling research focuses on a particular application rather than the general case. This is mainly because each application has its own characteristics and its own research challenges that are imposed by various hard and soft constraints. The safety regulations and labor negotiations vary sector by sector and country by country.

4.8 Port/Terminal Management

In most transport networks, intermediate nodes are indispensable parts. Intermediate nodes may represent depots, warehouses, distribution centers, airports, dry ports, and seaports. In particular, the seaport plays a vital interface role to connect seaborne transport and inland transport. This section provides a brief discussion on operations management issues at maritime container ports and terminals.

Two players are directly associated and responsible for port operations: the port authority and the terminal operator. The port authority normally focuses on the administration and management of the port infrastructures and the coordination and control of the activities of the different operators present in the port (Verhoeven 2010). The port authority outsources the cargo-handling activities to terminal operators who are responsible to provide handling equipment and other resources to handle ships and cargoes. There have been a large number of studies on container port/terminal productivity, which can be referred to the survey papers, Steenken et al. (2004); Stahlbock and Voss (2008); Bierwirth and Meisel (2010); Kim and Lee (2015).

From the planning-level perspective, container port/terminal management is often classified into strategic planning decisions and operational planning decisions. Strategic decisions include facility layout, berthing capacity, equipment selection, multimodal interfaces, IT-systems, and control systems. Operational decisions include berth allocation, crane assignment, stowage planning on vessel, storage and stacking in yard, equipment routing, and scheduling (Stahlbock and Voss 2008; Bierwirth and Meisel 2010).

From the container logistics perspective, maritime container terminals perform three types of functions (sub-systems): quayside operations, which focus on managing the interface with vessels including berth allocation, container loading to/unloading from vessels; yardside operations, which focus on managing container internal transport and storage within the port area; and landside operations, which focus on managing the interface with external trucks and trains for container receipt and delivery.

Port authority and terminal operators seek to provide efficient operations in all three sub-systems in order to attract ocean carriers and gain competitive advantages. The main objective of the port operations is to achieve maximum velocity of vessel turnaround, container movements, and make the best utilization of the key resources. This may be achieved by effectively controlling and integrating the three sub-systems of port operations and turning them into an efficient operating entity. In this regard, a number of studies have been conducted to integrate multiple logistics operations at container terminals, e.g., the simultaneous optimization of berth allocation and quay crane scheduling (Meisel and Bierwirth 2013; Vacca et al. 2013); joint optimization of berth allocation and yard management (Hendriks et al. 2013; Zhen et al. 2011); and integrated vehicle dispatching and storage yard management (Wu et al. 2013).

4.9 Emission Management

Transport is the second largest greenhouse gas (GHG)-emitting sector after energy (Buhaug et al. 2009). More specifically, road, international shipping, international aviation, domestic shipping and fishing, and rail transport contribute 21.3%, 2.7%, 1.9%, 0.6%, and 0.5% of global CO_2 emissions, respectively (Buhaug et al. 2009). Noting that GHGs significantly contribute to global warming and climate change and pose a danger to human health and welfare, much attention has been attracted to reduce emissions from the transport sector recently. For example, the European Union (EU) has policies in place to reduce emissions from a range of transport modes such as including aviation in the EU Emissions Trading System, and CO_2 emissions targets for cars and vans.

Shipping was the only transport mode for which GHG emissions were not regulated. Only recently, the MEPC adopted the Energy Efficiency Design Index (EEDI) for new ships (Psaraftis and Kontovas 2013). However, there are still no compulsory regulations for the existing ships and the targeted levels of emissions from shipping. Nevertheless, the International Maritime Organization has been promoting operational measures such as ship speed reduction, enhanced weather routing, optimization of logistics chains, adjustments for arrival times, better fleet planning, and quicker loading and discharging in order to reduce emissions from ships (Buhaug et al. 2009).

A large number of studies have investigated the impact of ship speed reduction on fuel consumption, operational cost, and CO_2 emissions (e.g., Notteboom and Vernimmen 2009; Cariou 2011; Ronen 2011). Psaraftis and Kontovas (2013) and Wang et al. (2013) reviewed the models involving ship speed as a key decision variable to minimize the fuel consumption (equivalently minimizing CO_2 emissions) or to minimize the total operational cost. Christiansen et al. (2013) highlighted that more studies have been devoted to sailing speeds and environmental impact of ships in the new millennium. Mansouri et al. (2015) provided a review to examine the potential of multi-objective optimization as a decision support tool to achieve the trade-off between environmental objectives and economic objectives in maritime transport. These review papers commonly pointed out that minimization of the environmental impact is becoming more important in maritime transport, which might be achieved through optimizing ship sailing speed at operational level and/or at tactical level in relation with other decisions.

A few studies considered the CO_2 emission problem together with ship routing and scheduling. For example, Song and Xu (2012) analyzed the CO_2 emissions from two alternative Asia–Europe services interfacing with the UK and identified which is preferable in different scenarios. Kontovas (2014) emphasized the need to incorporate the environmental dimension into the ship routing and scheduling problem and presented several conceptual approaches. Song et al. (2015) considered a joint tactical planning problem for the number of ships, the planned maximum sailing speed, and the liner service schedule in order to simultaneously optimize the expected cost, the service reliability, and the shipping emission under uncertain port times.

There are also several studies that incorporate emission performance into port/terminal management. Golias et al. (2010) attempted to maximize berth productivity and emissions production simultaneously. Du et al. (2011) jointly optimized berth allocation and vessel sailing speeds considering the vessel emissions at sea and in mooring periods. Hu et al. (2014) presented a nonlinear multi-objective mixed-integer programming model for the berth and quay-crane allocation problem treating vessel's arrival time as an additional decision variable. They showed that the model could improve vessels' fuel consumption and emissions, and utilization of berths and quay cranes without sacrificing service quality.

The above discussion mainly focused on the maritime transport sector. It should be noted that there are parallel bodies of research in other transport sectors with emission considerations. For example, green vehicle routing problem represents the research stream of vehicle routing with emission considerations. For the road transport sector, interested readers can refer to the recent survey papers, Lin et al. (2014) and Demir et al. (2014).

5 Implications for Managers

The previous section demonstrates that Production and Operations Management (POM) has been widely applied in various transport sectors. The models can generally offer managerial insights or decision support tools. The former provides managers knowledge to better understand the transport systems such as how KPIs may change with respect to system parameters or control parameters; whereas the latter assists managers to make business decisions, e.g., strategic and tactical decisions based on what-if scenario analysis, operational decisions based on real-time information.

There have been many successful applications of POM models/tools in transport industries (e.g., VRP, airline). However, some transport areas/sectors are lacking or lagging behind. For example, shipping lines rarely use planning tools to manage fleet sizing, ship redeployment, schedule design, empty container repositioning, and disruption management. The implication is that managers need to commit more effort and take the initiative. For example, managers could collaborate with researchers more closely so that the discrepancies between models and real transport systems can be minimized. Moreover, many companies are reluctant to provide data to researchers and are reluctant to change the legacy systems. There is a lot to be done from a manager's aspect.

6 Directions for Future Research

There are many research opportunities that remain or are emerging to be investigated. We preset two categories of future research opportunities: general POM modelling opportunities, and emerging ICT-driven opportunities.

6.1 General POM Modelling Opportunities

6.1.1 Objective Functions and Constraints

Existing literature often focused on a single objective in a specific aspect. More studies are required to simultaneously optimize multiple objectives. Taking the emissions as an example, there are various ways to embed emissions considerations into POM models. First, the objective function can include a component that represents the total emissions, which essentially internalizes the external cost of emissions. Second, by treating different types of KPIs as multi-objective optimization problems, we can seek Pareto optimal frontiers. Third, some KPIs could be converted into constraints by limiting the amount of emissions at each transport leg.

Soft performance indicators such as social responsibility and ethical performance (e.g., code of ethics, conforming to regulations) have gradually become important to business managers. It would be interesting to model such soft performance indicators and incorporate them into objective functions or constraints.

6.1.2 Decision Integration

The decisions in a transport system are essentially inter-dependent from a system perspective. Traditionally, the strategic, tactical, and operational decisions are tackled separately. It would be desirable to integrate some of these decisions into a single model, or a coupled model. Although a great effort has been committed in this direction, more research is required. It is worth noting that many sub-problems have already been NP-hard individually (e.g., network design, fleet deployment, and vehicle routing). Therefore, integrated models tend to be more challenging from the computational complexity perspective. Nevertheless, with the development of computational power, the problems that were unaffordable to solve in the past may become tractable.

6.1.3 Stochastic and Dynamic Operations

Uncertainty and dynamic operations are two intrinsic characteristics of transport systems. However, the strategic and tactical problems such as service network design, fleet sizing, and deployment often assume deterministic and stable situations; e.g., Pantuso et al. (2014) stated that very few papers explicitly treat uncertainty in the field of maritime fleet size and mix problems.

6.1.4 Solution Techniques and Heuristic Rules

The majority of realistic mathematical models for transport systems are in the form of integer programming or mixed integer programming due to the choice decisions (either of nodes, links, or paths), which leads to NP-hard. In the literature, linear functions and continuous variables were often used as an approximation of the nonlinear and discrete variables or a simplification of system behavior. One research direction is to evaluate the quality of the solutions obtained based on such approximation or simplification. Another direction is seeking to solve to optimality and/or find tighter bounds to the optimal solutions.

Metaheuristics have been widely applied to solve transport and logistics optimization problems. Apart from well-developed metaheuristics such as Genetic Algorithms, Simulated Annealing, Scatter Search, Tabu Search, and many new metaheuristics have emerged recently that are inspired by natural systems, e.g., Ant Colony Optimization, Particle Swarm Optimization, Bee Colony Optimization, Bacterial Foraging Optimization, Artificial Immune Systems, and Biogeography-based Optimization (Boussaid et al. 2013). There are research opportunities to apply these recently proposed metaheuristics in combination/comparison with classic ones.

Industry practice based heuristic rules are worth extracting and investigating. Such rules may be not optimal, but are intuitive and often yield reasonably good results. Empirical research is needed to gather data and extract rules. Using the practical rules as a reference base, with the help of machine learning techniques, it is possible to generate new rules that are more effective but still easy to implement. In addition, more knowledge about transport system behavior, e.g., customers' preference and industry's common practices, can be useful to formulate the problem more effectively.

6.2 Emerging ICT-Driven Opportunities

Emerging information technologies are important forces to create new research opportunities. We pointed out a few examples below.

Automation is a global trend that will have a huge impact on transport and terminal operations. Autonomous vehicles and robotics may transform the future of roads, personal transport, freight transport, and logistics. For example, container terminals are starting to implement automated equipment such as automated stacking cranes, automated rail mounted gantry cranes, and unmanned vehicle control systems.

"Internet of Things" and "Industrial Internet" have emerged in recent years. The underlying concept is to enable vehicles, travelers, equipment, facilities, and infrastructure to communicate with each other through various data streams by employing wired or wireless technologies (including smart devices). These may lead to two research directions. First, connected vehicles and travelers will be able to share data with all sorts of equipment and make better decisions on a real-time basis. Second, travelers may increasingly be able to procure mobility as a service, rather than purchase vehicles or make other long-term commitments to particular modes of travel, which will change the transport behaviors. The above research directions echo the concept of synchromodality in SteadieSeifi et al. (2014).

Big data and data mining can facilitate the management of transport and logistics. Transport industry and social media can generate huge amount of data. With the development of big data, data mining, and machine learning techniques, non-obvious travel patterns could be discovered, e.g., predicting unsafe transport operators, predicting traffic congestions and crashes, revealing traveler behaviors, and estimating real-time travel demands.

References and Bibliography

Agarwal, R. and O. Ergun (2008) "Ship scheduling and network design for cargo routing in liner shipping," *Transportation Science*, **42**: 175–196.

Arabeyre, J., J. Fearnley, F. Steiger and W. Teather (1969) "The airline crew scheduling problem: A survey," *Transportation Science*, **3**: 140–163.

Barnhart, C., P. Belobaba, and A.R. Odoni (2003) "Applications of operations research in the air transport industry," *Transportation Science*, **37**: 368–391.

Beaujon, G.J. and M.A. Turnquist (1991) "A model for fleet sizing and vehicle allocation," *Transportation Science*, **25**: 19–45.

Bell, W., L.M. Dalberto, M.L. Fisher, A.J. Greenfield, R. Jaikumar, P. Kedia, R.G. Macj and P.J. Prutzman (1983) "Improving the distribution of industrial gases with an on-line computerized routing and scheduling optimizer," *Interfaces*, **13**: 4–23.

Bendall, H.B. and A.F. Stent (2005) "Ship investment under uncertainty: Valuing a real option on the maximum of several strategies," *Maritime Economics & Logistics*, **7**: 19–35.

Bierwirth, C. and F. Meisel (2010) "A survey of berth allocation and quay crane scheduling problems in container terminals," *European Journal of Operational Research*, **202**: 615–627.

Boussaid, I., J. Lepagnot and P. Siarry (2013) "A survey on optimization metaheuristics," *Information Sciences*, **237**: 82–117.

Braekers, K., G.K. Janssens and A. Caris (2011) "Challenges in managing empty container movements at multiple planning levels," *Transport Reviews*, **31**: 681–708.

Brouer, B.D., J.F. Alvarez, C.E.M. Plum, D. Pisinger and M.M. Sigurd (2014) "A base integer programming model and benchmark suite for liner-shipping network design," *Transportation Science*, **48**: 281–312.

Brouer, B.D., J. Dirksen, D. Pisinger, C.E.M. Plum and B. Vaaben (2013) "The vessel schedule recovery problem (VSRP)—A MIP model for handling disruptions in liner shipping," *European Journal of Operational Research*, **224**: 362–374.

Brouer, B.D., D. Pisinger and S. Spoorendonk (2011) "Liner shipping cargo allocation with repositioning of empty containers," *INFOR*, **49**: 109–124.

Buhaug, Ø., J.J. Corbett, Ø. Endresen, V. Eyring, J. Faber, S. Hanayama, D.S. Lee, D. Lee, H. Lindstad, A. Mjelde, C. Pålsson, W. Wanquing, J.J. Winebrake and K. Yoshida (2009) *Second IMO Greenhouse Gas Study 2009*, International Maritime Organization, London.

Cariou, P. (2011) "Is slow steaming a sustainable means of reducing CO_2 emissions from container shipping?" *Transportation Research Part D*, **16**: 260–264.

Ceder, A. and N.H.M. Wilson (1986) "Bus network design," *Transportation Research Part B*, **20**: 331–344.

Cheung, R.K. and W.B. Powell (1996) "An algorithm for multistage dynamic networks with random arc capacities, with an application to dynamic fleet management," *Operations Research*, **44**: 951–963.

Christiansen, M., K. Fagerholt and D. Ronen (2004) "Ship routing and scheduling: Status and perspectives," *Transportation Science*, **38**: 1–18.

Christiansen, M., K. Fagerholt, B. Nygreen and D. Ronen (2013) "Ship routing and scheduling in the new millennium," *European Journal of Operational Research*, **228**: 467–483.

Christiansen, M., K. Fagerholt, D. Ronen and B. Nygreen (2007) "Maritime transportation." In: Barnhart, C. and G. Laporte (Eds.), *Handbook in Operations Research and Management Science*. Elsevier, pp. 189–284.

Clausen, J., A. Larsen, L. Larsen and N.J. Rezanova (2010) "Disruption management in the airline industry—concepts, models and methods," *Computers & Operations Research*, **37**: 809–821.

Coelho, L.C., J.F. Cordeau and G. Laporte (2014) "Thirty years of inventory routing," *Transportation Science*, **48**: 1–19.

Crainic, T.G. (2000) "Service network design in freight transportation," *European Journal of Operational Research*, **122**: 272–288.

Crainic, T.G. and G. Laporte (1997) "Planning models for freight transportation," *European Journal of Operational Research*, **97**: 409–438.

Crainic, T.G., M. Gendreau, and P. Dejax (1993) "Dynamic and stochastic models for the allocation of empty containers," *Operations Research*, **41**: 102–126.

Dang, Q.V., I.E., Nielsen and W.Y. Yun (2013) "Replenishment policies for empty containers in an inland multi-depot system," *Maritime Economics and Logistics*, **15**: 120–149.

Dantzig, G.B. and D.R. Fulkerson (1954) "Minimizing the number of tankers to meet a fixed schedule," *Naval Research Logistics Quarterly*, **1**: 217–222.

Dantzig, G.B. and J.H. Ramser (1959) "The truck dispatching problem," *Management Science*, **6**(1): 81–91.

Dejax, P. and T.G. Crainic (1987) "A review of empty flows and fleet management models in freight transportation," *Transportation Science*, **21**: 227–247.

Demir, E., T. Bektas and G. Laporte (2014) "A review of recent research on green road freight transportation," *European Journal of Operational Research*, **237**: 775–793.

Dong, J.X. and D.P. Song (2009) "Container fleet sizing and empty repositioning in liner shipping systems," *Transportation Research Part E*, **45**: 860–877.

Dong, J.X., C.Y. Lee and D.P. Song (2015) "Joint service capacity planning and dynamic container routing in shipping network with uncertain demands," *Transportation Research Part B*, **78**: 404–421.

Du, Y., Q. Chen, X. Quan, L. Long and R.Y.K. Fung (2011) "Berth allocation considering fuel consumption and vessel emissions," *Transportation Research Part E*, **47**: 1021–1037.

ERA (2014) "Railway safety performance in the European Union," European Railway Agency, France.

Ernst, A.T., H. Jiang, M. Krishnamoorthy, H. Nott and D. Sier (2001) "An integrated optimization model for train crew management," *Annals of Operations Research*, **108**: 211–224.

Ernst, A.T., H. Jiang, M. Krishnamoorthy and D. Sier (2004) "Staff scheduling and rostering: A review of applications, methods and models," *European Journal of Operational Research*, **153**: 3–27.

Farahani, R.Z., E. Miandoabchi, W.Y. Szeto and H. Rashidi (2013) "A review of urban transportation network design problems," *European Journal of Operational Research*, **229**: 281–302.

Freling, R., D. Huisman and A. Wagelmans (2003) "Models and algorithms for integration of vehicle and crew scheduling," *Journal of Scheduling*, **6**(1): 63–85.

Gelareh, S. and Q. Meng (2010) "A novel modeling approach for the fleet deployment problem within a short-term planning horizon," *Transportation Research Part E*, **46**: 76–89.

Golias, M.M., M. Boile, S. Theofanis and C. Efstathiou (2010) "The berth scheduling problem: Maximizing berth productivity and minimizing fuel consumption and emissions production," *Transportation Research Record*, **2166**: 20–27.

Gopalakrishnan, B. and E.L. Johnson (2005) "Airline crew scheduling: State-of-the-art," *Annals of Operations Research*, **140**: 305–337.

Guihaire, V. and J.K. Hao (2008) "Transit network design and scheduling: A global review," *Transportation Research Part A*, **42**: 1251–1273.

Hendriks, M. P.M., E. Lefeber and J.T. Udding (2013) "Simultaneous berth allocation and yard planning at tactical level," *OR Spectrum*, **35**: 441–456.

Hoff, A., H. Andersson, M. Christiansen, G. Hasle and A. Løkketangen (2010) "Industrial aspects and literature survey: Fleet composition and routing," *Computers & Operations Research*, **37**: 2041–2061.

Hu, Q.M., Z.H. Hu and Y. Du (2014) "Berth and quay-crane allocation problem considering fuel consumption and emissions from vessels," *Computers & Industrial Engineering*, **70**: 1–10.

Kim, D. and C. Barnhart (1999) "Transportation service network design: Models and algorithms." In: Wilson, N.H.M. (ed.) *Computer-aided transit scheduling*. Springer, Berlin, pp. 259–283.

Kim, K.H. and H. Lee (2015) "Container terminal operation: Current trends and future challenges," In Lee, C.Y. and Q. Meng (ed.), *Handbook of Ocean Container Transport Logistics—Making Global Supply Chain Effective*. Springer, New York, pp. 43–74.

Kohl, N., A. Larsen, J. Larsen, A. Ross and S. Tiourine (2007) "Airline disruption management—perspectives, experiences and outlook," *Journal of Air Transport Management*, **13**: 149–162.

Kontovas, C.A. (2014) "The green ship routing and scheduling problem (GSRSP): A conceptual approach," *Transportation Research Part D*, **31**: 61–69.

Lahyani, R., M. Khemakhem and F. Semet (2015) "Rich vehicle routing problems: From a taxonomy to a definition," *European Journal of Operational Research*, **241**: 1–14.

Lai, K.H., E.W.T. Ngai and T.C.E. Cheng (2002) "Measures for evaluating supply chain performance in transport logistics," *Transport Research Part E*, **38**: 439–456.

Laporte, G. (1992) "The vehicle routing problem: An overview of exact and approximate algorithms," *European Journal of Operational Research*, **59**: 345–358.

Lederer, P.J. and R.S. Nambimadom (1998) "Airline network design," *Operations Research*, **46**: 785–804.

Lenstra, J.K. and A.H.G.R. Kan (1981) "Complexity of vehicle routing and scheduling problems," *Networks*, **11**: 221–227.

Li, C., X. Qi and C.Y. Lee (2015) "Disruption recovery for a vessel in liner shipping," *Transportation Science*, **49**: 900–921.

Li, C., X. Qi and D.P. Song (2016) "Real-time schedule recovery in liner shipping service with regular uncertainties and disruption events," *Transportation Research Part B*, **93**: 762–788.

Lin, C., K.L. Choy, G.T.S. Ho, S.H. Chung and H.Y. Lam (2014) "Survey of green vehicle routing problem: Past and future trends," *Expert Systems with Applications*, **41**: 1118–1138.

Long, Y., L.H. Lee and E.P. Chew (2012) "The sample average approximation method for empty container repositioning with uncertainties," *European Journal of Operational Research*, **222**: 65–75.

Lourenco, H.R., J.P. Paixao and R. Portugal (2001) "Multiobjective metaheuristics for the bus driver scheduling problem," *Transportation Science*, **35**: 331–343.

Mandryk, W. (2009) "Measuring global seaborne trade," *International Maritime Statistics Forum*, New Orleans, 4–6 May 2009.

Mansouri, S.A., H. Lee and O. Aluko (2015) "Multi-objective decision support to enhance environmental sustainability in maritime shipping: A review and future directions," *Transportation Research Part E*, **78**: 3–18.

McKinnon A.C. (2007) "CO_2 emission from freight transport in the UK," Commission for Integrated Transport, London.

Meisel, F. and C. Bierwirth (2013) "A framework for integrated berth allocation and crane operations planning in seaport container terminals," *Transportation Science*, **47**: 131–147.

Meng, Q. and T. Wang (2010) "A chance constrained programming model for short-term liner ship fleet planning problems," *Maritime Policy and Management*, **37**: 329–346.

Meng, Q. and S. Wang (2011) "Optimal operating strategy for a long-haul liner service route," *European Journal of Operational Research*, **215**: 105–114.

Meng, Q., S. Wang, H. Andersson and K. Thun (2014) "Containership routing and scheduling in liner shipping: Overview and future research directions," *Transportation Science*, **48**: 265–280.

Meng, Q., T. Wang and S. Wang (2012) "Short-term liner ship fleet planning with container transshipment and uncertain container shipment demand," *European Journal of Operational Research*, **223**: 96–105.

Moin, N.H. and S. Salhi (2007) "Inventory routing problems: A logistical overview," *Journal of the Operational Research Society*, **58**: 1185–1194.

Mourao, M.C., M.V. Pato and A.C. Paixao (2001) "Ship assignment with hub and spoke constraints," *Maritime Policy and Management*, **29**: 135–150.

Nicholson, T.A.J. and R.D. Pullen (1971) "Dynamic programming applied to ship fleet management," *Operational Research Quarterly (1970–1977)*, **22**: 211–220.

Notteboom, T.E. and B. Vernimmen (2009) "The effect of high fuel costs on liner service configuration in container shipping," *Journal of Transport Geography*, **17**: 325–337.

Ortuzar, J. de D. and L.G. Willumsen (2011) *Modelling Transport*. (4th ed.), New York, John Wiley.

Pantuso, G., K. Fagerholt and L.M. Hvattum (2014) "A survey on maritime fleet size and mix problems," *European Journal of Operational Research*, **235**: 341–349.

Perakis, A. and D. Jaramillo (1991) "Fleet deployment optimization for liner shipping part 1. Background, problem formulations and solution approaches," *Maritime Policy and Management*, **18**: 183–200.

Powell, W.B. and T.A. Carvalho (1998) "Dynamic control of logistics queueing networks for large-scale fleet management," *Transportation Science*, **32**: 90–109.

Psaraftis, H.N. and C.A. Kontovas (2013) "Speed models for energy-efficient maritime transportation: A taxonomy and survey," *Transportation Research Part C*, **26**: 331–351.

Qi, X.T. and D.P. Song (2012) "Minimizing fuel emissions by optimizing vessel schedules in liner shipping with uncertain port times," *Transportation Research Part E*, **48**: 863–880.

Ritzinger, U., J. Puchinger and R.F. Hartl (2016) "A survey on dynamic and stochastic vehicle routing problems," *International Journal of Production Research*, **54**: 215–231.

Rodrigue, J.P., C. Comtois and B. Slack (2013) *The Geography of Transport Systems* (3rd ed.), New York, Routledge.

Ronen, D. (1993) "Ship scheduling: The last decade," *European Journal of Operational Research*, **71**: 325–333.

Ronen, D. (2011) "The effect of oil price on containership speed and fleet size," *Journal of Operational Research Society*, **62**: 211–216.

Song, D.P. (2005) "Optimal threshold control of empty vehicle redistribution in two depot service systems," *IEEE Trans. on Automatic Control*, **50**: 87–90.

Song, D.P. and J.X. Dong (2012) "Cargo routing and empty container repositioning in multiple shipping service routes," *Transportation Research Part B*, **46**: 1556–1575.

Song, D.P. and J.X. Dong (2013) "Long-haul liner service route design with ship deployment and empty container repositioning," *Transportation Research Part B*, **55**: 188–211.

Song, D.P. and J.X. Dong (2015) "Empty container repositioning," in *Handbook of Ocean Container Transport Logistics*, Lee, C.Y. and Q. Meng (eds.), Springer, New York. pp. 163–208.

Song, D.P. and C.F. Earl (2008) "Optimal empty vehicle repositioning and fleet-sizing for two-depot services systems," *European Journal of Operational Research*, **185**: 760–777.

Song, D.P. and J.J. Xu (2012) "CO_2 emission comparison between direct and feeder liner services: A case study of Asia-Europe services interfacing with the UK," *International Journal of Sustainable Transportation*, **6**: 214–237.

Song, D.P., D. Li and P. Drake (2015) "Multi-objective optimization for planning liner shipping service with uncertain port times," *Transportation Research Part E*, **84**, 1–11.

Song, D.P., J. Zhang, J. Carter, T. Field, M. Marshall, J. Polak, K. Schumacher, P. Sinha-Ray and J. Woods (2005) "On cost-efficiency of the global container shipping network," *Maritime Policy and Management*, **32**: 15–30.

Stahlbock, R. and S. Voss (2008) "Operation research at container terminals—a literature update," *OR Spectrum*, **30**: 1–52.

SteadieSeifi, M., N. Dellaert, W. Nuijten, T.V. Woensel and R. Raoufi (2014) "Multimodal freight transportation planning: A literature review," *European Journal of Operational Research*, **233**: 1–15.

Steenken, D., S. Voss and R. Stahlbock (2004) "Container terminal operations and operations research—a classification and literature review," *OR Spectrum*, **26**: 3–49.

Tierney, K., B. Skelsdottir, R.M. Jensen and D. Pisinger (2015) "Solving the liner shipping fleet repositioning problem with cargo flows," *Transportation Science*, **49**: 652–674.

Tran, K.N. and H.D. Haasis (2015) "Literature survey of network optimization in container liner shipping," *Flexible Service Manufacturing Journal*, **27**: 139–179.

Vacca, I., M. Bierlaire and M. Salani (2013) "An exact algorithm for the integrated planning of berth allocation and quay crane assignment," *Transportation Science*, **47**: 148–161.

Verhoeven, P. (2010) "A review of port authority functions: Towards a renaissance," *Maritime Policy and Management*, **37**: 247–270.

Wang, S. and Q. Meng (2012a) "Robust schedule design for liner shipping services," *Transportation Research Part E*, **48**: 1093–1106.

Wang, S. and Q. Meng (2012b) "Liner ship route schedule design with sea contingency time and port time uncertainty," *Transportation Research Part B*, **46**: 615–633.

Wang, S. and Q. Meng (2012c) "Sailing speed optimization for container ships in a liner shipping network," *Transportation Research Part E*, **48**: 701–714.

Wang, S. and Q. Meng (2012d) "Liner ship fleet deployment with container transshipment operations," *Transportation Research Part E*, **48**: 470–484.

Wang, S., Q. Meng and Z. Liu (2013) "Bunker consumption optimization methods in shipping: A critical review and extensions," *Transportation Research Part E*, **53**: 49–62.

Weide, O., D. Ryan and M. Ehrgott (2010) "An iterative approach to robust and integrated aircraft routing and crew scheduling," *Computers & Operations Research*, **37**: 833–844.

Wieberneit, N. (2008) "Service network design for freight transportation: A review," *OR Spectrum*, **30**: 77–112.

Woxenius, J. (2007) "Generic framework for transport network designs: Applications and treatment in intermodal freight transport literature," *Transport Reviews*, **27**: 733–749.

Wren, A. and J.M. Rousseau (1995) "Bus driver scheduling—an overview." In: Daduna, J.R., I. Branco and J.M.P. Paixao (Eds.), *Computer-Aided Transit Scheduling*. Springer, Berlin, Germany, pp. 173–187.

Wu, J., J. Lou, D. Zhang and M. Dong (2013) "An integrated programming model for storage management and vehicle scheduling at container terminals," *Research in Transportation Economics*, **42**: 13–27.

Yu, G. and X. Qi (2004) *Disruption management: Framework, Models and Applications*, Singapore: World Scientific Publisher.

Zhen, L., E.P. Chew and L.H. Lee (2011) "An integrated model for berth template and yard template planning in transshipment hubs," *Transportation Science*, **45**: 483–504.

31
POM AND RETAILING

Vishal Gaur

1 Introduction

The retailing sector is an important part of the economy of both developed and developing countries. In the U.S. economy, retail businesses (excluding motor vehicles and spare parts) represented $3.6 trillion in sales in 2014, contributed 5.8% to GDP, carried $366 billion in inventory, and provided direct employment to 15.6 million workers. E-commerce sales have been steadily growing faster than sales in brick-and-mortar stores. They have increased as a fraction of total retail sales from less than 0.2% in 1998 to 6.44% in 2014. The U.S. Bureau of Labor Statistics predicts that employment in retail is projected to grow at 7% per year between 2012–2022. The inventory productivity of retailers has improved over time; aggregate inventory turnover increased from 5.15 in 1994 to 6.87 in 2014. (We compile these statistics using data from Bureau of Economic Analysis (2016), Bureau of Labor Statistics (2016), and U.S. Census Bureau (2016).)

Retailing is a dynamic sector, affected by many different types of factors, such as the growth of online and mobile retailing, supply chain innovations such as Radio Frequency Identification (RFID) technology, regulatory changes in global trade such as the Multi Fibre Arrangement, developments in the digital technology industry, as well as concerns around worker safety, product contamination, quality enforcement, and fair trade. Retailing is conducted through a wide range of platforms used in different countries. These include *kirana* stores and kiosks in India and nanostores in Central and South America (which are millions of very small, family-owned and-operated stores); marketplaces such as Etsy (www.etsy.com) and Amazon marketplace; rental models (www.renttherunway.com/); pop-up stores (www.shopify.com/guides/ultimate-guide-to-pop-up-shops); and virtual stores (www.wpp.com/wpp/press/2012/oct/19/ecommerce-grocer-yihaodian-opens-stores-overnight/; see also Chapter 34 in this book).

The discipline of POM has contributed to the development of many aspects of retailing, such as inventory management, supply chain coordination, warehousing and logistics, revenue management, store operations, and customer service. Current research is seeking to address challenges such as omnichannel integration, sustainability, workforce management, and many problems at the interfaces of operations with finance and marketing. In this chapter, we first describe the past history of research and development in retailing, then characterize the state of retailing research and practice today, and finally make projections for future research and practice. Since retailing is a vast industry, it intersects with many topics in operations management, including supply chain management, services operations, operations-marketing interface, revenue management, and operations-finance interface. Our goal in this chapter is not to be comprehensive but to highlight those areas of research that have influenced the retailing industry (e.g., vendor-managed inventory) or are unique to retailing (e.g., assortment planning, shelf-space allocation, store execution). We also refer the reader to related contents in Chapter 6 on inventory management, Chapter 20 on POM and Marketing, and Chapter 34 on best practices in e-commerce supply chain management in this book.

2 A Historical Perspective of Research in Retail Operations

We classify the existing research in retail operations into inventory management, retail supply chains, customer service, pricing and clearance markdowns, shelf space management, assortment planning, and financial performance of retailing firms.

2.1 Inventory Management

Inventory management in retailing faces many challenges. One of these challenges is a proliferation in the amount of variety that retailers provide to customers. Variety makes it harder to forecast demand, plan inventory, manage shelf space and distribution centers, and manage relationships with suppliers. It also creates diseconomies of scale and scope, which increase cost and decrease profitability. Along with an increase in variety, retailers face a high incidence of stockouts and their attendant costs as shown by Corsten and Gruen (2003). These challenges have fueled research and the retailing industry has benefited from the vast advancements in inventory theory. In this section, we describe recent research on inventory management done in the context of retailing firms. The reader is referred to excellent books by Porteus (2002) and Zipkin (2000) for an in-depth treatment of inventory theory.

Inventory data in retailing at the store-SKU level is often inaccurate. Even when data is accurate, inventory gets misplaced in stores with surprising frequency. These two important problems, discovered by Raman et al. (2001), have wide-ranging implications for the usefulness of point-of-sale (POS) and inventory data for demand forecasting and inventory planning. They impose a high cost on the financial performance of retailers. They also highlight the importance of store execution and workforce management. Significantly, these problems are common across large and technologically advanced retailers. DeHoratius and Raman (2008) studied the drivers of discrepancies between system data and physical counts in stores in a retail chain and showed that inventory data inaccuracy occurs due to many factors including replenishment and sales processes in stores and distribution centers, store design, and variety. Researchers have designed new replenishment algorithms that address inaccuracy in inventory data (Kök and Shang 2007; DeHoratius et al. 2008). The management of inventory in retail stores is also exemplified by a case study on Wawa, a convenience store chain, by Krishnan and Fisher (2005). The case study shows that retail store inventory management is a complex task requiring process design, training, incentive alignment, and process discipline.

RFID technology holds the promise of reducing inventory data inaccuracy and misplaced SKUs. It can streamline processes in supply chains, improve labor productivity, bring about supply chain transparency, and improve in-store product availability. Research articles that have explored the value of RFID include Camdereli and Swaminathan (2010), Dutta et al. (2007), Gaukler et al. (2007), Hardgrave et al. (2013), and Lee and Ozer (2007). These papers have studied the value that RFID holds for retailers and manufacturers as well as mechanisms for sharing the costs of RFID. Gupta et al. (2009) conduct an extensive review of research on RFID and present directions for future research. They classify RFID research into two categories: research on the business value of RFID and that on the adoption and implementation of RFID. Large retail chains have experimented with the application of RFID in their supply chains. Ton et al. (2005) present a case study describing a pilot project at Metro Group, a large supermarket chain based in Germany, to implement pallet-level and case-level RFID with a subset of suppliers in some of its distribution centers.

Another topic that has received attention in the literature is store-level inventory management. Several researchers have studied decision models for the management of perishable inventory in retail stores (for example, Ketzenberg and Ferguson 2008; Ketzenberg et al. 2015; and Li et al. 2012). Akkas et al. (2016) measure the occurrence of product expiration in stores and identify its causes related to store execution, supply chain aging, and product characteristics such as case pack size and shelf life. Inventory management in vending machines has been studied by Ketzenberg et al. (2013). Van Donselaar et al. (2010) study the ordering behavior of retail store managers and discover that store managers deviate systematically from an automated replenishment system implemented in the store chain. Using inventory shipment and sales transaction data for several stores in a supermarket chain, they find that store managers prefer to change order quantities in the system to order slow-moving and large case pack items on the lean days of the week, which yields better use of labor time on lean days for replenishing shelves, so that attention can be focused on customer service on peak days. Their findings suggest gaps in the design of automated inventory replenishment systems.

Many researchers have focused attention on the inventory management of short lifecycle, seasonal, and fashion products. The length of selling season of such products typically ranges from a few weeks to less than six months. Thus, there is limited opportunity for inventory replenishment. Moreover, since the products are new, there is no historical demand information available to apply time series forecasting methods. The research on improving the profitability of such products has focused on developing new demand forecasting tools and quick response capability so that a retailer can create more accurate forecasts, update their forecasts as information is revealed, and replenish merchandise in the middle of a selling season. Murray and Silver (1966) and Hausman and Peterson (1972) were some of the early papers to study decision models for this problem, and Abernathy et al. (1999) conduct a field study of quick response capability in the apparel industry. Fisher and Raman (1996) present a multi-product model of capacitated production and inventory management for seasonal products and report results from a pilot project at a skiwear manufacturer. Key ideas in this paper are that early demand is an accurate predictor of demand in the rest of the season and that the standard deviation of forecasts issued by a panel of experts is a good measure of the demand uncertainty of an underlying product. Eppen and Iyer (1997a) present a Bayesian forecasting method that combines historical data and buyer judgment to update the demand forecast for a short lifecycle or fashion product and apply it for inventory management.

Many innovative methods for managing short lifecycle products have been studied in the literature, including backup agreements (Eppen and Iyer 1997b), reactive capacity (Raman and Kim 2002), and risk sharing and contracting with suppliers (Donohue 2000; Barnes-Schuster et al. 2002). Researchers have also conducted applied research on this topic (Fisher and Raman 1996; Caro and Gallien 2010). For example, Caro and Gallien (2010) describe work done in collaboration with the Spanish fast fashion retailer, Zara, focusing on the problem of allocating limited inventory over time from a centralized fulfillment center (or distribution center) to retail stores inventory. The authors conduct a pilot test of their algorithm at Zara. A key feature of their model is to incorporate the effect of broken sizes on demand. The problem of broken sizes occurs when a product is in-stock in some sizes and out-of-stock in others. For instance, a style of shirts may be available in Small and Extra-Large but stocked out in Medium and Large. Retailers prefer to remove such products from display to avoid customer dissatisfaction over not finding their sizes.

Researchers have also looked at methods for modeling and forecasting demand for short lifecycle products. Agrawal and Smith (1998) show that retail demand is represented well by a negative binomial distribution. Haksöz and Seshadri (2004) develop a sequential monotone likelihood ratio property for Bayesian updating of demand distributions that are stochastically increasing in early demand observations. Gaur et al. (2007) show using sales forecast data from equity analysts that the dispersion among experts' forecasts is useful as a metric to calibrate the uncertainty in the underlying sales. Gaur et al. (2013) show that stock market index returns contain information that can be useful for forecasting retail demand because demand for different types of retail firms is correlated with market indices to different degrees. Inventory management in retailing is also connected with supply chain coordination and pricing, which we discuss in subsequent sections.

2.2 Retail Supply Chains

There is a vast amount of literature on supply chain management that has led to improvements in the retailing industry. We briefly discuss this literature from the point of view of its impact on retailing.

The literature on the bullwhip effect identified practices in the industry that lead to poor performance of retailers and their suppliers (Lee et al. 1997). As a result, many programs have been implemented at consumer packaged goods companies and large retailers to improve supply chain coordination through methods such as forecast sharing, collaborating decision making, and vendor managed inventory. Researchers have documented these programs and their impact at Campbell Soup (Cachon and Fisher 1997), Barilla SpA (Hammond 1994), Proctor & Gamble (Sebenius and Knebel 2007), and other firms. Research in POM has also shown that information sharing in supply chains is valuable to both retailers and suppliers. For instance, Cachon and Fisher (2000) showed that sharing demand and inventory information enables a supplier to postpone the decision of allocating inventory across a network of stores, therefore enabling an improvement in the efficiency of inventory allocation. Subsequent research in this area has looked at the feasibility and implications of information sharing in different competitive settings, when a retailer is served by competing manufacturers as well as when a manufacturer supplies to competing retailers.

There are many methods that retailers can use to manage inventory in their supply networks. Researchers have studied pooling of inventory (Eppen 1979), transshipment (Robinson 1990), and fast shipments (Chen et al. 2016). DeHoratius and Raman (2007) examine the effect of store manager incentives with respect to sales performance and inventory shrinkage on the profitability of retail stores. Their study is based on data from a consumer electronics retail chain. Narayanan and Raman (2004) present a framework for aligning incentives in retail supply chains. They characterize the roles of hidden information, hidden actions, and badly designed incentives and then present methods to mitigate these problems. Finally, there is a vast amount of literature on coordination in decentralized supply chains, which has implications for retailing (Cachon 2003; Chen 2003). Researchers have also studied supply chain coordination and competition in the context of introduction of online channels (Cattani et al. 2006).

Although considerable research has been conducted in this area and there have been significant advancements in supply chain practice, supply chain coordination continues to remain a vexing problem for many retailers and their suppliers. This could be caused by the increasing complexity of supply chains, which requires scholars and practitioners to constantly remain one step ahead. Additionally, online retailing is transforming backend supply chains. Manufacturers that sell to Amazon.com experience different seasonality patterns of demand and information lead times than manufacturers that sell through traditional retail relationships. Coordination in the era of Amazon.com remains an exciting and open area of research.

2.3 Customer Service

Product availability and stockouts are a measure of customer service. Corsten and Gruen (2003) study the occurrence and implications of stockouts using data collected from CPG firms and supermarket chains in several countries. They show that stockouts occur frequently and are caused by reasons related to supply chain as well as retail store execution. Furthermore, customers who experience stockouts react in a variety of ways. They may substitute a different item, postpone the purchase, abandon the entire shopping cart, or even switch to a different store for their future shopping needs.

The implications of stockouts have been studied in different types of theoretical models. Balakrishnan et al. (2004) analyze a phenomenon called "stack them high, let them fly," in which the rate of demand occurrence is a function of the amount of inventory stocked by the retailer. The higher the inventory, the higher the demand rate. Their analysis uses a generalization of the EOQ model. A different approach is to model individual consumer behavior in which consumers choose which retailer to visit based on their expectations of service level provided by the retailer. Dana and Petruzzi (2001) analyze a rational expectations equilibrium between consumers and a retailer and determine the optimal inventory level for a retailer when consumers are sensitive to product availability. Bernstein and Federgruen (2004) consider a game-theoretic model in which retailers compete in the marketplace on their service levels and customers choose which retailer to visit based on their expectations of finding the product in stock at the retailer. In many situations, customers are unaware of the service levels provided by competing retailers, and they learn over time from past experiences, which then affects their future store visits. Gaur and Park (2007) study the implications of consumer learning on market shares and stocking levels of retailers competing in the marketplace.

Stockouts also lead to spillover demand, i.e., the demand in excess of the available inventory. Netessine and Rudi (2003) study a multi-item setting in which the spillover demand for an item is allocated to the other items. They analyze both centralized and decentralized optimal stocking decisions in this setting. Bassok et al. (1999) study inventory decisions for the practice of downward substitution, in which a retailer substitutes a higher-quality and higher-price product to meet excess demand for lower quality-lower price products. Finally, stockouts play a very critical role in assortment planning models. We discuss this implication of stockouts in Section 2.6.

2.4 Pricing and Clearance Markdowns

Department store markdowns soared from less than 5% of total sales in 1970 to more than 20% of total sales in 1997 according to data collected by the National Retail Federation (Fisher and Raman 2010: chapter 1). Thus, there has been considerable research in improving the management of markdowns in retailing. Gallego and van Ryzin (1994) develop an optimal markdown policy when demand follows a price-dependent Poisson process. Smith and Achabal (1998) present a model of a seasonal product in which the demand rate is an increasing function of the amount of inventory available. They develop an optimal markdown trajectory as a function of the remaining length of season and the amount of leftover inventory and test its performance at three major retail chains. Caro and Gallien (2012) develop a method for deciding clearance markdowns in a network of retail stores with varying demand rates and inventory availabilities and apply their method to the Spanish retail chain, Zara.

Recent researchers have also investigated the phenomenon that anticipation of markdowns can motivate consumers to behave strategically and wait for a better deal rather than purchasing immediately. Many approaches to manage strategic consumer behavior have been studied in the literature. Aviv and Pazgal (1998) show that when consumers are forward-looking, it may be optimal for a retailer to pre-commit to a price path. Cachon and Swinney (2009) show that quick response capability is more valuable to a retailer when consumers behave strategically, and Osadchiy and Vulcano (2010) analyze the implications of binding reservations.

2.5 Shelf Space Management

The productivity of shelf space is important for the profitability of a retailer. According to the 2007 U.S. Economic Census, there were 1,122,703 retail establishments in the United States and a total of 14.2 billion square feet of retail space. As reported by Farfan (2014), the amount of shelf space availability varies across countries: There was approximately 46.6 square feet of retail space per capita in the U.S. in 2007, two square feet per capita in India, 1.5 square feet per capita in Mexico, 23 square feet per capita in the United Kingdom, 13 square feet per capita in Canada, and 6.5 square feet per capita in Australia. Thus, retailers make large investment in shelf space, and a key decision is to allocate available shelf space among products.

The shelf-space allocation problem has a long history of research. One of the seminal papers in this area comes from Corstjens and Doyle (1981), who present a model in which products compete for limited shelf space but their demand is sensitive to the amount of shelf space allocated to each product. Cachon (2001) analyzes a model of joint optimization of retail shelf space, inventory, and transportation. Kök and Fisher (2007) incorporate shelf space constraints in an assortment planning problem. Competition for shelf space among manufacturers has also been studied in the literature. Martinez-de-Albeniz and Roels (2011) examine competition among manufacturers for retail shelf space. In their model, a retailer makes shelf space allocation decisions, and competing manufacturers make pricing decisions. They find that the incentives of retailers and manufacturers are misaligned, leading to suboptimal prices and shelf space allocations.

Shelf space allocation not only has demand implications, but it also has cost implications because the amount of shelf space allocated to a product limits the inventory of that product that the store can carry. For a slow-moving item with ample shelf space, this can increase inventory holding costs and product expiration. For a fast-moving product with limited shelf space, it can lead to stockouts and increased transportation cost. Van Donselaar et al. (2010) show that shelf space allocation has implications for the type of ordering policy followed by a retail store. Akkas et al. (2016) show that shelf space availability is related to the amount of product expiration. The cost implications of shelf space have not been fully studied in the literature and provide opportunities for future research.

2.6 Assortment Planning

Assortment planning can be defined as the decision of selecting which items to stock in a product category from a given set of possibilities and what product categories to carry in a retail store in order to maximize expected profit. Items within a category are typically substitutes, whereas items across categories are complements, e.g., chips and salsa or bread and jam. There has been a vast amount of theoretical and applied research on assortment planning in the past two decades.

Most of the papers in this area focus on assortment planning within a category. Researchers have also studied the problem of category management, although to a lesser degree. Kök et al. (2009) conduct a comprehensive review of the literature on assortment planning. We provide a brief summary of the main topics of research in this area.

Researchers have developed methods to decide the assortment for different types of customer choice behavior. Van Ryzin and Mahajan (1999) focus on the multinomial logit choice model, Smith and Agrawal (2000) use a model in which substitution rates are specified for different pairs of products, Gaur and Honhon (2006) focus on an attribute-based locational choice model, Cachon et al. (2005) incorporate consumer search in assortment planning, and Hopp and Xu (2005) study joint pricing and assortment planning decisions. Researchers have also extensively studied models of stockout-based substitution in assortment planning and developed heuristics and algorithms for different formulations of this problem. Work done in this area includes Mahajan and van Ryzin (2001), Kök and Fisher (2007), Goyal et al. (2016), and Honhon et al. (2010) as well as many other papers. An innovative problem studied by many researchers is that of dynamic assortment planning, in which a retailer changes the assortment over time and uses realized sales to learn about consumer demand. Research papers on this problem include Bernstein et al. (2015), Caro and Gallien (2007), Chen and Plambeck (2008), and Ulu et al. (2012).

Research in assortment planning has had a significant impact on practice. Such application involves the related problems of estimating demand and optimizing the product assortment. Anupindi et al. (1998) present a method to estimate demand rates and substitution parameters from censored demand data. This problem is complex because stockouts induce substitution, which changes demand rates of products over time. Musalem et al. (2010) also utilize similar data, and develop a method to estimate the parameters of a random utility model. The advantage of this approach is that the utility model is more parsimonious. Kök and Fisher (2007) estimate a multinomial logit choice model using data from a supermarket chain and conduct a pilot test of assortment planning. Fisher and Vaidyanathan (2012) study an interesting problem of localization of assortment. Using demand data for different subsets of products stocked in different stores, they estimate an attribute-based choice model and present a method to localize assortments to the demand characteristics in each store. Lee et al. (2016) apply choice estimation to data from a bookstore and conduct a controlled field experiment to evaluate the resulting improvement in stocking decisions and realized profit.

While all of the above papers deal with assortment planning for a category of substitutable products, a few research papers have studied the problem of planning assortments across several related product categories. A challenge in this problem is that the choice models for basket shopping consumers across a category of products are fairly complex. Cachon and Kök (2007) and Chong et al. (2001) are two research papers that propose choice models and analyze assortment planning for this problem. Category management has also been studied from the perspective of coordination between retailers and manufacturers, who may serve as category captains (Kurtuluş and Nakkas 2011). Assortment planning remains an area of vigorous research in different methods and applications. Recent research in assortment planning has looked at consumer behavior across brick-and-mortar and online channels (Dzyabura and Jagabathula 2016).

2.7 *Financial Performance of Retailing Firms*

Research in retailing is exciting, not only for the large variety of operational challenges faced by retailers, but also because data for retailers is readily available to assess their financial performance. Stock market investors and analysts closely watch many types of performance metrics used by retailers. These include inventory levels and write-downs, opening and closing of new stores, store traffic, comparable stores sales growth rate, profit margins, use of markdowns, and lifecycles of retail brands from growth to maturity and potential decline. In turn, retail managers can quickly assess the financial implications of their decisions by observing these same variables at a more detailed level across product categories, stores, or buyers.

Considerable research has been done on the inventory productivity of retailers. Inventory is linked to the financial performance of retailers because it provides signals for future performance and can be a source of information asymmetry between retailers and their investors regarding past performance (Gaur et al. 2014). Thus, research has addressed questions such as (i) what are the drivers of inventory productivity in retailing, (ii) how does inventory productivity of retail firms impact their earnings and stock returns, and (iii) do high- and low-inventory turnover retailers differ in the ways in which they manage demand uncertainty.

Specifically, Gaur et al. (2005) show that inventory turnover of retailing firms varies widely over time as well as across firms within retail business categories or segments. They propose a metric, adjusted inventory turnover, to measure performance changes by adjusting inventory turnover for correlations with contemporaneous gross margin, capital intensity, and sales surprise (i.e., the ratio of actual sales to forecast). For instance, a retailer that increases its inventory turnover while improving its gross margin or achieving a positive sales surprise would have performed better than another retailer that increases its inventory turnover with a deterioration in gross margin. Kesavan et al. (2010) devise a method to include historical inventory and gross margin data in time-series sales forecasting methods. Their work discovers that stock market analysts are biased because they do not pay adequate attention to abnormal inventory. Alan et al. (2014) and Kesavan and Mani (2013) take the next step in this research and show that inventory productivity and abnormal inventory of retailers are predictors of future stock returns and earnings. Finally, Kesavan et al. (2015) analyze the ability of high- and low-inventory turnover retailers (HIT and LIT, respectively) to manage demand uncertainty. They show that these two types of retailers respond differently to uncertainty; HIT retailers predominantly respond by adjusting their inventory levels (quantity response), whereas LIT retailers respond mainly by adjusting their prices (price response). Moreover, LIT retailers take longer lead time to incorporate new demand information in their inventory planning and are forced to make larger adjustments. As a result, the financial performance of LIT retailers is much more sensitive to abnormal inventory than that of HIT retailers.

Retailers can open and close stores at a rapid rate. An interesting problem created by store closings is that of liquidating inventory and managing a going-out-of-business sale. Craig et al. (2014) document the industry practice of inventory-based lending or asset-based lending, in which a retailer obtains a low-cost bank loan by using its inventory as collateral. Craig and Raman (2016) show that store liquidation has unique characteristics compared to end-of-season markdowns. They analyze data from a retailing firm and an inventory liquidation firm to assess the drivers of profitability in a store liquidation and develop an algorithm to optimize markdowns and transshipment of inventory across stores in order to maximize the total revenue generated from the sale.

3 Present Situation

The retailing industry is rapidly experiencing a transformation through several forces. In recent years, new research has emerged in retailing in store execution and workforce management as well as in online and omnichannel retailing. We discuss ongoing research in these developing areas as below.

3.1 Store Execution and Workforce Management

Fisher (2004) noted that a retail store performs both factory and sales functions. Several research articles and case studies have focused on problems in store execution and workforce management. Access to in-store data has encouraged research in this area. This research has led to an impact on practice as well as the discovery of new problems. One of these problems is that of assessing the impact of labor staffing on sales in retail stores (Fisher and Raman 2010: chapter 6). On the one hand, an increase in staffing is beneficial for better customer service, increased sales, and higher market share. On the other hand, staffing is expensive and requires the retailer to consider many factors, such as projections of store traffic and the mix of labor between full-time, part-time, and temporary workers. Perdikaki et al. (2012) use store traffic, labor staffing, and point-of-sale data from a retail chain to study the effect of traffic and staffing on characteristics of sales performance, such as customer conversion and basket value. Kesavan et al. (2014) use similar data to study the effect of labor mix, i.e., number of full-time, part-time, and temporary workers, on sales and profit. Mani et al. (2015) apply hourly data on store traffic, sales, and staffing in a mathematical model to identify time periods when retail stores are understaffed and measure the resulting impact on retail sales.

Solving a staffing problem also requires a retailer to estimate the elasticity of sales to additional staffing. This estimation problem is challenging due to endogeneity (i.e., staffing is planned in anticipation of sales) and data aggregation (i.e., retail store data are often too aggregated to observe cause and effect). Technology is coming to the rescue of POM researchers wanting to overcome this challenge. A wide variety of data from store traffic counters, video recordings, location sensing technology, and heat mapping are now available to measure how customers experience a retail store and interact with store employees. Researchers can employ these data to construct decision-support tools for retail store managers. For instance, Lu et al. (2013) combine video recognition data from retail stores with point-of-sale data to study the effect of waiting in queue on purchases. Digital snapshots were collected at the deli section of a supermarket and were analyzed by image recognition technology to track the number of customers waiting in line and the number of sales associates staffing the deli. This area offers rich opportunities for future research.

3.2 Online and Omnichannel Retailing

Online retailing is an important part of the retailing industry today. Between 2005 to 2015, online retail sales grew at a compounded annual growth rate of 14.1% whereas total retail sales (excluding motor vehicles and spare parts) grew at 2.9% per year. Thus, about one-third of the total growth in retail sales in the U.S. over the past ten years has occurred online. Amazon.com, a purely online retailer, is now among the ten largest companies in the U.S. by market capitalization. Brick-and-mortar retailers have also invested aggressively in expanding their online channels and in omnichannel retailing, i.e., a seamless integration of online and brick-and-mortar retail channels.

It is helpful to classify new research in this area into three types of topics: (i) *supply chain fulfillment* for online and omnichannel retailing, (ii) *customer experience*, and (iii) *merchandising*. We are beginning to see research on supply chain fulfillment. Whereas in a brick-and-mortar store, a customer visits a store to purchase a product, an online retailer has a network of fulfillment centers and can choose where to ship a product from to fulfill a customer's order. This decision can be based on several considerations, such as the transportation costs from the fulfillment centers to the customer, available inventory at the fulfillment centers, and whether it is a multi-item or a single-item order. Acimovic and Graves (2015) devise a heuristic to make fulfillment decisions by minimizing the sum of immediate and expected future fulfillment costs, and conduct a pilot test for an online retailer. Gallino and Moreno (2014) study the effect of supply chain fulfillment choices on the occurrence of demand. They consider the capability of buy-online-pickup-in-store (called BOPS or BOPUS) in the brick-and-mortar stores of a large retail chain. Using an interesting data set consisting of point-of-sale transactions from retail stores and the online channel of the chain, they apply a difference-in-difference method to compare the effect of introducing BOPS on sales in both channels. Interestingly, they find that introduction of this feature led to a reduction in online sales but an increase in store sales and traffic. Gao and Su (2016) conduct a theoretical analysis of the impact of BOPS on store operations. They show that although BOPS expands the market size for a retailer, not all products are well suited for BOPS.

The topic of customer experience has also been studied in a few recent papers. One aspect of customer experience is the practice of showrooming, in which customers receive information from stores and fulfillment takes place online. The concept of showrooming is illustrated by Warby Parker, an online eyewear retailer that opened brick-and-mortar showrooms in select markets to allow consumers to select products before placing their orders online. Warby Parker's showrooms carry only display inventory, and merchandise is stored in online fulfillment centers and shipped directly to customers' homes. Bell et al. (2014) study the effect of showrooming on the sales and profits of Warby Parker. They find that showrooming enabled the retailer to better match its channels with customer needs, thus reducing the occurrence of product returns, and increasing sales. Balakrishnan et al. (2014) analyze the implications of showrooming in a mathematical model of competition between a brick-and-mortar retailer and an internet retailer in which customers are heterogeneous and have uncertain valuations of the product.

The topic of online merchandising has been relatively less well studied. Dzyabura and Jagabathula (2016) propose a new consumer choice and assortment planning model that incorporates differences in choice behavior in stores and online. They test their model in controlled laboratory experiments and determine the optimal assortment of products that a retailer should carry online and in store to maximize its profits. This research is a promising start. New modeling and empirical research is needed in this area to help guide retailers in their merchandising decisions.

Online retailing provides opportunities to design new business models and to apply optimization and machine learning approaches to solve problems faced by retailers. Belavina et al. (2016)'s study the implications of revenue models for online groceries retailing for total sales, delivery cost, and food waste. They show that per-order payment model and subscription-based payment model fit different types of retailing depending on profit margins and geographic and demographic patterns. Ferreira et al. (2016) apply machine learning to historical sales data at an online retailer, Rue La La, in order to predict demand and set prices for products that the retailer has never sold before. They implement their algorithm as a decision support tool for the retailer and conduct field experiments to assess its performance. Acimovic and Graves (2015), discussed earlier in this section, is also an example of real-time optimization applied to online order fulfillment processes.

4 Directions for Future Research

Retailing is rich with opportunities for future POM research and application. In this section, we make five projections of important research directions in this industry.

4.1 Availability of Individual Customer-Level High-Frequency Data Will Drive Research in New Decision Models and Experiments

There are many kinds of data available in retailing: in-store data regarding point-of-sale transactions, customer behavior, store and workforce characteristics, fulfillment, and marketing and promotions; online shopping and clickstream data; public data about retailers; and macroeconomic, weather, and competitive data. Often, these data sets can be combined with each other to create informative decision models. These types of data are enabling researchers to apply analytical methods to retail decisions in new and innovative ways, as shown by Ferreira et al. (2016) in applying machine learning for demand forecasting and pricing at an online retailer, Kesavan et al. (2014) and Lu et al. (2013) for workforce management in a retail store, and Archak et al. (2011) for the analysis of online customer reviews.

The ready availability of data and the ability to make frequent changes also makes it possible to conduct field experiments in retail firms. Retailers frequently conduct experiments in their stores to test new merchandise, assess the design of store layouts, and test prices. However, these experiments used to be costly and often unreliable (Fisher et al. 2000). The design of experiments can be improved through detailed and high frequency data, the cost of experimentation can be brought down by the ability to isolate decisions across time, customers, and products, and the scope of application of experiments can be expanded to include targeted promotions, visual layout of websites and mobile displays, and inventory availability information. In the past, research has been done in brick-and-mortar retailing as a way to improve the design of experiments and test the reliability of their results (Fisher and Rajaram 2000; Gaur and Fisher 2005). Examples of the increasing use of field experiments in online retailing include Bell et al. (2014) and Gallino and Moreno (2014) and those in brick-and-mortar retailing include Caro and Gallien (2012) and Lee et al. (2016).

4.2 New In-Store Technologies Will Transform Retail Stores, Making Bricks and Clicks a Reality and Changing the Customer Experience

The type of retail technologies that have seen the most remarkable growth since 2010 is in-store traffic counting, scanning, and surveillance. There are several new startup ventures providing different kinds of technologies in this space. They are creating new kinds of structured and unstructured data that can be used to improve efficiency and quality in retail stores and are introducing new research problems in POM. They are also making it easier to use data and analytics to solve problems in innovative ways. Following are some examples:

- Axis Communications uses networked cameras in stores to count customers, measure traffic, and conversions. Information is available in real time, so that it can be used to conduct experiments in stores.
- Euclid Analytics collects and models customer location data to measure customer frequency and duration of visit and intensity of interaction.
- Hointer.com provides technology for effective and efficient operation of fitting rooms.
- LocationGenius collects location data from customer smartphones and integrates it with social media and customer demographics.
- Prism Skylabs uses heat-sensing technology in stores to provide analytics for planning store layout and pricing shelf space.
- RetailNext uses sensors to measure the effectiveness of displays and windows in retail stores.
- ShopKick is an app that customers can download on their smartphones and earn points when they walk into a store, scan merchandise, or make a purchase.

- Shopperception uses 3D sensor technology to detect how customers interact with products on retail shelves.
- ShopperTrak provides technology for traffic counting in stores, which can then be combined with POS data for optimizing staffing, conducting A/B tests, and measuring conversion.

Previously, brick-and-mortar retailers faced a data disadvantage compared to online retailers. They could only observe customer purchases, whereas online retailers could capture and archive the entire customer engagement with their online stores for those making a purchase as well as those who were just browsing. These technologies are plugging this data gap between brick-and-mortar and online retailers. They are also enabling customers to have a seamless engagement with retailers across multiple channels. Thus, brick-and-mortar retailers can adopt pricing, promotions, and store design tools in the same way as online retailers.

4.3 Emerging Retail Formats, Warehouse Logistics, and Package Delivery Methods Will Create More Opportunities for Research

The retailing industry has periodically seen the evolution of new formats. Formats evolved over the past century include supermarket stores, department stores, discount stores, category killers, warehouse clubs, and online retailers. New retail formats emerging in the recent years include mobile retailing, consumer-to-consumer marketplaces such as Etsy, pop-up stores, virtual stores by Yihaodian in China (Chapter 34 in this book), and a hyper-retail model in India. Retail formats have been an overlooked research opportunity in the past. There is need for new research on the lifecycles, economic viability, and social and market implications of these new formats. One research paper in this area is work by Blanco and Fransoo (2013) on nanostores in Latin American countries.

Similar to new retail formats, there has also been considerable development in the design of warehouses and order fulfillment processes consisting of picking, packing, and shipping. The growth of online retailing has particularly fueled innovations in this area. Warehouses can be designed for case-picking, or unit-picking, and for manual picking, conveyors, or robotic devices. Smart warehouses integrate with retailers' inventory management and demand forecasting systems to push product based on predictions of excess inventory and outages. Delivery to a customer's doorstep can be assisted by drones. Research can contribute to the design of algorithms for employing these technologies for order fulfillment.

4.4 Environmental Sustainability Will Grow as a Research Area in Retailing

Global warming and climate change are bringing an urgent focus to environmental sustainability in retailing. Different types of retail formats vary in their environmental implications. For instance, Cachon (2014) studies the carbon footprint implications of the design of a retail store network. Manufacturers and retailers need to coordinate with each other to reduce the cost and environmental implications of product expiration (Akkas et al. 2016). Some retailers, such as Wal-Mart and Whole Foods, are encouraging their suppliers to use environmentally friendly product and packaging designs as well as measure their carbon footprint. The design and effectiveness of these initiatives needs to be studied by POM researchers. Finally, online retail models can influence the frequency of customer shopping, and thus, there are environmental consequences of the design of such models (Belavina et al. 2016).

4.5 Merchandising and Sourcing Functions Will See Research in New Models

As we noted in Section 3, the digital revolution occurring in the retailing industry has influenced supply chain fulfillment and customer experience, but merchandising and sourcing functions have been largely left out. Merchandising in seasonal or short lifecycle products is done through a process called "open to buy" in which a retail buyer or merchant evaluates potential product offerings and makes procurement decisions over time given available cash. There has not been much research into the optimization of this process in the past. As retailers exploit data and technological tools in their customer engagement, there is need for research in improving the merchandising and sourcing functions.

5 Implications for Practitioners

POM research has had significant impact on practice through applied modeling-based and econometrics-based work. Some areas of practical impact discussed in this chapter are assortment planning, inventory management for short lifecycle products, supply chain coordination, field experiments in brick-and-mortar and online retailing, and clearance markdowns. In the past, retailing was characterized by long lead times and inaccurate and inaccessible data (Fisher et al. 2000). However, this is no longer the case. Retailers have shortened their lead times through making their supply chains more responsive and have become more data savvy. These changes have opened up the opportunity to apply analytical models for real-time decision making on pricing, assortments, and inventory management. In this section, we describe how the practitioner impact of POM has been measured in the literature.

One way to measure practical impact is to relate operational performance of retailers with their stock returns. Alan et al. (2014) show that higher inventory turnover is a predictor of higher stock returns, Kesavan et al. (2015) show that higher inventory turnover retailers have better ability to manage demand uncertainty than lower inventory turnover retailers, and Fisher et al. (1999) show that retailers with higher return on assets and lower standard deviation of return on assets achieve higher long-term average stock returns across a cross-section of firms. Hendricks and Singhal (2005) show the effect of supply chain disruptions on stock returns and equity risk.

Practical impact is also measured through the effect on profitability. Operational improvements have large financial benefits for retailers because net profits are a small fraction of sales for retailing firms and small improvements in gross margin or sales revenue translate into large increases in net profits. For instance, consider a retailer with a sales revenue of $100, cost of goods sold of $60, and fixed cost of $35. The fixed cost may include selling, real estate, marketing, depreciation and amortization, and corporate overhead expenses. Thus, the retailer has a 40% gross margin and a 5% net profit before tax. Suppose that the retailer implements a new tool for pricing or inventory management, which results in an increase in sales from $100 to $105 with an increase in cost of goods sold from $60 to $62, and no change in fixed cost. Then, the sales revenue increases by 5%, gross margin increases from 40% to 40.95% (given by $43/$105), and net profit increases from $5 to $8, an increase of 60%.

Another benefit of operational improvements is in improving the liquidity of a retailer. Cash is important for a retailer to manage its inventory and accounts payables. Consider an example of a retailer that has $100 in annual sales revenue, $60 in annual cost of goods sold, and $20 in average inventory. Thus, the annual inventory turnover of this retailer is 3.0. Suppose that the retailer improves its inventory turnover to 4.0 by reducing its required inventory from the average of $20 to an average of $15. This implies that the retailer's cash flow from operations increases immediately by $5 (= $20 −$15). This can be a substantial increase when compared to the cash flow impact of net profits of the retailer. Thus, operational improvements can have large benefits for a retailer in its profitability, cash flows, and stock returns.

6 Conclusions

The goal of this chapter has been to describe existing POM research on topics relevant to the retailing industry, identify present trends in research, and make a few projections for promising future directions of research. We have described theoretical modeling-based research, applied research, econometrics-based work, field experiments, as well as some important case studies.

The retailing industry has seen significant developments through POM research during the previous 20–25 years. These developments have occurred in inventory management, retail supply chains, pricing and markdown management, assortment planning, shelf space allocation, and financial management of retailers. Despite these developments, this industry continues to see explosive growth in research opportunities. Research areas that have gained importance in recent years include store execution, workforce management, and online and omnichannel retailing. In the future, there are new business models emerging in retailing, technology is enabling the capture of more data and more precise decision making, environmental sustainability is becoming an important consideration, and retailing is developing rapidly in emerging markets. At the same time, there continues to be a need for research on topics that have been hitherto under-studied, such as category management, merchandising, and coordination between online retailers and suppliers. In each of these areas, the retailing industry presents opportunities for doing theoretical modeling, data-based modeling, and empirical research, experimentation, as well as applied research.

Retailing is connected with many sectors of the economy, manufacturing, services, banking, technology, and transportation logistics. Consumer behavior observed in retail stores is often a signal of economic growth and a harbinger of macroeconomic news. Thus, POM research in retailing presents exciting opportunities that can be impactful not only in this industry but also in the rest of the economy.

Acknowledgments

The author is grateful to the editors Martin Starr and Sushil Gupta for feedback on an early version of this chapter, which greatly helped improve its content and focus.

References and Bibliography

Abernathy, F. H., J. T. Dunlop and J. H. Hammond (1999) *A Stitch in Time: Lean Retailing and the Transformation of Manufacturing—Lessons from the Apparel and Textile Industries*, Oxford University Press, Oxford, UK.

Acimovic, J. and S. C. Graves (2015) "Making Better Fulfillment Decisions on the Fly in an Online Retail Environment," *Manufacturing & Service Operations Management*, **17**(1): 34–51.

Agrawal, N. and S. Smith (1998) "Estimating Negative Binomial Demand for Retail Inventory Management with Unobservable Lost Sales," *Naval Research Logistics*, **43**(6): 839–861.

Akkas, A., V. Gaur and D. Simchi-Levi (2016) "Drivers of Product Expiration in Retail Supply Chains," Working Paper.

Alan, Y., G. Gao and V. Gaur (2014) "Does Inventory Turnover Predict Future Stock Return? A Retailing Industry Perspective," *Management Science*, **60**(10): 2416–2434.

Anupindi, R., M. Dada and S. Gupta (1998) "Estimation of Consumer Demand with Stock-Out Based Substitution: An Application to Vending Machine Products," *Marketing Science*, **17**(4): 406–423.

Archak, N., A. Ghose and P. Ipeirotis (2011) "Deriving the Pricing Power of Product Features by Mining Consumer Reviews," *Management Science*, **57**(8): 1485–1509.

Aviv, Y. and A. Pazgal (2008) "Optimal Pricing of Seasonal Products in the Presence of Forward-Looking Consumers," *Manufacturing Service Operations Management*, **10**(3): 339–359.

Balakrishnan, A., M. S. Pangburn and E. Stavrulaki (2004) "Stack Them High, Let 'em Fly": Lot-Sizing Policies When Inventories Stimulate Demand," *Management Science*, **50**(5): 630–644.

Balakrishnan, A., S. Sundaresan and B. Zhang (2014) "Browse-and-Switch: Retail-Online Competition under Value Uncertainty," *Production and Operations Management*, **23**(7): 1129–1145.

Barnes-Schuster, D., Y. Bassok and R. Anupindi (2002) "Coordination and Flexibility in Supply Contracts with Options," *Manufacturing & Service Operations Management*, **4**(3): 171–207.

Bassok, Y., R. Anupindi and R. Akella (1999) "Single-period Multiproduct Inventory Models with Substitution," *Operations Research*, **47** 632–642.

Belavina, E., K. Girotra and A. Kabra (2016) "Online Fresh Grocery Retail: A La Carte or Buffet?" *Management Science*, **forthcoming**.

Bell, D., S. Gallino and A. Moreno (2014) "How to Win in an Omnichannel World," *Sloan Management Review*, **56**(1): 45–53.

Bernstein, F. and A. Federgruen (2004) "A General Equilibrium Model for Industries with Price and Service Competition," *Operations Research*, **52**, 868–886.

Bernstein, F., A. Gürhan Kök and Lei Xie (2015) "Dynamic Assortment Customization with Limited Inventories," *Manufacturing & Service Operations Management*, **17**(4): 538–553.

Blanco, E. and J. C. Fransoo (2013) "Reaching 50 million Nanostores: Retail Distribution in Emerging Megacities," Working Paper 404, BETA Research School, Eindhoven University of Technology, Netherlands. http://cms.ieis.tue.nl/Beta/Files/WorkingPapers/wp_404.pdf

Bureau of Economic Analysis (2016) "Gross Domestic Product (GDP) by Industry," April, www.bea.gov/industry/index.htm

Bureau of Labor Statistics (2016) "Current Employment Statistics—CES (National) Tables," June, www.bls.gov/web/empsit/ceseeb1a.htm

Cachon, G. P. (2001) "Managing a Retailer's Shelf Space, Inventory, and Transportation," *Manufacturing & Service Operations Management*, **3**(3): 211–229.

Cachon, G. P. (2003) "Supply Chain Coordination with Contracts," in *Handbooks in OR and MS*, Volume 11, Supply Chain Management: Design, Coordination and Operations, pp. 229–339, Eds. A. G. de Kök and S. C. Graves, Elsevier, Amsterdam, Netherlands.

Cachon, G. P. (2014) "Retail Store Density and the Cost of Greenhouse Gas Emissions," *Management Science*, **60**(8): 1907–1925.

Cachon, G. P. and A. G. Kök (2007) "Category Management and Coordination in Retail Assortment Planning in the Presence of Basket Shopping Consumers," *Management Science*, **53**(6): 934–951.

Cachon, G. P. and M. L. Fisher (1997) "Campbell Soup's Continuous Replenishment Program: Evaluation and Enhanced Inventory Decision Rules," *Production and Operations Management*, **6**(3): 266–276.

Cachon, G. P. and M. L. Fisher (2000) "Supply Chain Inventory Management and the Value of Shared Information," *Management Science*, **46**(8): 1032–1048.

Cachon, G. P. and R. Swinney (2009) "Purchasing, Pricing, and Quick Response in the Presence of Strategic Consumers," *Management Science*, **55**(3): 497–511.

Cachon, G. P., C. Terwiesch and Y. Xu (2005) "Retail Assortment Planning in the Presence of Consumer Search," *Manufacturing & Service Operations Management*, **7**(4): 330–346.

Camdereli, A. and J. Swaminathan (2010) "Misplaced Inventory and Radio-Frequency Identification (RFID) Technology: Information and Coordination," *Production and Operations Management*, **19**(1): 1–18.

Caro, F. and J. Gallien (2007) "Dynamic Assortment with Demand Learning for Seasonal Consumer Goods," *Management Science*, **53**(2): 276–292.

Caro, F. and J. Gallien (2010) "Inventory Management of a Fast-Fashion Retail Network," *Operations Research*, **58**(2): 257–273.

Caro, F. and J. Gallien (2012) "Clearance Pricing Optimization for a Fast-Fashion Retailer," *Operations Research*, **60**(6): 1404–1422.

Cattani, K., W. Gilland, H. S. Heese and J. Swaminathan (2006) "Boiling Frogs: Pricing Strategies for a Manufacturer Adding a Direct Channel that Competes with the Traditional Channel," *Production and Operations Management*, **15**(1): 40–56.

Chen, F. (2003) "Information Sharing and Supply Chain Coordination," in *Handbooks in OR and MS*, Volume 11, *Supply Chain Management: Design, Coordination and Operations*, pp. 341–421, Eds. A. G. de Kök and S. C. Graves, Elsevier, Amsterdam, Netherlands.

Chen, H.-W., D. Gupta, H. Gurnani and G. Janakiraman (2016) "A Stochastic Inventory Model With Fast-Ship Commitments," *Production and Operations Management*, **25**(4): 684–700.

Chen, Li and E. Plambeck (2008) "Dynamic Inventory Management with Learning about the Demand Distribution and Substitution Probability," *Manufacturing & Service Operations Management*, **10**(2): 236–256.

Chong, J.-K., T.-H. Ho and C. S. Tang (2001) "A Modeling Framework for Category Assortment Planning," *Manufacturing & Service Operations Management*, **3**(3): 191–210.

Corsten, D. and T. Gruen (2003) "Desperately Seeking Shelf Availability: An Examination of the Extent, the Causes, and the Efforts to Address Retail Out-of-stocks," *International Journal of Retail & Distribution Management*, **31**(12): 605–617.

Corstjens, M. and P. Doyle (1981) "A Model for Optimizing Retail Space Allocations," *Management Science*, **27**(7): 822–833.

Craig, N. and A. Raman (2016) "Improving Store Liquidation," *Manufacturing & Service Operations Management*, **18**(1): 89–103.

Craig, N., C. F. Foley and A. Raman (2014) "The Inventory-Based Lending Industry," Harvard Business School Case 612-057, Cambridge, MA.

Dana, J. and N. Petruzzi (2001) "The Newsvendor Model with Endogenous Demand," *Management Science*, **47**(11): 1488–1497.

DeHoratius, N. and A. Raman (2007) "Store Manager Incentive Design and Retail Performance: An Exploratory Investigation," *Manufacturing & Service Operations Management*, **9**(4): 518–534.

DeHoratius, N. and A. Raman (2008) "Inventory Record Inaccuracy: An Empirical Analysis," *Management Science*, **54**(4): 627–641.

DeHoratius, N., A. J. Mersereau and L. Schrage (2008) "Retail Inventory Management When Records Are Inaccurate," *Manufacturing & Service Operations Management*, **10**(2): 257–277.

Donohue, K. L. (2000) "Efficient Supply Contracts for Fashion Goods with Forecast Updating and Two Production Modes," *Management Science*, **46**(11): 1397–1411.

Dutta, A., H. L. Lee and S. Whang (2007) "RFID and Operations Management: Technology, Value, and Incentives," *Production and Operations Management*, **16**(5): 646–655.

Dzyabura, D. and S. Jagabathula (2016) "Offline Assortment Optimization in the Presence of an Online Channel," Working Paper, NYU Stern School of Business, New York.

Eppen, G. D. (1979) "Note—Effects of Centralization on Expected Costs in a Multi-Location Newsboy Problem," *Management Science*, **25**(5): 498–501.

Eppen, G. and A. Iyer (1997a) "Improved Fashion Buying with Bayesian Updates," *Operations Research*, **45**(6): 805–819.

Eppen, G. and A. Iyer (1997b) "Backup Agreements in Fashion Buying—The Value of Upstream Flexibility," *Management Science*, **43**(11): 1469–1484.

Etsy (n.d.), https://www.etsy.com.

Farfan, B. (2014) "All 2014 Store Closings—US Retail Industry Chains to Close Stores," http://retailindustry.about.com/od/USRetailStoreClosingInfoFAQs/fl/All-2014-Store-Closings-US-Retail-Industry-Chains-to-Close-Stores.htm.

Ferreira, K. J., B. H. Lee and D. Simchi-Levi (2016) "Analytics for an Online Retailer: Demand Forecasting and Price Optimization," *Manufacturing & Service Operations Management*, **18**(1): 69–88.

Fisher, M. L. (2004) "To Me It's a Factory. To You It's a Store," *ECR Journal*, **4**(2): 8–18.

Fisher, M. L. and A. Raman (1996) "Reducing the Cost of Demand Uncertainty through Accurate Response to Early Sales," *Operations Research*, **44**(1): 87–99.

Fisher, M. L. and A. Raman (2010) *The New Science of Retailing*, Harvard Business School Publishing, Boston, MA.

Fisher, M. L. and K. Rajaram (2000) "Accurate Retail Testing of Fashion Merchandise: Methodology and Application," *Marketing Science*, **19**(3): 266–278.

Fisher, M. L. and R. Vaidyanathan (2012) "Which Product Should You Stock?" *Harvard Business Review*, **90**(11): 115–124. Reprint R00404.

Fisher, M. L., A. Raman and A. S. McClelland (2000) "Rocket Science Retailing is Almost Here—Are You Ready?" *Harvard Business Review*, **78**(4): 115–124.

Fisher, M. L., V. Gaur and A. Raman (1999) "Linking Finance and Operations in Retailing," Working Paper, Johnson School, Cornell University, Ithaca, NY.

Gallego, G. and G. van Ryzin (1994) "Optimal Dynamic Pricing of Inventories with Stochastic Demand," *Management Science*, **40**(8): 999–1020.

Gallino, S. and A. Moreno (2014) "Integration of Online and Offline Channels in Retail: The Impact of Sharing Reliable Inventory Availability Information," *Management Science*, **60**(6): 1434–1451.

Gao, F. and X. Su (2016) "Omnichannel Retail Operations with Buy-Online-And-Pickup-In-Store," *Management Science*, **forthcoming**.

Gaukler, G. M., R. W. Seifert and W. H. Hausman (2007) "Item-Level RFID in the Retail Supply Chain," *Production and Operations Management*, **16**(1): 65–76.

Gaur, V. and D. Honhon (2006) "Assortment Planning and Inventory Decisions under a Locational Choice Model," *Management Science*, **52**(10): 1528–1543.

Gaur, V. and M. L. Fisher (2005) "In-Store Experiments to Determine the Impact of Price on Sales," *Production and Operations Management*, **14**(4): 377–387.

Gaur, V. and Y.-H. Park (2007) "Asymmetric Consumer Learning and Inventory Competition," *Management Science*, **53**(2): 227–240.

Gaur, V., M. L. Fisher and A. Raman (2005) "An Econometric Analysis of Inventory Turnover Performance in Retail Services," *Management Science*, **51**(2): 181–194.

Gaur, V., N. Osadchiy and S. Seshadri (2013) "Sales Forecasting with Financial Indicators and Experts' Input," *Production and Operations Management*, **22**(5): 1056–1076.

Gaur, V., S. Kesavan and A. Raman (2014) "Retail Inventory: Managing the Canary in the Coal Mine!" *California Management Review*, **56**(2): 55–76.

Gaur, V., S. Kesavan, A. Raman and M. L. Fisher (2007) "Estimating Uncertainty Using Judgmental Forecasts," *Manufacturing & Service Operations Management*, **9**(4): 480–491.

Goyal, V., R. Levi and D. Segev (2016) "Near-Optimal Algorithms for the Assortment Planning Problem under Dynamic Substitution and Stochastic Demand," *Operations Research*, **64**(1): 219–235.

Gupta, S., C. Koulamas and G. J. Kyparisis (2009) "E-Business: A Review of Research Published in Production and Operations Management (1992–2008)," *Production and Operations Management*, **18**(6): 604–620.

Haksöz, Ç. and S. Seshadri (2004) "Monotone Forecasts," *Operations Research*, **52**(3): 478–486.

Hammond, J. (1994) "Barilla SpA (A)" Case Study 694046, Harvard Business School, Boston, MA.

Hardgrave, B. C., J. A. Aloysius and S. Goyal (2013) "RFID-Enabled Visibility and Retail Inventory Record Inaccuracy: Experiments in the Field," *Production and Operations Management*, **22**(4): 843–856.

Hausman, W. H. and R. Peterson (1972) "Multiproduct Production Scheduling for Style Goods with Limited Capacity, Forecast Revisions and Terminal Delivery," *Management Science*, **18**(7): 370–383.

Hendricks, K. and V. Singhal (2005) "An Empirical Analysis of the Effect of Supply Chain Disruptions on Long-Run Stock Price Performance and Equity Risk of the Firm," *Production and Operations Management*, **14**(1): 35–52.

Honhon, D., V. Gaur and S. Seshadri (2010) "Assortment Planning and Inventory Decisions under Stockout-Based Substitution," *Operations Research*, **58**(5): 1364–1379.

Hopp, W. J. and X. Xu (2005) "Product Line Selection and Pricing with Modularity in Design," *Manufacturing & Service Operations Management*, **7**(3): 172–187.

Kesavan, S. and V. Mani (2013) "The Relationship between Abnormal Inventory Growth and Future Earnings for U.S. Public Retailers," *Manufacturing & Service Operations Management*, **15**(1): 6–23.

Kesavan, S., B. R. Staats and W. Gilland (2014) "Volume Flexibility in Services: The Costs and Benefits of Flexible Labor Resources," *Management Science*, **60**(8): 1884–1906.

Kesavan, S., T. Kushwaha and V. Gaur (2015) "Do High- and Low-Inventory Turnover Retailers Respond Differently to Demand Shocks?" *Manufacturing & Service Operations Management*, **18**(2): 198–215.

Kesavan, S., V. Gaur and A. Raman (2010) "Do Inventory and Gross Margin Data Improve Sales Forecasts for U.S. Public Retailers?" *Management Science*, **56**(9): 1519–1533.

Ketzenberg, M. and M. Ferguson (2008) "Managing Slow-Moving Perishables in the Grocery Industry," *Production and Operations Management*, **17**(5): 513–521.

Ketzenberg, M., J. Bloemhof and G. Gaukler (2015) "Managing Perishables with Time and Temperature History," *Production and Operations Management*, **24**(1): 54–70.

Ketzenberg, M., N. Geismar, R. Metters and E. van der Laan (2013) "The Value of Information for Managing Retail Inventory Remotely," *Production and Operations Management*, **22**(4): 811–825.

Khan, H. (n.d.) "The Ultimate Guide to Pop-Up Shops," Shopify, www.shopify.com/guides/ultimate-guide-to-pop-up-shops.

Kök, A. G. and K. H. Shang (2007) "Inspection and Replenishment Policies for Systems with Inventory Record Inaccuracy," *Manufacturing & Service Operations Management*, **9**(2): 185–205.

Kök, A. G. and M. L. Fisher (2007) "Demand Estimation and Assortment Optimization under Substitution: Methodology and Application," *Operations Research*, **55**(6): 1001–1021.

Kök, A. G., M. L. Fisher and R. Vaidyanathan (2009) "Assortment Planning: Review of Literature and Industry Practice," Chapter 7 in *Retail Supply Chain Management: Quantitative Models and Empirical Studies*, Eds. N. Agrawal and S. A. Smith, Springer U.S. 99–153.

Krishnan, J. and M. L. Fisher (2005) "Store Level Execution at Wawa," Wharton School, University of Pennsylvania, Philadelphia, PA.

Kurtuluş, M. and A. Nakkas (2011) "Retail Assortment Planning Under Category Captainship," *Manufacturing & Service Operations Management*, **13**(1): 124–142.

Lee, H. L. and O. Ozer (2007) "Unlocking the Value of RFID," *Production and Operations Management*, **16**(1): 40–64.

Lee, H. L., V. Padmanabhan and S. Whang (1997) "Information Distortion in a Supply Chain: The Bullwhip Effect," *Management Science*, **43**(4): 546–558.

Lee, J.-K., V. Gaur, S. Muthulingam and G. F. Swisher (2016) "Stockout-Based Substitution and Inventory Planning in Textbook Retailing," *Manufacturing & Service Operations Management*, **18**(1): 104–121.

Lewis, R. (2015) "Retail in 2015: A Reality Check," Forbes.com. www.forbes.com/sites/robinlewis/2015/03/17/retail-in-2015-a-reality-check/#4353762a73b0.

Li, Y., B. Cheang and A. Lim (2012) "Grocery Perishables Management," *Production and Operations Management*, **21**(3): 504–517.

Lu, Y., A. Musalem, M. Olivares and A. Schilkrut (2013) "Measuring the Effect of Queues on Customer Purchases," *Management Science*, **59**(8): 1743–1763.

Mahajan, S. and G. van Ryzin (2001) "Stock Retail Assortments under Dynamic Consumer Substitution," *Operations Research*, **49**(3): 334–351.

Mani, V., S. Kesavan and J. M. Swaminathan (2015) "Estimating the Impact of Understaffing on Sales and Profitability in Retail Stores," *Production and Operations Management*, **24**(2): 201–218.

Martinez-de-Albeniz, V. and G. Roels (2011) "Competing for Shelf Space," *Production and Operations Management*, **20**(1): 32–46.

Murray, Jr., G. R. and E. A. Silver (1966) "A Bayesian Analysis of the Style Goods Inventory Problem," *Management Science*, **12**(11): 785–797.

Musalem, A., M. Olivares, E. T. Bradlow, C. Terwiesch and D. Corsten (2010) "Structural Estimation of the Effect of Out-of-Stocks," *Management Science*, **56**(7): 1180–1197.

Narayanan, V. G. and A. Raman (2004) "Aligning Incentives in Supply Chains," *Harvard Business Review*, **82**(11): 94–102.

Netessine, S. and N. Rudi (2003) "Centralized and Competitive Inventory Models with Demand Substitution," *Operations Research*, **51**(2): 329–335.

Osadchiy, N. and G. Vulcano (2010) "Selling with Binding Reservations in the Presence of Strategic Consumers," *Management Science*, **56**(12): 2173–2190.

Perdikaki, O., S. Kesavan and J. M. Swaminathan (2012) "Effect of Traffic on Sales and Conversion Rates of Retail Stores," *Manufacturing & Service Operations Management*, **14**(1): 145–162.

Pop-up stores. www.shopify.com/guides/ultimate-guide-to-pop-up-shops.

Porteus, E. (2002) *Foundations of Stochastic Inventory Theory*. Stanford Business Books, Stanford, CA.

Raman, A. and B. Kim (2002) "Quantifying the Impact of Inventory Holding Cost and Reactive Capacity on an Apparel Manufacturer's Profitability," *Production and Operations Management*, **11**(3): 358–373.

Raman, A., N. DeHoratius and Z. Ton (2001) "Execution: The Missing Link in Retail Operations," *California Management Review*, **43**(3): 136–152.

Robinson, L. W. (1990) "Optimal and Approximate Policies in Multiperiod, Multilocation Inventory Models with Transshipments," *Operations Research*, **38**(2): 278–295.

Sebenius, J. and E. Knebel (2007) "Tom Muccio: Negotiating the P&G Relationship with Wal-Mart (A)," Case Study 907013, Harvard Business School, Boston, MA.

Smith, S. A. and D. D. Achabal (1998) "Clearance Pricing and Inventory Policies for Retail Chains," *Management Science*, **44**(3): 285–300.

Smith, S. A. and N. Agrawal (2000) "Management of Multi-Item Retail Inventory Systems with Demand Substitution," *Operations Research*, **48**(1): 50–64.

Ton, Z., V. Dessain and M. Stachowiak-Joulain (2005) "RFID at the Metro Group," Case Study 606053, Harvard Business School, Boston, MA.

U.S. Census Bureau (2016) "Monthly and Annual Retail Trade Surveys 2014," March 7, 2016. www.census.gov/retail/index.html#arts.

Ulu, C., D. Honhon and A. Alptekinoglu (2012) "Learning Consumer Tastes through Dynamic Assortments," *Operations Research*, **60**(4): 833–849.

van Donselaar, K., V. Gaur, T. van Woensel, R. A. C. M. Broekmeulen and J. C. Fransoo (2010) "Ordering Behavior in Retail Stores and Implications for Automated Replenishment," *Management Science*, **56**(5): 766–784.

van Ryzin, G. and S. Mahajan (1999) "On the Relationship between Inventory Costs and Variety Benefits in Retail Assortments," *Management Science*, **45**(11): 1496–1509.

Virtual stores. www.wpp.com/wpp/press/2012/oct/19/ecommerce-grocer-yihaodian-opens-stores-overnight/.

WPP (2012) "E-Commerce Grocer Yihaodian Opens 1,000 Stores Overnight, www.wpp.com/wpp/press/2012/oct/19/ecommerce-grocer-yihaodian-opens-stores-overnight/.

Zipkin, P. H. (2000) *Foundations of Inventory Management*. McGraw-Hill.

PART VII

Expert POM Practitioners' Perspectives

32
POM FOR THE HOSPITALITY INDUSTRY

Lee Cockerell

1 POM for the Hospitality Industry

It is not magic that makes Walt Disney World® Resorts work. It's the way that the resorts work that makes it magical. The way that Walt Disney World® staff works entails the application of detailed planning systems and well-developed operating standards used alongside production and operations management systems and procedures.

Since operations management is the management of processes and systems that produce or deliver goods and services, operations management systems and processes directly affect the quality of products and services as well as the speed of delivery and consistency in the hospitality industry. In this chapter, I will refer to my work and experiences at Hilton Hotels, Marriott International, and the Walt Disney Company in order to talk about what I learned about the importance of well-developed systems and processes for providing world-class products and service.

2 Mapping Customer Service—Managing Systems and Processes

You can create magic in your organization by mapping the customer service touch points and then developing measurable standards of performance and implementing effective and detailed Production and Operations Management systems and processes. Well thought-out systems and processes are a vital part of managing an individual function and organizations as a whole. They are especially critical in hospitality where systems and processes have an immediate impact on the Guest/customer experience unlike in manufacturing where the impact to the customer is often far downstream.

3 Management Is About Control

Management is an interesting word, one that is often not fully understood by those bearing the title of manager or even by those hoping to become managers. Consider the responses I get when I ask individuals to define management. I often hear responses like "It means I am the boss." Other people say, "It means people who work in the organization have to do what I say" and so on. I have been teaching a time management course for over thirty-five years to help managers and aspiring managers to fully understand what the role of a manager really is. When I speak in front of these crowds, I tell them that management is the act of controlling events. Their role is not about bossing people around. It is not about making more money or having better benefits like company cars, bonuses, and healthcare. Management is about control. Great managers keep whatever they are responsible for under control. If they are a project manager, their responsibility is to keep that project under control in the areas of safety, quality, cleanliness, budgets, deadlines for completion, etc. The only way to keep any undertaking under control is to have a systematic way of completing every step along the way. One caution is to keep the customer central to all of the processes and systems you put into place so you don't over-process customer service to a point of creating hassles and aggravation.

4 Management Titles and POM Methods in the Hospitality Industry

As a function, operations management has changed significantly in recent years as a result of the increasing use of new technologies and detailed data now available in the hospitality industry. In the past, neither the term nor the title "operations management" were used very often in the hospitality business. In fact, in my entire forty-two-year career in hospitality, I had never heard operations management used as an approach to creating Production and Operations Management systems and processes. Most hospitality organizations use functional titles for each department such as front office manager, restaurant manager, executive chef, and housekeeping manager. Therefore, it is still true that in many organizations, the responsibility for developing effective systems and processes fall to these positions to create, monitor, maintain, and update as required.

In the early days of hospitality, checklists were one of the simplest operations management systems that managers found effective. Recipe cards, inventory, and production charts for culinary departments were other effective systems for controlling quality, cost, and consistency. The effectiveness of a clipboard with a detailed checklist shows that all operations management systems do not have to be complicated or require technology to be effective.

Operations management today is an area of management focused on designing and controlling processes, policies, procedures, rules, regulations, and guidelines to ensure the efficient delivery of goods and services to customers. Operations management focuses on productivity and continual improvement in order to ensure that just the right amount of resources are used to deliver customer expectations or to even exceed customer expectations the way that Walt Disney World® and other great brands do. Computers have dramatically improved the effectiveness and accuracy of data enabling organizations to put more efficient systems and processes into place.

5 Walt Disney World® Principles for Success

Walt Disney World® owes its success to six principles—all of which are based on well thought-out systems and processes to ensure effectiveness and consistency. These principles are:

1) Hiring and promoting excellent Cast Members (employees)
2) Training, testing, and enforcing training at every level
3) Creating measurable standards of performance and then developing and applying Production and Operations Management systems and processes throughout the organization to achieve those standards and to update them as required
4) World-class attention to detail with an attitude of "everything matters"

5) Effective storytelling and a high level of creativity
6) Creating a culture and environment where every Cast Member matters—and they know they matter.

5.1 Chain of Excellence at Walt Disney World®

Throughout this chapter, we'll look at anecdotes that show how these six principles create a reputation for Disney World as the best customer service organization in the world. Yet, these six rules can only explain in part why Disney World is the number one vacation destination in the world. The critical and fundamental reason Disney is so successful is because of strong leadership. This is true at every level. Disney World has what is called the "Chain of Excellence." As depicted in Figure 32.1, the chain starts at the top and is reflected on the bottom line (profit). In other words, great leaders create a positive and respectful environment so front-line employees wake up in the morning with the desire to serve and take care of the Guests/customers. This maximization of profits can only occur when employees have a positive attitude instead of just working for a paycheck. When this culture and environment of the "chain of excellence" is deeply rooted, operational excellence is achieved and strong profitability follows.

Great leaders always focus on others, not on themselves. They create a vision for excellence. They hire the right people, train and develop them, trust them, respect them, listen to them, and make sure to be there for them. As a result, these leaders get committed employees who work hard and give their best because they are involved with, appreciated for, and proud of the contributions they make within the organization. This kind of culture and environment yields immediate dividends in respect, cooperation, motivation, and productivity.

6 Great Leader Strategies at Walt Disney World®

The major contribution that I made at Disney was the development of Disney Great Leader Strategies (Cockerell 2008). In 1995, it became apparent that we were not moving quickly enough to implement the strong team focused leadership philosophy that we had communicated to the 7,000 managers at Disney the year before. We had been clear that management in the future would still need to get results but would instead be measured on how they got those results. They would need to move to a management style of leading that involved Cast Members at every level in decision making and implementation of work processes. In essence, managers would have to engage all Cast Members at every level by listening to them and taking seriously their recommendations on how to manage the business more effectively.

We had been very clear about the high involvement style of leadership that was expected going forward, but we were not making much progress in getting the managers to change their management style of command and control. At this point, we decided to make the expectations and basic concepts more clear. Drawing on everything that had been learned from triumphs and mistakes from bad, good, and great leaders, I took one year to define what came to be called Disney Great Leader Strategies (DGLS). This document became a sort of "bible" for teaching and helping

Figure 32.1 The Chain of Excellence

managers at all levels to become great leaders. These strategies also served as the foundation for the curriculum at the world-renowned Disney Institute (Kinni 2011), which conducts training and development programs for hundreds of organizations and hundreds of thousands of people a year around the world. Because these strategies were taught to all Cast Members, everyone from front-line Cast Members to upper management became fully committed to one common purpose.

7 The Disney World Purpose Statement

While we all have different roles in the show we have only one purpose and that is to make sure that every Guest who comes to Disney World has the most fabulous time of their life.

This simple statement communicates purpose clearly to everyone, and it emphasizes that it takes everyone doing an excellent job in order to ensure that the Guests have a world-class experience. When enacted, bottom-line results quickly followed: the percentage of returning Guests steadily increased, scores on leadership evaluations improved dramatically each year, and employee turnover dropped to the lowest level in the hospitality industry—which was a third of the industry average.

8 Creating Disney World Magic

The Disney Great Leader Strategies formed the basis of my first book, *Creating Disney Magic . . . 10 Common Sense Leadership Strategies from A Life at Disney*. These leadership strategies do not apply just to theme parks and resorts, and they don't work only for world-class brands like Disney. They can be effective in industries across the world, including restaurants, hospitals, airlines, bowling alleys, banks in London, or call centers in Bangalore.

I have taught these ten strategies to organizations around the world and never have found anyone who does not recognize their value once implemented. These ten strategies are:

1) Remember everyone is important (respect and inclusiveness).
2) Break the mold (organizational structure).
3) Make your people your brand (hiring and promoting the right people).
4) Create magic through training (training, testing, and enforcement).
5) Eliminate hassles (policies, procedures, and operating guidelines).
6) Learn the truth (know the facts).
7) Burn the free fuel (appreciation, recognition, and encouragement).
8) Stay ahead of the pack (stay relevant).
9) Be careful what you say and do (personal behavior).
10) Develop character (be honest, be trusted).

For this chapter, I want to focus on how the practice of the principles of operations management can move an organization from good to great (Collins 2001) or even from great to greater. To begin with, let us look at Strategy 5.

9 Eliminate Hassles (Policies, Procedures, and Operating Guidelines)

Strategy 5, which centers on eliminating hassles, gives many good examples of how operations management plays a key role in performance excellence. This strategy teaches the power of having well thought-out standards, policies, procedures, and operating guidelines. Even well-trained employees in a great culture and environment can't create magic without sound processes for getting the work done correctly and consistently. Effective processes make both routine (ordinary) events as well as extraordinary unpredictable events go smoothly. This frees employees up to do extra things with their time that help turn a good organization into a great organization that delivers world-class results.

On the other hand, ineffective processes create hassles, which can lead to alienated customers, frustrated employees, and a diminished bottom line. Without defined policies, procedures, and processes, effective systems training (which is vital to creating excellence) is impossible.

One of the main managerial responsibilities is to identify process problems and act quickly in order to fix them. Great leaders don't wait for complaints: they look for ways to improve how things are accomplished every day. This outlook occurs because the thought process around "We've always done it that way" could mean you've been doing "it" wrong all along. Here are some tips that worked like a charm at Disney from Strategy 5:

- When a problem arises, look for the process failure, not for someone to blame.
- Train employees to identify processes that interfere with getting their jobs done and then ask employees what you need to fix.
- Ask customers what they like and don't like about your business processes.
- Keep your processes up to date with the latest technology and relevant research.
- Check all new processes three to six months after introduction to see if they are working properly.
- Constantly ask, "Why do we do it that way?"
- Examine how well employees understand the processes you have in place. Check to determine if employees are able to explain the processes they use. *If you can't explain them, you don't understand them.*

10 Stay Ahead of the Pack

Another strategy that has special application to this chapter is Strategy 8, which focuses on staying ahead of the pack. In today's ever-changing world, unless you keep up with the times, you can't meet the responsibilities of leadership. That means constantly expanding your frame of reference in order to find new and better ways of doing things. Here are some ways to get ahead of the pack and stay there:

- Keep up with trends in your industry and in society as a whole.
- Be familiar with the most cutting-edge services and products.
- Go on "best practice trips" to learn from companies with great reputations.
- Go to the right meetings, read the right journals, and know the right people.
- Develop methods and surveys for learning what makes your customers tick.
- Ask your employees what your organization can do better.
- Ask your customers what your organization can do better.
- Encourage team members to keep their eyes and ears open in the workplace.
- Find out from team members as much as you can about the outside world.
- Check competitors' websites frequently.
- Pay frequent visits to your competitors in order to look for new ideas.
- Experience your own products and services from the customer's point of view.

It is essential to measure how well you are doing in "staying ahead of the pack." There are various functions in hospitality that can be compared with the competition and with your own organization over time.

To begin with, you require quality standard benchmarks. For example, do marketing and sales keep occupancy high? How good are the arrival and departure experiences? How satisfactory are the transportation services? Similarly, we ask questions about parking; registration (checking in and out); luggage services; communications (phone, fax, Wi-Fi); housekeeping and custodial; laundry; landscaping; engineering services (maintenance); food production (culinary); food and beverage management (restaurants, bars, catering, room service); guest services/concierge; security; pest management; recreation; pools, spas, and retail shops; entertainment; finance/accounting; ticket/tour sales; and IT, legal, and other areas that depend on the specific operation. At Disney, another major focus of applying effective systems is for acceptable queuing since waiting times are one of the biggest complaints. Improved systems in this area provide dramatic improvement of customer satisfaction.

11   The Four Keys Model

Disney has a culture of living Strategies 5 and 8 in addition to the other eight strategies in the Disney Great Leader Strategies guide. Truly, Disney has some of the best thinkers and implementers in the world including one of the best engineering departments. This includes brilliant industrial engineers who continually find more efficient and effective ways to do everything from cleaning a bathroom to putting the maximum number of Guests through an attraction. Their focus falls on keeping the entire operation clean as a whistle yet promoting safety as the number one focus for Guests and Cast Members.

The Four Keys is a model that has been used at Disney since Disneyland opened in 1955. Disney Cast Members world-wide are trained to use this model in their decision-making process. It is a model which has stood the test of time and is relevant for any organization. The "Four Keys" are as follows:

1) Safety
2) Courtesy
3) Show
4) Efficiency

Safety is Number 1 of the Four Keys at Disney. Number 2 is courtesy. Number 3 is "show" (how the place looks and how people perform), and Number 4 is efficiency. There are measurable standards of quality for each of these attributes. Safety would allow for no defectives. Safety must be 100%. Customers trust that standard. In the same sense, there is no excuse for a lack of courtesy. Some customers will have been affected if that standard has been abused. Show should be as good as it can get. Any scrap of paper should be picked up by a Cast Member and disposed of in the trash. Efficiency is more difficult to define, but inefficiency is usually easy to spot.

12   Learn to Tell a Good Story

Storytelling is one of the best methods of communication and teaching because everyone remembers a good story. The following five story examples will illustrate how applying standards and good Production and Operations Management methods creates world-class results in both products and services.

12.1 "Be Safe, Not Sorry!—Focused Attention Creates Positive Results"

Several years ago at Disney World, we started to put even more focus on Cast Member safety than we had in the past. We had always placed the maximum focus on Guest safety, but in some ways, we had come to believe that some accidents and incidents that Cast Members were involved in were not preventable. The lessons we learned here was that we should not get used to anything and that it is never too late to get better. There is no such thing as an accident, and truly, there are reasons and causes for everything we identify as an accident. Remove the cause, and you remove the accident/incident.

Over several months, we retrained all Cast Members on how to work safely in their own roles and how to be on the lookout for any safety issues they observed so that they could report them promptly to their manager. Also included in this modified version of training were clarifications for each Cast Member on how to work safely and how discipline (including potential terminations) would take place for not working safely. Managers were reminded that the most important part of their role was to make sure their team members were working safely, and they would be held responsible for injuries in their area of responsibility if they were not enforcing safe work practices.

As the head of operations, I implemented a process where I reviewed all injuries every morning and required the manager of the injured employee to contact me to explain in detail why the injury occurred and what was being done to make sure this kind of accident did not occur again. Accident and injury frequency declined by over 50% the first year. The new leadership, training, focus, clarity, and enforcement were all reasons why this new process was so effective. Focus and attention to detail are two of the most important talents of great managers in making improvements in processes and outcomes. There is a way to structure this situation: reflection (about the past) and anticipation (about the future) are two very powerful techniques anyone can use to first do it better the next time and second to avoid something altogether in the future.

12.2 "Quality over Quantity... Quality Always Wins Out!"

For many years, we let too many Guests into the parks on very busy days. As a result, we started to see declines in Guests' intent to return scores on surveys we provided them with. With our teams of industrial engineers, our team from the Consumer Insights department, and the operating managers, we learned that there was a maximum number of Guests who could be let into a park before the overall enjoyable experience began to decline. We refined that number to the "right" level and began to limit entrance once the maximum was reached. We did this by redirecting Guests to another park until we could once again open admissions for additional Guests. This new process improved Guests' experiences at the park enormously which in turn dramatically increased their intent to return.

As Walt Disney himself said, "Quality always wins out."

12.3 "Messy and Not Clean Look the Same to Guests/Customers"

At Disney, we interview and survey hundreds of thousands of Guests each year at various opportunities. We interview them both when they check in to a resort and when it comes time for them to check out. We also interview Guests in line for attractions and when they exit an attraction. We interview them as they enter a park and as they leave a park. We even interview them buying a turkey leg or an ice cream cone. And yes, we have even interviewed some Guests when they've come out of the bathroom.

After all, the bathroom is the one place in the parks where everyone that visits Disney goes for sure. This makes the bathroom a critical area to keep super clean. We learned from surveys that some Guests were rating a given fraction of our bathrooms as "dirty." We saw this trend especially on busy days. As we got deeper into the statistics, we figured out that we had to clean certain bathrooms every fifteen minutes instead of upholding our standard at the time of every twenty-five minutes. Additionally, we learned that when a Guest said the bathroom was dirty, it was, in fact, more likely to be messy from paper towels landing on the floor because the trashcan overflowed. It turns out that "messy" was interpreted as "dirty" and that "messy" is not magical. Once again, we improved our process and so the positive ratings went back up.

12.4 "9/11 Was the Saddest and Proudest Day of My Career"

We at Disney had prepared for a 9/11-esque incident long before that fateful day came to pass. One of the best POM processes we have at Disney World is to anticipate and be prepared for any crisis and unexpected event. We began a process of conducting crisis event simulations at least twice a year. We hired a company to put us through two or three simulations a year. These simulation exercises came when we least expected them, sometimes in the middle of the day and sometimes at three in the morning. We set a standard of being able to open our Emergency Command Center within 30 minutes of being notified of a crisis and getting all of the satellite command centers open across the property in the parks and resorts and other operating areas within 45 minutes. We practiced everything from tornadoes to hurricane preparation.

By the time 9/11 arrived in 2001, we were well prepared. The first plane hit the World Trade Center at 8:45 AM. The call went out to open our command center at 9:45 AM after the third plane hit the Pentagon. At 10:15 AM, our command center was open and staffed with all of the appropriate management. We quickly decided to close down operations and had all of the parks evacuated by 11:45 AM with over 75,000 Guests safely out of the parks, either sending them on their way home or back into their resort. Additionally, we sent Cast Members who worked as characters and entertainers in the parks to the resorts to entertain the children and others. Disney's very special use of resources to calm customers and their families when under crisis conditions is well known during hurricane episodes. It epitomizes the company's concern for both customers and employees under stressful conditions. The value carries over, and there is a big lesson for practitioners in Disney's success in such events.

During 9/11, we took extraordinary care of every Guest from giving them free meals to free rooms and free phone calls. Disney had systems in place for a crisis like this for years. We issued paper tickets to every Guest leaving the parks so they could return later when we reopened. All of these systems and preparation had taken place years before. It is not a matter of "if" you will have a crisis in your family or organization. It is a matter of "when" it will happen. Anticipate and plan now and you will be ready for whatever comes your way. While 9/11 was a sad and scary day, I was very proud of the great job every Cast Member did in looking after the safety and security of every single Guest and each other.

12.5 "How to Take the Wind Out of Hurricanes"

As many readers know (especially any Floridians), we experienced four major hurricanes in Florida in 2004 with three of them visiting Central Florida and Walt Disney World® Resorts. In fact, those hurricanes visited all of the businesses in Central Florida. Disney World leadership has known that it was not a question of "would another hurricane come to Orlando but when it would come." Since that date was unknown Disney followed an important management operations principle which is to "be prepared." The last major hurricane to affect Orlando was Hurricane Donna, back in the 1960s, long before Disney World came to Orlando.

When a large amount of time passes since the last crisis, most organizations and individuals become complacent. Anticipation is an important leadership behavior. I suggest leaders, including parents, sit down from time to time and anticipate what can happen to their systems. When you think about this, it is not difficult to come to a conclusion about most of the possibilities. If you schedule a group of your fellow team members to attend an "Anticipation Meeting," you will be surprised at all the things that your team members think about that you alone would not. As Ken Blanchard says, "None of us is as smart as all of us" (Blanchard and Bowles 2000).

Over the years, we had developed and exercised a very detailed annual defensive plan. First, we cleaned up the entire property by removing objects which could fly through the air in a hurricane and cause damage or injury. We also did a practice run by opening the central Operations Command Center as well as all of the satellite command centers across the property.

We then went through a mock hurricane exercise to make sure we were completely ready. We inventoried all supplies and materials and reviewed all of our procedures so every Cast Member knew exactly what to do to prepare for a hurricane when the command was given to get ready. While the damage to Florida was in the billions, Walt Disney World®'s damage was minor and was mostly the result of downed signs and trees. No one was injured even though there were thousands of Guests and Cast Members at Disney World during the various hurricanes.

13 The Concept of POM: Find the Best Way to Do Everything and Then Do It That Way

Systems matter. Seeing the big picture and making it the best it can be, is a large part of what the practice of Production and Operations Management is all about. Our responsibility as leaders is to figure out the best way to do something, train everyone how to do it best, and then enforce that training. When you find a better way in the future, go back and train everyone on the new way. And remember, it is never too late to find the better way. Excellence and continual improvement are components of a state of mind and the main responsibility of effective leaders. Without strong systems and procedures, no organization can deliver consistency in products and services. Any organization that delivers consistency at world-class levels will thrive in all parts of their business. The organizations that ignore the principles of Production and Operations Management may not survive. I especially like a quote (attributed to Southwest Airlines) that states, "There is a best way to land an airplane so let's all do it that way." That pretty much explains the concept of efficient Production and Operations Management.

The formula for excellence in any organization includes following time tested Production and Operations Management principles in addition to hiring the right people; following a strict cycle of training, testing, and enforcing training; and last but not least, creating a culture of excellence where everybody in the organization matters and they know they matter. Do these things, and excellence will follow in employee commitment and customer retention while providing a robust bottom-line.

References and Bibliography

Blanchard, K. and Sheldon Bowles. *High Five! The Magic of Working Together.* William Morrow 2000.

Cockerell, L. *Creating Disney Magic . . . 10 Common Sense Leadership Strategies from A Life at Disney.* Crown Business 2008.

Collins, J. C. *Good to Great: Why Some Companies Make the Leap and Others Don't.* William Collins 2001.

Kinni, T. *Be Our Guest: Perfecting the Art of Customer Service.* Disney Institute Book, 2011.

Walt Disney Quotes Business Quotes Comments. Available from: www.mywaltdisneyquotes.com/business-quotes/.

33
TRENDS IN GLOBAL SOURCING, PROCUREMENT, AND DISTRIBUTION RESEARCH AND PRACTICE

Edwin Keh

1 Global Trade's Role and Influence on Historical Developments

On top floor of a commercial building on a quiet street in the heart of Hong Kong's financial district stands the Club Lusitano, a social club for people of Portuguese and Macanese descent. Portuguese settlers and their descendants have been in Macau since the 1600s. Dominating the wall as you walk into the main dining room is a map with the main trade routes of the world circa the 1400s. Look closely at the map, and you will see that in the mid-1400s, all roads lead to Portugal. This era was the golden age of trade and discovery for Portugal.

The Portuguese didn't have global commerce to themselves for very long. Over the next two centuries, the Spanish, the Dutch, and the English sailed the world in search of new products to bring back home, new markets to trade with, and new lands to colonize.

Global sourcing has been a part of our human endeavor for many centuries. Trade has long since been the source of wealth, conflict, and adventure. While making a handsome profit, the Portuguese traders brought home spices and silks for the wealthy and curious. Classical global trade dealt mostly in the "exotic" (e.g., people, spices, and fabric) for the home market, while modern global trade has more practical and critical ends such as the more mundane daily necessities of life.

Trade among nations has been going on since ancient times. From as far back as 19th–20th centuries BCE, Assyrian and Arabian traders travelled long distances to the Far East for spices and silk. This continued for several centuries into the Middle Ages during which time the Portuguese got into the trade. With the formation of the Dutch East India Company around 1699, international trade became big business. National fortunes and prestige were measured by global trade ports and routes controlled by European nations.

The English and their East India Company (EIC) eventually overtook the Dutch. The British East India Company (the Company) blurred the lines between private enterprise, trade, and sovereign rule in India and other parts of Asia. The EIC was in business from 1600 to 1873. By the time that America was initially colonized, the EIC had both tens of thousands of employees and a private army of around 67,000 strong that served to protect its trade routes and manage and control its territories and markets. The EIC was the *de facto* ruler of India, parts of East Asia, and large territories in the Middle East/Central Asia. With this wide reach and their thousands of soldiers, the EIC controlled and managed the most important trade routes from Europe to the East.

By the 1700s, European countries were experiencing a great outflow of silver due to their citizens' great demand for spices, silks, and tea from China. However, Imperial China didn't have much demand of Western goods except for gold and silver. To deal with this and undermine Chinese market dominance, the EIC created a new demand for and a market in China for its new Indian narcotic: opium. Along with the EIC, Western powers waged two separate opium wars in the 1800s in China to ensure their ability to continue their own trade dominance. This controversial period of Western-dominated trade relations persisted till the beginning of World War Two.

2 The Modern Era of Global Trade

The modern era of Global trade began at the end of World War Two as Europe and Asia were rebuilding after the end of the fighting. Logistics was one of the reasons the Allies won the war as they both out-built and out-delivered the Axis Powers. The US Army Transportation Corp was the first to use standardized pallets and corrugated steel containers to speed up the movement of materials during the war. By 1955, the standardized intermodal container unit was developed, and the first purpose-built container ship set sail from Canada. Within ten years, the standardization of container sizes and stacking methods were established. Today, port capacity, shipping cargo holding capacity, and shipping terminal handling capacity are all measured in units of "Twenty Foot-Equivalent Units" (TEUs).

With the end of the wars that took place during the first half of the 20th Century, international trade grew steadily. Commodities such as oil and metal ores, grains, and other farm produce, industrial and heavy equipment for mining, farming, and transportation were the dominant goods traded.

With the improvements in transocean shipping and jet air travel, the world became smaller and more navigable. While Asia was portrayed as a source of the rare and "exotic" in the classic trade era, the continent is now a source of more common consumer-oriented products made affordable by the disparities in wages and opportunities.

Once limited to the adventurous and wealthy, overseas travel has become more reliable, faster, and more comfortable within the past century. Ocean and air travel went from being a risky form of adventure to the means for international tourism, global trade, and commerce.

Just as more global resources and commodities were consumed mostly in the West, an increasingly large amount of consumer product manufacturing moved from the West to the East. While the transition of globally manufactured goods entering Western economies began with the relative calm that followed the end of both World Wars, the major inflection point didn't come till the normalization of America's relationship with and recognition of the People's Republic of China during the last days of 1978. One indicator of the importance of the change in trade relationship between the United States and China is the fact that prior to Richard Nixon in 1972, no American president had ever visited China. Following that momentous visit, every American president since Nixon has visited China at least once.

Between the 1960s and the 1980s, the early benefactors of the modern era of global trade were the Asian neighbors of China. Beginning with post-war Japan, trade and manufacturing steadily moved East to Southeast Asia and South Asia. The "Asian Tigers," Hong Kong, Singapore, South Korea, and Taiwan, all experienced exceptionally high growth from the 1960s to the 1990s. These small economies had neither the land nor the population to satisfy the rapid increase in demand on their factories. China, with its vast land and huge labor force, became the natural destination for manufacturing.

With the opening of Modern China, a seemingly endless labor force became available for all sorts of production at labor prices that were many times below the minimum wages required in Western economies. Within two decades, all labor-intensive production migrated first to Southeast Asia and then to China.

3 Large-Scale Migration and Contract Manufacturing

The move to producing goods overseas heralded the birth of the huge global business of contract manufacturing—also sometimes referred to as outsourced production. From the 1970s, consumer products enjoyed three decades of deflationary prices globally. Just about every single household item marketed for the consumer cost less, but these items also had improved material quality and were available in significantly greater volumes with more choices and variety. Clothing, household furniture, electronic equipment, and other things once thought of as luxuries became disposable accessories. Inevitably, these price reductions came not only as result of cheaper labor but in many cases were made possible due to the usage of less reliable and less durable materials.

Three decades of favorable trade surpluses with the West also brought significant wealth to the East. Most of Southeast Asia and China went from agrarian economies to industrialized economies. Within a generation, modern cities began to appear all along the Pacific-facing coast. Small fishing villages became port cities, dirt roads became highways, and workshops became modern manufacturing facilities.

An example of recent rapid development in China is what happened to the small fishing village of Shenzhen, a village that was right across the border from Hong Kong. In the 1970s, this small fishing village had a population of about 75,000. In 1987, when I walked across the border of Hong Kong into Shenzhen, paved roads started to disappear about five blocks north of the border. Then with the opening of China, Shenzhen became one of the new "Special Economic Zones" that engaged in export contract manufacturing. The village became a factory town that today, is a world-class business city with a population of over 20 million people. From out of nowhere, a city with the population size of Australia appeared within less than forty years. Today, downtown Shenzhen is a banking and commercial center similar to New York or London.

From the 1980s onwards, hundreds of millions of people moved from the countryside of Asia into coastal cities in search of higher paying manufacturing jobs. The largest of these people movements was the move in China from western towns to eastern coastal cities. Unnoticed and largely undocumented, these were probably the largest migration of people ever in a single generation. Along with this movement came significant social changes. Extended families became fragmented, university education became more accessible, and international travel became possible. Household incomes, especially along coastal China and SE Asia, radically improved as global commerce ushered in an era of wealth creation at a pace that was breathtaking. However, along with these changes and the arrival of wealth and education came the seeds of demise of this very system of trade. We are once again at an inflection point at end of the first decade of the century.

4 The Forces Influencing the New Global Trade—An Inflection Point

Since the turn of this century, there have been several global forces at play. These include the dwindling army of cheap labor, the impact on the environment by the intensity of decades of rapid growth, the reduction of the labor wage differential arbitrage, and the emerging patterns of global consumption.

Since 1953, the Chinese economy has been centrally managed under a series of "5-year plans." With the opening of China to trade with the West in the 1980s, these operated in parallel and sometimes in tension with global market forces. Since the turn of this century, these plans increasingly call for significant growths in minimum wages and better social and retirement benefits. This is in order both to reduce the increasing wealth gap and to stimulate domestic consumption. The resulting double-digit "year on year" wage cost increases have reduced the China wage gap with the West. Chinese wage rates also set the bar for wage increases in the rest of the global manufacturing countries.

Meanwhile, the global population growth rate has been slowing down since the "baby boomer" era of the last century. Countries like Japan are aging rapidly and have steadily lowering birth rates. The Chinese government in the 1970s had concerns about its ability to feed its citizens. As a result, the government enacted the one-child policy in 1980 when the Chinese population exceeded 1 billion. In one generation, families and population growth slowed down dramatically. While on one hand, this meant fewer mouths to feed, it has also meant that there are fewer young workers coming into the marketplace. In late 2014, with an aging population and dwindling workforce, the Chinese government relaxed the one-child policy regulations in order to allow families to have two children.

The other change is rapid urbanization. More concentrated populations in the city means better access to healthcare and education, better employment opportunities, and greater access to information.

Single urbanized children have more resources invested in them. They have higher aspirations and are more ambitious to succeed economically. As result, fewer people are willing to settle for blue-collar factory work that has little career prospects. Wealth and opportunities have also gradually moved inland. So there is now less desire to move to coastal cities, as hometowns grew more prosperous. While there are still new young workers available across Asia (notably India, Indonesia, Bangladesh, and Vietnam) and Africa (specifically Ethiopia, Kenya, Nigeria), none can match the sheer numbers that the disappearing Chinese worker has left behind.

5 Pollution and Other Costs to Consuming and Manufacturing

Rapid industrialization has both a human and an environmental price tag. Cheap coal has meant the burning of more and more fossil fuel for electricity. Manufacturing processes leave behind dirty byproducts in the form of solid waste, polluted waters, and unhealthy emissions. The rapid depletion of nonrenewable resources and the increasing negative impact of industrial activities on our international community and the global environment have meant that this mode of production and trade is not sustainable. At the current scale of production, this consumption model is harming the very consumers it is supposed to be serving, leaving many to wonder if there is an alternative model available for our usage. As our current system of global sourcing creates wealth in these developing economies, there are more and more of the population that are also becoming middle-class consumers. By some estimates, the twenty years since 1985 saw the rise of 250–300 million Chinese citizens from the lower to the middle class. A consuming population equivalent to the American one came into existence. Serving a growing Chinese and increasingly global consumer population with the current model is unsustainable both because of resource constraints and the growing scale of the negative consequences this model is producing.

The success of outsourced production has resulted in wealth creation globally. As a result, wages in the developing economies and China have experienced steady annual increases. The global wage gap is getting narrower each year.

Sourcing production globally comes with new indirect and hidden costs. These costs include much longer and often more complex logistics supply chains, trade barriers to overcome, and international management challenges. In addition, there are unexpected risks associated with many parts of the world. These risks include political disruptions, currency fluctuations, and natural disasters. At home, these are compounded by market turbulences caused by faster fashion changes and the new fickleness of a social media-influenced consumer.

In recent times, for some industries, the pull to simplify sourcing and production activities by retreating back to local production is gaining momentum.

The other side of global wealth re-distribution is the rapid rise of the global middle-class consumer, taking over from the last generation of Western middle-class consumer. Just at the point at which we see global supply chains retreat back into domestic and regional patterns, the global picture becomes even more fragmented with the increased demand for goods from the newly arrived, third world middle class. The developing world has become wealthier and consumption is rising with that wealth. There is now a reverse pull on the global trade pattern by the demands of the new international markets. Everything from cell phones, apparel, automobiles, and commodities are growing in demand everywhere in the developing world. This is especially so in the loosely grouped countries of Brazil, Russia, India, China, and the lately added South Africa ("BRICS").

Whereas it was once upon time a simple East to West Trans-Pacific supply chain, we now have a multi-directional flow of goods, overseas and overland.

6   New Consumption Models and the Complex Cycles of Global Sourcing

To add to the challenge, there are also new consumption and retailing models emerging. These include, but are not limited to such models as:

- "Omni Channel" businesses sell across multiple platforms from various e-commerce platforms, mobile platforms, apps, traditional brick & mortar stores, and combinations of all of these to create continuous accessibility for consumers to their products.
- "O2O" or "Online to Offline" usually refers to buying online and picking up the goods in a physical store. Retailers use this to drive retail traffic into the stores with the hope of making additional sales. Consumers use this to save on delivery costs.
- "Pure play e-commerce" are purchases that are only available online from retailers and brands that have no physical stores. Consumers can do their purchases from the convenience of their computers or smart devices, retailers can save on the expenses of rent, payroll, distribution, and all the costs associated with a real store presence.
- "Socially Responsible Consumption" or "Ethical Consumption" is consumption based on one's values that either rewards or punishes companies based on their behavior and action in areas dealing with the environment, social responsibility, and ethical behavior among other various causes. This layers a new filter on top of the traditional judgment of a product or company by its price, esthetic, or quality.

These are all big trends that are skewing consumption and creating new market uncertainties and sometimes, structural mismatches.

At the same time, consumption cycles, volumes, and frequency are also going through changes. Retailers and brands are used to working with seasonal calendars. Christmas gift giving comes once a year, and that remains the most important buying season. Marketing campaigns, seasonal promotional calendars, and store planograms (visual plans and schematics of how products are displayed) determined sales volumes and sell through. There were seasons to the year, and annual cycles were how goods were bought and sold.

Global sourcing and production brought with it longer and more rigid production cycles. To take advantage of overseas material and far away labor costs, the supply chain got longer and more complex. From North Asia, production swept South and East into the smaller Asian countries, India, and on into the newly opened China and before moving further on in the Middle East and Africa. Increasingly, countries such as Ethiopia, Kenya, and Nigeria are being developed as sources of production. Raw materials have to be moved from one country to the next to take advantage of local labor supply. Different parts of the manufacturing processes are subcontracted farther and farther afield. All of these activities made production cycles longer, more complex, and more difficult to orchestrate.

Consumption patterns and habits don't usually stay still for long. While the United States is still the largest consumer market in the world, it also is going through changes. In the 1970s and '80s, the US retail landscape was disrupted by the arrival of the big box stores and specialty discounters. Customers began to have more choices as smaller communities gained better retail access. With more places to shop from, and a more diverse consumer base, demand volume was more difficult to predict and manage. At the same time, fashion cycles became faster as retailers responded with more frequent discounts, private label programs, and more market segmentations. Then in the 2000s, online stores and e-commerce became more and more important as a retail channel. The concurrent global growth of social media created more rapid dissemination of trends and instantaneous demand for goods. Consumers got used to products being ubiquitous and available on demand. Existing supply chain and procurement practices found it hard to meet the variable cycles of demand and the resulting growth in consumption velocity.

The new purchasing patterns, and the new need for smaller lots of more customized goods, strained the old system of production and logistics. For half a century, trade was calculated in units of containers (TEUs). Now, demand shifts, not with the regularity of the seasons or with the predictability of promotional calendars, but fluctuates with the fickleness of informal social popularity, the spontaneous outbursts of fads, and the unpredictable popular influences from multiple media and social sources. Retailers are now finding it necessary to produce more variety, frequent updates, and agile product changes just to keep up with the new marketplace.

7 Global Sourcing

In 1989, Hong Kong was the largest container port in the world. 4.5 million TEUs went through the port that year alone. By 2009, the largest container port in the world shifted to Singapore with the country handling an estimated 25.8 million TEUs of freight. In 2009, 4.5 million TEUs would not even put you in the top 20 largest ports in the world. As we can see, global trade volumes are growing exponentially.

Global sourcing is the broad international search for, and assessment of, appropriate capacity and capability of materials suppliers, manufacturers, and service vendors to produce and supply finished goods for a marketplace.

There are several major activities that take place in the process of making a product out of an idea. These start with putting form to an idea or a design. Designers and buyers work with a sourcing function to see how they can make a product or a line of products. Sourcing teams look at design ideas and make decisions about where to take these next as sourcing starts with technical design inputs. The goal is to achieve desired product performance, improve manufacturing process, and propose appropriate materials and specs for the product. These are usually iterative processes. Negotiations, trial and error, testing, and prototyping are all part of the process to get to the best possible product.

Communication barriers are usually one of global sourcing's major challenges. The various teams that work on the same project can be separated and located in multiple countries. Face-to-face meetings are infrequent and expensive, and there are usually only narrow windows for daily real time interaction due to the differences in time zones. Common means of electronic communications like email, a flat medium, and a compromise at best, has become the chief mode of communication as a matter of cost, expedience, and convenience.

Complicating this distant linkage are multiple barriers in languages and cultures. It is not uncommon for several nationalities to be involved in the sourcing activity. Miscommunications and misunderstandings are frequent issues. This is compounded by the fact that the sourcing team, manufacturers, materials suppliers, and other participants in the supply chain are often not the end users of the product. For example, one current popular manufacturing country of down jackets and snow parkas is hot and tropical Thailand. This makes it critical to spell out in great specificity the intent of use, requirements in performance, and the functional expectations of the end user.

Sourcing usually involves some element of innovation. A new product generally incorporates some change or updates to material, process, or function. While there may be some pattern or progression in the steps of innovation, a lot of times these novel inputs can be nonlinear, stem from multiple sources, and sometimes follow surprising directions. To the observer, design and sourcing can at times seem chaotic and confusing. Since some trial and error is involved in the development process the road to market at times can be longer than planned and may involve more than its expected share of failures.

In many organizations, the early processes in sourcing and development are where enterprise-level systems have a hard time keeping up. Large computer systems often offer limited support to the less than well-defined development process.

As a result, the other challenge is the difficulty to train and scale the sourcing and development functions. The innovative process is hard to teach in a standardized curriculum and hard to organize into a standardized process. Tribal learning and lengthy apprenticeships are oftentimes the only ways that people can become proficient in the development process.

As ideas move closer to becoming a viable product, the next step in the sourcing process is usually to make a sample or a prototype of the end product. This is useful for product design input and for review of aesthetics. Multiple generations of prototypes are usually made. The appropriate materials, their suitability, and the viability of the manufacturing process are all unknowns and still under consideration at this point.

8 Procurement

Procurement is the process of acquisition of specific goods and services. This involves determining who to do business with, agreeing on a price, agreeing on the terms of the sale, and agreeing to the specifications of the goods and services involved.

The selection of whom to buy from is usually determined by a set of purchasing criteria. These criteria usually include the qualifications of the seller and the acceptability of the products they are already producing. In many product segments, reputation, and word of mouth about the manufacturer are very important.

The price of a transaction is made up of various components and is also dependent on the terms of sale. The manufacturer's price may include the raw materials, various transportation costs, the cost of various material transformation processes, the labor costs, and the various profit margins and other costs along the way.

The buyer may also choose to acquire the raw materials separately and contract the manufacturer to do the assembly and other value-added processes. In this case, the price to the buyer is the sum of the materials; labor; transportation; and other costs such as tax, duty, financing or capital costs, and insurance.

Other pricing arrangements may include more services such as warranties of performance, guarantees for profitability, and trade financing for the purchases with very long payment terms. In footwear and apparel, it is not uncommon for payment to be made 30, 60, or even 90 days or more after delivery. Long payment terms mean, in effect, that the goods are most likely sold before payment.

How and on what terms purchasing is done may be a function of many considerations. These include not only various costs but also various perceived risks; time and speed desired; and market forces such as other competition, availability, and seasonality. Artificial Christmas trees are much cheaper to buy in January than November. Other cost components along the way may be the logistics costs of the finished goods, and the overheads of storage and distributions.

The quality standards and logistics terms are agreed to as part of the procurement process. Quality includes not only product performance quality but may include some social compliance in the manufacturing process, conforming to various ethical standards, and satisfying certain environmental requirements. Some of these may be legal requirements; others may be set by the buyers. While these may not impact the consumer's use or experience with the product, nonconformity may impact the reputation of the brand. The most famous of these may have been Nike's experiences in the 1990s when it was accused of operating sweatshops overseas.

The terms of sales determine the point of ownership and its associated risks and liabilities. For fast-depreciating goods and goods with fast obsolescence like some consumer electronics, fashion items, and perishables with short shelf lives, ownership risks are of significant considerations.

With international procurement, multiple countries may be involved. These transitions then may also be subjected to currency fluctuations, changes to multi- or bi-lateral trading agreements, and adjustments to logistics costs due to seasonal demands or fuel prices.

As product specifications are finalized, manufacturing decisions have to be made. There are several possible routes this can take. If there are internal manufacturing or production capabilities, sourcing can look to them for help in producing the product. More often than not, most firms have some internal or limited capabilities, but these capabilities may stop at the sample room or engineering, with bulk manufacturing outsourced to an outside manufacturer.

If there are some internal manufacturing and sampling capabilities, usually mock-ups, prototypes, and other production samples are put together to see if these ideas work or if there are needs for modifications and changes. Changes are often made, not only for design or production reasons, but also for costing and margin improvements. Some of these changes are made purely to circumvent or reduce import duties. For example, by adding a thin layer of felt on the bottom of canvas sneakers imported to the US, the footwear's classification changes from a fabric sneaker to house slipper and import duty drops from 37.5% to just 3%.

While engineering and design skills are important in global sourcing and purchasing, more often than not the ability to overcome various communication and cultural barriers is even more important. This ensures speedy progress in the specification of the product and in negotiations on the price and terms of the contract. As the design and engineering decisions are made, if outsourcing is involved, the critical decision is where and who will do the actual manufacturing.

Outsourcing of bulk manufacturing for many owners of brands and designs is a very common practice, especially when large volumes of products are manufactured. This is especially true for products that have fast fashion cycles, that require significant marketing investments, where value is created in the design process, and where there exist skilled contract manufacturers.

Right up to the 1960s, it was still very common for most companies to have everything from design to manufacturing functions under one roof. The Ford Motor Company owned their entire supply chain for the Model T. From the forests the company used for lumber to the mines it used for iron ore, Ford owned it all. The challenge with managing all of these activities is the difficulty of balancing manufacturing capacity to seasonal demand for goods, the complex task of managing very different companies, and the high costs of owning everything. Having everything under one roof also means that significant capital investments are necessary to start a new product. New workers have to be hired and trained. New factories have to be built and outfitted.

As contract manufacturing and overseas outsourcing gained favor, companies found that by divesting themselves of these "behind the scenes" activities and focusing their attention on the customer, they are more flexible to respond to consumer demands, they can introduce new products faster, and they can deploy resources to design and market even better products.

Specialized manufacturers have the advantage of being very skilled and experienced in a single, narrow type of product or component. As products become more complex, a level of specialization is critical for efficient production costs, continuous improvements to product, and rapid speed to market. More and more brands are broadening their product offerings. This helps brand owners maximize the value of their brand. IKEA for example sells wooden furniture, but it also sells electronics, bedding, and kitchen hardware as well as foods and plants. Many brands have become a one-stop solution or a convenient destination to serve the needs of their consumers. In the process, they need the support of many specialized manufacturers and suppliers.

The industries that have adopted outsource manufacturing the fastest are consumer product companies especially where production is most labor intensive. Apparel, footwear, and toys, for example, quickly embraced this new way of getting products made. Heavier industries like the automobile and aviation industries are slowly moving to outsourcing subcomponents and subassembly.

Contract manufacturers meanwhile have become better and better in their particular niches. In their area of manufacturing expertise, they now usually know more than their customers. This can result in better products for consumers, but sometimes this can also result in risks in product quality, as there are more and more opportunities for the specialized manufacturers to reduce material quality, manipulate manufacturing processes, and violate other quality requirements shielded, not only by their greater domain knowledge, but also by the separation of great distances between where things are made and where things are sold. As manufacturers also subcontract subassembly to other specialized manufacturers and producers, global procurement can at times be an opaque process with poor visibility to quality and production risks. There are now layer upon layer of submanufacturers and suppliers, some of these may be single points of failure, or bottlenecks or other hidden disruption risks.

If the brand owner has limited product development or production capabilities, they then will have to work with an external party such as an agent, a trading company, or an Original Equipment Manufacturer (OEM) or Original Design Manufacturer (ODM). An OEM will take technical specs and manufacture the product while an ODM will do more of the engineering design work. As more and more engineering skills gravitate to manufacturers, work seems to be divided between the creative/user interface activities and the engineering/production activities. The customer-facing activities fall mostly to the brand managers and retailers. The engineering, technical design, and production are then assigned to either an external vendor or to the manufacturer.

Up till the last few decades of the last century, there was an element of discovery and adventure in sourcing and procurement. As production for the Western markets flowed overseas eastwards and southwards, there were many unknowns to what was available and possible. New frontiers were waiting to be found by brave pioneers. New manufacturers were discovered, and new countries were explored as manufacturing went farther and farther afield. A lot of these early efforts were in an era when there were significant linguistic and cultural barriers.

As marketplaces become more mature and regulated, sourcing and procurement moved to a new phase of finding efficiencies and productivity in the material (use and yield) and product production processes. As markets matured and countries developed, there are now fewer new producers to be discovered. The more consolidated supply of manufacturers means that rather than trying to find a replacement for existing producers, the opportunities lie in working with existing manufacturers to help them become better at what they do. Many companies have also created clusters of manufacturers close to their own facilities so as to reduce logistics challenges while at the same time ensuring there is visibility and availability. An example of these manufacturing clusters would be the ones Toyota and other big Japanese automobile manufacturers have maintained over the last century. As more capital investments are made, and as clusters get bigger, some supply chains become less portable and more rigid.

The interface between the outside manufacturers and the brand owner is usually a buying or procurement function. In many companies, their buying office is also where most technical functions are housed. Purchasing also manages the interface and relationships with the production vendors of the company. These relationships today could be as impersonal as arm's-length blind auctions, or they could be so integrated into the company as to be indistinguishable where one company starts and the other ends. It is not uncommon to see different companies in some supply chains share office locations, access each other's system data, or have very integrated payment and financing systems.

9 Costing

Cost determination drives decisions about where and how to manufacture. There are multiple components that make up the cost of a product. These include all the direct costs of the raw material; the labor costs to process the material; transportation costs to move raw material and finished goods; and all taxes, tariffs, and import duties. Then there are the indirect costs. These include buying and selling agents' commission, manufacturers' profits, overheads, and energy costs like water and electricity. There are costs associated with risks such as currency fluctuations, transportation uncertainties, labor costs, and other unknowns associated with manufacturing in a foreign country.

If the manufacturing is done in-house, it may be easier to arrive at a true cost of ownership. This could be as simple as adding up the key cost components. Once there is a choice from multiple outside parties, costing becomes more complicated. Material costs can be skewed by different payment terms and other financial arrangements. Labor cost varies not only by countries but also by regions within countries. Labor costs are also a function of productivity, skill levels, raw material yield in processing, and percentage of reworks as a result of defects. A cheaper labor cost can also sometimes be offset by currency or transportation costs. If it takes longer to transport and make, it will mean fewer days of availability to sell or higher risks due to earlier commitments, and higher financing costs. It is always hard to make completely fair or accurate side-by-side cost comparisons. Sometimes, how costs are calculated will also have an impact on where goods are made.

"Open Book Costing" is an agreement by buyers and sellers to make all costs visible. A cost sheet with all the components that make up the cost is constructed. This usually consists of a bill of material, labor costs, and various overheads and profits. If the cost sheet is exhaustive then this is a good way to gauge true cost. However, in practice, it is very difficult to get to an exhaustive cost sheet. The process is also very time consuming.

A lot of consumer product companies use "FOB Price" as a means of comparing price. FOB, "Freight On Board" or "Free On Board," is usually how much the product costs up to the point that the goods are delivered to the port of export. This is a useful comparison when the choices are all from a similar part of the world. This gets more complicated if the comparisons are with manufacturers from different parts of the world where there may be differences in import duties and tariffs and where the shipping costs are significantly different.

So some companies that buy internationally use the cost of LDP for comparison. LDP or "Landed Duty Paid" is the cost of goods up to domestic import port, after overseas freight and duties are all paid. While this may take out some of the price variability for comparison, it still does not account for differences in transit times, risks, and differences in quality and reliability.

Some retailers use "Gross Margin Return on Investment" (GMROI) as a way of determining value. This tries to get at the profitability of inventory held. The challenge with this method is that often only an estimate of total inventory profitability can be made at any given time.

True total costs are often not known accurately till after goods have been shipped and sold.

10 Building Relationships Rather Than Making Transactions

Many companies now make high-level, longer-term procurement commitments to individual manufacturing vendors, geographical regions, or individual countries. These procurement frameworks are usually based on longer-term considerations such as relationship management, regional risk mitigation, and the consolidation of multiple purchasing commitments for raw material. By optimizing and leveraging groups of purchases, companies hope to gain better overall terms, enhance flexibility to respond to sudden market changes, and have better control and visibility over their general outsourced production activities.

Some purchases are done as entire packages of multiple items in a related family of products. These purchases could be items made from similar materials, from similar processes, or delivered at around the same time. There may also be purchases of subcomponents of products that are then assembled or customized before sales.

There are also multiple financial terms of purchase. Some customers take title as early as the raw materials stage. At the other extreme are companies who do not take title till the point of sale to customer. The control of material, the visibility of manufacturing processes, or cash flow are usually the deciding factors.

Managing dispersed teams engaged in complex activities is oftentimes difficult. Even a low-level quality inspector in a foreign country may have significant influence and authority over huge manufacturers. As a result, there are oftentimes opportunities for corrupt practices and other conflict of interest issues to emerge. Legal systems and enforcement still vary significantly from country to country.

With closer relationships in the supply chain comes greater accountability for all parties in the supply chain. Consumers are now calling for greater transparency and visibility as to how goods are manufactured and how workers engaged in manufacturing are treated anywhere in the process. Issues include fair wages, working hours, and workers' safety. Other concerns include the use of underage workers, forced or coerced labor, and dangerous working environments. Some of these concerns have resulted in negative press for various brands and companies. These once invisible issues have become concerns for all stakeholders in the supply chain.

The impact of our global supply chain activities on the environment is also a growing concern. How heavy a carbon footprint our supply chain leaves, how much environmental damage is done, what impact the use of certain materials have on our air, rivers, and land are questions more and more consumers care about. Increasingly, consumers are aware of the interconnectedness of the world. Consumption is not only a matter of convenience, but also an opportunity to demonstrate personal sustainability values and to tangibly support causes.

11 The Challenges of Distribution

Making products available to the consumer is the process of distribution.

Moving finished products from a global supply chain so that they are available to consumers can be complicated. The physical movement of goods oftentimes is the easier part of the task. Making sure the right product is at the right place at the right time is more challenging.

Many manufacturing countries have barriers of entry for various raw materials. Most have requirements for declaration of content and composition of materials, and international movements of materials oftentimes incur various duties, tariffs, and taxes.

Exporting finished goods after manufacturing is another set of requirements that demand documentation. Destination countries, apart from duties and tariffs, may also have import restrictions, annual import quotas, testing reports, certifications, provenance, and other documentation requirements. Importers usually also incur the ultimate liabilities for the nonperformance of products in their marketplace.

A series of multi-lingual documents are often necessary for the movement of raw materials to the point of manufacturing, and manufactured goods to the points of sale. Various service providers like customs brokers and import agents oftentimes provide specialized services to navigate the complicated rules and regulations from the various national jurisdictions.

Between the manufacturer and the points of sale there may be multiple locations of storage, consolidation, deconsolidation, warehousing, and staging. These steps are to get the product properly labeled, assorted, price tagged, and shelved for presentation to the potential consumer.

Since the turn of the century, the marketplaces for most products are international and moving through multiple channels. Where goods are positioned, so that they can be accessed for sale, is more and more important. Retailers need to place products so that they are accessible, grouped so that fulfillment is cost effective, and prepositioned so that fast deliveries are possible. Tracking, tracing, and inventory management of products now require specialized systems.

Consumer product supply chains have long adopted tools and hardware to track and manage inventory. In the 1970s, supermarket retailers were the first to adopt the barcode system as a way of managing inventory. This proved to be a runaway success. Barcodes are cheap and allowed for the management of large quantities of different items. Various forms of barcodes are still in use today.

The limitations to barcodes are that they are a visual system that requires direct line of sight for scanning. The tags themselves also have a limited data storage capacity. Since the turn of the century, RFID tags of various forms have been introduced as a more effective way of tracking inventory. RFID or Radio Frequency Identification tags have the advantage of being scannable at a distance without contact. Current systems also allow for very rapid scans of warehouses or containers full of different merchandise.

Machine readable inventory systems and technologies ensure real time visibility of products, traceability to source in case of quality issues, and a degree of inventory accuracy that was difficult to achieve in the past without those tools.

12 The Opportunities Ahead

Since the 1970s, as reliance on outsourced production grew, the prices that consumers paid for most of their household products, as part of their total house income, has lessened and remained flat to negative for the last few decades of the twentieth century. Apparel for the average American household went from 14% of household spending in 1900 to 4% in 2003. Labor and cost savings changed our attitudes to items such as apparel, household furnishings, and appliances from heirloom items to disposable commodities.

Apparel fashion cycles exploded from two collections a year to collections that are continuously arriving year round at the present time. Thanks to "fast fashion," a seemingly endless supply of faster and more frequent product cycles are now more expected than demanded. Consumer product companies grow by creating more demand at home and by opening new markets aboard. Success has meant markets growing exponentially. An increasingly prosperous global economy means greater amounts of middle-class consumers all around the world. Starting in the 1980s, we have more and more time, resources, and appetite for consumption thanks to decades of relative global peace, better farming methods, highly efficient global trade, and the eradication of more and more diseases and illnesses. Supply chains now have to satisfy growing consumption globally especially in large economies like China and India. These economies now challenge the dominance of Western markets. Global supply chains will have to be even more agile and responsive to serve global customers.

In this environment, business models, enterprise systems, and management skills will all need to adapt to the new opportunities. E-commerce and multi-channel businesses will mean even faster and nimbler supply chains. Once upon a time retail distribution used to stop at the shelves of the large retail stores. A few big box discount stores, a department store, or a regional mall can serve the needs of an entire community. Now, more and more consumers no longer go to a store to shop. With e-commerce now ubiquitous on smart devices, consumers expect the store to arrive at their doorstep and at their convenience. The challenge of "the last mile" is now even fiercer as everything speeds up and the consumer globally disperses. Consumers expect more convenience, better service, greater value, and greater variety from their purchases.

Modern cities and modern lifestyles are not possible without sophisticated global supply chains working seamlessly in the background. In parts of the world today, we are already experiencing the limits of yesterday's supply chain infrastructure for today's demands. Too much planning is being done to meet demand that exists and not enough is being done to meet demand that will be. The dynamics of our contemporary life, the growing size of our cities, and the expectations of new generations of connected global consumers require even more powerful, agile, and smart supply chains to adequately service and satisfy.

Just as the Portuguese traders of the 1400s set sail to seize the opportunities of their global supply to satisfying market demands, so modern-day businesses, traders, and operators of supply chains crisscross the globe to find their fortunes. The complexity and dynamics of modern global trade also opens up opportunities to study, explore, and research for innovations, improvements, and efficiencies. Markets are changing and evolving constantly, at rates faster and even more dramatic than ever.

The world today may seem smaller than that of the 1400s. However, the opportunities today loom ever larger.

13 Effective Global Supply Chain Operations—A Product and Process Characteristics-Based Decision-Making Framework

In a rapidly changing and evolving marketplace, the ability for globalized or dispersed supply chain teams to make optimum decisions in real time is critical. In the experience of many fast-growing businesses, the inability for rapid global collaboration is oftentimes one of the key limits to growth.

Communication tools, enterprise systems, and standardized processes all equip teams for their daily work. However, strategic and operational effectiveness also involves consistently making good decisions at all levels, setting the right priorities in every process, and globally driving towards the same goals. Between the hardware and tools that allow routine work to get done and enable the values and the mission of the business, there are also "decision-making frameworks" that allow for rapid analysis of circumstances and evaluation of possible courses of action. These "decision-making frameworks" are intended to rapidly provide consistent tactics and appropriate responses across the entire supply chain so that local and individual actions and decisions complement and reinforce each other globally without the need for frequent consultation.

Decision-making frameworks are a way to analyze situations and make choices for action. An effective analytical tool and applied decision-making framework that has been introduced to multiple global supply chains is the "Product and Process Characteristics Based Decision-making Framework." This tool, explained below, is based on and inspired by Kasra Ferdow's (2008) work.

13.1 Product Characteristics

If we look at the characteristics of manufactured products, the continuum runs from basic commodities to unique more complicated products as shown in Figure 33.1. Commodity Products are usually simple common products that are manufactured rapidly and in large quantities. These tend to be inexpensive, oftentimes seen as disposable in nature, and as consumables in use.

Unique Manufactured Products are assembled and engineered and often require multiple processing systems and materials. These are usually made in small numbers and are generally more expensive or difficult to make. Some degree of complexity is involved in their design and manufacturing process. Commodity Products are akin to white t-shirts or building bricks. A Unique Manufactured Product is a product valued for its special worth such as a luxury sports car or a designer leather handbag.

The key considerations here are how ubiquitous are these products? How frequently are their consumers influenced by fashion and social changes? How affordable are they?

13.2 Manufacturing Process Characteristics

The other continuum is the manufacturing process characteristics as shown in Figure 33.2. The focus is on what it takes to get the product made. What are the requirements of the production process? How are these products manufactured? What is necessary for the process? The extremes of this continuum are characterized by manufacturing environments that are either capital intensive or labor intensive.

Capital-Intensive manufacturing processes and environments usually require costly equipment. These are often large, heavy, and/or expensive. Steel mills, computer chip factories, and automobile assembly plants are all examples of Capital-Intensive manufacturing. Another way of gauging how Capital Intensive a manufacturing process is would be to look at the way equipment is depreciated. The bigger the percentage of equipment cost in the total manufacturing cost per unit, the more "Capital Intensive" is that process.

Figure 33.1 Product Characteristics

Capital Intensive Manufacturing

Labor Intensive Manufacturing

Figure 33.2   Manufacturing Process Characteristics

Capital-Intensive manufacturing is also characterized by its relative lack of mobility. Once a Capital-Intensive manufacturing plant is set up, it is usually difficult to change what, how, and where it produces. Capital-Intensive manufacturing tends to be rigid, inflexible, and not portable. A steel mill or an automobile plant would be hard to move or retool to make another product.

Labor-Intensive manufacturing on the other hand may require many workers, a high level of craftsmanship, a great deal of manual processes, or all of the above. Labor-Intensive manufacturing processes are usually difficult to automate, have a significant amount of variability, and use materials that are delicate, soft, irregular, and generally hard to manipulate.

If machines and tools are involved in Labor-Intensive manufacturing, these usually require many human operators. They can be viewed as an extension to the operators. These machines and tools tend to be lighter, less costly, and depend on operator skills to execute. With Labor-Intensive manufacturing, the workers, and not the machines usually make the difference in the quality, quantity, and velocity of manufacturing.

It was previously noted that Labor-Intensive manufacturing tends to be "portable." Where there are sources of workers, the manufacturing can be done. Moving the enterprise to take advantage of changes in politics, economics, or demographics tend to be more commonplace.

Examples of Labor-Intensive manufactured products are things like simple apparel (t-shirts or underwear), footwear, and various bags. These industries are known to move to where wages are lower, to where taxes and tariffs are more favorable, and to where labor supply is more plentiful. Labor-Intensive manufacturing operations tend to stay in one place if specialized skills are needed or if labor costs are stable or productivity is competitive.

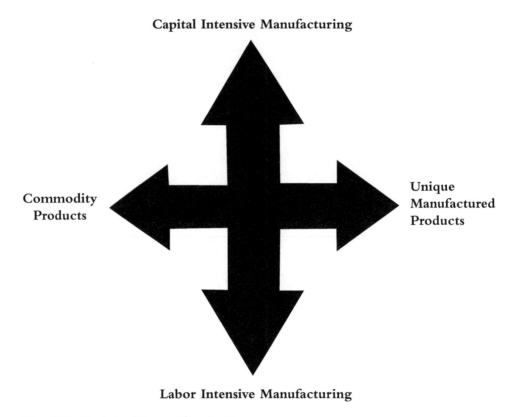

Figure 33.3   Product and Process Characteristics

If we look more at the emerging picture or framework of how the production processes and characteristics help us frame a view of our supply chain, we can begin to note some general characteristics important to all Commodity Products (versus) all Uniquely Manufactured Products, and how they differ from each other.

First observe that we can make certain statements that apply to Commodity Products and other statements that apply to Uniquely Manufactured Products (see Figure 33.4). Commodity Products, no matter how they are manufactured, are sensitive to market prices. Demand usually goes up when prices go down, and down when prices increase. Whether it's rolls of steel or packs of underwear, affordability influences the volume of consumption. Availability often is important. Since one commodity or product looks very much like the next, consumers will substitute one for the other based on price, availability, or convenience.

This is not usually true of Unique Manufactured Products where the demand and loyalty are more specific. Uniquely Manufactured Products are so scarce, differentiated, and desired that price is usually not the highest consideration. If, for example, a much-anticipated release of a new cell phone becomes available, demand for the phone will not fluctuate much if the price is 95% or 105% of the anticipated price. The key consideration for Unique Manufactured Products is the consumer demand for a specific (brand of) product. Lines forming outside retail stores in anticipation of low availability, or web sites groaning under heavy traffic on news of a new model; that's what's important. The other side of the coin for Unique Manufactured Products is that if the demand is low, price discounts are unlikely to help create much more demand.

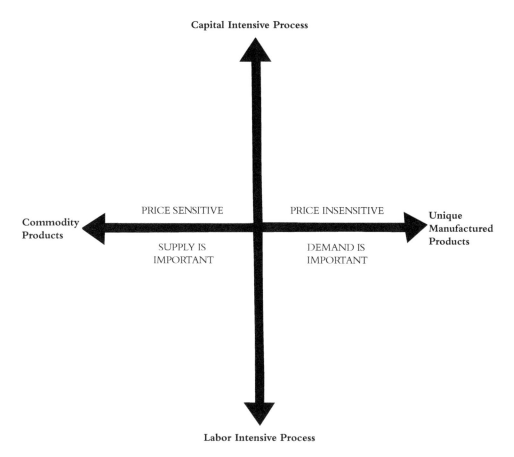

Figure 33.4 Shared Characteristics of All Commodity Products vs. the Shared Characteristics of All Uniquely Manufactured Products

The relative lack of portability of the Capital-Intensive process and the portability of the Labor-Intensive process also drives relationships in these supply chains (See Figure 33.5). To move Capital-Intensive (CI) supply chains takes time and significant expenses. So these relationships tend to be more stable, long term, and they require commitments from all parties in the supply chain to make the investments possible. CI Systems that are rigid and difficult to change are called "Sticky" supply chains.

Labor-Intensive (LI) supply chains on the other hand are usually more transactional. With their lower costs, higher volumes, or greater velocity, producers and production placements can change frequently and rapidly. Sourcing teams can move manufacturing suppliers, and manufacturing countries from season to season, or from order to order. Relationships in LI supply chains tend to be cost driven, short term, and indifferent, so there are few loyalties and frequent changes of producers. In other words, these supply chains are "Slippery" and more transactional.

If we accept that these characteristics are usually true in the different quadrants of the framework that we have just built, then we have constructed a picture of what is important in terms of our priorities, behavior, and investments based on what and how we are manufacturing (See Figure 33.6).

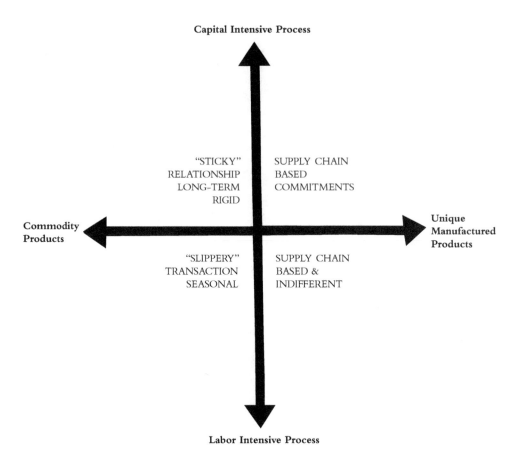

Figure 33.5 Shared Characteristics of All Capital-Intensive Processes vs. the Shared Characteristics of Labor-Intensive Processes

When we are manufacturing CI Commodities (such as steel or petroleum products), our priorities should be on process improvements. We will use new technologies and advanced operations to become the most efficient production plant in the world.

When making Capital-Intensive Uniquely Engineered products like cars or personal computers, we should work hard on managing and building manufacturing capabilities for all of our vendors in the supply chain. Car companies like Toyota, and manufacturers like Foxconn are examples of companies that have their key suppliers in very close proximity to their plants. They strive constantly to ensure their suppliers work with them to improve quality, reliability, and cost competitiveness in their products.

Labor-Intensive Uniquely Engineered product supply chain managers, on the other hand, should spend a lot of time in their (consumer) user facing activities (i.e., relationship management). They want their users to have very positive experiences; they want user interfaces to be friendly and seamless. They also should spend a lot of time on innovations for their products while developing Intellectual Property (IP) protection. An Apple iPhone, or a Louis Vuitton handbag, are examples of products of Labor-Intensive Uniquely Engineered supply chain products.

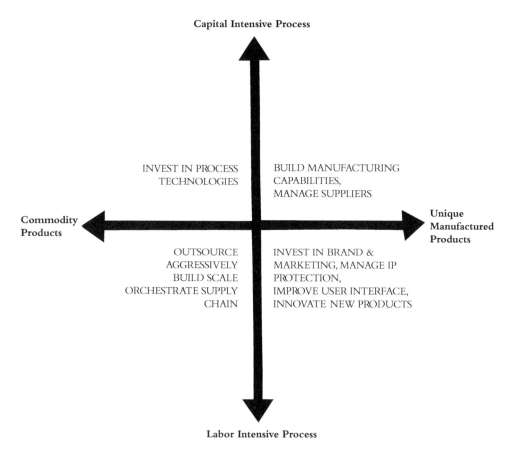

Figure 33.6 Important Priorities for the Different Types of Manufacturing Processes and Products

Finally, LI Commodity Product supply chain operators usually work hard to globally orchestrate their supply chains. They want to make the cheapest products by creating globally portable (agile) supply chains. They will buy materials at the lowest possible price, move these to the lowest cost labor markets for assembly, and then look for cost reduction opportunities in duties, taxes, and other bi-lateral trade advantages. Also, they want to build scale to take advantage of leveraged volume production efficiencies. The types of products that Walmart makes and sells would be mostly Labor-Intensive Commodity Products.

Supply chain leaders, to effectively manage their supply chain, need to begin with a clear understanding of their production processes and product characteristics. Then, they can drive priorities, investments, and behaviors to optimize their global supply chains.

The best (in-class) supply chains have managers who consistently follow this procedure of aligning product and process characteristics. Walmart aggressively outsources production and is always striving for better prices, Designer and luxury brands like LVMH fiercely protect their Intellectual Properties. BMW works diligently on its supply chain's engineering prowess. In which quadrant one sits impacts all decisions about where to make the product, whether to outsource production, and how transactions and relationships are managed.

14 Implications for Future Research

As supply chains spread out, to make and sell globally, the resulting competition may now be the best in the world. A method for evaluating the strength of existing supply chains would be valuable. In that regard, post mortems on supply chains and companies that failed in recent years, as well as a study of supply chains that are more successful than their peers, both point to shared and common reasons in most cases. Researchers could provide measurable evidence as well as helping to identify best practices for both CI and LI types of systems. It would certainly help to validate the belief that supply chain managers who understand where they "sit" and who consistently act appropriately for their product and process combinatorial characteristics tend to be most successful.

This research effort would help to validate the belief that for managers and practitioners in global supply chains it is worth their time to identify where their supply chain product and production process characteristics place them. It is likely to fine-tune the categories of CI and LI as well as demonstrating that they are changing as technology develops. For example, the impact of robots on the definition of Labor-Intensive work offers great research opportunities. Similarly, advances in flexible manufacturing systems (that lead to mass customization) will have an as yet unknown impact on what is considered normal output of Capital-Intensive manufacturing systems.

The kinds of research described above will alter the decision-making details as shown in Figures 33.1 through 33.6. With greater understanding, managers will be able to better assess whether they are spending their time and resources on the right things. They can manage their supply chain vendor relations appropriately. This vendor and supplier inclusion provides another dimension for researchers. How extensive should the examination of total supply chain involvement become? Additionally, it raises questions about how many suppliers a producer should have at any one time. With few, the emphasis on alignment can be intense. As the number of suppliers increase, the ability to "sit" in the same quadrant diminishes.

Finally, in the real world, there is another (future) complication as an increasing number of supply chains develop multiple product and production process characteristics of alternate types. Thus, one finds Basic Commodity Products being sold side-by-side with Uniquely Manufactured Products. Walk through a general retail outlet, or scroll through most web sites, and numerous instances will be found where limited edition fashion products are being offered alongside of basic year-round items. To deal with such situations, supply chain management dexterity and a deep understanding of supply chains is critical, but it must be informed by suitable research.

In concluding this section on implications for future research, it may be essential to delve far deeper into the relationship of the product and process characteristics to improve the decision-making process. We are but at the beginning of understanding some of the more interesting implications and things are changing very rapidly. Even without the technology shifts, there should be numerous opportunities to refine the model and develop more useful tools to support improved decision making and assessment tools to better understand supply chain performance.

References and Bibliography

Bell, D., G. Santiago, and A. Moreno (2014) "How to Win in an Omni Channel World," *MIT Sloan Management Review*, **56**(1): 45.

De Souza, R., M. Goh, M. Kumar, and J. Chong (2011) *Combating Supply Chain Disruptions: Lessons Learned from Japan*. Logistics Institute, Asia Pacific, www.go2uti.com/documents/10157/100902/TheLogisticsInstituteAsiaPacific-CombatingSupplyChainDisruptions-WhitePaper.pdf.

Donkin, R. A. (2003) *Between East and West: The Moluccas and the Traffic in Spices Up to the Arrival of Europeans*. Diane Publishing Company, Collingdale, PA.

Drake, M. (2012) *Global Supply Chain Management (The Supply and Operations Management Collection)*. Business Expert Press, Amazon Digital Services LLC, New York.

Fairbanks, J. K. (1965/1973). *East Asia: The Modern Transformation*. Second edition. Houghton Mifflin, Boston, MA.

Farrell, D., E. Beinhocker, U. Gersch, E. Greenberg, E. Stephenson, J. Ablett, M. Guan, and J. Devan (2006, November) *From "Made in China" to "Sold in China" The Rise of the Chinese Urban Consumer*. McKinsey Global Institute, San Francisco, CA.

Ferdows K. (2008) "Managing Evolving Global Production Networks." In R. Galavan, S. Murray, C. Markides, ed. *Strategy, Innovation, and Change*. Oxford University Press, Cambridge, MA, 149–162.

Fisher, M. and A. Raman (2010) *The New Science of Retailing: How Analytics are Transforming the Supply Chain and Improving Performance*. Harvard Business Review Press, Boston, MA.

Fisher, M., J. Hammond, W. Obermeyer, and A. Raman (1994) "Making Supply Meet Demand in an Uncertain World," *Harvard Business Review*, **72**(3): 83–92.

Golini, R. and M. Kalchschmidt (2011) "Managing Inventories in Global Sourcing Contexts: A Contingency Perspective," *International Journal of Production Economics*, **165**: 64–78.

Golini, R. and M. Kalchschmidt (2011) "Moderating the Impact of Global Sourcing on Inventories through Supply Chain Management," *International Journal of Production Economics*, **133**(1): 86–94.

Jain, N., K. Girotra, and S. Netessine (2014) "Managing Global Sourcing: Inventory Performance," *Management Science*, **60**(5): 1202–1222.

Koehler, J. (2015) *Darjeeling: The Colorful History and Precarious Fate of the World's Greatest Tea*. Bloomsbury Publishing USA, New York.

Kusaba, K., R. Moser, and A. M. Rodrigues (2011) "Low-Cost Country Sourcing Competence: A Conceptual Framework and Empirical," *Journal of Supply Chain Management*, **47**: 73–93.

Lee, H. L. (2010) "Don't Tweak Your Supply Chain—Rethink It End to End," *Harvard Business Review*, **88**(10): 1–22.

Lloyd's List Intelligence (2015) www.lloydslist.com/ll/sector/containers/article504607.ece

Lo, C.-P., S.-J. Wu, and S.-Y. Hsu (2014) "The Role of Overseas Chinese-Speaking Regions in Global Sourcing," *China Economic Review*, **30**: 133–142.

MacMillan, M. (2008) *Nixon and Mao: The Week That Changed the World*. New York: Random House Trade Paperbacks.

Shah, J. (2009) *Supply Chain Management: Text and Cases*. Pearson Education, India.

Steven, A. B., Y. Dong, and T. Corsi (2014) "Global Sourcing and Quality Recalls: An Empirical Study of Outsourcing-Supplier Concentration-Product Recalls Linkages," *Journal of Operations Management*, **35**(5): 241–253.

Van Meighem, J. A. and G. Allon (2015) *Operations Strategy: Principles and Practice*. Dynamic Ideas LLC.

34
BEST PRACTICE
Supply Chain Optimization at Yihaodian

Gang Yu and Ping (David) Yang

1 Introduction

Founded in July 2008, Yihaodian (YHD) is a leading Business to Consumer (B2C) e-commerce company in China. In this chapter, we introduce the company's supply chain strategy and its innovations on supply chain models. We focus on supplier logistics centers, pallet pooling services, aggregated supplier delivery, and cross docking logistics. Due to its advanced supply chain design, Yihaodian accomplishes eighteen inventory days-on-hand and 8% stock-outs leading the e-commerce retailers.

2 Company Overview

Yihaodian (YHD) is the first online supermarket in China. Growing at a Compound Monthly Growth Rate (CMGR) of 28% in its first four years, the company exceeded $2 billion in Gross Merchandise Volume (GMV) by the end of 2013.

YHD differentiates itself by building all of its own back-end systems. With a technology team of approximately 1,000 people, YHD has independently developed numerous supply chain management systems and technology, obtaining multiple patents and 124 software copyrights. This has become a key competitive advantage for the company. At the same time, YHD has also insisted on building its own fulfillment network.

The company currently has six distribution centers located in Shanghai, Beijing, Guangzhou, Wuhan, Chengdu, and Quanzhou that serve all areas of Mainland China. These distribution centers have a total storage space surpassing 220,000 square meters. In addition, YHD established 254 local distribution hubs within major cities in China to handle last-mile delivery. The company plans to continue adding distribution hubs in other cities to fulfill most orders with its own delivery network.

In May 2011, YHD formed a strategic partnership with Walmart and was acquired by the retail giant in July 2015. Powered by Walmart's extensive offline retail network, YHD has become the largest online supermarket in China, selling millions of products online including food and beverages, beauty products, cleaning, baby care, electronics, furniture, health and wellness, shoes, and apparel. Moreover, YHD provides various value-added services to its customers, suppliers, and logistics providers such as e-commerce, marketing, and online software; YHD is in a leading position in terms of providing data support and service applications for its customers. YHD's main competitors are Tmall and JD. According to the 2015 China Digital Power Study by Kantar Retail, a report to benchmark China's e-commerce industry, YHD (66.7%) took third place after JD (73.9%) and Tmall (71.3%) in "The Best of the Best" ranking. YHD's advantage in the online retail industry is hard to replicate given its history, support from Walmart, and unique business model.

3   Industry Landscape and YHD's Supply Chain Strategy

For retailers, regardless of what the front-end looks like, how the products are presented, whether it is online or offline, and what marketing methods are deployed, the core business of retail is to deliver a desired product to the customer at a certain time and location while ensuring its quality. This fulfillment process cannot be realized by the front-end of the business, but relies upon a well-established supply chain system. Therefore, supply chain management should be hailed as every retail business' core competency.

Tmall and Jingdong Mall (JD), the two largest B2C online retailers in China, are the best examples of this point, both having invested heavily in their respective supply chain systems. Cainiao Network, a subsidiary of Tmall, strives to build an intelligent logistics network with a registered capital of $1 billion and three rounds of financing totaling $48 billion. Cainiao focused its efforts on the integration and transfer of information across all parts of the supply chain, so the actual products and materials could be moved around less frequently to improve efficiency. Even online e-commerce platforms as large as Alibaba have not given up on building their own logistics network.

On the other hand, JD takes building its own supply chain system even more seriously. In the beginning of 2009, JD decided to form its own logistics company. Upon receiving a $150 million investment from the Tiger Global Fund in January 2010, Liu Qiangdong, JD's CEO, announced that half of the investment would be spent on building its own fulfillment network. This network included three more distribution centers in Beijing, Shanghai, and Chengdu totaling more than 100,000 square meters, fifteen to twenty secondary distribution centers, and hundreds of local distribution hubs across more than fifty cities. In March 2010, JD announced the completion of its four distribution centers covering China's Northern, Eastern, Southern, and Southwestern regions. In April 2011, JD completed a $1.5 billion C-round financing and planned to use most of the funding on the development of its supply chain and technology systems. The company announced a plan to build seven primary distribution centers in 2011, before spending an additional $1 billion on logistics in the next three years. By that time, 70% of its 2009 B-round financing of $21 million had already been invested in logistics. JD's independent supply chain system enabled the company to provide "personalized" services for its customers.

From a strategic standpoint, YHD shares the same view with its competitors in that a well-established supply chain is an important competitive advantage for any e-commerce retailer. However, YHD's case is slightly different given the nature of its core product selections—grocery and general merchandise items. On one hand, customers frequently consume and purchase these fast-moving consumer goods (FMCG). As a result, customer acquisition costs tend to be low while retention tends to be high. On the other hand, these items can be bulky, heavy, and prone to damage, while at the same time constrained by short shelf lives and limited margins. As a result, supply chain management is even more important for a retailer like YHD as any development in its supply chain system would become YHD's best entry barrier against future competitors.

In light of the above, YHD has always placed supply chain management at the forefront of its strategic focus. Inventory days-on-hand and stock-outs are usually to measure the performance of its e-commerce supply chain. For example, through continually optimizing its supply chain process, YHD reduced its inventory days-on-hand from 60 days to 18 days, as compared to 30 or more days for traditional retailers. (For comparison purposes, JD's inventory days-on-hand is about 38 days.) Stock-outs were reduced to 8% for self-run products and 3% for top-selling products. Moreover, while an average distribution order (DO) for YHD often contained more SKUs than that of a competitor (about 6 times that of JD's), YHD was still able to achieve an average warehouse picking time of only 50 seconds. (Warehouse picking time is the time from starting the first SKU to the completion of picking all the SKUs in this order.) Such achievements cannot be realized without YHD's continual investment in supply chain optimization and innovation as outlined below.

4 Supply Chain Models and YHD's Innovation

To understand supply chain management and its optimization, we must first understand the structure of a supply chain and its constituents. In general, a traditional supply chain model can be expressed as shown in Figure 34.1.

From Figure 34.1, we can see that, in order for a product to reach a customer, multiple transfers of the product are needed which will inevitably translate into costs. The depiction above is

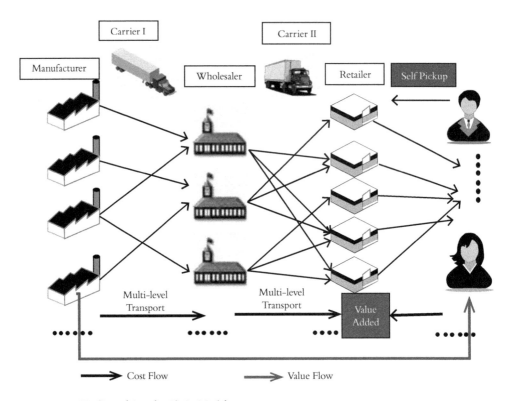

Figure 34.1 Traditional Supply Chain Model
Source: YHD.com

Best Practice: Supply Chain Optimization

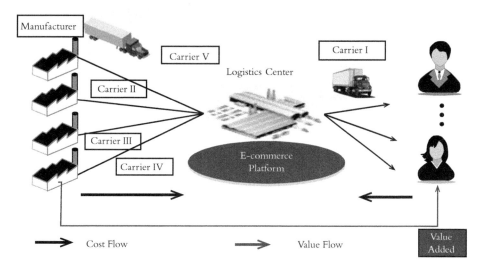

Figure 34.2 E-commerce Supply Chain Model
Source: YHD.com

actually a best-case scenario. In reality, a traditional retail supply chain often includes even more layers of transfers between manufacturers and wholesalers, as well as between wholesalers and retailers. Such processes can be very costly in terms of shipping, handling, labor, and warehouse leasing, all of which ultimately pass onto customers. Comparing the cost flow and value flow of this model, cost is easily incurred during the process of delivering a desired product to a customer, very often on non-value-added processes.

As a contrast, e-commerce promises to disrupt the traditional model by minimizing non-value-added processes while maintaining a responsive and scalable supply chain system utilizing advanced IT technologies. For example, additional storage and picking cost in the distribution center can be avoided if the cross-docking logistics are applied. The e-commerce supply chain model is shown in Figure 34.2.

In Table 34.1, we compare the cost structure of a traditional retailer's supply chain versus an e-commerce retailer's supply chain.

Needless to say, today's e-commerce retailers have not yet achieved the ideal cost structure outlined above. This is why YHD continued to optimize its supply chain and logistics system within the past few years.

4.1 Supplier Logistics Center (SLC)

With the rapid development of e-commerce and the constant expansion of online product offerings, online retailers are increasingly under pressure to expand their warehousing capacity. YHD already operates multiple warehouses reaching almost 400,000 square meters. Simply adding more space to deal with the increased demand and SKUs is by no means practical. SLC is one way to deal with YHD's limited space by aggregating supplier inventory into a third-party operated logistics center located near a YHD fulfillment center. Currently this logistics center is exclusive for YHD. The SLC model is shown in Figure 24.3.

Table 34.1 Cost Structure Comparison between Traditional Retailer Supply Chain and E-Commerce Retailer Supply Chain

Cost	Traditional Retailers	E-commerce Retailers	Explanation
Multiple inventory	High	Low	A traditional supply chain contains multiple layers with each layer holding its own inventory; e-commerce replaces this with one large, centralized distribution center.
Multiple transportation cost	High	Slightly lower	In a traditional model, transportation cost is high due to multiple transfers and the lack of an economy-of-scale; e-commerce solves this problem with a centralized distribution center.
Multiple inventory management	High	Slightly lower	Inventory management cost is saved in the e-commerce model mostly due to the reduction of labor.
Channel handling cost	High	Slightly lower	Handling cost at each channel is reduced in the e-commerce model due to the simplification of the supply chain process.
Store rent	High	Extremely low	E-commerce uses virtual storefronts and reduces overall and marginal cost significantly.
Store staff	High	Slightly lower	In general, e-commerce platforms have a cost advantage.
Last mile	Extremely low	Slightly higher	Traditional retailers essentially transferred last mile delivery costs to customers; e-commerce retailers need to deliver the products, and costs can be particularly high where the fulfillment network is not well established.

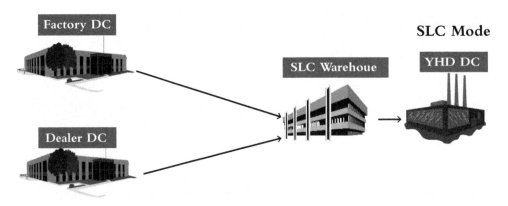

Figure 34.3   SLC Model
Source: YHD.com

SLC essentially aggregates suppliers to a location near a YHD fulfillment center. There are several benefits to this aggregation. The first benefit is an increased turnover due to lower safety stock levels at YHD's own fulfillment center. SLC shortened the distance between suppliers and YHD, thereby shortening the distance between suppliers and end customers. As a result, YHD can carry less inventory and set lower safety stock levels, resulting in improved turnover and days-on-hand. YHD reduced SLC inventory days-on-hand from 18 days to 9 days.

The second benefit is the economy of scale and increased efficiency from letting the SLC operator handle front-end supplier logistics. The SLC not only shares inventory risk with YHD such as high inventory level or stock-out but also saves YHD from having to deal with multiple suppliers. YHD is able to simplify its front-end logistics without sacrificing product variety.

Next is the benefit of rapid response and a lower risk of stock-outs. Another advantage that comes with bringing suppliers closer to its end customers is rapid response. In order to attract customers, online retailers often offer promotions that are sometimes in response to a competitor move and can be quite unpredictable; this may result in either frequent stock-outs or unreasonably high safety stock levels. SLC facilitates communication between suppliers and YHD and enhances YHD's rapid response capability given its proximity to a YHD fulfillment center.

The impact of an SLC is quite noticeable. Compared to a supplier lead-time of ~6 days, SLC can deliver to a YHD fulfillment center within 6 hours. Moreover, YHD's days-on-hand is merely 18 days, while goods tend to stay at the SLC for about 9 days. All of these contribute to improved cash flow for YHD.

It is worth noting that the SLC model does not entail a complete transfer of supplier inventory; a supplier only keeps a portion of its inventory at the SLC where it is closer to the customer. The SLC provides operational and storage services at a reasonable cost, while in the process eliminating various non-value-added services for the supplier. Non-value-added services can be found in the second paragraph in Section 4.2.

On the back-end, YHD created a customized version of its Warehouse Management System (WMS) for the SLC's third party operator. This WMS is also connected to YHD's internal PMS (Purchase Management System) and WMS (Warehouse Management System), allowing for constant information sharing and rapid response.

4.2 Pallet Pooling Service

YHD partners with pallet suppliers and upstream product suppliers so that goods are delivered to YHD's fulfillment center already placed on top of standardized pallets. Instead of unloading each cotton box individually from the delivery truck, pallet pooling allows the entire pallet of boxes to be unloaded and then moved around in the warehouse. Once the pallet is unloaded, another standardized pallet will be returned to the supplier and carried back to the supplier's warehouse. Inbound quality assurance will be conducted inside the warehouse after receiving the products. In case of damages and quality issues, a guaranteed remedy will be made.

The cost of unloading and moving the products is a type of channel handling cost as mentioned in Table 34.1; such processes are deemed non-value-added and can be extremely costly. Pallet pooling effectively solves this problem. In general, product transfers between different channels (e.g., suppliers and YHD) generate the following costs: unloading, checking, testing, warehousing, and transferring. These costs have a linear relationship with the number of operation units. If the operation unit is a box, then the costs linearly increase with the number of boxes. If the operation unit is a pallet, then the costs linearly increase with the number of pallets.

Therefore, by reducing the operation unit from multiple boxes to a single pallet, YHD's pallet pooling services can reduce channel handling costs significantly. Moreover, since pallets can be

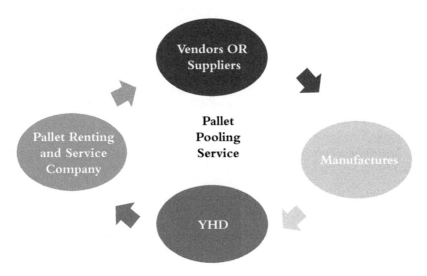

Figure 34.4 Pallet Pooling Service
Source: YHD.com

moved around with machines, labor costs associated with the process are also reduced. Not surprisingly, this innovation has increased efficiency for YHD by 90% and reduced product damage by 50%. YHD's pallet pooling service is demonstrated in Figure 34.4.

YHD's pallet pooling service benefits suppliers in several different ways:

- First, the pallet-pooling service dramatically reduced loading time and provided a more flexible delivery schedule. For a 12.5-meter (41-foot) van, loading time can be reduced from 3–4 hours to merely 20–30 minutes with pallet pooling, increasing efficiency by more than 90%. With the loading docks no longer under pressure, a supplier can choose from more available time slots and enjoy more flexible scheduling.
- Next, it prioritized "Green Channel" for suppliers using pallet pooling. On the loading docks, YHD grants priority to suppliers that have signed up for pallet pooling, accelerating turnover of the vehicles.
- Third, there is a reduced labor cost for suppliers given the use of equipment for transporting pallets. YHD provides the equipment for suppliers to unload and move the pallets, reducing the labor needed; a supplier can also hire temporary workers at YHD's fulfillment center. All of these reduce handling costs for a supplier.
- Finally, they benefit from better preservation of goods and less damage incurred in the unloading and moving process. Pallet pooling and the associated mechanized operations allows for better protection of the products and less damage and loss. For example, product damage for a liquor business was reduced from 2% to below 1% after pallet pooling. Pallet pooling creates real value for a supplier in addition to improving efficiency.

In addition, YHD also benefited from this service due to higher utilization of its loading docks and lower labor costs. For YHD, setting up the pallet pooling service and getting its suppliers onboard was no easy task. Major issues include standardization of the pallets, recycling, quality control, cost allocation, and maintenance. In order to solve these problems, YHD decided to partner with a third-party pallet provider that will be responsible for operating, recycling, and maintaining the pallets. All pallets belong to the company, and YHD leases the needed pallets from this company and returns any unused pallets at the nearest recycling station. The cost is allocated according to the occupied time of different partners. With pallet pooling among the manufacturer, logistics provider, and YHD, the total number of pallets needed in aggregate has been reduced, and each party is spared from having to manage its own pallets.

Moreover, YHD used various incentives such as the "Green Channel" mentioned earlier to encourage suppliers to sign up. Participating suppliers include P&G, Unilever, Nestle, Suntory, Coca-Cola, Kimberly-Clark, Kao, and Pepsi. YHD's own experience dictates that for pallet pooling within a 150 kilometers radius, savings can reach as high as 15%–20% of the total logistics cost.

4.3 Aggregated Supplier Delivery

Aggregated supplier delivery is another one of YHD's programs that relate to front-end logistics integration. For suppliers with smaller scale and less frequent deliveries, pallet pooling may not be as desirable or practical. YHD aggregates these suppliers' orders and recommends a logistics provider to collect each individual order and deliver them together to YHD's fulfillment centers. This is particularly valuable for suppliers that are smaller in scale and do not have delivery capabilities. Figure 34.5 demonstrates the difference between a traditional delivery model and YHD's innovative solution.

Specifically, aggregated delivery adds the most value for two types of suppliers. First, we look at suppliers that used to deliver to YHD directly yet had limited scale. Suppliers of this type tend to be small, and direct delivery can be very costly without the benefit of scale. With the aggregated delivery program, a third-party logistics provider will pick up the products from the supplier and deliver them to YHD. This saves the supplier from having to invest in its own delivery network, effectively reducing its fixed cost. Moreover, the supplier no longer has to deal with the hassles of scheduling and queuing, as well as any potential issues that may come up during delivery.

Second are the suppliers that used to deliver products to YHD via transshipment. These suppliers are typically of even smaller scale, and used to deliver their products to an LTL (Less-Than-Truckload) freight company who will then deliver to YHD. Conceptually, the LTL freight company is similar to the logistics provider chosen by YHD in the aggregated delivery model. However, the LTL freight company cannot achieve economy of scale with YHD since it is delivering to multiple destinations. Also, different LTL freight companies may have different service

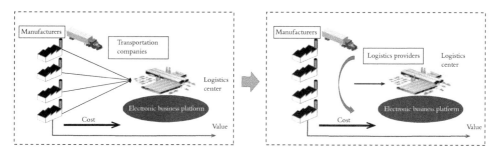

Figure 34.5 The Shift from the Traditional Delivery Model to YHD's Aggregated Delivery Model
Source: YHD.com

capabilities and delivery standards, making it hard for YHD to monitor performance. These issues often result in problems such as delays and product damage, incurring additional costs for YHD.

With the implementation of the aggregated delivery program, YHD has achieved the following things:

- It has achieved reduced communication friction between YHD and suppliers. Suppliers and logistics providers used to make appointments with YHD via email, sometimes resulting in miscommunication or delayed responses. In lieu of emailing back and forth, YHD built a supplier portal (SP) where logistics providers and suppliers can schedule appointments with YHD through a shared online system free of charge. After as many as thirty rounds of modifications to further optimize this system, the SP currently does not require any human intervention and allows for real-time information sharing between suppliers/logistics providers and YHD.
- Next, the company has achieved real time feedback on the status of a purchase order. Historically, suppliers and YHD do not have the capability to track the fulfillment status of a purchase order. YHD made such a large number of purchase orders on a daily basis that it would be impossible for anyone to track the progress of each individual order. On the SP platform, such information can be updated in real time without any human intervention. This allows employees and managers to monitor all orders simultaneously and make timely decisions.
- Third, the company has achieved a more efficient appointment system. Before the implementation of this program, suppliers made appointments offline, and the delivery schedule was controlled manually; suppliers did not know how to use YHD's Supplier Portal, and YHD did not have enough information on the amount of cargo delivered unless this was communicated in the email. This often resulted in logistics providers making inappropriate delivery reservations. Nowadays, with such information readily available on the SP, YHD is more informed of the amount of cargo and other logistical details beforehand, and is in a better position to evaluate whether or not a logistics provider's reservation is reasonable. For example, after checking the SP, YHD may suggest the logistics provider to reserve the loading dock for more or less than half a day.
- Fourth, the company attained economy of scale by aggregating supplier orders (as mentioned above).

4.4 Cross-Docking Logistics (CDL)

CDL is a well-known logistics strategy invented by Walmart to increase supply chain efficiency from the 1980s. The idea is to use fulfillment centers not for storage but as a connection point between manufacturers and retailers/customers. YHD is the first e-commerce company in China to use this technique:

> In essence, CDL entails products 'passing through' the fulfillment center without being stored or picked. The products are unloaded from incoming trucks and directly entered into the CDL system; on the outbound docks, the products are sent to pallets and delivery trucks via a conveyer belt with little or no storage in between.
>
> (Boysen and Fliedner 2010)

It is generally believed that in a CDL supply chain system, fulfillment centers act as coordination points instead of storage points. In a typical CDL system, the goods are sent from the manufacturer to the fulfillment center and then transferred to outbound trucks to be shipped to retailers as soon as possible. The goods typically spend very little time in the fulfillment center, usually not more than twelve hours. The model adopted by YHD is often referred to as terminal cross-docking logistics, whereby products received from suppliers are not stored but are instead sent to its designated destination. Terminal CDL categorizes and merges orders according to the departing trucks and requires orders from two or more vendors be sent to the designated destination at the same time. As a result, order arrival time as well as the designated locations must be well coordinated.

Generally speaking, YHD uses Shanghai and Guangzhou as coordination centers and designates Wuhan, Quanzhou, and Chengdu as terminal destinations. The benefit of CDL is relatively straightforward for YHD: goods received from suppliers are not stored but directly sent to outbound areas or onto outgoing trucks. YHD's CDL may take various forms depending on the fulfillment center's operating environment.

PMS is YHD's internal IT system that handles CDL. Each team takes an order from PMS and completes the order as commanded. Assuming Wuhan is the terminal destination, we will explain how YHD's IT system supports CDL. First, YHD's procurement staff sends out a purchase order that may be fulfilled by multiple suppliers. Then, PMS chooses a supplier considering factors such as cost and supplier lead times. PMS also needs to determine whether or not to use CDL for this order based on YHD's delivery lead times and the availability of trucks. For example, for a core product such as imported milk, CDL may take too long and the system may choose direct delivery instead. Once PMS has chosen to use CDL for a particular order, this order will be labeled accordingly with the same information updated in WMS. The WMS' staff will be able to see the CDL nature of this order (receipt only, no storage), and TMS staff will receive an order to prepare for delivery. Finally, TMS can issue in-transit information and update this in PMS for YHD's procurement staff to monitor and intervene if needed.

It is clear that YHD's use of CDL relies heavily upon its internally developed IT system. Without such a system, CDL may cause excessive inventory or frequent stock-outs. YHD's current model maximized the benefits of centralized procurement while at the same time reduced the cost of directly delivering from the Shanghai fulfillment center.

5 Performance Improvements

After the implementation of the aforementioned supply chain innovations such as SLC, pallet pooling, aggregated delivery, and CDL, YHD has achieved significant performance improvements:

- Improved inventory turnover and decreased days-on-hand from 48 days to 18 days; goods stay at the SLC for only 9 days, improving YHD's overall cash flows
- Reduced stock-outs from 16% to 8%; stock-outs for top-selling products also reduced from 9% to 3%
- Reduced lead time; SLC lead time is only 6 hours versus 6 days for a supplier
- Improved loading efficiency; for a 12.5-meter van, loading time is reduced from 3–4 hours to 20–30 minutes, representing a 90%+ increase in efficiency
- Lower loading and picking costs saved through cross docking.

6 Future Development

Although significant value has been generated through supply chain optimization, there is still tremendous room for improvement. YHD is working on the following areas.

6.1 Collaborative Planning, Forecast, and Replenishment (CPFR)

CPFR requires a retailer to make forecasts and plans along with its various partners (e.g., suppliers), so that cost savings may be achieved through more accurate forecasting and faster replenishment. YHD collaborates with its suppliers to establish sales targets and procurement plans, and attempts to reach a middle ground when demand predictions differ. For online retailers, frequent promotions further distort the demand curve (Figure 34.6) and requires YHD to build an even more efficient collaboration channel with its suppliers, to offer more predictable promotions and update suppliers in real time when exceptions occur. Furthermore, YHD built the Supplier Portal for information sharing with suppliers online. Up to date, more than 5,000 suppliers have joined the platform.

With the rapid geographic expansion of YHD's business, multi-level inventory is creating new challenges for the company. YHD's target is to fulfill 80% of orders with local fulfillment centers. The rest of their orders will be fulfilled by larger fulfillment centers in Shanghai, Guangzhou, and Beijing. However, due to demand fluctuations, a large portion of the orders are currently being split into multiple distribution orders. Moreover, many suppliers do not have the capability to ship nationally. All of the above increased operational costs for YHD. Therefore, YHD will continue to collaborate with suppliers to solve these supply chain challenges. Currently, YHD is considering integrating its procurement function with that of Walmart's.

6.2 Data-Driven Supply Chain Management

With the invention of the "November 11" and "December 12" promotional days in China (similar to "Black Friday" in the US), unexpectedly high demand spikes created significant supply chain pressures for online retailers. YHD strives to provide the best customer experience despite such uncertainties in the online retailing industry.

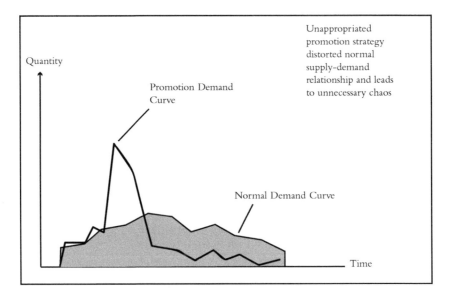

Figure 34.6 The Demand Curve

Source: YHD.com

Best Practice: Supply Chain Optimization

YHD currently has more than 400,000 square meters of fulfillment center space with 3 million SKUs and 70 million users. In addition to its scale, YHD's integrated supply chain also involves many processes such as procurement, stocking, delivery, and returns that are all interconnected. The scale and complexity of the system represents significant challenges for a supply chain manager.

First, the massive amounts of highly complex data may cause managers to lose focus. A manager may have access to numerous reports on the quality and efficiency of each supply chain process and business unit, such as warehouse shipping-out efficiency reports and warehouse order split rate reports. The more data there is, the harder it is for a manager to stay focused and uncover the most important issues.

Second, due to the size and complexity of a supply chain system, managers may only see a small part of a bigger picture. In order to make a decision, multiple data points must be viewed together. For example, efficiency data must be viewed together with the incurred cost, and it must be viewed in comparison with similar data from a competitor.

Third, data may be difficult to analyze due to the lack of comparison. For example, a 10% split rate of orders is actually reasonable among all the warehouses, but the same number between two warehouse is not acceptable according to the historical data. Without historical data or other information to validate, managers may not be able to make well-informed decisions.

Data-driven supply chain management is YHD's solution to the aforementioned problems. YHD has built its own big data platform to 1) aggregate, combine, and present the data in a graphical manner for managers to make quick decisions, 2) mine data and identify correlations between data points to inform managers of connections between various aspects of the supply chain process, 3) monitor each step of the supply chain process in real time, and 4) formulate supply chain strategies based on a holistic view of the entire system (Figure 34.7).

YHD's success is largely related to the optimization of its supply chain system. Supply chain optimization is especially important to YHD whose products are bulky, heavy, and prone to damage, yet constrained by short shelf lives and limited margins. Just like a traditional retailer, the

Visualization of the efficiency

- Compliance efficiency analysis
- Bottleneck analysis for warehouse

Supply chain surveillance room

- Cost/quality/efficiency synthesis display
- Dashboard for warehouse manager
- Dashboard for purchase manager
- Dashboard for delivery manager

Historic data mining

- Supply chain key performance
- Configuration for warehouse operation (tasks, staff, etc.)

Synthesis evaluation system

- Auto-PO effect evaluation system
- Sale forecast effect evaluation

Figure 34.7 The Plan for the Data Analysis Platform

Source: YHD.com

essence of e-commerce remains to be the delivery of the right products to the right customers at the right place and the right time, and supply chain management is a critical component of this process. YHD's practice to continually optimize its supply chain has proven its great value, and such value cannot be achieved without leadership vision, constant innovation, and a desire for relentless improvement.

References and Bibliography

Boysen, N. and M. Fliedner (2010) "Cross Dock Scheduling: Classification, Literature Review and Research Agenda," *Omega*, **38**: 413–422.

Gupta, S., C. Koulamas and G. J. Kyparisis (2009) "E-Business: A Review of Research Published in *Production and Operations Management* (1992–2008)," *Production and Operations Management*, **18**(6): 604–620.

PART VIII

POM—The Next Era

35
THE EVOLUTIONARY TRENDS OF POM RESEARCH IN MANUFACTURING

Tinglong Dai and Sridhar Tayur

1 Introduction: Creating Wealth and Happiness, Massively

What are we talking about when we speak of "manufacturing"? The U.S. Census Bureau defines the manufacturing sector as the collection of "establishments engaged in the mechanical, physical, or chemical transformation of materials, substances, or components into new products," which does not seem satisfying to readers who wonder, "What exactly is the *purpose* of manufacturing?"

Manufacturing has created wealth and happiness in a massive way and has been responsible for achieving a global improvement in the quality of human life. In his "Report on Manufactures" (1791, p. 240), Alexander Hamilton wrote that:

> Not only the wealth; but the independence and security of a Country, appear to be materially connected with the prosperity of manufactures. Every nation, with a view to those great objects, ought to endeavour to possess within itself all the essentials of national supply. These comprise the means of subsistence, habitation, clothing, and defence.

The simultaneously complementary and substitutive relationship between manufacturing, technology, labor, and capital complicates the situation. The manufacturing sector contributed just 11% of the value added to U.S. GDP in 2012, a significant decline from 25% in 1970. The decline in the importance of the manufacturing sector is global: it contributed to 16% of the value added to the world's GDP in 2012, down from 27% in 1970.

However, we should not underrate the importance of manufacturing to the economy and society for at least two reasons. First, the manufacturing sector has been a traditional source of abundant middle-class jobs. In the case of the United States, the sector is credited with providing steady income to millions of households, allowing them to afford decent living standards, support children's education, and, collectively, form the largest consumer market in the world, which is crucial to the continued prosperity of the manufacturing sector. Second, the manufacturing sector sustains and regenerates itself through technological advances: shaped by technology, manufacturing drives technological innovations through, among other means, investing in research and development activities. Combining both aspects, we see a virtuous cycle in which technology drives the refinement and expansion of the manufacturing sector, which creates jobs, enables better lives for many, and propels more innovative technology.

Will this virtuous cycle sustain? At this crossroad of history, we do not have the answer, but the past offers some definitive signs of hope. Edmund Phelps, in the book *Mass Flourishing: How Grassroots Innovation Created Jobs, Challenge, and Change* (2013, p. 1), concludes, "Over most of human existence, the actors in a society's economy seldom did anything that expanded what may be called their economic knowledge—knowledge of how to produce and what to produce." Figure 35.1 shows a population-weighted economic and human history of the past two thousand years. It provides visual evidence of the dramatic effect of the flourishing of manufacturing: prior to the Industrial Revolution, the wealth created or the number of years that people lived remained stable for centuries. The world began to change dramatically at a rapid pace only after the inception of manufacturing in the 18th century.

In this chapter, we seek to provide a targeted view of the manufacturing sector—with a focus on massively produced consumable goods such as chemicals, consumer packaged goods (CPGs), automobiles, industrial machinery/components, pharmaceuticals, medical devices—and the sector's relationship with POM, which inevitably involves discussing technology. Indeed, the influence of POM over manufacturing is largely through its mastery and command of technology. We are interested in examining the way that manufacturing creates massive wealth and happiness, and are therefore mindful of whether the development of manufacturing improves or impairs social welfare.

In the rest of the chapter, we will move on to discussing the role of technological innovation in manufacturing, distribution, and logistics, as well as how POM orchestrates technologies in improving and transforming the manufacturing sector. We then outline practical problems in operations management (PPOMs) in the manufacturing sector, which allows us to trace POM in the evolution of the manufacturing sector. Lastly, we weigh the labor-versus-capital tension and close with thoughts on the impact of POM on society and global trade, as well as on relevant research opportunities for young scholars.

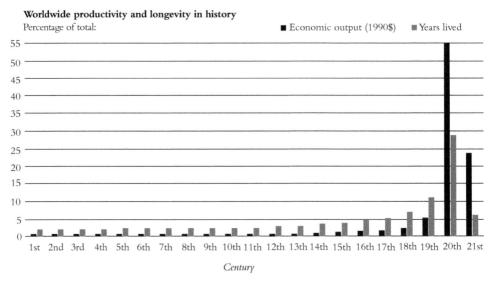

Figure 35.1 Worldwide Productivity and Longevity in History. The *y*-axis Shows the Percentage That Each Century's Population-Weighted History Accounts for the Entire Human History.

Source: Adapted from Economist (2011)

2 Modern Manufacturing: An Orchestration of Technologies

The word "manufacture," coined in the 1560s from Latin *manu* (hand), originally referred to handcrafted products. By this definition, many notions associated with modern manufacturing do not apply: specialization is rare, collaboration is seldom required, knowledge sharing is almost non-existent, and economy of scale is lacking. In fact, diseconomy of scale may be the norm in the case of handcrafted production, because excessive unorganized manual labor often leads to fatigue and boredom.

The past four and a half centuries have witnessed the "ecological extinction or near extinction" of handcrafted production in the manufacturing sector (Fraser 2015). Most saliently, this is due to technological advances that include the invention of steam engines, availability of long-distance mass-transportation tools, electrification of industries and households, invention of the computer, not to mention the development of telecommunication, Internet, and mobile devices in recent years. What is not as salient in the pathway leading to modern manufacturing, however, is the changes in the *operations*.

An early identification of such changes is in *Capital, Volume I* (Marx 1912, p. 371), which involves two aspects: increased scale of labor ("the union of various independent handicrafts, which become stripped of their independence and specialized to such an extent as to be reduced to mere supplementary partial processes in the production of one particular commodity") and specialization of and isolation among job functions ("An artificer, who performs one after another the various fractional operations in the production of a finished article, must at one time change his place, at another his tools. These gaps close up so soon as he is tied to one and the same operation all day long").

We have witnessed the historical and inevitable shift from handcrafted production to an automated, massive production that has become the principal way that our society creates products crucial to its citizens' wealth and happiness. Yet our materialistic abundance, in certain cases, may lead to "excess and a lack of taste, a trend exemplified by living in custom built, faux French mansions, and driving Hummers, civilian version of a military assault vehicle" (Smil 2013, p. 2). The ongoing "maker movement" (Morozov 2014), a response to the banal aspect of modern manufacturing that may feel ironic to historians, emphasizes handcrafted and individualistic products. Will the word "manufacturing" ever return to its original root? We do not know the answer, but one thing we are certain of is that the renaissance of individual, handcrafted production—if materialized—will be empowered by technology (specifically, additive technologies such as 3D printing).

But what *is* technology? In *The Nature of Technology*, Arthur (2009, p. 53) characterizes the essence of technology as "a programming of phenomena for a purpose . . . an orchestration of phenomena to our use." Arthur continues, saying that "more than anything else technology creates our world. It creates our wealth, our economy, our very way of being." In other words, the purpose of manufacturing is no different from the function of technology and is achieved essentially through an orchestration of technologies.

Consider how technologies such as the steam engine, electric power transmission, computers and programming languages, the Internet, the iPhone, wearable devices, and 3D printers shaped the manufacturing sector. Technology, when orchestrated for the purpose of manufacturing, permanently transforms the latter and then dictates the evolution of trade flows and work patterns. But what tool does a manufacturing manager have in orchestrating technology?

3 What Is Orchestrating Technology?

Technological revolutions do not simply change the way people make products. They also call for, and inevitably are followed by, changes in the way that physical, financial, information, and human resources are organized and managed. Such changes need an orchestrator, that is, operational innovations (hereafter, Production and Operations Management as represented by POM). Even the least attentive historian would be cognizant of the fact that, with every tide of technology innovations, *operational* innovations emerge. Examples include, Newton's seminal industrial engineering initiatives, Frederick Taylor's scientific management (albeit questioned by historians, e.g., Lepore 2009), Ford's invention of the assembly line system, Toyota Production Systems, the invention of operations research, W. Edwards Deming's quality control movement, the emergence of supply chain management, and the contemporary Enterprise Inventory Optimization software.

But what is "operation"? The *Random House Dictionary* defines "operation" as the "power to act." This definition precisely captures the relationship between operational innovation and technology innovation: POM provides the *power* necessary for technology to transform manufacturing to meet the needs of end consumers. What gives modern capitalism its dynamism that separates it from the early mercantile capitalism? The answer, according to Phelps (2013), is strikingly simple: ideas. The field of knowledge known as POM provides and *is made up of*, ideas for organizing manufacturing activities. POM is full of ideas for creating and updating a firm's business model to act on ever-shifting risk curves (Girotra and Netessine 2014).

POM's tendency to *act* has shaped the trajectory of the evolution of its theory and practice: for most of its history, the practice of POM has been far ahead of its theoretical foundations and academic formulations. Consider, for example, the *kanban* practice that the Japanese manufacturing sector started experimenting with in 1947, two years before the founding of the Graduate School of Industrial Administration (GSIA) of the Carnegie Institute of Technology, a major birthplace of systematic, quantitative approaches to addressing real business problems, a.k.a., management science (Khurana 2010). The practice did not begin to draw worldwide attention and mimicry until the 1980s. Only at that time did rigorous, theoretic studies—including Deleersnyder et al. (1989); Mitra and Mitrani (1990); Tayur (1992; 1993); Veatch and Wein (1994)—start flourishing in major POM theory outlets.

POM textbooks contain a great deal of information about operational innovations before the 1990s. Knowledge or consensus regarding what has happened since that time, however, has been scant. Paul Krugman (2015) attributes "the big productivity gains of the period from 1995 to 2005" to "things like inventory control." The same period marks the inception and development of the enterprise of inventory optimization *software*. Therefore, a significant portion of the rest of the chapter will be devoted to the practical impacts of inventory control, among other problems related to product portfolio choice, planning for flexibility and responsiveness, production planning, and logistics of manufacturing companies.

4 Operational Innovations and PPOMs

We now discuss a number of fundamental PPOMs, as listed in Table 35.1, which are motivated by operational innovations and verifiably address manufacturing executives' concerns. These problems may be issues inside the factory, outside the factory, or at interfaces between the inside and outside of the factory.

We wish to emphasize that the eight PPOMs identified herein are by no means exhaustive of the whole range of problems that POM encounters in its role as it influences and transforms the manufacturing sector. Rather, these eight PPOMs represent part of the best efforts made by the POM community to understand the complex and fascinating operational details in the manufacturing sector and to implement some of the most intellectually exciting and practically applicable ideas. Other important areas where PPOMs exist, such as quality control and standardization,

Table 35.1 Practical Problems in Operations Management (PPOMs)

Category	Application Areas	Selected POM Contributions
Inside the factory	PPOM-1: Production and inventory control	Simon (1952), Wagner and Whitin (1958), Stecke (1983), Roundy (1985), Bowman and Muckstadt (1993), Glasserman and Tayur (1995), Jordan and Graves (1995), Anupindi and Tayur (1998), Kapuściński and Tayur (1998), Markowitz et al. (2000), Levi et al. (2006)
	PPOM-2: Employment planning	Holt et al. (1955), Schild (1959), Hanssmann and Hess (1960), Buffa (1972)
	PPOM-3: Management of *kanban*-controlled systems	Deleersnyder et al. (1989), Mitra and Mitrani (1990), Tayur (1992, 1993), Veatch and Wein (1994)
Outside the factory	PPOM-4: Network design and flexibility	Lee and Billington (1993), Huchzermeier and Cohen (1996), Rao et al. (2000), Graves and Willems (2000, 2005)
	PPOM-5: Inventory placement and logistics with non-stationary demand	Bradley and Arntzen (1999), Chen and Song (2001), Graves and Willems (2008), Tardif et al. (2010)
Interface between the inside and the outside of the factory	PPOM-6: Inventory management with service-level requirements	Gerchak et al. (1988), Glasserman and Tayur (1995), Ettl et al. (2000), Troyer et al. (2005), Keene et al. (2006)
	PPOM-7: Product design	Lee (1996), Lee and Tang (1997), Swaminathan and Tayur (1998), Yunes et al. (2007), Dai et al. (2016)
	PPOM-8: Lead-time quotation	Duenyas and Hopp (1995), Anupindi and Tayur (1998), Tayur (2000), Keskinocak et al. (2001), Plambeck (2004), Kapuściński and Tayur (2007)

are not covered here, but will be detailed in other chapters of the volume. Likewise, due to space limits, we are not able to cover the following topics: (1) sustainability-related issues, such as remanufacturing, reverse logistics, and carbon footprint; (2) ethical and political issues, such as counterfeiting, child labor, conflict minerals, and supply-base issues; and (3) planned obsolescence and the associated innovations leading to shorter shelf life and fast fashion alterations. In addition, we do not consider largely strategic-level considerations such as (1) capacity options, (2) quantity discounts, and (3) contracting and incentive design. Lastly, because we have a contemporary, managerial focus, we refrain from referring to the earliest production and inventory models (e.g., Harris 1915) in discussing the PPOMs.

4.1 POM Inside the Factory

Massive production, empowered by the uses of standardized components (invented in the late 19th century) and moving assembly lines (invented in the early 20th century), introduced formidable managerial challenges that did not exist during the preceding centuries dominated by handcrafted production. Any plant manager in a modern manufacturing firm naturally faces three basic and practical problems: (1) when and at what rate to produce and store inventory; (2) how to hire, fire, and deploy workers; and (3) how to coordinate various production stages.

These practical problems correspond to three areas of POM applications, namely, PPOM-1 (production and inventory control), PPOM-2 (employment planning), and PPOM-3 (management of *kanban*-controlled systems). In fact, Warren Buffett, arguably the foremost capitalist of our time, may be said to be a master of addressing these PPOMs (at least the first two), according to his biographer Alice Schroeder (2008, pp. 213–216). In early 1962, Buffett acquired the rights of control of Dempster Mill Manufacturing Company based in Beatrice, Nebraska. Buffett coached Lee Dimon, a former purchasing manager who accumulated such an excessive amount of windmill-parts inventory that "the company's bank prepared to seize the inventory as security for its loan, then grew alarmed enough to make noises about shutting Dempster down." Buffett and his partners "swept through the place like a swarm of boll weevils and slashed inventory, sold off equipment, closed five branches, raised prices for repair parts, and shut down unprofitable product lines. They laid off a hundred people." The results were impressive: by year-end 1962, Dempster became profitable, and "the bank was happy."

Undoubtedly, PPOM-1 dominated much of POM theory from the 1950s the until the 2000s, not only for its apparent relevance to practice, but also for its irresistible intellectual appeal. Nobel winners Kenneth Arrow and Herbert Simon were among the founding fathers of the production and inventory theory and established what is well known as the base-stock policy that much of today's production and inventory control practice still uses today. Interestingly, until the early 1990s, almost four decades after the birth of the production and inventory theory, a practically efficient method to compute the optimal base-stock level for industry-level problems still did not exist. The necessity drove another level of academic excitement, represented by the application of infinitesimal perturbation analysis (IPA) to design efficient recursive methods that allow industry-scale applications (Glasserman and Tayur 1995).

A major concept in addressing PPOM-1 is flexibility—the ability of a factory or production line to manufacture multiple products, which allows maximum utilization of limited production capacity. The corresponding POM practice, namely, flexible manufacturing systems (FMSs), started in the late 1970s. A few years later, Stecke (1983) identified five production-planning problems, including (1) part-type selection problems, (2) machine-grouping problems, (3) production-ratio problems, (4) resource-allocation problems, and (5) loading problems. To show POM was actually helpful in guiding the then-brand-new practice of FMSs, Stecke (1983) applied her algorithms to a production facility at the Caterpillar Tractor Company in Illinois.

Jordan and Graves (1995) examine the flexibility of making products at different plants or lines from a different angle: "How much process flexibility is needed?" More specifically, "Can the benefits of total flexibility be achieved with something less than total flexibility?" Their approach, even by today's standards, was radically refreshing. Jordan and Graves (1995, p. 578) wrote that:

> We have not developed an optimization model. . . . Complex models have their place, especially for guiding specific decisions. However, simple models—if focused on the right questions—can often reveal new principles that can greatly improve management decision-making.

In their own writing, Anupindi and Tayur (1998) expressed the same view, writing that, "A crucial aspect of our approach is that we insist on a systematic way of managing the critical stage: a cyclic schedule. . . . We recognize that our production strategy may not be optimal. However, it is simple and can be implemented easily on the shop floor." Conceptually relevant to this flexibility is the so-called stochastic economic lot scheduling problem (SELSP), which arises when a single machine can make multiple types of products (i.e., satisfy multiple types of demand) but has to make one type at a time. The demand for each type of product arrives in a random fashion, and each switch of product type incurs a setup time.

The SELSP problem is among the most technically challenging topics in PPOM-1. The exact optimal solution to SELSP is intractable due to its large state space. Nevertheless, POM researchers have studied it using various creative approaches. For example, Bowman and Muckstadt (1993) used a Markov chain approach and considered a finite number of schedules. A more practical cyclic scheduling strategy, however, involves a fixed production sequence. Anupindi and Tayur (1998) focused on the case of a fixed production sequence and derived the cyclic schedule under which the switch to each product was only triggered by its own inventory level. Markowitz et al. (2000) developed a heavy-traffic approximation to obtain the optimal fixed production sequence in which the switching decision depends on the inventory levels of all the products.

Although fears of a jobless future in which automated robots rather than humans operate manufacturing have long existed (Ford 2015), manufacturing simply cannot function without some level of human involvement. PPOM-2 (employment planning) addresses the issue of hiring workers and scheduling them according to the needs of production. One fundamental difference separating this decision from production and inventory control is that human beings, unlike machines, are inherently flawed and need to rest at a certain point in time. Frederick Taylor (1914) was not the first to understand and formalize human limits, but he was certainly the first to attempt to systematically address them. Taylor contends that workers need to overcome the tendency to work below their capacity ("soldiering") to become "first-class men." Irrespective of whether Taylor indeed "fudged his data, lied to his clients, and inflated the record of his success" (Lepore 2009, p. 114), his stopwatch system brought him global fame. It led to what may have possibly been the only U.S. legislation effort to endorse and publicize POM theory and made him and his theory an indispensable part of business education. All these accolades, unfortunately, did little to help change capitalism's reputation of cruelty and heartlessness.

Consider a factory facing seasonable demand and that would thus have fluctuating inventory and capacity utilization throughout a year. Assuming a fixed workforce size, PPOM-1 helps optimize the production and inventory decisions. PPOM-2, on the other hand, addresses the issue of employment planning in one of two ways: first, make hiring and firing decisions dynamically. According to *laissez-faire* capitalism, the factory can hire and fire workers flexibly depending on the needs of production over time: hire more to meet increased demand and lay off workers to meet decreased demand. Yet, in the real world, hiring, and particularly firing, can be very costly, time-consuming, and distressing. Thus, sophisticated planning is in order. Second, maintain a largely fixed workforce size but absorb demand fluctuations with overtime work and possibly part-time workers. Holt et al. (1955, p. 5) contend, "Order fluctuations should, in general, be absorbed partly by inventory, partly by overtime, and partly by hiring and layoffs, and the best allocation among these parts will depend upon the costs in each particular factory."

Jointly, PPOM-1 and PPOM-2 aid in a factory's production, inventory, and employment management. A sizable factory often consists of multiple production stages (cells), and coordination between these stages can be a major challenge; failure to coordinate leads to frequent blocking and starving at various stages, requiring (sometimes excessive) inventory buffering.

Assuming some uncertainty in the production process, achieving "just-in-time" production in a literal sense is impossible. Is there a practical way to partially achieve it? The *kanban* approach, developed in 1947 in Japan by Taiichi Ohno in the Toyota Motor Corporation, provides an answer (Monden 2011). A *kanban* is simply a card, and each production unit has a fixed number of *kanbans*. The circulation of *kanbans* provides an informative signal regarding each unit's inventory status; each machine will remain idle, even with all the necessary parts, until the next machine is ready to receive the next batch of parts. A *kanban* provides a revolutionary "pull" alternative to the more traditional "push" manufacturing system, in that it insists customer demands drive production, and each cell's production is driven by the downstream cell's requirements. The "pull" approach minimizes human-made interruptions and delays and enables a smooth production process in which materials flow through the entire sequence smoothly following customer orders.

The *kanban* system has been highly successful and has found numerous applications in manufacturing firms worldwide. Tayur (2000) tells of four employees of an Ohio laminate plant who approached him in the summer of 1992 to help them implement a *kanban* system in their plant. When he asked them why they wanted a *kanban* system, they answered simply and firmly, "It will make us profitable again." In a separate episode, Steve Jobs, in 1986, insisted on following the *kanban* system in designing the product line for the NeXT computers. According to Isaacson (2011, p. 225):

> [Jobs] insisted on building his own fully automated and futuristic factory, just as he had for the Macintosh. . . . Empty circuit boards were fed in at one end and twenty minutes later, untouched by humans, came out the other end as completed boards. The process followed the Japanese principle known as *kanban*, in which each machine performs its task only when the next machine is ready to receive another part.

The transition from "push" to "pull" not only challenges traditional managerial thinking, but also defies the classical queuing network models, in which each stage of a tandem queue is often triggered by its preceding stage. The classical sample path techniques become unreasonably cumbersome, and a new technique is needed. Tayur (1992, p. 298) joyously announced that, "Fortunately, such a technique has recently become available."

4.2 POM Outside the Factory

A factory never exists for its own purpose. Adam Smith recognizes this fact in *The Wealth of Nations* (1776, chapter V), writing, "If [an item] was produced spontaneously, it would be of no value in exchange, and could add nothing to the wealth of the society." Although large-scale production was made possible by the invention of automated assembly lines, its existence was driven by modern freight transportation networks. These networks overcame geographic disconnections between different markets and generated sizable factory orders, making large-scale production a necessity.

PPOM-4 (network design and flexibility) aims to address the following question: what are the best locations for suppliers, production sites, assembly lines, and distribution centers to satisfy customer demand? In other words, what is the best configuration of a firm's supply chain network? The solution to PPOM-4 often requires a network way of thinking.

Lee and Billington (1993, p. 835) study the problem of managing material flows at the Hewlett-Packard Company (HP). They recognize that inventories stored at different locations have different cost structures and abilities to meet customer orders. Hence, HP needs to control inventories "along the chain while maximizing customer service performance." A more treacherous challenge, however, is the decentralization in decision making, because many firms "have intentionally decentralized operational control of their business units or function," which makes information flows "restricted or costly so that complete centralized control of material flows may not be feasible."

Among POM researchers' efforts to facilitate the implementation of centralized model outputs in decentralized, multi-agent settings, Tayur (2013, p. 6851) coined the term "management mechanics," a comprehensive modeling method building on "staged optimization":

> A modeling framework and solution proposal should allow for partial changes in the decisions in a sub-network holding the rest somewhat constant, and then, increase the range and scope of decisions being changed. What is needed is a comprehensive model that allows for what I call "staged optimization" deliberately restricting some variables to be within a certain range for the time being. That is, a controlled release in concert with the organization's capacity to absorb change, in rhythm with their existing processes and compatible with their IT systems.

Another vexing operational challenge outside the factory is the logistics network planning under *non-stationary* demand (a.k.a. seasonal demand) (PPOM-5). Bradley and Arntzen (1999) report "severe end-of-quarter demand spikes" at an electronic firm, and refer to the demand pattern as "the hockey-stick pattern." Similar to PPOM-2 (employment planning), an obvious tradeoff exists between capacity expansion and inventory buffering. Interestingly, regarding the actual decision-making mechanisms at the firm, different entities manage these two levers. To be able to influence the firm's capacity decision making, Bradley and Arntzen (1999) wrote, "It was crucial that our analysis convinces managers responsible for capacity decisions that the implications of our model regarding capacity investment were appropriate."

One approach to handling non-stationary demand is to model the demand process as a Markov-modulated Poisson demand process and find optimal safety stock levels at various inventory nodes (e.g., Chen and Song 2001). Graves and Willems (2008), on the other hand, develop a discrete-time model with several key assumptions and show that a constant-service-time policy is near optimal and "has obvious implementation advantages." Tardif et al. (2010, p. 5) solve PPOM-5 by redesigning Deere & Company's outbound distribution network to better serve its extensive distribution network consisting of 2,500 independent dealers. To keep the logistics costs low and maintain service requirements for Deere's highly seasonable products, the company deployed different tactics during the peak and off-peak selling and shipping seasons. While recognizing the value of formally treating the "trade-offs between transportation, warehousing, and inventory replenishment decision."

4.3 Interface Between the Inside and the Outside of the Factory

The activities inside and outside the factory are inherently connected and interact. Therefore, when making operational decisions, a modern manufacturing manager should not pretend those decisions are isolated. PPOM-6 (inventory management with service-level requirements) significantly extends the scope of PPOM-1 (production and inventory control) in that it deviates from the hidden critical assumption that the demand is outside the firm's control. Instead, PPOM-6 aims to directly incorporate and influence product availability through improving the production, inventory, and distribution decisions.

An industry-scale implementation at Caterpillar (Keene et al. 2006), which has a complex product line and faces competition in a global marketplace, aims to increase the firm's product availability. This goal entails answering the following questions:

(1) What product availability is possible and at what cost and inventory levels?
(2) What inventory reduction is possible?
(3) What mix and deployment of inventory will enable BCPD (the Building Construction Products Division) to improve and stabilize product availability while minimizing total chain inventory?
(4) Does BCPD have the data and systems it needs to optimize inventory and meet its product availability objectives?

The outcome of the project demonstrates the power of POM in manufacturing: the standard deviation of product availability was halved, whereas the mean lead times shrank by 20%.

Among the POM researchers and practitioners' efforts in bridging the inside of the factory with the outside, PPOM-7 (product design) reflects a radical way of thinking: the lever here is not simply inventory, capacity, or network configuration. Rather, it aims to fundamentally change the design of the product in order to serve customers better at lower costs. As with several PPOMs mentioned previously, this problem emerges only because today's factories face a multitude of demands from aspiring customers. Lee (1996, p. 151) states that "product proliferation creates a major operational challenge to managers of a manufacturing enterprise. It's difficult to forecast demands accurately, leading to high inventory investment and poor customer service."

Specifically, what is the best way to avoid inventory wastage due to product proliferation? The answers may involve PPOM-4, PPOM-5, and PPOM-6, as well as changing the manufacturing process itself. Lee and Tang (1997) formalize the concept of delayed differentiation according to which managers would not commit work-in-process (inside the factory) to a particular custom option until a later point, so that the firm can gain better demand information (from outside the factory). The so-called "vanilla boxes" (i.e., an assembly process using semi-finished products) idea, emerging out of IBM's product-development practice and studied by Swaminathan and Tayur (1998), proposes planning inventories in advance to react to market demand responsively, while maintaining an array of customer options.

Lastly, PPOM-8 (lead-time quotation, i.e., providing customers with quotes of lead times for make-to-order operations, also called "due-date setting") is relevant to the Internet age in which customers desire more product choices shipped at a faster pace. This requirement would naturally influence what is happening inside the factory. Keskinocak et al. (2001, p. 266) consider a factory making orders of customized tools for steel mini-mills to produce specialty steel. Because little uncertainty exists in the actual production process for each family of products, the authors argue,

> [T]he key challenge in managing this business is thus not in manufacturing, but rather in the interface between manufacturing and customer service representatives (CSRs), the functional group that accepts orders and guarantees lead times to the customers who demand customized rolls and whose order process is not easily predictable.

This consideration needs to be directly factored into the factory's objective function because the revenues decrease the quoted lead-time.

In general, the manufacturer can quote multiple lead times for differentially patient customers. Plambeck (2004) observes that among BMW customers, those in Germany can often wait for one or two months, whereas those in the United States and Europe are reluctant to wait for more than one week. Thus, the factory's problem goes beyond production scheduling and entails capacity and pricing decisions.

5 Capital Versus Labor

Consider the following encounter between PPOM-2 and PPOM-3 (Isaacson 2011, p. 184) that is centered on the "Cuba-admiring wife of France's socialist president François Mitterrand" Danielle's visit to the Apple factory, accompanied by Steve Jobs:

> [Mitterrand] asked a lot of questions, through her translator, about the working conditions, while Jobs . . . kept trying to explain the advanced robotics and technology. After Jobs talked about the just-in-time production schedules, she asked about overtime pay. He was annoyed, so he described how automation helped him keep down labor costs, a subject he knew would not delight her. "Is it hard work?" she asked. "How much vacation time do they get?" Jobs couldn't contain himself. "If she's so interested in their welfare," he said to her translator, "tell her she can come work here any time."

It is fair to say the tension between labor and capital has *always* been a focal point of the manufacturing sector over its course of evolution. Inherently, according to Karl Marx (1973, p. 325),

> Capital and labour relate to each other here like money and commodity; the former is the general form of wealth, the other only the substance destined for immediate consumption. Capital's ceaseless striving towards the general form of wealth drives labour beyond the limits of its natural paltriness.

Industrial capitalism—as opposed to *merchant capitalism* from the 1550s to 1800s: "someone with wealth might become a merchant, investing in wagons or boats to transport goods to places where prices were higher" (Phelps 2013, p. 2)—started around the early 18th century, and reached its peak in the late 19th century. Mark Twain coined the term "the gilded age" to refer to the period around 1870–1900 that featured an unprecedented level of wealth in a society that was driven largely by *"Beautiful credit! The foundation of modern society."*

Ironically, almost two centuries later, the fact that we are now living in "the second gilded age" is striking (Fraser 2015). The increasing level of economic inequality—more low- and high-income individuals in the population but fewer in the middle-income range—is disconcerting. Why does inequality matter to the future of manufacturing? The prosperity of manufacturing creates a solid base of middle-class consumers who, in return, drive the demand for more and better products. This virtuous loop that has powered the manufacturing sector for more than a century will lose its magic without a sufficiently large proportion of the workforce having solid earning powers.

As we previously discussed in PPOM-2, managing a workforce has traditionally involved no more than hiring, firing, and deploying. In the past decades, robotics has significantly enhanced automation and reduced the need for blue-collar workers. Another technology significantly influencing today's labor practice is real-time productivity monitoring, the technology underlying which is enormously attractive for its newness, as stated by David Cozzens, the CEO of Telogis, a company specializing in providing telematics to commercial trucking fleets (Kaplan 2015). Cozzens acclaimed, "It was big data. It was the Internet of things. It was cloud computing; it was mobile; it was really a new market, with low penetration" (pp. 23–28).

Firms are leveraging real-time productivity-monitoring tools to track their employees' performance on an hourly or more frequent basis, which, ironically, has driven the emergence of a new oxymoron—permanent part-time jobs.

The so-called "sharing economy," epitomized by Uber, has also led to dramatic changes in the form of labor, which may be phrased as "uber-ized" workers. Although this solution seems novel, it does not come with benefits such as health insurance or social security that are crucial in maintaining a middle-class lifestyle. In addition, much of the sharing economy reduces demand for durable products, which in itself is not good news for the manufacturing sector. The technology and operational innovations may look fancy, but Fraser (2015, p. 326) wrote, "How odd this fancy seems. Our new system of flexible global capitalism, including the American branch, is increasingly a sweatshop economy."

Before making any attempt to address economic inequality, we need to weigh the following question: will the ever-increasing economic inequality jeopardize the future of manufacturing? Economists and political philosophers agree that excessive economic inequality is simply a symptom, and directly tackling the symptom may backfire (Allen 2015). Increased economic inequality is often either transitory or even beneficial to society. On one hand, Simon Kuznets (1955) famously proposed an inverted-U curve outlining the relationship between productivity and economic inequality: increased income per capita in a society initially leads to higher economic inequality; once the income hits a threshold, the opposite is true. John Rawls (2009), on the other hand, contends that management practices widening economic inequality are moral if they benefit (or do not harm) the least advantaged group in absolute terms. These insights may guide the POM community as we reckon social-welfare implications of various technological and operational developments in the manufacturing sector.

6 Implications for Managers

Undoubtedly, managers have always been eager learners of well-known POM practices—as we have illustrated in the cases of Steve Jobs' just-in-time experiments at Apple and Warren Buffett's inventory-management efforts at Dempster. Yet, managers often undervalue POM theory for at least two reasons. One, as mentioned previously, the theoretic development of POM often trails POM practice. Therefore, a significant proportion of POM studies, although truthfully reflective of POM practice, do not contain sufficiently refreshing "new news."

The good news is that the academic field of POM, by observing and improving practice while also keeping a healthy distance, can attract some of the most intelligent minds. "The price to be paid for keeping good scientists," as Simon (1976, p. 347) points out, is that "a certain part of their activity will simply result in good science, not particularly relevant to the specific concerns of business." In our view, the price is perfectly reasonable and provides managers with the advantage of a never-ending stream of first-class researchers who, from time to time, make important breakthroughs (e.g., stochastic inventory models and computational techniques) influencing worldwide practice.

For instance, the rise of private equity (PE) funds has made the role of POM more visible, because POM can be effectively utilized to orchestrate technologies to improve a manufacturing firm's profitability and thus return on assets. In an interview (Camm and Tayur 2010, p. 449), Tayur provides an example of a capital-driven, POM-empowered bailout effort of a dying factory:

> One particular company was an amazing experience in which we repurposed a foundry that was making parts for the automotive industry . . . into making parts for wind energy. Our investment of $3 million in 2002 returned over $34 million in 2008.

Nearly half of this return can be tied to OM projects—which improved capacity flexibility, reduced scrap, and institutionalized lean practices—and strong inventory-control techniques.

The future of manufacturing will crucially depend on practitioners' and researchers' co-creation of POM theory and practice: a rigorous academic discipline attracts the best and brightest minds to advance the theory, while the close collaboration between practitioners and researchers ensures the manufacturing sector continues to shape and enrich the discipline, which, in return, helps manufacturing regenerate itself and flourish.

7 Conclusion: The Future of POM and Manufacturing

A manufacturing revolution is underway due to major technological advances. In this section, we outline several new patterns in the future of manufacturing and their implications on POM research.

First, additive manufacturing technologies (e.g., 3D printing) and direct-to-consumer distribution through the Internet will change the work patterns of manufacturing organizations, such as medical-equipment manufacturers (Rifkin 2014). These technologies may fundamentally change the global landscape of the manufacturing sector. For example, 3D printing will mean a reduced need for outsourcing small, complex specialty products to suppliers in developing countries, which provides dual advantages in that (1) the manufacturer can function with *zero* finished-product inventory and (2) the manufacturer can produce close to where demand exists. For POM researchers, this paradigm-shift calls for not only a new set of quantitative modeling tools but also empirical studies identifying effective managerial practices.

Additive manufacturing technologies, due to their unprecedented and ever-increasing affordability, will also empower the maker movement, a.k.a. the "third industrial revolution," that promotes "good taste and self-fulfillment through the creation and the appreciation of beautiful objects" (Morozov 2014, p. 69). To use Maslow's theory of a hierarchy of needs, this movement will facilitate a transition from producing abundant generic products satisfying customers' basic needs (physiological and safety) to empowering "prosumers" (as opposed to customers) who create and manufacture, driven by their own needs for belongingness/love, esteem, self-actualization, and self-transcendence. The purpose is not to substitute higher-level needs with industry products but rather to complement, enrich, and elevate an individual's pursuit of such needs. Can POM go beyond firms' profit maximization and help individuals reach their personal goals? In addition to journal and conference publications, can POM researchers publicize their intellectual findings in more tangible and accessible ways, such as mobile applications and software from which consumers can readily benefit?

Second, the Internet of Things (IoT), the formation of an interconnected computer network of machines and locations through wide availability of affordable sensors, will be a major shaper of the future of manufacturing. Thanks to the popularity of smartphones, wearable devices (e.g., Apple Watch, Google Glasses, activity trackers), and RFID, IoT has been available even in some of the least materialistically rich countries. IoT makes the world of manufacturing more tractable and transparent, and has potential applications to manufacturing operations such as quality control. IoT also provides the *ubiquitous computing* capability that may alter the workings of the enterprise inventory optimization system. POM researchers may start revisiting some of the commonly made assumptions, especially those regarding information-sharing mechanisms between firms: are the traditionally accepted principal-agent theory, and more broadly, informational economics models (e.g., Plambeck and Zenios 2003; Dai and Jerath 2013, 2016a, 2016b), applicable to new realities?

Third, an increasingly robotized manufacturing sector kills traditional blue-collar jobs that previously had to be performed by human beings, but creates middle-class jobs that never existed before. With skyrocketing labor costs in China and the continued lack of sophisticated infrastructure in much of the underdeveloped world necessary for global manufacturing, the trend will become global. Today, major manufacturing firms in China's Pearl River Delta Region, which makes the majority of the world's apparel, electronic, and high-tech products, have switched to fully or partially automated facilities. This will contribute to widespread structural unemployment over many parts of the world, at least for the foreseeable future. Does POM have a role in shaping a better future for manufacturing by helping to provide abundant and well-paid manufacturing jobs? Extensive studies allude to conditional positive answers in the retail sector, and some of the ideas may be applicable to manufacturing (Zeynep 2014). POM researchers can participate in the public discourse on speeding up automation in manufacturing by helping to craft operational strategies that make structural unemployment, as the society transitions to a more knowledge-intensive economy, less painful.

Fourth, after being leapfrogged by emerging economies in various technological and operational frontiers, the United States and Europe are set to become the "new emerging economy" (Zweig 2013), with better infrastructure, rule of law, and globally competitive human costs, leading to the booming of backshoring. This transition is largely driven by technological innovations and will drive the need for operational innovations, in both theory and practice.

Today's economy, to quote Arthur (2009, p. 209), "is becoming generative. Its focus is shifting from optimizing fixed operations into creating new combinations, new configurable offerings." POM should continue to play the role of orchestrating technologies in building a better future for manufacturing. We echo the sentiments of Ovid at the end of this chapter, "Let others praise ancient times; I am glad I was born in these."

References and Bibliography

Allen, D. (2015) "Equality and American Democracy." *Foreign Affairs* (December 14): 23–28.
Anupindi, R., and S. Tayur (1998) "Managing Stochastic Multiproduct Systems: Model, Measures, and Analysis." *Operations Research* **46**(3): S98–S111.
Arthur, W. B. (2009) *The Nature of Technology: What It Is and How It Evolves.* Simon and Schuster, New York.
Bowman, R. A., and J. A. Muckstadt (1993) "Stochastic Analysis of Cyclic Schedules." *Operations Research* **41**(5): 947–958.
Bradley, J. R., and B. C. Arntzen (1999) "The Simultaneous Planning of Production, Capacity, and Inventory in Seasonal Demand Environments." *Operations Research* **47**(6): 795–806.
Buffa, E. S. (1972) *Operations Management: Problems and Models.* John Wiley & Sons, London.
Camm, J. D., and S. Tayur (2010) "Editorial: How to Monetize the Value of OR." *Interfaces* **40**(6): 446–450.
Chen, F., and J.-S. Song (2001) "Optimal Policies for Multiechelon Inventory Problems with Markov-Modulated Demand." *Operations Research* **49**(2): 226–234.
Dai, T., and S.-H. Cho, and F. Zhang (2016) "Contracting for On-Time Delivery in the U.S. Influenza Vaccine Supply Chain." *Manufacturing & Service Operations Management* **18**(3): 332–346.
Dai, T., and K. Jerath (2013) "Salesforce Compensation with Inventory Considerations." *Management Science* **59**(11): 2490–2501.
Dai, T., and K. Jerath (2016a) "Impact of Inventory on Quota-Bonus Contracts with Rent Sharing." *Operations Research* **64**(1): 94–98.
Dai, T., and K. Jerath (2016b) "Salesforce Contracting under Supply Uncertainty." Johns Hopkins University Working Paper.
Deleersnyder, J.-L., T. J. Hodgson, H. Muller-Malek, and P. J. O'Grady (1989) "Kanban Controlled Pull Systems: An Analytic Approach." *Management Science* **35**(9): 1079–1091.
Duenyas, I., and W. J. Hopp (1995) "Quoting Customer Lead Times." *Management Science* **41**(1): 43–57.
Economist (2011) "Two Thousand Years in One Chart." *The Economist* (June 28th), www.economist.com/blogs/dailychart/2011/06/quantifying-history (accessed October 22, 2016).

Ettl, M., G. E. Feigin, G. Y. Lin, and D. D. Yao (2000) "A Supply Network Model with Base-Stock Control and Service Requirements." *Operations Research* **48**(2): 216–232.

Ford, M. (2015) *Rise of the Robots: Technology and the Threat of a Jobless Future*. New York: Basic Books.

Fraser, S. (2015) *The Age of Acquiescence*. New York: Little, Brown and Company.

Gerchak, Y., M. J. Magazine, and A. B. Gamble (1988) "Component Commonality with Service Level Requirements." *Management Science* **34**(6): 753–760.

Girotra, K., and S. Netessine (2014) *The Risk-Driven Business Model: Four Questions That Will Define Your Company*. Cambridge, MA: Harvard Business Press.

Glasserman, P., and S. Tayur (1995) "Sensitivity Analysis for Base-Stock Levels in Multiechelon Production-Inventory Systems." *Management Science* **41**(2): 263–281.

Graves, S. C., and S. P. Willems (2000) "Optimizing Strategic Safety Stock Placement in Supply Chains." *Manufacturing & Service Operations Management* **2**(1) 68–83.

Graves, S. C., and S. P. Willems (2005) "Optimizing the Supply Chain Configuration for New Products." *Management Science* **51**(8): 1165–1180.

Graves, S. C., and S. P. Willems (2008) "Strategic Inventory Placement in Supply Chains: Nonstationary Demand." *Manufacturing & Service Operations Management* **10**(2): 278–287.

Hamilton, A. (1791) "Report on Manufactures." Communicated to the United States House of Representatives, www.constitution.org/ah/rpt_manufactures.pdf (last accessed: October 22, 2016).

Hanssmann, F., and S. W. Hess (1960) "A Linear Programming Approach to Production and Employment Scheduling." *Management Science* **MT-1**(1): 46–51.

Harris, F. W. (1915) *Operations Cost, Factory Management Series*. Chicago, IL: Shaw.

Holt, C. C., F. Modigliani, and H. A. Simon (1955) "A Linear Decision Rule for Production and Employment Scheduling." *Management Science* **2**(1): 1–30.

Huchzermeier, A., and M. A. Cohen (1996) "Valuing Operational Flexibility under Exchange Rate Risk." *Operations Research* **44**(1): 100–113.

Immelt, J. (2013), CEO and Chairman, General Electric, is interviewed by the Economist's (writer) Greg Ip, at (the conference) Manufacturing's Next Chapter, presented by the Atlantic (magazine), February 7.

Isaacson, W. (2011) *Steve Jobs*. New York: Simon & Schuster.

Jordan, W. C., and S. C. Graves (1995) "Principles on the Benefits of Manufacturing Process Flexibility." *Management Science* **41**(4): 577–594.

Kaplan, E. (2015) "The Spy Who Fired Me: The Human Costs of Workplace Monitoring." *Harpers* (March): 31–40.

Kapuściński, R., and S. Tayur (1998) "A Capacitated Production-Inventory Model with Periodic Demand." *Operations Research* **46**(6): 899–911.

Kapuściński, R., and S. Tayur (2007) "Reliable Due-Date Setting in a Capacitated MTO System with Two Customer Classes." *Operations Research* **55**(1): 56–74.

Keene, S., D. Alberti, G. Henby, A. J. Brohinsky, and S. Tayur (2006) "Caterpillar's Building Construction Products Division Improves and Stabilizes Product Availability." *Interfaces* **36**(4): 283–295.

Keskinocak, P., R. Ravi, and S. Tayur (2001) "Scheduling and Reliable Lead-Time Quotation for Orders with Availability Intervals and Lead-Time Sensitive Revenues." *Management Science* **47**(2): 264–279.

Khurana, R. (2010) *From Higher Aims to Hired Hands: The Social Transformation of American Business Schools and the Unfulfilled Promise of Management as a Profession*. Princeton, NJ: Princeton University Press.

Krugman, P. (2015) "The Big Meh." *New York Times* (May 25): A19.

Kuznets, S. (1995) "Economic Growth and Income Inequality." *American Economic Review* **45**(1): 1–28.

Lee, H. L. (1996) "Effective Inventory and Service Management through Product and Process Redesign." *Operations Research* **44**(1): 151–159.

Lee, H. L., and C. Billington (1993) "Material Management in Decentralized Supply Chains." *Operations Research* **41**(5): 835–847.

Lee, H. L., and C. S. Tang (1997) "Modelling the Costs and Benefits of Delayed Product Differentiation." *Management Science* **43**(1): 40–53.

Lepore, J. (2009) "Not So Fast." *The New Yorker* (October 12): 114–122.

Levi, R., R. O. Roundy, and D. B. Shmoys (2006) "Primal-Dual Algorithms for Deterministic Inventory Problems." *Mathematics of Operations Research* **31**(2): 267–284.

Manyika, J., M. Chui, J. Bughin, R. Dobbs, P. Bisson, and A. Marrs (2013) *Disruptive Technologies: Advances that Will Transform Life, Business, and the Global Economy*. Vol. 180. San Francisco, CA: McKinsey Global Institute.

Markowitz, D. M., M. I. Reiman, and L. M. Wein (2000) "The Stochastic Economic Lot Scheduling Problem: Heavy Traffic Analysis of Dynamic Cyclic Policies." *Operations Research* **48**(1): 136–154.

Marx, K. (1912) *Capital: A Critique of Political Economy, Volume 1*. Chicago, IL: Charles H. Kerr & Company.
Marx, K. (1973) *Grundrisse*. London: Penguin Group.
Mitra, D., and I. Mitrani (1990) "Analysis of a Kanban Discipline for Cell Coordination in Production Lines. I." *Management Science* **36**(12): 1548–1566.
Monden, Y. (2011) *Toyota Production System: An Integrated Approach to Just-in-Time*. Boca Raton, FL: CRC Press.
Morozov, E. (2014) "Making It." *The New Yorker* (January 13): 69–71.
Phelps, E. S. (2013) *Mass Flourishing: How Grassroots Innovation Created Jobs, Challenge, and Change*. Princeton, NJ: Princeton University Press.
Plambeck, Erica L. (2004) "Optimal Leadtime Differentiation via Diffusion Approximations." *Operations Research* **52**(2): 213–228.
Plambeck, E. L., and S. A. Zenios (2003). "Incentive Efficient Control of a Make-to-Stock Production System." *Operations Research* **51**(3): 371–386.
Rao, U., A. Scheller-Wolf, and S. Tayur (2000) "Development of a Rapid-Response Supply Chain at Caterpillar." *Operations Research* **48**(2): 189–204.
Rawls, J. (2009) *A Theory of Justice*. Boston, MA: Harvard University Press.
Rifkin, J. (2014) *The Zero Marginal Cost Society: The Internet of Things, the Collaborative Commons, and the Eclipse of Capitalism*. New York: Palgrave Macmillan.
Roundy, R. (1985) "98%-Effective Integer-Ratio Lot-Sizing for One-Warehouse Multi-Retailer Systems." *Management Science* **31**(11): 1416–1430.
Schild, A. (1959) "On Inventory, Production and Employment Scheduling." *Management Science* **5**(2): 157–168.
Schroeder, A. (2008) *The Snowball: Warren Buffett and the Business of Life*. New York: Bantam Books.
Simon, H. A. (1952) "On the Application of Servomechanism Theory in the Study of Production Control." *Econometrica* **20**(2): 247–268.
Simon, H. A. (1976) *Administrative Behavior: A Study of Decision-Making Processes in Administrative Organization*. New York: Free Press.
Smil, V. (2013) *Made in the USA: The Rise and Retreat of American Manufacturing*. Cambridge, MA: MIT Press.
Smith, A. (1776) *The Wealth of Nations*. London: W. Strahan and T. Cadell.
Stecke, K. E. (1983) "Formulation and Solution of Nonlinear Integer Production Planning Problems for Flexible Manufacturing Systems." *Management Science* **29**(3): 273–288.
Swaminathan, J. M., and S. R. Tayur (1998) "Managing Broader Product Lines through Delayed Differentiation using Vanilla Boxes." *Management Science* **44**(12): S161–S172.
Tardif, V., S. Tayur, J. Reardon, R. Stines, and P. Zimmerman (2010) "OR Practice-Implementing Seasonal Logistics Tactics for Finished Goods Distribution at Deere & Company's C&CE Division." *Operations Research* **58**(1): 1–15.
Taylor, F. W. (1914) *The Principles of Scientific Management*. New York: Harper.
Tayur, S. R. (1992) "Properties of Serial Kanban Systems." *Queueing Systems* **12**(3–4): 297–318.
Tayur, S. R. (1993) "Structural Properties and a Heuristic for Kanban-Controlled Serial Lines." *Management Science* **39**(11): 1347–1368.
Tayur, S. (2000) "Improving Operations and Quoting Accurate Lead Times in a Laminate Plant." *Interfaces* **30**(5): 1–15.
Tayur, S. (2013) "Planned Spontaneity for Better Product Availability." *International Journal of Production Research* **51**(23–24) 6844–6859.
Tayur, S. (2015) "Why I am an Academic Capitalist." Plenary speech at POMS 26th Annual Conference 2015, Washington, D.C. (May 8).
Troyer, L., J. Smith, S. Marshall, E. Yaniv, S. Tayur, M. Barkman, A. Kaya, and Y. Liu (2005) "Improving Asset Management and Order Fulfillment at Deere & Company's C&CE Division." *Interfaces* **35**(1): 76–87.
Twain, M., and C. D. Warner (1873) *The Gilded Age: A Tale of Today*. London: Penguin.
Veatch, M. H., and L. M. Wein (1994) "Optimal Control of a Two-station Tandem Production/Inventory System." *Operations Research* **42**(2): 337–350.
Wagner, H. M., and T. M. Whitin (1958) "Dynamic Version of the Economic Lot Size Model." *Management Science* **5**(1): 89–96.
Yunes, T. H., D. Napolitano, A. Scheller-Wolf, and S. Tayur (2007) "Building Efficient Product Portfolios at John Deere and Company." *Operations Research* **55**(4): 615–629.
Zeynep, T. (2014) *The Good Jobs Strategy*. Boston, MA: Houghton Mifflin Harcourt.
Zweig, J. (2013) "Here Comes the Next Hot Emerging Market: The U.S." *Wall Street Journal* (August 24): B1.

36
FUTURE TRENDS FOR RESEARCH AND PRACTICE IN THE MANAGEMENT OF GLOBAL SUPPLY CHAINS

Henrique L. Correa

1 Introduction

In Chapters 1 and 2, a discussion about the remarkable POM history was developed in an attempt to set the stage for the chapters that follow and to help managers and researchers understand better the path of evolution and the current state of the POM field but also to help POM professionals, students, and researchers to be better prepared for the future.

In this chapter, we go one step further—we make an attempt to anticipate future trends for the area of supply chain management (SCM) that will likely impact SCM research and practice. We understand that it is always risky to try to predict trends for most areas of knowledge. However, we consider that by discussing some relevant trends in development in today's world that influence supply chain management and by analyzing said potential of these trends to shape the future, we may help POM managers better prepare for what is to come. Then, based on the discussed trends and on the extant literature, we discuss the most relevant avenues and opportunities for future research in SCM, with an emphasis on the management theories that most likely can offer support for the development of the identified research opportunities.

1.1 Increase in Volatility

With global supply chains crossing borders, alongside the growing need for integration of decision-making processes, the chains are interconnected and their members are more interdependent. This interdependence means that an alteration in any link in the chain has an influence on practically all the other links (Kleindorfer and Saad 2005). The possibility of a catastrophic interruption in one or more links of the chain is a constant source of concern for managers today. The worry is not just concerning random natural phenomena like tsunamis, floods, or earthquakes that render plants or other facilities inoperative. Numerous other factors (Sheffi 2002; Christopher 2004) have caused substantial disruptions with a global panorama: strikes, sabotage, terrorism, exchange rate and commodity price fluctuations, economic crises affecting demand in certain regions, besides the entry of billions of people into the consumer markets, with the expansion of emerging countries causing a boom and placing great pressure on natural resources. The result is a greater and growing volatility tendency in environments where global supply chains operate.

1.2 Increase in Complexity

Supply chains have had to contend with an unprecedented diversification and customization of products. According to Mik et al. (2011), the manufacturers of cell phones launched 900 more models in 2009 than they had launched in 2000 when cell phones were already an established technology. The number of different products, like drinks, cereal, and confectionery products, experienced an increase of more than 25% between 2004 and 2006 alone. This trend continues.

At the same time, the emergence of developing countries has created a massive number of middle-class consumers, making these consumer markets highly attractive to both domestic and multinational companies. However, the distribution of products in developing countries has great challenges like bad quality infrastructure in transportation and communication, difficulty of access to large sections of the population living in remote or non-urbanized regions, and non-existent or embryonic distribution structures (as in India and China, for example). This substantially increases the complexity and uncertainty of the global supply chains that serve these markets (Dobberstein et al. 2005).

Another contributor to the complexity of global supply chains is the tendency for an increase in commercial "returns" and manufacturer's "recalls" that require the development of complex solutions for the reverse or closed-loop supply chains (Souza 2013; Ferguson and Souza 2010). The reason for an increase in returns is related to two factors. The first concerns the fact that markets are becoming more competitive and the policy of "no questions asked" for returns tends to be adopted as a competitive differential or, as it is in the U.S., a *sine qua non*. In the U.S., it is estimated (Blackburn et al. 2004) that around 6% of products sold by big retail stores such as Wal-Mart, Target, and Costco are returned for a great variety of reasons. In Europe, this percentage falls to around 1%, and in other countries, the percentage is even lower, but the tendency is for continued expansion of this effect. The second factor is the growth of e-tailing (internet business-to-consumer commerce). Today, products such as shoes and clothes are increasingly bought on the internet. As they are products that are intended to fit the body type of clients, up to 50% of these items are returned.

1.3 Increase in the Influence of Organized Society and Governments to Make Organizations Pursue the Triple Bottom Line (3BL)

Encouraged by the internet and its instruments, organized society through NGOs and government bodies started to demand that corporations and their supply chains assume greater responsibility for the environmental sustainability of the planet and for their social impact. As a consequence, many organizations are now adjusting their objectives accordingly; from aiming to maximize their results only in the traditional single "bottom line" (profit), some progressive companies are now striving to maximize their performance in the "triple bottom line" (3BL). The 3BL consists of 1) economic prosperity (profit), 2) environmental sustainability (planet), and 3) social responsibility (people). It has become clearer that profit should not be the only defining element of success in companies and economies. It is also important to consider the future of people (internal and external to the organization) and the planet. These concerns have increased because countries such as Brazil, Russia, India, China, and South Africa (the BRICS countries are great economies experiencing accelerated growth) and others have grown at unprecedented rates, causing drastic increases in the consumption of the natural resources required to meet the needs of consumers. Furthermore, there are other potentially harmful effects of the current model of fast economic growth; to meet the energy and other production resource needs for accelerated growth, many companies have produced increasing quantities of polluting emissions which have not only polluted the air, water, and ground, but as scientists argue, have also been responsible for global warming.

At the same time, the disposition of products, wrappings, and other materials after their use has filled landfills at a rate that is no doubt unsustainable in the long term. To counter this, society has been reorganizing itself. Companies are pressured to change their processes and even their business models to reflect a greater concern with environmental sustainability and social responsibility. Furthermore, actions in production processes have implications for supply chains. The pressure to reduce the generation of waste calls for an increase in reuse and recycling. The management of reverse supply chains needed to implement reuse and recycling will be crucial for the supply chains of the future.

Some analysts believe that as long as societies use their pressure mechanisms to force companies to bear the real cost of their production processes, there will be a substantial change in the configuration of global supply chains. One example is the price of fuel. In most countries fuel prices do not include any charges or taxes to repair the environmental damage caused by its extraction, transport, and burning. If and when governments start to charge fuel-consuming companies for these damages, fuel and energy costs will multiply thereby rendering, for example, global sourcing less viable, as it depends on transcontinental transport, a recognized big fuel consumer. If this happens, in the medium- to long term we can expect a reversal in global sourcing with a possible tendency for re-insourcing and near-sourcing with a return to more intensive use of local or near suppliers, therefore, breaking global supply chains into more regional ones. This would have the side effect of reducing, to a point, the complexity of global chains today.

2 Implication of the Identified Trends for Practitioners

Considering these three tendencies, some competencies seem relevant for the management of future supply chains.

2.1 Competencies to Deal with the Rise in Supply Chain Volatility

To face volatile markets and supply conditions, the ability to act quickly is fundamental for companies—both in regards to internal production and also the external environment (the supply chain and its flows). In developing such supply chains, chain managers must develop greater flexibility and adaptability (Engelhardt-Nowitzki 2012). On the one hand, supply chain management must develop competencies to integrate their partner companies' information systems to ensure the sharing of relevant information and the coordination of decision processes (Jin et al. 2014; Correa 2014) and performance improvement initiatives (Iida 2012) across these companies' borders. The discussion about the bullwhip effect causes and possible solutions in Chapter 2 illustrates some ways in which supply chain managers have to deal with supply chain volatility.

On the other hand, it is important for supply chains to develop the competencies pertinent to the broad area of risk management. Not only the risk management associated with traditional accidental disruption factors such as defects, delays, and suppliers going out of business and random (such as natural) phenomena. There are also less obvious risk factors such as fluctuations in the prices of commodities and fuel, the financial and contextual situation of suppliers and customers (Wiengarten et al. 2013) and ethical and legal questions concerning members of the chain (Sheffi 2005). See Sheffi (2015) for more discussion on this important theme.

2.2 Competencies to Deal with the Increase in Supply Chain Complexity

To deal with the expected increase in complexity, chain managers must develop competencies to adopt and manage innovative solutions, as the levels of complexity today and of the future are unprecedented. These competences start from understanding the drivers of supply chain complexity (Bode and Wagner 2015), for instance, intrinsically complex products, proliferation of products, complex supply chains, and complex distribution. Perhaps before dealing with increased complexity, managers can determine whether or not the complexity can be simplified. For example, the enormous diversity of products, assumed to be necessary in some companies, may be seen as counterproductive in the eyes of the client (some clients are put off when they have excessive options and some give up buying). However, for many industries, the increase in product variety appears inevitable and consequently some additional competencies may be useful.

2.2.1 The Use of Postponement

To accommodate the growing complexity brought about by product proliferation and the consequent increased risks of supply chain disruption, it is important to develop competencies related to the use of postponement (Yang and Yang 2010). Postponement means delaying the completion of the final product until after the client's order has been received. This often results in performance improvement in many industries, in terms of inventory reduction and customer service (see e.g., Wong et al. 2011). One example can be the supply chains that sell wall paint. These chains wait for the client order in the retail store to come in before mixing the twelve or so standard colors. By doing so, they are able to transform these few simple shades into millions of possible final products. This involves innovative forms of designing products, of producing them, and of allocating production activities to the parties in the chain. In some situations, it will be necessary to redesign the chain but this, strategically, may be worth it.

2.2.2 Integration of Decision-Making Processes and Increased Collaboration

Another crucial skill to deal with greater complexity is the ability to integrate decision-making processes (Prajogo and Olhager 2012) and increase collaboration (Cao et al. 2010 provide a comprehensive literature review of supply chain collaboration) in the chain by increasing information sharing, decision-making coordination (Jin et al. 2014), and aligning incentives within the chain. For this, high levels of trust are necessary. There are several ways to build trust and reduce supply chain complexity as perceived by companies:

- Decisions of outsourcing that observe the strategic implications about when to outsource and when to internally produce, and by doing so "distributing" the complexity among partners;
- Carefully selecting key partners in the chain to whom activities are outsourced, considering multiple aspects that include supplier location;

- Establishing long-lasting relations with the key-partners with whom the sharing of information and the integration of decision-making processes are intensified; and,
- Developing contractual forms and relationships with partners in the chain that better distribute risks and returns, in such a way that incentives of the chain partners are aligned (Narayanan and Raman 2004) resulting in less need for complex conflict resolution.

2.2.3 The Use of New Technologies

For some markets, new technologies such as three-dimensional printing (3D printing) or additive manufacturing can also offer very attractive options for dealing with complexity in supply chains. Unlike machining processes, which are subtractive, 3D printing is additive. Drawing on a computer-aided design file, an object is divided into paper-thin cross-sectional slices, which are then each printed out of liquid, powder, plastic, or metal until the object is complete. 3D printing is ideal for one-off batches of physical models, prototypes, tooling components, and spare parts in many industries (Jong and Brujin 2013), which require complex and frequently inefficient supply and distribution systems if these products are centrally produced and then distributed using conventional methods. For instance, think about the spare parts industry for an aircraft manufacturer. Hundreds of thousands of parts must be available when needed so that repairs can be done quickly to airplanes thereby reducing the time that they remain grounded. The complexity of dealing with this daunting stock management and logistical problem can be substantially reduced if the plans of the parts (instead of the parts themselves) are stocked in servers and electronically downloaded by locations whenever and wherever said parts are required to be "printed out" locally, to order, quickly, simply, and cheaply. 3D printing has great potential for use by supply chains that produce and deliver items that are required in great variety but in very small quantities, dispersed over a broad geographic area. 3D printing has a great potential to affect low-volume supply chains, possibly creating new business models and supporting new supply chain configurations (Cautela et al. 2014).

2.2.4 Segmentation of Supply Chains

One last competence worth mentioning in relation to complexity is related to operational focus. As discussed in Chapter 2, trade-offs are manifested in supply chains. The use of the same supply chain structure (the same logistics footprint—plants and warehouses, the same structure of transport) to produce and distribute products that compete in very different ways in the market can cause an unnecessary increase in complexity for the chain. The segmentation of the supply chain of a company based upon characteristics of the products they produce and distribute can not only increase the operational focus but also reduce complexity.

Fisher (1997) suggests that innovative products (with unpredictable demand, shorter life cycles, and frequent product launches) should be served by responsive (agile and flexible even if less efficient) chains; functional products (with more stable demand, longer life cycles and less frequent product launches) should be served by efficient chains (even if less flexible and responsive). See Chapter 2 for further insight. If a company has both innovative and functional products, according to this logic, it should be able to segment them accordingly and have each of them to be produced and distributed by separate, less complex, and more focused supply chains that are either responsive or efficient.

2.3 Competencies to Deal with the Increase in Pressure for 3BL

3BL requires that companies and supply chains incorporate the "Reduce, Reuse, Recycle" approach. These concerns have become an integral part of the supply chain (Mishra et al. 2012).

"Reducing" the use of resources requires a skill set that is very familiar to operations managers (e.g., lean thinking, Womack and Jones 2004) but also one that can contribute to improved environmental sustainability. Companies that have considerably reduced their environmental footprint (for example the Subaru plant in Indiana that is proud of having reduced the amount of waste sent to landfills to zero through the application of Reduce, Reuse, Recycle principles) have become masters in taking "lean" principles to the extreme. The goals are the same: waste reduction and continuous improvement. The unnecessary use of resources and the generation of emissions, waste, and solid residue are nothing more than wasteful. The use of "lean" principles can help chains to achieve higher levels of environmental sustainability. If this approach is used, the attainability of "green" (environmentally sustainable) supply chains and profitability can be seen as congruent, not conflicting, goals (Kumar et al. 2012).

The "Reuse and Recycle" parts require supply chain managers to develop competencies, governance structures, and collaboration with supply chain partners (Blome et al. 2014) in the management of the required reverse and closed-loop flows (Aitken and Harrison 2013). Reverse logistics and closed-loop supply chains are now essential in order to ensure that less non-renewable resources are extracted from nature and that less polluting material is sent into the air, water, and landfills. Many supply chains and corresponding logistics have always been developed to guarantee efficient unidirectional flows of materials from raw materials to the end consumer.

Building the reverse closed-loop logistics for flows to take products back after the end of their economic life to re-enter the supply chain as secondary input material poses new challenges for supply chain managers (Liekens and Vandaele 2012). For instance, how is it possible to make sure that consumers properly dispose of their products after use? How can a company reduce the uncertainty of the supply of used products in recycling operations? How can a company deal with different conditions of products that consumers want to recycle? How can a manager design logistical systems that, instead of taking products from a few units (manufacturers) to many (consumers), take used products from many (consumers) to a few units (recycling centers)? How can the economics of reverse and closed loop flows be reconciled so that viability is achieved? Those are only some of the challenges posed by the increased importance of reverse flows in supply chains. A comprehensive literature about reverse logistics and closed-loop supply chains can be found in Govindan, Soleimani, and Kannan (2015).

One skill that may be important in responding to the increase in internal and external pressure for 3BL objectives is that of seeking, developing, and maintaining productive and collaborative partnerships with key pressure groups such as NGOs and government bodies. Partnership and collaboration with NGOs such as Greenpeace, for example, in some instances have proved to be more effective than confrontation. McDonald's has responded to boycotts and accusations of indirectly causing deforestation in a positive way, working in partnership with Greenpeace and other NGOs, as much from a perspective of resolving problems as from public relations (Goldberg and Yagan 2007).

Another useful competency in terms of guaranteeing social responsibility, not only of the company in focus, but also of partners in the chain is the mapping out and management of risk factors, for example, of partners using child labor or placing workers in inhumane working conditions. This should include not only direct suppliers but also suppliers' suppliers. For instance, the findings of Awaysheh and Klassen (2010) suggest that there is a relationship between supply chain structure and suppliers' socially responsible practices. The supply chain managers of the future need to have a profound understanding of such issues.

3 Directions for Research in Supply Chain Management

The debate over rigor versus relevance in research continues among supply chain researchers and practitioners. According to Thomas et al. (2011), some people believe that the relevance of academic research is more important. They want to avoid becoming overly rigorous or practically irrelevant. At the other end of the spectrum, some people suggest that rigor needs to come first to prevent the dissemination of bad research. Between the two ends, a third view contends that both rigor and relevance are needed so that research is both interesting to many constituencies and trustworthy. We believe that the third view represents what we as researchers need to do if we want the discipline of supply chain management to maximize its contribution to society.

Managerially relevant research is "knowledge that managers can use to better understand phenomena relating to that which they manage" (Carter 2008, p. 78). Academically rigorous research tries to cultivate a deeper understanding of a concept by applying valid and reliable research methods and approaches while examining the implications of important theories for that concept. As Connelly et al. (2013, p. 227) put it,

> Building theory in this way is valuable, in part, because doing so allows scholars to describe a concept in vivid detail, explain its importance, position it within the field of study, identify its implications and predict how it affects and is affected by related phenomena and ideas (Dubin 1978; Kerlinger 1986). Applying one theory provides a basis to develop research questions, explore relationships, and create ideas that describe, explain, and predict, but broader approaches can offer even greater potential.

In this section, an attempt is made to draw from a number of contributions found in the literature to describe some opportunities for future research (that hopefully ends up being both rigorous and relevant) in the field of global supply chain management. In order to do that, we reviewed some papers published since 2008 (Connelly et al. 2013; Carter and Easton 2011; Pagell and Shevchenko 2014; Parente et al. 2008; Sodhi et al. 2011; Daugherty 2011; Melnyk et al. 2014; González-Loureiro et al. 2015; Stank et al. 2011; Sanders and Zacharia 2013) that have proposed agendas for future supply chain management research. We will also discuss some relevant theories that could shed light on and support the proposed research opportunities.

3.1 Supporting Theories

In our literature research, the following theories are found to be related to and useful for several aspects of global supply chain management:

- *Real options theory (ROT)*: *ROT* is an alternative framework in the theory of investment decisions which modifies the traditional Expected Net Present Value theory. It explores the important consideration of including opportunity and risk when exploring factors that affect companies' performance (Connelly et al. 2013; Amram and Kulatilaka 1999; Contractor et al. 2011).
- *Internationalization theory (IT)*: a set of theories that aim to explain why some firms pursue foreign direct investment and others do not (Connelly et al. 2013; Hymer 1976; Dunning 2003).
- *Transaction cost economics (or theory) (TCE)*: Transaction costs are the total expenses, both direct and indirect, of carrying out an exchange, whether it is between firms or within a firm. *TCE*

suggests that sourcing (the "make or buy" decision) decisions are made by firms in a way that transaction costs are minimized (Connelly et al. 2013; Williamson 2008).

- *Agency theory (AT)*: studies contracting in terms of "principals" who hire "agents" to carry out activities on their behalf, focusing on potential information asymmetry and conflicting interests with some possibility of moral hazard (Connelly et al. 2013; Eisenhardt 1989).
- *Resource dependence theory (RDT)*: analyzes how companies seek to maintain control of vital resources. They establish relationships with others to acquire those resources when they lack them thereby losing total control over its destiny; they then seek to alter those relationships to minimize dependency (Connelly et al. 2013; Medcof 2001).
- *Social network theory (SNT)*: centers on the relationships (or ties) a firm has with surrounding firms. According to *SNT*, firms' decisions are based, in large part, on information and influence that arise from their social network (Connelly et al. 2013; Thoreli 1986).
- *Institutional theory (InsT)*: describes how pressures to gain legitimacy arise from both formal (e.g., regulatory bodies) and informal (e.g., social influences from actors such as the media, NGOs, or trade associations) institutions and how they influence a firm's decision making (Connelly et al. 2013; Suchman 1995).
- *Game theory (GT)*: game theory's utility relates to changing viewpoint: from decisions made by competitors as exogenous towards the endogeneity of decisions within a system. In such a system, all incumbents seek the common benefit instead of the individual one (González-Loureiro et al. 2015; Smith 1982).
- *Stakeholder theory (ST)*: analyzes how organizations manage issues related to their morals and values while seeking to maximize their performance in trying to balance and meet all their stakeholders' goals and expectations (González-Loureiro et al. 2015; Freeman 1984; Donaldson and Preston 1995).

3.2 Proposed Research Directions in Supply Chain Management

Some directions for further research are proposed here, with theories that might support them, whenever appropriate. The same structure that we used in Section 1 of this chapter will be used here to classify the topics that represent future trends in supply chain management: increased volatility, increased complexity, and increased pressure for 3BL.

3.2.1 Future Research Related to Increased Volatility

At a strategic level, Melnyk et al. (2014) offer directions for further research in terms of supply chain design in relation to the recognition that supply chains do not always remain static:

- What type of supply chain features foster supply chains that can easily adapt and change? Correspondingly, what types of features inhibit changes in supply chain design?
- What factors signal (trigger) the need for supply chain redesign?
- What types of technique, procedure, or analytics can be used to improve supply chain redesign?

At a tactical level, volatility is affected by the bullwhip effect. Although solutions to mitigate the bullwhip effect have received attention from the literature (Lee et al. 1997), implementing those technical solutions is still difficult for many companies and their supply chains. Researchers can provide a great service to practitioners if they focus on the implementation of actions that mitigate the bullwhip effect. Coordination and collaboration are key aspects here. Theory supported exploration of successful and unsuccessful cases in which more and better collaboration and cooperation were achieved would be very instructive. A variety of theories that could lend their support, depending on the approach and research question: Game theory (*GT*)—in analyzing how to turn win-lose into win-win relationships in the supply chain—and Agency theory (*AT*)—in aligning incentives among partners in the supply chain for a "common good."

Additionally, one of the most important opportunities for further research on increased levels of volatility in supply chains is supply chain risk management (SCRM). In their survey with supply chain researchers, Sodhi et al. (2011) found three gaps pertinent to future research in supply chain risk management: (1) no consensus on the definition of SCRM, (2) lack of research on response to supply chain risk incidents, and (3) a shortage of empirical research on SCRM. To close the gaps, they also suggest more involvement of researchers with industry for case studies and event based (such as critical incident) research; they also call for more conceptual work on which to base the empirical research. Real options theory (*ROT*) could offer support because of the categories it covers (e.g., risk). Institutional theory (*InsT*) could be useful in helping with the inclusion of formal and informal actors who insist that companies understand and mitigate supply chain risks. Agency theory (*AT*) can offer support because managing risk in supply chains requires including the consideration of several tiers of suppliers and customers, many of which can be considered "agents" of the company in analysis.

3.2.2 Future Research Related to Increased Complexity

Supply chains continue to become increasingly complex over time. As companies outsource their activities to expert companies, the interfaces between a company and its partners in the supply chain grow not only in number but in complexity of the relationships established because in supply chains, in many situations, collaboration and cooperation between partners is preferable to conflict. Here, Daugherty (2011) offers some suggestions for future research on supply chain relationships, motivated by some accounts in the literature that "successful collaborative relationships between a firm and its core suppliers is still rare." Daugherty argues that research is needed to look at current buyer-seller relationships.

Here are some research questions (based on Daugherty 2011; Stank et al. 2011; and others) and theories related to managing relationships in global supply chain management:

- Are the problems (with supply chain relationships) encountered due to temporary or cyclical influences such as the economy or are our partnership/alliance models flawed? (TCE, AT, RDT theories)
- How do we extend current collaborative relationships to look beyond one buyer and one seller to encompass multiple tiers of suppliers and multiple tiers of customers? (AT, SNT theories)
- What are the trends in outsourcing? How can effective sourcing contracts be crafted? What types of outsourcing arrangements yield the greatest enhancements to service productivity and success? (TCE, RDT, GT theories)
- How do cultural differences affect day-to-day interactions and the success of long-term relationships? (IT, ST theories)
- Buyer-seller partnerships or alliances do not involve equal partners. Given that, what can be done to improve chances of relationship success and protect the less powerful partner? (ST, GT, AT theories)
- How can the performance of partners and partnerships in the supply chain be measured so that trust is fostered, accountability is present, and incentives are aligned (Stank et al. 2011)? (GT, ST, AT theories)

The issue of governance also becomes crucial as complexity increases in supply chain management. González-Loureiro et al. (2015, p. 171) suggest that more research is needed about "the internal organization of the supply chain: which organization must take the leading role and how to distribute the coordination efforts?" According to the authors, "there is a need to broaden the perspective from the (individual) firm to the supply chain as an informal form to organize the industrial economic activity, i.e., the idea of the extended firm." Here theories such as *InsT*, *AT*, *RDT*, and *ST* could be of help.

3.2.3 Future Research Related to Increased 3BL Performance

Carter and Easton (2011) offer future research directions that will support companies and their supply chains to increase their 3BL performance, based on their extensive literature review of the topic. They notice that researchers in the field commonly use multi-industry samples and that this may represent an important research opportunity: to take deeper dives into individual industries (e.g., service supply chains) as sampling frames so that specific types of sustainability activities that are germane to those industries are identified and also industries in which the boundaries of specific theories might be extended or shown not to apply.

Supply chain managers are in a particularly advantageous position to impact—positively or negatively—environmental and social performances (Carter and Easton 2011). Although they adopt the terminology "Sustainable Supply Chain Management" (SSCM) and call for further research on the issue, Pagell and Shevchenko (2014) argue that sustainable supply chain management should have no future. Their intention is to state that all supply chains will use SSCM in the future. Therefore, the term becomes redundant. In other words, they think that in the future the "un-sustainable" supply chains will not be around anyway.

In their literature search, Carter and Easton (2011, p. 55) also observe one striking result was the "relative dearth in the use of a theoretical lens to examine problems of interest in the sustainability arena." They also observe that there is an encouraging trend toward integrating theory in SSCM research. They observe that of the theories that have been used Stakeholder theory (*ST*) is the most prevalent and that Transaction cost economics (*TCE*) is one of the lesser used theories in the SSCM literature that they reviewed. Pagell and Shevchenko (2014) offer some insights in terms of SSCM future research directions. First, they argue that the extant research has frequently asked the question "does sustainability pay?" However, this is the wrong question going forward. The question should be "how to create supply chains that are sustainable?"—what requires more multi-disciplinary research that explicitly looks at the supply chain from the perspective of other stakeholders, such as government, NGOs, communities, and the natural systems where the chain operates. Here, Stakeholder theory (*ST*) can be of help. Pagell and Shevchenko (2014) also see great research opportunities when it comes to "measurements" in SSCM: measuring a single link in the chain and not the impact of the entire chain according to the authors is very challenging but absolutely necessary and under-researched. Here, theories such as *AT*, *SNT*, and *IT* could offer interesting insights.

4 Conclusion

The evolution of the management of global supply chains is occurring in a more accelerated form than in previous phases of POM's evolution (see Chapters 1 and 2), and the levels of volatility, complexity, and social pressure on supply chains today and in the future do not have historical precedence, requiring all the competencies needed in the previous phases of evolution and some additional ones. It is important that companies are conscious of what these are for their specific environment and that they prepare, arming themselves with them, to face the challenges ahead.

Acknowledgements

I would like to thank my Graduate Assistant Bryan Basnight for his help with the literature review and formatting of this chapter.

References and Bibliography

Aitken, J. and A. Harrison (2013) "Supply governance structures for reverse logistics systems." *International Journal of Operations & Production Management*, **33**(5): 745–764.

Amram, M. and N. Kulatilaka (1999) *Real Options: Managing Strategic Investment in an Uncertain World*. Harvard Business School Press: Boston, MA.

Awaysheh, A. and R.D. Klassen (2010) "The impact of supply chain structure on the use of supplier responsible practices." *International Journal of Operations & Production Management*, **30**(12): 1246–1268.

Blackburn, J., V. Daniel, R. Guide, Gilvan C. Souza and Luk Van Wassenhove (2004) "Reverse supply chains for commercial returns." *California Management Review*, **46**(4): 5–22.

Blome, C., A. Paulraj and K. Schuetz (2014) "Supply collaboration and sustainability: A profile deviation analysis." *International Journal of Operations & Production Management*, **35**(4): 639–663.

Bode, C. and S.M. Wagner (2015) "Structural drivers of upstream supply chain complexity and the frequency of supply chain disruptions." *Journal of Operations Management*, **36**: 215–228.

Cao, M., M.A Vonderembse, Q. Zhang and T.S. Ragu-Nathan (2010) "Supply chain collaboration: Conceptualization and instrument development." *International Journal of Production Research*, **48**(22): 6613–6635.

Carter, C.R. (2008) "Knowledge production and knowledge transfer: Closing the research–preactice gap." *Journal of Supply Chain Management*, **44**(2): 78–82.

Carter, C.R. and Easton, P.L. (2011) "Sustainable supply chain: Evolution and future direction." *International Journal of Physical Distribution and Logistics Management*, **41**(1): 46–62.

Cautela, C., P. Pisano and M. Pironti (2014) "The emergence of new networked business models from technology innovation: An analysis of 3-D printing design enterprises." *International Entrepreneurship and Management Journal*, **10**(3): 487–501.

Christopher, M. (2004) "Building the resilient supply chain." *International Journal of Logistics Management*, **15**(2): 1–14.

Connelly, B.L., D.J. Ketchen and T.M. Hult (2013) "Global supply chain management: Towards a theoretically driven research agenda." *Global Strategy Journal*, **3**(3): 227–243.

Contractor F.J., J.A. Woodley and A. Piepenbrink (2011) "How tight an embrace? Choosing the optimal degree of partner interaction in alliances based on risk, technology characteristics, and agreement provisions." *Global Strategy Journal*, **1**(1): 67–85.

Correa, H.L. (2014) *Global Supply Chain Management*. Atlas: São Paulo, Brazil. https://itunes.apple.com/us/book/global-supply-chain-management/id899237729?|=pt&ls=1&mt=11. Accessed October 22, 2015.

Daugherty, P.J. (2011) "Review of logistics and supply chain relationship literature and suggested research agenda." *International Journal of Physical Distribution and Logistics Management*, **41**(1): 16–31.

Dobberstein N., C.S. Neumann and M. Zils (2005) "Logistics in emerging markets." *McKinsey Quarterly*, February: 15–17.

Donaldson, T. and L.E. Preston (1995) "The stakeholder theory of the corporation: Concepts, evidence, and implications." *Academy of Management Review*, **20**(1): 65–91.

Dunning, J.H. (2003) "Some antecedents of internationalization theory." *Journal of International Business Studies*, **34**(2): 108–115.

Eisenhardt, K.M. (1989) "Agency theory: An assessment and review." *Academy of Management Review*, **14**(1): 57–74.

Engelhardt-Nowitzki, C. (2012) "Improving value chain flexibility and adaptability in build-to-order environments." *International Journal of Physical Distribution & Logistics Management*, **42**(4): 318–337.

Ferguson, M.E. and G.C. Souza (2010) *Closed-Loop Supply Chains: New Developments to Improve the Sustainability of Business Practice*. CRC Press (Taylor and Francis): Boca Raton, FL.

Fisher, M. (1997) "What is the right supply chain for your product?" *Harvard Business Review*, March–April: 105–116.

Freeman, R.E. (1984) *Strategic Management: A Stakeholder Approach*. Boston, MA: Pitman.

Goldberg, R.A. and J.D. Yagan (2007) "McDonald's Corp.: Managing a sustainable supply chain." Case study. Product number 907414-PDF-ENG. Harvard Business School Publications: Boston, MA.

González-Loureiro, M., M. Dabic and T Kiessling (2015) "Supply chain management as the key to a firm's strategy in the global marketplace: Trends and research agenda." *International Journal of Physical Distribution and Logistics Management*, **45**(1/2): 159–181.

Govindan, K., H. Soleimani and D. Kannan (2015) "Reverse logistics and closed-loop supply chain: A comprehensive review to explore the future." *European Journal of Operational Research*, **240**(3): 603–626.

Hymer, S.H. (1976) *The International Operations of National Firms*. MIT Press: Cambridge, MA.

Iida, T. (2012) "Coordination of cooperative cost-reduction efforts in a supply chain partnership." *European Journal of Operational Research*, **222**(2): 180–190.

Jin, Y., M. Vonderembse, T.S. Ragu-Nathan and J.T. Smith (2014) "Exploring relationships among IT-enabled sharing capability, supply chain flexibility, and competitive performance." *International Journal of Production Economics*, **153**: 24–34.

Jong, J.P.J. and E. de Brujn (2013) "Innovation lessons from 3-D printing." *MIT Sloan Management Review*. **54**(2): 43–53.

Kleindorfer, P.R. and G.H. Saad (2005) "Managing disruption risks in supply chains." *Production and Operations Management*, **14**(1): 53–68.

Kumar, S., S. Teichman and T. Timpernagel (2012) "A green supply chain is a requirement for profitability." *International Journal of Production Research*, **50**(5): 1278–1296.

Lee, H., V. Padmanabhan and S. Whang (1997) "The bullwhip effect in supply chains." *Sloan Management Review*, **38**(8): 93–102.

Liekens, K. and N. Vandaele (2012) "Multi-level reverse logistics network design under uncertainty." *International Journal of Production Research*, **50**(1): 23–40.

Medcof, J.W. (2001) "Resource-based strategy and managerial power in networks of internationally dispersed technology units." *Strategic Management Journal*, **22**(11): 999–1012.

Melnyk, S.A., R. Narasimhan and H.A. De Campos (2014) "Supply chain design: Issues, challenges, frameworks and solutions." *International Journal of Production Research*, **52**(7): 1887–1896.

Mik, Y., A. Niemeyer and B. Ruwadi (2011) "Building the supply chain of the future." *McKinsey Quarterly*, January: 1–10.

Mishra, N., V. Kumar and F.T.S. Chan (2012) "A multi-agent architecture for reverse logistics in a green supply chain." *International Journal of Production Research*, **50**(9): 2396–2406.

Narayanan, V.G. and A. Raman (2004) "Aligning incentives in supply chains." *Harvard Business Review*, November: 94–102.

Pagell, M. and A. Shevchenko (2014) "Why research in sustainable supply chain management should have no future." *Journal of Supply Chain Management*, **50**(1): 44–55.

Parente, D.H., P.D. Lee, M.D. Ishman and A. Roth (2008) "Marketing and supply chain management: A collaborative research agenda." *Journal of Business & Industrial Marketing*, **23**(8): 520–528.

Prajogo, D. and J. Olhager (2012) "Supply chain integration and performance: The effects of long-term relationships, information technology and sharing, and logistics integration." *International Journal of Production Economics*, **135**(1): 514–522.

Sanders, N.R. and Z.G. Zacharia (2013) "The interdisciplinary future of supply chain management research." *Decision Sciences*, **44**(3): 413–429.

Sheffi, Y. (2002) "Supply Chain Management under the threat of international terrorism." *International Journal of Logistics Management*, **12**(2): 1–11.

Sheffi, Y. (2005) *The Resilient Enterprise*. MIT Press: Cambridge, MA.

Sheffi, Y. (2015) *The Power of Resiliency*. MIT Press: Cambridge, MA.

Smith, J.M. (1982) *Evolution and the Theory of Games*, Cambridge University Press: Cambridge, UK.

Sodhi, M.S., B.G. Son and C.S. Tang (2011) "Researchers' perspective on supply chain risk management." *Production and Operations Management*, **21**(1): 1–13.

Souza, G.C. (2013) "Closed-loop supply chains: A critical review and future research." *Decision Sciences*, **44**(1): 7–38.

Stank, T.P., J.P. Dittmann and C.W. Autry (2011) "The new supply chain agenda: A synopsis and directions for future research." *International Journal of Physical Distribution & Logistics Management*, **41**(10): 940–955.

Suchman, M.C. (1995) "Managing legitimacy: Strategic and institutional approaches." *Academy of Management Review*, **20**(3): 571–610.

Thomas, R.W., C.C. Defee, W.S. Randall and B. Williams (2011) "Assessing the managerial relevance of contemporary supply chain management research." *International Journal of Physical Distribution & Logistics Management*, **41**(7): 655–667.

Thoreli, H.B. (1986) "Networks: Between markets and hierarchies." *Strategic Management Journal*, **7**(1): 37–51.

Wiengarten, F., M. Pagell and B. Fynes (2013) "The importance of contextual factors in the success of outsourcing contracts in the supply chain environment: The role of risk and complementary practices." *Supply Chain Management: An International Journal*, **18**(6): 630–643.

Williamson, O.E (2008) "Outsourcing: Transaction cost economics and supply chain management." *Journal of Supply Chain Management*, **44**(2): 5–16.

Womack, J. and D. Jones (2004) *Lean Thinking*. The Free Press: Simon & Schuster, New York.

Wong, H., A. Potter and M. Naim (2011) "Evaluation of postponement in the soluble coffee supply chain: A case study." *International Journal of Production Economics*, **131**(1): 355–364.

Yang, B. and Y. Yang (2010) "Postponement in supply chain risk management: A complexity perspective." *International Journal of Production Research*, **47**(7): 1901–1912.

37
CONCLUSIONS
Evaluation and Prognostications for the POM Domain

Sushil K. Gupta, Martin K. Starr, and Aleda Roth

1 Summing Up the Accomplishments

POM, as it exists today, has treaded many eras and crossed many milestones during its amazing journey through eons of time beginning with the Stone Age (9300 BCE) to the Information Age (1950 CE). "Power" is the hub of all progress and development in the world. POM has witnessed, and has been a partner for transition from coal power to petroleum to atomic energy and now is a big player in the progress towards harnessing natural energy—the sun, the wind, and the storms. Readers are advised to re-read Chapter 1 of this book for more details.

The development of power sources has accelerated industrial progress that includes, among other things, manufacturing, transportation, electrification, and telecommunication. POM is transforming healthcare delivery systems, agriculture, hospitality, logistics, and disaster management. POM has even helped in improving commercial operations—marketing and retailing.

Tools of the trade such as forecasting, production planning, inventory management, scheduling, quality control, and facilities planning, have been shown to apply to a diverse set of operations; and to help with the development of strategic plans.

Along with growth in POM, the other management disciplines—accounting, finance, marketing, and human resources, etc.—grew side by side. POM has learnt to live and interact with these disciplines. Developments continue to take place in science and technology, product development, process capabilities, alternate sources of energy, interaction among different business partners for improved supply chains, logistics clusters, lean operations, and agile systems. Project Management is becoming an important area of development.

Data analytics and operations management are intimately connected. Data collection and data analysis capabilities are improving with developments in computer technology. POM also had its share of influence on military operations and is now influencing startup companies, nonprofit organizations, sustainability, and social responsibility. Human behavior has become an important topic of study since it plays an important role in the implementation of POM decisions and strategies.

The Routledge Collection, with the dedicated efforts and experiences of seventy authors spread across thirty-seven chapters divided into the book's eight parts, is a remarkable compendium of POM progress through eons of time and reflections from an enigmatic future.

In the next two sections, we step into unknown and unchartered territory in order to reflect what POM can do. POM has slowly and steadily found its way into service industries. Section 2 is devoted to a discussion of how POM steps out of the manufacturing boundary and permeates in the service arena. In Section 3, we will sum up and integrate the POM domain in terms of the three major areas of the survey that we sent out to the authors of the POM Companion. This proverbial three-legged stool is supported by TRP—Teaching, Research, and Practice. The survey respondents offer their reflections of our TRP future.

2 Reflections on the New Service Economy

The aim of this section is to re-engage strategic thinking in service operations by examining several of the underlying forces that are reshaping service business environments and are influencing major discontinuities from business as usual. The rapidity of technological change, the accelerated growth and timeliness of information exchange and digital media, and the widening reach to customers anywhere and anytime, challenges traditional service operations strategy and at the same time affords unprecedented opportunities for creating new knowledge and changing mindsets about service research and practice. In fact, we now are on the cusp of a major paradigm shift that is irreversibly altering the landscape of businesses globally (Roth et al. 2016). The past decade has witnessed an unparalleled escalation of market, social, and technological forces leading to the new service economy. The new service norms are heightened levels of customer experience content in ordinary services offerings, the morphing of existing services and service sectors, the servitization of goods, the creation of entirely new business models, and much more.

Understanding this new service economy is essential, as it plays such a prominent role in the value-added in developed economies, and is increasingly making major inroads into the developing world as a major component of their gross domestic product (GDP). Value-added components of GDP are often classified into the respective contributions made by three broad sectors of an economy: services; industry (i.e., durable and nondurable goods, mining, energy production, and construction); and agriculture (i.e., agriculture, fishing, and forestry). For semantic clarity, the service sector is typically broken down into subsectors, including wholesale and retail trade, leisure and hospitality, utilities, transportation and warehousing, information and communications, financial activities, professional and business services, education, government, and all other private activities that are not goods-producing. In the pace-setting U.S. economy, services accounted for 80.1% of the jobs in 2014 (Bureau of Labor Statistics 2015). However, the value-added of the service sector to global GDP and related labor force participation was estimated to be 62.4% in 2015 and 43.1% in 2011, respectively. By contrast with services, similar statistics for the industrial "goods" sector were about half, i.e., 31.1% and 22.2%, respectively (Central Intelligence Agency 2016). While agriculture accounted for 6.5% of value-added, the labor force participation rate was relatively high at 34.6%. Nonetheless, a case can be made that the current economic classifications are somewhat outdated, as services are also an increasing component of both industrial and agricultural sectors.

While the service economy matters to most economies in the world in terms of employment and value-added percent of gross domestic product (GDP), these metrics do not reveal the depth of the evolutionary transformations and paradigm shifting undercurrents of creative destruction in traditional services. Arguably, over the past three decades, service operations have done a magnanimous job in advancing and solving both tactical and mid-term problems, such as revenue management, scheduling, capacity planning, service quality, etc. However, despite the urgency, much less research has been conducted in setting strategic directions for service operations management. Service strategies are particularly valuable in creating resilient and adaptive delivery system designs, which are needed to tackle the implications of emerging issues for service research, teaching, practice, and policy.

In this context, this section highlights the following six evolutionary trends using the lens of service operations strategy and design for customer experience:

- The rise of the experience economy
- Increasing the service component of business to business (B2B) services
- Propelling new business models through technology-enabled, service encounters and platforms
- Finding symbiosis across service sectors
- Expanding sources of new service design and innovation
- Gaining momentum towards response service operations.

In our view, these forces typically remain well below the radar screen in current service operations strategy research. However, because of their evolutionary significance for advancing and steering the future course of service operations, more rigorous academic scrutiny is warranted.

These trends also reinforce the urgency of leapfrogging ahead of the curve by taking a more futuristic perspective of services. When compared to manufacturing, service operations strategy is still in its infancy. While there is some similarity with manufacturing strategy formulation, the strategic design of service delivery systems is inherently different and typically far more complex. Classical service operations management distinguishes delivery of services from goods production on five interrelated dimensions: intangibility, customers as co-producers in the delivery system, heterogeneity, perishability, and simultaneity (Fitzsimmons et al. 2014; Heskett et al. 1990; Sasser et al. 1991).

First, service strategy must account for the inherently intangible nature of services, which creates a conundrum for design and execution. Services are concurrently difficult to copy, to patent, and to convey their value to customers and stakeholders. Take, for example, the following situation: how do service firms of different types design their operating systems to effectively handle customers' implicit and explicit "feelings," such as relief from pain or WOW effects, etc.? (See, for example, Baglieri and Karmarkar 2014; Voss et al. 2008; Roth and Menor 2003; Pine and Gilmore 1998.)

Second, customers are co-producers in service systems. When compared to their employees, service providers have much less control over the "quality" of customer input (Chase and Apte 2007; Roels et al. 2014). Therefore, strategic decisions need to be made regarding the physical and virtual design of the operating systems to account for variation in customers' abilities, willingness, and appropriateness to participate in some or all parts of the service process (Froehle et al. 2007).

Third, service operations strategies must take into consideration the fact that the heterogeneity (e.g., the added system variation) in each service encounter interaction between customers and employees is different (Frei 2006). Notably, human factors play a significant role in understanding differences from customer to customer as well as among their employees (Chase and Dasu 2001; Dixon and Verma 2013; Secchi et al. forthcoming).

Fourth, many services like hotel rooms, airline seats, and doctor appointments are perishable in that they are subject to time-perishable capacity. As a result, designers must carefully develop approaches to ensure target utilization levels. Fifth, the notion of simultaneity in consumption and production implies that services cannot be stored or inventoried for use at a later date, so matching supply and demand is crucial (Fisher et al. 1994). Hence, when not occupied or in use at the allotted time, that particular revenue opportunity is gone forever; on the flip side, when demand exceeds available capacity, sales are also foregone.

As described above, each of the basic characteristics of services depend on the "appropriate" behavior of people within the operating systems and, especially, on the alignment of a myriad of customer and employee behavioral factors. Unlike marketing science, the human side of operations is not well understood in classical service operations strategy (Roth and Jackson 1995; Huete and Roth 1988; Roth et al. 1995), with perhaps some exceptions around the customer contact model (Chase 1981), employee job design, and technological adoption (Boyer et al. 2002; Hitt et al. 2002; Xue and Harker 2002). Yet today more than ever before, the interplay among the behavioral components, when combined with the dynamic interaction with market forces and the dizzying speed of technological progress, is game changing for service design and delivery. Take for example, the exploration of behavioral and design synergies between hospitality and healthcare services to improve the effectiveness of senior housing and care (Negrea 2016). Furthermore, the six evolutionary trends also impact the globalization of services between and among developed and emerging market countries. Consider, for example, that while the U.S. service sector holds 77.8% of the country's GDP, the fastest compound annual growth within the service sector GDP from 2001–2012 was observed in China (10.9%), India (9%), and, at a distant third, Russia at 5.4% (Bhargava 2015). The rise of global services indicates even more service design complexity because of the cultural and business interchanges among customers, providers, and governments.

Given all of the above, there is a need to explore the evolutionary trends and their implications for service operations strategy and design for customer experience. The future is here.

3 TRP—The Three Legs of the POM Stool

We sent a survey (see the survey instrument in the Appendix) to the first author of each chapter with a request to forward the survey to their coauthors. We received thirty-four responses, a good response rate that enables us to draw meaningful conclusions. The survey was sent on June 23, 2016, with a response date of July 7, 2016, and most respondents met the deadline, which shows their enthusiasm for the Routledge project.

The responses that we received were incredible for two reasons. First and foremost, there was a major amount of agreement on what should be done in all three TRP areas. Second, these responses were uniformly in favor of significant change. While they did not all agree on the time frame, a major portion of the respondents did reject the status quo and proposed opportunities for future improvement and change. That is important because we are hearing the voices and goals both from future leaders of POM and those who have created the foundation these future leaders are building upon.

Teaching will be expanded to include POM Teaching and Learning (Section 3.1), since that title better encompasses the relevant system. Research will be expanded to include Research and Modeling (Section 3.2), because (again) that title provides a more complete view of the intended system. Finally, practice will be expanded to include public policy, thus, leading to a rewording as follows: New POM Practice Domains (Section 3.3). This change is for the same reasons as in the prior cases.

3.1 *POM Teaching and Learning*

The responses to the questions on POM teaching and learning can be grouped in the following categories:

- POM in business schools
- Curriculum

- Teaching material
- Technology/online (could be called pedagogy)
- Systems approach/interdisciplinary teaching
- Experiential learning.

3.1.1 POM in Business Schools

There is evidence of increased student interest in POM courses in the U.S. Of course, every trend is biased by the selected starting point. If we chose the decade of the 1960s (when jobs in manufacturing, especially those held by engineers with MBA's were very attractive and widely respected), the present-day picture would not be as good. There is also evidence that the popularity of POM courses varies a great deal geographically. We believe that research is required to determine where POM courses are in demand and why they are favored in those locations. From such research, there may be useful information that can be transferred across borders.

The dynamics of the POM field of study must be understood as technological changes disrupt traditional present-day conceptions of how to make and deliver goods and services. The growing presence of artificial intelligence and robotics will affect many applications, with respondents noting in particular the effects on manufacturing, financial services, healthcare, and agriculture. It was noted that as manufacturing returns to the U.S. and Europe, the production aspects will again become important, although it will need to have a much stronger integration with the technology and management information system (MIS) areas, since so much of production will be automated.

Another factor that must be considered is the rebranding of POM as Supply Chain Management (SCM). There are manifest opinions about SCM being a subset, albeit of critical importance, of the POM field. Here too, research is warranted to determine how SCM deals with subjects such as quality (e.g., statistical quality control and Six Sigma) and process improvement (such as *Kaizen*, *Poka-yoke*, aggregate scheduling, job sequencing, and work shift assignments). In addition to finding out how various schools around the globe are dealing with SCM there are pragmatic issues about how it should be positioned.

Overall, we conclude that (presently) students prefer studying service systems to manufacturing. As a concentration, there is a low preference for POM. We believe that this is attributable to the (seemingly justified) belief that marketing and financial jobs enjoy more glamour and higher pay scales. Those MBA students who are inspired by POM topics (often via an SCM concentration) do well and go on to get good positions in industry. With new disruptive technologies, it may be possible for the POM field to return to the old days when corporate management placed highest value on engineers with MBA degrees.

3.1.2 Curriculum

Respondents indicated that POM courses dealing with process management are disappearing from the core, often being replaced by Supply Chain Management courses. In some business schools, POM teaching is restricted to a Decision Science approach to the Operations Management field. We also see POM teaching being extended to other domains including healthcare, service industries, and data analytics (OR and statistics), but such extensions do not appear to represent a widely accepted broad-based pattern.

There is a general feeling amongst respondents that POM is not being taught as well as it might be (poor curricula) at both business schools and engineering colleges. When students have a required POM course, they are seldom enthusiastic about going further with electives. Survey respondents suggested that the traditional POM curriculum does not inspire student excitement or career confidence. Perhaps this is reinforced because few curricula provide attractive electives. One respondent said that a relatively popular elective may result from POM and information technology working together.

Another respondent, emphasizing the role of information systems and service organizations, stated the following:

> I think especially in the USA, we should be predominantly service oriented in our OM teaching and also move closer to Information Systems. Service operations depend more on the underlying information systems, than manufacturing operations. For example, in our modules on TQM, we should deal with quality control and TQM of customer databases as well as with quality control of corporate information systems. In service industries this is of the utmost importance.

Consider the comment that curriculum content is determined by extant published research with some sprinkling of academic "practice" gleaned from cases, on-going research, and a smattering of consulting. For both undergraduate and MBA students, the ratio needs to change making "practice" a larger part of the pie. How to achieve this state of affairs is a relevant research question. In the U.S., relatively few professors are deeply engaged in POM practice. This is unlike Europe, where there is institutional pressure to demonstrate application relevance.

It is stated that practice is often brought into the class through guest lecturers from industry, rather than first hand personal experiences. Further, textbook content (written by professors) is mostly academic, often times replete with techniques that are obsolete or embodied in available software. An innovative and path-breaking textbook would be viewed with alarm by teachers and their Ph.D. students who have been trained in the conventional wisdoms in the traditional ways.

To be effective, we need both mathematical techniques of POM and an understanding of the management practices of our practitioners, e.g., doctors, lawyers, and farmers. We should avoid POM teaching in which quantitative "silos" overwhelm qualitative ones. Support an integrative approach which provides linkages to strategy, finance, marketing, and other areas. Most MBA students now leave with an inadequate understanding and appreciation of what it means to manage and schedule work and processes, forecast, manage inventory and capacity strategically, improve processes, and integrate processes. Most shocking is that few POM courses teach students about the job of a Chief Operating Officer.

3.1.3 Teaching Materials

This section on Teaching Materials is meant to include curriculum matters while making an effort to take a bigger look at the issues involved. A number of respondents' observations differ markedly. We conclude that some institutions have changed while others have not. This seems to indicate a need for research to determine who is doing what and how many of each kind prevail.

One respondent group observed that in the last three decades, significant changes have occurred in POM teaching. The responses stated that notable among these changes is an increased focus on *applications* rather than on *methodology*. These respondents (although not uniformly) went on to laud the use of online mechanisms for content delivery. Some also commended the integration of unique learning formats (technology based tools, gaming, simulations, and flipped classrooms) and the design of POM courses which integrate concepts from other functional areas (e.g., Marketing, Finance, and Entrepreneurship).

In contrast, another respondent group observed that POM teaching remains too grounded in traditional subject areas. Those respondents (uniformly) stated that delivery systems need major transformation. For them, a significant percent of present POM teaching is based on past and increasingly archaic industry practices. This group derided outmoded case studies, saying that we need research and development of teaching materials for new and more relevant areas. Some said that POM teaching must now adapt materials for developed and developing countries.

Another respondent said that the optimal teaching style may depend on the characteristics of individuals in the student body—what type of jobs are various segments of the student body looking for? How many POM students will end up in consulting, or in general management, or as an entrepreneur in a home business, or on Wall Street in the finance world? Each scenario demands a calculated difference in what the optimal content of a POM course would be. An answer that cuts to the heart of the matter stated that we should focus on "teaching students to be operations managers" rather than focusing on "teaching students operations management."

This same theme has appeared repeatedly which urges that we get students to analyze real operations (e.g., restaurants, hospital wards, retail outlets, manufacturing, etc.), and provide managers with a "consulting report" detailing their recommendations (technical aspects and their implementation) which must use techniques that students have discussed in class.

One respondent, who uses many different *Wall Street Journal* articles as mini-cases for class discussion and does not do much online, said,

> We really focus on doing the face-to-face, classroom interaction well, and I think there will continue to be a place for this. The students learn a lot though the in-class discussions and interactions that would be difficult to replace with a virtual classroom, given current technology.

3.1.4 Technology and Online

When it comes to teaching technology, some institutions have made a lot of progress, through the introduction of online and blended learning systems. How we teach is well served, but what we teach needs attention and revision. Another respondent stated that there are accelerating trends toward more active classrooms using technology in various new ways. Blending was mentioned as was "flipping the classroom."

One respondent said that we must discourage students from sitting in our classrooms thumbing smartphones to find answers without interaction and discussion. Classes should be taught in a blended teaching manner using technology, videos, and case studies. Let us face the challenge of digitalization of education and share with each other new learning processes that characterize millennials. Pedagogical research should be done in order to understand which new teaching methodologies would be more appropriate to the new generations and for the newer subjects of POM.

Teaching online creates both challenges and opportunities. The opportunities include the ability to use multiple media (video cases, podcasts, hyperlinks to external sites, etc.) and these mixed pedagogy approaches appeal to different learners in multiple ways. Other opportunities are online assessment, e.g., multiple-choice questionnaires. The challenges include students gaming the system—cheating in online assessment—as well as ensuring and controlling that all students actually engage with the material.

One respondent strongly recommended computer based business games to teach both POM and SCM. The respondent stated,

> I also like to use Skype and WebEx to invite executives from all around the world to speak to our students without having to fly them in. This is a cheap and effective way

to provide students with the opportunity to both learn from real high level operations managers and also build their professional networks.

We should make much better use of blended teaching and normative experiential learning. Massive Open Online Courses (MOOCs) and Open Source content will become increasingly important and accessible, so universities will need to respond by adding value and keeping abreast with latest thinking. Next generation students will expect to learn very differently, and as a result, new ways of teaching will have to be developed. Gamification and business games have begun to replace traditional lectures.

In terms of delivery, we need to take advantage of blended teaching systems that utilize technology and social media wherever possible. Integration of lectures with smartphones and tablets is a trend that should pick up and accelerate within the next few years. Hands-on projects with real world companies are another trend that leading pedagogical programs will increasingly reflect over time.

3.1.5   Systems Approach/Interdisciplinary Teaching

To achieve the many benefits of using the systems approach, the teacher must illuminate the entire picture. This includes multiple goals, and all relevant drivers of the outcomes. We must invoke cross-disciplinary management of the problem rather than staying within one department. Operations management choices affect and are affected by choices made in other areas of the business. One respondent said,

> Because my managerial course was (for no good reason) scheduled as the last core (compulsory) course in our MBA program, I was forced to think about it more as a capstone course, which in hindsight has done a lot to improve it on this front!

We must not forget that our roots lie in the area of decision making. Mathematical models, which are more easily accessed with new technology, can still be used as tools to provide information as an input for a final decision.

Another respondent stated,

> Decisions are not made in a vacuum, but are driven by strategy, the markets, financial justifications, and such. At a minimum, such integration needs to be added. POM is critical yet I don't think we link these decisions to current events and "relatable" issues.

Another person said that much of the POM teaching material is dated and does not reflect the convergence of functions. HR is still taught separately and should be much more closely related in a socio-technical systems approach, as should operations strategy and management accounting.

3.1.6   Experiential Learning

Several respondents said that classroom teaching of POM is important but so are current real life examples. In the words of one of the respondents, "Every student in almost every major should understand the impact of practicing POM approaches in solving business problems." To meet this educational challenge, it would be useful to stress the role of experiential learning. The students have to be given real-life examples and stories of how different approaches to POM have made significant differences in the outcome of organizations solving business problems. In other words, learning to do what needs to be done on the job. Ways of approaching this include mentoring, internships, group consulting projects, debates, and field trips. Cases might qualify if taught by teachers who have actual consulting experience that they can share in the classroom or online.

It is important to take students to visit organizations that practice using sound POM methods. Plant visits to disorganized companies may be illuminating for a brief period unless the project includes introducing good organizational systems. In that case, students get to deal with real problems and have an opportunity (longer term) to see real examples of POM thinking being implemented. They begin to understand the impact of POM methods. One respondent stated that "our research has shown that dialogue and reinforcement are critical for learning." Another urged integrating POM experiences with other disciplines.

In this regard, it was noted that field trips which reflect POM operations across supply chains should be constructed. Research might be useful to define how best to do this kind of exercise. It comes to mind that class projects that bring suppliers and producers into the evaluation and judging process have been shown to be enjoyed by all participants in such an endeavor. In addition, POM field trips (to actual cross supply chain operations) ought to be an integral and regular part of the learning program. Some schools do this well, but they are in the minority

The POM community needs to focus on the employability of POM students, which is often ignored, to attract students to the discipline. If certain courses such as supply chain management seem to be important to recruiters, then students will opt for them. Our field needs research to determine what managers in a variety of industries consider important in their employment profiles. The following comment is on target: "Recruiters want today's MBA students to study POM topics in the context of new industries such as digital technology, new physical technologies, new types of services (such as belonging to the shared economy), marketplaces, and networks, and so on." It seems like a good idea for POM researchers to find out what recruiters want today (in quite specific locales) and what they will likely be wanting the day after tomorrow.

3.2 Research and Modeling

For research projections, the responses can be divided into four interconnected groups: Models and Methodology, Interdisciplinary Research, Research Domains, and Publications Outlets.

3.2.1 Models and Methodology

Decision making needs to be bolstered with decision support systems that combine models and empirical studies. A number of times, it was urged that heuristic methods and systems dynamics be more broadly applied. Additionally, simulations were lauded by various people as permitting inclusion of a larger number of variables thereby achieving more complex models of realistic situations. Research on larger, integrated processes was suggested to aid in coping with the nature of complex adaptive systems. Technology users need to work closely with technology developers. It was stressed that each area of application has many unique uses of technologies.

Prescriptive (modeling) and descriptive (empirical) studies can be better coordinated and blended. We need research on how to blend these methodologies instead of choosing one or the other.

Here is a list of various disparate comments that were made about research methodology:

- Rigorous methodology is essential, but it must be open and applied to real problems.
- Methods that include behavioral elements as well as competition and strategic organizational choices (e.g., merger, entry, and exit) are needed.
- Longitudinal survey methods and behavioral testing for refinement of model assumptions are required.
- Can we learn anything from innovations in other fields such as medicine and biotechnology?
- Keep track of how many times "practice" followed POM prescriptions for implementation.
- Industry 4.0 methods should be understood and absorbed by POM.
- Quality control should be applied to customer databases and corporate information systems. This is particularly important for service industries.
- Multi-method systems (and triangulation) need to be developed, coordinated, used, tested, and improved. Blended methodologies and blended research methods are emerging with machine learning and operations analytics. (Note that **triangulation** is a powerful technique that facilitates validation of data through cross verification from two or more sources. In particular, it refers to the application and combination of several research methods in the study of the same phenomenon.)
- Supply chains information flows require methods to facilitate and enhance them. Knowledge outsourcing has complexity that does not exist in component flows.
- Environmental POM and Sustainability Methodologies are essential teaching and research topics that tend to get short shrift.

Contrary to the current hype, many of our survey respondents share the opinion that "Big Data" as a term will not survive for much longer. Data-based studies show the world as it is: there must be models that can show the direction to improvements (optimization is never mentioned). Predictive analytics (based on existing data) may show trends and is valuable.

3.2.2 Interdisciplinary Research

Many respondents mentioned an interest in interdisciplinary research as an avenue that must be expanded as it is necessary to build bridges among disciplines. Siloes in organizations and in journals inhibit interdisciplinary efforts. Collaborative research between functions in all kinds of organizations would provide needed insights. This might apply to better supply chain decisions and communication. Connections to IT and the cloud must be developed for OM (this was said in different ways by different respondents). Here, we cite statements from two respondents about interdisciplinary research:

> There is a great push toward interdisciplinary research, though still difficult from a publishing standpoint as journals are 'siloed', Nevertheless, I think many of the contemporary research problems we see in practice can only be addressed through some type of interdisciplinary approach. How this is done and structured are certainly challenges. Along these lines, there is a greater push toward multi-method research to provide greater methodological rigor.
>
> Our experience has shown that inter-disciplinary research can provide new and powerful insights into a domain. For example, rather than simply thinking about a farmer's adoption of a technology, one thinks about the innovation network operating around that technology or suite of technologies. New technologies will open up opportunities for POM, but we need to be working with the technology developers and the technology users to have impact here.

3.2.3 Research Domains

More studies are needed that relate OM to entrepreneurship, POM cases connected to multidisciplinary learning, and Omni-Channel Fulfillment methods. The impact of developments in advances, such as 3D printing, driverless cars, the Internet of Things (I of T), robotics, and artificial intelligence (AI) on POM, needs to be assessed. Several other research areas include waste management systems, agriculture, and processed food supply chains, methods that apply to shared economy applications. Better methods are needed for visualization and communication such as finding the best way to convey information in a picture (e.g., using diagrams) or understanding how software can be made more effective for visualization. This type of thinking is a relatively new area that must be supported because our brightest young scholars are telling us to "pay attention." Methodology for the use of social networks needs to be developed.

3.2.4 Publications Outlet

One of the respondents mentioned the lack of high-quality journals (the respondent calls these "4★ POM journals") compared to other disciplines, writing,

> This reduces the scope for REF return in OM, which has meant that universities have invested in departments, such as strategy and marketing, where they can get a higher REF return, so P/OM has suffered in attracting the investment, and credibility, it deserves.

The Research Excellence Framework (REF) is the successor to the *Research Assessment Exercise*, a method of assessing the research of British higher education institutions. It took place in 2014 to assess research carried out during the period 2008–2013 inclusive. The results were published on December 18, 2014.

3.3 New POM Practice Domains

Responses to POM practice are categorized in the following three groups: emerging areas, geographical expansion, and POM and the public sector.

3.3.1 Emerging Application Areas

The emerging area mentioned the most was that of disaster management. The second most notable mention was the use of cross-functional efforts; also termed as integration of POM with other areas by one of the respondents. This matches with what was mentioned in research as well. POM should develop applications to data products as compared to the traditional application to physical products. In the same vein is the feeling that POM should be used for the management of information flows.

There is a theme that runs across many answers to many parts of the survey: there can be greater application to non-profit and government sectors. Also, there is a need for assisting start-ups and engagement with a broader range of services, especially related to the sharing economy (e.g., Uber) and financial services.

Only mentioned once but still entirely relevant are: agriculture and processed food supply chain, Internet of Things, autonomous vehicle design and manufacture, office robotics, R&D, solid waste management, sustainability (especially reverse supply chains), risk management of supply chains, distributed manufacturing industry, political campaigns, and entertainment.

Finally, there is a European awareness of Industry 4.0, with one respondent mentioning the (related) idea of a circular economy. The *circular economy* is a generic term for an industrial *economy* that produces no waste and pollution, by design or intention, and in which material flows are of two types: biological nutrients, designed to reenter the biosphere safely, and technical nutrients, which are designed to circulate at high quality in the production system without entering the biosphere. This is in contrast to a Linear Economy, which is a take, make, and dispose model of production.

One respondent talks about the "dark side of supply chains," which refers to things like counterfeiting products and the use of child labor.

3.3.2 Geographical Expansion

Many issues arose under various questions that relate to geography. The major one is the difference between developed and less developed countries for implementation differences often stemming from quite different approaches in a variety of cultures. One gets the feeling that these problems are glossed over even though they are blocking good communications along the supply chain. In the same regard, the visibility of supply chain partners is often not possible because of cultural issues and, consequently, supply chain risk is high and needs to be managed (e.g., risk management of supply chains).

There is a real need for public sector involvement of POM in developing countries because there is great waste (especially in poor countries). There are also serious issues concerning protection of knowledge transferred to developing countries.

POM techniques have greater clout in small countries if those smaller countries will allow applications. Two points about the smaller countries may be noted. First, a lack of managers with a POM education can be a major impediment to success. Second, these countries also often lack adequate infrastructure, which means that local laws can be overlooked and misunderstood.

Finally, and this is a cross-over between geography and teaching, we need more cases that reflect the realities of global supply chains. Of interest is the impact of new technology on emerging economies, for example, the use of drones and robots.

3.3.3 POM and the Public Sector

There are two interpretations that were made by respondents. First is the degree to which POM methods can be applied to the public sector. Second, how does public policy impact POM's work in the private and the not-for-profit sectors?

3.3.3.1 REGARDING THE FIRST POM INTERPRETATION

Although no one seems to have a plan for POM to get involved, most everyone thought it was logical for POM methods to be applied to many public sector applications. Some respondents believe it has already occurred to a limited degree and would like to see more applications of POM methods. This seems like an opportunity that we should research and even consider involving the Production and Operations Management Society (POMS) to promote public sector applications.

It is expected that POM will move into the public sector, but current usage is low. Public sector research requires non-traditional objective functions. Interest in non-traditional objective functions seems to be growing. It was also pointed out that public sector policy may need new insights about leadership in the public sector.

Military systems have been there for years. The field was born in war. It started as OR and whatever you call it, many POM methods are used by the military which is a public sector application. However, most (academic) research journals seem disinterested in applied work.

Two respondents had the following interesting comments: Research is needed to apply POM to NGOs and that will happen. Change the objective functions and develop multi-criteria objective functions. The National Academies have organized discussions of using POM for building peace in various hot spots. POM is moving into healthcare. See the South Korea Trauma Center Network (Cho et al. 2014).

3.3.3.2 Regarding the Second POM Involvement

The answer to the question, "How is POM as a field affected by public policy?" depends on which country we are we talking about. One respondent mentioned that "tariff structures and economic trading blocs" will affect many POM practices. That certainly includes the relevant supply chains. One said that Brexit will change the system that POM needs to deal with. Overall, the concern was with impact on practitioners. There was a good deal of concurrence that as researchers, we need to define the problems faced by practitioners.

Other issues raised included minimum wage laws, safety rules and regulations, supply chain identities, cybersecurity, and info flows across firms. Standardization by public policy can make a big difference (e.g., for pallets) as pallet standardization will increase speeds of delivery of services, improve product quality, and benefit the environment.

Additionally, it was stated that POM can play an important role with respect to energy policies and sustainability decisions. We should actively monitor trends in public policy since these decisions will impact research funding. Funding also impacts POM practitioners (for example, with respect to road, bridge, and building infrastructures, to health services, to military bases and logistics, and to bi-lateral trade). Will Triple Bottom Line (3BL) become institutionalized by public sector policy?

Finally, public sector policy may play a lesser role in a globalized world. Will UN policy affect POM? One reply said: 3BL will require greater accountability and will put more pressure on OM practitioners.

4 Conclusions

It was interesting to see the degree to which congruence and convergence occurred among the respondents of the survey. We tried to reflect (in general terms) who concurred with whom, and vice versa. Research is necessary in order to further develop the emerging patterns of agreement and to diagnose the causes and cures for disagreements.

For example, services and manufacturing are still vying for investment funds in different geopolitical settings. Services are becoming a more important sector of all economies. However, there are those who advocate being entirely committed to services with a zero-manufacturing base. Others proclaim that without manufacturing, a society is off-balance. The resolution of the ideal ratio will not be fixed in time. It is a dynamic parameter that varies over time according to geographic and technological factors. It shifts with the wealth of nations in their infrastructure and their institutional accomplishments in education and culture. There is no doubt about the fact that manufacturing will not disappear but it will change. As robotic technology emerges, new patterns will characterize global shifts. All people continue to need clothes and shoes to wear. but where will they be made in the next decade, by whom, and how?

It is likely that many new forms of fabrication will appear in the U.S. and Europe as well as Asia (and let us not overlook South America, Africa, and even the depths of outer space) to replace outsourcing with domestic sourcing. From each country's point of view, there are only two forms of sourcing. Either make products locally (domestically) or in a different country where wage rates are so much lower that extra costs of transportation are irrelevant. This should be a simple decision, if, and only if, you can prognosticate correctly the costs, prices, and demand levels of all consumer products.

Theoretical history is science fiction, another name for the prognostication of future events. History has many data points that indicate how the interests of the citizenry will play an important role. Advocates of Brexit exemplify this effect. Political leadership in many countries including the U.S. are determined to play an important role.

We sum up our findings by quoting some capstone conclusions of the broad field of respondents to our survey.

First, the POM field is outreaching to many application areas where operations research is well-known, statistical techniques are widely applied, data analytics has been increasingly applauded, but POM is relatively unknown. This tells us that how we in the field define ourselves, determines how others see us. It would help if a broader definition of operations management was developed. It must include manufacturing as presently practiced and as it is likely to be practiced in the future. But greater degrees of AI and automation using robotics will substantially impact services as well. It must include the evolving fields of services in hospitals and hospitality venues, in sports arenas and entertainment centers, in restaurants and theaters, museums and concert halls. It must also include stadiums and libraries as well as police stations and Courts of Law.

Second, POM principles in not-for-profit and government organizations are founded on different objective functions. POM is not wedded to the profit function. There are so many signs that it is growing up and getting wings. Otherwise, it would become irrelevant with co-operatives, volunteer-based organizations, and evolving organizational structures related to a sharing economy (e.g., Uber, AirBnB, Vizeat, etc.).

Third, we sensed the urgency of our respondents to develop robust POM approaches that can be used successfully under both developed and developing world perspectives. Following that, we found that while many concepts are evolving rapidly outside the current boundary of POM, they will have huge implications for POM in general. These trends include mobile-payment systems; Fin Tech—Smart: cities, homes, and service systems, the Internet of Things, wearable technologies, and the embedding of sensors in almost everything. More focus needs to be on "value-creation" in general and linkages with theories from other disciplines (e.g., Service-Dominant Logic from Marketing).

Finally, the development of any discipline requires constant guiding and monitoring. POM is no exception. There have been informal overseers and authorities to guide its development since the very beginning. The origins of various government and international agencies (e.g., U.S. Food and Drug Administration, and the International Organization for Standardization—ISO) can be traced back to the artisan craft guilds, beginning around 1500 CE that came into being for compliance of product standards in each trade. The current era also witnessed the creation of many professional organizations to foster research and practice in POM. Some of these include: the Production and Operations Management Society (POMS), the Manufacturing and Service Operations Management Society (MSOM), the European Operations Management Association (EuROMA), the American Production and Inventory Control Society (APICS), and the Japanese Operations Management and Strategy Association (JOMSA).

References and Bibliography

Baglieri, E., & Karmarkar, U. (2014) *Managing Consumer Services: Factory or Theater?* Springer International Publishing, Cham, Switzerland.

Bhargava, Y. (2015) "India has second fastest growing service sector," *The Hindu*, February 23. www.thehindu.com/business/budget/india-has-second-fastest-growing-services-sector/article6193500.ece

Boyer, K. K., Hallowell, R., & Roth, A. V. (2002) "E-services: Operating strategy—a case study and a method for analyzing operational benefits." *Journal of Operations Management*, **20**(2): 175–188.

Bureau of Labor Statistics (2015) "Industry employment and output projections to 2014," Monthly Labor Review of the United States Department of Labor, December 2015. www.bls.gov/emp/ep_table_201.htm

Central Intelligence Agency (2016) *The World Factbook*. www.cia.gov/library/publications/the-world-factbook/geos/xx.html. Accessed May 26, 2016.

Chase, R. B. (1981) "The customer contact approach to services: Theoretical bases and practical extensions," *Operations Research*, **29**(4): 698–706.

Chase, R. B., & Apte, U. M. (2007) "A history of research in service operations: What's the big idea?" *Journal of Operations Management*, **25**(2): 375–386.

Chase, R. B., & Dasu, S. (2001) "Want to perfect your company's service? Use behavioral science," *Harvard Business Review*, **79**(6): 78–84.

Cho, S. H., Jang, H., Lee, T., & Turner, J. (2014) "Simultaneous location of trauma centers and helicopters for emergency medical service planning," *Operations Research*, **62**(4): 751–771.

Dixon, M., & Verma, R. (2013) "Sequence effects in service bundles: Implications for service design and scheduling," *Journal of Operations Management*, **31**(3): 138–152.

Employee Projections [online] (2015) *U.S. Bureau of Labor Statistics*. Available from: www.bls.gov/emp/ep_table_201.htm. Accessed 27 Jul 2016.

Fisher, M. L., Hammond, J. H., Obermeyer, W. R., & Raman, A. (1994) "Making supply meet demand in an uncertain world," *Harvard Business Review*, **72**(2): 83–103.

Fitzsimmons, J., Fitzsimmons, M., & Bordoloi, S. K. (2014) *Service Management: Operations, Strategy, Information Technology*. 8th Edition, McGraw-Hill Higher Education, New York.

Frei, F. X. (2006) "Breaking the trade-off between efficiency and service," *Harvard Business Review*, **84**(11): 92.

Froehle, C. M., & Roth, A. V. (2007) "A resource-process framework of new service development," *Production and Operations Management*, **16**(2): 169–188.

Heskett, J. L., Sasser, Jr., W. E., & Hart, C. W. L. (1990) *Service Breakthroughs: Changing the Rules of the Game*. The Free Press, New York.

Hitt, L. M., & Frei, F. X. (2002) "Do better customers utilize electronic distribution channels? The case of PC banking," *Management Science*, **48**(6): 732–748.

Huete, L. M., & Roth, A. V. (1988) "The industrialization and span of retail banks' delivery systems," *International Journal of Operations & Production Management*, **8**(3): 46–66

Morgan, I., & Rao, J. (2003) "Making routine customer experiences fun," *MIT Sloan Management Review*, **45**(1): 93–95.

Negrea, S. (2016) "Exploring ideas from hospitality, health Management, and design for senior housing and care: Insights from 2016 CIHF Living Roundtable," *Cornell Institute for Healthy Futures*, **1**(1): 4–11.

Pine, B. J., & Gilmore, J. H. (1998) "Welcome to the experience economy," *Harvard Business Review*, **76**(4): 97–105.

Roels, G. (2014) "Optimal design of coproductive services: Interaction and work allocation," *Manufacturing & Service Operations Management*, **16**(2): 578–594.

Roth, A. V., & Jackson III, W. E. (1995) "Strategic determinants of service quality and performance: Evidence from the banking industry," *Management Science*, **41**(11): 1720–1733.

Roth, A. V., & Menor, L. J. (2003) "Designing and managing service operations: Introduction to the special issue," *Production and Operations Management*, **12**(2): 141–144.

Roth, A. V., Julian, J., & Malhotra, M. K. (1995) "Assessing customer value for reengineering: Narcissistic practices and parameters from the next generation," *Business Process Change: Reengineering Concepts, Methods, and Technologies*. Harrisburg, PA: Idea Group Publishing, 453–473.

Roth, A., Singhal, J., Singhal, K., & Tang, C. S. (2016) "Knowledge creation and dissemination in operations and supply-chain management," *Production and Operations Management*, **forthcoming**.

Sasser, Jr., W. E., Hart, C. W., & Heskett, J. L. (1991) *The Service Management Course: Cases and Readings*. The Free Press, NY.

Secchi, E., Roth, A., and Verma, R. (2017) "The impact of service improvisation competence on customer satisfaction: Evidence from the hospitality industry," *Production and Operations Management Journal*, **forthcoming**.

Voss, C., Roth, A. V., & Chase, R. (2008) "Experience, service operations strategy, and services as destinations: Foundations and exploratory investigation," *Production and Operations Management*, **17**(3): 247–266.

Xue, M., & Harker, P. T. (2002) "Customer efficiency concept and its impact on e-business management," *Journal of Service Research*, **4**(4): 253–267.

Appendix

Survey of the Contributors to the Routledge "Companion"

We will not use the typical 10-point scale. Please write us about each of these three major topics.

We will do our best to analyze your meanings and use Delphi concepts to interpret your intent.

POM Teaching
Focus on some of the following issues.
Give an assessment of POM Teaching. Is the POM field being taught properly? Or, alternatively, what can be done to improve how we teach POM?
In-class?
On-line?
Blended teaching systems?
Using technology?
POM Research
What new research directions do you envisage for the POM research domain?
Methodologically
Models (either or both: quantitative and qualitative)
Empirical studies
Blended methods
Technology (Robotics, 3D printing, etc.)
Big Data Analytics and Computing
POM Practice

The focus is at organizational, national, and international levels.

What are the emerging areas in which POM can be used? For example, applications of POM have been identified in many emerging fields in the "Companion." These include, among others, disaster management, sports, agriculture, and telecommunications.

What are your views on the geographical expansion of POM practice? Can you apply this to Manufacturing and Service? Will there be geographic differentials in adoption of POM methods?

What is the role of public policy in POM's future?

Will POM methods find their ways in the public sector (government and its agencies; e.g., public health, IRS, FEMA, UN, and WHO etc.) and nonprofit sector (e.g., Red Cross, NGOs, social, health, and educational services)?

INDEX

Note: Page numbers in **bold** refer to **figures**; Page numbers in *italics* refer to *tables*

absorptive capacity 201, 204–207, 209
access block 434, 436
accomplishments 676–677
accounting 242, 313, 345–354, 356, 358, 377, 381, 392, 521, 606, 676, 683; cost 242; information technology advances 358
activity scheduling 215–216
Activity-Based Costing (ABC) 242, 346, 348, 355; hierarchy 355–357
actors: non-state 503–504
adaptability 21, 215, 224, 227, 551, 556, 665
additive manufacturing technologies 181, 185, 199, 659, 667
Advanced Manufacturing Technologies (AMT) 180
Advanced Micro Devices (AMD) 198
Advanced Research Projects Agency Network (ARPANET) 12
advances in science and technology 197–200, 202–210
advertisement 46, 291, 294–298; scheduling 297
advertising: cooperative 385; online 296–298
aerotropolis 311
affect heuristic 332
agency costs 360, 362, 370
agency theory (AT) 346–348, 670–672
agglomeration 309–310, 313, 316, 318, 322, 419; versus dispersion 311
Aggregate Inventory Analysis 101, 108–109, 122–123
aggregate production planning 65, 77–79, 102; dimensions 63–64; disaggregation 71–75; evaluation of early models 70; historical perspective 66–71; importance 63; in practice 75–77

aggregated supplier delivery 632, 639–640
Agile Manifesto 244
Agile Manufacturing (AM) 173–174, 242–244, 246, 248
agile PM 220, 224
aid provisioning 510, 513–514, 517–520, 522
Air Logistics Park Singapore (ALPS) 314
air transport 559
Airbnb 20, 255, 257, 267, 269, 689
algorithm design 292–293
aligned domains 329–335, 337
alignment of incentives 18, 26, 34–35
all-unit discount 106, 116
alliances: competitor 204–205, 207–208; and partnerships 204–205, 207–209
allocation 520–521; bases 354–355
Amazon 14, 145, 163, 169, 199–200, 266, 268–269, 296, 375–376, 529, 531, 579, 583, 587
American National Standards Institute (ANSI) 10
American Production and Inventory Control Society (APICS) 13, 121, 123, 689
American Society for Quality (ASQ) 129–130
Americans with Disabilities Act (ADA, 1990) 166
amplification effect *see* bullwhip effect
analytics: predictive 56, 162, 164, 301, 337, 685
anchor product position 279
anchoring and insufficient adjustment heuristic **31**, 332
ant colony algorithm 71, 153, 573
anti-value 223
Anticipatory Protection 287
APICS (American Production and Inventory Control Society) 13, 121, 123, 689
Apple 32, 304, 385, 628, 657–659

Index

appointment: overbooking 94–95; scheduling 83, 92, 94–95, **96**
approximation algorithm 85–88
arbitrage 363
architecture 3, 217, 222, 224
architecture frameworks (AFs) 223–224
ARENA Software 437
arsenals 497–498
Asian Tigers 612
assembly line 6–8, 10, 25, 82, 97, 128, 148–149, 170, 179, 497, 650, 652, 654
assortment planning 580, 583–585, 588, 591–592
asymmetric information 28, 219, 285–286, 296, 365, 586, 670
attribution bias **331**, 332
auctioning strategies 298
audience targeting 297–298
automation 19, 145, **148**, 155–158, 160–161, 164, 166, 174, 179–180, 235, 241, 298–299, 356–357, 574, 657, 660, 689
availability heuristic 332
availability/familiarity bias 331

backorder costs 67, 379
backordering 103
Balanced Scorecard 346, 348–349, 351–352
batch-picking 160
Bayesian networks (BN) 530
behavior 221; designing for 335–337; opportunistic 29, 31, 38, 205
Behavioral Operations (BeOps) 327–329, 332, 339–340
benchmarking 121, 455
Bessemer 11
best practices 173, 224, 239, 247, 264, 317, 398, 405–407, 455, 580, 605, 609, 630; in design for OM tools 337–338; in Human Resources (HR) 403–404; in Human Resources Management (HRM) 395–397; and manufacturing 178–179
biases 50–54, 258, 330–333, 335–339, 378
big data 58, 162, 291, 298, 305, 459, 505, 532–533, 539, 574, 643, 657, 685; analytics 45, 56–57, 174, 185; and city planning 299–300
black swan theory 56–57
blue-collar jobs 317, 614, 657, 660
bounded rationality 328–330, **331**, 332
Brexit 19, 688–689
bricks and clicks 589–590
BRICS 322, 615, 664–665
broken-leg cues 54
Bronze Age 4
Brooklyn Bridge 11
brown products 279–281
brownfield: versus greenfield 199–200
budget 64, 73, 106, 109, 120, 122, 131, 203, 214, 224, 298, 434, 480, 491, 501, 514–515, 520, 602

bullwhip effect 17–18, 20, 35–38, 46–47, 107, 328–329, 345, 582, 665, 670
business: improvement systems 125–126, 242–244, 246–247; Omni Channel 615; plan 57, 63–64, 73, 73–74, 76, 263, 265, 378, 401; schools 121, 679–680
business model innovations (BMIs) 256, 262, 264, 266–269
buy-online, pick-up in store (BOPS) 377, 588

caching 531–533, 539
Can Manufacturing and Marketing Coexist? (Shapiro) 374
Canadian Association of Emergency Physicians (CAEP) 434
Canadian Triage Acuity Standards (CTAS) 437
cannibalization 281–284
capabilities: manufacturing 171, 175–177, 201, 263, 628, *see also* process capabilities
capability planning 379–380, 387
capacity: constraints 120, 262, 281, 348; management 244, 256–257, 265, 268, 416, 564; planning 16, 354, 528–529, 531, 565, 677; pricing 534
capacity allocation 329, 533–534; and sharing 529–530
capital: structure 368; versus labor 657–658; working 47, 102, 120, 361
Capital Asset Pricing Model (CAPM) 363, 368
capital investment 63, 73, 178, 309, 366, 394, 430, 452, 459, 503, 528, 619–620
Capital (Marx) 649
capital-intensive manufacturing 624–625, **626**, 627–628, **629**, 630
capitalism: industrial 657; *laissez-faire* 653; merchant 657
capitation 429
carbon emissions 164–165, 276, 277, 278, 286, 288, 319, 558, 590, 621, 651
care *see* healthcare; preventive care
cargo routing problem 565–566
carrying costs 109, 111–112, 114–115, 121, 314
causal forecasting 52, 55
cause-and-effect diagram 130, 136, **137**
Centre for Research on the Epidemiology of Disasters (CRED) 545
Chain of Excellence Model 603
channel: coordination 360, 367, 385; dynamics 383–385
check sheets 138
China: outsourcing to 16–18; Special Economic Zones 16, 322, 613
circular economy 184–185, 256, 687
city: energy needs 299–300; planning 298–300; smart 291, 298–301, 305; transportation 299
civilian operations management 497–498, 500–501

Index

Classification and Regression Trees (CARTs) 512, 530
clearance markdowns 580, 583–584, 591
closed-loop supply chains 184–185, 334, 452, 664, 668
cloud computing 162–163, 300, 302, 527–528, 531, 533–536, 539, 657, 685
clusters *see* logistics clusters
Code of Hammurabi (1754 BC) 128
cognitive limitation 328–330, **331**, 332–333
cognitive psychology 329–333
collaboration 164, 312–314, 322, 666–668, 670–671; horizontal 312, 322; intra-cluster 312–314
Collaborative Planning, Forecasting, and Replenishment (CPFR) 57, 379, 642
collaborative relationships 28, 671
collections process 282–283
collective producer responsibility (CPR) 286
combat 498–500, 502–503
combining forecasts 52–55
commercial returns 664
Commodity Products 48, 199, 624, 626, **627**, 628–630
communication 35–38
competencies 169, 171–172, 175–176, 185, 386, 393, 397–398, 403, 665–669, 672; core 30–31
competition 25, 28, 30–32, 161, 281, 605–606
competitive priorities 171–172, 175, 177, 182
competitive ratio 85
competitor alliances 204–205, 207–208
completion time 84–88, 97
complex adaptive systems (CAS) 222, 224, 684
complexity 214, 216–217, 219–224, 226, 256, 287, 313, 328–330, 332, 334, 338–339, 387, 433–434, 436–437, 505, 623–624, 643, 664–667, 670–672, 679
component commonality 281–282
Compound Monthly Growth Rate (CMGR) 632
computational complexity 84–85, 573
concept of POM 609
concurrent engineering 217
conflict 500–505
connected hub structure 563
connectivity 162, 320–321, 531–532, 536, 538
connectivity-based analytics (CBA) 256–257, 264–265, 267–271
constant work-in-process (CONWIP) 16, 166
constraints 64–65, 68–76, 258, 262–263; capacity 349–352; and objective function 572–573; operational 255–258, 262, 264–265, 267, 270–271
consumer: behavior 377, 520, 583–585, 592; demand 34–38, 77, 378–379, 528, 585, 619, 626; green 279–280; knowledge 383–385
consumption: environmental impact 614–615; new 615–616; stock-dependent 101, 107, 122; tax 286

content delivery network (CDN) 533–534
content distribution 533
contextual information 54–55
contingency plans 200, 467–468, 470, 472–473, 477–480, 487, 492–493, 561
continuity bias 336
continuous review policy 103
contract manufacturing 17, 613, 618–619
control 468–470, 472–473, 475–477, 479–482, 485, 489–493, 601–602; charts 129, 138, **139**, 499; process 468–469, 473, 480–493; responses 468–469, 479, 482, 484–485, 487–488, 491–492
CONWIP (constant work-in-process) 16, 166
cooperation 25–26, 28, 31
cooperative advertising 385
coopetitive development 204–205, 207
coordinated replenishment 115, 122
coordination 35–38, 216–217; channel 360, 367; cross-functional 399–400; organizational 216–217; risk 329
core competencies 30–31, 161, 175, 386, 633
corporate social responsibility (CSR) 121, 145, 277, 374, 382, 385–387, 418
corporate support 511
corridor route structure 562, *563*
cost accounting 242
cost measurement 346; accuracy of 356–357; dynamic 358; mechanics of 354–356; and operations 354–357
costing 357, 618, 620–621
costs: agency 360, 362, 370; backorder 67; carrying 103; disposal 285–287; distress 367, 370; of hiring and firing 67; ordering 103–105, 109, 111–112, 115–116, 356, 361; product variety 350, 356–357; shortage 103–104, 112, 121; transaction 29, 29–31, 30–31, 204, 362, 669–672
Council of Supply Chain Management Professionals (CSCMP) 557
Coverage Analysis 110–111, 121–123
crashing 91–92, 216, 222
Creating Disney Magic (Cockerell) 604
crew scheduling and rostering 562, 569–570
crisis management 18–19, 538, 608–609
Critical Path Method (CPM) 90–91, 216
Crosby, Philip B. 8, 15, 128, 131
cross-docking logistics (CDL) 635, 640–641
cross-functional coordination 399–400
crowdsourcing 58, 262, 300
cube-per-order index policy 158–159
cumulative model 176–177
current issues in POM 397–400
current moment bias **331**, 332
curriculum 215, 500, 604, 617, 679–681
customer: experience 161, 163, 414, 587–591, 601, 642, 677–679; quality expectations 125, 127, 134, 144; segmentation 283, 375–378, 417, 419
customer environmental awareness (CEA) 281–282

695

Index

customer service 53, 64, 71, 75–76, 79, 257, 317, 561, 579–581, 583, 587, 601–603, 655–656, 666
Customer Service-Managing Systems and Processes 601
customer-level high-frequency data 589
customization 26, 161, 173–175, 181, 198, 248, 314–315, 630, 664
cycles 48
cyclicality 222, 468, 671

data 291–296, 298–305; analytics 20, 162, 256, 291, 296, 301–302, 304–305, 394, 405, 407, 456, 527, 676, 680, 689; customer-level high-frequency 589; from mobile platform 294–295; in sport 455–456, see also big data
Data Analysis Platform **643**
Data Envelopment Analysis (DEA) 278
data mining 145, 162, 295–296, 304, 555, 574
data science 298
data-driven supply chain management 642–644
data-rich forecasting 378–379, 387
decentralized system 15, 17–18, 282, 285–286, 300, 432, 522, 529, 582–583, 655
decision: integration 573; manufacturing 177–179, 618; operational 361–362, 362–367, 368; rules 66–71, 106, 110–111, 332, 356, 470, 475, 477, 480, 493, 505; variables 63, 65–68, 71, 85, 93, 103–104, 106, 111–112, 115, 349, 563, 566–567, 571–572, see also operational decisions
decision point recognition 468, 484–487
decision-making 164, 173, 181, 207, 257–258, 299–300, 302, 310, 328, 330, 332–334, 345, 394, 400, 439–440, 452, 468, 472, 487, 568, 582, 591–592, 623–630, 652, 655; processes 27–28, 75–76, 82, 328, 330, 332–333, 378, 467, 469, 553, 663, 666–667
decomposition 75, 222, 570
dedicated storage policy 158, 166
definition of quality 125, 131
delayed differentiation 656
demand: consumer 34–38; curve **642**; lumpy 38, 58; management 46–47, 416; non-stationary 655–656; variability 117–120, 198
demand-side platforms (DSPs) 298
Deming, William Edwards 8, 13, 15, 128–131, 238, 243, 245, 497, 650
derivative NPD projects 202–203, 206–207, 209
descriptive research: versus normative research 467–468
design 277; eco- 284–285; network 527–528, 654, 656; product 65, 131, 198, 201–202, 209, 217, 222, 267, 277–281, 285, 355, 380, 617, 656; schedule 565–567, 572; of sport operations 451–452; static route 563; warehouse 158–160, 164, 166
Design of Experiments, The (Fisher) 129
Design for Manufacture and Assembly (DFMA) 142

design for manufacturing (DFM) 5
design for product recovery (DfR) 286
design structure matrix (DSM) 217
deterministic scheduling 83–84, 97
developing countries 276, 448, 519, 579, 659, 664, 682, 687
development: product 15–16, 78, 205, 209, 217, 277–278, 280, 282, 619, 656, 676
device manufacturing 303
devices 294–296, 298–299, 303, 304
diagnosis 468, 482, 484–485, 487–489
differentiation: delayed 656
digital technologies 179–181, 185, 256–257, 271, 579, 684; new 264–266
dimensions of aggregation 63–64
direct link structure 562, *563*
directions for research 669–672
disaggregation 45, 63, 70–75
disaster management (DM) 4, 15, 537, 539, 556, 676, 686; achievement of excellence 544–547; context 543–544; cycle **544**, 548; future projections 551–552; past history 547–548; potential applications in 300–301; present situation 548–550; present taxonomies 548–550; present typologies 550; research 553–555
disaster recovery 300–301, 518, 536–537, 539, 548
discount: quantity 102, 106, 116–117, 651
disjunctive graph 90, **91**
Disney Great Leader Strategies (DGLS) 603–604, 606
dispersion 182, 208, 322, 582; versus agglomeration 311
disposal costs 285–287
disruption 10–14, 18, 20–21, 39–40, 58, 122, 126, 200, 204, 247, 270, 369, 383, 386–387, 435, 543, 562, 591, 615, 619, 663, 665–666; management 419–420, 562, 568–569, 572
distress costs 367, 370
distribution: challenges 622; global 622; plans 74–75; product 377, 517–520; of product and service 517–520
division of labor 5–7, 10–11, 14, 20, 497
do-it-yourself 404
domain knowledge 53–55, 619
donation 511–516, 519–520
downside risk 473, 479, 493
Drum, Buffer, Rope (DBR) 244
dynamic capabilities theory 381–382, 386–387
dynamic cost measurement 358
dynamic packet routing (DPR) 528
dynamic packet transmission (DPT) 528
dynamic problem 83–84
dynamic route design 563

e-commerce 160, 164, 266, 292, 319, 579–580, 615–616, 623, 632–635, *636*, 640, 644; supply chain model 634–635, *636*
e-tailing 664

e-waste 276, 278, 285–286
Earliest Due Date (EDD) 89
earned value management (EVM) 216, 219, 223
East India Company (EIC) 611–612
eco-design 284–285
eco-efficiency 279
economic inequality 657–658
Economic Order Quantity (EOQ) 101, 103, 105–106, 108, 110–115, 117, 120, 123, 356–357, 360–362, 364, 583
economic problems 293–294
economic prosperity 27, 664
economies of scale 12, 14, 26, 102, 199–200, 257, 310, 319, 580, 637, 639–640, 649
economy: sharing 20, 169, 184, 267, 658, 686, 689
EDD (Earliest Due Date) 89
education 318; online 536
Edwards, George D. 8, 128–129
efficiency 25–26, 28–29, 32–33, 86, 128, 164–165, 182, 198–199, 234, 239, 245, 257, 285–286, 309, 313, 316–317, 319–321, 323, 331, 333, 338, 361, 367, 377, 382–383, 386, 392, 407, 418–419, 427, 434, 450, 456, 460, 497–498, 500, 504, 513–514, 516–518, 521–522, 529, 557–558, 561, 582, 589, 606, 633, 637–638, 640–641, 643; eco- 279
Efficient Consumer Response (ECR) 379
efficient supply chain 32–33, 361, 367, 640
eliminating hassles 604–605
embedded sub-plans 477
emergency care 428–430, 433–440, 537
emergency departments (EDs) 428, 433–434, 440; management challenges 434–435; process flow **435**; simulation of 435–436; triage 436–439
emergent opportunities 264–271
emerging application areas 686–687
emissions 18, 142, 164, 276, 278, 286, 316, 558, 560, 567–568, 573, 614, 665, 668; management 562, 571–572
empirical research 171, 206–207, 216, 218, 224, 240, 293, 385, 455, 470, 493, 573, 588, 592, 671; methodologies 183
empirical results 13, 201, 207, 360–361, 366, 368–369
Employee Life Cycle (ELC) 401, 403, 405, 407
employee value proposition (EVP) 394
employees: role of 415–416
employment planning 77, 652–653, 655
empty container management 562, 567–568
empty container repositioning (ECR) 568, 572
empty vehicle management 562, 567–568
end-of runway location 315–316
energy 291, 299–302, 305; consumption 164, 301–302; management 291, 301–302
Energy Efficiency Design Index (EEDI) 571
energy efficient manufacturing 164–165
Engelberger, Joe 7

entrepreneurship 218, 255–258, *259–261*, 262–263, 265, 267–271, 686
environment 468, 470, 487, 489–493
environmental attributes 278–281
environmental awareness 281–282
environmental innovation 316, 322
environmental legislation 277–278, 284–288
environmental performance 165, 281; and green product design 278–279
environmental quality 280, 282
environmental regulations 278, 285–286
environmental sustainability 15, 18–19, 27, 181, 590, 592, 664–665, 668; in POM and Marketing 385–386
EOQ (Economic Order Quantity) 101, 103, 105–106, 108, 110–115, 117, 120, 123, 356–357, 360–362, 364, 583
Ethical Consumption 615
Etsy 579, 590
European Operations Management Association (EurOMA) 13, 689
European Railway Agency (ERA) 559
European Union (EU) 284, 550, 571
everyday low prices (EDLP) 38
evolution of POM 3–4
exact algorithm 85–86, 566
Exchange Curve 108–110
exchange problems 501–502
experiential learning 680, 683–684
explanatory survey 400–401
Extended Producer Responsibility (EPR) 285–286
External HR Consultants (EXCs) 396, 407
external knowledge 197, 201, 209–210; leveraging 207–208; managing 204–206

Facebook 169, 200, 292
facilities: design and planning 147, 160–167; layout 152–154
factory 652–657
familiarity bias 331
fee for service 429
feed: budgeting 470, 472, 475; planning 472–473, **474**
Feigenbaum, Armand 8, 128, 130–131, 238, 497
Fence-Sitters 280
50 years of OR in sport 443, *444–447*
finance 320–321; empirical results in 368–369
financial asset prices 368
financial considerations 256, 265, 361, 367
financial markets 345, 360–370
financial performance of retailers 580, 585–586
financing needs 361–362
firm value 369, 381, 383, 387
firms: non-competing 205–206, 208; retail financial performance of 585–586
Fisher, Ronald Alymer 8, 128–129
fixed-position layout 152

fleet sizing and deployment 557, 561–562, 564–565, 568, 572–573
flexibility 16, 19, 26, 32, 73, 112, 143, 173–177, 180, 184, 199, 208, 224, 239, 244, 246, 262–263, 266, 310, 319, 338, 368–369, 403, 417, 430, 473, 477, 492, 518, 528, 556, 558, 560–561, 567, 621, 650, 652–653, 665
flexible manufacturing systems (FMS) 15–16, 180, 630, 652
flexible technologies 180, 198
flow: patterns 149, **150**; process chart 149–151
Flow Accounting 242
follow the leader heuristic **331**, 333
Ford, Henry 6–8, 25, 128, 170, 179
forecast: combining 52–55; errors 47, 52–53, 57–58
forecasting 4, 17, 20, 34, 37, 58–59, 65, 69, 73, 76, 78, 93, 220, 283, 287, 329, 332–333, 336, 374, 378–379, 382, 387, 413, 416, 419, 443, 448, 456, 479, 505, 512, 518, 546, 580–582, 586, 589–590, 642, 656, 676, 681; causal *50*, 73; data-rich 378–379; future of 55–57; impact on costs 47; introduction to 45–47; judgmental 51, 53–55; methodologies 50–55; process of 47–50; quantitative *50*, 52–53, 55; rule-based 54–55; statistical 45, 50–55; time series 52, 55; versus planning 45–46
formal planning 470, 472–475, 493
forward supply chains 281–282
foundation support 511
franchising 417–419
Freight on Board (FOB) Price 620–621
frequency histograms 136, **138**
functional products 32–33, 279, 667
fundamental planning tool 470
Fundamental Theorem of Asset Pricing 363
fundraising 511–514, 516, 520–522
future projections: disaster management 551–552; military 502–504; quality management 143–144; sports operations management 456–460
future research 40, 670–672; aggregate production planning 77; content delivery network (CDN) 534; data analytics 305; facilities design and planning 166–167; global research and practice trends 630; global supply chain management 40; healthcare 303–304, 440; healthcare operations 538; hospitality 421–423; HR and POM 407–408; human behavior in operations 339–340; increased 3BL performance 672; increased complexity 671–672; increased volatility 670–671; inventory management 122–123; lean operations management 244–247; lean production 247; logistics clusters 322–323; management accounting and OM 358; mobile technology 295–296; network infrastructure 531; not-for-profit operations management 521–522; OM and cloud computing 535–536; POM for disaster management 555–556;
POM and finance 370; POM and Marketing 387; POM and military 505; POM and retailing 588–591; POM and transport and logistics 572–574; process capabilities and leveraging advances 206–208; project design and management 224–226; recommender systems 292–293; scheduling in manufacturing and services 97–98; smart cities 300–301; sustainable operations 287–288; telecommunications and OM 539; telecommunications in operations 537
future trend 663, 665–669

game theory (GT) 205, 376, 499–500, 503–504, 531, 554, 583, 670–671
Gantt chart 95, 223
Genchi Gembutsu 238
General Motors (GM) 15, 200, 331–332
generalized second-pricing (GSP) 298
geographic implications 396–397
geographical expansion 686–687
gilded age 657
global competition 15–16, 107, 123, 319
global distribution 17, 19, 622
Global Entrepreneurship Monitor (GEM) 255
global forces 15
global manufacturing strategy 16–17, 181–183, 614, 660
global objectives 27
global procurement 617–620
global sourcing 16, 611, 614, 616–618, 665; complex cycles of 615–616
global supply chains 17–19, 27, 34–35, 38, 40, 127, 181, 311, 319, 322, 395, 615, 621–622, 630, 663–665, 669–672, 687; effective operations 623–629
global trade 10, 319, 322, 579, 615–616, 623, 648; and historical developments 611–612; modern 612–613; new 613–614; processes 19
globalization 38, 122, 169, 185, 319–321, 398, 679
goal programming (GP) 70–71, 74–75, 122
goal setting theory 334
Goal, The (Goldratt and Cox) 244
goals 34, 65, 71, 75–76, 169–171, 173, 175–177, 179–180, 182, 207, 217, 219–220, 222–224, 263, 312, 326, 333–334, 362, 393, 395–397, 402, 427, 453, 460, 468–469, 472, 476–477, 518, 551, 557–558, 561, 623, 659, 668, 670, 679, 683
Goldratt, Eliyahu 203, 244
Google 165, 200, 294, 297, 299, 504, 659
Gosset, William Sealy 8, 128–129, 135
governance 218, 299, 668, 672
government 24, 27, 160, 216, 244, 248, 257, 302–303, 309, 311–312, 319–322, 419, 427, 430, 432, 510–512, 519, 522, 536, 538, 548, 614, 664–665, 668, 672, 677, 679, 686, 689; support 512
Great Leader Strategies 603–604, 606
green consumers 279–280

green products 277–282, 285, 287
greenfield: versus brownfield 199–200
Greening 280–281
Gross Margin Return on Investment (GMROI) 621
Gross Merchandise Volume (GMV) 632
Gross Value Added (GVA) 450, 459
group: influences 333–334; social dynamics 399
group-technology layout 152
Guide to the Project Management Body of Knowledge (PMBOK) (PMI) 215, 217
guilds 5, 128, 689

Hamilton, Alexander 647
happiness 647–649
hassles: eliminating 604–605
Hayes and Wheelwright framework 171–172
Health Information Exchange (HIE) 302–303, 537–538
healthcare 4, 6, 11, 14–15, 20, 45–46, 82–83, 92, 94, 162, 198, 202, 239, 241, 264, 266, 269, 291, 302–305, 358, 403, 414, 427–440, 443, 453, 460, 511, 527, 537–538, 602, 614, 659, 676, 679–680, 688; existing research in 302–303; future research 303–304; and information technology 302; and online communities 303
hedging 361, 366–369, 529
Heijunka 235
Hershey's 200
heuristic algorithm 85–86, 566
heuristic rules 573–574
heuristics 69–70, 75, 86, 94, 216, 258, 297, 330, **331**, 332–333, 335, 469, 472, 475–478, 480, 485, 492–493, 528, 532–533, 554–555, 564, 566, 585
Hierarchical Production Planning (HPP) 74
high-end warfare 503
high-inventory turnover (HIT) retailers 586
high-speed delivery 163
hiring and firing costs 66–68
historical developments 611–612
historical evolution of SCM 25–27
historical perspective: aggregate production planning 66–71; retail operations 580–586; value of 4–5
history of QM development 128–131
holistic production system (HPS) 6
Holt-Modigliani-Muth-Simon (HMMS) Model 66, 68–69, 360
homeland security 303, 538–539
horizontal collaboration 312, 322
Hoshin Kanri 238
hospitality industry 4, 82, 255, 267, 379, 413, 415–417, *422–423*, 601, 604, 606, 676–677, 679, 689; essence of 414; lean thinking and sustainable operations 420; management of 418–419; and management titles 602; and new media 420–421; product and service innovation 414
House of Quality 133–134
How to Operate QC Circle Activities (Ishikawa) 130
hub-and-spoke structure 562, *563*, 564
Hulu 296
Human Capital Analytics (HCA) 394
human capital research 394
Human Capital Resources (HCR) 392–393
Human Resources (HR) 79, 164, 215, 218, 221, 392–408, 448, 521, 562, 650, 676; and POM 393–400; and talent 404–407
Human Resources Management (HRM) 173, 179, 240, 392–393, 398–399, 405–408; best practices 395–397; current trends 394–395
humanitarian operations 382, 536–537, 539, 553
Hungarian Method 87
hybrid layout 152

IBM 7, 20, 56, 299, 385, 656
ICT-driven opportunities 572, 574
idiosyncratic risk 363–364
implementation 468, 476–481, 486–487, 489, 492–493
in-store technologies 589–590
incandescent bulbs 9
incentive compatibility (IC) constraint 347
incentive misalignment 34–35
incentives 16–18, 26, 35, 46, 58, 185, 200, 202–203, 206, 208–209, 221, 226, 279, 285–286, 301, 303, 314, 321–322, 345–354, 358, 366, 369, 415–416, 429, 516, 519, 529, 582, 584, 639, 666–667, 671
incremental discount 106, 116
individual producer responsibility (IPR) 286
individual rationality (IR) constraint 347
individual support 511
industrial capitalism 657
industrial clusters 310–312, 316, 322
Industrial Revolutions 4, 10–15, 19, 497–498, 648, 659; First (IR 1.0) 4, 10–11; Second (IR 2.0) 4, 11–12; Third (IR 3.0) 4, 12–13, 15, 17, 20–21, 659; Fourth (IR 4.0) 4, 12–15, 18–19
industrial-type transport 560–561
Industry 4.0 12–14, 19–20, 174, 685, 687
industry landscape 633–634
infinitesimal perturbation analysis (IPA) 652
influences: social 333–334, 670
informal planning 470–472
information: access 45, 55–56, 218; asymmetry 28, 219, 285–286, 296, 365, 586, 670; contextual 55; inputs 63–65; sharing 57–58, 108, 205, 294, 313–314, 335, 345, 399–400, 582, 637, 640, 642, 659, 666
Information Age 4, 676
Information Systems (IS) 218, 223, 399–400, 531, 537, 665, 681, 685

information technology 17, 20, 64, 77, 197–200, 203–204, 208–209, 258, 264, 268, 317–318, 358, 395, 511, 536, 574, 681; and healthcare 302; role of 180
information technology-worker system 203–204, 206–207, 209
InnoCentive 205
innovation 32, 45, 51, 172, 174–175, 197, 199, 210, 214, 218, 220, 224, 235, 239, 241, 244, 247, 263–264, 266–267, 271, 277, 279, 310–312, 316–317, 322, 355, 382, 387, 393–396, 399, 403, 414–415, 419, 452, 459, 497, 504, 579, 590, 617, 623, 628, 632, 634–641, 644, 647–648, 650–651, 658, 660, 678, 685; in green product design 280; management 217; operational 255–257, 264–271, 650, 658, 660; product 45, 175, 414; service 264, 414; technological 51, 218, 647–648, 650, 658, 660
innovative products 32–34, 279, 667
Input-Process-Output (IPO) 330, **331**, 362
Institute of Management Sciences, The (TIMS) 13
institutional theory (InsT) 670–672
integer programming 89, 93–94, 528, 532, 535, 563, 565, 573
integration 26–27, 29, 52–54, 173–174, 176, 178, 180, 183, 197–198, 200, 215, 223, 263–264, 266, 269, 375–379, 381, 387, 393, 395, 399, 428, 502, 573, 579, 587, 633, 639, 663, 666–667, 680–681, 683, 686
integrative model 176–177
Intel 31, 385
inter-cluster innovation transfer 316–317
interchangeable parts (IP) 7–8, 497
interconnection 174, 527–528, 531
interdisciplinary research 684–685
interdisciplinary teaching 680, 683
interface 15, 74, 95, **96**, 169, 256–258, 268, 270, 303, 338, 340, 346, 358, 374, **375**, 376–381, 383–387, 398, 414, 530, 536, 570–571, 579–580, 619–620, 628, 650, 655–657, 671
intermediate product quality 353–354
intermediate targets 475, 477–479
Internal HR Consultants (INCs) 395–396, 405, 407
internal knowledge 197, 205, 209–210, 312; leveraging 206–207; managing 200–204
internal manager-clients (IMCs) 395–396, 405, 407
International Disaster Database (EM-DAT) 545, 548
International Electrotechnical Commission (IEC) 10
International Maritime Organization (IMO) 571
International Motor Vehicle Program (IMVP) 235, 241
International Paralympic Committee (IPC) 453
International Society for Inventory Research (ISIR) 121, 123

international trade 182, 319–322, 611–612
internationalization theory (IT) 669, 671–672
Internet of Things (IoT) 19, 161–162, 174, 181, 185, 247, 530, 574, 657, 659, 686, 689
intra-/inter-firm issues 378–381
intra-cluster collaboration 312–314
Introduction to Operations Research (Churchman et al.) 13
intrusion detection system (IDS) 530–531
inventory 13, 15–17, 25, 32, 34–37, 45–48, 51, 53, 56–58, 64–71, 73, 75–76, 101–123, 141, 160, 164, 235, 239, 242, 244, 256, 258, 262–263, 267, 293–294, 301, 312, 314, 329, 332–333, 352, 356, 360–362, 365, 367, 374–380, 383–384, 386, 416, 451, 467, 497, 502, 518, 520, 522, 528, 546, 558, 562, 565–568, 579–592, 602, 621–622, 632, 634–635, 637, 641–642, 650–656, 658–659, 666, 676, 681; and backorder costs 66–68; functions 102; policy 36–37, 101, 103–104, 106–107, 109–111, 114–115, 123; problem formulation 103–106; research 101, 105–111, 121, 123; routing problem 562, 565–566; volatility 376–377
inventory management 45, 70, 101–103, 106–111, 120–123, 256, 329, 332–333, 375–378, 384, 467, 546, 558, 565–566, 579–582, 590–592, 622, 655–656, 658, 676; scientific 110–111, 120–122; and supply process 518–520
inventory models 13, 101, 103–107, 109, 114, 121–123, 360, 518, 651, 658; with quantity discounts 116–117; taxonomy of **105**; types of 111–120
invisible hand 5
IR 1.0 (First Industrial Revolution) 4, 10–11
IR 2.0 (Second Industrial Revolution) 4, 11–12
IR 3.0 (Third Industrial Revolution) 4, 12–13, 15, 17, 20–21, 659
IR 4.0 (Fourth Industrial Revolution) 4, 12–15, 18–19
Iron Age 4
Ishikawa diagram (cause & effect) 130, 136, **137**
Ishikawa, Kaoru 8, 128, 130, 238, 497
ISO 9001 2015 125, 132–133
iteration 90, 183, 217, 222, 226, 244, 338

Japanese effect 13, 15–16
Japanese Operations Management and Strategy Association (JOMSA) 689
Japanese Production Management (JPM) 126
Japanese Union of Scientists and Engineers (JUSE) 130
Jidoka 235
job scheduling 297, 534–535
job shop: scheduling 71, 82, 86–91, **96**, 219
jobless future 653
jobs 5–6, 14, 55, 73, 83–90, 95, 97, 169, 255, 311, 317–318, 402, 404, 413, 533–535, 605, 613, 647–648, 654, 657–658, 660, 677, 680, 682

joint capability planning 379–380, 387
judgmental forecasting 50–51, 53–55
Juran, Joseph M. 8, 128–130, 238, 497
Juran on Leadership for Quality (Juran) 130
just-in-time (JIT) 101–102, 107–108, 114, 128, 173, 235, 239–240, 246, 294, 314, 559, 654, 657–658
Just-in-Time for Today and Tomorrow (Ohno) 130
just-world bias 337

kaizen 21, 141, 235–236, 238, 680
kanban 16, 141, 166, 235, 650, 652, 654
Kauffman Foundation 255
key performance indicators (KPIs) 336, 458–459, 561, 572–573
kirana stores 579
kitting 314–315
Kiva robots 14
knowledge: consumer 383–385; development and transfer 200–203, 205–206, 208–209; domain 55; external 204–206, 207–208; internal 200–207; management 145, 221, 223, 397, 407–408; outsourcing 205–206, 208–209, 685; process 200–202; product 200–202; proprietary 198–199, 203, 205; workers 200, 206

labor: division of 5–7, 10–11, 14, 20; sharing 313; versus capital 657–658
labor-intensive manufacturing 14, 613, 624–625, **626**, 627–630
laissez-faire capitalism 653
Landed Duty Paid (LDP) 621
large-scale migration 613
large-scale surveys 183–184
law enforcement 300
Law of Pragnanz 337
lead time 38, 48, 75, 77, 101, 106, 111, 117–120, 123, 127, 158, 161, 234, 239, 242–244, 276, 295, 314, 317–318, 536, 583, 586, 591, 637, 641, 656; quotation 656
Leadership in Energy and Environmental Design (LEED) 165
leading hand (*Gemba-cho*) 130
Lean 107, 120, 131, 141–142, 223, 234–236, 239–248, 256, 258, 385–386, 546, 581, 659, 668, 676
Lean Accounting 242
Lean Production 128, 130, 173, 234, 399, 504; contemporary and future research 244–247; emergence of 235–239; evolution of research 239–244; in hospitality 420
Lean Six Sigma (LSS) 131, 141–142, 243, 246
Lean Thinking (Womack and Jones) 239–240
learning 16, 30, 70, 72, 126, 143, 145, 162, 200–201, 220–221, 226, 238, 278, 304, 310, 338–339, 346, 351, 393, 395, 397, 403–404, 407–408, 414, 448, 456, 469–470, 477, 482, 484–485, 492–493, 530, 536–537, 574, 583, 588–589, 605, 617, 685–686; experiential 680, 683–684; online 680, 682–683; organizational 145, 338, 397, 407–408; and teaching 679–684
legislation: environmental 277–278, 284–287
Less-Than-Truckload (LTL) freight 639–640
Let's Talk Quality (Crosby) 131
leverage 58, 144, 199, 201–202, 204, 207, 209–210, 218, 265, 267–268, 271, 330, 339, 366–368, 404, 407, 629
life-cycle assessment 284–285
limits of control *see* control
Linear Decision Rules (LDR) 66–71, 74, 505
Linear Programming (LP) 68–71, 84, 89, 91–94, 349–350, 363, 500, 528, 564–565
liner-type transport 560–561
liquidity 360–362, 369, 591
List Scheduling (LS) 88
location determination of users 295
logistics 13, 15, 17, 31, 38, 76, 78, 128, 157, 182, 266, 287–288, 309–323, 369, 405, 455, 498, 502–503, 511, 518, 520, 537, 546, 553, 556–558, 561–574, 579, 592, 612, 614, 616, 618, 620, 632–633, 635, 637, 639–641, 648, 650–651, 655, 667–668, 676, 688; and materials handling 160–164; reverse 78, 185, 375–378, 380–381, 387, 651, 668; warehouse 590
logistics clusters 309–312, 313–323, 676; decline of 319–320; development of 312, 321; future of 318–320; growth of 319; industrial 310–311; map **310**
logistics clusters benefits: innovation 316–317; intra-cluster collaboration 312–314; jobs 317–318; value-added services 314–316
Longest Processing Time (LPT) 88–89
loss aversion 330–331
lost sales 103, 106, 114, 122, 332
low-cost intelligent robotics (LCIR) 264, 266–268, 271
low-inventory turnover (LIT) retailers 586
LPT (Longest Processing Time) 88–89
lumpy demand 38, 58

Machine That Changed the World, The (Womack et al.) 234, 238, 241, 420
McKay stitching machine 11
McKinsey & Company 77, 169
make or buy decision 28–31, 380, 670
maker movement 649, 659
makespan 86, 88–92, 97
Malcolm Baldrige National Quality Award 129, 132, 143
management 601–602; capacity 416; of donative funds 511–512, 514, 520; knowledge 145, 221, 223, 397, 407–408; mechanics 655; portfolio 203, 206, 217–218, 224, 522; process 126, 395, 601, 680; revenue 198, 336, 416–417, 421, 511,

514–515, 522, 579–580, 677; risk 38–39, 57–58, 127, 142, 216, 219–221, 223, 226, 257, 366, 369, 385, 419–420, 492, 665, 668, 686; scientific inventory 110–111, 120–122; speed 562, 567; strategic 170, 172, 184, 393; strategic human resources 392–393, 400–403, 408; tactical 468–475, 478, 480, 484, 489, 492–493; titles 602; total quality 125–126, 130, 142, 235, 238–240, 243; workforce 516, 579–580, 586–587, 589, 592; yield 255, 257, 262, 265, 268, 270, 416–417, 453, 459, *see also* supply chain management (SCM)

Management Coefficients Model (MCM) 69–70
management science 215, 497, 500, 553, 650
manufacturing 4–6, 8, 10–12, 14–19, 26, 47, 63, 65, 68, 73–75, 77–79, 82–84, 97, 107, 126, 131, 144, 147, 152–153, 161, 166, 169–185, 197–201, 203, 208–209, 234–236, 239, 241–245, 247–248, 255, 257–258, 262–264, 266, 276–277, 279, 281–287, 311, 314, 317, 320, 351, 356, 358, 397, 404–405, 414, 514, 528, 558–559, 592, 601, 612–614, 616–622, 624–625, 627–628, 630, 647–660, 667, 676–678, 680–682, 686, 688–689; capabilities 171, 175–177, 201, 263, 628; capital-intensive 624–625, **626**, 627–628, **629**, 630; contract 613; decisions 177–179, 618; energy and resource efficient 164–165; environmental impact 614–615; future of 659–660; importance of 647; improvement programs 178–179; labor-intensive 624–625, **626**, 627–630; modern 649; networks 16, 182–183; process characteristics 624–629; robotized 660; scheduling in 86–92; smart 174; strategic role of 170–171; technology 19, 176, 179–181, 185, 197–201, 647, 659

manufacturing operations 17, 178, 182–183, 242, 266, 276, 287, 625, 649, 659, 681; strategic goals 175–177; strategic role 170–171

manufacturing paradigm 172–174; most relevant 173–174; versus strategic choices 174

Manufacturing and Service Operations Management Society (MSOM) 689

manufacturing strategy 15–16, 169–185, 678; configurations 177; content 171–172, 178; how to research 183–184; infrastructural decisions 177–179; key concepts 171–172; new challenges for 184–185; process 171–172; structural decisions 177–179; and technological evolution 179–181

Manufacturing—missing link in corporate strategy (Skinner) 170
markdowns: clearance 583–584
market: financial 362–367; perfect 360–361; secondary 281–282; segments 26, 265, 279–281, 284, 376–377, 387, 616
marketing: capabilities 386; interface 378–381, 383–386

Marx, Karl 657
mass customization 161, 173–174, 198, 248, 314, 630
Mass Flourishing (Phelps) 648
mass production 8, 11–12, 25–26, 128, 161, 170, 179, 235, 239, 242, 244, 248
master production schedule (MPS) 73–74
material requirements plan (MRP) 73–74, 180
materials handling 155–157, 160, 163, 166; and logistics 160–164; principles of 157
materials handling devices (MHDs) 158, **159**; automated 156–157; types of 155
maximum lateness 89–90
media: new 420, 421
merchandising 198, 283, 315, 581, 587–592, 622, 632–633
merchant capitalism 657
metaheuristics 86, 566, 573
methodology: and models 684–685
micro-level process integration 378–379
migration: large-scale 613
milestones 4–10, 12, 15, 92, 478–479, 487–489
military 4–5, 13–14, 123, 215, 497–505, 676, 687–688; operations management 497–498, 500–501; past history 498–501; present situation 501–502
Military Operations Research Society (MORS) 500
min-max 84, 86
min-sum 84, 86
mobile apps 296–298, 421
mobile computing 161
mobile network service 291, 296
mobile phones 17, 291, 295–296, 298, 382
mobile platform 294–296, 615
mobile technology 295–296
mobility: upward 317–318, 318, 322
modeling: and research 684–686
models: and methodology 684–685
Modern Production Management (Buffa) 13
modularity 8, 17, 222, 287, 528
Moneyball (Lewis) 456, 458
monitoring 56, 135, 144, 181, 198, 214, 218, 278, 304, 362, 421, 468, 472, 482–486, 488–489, 491–493, 513, 538–539, 550, 657–658, 689; factors 482–483; methods 483–484; network 485; process 468, 482, 484–485, 493
muda, mura, muri 235
multi-agents 349, 655
multi-channel retailing 374–378, 387
multi-period capacity and flow application (MPCFA) 528
multi-tasking 348, 350, 352

NAFTA 19
nanostores 579, 590
natural resources 18, 164, 276, 665

Nature of Technology, The (Arthur) 649
nearshoring 183, 185
Netflix 293–294, 296
netwar 503
network: infrastructure 527–531, 539; operations 531–536, 539; risk management 530–531
network design 164, 270, 282–283, 287, 433, 527–529, 531, 561–564, 566–568, 570, 573; and flexibility 654, 656; security 530–531, 539
new challenges for manufacturing strategy 184–185
new digital technologies 264–266
new emerging economy 660
new media 420–421
new product development (NPD) 16, 78, 200–203, 205–207, 209, 278, 381–382, 399–400, 448; and process capabilities 197–198
new product introduction 63, 73, 198, 284–285
new service economy 677–679
new technologies 46, 166, 174, 176, 181, 185, 266, 278, 379, 421, 519, 527, 602, 628, 667, 683, 685, 687; digital 264–266
New United Motor Manufacturing, Inc. (NUMMI) 15, 236
news vendor model 360, 362–368
NGO 27, 510, 664, 668, 670, 672, 688
9/11 608
no-show 94–95
non-competing firms 205–206, 208
non-state actors 503–504
non-stationary demand 655–656
normative research: versus descriptive research 467–468
not-for-profit operations 244, 510–522, 687, 689
NP-Hard 84–85, 87–90, 93, 97, 216, 297, 527–528, 532, 534, 566, 573
NUMMI (New United Motor Manufacturing, Inc.) 15, 236

objective function 70–71, 83–85, 87, 97, 112, 270, 431, 567, 656, 687–689; and constraints 572–573; and rules 67–68
observe, orient, decide, act (OODA) loop 503–504
Occupational Safety and Health Administration (OSHA) 166
Ohno, Taiichi 8, 128, 130, 141, 235, 242, 497, 654
Omni Channel businesses 615, 686
omnichannel retailing 579, 586–588
online advertising 296–298
online communities 303–304, 421
online education 536
online retailing 270, 293, 376, 387, 583, 587–592, 633, 635, 637, 642
online teaching and learning 680, 682–683
Online to Offline (O2O) 615
online travel agents (OTAs) 417, 420–421
Open Book Costing 620

Operating Guidelines 604–605
operational constraints 255–258, 262, 264–265, 267, 270–271
operational decisions 74, 107, 218, 256–258, 263, 265, 270, 314, 332, 360, 369–370, 376, 428, 555, 570, 572–573, 655; and financial asset prices 368; and financial markets 362–367; and financing needs 361–362
Operational Excellence (OE) 131, 234, 239, 244–248, 603
operational innovations (OIs) 255–257, 264–271, 650, 658, 660
operational processes 328, 333, 339, 415
Operational Research Society 13
operations 400–401, 403, 421, *422–423*; and cost measurement systems 354–357; cost of 417–418; empirical results in 368–369; optimization of 346–354; planning 72–74; practices 399; Research Society of America (ORSA) 13; strategy 16, 26, 45, 63–64, 73, 77, 183, 452, 454, 459, 677–679, 683; and telecommunications 536–539
Operations Management, Entrepreneurship, and Value Creation (Kickul et al.) 257
operations management (OM) 3, 13, 19, 26–27, 68, 75, 126, 128, 130, 142, 166, 197, 205, 215, 239, 242–247, 255–258, 262, 264, 271, 291, 304, 326–327, 329, 332, 340, 345–346, 348–354, 356–358, 361, 367, 374, 379, 392, 399, 404–405, 413–414, 421, 429, 443, 448, 450–452, 455–456, 458–460, 502, 510–512, 519–522, 527, 539, 543, 553, 570, 580, 601–602, 604, 607, 668, 676, 678, 680, 682–683, 689; of caching 531–533; civilian and military contexts 497–498, 500–501; of cloud computing 534–536; and cost measurement accuracy 356–357
operations/supply chain (O/SC) management 277–278, 450
opportunistic behavior 29, 31, 38, 205
opportunities: emergent 264–271; ICT-driven 574; research 4, 27, 40, 58, 78, 144–145, 207–208, 210, 257, 269, 288, 322, 329, 383, 387, 457, 505, 522, 555, 572–574, 592, 630, 648, 663, 669, 672
opportunity management 224–226
optimal appointment schedules 95
Optimal Policy Curve 108–111, 121–123
optimization 66, 71, 85–86, 95, 98, 101, 104–106, 120, 122, 153, 164, 206–208, 216, 218–220, 245, 257, 291–292, 297, 301–302, 346–348, 362, 365, 367, 432–434, 501–502, 505, 527, 532–535, 566–567, 571, 573, 584, 588, 591, 634, 641, 643, 650, 652, 655, 659; problems 86, 284, 297, 301, 347, 365, 367, 501–502, 532–533, 573; staged 655
option valuation 368
order: picking 158–160, 166–167; quantities 17, 37, 46, 103, 106–107, 116, 282, 329, 361, 581

ordering cost 103–105, 109, 111–112, 115–116, 356, 361
organization 221–222
Organization for Economic Co-operation and Development (OECD) 427
Organizational Capabilities (OC) 381, 386, 397, 407
Organizational Capital Resources 393
organizational coordination 216–217
organizational development (OD) 394–395
Organizational Learning (OL) 145, 338, 397, 407–408
organizational performance 143, 395–400, 448
organized society 664–665
Original Design Manufacturer (ODM) 619
Original Equipment Manufacturer (OEM) 281–284, 286–287, 619
output consequence 381–383
outsourcing 12, 14, 24–26, 28, 30–31, 65–66, 76, 108, 161, 205–206, 209, 221–222, 270, 276, 283, 380, 387, 404, 531, 570, 613–614, 618–619, 621–622, 629, 659, 666, 671, 685, 688; to China 16–18
overbooking 94–95
overlapping 16, 200, 216–217, 222
overtime wages 66–68
ownership structure 417–418

package delivery methods 590
pallet pooling service 632, 637–639, 641
Panama Canal 11, 163, 309, 318
Parametric Production Planning (PPP) 69–70
Pareto chart 136, **137**
Pareto Principle 108–109, 238
partially observable Markov decision process (POMDP) 433
partnering 221–222
partnership 31, 35, 204, 262–263, 270, 395, 401–404, 407–408, 417, 522, 632, 665–668, 671; and alliances 204–205, 207–209
Patient Protection and Affordable Care Act (PPACA, 2010) 202, 302
people 221
perfect market 31, 360–361
performance: evaluation for nonprofits 520–521; improvements 173, 176, 199–200, 292, 641, 665–666; KPIs 458–459, 561; measurement 35, 178, 345–354, 358, 417, 453, 554; organizational 396–397, 399–400; worst-case ratio 85, 87–89
periodic review policy 103–104, 115–116, 518
personnel scheduling (or shift scheduling) 82–83, 92–94
Physical Capital Resources 392–393
pipeline transport 558–559, *560*
Pirandello principle 498
plan structure 475–480, 492–493
plan-do-check-act (PDCA) 129, 140, 143, 238, 241, 243, 502, 504

planned giving 512
planning 15–17, 33, 40, 47, 57, 59, 63–79, 101–103, 117, 119–120, 125, 130, 133–134, 144, 147, 152–153, 157, 160, 164–166, 175, 179–180, 215, 218, 220–226, 244, 258, 263, 299, 304, 309, 332, 339, 354, 358, 378, 394, 400–402, 419, 450–451, 452, 456, 458–460, 467–470, 472–473, 475–480, 484, 489, 492–493, 497–499, 501–504, 512–513, 516–518, 521, 527–529, 531, 546, 558, 561–565, 568–572, 580, 583–586, 588–589, 591–592, 601, 623, 650, 653, 655–656, 676–677; assortment 584–585; capability 379–380; capacity 528–529; city 299–300; employment 77, 652–653, 655; feed 472–473, **474**; formal 472–475; heuristics 469–470, 472, 475–478, 480, 485, 492–493; horizon 64–70, 75–77, **468**, 469, **476**, 478, 503, 528–529; informal 470–472; predictive schedule 477–478; process 46, 103, 468–475, 563; resource 72; versus forecasting 45–46; warehouse 164, *see also* aggregate production planning
plant location 182
platform economics 267, 269–270
policy 35, 38, 47, 55, 77, 104, 106, 110, 121–122, 158–160, 172, 178, 222, 263, 283, 285, 295–296, 299–300, 304, 322, 327, 357, 369, 375–376, 378, 380, 384, 397, 414, 427, 433–434, 510, 518–520, 522, 532, 538, 561, 568, 571, 602, 604–605, 688; implications 286–288; warehouse storage 158–160; work 222
pollution 162, 165, 256, 614–615, 687
polynomial time 84–85, 87–89, 91–93, 528–529
POM for the Hospitality Industry 601
POM and Marketing Capabilities 386
POM and Marketing Interface 378–381, 383–386
POM Methods 602
POM and Shareholder Wealth 381–383
pop-up stores 579, 590
port management 570–571
portfolio management 203, 206, 217–218, 224, 522
postponement 58, 666; and customization 314–315; strategy 17
practical problems in operations management (PPOMs) 648, 650–657
precedence 40, 89, 91, 222, 566, 672
predictive analytics 56, 162, 164, 301, 337, 685
predictive planning schedule 477–478
preemption 89, 219, 284
preventive care 428–433, 440; designing 431–432; extended models for 432–433; processes 430–431
prices: financial asset 368
pricing 20, 262, 265, 267–268, 279, 281, 286, 295, 297–298, 354, 363, 365, 376, 378, 380, 416–417, 448, 450, 513, 518, 520, 522, 529, 534, 536, 561, 580, 582, 585, 589–592, 618, 657; capacity 534; and clearance markdowns 583–584; and revenue management 514–515
Principles of Scientific Management, The (Taylor) 128

printing: 3-D 649, 659, 667
priority rule 84–85, 87–88, 95, 97, 216
privacy 298, 302–304, 414, 434
private equity (PE) 658
probabilistic inventory models 117–120
problems 83–84, 293–294, 501–502; scheduling 83–93, 95, 97, 297, 534–535, 567, 569–570, 572; supply chain 293–294
procedures 4, 7, 14, 46, 54–55, 90, 95, 197, 303, 394, 433, 436, 452, 473, 477, 601–602, 604–605, 609
process: architecture 217, 222; characteristics 202, 242, 623–630; coordination 374, 378–381, 386; design 277; development 199–200, 209, 277–278, 278–281, 287; flowchart 136; knowledge 200–202; layout 152; management 126, 395, 601, 680; operational 328, 333, 339, 415; project 215–217, 222–223
process capabilities 139, 207–210, 676; advances in 199; and external knowledge 204–206; greenfield versus brownfield 199–200; and internal knowledge 200–204; and new product development (NPD) 197–198; and profitability 198–199
process design 4–5, 133, 185, 200–202, 206, 209, 277, 287, 348, 428–429, 433, 448, 456, 458, 580
processing time 83–84, 86–92, 94, 97, 199
procurement 75, 102–103, 106, 110, 112, 114–116, 119–121, 205, 215, 329, 355–356, 360, 376, 378, 382, 501–503, 518–520, 522, 591, 616–621, 641–643
Producer Pays 286
product 4, 64; characteristics 182, 581, 624, 629; competition 281; design 65, 131, 198, 201–202, 209, 217, 222, 267, 277–281, 285, 355, 380, 617, 656; development 15–16, 78, 205, 209, 217, 277–278, 280, 282, 619, 656, 676; distribution 377, 517–520; families 64–65, 73–74, 76–77; green 278–282; innovation 45, 175, 414; intermediate quality 353–354; knowledge 200–202; layout 152; offering 198, 262, 280–282, 357, 379, 517–518, 591, 619, 635; portfolio 198, 206, 209, 217, 650; remanufactured 282–284, 287, 377–378, 380; returned 377–378; short lifecycle 581–582, 591; variety cost 356–357, *see also* new product development (NPD)
Product Service Systems (PSS) 174, 247
production: costing 620–621; decision-making 623–629; and inventory control 652–653, 655; mass 8, 11–12, 25–26, 128, 161, 170, 179, 235, 239, 242, 244, 248; smoothing 66
Production and Operations Management Society (POMS) 13, 121, 123, 687, 689
productivity 6–7, 14, 65, 160, 180, 239, 258, 263, 265–266, 310–311, 353, 394, 396, 399, 404, 475, 492, 570, 572, 579–580, 584, 586, 602–603, 620, 625, 650, 657–658, 671

professional perspective 400–404
professional societies 121–123, 215
profit sharing 283, 351
profitability 32, 47, 79, 144, 162, 198–199, 263, 267, 277, 283, 285, 313–314, 368, 376, 379, 458, 511, 580–582, 584, 586, 591–592, 603, 618, 621, 658, 668
program evaluation and review technique (PERT) 215–216
program management 225
progress 223
project 214, 220–221; crashing 91–92; process 215–217, 222–223
Project Management Institute (PMI) 215
project management offices (PMOs) 225
project management (PM) 11, 46, 91, 214–215, 217, 225, 244, 331, 336, 399–400, 448, 456, 676; current research 219–223; future research 224–226; methods 220–221; past research 215–219; tool development 216
project manager 214, 217–222, 224–226, 243, 602
project portfolio management (PPM) 217–218
project process 215–217, 222–223
projections *see* future projections
proprietary knowledge 198–199, 203, 205
prosperity: economic 27, 664
public sector 239, 241, 248, 510–511, 686–688
publications outlet 684, 686
pull production 346, 348–349, 358, 654; versus push production 352–354
purchase 28–29, 32, 36, 73, 103, 108, 112, 116–117, 121, 125, 155, 160–162, 292–293, 295, 315, 362–363, 376–378, 380–381, 417–418, 475, 515, 517, 531, 565, 568, 574, 583, 587, 589–590, 615, 618, 621, 623, 633, 640–641
Purchase Management System (PMS) 637, 641
pure play e-commerce 615
push production 346, 348–349, 654; versus pull production 352–354

QC Circle Koryo (Ishikawa) 130
quadratic assignment problem (QAP) 153
qualitative forecasting *50*
quality 4–5, 8–9, 11, 13–16, 26, 31, 39, 56, 71, 73–74, 85–86, 89, 107, 120, 125–133, 135–136, 140–145, 173, 175–178, 180–181, 198, 205, 208–209, 215, 219–220, 223–225, 234, 236, 238–239, 243, 245, 255–258, 266–269, 279–280, 282–285, 302–304, 347–348, 351–353, 358, 377, 380, 383, 394, 396, 398–400, 402, 414–415, 427, 430, 433–434, 443, 448, 450–451, 453–456, 467, 497–498, 504, 514–516, 519, 536–538, 551, 557, 561, 572–573, 579, 583, 589, 601–602, 606–607, 607, 613, 615, 618–619, 621–622, 625, 628, 633, 637–638, 643, 647, 650–651, 659, 664, 676–678, 680–681, 685–688; culture 129, 142–143; definition 125; environmental 280,

Index

282; intermediate product 353–354; recovery plans 142; risk management 142; service 131–132, 142–144, 267–268, 414–415, 453–454, 572, 677
Quality Control (Feigenbaum) 130
Quality Control Handbook (Juran) 130
Quality Function Deployment (QFD) 133–134, 143
quality improvement (QI) stories 125, 130–131, 140–141, 143–144, 238, 383, 454
Quality is Free (Crosby) 15, 131
Quality Management (QM) 8, 125, 132, 135, 141, 144–145, 238, 255–257, 269, 415; achieving excellence 127; history of 128–131; imperatives 127; present situation 132–143; successes and failures 126–127; themes 142–143
Quality and Me (Crosby) 131
Quality Planning and Analysis (Juran) 130
quantitative forecasting 50, 52–53, 55
quantity discount 102, 106, 116–117, 651

radical NPD projects 202–203, 206–207, 209
Radio-Frequency Identification (RFID) 25, 56, 162, 181, 377, 538, 579–581, 622, 659
rail transport 558–559, 560, 566–571, 574
random storage policy 158, 166
randomness 48, 97, 345
Rawls, John 658
real estate 419, 591
real options theory (ROT) 669, 671
real-time bidding (RTB) 297–298
recall 18, 131, 142–144, 303, 331–332, 380, 386, 664
recommender systems 291–294
recovery: disaster 536–537
recycling 276–277, 279, 285–286, 521, 638–639, 665, 668; subsidy 286
reduce 665, 668
reflection effect 331
refurbishing 282, 285, 318, 380
regional science 311–312, 314–317, 320, 322–323
regular time wages 66, 68
regulation 9, 19, 166, 285–286, 311–312, 316, 319–322, 358, 414, 468, 477–478, 492, 519, 569–571, 573, 602, 614, 622, 688; and taxes 321
relationship building 516, 621
relief item inventory management 518
remanufactured products 282–284, 287, 377–378, 380
remanufacturing 18–19, 184, 277, 281–284, 286–287, 651
Reorder Point 103, 111, 117–118, 356
replenishment 25, 34, 37, 46, 56–57, 104, 106–107, 111, 113, 115, 119, 122, 198, 276, 379, 580–581, 642, 655
Report on Manufactures (Hamilton) 647
request routing 533

rescue operations 536–537, 548
research 669–672; descriptive versus normative 467–468; domains 327, 329, 684, 686; empirical 183, 218; future 40, 670–672; in healthcare 302–304; human capital 394; implications 58, 267–270; interdisciplinary 684–685; inventory 106–111; and modeling 684–686; opportunities 4, 27, 40, 58, 78, 144–145, 207–208, 210, 257, 269, 288, 322, 329, 383, 387, 457, 505, 522, 555, 572–574, 592, 630, 648, 663, 669, 672; questions 171, 218, 225, 291, 304, 397, 400–401, 669, 671
research and development (R&D) 17, 127, 202–203, 205, 225, 266, 380, 539, 579, 647, 682, 686
Research Excellence Framework (REF) 686
reshoring/backshoring 183, 185
resource: allocation 203, 206, 221, 226, 433, 470, 516, 520, 535, 652; constraints 91, 105–106, 216, 265, 286, 297, 614; leveling 216; loading 216; management 102, 514–517; natural 276; optimization 535; planning 73–74, 401, 513, 516; profiles 74–75, *see also* Human Resource Management (HRM); Human Resources (HR)
Resource Constrained Project Scheduling (RCPS) 82, 86, 91–92, 216
resource dependence theory (RDT) 670–672
resource efficient manufacturing 164–165
resource-based view (RBV) 29–30, 381–382, 393, 448
responsibility: social 18–19, 27, 385–386, 395, 573, 615, 664–665, 668, 676
responsive supply chain 32–33
retail 18, 25, 32, 34–38, 48, 56, 160, 163–164, 198–199, 239, 269–270, 281–283, 300, 304–305, 309, 311, 313–315, 320–321, 367, 369, 374–380, 383–385, 387, 579–592, 615–616, 621–623, 626, 630, 632–635, 636, 637, 640–644, 660, 666, 676–677, 682; competition 281; display arrangement 314–315; financial performance of firms 580, 585–586; formats 590; operations 291–294, 580–586; present situation 586–588; stores 56, 164, 281, 315, 377, 580–582, 584, 587–589, 589–590, 592, 623, 626, 664; supply chains 580, 582–583, 592, 635; technologies 589
retailers: financial performance 585–586; high-inventory turnover (HIT) 586
retailing: multi-channel 374–378, 387; online 270, 293, 376, 387, 583, 587–592, 633, 635, 637, 642
Rethink Robotics 257, 266
returned products 287, 377–378, 380
reuse 665, 668
revenue management 198, 336, 416–417, 421, 511, 522, 579–580, 677; and pricing 514–515
reverse logistics 185, 375–378, 387, 651, 668; and sustainability 78, 380–381
reverse supply chains 122, 277, 281–283, 380, 665, 686
rework 126, 131, 143, 217–218, 221–222, 226

706

Index

RFID (Radio-Frequency Identification) 25, 56, 162, 181, 377, 538, 579–581, 622, 659
risk: assessment 38–40; coordination 329; downside 473, 479, 493; idiosyncratic 363–364; management 38–39, 57–58, 127, 142, 216, 219–221, 223, 226, 257, 366, 369, 385, 419–420, 492, 665, 668, 686; premium 351–352, 364, 369, 420; systematic 360, 369; upside 473, 479, 493
risk-neutral equivalence 363–364
road transport 558–560, 563, 567–568, 571–572, 574
robotics 7, 12, 14, 20, 161, 199, 256, 264, 538, 574, 657, 680, 686, 689; low-cost intelligent (LCIR) 264, 266–268, 271
robotized manufacturing 660
robustness 97–98, 106, 111, 241, 567
role mining problems (RMP) 530
role refinement problems (RPPs) 531
role-based access control (RBAC) 530
routing and scheduling 561–562, 565–567, 570–572
rule-based forecasting 54–55
run charts 135

safety 185, 220–221, 239, 269, 382, 400, 453, 519, 537–538, 557, 569–570, 579, 602, 606–608, 621, 659, 688; stock 40, 46, 65, 117–119, 123, 637, 655
sales: lost 103, 106, 114, 122, 332
Sales and Operations Planning (S&OP) 73, 75–79, 374, 378
Salveson, Mel 13
sandcone model 176
scatter diagrams 138, **139**
schedule design problem 565–567, 572
scheduling 7, 15, 20, 45–47, 71–75, 82–95, **96**, 97–98, 214–216, 219, 244, 258, 297, 354, 356, 433, 443, 452–453, 456, 459, 516, 534–535, 546, 557, 561–562, 561–563, 565–567, 569–572, 570–572, 638–639, 653, 657, 676–677, 680; crew 569–570; deterministic 83–84, 97; job 534–535; job shop 71, 82, 86–91, **96**, 219; machine 82, 86–87, 89–91; in manufacturing 86–92; parallel machine 86–89; personnel (or shift) 92–94; problems 83–93, 95, 97, 297, 534–535, 567, 569–570, 572; in services 92–95; single machine 84–90; stochastic 83–84, 97–98; system 94–96
Science and Art (S&A) 3
scientific inventory management 110–111, 120–122
Search Decision Rule (SDR) 70
search problems 501–502
seasonality 48, 74, 160, 318, 583, 618
second gilded age 657
secondary market 281–282

security 56, 58, 298, 414, 453, 503, 505, 530–531, 534, 537–539, 557, 606, 608, 647, 652, 658
segmentation 31–35, 280, 283, 375–378, 417, 512, 616, 667
Selective Inventory Management (SIM) 101, 108
sensors 56, 161–163, 181, 201, 247, 266, 502, 530, 589, 659, 689
service: customer 583, 601; distribution 517–520, 522; fee for 429; innovation 264, 414; network design 562–564, 566–568, 570, 573; offering 247, 315, 458, 517–518, 522; quality 131–132, 142–144, 267–268, 414–415, 453–454, 572, 677; sector 7, 264, 355–356, 358, 677–679
service level agreement (SLA) 532, 535
service-level requirements 655–656
services 4, 6–7, 9–11, 15, 17, 20, 24, 26–30, 34, 53, 63–65, 68–69, 71, 73, 75–79, 82–84, 92, 94, 97, 118–120, 123, 125, 127, 130–133, 140, 142–144, 147, 152–153, 161, 163–166, 174, 197–200, 202, 204–205, 208–209, 214, 234, 236, 239, 241, 244–245, 247–248, 255–258, 263–265, 267–269, 277, 293–296, 319–320, 322, 336, 354–356, 358, 374–377, 378–380, 387, 396, 398–399, 401, 403–404, 414–416, 418–419, 429–433, 437, 440, 450–455, 458–459, 502, 510–512, 514–515, 517–520, 522, 528–530, 532–534, 536–538, 548, 551, 557–558, 560–574, 579–581, 583, 587, 592, 601–603, 605–607, 609, 616–618, 622–623, 632, 633, 637–639, 655–656, 666, 670–672, 677–681, 684–686, 688–689; and division of labor 6–7; scheduling in 92–95; value-added 314–316, 314–317, 322, 632, 637
set biases 336, 338–339
setups 74–75
shareholder wealth 381–383, 385–386
sharing 529–530, 536; economy 20, 169, 184, 267, 658, 686, 689
shelf space management 580, 584
Shewhart Cycle 129
Shewhart, Walter A. 8–9, 129, 135, 238, 243, 497, 502, 504
Shifting Bottleneck Heuristic (SBH) 86, 90–91
Shingo, Shigeo 235, 246
shipping port 156–157
short lifecycle products 581–582, 591
shortage cost 103–104, 112, 121
Shortest Processing Time (SPT) 87
Simon, Herbert 328, 469, 472, 489, 652, 658
simulation 75, 94, 106–107, 201, 210, 222, 291–292, 300, 433, 435–437, 440, 472, 493, 498, 520, 554, 564–565, 608, 681, 684
Single Minute Exchange of Die (SMED) 15–16, 246
site selection 320–321
Six Sigma 129, 131, 140–142, 223, 225, 242–243, 246, 420
slow streaming 567

slow-moving items 119–120, 584
smart cities 291, 298–301, 305
smart manufacturing 174
Smith, Adam 5–6, 10, 654
social control theory 334
social influences 333–334, 670
social network theory (SNT) 670–672
social responsibility 18–19, 27, 395, 573, 615, 664–665, 668, 676; in POM and Marketing 385–386
Socially Responsible Consumption 615
software 31, 49, 51–52, 122, 152–154, 162–163, 166, 199–200, 203, 206, 216, 219–220, 225–226, 244, 258, 265–267, 299, 313, 320, 403, 418, 456, 504, 533, 536, 566, 632, 650, 659, 681, 686
solution methodologies 71, 85–86, 88–89, 91
solution techniques 563–564; and heuristic rules 573–574
sourcing 16–17, 46, 178, 181, 264, 266, 269, 320, 502, 518–519, 591, 611, 614–620, 627, 665, 670–671, 688
Special Economic Zones (China) 16, 322, 613
speed management 562, 567
sport 457–460; attendance 455; characteristics 450–452, 454, 457; data in 455–456; fans' expectations 454; industry 443, 450, 452, 455, 457–459; literature review 448, 450, 456–457; past history 443–450; present situation 450–456
sport operations 443, 448, 450; design of 451–452, 458–459; improvement of 451, 453–455, 458, 460; planning and control of 451–453, 458–459
sports value framework (SVF) 458
staged optimization 655
stakeholder 24, 27, 47, 76–77, 162, 215, 219, 225, 225–226, 286–288, 298, 303, 320, 385–386, 402, 427, 429, 450, 453–454, 460, 517, 522, 551, 621, 672, 678; management 215
stakeholder theory (ST) 670–672
standardization 8–10, 119, 123, 128, 141, 157, 163, 170, 179, 224, 397, 612, 638, 650–651, 688
startup operations 255–264, 267, 269, 271
State Counter Disaster Organization Act (1975) 547
static problem 83–84
static route design 563
statistical forecasting 45, 50–55
Statistical Methods for Research Workers (Fisher) 129
Statistical Process Control (SPC) 129, 135–140, 238
Statistical Quality Control (SQC) 8–10, 243, 680
Statistical Tables (Fisher) 129
stochastic and dynamic operations 573
stochastic economic lot scheduling problem (SELSP) 653
stochastic scheduling 83–84, 97–98
stock: safety 40, 46, 65, 117–119, 123, 637, 655
stock dependent consumption 101, 107, 122

stock keeping units (SKUs) 45, 52, 56, 78, 158, 160, 270, 580, 634–635, 643
Stone Age 4, 676
Storage Capacity Allocation Problem 534
storage policies: warehouse 158–160
store execution 580–581, 583, 586–587, 592
stores: pop-up 579, 590; retail 56, 164, 281, 315, 377, 580–582, 584, 587–589, 589–590, 592, 623, 626, 664; virtual 579, 590
strategic choices 179, 477; versus manufacturing paradigm 174
strategic configurations 177
Strategic Human Resources Management (SHRM) 392–393, 400–403, 408
strategic management (SM) 170, 172, 184, 393
strategic role of manufacturing 170–171
Strategically Flexible Production 173
strategy 4, 16–17, 20, 26, 28–32, 45, 47, 63–66, 73, 77–78, 94, 102, 111, 119, 121–122, 128, 132, 142–143, 169–185, 200, 243, 246, 263–265, 280, 282–283, 287, 297–298, 315, 329, 345, 351, 358, 361–362, 379–380, 382, 385, 392, 401, 404, 407, 414, 417, 432, 437, 443, 448, 452–454, 456, 458–460, 497–498, 503, 515, 517–518, 529, 546, 604–605, 632, 640, 653, 677–679, 681, 683, 686; auctioning 298; operations 16, 26, 45, 63–64, 73, 77, 183, 452, 454, 459, 677–679, 683
structural equation modeling (SEM) 394, 397
structural models 222–223
sub-cluster development and jobs 317–318
subsidy programs 519–520
sufficient statistic condition 347–349
Sunk-Cost Fallacy 331
supplier logistics center (SLC) 632, 635–637, 641
supply: network alliances 204, 207; options 63, 65–66; process 518–520; variability 102, 117–120, 122
supply chain 5, 15, 17–19, 24–40, 45–47, 56–58, 78–79, 101, 107, 125, 127, 144–145, 157, 160, 163, 181, 183, 185, 198, 208, 239, 246, 256–258, 264, 266–267, 269–270, 277–278, 281–288, 291, 298, 303, 309, 311, 319–320, 322, 326, 328–329, 331–334, 336, 361, 367–370, 374, 376–384, 386–387, 393–395, 397–398, 404–405, 407, 420–421, 429, 448, 450, 514, 518, 531, 543, 546, 551, 557–558, 568, 579–583, 587–588, 591–592, 614–618, 620–624, 626–630, 632–635, 640–644, 650, 654, 663–672, 676, 684–688; and bullwhip effect in 35–38; closed-loop 664, 668; complexity 666–667; disruption 18, 369, 386, 591, 666; forward 281–282; fulfillment 587–591; global 27, 623–629, 630, 669–672; management (SCM) 24, 76, 107, 122, 257–258, 277, 320, 383, 386, 395, 397–398, **406**, 407–408, 421, 448, 456, 553, 557, 566, 580, 582, 630, 632–634, 650, 663, 665, 680, 682, 684; models 634–641; operations 17, 367, 393, 623–629, 684; problems 293–294;

reverse 122, 277, 281–283, 282–283, 380, 665, 686; risk assessment in 38–40; segmentation 31–35, 667; strategy 633–634; structure 57, 246, 281, 283, 285, 667; sustainability in 277; visibility 78–79, 163; volatility 665–666

supply chain management (SCM): essential concepts 28–40; future research 669–672; historical evolution of 25–27; successful 27–28; supporting theories 669–670

supply chain risk management (SCRM) 18, 369, 671

support: technical 203–204, 206, 209

surveys: conclusions 402–404; large-scale 183–184

sustainability 15, 18–19, 27, 79, 126, 162, 175, 177, 179, 181, 184–185, 241, 248, 262, 287, 321, 374, 385, 387, 402, 407, 459, 478, 538, 561, 567, 579, 590, 592, 621, 651, 664–665, 668, 672, 676, 685–686, 688; focus on 276; in hospitality 420; and operations/supply chain (O/SC) management 277–278; and product/process design 277; and reverse logistics 78, 380–381; in supply chains 277, *see also* environmental sustainability

Sustainable Supply Chain Management (SSCM) 281, 672

Sustained Competitive Advantage (SCA) 392–394, 400, 402–403, 405, 407–408

system dynamics 107, 217, 222, 329, 334–335, 400, 433

System Dynamics Understanding (SDU) 400

system management 244, 601

Systematic Layout Panning (SLP) 152–153, **154**

systematic risk 360, 363, 369

systems: approach 197–198, 234, 239, 246, 482–483, 680, 683; thinking 218, 245, 329, 334–335, 400; views 222–223

tactical management 468–475, 478, 480, 484, 489, 492–493

Taguchi, Genichi 15

Takt time 235

targets 71, 78, 133–134, 203, 235, 279, 284, 427, 468–470, 475–481, 489, 491–493, 502, 550, 571, 642; intermediate 475, 477–479; terminating 469, 475, 478–479, 492

tax 16, 20, 182, 285–286, 312, 320–322, 360, 362, 364–367, 370, 511, 591, 617, 620, 622, 625, 629, 665; consumption 286; effects 364–367, 370

taxi-type transport 560

Taylor, Frederick W. 25, 128, 497–498, 650, 653

teaching 129, 143, 170, 245, 345, 398, 404, 510, 537, 601–604, 606, 677–685, 687; interdisciplinary 680, 683; materials 345, 680–683; online 680, 682–683

Teaching, Research, and Practice (TRP) 677, 679–688

teams 221

technical support 203–204, 206, 209

technological evolution 24–25; and manufacturing strategy 179–181

technological innovations 51, 218, 647–648, 650, 658, 660

Technological Revolution 11, 649

technology 3–4, 12, 17, 20–21, 24–26, 30, 45, 53, 57, 68, 77, 108, 131, 142, 148, 152, 161–162, 166, 176, 178–180, 185, 197–210, 247, 255–256, 258, 263–269, 278–279, 295, 298–299, 339–340, 349, 366, 382, 402–403, 407, 414, 417, 436, 456–457, 459, 501, 504, 519, 527–528, 531, 534, 536–538, 547–548, 557–558, 579–580, 587, 589–590, 592, 602, 605, 630, 632–633, 647–650, 657–658, 664, 667, 676, 678, 680–685, 687–688; challenges 298; digital 180–181, 264–266; flexible 180; information 180, 197–200, 203–204, 208–209, 302; manufacturing 19, 176, 179–181, 185, 197–201, 647, 659; mobile 295–296; new 46, 166, 174, 176, 181, 185, 266, 278, 379, 421, 519, 527, 602, 628, 667, 683, 685, 687; retail 589; teaching and learning 680, 682–683

tele-medicine 537–538

telecommunications 17, 27, 199, 201, 203, 295–296, 527–528, 536–539, 649, 676

ten principles of materials handling 157

terminal management 562, 570–572

terminating targets 469, 475, 478–479, 492

Tesla Factory 14–15

theory 9, 29, 59, 83, 94, 104, 128–129, 169–170, 172, 176, 183, 206, 218, 220, 222, 240–242, 245, 248, 267, 269, 328, 334, 346, 348, 361–362, 368, 374, 381–382, 385, 387, 394, 443, 448, 450, 458, 467, 493, 498, 503–504, 555, 580, 650, 652–653, 658–660, 669–672; building 183, 218–219, 240, 267

Theory of Constraints (TOC) 242–244, 246

Third Industrial Revolution, The (Rifkin) 12

third-party logistics (3PL) 38, 161, 266, 309, 313, 315

3D printing 166, 199, 649, 659, 667, 686

3Rs 255–258, 262, 264–265, 267, 270–271

Throughput Accounting (TA) 242

throughput maximization 346, 348–352

time 64; polynomial 84–85, 87–89, 91–93, 528–529; total completion 85–88; total weighted completion 84–87, **88**

time series forecasting 52, 55

time-cost tradeoff 216, 222

Time-Driven Activity-Based Costing (TD-ABC) 348, 355–356

Today and Tomorrow (Ford) 128

tolerance ranges 7–8, 10

total completion time 85–88

Total Productive Maintenance (TPM) 173, 234–235, 238–241

Index

Total Quality Control (TQC) 234, 238
Total Quality Management (TQM) 125–126, 130, 142, 235, 238–240, 243
total weighted completion time 84–87, **88**
Toyota Kata 241
Toyota Production System (Ohno) 130
Toyota Production System (TPS) 15, 128, 130–131, 131, 141, 180, 234–239, 241, 245, 247–248, 497, 650
trade: credit 367, 369; global 19, 611–614; international 182, 319–322, 611–612
trade-offs 26–27, 175–177, 205, 279, 282, 284, 293, 356, 503, 517, 520, 655, 667
traditional costing methods 354–355
training 8, 64–65, 77, 120, 126, 128–130, 144, 162, 198, 200, 202, 204, 239, 241, 267, 312–313, 317–318, 392–394, 396, 398–399, 401–402, 407–408, 414, 416, 418, 439, 456, 499, 503, 516–517, 521, 530, 546, 580, 602, 604–605, 607, 609
transaction cost economics (TCE) 29, 669–672
transaction costs 29–31, 204, 362, 669–670
transactions 14, 29, 158, 198, 265, 294, 380, 588–589, 621, 629
transport: liner-type 560–561; modes and features 558–560; pipeline 558–559, *560*; rail 558–559, *560*, 566–571, 574; road 558–560, 563, 567–568, 571–572, 574; systems 560–561, 572–573; taxi-type 560; water (maritime) 558–560
transportation 11, 14, 16–17, 19, 27, 37–38, 46, 68, 82, 87, 92, 97, 147, 161, 164, 182, 255, 264–265, 282, 287, 291, 299, 309, 311–317, 319–322, 431, 455, 500, 502–503, 548, 555, 557–558, 561–572, 563–564, 567–569, 584, 587, 592, 606, 612, 617, 620, 649, 654–655, 664, 676–677, 688; capacity sharing 312–313; city 299
travel agents: online 417, 420–421
trend 12, 19, 34, 37, 48, 50–52, 55–56, 65, 101–102, 135, 160–167, 183, 199, 256, 270, 294, 304, 310–311, 319, 321, 339, 376, 394–395, 397, 401, 403, 407, 433, 456, 574, 592, 605, 608, 615–616, 649, 660, 663–672, 678–680, 682–683, 685, 688–689; biases 336–338
triage 434–439
triple bottom line (3BL) 27, 664–665, 668–670, 672
Twenty Foot-Equivalent Units (TEUs) 612, 616
Twitter 292, 303

Uber 20, 169, 255–257, 264–270, 658, 686, 689
ubiquitous computing 659
Uddevalla 6
uncertainty 28–29, 71, 78, 102, 120, 174, 198, 202–203, 205–209, 215, 219–221, 221, 223, 226, 283–284, 301, 332, 338–339, 378–379, 451, 453–454, 458–459, 467–470, 473, 480, 485, 489, 492, 513–515, 519, 528–529, 531, 535, 551, 565, 567, 569, 573, 581–582, 586, 591, 654, 656, 664, 668; market and technical 203, 205, 207, 209
Unique Manufactured Products 624, 626, **627**, 628, **629**, 630
Unique Selling Proposition (USP) 403
unknown unknowns (unk-unks) 221
unk-unks *see* unknown unknowns
upside risk 473, 479, 493
upward mobility 317–318, 322
urbanization 161, 614
US Antisubmarine Warfare Operations Research Group (ASWORG) 499
US Green Building Council (USGBC) 165

value 214, 216–217, 219–220, 222–223, 225–226
value-action gap 279
value-added services 314–317, 322, 632, 637
Vanguard Method 245
vanilla boxes 656
vehicle routing problem (VRP) 558, 561–562, 564–566, 570, 572–573
vendor-managed inventory (VMI) 34, 108
virtual stores 579, 590
volatility 28, 35, 37–38, 40, 46, 64, 121, 173, 348, 364, 376–377, 387, 663–666, 670–672
volunteer management 516–517
Volvo 6
vulnerability 39–40, 547

wages: overtime 66–68; regular time 66, 68
Wal-Mart 25, 37, 163, 277, 375, 531, 590, 629, 632–633, 640, 642, 664
Walt Disney World 601–609
Walt Disney World® Magic 604
war/warfare 497–505
Warby Parker 375–376, 588
warehouse: capacity sharing 313; design 158–160, 164, 166; logistics 590; planning 164; storage policies 158–160
Warehouse Management System (WMS) 637, 641
Waste Electrical and Electronic Equipment (WEEE) 284
water (maritime) transport 558–560
Watson (supercomputer) 7, 20, 56, 299
wealth 5, 10, 240, 381–383, 385–386, 611–615, 647–649, 654, 657, 688; shareholder 381–383, 385–386
Wealth of Nations, The (Smith) 5–6, 10, 654
weapons 497–499, 501–503
wearable computing 161
Weighted Shortest Processing Time (WSPT) 84, 86–87
white-collar jobs 214, 317
Whitney, Eli 7–8
wireless mesh network (WMN) 538
wireless sensor network (WSN) 530

Index

work policy 222
workforce 47, 64, 64–76, 162, 169, 173, 185, 197, 200, 203–204, 206–209, 241, 345, 401–403, 407, 521, 614, 653, 657; change 162; management 516, 579–580, 586–587, 589, 592
working capital 47, 102, 120, 361
Workplace Management (Ohno) 130
World Class Manufacturing 173
World Trade Organization (WTO) 319
World Travel and Tourism Council (WTTC) 413
worst-case performance ratio 85, 87–89

Yelp 292
yield management 255, 257, 262, 265, 268, 270, 416–417, 453, 459
Yihaodian (YHD) 642–644; company overview 632–633; innovation 634–641; supply chain strategy 633–634

Zero Defects 131
Zipcar 257, 264–266
zone-picking 160
zoning 320–321

Taylor & Francis eBooks

Helping you to choose the right eBooks for your Library

Add Routledge titles to your library's digital collection today. Taylor and Francis ebooks contains over 50,000 titles in the Humanities, Social Sciences, Behavioural Sciences, Built Environment and Law.

Choose from a range of subject packages or create your own!

Benefits for you
- » Free MARC records
- » COUNTER-compliant usage statistics
- » Flexible purchase and pricing options
- » All titles DRM-free.

Benefits for your user
- » Off-site, anytime access via Athens or referring URL
- » Print or copy pages or chapters
- » Full content search
- » Bookmark, highlight and annotate text
- » Access to thousands of pages of quality research at the click of a button.

REQUEST YOUR **FREE** INSTITUTIONAL TRIAL TODAY

Free Trials Available
We offer free trials to qualifying academic, corporate and government customers.

eCollections – Choose from over 30 subject eCollections, including:

Archaeology	Language Learning
Architecture	Law
Asian Studies	Literature
Business & Management	Media & Communication
Classical Studies	Middle East Studies
Construction	Music
Creative & Media Arts	Philosophy
Criminology & Criminal Justice	Planning
Economics	Politics
Education	Psychology & Mental Health
Energy	Religion
Engineering	Security
English Language & Linguistics	Social Work
Environment & Sustainability	Sociology
Geography	Sport
Health Studies	Theatre & Performance
History	Tourism, Hospitality & Events

For more information, pricing enquiries or to order a free trial, please contact your local sales team:
www.tandfebooks.com/page/sales

The home of Routledge books

www.tandfebooks.com